Advance Praise for *Adobe InDesign CS3 One-on-One*

"Deke McClelland is a joy to watch present and in many ways more of a joy to read. Deke is best known for his work in Photoshop; however, one of Deke's best-kept secrets is his understanding of Adobe InDesign. Adobe InDesign CS3 has tons of little nuances and hidden features. Deke helps you uncover them all. Having used InDesign since version 1.0, I'm often surprised when I can learn a tip or trick that I hadn't seen before. When I read Deke's books, I always learn something new."

—Terry White
Director, Creative Pro Sales, Adobe Systems, Inc.

"Deke McClelland's *Adobe InDesign CS3 One-on-One* is an effective and thorough way to learn how to get the most out of Adobe InDesign in a step-by-step, hands-on fashion. There's no substitute for learning by doing, and if you're looking for a 'hands-on' tutorial to learn how to tap into all the power of InDesign, this is the book for you."

—Tim Cole
Senior InDesign Evangelist, Adobe Systems, Inc.

"This book is not only enjoyable and approachable, it's a valuable reference for just about anybody. Whether you're going through lessons step by step or merely skipping from one 'Pearl of Wisdom' to the next, you'll find it well worth the price."

—Terri Stone
Editor in Chief of *InDesign Magazine* and *Creativepro.com*

Advance Praise for *Adobe InDesign CS3 One-on-One*

"The wealth of knowledge that is Deke McClelland is yours once again. Harness and reap the benefits of Deke's lessons, explanations and demonstrations on InDesign CS3 to really take you to the next level."

—Steve Holmes
Creative Director, Energi Design (San Francisco)
www.clickenergi.com

"I love the combination of video and clear, step-by-step text! Deke's you-can-do-it attitude is great!"

—David Blatner
Co-host, *InDesignSecrets.com*

Adobe InDesign CS3

one-on-one™

Also from Deke Press

Adobe Photoshop CS3 One-on-One
Photoshop Elements for Windows One-on-One

Upcoming titles from Deke Press

Photoshop Channels and Masks One-on-One
Adobe Illustrator One-on-One

Adobe InDesign CS3

one-on-one™

DEKE McCLELLAND

deke™ PRESS

O'REILLY®

BEIJING • CAMBRIDGE • FARNHAM • KÖLN • PARIS • SEBASTOPOL • TAIPEI • TOKYO

Adobe InDesign CS3 One-on-One

by Deke McClelland

Printed in the United States of America.

This title is published by Deke Press in association with O'Reilly Media, Inc., 1005 Gravenstein Highway North, Sebastopol, CA 95472.

O'Reilly Media books may be purchased for educational, business, or sales promotional use. Online editions are also available for most titles (*safari.oreilly.com*). For more information, contact O'Reilly's corporate/institutional sales department: 800-998-9938 or *corporate@oreilly.com*.

Managing Editor:	Carol Person
Content Cornucopia:	Colleen Wheeler
Associate Editor:	Susan Pink, Techright
Indexer:	Julie Hawks
Technical Editor:	Ron Bilodeau
Manufacturing Manager:	Sue Willing
Publicist:	Sara Peyton
Night Editors:	Dan Brodnitz, Steve Weiss
Cover, Project, and Interior Designer:	David Futato
DVD Management:	Tanya Staples
Video Producer:	Max Smith
Live-Action Video; Desktop Editors:	Scott Erickson, Mike Harrison
Video Testers:	Brian Coyle, Cassie Ross, Michelle Carr
Operations Manager:	Karen Gauthier

Print History:

December 2007: First edition.

Special thanks to Galen Fott, Jim Felici, Michael Ninness, Lynda Weinman, Bruce Heavin, Megan O. Andersen, Jenn Cornelius, Paavo Stubstad, David Rogelberg, Sherry Rogelberg, Stacey Barone, Linda Thornton, Kevin O'Connor, David Blatner, Anne-Marie Concepcion, Mordy Golding, Barry Anderson, Celeste Forevary, Jeremy Doak, Laura Adair, Julie Delany, Betsy Waliszewski, Michele Filshie, and Tim O'Reilly, as well as Garth Johnson, Megan Ironside, Val Gelineau, Addy Roff, and the gangs at iStockphoto.com, PhotoSpin, NAPP, Peachpit Press, Microsoft, and Adobe Systems. Extra special thanks to our relentlessly supportive families, without whom this series and this book would not be possible. In loving memory of Marjorie Baer.

This book was typeset using Adobe InDesign CS3 and the Adobe Futura, Adobe Rotis, and Linotype Birka typefaces.

0-596-52976-7
978-0-596-52976-5

[C]

RepKover™ This book uses RepKover™, a durable and flexible lay-flat binding.

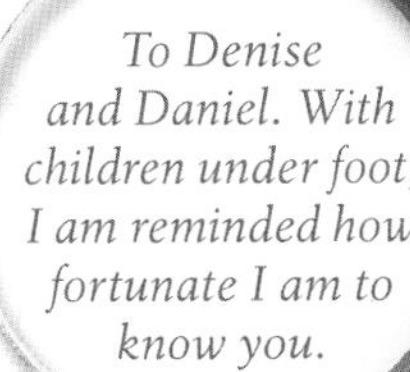
To Denise
and Daniel. With
children under foot,
I am reminded how
fortunate I am to
know you.

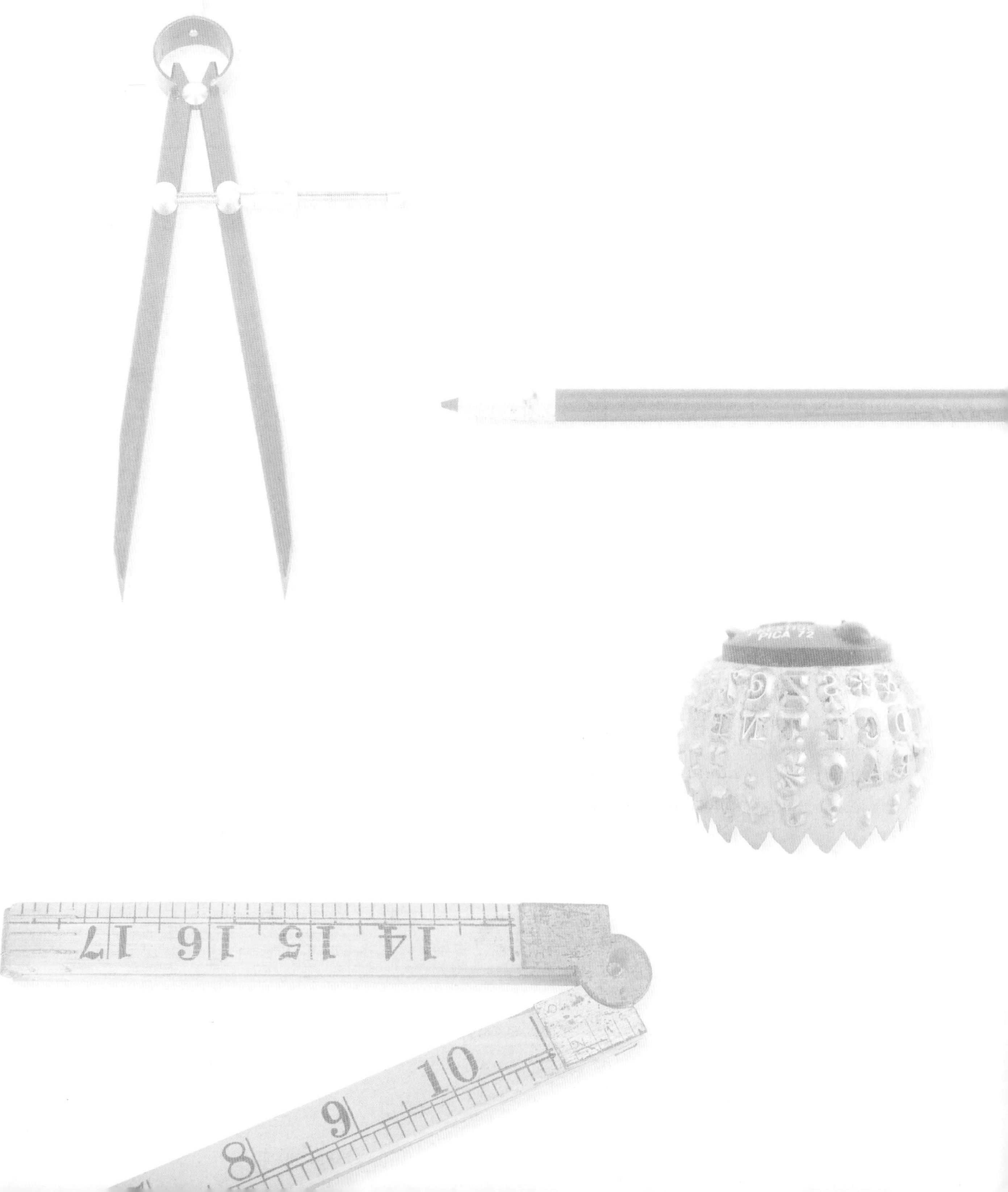

PICA 72

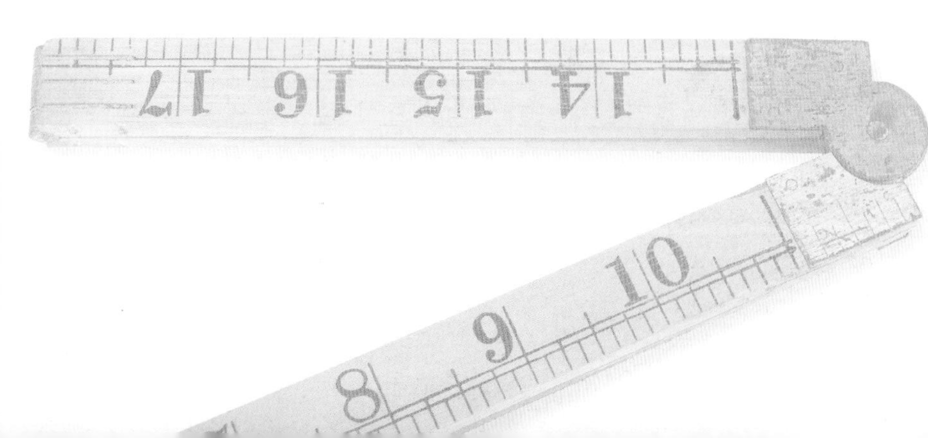

CONTENTS

PREFACE

HOW ONE-ON-ONE WORKS

Welcome to *Adobe InDesign CS3 One-on-One*, the eighth in a series of highly visual, full-color titles that combine step-by-step lessons with more than two hours of video instruction. As the name *One-on-One* implies, I walk you through InDesign just as if I were teaching you in a classroom or corporate consulting environment. Except that instead of getting lost in a crowd of students, you receive my individualized attention. It's just you and me.

I created *One-on-One* with three audiences in mind. If you're an independent designer or graphic artist—professional or amateur—you'll appreciate the hands-on approach and the ability to set your own pace. If you're a student working in a classroom or vocational setting, you'll enjoy the personalized attention, structured exercises, and end-of-lesson quizzes. If you're an instructor in a college or vocational setting, you'll find the topic-driven lessons helpful in building curricula and creating homework assignments. *Adobe InDesign CS3 One-on-One* is designed to suit the needs of beginners and intermediate users. But I've seen to it that each lesson contains a few techniques that even experienced users don't know.

Read, Watch, Do

Adobe InDesign CS3 One-on-One is your chance to master Adobe's revolutionary layout application under the guidance of a professional trainer with more than twenty years of hard-won, in-the-trenches computer design and imaging experience. Read the book, watch the videos, do the exercises. Proceed as quickly or slowly as you like and experiment as you see fit. It's the best way to learn.

Figure 1.

The goal: Start with this base document . . . Figure 2.

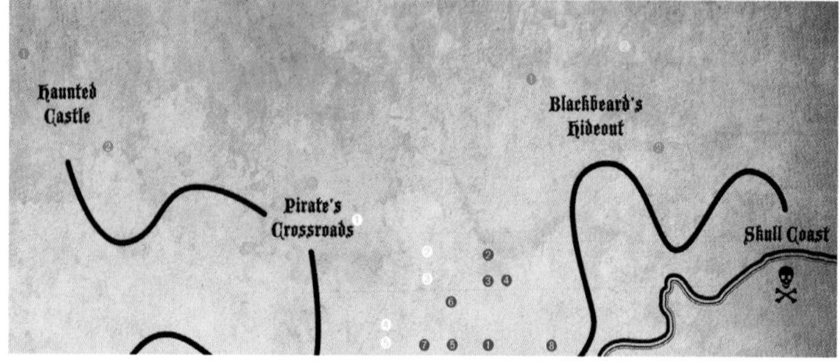

and complete this fully realized project. No head scratching allowed!

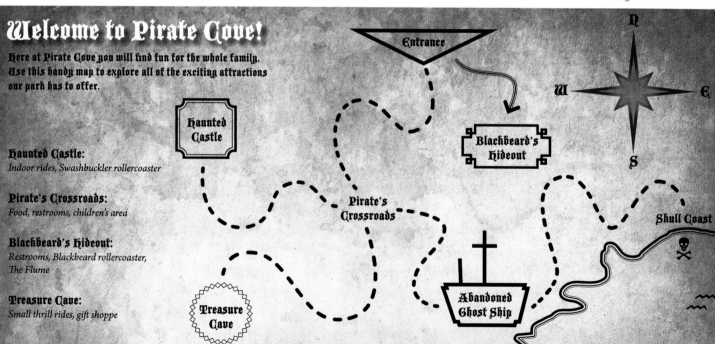

Adobe InDesign CS3 One-on-One contains twelve lessons, each made up of three to six step-by-step exercises. Every book-based lesson includes a corresponding video lesson (see Figure 1), in which I introduce the key concepts you'll need to know to complete the exercises. Best of all, every exercise is project-based, complete with exhaustively tested sample files (for example, see Figure 2), culminating in an actual finished document worthy of your labors (such as the whimsical but rigorous Figure 3). The exercises include insights and context throughout, so you'll know not only what to do but, just as important, why you're doing it. My hope is that you'll find the experience entertaining, informative, and empowering.

All the sample files required to perform the exercises are included on the DVD-ROM at the back of this book. The DVD also contains the video lessons. (This is a data DVD, not a video DVD. It won't work in a set-top device; it works only with a computer.) Don't lose or destroy this DVD, drop it, or loan it to a friend. It is as integral a part of your learning experience as the pages in this book. Together, the book, sample files, and videos form a single comprehensive training package.

Figure 3.

One-on-One Requirements

The main prerequisite to using *Adobe InDesign CS3 One-on-One* is having Adobe InDesign CS3 (also known as InDesign 5, because it's the fifth version of the software) installed on your system. You may have purchased InDesign CS3 as a stand-alone package (see Figure 4) or as one element in the Design Standard, Design Premium, or Master Collection version of Adobe's ambitious Creative Suite 3. Although many of the topics covered in this book are common to InDesign CS2 and earlier, you'll need InDesign CS3 to open the sample files. Also worth noting, I and my Elite Team—I've been at this for 22 years, and I've got to say, my current crew is second to none—tested all exercises with Adobe InDesign CS3 but not with older versions.

Figure 4.

Adobe InDesign CS3 One-on-One is cross-platform, meaning that it works equally well whether you're using InDesign installed on a Microsoft Windows–based PC or an Apple Macintosh. Any computer that meets the minimum requirements for InDesign CS3 also meets the requirements for *Adobe InDesign CS3 One-on-One*. If you own a PC, you will need an Intel Pentium 4, Xeon, or Core Duo processor running Windows Vista or XP with Service Pack 2. If you own a Mac, you need a PowerPC G4 or G5, or a multicore Intel processor running Mac OS X 10.4.8 (Tiger), 10.5 Leopard, or higher.

Regardless of your chosen (or job-imposed) platform, your computer must meet the following *minimum* requirements:

- 1GB of RAM (2GB even better)
- 5GB of free hard disk space (4.5GB for InDesign and the Suite and the remaining 500MB for the *One-on-One* video and project files)
- 16-bit color video card with 64MB of video RAM
- Color monitor with 1024-by-768 pixel resolution
- DVD-ROM drive
- Broadband Internet connection for extras (but if you're working unfettered—in a plane, pub, subway, or pachinko parlor; on an Antarctic cruise or Day 6 of a safari; while repairing the Space Station or just floating in a hot-air balloon—you can most assuredly do without)

To play the videos, you will need Apple's QuickTime Player 7.0 or later. Many PCs and all Macintosh computers come equipped with QuickTime; if yours does not, install QuickTime using the link provided on the DVD-ROM included with this book.

Arno Pro
Light Display, *Light Italic Display*, Display, *Italic Display*, Regular, *Italic*, Caption, *Italic Caption*, Semibold Display, *Semibold Italic Display*, **Semibold**, ***Semibold Italic***, **Semibold Caption**, ***Semibold Italic Caption***, **Bold Display**, ***Bold Italic Display***, **Bold**, ***Bold Italic***, **Bold Caption**, ***Bold Italic Caption***

Bell Gothic Standard
Bold, **Black**

Bickham Script Pro
Regular, Semibold, Bold

Birch Standard Regular

Blackoak Standard Regular

Brush Script Standard

Chaparral Pro
Light*, *Light Italic**, Regular, *Italic*, Semibold*, *Semibold Italic**, **Bold**, ***Bold Italic***

CHARLEMAGNE
REGULAR **BOLD**

Cooper Standard
Black, *Black Italic*

ECCENTRIC STANDARD

Adobe Caslon Pro
Regular, *Italic*, Semibold, *Semibold Italic*, **Bold**, ***Bold Italic***

Garamond Premier Pro
Regular, *Italic*, Semibold, *Semibold Italic*

Adobe Garamond Pro
Regular, *Italic*, **Bold**, ***Bold Italic***

Giddyup Standard

Hobo Standard Medium

Letter Gothic Standard
Medium, *Slanted*, **Bold**, ***Bold Slanted***

LITHOS PRO
EXTRA LIGHT, LIGHT, REGULAR, **BOLD**, **BLACK**

MESQUITE STANDARD MEDIUM

Minion Pro
Regular, *Italic*, Medium, *Medium Italic*, Semibold, *Semibold Italic*, **Bold**, ***Bold Italic***, **Bold Condensed**, ***Bold Condensed Italic***

Myriad Pro
Light*, *Light Italic**, Regular, *Italic*, Condensed, *Italic*, **Semibold**, ***Semibold Italic***, **Bold**, ***Bold Italic***, **Bold Condensed**, ***Bold Condensed Italic***

Nueva Standard
Condensed, *Condensed Italic*, **Bold Condensed**, ***Bold Condensed Italic***

OCR A Standard

ORATOR STANDARD
MEDIUM, *SLANTED*

Poplar Standard Black

Prestige Elite Standard

ROSEWOOD STANDARD

STENCIL STANDARD

Tekton Pro
Bold, *Bold Oblique*, Bold Condensed, Bold Extended

TRAJAN PRO
REGULAR, **BOLD**

*Hand-install from CS3 Content DVD

Figure 5.

Finally, you'll want to install the *One-on-One* lesson files, color settings, and keyboard shortcuts from the DVD-ROM that accompanies this book, as explained in the next section.

All sample files use the fonts pictured in alphabetical order in Figure 5. These fonts are included with most versions of Creative Suite 3. (They may not ship with certain educational and foreign editions.) Most of the fonts in the figure install automatically. Only six styles have to be installed by hand, as I will explain in the next section.

One-on-One Installation and Setup

Adobe InDesign CS3 One-on-One is designed to function as an integrated training environment. Therefore, before embarking on the lessons and exercises, I ask you to install a handful of files onto your computer's hard drive. These are:

- QuickTime Player software (if it isn't already installed)
- All lesson files used in the exercises (340MB in all)
- *One-on-One* Creative Suite color settings
- Custom dekeKeys—InDesign keyboard shortcuts
- Six typefaces included with Creative Suite 3

Except for the fonts, all of these files are provided on the DVD-ROM that accompanies this book. The fonts are included on the disk labeled Contents that comes with Creative Suite 3. To install the files, follow these steps:

1. ***Insert the* One-on-One *DVD.*** Remove the DVD from the back cover of the book and place it in your computer's DVD drive. Then do one of the following, depending on your platform:

   - On the PC, Windows will most likely display a dialog box asking you what action you'd like to perform on the disk. Scroll down the list and click **Open Folder to View Files Using Windows Explorer**.
   - On the Mac, double-click the DVD icon on your computer's desktop.

   Figure 6 shows the contents of the DVD. Although this screen shot happens to come from a Mac, you'll see the same six files on a PC, albeit in list form or with different icons.

2. ***If necessary, get QuickTime.*** If you already have QuickTime (it comes preinstalled on all Macintosh computers and some Windows-based PCs), skip to Step 3. If you don't or you're not sure, double-click the file *IDcs3 Videos.html* on the DVD to open the *InDesign CS3 One-on-One* page in your default Web browser. Near the bottom of the screen are two small lines of type, magnified in Figure 7. The first one ends with a link, *www.apple.com/quicktime*. Click it (or just enter that URL into your browser if you prefer) to open a new window to Apple's QuickTime site. Follow the on-screen instructions to download and install the software. After you finish installing QuickTime (if you are asked to restart your system, do so), proceed to the next step.

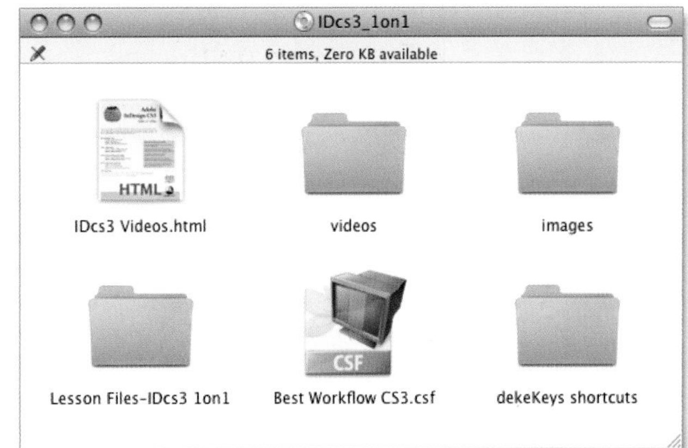

Figure 6.

Figure 7.

3. ***Copy the lesson files to your desktop.*** Return to your computer's desktop (called the Explorer under Windows, and the Finder on the Mac). Inside the window that shows the contents of the DVD, locate the folder called *Lesson Files-IDcs3 1on1*. This folder contains all twelve lessons' worth of sample files—including InDesign documents, linked graphics, even a Microsoft Word document—that you'll be using throughout the exercises in this book. Drag the folder to the desktop to copy it, as you see me doing in Figure 8.

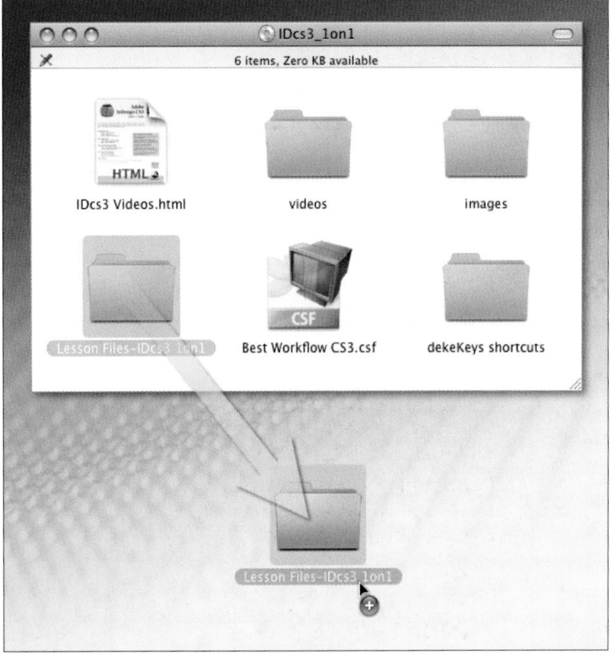

Figure 8.

You don't absolutely have to copy the folder to the desktop; in fact, you can put it anywhere you want. But be advised, if you put it somewhere other than the desktop, I leave it up to you to find the *Lesson Files-IDcs3 1on1* folder and the files therein for yourself. 'Nuff said.

---

4. ***Copy the color settings to your hard drive.*** On the DVD, locate the Adobe CS3 color settings file called *Best workflow.csf*. Copy this file to one of three locations on your hard drive, depending on your platform and operating system. (Note that, in the following, user indicates your computer login name.)

   - Under Windows Vista, the location is *C:\Users*user*\AppData\Roaming\Adobe\Color\Settings*
   - Under Windows XP, it's *C:\Documents and Settings*user*\Application Data\Adobe\Color\Settings*

- On the Mac, regardless of your operating system, choose **Go→Home** and copy the color settings to the folder *Library/Application Support/Adobe/Color/Settings*.

If you can't find the *Application Data* folder on the PC, it's because Windows is making the system folders invisible. Choose **Tools→Folder Options**, click the **View** tab, and turn on **Show Hidden Files and Folders** in the scrolling list. Also turn off the **Hide Extensions for Known File Types** and **Hide Protected Operating System Files** check boxes and click the **OK** button.

5. ***Install the dekeKeys keyboard shortcuts.*** Open the *dekeKeys shortcuts* folder on the DVD. There you'll find two versions of my custom dekeKeys keyboard shortcuts, one for the Mac and one for Windows. Copy the file that corresponds to your platform in one of the following three folders:
   - Under Windows Vista, it's *C:\Users*user*\AppData\Roaming\Adobe\InDesign\Version 5.0\InDesign Shortcut Sets*.
   - Under Windows XP, it's *C:\Documents and Settings*user*\Application Data\Adobe\InDesign\Version 5.0\InDesign Shortcut Sets*.
   - On the Mac, choose **Go→Home** and then make your way to *Library/Preferences/Adobe InDesign/Version 5.0/InDesign Shortcut Sets*.
6. ***Start InDesign.*** If InDesign CS3 is already running on your computer, skip to Step 7. If not, start the program:
   - On the PC, go to the **Start** menu (⊞ under Windows Vista) and choose **Adobe InDesign CS3**. (The program may be located in the **Programs** or **All Programs** submenu, possibly inside an **Adobe** submenu.)
   - On the Mac, choose **Go→Applications** in the Finder. Then open the *Adobe InDesign CS3* folder and double-click the *Adobe InDesign CS3* application icon.
7. ***Change the color settings to Best Workflow.*** Now that you've installed the color settings (Step 4), you have to activate them. Assuming that you own the full Creative Suite 3 package (regardless of the edition), you'll need to synchronize the color settings across all Adobe applications. Launch the Bridge application by choosing **File→Browse**. Inside the Bridge, choose **Edit→Creative Suite Color Settings** or press the keyboard shortcut, Ctrl+Shift+K (⌘-Shift-K on the Mac). Select the **Best Workflow CS3** item in the scrolling list, as in Figure 9. (If you don't see it, turn on the Show Expanded List of Color Settings Files check box.) Then click **Apply**. From now on, all your CS3 applications will display consistent color and the colors of your documents will match (or very nearly match) those shown in the pages of this book.

Figure 9.

If you own a stand-alone version of InDesign, Choose Edit→Color Settings. Inside the Color Settings dialog box, click the Settings pop-up menu and choose Best Workflow. (If you plan on accepting a lot of CMYK graphics from outside sources, you may also want to set the second CMYK option to Preserve Embedded Profiles, which converts imported images from one color space to another. Otherwise, don't worry about it.) Then click the OK button.

8. *Change the keyboard shortcuts to dekeKeys.* To load the dekeKeys keyboard shortcuts, return to InDesign, choose **Edit→ Keyboard Shortcuts**. At the top of the **Keyboard Shortcuts** dialog box, click the **Set** pop-up menu and choose **dekeKeys IDcs3 1on1** (**Win** or **Mac**), as in Figure 10. Then click the **OK** button. This loads a few keyboard shortcuts for some of InDesign's most essential functions, and ensures that you and I will be on the same page throughout the exercises. (I do override a couple of InDesign's default shortcuts, but nothing that you'll miss.)

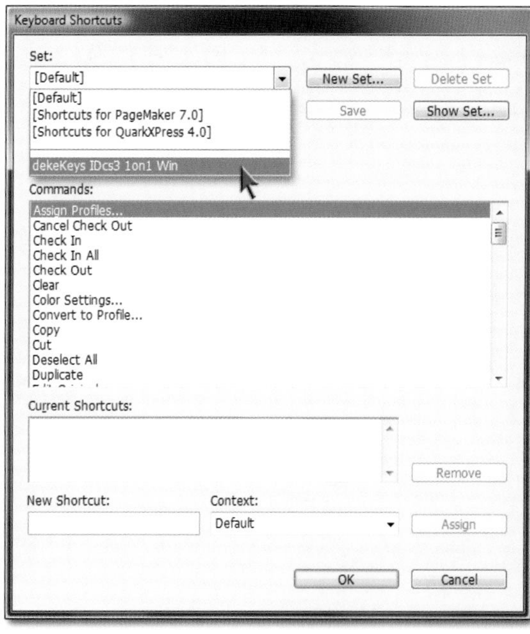

Figure 10.

9. *Quit InDesign.* You've come full circle. On the PC, choose **File→Exit**; on the Mac, choose **InDesign→Quit InDesign**. Quitting InDesign not only closes the program but also saves the changes you made to the color settings and keyboard shortcuts.

10. *Eject my DVD and put in Adobe's.* Now we need another DVD. Eject the *Adobe InDesign CS3 One-on-One* DVD and put it in a safe place (such as the sleeve on the back cover of this book). Keep it handy; you'll need it again in the next section. Then locate your copy of Adobe Creative Suite 3. The Suite includes at least two disks, one labeled *Application* and the other *Content*. Insert the *Content* disk in your computer's DVD drive and open it so you can see its contents.

If you don't have access to the full Creative Suite, don't sweat it. You can still open the sample files included with this book, but you may encounter a few warnings telling you that you're missing certain fonts. Just click the OK button and work inside the file as you normally would. Some of your results won't look the way they do in the book, but you'll still be able to gain some practical, hands-on experience with InDesign.

11. *Install six fonts included with CS3.* Navigate to the *Fonts* subfolder inside the *Goodies* folder. Therein, you'll find a

treasure trove of more than 150 professionally designed typefaces, many of which are installed by default, some of which are not. We're interested in six: four styles of Chaparral Pro (Light, Light Italic, Semibold, and Semibold Italic) and two styles of Myriad Pro (Light and Light Italic). To load them on your system:

- On the PC, go to the **Start** menu (⊞ under Windows Vista) and choose **Control Panel**. Locate the **Fonts** item (you have to go to Classic View to see it) and open it. Then copy the fonts from the DVD to this folder window.
- On the Mac, copy the fonts to one of your many fonts folders. I recommend the folder *Library/Fonts*, because this is where the Creative Suite puts the fonts it automatically installs.

You can copy other fonts if you like. But bear in mind that many of the fonts are already installed, so you may get replacement warnings. Consult Figure 5 on page xvi to recall which fonts are already in your system.

Congratulations, you and I are now in sync. Just one more thing: If you use a Macintosh, the system intercepts a few important InDesign keyboard shortcuts, which you'll want to modify according to the following tip. If you use a PC, feel free to skip the tip and move along to the next section.

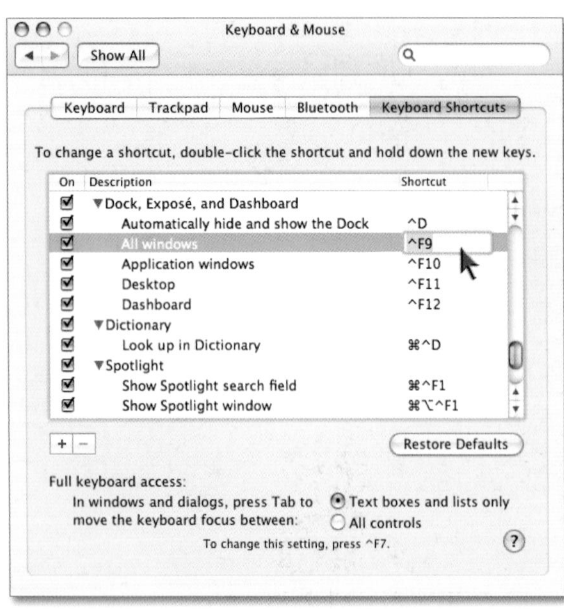

Figure 11.

Adobe intends for the F9, F10, F11, and F12 keys to display or hide some of InDesign's most common palettes. Meanwhile, pressing ⌘ and Option with the spacebar should access the zoom tool. But in recent versions of OS X , these keys tile or hide windows according to Apple's Exposé or invoke search functions via Apple's Spotlight. To rectify these conflicts, choose **System Preferences** from the menu. Click **Show All** at the top of the screen, click the **Keyboard & Mouse** icon, and click the **Keyboard Shortcuts** button. Scroll down the shortcuts until you find one called **All Windows**. Click the **F9** shortcut to highlight it. Then press Control-F9 (which appears as **^F9**, as in Figure 11). After that, reading down the list, replace F10 with Control-F10, F11 with Control-F11, and F12 with Control-F12. Next, click **⌘Space** and replace it with ⌘-Control-F1; click **⌘⌥Space** and replace it with ⌘-Control-Option-F1 (which shows up as **⌘⌥^F1**). Finally, click the ⊗ in the upper-left corner of the window to close the system preferences. From now on, the palette and zoom tool shortcuts will work according to Adobe's intentions, as well as the directions provided in this book.

If you run into other system-level conflicts with InDesign for the Mac, most likely you'll want to use the Keyboard Shortcuts section of the Keyboard & Mouse system preferences to solve them.

Playing the Videos

At the outset of each of the lessons in this book, I ask you to do something most books don't ask you to do: Play a companion video lesson from the DVD-ROM. Ranging from 7 to 20 minutes apiece, these video lessons introduce key concepts that make more sense when first seen in action.

Edited and produced by the trailblazing online training company lynda.com, the video lessons are not traditional DVD movies. They're better. A standard DVD movie maxes out at 720-by-480 nonsquare pixels, of which only 720-by-240 pixels update at a time (an antiquated and generally unfortunate phenomenon known as *interlacing*). We have no such restrictions. Our movies play at resolutions as high as 880-by-660 pixels (see Figure 12), and every pixel updates at the same rate. The result is a high-quality, legible screen image, so that you're never squinting in an attempt to figure out what tool

Figure 12.

or command I'm choosing. And thanks to lynda.com's considerable experience supplying movies over slow Internet connections, every movie plays smoothly, even on older-model computers. This is video training at its finest.

PEARL OF WISDOM

Readers frequently ask me if the videos are excerpted from one of my full-length video series. The question comes up so often that I'm going to answer it preemptively: No. Every minute of the nearly 3 hours of video on the DVD is unique to this book. (The total length of the videos comes to 2 hours and 54 minutes. I know, the cover says "over 2 hours" and it's really just 6 minutes shy of 3. Better to under-promise and over-deliver. Besides, I didn't want to overwhelm you.)

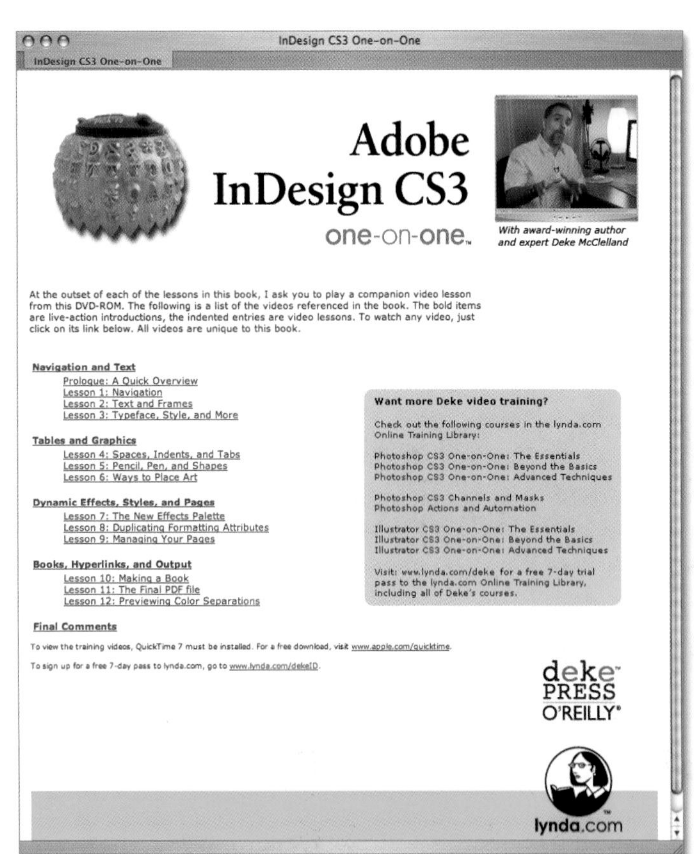

Figure 13.

To watch a video, do the following:

1. ***Insert the One-on-One DVD.*** The videos reside in a folder called *videos*. You can copy that folder (which weighs in at 560MB) to your hard drive and play the videos inside QuickTime if you like. But that's by no means necessary, nor do I encourage it. I designed the videos to play from a simple Web page interface directly from the DVD, as these steps explain.

2. ***Launch the video interface.*** Open the DVD so you can see its contents. Then double-click the file named *IDcs3 Videos.html* to open the *InDesign CS3 One-on-One* page in your default Web browser, as pictured in Figure 13.

3. ***Click the link for the video lesson you want to watch.*** The left side of the page offers a series of eighteen links, each of which takes you to a different video. Click one of the five bold items to watch a live-action segment from your cordial host, me. The indented links take you to one of the thirteen video lessons, twelve of which accompany the twelve lessons in this book; the thirteenth goes with this very Preface. You can watch the video lessons in any order you like. However, each makes the most sense and provides the most benefit when watched at the outset of the corresponding book-based lesson.

4. *Watch the first introductory video.* Click the **Navigation and Text** link to watch the first welcoming message. It explains a bit more about how the book and video lessons work with each other. Plus, it permits me to talk to you live and in person (by which I mean prerecorded and on a computer screen).

5. *Watch the video lesson at your own pace.* Use the play controls under the movie to play, pause, or jump to another spot in the movie. You can also take advantage of the following keyboard shortcuts and hidden tricks:

   - Click inside the movie to pause it. Double-click to start the movie playing again.
   - You can also pause the video by pressing the spacebar. Press the spacebar again to resume playing.
   - I don't know why you'd want to do this, but you can play the video backward by pressing Ctrl+← (⌘-← on the Mac). Or Shift-double-click in the movie.
   - Drag the circular playhead (labeled in Figure 14) to shuttle back and forth inside the move. Or just click in the timeline to move to a specific point in the video.
   - Press the ← or → key, respectively, to pause the movie and go backward or forward one frame.

Figure 14.

- Press Ctrl+Alt+← (Option-←) to return to the beginning of the movie.
- Use the ↑ or ↓ key, respectively, to raise or lower the volume.

Here's a really weird one: Press the Alt key (Control on the Mac) and drag in the frame controls in the bottom-right corner of the window to change the playback speed.

That last technique is an undocumented trick dating back to the early days of QuickTime. It's hard to predict, but with a little bit of experimenting, you can fast-forward over the tedious stuff (when will I stop yammering?) or slow down the really useful information that otherwise goes by too fast.

PEARL OF WISDOM

One final note: Unlike the exercises inside the book, none of the video lessons include sample files. The idea is, you work along with me inside the book; you sit back and relax during the videos. And that's an order.

---

6. ***Play the first video.*** Before going any further, I urge you to watch the 12-minute 54-second video that accompanies the Preface. To do just so, click **Prologue: A Quick Overview** under the **Navigation and Text** heading, as I've illustrated in Figure 15. This video lesson provides you with a brief overview of how InDesign works and what it can do. It's the perfect way to kick things off.

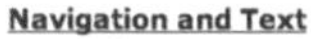

Navigation and Text
- Prologue: A Quick Overview
- Lesson 1: Navigation
- Lesson 2: Text and Frames
- Lesson 3: Typeface, Style, and More

Tables and Graphics
- Lesson 4: Spaces, Indents, and Tabs
- Lesson 5: Pencil, Pen, and Shapes
- Lesson 6: Ways to Place Art

Dynamic Effects, Styles, and Pages
- Lesson 7: The New Effects Palette
- Lesson 8: Duplicating Formatting Attributes
- Lesson 9: Managing Your Pages

Books, Hyperlinks, and Output
- Lesson 10: Making a Book
- Lesson 11: The Final PDF File
- Lesson 12: Previewing Color Separations

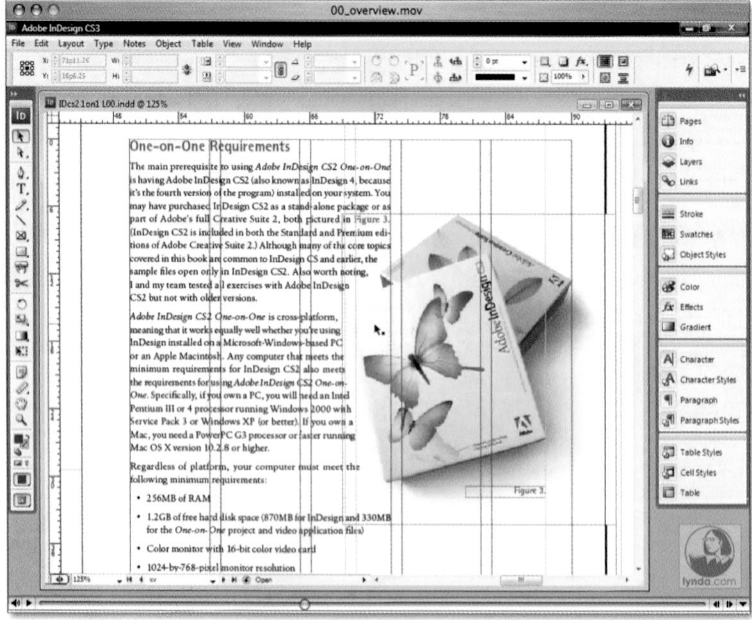

Figure 15.

Structure and Organization

Each of the lessons in the book conforms to a consistent structure, designed to impart skills and understanding through a regimen of practice and dialog. As you build your projects, I explain why you're performing the steps and why InDesign works the way it does.

Each lesson begins with a broad topic overview. Turn the page, and you come to a section called "About This Lesson," which lists the skills you'll learn and directs you to the video-based introduction.

Next come the step-by-step exercises, in which I walk you through some of InDesign's most powerful and essential page-layout functions. A DVD icon appears whenever I ask you to open a file from the *Lesson Files-IDcs3 1on1* folder that you installed on your computer's hard drive. To make my directions crystal clear, command and option names appear in bold type (as in, "choose the **Open** command"). The first appearance of a figure reference appears in colored type. More than 900 full-color, generously sized screen shots and images diagram key steps in your journey, so you're never left scratching your head, puzzling over what to do next. And when I refer you to another step or section, I tell you the exact page number to go to. (Shouldn't every book?)

To make doubly sure there are as few points of confusion as possible, I pepper my descriptions with the very icons you see on screen, critical icons like 👁, *fx*, ◰, and 🔒. So when I direct you to add a page to your document, I don't tell you to click the Create New Page icon at the bottom of the Pages palette. (The only time you see the words *Create New Page* is when you hover your cursor over the icon, which is possible only if you have the experience to know what icon I'm talking about before I even mention its name.) Instead, I tell you to click the ◳ icon, because ◳ is what it is. It meant hand-drawing nearly 400 icons to date, but for you, it was worth it.

PEARL OF WISDOM

Along the way, you'll encounter the occasional "Pearl of Wisdom," which provides insights into how InDesign works and how it fits into the larger worlds of page layout and electronic publishing. While this information is not essential to performing a given step or completing an exercise, it may provide you with valuable context, help you understand why Adobe chose to implement a function the way it did, and even rewire your brain a bit so that you can get more work done with less effort.

More detailed background discussions appear in independent sidebars. These sidebars shed light on the mysteries of color, bit depth, resolution, and other high-level topics that are key to understanding InDesign.

A colored paragraph of text with a rule above and below it calls attention to a special tip or technique that will help you make InDesign work faster and more smoothly.

Some projects are quite ambitious. My enthusiasm for a topic may even take us a bit beyond the stated goal. In such cases, I cordon off the final portion of the exercise and label it "Extra Credit."

EXTRA CREDIT

If you're feeling oversaturated and utterly exhausted, the star icon is your oasis. It's my way of saying, you deserve a break. You can even drop out and skip to the next exercise. On the other hand, if you're the type who believes quitters never prosper (which they don't, incidentally), by all means carry on. You'll be rewarded with a completed project and a wealth of additional tips and insights.

Each lesson ends with a section titled "What Did You Learn?" which features a multiple-choice quiz. Your job is to choose the best description for each of twelve key concepts outlined in the lesson. Answers are printed upside-down at the bottom of the page.

FURTHER INVESTIGATION

Finally, every so often you'll come across a "Further Investigation" marker, which includes information about further reading or video training. Often times, I refer you to the lynda.com Online Training Library, which contains tens of thousands of movies, more than a thousand of them by me. And all available to you, by subscription, every minute of every waking day.

Just to be absolutely certain you don't feel baited into making yet another purchase, I've arranged a time-limited back door for you. Go to *www.lynda.com/dekeID* and sign up for the 7-Day Free Trial Account. This gives you access to the *entire* Online Training Library, including all the movies in my "Further Investigation" recommendations. But remember, your seven days start counting down the moment you sign up, so time your Free Trial wisely.

Then again, if you find the service so valuable you elect to subscribe, we're happy to have you. It's all good.

The Scope of This Book

No one book can teach you everything there is to know about InDesign, and this one is no exception. But I do manage to tackle what I consider to be the most important functions. For those of you who are looking for information on a specific aspect of InDesign, here's a brief list of the topics and features discussed in this book:

- Lesson 1: Ways to start a document, including opening an InDesign document, creating a new document, setting up guides, and saving a document; customizing the interface, working with palettes, and saving workspaces; and managing documents and assets from the Adobe Bridge
- Lesson 2: Adding text to a document, including flowing text between multiple frames, editing and selecting text, the Check Spelling command, and the path type tool
- Lesson 3: Formatting attributes, including font, type size, leading, color, paragraph spacing, alignment, justification, hyphenation, and paragraph composition, as well as glyphs and OpenType
- Lesson 4: Assembling lists and tables, including drop caps, tabbed lists, hanging indents, automatic bullets and numbering, line breaks, and spacing characters; the Tabs palette; and the Table function
- Lesson 5: Drawing tools and path attributes, including the line, pencil, pen, and shape tools; the Color, Swatches, Stroke, Gradient, Align, and Pathfinder palettes; and the Compound Paths command
- Lesson 6: Working with imported artwork, including cropping, the scale and free transform tools, the Transform and Text Wrap palettes, inline graphics, and anchored objects
- Lesson 7: Applying transparency, including the Effects palette, blend modes, the Drop Shadow, Glow, and Feather commands, clipping paths, alpha channels, layered PSD images, and the Flattener Preview palette
- Lesson 8: Style sheets, including the eyedropper, paragraph styles, the Based On and Next Style options, quick apply, character styles, nested style sheets, cell styles, table styles, and object styles

- Lesson 9: Document structure, including page numbering, sections, master pages, layers, the Structure bay, the Tags palette, and XML automation
- Lesson 10: Long-document functions, including making books, file synchronization, the Table of Contents command, and the Index palette
- Lesson 11: Creating an interactive PDF document, including the Bookmarks, Hyperlinks, and State palettes, embedding sounds and movies, and the Export command
- Lesson 12: Print functions, including the Print command, overprinting, and the Trap Presets palette, as well as the Preflight and Package commands

To find out where I discuss a specific feature, please consult the Index, which begins on page 511.

While I cover almost every single aspect of InDesign—more than any other tutorial guide on the market—a few specialized topics fall outside the scope of this book. These include footnotes, baseline grids, scripting, the Library palette, snippets, Version Cue (included as part of the Creative Suite), and cross-media export to XHTML and Dreamweaver.

FURTHER INVESTIGATION

If these topics are of interest to you, you'll find plenty of information available online and on demand at lynda.com. Of particular interest are InDesign training videos from my esteemed colleagues David Blatner, Anne-Marie Concepcion, Taz Tally, Ted LoCascio, and Brian Wood. (Not to mention, more than 150 hours of Photoshop and Illustrator training from yours truly). You won't believe how much quality information is available at your beck and call for the price of a click. Go to *www.lynda.com/dekeID* and sign up for your seven days.

I now invite you to turn your attention to Lesson 1, "Starting a Document." I hope you'll agree with me that *Adobe InDesign CS3 One-on-One*'s combination of step-by-step lessons and video introductions provides the best learning experience of any InDesign training resource on the market.

LESSON 1

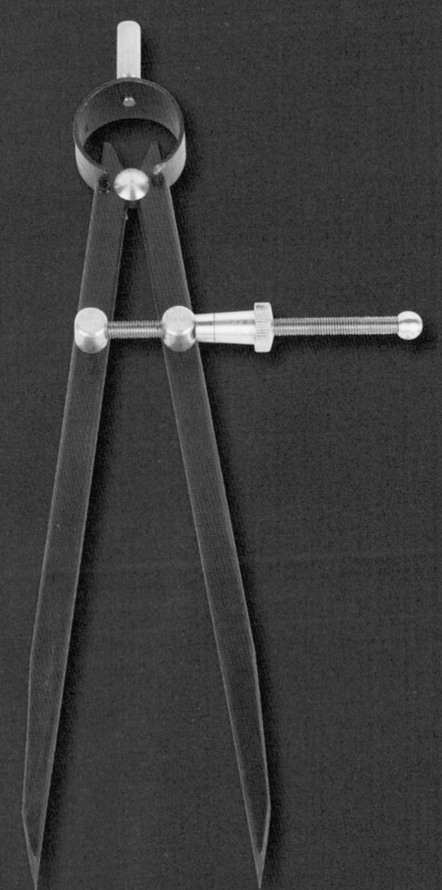

STARTING A DOCUMENT

EVEN BY computer industry standards, publishing is a volatile business. Adobe's PostScript printing language gave us the ability to combine text and graphics without traditional paste-up, but has since conceded cutting-edge functions such as transparency to the more flexible Portable Document Format (PDF). PageMaker single-handedly created a multimillion-dollar industry, only to watch QuarkXPress charm away its professional design audience just a few years later. Apple, the sole supplier of early publishing machines, now garners most of its revenue from its consumer products and media sales. Even the industry's original moniker, *desktop publishing*, has fallen out of favor. Amateurs engage in desktop publishing; professionals operate in the more refined realms of document production, print media, electronic publishing, and page design.

So I guess it figures that more than 20 years after the publishing revolution began, it appears primed for another coup, this time in the form of InDesign. Nearly a decade since Adobe released what many gleefully termed its "Quark killer," XPress remains in heavy use. But despite recent advances, relatively few of Quark's customers are upgrading, robbing the program of its fuel for innovation. Meanwhile, InDesign is on a slow but steady march, expanding its base of users one print house, advertising agency, and periodical at a time. And now, depending on what report you read, InDesign has finally become the dominant application. Whether that's true or not, three things are for sure: PageMaker is dead, XPress is withering, and InDesign is the tool with a future.

Fortunately, the tool with a future just so happens to be a first-rate piece of software. By most accounts, InDesign is several times more capable than QuarkXPress and equally more efficient in its approach. That's why I want you to put this book down—if not now, well then, when you get a moment—and pat yourself on the back. You made a wise decision the day you decided to take on InDesign.

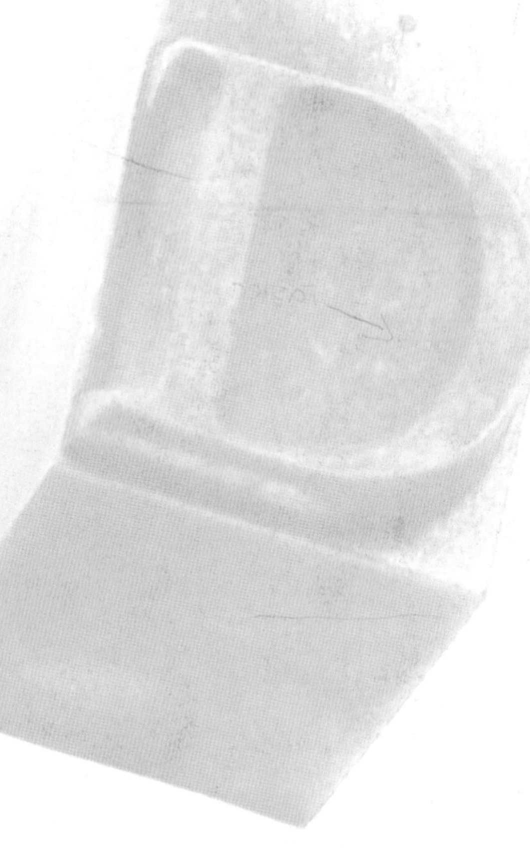

ABOUT THIS LESSON

Project Files

Before beginning the exercises, make sure you've copied the lesson files from the DVD, as directed in Step 3 on page xvii of the Preface. This should result in a folder called *Lesson Files-IDcs3 1on1* on your desktop. We'll be working with the files inside the *Lesson 01* subfolder.

Before you can take advantage of InDesign's state-of-the-art page-composition functions, you must know how to open a file, set up a new document, adjust columns and guides, and save your work to disk. In this lesson, you'll learn how to:

- Open a document created in InDesign . . . . page 6
- Make a spanking new document . . . . page 11
- Change margins, columns, and ruler guides . . . . . page 15
- Save the positions of palettes and other interface elements . . . . page 24
- Use the Adobe Bridge to organize and manage your digital assets . . . . page 29
- Save your finished document as a native InDesign or template file . . . . page 39

Video Lesson 1: Navigation

Another topic I urge you to master as soon as possible is navigation. Not *doing* anything to a document, mind you, just moving around inside it: magnifying an area, panning to a different part of a page, and so on. Navigation is the topic of the first video lesson on the DVD. To watch this video, insert the DVD and double-click the file *IDcs3 Videos.html*. After the page loads in your Web browser, click **Lesson 1: Navigation** under the **Navigation and Text** heading. The movie lasts 19 minutes and 20 seconds, during which you'll learn these shortcuts:

Operation	Windows shortcut	Macintosh shortcut
Typical or High Quality display mode	F2, F3*	F2, F3*
Zoom in or out	Ctrl+= (plus), Ctrl+− (minus)	⌘-=, ⌘-−
Zoom to 100 percent or fit page	Ctrl+1 (one), Ctrl+0 (zero)	⌘-1, ⌘-0
Fit spread or pasteboard in window	Ctrl+Alt+0, Ctrl+Shift+Alt+0	⌘-Option-0, ⌘-Shift-Option-0
Zoom in with magnifying glass	Ctrl+spacebar-click or drag	⌘-spacebar-click or drag
Zoom out with magnifying glass	Ctrl+Alt+spacebar-click	⌘-Option-spacebar-click
Scroll with hand tool	Alt+spacebar-drag in document	Option-spacebar-drag in document
Cycle between open document windows	Ctrl+~ (tilde)	⌘-~
Highlight zoom value	Ctrl+Alt+5	⌘-Option-5
Switch to previous or next page spread	Alt+Page Up, Alt+Page Down	Option-Page Up, Option-Page Down
Go back or forward to last viewed page	Ctrl+Page Up, Ctrl+Page Down	⌘-Page Up, ⌘-Page Down
Hide or collapse toolbox and/or palettes	Tab, Shift+Tab, Ctrl+Alt+Tab	Tab, Shift-Tab, ⌘-Option-Tab

* Works only if you loaded the dekeKeys keyboard shortcuts (as directed on page xix of the Preface).

What Is InDesign?

Like any page-composition program, InDesign lets you combine elements from a variety of sources to make multipage documents. You can import text from a word processor or enter text directly in InDesign. You can import photographs and high-resolution line art, as well as create artwork with InDesign's drawing tools. In this regard, InDesign is a kind of page-making mill. You pour text and graphics into its hopper, mix them together using your carefully practiced design skills, and eventually produce fully rendered pages, like the one pictured at the end of Figure 1-1.

Once the raw materials are in the hopper, InDesign invites you to place them on the page. You can establish regular columns of type or adjust each column independently. You can align text and graphics using a variety of grids and guidelines. You can wrap text around graphics, place text along curved lines, and even insert graphics into text blocks as if they were letters entered from the keyboard. And all the while, text and graphic objects are independently editable. You have only to drag an object to move it to a new location, scale it, or slant it to a more interesting angle.

Although InDesign is more than adequate for designing single pages, it really comes to life when laying out multipage documents. You can add and reorder pages with ease, automatically number pages, and repeat regular design elements from one page to the next. When constructing long documents like books, InDesign helps you generate a table of contents and an index. And you can even create automated templates to expedite the layout of newsletters and other periodicals.

Most InDesign documents are bound for print, so it makes sense that the program is well versed in outputting full-color pages and separating inks for commercial reproduction. But print isn't your only option. InDesign exports directly to PDF, ideal for designing interactive documents with bookmarks, hyperlinks, and other navigation functions. You can also export tagged files that can be used as the basis for Web pages.

Plainly put, there's no better program for designing documents. InDesign allows you to control every phase of the page-layout process with glorious precision and unparalleled control. As proof of my commitment, I submit to you this very document. I used InDesign to create every page of this book—not to mention a few thousand pages before them.

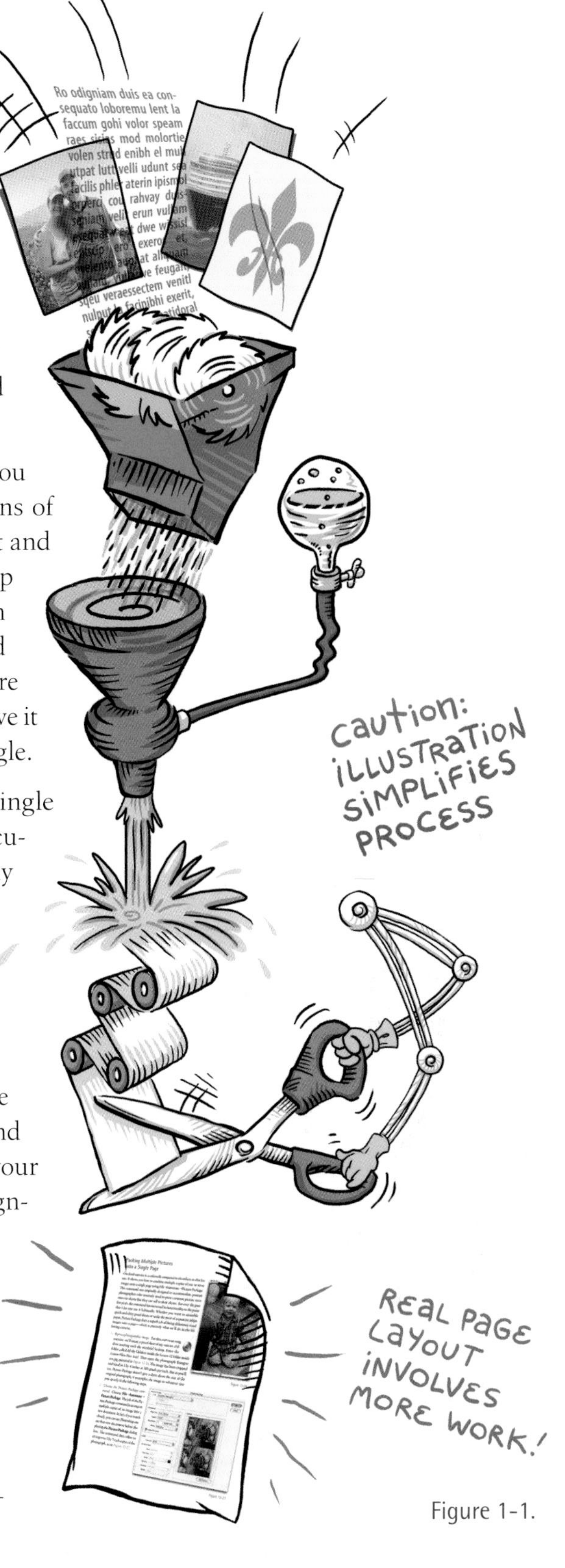
caution: illustration simplifies process
Real page layout involves more work!

Figure 1-1.

Opening an InDesign Document

Opening an InDesign document is pretty much like opening a document in any application, Adobe or otherwise. It all begins with the Open command. That said, there are a few possible stumbling points, which this exercise shows you how to circumnavigate.

Figure 1-2.

1. ***Get to the Open a File dialog box.*** Choose **File→Open** from the menu bar. Alternatively, you can press Ctrl+O (⌘-O on the Mac). Either way, you get the **Open a File** dialog box. Figure 1-2 shows the dialog box as it appears on the Mac under OS X Leopard (10.5).

PEARL OF WISDOM

When you first launch InDesign, you'll get the infamous welcome screen, just as you do the first time you open any Creative Suite application. In the past, you were probably justified in getting rid of it as fast as you could turn off the Show This Dialog at Startup check box. But the CS3 welcome screen is moderately useful, so you might want to spend a few minutes inspecting its options. Not only do you get a handy list of recently opened files and new document types, but there are links to some helpful resources and community sites as well. If these seem like options you'll use, great; if not, turn on the **Don't Show Again** check box to dismiss the screen forever, and then choose **File→Open** as indicated above. (And it's not really *forever* forever; you can revisit the screen any time you like by choosing Help→Welcome Screen.)

2. ***Navigate to the Lesson 01 folder.*** Assuming you installed the lesson files on your desktop, here's how to get to the *Lesson 01* folder:

   - Click the **Desktop** icon located along the left side of the dialog box to display the files and folders on your computer's desktop. (If you don't see a Desktop icon on the Mac, press ⌘-D instead.)
   - Locate and double-click the *Lesson Files-IDcs3 1on1* folder.
   - Finally, double-click the *Lesson 01* folder. You're in like Flynn.

3. ***Select a file.*** Click the file called *Grand opening.indd* to select it. In this opening exercise about opening files, it seems appropriate to open a document about an opening. Assuming you're open to that, of course.

If you're using a Windows-based PC and you don't see the document you want, you probably need to change the setting in the Files of Type pop-up menu at the bottom of the dialog box, as in Figure 1-3. Although this menu is useful for narrowing the choices in a folder full of files—you can view just QuarkXPress documents, for example—it may prevent you from seeing the InDesign document you want. For day-to-day work, the default setting of All Readable Files is your best bet.

4. ***Specify how you want to open the file.*** You can specify how you want to open a document using the round radio buttons in the bottom-left corner of the Open a File dialog box. These options generally come into play when you are working with a *template*, which is a special kind of InDesign file that serves as the starting point for a series of similar documents. For instance, if you publish a weekly newsletter, you can create a template that contains the basic layout settings and formatting attributes.

   Here's a rundown of how the three radio buttons (labeled Open As on the PC) work:

   - Most of the time, you'll leave the Normal radio button (called Open Normal on the Mac) selected. If you are opening a standard InDesign (*.indd*) file, the program opens the original file. When opening a template (*.indt*), InDesign opens an untitled copy of the file so that the original template is preserved.
   - To make changes to a template file, select the Original (or Open Original) radio button.
   - To work with a copy of an InDesign file and preserve the original, select the Copy radio button (named Open Copy on the Mac).

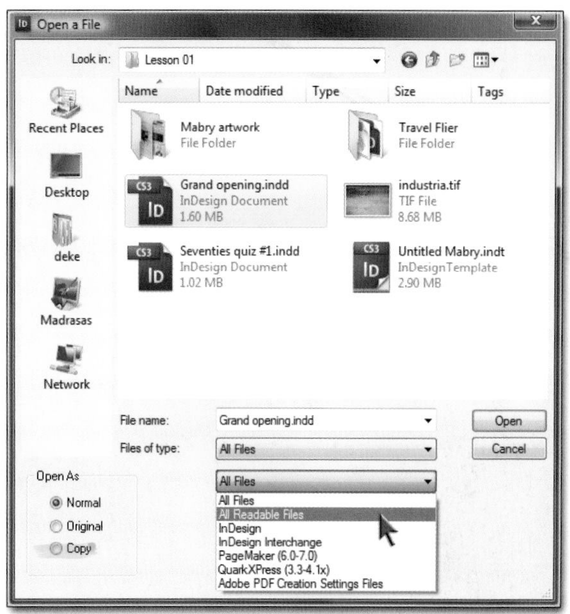

Figure 1-3.

PEARL OF WISDOM

If you're used to templates in, say, Microsoft Word—which lets you assign a template to an existing file or use it to fill out fields in a form—lower your expectations. In InDesign, a template is a file that opens untitled, thus protecting the original. End of story.

For our purposes, select **Normal** on the PC or **Open Normal** on the Mac. (Note that selecting Original, or Open Original on the Mac, would produce the same result because *Grand opening.indd* is not a template file.)

Interface and Document Window

The first time you run InDesign CS3, the interface is so minimized you hardly know it's there. But a few minutes of poking around unleashes a Pandora's Box, bursting with all varieties of tools, icons, and other gizmos. The following list explains some of the more pivotal interface elements—all labeled in the figure below.

- **Cursor:** The cursor tracks mouse movements and changes to reflect the active tool or operation. Keep an eye on it and you'll have a better sense of what you're doing.
- **Cluster bar:** I call a set of stacked palettes represented by side-by-side tabs (such as Pages, Layers, and Navigator below) a *cluster*. The light gray area above the tabs is the cluster bar. Drag the bar to move a cluster. Click the bar to collapse or expand a cluster.
- **Control palette:** The horizontal palette along the top of the screen provides access to InDesign's most commonly used options. The palette is context sensitive, changing to accommodate the selected object or active tool.

Press Ctrl+Alt+6 (⌘-Option-6) to hide or show the control palette. Press Ctrl+6 (⌘-6) to highlight the first numerical value. Then press Tab to advance or Shift+Tab to back up.

- **Docking pane:** A docking pane contains many palette clusters, stacked one atop the other. Drag a cluster bar and drop it onto a docking pane to add palettes to the pane. Drop a palette next to a pane to begin a new pane.
- **Document window:** Each open document appears in a separate window. This is where you edit text, position graphics, and assemble your pages.
- **Guides:** The colored lines in the document window are nonprinting "magnetic" guides, meaning that objects snap into place when dragged close to them.
- **Menu bar:** Click a name in the menu bar to display a list of commands. Click a command followed by three dots (such as Export...) to display a *dialog box*. Otherwise, the command works right away.

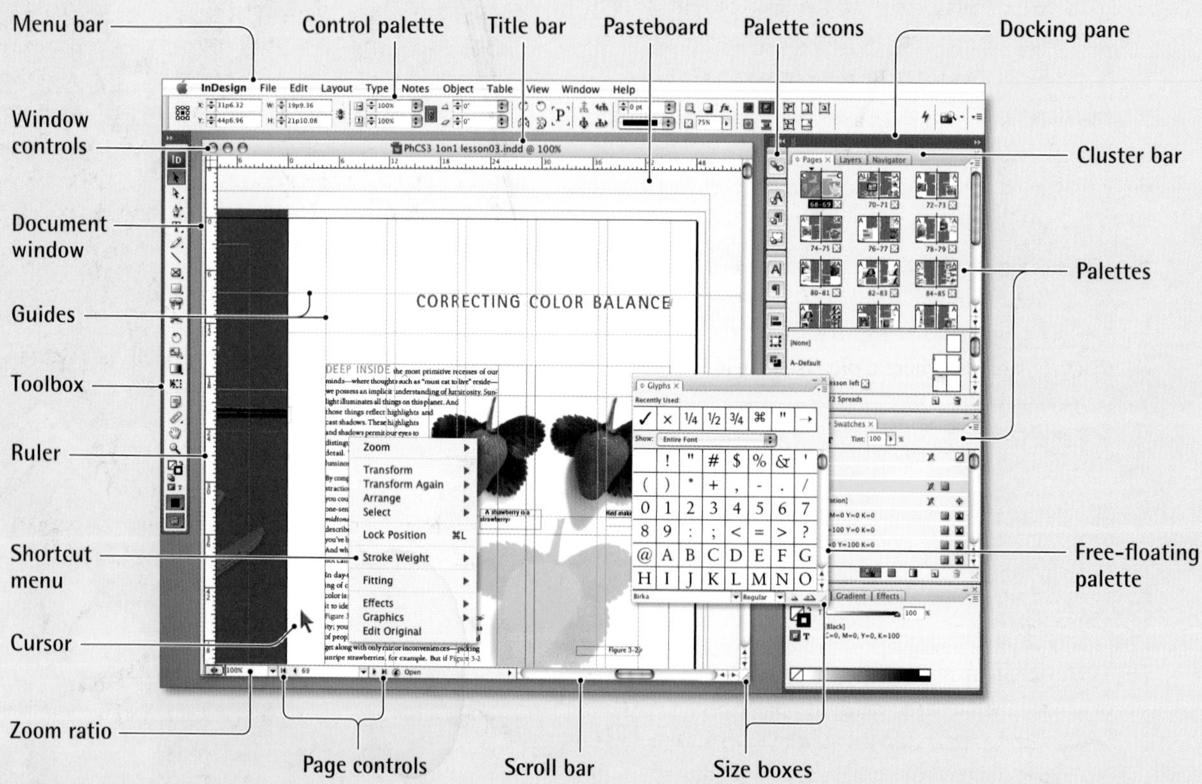

- **Page controls:** The controls in the bottom-left corner of the document window let you switch pages, either sequentially or by entering a specific page number.

Shift+Page Down takes you to the next page; Shift+Page Up goes to the previous one. For a specific page, press Ctrl+J (⌘-J), type a number, and press Enter or Return.

- **Palettes:** A palette is a window of options that remains visible as you work. (In CS3, Adobe inexplicably and inaccurately calls these *panels*; but they remain, as ever, palettes.) To switch between palettes, click a named tab. Move a palette by dragging its tab. Drop a palette outside a docking pane to make it free-floating. Click the tiny ▾≡ in the top-right corner to bring up the palette menu.

Drag the left edge of a palette to make a pane wider or narrower. Drag the bottom edge to make it taller or shorter. InDesign scales neighboring palettes to accommodate.

- **Palette icons:** When you collapse a docking pane, InDesign shows its palettes as icons. Click an icon to temporarily display or hide the palette. Drag the left edge of the pane to hide or show palette names next to the icons.
- **Pasteboard:** The blank area beyond the pages in the document window is called the pasteboard. Think of the pasteboard as your junk drawer; it's a great place to stash text and graphics you might need later.
- **Ruler:** Press Ctrl+R (or ⌘-R) to frame the document window with two rulers, one above and one to the left. Tick marks track your movements. In the U.S., the default unit of measure is *picas*, where a pica is ⅙ inch.

To change the unit for a single ruler, right-click it and select a different setting. To cycle both rulers from one unit to the next, press Ctrl+Shift+Alt+U (or ⌘-Shift-Option-U).

- **Scroll bars:** Located opposite the rulers, the scroll bars let you pan the document horizontally or vertically to display hidden areas.
- **Shortcut menu:** Click the right mouse button to display a menu of options. (On the Mac, you can press the Control key and click.) Like the control palette, the shortcut menu changes to suit a selected object or the active tool.
- **Size box:** Drag the bottom-right corner of a window or scalable palette to make it bigger or smaller.
- **Title bar:** The title of the last-saved version of a file appears at the top of the document window. Click the title bar to make a document active so you can edit its contents; drag the title bar to move a document window.

To switch between open windows from the keyboard, press Ctrl+[~] (⌘-[~]). On a U.S. keyboard, the [~] key is located in the upper-left corner of the keyboard, next to the [!].

- **Toolbox:** Click an icon in the toolbox to select a tool; then use the tool in the document window. A small black triangle at the bottom-right of an icon means multiple tools share a single *slot*; click and hold the icon to display a flyout menu of alternate tools. Or press Alt (or Option) and click a slot to cycle between tools.

Press the Tab key to hide the toolbox and all palettes. Press Tab again to bring them back. To hide or show all palettes except the toolbox and control palette, press Shift+Tab. To expand or collapse palettes attached to the sides of the screen, press Ctrl+Alt+Tab (⌘-Option-Tab on the Mac).

- **Window controls:** The title bar contains three controls that let you hide (min), size (max), and close a document window. As illustrated below, the Mac controls are on the left; the Windows controls are on the right.

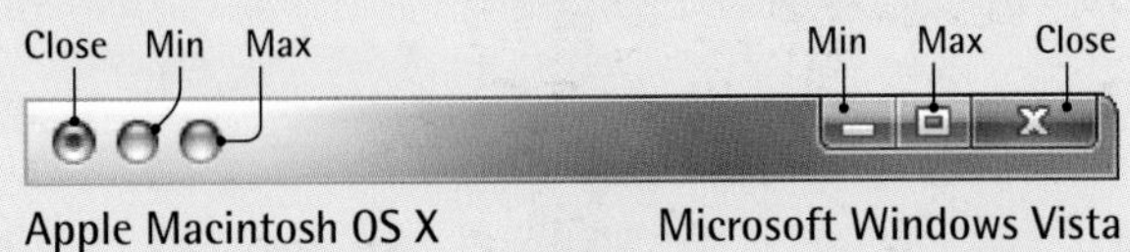

- **Zoom ratio:** The percentage value in the bottom-left corner of the document window lists the magnification of the document on screen. Raise the value to zoom in; lower the value to zoom out. For more information, watch Video Lesson 1, "Navigation," on the DVD (see page 4).

To highlight the zoom ratio value, press Ctrl+Alt+5 (or ⌘-Option-5). Then type a value between 5 and 4,000 percent and press Enter or Return. When the value is highlighted, press the ↑ or ↓ key to zoom in or out by 25 percent increments.

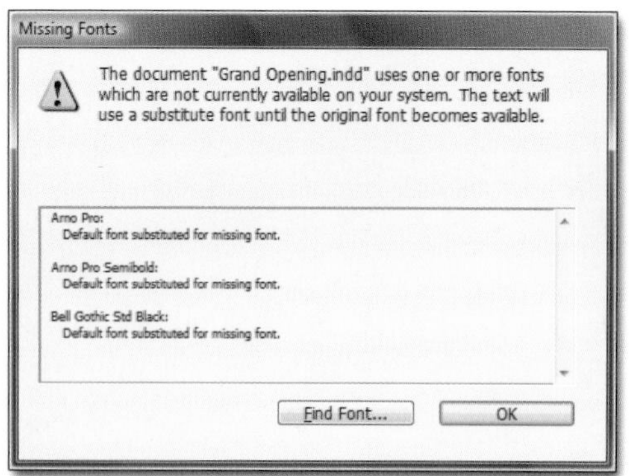

Figure 1-4.

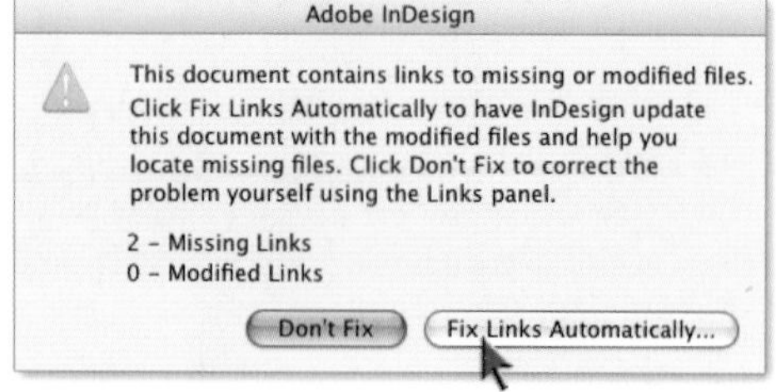

Figure 1-5.

Figure 1-6.

5. ***Open the document.*** Click the **Open** button or press the Enter or Return key to open the document in InDesign. If the document appears on screen, all is well. But be aware that InDesign might ask you to respond to an alert message or two before opening the file:
   - For example, if you own the stand-alone version of InDesign CS3, it's possible that the program will complain that one or more fonts used in the document are missing from your system, as in Figure 1-4. If so, click **OK** to tell InDesign to substitute whatever fonts it deems appropriate.
   - If you established your own color settings—something other than what I asked you to do in the Preface (see Step 7, page xviii)—InDesign may greet you with the **Profile or Policy Mismatch** message. If so, just click **OK** to make it go away. If not (as is more likely), no worries.
6. ***Fix any missing or modified links.*** There's also a good chance you'll encounter the alert message shown in Figure 1-5. When you import a graphic into a document, InDesign avoids any unnecessary duplication of information by creating a link to the graphic file on disk. But if the graphic file has been moved since the last time the InDesign document was saved—as invariably occurs when copying files from a DVD to your hard drive, for example—InDesign may get confused and be unable to find the graphic. If that happens, do the following:
   - Click **Fix Links Automatically** to tell InDesign to hunt down the graphic file and reestablish the links on its own.
   - If clicking the button takes you to a **Find** dialog box, look for *Industria.tif* in the *Lesson 01* folder. When you find it, select the file and click **Open**. A few moments later, InDesign displays the document in a new window, as in Figure 1-6.

I'll be asking you to open and modify lots of documents in this book. When you arrive at the successful conclusion of an exercise, as you have now, you may do with the document as you will. You can inspect it, modify it, or ignore it altogether. To tidy up your screen and move on, click the ☒ icon in the title bar (⊗ on the Mac). Or you can choose **File→Close**.

Setting Up a New Document

All layout programs let you create new documents, but few let you do so as meticulously as InDesign. InDesign's controls permit you to establish a solid foundation, which in turn serves as the backbone for a successful design. Armed with a structure of margins, columns, and bleeds, you have everything you need to structure your content, solve problems, and concentrate your creative energies. Without that foundation, all you have is an empty page.

The goal of the next exercise is to create a new multipage document. For the sake of example, we'll create a document that subscribes to the page dimensions and margins at work in this very book.

1. *Choose the New command.* Choose **File→New→Document** or press Ctrl+N (⌘-N on the Mac). InDesign displays the **New Document** dialog box, as in Figure 1-7.

2. *Enter the number of pages.* Ever helpful, InDesign highlights the first option, **Number of Pages**, so you can dig right in. Change the value to 12.

   Why 12? First, it's an even number, so the document will start on a right-hand page and end on a left one. Second, if you don't know exactly how long a final document will run, 12 pages give you room to experiment without running so long that you have to delete a lot of pages later. In other words, it's an educated shot in the dark.

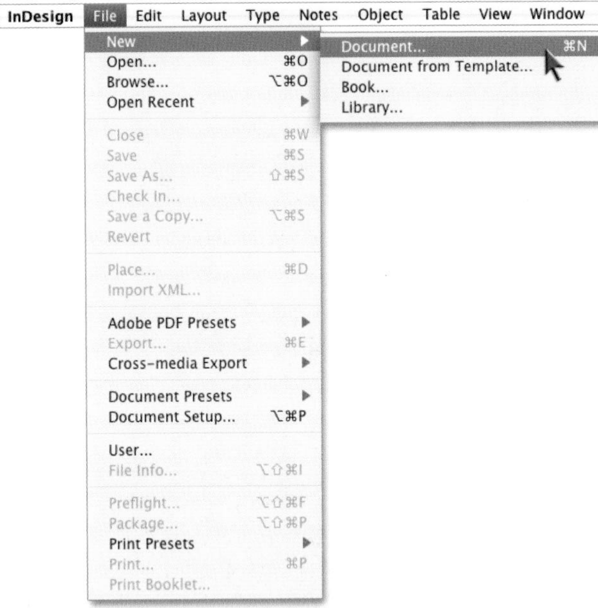

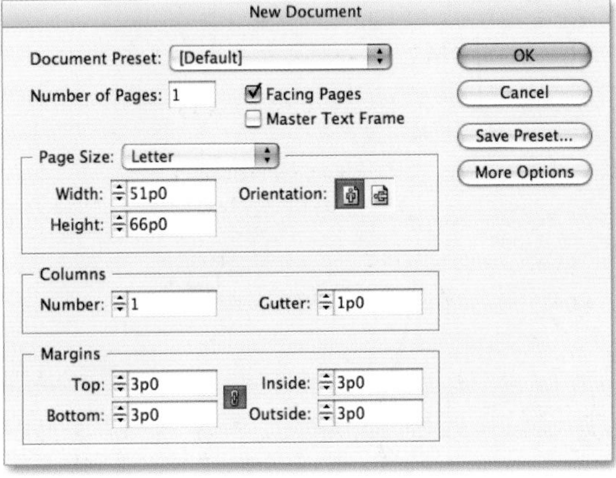

Figure 1-7.

PEARL OF WISDOM

Bear in mind, every value that you enter into the New Document dialog box can be modified later. You can add or delete pages, change margins and columns, and even set up new pages with independent margins and columns. So if you have only a vague idea of how you want to set up your new document, don't fret. Just rough in some numbers and consider the resulting document a work in progress.

3. *Turn on Facing Pages.* As illustrated in Figure 1-8 on the next page, your everyday multipage publication comprises many pairs of facing pages. Examples include newsletters, magazines, books—anything printed on both sides of a page and bound or folded along a spine. The left-hand page bears an even page number, and hence is called the *even page*; the one

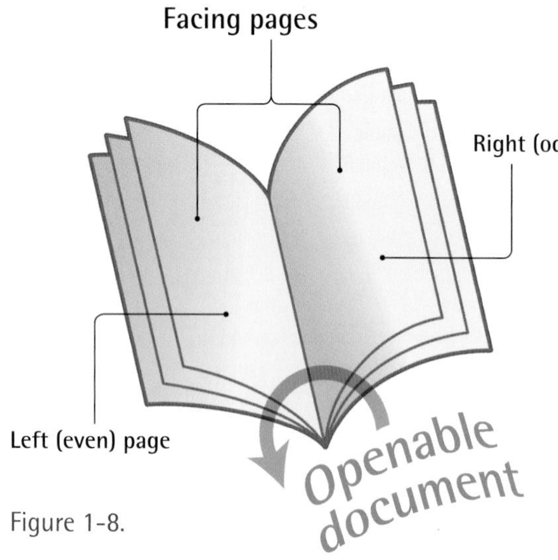

Figure 1-8.

on the right sports an odd number, making it the *odd page*. If you intend to create such a document, select the **Facing Pages** check box. When this option is on, InDesign makes each pair of pages symmetrical. This means the two inner margins (the right margin on the even page and the left on the odd) are the same, as are the outer margins (left on even, right on odd).

PEARL OF WISDOM

About the only time you want to turn off Facing Pages is when: 1) your final document includes strictly single-sided pages, as in the case of a legal contract, or 2) you plan to output the file to PDF and distribute it electronically, in which case the traditional spine-bound document metaphor (Figure 1-8) doesn't apply. When Facing Pages is off, InDesign treats each page the same, with consistent left and right margins, unless you specify otherwise.

4. ***Leave Master Text Frame turned off.*** InDesign lets you create automatic text boxes, called *frames*, to house the text in your document. But it's so easy to create frames as you enter or import text that there's little advantage in having InDesign set them up in advance. To see the Master Text Frame check box in action, watch Video Lesson 2, "Text and Frames," on the DVD (see page 48). But for the present, leave the option off.

5. ***Adjust the page dimensions.*** If you want your pages to conform to a common paper format, such as letter, A4, or tabloid, choose the size from the **Page Size** pop-up menu. But don't think those choices are the only ones available. Although your inkjet or laser printer may limit you to certain paper formats (most can't accommodate tabloid, for example), commercial printers can trim paper to any size you like, provided that the page fits on the press. Meanwhile, if you intend to publish your document to PDF and have no plans to print it, why then no paper, no problems.

   The pages in this book measure 8 inches wide by 9¾ inches tall, slightly narrower and shorter than a letter-sized page but quite large by book standards. To create such a page, enter the desired dimensions into the **Width** and **Height** option boxes. Only problem is, InDesign's default units of measure are *picas* and *points*. A pica is ⅙ inch; a point is $^1/_{12}$ pica, or $^1/_{72}$ inch. The default Width value of 51p0 means 51 picas and 0 points, which translates to 8½ inches.

PEARL OF WISDOM

If you don't like picas, you can choose Edit→Preferences (on the Mac, InDesign→Preferences) and click Units & Increments to switch to inches or some other unit. But I urge you not to, if only to strike accord with the rest of the design community. Picas and points are the standard for page layout in the U.S. and England, and they enjoy wide support across all varieties of design applications and hardware.

And besides, why switch when you can convert from inches on-the-fly? Here's how. Press the Tab key one or more times to advance to the Width value. Then type 8 inches (8in or 8i for short). Press Tab to advance to the Height value. The moment you do, InDesign converts your inches to picas, making the Width value 48p0, or 48 picas. Next, enter 9.75 inches (or 9.75in) and press Tab again. The Height value becomes 58p6, which is 58 picas 6 points, or 58.5 picas.

Just for fun, Figure 1-9 shows the many other ways to enter alternative measurements, including millimeters and ciceros. (Like a pica, the European *cicero* comprises 12 points, but each point—sometimes called a *didot*—is about 1/68 inch.) Note that you can spell out units or use a number of abbreviations. You can also perform small bits of math.

9.75 inches	702 points	247.65 millimeters
9.75inches	702 point	247.65mm
9.75 inch	702pt	24.765 centimeters
9.75inch	picas 702	24.765cm
9.75 in	pica 702	24cm+7.65mm
9.75in	pica702	24765/100mm
9.75i	p702	54.9 ciceros
9.75"	9i+4.5p	54.9 cicero
9"+.75"	9i+4p6	54.9c
10"-0.25"	9i+54pt	54 cicero 10.8
39/4"	9i+p54	54cicero10.8
39*0.25"	10i-1.5p	54c10.8
58.5 picas	10i-1p6	ciceros 658.8
58.5 pica	10i-18pt	cicero658.8
58.5pica	10i-p18	c658.8
58.5p		
58 pica 6		
58pica6		
58p 6		
58p6		

50 different ways to say "9 3/4 inches" in InDesign

Figure 1-9.

6. ***Specify two columns.*** The **Columns** values determine how many columns of type you intend to place on a page. InDesign automatically flows text into these columns, but you can modify the dimensions of a text frame and adjust the column guides any time you like.

   This book employs a loose two-column design with text on the inside of the page and graphics on the outside. So tab down to the next section and change the **Number** value to 2. The **Gutter** value defines the distance between columns; leave this set to 1p0, or 1 pica. Note that InDesign delivers columns of equal width. If you want to create columns of different widths, like the ones in this book, you'll have to adjust the columns manually, as I explain in the next exercise ("Adjusting Margins and Guides," page 15).

7. ***Increase the margins.*** The **Margins** values define the amount of room between the far edge of your content and the perimeter of the page. When Facing Pages is active

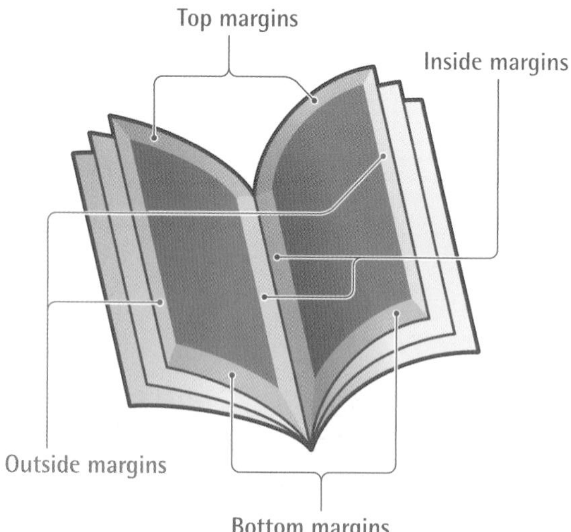

Figure 1-10.

(Step 3, page 11), InDesign calculates inside and outside margins, as well as top and bottom margins (see Figure 1-10). If Facing Pages is off, you must set the left and right margins.

The default Margins values of 3 picas (½ inch) apiece give a design room to breathe and guarantee that nothing will get clipped when the final pages are trimmed. This book includes a roomier bottom margin to accommodate the page number, as well as some extra space along the inside margin to account for the area lost in the deep furrow where the pages meet the spine. So change both the **Bottom** and **Inside** values to 4p6 (¾ inch) while leaving **Top** and **Outside** set to 3p0.

Oh, but easier said than done. By default, InDesign likes to keep all four of these settings the same. Convince it you know what you're doing by clicking the icon to the right of the Top and Bottom options to break the chain. The icon becomes a broken icon, indicating that the four measurements can be set independently.

---

8. ***Expand the dialog box.*** Click the **More Options** button in the upper-right area of the dialog box to reveal the Bleed and Slug options (see Figure 1-11), which permit you to increase the size of the printable area of a page beyond its strict Page Size boundaries.

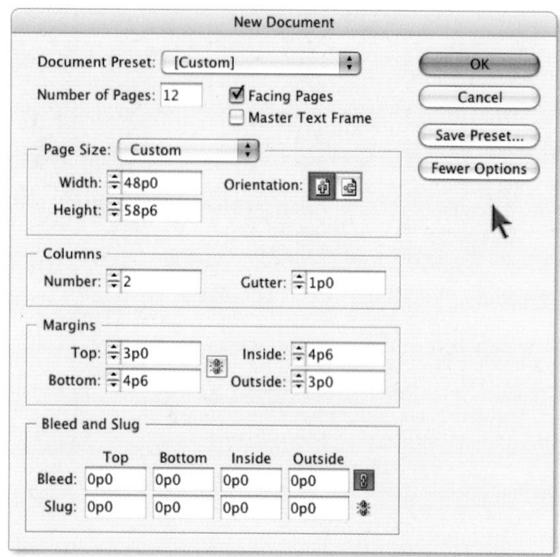

Figure 1-11.

PEARL OF WISDOM

If you want a text or graphic object to extend all the way to the edge of a page—like the big, colorful artwork at the outset of each lesson in this book—you have to add an extra margin outside the page boundary called a *bleed*. This gives your commercial printer some wiggle room when trimming the page, so that the finished product doesn't end up with a tiny sliver of exposed, uninked paper. The *slug* is an additional area beyond the bleed that contains project titles, handling instructions, and any other stuff you want to communicate to your commercial printer. In Figure 1-12 on the facing page, the slug boundary appears as a thin blue line, the bleed boundary is red, and the trim size is yellow. Nothing beyond the trim size (as indicated by the crop marks) will appear in the final product you receive back from the printer.

---

9. ***Set all Bleed values to 1 pica.*** Typical bleeds range from 0.5 to 1.5 picas. We'll split the difference. Check to make sure that the icon to the right of the Bleed settings is active. Then change one of the values to 1p0 and press the Tab key to update the others.

10. ***Set all Slug values to 3 picas.*** Click the link icon to the right of the final **Slug** option to turn on the link. Then change any Slug value to 3p0 (or 0.5in) and again press the Tab key.

11. ***Save your settings as a new document preset.*** After putting this much work into adjusting settings in the New Document dialog box, you don't want to lose them. To save your settings—even if you think there's just a hint of a chance that you might want to use them again—click the **Save Preset** button. Then name the new preset "One-on-One," as in Figure 1-13, and click the **OK** button. A new option called One-on-One appears in the Document Preset pop-up menu at the top of the dialog box. In the future, choosing that option loads all the settings you applied in this exercise.

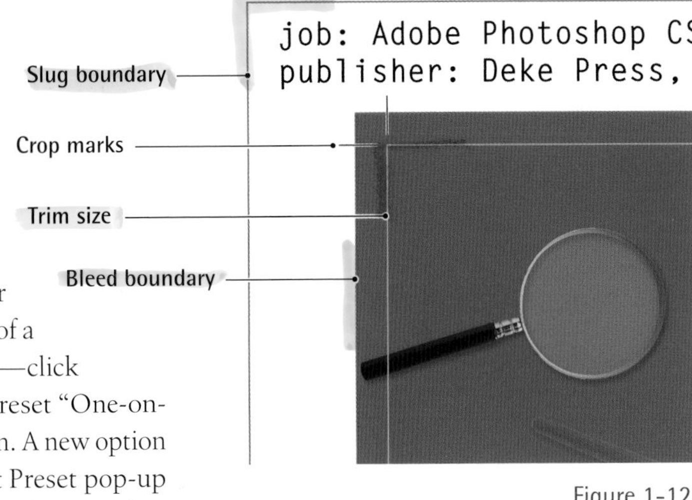

Figure 1-12.

12. ***Click the OK button.*** Or press the Enter or Return key to accept your settings and create a blank document inside a new document window. Your document should look like the one in Figure 1-14 on the next page, with purple page margins, a red bleed boundary, and a blue slug boundary.

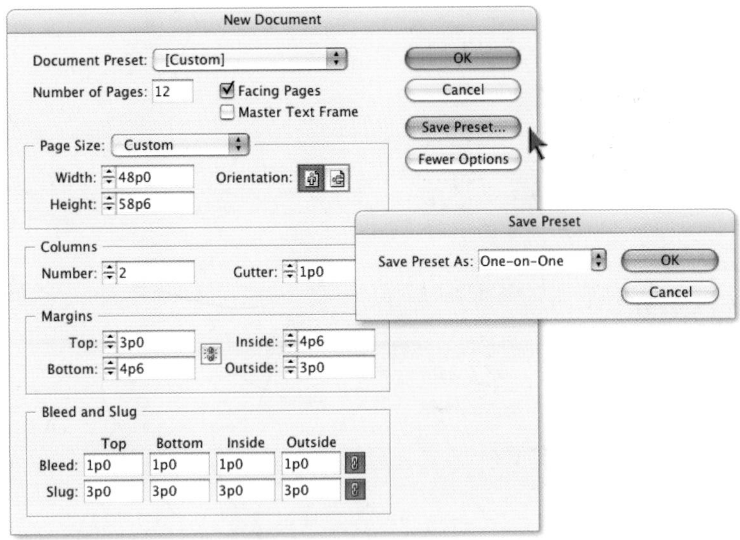

Figure 1-13.

Now that you've created a pristine new document—complete with page dimensions, margins, and bleed and slug boundaries—you'll learn a few ways to change it in the next exercise.

Adjusting Margins and Guides

As mentioned, every page attribute that you specify in the New Document dialog box can be changed long after you create a document. But instead of adjusting everything from a single dialog box, as in the preceding exercise, you have to flit back and forth between a few. One dialog box affects the entire document, another changes one or two active pages, and a third offers access to options that aren't even available in the New Document dialog box.

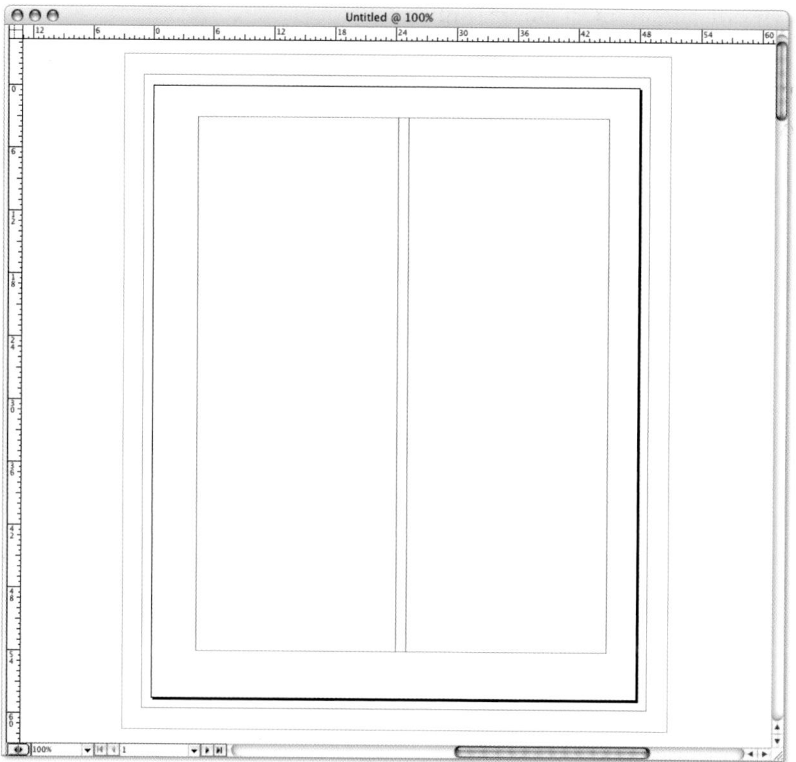

Figure 1-14.

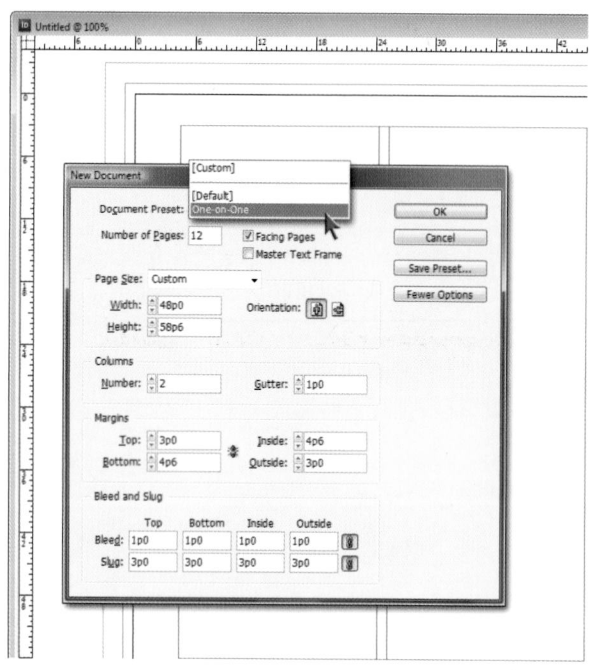

Figure 1-15.

In this exercise you use one of those dialog boxes to explore how to change margins, columns, page numbers, and custom guidelines in the new document you just created so that it matches the layout used for this book.

1. ***Create a new document.*** If the new document from the preceding exercise remains open, skip to Step 2. Otherwise, choose **File→New→Document** to display the **New Document** dialog box. Then choose **One-on-One** from the **Document Preset** pop-up menu to load the settings you saved in Step 11 on the preceding page (see Figure 1-15). To create the document, click **OK**.

In saving the preset back in Step 11 of the preceding exercise, you also updated the default settings. To bypass the New Document dialog box and put these settings into play, eschew File→New and press Ctrl+Alt+N (⌘-Option-N) instead.

---

2. ***Choose the Margins and Columns command.*** The first page of a document is generally where you put the title of the publication or chapter, so it's the one page where the margins and guides are likely to vary. Your new document is no exception. With the first page visible in

the document window, choose **Layout→Margins and Columns**. Alternatively, if you loaded my dekeKeys shortcuts, as suggested on page xix of the Preface, you can access the command from the keyboard by pressing the shortcut Ctrl+/ (⌘-/ on the Mac). As shown in Figure 1-16, the **Margins and Columns** dialog box contains only the options from the New Document dialog box that are applicable to a single page at a time.

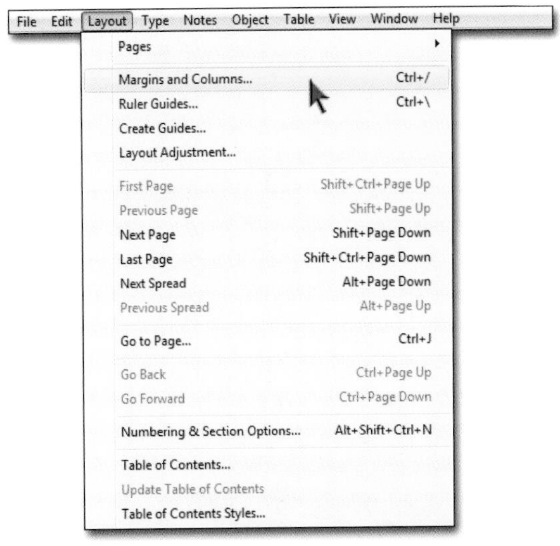

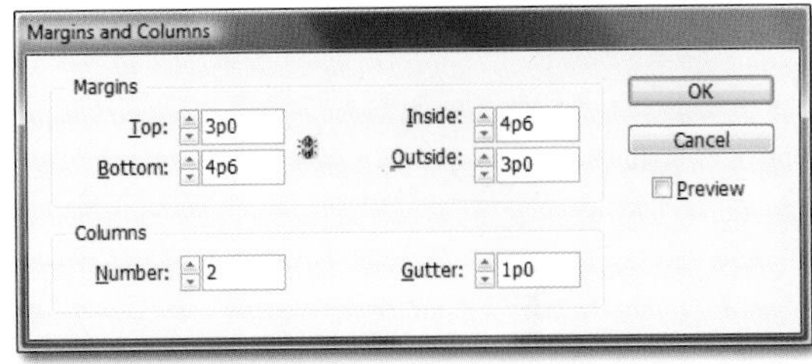

Figure 1-16.

3. ***Increase the Top margin value.*** Make the top margin larger by changing the **Top** value to 2.75in. Press Tab and InDesign converts this value to its equivalent in picas, 16p6.

Before clicking the OK button, you can preview the effect of your change by turning on the Preview check box. As witnessed in Figure 1-17, this is a fantastic way to gauge the result of your changes before making a commitment.

Click **OK** to accept the change. The resulting margin boundaries will house the body text. The chapter title will sit in the empty area above the body text.

4. ***Add two vertical ruler guides.*** In clearing a space for the chapter title, you've also removed all constraints to the placement of text. Fortunately, you can establish custom constraints by adding *ruler guides*, or just *guides* for short. As in QuarkXPress, Photoshop, and other programs, you create a ruler guide by dragging from one of the two rulers, hence the name. But that's where the similarities end. As you'll see over the next few steps, InDesign implements the humble ruler guide better than any other program on the market.

   We'll start by adding two vertical guides, one along the left margin and the other along the right.

   - Drag from the middle of the vertical ruler on the left side of the document window until your cursor snaps into alignment with the left margin. At the moment of the snap, your cursor changes from black to white, as in Figure 1-18 on the next page. You can also monitor the X value on the left side of the control palette at the top of your screen. When the guide is properly aligned, the value will read 4p6, the location of the inside margin.

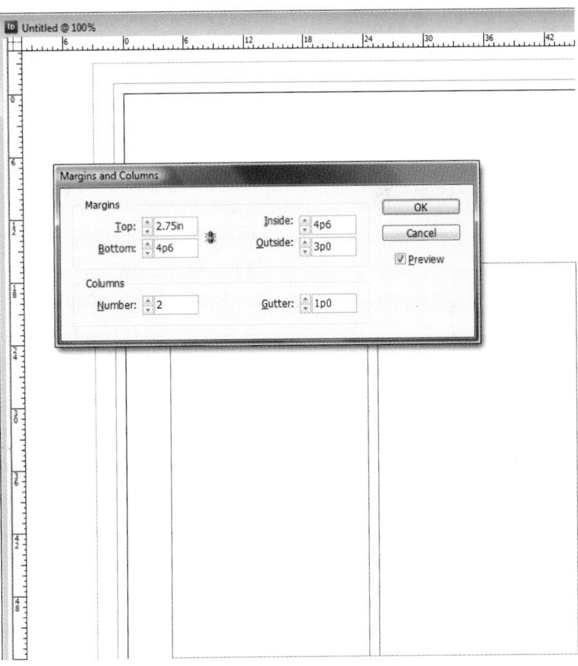

Figure 1-17.

- Drag another guideline from the vertical ruler so that it snaps into alignment with the right page margin. The newly black X value in the control palette will read 45p0.

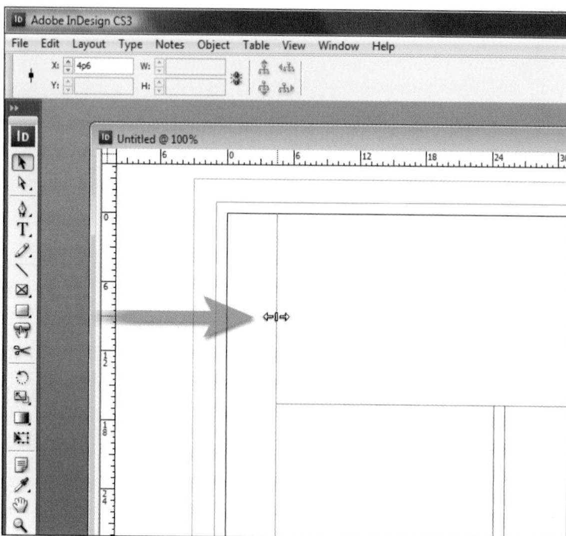

Figure 1-18.

PEARL OF WISDOM

If the guide does not snap and your cursor does not turn white, click the View menu, choose Grids & Guides, and check to see whether the Snap to Guides command has a check mark in front of it. If it doesn't, choose the command. The Snap to Guides command controls not only whether objects snap into alignment with a guide but also whether a guide snaps into alignment with selected objects and other guides as you drag it.

5. ***Make a horizontal guide.*** Now to constrain the top and bottom of the title text. Drag a guide from the horizontal ruler at the top of the screen and drop it at the point where the Y value in the control palette reads 8p6.

To snap the guide into alignment with the regular tick-mark increments in the ruler, press the Shift key as you drag the guide. The Shift key does not have to be down when you start dragging (in other words, you can press it mid-drag), but it does have to be down when you release the mouse button. Because the guide is snapping, your cursor will again appear white, as in Figure 1-19. The number of tick marks increases as you magnify a document, and more tick marks mean more snap points when Shift is held down.

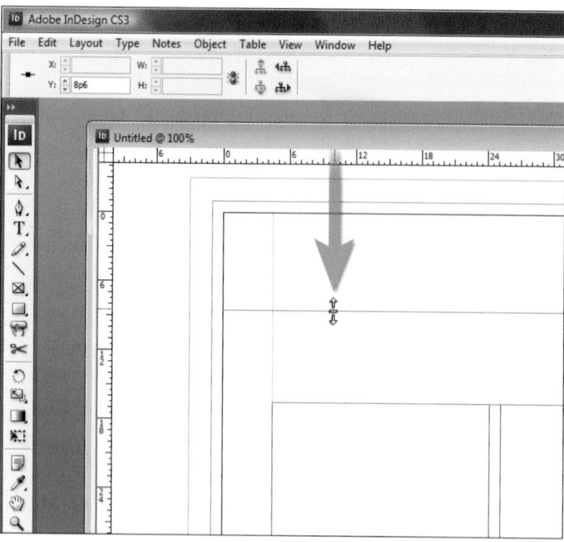

Figure 1-19.

If you're still having problems getting the guide into position, here are a few other tricks to try:

- After releasing the guide, press the ↑ or ↓ key to nudge the guide up or down, respectively, in 1-point increments. Press Shift+↑ or Shift+↓ to move the selected guide in 10-point increments.
- Highlight the **Y** value in the control palette and change it to 8p6. Then press Enter or Return to move the guide.

Note that the guide has to be selected for these techniques to work. A selected guide is colored a medium blue (as opposed to the deselected guides, which are cyan). If the guide is not selected, click it with the black arrow tool.

6. ***Create another horizontal guide.*** Now let's create a bottom guide for the chapter title. We can do this in two ways. One is the ho-hum way we've been doing things. Drag the guide from the horizontal ruler, press Shift if necessary, and drop the guide when the Y value reaches 13p0. But if you're looking for something new, try this technique instead:

   - First, make sure the horizontal guide you created in Step 5 is selected.
   - Highlight the **Y** value in the control palette.
   - Change the value to 13p0.
   - Press Alt+Enter (Option-Return on the Mac). InDesign clones the guide to the new position.

   Our next chore is to adjust the width of the columns. As you might have noticed, while the page you're currently reading is divided into two columns—one for standard text like the stuff you're reading and the other for graphics and special text—the main text column is several picas wider. Although the Margins and Columns command is limited to regular columns, you can create uneven columns by dragging the column guide in the document window. But this approach has two problems: First, unlike ruler guides, column guides don't remain selected when you click them, so you can't nudge the guides from the keyboard or specify a precise numerical position in the control palette. Second, changing the location of a column guide on one page affects that page only, hamstringing your ability to make global edits. Like the problems, the solutions are twofold: Recruit ruler guides for their precision and master pages for their global influence, as the following steps explain.

7. ***Go to the master page.*** Behind every page is a master page. The purpose of the *master page* is to convey recurring objects such as page numbers and, happily for us, guides. To access the master page, click the ▾ icon to the right of the page number in the bottom-left corner of the document window. As shown in Figure 1-20, this displays a pop-up menu of pages. Choose the last option, **A-Master**.

To go to the master page even faster, press Ctrl+J to highlight the page value, type the letter A, and press the Enter key. (On the Mac, press ⌘-J, A, and Return.)

PEARL OF WISDOM

This trick is so important, I'm putting it in a *Pearl* frame all by itself, off the beaten path where you can't help but see it. To hide all nonprinting elements—including frames, guides, boundaries, and the contents of the pasteboard—click and hold the icon at the bottom of the toolbox (▢) and choose the Preview option. To bring the guides back, click that icon again (now it looks like ▣) and choose Normal. Or better yet, just press the W key (the last letter in *preview*) to switch back and forth between the two modes. (This assumes no text is active.) It may not be the most logical shortcut, but memorize it anyway. When I'm working in InDesign, I probably press the W key a few hundred times a day.

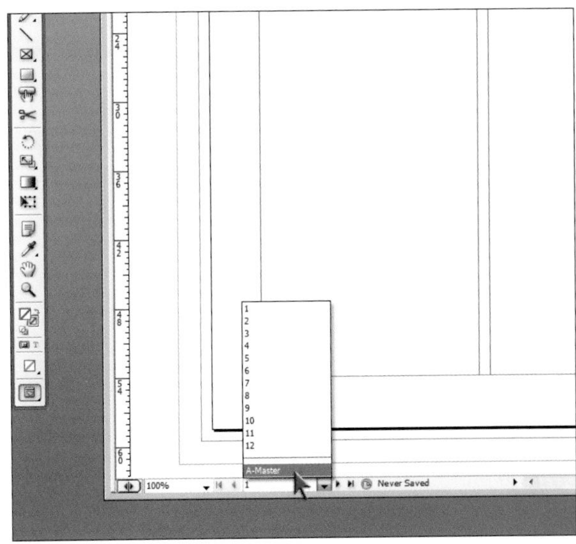

Figure 1-20.

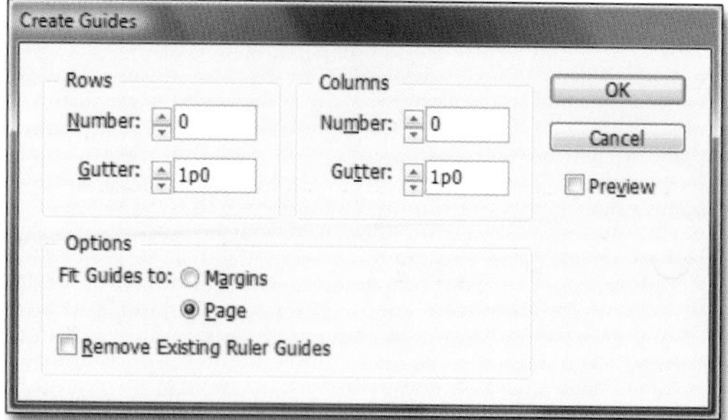

Figure 1-21.

Whatever your method, you should now see a pair of humble-looking but powerful master pages. For a detailed examination of master pages, read "Setting Up Master Pages," which begins on page 380 of Lesson 9. In the meantime, know this: Any change made to these master pages will affect every page in this document.

8. ***Choose the Create Guides command.*** If you were to scrutinize the printed page you're currently reading, you might notice that the outside graphics column is two-thirds as wide as the inside text column. Two parts graphics to three parts text adds up to five parts. So to exactly align our uneven columns, we need to divide the page into fifths. As luck would have it, InDesign can do this for us by automatically laying down guides. To take advantage of this wonderful function, choose **Layout→Create Guides** to display the **Create Guides** dialog box, as shown in Figure 1-21.

9. ***Create five columns of guides.*** The Create Guides dialog box lets you create a series of ruler guides—horizontal, vertical, or both—at regular increments. The guides may even include gutters, like column guides. Here's how I want you to fill out the options in the dialog box:

   - First, turn on the **Preview** check box. You'll want to see what you're doing.
   - Our design demands regular columns, so Tab your way to the **Columns** options and change the **Number** value to 5. The Gutter value is fine at 1p0.
   - The guides need to fit inside the margins. So set the **Fit Guides To** option to **Margins**.

   You should get the results shown in Figure 1-22 on the facing page. When you do, click **OK** to make those guides.

10. ***Move the column guides into alignment.*** Drag either edge of the purple column guide (the two lines make one guide) in the middle of the left master page so it snaps into alignment with the dual ruler guides just to the left of it, as in Figure 1-23. (In the figure, the guides turn red as they snap into alignment with the ruler guides. If you can't move the column guide, choose View→Grid & Guides→Lock Column Guides to unlock it.) Next scroll to the right master page and drag its column guide to the right. You should end up with two outer columns that are two-thirds as wide as the inner columns.

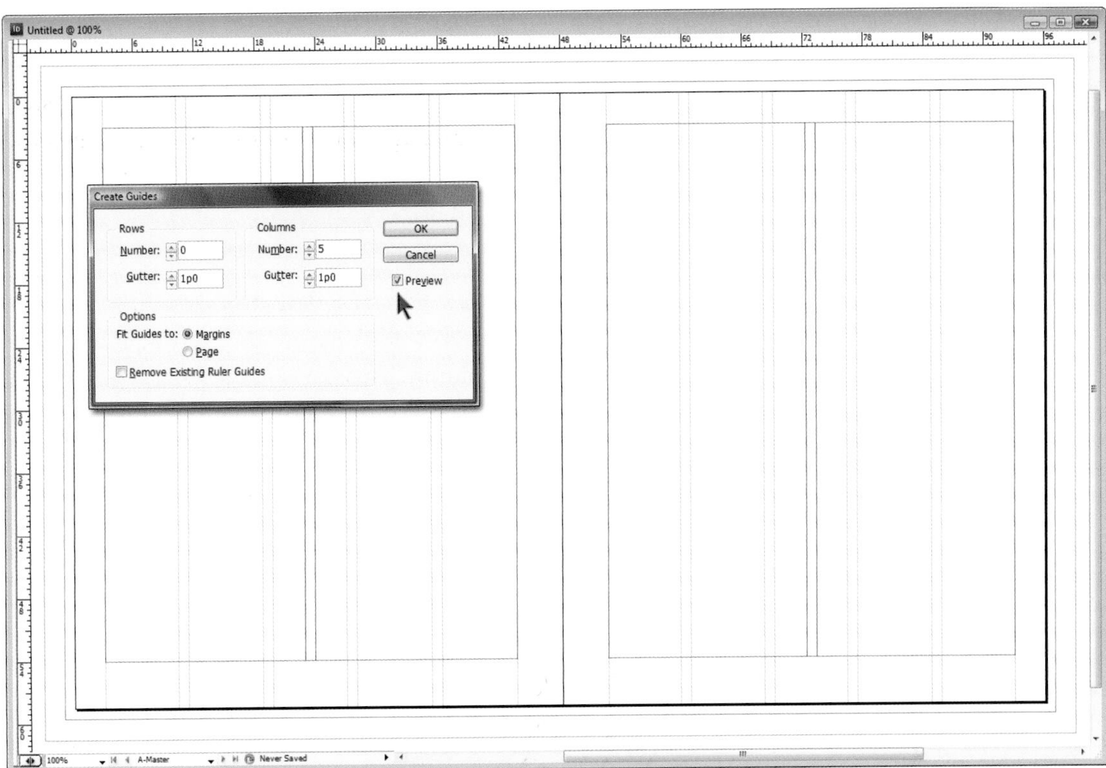

Figure 1-22.

PEARL OF WISDOM

Now that the column guides are positioned properly, we don't really need the cyan-colored ruler guides anymore. And leaving them in place might prove a little confusing because they clutter up the page. One solution is to delete them. But I hate to delete anything I've created. As I've learned from hard experience, something you need once is something you might well need again. Fortunately, you can hide the guides and still keep them around in a few ways. Here's my favorite:

11. ***Select all the ruler guides.*** As you may have gathered by now, InDesign treats guides as selectable objects that you can move, modify, and delete independently of each other. For example, you can select any one of the cyan guides by clicking it. You press Shift and click to select multiple guides.

    For our part, we'll change all the guides across both master pages. But Shift-clicking 20 separate guidelines is too much work. Fortunately, InDesign provides an excellent shortcut.

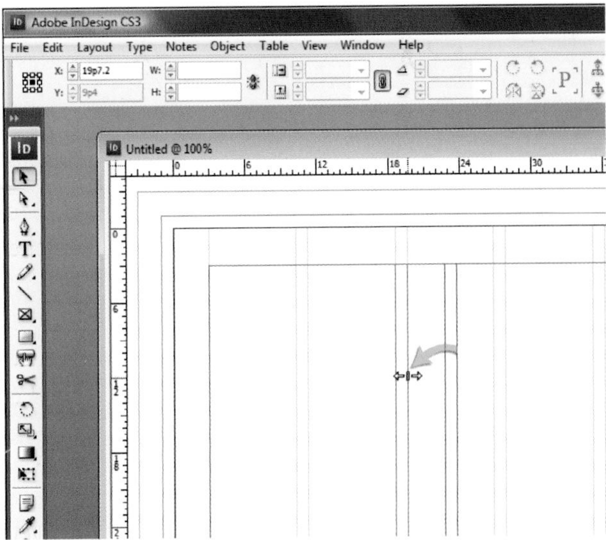

Figure 1-23.

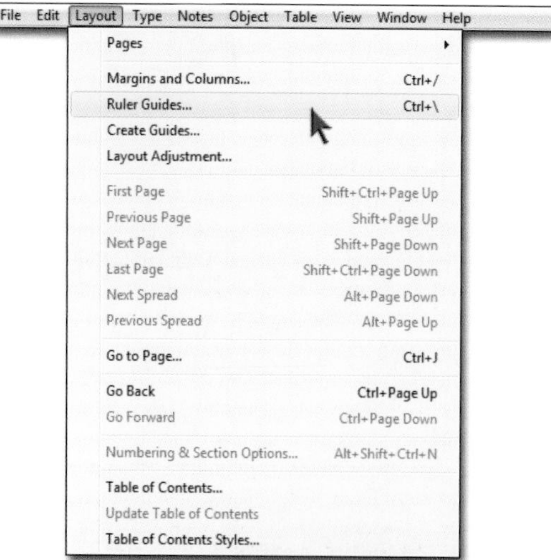

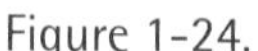

Figure 1-24.

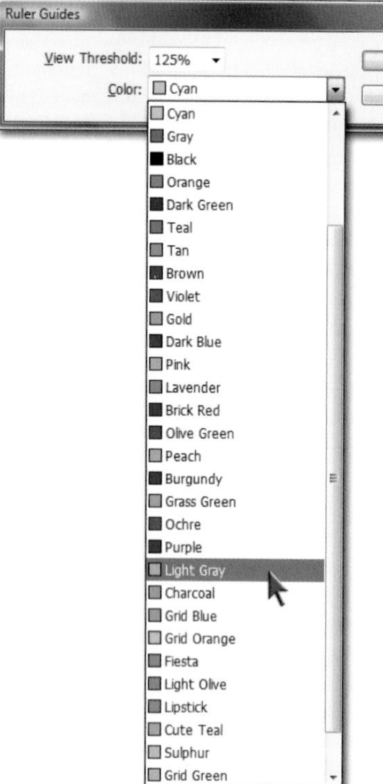

Figure 1-25.

To select all ruler guides on the active page or *page spread* (a pair of facing pages), press Ctrl+Alt+G (⌘-Option-G on the Mac). Even if the pages contain text and graphics, InDesign selects only the ruler guides.

Note that the menu option has no menu command. Like so many things in InDesign, the shortcut *is* the feature.

12. ***Choose the Ruler Guides command.*** This is the point at which you could delete the guides just by pressing the Backspace or Delete key. But let's modify them instead. Choose **Layout→Ruler Guides**. Or, if you loaded the dekeKeys shortcuts as I recommended in the Preface, you can take advantage of the shortcut Ctrl+\ (⌘-\ on the Mac). InDesign displays the small **Ruler Guides** dialog box shown in Figure 1-24.

13. ***Change the color and visibility of the guides.*** Make two adjustments to this dialog box:

    - Change the **View Threshold** value to 125 percent. This tells InDesign to display the guides when you magnify the document to 125 percent or greater. When zoomed farther out—say, to 100 percent—the guides are invisible. Because the guides are out of sight doesn't mean they're gone. Objects will continue to snap to the guides at all zoom ratios.
    - Click the **Color** pop-up menu and choose the most unobtrusive color possible, **Light Gray** (see Figure 1-25). Even when you do see the guides, they won't attract attention.

    When you're finished, click **OK** to accept your changes. If you're zoomed out, the guides will disappear. If you're zoomed in to 125 percent or closer, the guides remain medium blue because they're selected. Choose **Edit→Deselect All** or press Ctrl+Shift+A (⌘-Shift-A) to see their true coloring.

14. ***Add two full-spread ruler guides for the page numbers.*** Note that your changes affect the selected guides only. All other ruler guides, past and future, remain cyan. To see what I mean—and learn another cool trick—let's add a couple more guides. Drag a horizontal guide from the top ruler to the bottom of the page, where the Y value in the control palette reads 55p0. (Because no guide was previously selected, the Y value is faint.) Midway into the drag, press and hold the Ctrl key (or ⌘ on the Mac).

Pressing Ctrl (or ⌘) extends the guide across both pages in the spread. Be sure to hold the key until after you release the mouse button. You can achieve this result by dragging the guide into the pasteboard.

Then, with the newest guide selected, highlight the **Y** value (55p0) in the control palette, change it to 56p6, and press Alt+Enter (or Option-Return). Pictured in Figure 1-26, the result is two guides that span the entire master page spread and define the upper and lower boundaries of the page numbers.

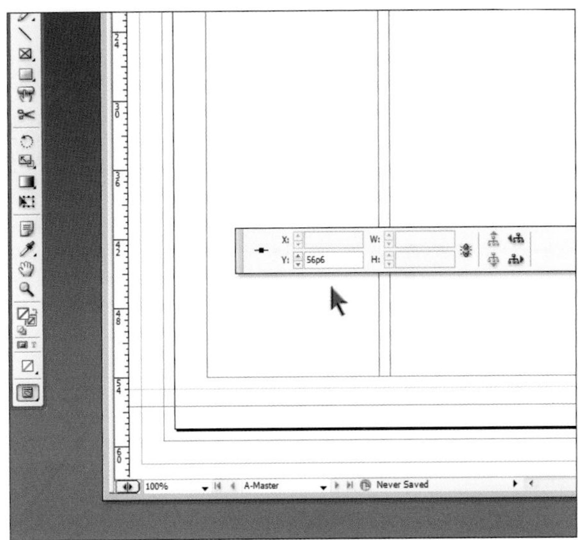

Figure 1-26.

15. ***Return to the main document.*** Switch to page 2 (see Figure 1-27). On the PC, you can press Ctrl+J, type 2, and press Enter. On the Mac, press ⌘-J, 2, Return. Then choose **View→Fit Spread in Window** to see both pages 2 and 3. The columns are wide on the inside and a bit narrower on the outside, the twenty gray ruler guides are hidden, and two page number guides grace the bottom of the document. Zoom in and you'll see the gray guides suddenly pop into view at 125 percent. True to our expectations, changing the guides on the master page has affected all other pages as well.

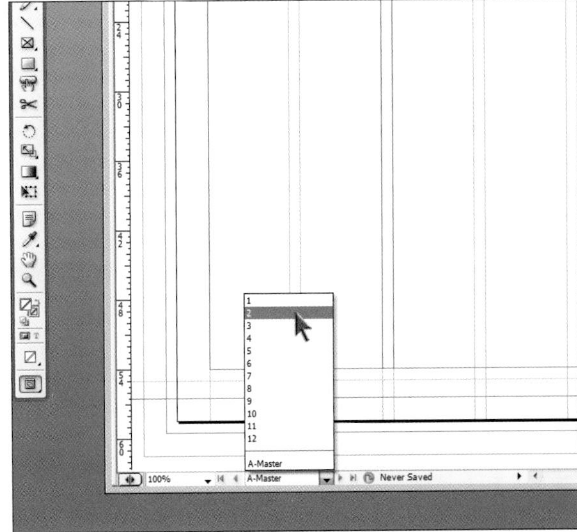

Figure 1-27.

16. ***Fix the first page.*** Well, actually, *one* page hasn't been affected, and like this book, it goes by the name *One*. Choose **Layout→First Page** or press Ctrl+Shift+Page Up (⌘-Shift-Page Up on the Mac) to go to page 1. You'll notice that, despite all our efforts, the columns remain resolutely equal in width. In the course of changing the top margin of this page back in Step 3 (page 17), we broke the link between the page 1 column guides and the guides on the master pages. Alas, such is life—and so we must repeat a bit of work.

    First, zoom in close enough to see the gray ruler guides. Then drag the purple column guide so it snaps into alignment with the pair of gray ruler guides immediately to the right of it, as in Figure 1-28 on the next page. Just like that, problem solved.

17. ***Recolor the title guides.*** To better set off the chapter title boundaries, I suggest we change the color of the two horizontal guides at the top of page 1.

    - First, drag around the guides with the black arrow tool to select them, as demonstrated in Figure 1-29.

When you drag in an empty portion of a document, you create a dotted rectangular *marquee*; anything partially inside the marquee becomes selected. The marquee can contain guides only; if an object falls inside the marquee, the guides are ignored and the object is selected.

- Next, choose **Layout→Ruler Guides** or press Ctrl+⌨ (⌘-⌨). Change the **Color** to **Gold** and click **OK**. Click anywhere off the guides to deselect them and see their new color.

This seemingly simple action lets you create color-coded guides. Now if you tell your fellow layout artists, "Use the cyan guides to position the page number and the orange guides for the title," they'll know exactly what you mean. (They look orange anyway.)

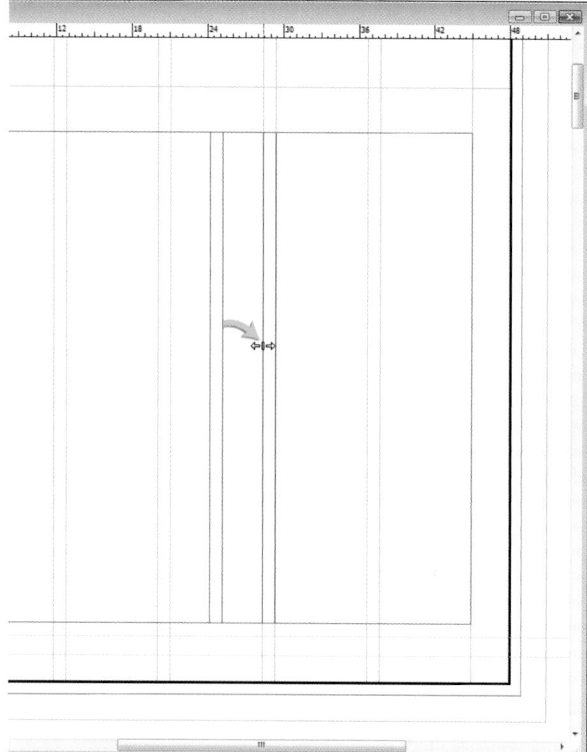

Figure 1-28.

You've put in a lot of work, so you might want to save your document. Choose File→Save As, enter a name, and click the Save button. (For more information, read "Saving Your Document" on page 39 of this lesson.)

PEARL OF WISDOM

In the fever of laying out a page, when you're selecting this and dragging that, it's easy to snag a ruler or column guide and accidentally move it out of position. The solution is to lock them in place, and the thoughtful people at Adobe allow you to lock column guides separately from the ruler guides. (Why is that a good thing? You probably won't fiddle with column guides after you place them, but you probably will want to adjust ruler guides.) Just trot off to the View→Grids & Guides menu and choose the lock of your choice.

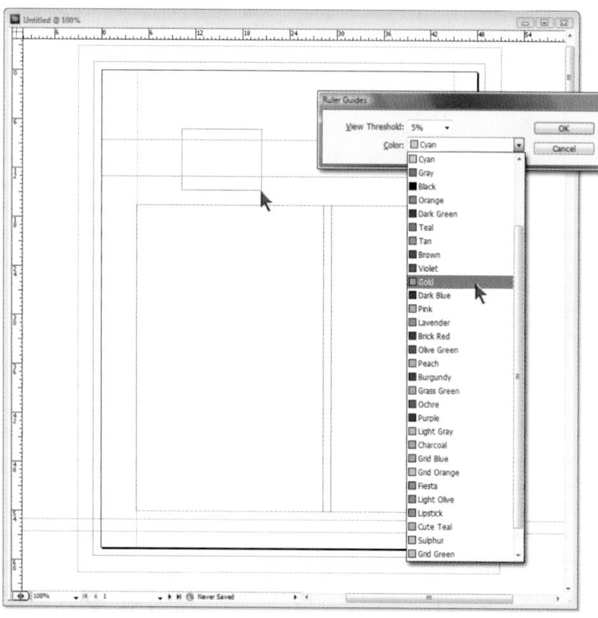

Figure 1-29.

Creating Custom Workspaces

Like most Adobe software, InDesign's interface can be described as palette intensive. Lurking under the Window menu are 39 palettes, (though mercifully less than half appear on screen by default). A palette can either stand on its own or be nested with other palettes inside a *docking pane*. InDesign's default workspace places five clusters of nested palettes on the right side of the screen in a single docking pane. As you can see in Figure 1-30, they appear as icons and palette titles. Clicking any of the icons temporarily expands the corresponding palette until you click to send it back in line. If this default palette setup doesn't suit you, not to worry. InDesign lets you create and save your own custom workspaces so that you can have different palette arrangements for different tasks.

By way of example, this exercise shows you how to set up and save a custom workspace well suited for the work you'll be doing in InDesign as you go through this book. You'll also learn how to switch between a custom workspace and the default.

PEARL OF WISDOM

When shooting the figures for this exercise, I maintained a screen resolution of 1024 by 768 pixels, which is definitely on the skimpy side when using InDesign. I hope you're using a monitor with a higher resolution, and possibly even two monitors, one for the document window and another for palettes. In other words, the figures in this exercise demonstrate a sort of worst-case scenario. So if your screen doesn't look exactly like mine, that's probably a good thing.

1. ***Restore the default palette locations.*** Assuming you haven't done any palette redecorating that you care to keep, let's get on the same page by choosing **Window→Workspace→Default Workspace**. Shown in Figure 1-31, this command resets all palettes to just icons and names, as if you were starting InDesign CS3 for the first time.

2. ***Open a sample document.*** To ensure that we're *literally* on the same page, open the file named *Seventies quiz.indd* located in the *Lesson 01* folder inside the *Lesson Files-IDcs3 1on1* folder. The document appears in Figure 1-32.

3. ***Zoom in on the area above the text.*** Let's say we want to draw near the top of the document, and we want to be zoomed in close to do detail work. Press Z to get the zoom tool, and then click in the upper-left corner of the document directly below the first *e* in *We all loved*. (The exact position isn't all that important; the *e* is just a landmark so that you and I are seeing more or less the same thing.) Keep clicking until you're zoomed in to 400 percent, as in Figure 1-33 on the next page. In my case, it took six clicks, but your experience might be different.

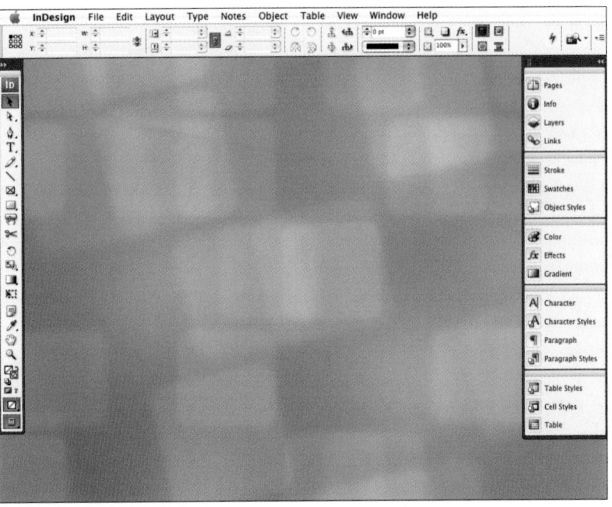

Figure 1-30.

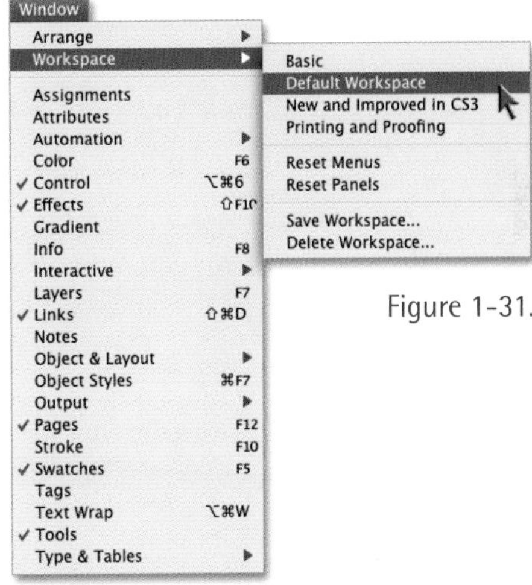

Figure 1-31.

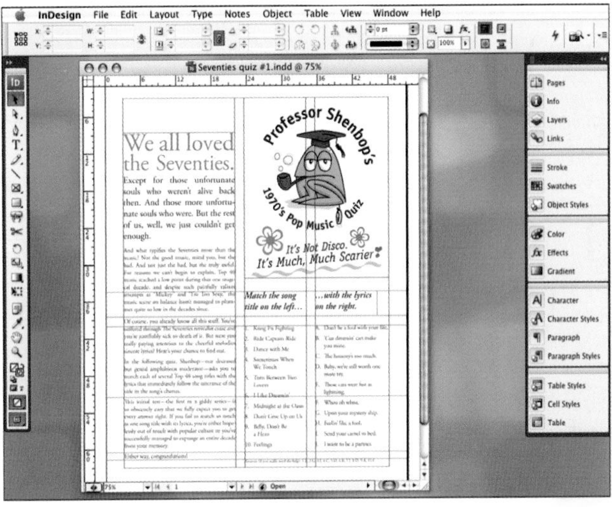

Figure 1-32.

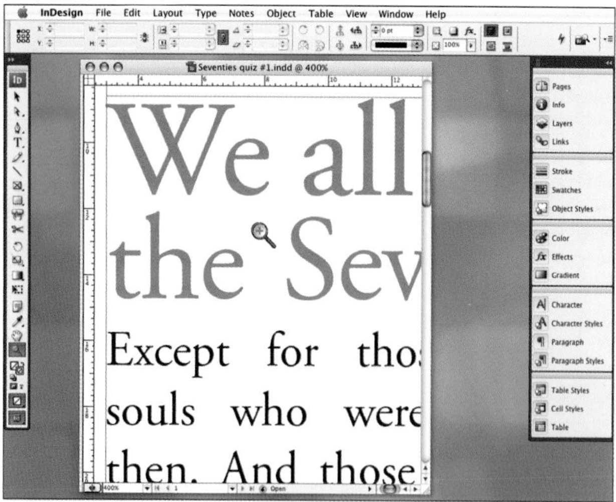

Figure 1-33.

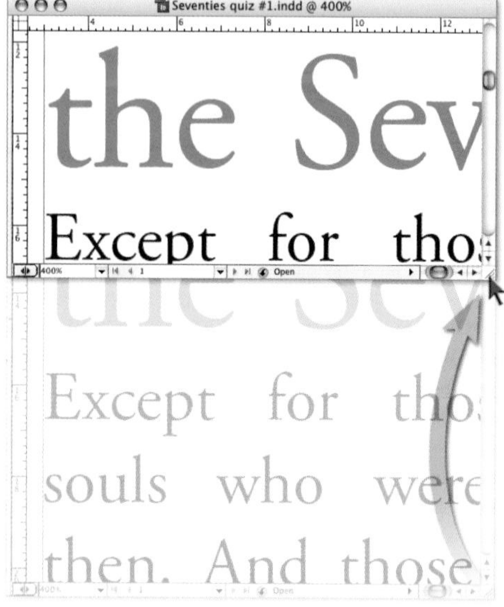

Figure 1-34.

Figure 1-35.

4. ***Resize the document window.*** Click the size box in the lower-right corner of the document window and drag it upward so that only a small amount of the introductory text is visible, as shown in Figure 1-34.

5. ***Expand the docking pane to reveal the palettes.*** The default view gives you an icon and name for each of the default palettes. To start, you have five clusters of light gray palettes nestled inside a larger dark gray *docking pane*, which is anchored to the right edge of your screen. Click the double-arrow (◂◂) or anywhere else along the top of the docking pane to expand the pane and see the full contents of the front palette from each cluster, with tabs for the other palettes visible behind them.

6. ***Move and close the Info palette.*** You can switch any palette to the familiar free-floating form by dragging its tab and dropping it in the wide open, outside the docking pane. In this case, I want you to drag the **Info** palette (between Paper and Layers) to the middle of your screen. We don't need the Info palette for our custom setup, so close it by clicking the wee × in the top-right corner of the palette.

7. ***Close the three palettes in the Table cluster.*** You could drag each of these palettes—Table Styles, Cell Styles, and Table—to the middle of the screen and close it independently. But there's an easier way: Click the light gray area above the **Table Styles** tab—which I call the *cluster bar*, for lack of a better term—and drag the entire cluster of table-related palettes out of the docking pane, as in Figure 1-35. This moves all grouped palettes together. Now click the × in the top-right corner to kill three birds with one stone. Good night, birds.

8. ***Move the Links palette to a new docking pane.*** In addition to making palettes free-floating, you can move them into new docking panes. Drag the tab for the **Links** palette out toward the workspace. As you cross over the left edge

of the docking pane, you'll see a blue vertical bar, as on the left side of Figure 1-36. The moment you see this bar, release. This puts the Links palette in a new docking pane (right side, Figure 1-36) and gives it lots of room to expand (which it is inclined to do, as you'll see later in the book).

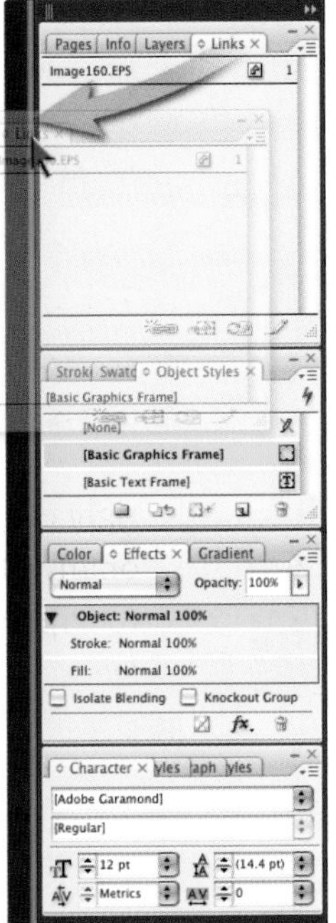

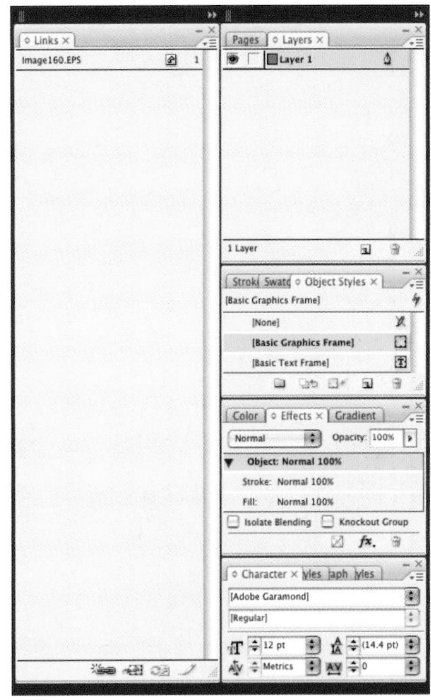

Figure 1-36.

9. ***Collapse the Links palette to icons.*** By now, you may be encroaching a bit too radically on your document window real estate. So reduce the width of the Links palette by clicking the ▸▸ icon (or the top of its docking pane) to collapse the pane to a chain icon and the word *Links*. To see the chain icon by itself, drag the left edge of the pane as far as you can to the right.

10. ***Start a new cluster beginning with the Object Styles palette.*** Drag the **Object Styles** palette away from its strange bedfellows Stroke and Swatches to just under the Links palette icon. Drop it when you see a blue horizontal bar along the bottom of the chain icon, as in Figure 1-37. InDesign adds the palette to the second dock and collapses it to an icon.

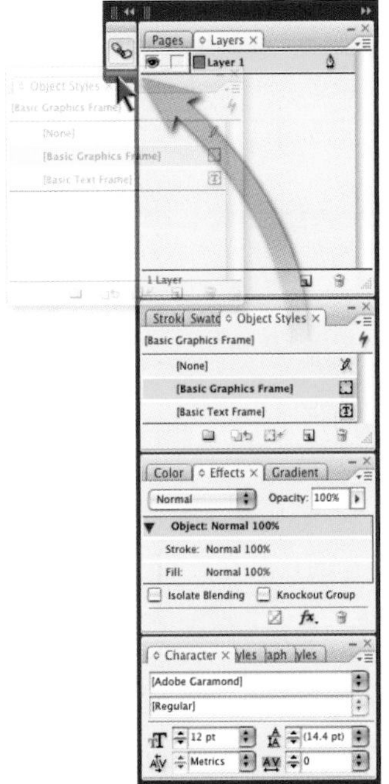

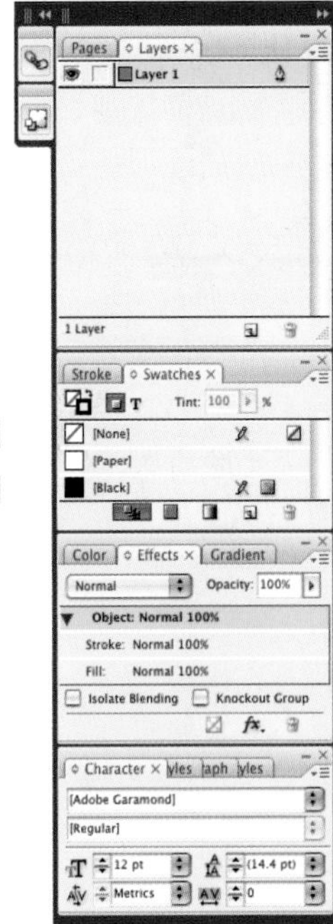

Figure 1-37.

11. ***Add the Character Styles and Paragraph Styles palettes to the Object Styles cluster.*** First, dispose of the **Character** and **Paragraph** palettes (the ones *without* the word Styles) by selecting the corresponding tab and clicking the × to the immediate right of the palette title. Then drag the cluster bar for the remaining **Character Styles** and **Paragraph Styles** palettes to just above the Object Styles icon. You should see the frame around the icon turn blue, as well as a blue bar above the icon, indicating that you are about to join the three palettes into a single, logical Styles cluster, as in the small and intimate Figure 1-38.

Figure 1-38.

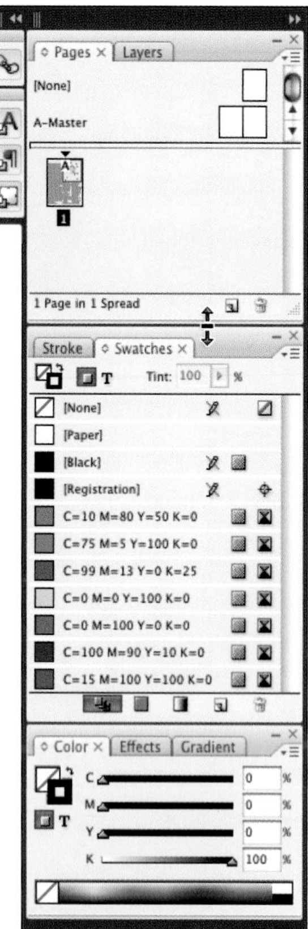

Figure 1-39.

12. ***Adjust the height of the palettes.*** Back in the far-right docking pane, click the **Pages** and **Color** tabs to bring those palettes forward. Then hover your cursor over the horizontal divider line between the **Pages** and **Swatches** palettes so that your cursor becomes a double-headed arrow, as in ↕. Drag the divider line up to extend the Swatches palette and shrink the Pages palette. Increase the height until you can conveniently see all the swatches at once, as in Figure 1-39.

13. ***Rearrange the other palettes as you see fit.*** You now have fewer palettes on screen than by default, but they're more than enough to get us started. Still, you may want to make some adjustments to better exploit your screen real estate. Here are a few techniques you can use:

    - Expand or reduce the width of a docking pane by dragging the left edge of the pane.
    - Click the ♦ icon in the tab to cycle between different expansion settings. Or double-click the palette's tab. (The latter technique gives you extra options when the palette is free floating.)
    - Collapse a palette to only tabs by clicking the cluster bar above the palette title. Click again to restore the palette.
    - To bring back a hidden palette, choose its name from the Window menu. All palettes are listed in alphabetical order, although many are squirreled away inside submenus.
    - Note that you can't drag a docking pane, but you can create a new one—on the other side of the screen, for example—by dragging a palette there and waiting for the familiar blue vertical bar.

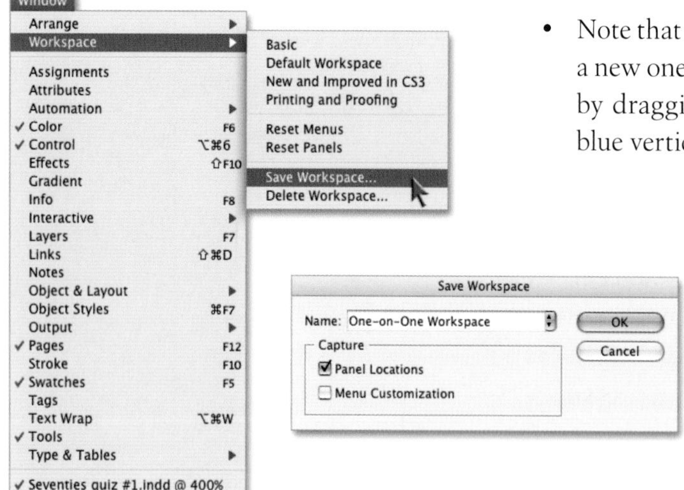

Figure 1-40.

14. ***Save your altered workspace.*** Now that you have your palettes arranged just the way you want them, save which palettes are visible as well as their position and scale by choosing **Window→Workspace→Save Workspace**. Name the workspace "One-on-One Workspace" (see Figure 1-40) and then click the **OK** button.

15. ***Again restore the default workspace.*** Having saved your drawing workspace, you can now switch between it and any other workspace, including InDesign's default.

Choose **Window→Workspace→Default Workspace**. Your custom palette configuration vanishes, replaced by the original arrangement.

16. ***Bring back the One-on-One workspace.*** Now comes the real test. Choose **Window→Workspace→One-on-One Workspace** and, presto, your saved workspace reappears, ready for you to make your way through this book.

To delete a saved workspace, choose Window→Workspace→Delete Workspace. Then choose the name of the workspace you want to delete from the Name pop-up menu and click Delete.

Although the Save Workspace command might seem to give you complete control over the interface, it actually has no bearing on the document window itself. Try this: Resize the document window, and zoom out from the page so it looks approximately the way it did in Figure 1-32 on page 25. (You zoom out by Alt- or Option-clicking with the zoom tool.) Then switch back and forth between the Default Workspace and One-on-One Workspace configurations. Throughout, the window remains unaffected. In InDesign and other Adobe CS3 applications, the workspace is all about palettes; settings applied to the document window, such as zoom level and position, are stored with the document file itself.

Using the Bridge with InDesign

When creating documents, you need tools for keeping track of all the *digital assets*—a utilitarian name for the images, artwork, and other bits and pieces—that go into them. Windows Explorer and the Macintosh Finder are supposed to do this, but for the demanding InDesigner, these general-purpose organizers are no more than blunt instruments. Which leads us to another bright idea from Adobe: a digital asset manager (DAM) called the Bridge. Originally developed as a method for previewing images in Photoshop (and called the File Browser), the Bridge has become a central hub for the entire Creative Suite and an essential asset manager for InDesign. And it's included with every commercially sold version of InDesign.

From its name, you might guess that the Bridge links the various programs in the suite, spanning the chasms between them, and that's true. But a better analogy might be the bridge of the *Starship Enterprise*. From here, you can explore the entire universe, including those parts that belong to the CS3 Federation, and beyond.

The suspense must be killing you. So here, in a nutshell, are some of the things it does. The Bridge lets you:

- See all your files, on any disk or device that your computer is connected to. The Bridge can generate scalable previews of documents created with most Adobe applications or saved in recognized file formats. Unsupported formats appear as icons.
- Open files by double-clicking their thumbnails.
- Move and copy files between your hard disks, removable media, and networked volumes.
- Assign rankings and keywords to files, which you can then use to sort through large quantities of photos, illustrations, and other assets.
- View and edit a document's *metadata*, which comprises a host of valuable information about each file: who made it and when, what it contains, where it came from, and much more.
- Synchronize color settings across all Creative Suite applications so that the individual applications display and print colors similarly. (This feature works only if you own one of the many varieties of CS3.)
- Follow electronic links to the outside world, such as online Adobe help, training videos, and user forums, as well as an open door to Adobe's Stock Photo service.
- New to Bridge 2.0 (the version that ships with CS3), you can combine related files into a *stack*, which you can collapse or expand like an accordion file.
- Import assets into InDesign with a simple drag and drop. You can even shrink the Bridge to a compact widget, permitting you to view the Bridge and InDesign simultaneously.

I can't tell you everything about the Bridge—that could fill another book—but I can provide you with a good start. In this lesson, you'll use the Bridge to organize assets, find files, and import a few images into an InDesign document. By the end, you should have a fair sense of what the Bridge can do for you.

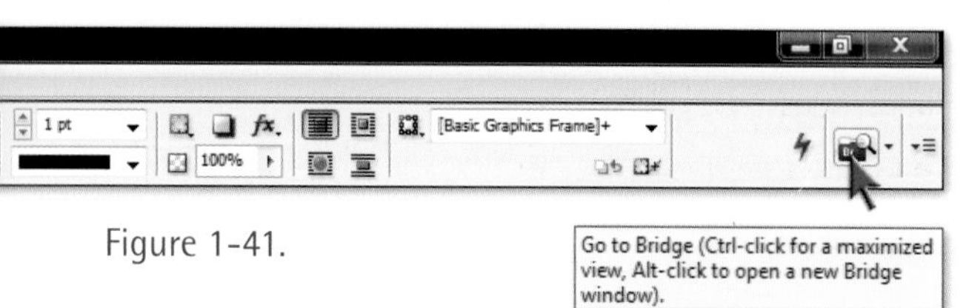

Figure 1-41.

1. ***Start the Bridge.*** To open the Bridge from InDesign, choose **File→Browse**. Or you can press Ctrl+Alt+O (on the Mac, ⌘-Option-O) or click the folder icon with the tiny magnifying glass on the right side of the control palette, as in Figure 1-41. The launch process begins.

2. ***Navigate to the Travel Flier folder.*** By default, the Bridge window presents you with a large *assets browser* (called the Content panel) surrounded by six movable panels, all labeled in black in Figure 1-42. (The violet labels show ancillary options.) The top-left section contains tabs that let you switch between the Favorites and Folders panels. The Favorites panel gives you instant access to commonly used folders, as well as a few links that Adobe thinks you'll find useful. The Folders panel lets you navigate to a specific folder on your hard disk or other media that contains your digital assets. With that in mind, here's what I want you to do:

   - If it isn't already selected, click the **Favorites** tab.
   - Click the blue **Desktop** icon.
   - The **Content** panel shows the files and folders on your computer's desktop. However sloppy a desktop housekeeper you might be, the Bridge alphabetizes everything for you in tidy rows. Find the folder called *Lesson Files-IDcs3 1on1* and double-click it. (This step assumes you copied the folder to your desktop. If you put the lesson files elsewhere or left them on the DVD, go there instead.)

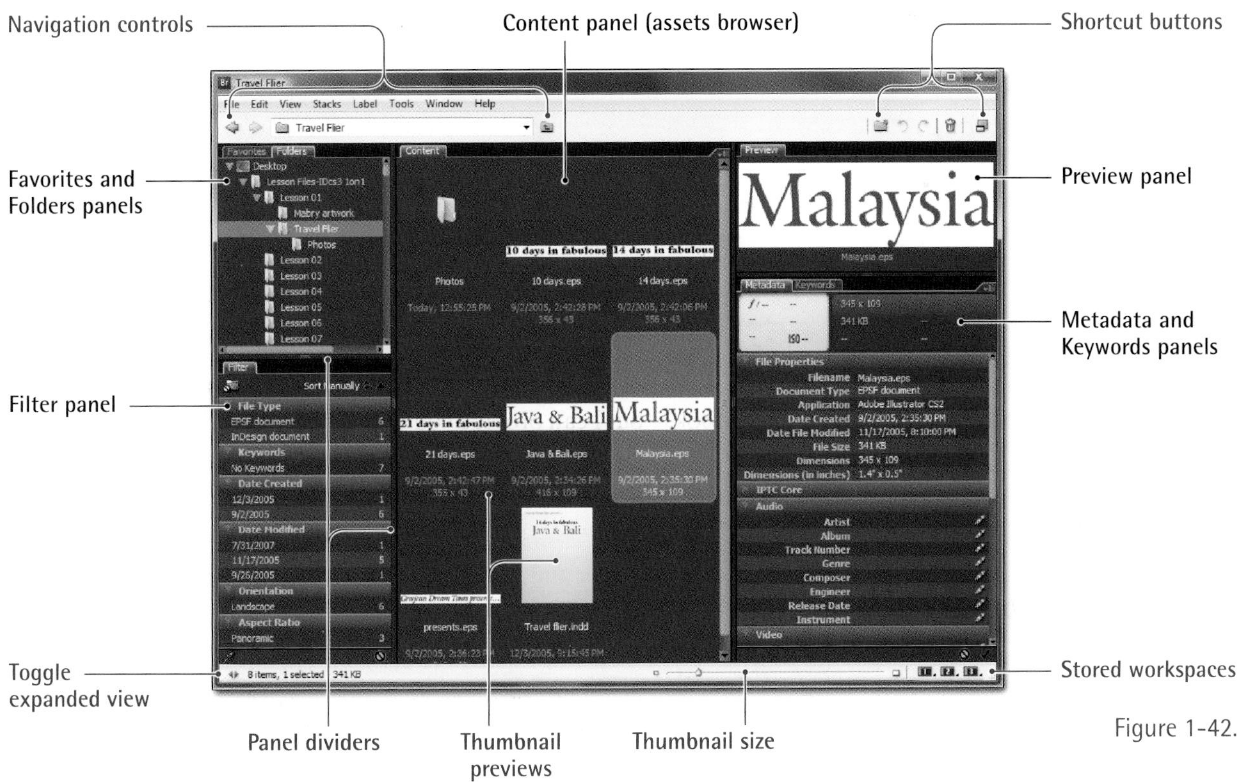

Figure 1-42.

- Click the **Folders** tab to switch to the *folder tree*, thus termed because it branches off into folders and subfolders.
- Click the "twirly" triangle (▶) in front of *Lesson Files-IDcs3 1on1* to expand it. Then click the ▶ in front of the *Lesson 01* folder to open it as well.
- Finally you'll find a folder called *Travel Flier*. Click that folder to fill the assets browser with a *Photos* folder, a handful of text illustrations, and a single InDesign document, all of which appear in Figure 1-42 on the preceding page.

If the folder tree becomes too pinched, you can widen it by dragging one of the vertical panel dividers, labeled in the figure. You can also increase the height of the panel by dragging a horizontal divider.

The *Travel Flier* folder illustrates how you might use a folder to hold documents, assets, and other folders. In this case, the files and folders add up to a one-page travel handout.

To increase the size of the thumbnails, drag the slider in the bottom-right corner of the window (labeled *Thumbnail size* in Figure 1-42) to the right. You can also press Ctrl+[+=] (⌘-[+=]) to zoom in incrementally from the keyboard.

---

3. ***Add the folder to the Favorites list.*** We're going to be using the Travel Flier folder a lot. To make it easy to access, let's add it to the Bridge's Favorites list. Right-click the folder's icon and choose **Add to Favorites** from the pop-up menu. Although it's currently hidden, the folder has been added to the Favorites panel. We'll come back to it shortly.
4. ***Switch to the Vertical Filmstrip workspace.*** Our next task is to evaluate a few photographs and decide which ones are good enough to add to our InDesign document. And that means being able to view and compare images inside a generously allotted Preview panel.
   - Double-click the folder named *Photos* to view a collection of vacation snapshots from designer Jim Felici.
   - Click and hold the [2] icon in the bottom-right corner of the Bridge window and then choose the **Vertical Filmstrip** command. As you can see in Figure 1-43 on the facing page, the Bridge displays a slim Contents panel along the right side of the screen with a large Preview panel in the middle, great for evaluating photos and other artwork in detail.

PEARL OF WISDOM

If you're familiar with the previous version of the Bridge, you may wonder why Adobe swapped the sensible thumbnail and filmstrip icons for the meaningless 1, 2, and 3? Because 1, 2, and 3 can be any workspaces you want them to be. By choosing Vertical Filmstrip from the 2 button, you set 2 to be Vertical Filmstrip. (By default, 2 is Horizontal Filmstrip, which in my experience is ill suited to modern wide-format LCD screens.) Now you have only to click the 2 to return to this flexible photo-review mode.

Figure 1-43.

5. ***Restore the Metadata and Keyword panels.*** Although the filmstrip workspace is great for viewing the photo collection, we've lost the Metadata and Keyword panels, which are useful to have around:

   - *Metadata* is all the information that travels along with a file, including details about who and what created it, file size, and when it was last modified.

   - *Keywords* are labels that you add to a file to describe its contents. Later, you can search for those labels, making it easier to find images and other assets that have slipped from your memory, as they invariably do.

   Choose **Window→Metadata Panel** and **Window→Keywords Panel** to bring back the two panels. The Bridge puts them on the right side of the window, encroaching on the assets browser. We'll fix that obvious problem in the next step.

FURTHER INVESTIGATION

The Bridge offers lots of ways to rate, label, and filter your assets, add keywords to them, edit metadata, and otherwise intelligently manage your assets. These are tools particularly popular with photographers. For a more in-depth look at the Bridge, check out my book *Adobe Photoshop CS3 One-on-One*. Or start your complimentary 7-Day Free Trial Account at *www.lynda.com/deke* (as introduced on page xxvi of the Preface), navigate to my introductory Photoshop series *Photoshop CS3 One-on-One: The Essentials*, and catch my hour-long Chapter 3, "The New and Improved Bridge."

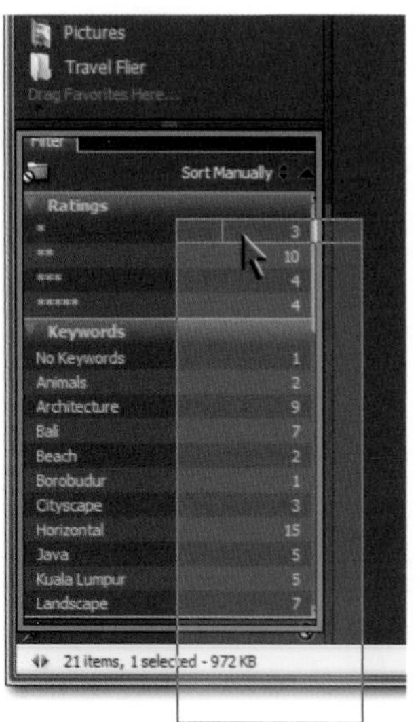

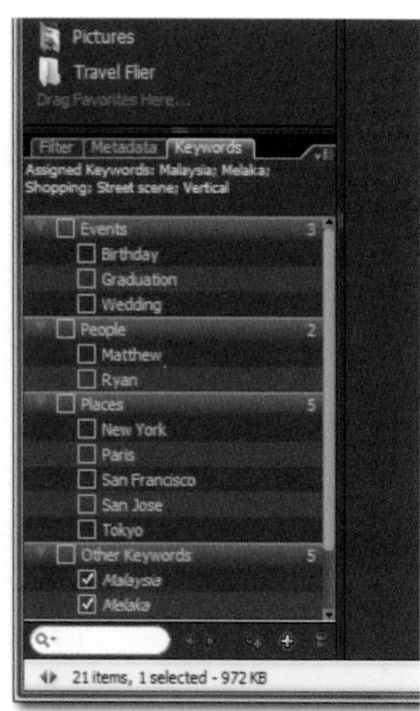

Figure 1-44.

6. ***Move the Metadata and Keywords panels to the bottom-left pane.*** You can move any panel into a new pane by grabbing its tab and dragging it. Drag the **Metadata** panel down to the bottom-left corner of the window, until you see a heavy blue outline around the **Filter** panel, as in the first example in Figure 1-44. Do the same with the **Keywords** panel. The result appears in the second example in the figure.

7. ***Save the new workspace.*** After getting everything the way you want it—for my part, I clicked the **Folders** tab to bring that panel to the front and enlarge the overall size of the Bridge window to give myself room to work—you'll want to save your workspace for future use. Then do the following:

   - Click and hold the [3] icon and choose the **Save Workspace** command, as in Figure 1-45.
   - Name the workspace something like "Better Filmstrip" and click the **Save** button.

   In this one step, you've managed to save your workspace and save it off to the [3] icon. Now anytime you click [3], the Bridge will switch you to the Better Filmstrip workspace.

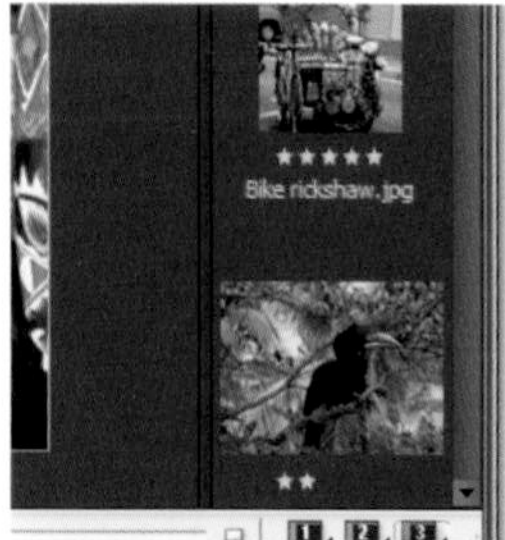

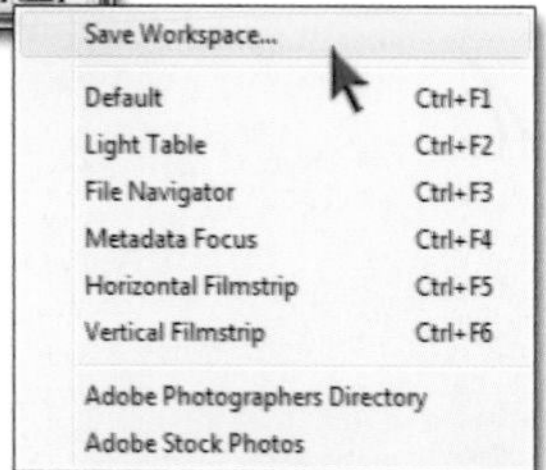

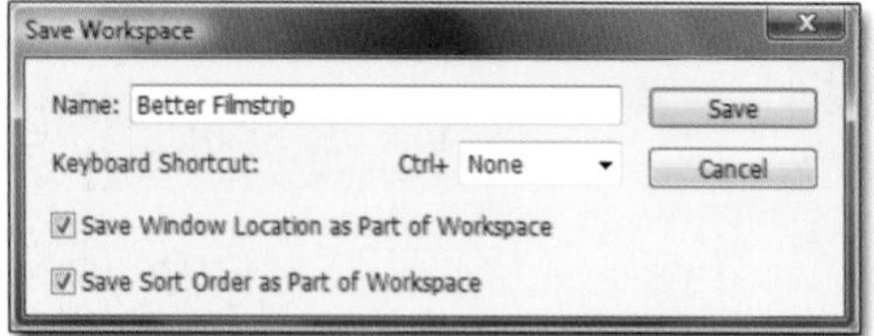

Figure 1-45.

If the Bridge does something crazy like switching panels around after you save the workspace (a persistent bug as I write this), just click [3] again and see if that doesn't solve the problem. Worst-case scenario, you'll have to click and hold [3] and choose Better Filmstrip. You should *not* have to manually reposition panels.

8. ***Sort the files by their ratings.*** Notice that I've assigned a few star ratings to the photos. The Bridge's Filter panel lets you employ ratings and other criteria (keywords, orientation, file format) to separate the wheat from the chaff. By way of example, here's how to sort the images according to rating, from highest to lowest:

   - Click the tab for the **Filter** panel to bring it in front of Metadata and Keywords.
   - In the **Filter** panel, click the ⬍ icon to the right of **Sort by Filename** (or however it reads for you)

and choose **By Rating** from the ensuing pop-up menu, as demonstrated in Figure 1-46. This sorts the images by the number of stars they've received, from fewest to most.

- To see the images with the most stars at the top of the filmstrip, click the ▲ to the right of the ⬍ to reverse the order from ascending to descending, which in Bridge parlance means high ratings declining into lower ones.

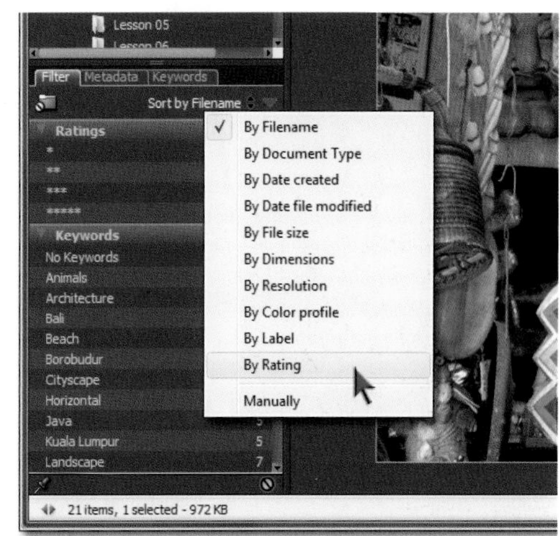

Figure 1-46.

PEARL OF WISDOM

You don't have to accept the Bridge's automatic sort order. You can make files appear in the Content panel wherever you want them. Just drag a thumbnail to move it to a new position, as in Figure 1-47 below. The colorful horizontal line indicates the file's new position when you release the mouse button. The thumbnails will remain reordered until you choose a new command from the Filter panel's ⬍ pop-up menu.

9. ***Show only the images from Bali.*** For purposes of the travel flier, your job is to pick out some images that might successfully entice travelers to exotic Bali, Indonesia. The first order of business, then, is to hide all images that *aren't* from Bali by clicking the keyword **Bali** in the **Keywords** section of the **Filters** panel (which automatically lists all keywords that I have added to my images). The Bridge helpfully omits all photos tagged as coming from Java, Malaysia, and Singapore so that only those from Bali are left.

10. ***Stack three photos.*** The Bridge lets you create groups of related files called stacks. These might be photos shot with the same model, framing, or lighting in anticipation of a single use. In our case, we'll stack similarly ranked images:

    - Select the trio of ★★★ images—*Terrace.jpg*, *Sanur beach.jpg*, and *Courthouse.jpg*—by clicking the first one and Shift-clicking the third. All three images appear in the Preview panel.

    - Choose **Stacks→Group as Stack** or press Ctrl+G (⌘-G). As seen in Figure 1-48, the Bridge appends a number (③) to identify the quantity of files in the stack.

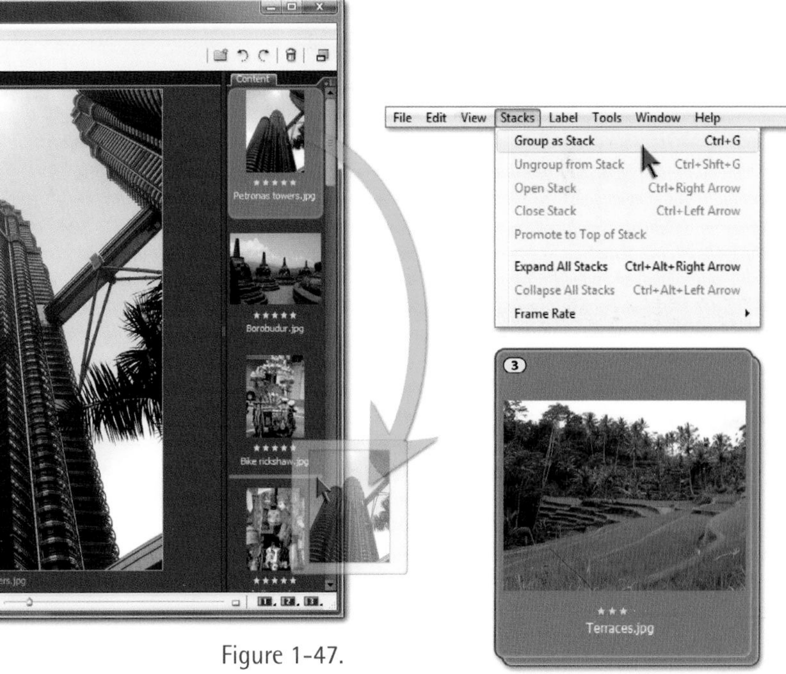

Figure 1-47.

Figure 1-48.

11. ***Switch to the compact mode.*** Now that you've isolated a few evocative photos, let's use them to build a simple page. Our plan is to drag the images directly from the Bridge window into an InDesign document. To shrink the Bridge window so you can see it and InDesign at the same time, choose **View→Compact Mode** or press Ctrl+Enter (⌘-Return). You can also click the ◻ icon, labeled in Figure 1-49. The forward Bridge window shrinks to a fraction of its previous size, revealing the assets browser, a few navigation controls, and nothing more. You can resize the Bridge window by dragging the bottom-right corner of the interface.

Figure 1-49.

12. ***Open an InDesign document.*** The Bridge is also a perfectly good place from which to open a variety of document types, including InDesign. Go back one step in your Bridge browsing history by clicking the ◁ button in the top-left corner of the newly shrunken window. Scroll down to the *Travel flier.indd* document and double-click it. A second or two later, you're back in InDesign, but with a difference: The compact Bridge window remains in front, like an über palette that is capable of floating even above other palettes, as in Figure 1-50.

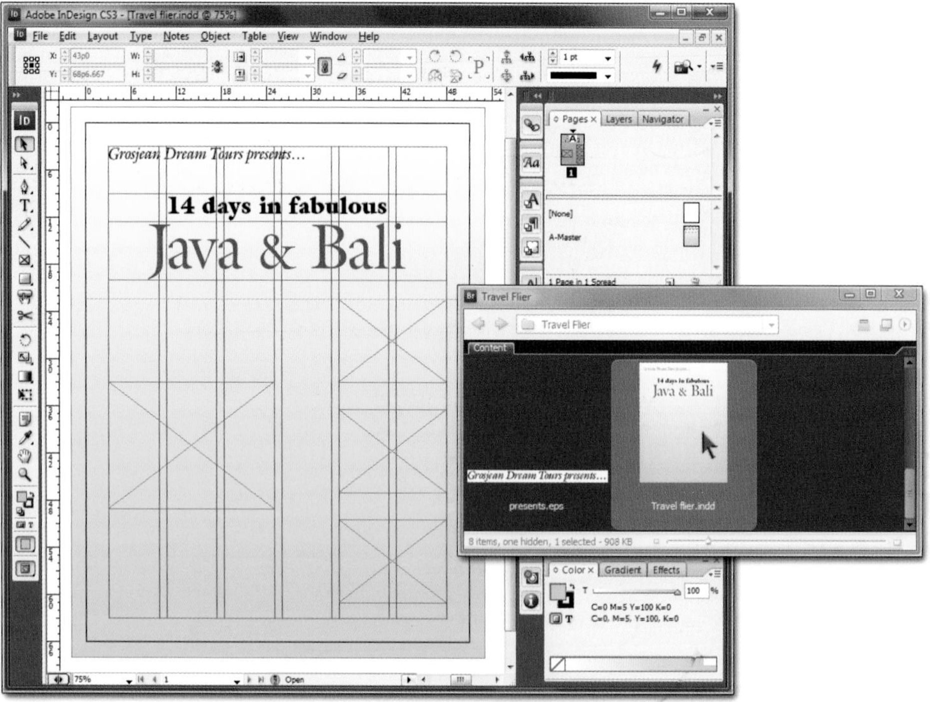

Figure 1-50.

13. ***Drag an image thumbnail into the InDesign document.*** Aside from some imported text objects, the *Travel flier.indd* document is largely empty, awaiting those vacation photos you've winnowed out in the Bridge. Click the ⇨ button in the top-left corner of the Bridge window to return to the *Photos* folder. Scroll down a few rows to the *Borobudur.jpg* thumbnail, which features an evocative image of the famous ninth-century Buddhist Mahayana monument in Java. (Even though this is a ★★★★★ image, it isn't from Bali so the Bridge shows it after the Bali photos.) Drag the thumbnail from the Bridge into the InDesign window and drop it onto the large red box with an ✕ through it on the left side of the page, as illustrated in Figure 1-51. (Note that I've collapsed InDesign's palettes to make the figure a bit more legible.)

Figure 1-51.

14. ***Fit the image to the frame.*** When you drag the image over, it comes in too big for its frame. To adjust its size, click the image to select it and switch applications. (The Bridge window remains in front. If that bugs you, feel free to move it out of the way.) Right-click and choose **Fitting→Fill Frame Proportionally** to instruct InDesign to scale the photo so it fits the frame, as in Figure 1-52 on the next page. (I designed the frames to match the proportions of the photos, so cropping isn't necessary.) For the full story on placing graphics, stay tuned for Lesson 6, "Importing and Modifying Artwork."

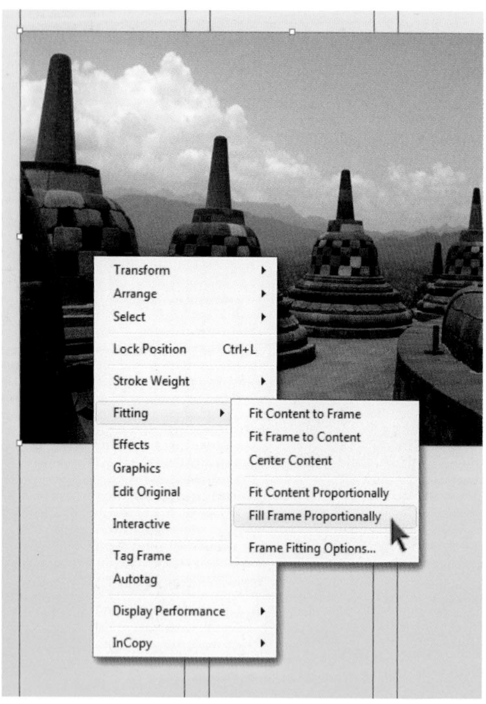

Figure 1-52.

15. ***Import the entire stack of smaller images*** You don't have to stick to placing just one image at a time. New in InDesign CS3, you can load your cursor with multiple images in the Bridge and drop them in one at a time when you get back to InDesign. Return to the compact Bridge window and scroll up to the stack of Bali images you created in Step 10 (which goes by the name of the first image, *Terraces.jpg*). Then do the following:

    - Press the Alt key (Option on the Mac) and click the stack thumbnail to select all the images in the stack, as indicated by a double outline around the thumbnail. (Merely clicking in the thumbnail selects the pictured image only, in this case, *Terraces.jpg*.)
    - Drag the stack and drop it into the InDesign document. When you do, InDesign changes the cursor to a with a parenthetical 3 and a postage stamp–sized preview of the first image, as in Figure 1-53. (If you don't see the preview, click in InDesign to bring the application to the front.) The 3 tells you that your cursor is loaded with three images.
    - Click in one of the small frames on the right side of the page to drop the image in place. Then move to the next frame and click to place the next image. After each click, you get a preview and reminder of how many images remain to be placed. No number means there's just one image left.

If you want to place an image out of sequence, you can toggle through the order by pressing an arrow key on your keyboard.

I preset the frames so that all images resize to their new homes automatically, as in Figure 1-54 on the facing page. You'll learn about this and many more placing options in Lesson 6.

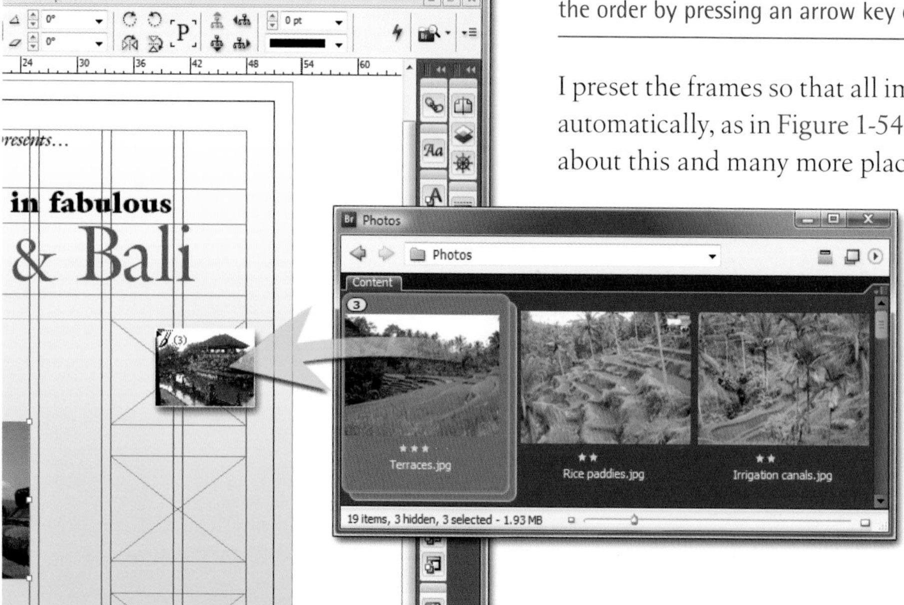

Figure 1-53.

16. ***Restore the Bridge to its default workspace.*** The Bridge's memory is uncanny and complete. If you quit the Bridge and open it back up again, it will appear exactly as it was when you left it. So if you're not the only one using the program on your machine, you might want to do your colleagues a favor before you quit and reset the workspace. Here's how:

    - Click the compact Bridge window to switch to the Bridge application.
    - Click the ▭ icon in the top-right corner of the window or press Ctrl+Enter (⌘-Return) to expand the window so it once again displays the menu bar.
    - Return to Adobe's factory-defined default workspace by clicking the ▣ button in the bottom-right corner of the window, which is still set to the default workspace. Alternatively, you can press the keyboard shortcut, Ctrl+F1 (⌘-F1). The Bridge restores the Content and Preview panels to their original locations.
    - Quit the Bridge by choosing **File→Exit** (**File→Quit** on the Mac). The operating system returns you to InDesign.

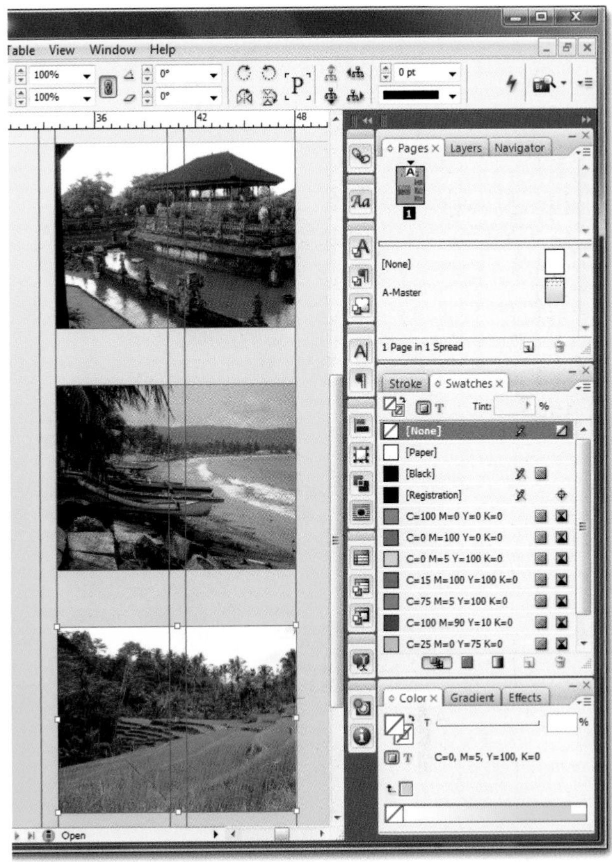

Figure 1-54.

Feel free to save your work on *Travel flier.indd*, as described in the very next exercise. But feel equally free to give it the heave-ho and close the document without saving. For now, it's not important that you save your work; it's important that you *do* the work and come to grips with some of the basic functions inside InDesign CS3.

Saving Your Document

InDesign is packed with state-of-the-art functions that make other layout applications look as archaic as a box of Gilbert O'Sullivan eight-tracks in the trunk of an AMC Gremlin. But if I had to choose the most critical command in the program, it would be the Save command. Without File→Save, you couldn't preserve your work. Your only choice would be to do the same old thing over and over again, just like we did in the days before digital.

So it is with a mixture of delight and relief that I confirm that, yes, InDesign offers a Save command and, yes, you'll learn how to use it in this exercise. Not only that, InDesign has the quite fortunate habit of automatically saving your work to a separate backup file behind your back (see "InDesign Saves Your Sanity," page 42). Here's how saving works:

1. ***Open a document.*** **Choose File→Open** or press Ctrl+O (⌘-O on the Mac). Open the file *Untitled Mabry.indt* in the *Lesson 01* folder inside *Lesson Files-IDcs3 1on1*. (If you get the modified links message, click the Fix Links Automatically button to refresh the graphics.) This file, from a book I wrote a while back called *Adobe Master Class: Design Invitational* (Peachpit Press, 2002), contains six pages that feature the work of designer Michael Mabry, as pictured in Figure 1-55. (The pages themselves were designed and executed by Andrew Faulkner.) Imagine that you just created this file or opened it from a QuarkXPress document. Now you're ready to save it for posterity.

Assignment:
Create a large-format poster with fluid text shapes

Applications used:
Adobe Photoshop,
Adobe InDesign

As creative professionals, many of us enter the computer, adopt its tools, and never come back out again. It's as if we're the remnants of an indigenous tribe whose elders express concern because we've stopped speaking the old language and lost touch with the old ways. We're all computer, all the time.

Michael Mabry senses that The Machine wants to suck him in and rob him of his ancestral traditions. So in his own quiet way, he rages against it. A self-professed "nontechnological technology guy," he sees himself as having one foot in the old world and the other in the new. "I guess I look at the computer as a necessary evil, really. I try to make it as invisible as possible, and there are times when I go to great lengths to avoid it. I don't want it to get in the way of what I'm doing. But like most designers, I definitely need it to do business today."

Michael Mabry

Page Design

Michael Mabry: Page Design 49

Figure 1-55.

PEARL OF WISDOM

Because this file was last saved as a template (hence the *.indt* extension), InDesign opens an untitled copy of the file. This prevents you from accidentally saving over the original. More importantly where this exercise is concerned, it exactly simulates the experience you would have if you were to create a new document or open a QuarkXPress file—so far as InDesign is concerned, the document has never been saved.

2. ***Consult the File Handling preferences.*** This step is not essential to saving a file; it merely establishes a few preferences and provides you with some information about how your system is configured. Choose **Edit→Preferences→File Handling** (under the **InDesign** menu on the Mac). Pictured in Figure 1-56, these options control how InDesign saves its files. Here's how the options work:

   - The first option, **Document Recovery Data**, determines where InDesign stores its auto-saved documents. To learn more, read the sidebar "InDesign Saves Your Sanity" on the next page.
   - As long as we're here, make sure the **Always Save Preview Images with Documents** check box is on. This embeds a thumbnail preview so you can identify a file at a glance from within the Bridge as well as from the Open dialog box. You even get to choose the thumbnail size you prefer, as measured in pixels. The default Medium is relatively small. I like to see my thumbnails with more clarity, so I set the **Preview Size** option to **Extra Large 1024 × 1024**.
   - Personally, I also turn off the **Relink Preserves Dimensions** at the bottom of the dialog box. This prevents InDesign from automatically scaling an updated graphic when it's a different size than its predecessor (something it started to do in CS2). No doubt some designers believe that the size of the frame should dictate the size of the imported image; I believe exactly the opposite. Good thing we have this check box so we can reconcile our differences without resorting to violence.

   Click the **OK** button to exit the dialog box and accept your changes (assuming you made any).

3. ***Choose the Save command.*** Press Ctrl+S (⌘-S) or choose **File→Save**. If the document had been saved before, InDesign would update the file on disk. But because it hasn't, the **Save As** dialog box appears, as in Figure 1-57.

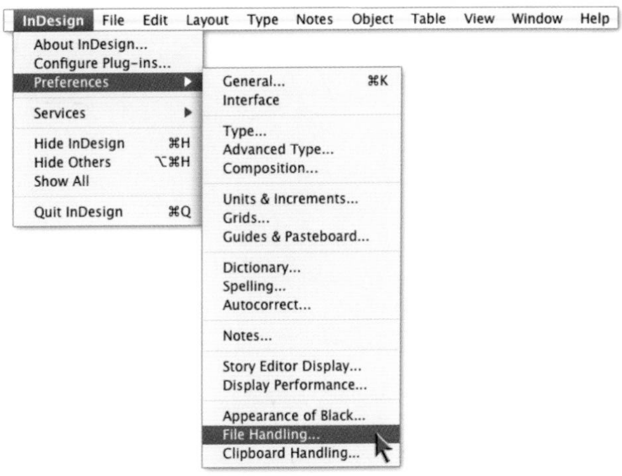

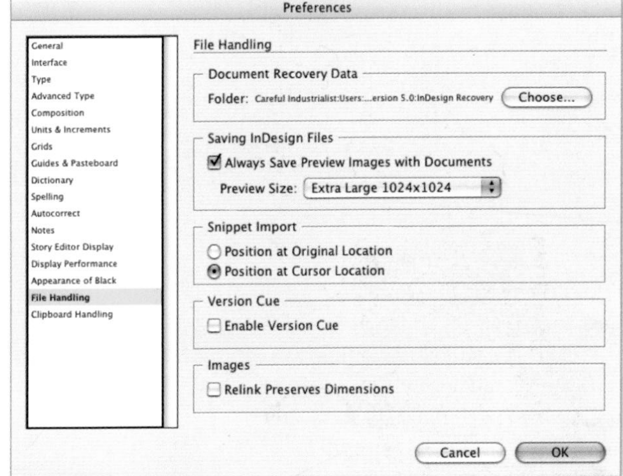

Figure 1-56.

Figure 1-57.

InDesign Saves Your Sanity

These days, operating systems seldom crash. It's a rare day when you see the "blue screen of death" on the PC or a restart message on the Mac. (It's a very bad day, but it's still thankfully rare.) But while the operating system does a splendid job of protecting itself (and you in the process), applications still go down. Even an application as virtuous as InDesign encounters the occasional fatal error. And when the program goes down, your data goes with it.

At least, that's how it works in a normal program. Fortunately for us, however, InDesign is anything but normal. The entire time you work, InDesign is thinking, "I could mess up—you never know, I could mess up!" while furiously anticipating just such a mishap. Every time you perform what InDesign regards to be a critical event—often something as simple as drawing a rectangle or adding a page—the program saves a backup of the file to its top-secret *InDesign Recovery* folder. That way, when the worst happens (as it inevitably does), you have something to work from. The recovered file may not reflect every last edit you performed, but it's typically no more than a few operations behind. So instead of losing, say, several hours of work, you lose two or three minutes.

To see it for yourself, try this:

1. Close all open documents. (Otherwise, InDesign is faced with the proposition of recovering multiple documents, which works but takes extra time.)

2. Create a new document. Just to keep things simple, make it one page long.

3. Select the pencil tool. It's the fifth tool down in the single-column toolbox. It's not a particularly useful tool, but it is easy to use, which suits our purposes.

4. Scribble in the document window. The figure below gives you an idea of what I have in mind. But it really doesn't matter—just have fun.

5. Select a line weight and style. See those two pop-up menus on the right side of the control palette? One reads 1 pt and the one directly below looks like a black bar. Use these options to select different thicknesses and styles for your doodling.

6. Add a blank page. Press Ctrl+Shift+P (⌘-Shift-P) to add a new blank page to the document. (I'll introduce the corresponding command in Lesson 9, but for now just press the keys.)

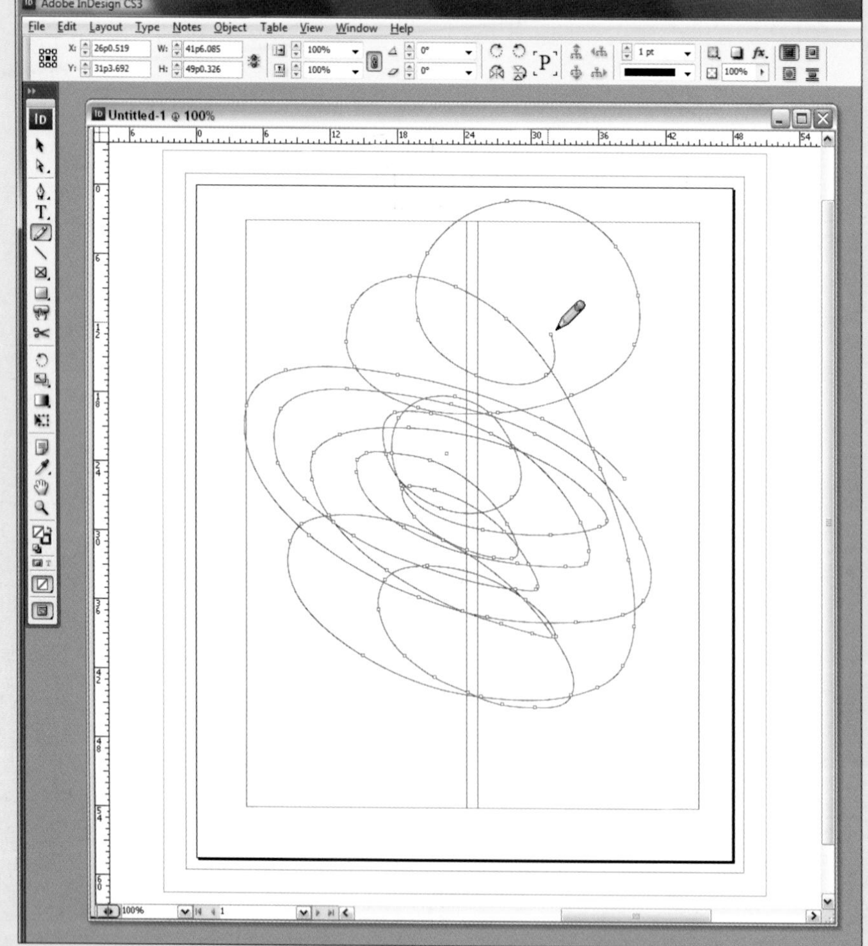

7. Repeat the last three steps several times. Draw a squiggle with the pencil, modify the outline from the control palette, and add another page by pressing Ctrl+Shift+P (or ⌘-Shift-P).

8. Simulate a crash. We'll do that by force-quitting the application. On the PC, press Ctrl+Alt+Delete to call up the Task Manager window. (Under Windows Vista, you also have to click the Start Task Manager button.) Select Adobe InDesign CS3 from the Applications list and click End Task. An alert message will appear, asking whether you want to save the file. Ignore it! Shortly thereafter, Windows complains that "The system cannot end this program because it is waiting for a response from you." Click the End Now button to abruptly terminate InDesign, as shown on the right. Close the Task Manager by clicking the ☒ icon in the title bar.

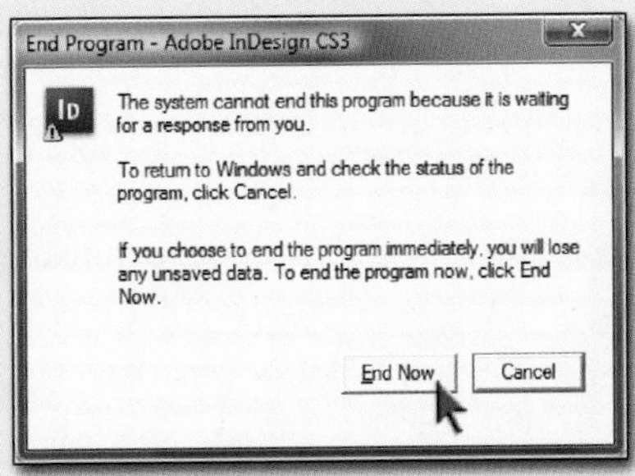

On the Macintosh, things work a bit differently. First, to force-quit InDesign, press ⌘-Option-Escape. Then select InDesign from the list and click the Force Quit button, as in the figure on the right. When the alert message appears, click Force Quit again. Then close the Force Quit window by clicking the ⊗ on the left side of the title bar.

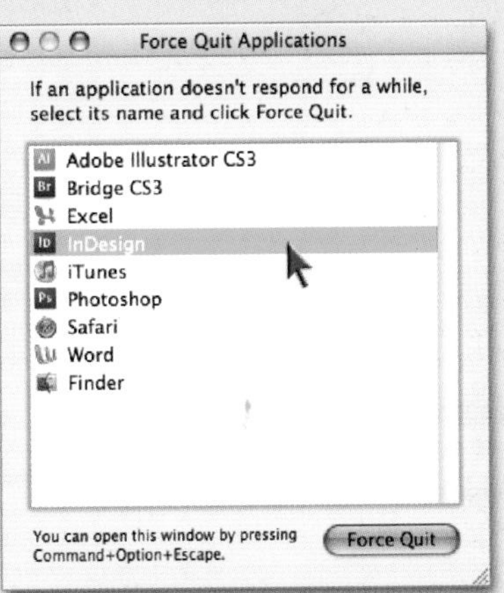

9. Wait for the application to completely empty out of memory. Give it a couple of minutes just to be on the safe side. Then restart InDesign. During the startup process, the application might display a message like the one on the right, asking if you want it to automatically recover files. In this case, click Yes. If you don't see the message, it just means InDesign has set about recovering unsaved files without your consent.

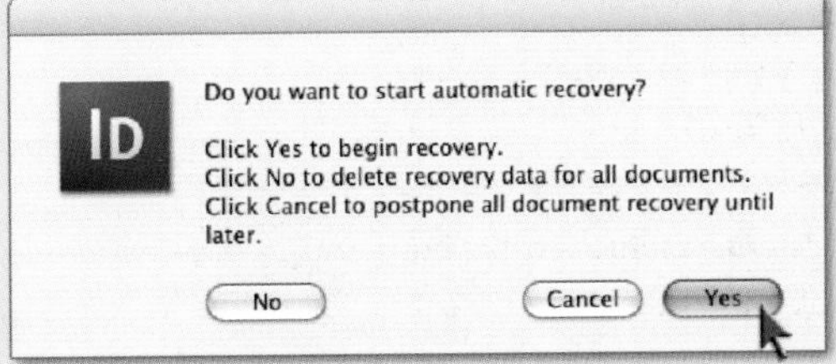

In a few moments, you will see a recent version of your document. It may contain one page; it may contain many pages. It may include all your pencil squiggles, or it may include only the very first squiggle. Whatever the case, it's welcome news: InDesign managed to save something, which is more than you saved. It's still no substitute for saving your documents on a regular and frequent basis, but it's a heck of an insurance policy.

PEARL OF WISDOM

Typically, you can save a document by closing it. Just click ☒ or ⊙ in the title bar or choose File→Close. When asked to save the document, click Yes or Save and away you go. But if you ask me, relying on a force-save is a trifle cavalier. If you accidentally click No or Don't Save—or press the N or D key—*you lose your changes with no way to get them back!* My suggestion: When you want to close a document, first choose File→Save.

4. ***Choose the desired format.*** Leave the **Save as Type** option (called **Format** on the Mac) set to **InDesign CS3 Document**. This saves the pages as an everyday native file that opens as a titled document. (The other option, InDesign CS2 Template, saves the file as a template that opens untitled, as this one did, thus making the original harder to overwrite.)

5. ***Specify a name and location.*** I recommend that you save the file inside the same *Lesson 01* folder that contains the *Untitled Mabry.indt* document. This keeps the file in close proximity to the linked images in the *Mabry artwork* folder. Then even if you copy the *Lesson 01* folder to a different location, all the links will remain intact.

   You can name the file as you like, with one proviso: Leave the extension set to *.indd* for an InDesign document or *.indt* for an InDesign template. It's difficult to override this extension on the PC, but it's easy on the Mac. *Don't do it!* Files without extensions won't successfully transport across platforms (via email or servers), they go unrecognized by Windows, and they might not work properly under future versions of the Mac OS.

6. ***Click the Save button.*** Or press Enter or Return to save the file to disk. From this point on, you can update the file to reflect any changes you make by choosing File→Save. To again invoke the Save As dialog box—whether to save a different version of the document or store it in a different location—choose **File→Save As** or press Ctrl+Shift+S (⌘-Shift-S on the Mac).

The Save As command has one other bonus: It rebuilds the file and makes it more efficient. When you choose File→Save, InDesign appends the new information onto the old. This saves time and makes for a more efficient working experience, but it also balloons the file over time, causing it to grow incrementally larger with every press of Ctrl+S. To streamline the file, periodically choose File→Save As. (I generally add a version number to the end of the filename, such as "-1" or "-2.") If it's been a long time since your last Save As, it's not unusual to see the file size drop by half or more.

PEARL OF WISDOM

Page-layout apps in general and InDesign in particular are notoriously bad about backward compatibility. A standard InDesign CS3 file cannot be opened in CS2 or earlier. But you can export files to a format that is openable, if not entirely compatible, with InDesign CS and CS2. To do this, choose File→Export or press Ctrl+E (⌘-E). In the Export dialog box, change the Save As Type (or Format) setting to InDesign Interchange. This creates a file with the extension *.inx*, which InDesign CS and CS2 can open. One caveat. For this trick to work, you also have to update your older version of InDesign. From inside the CS and CS2 applications, choose Help→Updates, log onto Adobe's Web site, and download the appropriate update. Don't expect features that are new to CS3 to survive the transition, and be prepared for a few other possible gotchas in the process. But at least your transition to InDesign CS3 doesn't entirely doom you to a fate of forward obsolescence. Or would that be an overabundance of relevance? Thanks to *.inx*, we may never know.

WHAT DID YOU LEARN?

Match the key concept in the numbered list below with the letter of the phrase that best describes it. Answers appear upside-down at the bottom of the page.

Key Concepts

1. Template
2. Profile or Policy Mismatch
3. Control palette
4. Docking pane
5. Fix Links Automatically
6. Facing Pages
7. Pica
8. Bleed
9. Slug
10. Ruler guide
11. The Bridge
12. InDesign Interchange

Descriptions

A. A file-management system that comes with InDesign that you can use to find, rename, move, rank, and assign keywords to files.

B. New to CS3, this interface element houses clusters of palettes that are locked into vertical columns.

C. A button that seeks to reestablish connections to all graphic files that have been moved or modified since the last time an InDesign document was saved.

D. Also known as *.inx*, this file format facilitates compatibility between InDesign CS3 and its predecessors InDesign CS and CS2. For a full description, direct your attention twelve inches to the west.

E. This special kind of InDesign file contains page specifications and placeholder frames that serve as the starting point for a series of similar documents.

F. This alert message warns you that you're about to open a document that uses a different color space than the one you specified in the Color Settings dialog box.

G. Nonprinting horizontal and vertical lines that serve both as visual markers and magnetic alignment tools.

H. A context-sensitive palette, located by default at the top of the screen, that changes to accommodate the selected object or active tool.

I. A unit of measurement equal to 12 points, or $1/6$ inch, which you can annotate inside a numerical option box by entering the letter *p*.

J. An area outside the page boundary that holds the excess from artwork and other objects; this excess is intended to extend to the very edge of the page and will be cut away when the pages are trimmed.

K. A portion of the pasteboard outside the bleed that holds printing information such as project titles and handling instructions.

L. A setting that lets you see pages side-by-side, as in a book or magazine, and creates mirror-image margins and column structures for them.

Answers

1E, 2F, 3H, 4B, 5C, 6L, 7I, 8J, 9K, 10G, 11A, 12D

LESSON 2

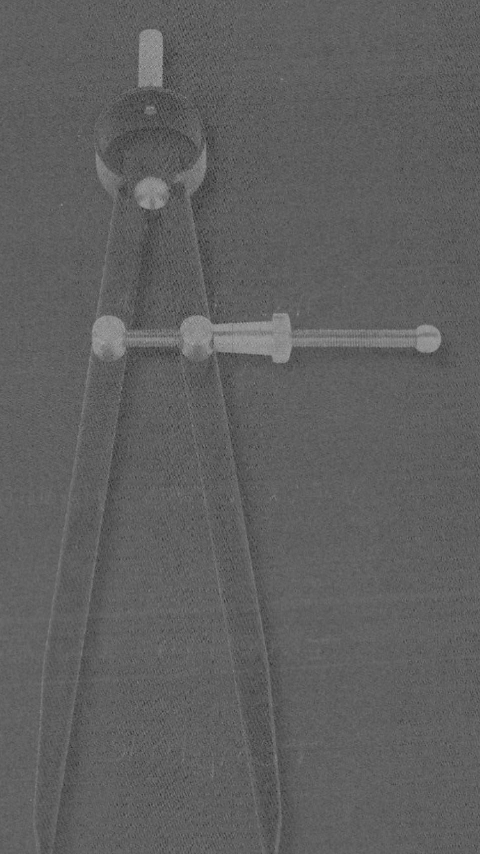

CREATING AND FLOWING TEXT

WHEN IT COMES to working on computers, most serious writing—including the writing I'm writing right now—takes place in a word processor such as Microsoft Word. I'm going to climb out on a limb and guess that you use Word, too. InDesign and Quark may keep butting heads for a while yet, but Word managed to shake off serious competition years ago. And while Microsoft's reputation for creating intuitive, reliable software isn't exactly stellar, they got a lot of things right in the case of Word.

Heck, Microsoft even crammed a fair amount of actual page-layout features into the program. But I'm going to climb out even further on this limb here and guess that you don't use them. Maybe, just *maybe*, you've created a two-column spread in Word, but that's probably it. And frankly, congrats to you for getting that far. Word's page-layout capability reminds me of Samuel Johnson's comment about a dog walking on its hind legs: "It is not done well; but you are surprised to find it done at all."

I bring this up because Word has shaped many people's notions of how computer applications should handle text. Word processors make it easy for you to quickly enter and edit text. They'd better; that's their main reason for existing. But when it comes to controlling how that text appears on the printed page, a word processor pretty much expects you to create single columns of text that flow in regular procession from one page to the next.

Not so with InDesign. To say that InDesign makes easy work of composing multicolumn documents is true, but it doesn't begin to tell the story. As we saw in the previous lesson, you can specify different column settings on different pages and even make neighboring columns different widths. But the real genius of InDesign and other layout programs is that you don't have to adhere to your column settings at all. Every character of type exists inside an independent, free-floating container called a *frame*. That frame can be rectangular,

ABOUT THIS LESSON

Project Files

Before beginning the exercises, make sure you've copied the lesson files from the DVD, as directed in Step 3 on page xvii of the Preface. This should result in a folder called *Lesson Files-IDcs3 1on1* on your desktop. We'll be working with the files inside the *Lesson 02* subfolder.

In this lesson, we'll look at the many ways to create, import, edit, and correct text in InDesign. You'll learn how to:

Video Lesson 2: Text and Frames

Adding text to a document is a matter of drawing frames, placing a Word file, and entering or modifying text with the type tool. If you're familiar with early layout applications such as PageMaker or QuarkXPress, this may sound like child's play. But like any program, InDesign throws a few curve balls, enough to occasionally frustrate even seasoned users.

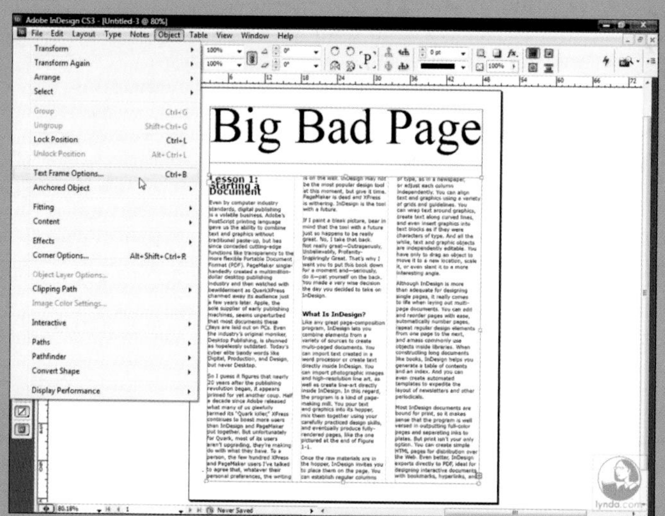

To get a feel for how you import and adjust text in InDesign, watch the second video lesson included on the DVD. To view this video, insert the DVD and double-click the file *IDcs3 Videos.html*. Then click **Lesson 2: Text and Frames** under the **Navigation and Text** heading. During this 14-minute 57-second movie, you'll learn the following shortcuts:

Operation	Windows shortcut	Macintosh shortcut
Create a new document	Ctrl+N	⌘-N
Change the number of columns	Ctrl+/ (slash)*	⌘-/*
Increase or reduce the type size	Ctrl+Shift+>, Ctrl+Shift+<	⌘-Shift->, ⌘-Shift-<
Accept text edits and select arrow tool	Esc (Enter on keypad*)	Esc (Enter on keypad*)
Place text into a document	Ctrl+D	⌘-D
Change selected text frame options	Ctrl+B	⌘-B
Select all text in a story	Ctrl+A	⌘-A
View and edit text in the Story Editor	Ctrl+Y	⌘-Y

* Works only if you loaded the dekeKeys keyboard shortcuts (as directed on page xix of the Preface).

geometric, elliptical, or any shape you like, as Figure 2-1 illustrates. You can move and scale the frame just by dragging it. And you can drop the frame literally anywhere on the page. I commend Word and other word processors for their text-editing prowess. But when it comes time to put that text on the page, I simply couldn't manage without a program like Adobe InDesign.

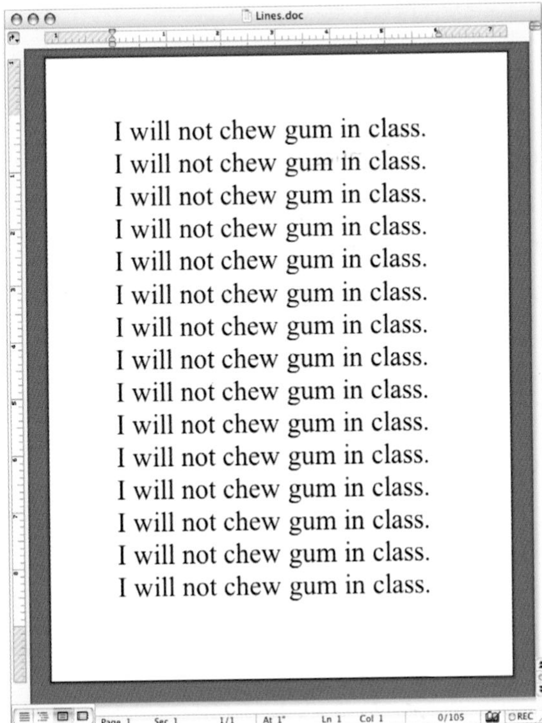

A single column of type in Word

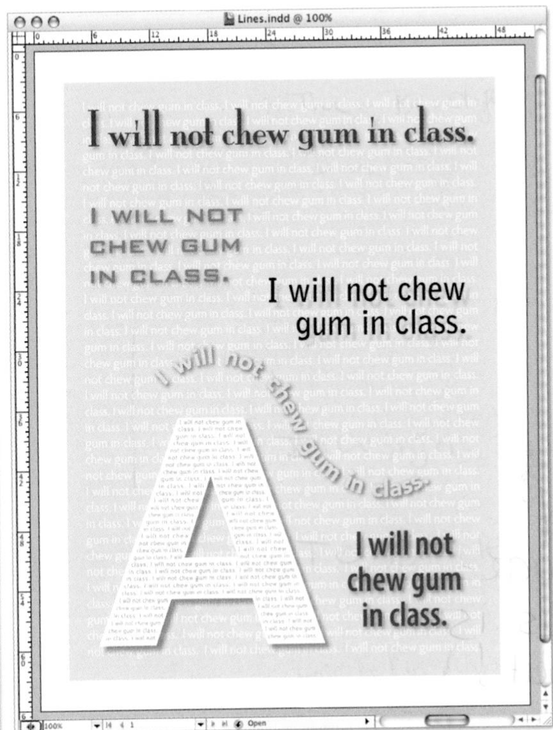

Text arranged in free-form frames in InDesign

Figure 2-1.

The Mechanics of Frames

If you come from QuarkXPress or PageMaker, you know that text frames are nothing new. The programs use different terminology—Quark calls them *text boxes* and PageMaker calls them *text blocks*—but they're one and the same. (I still use the term *text block* to mean a frame that's filled with text.) For those to whom page layout is a new experience, a few words about how frames work: InDesign regards the text frame as an independent object, just like a line or shape. The main difference is that instead of being filled with color, it's filled with type. Double-click inside the frame and start typing away. Or, if you've already typed the text in a word processor, import the text from a file on disk, or copy it from the word processor and paste it into InDesign. The text automatically wraps from one line to the next inside the confines of the frame.

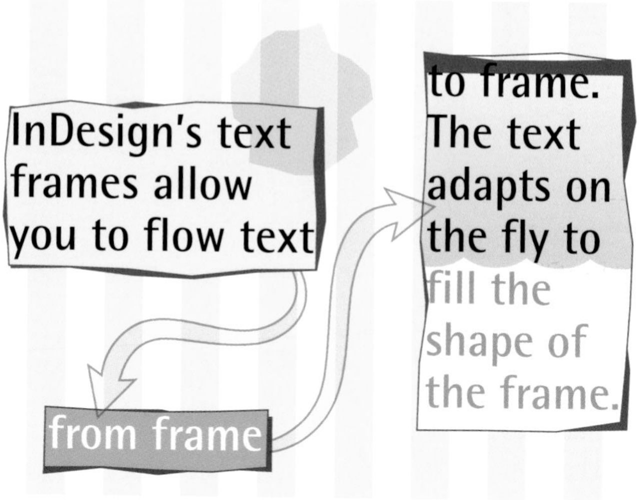
InDesign's text frames allow you to flow text
from frame
to frame. The text adapts on the fly to fill the shape of the frame.

Figure 2-2.

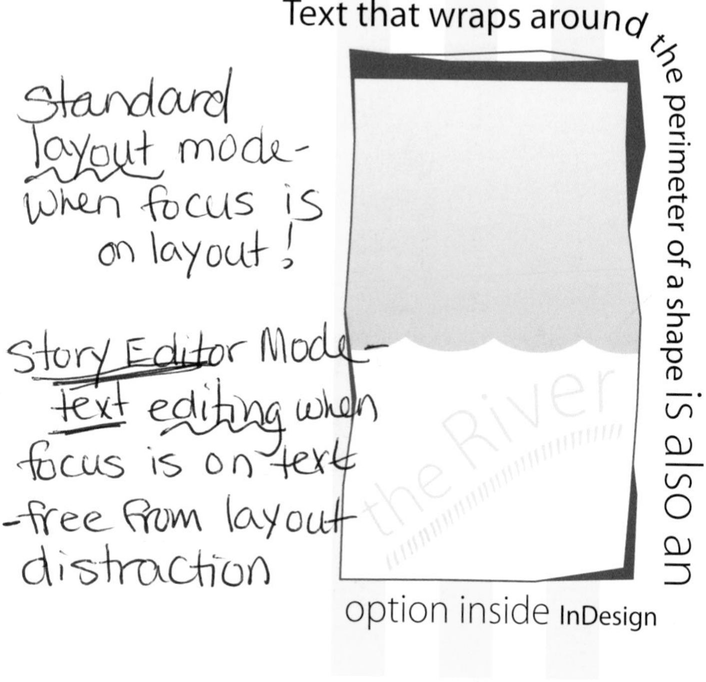
Text that wraps around the perimeter of a shape is also an option inside InDesign
the River

Figure 2-3.

It's rare that a single text frame can contain all the text in a document, so you can draw many text frames and link them. *Linking* means a long text document can flow from one frame to another to create multiple columns and pages of type. You can draw and link frames manually, as in Figure 2-2. Or you can watch your text roar through scores of columns and pages with a single click.

Whether empty or full, a text frame can be edited to suit your shifting layout needs. The black arrow in the toolbox lets you change the size of the frame; the white arrow lets you change its shape (everything from square to round). Either way, InDesign rewraps and reflows the text immediately and automatically, permitting you to concentrate on the page design without having to fuss over each and every character of content. And while text usually flows inside the frame, it doesn't have to. You can also wrap text around the perimeter of a frame, as illustrated in Figure 2-3.

When it comes time to fuss over the content—sadly, misspellings and typos are a fact of life—InDesign is good at that, too. You can edit the text directly inside a frame, great for staying abreast of how your changes affect flow and hyphenation. Or you can switch to the Story Editor, a bare-bones text-editing environment that InDesign inherited from its progenitor, PageMaker. The Story Editor not only allows you to focus on your text, free from the distractions of layout, but also works quickly, saving InDesign's rewrap and reflow calculations until the editing is complete. And like any self-respecting layout program, InDesign lets you spell check your text, both in the standard layout and Story Editor modes.

InDesign's combination of flexible, frame-based layout and eternally editable text makes it a cinch for you to "suit the action to the word, the word to the action," as the melancholy Hamlet put it. (Alas! Had he only lived to be a digital compositer. Where be your gibes now; your gambols, your songs?) Absorb the information presented in this lesson and you'll be one big step forward on the road to mastery of InDesign. But enough words, already. Let's get down to action.

Flowing Text into Frames

It's easy enough to enter text into a lone frame, as I demonstrate in Video Lesson 2, "Text and Frames." (If you haven't watched the video, this is a good time to do so.) The trick is making text flow from column to column in multiple frames. *Flow* is the perfect word, too. Text in InDesign courses like a tenacious little river, filling every vessel it contacts. It swells to fill wide frames and dribbles through narrow ones. The similarities between text and liquid are so downright palpable that many designers refer to the act of importing text into linked frames as "pouring a document."

This exercise shows you how to import text from a Word file and flow that text through a multicolumn InDesign document. The goal is to lay out a cookie recipe for publication in a food magazine. In the process, you'll learn how to draw text frames, link them together, and auto-pour long documents.

1. ***Open a document.*** Open the file named *Cookie recipe 1.indd* located in the *Lesson 02* folder inside *Lesson Files-IDcs3 1on1*. Figure 2-4 shows the first page of this two-page document. The page contains a single photo; the text eagerly awaits.

2. ***Select the type tool and draw a text frame.*** We need to draw a text frame to hold the title of the recipe and the byline at the top of the first page. Press T to get the type tool and drag to draw a rectangle from the upper-left corner of the first column to the intersection of the cyan guide and the right margin, as in Figure 2-5. The frame should snap to the guides. (If not, choose **View→Grids & Guides→Snap to Guides** to turn snapping on.) You should see a blinking insertion marker in the upper-left corner of the resulting text frame.

Figure 2-4.

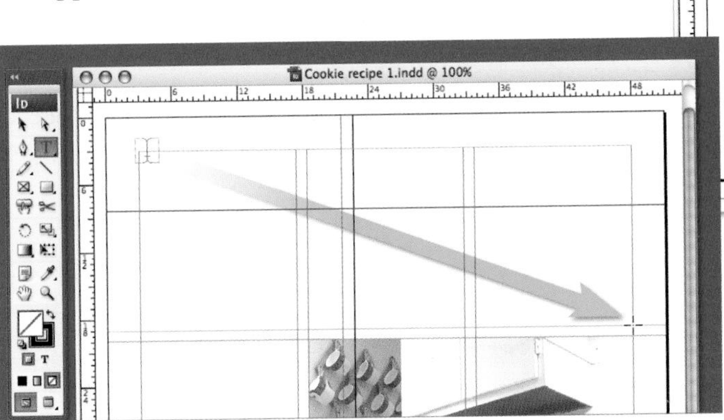

Figure 2-5.

Because you drew the text frame with all its edges aligned to columns and guides, you can't see the frame itself. If you like, choose View→Grids & Guides→Hide Guides or press Ctrl+; (⌘-; on the Mac) to hide the guides so you can see the frame. Just make sure you choose the command again to turn the guides back on before continuing.

3. ***Place a document from a word processor.*** Choose **File→Place** or press Ctrl+D (⌘-D) to display the **Place** dialog box. Go to the *Lesson 02* folder and select the *Puppet text.doc* file. Turn on the **Show Import Options** check box and click the **Open** button. (Or leave the check box off and Shift-click Open.) InDesign displays the **Microsoft Word Import Options** dialog box (see Figure 2-6), which presents you with a wealth of options, including the following:

- If your document contains a table of contents, footnotes, endnotes, or an index, use the four Include check boxes to specify whether or not you want to import these elements. Our document doesn't contain this stuff, so it doesn't matter if the options are on or off.

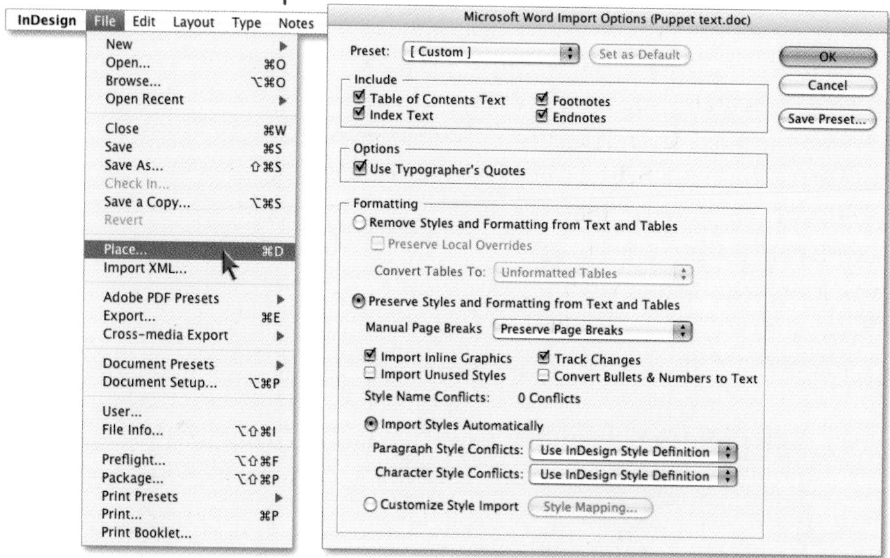

Figure 2-6.

- The **Use Typographer's Quotes** check box lets you choose to convert any straight quotes in your Word file into typographer's quotes (also known as "curly" quotes, because they typically curl around the text inside the quotes). This check box also replaces straight apostrophes with curled ones. Leave it turned on.

- The Formatting radio buttons control whether InDesign respects or ignores the font, type size, and other attributes applied inside the word processor. We want to retain the formatting used in this document, so leave **Preserve Styles and Formatting from Text and Tables** turned on.
- Word and other word processors let you insert page breaks to define where one page ends and another begins. But Word pages almost never correspond to InDesign pages. To let your documents flow freely, set the **Manual Page Breaks** option to **No Breaks**.
- Most of the remaining options determine how InDesign imports and formats style sheets from a Word document. For example, if a Word style conflicts with one in your InDesign document, you can choose to resolve it in InDesign's favor, since InDesign offers more precise typographic control. This particular Word document contains a couple of styles but none that conflict with InDesign, so you can safely ignore these options. For complete, authoritative information on style sheets, read Lesson 8, "Using Style Sheets."

To recap, set Manual Page Breaks to No Breaks and leave the other options as is. Then click **OK**. The first part of the text appears within the frame you drew in the last step, which results in a filled text block. Of course, this cookie recipe consists of more than a title and a byline. InDesign tells you that there's more to come by expressing the *out port*—the box in the lower-right corner of the text block, labeled in Figure 2-7—as a red ⊞. This indicates that the entirety of the text—known in InDesign parlance as the *story*—doesn't fit inside the text frame. Think of the out port as a faucet that has been turned off so that the

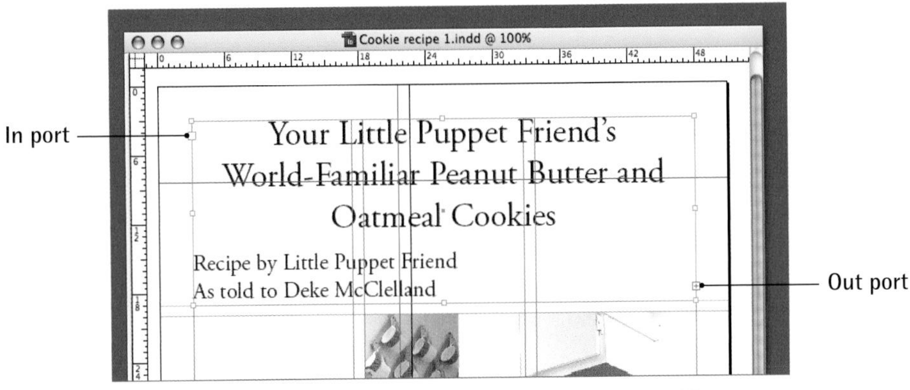

Figure 2-7.

story can't flow any further. Your job is to open the faucet and give the story another container to flow into.

4. ***Select the black arrow tool.*** Click the black arrow in the upper-left corner of the toolbox. Adobe calls this the selection tool, because selecting is what it does. But I prefer to call it what it is, the black arrow tool.

If you loaded my dekeKeys keyboard shortcuts as directed on page xix of the Preface, you can get to the black arrow at any time by pressing the Enter key on the numeric keypad. If you remember none of my other keyboard shortcuts, remember this one: It really will save you scads of time (although I must admit, scads are difficult to measure).

---

5. ***Select the text frame's out port.*** Click the text frame's out port (the red ⊞). The cursor changes to a loaded text cursor with a blue link icon and the first lines from the story, which tells you that you are armed with text that's ready to be placed.

6. ***Draw a second text frame.*** Position the cursor at the intersection of the left edge of the left column and the magenta ruler guide (directly below the cyan one). The black arrow in the loaded text cursor turns white when the cursor is next to a guide, as in the white-arrow cursor. This color change means that you are about to create a text frame that snaps into alignment with the guide. With the cursor positioned as I've described, drag to draw a second text frame within the first column. As Figure 2-8 shows, the text automatically flows from the first text frame into the second. The upper-left corner of this second frame sports a blue *in port*. The in port contains an arrowhead (▶), which shows that text flows from another text frame into this one. You'll also see that this frame ends with a red ⊞ out port, signifying that still more text is waiting to flow.

   Before we let this dammed text flow—note the spelling on that one—take a moment to click inside the first text block. The first frame's out port is now a blue ▶ arrow, which indicates that text flows out of it into another text frame. This frame also has an in port, but because the frame is the first text block in the string of blocks that will contain this story, the in port is empty.

7. ***Load the text cursor and go to page 2.*** Let's continue the text flow on the second page of the document. Click in the second text frame's out port to load the text cursor,

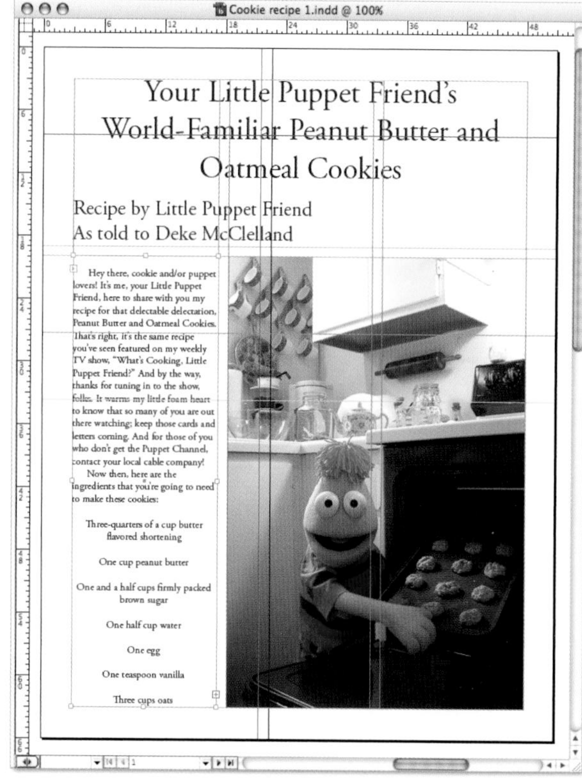

Figure 2-8.

press Ctrl+J (⌘-J) to highlight the page number in the lower-left corner of the document window, type 2, and press Enter or Return to go to page 2.

8. *Create a new text frame.* This time, instead of dragging to draw a text frame, click the cyan guide somewhere in the first column. As Figure 2-9 shows, InDesign creates the text frame automatically, positioning the top of the frame at the point where you clicked and pouring text into the remaining length of the column.

PEARL OF WISDOM

Modeled after a function introduced by the first incarnation of PageMaker but inexplicably never added to QuarkXPress, automatic frame making is InDesign's alternative to drawing frames by hand. You can use this trick anytime you want a text block to be the same width as a column—as in Step 6, for example. But if you intend to violate columns, as you did in Step 2, drawing the frame by hand is your only option. My recommendation: Let InDesign be in charge of frames when you can; draw frames when you must.

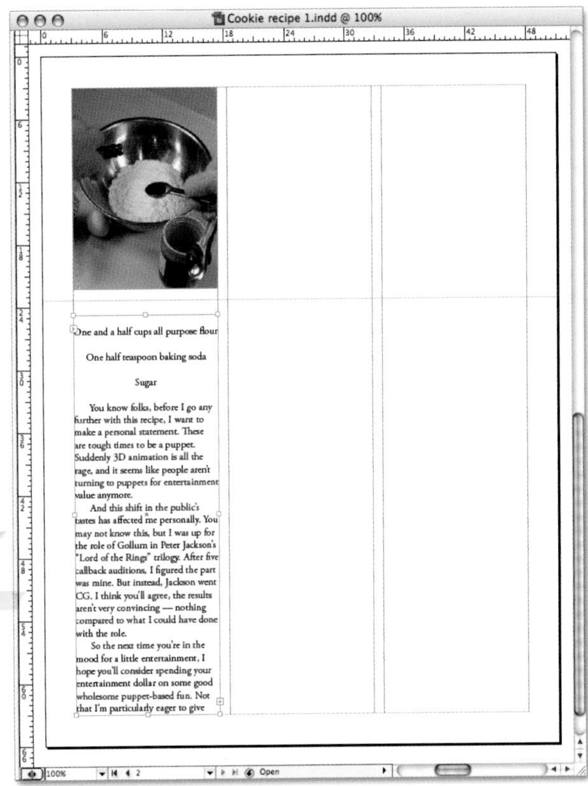

Figure 2-9.

9. *Display the text threads.* As you might imagine, with text flowing from one page to the next, potentially skipping pages and intertwining with other stories, it may become difficult to follow how a single article flows from one frame to the next. Choose **View→Show Text Threads** or press Ctrl+Alt+Y (⌘-Option-Y on the Mac) to display blue lines between the out ports and in ports of linked, or *threaded*, text blocks. The blue lines make it easy to follow the flow of a story, as in Figure 2-10 on the next page.

If it took you a while to find the Show Text Threads command in the View menu, try this nifty trick: Press Ctrl+Shift+Alt (that's ⌘-Shift-Option on the Mac) and click View to alphabetize the commands in the menu. This technique works with all menus, but Adobe added it with the convoluted View menu in mind.

As you can imagine, it would take quite a while to lay out a large amount of text by clicking or dragging to create a text frame, clicking the frame's out port to load the cursor, clicking or dragging to create another text frame, clicking that frame's out port, and so on. Luckily, InDesign gives you several ways to speed the process along.

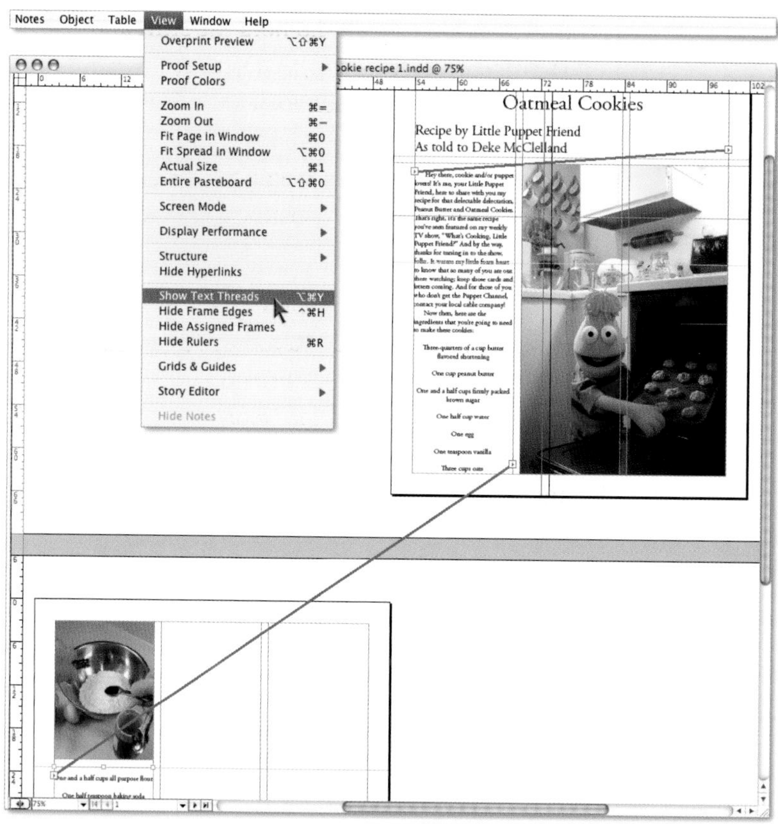

Figure 2-10.

10. *Load the text cursor.* Then click the last frame's out port.

11. *Select the top of the second column on the second page.* Press the Alt (or Option) key to change the cursor to the *semi-autoflow* cursor (⤵). To see exactly what it does, click while keeping Alt (or Option) down. The second column fills with text, as shown in Figure 2-11, but nothing more. What's so automatic about that? Release the key and take a look at your cursor. It's already loaded and ready for you to continue pouring text. No need to click the out port first. You saved yourself one whole click!

12. *Choose the Undo Place command.* All right, so maybe saving a single click doesn't measure up to your idea of state-of-the-art automation. Fortunately, InDesign has a few more tricks up its sleeve. First choose **Edit→Undo Place** or press Ctrl+Z (⌘-Z) to undo the last operation. And voila, you still have a loaded text cursor. I don't know about you, but I'm impressed.

What if you *don't* want InDesign to reload your cursor? To regain the black arrow tool, press the Esc key or just press Ctrl+Z (⌘-Z) again.

---

13. *Fill the remaining columns.* Press and hold the Shift and Alt keys (Shift and Option on the Mac). This time, you get the *autoflow document* cursor, which looks like . With the keys still down, click at the top of the second column. As illustrated in Figure 2-12, the flowing text fills all the remaining columns in the document. You have to admit, *this* is automation.

14. *Choose Undo Place again.* Oh, but take a look at the bottom of the last column: We still have a red out port (⊞). Obviously, my verbose Little Puppet Friend (I call him LPF) has given a lengthy cookie recipe, more than these two pages can accommodate. This brings us to InDesign's third text-flowing shortcut. To see it in action, I ask you to once again press Ctrl+Z (or ⌘-Z) to undo the last action and reload that cursor.

15. *Shift-click at the top of the second column.* Press and hold the Shift key to get yet another variety of the loaded text cursor, this time with a solid loopy arrow, as in . This is the Superman of text flow functions, the *autoflow* cursor. Still pressing Shift, click at the top of the second column and as quick as you can say "Houdini never did this," InDesign not only fills all the columns to the end of the document but actually creates a brand new page to accommodate the overflow text, as shown in the large Figure 2-13 on the next page. If LPF had written a novel instead of a cookie recipe, InDesign would have added as many pages as needed to contain the text, automatically generated the necessary frames, and threaded the text through them. Conclusion: Shift-clicking is the finest method for roughing out text into pages yet divined by man, woman, or puppet.

16. *Save your document.* If you want to make sure you're at the end of the article, click the final column on the new third page, and notice the empty out port at the bottom of the column. This signifies that, indeed, that's all he wrote. Then choose **File→Save As**. Name your modified document "My cookies 1.indd," and save it in the same *Lesson 02* folder inside *Lesson Files-IDcs3 1on1*.

Incidentally, if you're planning to speed directly into the next exercise, keep this document open. We're not finished with it yet. (If you accidentally close it without saving, don't worry because I have you covered. But I reckon that you might as well follow through with your own file if you can.)

Figure 2-11.

Figure 2-12.

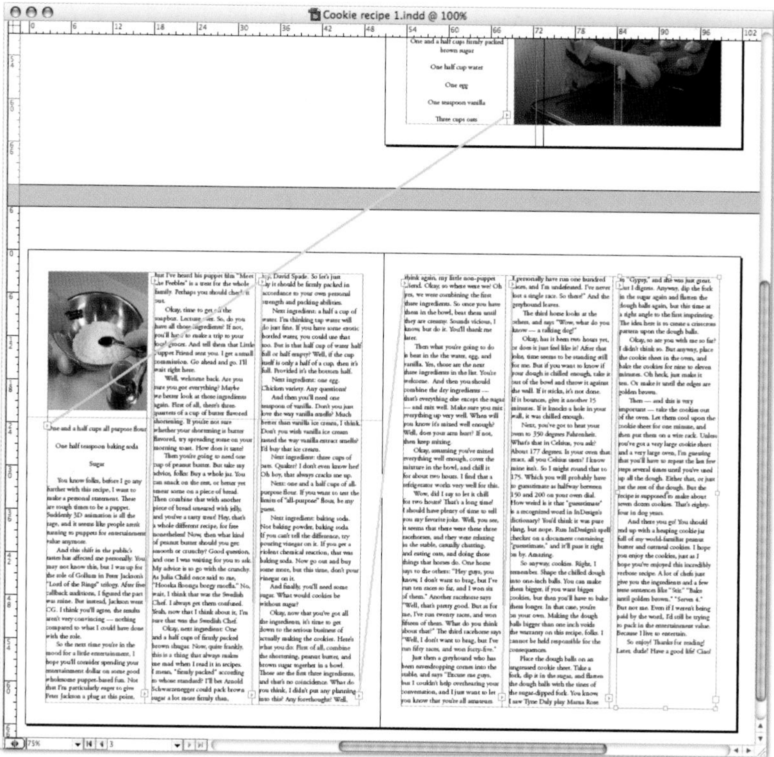

Figure 2-13.

Adjusting Text Blocks

InDesign's text frames are infinitely adjustable, so if everything isn't perfect when you first lay out your frames, you can go back and tinker with them until they're exactly right. In the following steps, we'll adjust the text blocks we created in the preceding exercise. And with a song in our hearts, we'll see how that Ol' Text River, he just keeps flowin' along, even into nonrectangular text frames.

1. *Open a document.* This exercise picks up where the last one left off. So if you still have open the *My cookies 1.indd* document you saved in the preceding exercise, you can skip to Step 2. If you didn't work through the last exercise, I have you covered. Open the file *Cookie recipe 2.indd* located in the *Lesson 02* folder inside *Lesson Files-IDcs3 1on1*.

2. *Crop the graphic on the first page.* We have to make some serious adjustments to the text on the opening page, but first you need to resize the frame for the graphic. That's right, just like text, graphics reside inside frames. And by resizing the frame, you crop the photograph. (For complete details on cropping graphics, see "Cropping and Scaling Artwork" on page 227 in Lesson 6.)

If the black arrow tool is active, great; if not, select it now. Then click the graphic to activate its frame. Small white boxes called *handles* appear in the corners and in the middle of each side of the frame. You can click and drag these handles to change the size of the frame.

Move your cursor over the handle at the top-center of the frame. When the cursor turns into a two-headed arrow, drag downward until the top edge of the frame snaps to the yellow guide. Then drag the middle handle on the left side of the frame to the right until it snaps to the vertical black guide. Figure 2-14 demonstrates both operations.

Figure 2-14.

3. ***Scale the text block in the first column.*** Click the bottom-left text block—the one that begins *Hey there, cookie and/or puppet lovers*—to activate it. Then drag the handle on the right side of the frame to the right until it snaps to the red guide. The text reflows to accommodate the larger frame. Drag the top handle down until it snaps to the yellow guide. Figure 2-15 shows your document after these changes.

Figure 2-15.

4. ***Make the top text block bigger.*** I want the first couple of paragraphs to appear in the top text block. To accomplish this, we'll enlarge the top frame. Click the frame to select it. Then drag the handle on the bottom edge downward until it snaps to the green guide. The last line in the top text block should begin *Now then, here are the ingredients*, with *Three-quarters of a cup butter flavored shortening* leading off the bottom block. Figure 2-16 on the next page shows what I'm talking about.

5. ***Move the top text block down.*** There's too much space between the top text block and the other elements on the first page, so let's move the entire text block down. With the top text block selected, click inside it and drag down until the top edge snaps to the dark blue guide, as in Figure 2-17. You can press the Shift key while you drag to help constrain the movement of the frame straight downward. (The Shift key constrains

Figure 2-16.

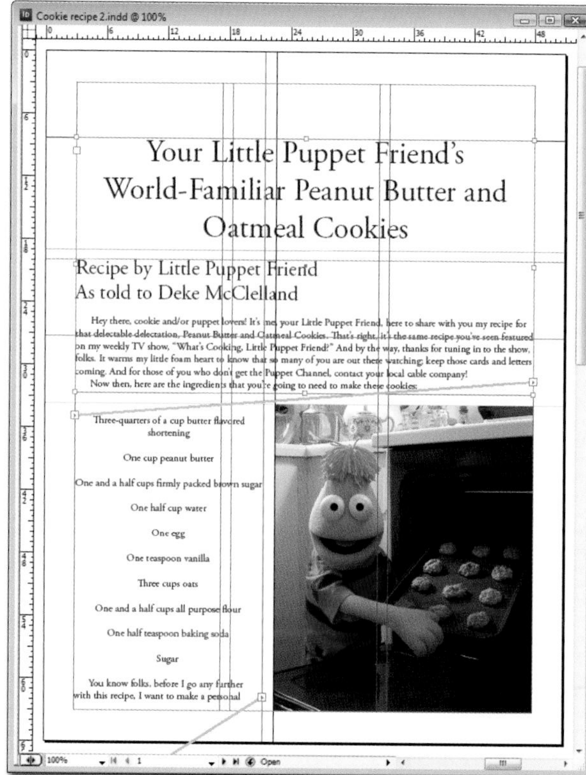

Figure 2-17.

the angle of a drag to a multiple of 45 degrees, so you still have to make some effort to drag in a vertical direction.) But because View→Snap to Guides is turned on, it's just as easy to drag the frame straight down without using Shift.

If you need to move more than one text block at a time, select the additional text blocks by Shift-clicking on them with the black arrow tool. Meanwhile, Shift-clicking a selected text block deselects it. You can also drag in an empty area of the document window to draw a rectangular marquee. Any objects even partially inside the marquee become selected.

---

6. ***Delete the bottom-left block on the first page.*** I have something else in mind for the bottom-left text block: I want to replace its rectangular frame with an oval one. Rather than converting the rectangle to an ellipse—an arduous, inexact process at best—we're better off deleting the rectangle and drawing the ellipse in its place. Select the bottom-left text block and press the Backspace or Delete key. The frame disappears, but as Figure 2-18 illustrates, the text remains intact, flowing from the top block into the first frame on the next page. (You may want to scroll down to observe this. Clicking a text frame makes the text threads visible.)

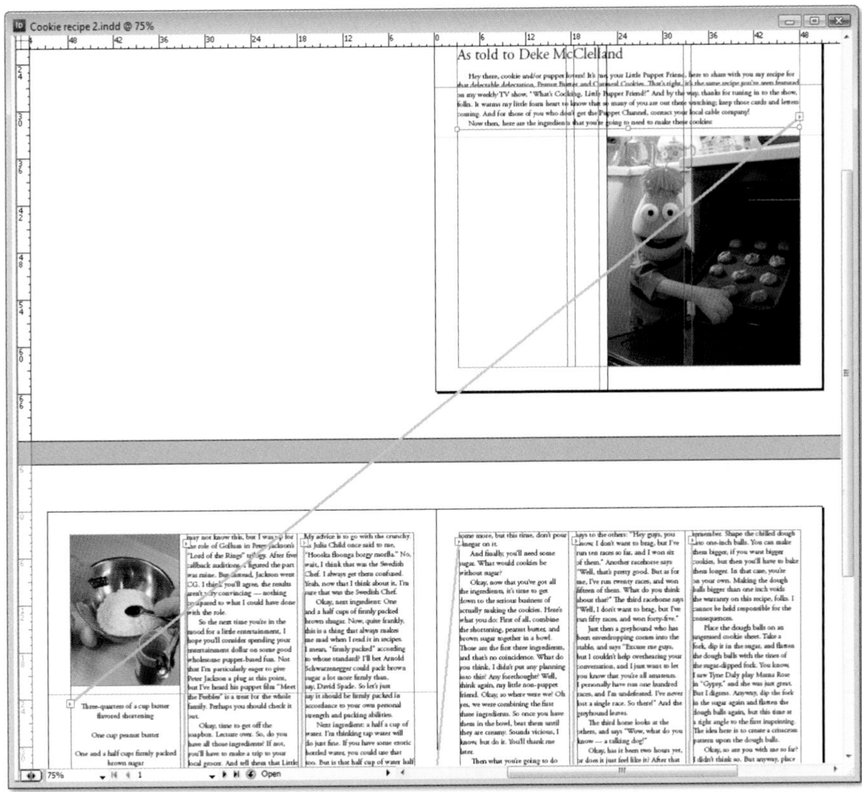

Figure 2-18.

7. *Select the ellipse tool.* InDesign provides two tools that let you draw oval text frames: the ellipse frame tool and the standard ellipse tool. As shown in Figure 2-19, the ellipse frame tool is located in the frame tool flyout menu (green in the figure); the ellipse tool shares a flyout menu with the shape tools (blue). You can select the latter tool from the keyboard by pressing the L key.

   As I mentioned, either tool is perfectly capable of creating a frame for holding text. The only difference is that, by default, the ellipse tool draws a frame with a visible border, called a *stroke* and the ellipse frame tool does not. I want a frame with a border, so press the L key to select the standard ellipse tool.

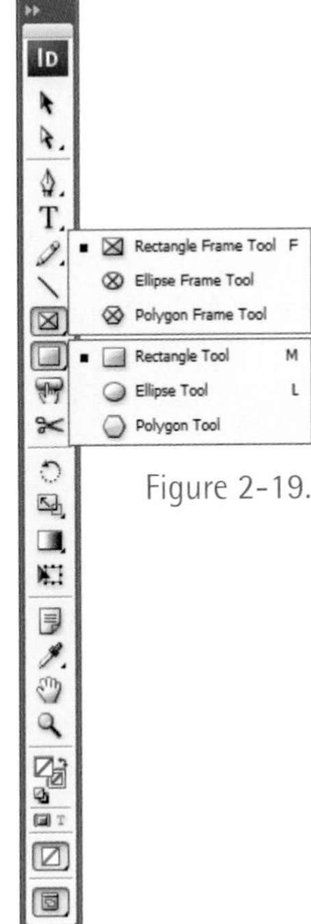

Figure 2-19.

8. *Draw an oval frame in place of the deleted frame.* To draw the oval frame, begin dragging at the intersection of the yellow and red guides, as in Figure 2-20 on the next page. Then drag down and to the left until the cursor is even with the lower-left corner of the first column. When you release the mouse, the oval appears.

9. *Click the text frame's out port.* Now that we have an elliptical frame in place, I'd like you to reflow the text into the frame. To make this happen, first press the V key (or Enter on the keypad if you loaded my shortcuts) to return to the black arrow tool. Click

Figure 2-20.

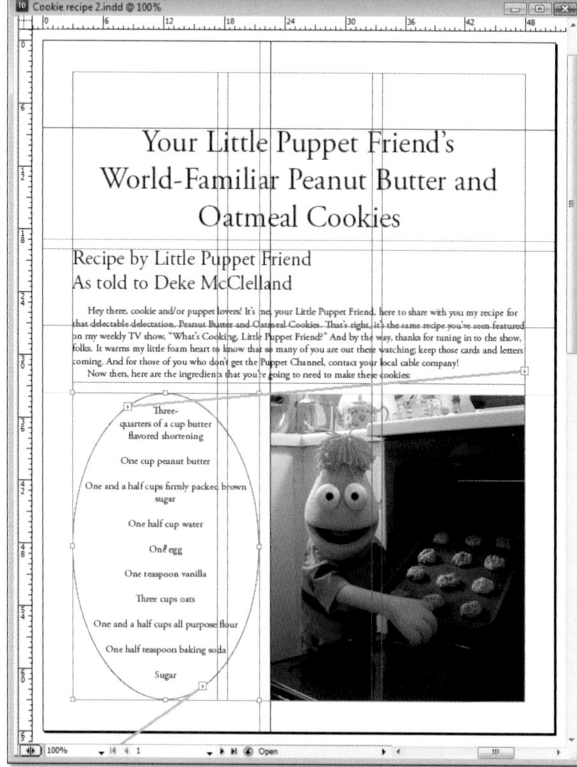

Figure 2-21.

the top text block, and then click its out port. Once again, you have loaded your cursor.

Pressing the V key is InDesign's shortcut for the black arrow tool. This may make you wonder: If V already exists, why did I go to the trouble of creating my own shortcut, Enter? Consider for a moment what happens if text is highlighted. Pressing V replaces the type with a lowercase *v*. The Enter key works whether text is active or not, making it my shortcut of choice for the black arrow tool.

---

10. ***Flow the text into the oval frame.*** If you hover your cursor over the text block on which you just clicked, you'll notice that the cursor changes from into a broken chain. This tells you that another click of the mouse will break the link to all subsequent frames. After that, you can flow the text in a different direction.

 That's one way to steer the text into the oval, but it would involve reflowing the article onto the second page. Here's a better technique: Move the cursor into the oval. You should see yet another variation of the loaded cursor that looks like . This *area text* cursor indicates that you are about to flow text into an existing shape. Click in the oval to fill it with text, as in Figure 2-21. The ingredient list flows up from the second page and perfectly fills the oval frame.

11. ***Save your document.*** Choose **File→Save As** and name your document "My cookies 2.indd." As before, save it in *Lesson 02* in *Lesson Files-IDcs3 1on1*.

Editing Your Text

Now that you've placed some text and had a crack at creating and modifying frames, it's time we took a look at ways to edit the text inside those frames—fix typos, add words, that kind of thing. InDesign provides two methods of doing this: You can edit text directly in the document window, or you can switch to the pared-down Story Editor. Either way, InDesign makes the process as straightforward and obvious as reasonably possible. What isn't obvious is the plethora of handy shortcuts that permit you to edit with greater speed and less cursing. This exercise shows off some of InDesign's best text-editing techniques.

1. ***Open a document.*** As before, this exercise is a continuation of its predecessor. If you still have *My cookies 2.indd* open, wonderful. You might want to press Ctrl+; (or ⌘-;) to hide the guides, because we don't need them anymore. Then move on to Step 2. Otherwise, open the file named *Cookie recipe 3.indd* located in the *Lesson 02* folder inside *Lesson Files-IDcs3 1on1*, which has the guides turned off by default. (Do you see how I help you?)

2. ***Identify the text to be deleted.*** As I read through LPF's recipe, I see that he didn't exactly stick to the topic of making cookies. We'll edit out one of his more egregious tangents, which starts with the first paragraph on the second page and ends two sentences into the fourth paragraph. In fact, let's work from the bottom up, deleting those two offending sentences first.

3. ***Delete the first two sentences of the fourth paragraph on the second page.*** Scroll to the bottom-left corner of the second page of the document until you see the paragraph that begins *Okay, time to get off the soapbox*. Double-click inside the text to switch to the type tool and position the blinking insertion marker. Then select the first two sentences of this paragraph using one of the following techniques:

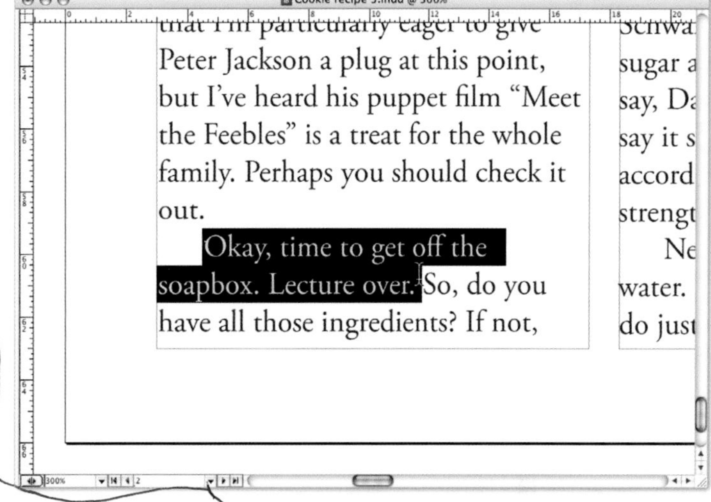

Figure 2-22.

   - Drag from the left edge of the *O* in *Okay* to the left edge of the *S* in *So*. Be sure to select the period and space between *over* and *So*. The first two sentences should now appear highlighted, as in Figure 2-22.
   - Click in front of the *O* in *Okay*. Then press the Shift key and click in front of the *S* in *So*. This selects the entire range of characters between the click and Shift-click points.
   - Double-click the word *Okay*, keeping the mouse button down on the second click. (That's a click-press, as opposed to a standard double-click.) Now drag to select the text in whole-word increments. Drag down one line and to the right until you've selected the first two sentences, including the space before *So*.

   After you have the sentences selected, press the Backspace or Delete key to remove them.

4. ***Delete the third paragraph.*** To make things more interesting—and to demonstrate some useful techniques—I'd like you to select and delete the first three paragraphs on the second page using only the keyboard. Start with the third paragraph:

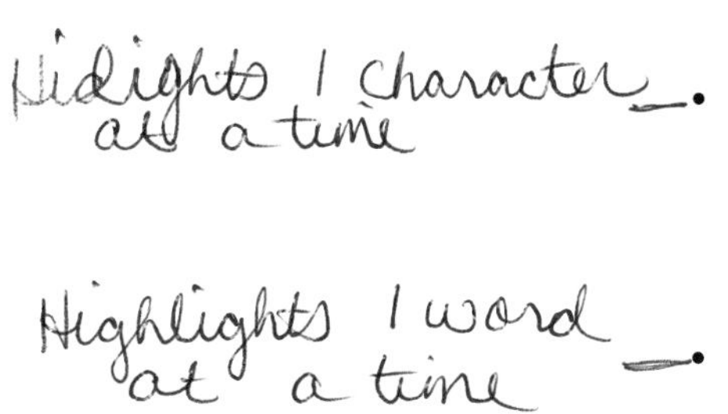

   - At this point, the insertion marker should be blinking immediately in front of the word *So*. Press the ↑ key once to move the insertion marker to the end of the third paragraph, after the word *out*.
   - Now, hold the Shift key and press ←. This highlights the period at the end of the paragraph. Press Shift+← again to select the letter *t*. Keep pressing Shift+← to expand the selection one character at a time.
   - Finding this agonizingly slow? Try adding the Ctrl key (⌘ on the Mac) to the mix. Press Ctrl+Shift+← (or ⌘-Shift-←) to select an entire word at a time.
   - If you select too many words, you can deselect a few by pressing Ctrl+Shift+→ (or ⌘-Shift-→). Watch out though: If you go too far in your eagerness to deselect, you'll start selecting words in the fourth paragraph.

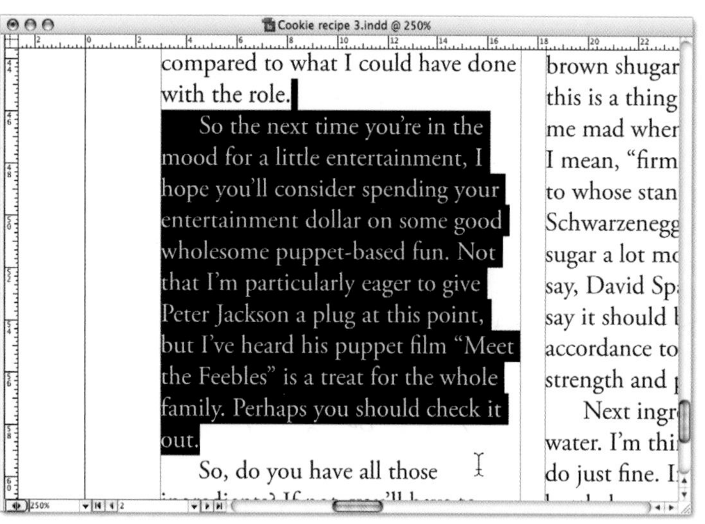

Figure 2-23.

   - Another trick to try: Press Shift-↑ to expand the selection a line at a time.
   - Press Shift-↑ until you've selected part of the first line in the paragraph, *So the next time you're in the*. Then press Ctrl+Shift+← (or ⌘-Shift-←) several times to expand the selection past the word *So*, past the indent, to the sliver of space after the period that represents the carriage return at the end of the second paragraph.

   Your selection should look like the one in Figure 2-23, with a little bit of highlight poking above the first line in the selection. Press Backspace or Delete to delete the text.

5. ***Delete the first two paragraphs.*** You should see the insertion marker pulsing away after the period at the end of the second paragraph. Now let's select and delete the first two paragraphs on this page even more quickly than we removed the third one:

   - Press Ctrl+Shift+↑ (⌘-Shift-↑ on the Mac) to select the entire second paragraph.

- Press Ctrl+Shift+↑ (⌘-Shift-↑) again to select the first paragraph as well, as shown in Figure 2-24.
- With the first two paragraphs selected, press Backspace or Delete.
- Press the → key and then press Backspace (or Delete) to eliminate the blank line at the top of the text frame. Or press the forward delete key, labeled Delete on the PC (⌦ on the Mac).

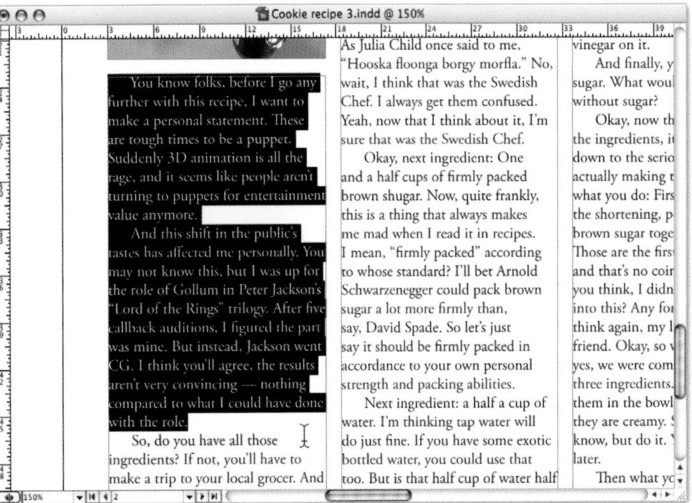

Figure 2-24.

Another way to edit text is to move it. After selecting a passage of text, you can drag it to a new location. Problem is, the function is turned off by default. During the testing phase, users found that it was too easy to move text by accident. If you're worried you too might become the victim of accidental drag-and-drops, skip to Step 8 on the next page. Otherwise, join me in trying the feature out for yourself.

6. *Turn on drag-and-drop text editing.* Choose **Edit→Preferences→Type** (on the Mac, **InDesign→Preferences→Type**), or press Ctrl+K, Ctrl+3 (⌘-K, ⌘-3). Then turn on the **Enable in Layout View** check box, which I've circled in Figure 2-25. I also want you to turn off **Adjust Spacing Automatically When Cutting and Pasting Words**, highlighted blue in the figure. This deactivates InDesign's auto-spacing function, which can make a mess when dragging text. Click **OK**. Now you're ready to drag and drop text.

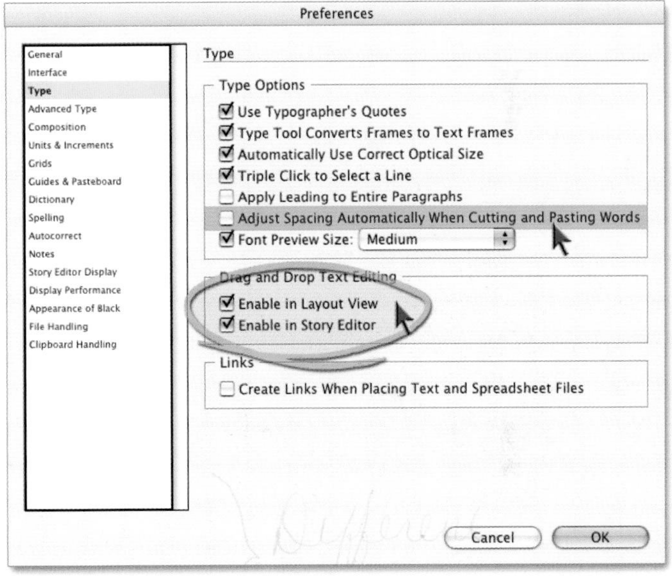

Figure 2-25.

7. *Locate and then move a paragraph by dragging it.* Our Little Puppet Friend made a mistake (it's hard to concentrate when your head is stuffed with someone else's hand) and wrote a paragraph in the recipe out of order compared with the list of ingredients on the first page. Rather than directing your attention to paragraph X in column Y, let's do a search. Choose **Edit→Find/Change** or press Ctrl+F (⌘-F). I happen to know that LPF has problems keeping his oats in order, so enter "oats" into the **Find What** field. To scan the whole recipe, change the **Search** setting to **Story**. Then click **Find**, as in Figure 2-26.

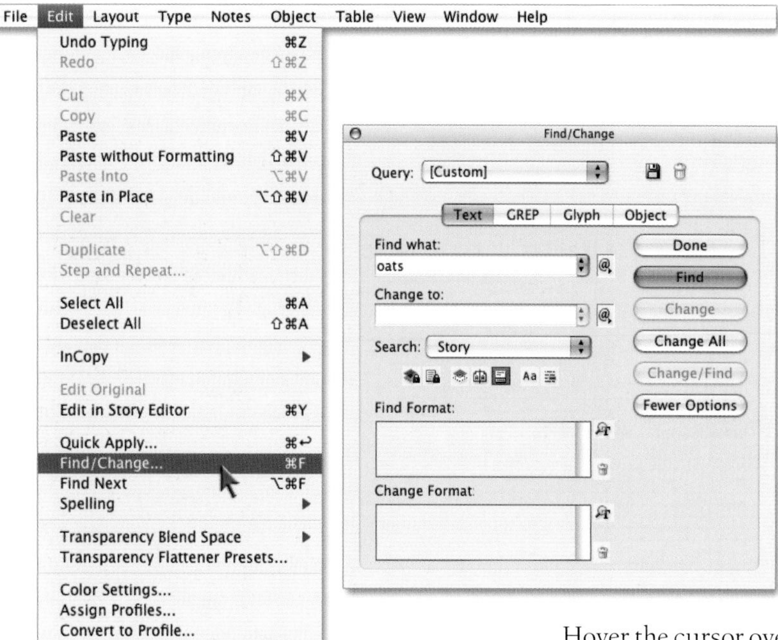

Figure 2-26.

InDesign delivers you to the word *oats* in the second column near the bottom of the second page. Click **Done** to close the dialog box. This is the right place, but we want to move the whole paragraph. So click four times in a row on *oats* or one of its neighbors to select the paragraph. If you're having problems making that work, drag over the entire paragraph, making sure you pick up the indent at the beginning and the little sliver of space at the end.

By default, double-clicking with the type tool on a word selects the word, triple-clicking selects the line of type, 4×-clicking selects the paragraph, and 5×-clicking selects the entire story.

Hover the cursor over the selected text so it turns into an arrowhead with a small T, as in ▶T. Then drag the paragraph. As you drag, a vertical bar shows the position at which the text will drop. Drag the text to the beginning of the previous paragraph, so the bar precedes the indent (see Figure 2-27), and then release the mouse button. In a flash, the paragraph moves to its new home.

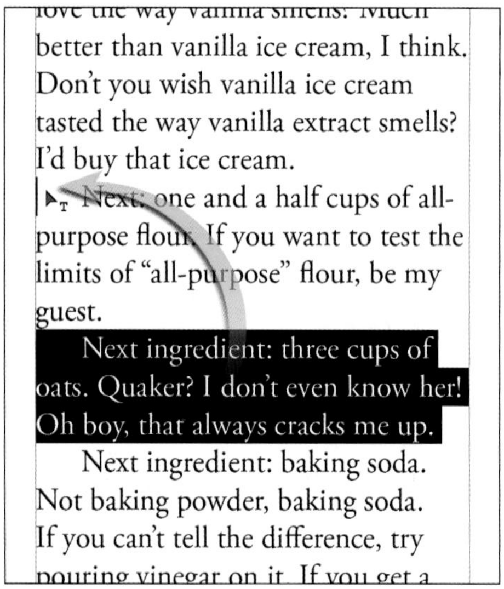

better than vanilla ice cream, I think. Don't you wish vanilla ice cream tasted the way vanilla extract smells? I'd buy that ice cream.

Next: one and a half cups of all-purpose flour. If you want to test the limits of "all-purpose" flour, be my guest.

Next ingredient: three cups of oats. Quaker? I don't even know her! Oh boy, that always cracks me up.

Next ingredient: baking soda. Not baking powder, baking soda. If you can't tell the difference, try

Figure 2-27.

You can drag text from one text block to another, from one page to another, between InDesign documents, and even between InDesign and another application. Yes, it's very cool.

8. ***Switch to the Story Editor.*** As you're editing, InDesign may seem a little sluggish compared to, say, a word processor. If you think about it, this is perfectly understandable; an edit you make early in a lengthy story can cause changes that ripple throughout many frames and pages. InDesign has a lot to keep track of, so it can be excused for being a little slow to respond. For heavy editing tasks, often the more practical route is to switch to the Story Editor. Plus, it makes navigation a snap, as we shall see.

To switch to the Story Editor, choose **Edit→Edit in Story Editor** or press Ctrl+Y (⌘-Y on the Mac). InDesign displays the **Story Editor** window featured in Figure 2-28. Bear in mind, the Edit in Story Editor command is available only when a text frame is selected or an active insertion marker is in the text. The active insertion marker is necessary to tell the Story Editor what story you want to edit. If the command appears dimmed, click inside the story and try again.

The Story Editor has no fonts, no styles, no hyphenation, just plain old text that you can edit without waiting for InDesign to adjust the layout in response to your changes. InDesign divides the window into two panes: the one on the right displays the text; the one on the left lists leading measurements (the vertical space consumed by the type) and style sheets. For the present, we're going to ignore both, but you'll be well versed with them by the time you complete this book.

To give yourself more room to work, you can drag the vertical divider line to the left. Or more simply, choose View→Story Editor→Hide Style Name Column and have done with the leading measurements and styles in one quick action.

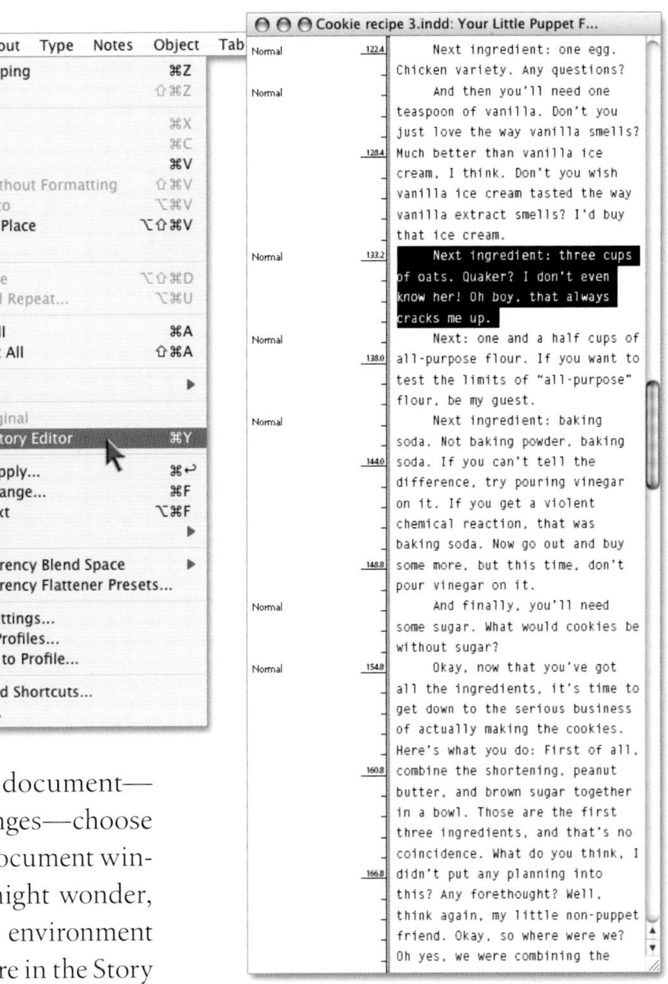

Figure 2-28.

If you want to see how your edits affect the document—which updates periodically to reflect your changes—choose Window→Arrange→Tile Vertically to see both document window and Story Editor at the same time. You might wonder, doesn't viewing the frills from inside a no-frills environment sort of defeat the purpose? Not really. When you're in the Story Editor, it has precedence; the document window updates only when it senses a lull in activity. Your edits occur immediately no matter what may be happening in the background.

9. *Display the Preferences dialog box.* If nothing else, text in the Story Editor should be easy to read. If you're experiencing eye fatigue or simply don't like the way the type looks, you can customize its appearance. Choose **Edit→Preferences→Story Editor Display** (on the Mac, **InDesign→Preferences→Story Editor Display**) to display the **Story Editor Display** panel of the **Preferences** dialog box (see Figure 2-29). It's worth visiting if only to see the deathless line of prose *Sphinx of black quartz judge my vow*, which not only contains all 26 letters in the alphabet but also updates to show you how the Story Editor text will appear after you change settings.

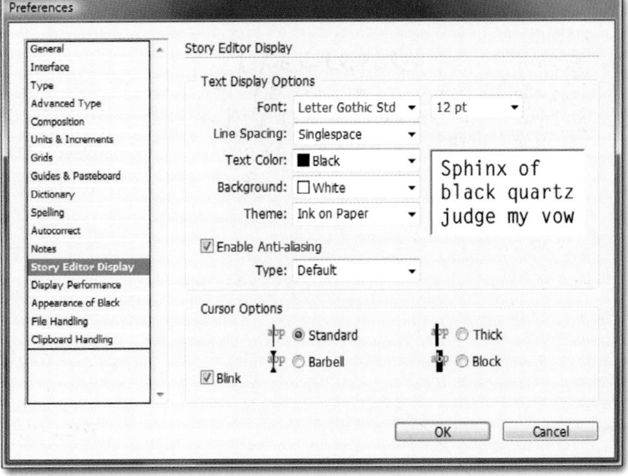

Figure 2-29.

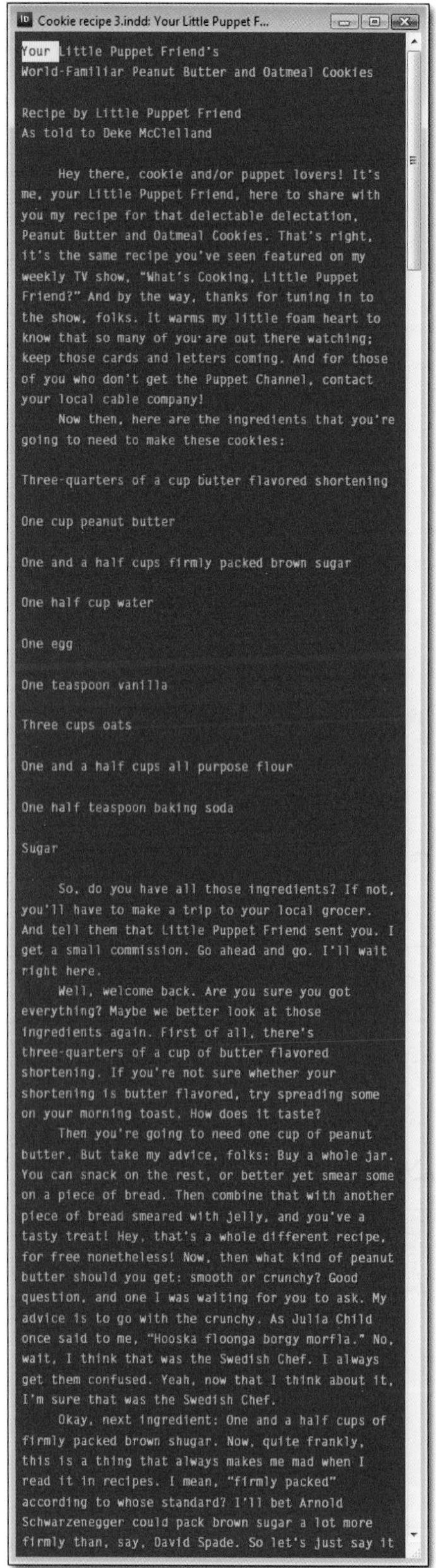

Figure 2-30.

10. ***Set the theme to Classic System.*** The **Theme** pop-up menu lets you choose between four preset text color and background combinations. Choose **Classic System**, which emulates the ancient terminal systems used by newspaper editors and the like. (Personally, I like it because it reminds me how happy I am that I don't have to use DOS ever again.) Then click **OK** to exit the Preferences dialog box. The Story Editor updates to reflect your changes, as in Figure 2-30.

11. ***Position the cursor at the beginning of the story.*** Now we'll make an editorial change in the Story Editor and learn another keyboard shortcut in the process. As you've probably noticed, the highlighted text is automatically carried over from the layout view into the Story Editor, with the window scrolled so that the insertion marker appears at the top. But I don't want you to change this text. I want you to make a change to the very beginning of the story. And the easiest way to get there is to press Ctrl+Home (⌘-Home on the Mac).

On full keyboards, the Home key is located at the top of a group of six keys between the standard alphanumeric keys and the numeric keypad. If your keyboard lacks such keys, Home may be doubled up with the 7 on the keypad. In this case, tap the Num Lock key on the numeric keypad to turn it off. Then press Ctrl and 7 on the keypad. (Num Lock toggles keys on the keypad between numbers and navigation commands, such as Home and End.) On Apple's MacBook Pro, you press ⌘-Fn-←. Other notebooks hide the Home key elsewhere or abandon it entirely.

Note that this and other editing shortcuts work equally well in the document window and the Story Editor. Pressing the Home key without the Ctrl (or ⌘) key moves the insertion marker to the beginning of the current line.

12. ***Delete the first word in the title.*** Press Ctrl+Shift+→ (or ⌘-Shift-→) to select the word *Your* and the space after, as you can see at the top of Figure 2-30. Then press Backspace or Delete to delete it.

13. ***Advance the cursor to the end of the story.*** Ctrl+Home takes you to the beginning of a story, so it only stands to reason that you can press Ctrl+End (⌘-End) to go to the end.

14. ***Replace the last two words.*** Press Ctrl+Shift+← (⌘-Shift-← on the Mac) four times to make the selection—one each for the exclamation points and once each for the words *life* and *Ciao*. Then type the phrase, "wholesome glass of milk with the cookies!" The new entry replaces the selected type.

15. ***Scroll to the same point in the document window.*** Choose **Edit→Edit in Layout** or press Ctrl+Y (⌘-Y on the Mac) to send the Story Editor to the back and display the newly edited text in the document window. InDesign even auto-scrolls to the most recently modified text, which happens to be in the third column of page 3, as in Figure 2-31.

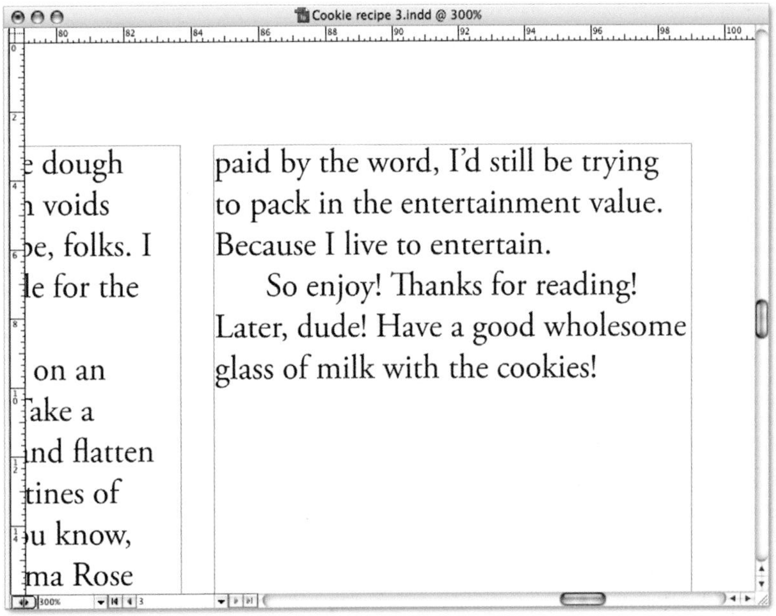

16. ***Save your document.*** I expect you know the drill by now, but I'm going to tell you anyway. Choose **File→Save As**, name the document "My cookies 3.indd," and save it in the *Lesson 02* folder. We're finished with the Story Editor, so if you like, you can close it. Bring the Story Editor to the front by pressing Ctrl+Y (⌘-Y). Then click the ☒ icon (⊗ on the Mac) in its title bar to close it. Or leave it running in the background—it won't hurt a thing.

Figure 2-31.

PEARL OF WISDOM

The Story Editor shows you all the text in a story, regardless of how many frames it fills. Or overfills, for that matter. And that's as it should be. After all, you want to see all your text. But you want to see whether it goes too long as well. In the layout view, you can spot overflow text by the appearance of the red out port (⊞). In the Story Editor, overflow text is flanked by a vertical red bar, as in Figure 2-32. The difference: The Story Editor shows how much text is running over; the layout view does not. If you have lots of overset copy, you have lots of layout work ahead of you. If there's just a dribble, you can edit the text to draw the overset material back into the last frame of the story. It's just another reason to at least occasionally turn your attention to the remarkable Story Editor.

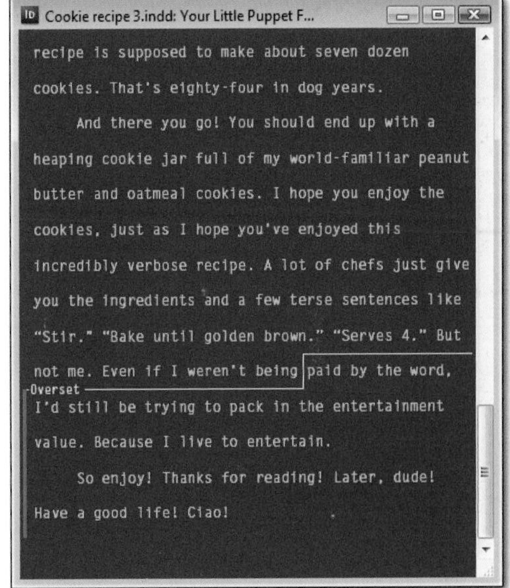

Figure 2-32.

Checking Your Spelling

InDesign lets you check the spelling of your text. If your text was written in a word processor, I hope you already checked the spelling there. But the Story Editor provides an open invitation for last-minute tinkering and rewriting. And when rewriting occurs, spelling mistakes can sneak in. So it's a good idea to submit your text to a final spell check.

PEARL OF WISDOM

I'll be brutally honest: I'm not a fan of InDesign's spell checker. You can't instruct it to ignore words in all caps, hyphenated words, filenames, or Web addresses. It mistakes parentheses and other special characters for the beginnings of sentences. Plus, the dictionary lacks a troubling number of routine words, such as *editable*, *hyperlinks*, *multipage*, *workspaces*, *inkjet* (!), *email* (!!), *QuarkXPress* (no surprise there), *Microsoft* (wow, that's just petty), *Deke* (et tu, InDesign?), and my favorite, *CS*. As a result, it wastes a great deal of your time flagging errors that aren't errors. I am at least thankful it recognizes *InDesign*. On the plus side, you can add words to a custom dictionary that is shared by fellow CS3 applications. You can even instruct the program to check the spelling of words as you type them into a document.

Anyhoo, better a finicky spell checker than none at all. Let's see how to use it.

1. ***Open a document.*** This is the last exercise in this lesson that picks up where the last one left off. If you have ready access to the file you saved in Step 16, *My cookies 3.indd*, open it. Otherwise, you can use *Cookie recipe 4.indd*, located in the *Lesson 02* folder inside *Lesson Files-IDcs3 1on1*.

2. ***Activate the story.*** Armed with the type tool, click anywhere in the story. Then press Ctrl+Home (⌘-Home) to move the blinking insertion marker to the very beginning of the story so you can spell check the document from word one.

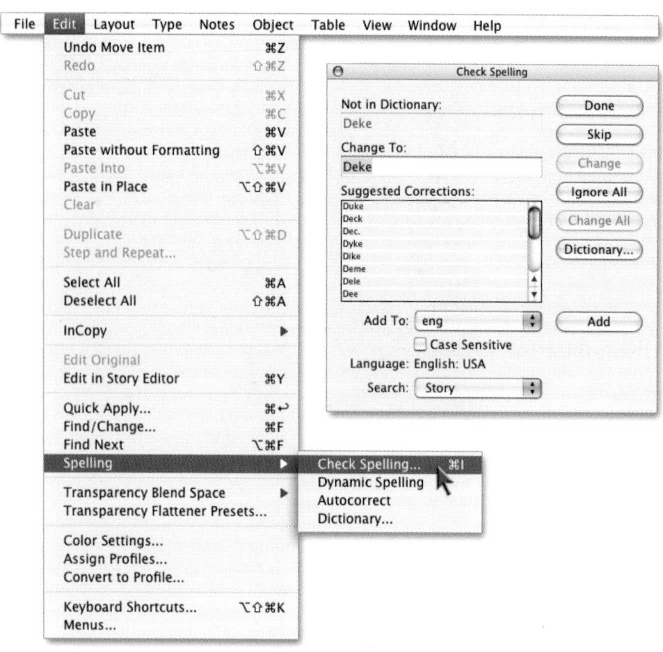

Figure 2-33.

3. ***Choose the Check Spelling command.*** Either choose **Edit→Spelling→Check Spelling** or press Ctrl+I (⌘-I on the Mac) to display the **Check Spelling** dialog box, pictured in Figure 2-33. Almost immediately, InDesign CS3 locates and selects the first questionable word in the story—my name, naturally.

4. ***Set the search parameters.*** Before you correct my name, your first order of business is to tell InDesign exactly what you want to spell check by choosing an option from the Search pop-up menu. You can choose to search the Story (that is, all text in a series of threaded text blocks), the entire Document (which might contain several stories), All Documents that you have open, or from the insertion marker To End of Story. If you have text selected when you choose the Check Spelling command, a fifth option, Selection, appears. When I use

the spell checker for day-to-day work, I set it to Selection, so I can easily check a single selected word without scrolling elsewhere inside my document. But we're performing a big end-of-document-creation spell check, so set the **Search** option to **Document** to check the whole thing.

5. ***Select the first suggested correction and click Skip.*** The Check Spelling dialog box offers a number of possible alternative spelling to my name, virtually all of which I was called at some point in junior high. Click the first item in the **Suggested Corrections** list, **Duke**. The following buttons become active:

   - The Start button changes to Skip, which ignores this word and moves on to the next suspect word.
   - Change swaps the currently selected occurrence of *Deke* with *Duke*.
   - Ignore All skips *Deke* in this and every other document until the next time you quit and restart InDesign.
   - Change All changes this and all future occurrences of *Deke* to *Duke*, again until you quit and restart InDesign.

   The thing is, although I do rather remind myself of John Wayne—check out the videos, I'm the spitting image—I have no desire to change my name to *Duke*. And if you scroll down the list, it only gets worse. So do me a big favor, and click the **Skip** button to move on. You could also click Ignore All, but as it just so happens, there are no more occurrences of *Deke* in this story.

6. ***Click Skip again.*** InDesign moves on to the next unfamiliar word, which happens to be my last name, *McClelland*. While there's something admittedly thrilling about being *Mainlined* by *Mescaline* in the *Motherland* (a few of the suggestions on display in Figure 2-34), I'm a bit too busy at the moment to indulge. Click **Skip** to move on.

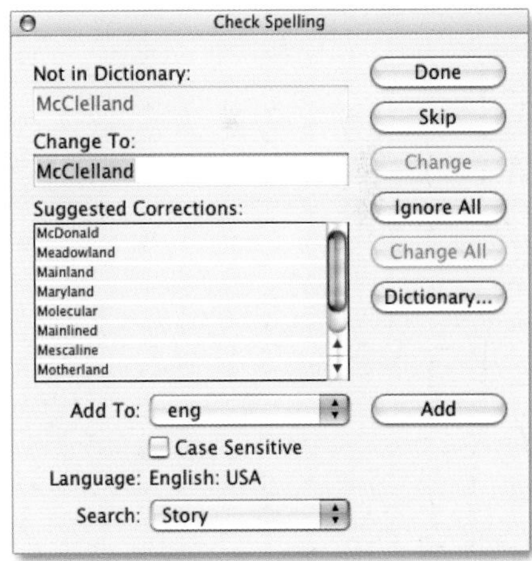

Figure 2-34.

7. ***Click Skip four more times.*** This bypasses the Swedish-gibberish quote and brings up the next unfamiliar word, *shugar*.

8. ***Correct the misspelling.*** It's unusual to see a renowned cookie expert misspell such a sweet word, but puppets are notoriously bad typists. To set the record straight, click the first choice, **sugar**, in the **Suggested Corrections** list. Just in case *shugar* pops up again, click **Change All** to correct all occurrences of the word. A message appears, telling you that there was only one instance of *shugar* in the document. Click the **OK** button to confirm and move on.

9. ***Add* Schwarzenegger *to the dictionary.*** The spell checker next questions the word *Schwarzenegger.* I suspect that Adobe, a California corporation, has heard of this guy, but proper nouns are not InDesign's strong suit. Still, the name has rather pervaded the public consciousness, so I reckon it ought to be part of the dictionary. The fast and easy way to accomplish this is to simply click the Add button. This adds the word to the current dictionary and continues your spell check.

   Alas, simple is not always best. The better choice is to click the **Dictionary** button. The **Dictionary** dialog box contains a lot of options, and we need them all to properly add the famous muscleman's name. So here's a quick rundown:

   - The Target pop-up menu lets you specify whether you want to store your changes in the *user dictionary*—specifically, in a file called *added.clam* buried several folders deep along with the system files on your hard drive—or directly in any open document so that others who open that file will also have access to your saved words.
   - The Language option lets you select the language you're working in. Or at least, so goes the theory. For the reality, see the "Pearl of Wisdom" on the left.
   - The Dictionary List pop-up menu contains three settings. Select the first, Added Words, to add an unfamiliar word to the custom dictionary. Select the second option, Removed Words, to force InDesign to question a word that is in its main dictionary but you consider to be wrong. For example, InDesign likes to spell the word *email* as *e-mail*. If you disagree, you'd add *email* to the Added Words list and *e-mail* to the Removed Words list. Select the last option, Ignored Words, to view and modify any words that you have told InDesign to ignore during the current session.
   - The Word option shows the word in question, the one you are poised to add, remove, or hyphenate. You can use that word or enter another.
   - Click the Hyphenate button to ask InDesign to automatically hyphenate your word. If you click Hyphenate using the German: 2006 Reform dictionary (arguably the closest match for the native Austrian), you get *Schwar~~zen~~eg~~ger*. The tilde (~) characters indicate potential hyphens, with fewer tildes getting the higher priority. You can edit the tildes if you like; any number from one to three is acceptable.

PEARL OF WISDOM

You may find that the Language option offers just one language, the native language for your country (such as English: USA or German: 2006 Reform). To access another language—or a specialized variation such as English: USA Medical—you must first assign it to the text as a character-level formatting attribute. Select some text with the type tool and choose the desired language from the control palette. Amazingly, you can do this with the Dictionary dialog box open. But you'll have to click Done and then click the Dictionary button again to gain access to the new language in the Language pop-up menu.

To request that a word *never* be hyphenated automatically, enter a tilde in front of the word, as in *~Schwarzenegger*. I don't recommend that with a word this long, but it might make sense with *~InDesign*, which becomes difficult to read when split.

- Turn on the Case Sensitive check box to add the word to the dictionary with its capitalization intact, perfect for proper nouns like this one.

Here's what I want you to do:

- Set the **Language** option to the language you use most often. Leave **Target** set to its default (**eng** for English, for example) so InDesign saves the word to the user dictionary.
- Make sure **Dictionary List** is set to **Added Words**.
- Change the spelling of the contents of the **Word** option box to *Schwar~ze~~neg~~~ger*. Again, the word is more likely to be hyphenated where there are fewer tildes.
- Turn on the **Case Sensitive** check box.
- Click the **Add** button to add our new vocabulary word to the list under the Word option, as in Figure 2-35.
- Finally, click the **Done** button to return to the Check Spelling dialog box.

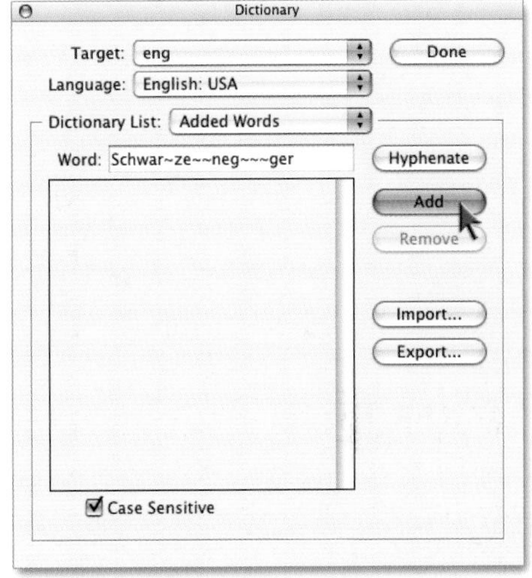

Figure 2-35.

10. ***Prod InDesign to move along.*** Seems like InDesign should go ahead and continue to check the document after you leave the Dictionary dialog box, but you have to give it a little nudge. Click **Skip** and the **Check Spelling** dialog box goes on about its business.

11. ***Fix the repeated words.*** The next point of business happens to be *the the*—not the 1980s British pop-music act, but rather an all-too-common instance of a repeated word. As shown in Figure 2-36, the option at the top of the dialog box changes from Not in Dictionary to Repeated Word, and the Add button becomes dimmed. (You can't add a repeated word to the dictionary.) Select **the** in the **Suggested Corrections** list and click **Change**. The double world becomes one.

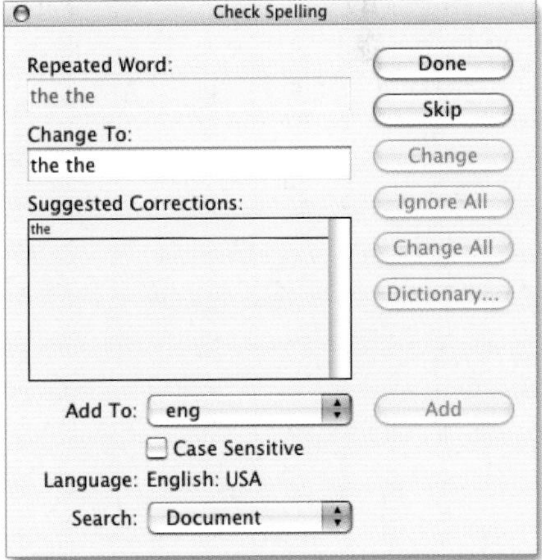

Figure 2-36.

12. ***Add* ungreased *to the dictionary.*** After making the correction, the spell checker moves to the word *ungreased*. According to *Webster's* and other sources, this is not a word. Strunk and White urged us to avoid made-up words when plain words will do. But no other word will do. The cookie demands a baking

sheet free of grease, thus ungreased it must be. So click the **Dictionary** button to bring up the **Dictionary** dialog box. I'm not sure I'm ready to add this word to the user dictionary—this is one of those words that raises eyebrows outside the culinary world—so it's best to keep it inside this document. Choose your document's name from the **Target** pop-up menu. Click **Add** to sanctify the word inside this file, and click **Done** to return to the **Check Spelling** dialog box.

13. ***Click Skip three times.*** The first click of the **Skip** button tells the spell checker to keep searching the document. The next two clicks skip past more proper nouns that you're unlikely to use again—unless you're a big "Cagney and Lacey" fan, that is.

14. ***Wrap it up.*** A moment later, InDesign tells you that the spell check is complete. Click **OK** to dismiss the message, and then click **Done** to close the Check Spelling dialog box. My friend, you are finished.

EXTRA CREDIT

Ideally, Check Spelling would be one of the last commands you apply to a document, right before you send it off to the printer. But you tend to use it during a document's middle age, when you're trying to get the text more or less in order. It's during that final phase, when you're making last-minute tweaks, that it's most tempting to give Check Spelling the slip. After all, who wants to go through the tedious task of clicking the Skip button a few dozen times just to discover one or two spelling mistakes? Fortunately, there's a better way. InDesign can play proofreader as you type, flagging your spelling errors as fast as you can make them. Called *dynamic spell checking*, it's cheap insurance against embarrassing bungles. To learn more, read on.

15. ***Spell check as you type.*** To activate the dynamic spell checker, choose **Edit→Spelling→Dynamic Spelling**. A check mark in front of the command shows that it's on.

16. ***Experiment with a few misspellings.*** You should see a couple of proper nouns underlined in red squiggles. If not, wait a few seconds for InDesign to catch up with you. (The dynamic spell checker always starts at the beginning of the document and works its way, sometimes ploddingly, forward. To spur it on, press the W key a couple of times to enter and escape the preview mode.) If you don't see the red underlines, try typing a few choice misspellings of your own. You might also try repeating a word or adding a lowercase letter to the beginning of a sentence, both of which receive green underlines, as in Figure 2-37 on the facing page.

17. ***Document one of your favorite typos.*** InDesign can also keep a record of your most common typing errors and correct them on-the-fly. Me, as accustomed as I should be to the word *paragraph*, my fingers seem to prefer *pargaraph*. To register your own orthographic *bêtes noires*, choose **Edit** (on the Mac, **InDesign**)→**Preferences**→**Autocorrect** or press Ctrl+K, Ctrl+0, ↓ (⌘-K, ⌘-0, ↓). Then click the **Add** button. Enter a favorite typo into the first blank and its proper spelling in the second, as in Figure 2-38. Dynamic spell checking doesn't work in the Preferences dialog box, so pay attention—make a spelling error here, and you've created a formidable typo generator! When you finish, click **OK** to save the correction.

The autocorrect feature can also be a fabulous method for translating shorthand. For example, let's say you're sick and tired of entering the word *InDesign*. (Where I came up with that, I'll never know.) Click the Add button. Set the Misspelled Word blank to "ig" (since *id*, *is*, and *in* are already legitimate words) and Correction to "InDesign." Then click OK. Now whenever you type "ig," *InDesign* is what you'll get.

Click the **OK** button again to escape the Preferences dialog box.

18. ***Autocorrect your favorite typo.*** Choose **Edit→Spelling→Autocorrect** to activate the autocorrect function. Then enter the misspelled word you documented in the preceding step. The moment you press the spacebar, InDesign corrects the word automatically. How much better could it be?

That's it for the cookie recipe. Feel free to save your changes—after all, you fixed the spelling of a word, deleted a repeated word, and added a word to the document's internal dictionary. After you've saved the file, close the file in anticipation of the next exercise.

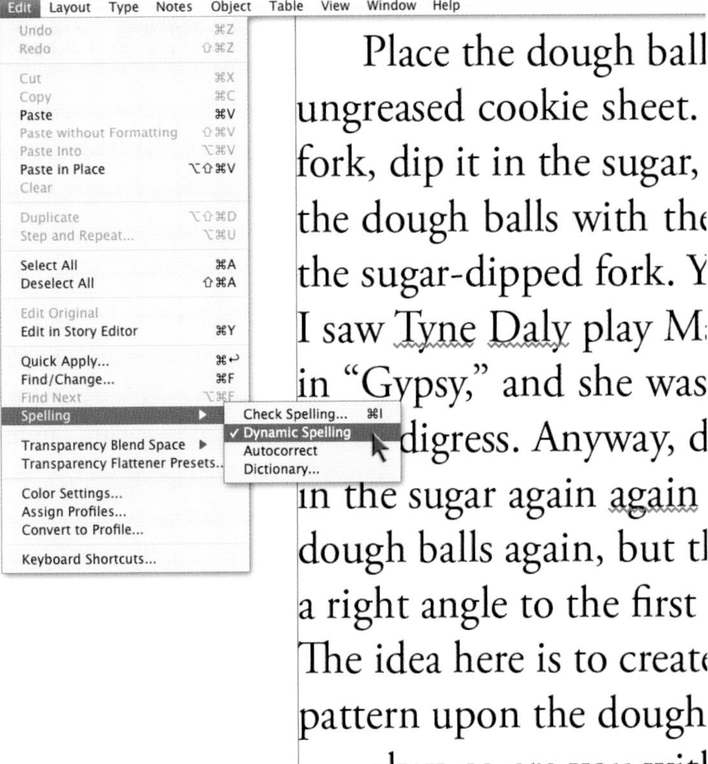

Figure 2-37.

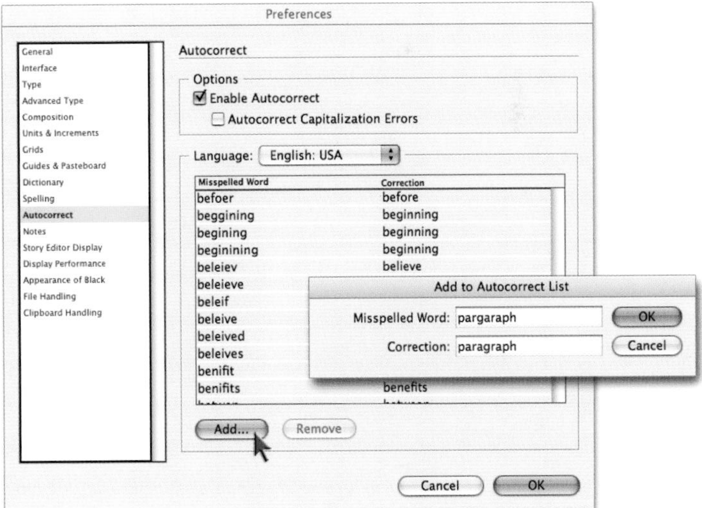

Figure 2-38.

Joining Type to a Curve

In addition to placing text inside a rectangular frame or another shape, you can flow text around the outside of a shape. Figure 2-39 offers a few examples. For the sake of comparison, the central text is set inside an oval. The rest flows around curves. In Adobe parlance, these curves are *paths*, so each line of type is called *type on a path*, or just plain *path type*. In all, Figure 2-39 contains ten independent lines of path text—two in white, two dark green, and six in black.

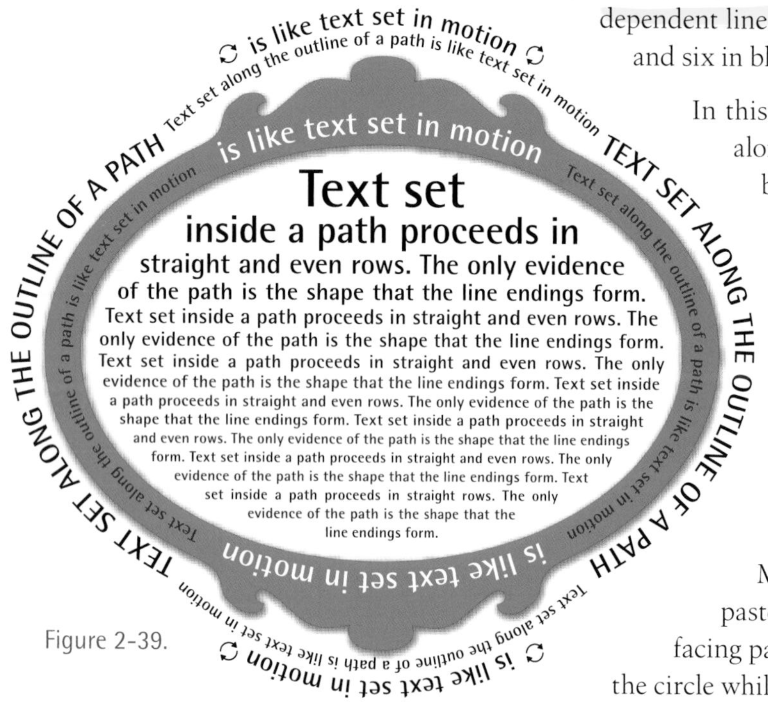

Figure 2-39.

In this exercise, you'll create two lines of type, one along the top of a circle and the other along the bottom. In addition to binding text to the shape, you'll learn how to move the text along the path outline, flip it to one side of the path or the other, and space the letters to keep them legible.

1. ***Open a document.*** Open the file *Professor Shenbop.indd* in the *Lesson 02* folder in *Lesson Files-IDcs3 1on1*. Here we see a cartoon frog with a pull-string surrounded by a red circle. Meanwhile, two lines of type lay waiting in the pasteboard above the page (see Figure 2-40 on the facing page). Our goal is to take this text and join it to the circle while keeping the text upright and legible.

2. ***Hide the frame edges and path outlines.*** See those blue lines running around and through the objects in the illustration? These *frame edges* mark text frames and the path outlines. Normally, I like them, but here they're distracting. To hide them, choose **View→Hide Frame Edges** or press Ctrl+H. (Mac users, do *not* press ⌘-H. It hides the application.)

3. ***Activate the text in the pasteboard.*** Double-click the word *Professor* at the top of the pasteboard. (You may have to scroll up to see it.) If the black arrow tool was active, this switches you to the type tool and activates the text. If the type tool was active, double-clicking highlights the word. Either way, you're set.

4. ***Select the first line of type.*** Select the entire line *Professor Shenbop's*. You can do this in a few ways:

   - Click in front of the *P* in *Professor* and then Shift-click after the final *s* in *Shenbop's*.

- Double-click a word; on the second click, hold the mouse button and drag to highlight the other word.
- Triple-click inside a word to select the entire line.

Or don't click at all. Just press Ctrl+Shift+\ (⌘-Shift-\ on the Mac) to extend an existing selection to include an entire line of type. It's a weird keyboard shortcut but extremely useful if you can remember it.

5. *Copy the selected text.* In some programs, you join text to a path by creating the text and the path independently and then combining the two. In Adobe apps, you enter the text directly onto the path. To use existing text, like the stuff we have here, you have to copy the text and then paste it onto the path. To start the process, choose **Edit→Copy** or press Ctrl+C (⌘-C on the Mac) to copy the text to InDesign's clipboard.

Figure 2-40.

PEARL OF WISDOM

Our next task is to prepare the circle to receive the text. Because we have two lines of type—one for the top of the circle and the other for the bottom—we need two separate paths. (Sadly, InDesign won't let you join two lines of type to one circle.) The trick: Cut the circle into two halves, one upper and one lower. That's a job for the scissors tool.

6. *Select the scissors tool in the toolbox.* Press Ctrl+Shift+A (⌘-Shift-A) to invoke the **Deselect All** command and deselect the text. Then click the scissors tool in the toolbox, as in Figure 2-41, or press the C key. The purpose of the scissors tool is to snip apart path outlines.

7. *Snip the circle.* Now to snip both the left and right sides of the circle, thus separating the top and bottom halves. Sounds simple enough, but you have to do it just right:

   - First, move the scissors tool cursor over the inside edge—I repeat, the *inside* edge—of the leftmost point in the circle. (If you're keeping an eye on the control palette, move the cursor until the dimmed coordinate values read X: 5p2, Y: 12p0.) When the cursor changes from a cross to a tiny bull's-eye (as in ⌖), click. The red outline shifts inward, from outside the thin blue line—which is the path of the circle—to inside the line. Blue lines also appear. These are the control handles. I discuss control handles in Lesson 5, "Drawing inside InDesign." For now, don't worry about them.

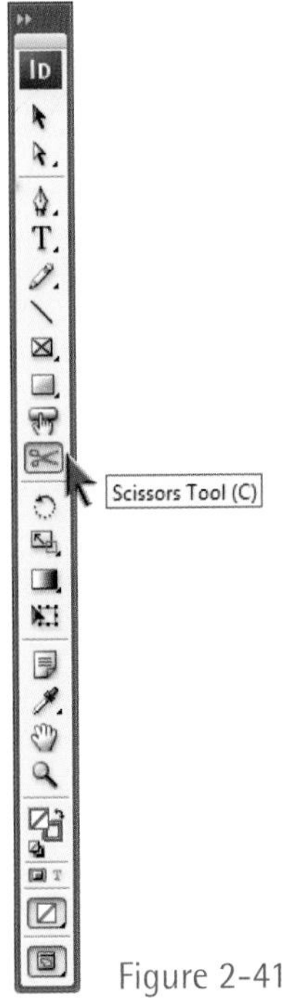

Figure 2-41.

- Now click the rightmost point in the circle, which has shifted to the outside edge. Again, watch for the cursor to change before you click.

The orange arrows in Figure 2-42 show the proper click points. This screen shot was taken after creating the points, so the red outline has already shifted to the inside of the blue path.

8. ***Select the type-on-a-path tool.*** Click and hold the type tool icon in the toolbox to display a flyout menu, and then choose the type-on-a-path tool, as in Figure 2-43. Or Alt-click (Option-click) the type tool icon. Or just press the keyboard shortcut Shift+T. However you do it, you'll arm yourself with the tool used to put type along a curve in InDesign.

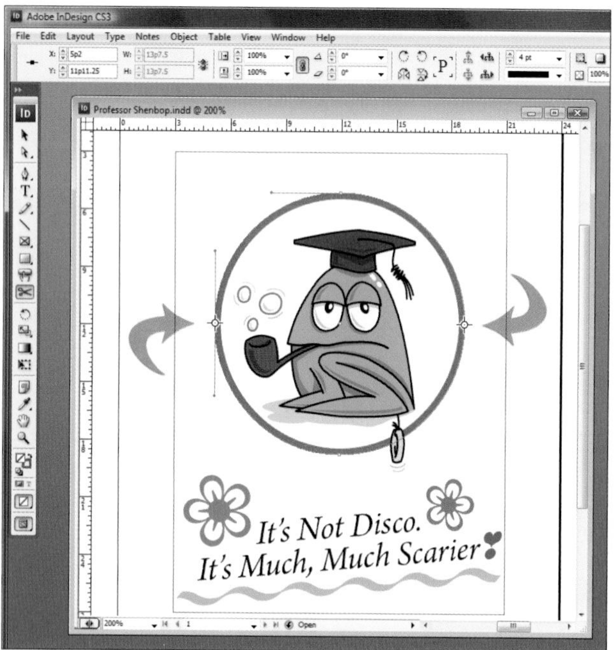

Figure 2-42.

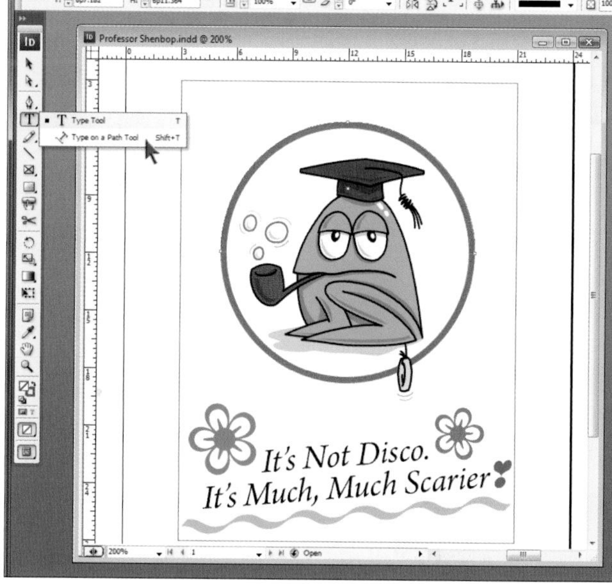

Figure 2-43.

9. ***Click anywhere along the top half of the circle.*** Move your cursor to the outside edge of the top of the circle. When a plus sign appears next to the cursor (⁺), click. The path is now ready to accept text.

10. ***Paste the copied text.*** It's been five steps since you copied the text, but that doesn't matter. The clipboard retains its information until the next time you choose Edit→Copy or Cut. So choose **Edit→Paste** or press Ctrl+V (⌘-V) to paste the text along the top half of the circle.

PEARL OF WISDOM

Unexpectedly, InDesign pastes the text upside-down and along the inside of the circle, as in Figure 2-44. The reason: Every path outline has a direction, and apparently InDesign thinks this particular path goes counterclockwise. So the text goes under the hump instead of over it. Fortunately, this minor irritation is easily fixed.

11. ***Switch to the black arrow tool.*** When it comes to flipping text across a path, the black arrow is your tool. If you loaded my dekeKeys shortcuts as directed on page xix of the Preface, press the Enter key on the numeric keypad. Otherwise, click the black arrow in the upper-left corner of the toolbox.

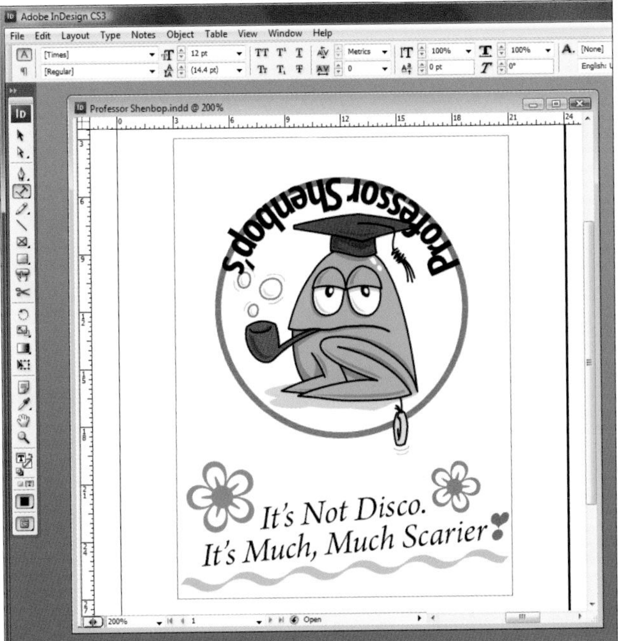

Figure 2-44.

12. ***Flip the text to the other side of the path.*** If you look very closely at the handle (the blue square) centered atop the rectangular bounding box around the text, you should see a tiny blue crossbar that intersects the end of the capital *S* in *Shenbop's*. (It's actually a little ⊤, but it's hard to make out because of the bounding box.) This all-too-subtle indicator lets you control which side of an object the text is on. To flip the text, drag the tiny crossbar upward. As illustrated in Figure 2-45 on the next page, this sends the text to the other side of the hump.

Can't locate the crossbar? Just don't feel like monkeying with it? Do I have the solution for you: Choose **Type→Type on a Path→Options**. When the dialog box appears, select the **Flip** check box (if necessary, turn on **Preview** to make sure the text flips), and click **OK**.

13. ***Make the outline transparent.*** Now that you've flipped the text, the next problem is the thick red outline, which should not be there. To get rid of it, click the red control near the bottom of the toolbox, as indicated by the purple arrow cursor in Figure 2-46 on the facing page. This shifts the focus to the border, or *stroke*, of the path. Then choose ☐ **Apply None** from the second-to-last control in the toolbox, as indicated by the green cursor in the figure, to change the outline to transparent.

Drag this tiny doohickey upward

...to flip the text to the other side

Figure 2-45.

From the keyboard, press the X key to switch the focus to the stroke and then press the / key to make the stroke transparent. If you still see a few weird red lines, choose Edit→Spelling→Dynamic Spelling to turn off the warnings for the word Shenbop. For more information on strokes, see "Fill, Stroke, Color. amd Gradients" on page 190 of Lesson 5.

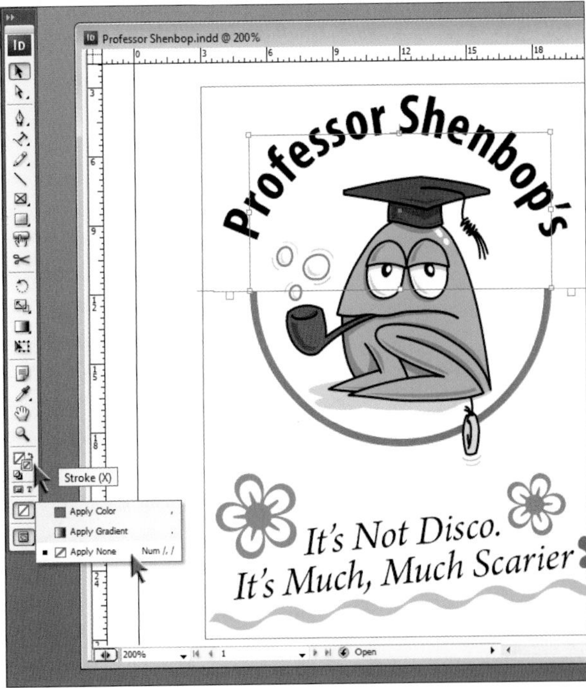

Figure 2-46.

One line of path type down, one more to go. So far, you've attached type to a path and accounted for one potential problem that may occur when adding type to a convex curve, where the text is on the outer surface of the arc.

EXTRA CREDIT

Now we'll take a look at the special issues that might arise when adding text to a concave curve, where the text needs to go on the inner surface of a curve. However, if you've had enough path type for now, skip ahead to "What Did You Learn?" (page 87). But if you're still itching to learn more—and I hope you are because some good stuff is coming up—keep reading.

14. ***Repeat the previous steps on the bottom half of the circle.*** Specifically, repeat Steps 4, 5, 9, and 10. Needless to say, I wouldn't think of asking you to go back and reread those paragraphs. So here's the skinny:

   - Select the type-on-a-path tool in the toolbox. If you like keyboard shortcuts, press Shift+T.
   - Select the second line of type in the pasteboard, the one that reads *1970's Pop Music Quiz*. Notice that the type-on-a-path tool is equally adept at selecting normal text as it is at creating and editing path type.
   - Press Ctrl+C (or ⌘-C) to copy the text.
   - Click anywhere along the bottom half of the circle. (Make sure the type-on-a-path cursor shows a plus sign, as in ⌶, before you click.)
   - Press Ctrl+V (or ⌘-V) to paste the text.

At this point, your document should look like the one shown in Figure 2-47. For now, we'll leave the red stroke intact; it serves as a helpful point of reference. Although the bottom line of type flows in the proper direction, left to right, InDesign has aligned it to the

Figure 2-47.

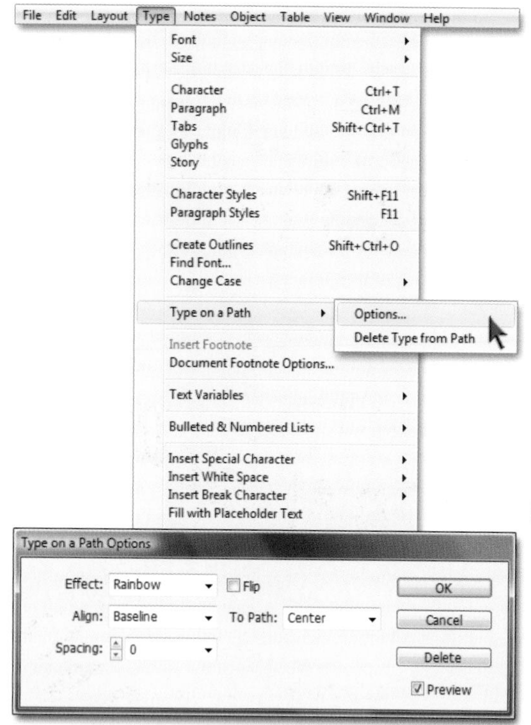

Figure 2-48.

inside of the half circle rather than the outside. As a result, the letters appear squished, not to mention directly under Shenbop's nether regions. A remedy is at hand.

15. *Open the Type on a Path Options dialog box.* Choose **Type→Type on a Path→Options** to display the dialog box pictured in Figure 2-48. The options to which the command name refers permit you to change how InDesign aligns text to a curve.

Strictly speaking, the command has no keyboard equivalent, but it does have a hidden shortcut. Double-click the type-on-a-path icon in the toolbox and up comes the Type on a Path Options dialog box.

---

16. *Align the letters by their ascenders.* First, make sure the **Preview** check box is on. Then select **Ascender** from the **Align** pop-up menu. This aligns the topmost portions of the letters with the path, shifting the characters below the circle, as in Figure 2-49. Granted, this setting drops the letters too far, but it's the only Align option that comes close to satisfying our needs. Fortunately, you can fine-tune the vertical alignment after you leave the dialog box.

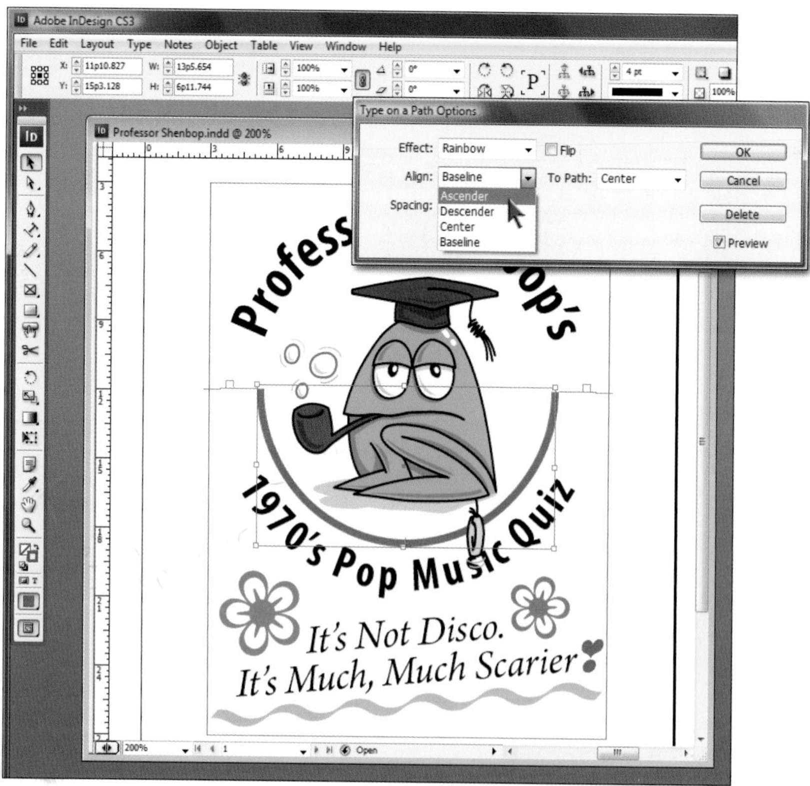

Figure 2-49.

17. *Bring the letters together.* Shifting the characters down produces the side effect of spreading them farther apart. As a result, we have too much space between one character and the next. To squish them together a bit, change the **Spacing** value to –5.

18. *Leave the Effect option set to Rainbow.* While **Rainbow** might sound like an ethereal, impractical setting, it's actually the most buttoned-down path type effect you can apply. Figure 2-50 illustrates all five options available in the **Effect** pop-up menu. Skew is sometimes useful for simulating text wrapping around an object. But for this example, Rainbow is the way to go.

19. *Click the OK button.* Or press Enter or Return to accept your changes. Things are certainly looking better, but some issues remain. The text needs to be closer to the line, and the words need to be spaced around the yellow ring attached to the pull-string coming out of Shenbop's . . . foot. Let's start things off by adding some space.

20. *Increase the space before* Quiz. Press the T key to get the type tool or Shift+T for the type-on-a-path tool—either tool works. Then highlight the space character between *Music* and *Quiz*. Currently, this is a standard, everyday space created with the spacebar. But InDesign gives you several other spaces to choose from. For the thickest space possible, right-click the selected space (or Ctrl-click if your Macintosh mouse has just one mouse button). Then choose **Insert White Space→Em Space**, which inserts a space as wide as the type size, as in Figure 2-51 on the next page. This is 24-point type, so the space is exactly 24 points wide. (To learn more about fixed-width spaces and other special characters, read the "Dashes, Spaces, and Breaks" exercise, which begins on page 149 of Lesson 4.)

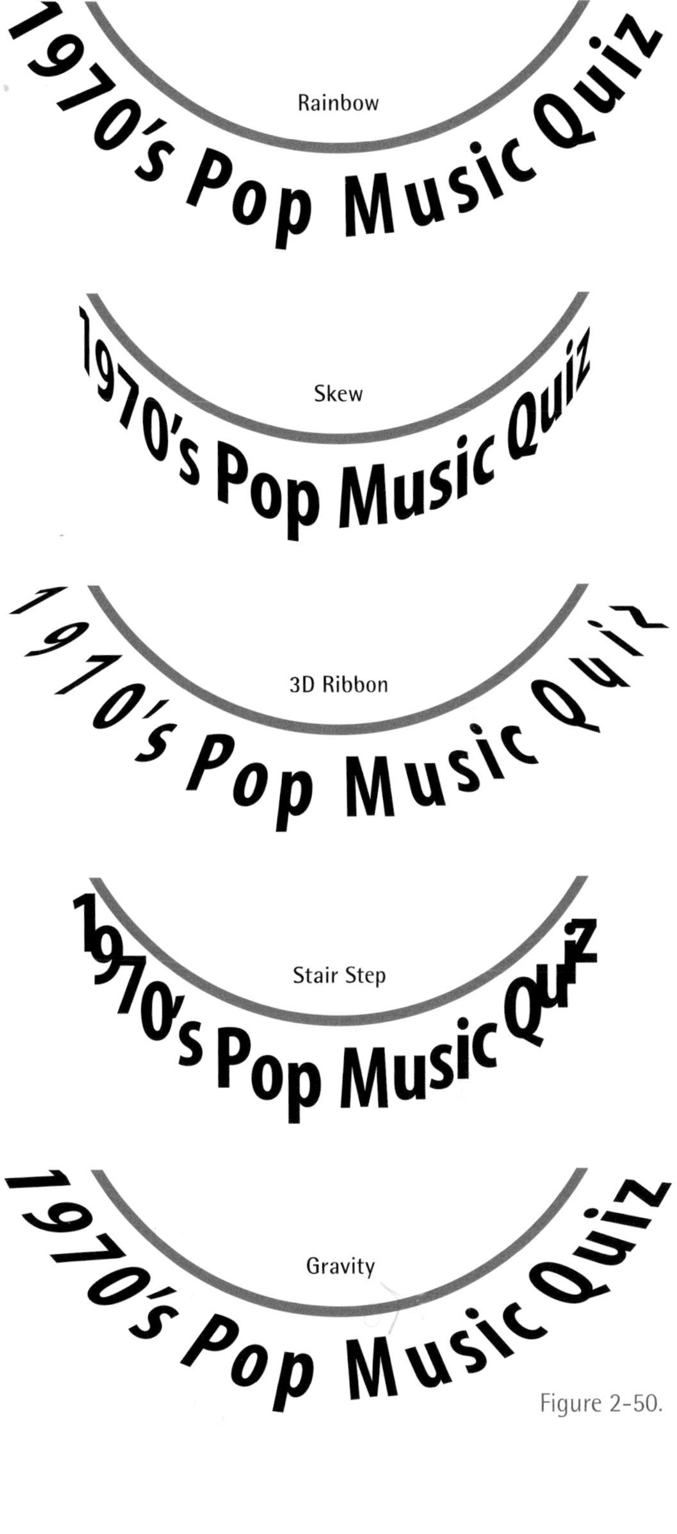

Figure 2-50.

21. ***Adjust the baseline shift.*** Now it's time to move the text closer to the line. Press Ctrl+Shift+\ (or ⌘-Shift-\) to select the entire line. Then go to the control palette at the top of the screen. Click the icon that looks like a capital letter *A* paired with a superscript one ($\mathbf{A}^{a}$) to select the baseline shift value, which lets you nudge characters up or down. Change the value to 7 and press Enter or Return. The letters move up 7 points until they just barely touch the red path, as in Figure 2-52 on the facing page. Notice that the letters also scoot closer together, which happens to work out perfectly.

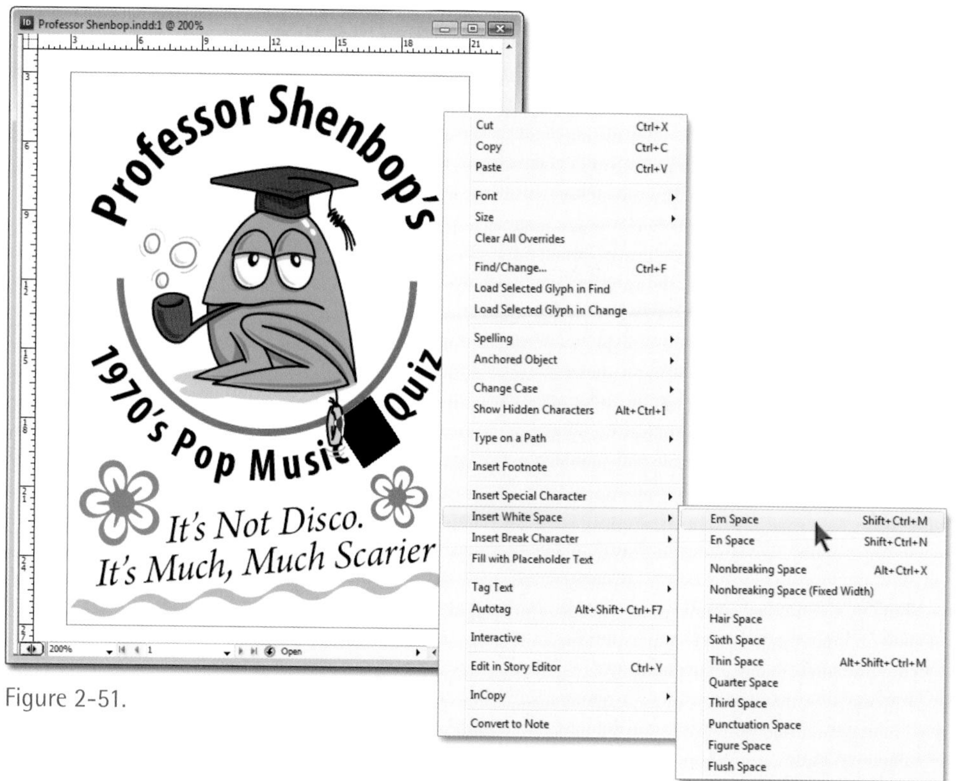

Figure 2-51.

22. ***Switch back to the black arrow tool.*** The text is joined nicely to its path, and the em space permits plenty of room for the ring. Only problem is, the space isn't aligned with the ring. You need to move the type slightly to the left, which you can do with the black arrow tool. Either click the black arrow icon in the toolbox or (assuming you loaded dekeKeys as advised back on page xix of the Preface) press Enter on the keypad.

23. ***Drag the end bar.*** See the blue bars at both ends of the red half circle? These are the equivalent of column markers, the points at which the text begins and ends on the path. But they also

Figure 2-52.

permit you to move text along the path. For example, to move the text to the left, drag the right bar down and to the left, as demonstrated in Figure 2-53. A simple adjustment or two moves the space directly over the ring.

Alternatively, you can move text by using the tiny crossbar (⊤), introduced in Step 12 (see page 79). After (and only after) you move in one of the end bars, you can drag the crossbar (presently located above the M) to move the text back and forth. Just be careful not to drag the bar to the other side of the path or you'll flip the text.

Figure 2-53.

24. ***Make the outline transparent.*** The final step is to get rid of the thick red outline. Thanks to Step 13, the stroke should still be active. So just press [/] to make it invisible.

Figure 2-54 shows the final piece of artwork. Notice that I adjusted the top line of type, *Professor Shenbop's*, by dragging the left end bar up and to the right to make the text more symmetrical with the lower curved line of type. The amount of empty space on either side of the charismatic Shenbop is equal. (Did I mention that he's dead? World's first, possibly only, cartoon taxidermied frog—I'm quite proud of that.) The text is a bit off-kilter, which I regard as perfect for my kooky illustration.

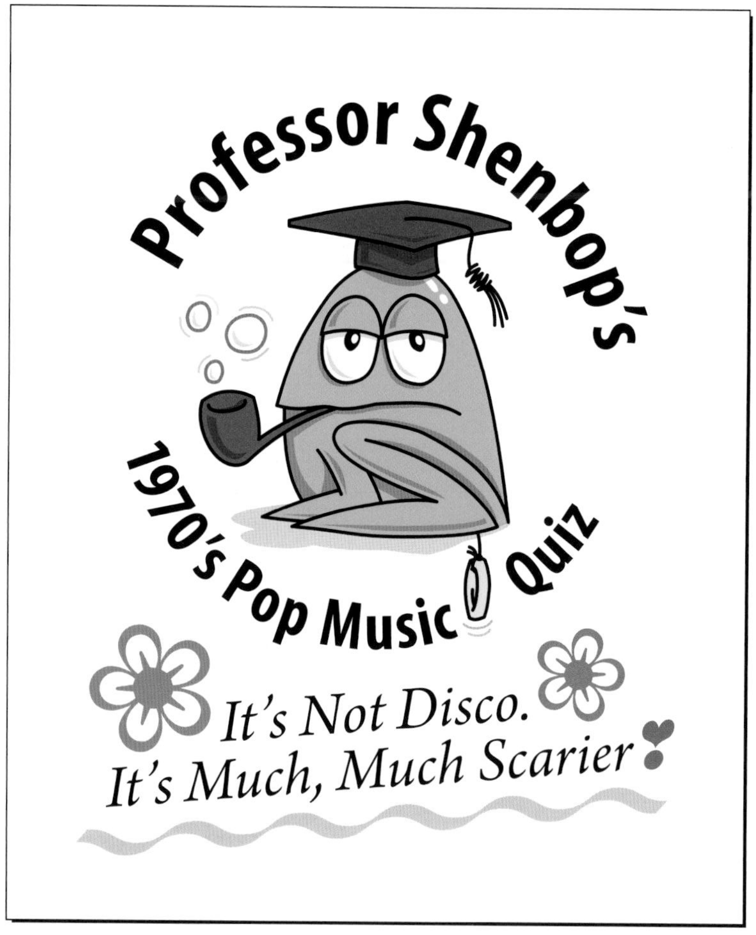

Figure 2-54.

WHAT DID YOU LEARN?

Match the key concept in the numbered list below with the letter of the phrase that best describes it. Answers appear upside-down at the bottom of the page.

Key Concepts

1. Frame
2. Place
3. Typographer's quotes
4. Out port
5. Story
6. Text threads
7. Autoflow
8. Handles
9. Area text
10. Story Editor
11. Dynamic Spelling
12. Path type

Descriptions

A. Located in the lower-right corner of a text block, this box shows whether the frame hides overflow text (⊞) or passes it to another frame (▶).

B. InDesign's ability to flow all text from a story in a single click—whether into frames or empty columns—and even generate pages.

C. This command permits you to import all varieties of content into InDesign, including text from a word processor and graphics.

D. Type set inside an existing shape, regardless of the tool used to draw the shape in the first place.

E. A command that highlights typing mistakes as you type.

F. Small boxes appearing around a frame that you drag to change the size of the frame.

G. InDesign's built-in text processor, which omits formatting in an attempt to streamline the correction process and permits you to focus on content exclusive of design.

H. Text that follows the contours of a curve.

I. Punctuation marks that curl or bend toward the text they bracket, as opposed to remaining invariably straight.

J. An independent, free-floating container that may contain text or an imported graphic.

K. A continuous body of text that may exceed the confines of a frame or page and flow from one text frame to another.

L. When turned on, these nonprinting lines show how text flows from one frame to another.

Answers

1J, 2C, 3I, 4A, 5K, 6L, 7B, 8F, 9D, 10G, 11E, 12H

LESSON

3

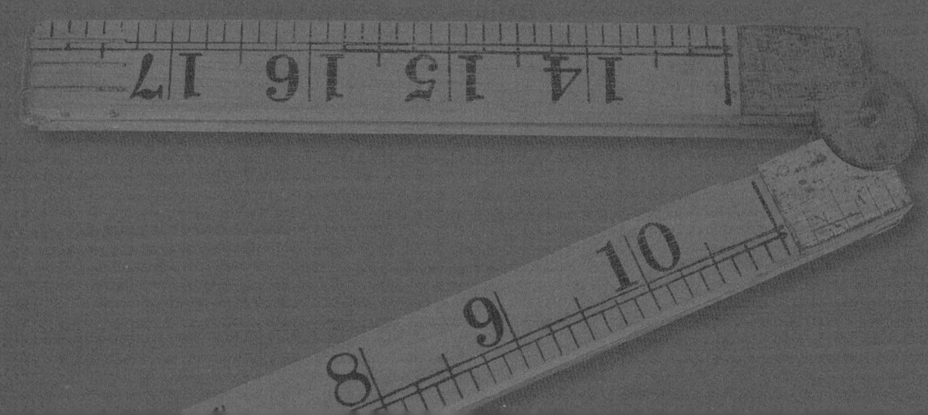

BASIC TEXT FORMATTING

IF YOU'RE NEW to page design, or merely a pragmatist at heart, you might have difficulty understanding why so many people devote so much time and effort to changing the appearance of a handful of letters. If you've seen one typeface, you've seen them all. Why not just enter the text, print it, and be done with it?

Even in my capacity as a gung-ho type enthusiast (read: type nerd), I have to admit that the differences between one typeface and another are at times incredibly subtle. Consider Figure 3-1. Here we have uppercase O's from seven different sans serif fonts. (To learn more about serif and sans serif typefaces, see the sidebar "The Look of Type" on page 98.) A type nerd like me could draw you a diagram to explain how remarkably diverse these letters are, hailing from as many as three distinct sans serif traditions: Grotesque, Geometric, and Humanist (see Figure 3-2 on page 91). But to the untrained eye, the letters are just a bunch of ovals. Some look like hula hoops; others look more like donuts. But they're all ovals. The overwhelming majority of your readers can't tell a Grotesque O from a Humanist O, and furthermore they probably don't care. It makes you wonder why Max Miedinger put so much care into creating his ubiquitous typeface Haas-Grotesk (renamed Helvetica in 1960)—and why in the world I know that he did.

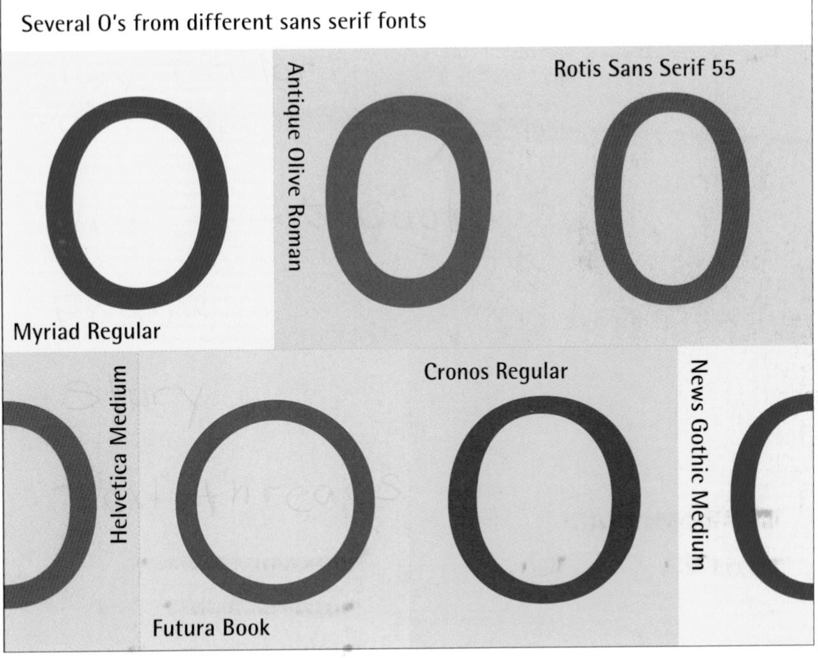

Figure 3-1.

ABOUT THIS LESSON

Project Files

Before beginning the exercises, make sure you've copied the lesson files from the DVD, as directed in Step 3 on page xvii of the Preface. This should result in a folder called *Lesson Files-IDcs3 1on1* on your desktop. We'll be working with the files inside the *Lesson 03* subfolder.

This lesson introduces you to InDesign's state-of-the-art character and paragraph formatting controls. We'll also take a look at Adobe's OpenType font technology. You'll learn how to:

Video Lesson 3: Typeface, Style, and More

Like any publishing program, InDesign divides its formatting capabilities into two groups: those that affect individual characters of type (as well as the relationship between characters) and those that affect entire paragraphs at a time. The notion is so ingrained that InDesign's text formatting palettes bear the names Character and Paragraph.

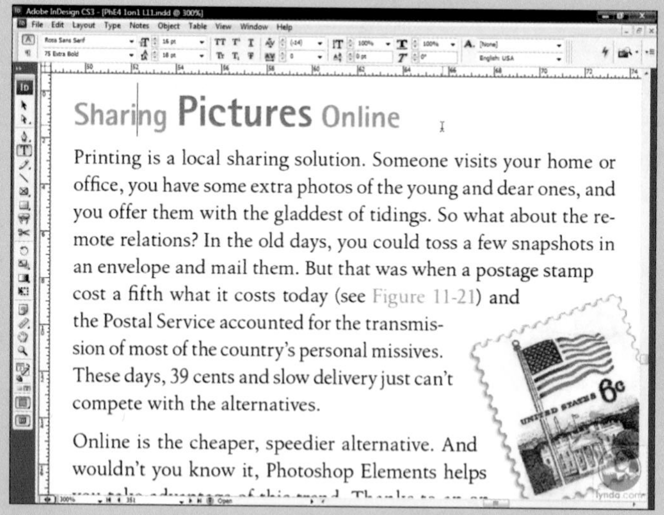

To see how these palettes work, watch the third video lesson on the DVD. Insert the DVD, double-click the file *IDcs3 Videos.html*, and click **Lesson 3: Typeface, Style, and More** under the **Navigation and Text** heading. This 13-minute 50-second movie shows you how to apply some basic formatting options and acquaints you with the following shortcuts:

Operation or palette	Windows shortcut	Macintosh shortcut
Center, right-align, or left-align text	Ctrl+Shift+C, R, or L	⌘-Shift-C, R, or L
Switch options in the control palette	Ctrl+Alt+7, or F4*	⌘-Option-7, or F4*
Hide or show the control palette	Ctrl+Alt+6, or Ctrl+F4*	⌘-Option-6, or ⌘-F4*
All caps, underline, bold, or italic	Ctrl+Shift+K, U, B or I	⌘-Shift-K, U, B or I
Restore regular, or Roman, style	Ctrl+Shift+Y	⌘-Shift-Y

* Works only if you loaded the dekeKeys keyboard shortcuts (as directed on page xix of the Preface).

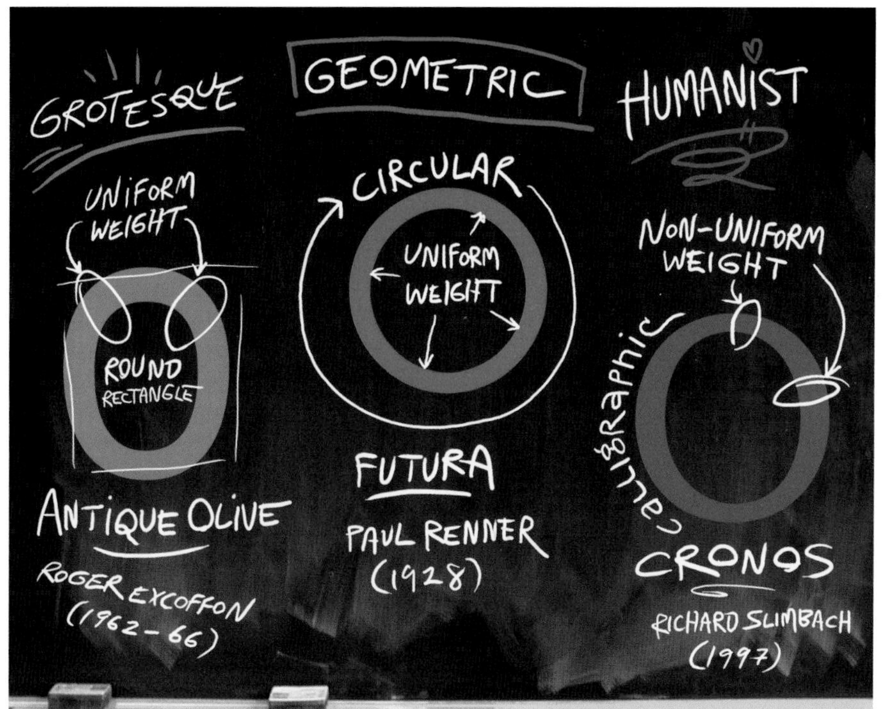

Figure 3-2.

Well, I'm here to tell you, Miedinger and the others did what they did because the appearance of type can determine whether or not it gets read. While single letters are endlessly entertaining to us type nerds, fonts and other type characteristics take on real meaning when applied to larger passages of text. By way of example, Figure 3-3 on the following page shows each of the typefaces from Figure 3-1 applied to a full sentence. (Believe it or not, the size specifications are consistent throughout.) Suddenly it becomes evident just how much a typeface—in addition to color and other factors—can affect our perception of what we read. Each face imbues a page with its own particular weight, texture, and style, which in turn affect the appeal, mood, and legibility of your text. Much as I love graphics, text is the reason most printed documents (including this one) exist. And that makes the humble font the single greatest contributor to the look and feel of a page.

Applying Formatting Attributes

To *format* type is to define its appearance. Therefore, the specific physical traits of type are called *formatting attributes*. InDesign's extensive and far-flung formatting options control everything from the way a single letter looks to the relationship between neighboring letters. In addition to typeface, examples include the slant or thickness of a letter

Helvetica Medium

Meanwhile, each of those same fonts appl
phrase or sentence imparts a unique look a

Myriad Regular

Meanwhile, each of those same fonts applied t
phrase or sentence imparts a unique look and fe

Futura Book

Meanwhile, each of those same fonts applied to a
phrase or sentence imparts a unique look and feel.

Antique Olive Roman

Meanwhile, each of those same fonts a
phrase or sentence imparts a unique lo

Cronos Regular

Meanwhile, each of those same fonts applied to a
phrase or sentence imparts a unique look and feel.

Rotis Sans Serif 55

Meanwhile, each of those same fonts applied to a
phrase or sentence imparts a unique look and feel.

News Gothic Medium

Meanwhile, each of those same fonts applied
phrase or sentence imparts a unique look and

Figure 3-3.

(style), its height (type size), the distance from one row of type to the next (leading), how the rows line up with each other (alignment), and the placement of tabs and indents.

To format text, you must first select it with either the black arrow tool or the type tool:

- If you select a text block with the black arrow tool, InDesign changes all type inside it. (Note that this works with an unthreaded text block only; threaded text must be selected with the type tool.) The control palette doesn't offer any type functions when the black arrow is active, so you'll have to apply your formatting attributes from the Character and Paragraph palettes. Before changing the color of your type, be sure to click the T icon at the bottom of the toolbox, as in Figure 3-4. Otherwise, you'll change the color of the frame instead (which also has its uses, as you'll see in the first exercise).

Figure 3-4 shows the wider two-column toolbox, which enlarges the fill and stroke icons at the bottom of the palette so they're easier to read. Remember, you can change the width of the toolbox by clicking the ▸▸ icon at the top of the docking pane.

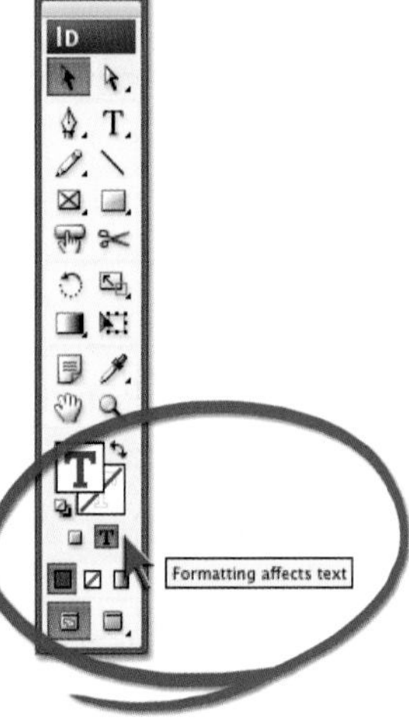

Figure 3-4.

- If you select one or more letters with the type tool, the kind of formatting you apply affects the results. Choosing a font, a type size, or another *character-level attribute* affects the selected letters or words only. Changing the alignment, the indent, or another *paragraph-level attribute* affects the entire paragraph, regardless of how much of that paragraph is selected. For more information on character versus paragraph formatting, watch Video Lesson 3, "Typeface, Style, and More," on the DVD (see page 90).

After selecting your text, you can apply formatting attributes from the control palette, the Type menu, or one of nine—count them, *nine*—other palettes. And even then, you have to use other palettes to color or add effects to your text. If this sounds extreme, bear in mind two things. First, there's a lot of duplication. You can change the type size from six locations and the font from seven. Fortunately, this book focuses on the *best* methods (not all methods). Second, InDesign's range of formatting attributes goes well beyond those included in QuarkXPress and PageMaker. The formatting attributes are so vast, in fact, that we'll spend this and the next two lessons exploring them.

Font, Size, and Color

While a skilled writer can pack a string of words with nuance, emotion, and meaning, a skilled designer can take those words and amplify their effect through careful use of typeface, size, and color. These three components are vital tools for enhancing legibility and drawing attention to important words and phrases in your document. Luckily, InDesign gives you plenty of ways to apply these crucial formatting attributes, as we'll see in this next exercise.

1. ***Open a document in need of help.*** Open the file *Seventies quiz #1.indd*, which you'll find in the *Lesson 03* folder inside *Lesson Files-IDcs3 1on1*. As pictured in Figure 3-5, the first column of type features an odd color scheme, sure to discourage even the most eager reader. Although you may never encounter a formatting blunder of this magnitude in your workaday routine, learning how to fix it provides us with a swell introduction to InDesign's text-coloring capabilities.

2. ***Select the ugly text frame on the left.*** Get the black arrow tool from the toolbox and click the text frame to select it.

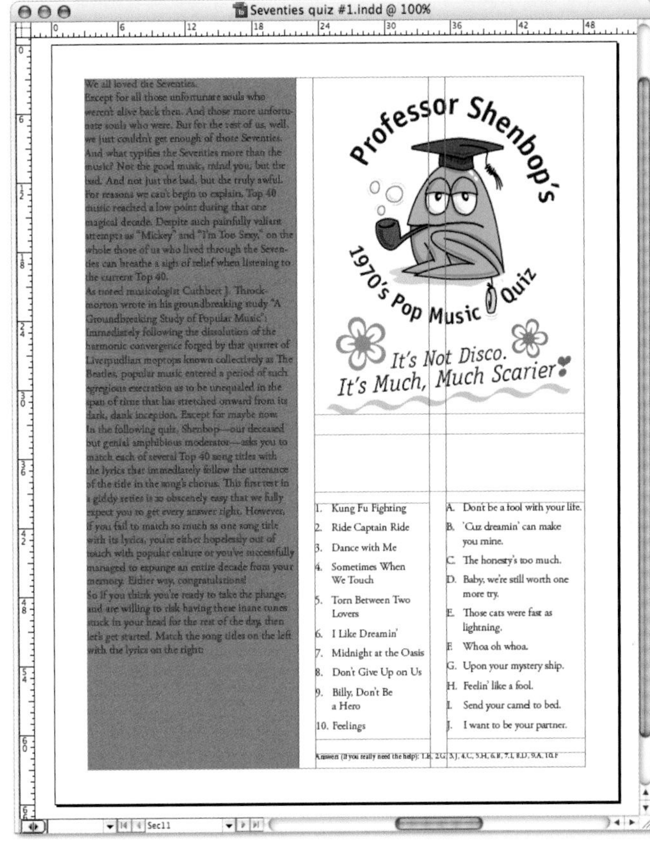

Figure 3-5.

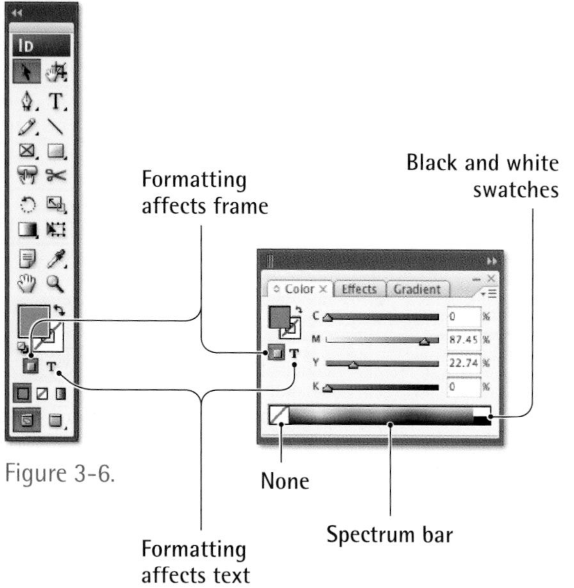

Figure 3-6.

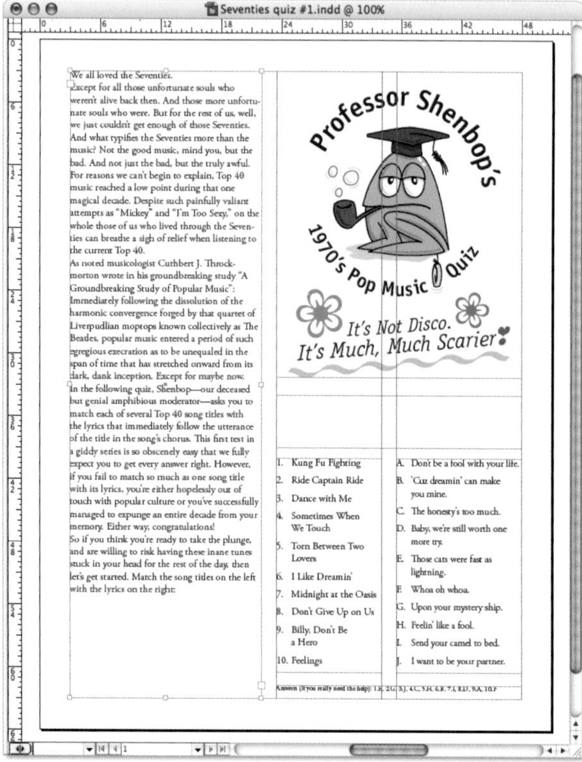

Figure 3-7.

3. ***Change the background color of the text frame.*** Our first point of business is to get rid of that ghastly pink background. Choose **Window→Color** or press F6 to access the **Color** palette. Figure 3-6 shows a labeled version of the palette, along with the corresponding options in the toolbox. You can use either the palette or the toolbox to perform the following:

   - Click the pink fill icon (◪). This makes the interior of the text frame active.
   - Below the pink fill icon are two small icons. The ▣ icon affects the interior of the frame; the [T] icon affects the text. The ▣ icon should be selected; if it isn't, click it.
   - Click the ⊘ icon in the bottom-left corner of the Color palette, or press the [/] key. The pink in the text frame goes away.

4. ***Change the color of the text to black.*** Click the [T] icon below the ◪ icon in the Color palette or toolbox to modify the text inside the frame. Then click the black swatch in the lower-right corner of the Color palette. The text turns black, as in Figure 3-7.

5. ***Select the first line of text.*** Having changed the entire text block, let's look at a few ways to format individual words and lines of type. To accomplish this, you'll need the type tool. Double-click the text frame to automatically switch to the type tool and position the blinking insertion marker. Now triple-click any word in the first line of text to select the entire line.

6. ***Bring up the Character palette.*** One way to apply character-level formatting attributes is to use those options in the control palette that I've labeled in Figure 3-8. Depending on which icon is active in the top-left corner of the screen ([A] or [¶]), the character options appear in the left half of the palette ([A]) or the right ([¶]). You can switch between the two by clicking the icons or pressing InDesign's shortcut, Ctrl+Alt+7 (⌘-Option-7). To make your control palette look like the one in the figure, click the [A].

   The control palette is convenient, but for the time being, we'll focus on the Character palette, which is more concise. Choose **Type→Character** or press Ctrl+T

(⌘-T on the Mac) to display InDesign's **Character** palette, also labeled in Figure 3-8. Happily, the first option in the palette—the font name—is already highlighted.

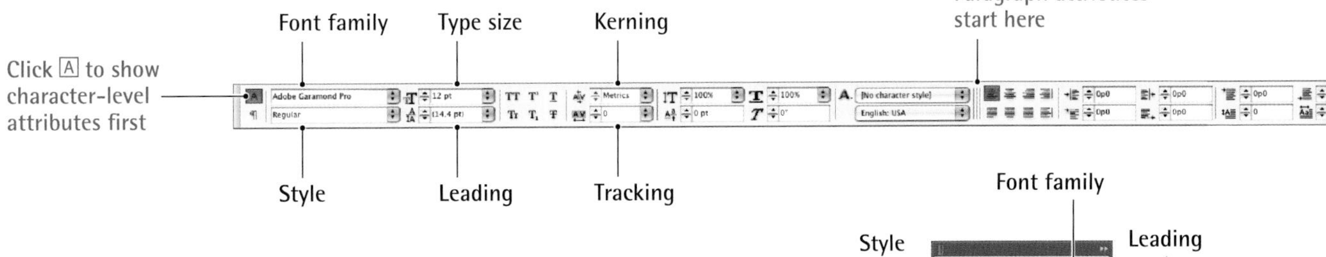

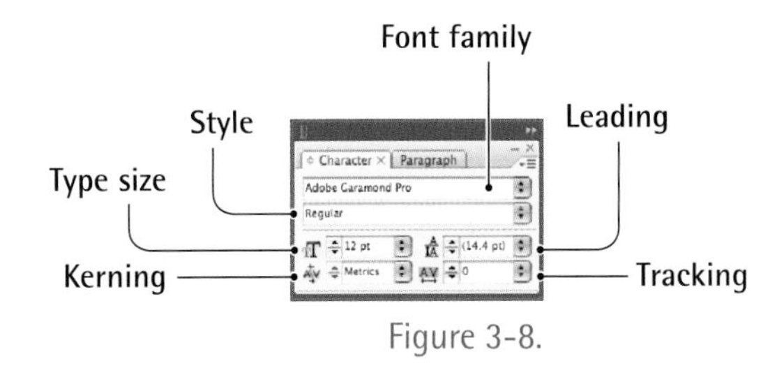

Figure 3-8.

7. *Change the font to Jenson or Arno.* This may seem like a indecisive instruction, but with CS3, Adobe switched out the fonts that ship with the Creative Suite. So, with the font name in the Character palette highlighted, do one of the following:

   - If you previously installed InDesign CS or CS2 on your machine, type "adobe jenson pro." Probably, you need only type "adobe j" before the Character palette fills in the rest for you.
   - If CS3 is the first version of the program that got installed on your computer, type "arn" to select the font Arno Pro.

   Press Tab to apply the font. I'll be using Jenson (see Figure 3-9), but the two are similar.

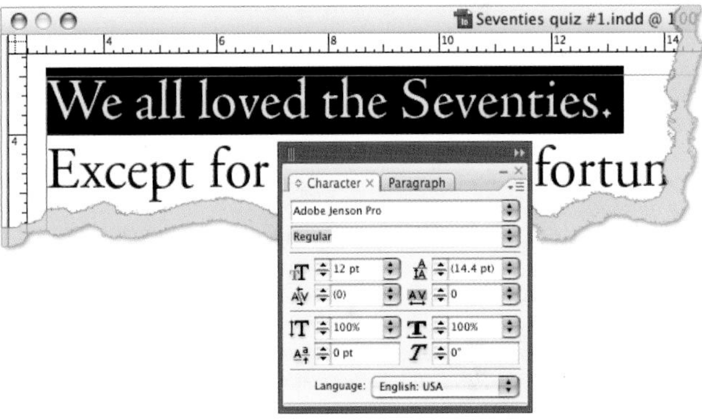

Figure 3-9.

PEARL OF WISDOM

I don't think anyone knows what half the fonts on his or her system look like. Which is why InDesign lets you preview your collection. Click and hold the ▾ or ⬍ arrow to the right of the font name to display the font pop-up menu and there they are. To enlarge the font previews, choose Edit→Preferences→Type (on the Mac, InDesign→Preferences→Type), set the Font Preview Size option to Large, and click OK. If you see the message *building* in the font pop-up menu, it means InDesign is working on the font preview. Just give it another minute or two and try again.

8. *Change the type style to Bold.* Choose **Bold** from the second pop-up menu in the Character palette (labeled Style in Figure 3-8) or press Ctrl+Shift+B (⌘-Shift-B on the Mac). Either way, the selected text becomes bold, as in Figure 3-10.

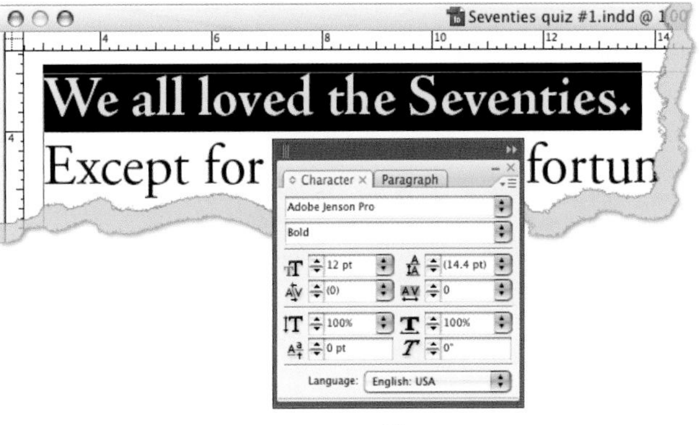

Figure 3-10.

9. ***Increase the type size to 30 points.*** Choose **30 pt** from the type size (TT) pop-up menu. Or type 30 in the option box and press Enter or Return.

Alternatively, you can change the type size from the keyboard. Press Ctrl+Shift+> or Ctrl+Shift+< (that's ⌘-Shift-> or ⌘-Shift-< on the Mac) to enlarge or reduce text, respectively, in 2-point increments. Add the Alt (or Option) key to increase or decrease the type size by five times that amount, or 10 points by default.

---

10. ***Decrease the leading to 30 points.*** Increasing the type size bumped the text to two lines. Now we have the option of modifying the vertical distance between those two lines, which is known as *leading*. (See the upcoming sidebar on page 98, "The Look of Type," for a thorough discussion of leading and other key formatting terms.) By default, InDesign applies Auto leading, which is equal to 120 percent of the type size. For instance, the Auto leading for our 30-point text is 120 percent of 30, or 36 points, as the $\stackrel{A}{IA}$ value in your Character palette should show.

A glance at the Character palette confirms whether or not Auto leading is in effect. If the $\stackrel{A}{IA}$ value appears in parentheses, Auto leading is on; otherwise a manual leading value prevails. Auto leading changes automatically with the type size; manual leading does not.

Large text such as a headline often looks best when the leading matches the type size, a treatment known as *solid* leading. You can achieve this by performing either of the following:

- Select the $\stackrel{A}{IA}$ value and change it to 30 points. Press Enter or Return to apply the value.
- Pressing Alt+↓ (or Option-↓) expands the leading in 2-point increments; Alt+↑ (or Option-↑) reduces the leading, again by 2 points. So to reduce the leading from 36 to 30 points, press Alt+↑ three times in a row. Your headline should now look like the one in Figure 3-11.

Figure 3-11.

When adjusting leading from the keyboard, add the Ctrl (or ⌘) key to scale the increment by a factor of five. For example, pressing Ctrl+Alt+↓ increases the leading by 10 points. To restore Auto leading, press Ctrl+Shift+Alt+A (⌘-Shift-Option-A on the Mac). Consult the "Formatting Shortcuts" sidebar on pages 104 and 105 for this and other handy keyboard shortcuts.

PEARL OF WISDOM

If you come from QuarkXPress, you may find it disconcerting that the leading option is located in the Character palette rather than the Paragraph palette. The reason is that InDesign lets you apply leading on a line-by-line basis. Personally, I prefer this approach because it makes it easier to squeeze or expand lines to better fit the length of a column. But I know Quark devotees who absolutely have a conniption over this. If you feel a conniption coming on, spare yourself a fit and do the following: Press Ctrl+K followed by Ctrl+3 (⌘-K, ⌘-3 on the Mac) to display the Type panel of the Preferences dialog box. Then turn on the Apply Leading to Entire Paragraphs check box. Now InDesign will apply leading to entire paragraphs, just like Quark.

---

11. *Bring up the Units & Increments panel of the Preferences dialog box.* By default, InDesign's formatting shortcuts change the type and leading values in 2-point increments. While this is appropriate for grand, sweeping changes, my experience suggests that 2 points is too much for everyday work. So let's change it. Press Ctrl+K and then Ctrl+6 (⌘-K, ⌘-6) to display the **Units & Increments** panel of the **Preferences** dialog box, as in Figure 3-12.

12. *Change the Size/Leading value to 0.5 pt.* Tab your way down to the **Size/Leading** value and change it to 0.5 point, which gives you finer control when making keyboard modifications. After you make the change, click the **OK** button to exit the Preferences dialog box.

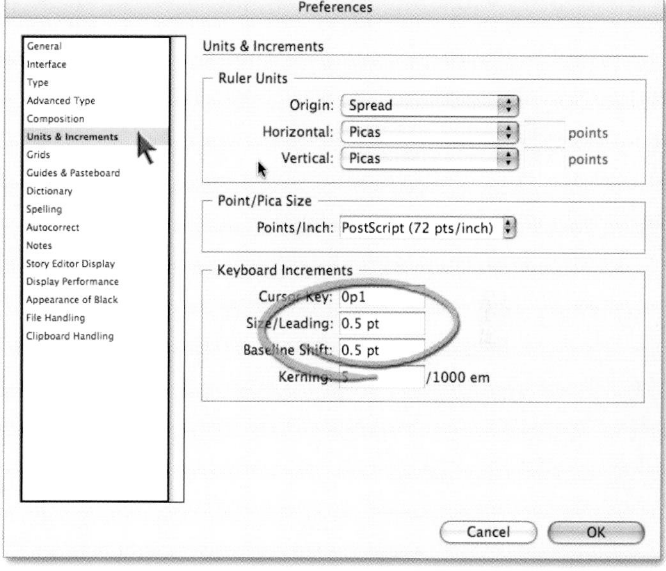

Figure 3-12.

13. *Highlight the paragraph below the headline.* Quadruple-click with the type tool somewhere in the first paragraph below the headline. This selects the entire paragraph.

14. *Increase the type size to 15.5 points.* Having set the Size/Leading value in the Preferences dialog box to 0.5 point, the fastest way to increase the type size from 12 to 15.5 points is to:

    - Press the shortcut Ctrl+Shift+Alt+> (or ⌘-Shift-Option->) to raise the type size by 2.5 points, or to 14.5 points.
    - Then press Ctrl+Shift+> (⌘-Shift->) twice to nudge the type the last extra point. The result appears in Figure 3-13.

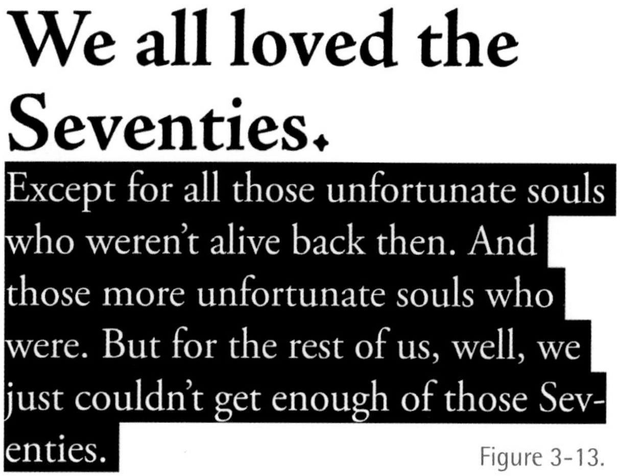

We all loved the Seventies.

Except for all those unfortunate souls who weren't alive back then. And those more unfortunate souls who were. But for the rest of us, well, we just couldn't get enough of those Seventies.

Figure 3-13.

The Look of Type

Subtle crafts demand meticulous tools, and typography has more meticulous tools than you can shake a finely carved stick at. Let's begin at the beginning, with fonts—specifically, the two fonts that ushered in desktop publishing, Times and Helvetica, both pictured below. In Times, the lines of each character change gradually in thickness and terminate in tapering—or *bracketed*—wedges called *serifs*. Created in 1931 by Stanley Morison for *The Times* of London, the font was designed as a revival of the 18th-century Transitional serif faces. Meanwhile, the "naked" sans serif Helvetica drew its inspiration from the turn of the previous century. With its uniform strokes and disdain for ornamentation, Helvetica came to dominate typesetting and remains one of the top-ten selling fonts to this day. It even inspired its own revival, Robin Nicholas's 1982 Arial, now an online standard.

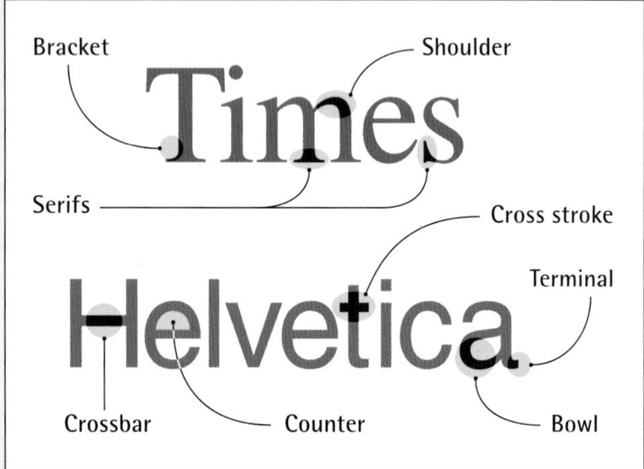

The number of fonts available to digital publishers has grown exponentially over the last 20 years. In addition to a few thousand serif and sans serif faces, you can choose from slab serif, monospaced, blackletter, script, display, symbol—the list goes on and on. Fortunately, even the wackiest of these fonts subscribes to a few basic formatting conventions.

For example, regardless of font, type is measured in points, from roughly the top of the highest letter to the bottom of the lowest. But that doesn't mean that 12-point text set using one typeface matches the size of another—in fact, far from it. To show why, the illustration at the top of the opposite page shows three lines of 52-point type. Only the font changes, from Century Old Style on top to Künstler Script and finally the display face Tekton. The first line appears the largest thanks to its relatively tall lowercase letters. Like most script faces, Künstler offers short lowercase letters and thus appears the smallest.

When gauging type size, bear in mind the following:

- Each row of characters rests on a common *baseline*. The parts of characters that drop below the baseline—as in *g*, *j*, *p*, *q*, and *y*—are called *descenders*.
- The line formed by the tops of most lowercase letters—*a*, *c*, *e*, and others—is the *x-height*. Those characters that fit entirely between the baseline and x-height are called *medials*. Large medials usually translate to a larger looking font and remain legible at very small sizes.
- The portions of lowercase letters that rise above the x-height—*b*, *d*, and the rest—are called *ascenders*. Two letters, *i* and *t*, do not rise to full height and are considered medials.
- The unlabeled white lines in the upper-right illustration indicate the *cap heights*, which mark the top boundary of the capital letters. When working with a standard text face such as Century Old Style (as well as Times, Helvetica, and their ilk), the cap height falls slightly below the ascenders. Künstler Script raises the cap height well above the ascenders; the display face Tekton makes caps and ascenders the same height.

In the old days of metal typesetting, *point size* was calculated by measuring the piece of lead that held the letter. This meant the size was slightly larger than the largest character of type. Typesetters added room between lines of type by inserting additional blank strips of lead. Now that everything's digital, the lead is gone but not forgotten. Designers still call line spacing *leading* (pronounced "ledding"). And while modern type houses can size their characters any way they want, the actual height of the characters is typically smaller than the prescribed size. For example, in the upper-right illustration, each colored bar is exactly 52 points tall; the characters fit inside the bars with a few points to spare.

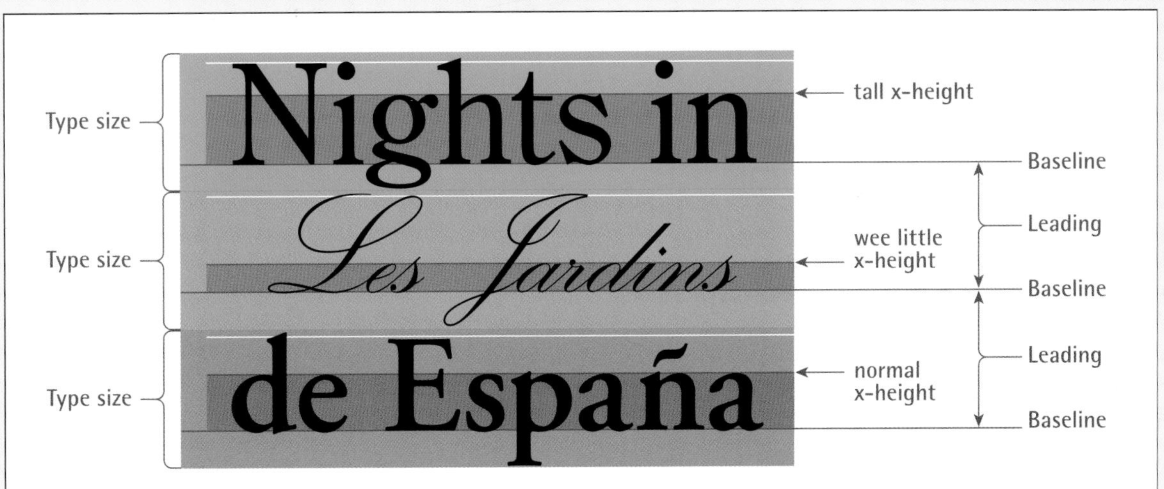

In addition to height, you can measure type by its width and weight. The difference is that you don't typically scale these attributes numerically. Rather, you select from predefined styles, such as those pictured for the fonts Myriad and Moonglow to the right. Because few fonts include width variations, InDesign lets you stretch or squish the letters manually. But doing so can make the text look ridiculous. As indicated by the brown text in the right-hand figure, scaling the width of a letter changes the proportions of its strokes as well as its proximity to other letters. If you choose to stretch, I recommend going no narrower than 80 percent and no wider than 125 percent.

Myriad, Width	Myriad, Weight
Condensed	Light
Regular	Regular
Semi-extended	**Semibold**
Stretched	**Bold**
	Black

Moonglow, Width	Moonglow, Weight
CONDENSED	LIGHT
REGULAR	REGULAR
EXTENDED	**SEMIBOLD**
MOONGLOW SQUISHED	**BOLD**

Most font families include at least one italic or oblique style. These slanted variations are used to stress foreign or unfamiliar phrases, as well as titles of books and other publications. Although InDesign also offers underlines, they aren't commonly used. (You may notice that underlines do not appear in this book, for example.) These days, the underline is relegated to marking hyperlinks, such as those on the Web, and that's about it. So in virtually all cases, if you're tempted to underline, use italics instead. If an italic style is not available, InDesign lets you slant text manually by entering a skew value in the control palette (as I show in Video Lesson 3, "Typeface, Style, and More," on the DVD). A value of 12 degrees or less is generally sufficient.

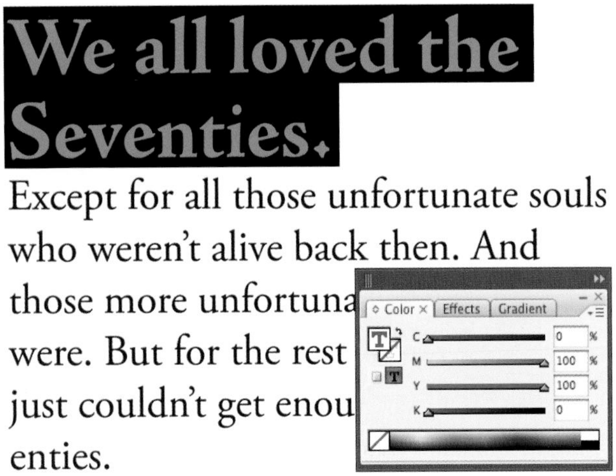

15. ***Change the headline to red.*** As a final touch, let's assign the headline a bold, vibrant, 1970's color. Quadruple-click anywhere in *We all loved the Seventies* to select the entire headline. Go to the **Color** palette, click the ▾≡ icon in the palette's top-right corner, and choose CMYK so that you see four slider bars, one each for C, M, Y, and K, as in Figure 3-14. Also make sure the text fill icon is active, as in T. Leave the Cyan (**C**) value set to 0; change the Magenta and Yellow (**M** and **Y**) values to 100 percent; then change the Black (**K**) value to 0. Press Enter or Return to apply the color.

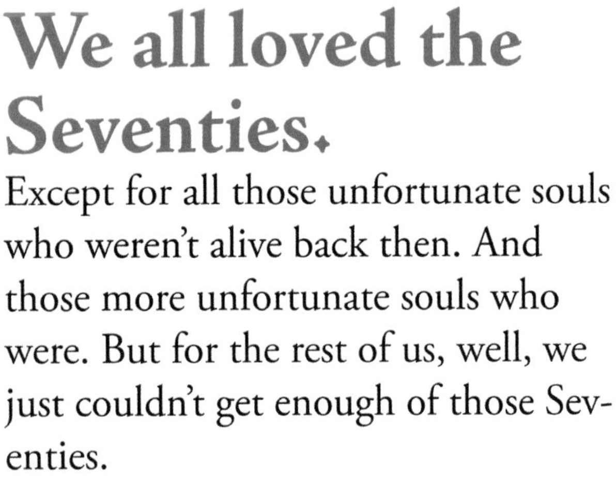

We all loved the Seventies.

Except for all those unfortunate souls who weren't alive back then. And those more unfortuna… were. But for the rest … just couldn't get enou… enties.

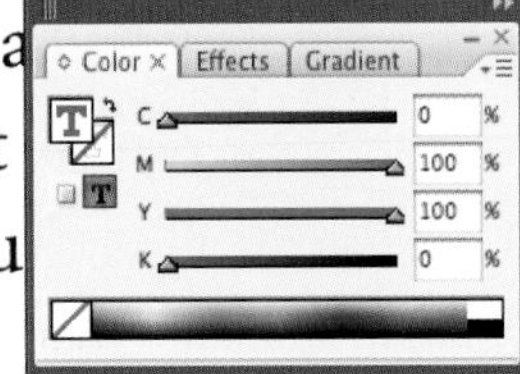

Figure 3-14.

16. ***Deselect the text.*** Press Ctrl+Shift+A (⌘-Shift-A on the Mac) to deselect the text and see the results of your changes. As Figure 3-15 shows, the revised headline is a lovely ruby red, just the sort of color you'd expect from Lipps, Inc. or some similar ultra-funky, chart-topping, dead-the-second-the-decade-ended act of the Seventies.

We all loved the Seventies.

Except for all those unfortunate souls who weren't alive back then. And those more unfortunate souls who were. But for the rest of us, well, we just couldn't get enough of those Seventies.

Figure 3-15.

That's not to say the text looks *good*, necessarily. It has spacing problems, the lines break badly—in short, it's a mess. Which is why we'll continue to work on this very document in the next exercise.

Kerning and Tracking

In the preceding exercise you learned, among other things, how to adjust the vertical space between lines of text. In this exercise you'll work on controlling the horizontal space within lines of text using two strangely named properties, kerning and tracking. In publishing, *kerning* changes the space between two adjacent characters of type; *tracking* affects a range of selected characters at a time. It works like this:

- Every character of type includes a fixed amount of left and right space, called *side bearing*. The side bearing is defined in the font; you can't change it. Together, the right bearing of one character and the left bearing of the one that follows it determine the base spacing between two characters of type.
- The base spacing satisfies most pairs of characters, but when it doesn't, kerning is there to compensate.

For example, consider the classic *WA* combo illustrated in Figure 3-16. The letters slant parallel to each other, resulting in a big gap between them. *WA* is such a well-known combo that the font contains instructions to kern it automatically. Hence, *WA* is termed a *kerning pair*.

- If you don't like InDesign's automatic kerning—or none was applied—you can enter a custom kerning value to override the space between a pair of characters. Measured as a fraction of an em space (that is, a fraction of the width of the active type size), the kerning value is added to or subtracted from the bearing space.
- Finally, you heap tracking on top of the side bearing and kerning settings to adjust the spacing of many characters at a time. Like kerning, tracking is measured in fractions of an em space, so it automatically adjusts to suit changes in type size.

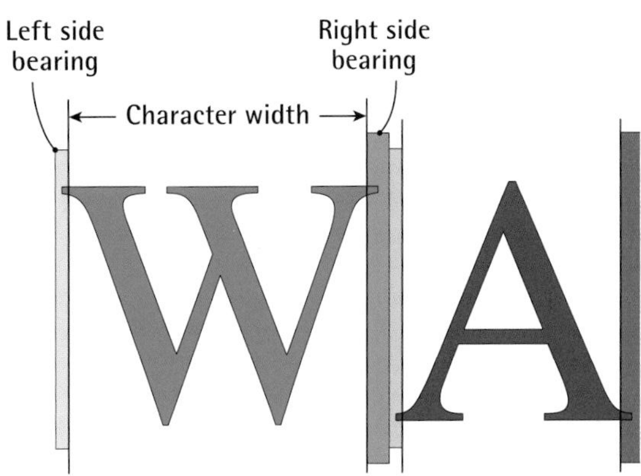

Figure 3-16.

Together, kerning and tracking let you fine-tune a font's already good default character spacing to create more attractive, easier-to-read text, as I shall demonstrate in the following exercise.

1. ***Open a document.*** Open the next file I've prepared for you, *Seventies quiz #1a.indd* in the *Lesson 03* folder inside *Lesson Files-IDcs3 1on1*. (This document uses Arno Pro to make it compatible with CS3 systems.) Or if you just completed the preceding exercise, you can simply forge ahead with the file you have open. Either way, your document should look like the one shown in Figure 3-17.
2. ***Select the first column of text.*** We'll start by modifying the spacing of all the text in the left column. So get the black arrow tool and click the left frame.
3. ***Magnify the red headline at the top of the column.*** Although we're going to adjust the kerning for *all* the text in the frame, spacing changes can be subtle, so I recommend that you zoom in on a representative portion of the text to better see what's going on. Get the zoom tool and drag to draw a marquee around the headline and the following paragraph. You should be able to achieve a zoom similar to the one pictured in Figure 3-18 on the next page.

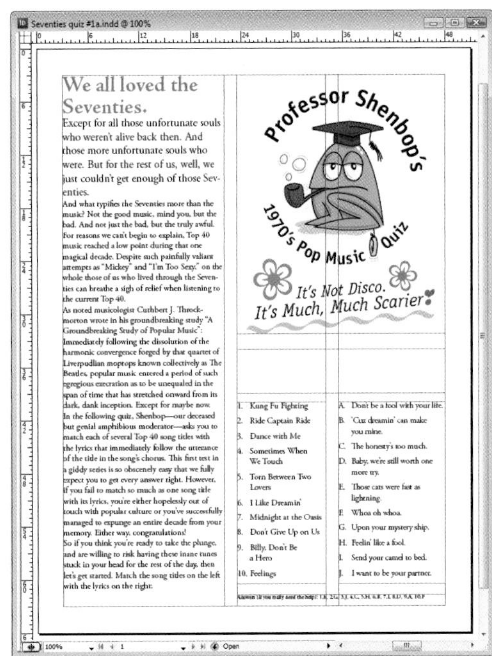

Figure 3-17.

4. ***Apply optical kerning.*** Virtually all type designers embed kerning specifications directly into their fonts. This *metrics kerning* ensures that well-known kerning pairs—such as *Av*, *Ye*, and even *r.* (that is, an *r* followed by a period)—are not

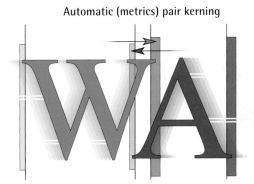

Figure 3-18.

interrupted by unintended gaps. Like other publishing programs, InDesign abides by a font's metric kerning specifications by default. But while metric kerning is the industry standard, it relies heavily on the skills and thoroughness of the font designer. Some fonts (such as Adobe's OpenType collection) contain thousands of carefully defined kerning pairs. Others describe only the most obvious pairs and give those minimal attention.

If you're working with a badly kerned font—and for the moment, I'd like you to pretend you are—InDesign provides an alternative. Inside the **Character** or control palette, choose **Optical** from the kerning (AV) pop-up menu. This applies Adobe's exclusive *optical kerning* function, which automatically evaluates character outlines to produce what InDesign considers to be the most attractive results possible. The program doesn't always get it exactly right, but it's a big improvement over bad metrics kerning. Case in point: The text you're reading now is set in Linotype's Birka, which is a prime example of a stylish, even delicate, legible typeface with rotten kerning info. No problem with optical kerning. While I hand-tweaked a few characters here and there, most of what you see was kerned automatically by InDesign.

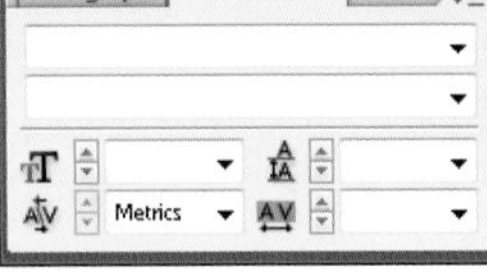

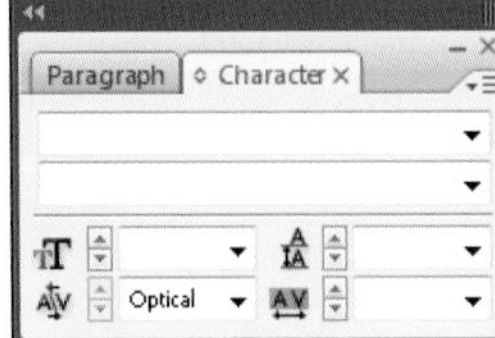

Figure 3-19.

When you choose the Optical option, you'll see a slight shift in the letters. Figure 3-19 demonstrates the kerning shift applied to the headline. The cyan letters show metrics positioning, the red letters show optical, and the dark areas show overlap. Frankly, this is a modest adjustment, and some might argue a bad one. The product manager of Adobe's Western Type Department recommends metrics kerning for all Adobe OpenType fonts. Optical kerning is a demanding operation that can slow InDesign's performance, and OpenType fonts already include all the kerning pairs you'll need. But OpenType fonts are all you and I have in common, and I want you to see the feature in action.

PEARL OF WISDOM

If you are using a script font such as Bickham Script Pro, do *not* use optical kerning! The characters in a script font are drawn and kerned specifically to emulate cursive writing so that the characters touch when metrics kerning is applied; optical kerning destroys this handwritten effect.

5. ***Decrease the kerning keystroke increment.*** All right, so much for automatic kerning; let's get down to the manual stuff. But before we do, I want you to reduce InDesign's clunky kerning increments. Press Ctrl+K and then Ctrl+6 (⌘-K, ⌘-6 on the Mac) to access the **Units & Increments** panel of the **Preferences** dialog box. Tab down to the **Kerning** value and lower it from 20/1000 em space—equal to a relatively whopping 0.6 point in the case of our 30-point headline—to 5/1000 em. To do so, you just need to enter 5. Then click **OK**. This will result in more precise keyboard kerning adjustments, as you'll experience in the next step.

6. ***Adjust the kerning of the word* We.** Kerning problems most frequently appear when using letters with negative space, which is especially prevalent among capital letters such as *L*, *T*, and *V*. In our case, the negative space in *W* creates a bit of an empty pocket inside the word *We*. Get the type tool and click between the letters *W* and *e*, as in Figure 3-20. Notice that the A/V value in the Character palette appears as (–89) for Jenson or (–45) for Arno Pro. (If you see something else, you neglected to apply Optical kerning in Step 4.) The parentheses tell you that InDesign automatically applied this value, using either metrics or optical kerning.

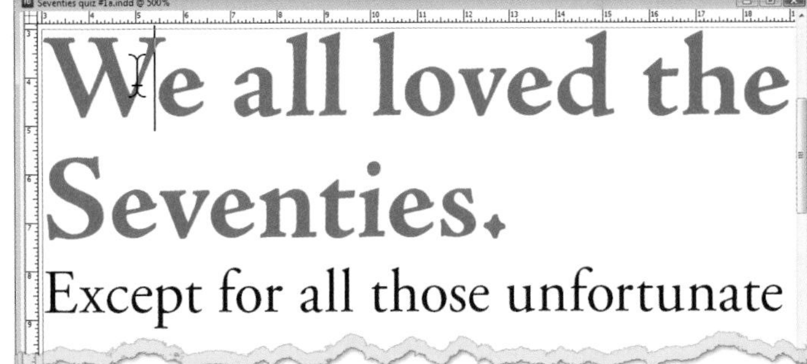
We all loved the
Seventies.
Except for all those unfortunate

Figure 3-20.

To nudge these letters closer together, do the following:

- Press Alt+← (Option-← on the Mac) to move the *e* exactly 5/1000 em space toward the *W*. When the type size is set to 30 points, 5/1000 em is 0.15 point, or 1/480 inch. That's a small nudge, all right. Perhaps too small.
- Press Ctrl+Alt+← (or ⌘-Option-←) to nudge the letters five times the specified kerning increment, or 25/1000 em.

Most of the time, you'll want to kern characters closer together. But for those occasional times when you need to kern letters apart, pressing Alt+→ (Option-→ on the Mac) does the trick. Press Ctrl+Alt+→ (⌘-Option-→) to multiply the increment by a factor of five.

Formatting Shortcuts

When it comes to formatting, InDesign is shortcut crazy. And for good reason—shortcuts let you experiment with various text settings while keeping your eyes on the results. Quite simply, by assigning a few keyboard shortcuts to memory, you can dramatically increase how fast you work. Assuming you have a rough feel for the location of keys on the keyboard, you can adjust formatting settings almost as fast as you can think of them.

I should note that I'm not asking you to do anything I wouldn't ask of myself. This is not a comprehensive list that I've assembled by pouring through menus and help files. These are the shortcuts that I use routinely, all lodged in the nether regions of my brain. Sure I had to displace some information—my home phone number, my kids' birthdays, what my mom looks like—but it was worth it.

Before trying out these shortcuts for yourself, I recommend that you confirm the keyboard increments in the Preferences dialog box. Choose Edit→Preferences→Units & Increments (InDesign→Preferences→Units & Increments on the Mac) or press Ctrl+K, Ctrl+6 (⌘-K, ⌘-6). Then Tab your way down to the Keyboard Increments options. As I mentioned in the previous exercises, I recommend setting Size/Leading to 0.5 point and Kerning to 5/1000 em. I also suggest you change Baseline Shift to 0.5 point, as shown below. Then click the OK button to confirm.

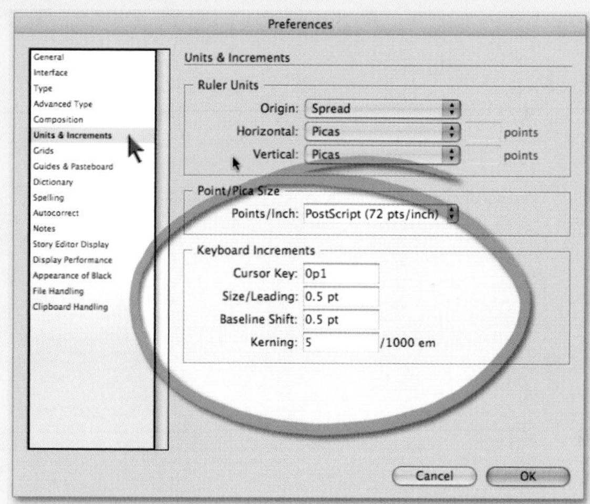

Whatever values you decide on, bear in mind that they're editable and you can change them anytime you like. Because these increments are variables, I refer to them in the following table by their initials—*SI* for the Size/Leading increment, *BI* for the Baseline Shift increment, and *KI* for the Kerning increment. In all cases, text has to be selected for the keyboard shortcuts to work.

Operation	Windows shortcut	Macintosh shortcut
Apply bold type style (when available)	Ctrl+Shift+B	⌘-Shift-B
Apply italic type style (when available)	Ctrl+Shift+I	⌘-Shift-I
Underline selected text	Ctrl+Shift+U	⌘-Shift-U
Strikethrough selected text	Ctrl+Shift+/ (slash)	⌘-Shift-/ (slash)
Change text to all caps	Ctrl+Shift+K	⌘-Shift-K
Change text to small caps	Ctrl+Shift+H	⌘-Shift-H
Superscript selected text	Ctrl+Shift+= (plus)	⌘-Shift-= (plus)
Subscript selected text	Ctrl+Shift+Alt+=	⌘-Shift-Option-=
Restore regular or plain style	Ctrl+Shift+Y	⌘-Shift-Y
Increase type size by SI	Ctrl+Shift+. (period)	⌘-Shift-. (period)
Increase type size by 5× SI	Ctrl+Shift+Alt+.	⌘-Shift-Option-.

Operation	Windows shortcut	Macintosh shortcut
Decrease type size by SI	Ctrl+Shift+, (comma)	⌘-Shift-, (comma)
Decrease type size by 5× SI	Ctrl+Shift+Alt+,	⌘-Shift-Option-,
Increase leading by SI	Alt+↓	Option-↓
Increase leading by 5× SI	Ctrl+Alt+↓	⌘-Option-↓
Decrease leading by SI	Alt+↑	Option-↑
Decrease leading by 5× SI	Ctrl+Alt+↑	⌘-Option-↑
Reinstate Auto (120%) leading	Ctrl+Shift+Alt+A	⌘-Shift-Option-A
Increase baseline shift by BI	Shift+Alt+↑	Shift-Option-↑
Increase baseline shift by 5× BI	Ctrl+Shift+Alt+↑	⌘-Shift-Option-↑
Decrease baseline shift by BI	Shift+Alt+↓	Shift-Option-↓
Decrease baseline shift by 5× BI	Ctrl+Shift+Alt+↓	⌘-Shift-Option-↓
Increase kerning/tracking by KI	Alt+→	Option-→
Increase kerning/tracking by 5× KI	Ctrl+Alt+→	⌘-Option-→
Decrease kerning/tracking by KI	Alt+←	Option-←
Decrease kerning/tracking by 5× KI	Ctrl+Alt+←	⌘-Option-←
Increase word kerning by KI*	Ctrl+Alt+\ (backslash)	⌘-Option-\ (backslash)
Increase word kerning by 5× KI*	Ctrl+Shift+Alt+\	⌘-Shift-Option-\
Decrease word kerning by KI*	Ctrl+Alt+Backspace	⌘-Option-Delete
Decrease word kerning by 5× KI*	Ctrl+Shift+Alt+Backspace	⌘-Shift-Option-Delete
Restore kerning to Metrics and tracking to 0*	Ctrl+Alt+Q	⌘-Option-Q
Reset horizontal scale to 100%*	Ctrl+Shift+X	⌘-Shift-X
Reset vertical scale to 100%*	Ctrl+Shift+Alt+X	⌘-Shift-Option-X
Toggle automatic hyphenation	Ctrl+Shift+Alt+H	⌘-Shift-Option-H
Toggle typographer (curly) quotes	Ctrl+Shift+Alt+' (quote)	⌘-Shift-Option-' (quote)
Left-align paragraph	Ctrl+Shift+L	⌘-Shift-L
Right-align paragraph	Ctrl+Shift+R	⌘-Shift-R
Center-align paragraph	Ctrl+Shift+C	⌘-Shift-C
Justify all lines except last one	Ctrl+Shift+J	⌘-Shift-J
Justify that last line, too	Ctrl+Shift+F	⌘-Shift-F

* Okay, I admit, even I have a hard time remembering a few of these. You have my permission not to worry about the shortcuts marked with an asterisk, guilt free. As for the others, you have some memorizing to do!

The AV value changes to –119 for Jenson or –70 for Arno. The parentheses go away, so you know manual kerning is in force.

7. ***Kern the rest of the headline to taste.*** Why did I have you reduce the Kerning value in Step 5 only to multiply it by five a moment later? Because other letter pairs require smaller adjustments:

   - Click between the *o* and *v* in *loved*. Then press Alt+← (Option-←) twice to reduce the spacing by a slim 10/1000 em.
   - Then press the → key to move the insertion marker between the *v* and *e*, and press Alt+← (Option-←) twice again.
   - Next, click between the first *e* and the *v* in *Seventies*. These letters are more widely spaced, so press Ctrl+Alt+← (⌘-Option-←) to move them together. If that's too much, press Alt+→ (Option-→) to nudge them slightly apart.

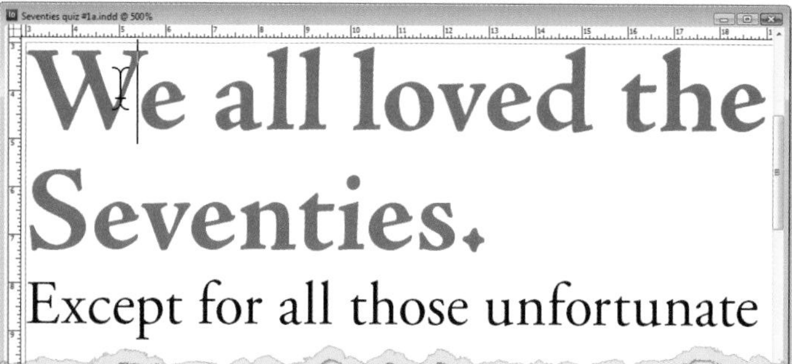

We all loved the
Seventies.
Except for all those unfortunate

Figure 3-21.

Figure 3-21 shows the results of these kerning changes.

8. ***Adjust the tracking in the paragraph below the headline.*** Mind numbed by the sheer tedium of it? That's manual kerning for you—subtle, meticulous, and rarely exciting. Fortunately, you can affect multiple letters at a time using tracking. It's not any more exciting, but it tends to go faster. Professional designers typically use tracking for one of two purposes:

   - As characters grow, so does the space between them. As a result, headlines and other large text may appear more loosely set than, say, body copy. To offset this, track the letters in a headline closer together. (Quark and PageMaker go so far as to let you customize default tracking according to type size; InDesign does not.)
   - You can also use tracking to shift characters from one line of text to another, an operation known as *copyfitting*. Consider the partial word *enties* at the end of the first paragraph. Tightening the tracking will unite it with the line above.

   Quadruple-click inside this first paragraph to select the entire thing. The same keyboard tricks that kern letter pairs track text as well, and by the same increments. So press Alt+← (Option-← on the Mac) twice to track the letters 10/1000 closer than they were before. Note the AV values in the Character and control palettes change to –10. Your text should end up looking similar to Figure 3-22.

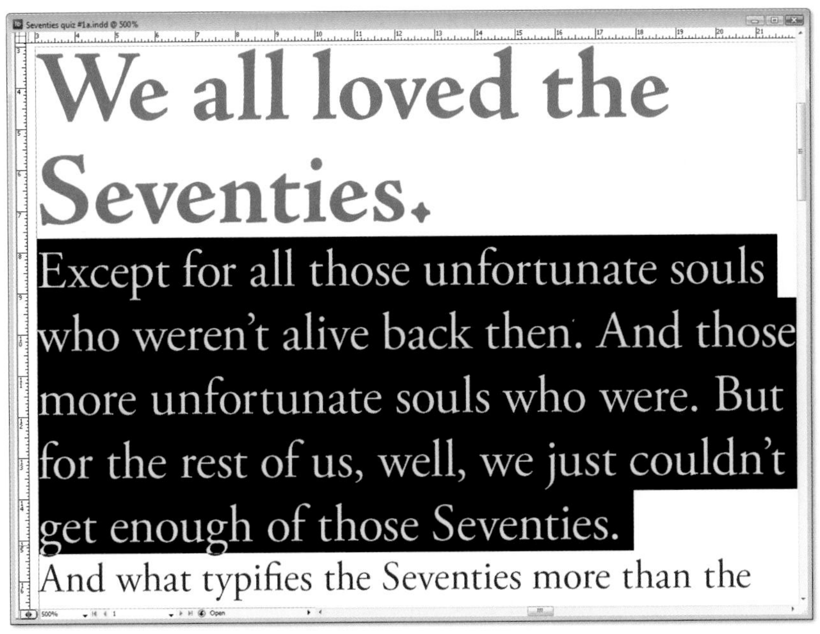
We all loved the Seventies.
Except for all those unfortunate souls who weren't alive back then. And those more unfortunate souls who were. But for the rest of us, well, we just couldn't get enough of those Seventies.
And what typifies the Seventies more than the

Figure 3-22.

Paragraph Spacing and Alignment

Although the niceties of kerning and tracking are essential for regulating the relationship between letters and words, they rank among the subtlest adjustments you can apply in InDesign. In stark contrast, our next topics are as obvious as the entire paragraphs they influence. First, we'll look at *paragraph spacing*, which adds vertical space between one paragraph and its neighbor. Then, we'll modify the alignment of text to create centered and justified paragraphs. Finally, we'll use InDesign's Keep Options command to glue neighboring lines of type together, thus avoiding those lonely casualties of page layout, widows and orphans.

1. ***Open a document.*** If you still have the file from the preceding exercise open, you're good to go. Otherwise, open the file titled *Seventies quiz #1b.indd* located in the *Lesson 03* folder inside *Lesson Files-IDcs3 1on1*. (Again, in my document, the red headline is set in Arno Pro.) As shown in Figure 3-23, the body copy in the left column suffers from what might be called "clumpiness," if only that were a word. The lines of text run together with nary an indent to indicate where one paragraph ends and the next begins. It's forbidding. It's unappealing. No one wants to read a clump. Fortunately, InDesign gives you all the tools you need to separate the paragraphs and make the clump go away.

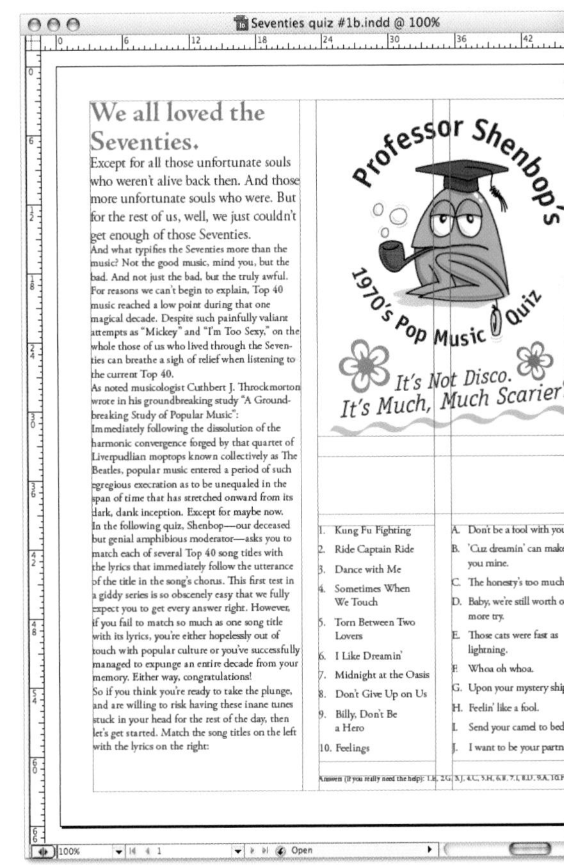
Seventies quiz #1b.indd @ 100%
We all loved the Seventies.
Professor Shenbop's
1970's Pop Music Quiz
It's Not Disco. It's Much, Much Scarier

Figure 3-23.

2. *Bring up the Paragraph palette.* If the **Paragraph** palette appears grouped with the Character palette, click the **Paragraph** tab to bring it to the fore. If you closed the palette as I had you do in the "Creating Custom Workspaces" exercise on page 24 of Lesson 1, choose **Type→Paragraph** or press Ctrl+Alt+T (⌘-Option-T) to bring it back. To keep things tidy, drag the palette into the same cluster as the Character palette.

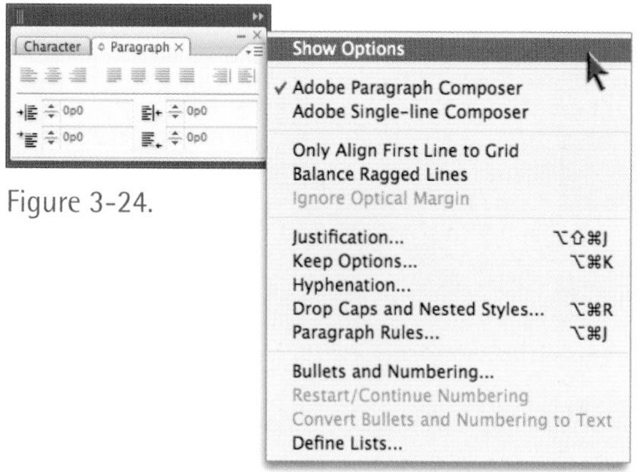

Figure 3-24.

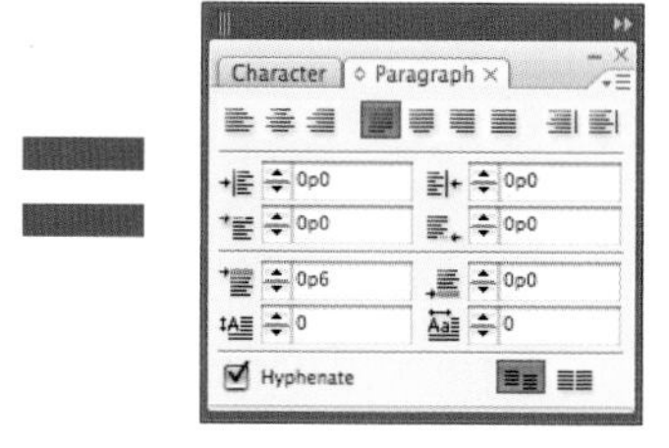

If you're missing some of the options shown on the right side of Figure 3-24, click the ▾≡ icon and choose Show Options to expand the palette to its full size. Or, if the palette is free-floating, click the ♦ arrow next to the word Paragraph twice.

Alternatively, you can use the paragraph options in the control palette. If you click the ¶ icon in the top-left corner of the screen, these options appear on the left side of the palette. Otherwise they follow the character options, just as they did back in Figure 3-8 (page 95). You can also press Ctrl+Alt+7 (⌘-Option-7) to swap the options. Frankly, that shortcut has never made much sense to me, which is why I've provided you with a different one: If you loaded my dekeKeys shortcuts as suggested on page xix of the Preface, press the F4 key to toggle back and forth.

3. *Apply paragraph spacing to the text in the left column.* One way to rid your text of clumpiness is to add an indent to the first line of each paragraph. You can do that the old-fashioned way, by inserting a tab character like you would if using a typewriter. But that means pressing the Tab key at the outset of each and every paragraph. If first-line indents are your goal, you're better off entering a positive value into the first-line indent option (second option on the left, ⁺≡, in the Paragraph palette).

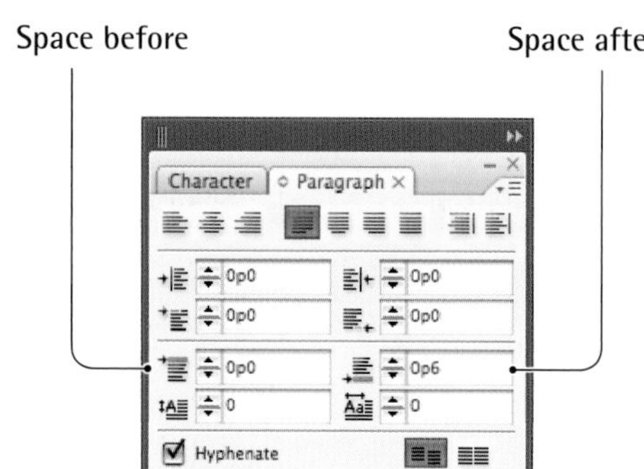

Figure 3-25.

PEARL OF WISDOM

The other way to set off paragraphs is to insert vertical space between them. The Paragraph palette offers two options for inserting paragraph space. As labeled in Figure 3-25, one option adds space before a paragraph; the other adds space after. In a way, the two options are redundant: both spacings appear between paragraphs and neither affects the positioning of text with respect to the frame. So 1 pica of space after one paragraph looks the same as 1 pica of space before the next. Why does InDesign go to the trouble of supplying two options? To accommodate style sheets. For example, you might create a Headline style that combines before and after spacing to add extra space above and below all headings in a document. For more info, see Lesson 8, "Using Style Sheets."

Just as I use paragraph spacing to set off the paragraphs in this book, you'll use it to separate the paragraphs in the first column of text. With the black arrow tool, click the first column in the document to select it. Then go to the Paragraph palette and enter 0p6 in the space after (₋≣) option box. Press the Enter or Return key to apply 6 points of space between each paragraph in the frame and the paragraph that follows it, as in Figure 3-25.

4. ***Add more space after the headline and first paragraph.*** While 6 points of space between paragraphs works nicely for the main body copy, the headline and first paragraph remain cramped. Press T to get the type tool. Then drag from anywhere in the headline to anywhere in the first paragraph to select portions of each. Then raise the ₋≣ value in the Paragraph palette to 1 pica.

5. ***Run overflow text into the empty frame.*** The added space forces the text to overflow the first column. Switch to the black arrow tool, click the left text frame's out port (⊞), and move the cursor over the empty text frame below the graphic on the right side of the document. When you see the elaborate link cursor—which includes a black 🔗 with a blue ⬚ and a preview of the first lines of text in the story, as in Figure 3-26—click. One line of text flows from the left column into the newly threaded frame on the right. In the publishing world, it's considered bad form to leave the last line of a paragraph dangling all alone at the top of a column. They even have a word for it: *widow*. But other changes we make may fix the problem.

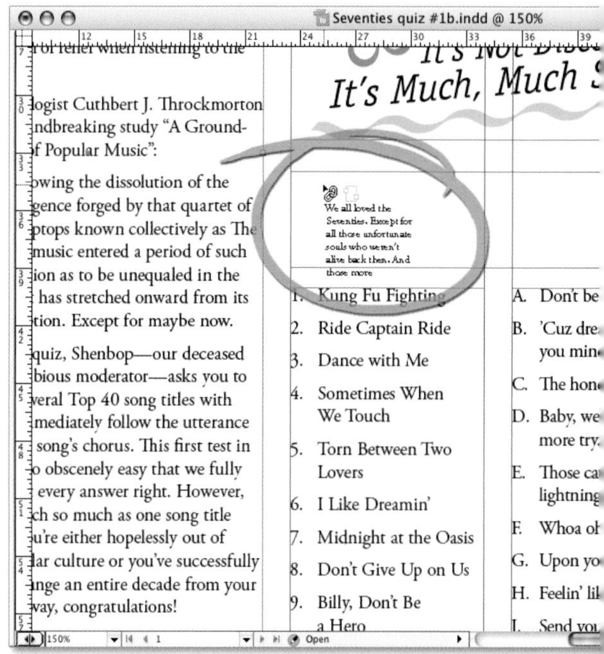

Figure 3-26.

6. ***Indent the left side of the fourth paragraph.*** The fourth paragraph in the left column is actually a long, painfully unfunny quote. I want you to offset this block quote by indenting the left and right sides. Using the type tool, click anywhere in the fourth paragraph, the one that begins with the word *Immediately*. Enter 3 into the first option box (→≣) in the Paragraph palette and press the Tab key to indent the paragraph 3 picas to the left. This also advances you to the right indent option (≣←); enter 3 and press Enter or Return. The result is the effect pictured in Figure 3-27.

7. ***Select all the body copy in the left column.*** The quote text continues to look unbalanced because of the ragged margin along the right side of the column. Therefore, we'll balance the body copy by justifying it. Using the type tool, select

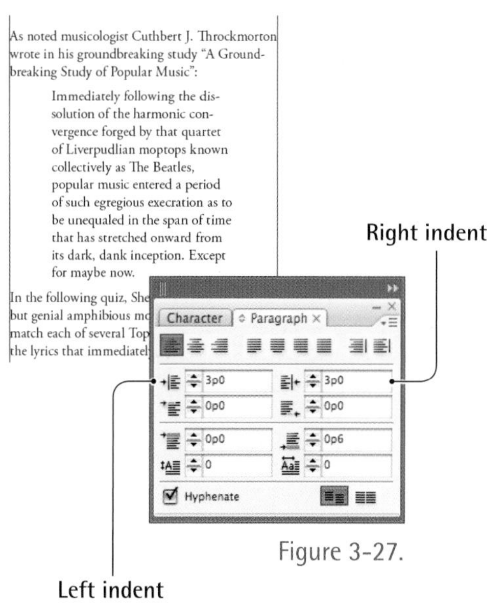

Figure 3-27.

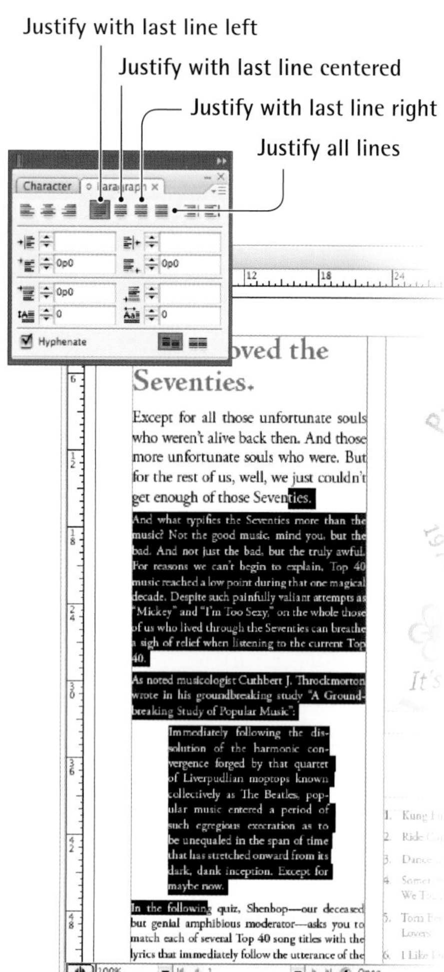

Figure 3-28.

portions of all paragraphs in the left column *except* the red headline. You don't have to be exact when making this selection. As long as a single character in the first and last paragraphs is selected, you're good to go.

8. ***Justify the selected text, with the last line flush left.*** Notice that the first of the seven alignment icons at the top of the Paragraph palette (▤) is active. This tells you that the selected text is left aligned, or *flush left*, which means that each line in a paragraph begins at the same left edge. Let's change this so that the left and right edges are aligned, creating nice even edges on both sides of the text block. To do so, click the fourth icon (▤) at the top of the Paragraph palette, or press Ctrl+Shift+J (⌘-Shift-J on the Mac). Shown in Figure 3-28, the resulting text is said to be *fully justified*, or just plain *justified*. InDesign modifies the spacing between and within words to line up the left and right edges of the text.

PEARL OF WISDOM

Notice that the last line of each selected paragraph is still aligned left. But it doesn't have to be that way. The fifth, sixth, and seventh icons at the top of the Paragraph palette likewise justify text but offer different options for dealing with the last line of a paragraph. The last of these icons, ▤, spreads the words in the last line until they too appear justified. Such a paragraph is said to be *force justified*. You can force justify text from the keyboard by pressing Ctrl+Shift+F (or ⌘-Shift-F). But don't do that here; we'll stick with the last line flush left.

9. ***Center align the overflow text.*** You may not have noticed, but our modifications in the last three steps have moved an entire paragraph to the second column, thus reuniting the widow with the rest of her family. Inasmuch as this warms my heart, I have a nagging feeling that the family could use some help. Click anywhere inside the restored paragraph and then click the second alignment icon (▤) in the Paragraph palette. Or press Ctrl+Shift+C (⌘-Shift-C on the Mac). Figure 3-29 shows how this centers the text.

As long as I'm handing out shortcuts, I might as well toss in a couple more: Press Ctrl+Shift (⌘-Shift on the Mac) plus a letter to align text. Thus, Ctrl+Shift+L (⌘-Shift-L) aligns text to the left; Ctrl+Shift+R (⌘-Shift-R) aligns it to the right.

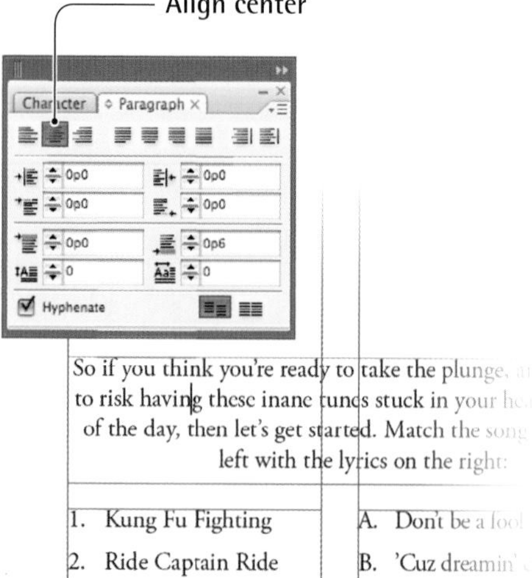

Figure 3-29.

10. ***Balance the red headline.*** The headline looks uneven to me. Fortunately, a special InDesign command can fix it. Click anywhere in the headline with the type tool. Then click the ▾≡ icon

in the Paragraph palette and choose **Balance Ragged Lines**. As pictured in Figure 3-30, InDesign bumps the word *the* down to the second line, thus evening out the first and second lines.

Figure 3-30.

If you loaded my dekeKeys shortcuts (as directed in Step 8 on page xix of the Preface), press Ctrl+Alt+B (⌘-Option-B) to choose Balance Ragged Lines.

---

11. ***Select the last three lines in the second paragraph.*** Justified type produces a crisp, tidy document. But for us, it creates a problem in the second paragraph. See that tiny *40* on its own line at the end of the paragraph? Let's fix this poor widow using *word kerning*, which changes the space between words without affecting the space between the letters within the words. (Specifically, word kerning adjusts the distance between the first letter in a word and the space before it.)

    Word kerning is a character-level attribute. So start by selecting the last three lines of the second paragraph of body copy as follows:

    - Click anywhere in the third-to-last line in the second paragraph.
    - Press Ctrl+Shift+\ (⌘-Shift-\ on the Mac) to select the entire line.
    - Press Shift+↓ twice to select each of the remaining lines in the paragraph, as in Figure 3-31.

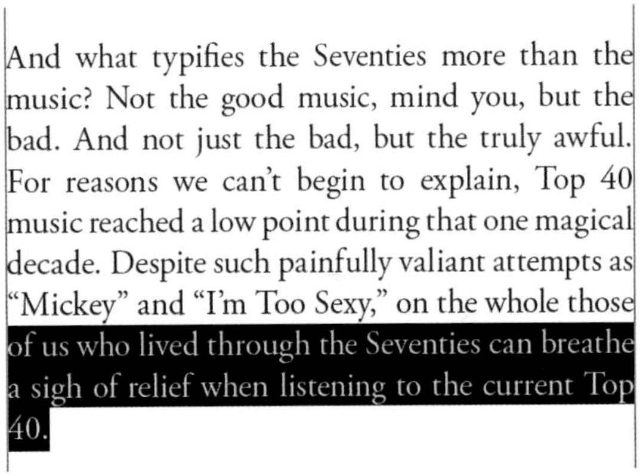

And what typifies the Seventies more than the music? Not the good music, mind you, but the bad. And not just the bad, but the truly awful. For reasons we can't begin to explain, Top 40 music reached a low point during that one magical decade. Despite such painfully valiant attempts as "Mickey" and "I'm Too Sexy," on the whole those of us who lived through the Seventies can breathe a sigh of relief when listening to the current Top 40.

Figure 3-31.

12. ***Tighten the word kerning.*** Word kerning is another of InDesign's secret features. You change it by keyboard shortcut only, using the same increment that you specified for the Kerning value in the Preferences dialog box (see Step 5 on page 103). Here's how:

    - To spread the selected words from their preceding spaces, press Ctrl+Alt+\. (⌘-Option-\ should work on the Mac; if not, also press Control.)
    - To tighten word kerning, press Ctrl+Alt+Backspace (or ⌘-Option-Delete). PC users, take note: that's Ctrl+Alt+Backspace, *not* Ctrl+Alt+Delete (which force-quits applications)!
    - To increase the kerning increment by a factor of five, add the Shift key.

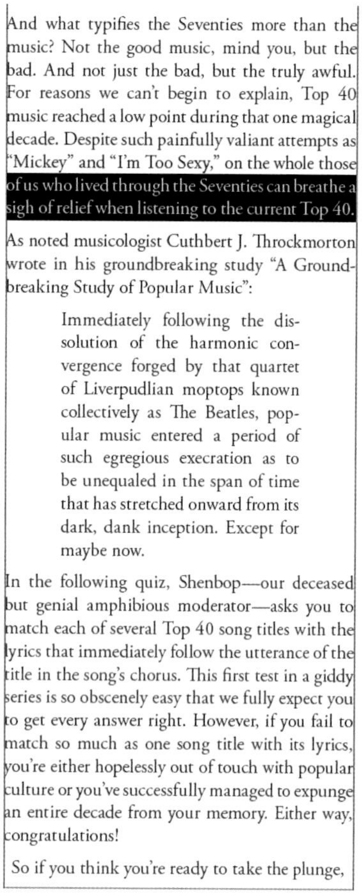

And what typifies the Seventies more than the music? Not the good music, mind you, but the bad. And not just the bad, but the truly awful. For reasons we can't begin to explain, Top 40 music reached a low point during that one magical decade. Despite such painfully valiant attempts as "Mickey" and "I'm Too Sexy," on the whole those of us who lived through the Seventies can breathe a sigh of relief when listening to the current Top 40.

As noted musicologist Cuthbert J. Throckmorton wrote in his groundbreaking study "A Groundbreaking Study of Popular Music":

> Immediately following the dissolution of the harmonic convergence forged by that quartet of Liverpudlian moptops known collectively as The Beatles, popular music entered a period of such egregious execration as to be unequaled in the span of time that has stretched onward from its dark, dank inception. Except for maybe now.

In the following quiz, Shenbop—our deceased but genial amphibious moderator—asks you to match each of several Top 40 song titles with the lyrics that immediately follow the utterance of the title in the song's chorus. This first test in a giddy series is so obscenely easy that we fully expect you to get every answer right. However, if you fail to match so much as one song title with its lyrics, you're either hopelessly out of touch with popular culture or you've successfully managed to expunge an entire decade from your memory. Either way, congratulations!

So if you think you're ready to take the plunge,

Figure 3-32.

It's a crazy keyboard shortcut, one I have problems remembering. But every so often, it comes in handy. And now's one of those times. With the last three lines highlighted, press Ctrl+Shift+Alt+Backspace (or ⌘-Shift-Option-Delete) twice in a row to reduce the word kerning to –50. (You can confirm this by clicking before the first letter of any of the kerned words and checking the AV value in the Character palette.) The reduced spacing causes the *40* to join the line above it.

13. ***Choose the Keep Options command.*** Alas, what's good for the widow doesn't always benefit the rest of the text family. As Figure 3-32 shows, our latest adjustment has created a new problem. The first line of the final paragraph has flowed out of the text frame on the right and into the bottom of the left column. This single stranded first line of a paragraph is known as an *orphan*, because it has been abandoned by its family—i.e., the other lines in the paragraph.

PEARL OF WISDOM

I should say, considerable disagreement exists over the exact definitions of widows and orphans. After consulting with a half-dozen type experts—all of whom voice slightly different opinions—I've decided to defer to Adobe's definition: Whatever the circumstances, an orphan is one or more abandoned lines at the beginning of a paragraph (and thus, the end of a column); a widow comes at the end of a paragraph (and thus, the beginning of a column). Whatever *you* decide to call them, one thing's for sure: InDesign, tenderhearted application that it is, gives you ways to help the poor widows and orphans of the text world.

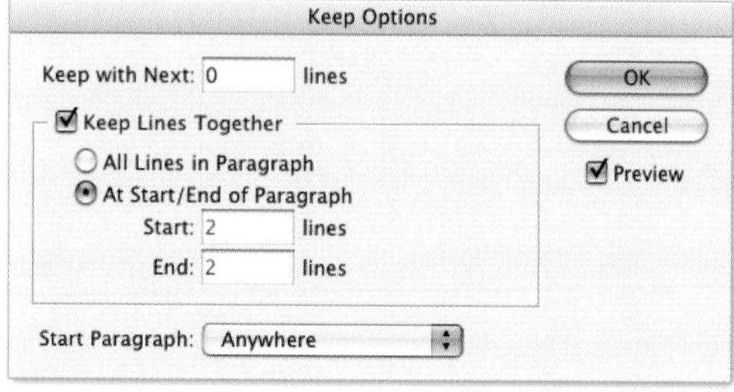

Figure 3-33.

Semantics aside, how do you fix the orphan? For starters, click either in the lone line at the bottom of the left column or in the overflow text block on the right. Then click the ▾≡ icon in the corner of the Paragraph palette and choose the **Keep Options** command, or press Ctrl+Alt+K (⌘-Option-K on the Mac). Up comes the **Keep Options** dialog box, as in Figure 3-33.

14. ***Turn on Keep Lines Together.*** The simple act of turning on the **Keep Lines Together** check box is enough to reunite our orphan with its family. (To see it happen, turn on the **Preview** check box.) But you probably want to know how all the options in this dialog box work, so here's a brief rundown:

    - The first option, Keep with Next, glues the last line of a paragraph to as many as five lines in the paragraph that follows it. Use this option to keep headlines with the text that follows them.

- After selecting Keep Lines Together, turn on All Lines in Paragraph to prevent the paragraph from breaking between frames and keep it whole.
- Next, At Start/End of Paragraph lets you specify how many lines will stick together at the beginning or end of the paragraph. In our case, the default Start setting of 2 lines means that no fewer than two lines in the selected paragraph can break away from the others. There isn't room for two lines at the end of the left column, so the entire paragraph flows to the frame below the graphic.
- The Start Paragraph option lets you decide where the reunited paragraph should appear. I rarely use this option, and any of the first three settings will give you the result pictured in Figure 3-34.

Click **OK** to accept the changes to the selected paragraph. You are now done with this document. Feel free to close it. Save your changes or not; it's up to you.

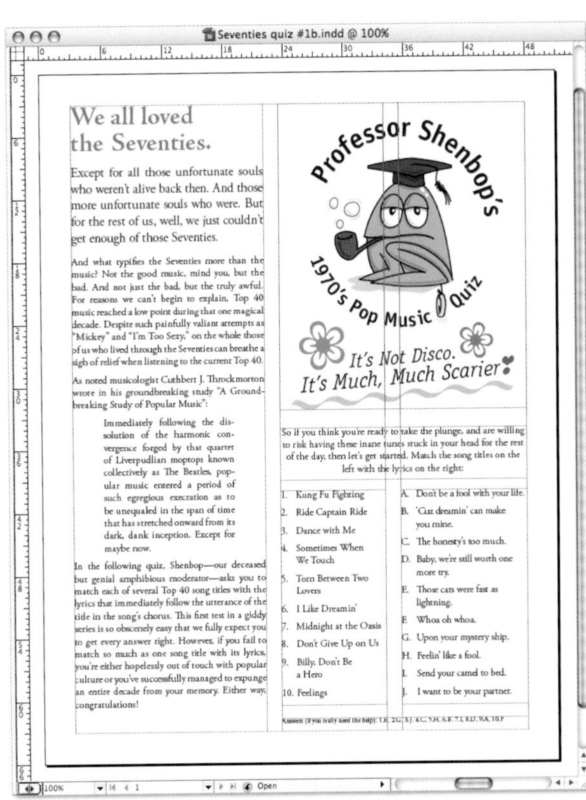

Figure 3-34.

Hyphenation and Composition

Like most other design programs, InDesign automatically hyphenates text to make lines wrap more neatly. But unlike those other programs, it does so more intelligently, often evaluating multiple lines at a time before making its hyphenation decisions. Plus, InDesign gives you an enormous amount of control over the process, permitting you to not only increase or decrease the frequency of hyphenation, but even adjust spacing and change the general "color" of a paragraph. (Densely packed letters make for a dark paragraph; spread out letters make for a light one.)

To some, adjusting hyphenation may sound like a dreadfully dull way to while away a perfectly good half hour. And to be perfectly honest, even I, King of the Control Freaks, resort to hyphenation adjustment only when InDesign's default hyphenation doesn't look right. But I have to admit, there's something very satisfying about taking command of even a mundane process when that process is executed as expertly as InDesign's hyphenation engine.

In this exercise, we'll take a few paragraphs and change the amount of hyphenation and spacing that InDesign applies. At all times, it's InDesign's hyphenation and justification engine that's making the real decisions; we're just overseeing the process. The idea is, while you can wrest away control and hyphenate words manually, it's far more efficient to let InDesign do the heavy lifting, subject to your occasional oversight. Also note that, although InDesign hyphenates flush-left type (as well as centered and flush-right), we'll be working with justified type. The reason: Justification includes some additional compositional controls that I want you to see.

1. ***Open a document.*** Open the file *Page 375.indd* in the *Lesson 03* folder inside *Lesson Files-IDcs3 1on1*. Pictured in Figure 3-35, this single-page document is nothing less or more than page 375 from the very first book in this series, *Adobe Photoshop CS One-on-One*. It contains three paragraphs of body copy. The paragraphs look okay, but if you examine them closely, you'll see a few minor but vexing problems. Highlighted in Figure 3-35, these problems fall into three categories:

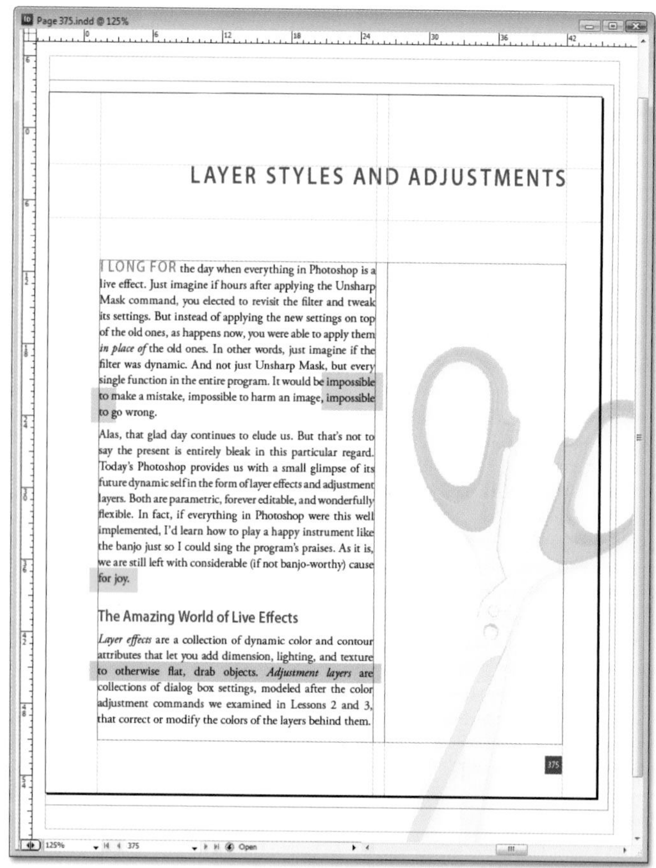

LAYER STYLES AND ADJUSTMENTS

I LONG FOR the day when everything in Photoshop is a live effect. Just imagine if hours after applying the Unsharp Mask command, you elected to revisit the filter and tweak its settings. But instead of applying the new settings on top of the old ones, as happens now, you were able to apply them *in place of* the old ones. In other words, just imagine if the filter was dynamic. And not just Unsharp Mask, but every single function in the entire program. It would be impossible to make a mistake, impossible to harm an image, impossible to go wrong.

Alas, that glad day continues to elude us. But that's not to say the present is entirely bleak in this particular regard. Today's Photoshop provides us with a small glimpse of its future dynamic self in the form of layer effects and adjustment layers. Both are parametric, forever editable, and wonderfully flexible. In fact, if everything in Photoshop were this well implemented, I'd learn how to play a happy instrument like the banjo just so I could sing the program's praises. As it is, we are still left with considerable (if not banjo-worthy) cause for joy.

The Amazing World of Live Effects

Layer effects are a collection of dynamic color and contour attributes that let you add dimension, lighting, and texture to otherwise flat, drab objects. *Adjustment layers* are collections of dialog box settings, modeled after the color adjustment commands we examined in Lessons 2 and 3, that correct or modify the colors of the layers behind them.

375

Figure 3-35.

- The pink boxes highlight *stacks*, in which identical words appear directly on top of each other. Stacks call attention to how the text wraps and can even cause a reader to skip a line of text.
- The yellow box highlights a couple of stray words at the end of a paragraph, similar to the lone *40* that we encountered in the preceding exercise. Because the stray words occur at the end of a paragraph, they are considered to be widows, albeit ones that the Keep Options don't address. In the last exercise, we fixed the placement of *40* using word kerning. But there's more than one way to fix a widow, as you will soon see.
- The green box highlights a line of type that is much more loosely spaced than those immediately above and below it. Such inconsistencies in spacing look sloppy. And when the space between words grows larger than the space between lines of type, it may hinder readability.

As I said, these problems are minor, the design equivalent of forgetting to dot your *i*'s and cross your *t*'s. So no biggie, right? Except that you'd look like a twit if you didn't dot your *i*'s and cross your *t*'s, and the same is true in the design world if you left these problems in place. So let's fix them by adjusting the hyphenation and composition of the paragraphs.

2. ***Select the text.*** Hyphenation is a paragraph-level formatting attribute. If you want to adjust a single paragraph, click inside the paragraph with the type tool. Because we want to fix all the text, select the text block with the black arrow tool.

3. ***Choose the Hyphenation command.*** You can choose the command in two ways.

   - If the type tool were active, you could click the ▾≡ icon on the far right side of the control palette to display the panel options, and choose Hyphenation.
   - In your case, the black arrow tool is active and the control palette shows transformation options. So go to the **Paragraph** palette, click the ▾≡ icon in the top-right corner, and choose **Hyphenation**.

   Both alternatives are illustrated in Figure 3-36.

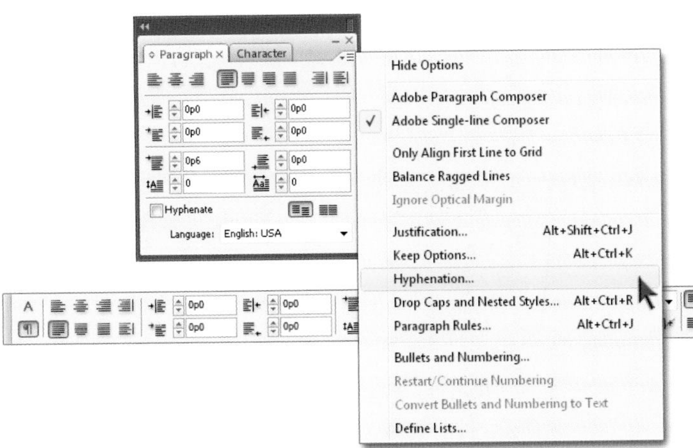

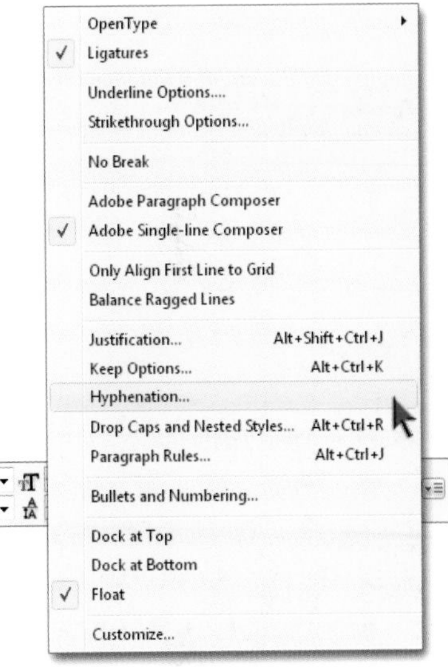

Figure 3-36.

4. ***Turn on the Hyphenate check box.*** Pictured in Figure 3-37, the **Hyphenation Settings** dialog box controls several aspects of hyphenation, including whether the feature is turned on. If this were a new document, hyphenation would be active by default. But I've specifically turned it off so you can see how to turn it on manually, which you do by clicking the **Hyphenate** check box. To see the difference hyphenation makes, turn on the **Preview** check box as well.

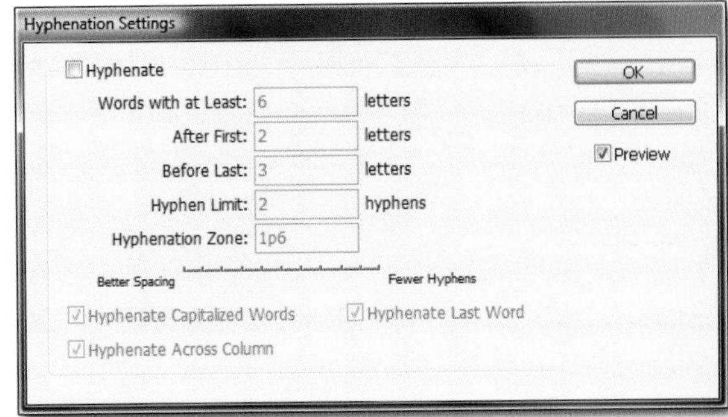

Figure 3-37.

InDesign lets you turn automatic hyphenation on and off without setting foot in the Hyphenation Settings dialog box. There's the Hyphenate check box in the control palette. Or press the shortcut Ctrl+Shift+Alt+H (or ⌘-Shift-Option-H).

5. *Move the slider triangle closer to Better Spacing.* The Hyphenation Settings dialog box is loaded with settings, but few of them are worth worrying about. The big exception is the slider bar just below Hyphenation Zone, which lets you adjust the frequency of hyphenation. The rationale goes like this: Hyphenation interrupts the flow of a word, so you want to use hyphens sparingly. But even word spacing looks better, and word spacing is improved by hyphenation. So InDesign gives you the option of finding your own happy marriage.

   For this exercise, I recommend that you move the slider triangle about four ticks from the extreme **Better Spacing**, as I have in Figure 3-38. (If you're having problems getting it exactly right, don't fret. A tick mark one way or the other won't make much difference.) This setting favors consistent word spacing and permits InDesign as many hyphens as it needs, provided no more than two hyphenated lines appear in a row.

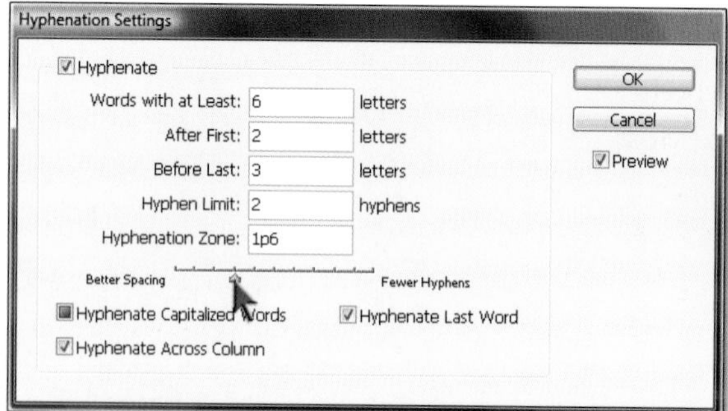

Figure 3-38.

6. *Raise the Hyphen Limit value.* Now you might ask, "No more than two hyphenated lines in a row—where does that come from?" The answer is the one remaining useful option, **Hyphen Limit**, which is set to 2. Before you change it, take a look at the second-to-last line of type in the document window, the one near the bottom of the page that begins with the partial word *ment*. The line is a bit loose, but InDesign is prohibited from fixing it by the Hyphen Limit.

   The solution: Lift the prohibition. Change the value to 3 and press Tab to advance to the next option. Just like that, the line tightens and hyphenates. Figure 3-39 shows before and after views.

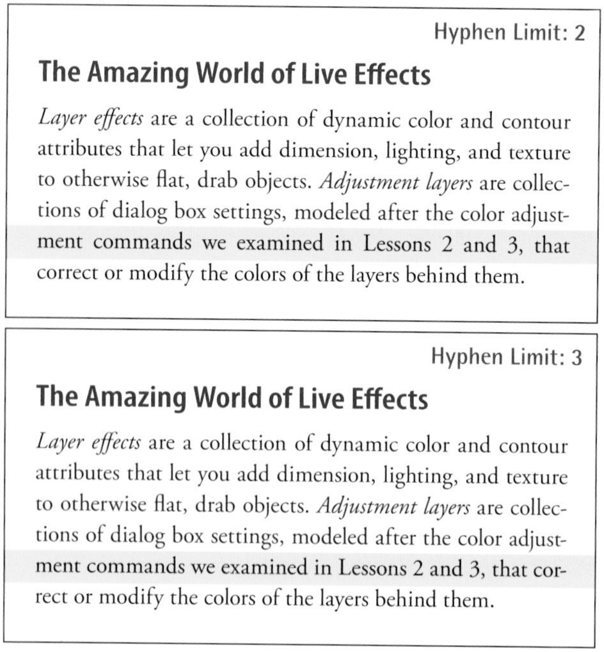

Hyphen Limit: 2

The Amazing World of Live Effects

Layer effects are a collection of dynamic color and contour attributes that let you add dimension, lighting, and texture to otherwise flat, drab objects. *Adjustment layers* are collections of dialog box settings, modeled after the color adjustment commands we examined in Lessons 2 and 3, that correct or modify the colors of the layers behind them.

Hyphen Limit: 3

The Amazing World of Live Effects

Layer effects are a collection of dynamic color and contour attributes that let you add dimension, lighting, and texture to otherwise flat, drab objects. *Adjustment layers* are collections of dialog box settings, modeled after the color adjustment commands we examined in Lessons 2 and 3, that correct or modify the colors of the layers behind them.

Figure 3-39.

7. *Click OK.* That's all the good we can do in this dialog box. Click the **OK** button to close the dialog box and apply the hyphenation settings to the active text.

   Okay, if I were you, I'd be protesting, "Hey, how about those other options?" So here's the deal:

   - The first three are self-evident. By default, InDesign is limited to hyphenating words at least six letters long, with the hyphen occurring after the first two letters and before the last three. I suggest you leave these options at their default settings.

- As for Hyphenation Zone, it determines the maximum distance between a potential break and the right edge of the text frame. Again, I recommend you leave this one alone.
- Hyphenate Capitalized Words permits the splitting of names, trademarks, and other proper nouns. I usually turn it on for body copy, where hyphenation tends to be democratic, and off for headlines, which tend to read better without hyphens.
- Hyphenate Last Word regulates a typographic phenomenon known as the *hyphenated widow*, in which part of a word drops to the last line of a paragraph. I usually turn it off.
- The final option, Hyphenate Across Column, controls whether a single word can be split between columns or frames. Most editors agree such hyphenation is bad form, and I have to agree. Which is why I personally turn it off.

EXTRA CREDIT

The text is considerably improved, and all our problems—stacks, looseness, and the widow—are solved. In fact, under normal conditions, you might figure this is good enough and move on. But these aren't normal conditions. I'm still not quite satisfied with the text, and when teacher's not happy, no one's happy. Namely, even though I just sanctioned three hyphens in a row, I am secretly troubled by it. More to the point, I mark this as Extra Credit because from here on, we embark upon some very subtle adjustments. But one day, I assure you, you'll be glad you have these tools under your belt.

8. ***Choose the Justification command.*** With the text selected with the black arrow, click the **Paragraph** palette's ▾≡ doohickey and choose **Justification**. Or press Ctrl+Shift+Alt+J (⌘-Shift-Option-J) to display the **Justification** dialog box, pictured in Figure 3-40. Most of these options control how InDesign automatically spaces and arranges characters in justified paragraphs. And one option, Composer, controls flush-left and otherwise-aligned text as well.

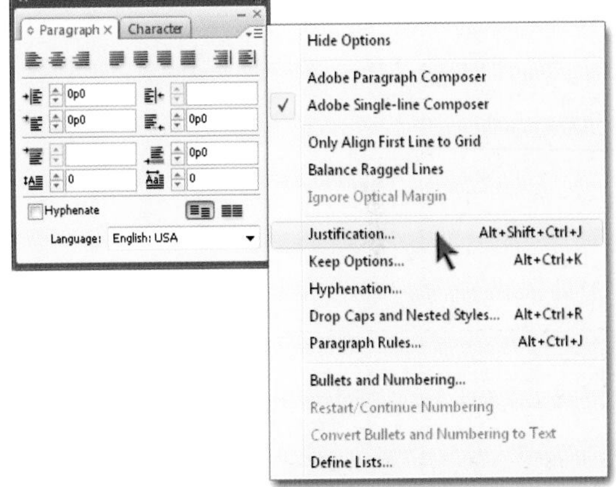

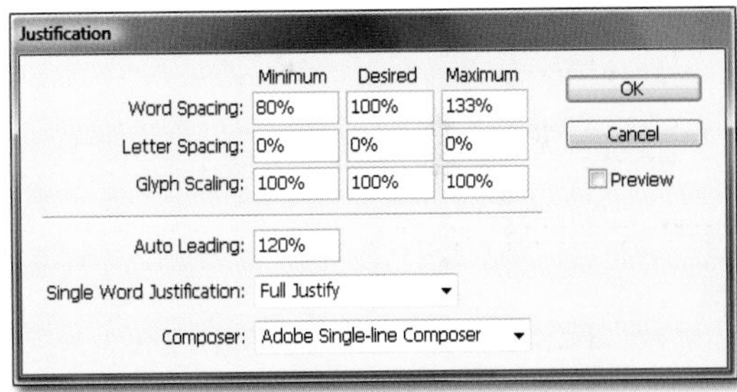

Figure 3-40.

9. ***Turn on Adobe Paragraph Composer.*** Click the **Composer** pop-up menu, which is currently set to Adobe Single-line Composer, and choose **Adobe Paragraph Composer**. Then turn the **Preview** check box on and off and watch what happens in the document window. The stacked words *impossible* hyphenate differently, and the word *it* falls to the second-to-last line in the second paragraph. What's going on?

   - Before we changed to the Paragraph Composer, InDesign distributed letters according to the Single-line Composer,

Single-line Composer

The Amazing World of Live Effects

Layer effects are a collection of dynamic color and contour attributes that let you add dimension, lighting, and texture to otherwise flat, drab objects. *Adjustment layers* are collections of dialog box settings, modeled after the color adjustment commands we examined in Lessons 2 and 3, that correct or modify the colors of the layers behind them.

Paragraph Composer

The Amazing World of Live Effects

Layer effects are a collection of dynamic color and contour attributes that let you add dimension, lighting, and texture to otherwise flat, drab objects. *Adjustment layers* are collections of dialog box settings, modeled after the color adjustment commands we examined in Lessons 2 and 3, that correct or modify the colors of the layers behind them.

Figure 3-41.

which evaluates each line of text independently, as in PageMaker, QuarkXPress, and other layout applications. The result can be a wide variation in the spacing of justified lines or ragged endings of flush-left lines.

- InDesign's solution is the Paragraph Composer, which looks at all lines in a paragraph when distributing letters in any one of them. This creates more consistent spacing from one line to the next.

Sometimes, the Paragraph Composer makes an enormous difference, which is why it's active by default. (I turned it off for this document so you could see how it works.) And had you applied the Paragraph Composer before choosing Hyphenation in Step 3, you would have seen a big shift in the last paragraph. As illustrated in Figure 3-41, prior to Step 3, the third and fifth lines were extremely loose. Even without the aid of hyphenation, the Paragraph Composer managed to equalize the spacing, bringing the words highlighted in blue up a line.

In our post-Step 8 world, however, things are subtler. The Paragraph Composer affects at most four lines of type. The moral: When working with little or no hyphenation, turn on the Paragraph Composer; when permitting liberal hyphenation, as we are, experiment to see which setting works best.

Also bear in mind, the Paragraph Composer is a computationally intensive operation. So if you find InDesign behaving sluggishly, you might try switching to the computationally simple Single-line Composer. It usually quickens InDesign's performance—particularly when entering text from the keyboard—and the line spacing is no worse off than in QuarkXPress.

For our purposes, however, leave the Paragraph Composer on. Every little spacing aid helps.

10. ***Adjust the Letter Spacing and Glyph Scaling values.*** The top of the Justification dialog box is occupied by a series of Minimum, Desired, and Maximum values that control the range of spacing InDesign can use to balance justified type. By default, InDesign permits fluctuations only in word spacing. But you can also allow it to vary letter spacing (the line-by-line tracking) and glyph scaling (the width of individual letters and other characters).

I'd like you to change the following settings, highlighted in yellow in Figure 3-42:

- Click in the first **Letter Spacing** value. Then press the ↓ key to reduce the value to -1 percent. Right away, you'll see several lines shift. The results are better hyphenation and spacing in the second paragraph but a return of the stacks in the first. We'll fix this in a moment.
- It's always nice to have symmetry. So Tab your way to the third Letter Spacing value and press ↑ to raise it to 1 percent. Hmm, no change whatsoever—okay, it was worth a shot.
- Now Tab your way to the third and final **Glyph Scaling** value and press the ↑ key three times to raise the value to 103 percent. Huge difference! Much better hyphenation than anything we've seen so far plus a solution to the newest widow.

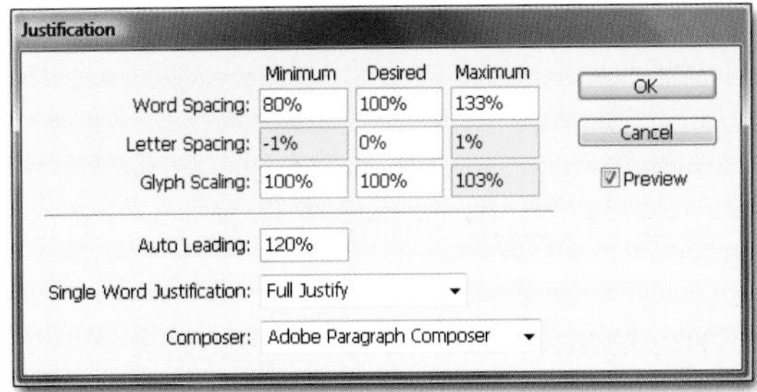

Figure 3-42.

Isn't this exciting? I tell you, you're a born layout artist if you feel your heart flutter just a little bit when you see these kinds of changes. If not, it just means you're normal, and people tell me that's okay, too.

11. *Click OK.* Once your settings match those pictured in Figure 3-42, you are welcome to click the **OK** button.

12. *Eliminate the stack manually.* We've gone as far as we can with InDesign's automated controls. That means we'll have to fix those pesky stacks manually. And we'll do so using a line break. Double-click inside the text to switch to the type tool. Then select the space between the words *on* and *top* in the fourth line of the first paragraph. To swap the space for a line break, right-click in the text frame and choose **Insert Break Character→Forced Line Break**. InDesign knocks the word *top* to the next line without creating a new paragraph. Other lines adjust automatically, making the stack go away. Figure 3-43 shows a magnified version of the final page.

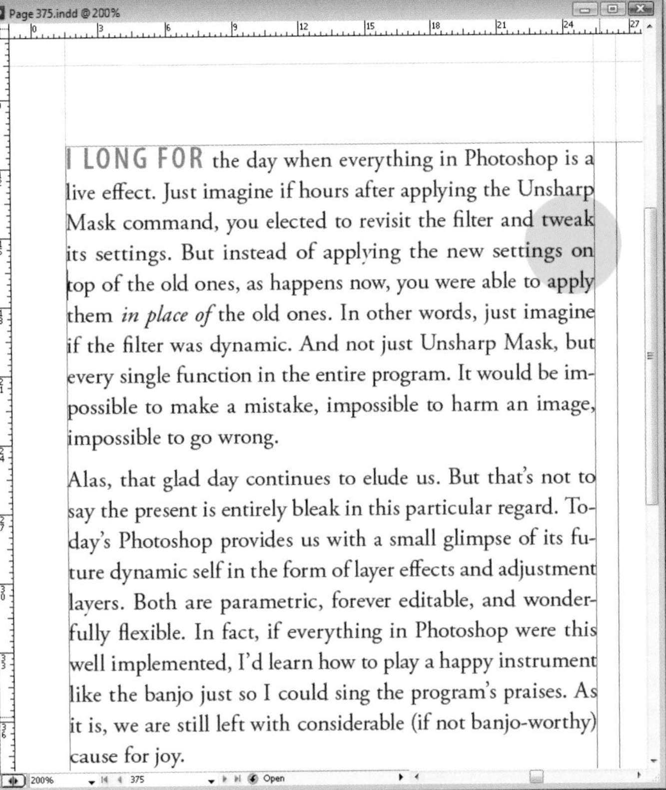

I LONG FOR the day when everything in Photoshop is a live effect. Just imagine if hours after applying the Unsharp Mask command, you elected to revisit the filter and tweak its settings. But instead of applying the new settings on top of the old ones, as happens now, you were able to apply them *in place of* the old ones. In other words, just imagine if the filter was dynamic. And not just Unsharp Mask, but every single function in the entire program. It would be impossible to make a mistake, impossible to harm an image, impossible to go wrong.

Alas, that glad day continues to elude us. But that's not to say the present is entirely bleak in this particular regard. Today's Photoshop provides us with a small glimpse of its future dynamic self in the form of layer effects and adjustment layers. Both are parametric, forever editable, and wonderfully flexible. In fact, if everything in Photoshop were this well implemented, I'd learn how to play a happy instrument like the banjo just so I could sing the program's praises. As it is, we are still left with considerable (if not banjo-worthy) cause for joy.

Figure 3-43.

Note that I've highlighted the point at which you should have inserted the line break in the figure. I also turned on Type→Show Hidden Characters, which shows spaces and breaks as pale blue symbols. For more information on line breaks and hidden characters, see the exercise "Dashes, Spaces, and Breaks" on page 149 of Lesson 4.

Accessing Special Characters

As I first mentioned on page xvi of the Preface, InDesign ships with several fonts from Adobe. They all happen to be OpenType fonts, which generally contain a wider selection of characters than their more common, non-OpenType counterparts. OpenType fonts offer special intelligence that connects character variations—including such accented *diacritics* as *a*, *á*, *â*, and so on—so that InDesign can find the exact letter or symbol to fit your needs. For a peek under the OpenType hood, read the sidebar "OpenType, Unicode, and Glyphs" on page 124. But frankly, it's not essential that you understand the technical stuff. All that really counts is that you know how to use an OpenType font, as you will after this exercise.

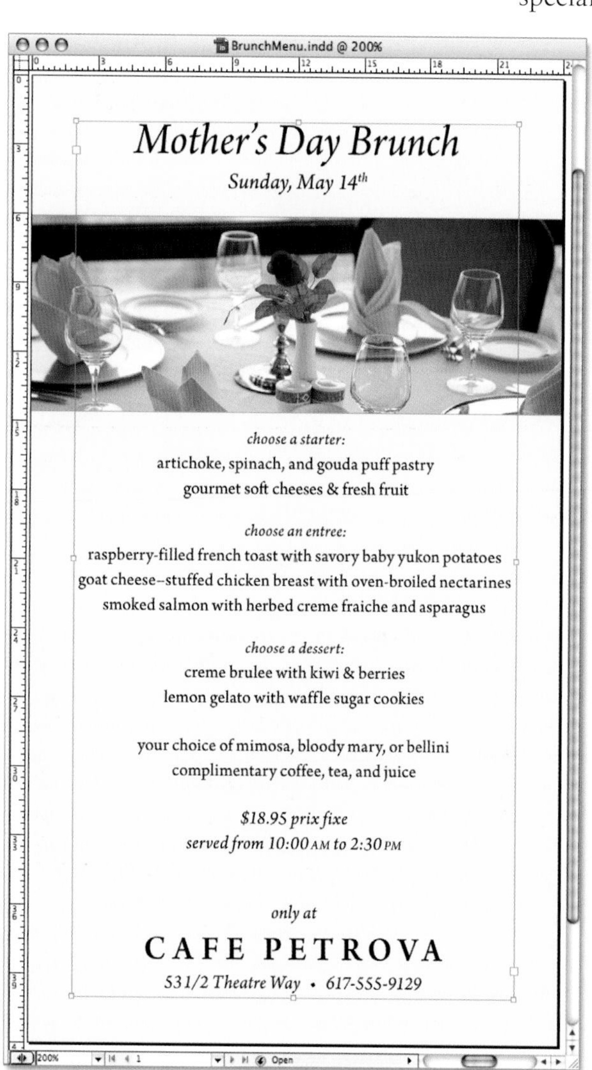
BrunchMenu.indd @ 200%
Mother's Day Brunch
Sunday, May 14th
choose a starter:
artichoke, spinach, and gouda puff pastry
gourmet soft cheeses & fresh fruit
choose an entree:
raspberry-filled french toast with savory baby yukon potatoes
goat cheese–stuffed chicken breast with oven-broiled nectarines
smoked salmon with herbed creme fraiche and asparagus
choose a dessert:
creme brulee with kiwi & berries
lemon gelato with waffle sugar cookies
your choice of mimosa, bloody mary, or bellini
complimentary coffee, tea, and juice
$18.95 prix fixe
served from 10:00 AM to 2:30 PM
only at
CAFE PETROVA
531/2 Theatre Way • 617-555-9129
200%
Open

Figure 3-44.

In the next steps, we'll take a document with no special character treatments (see Figure 3-44) and go fairly nuts exploiting the letter-swapping capabilities of OpenType. Specifically, we'll add ligatures, small caps, fractions, ordinals, and more. If you don't know what some of these things are, don't worry. You will soon.

1. ***Open a document.*** Open the document *BrunchMenu.indd* contained in the *Lesson 03* folder inside *Lesson Files-IDcs3 1on1*. Pictured in Figure 3-44, the document features a prix fixe menu for a Mother's Day brunch at a certain world-renowned and entirely fictional café. The design comes from our own David Futato, the guy responsible for the look of the *One-on-One* book series. The image hails from iStockphoto contributor Nilgun Bostanci.

2. ***Bring up the Character palette.*** Click the big text block with the black arrow tool to select it. Then choose **Type→Character** or press Ctrl+T (⌘-T) to display the **Character** palette, which provides access to most of InDesign's automatic OpenType functions. The palette shows that the selected text is set entirely in the OpenType font Arno Pro.

3. *Turn on Ligatures.* Although the menu looks fairly polished, it's not nearly as elegant as it might be if we employed the full power that OpenType fonts in general and Arno (or Jenson) in particular make available. Counting lowercase letters, capitals, numbers, punctuation, and the various styles, the menu contains perhaps 100 unique character variations, or *glyphs*. Meanwhile, the four type styles used in the document comprise more than 10,000 glyphs. That's at least 100 glyphs for every 1 glyph we're using.

   Some of those unused glyphs are conjoined letters called *ligatures*. The idea is that some letters look wrong when positioned next to each other, usually because they overlap or almost touch in ways that type designers over the years have found unappealing. Figure 3-45 illustrates a handful of these letter combinations, both as separate characters (top) and as ligatures (bottom). The black characters are common ligatures; the blue ones are discretionary, old-fashioned ligatures.

   All letters expressed as independent characters

   With effort, the fly caught up with the wasp. "Make haste!" cried the junior insect. "The officers have finally amassed their armies between the orange juice and the waffles!"

   Certain combinations fused into ligatures

   With effort, the fly caught up with the wasp. "Make haste!" cried the junior insect. "The officers have finally amassed their armies between the orange juice and the waffles!"

   Figure 3-45.

   Most programs require you to enter ligatures manually, which means resorting to the Character Map utility on the PC or pressing some obscure key combinations on the Mac. InDesign swaps out ligatures on-the-fly, and even spell checks them properly. (Okay, so there's an unexpected advantage of the otherwise uninspiring Adobe spell checker.) All you have to do is turn on the Ligatures function.

   To do so, click the ▾≡ icon in the top-right corner of the Character palette and choose the **Ligatures** command from the palette menu, as in Figure 3-46. You'll see a slight movement across your document as InDesign replaces various pairs of letters. including the *ff* in *stuffed*, the *fi* in *filled*, the *Th* in *Theatre*, and even the *ffl* in *waffle*.

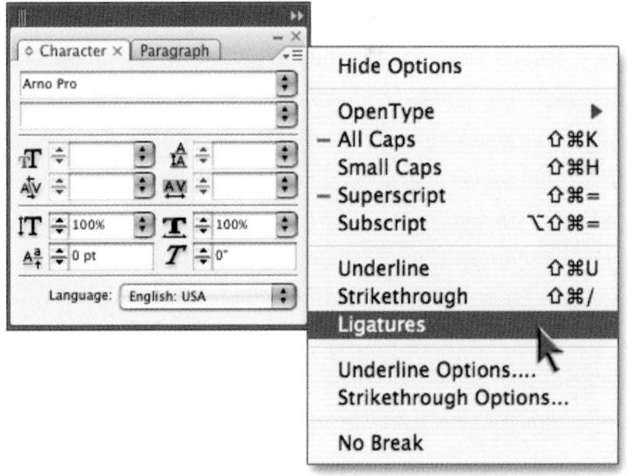

Figure 3-46.

4. *Turn on Discretionary Ligatures.* As you will have noted from Figure 3-45, standard ligatures are universally useful (which is why, if this were a new document, ligatures would be on by default); discretionary ligatures aren't. These precious glyphs would look ridiculous in a business publication. But in a menu for a classy joint like ours, discretionary ligs are just the ticket.

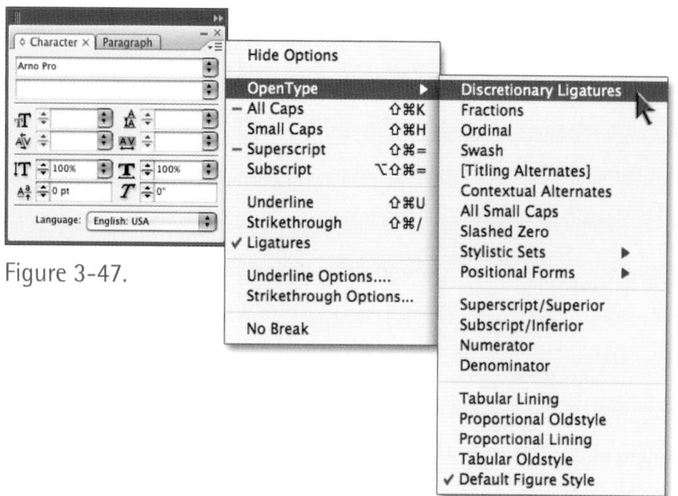

Figure 3-47.

Again click the ▾≡ at the top of the Character palette and choose **OpenType→Discretionary Ligatures**, as in Figure 3-47. Notice the old-world flourish, especially in the entrée section with the *sp* in *raspberry*, the *st* in *toast*, and the *ct* in *nectarine*.

PEARL OF WISDOM

All commands in the OpenType submenu are exclusively applicable to selected text set in an OpenType font. Any command in brackets, such as [Titling Alternates] in the case of Arno Pro, does not apply to this specific typeface. So, when using a non-OpenType font, *all* OpenType commands appear in brackets.

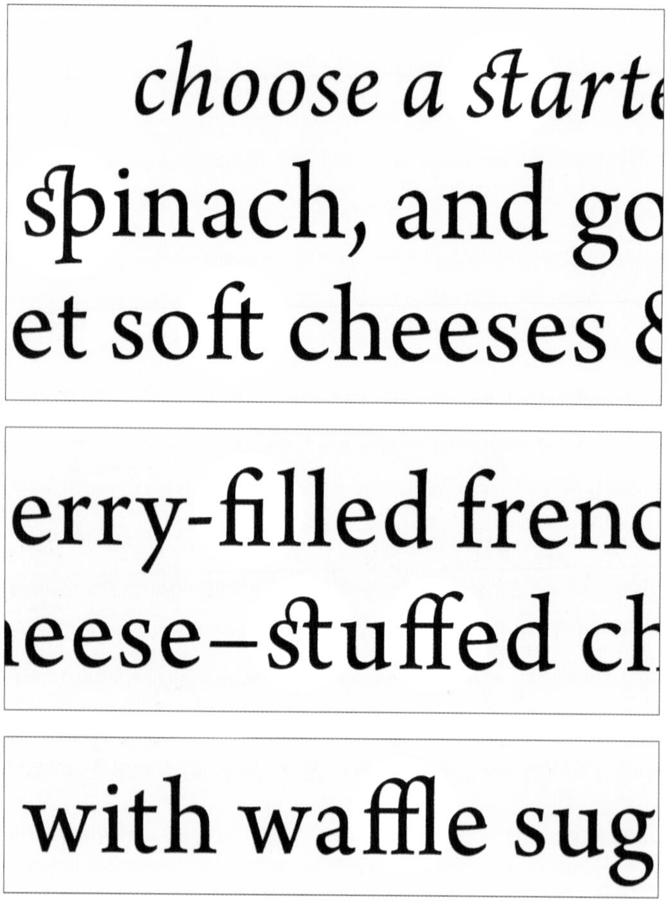

5. ***Switch out the* ft *in* soft.** The second line below the image features the line *gourmet soft cheeses & fresh fruit* with the *f* and *t* in *soft* fused into a discretionary ligature. Thing is, I like the primary ligature for these letters better. Double-click in the text to switch to the type tool and double-click the word *soft* to select it. (You could select just the *ft*, but there's no reason to be so careful.) Then click the ▾≡ in the Character or control palette and choose **OpenType→Discretionary Ligatures** to turn it off. The discretionary ligature gives way to the standard ligature. Figure 3-48 shows a few details from the document, featuring both standard and discretionary ligatures created in this and the last two steps.

choose a start

spinach, and go

et soft cheeses &

erry-filled frenc

eese–stuffed ch

with waffle sug

Figure 3-48.

6. ***Add some small caps.*** Now we move on to another popular alternative letter, the x-height capital, or *small cap*. These are dwarfish capital letters that stand as tall as lowercase characters, most commonly used to call out common abbreviations, such as 7AM, AD 456, and AKA Lloyd the Impaler.

The *AM* and *PM* in the third-to-last line on the page are already set in small caps, but these are fake small caps, created by reducing the type size of capital letters. If you look closely, you'll notice that the weight of the small caps is far lighter than that of the characters around them, even though the type style (Italic) is the same. Simple reason: Reducing the size of letters reduces their weight. Solution? Do as follows:

- Still armed with the type tool, click between the space after the *10:00* and the following *AM*.
- Type "am" in lowercase letters. Notice how much thicker these letters are?
- Select the letters you just typed and choose **Small Caps** from the Character palette menu.
- Press the forward Delete key (on the Mac, the key is marked with a ⌦) twice to delete the old, puny small caps.
- Click between the *2:30* and *PM*. Type "pm."
- Select the weightier lowercase *pm* and avail yourself of another method for making small caps: Click the Tт icon in the control palette or press the shortcut Ctrl+Shift+H (⌘-Shift-H). When using an OpenType font that offers small cap glyphs, as this one does, InDesign replaces the characters with the proper glyphs.
- Delete the bad, wimpy old *PM*. The new glyphs match the weight of surrounding characters, as Figure 3-49 illustrates.

Note that the Tт icon produces the desired effect only if designer small caps are available, either from an OpenType font or from a specialty font such as one from Adobe's Expert Collection. If such glyphs are not available, InDesign merely capitalizes the letters and decreases their size.

7. *Set the fraction.* At the bottom of the menu is the address, which includes an improperly set fraction. Select the fraction *1/2* with the type tool, and then choose **OpenType→Fractions** from the Character palette menu. That's all it takes to replace a bad fraction with the proper prebuilt glyph. Figure 3-50 shows the difference. I usually kern the fraction away from any normal numbers that precede it to give it a little room to breathe. In the case of Figure 3-50, however, the natural character spacing looks just fine.

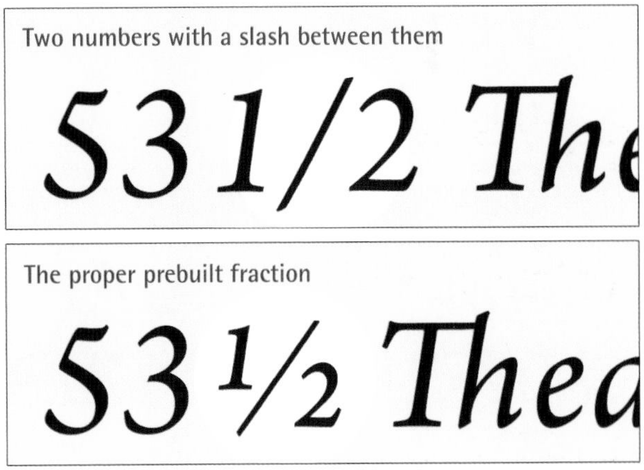

Fake Small Caps

to 2:30 PM

Designer OpenType Small Caps

to 2:30 PM

Figure 3-49.

Two numbers with a slash between them

53 1/2 The

The proper prebuilt fraction

53 ½ Thea

Figure 3-50.

OpenType, Unicode, and Glyphs

Like any revolutionary technology, OpenType makes your life easier in proportion to the effort you put in. With OpenType, a little learning goes a long way. And by little, I mean very little. Read this spread and you'll be up to speed.

OpenType serves three purposes: It expands the character set, it simplifies the installation process, and it permits applications to associate letter variations with their base characters. Before OpenType, most Western fonts were limited to 1 byte (8 bits) of data per character, which meant that a single font could offer no more than 256 *glyphs*, or character variations. By typewriter standards that's a lot, but by modern typesetting standards it's unacceptably low. By themselves, the letters (capital and lowercase), numbers, and punctuation shown on a U.S. typewriter or computer keyboard add up to 92 glyphs. Throw in some extra punctuation, a few fractions, the occasional symbol, and the bevy of accented letters used in the U.S., Europe, and elsewhere, and you hit the ceiling fast. The figure below shows samples of the italic style from Arno Pro. A *single* character offers 231 glyphs (and that's just by my reckoning). A 1-byte font simply can't handle this much variety.

The solution is the 2-byte (16-bit, or double-byte) *Unicode* specification. By assigning 2 bytes

Font: Arno Pro Italic, **Character:** A, **Glyphs:** 231 (at last count)

AaaAaA ÁááÁáÁ ÂââÂâÂ ÄääÄäÄ

ÀààÀàÀ ÅååÅåÅ ÃããÃãÃ ĂăăĂăĂ

ẠạạẠạẠ ẢảảẢảẢ ẤấấẤấẤ ẦầầẦầẦ

ẨẩẩẨẩẨ ẪẫẫẪẫẪ ẬậậẬậẬ ẮắắẮắẮ

ẰằằẰằẰ ẲẳẳẲẳẲ ẴẵẵẴẵẴ ẶặặẶặẶ

ĀāāĀāĀ ĄąąĄąĄ ǺǻǺǺ ΆάᾺΆ ΑιΑΙ

ΑιἀἈιἈἈιἈιἁἉιἉἉιἉιἄἌιἌἌιἌιἅἍιἍἍιἍι

ἂἊιἊἊιἊι ἃἋιἋἋιἋι ἆἎιἎἎιἎι ἇἏιἏἏιἏι

ᾳᾼᾼᾲᾺᾺᾀᾈᾈᾁᾉᾉᾄᾌᾌᾅᾍᾍᾂᾊᾊᾃᾋᾋᾆᾎᾎᾇᾏᾏ

ΛʌʌΛ ЉљљЉ ÆææÆ ǼǽǽǼ RAKAª

per character, a Unicode-compatible font may comprise as many as 65,536 glyphs, enough to represent the most common characters in virtually every major language in use today, including Greek, Farsi, and Japanese. Font standards that support Unicode, such as OpenType, organize characters by address. For example, a lowercase, unaccented *a* is always character 0061. (If the font lacks an *a*, the address is blank.) This way, your character remains intact when you switch fonts. Even better, you can plug in a foreign keyboard—one with accented characters, for example—and the font will respect each key to the best of its ability.

But OpenType doesn't stop there. An OpenType font associates glyphs with their base characters. So an OpenType-aware program knows that an uppercase A, a lowercase *a*, a small cap A, a swash *A*, and many others are variations of one letter. The spell checker sees them as *A*'s, and is even smart enough to decipher accents, just as it should. And if the program is as clever as InDesign, it can swap out glyphs and suggest alternatives automatically. To see this feature in action, work through the exercise "Accessing Special Characters," which begins on page 120.

Finally, OpenType fonts are more compact than their predecessors. A single OpenType file includes everything you need to use a typeface on your computer. So where an older font may require you to install separate screen, printer, and metrics files—not to mention extra files to hold overflow glyphs such as small caps and swashes—the OpenType font presents you with a single file (see below). This one file is also cross-platform, so it serves PCs and Macs alike—and it does so with identical kerning metrics, which means there's no danger of having text reflow when you change platforms.

Incidentally, all the typefaces that ship with InDesign CS3 (as well as the many editions of the Creative Suite) are OpenType fonts. A font name that has the word *Pro* contains a wider variety of glyphs, including a large supply of accented letters. A font name that contains *Std* (for "standard") is more modest.

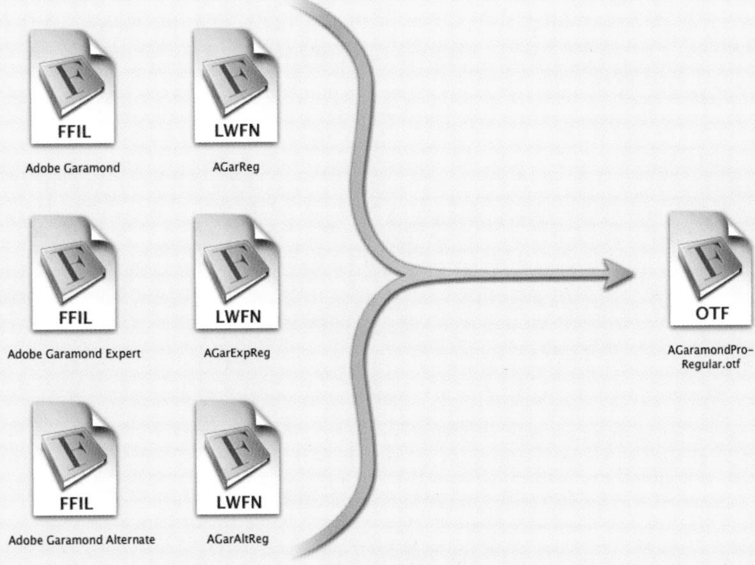

PEARL OF WISDOM

OpenType fonts aren't the only ones that include fractions. In fact, most fonts include the fractions ½, ¼, and ¾. But unless you're using an OpenType font, you can't choose OpenType→Fractions to get to them. Instead, you select the fractions from the Glyphs palette, which I introduce in Step 11 on page 127. Alternatively, on the PC, you can access fractions by pressing Alt and typing a sequence of numbers on the numeric keypad. Hold down the Alt key while typing 0-1-8-9 on the keypad (not along the top of the keyboard) to get ½. Alt+0-1-8-8 gets you ¼; Alt+0-1-9-0 gets you ¾. (There are no fraction keystrokes on the Mac.)

Some OpenType fonts let you create much more complicated fractions than these. For example, just for fun, try selecting the entire address, *531/2*, and choosing OpenType→Fractions. The result is the fraction $^{531}/_{2}$, which is precisely the kind of address that most restaurant owners try to avoid.

8. ***Add some real ordinals.*** Now it's time for another strange-sounding type treatment, the ordinal. In typesetting, an *ordinal* is a superscripted sequence of letters following a number, such as the *st* in 1st. Click between the *14* and *th* in the date at the top of the page. Notice that the *th* is a fake ordinal, created by superscripting standard text. As with fake small caps, the weight is all wrong. To fix the problem:

   - Type *th* in lowercase letters.
   - Select the letters you just typed and then choose **OpenType→Ordinal** from the Character palette menu. Again, InDesign finds the designer-approved ordinal glyphs provided by Arno Pro. The glyphs match the weight and letter spacing of the surrounding text, as in Figure 3-51.
   - Delete the bad old fraudulent ordinals.

Fake ordinals (really subscripts)

, May 14th

Designer OpenType Ordinals

, May 14th

Figure 3-51.

The OpenType→Ordinal command is a little too smart for its own good. If you swap the *th* for something else that could be an ordinal, such as *st*, *nd*, or *rd*, InDesign refuses to participate. Unless the ordinal precisely goes with the preceding number, InDesign recognizes it as a fraud. Consider it a safety mechanism: If the Ordinal command doesn't work, at least you know you mistyped either the number or the ordinal. I mean, no one wants to see an accidental *3th*, right?

---

9. ***Set the phone number in oldstyle numerals.*** Forgive me; having transported you from the bottom of the page to the top, I am now about to send you back to the bottom. There, next to the address, you'll find a phone number. Select the entire thing and choose **OpenType→Proportional Oldstyle** from the Character palette menu. This replaces the standard numbers (sometimes called *capital numbers* because they are all the same height and sit on top of the baseline) with oldstyle numerals of differing heights with descenders. You can see the difference in Figure 3-52. I've heard type experts argue that oldstyle numerals are more legible in text because of their height variation. But I imagine most readers regard the numbers as antique or pretentious, the latter of which suits this document but may not work for others.

Standard ("capital") numbers

617-555-9

Oldstyle numbers

617-555-91

Figure 3-52.

PEARL OF WISDOM

To restore standard numbers, choose one of the two commands with Lining in their titles in the OpenType submenu. Incidentally, the difference between Tabular Lining and Proportional Lining has to do with spacing. Choosing a Tabular command assigns every number the same width, so they line up in a table, as when adding columns of numbers. The Proportional command assigns less space to a skinny number such as 1 than to a wide number such as, well, everything else. Proportional is typically the better choice when setting numbers inside lines of type.

10. ***Replace the initial capital M with a swash.*** Many italic OpenType fonts include cursive characters with additional flourish, known as *swash characters*. While it's easy to go too nuts with swashes—I'll show you how in just a moment!—they can be useful at the outset of a line or paragraph. To try one on for size, select the *M* at the beginning of *Mother's* at the top of the document and then choose **OpenType→Swash** from the Character palette menu. Figure 3-53 features magnified before and after views.

11. ***Bring up the Glyphs palette.*** One of the problems with selecting swash characters is that you never know if a specific character has a swash form (most don't) or what that swash will look like until you choose OpenType→Swash. Fortunately, InDesign provides a previewing tool that shows you every single character the font offers. Choose **Type→Glyphs**—or,

Figure 3-53.

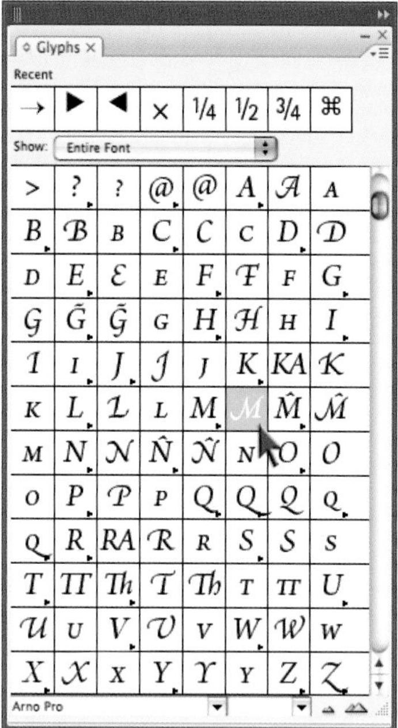

Figure 3-54.

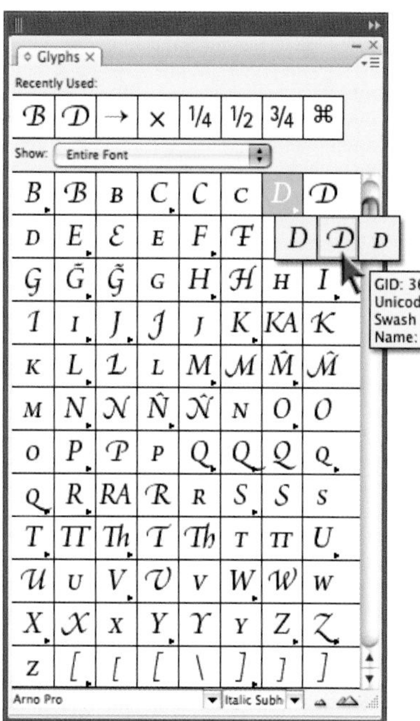

Figure 3-55.

assuming you loaded the dekeKeys shortcuts (page xix), press Ctrl+F12 (⌘-F12 on the Mac)—to display the **Glyphs** palette. Unlike other InDesign palettes, this one comprises a grid of cells, each of which contains a glyph from the active font. If the capital *M* is still highlighted in your document, you will see the *M* surrounded by a bevy of other capital letter variations, as in Figure 3-54.

The Glyphs palette accommodates standard and OpenType fonts alike. Because it shows each and every glyph—including many that are not available from PC or Mac keyboards—it's especially great for locating characters in non-Roman or symbol fonts. Some things to know about this incredibly useful palette:

- To insert a glyph into the active text block, double-click its cell in the palette.
- To examine a different typeface or style, select it from one of the two pop-up menus at the bottom of the palette.
- To examine a glyph more closely, click the big mountain icon (△) in the bottom-right corner of the palette. To zoom out, click the little mountain icon (△) to the left of that.
- Drag the size box in the bottom-right corner to expand the palette and see more glyphs at a time. You can also drag the edges of the palette—top, bottom, left, or right.
- If you find yourself using a small collection of glyphs over and over again, you're in luck. In InDesign CS3, the Glyphs palette starts off with a handy list of Recently Used glyphs that is independent of any particular font. Shown in Figure 3-54, my Recently Used list includes →, ⌘, and other glyphs that appear countless times in this book.

There's some other stuff, but that's good enough for now.

12. ***Replace the D in Day with a swash.*** Using the type tool, select the *D* in the word *Day*. Doing so scrolls the Glyphs palette up to the top of the character set, where the capital *D* lives. Click and hold the D cell to display a menu of alternatives, which includes a small cap and a swash variation. This little menu shows us not only that a swash exists for this character but also what it looks like (see Figure 3-55). Choose the swash character to replace the selected *D* in the document.
13. ***Swash the entire first line.*** On further reflection, I like the *M* and *D* swashes so much, I reckon we might as well go ahead and swash the first line. Press Ctrl+Shift+□ (or ⌘-Shift-□) to

select the entire line of type. Then choose **OpenType→Swash** from the **Character** palette menu. InDesign replaces all occurrences of *B*, *h*, and *y* with swash variations *B*, *h*, and *y*. The other letters lack swash variations, so they remain unchanged.

14. ***Go alternate character crazy.*** If you enjoy this sort of thing, you can assign swashes and other alternates to characters all over this document. Here are a few suggestions:

    - Replace the two &'s (called *ampersands*) with &'s.
    - Swap the $ for a raised ordinal variety.
    - Trade the *e* at the end of *prix fixe* with a decorative *e*.
    - Select the *Th* ligature at the outset of *Theatre* and swap it for the swash ligature, *Th*.

15. ***View just the ornaments.*** Most of Adobe's large, serifed OpenType font families include *ornaments*, which are tiny graphics such as leaves, flowers, swirls, and other representational forms. To see just the ornaments included with Arno Pro Italic, click in the final line of type with the type tool. Then click the **Show** pop-up menu at the top of the Glyphs palette—the one that reads **Entire Font**—and choose **Ornaments**. With that, InDesign shows just the ornaments, 57 in all, as in Figure 3-56.

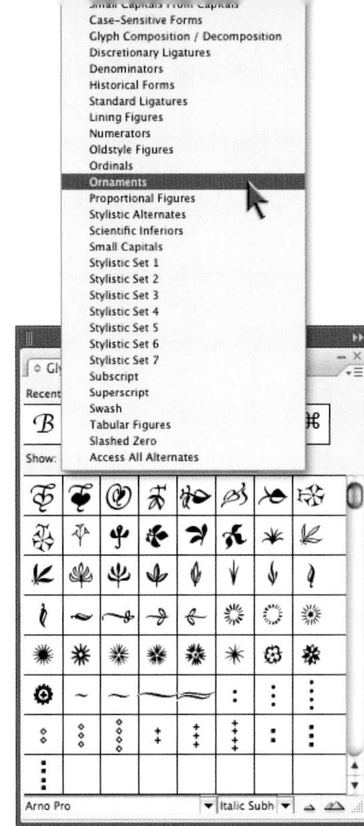

Figure 3-56.

16. ***Replace the bullet with an ornament.*** Select the bullet between the address and the phone number at the bottom of the menu. Then double-click one of the botanical ornaments in the Glyphs palette. I'm partial to the ❧, as witnessed in Figure 3-57. As I always say, nothing says elegance like an ornamental leaf.

17. ***Make and fill a custom glyph set.*** You don't have to rely on the Recently Used row to gather glyphs that you use often. If you really like that particular leaf ornament, for example, right-click the symbol in the **Glyphs** palette, choose **New Glyph Set**, and name the symbol something appropriate like "Menu Embellishments." Right-click another favorite and choose **Add to Glyph Set→Menu Embellishments**.

Nothing says you have to limit a glyph set to a single font. I use a multifont set to lay out this book. That way, I don't have to hunt through a dozen or so typefaces with several hundred glyphs apiece to find the symbols I use most often; they're all right there in one location.

Figure 3-57.

Mother's Day Brunch
Sunday, May 14th
choose a starter:
artichoke, spinach, and gouda puff pastry
gourmet soft cheeses & fresh fruit
choose an entrée:
raspberry-filled french toast with savory baby yukon potatoes
goat cheese-stuffed chicken breast with oven-broiled nectarines
smoked salmon with herbed crème fraîche and asparagus
choose a dessert:
crème brûlée with kiwi & berries
lemon gelato with waffle sugar cookies
your choice of mimosa, bloody mary, or bellini
complimentary coffee, tea, and juice
$18.95 prix fixe
served from 10:00 AM to 2:30 PM
only at
CAFÉ PETROVA
53½ Theatre Way 617-555-9129

Figure 3-58.

18. ***Add the appropriate accent marks.*** The only thing that could possibly make our menu any more tasteful is to properly acknowledge the French words (which after all are so yummy). The Glyphs palette is the place to find letters with the needed diacritical marks.

    - Start by selecting the second *e* in *entree*, which should be an *e* with a grave accent, as in *é*. Unfortunately, InDesign doesn't group accented characters with the base letter. So change the **Show** menu in the Glyphs palette to **Basic Latin and Latin 1**. Scroll down past the "naked" letters until you get to the accented characters. Then double-click the *é*.
    - Change the *E* in *CAFE* to an *É*.
    - If you're enjoying yourself, go all the way. The proper spellings for the creams are *crème fraîche* and *crème brûlée*.

    One might grouse that there's a certain tedium to hand-selecting diacritics from the Glyphs palette. But I prefer to think of it as Zen. We're putting our document in order, one painstaking character at a time.

19. ***Switch to Metrics kerning.*** After examining the document, I have just one concern: The letter spacing is irritatingly uneven. The kerning for the entire document is set to Optical. Yet we're working with one of Adobe's most elaborately realized fonts; surely its built-in metrics must be better. To find out, select the black arrow tool and click the central text block to select it. Then click the pop-up menu in the **Character** palette and choose **Metrics**. The text realigns, producing a subtle but undeniable elevation in quality.

After all that work, I really ought to be hungry. But one look at the final document (see Figure 3-58), with its crisp, sparkling letterforms as impeccable as its stemware, and I find myself strangely drawn not to the food, but to the beverages. Any and every one on the list.

The Power of the Indent

Everything in this lesson stems from one of the most basic formatting options we've witnessed so far, the indent. Remember how you indented the left and right edges of the quotation in the "Paragraph Spacing and Alignment" exercise in Lesson 3 (page 107)? Couldn't have been easier, right? And yet, thanks to this humble indent, a line of text doesn't have to align precisely with the edges of the frame. As shown in Figure 4-2, each and every paragraph—nay, each and every line—can float inside the frame just as the frame floats on the page.

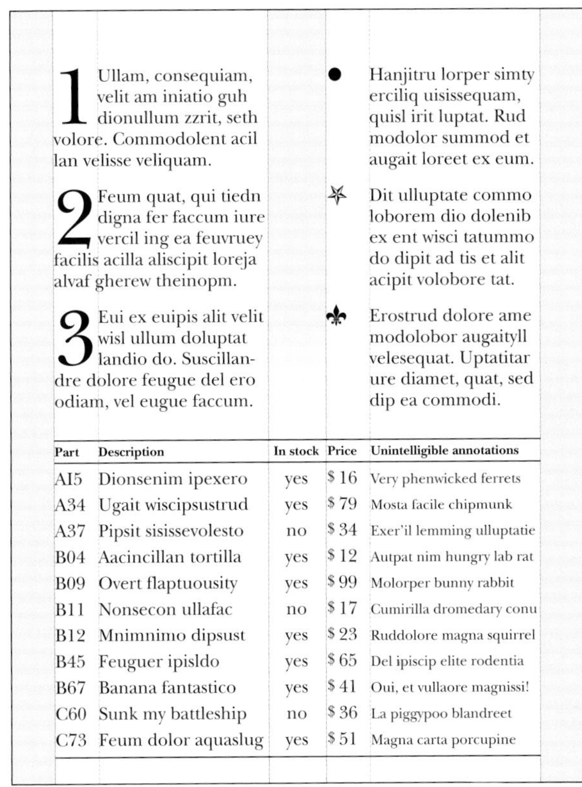

1 Ullam, consequiam, velit am iniatio guh dionullum zzrit, seth volore. Commodolent acil lan velisse veliquam.

● Hanjitru lorper simty erciliq uisissequam, quisl irit luptat. Rud modolor summod et augait loreet ex eum.

2 Feum quat, qui tiedn digna fer faccum iure vercil ing ea feuvruey facilis acilla aliscipit loreja alvaf gherew theinopm.

Dit ulluptate commo loborem dio dolenib ex ent wisci tatummo do dipit ad tis et alit acipit volobore tat.

3 Eui ex euipis alit velit wisl ullum doluptat landio do. Suscillandre dolore feugue del ero odiam, vel eugue faccum.

Erostrud dolore ame modolobor augaityll velesequat. Uptatitar ure diamet, quat, sed dip ea commodi.

Part	Description	In stock	Price	Unintelligible annotations
AI5	Dionsenim ipexero	yes	$ 16	Very phenwicked ferrets
A34	Ugait wiscipsustrud	yes	$ 79	Mosta facile chipmunk
A37	Pipsit sisissevolesto	no	$ 34	Exer'il lemming ulluptatie
B04	Aacincillan tortilla	yes	$ 12	Autpat nim hungry lab rat
B09	Overt flaptuousity	yes	$ 99	Molorper bunny rabbit
B11	Nonsecon ullafac	no	$ 17	Cumirilla dromedary conu
B12	Mnimnimo dipsust	yes	$ 23	Ruddolore magna squirrel
B45	Feuguer ipisldo	yes	$ 65	Del ipiscip elite rodentia
B67	Banana fantastico	yes	$ 41	Oui, et vullaore magnissi!
C60	Sunk my battleship	no	$ 36	La piggypoo blandreet
C73	Feum dolor aquaslug	yes	$ 51	Magna carta porcupine

Figure 4-2.

Now take the simple indent and imagine it repeated multiple times inside a single line of type. Instead of indenting just the beginning or end of a line, you can indent a single word or character. Plus, you can move the type to a specific location, relative either to the edge of the frame or another character. The only thing you can't do is make one character overlap another. If this threatens to happen, InDesign bumps the text to the next indent or wraps it to the next line.

As you can see, InDesign's indenting capabilities can pop up literally anywhere inside a paragraph. The next five exercises explain when these specialized indents are useful and how to apply them.

Adding a Drop Cap

Let's start things off with the ever-popular drop cap. Contrary to the latter half of its name, a *drop cap* doesn't have to be a capital letter. It can be any character—a lowercase letter, a number, a punctuation mark, or a symbol. But it does have to drop. As illustrated in Figure 4-3 on the next page, the traits that distinguish a drop cap from the rest of the pack are its large size and the way it drops down to consume multiple lines of type.

A drop cap may also comprise multiple characters. But without exception, drop caps appear at the beginning of a paragraph, and typically at the outset of a chapter or story. InDesign expresses the drop cap as a paragraph-level formatting attribute even though it affects just a few isolated characters.

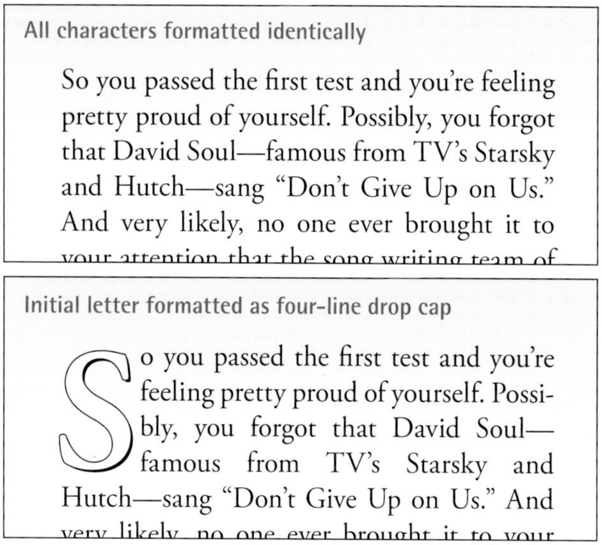

All characters formatted identically

So you passed the first test and you're feeling pretty proud of yourself. Possibly, you forgot that David Soul—famous from TV's Starsky and Hutch—sang "Don't Give Up on Us." And very likely, no one ever brought it to your attention that the song writing team of

Initial letter formatted as four-line drop cap

So you passed the first test and you're feeling pretty proud of yourself. Possibly, you forgot that David Soul—famous from TV's Starsky and Hutch—sang "Don't Give Up on Us." And very likely, no one ever brought it to your

Figure 4-3.

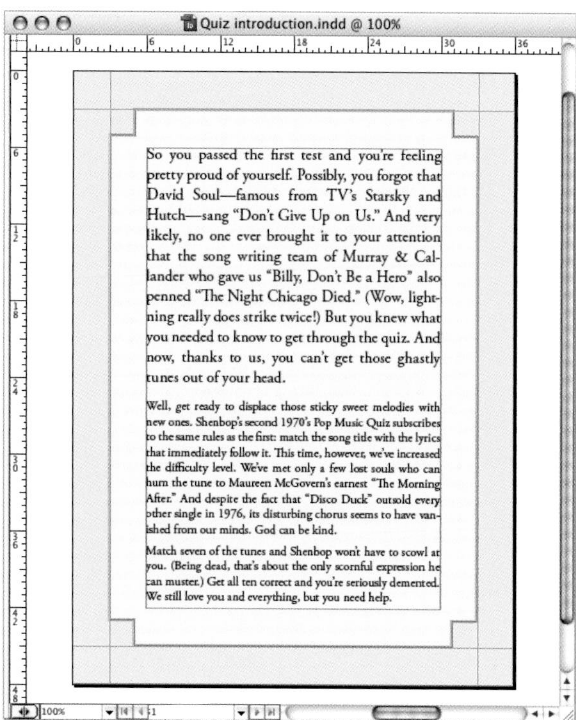

Figure 4-4.

PEARL OF WISDOM

In case you're scratching your head and thinking, "What does a drop cap have to do with lists and tables," take another peek at Figure 4-2 on the preceding page. The numbered list in the upper-left corner is actually a series of paragraphs that begin with drop caps. The enlarged numbers displace several lines of type and shift those lines rightward, exactly as if I had indented them. In this exercise, you'll be applying the drop cap to a single paragraph. But were you to apply just the first four steps in the exercise to several paragraphs in a row, you'd have yourself a list.

In this exercise, you'll enlarge the first word of a paragraph and drop it down to fill three lines of type. You'll also apply some specialized formatting attributes that fall outside, but nicely augment, InDesign's limited drop cap capabilities.

1. ***Open a document.*** Go into the *Lesson 04* folder inside *Lesson Files-IDcs3 1on1* and open the document *Quiz introduction.indd*. Pictured in Figure 4-4, this small-format document contains three paragraphs of type, the first set larger than the others. This first paragraph will contain our drop word.

2. ***Select the first paragraph.*** Double-click somewhere inside the first paragraph with the black arrow tool to switch to the type tool and insert the blinking insertion marker.

3. ***Bring up the Paragraph palette.*** Click its tab or press Ctrl+Alt+T (⌘-Option-T on the Mac). If the **Paragraph** palette is partially collapsed, expand it by clicking the ⇕ next to the word **Paragraph**. (Alternatively, you can work inside the control palette. To see the paragraph options on the left side of the palette, click the ¶ icon.)

4. ***Change the height of the drop cap to three lines.*** Whether you're using the Paragraph or control palette, click the icon that looks like a drop cap *A* (↕A≡). This option controls the size of the drop cap as measured in lines of type. Change the value to 3 and press the Tab key.

5. *Change the number of characters to 2.* By pressing Tab, you both enlarge the first letter of the paragraph, an *S*, and advance to the option box. This option box determines the number of letters in the drop cap. Change this value to 2 and press the Enter or Return key. InDesign enlarges both letters in the word *So*, as in Figure 4-5.

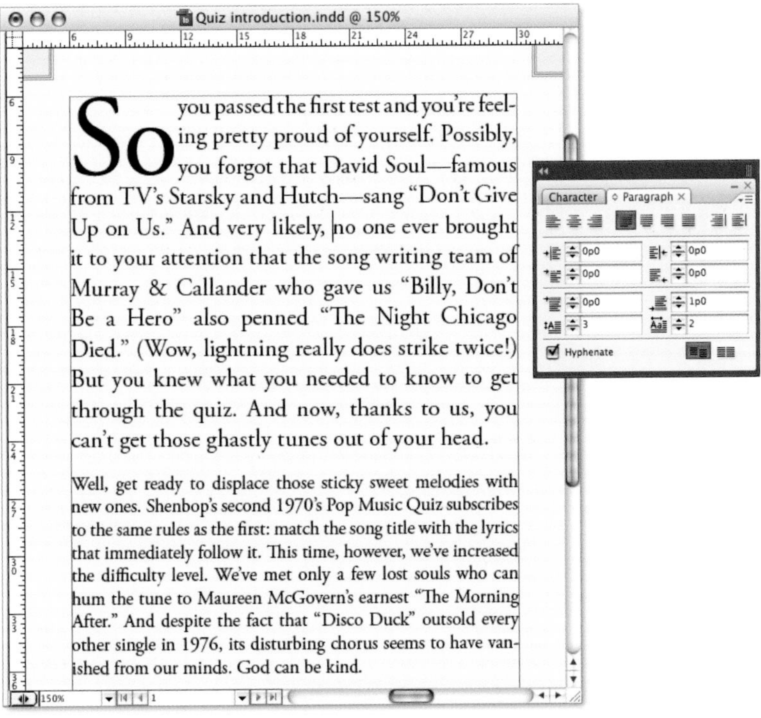

Figure 4-5.

That's really all there is to it. With no more effort than that, you tell InDesign to not only enlarge the first word to fill three lines of type but also indent the first three lines to avoid any overlap. Better yet, the effect is dynamic—if you change your mind, just enter new values and the drop cap updates.

PEARL OF WISDOM

Although InDesign's automated drop cap functions are great, it's unlikely you'll want to stop there. For example, what if you want to assign the characters a different font or color? Or perhaps give them outlines and shadows, as we saw back in Figure 4-3? That requires some additional work.

6. *Select the drop word.* Using the type tool, double-click the word *So* to select it. From here on out, we'll modify these characters by applying character-level formatting attributes as well as a handful of graphics functions.

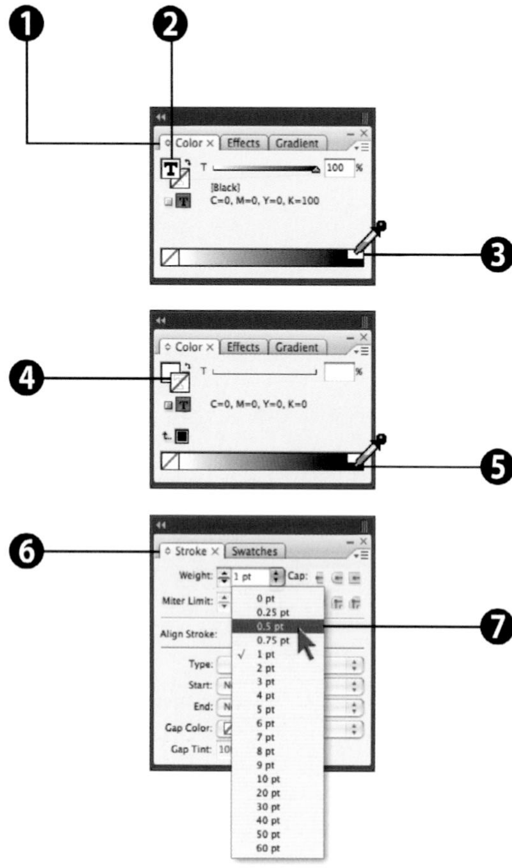

Figure 4-6.

7. ***Change the word to all caps.*** As I mentioned earlier, drop caps can be any characters. But they're called drop *caps* for a reason—whatever they can be, they usually look best when set in capital letters. To change the word *So* to all caps, click the [A] in the control palette to switch to the character attributes and then click the [TT] button. Or more simply, press the keyboard shortcut Ctrl+Shift+K (or ⌘-Shift-K).

8. ***Assign a white fill and a black stroke.*** The big round *O* makes the drop cap appear a bit heavy. To lighten it, we'll fill it with white and give it a thin black outline. Here's how:

   - Display the **Color** palette by clicking the Color tab (labeled ❶ in Figure 4-6) or by pressing the F6 key.
   - Click the black T in the upper-left corner of the palette (❷) to make the fill active. Then click the white swatch on the far right side of the gradient strip (indicated by the ❸). This makes the fill white.
   - White text against a light background doesn't show up too well, so we need to add an outline. Click the lightly outlined T with a red slash through it (labeled ❹ in the figure) to make the stroke active. Then click the black swatch at the end of the gradient strip (❺). The result is a beautiful black outline and a return to visibility for the drop caps.
   - Click the **Stroke** tab (❻) or press F10 to switch to the **Stroke** palette. Then change the **Weight** value to 0.5 points (labeled ❼ in Figure 4-6).

EXTRA CREDIT

You now have two big white letters with very thin black outlines. And if that looks good to you, then you have my permission to skip the rest of the exercise and fast-forward to "Lists and Hanging Indents" on page 141. But let's say you want to go further. Specifically, let's say you want to add a drop shadow. Unfortunately, InDesign doesn't let you add drop shadows to a single word inside a paragraph. But it does let you add a drop shadow to a graphic. So the trick is to first convert the text to a graphic and then add a drop shadow, as in the remaining steps.

9. ***Convert the selected letters to graphic outlines.*** Choose **Type→Create Outlines** or press Ctrl+Shift+O (⌘-Shift-O on the Mac). This changes the letters into full-fledged graphics, like those we'll be learning about in Lesson 5, "Drawing inside InDesign." You can no longer edit the type from the keyboard—whether to fix a typo or change the typeface—but you can add a drop shadow.

10. ***Select the* S *with the black arrow tool.*** To manipulate the graphic letters, you must first select them using the black arrow tool. And because they're housed inside a text block, you can select them only one at a time. It's a drag, frankly, but that's the way it is. So here goes: Assuming you loaded dekeKeys as instructed in the Preface (see page xix), press the Enter key on the keypad to switch to the black arrow tool. (If you didn't load dekeKeys, press Esc.) Then click the outline of the *S* to select it.

11. ***Add a drop shadow.*** Choose **Object→Effects→Drop Shadow** or press Ctrl+Alt+M (⌘-Option-M). When the **Effects** dialog box appears, the **Drop Shadow** settings will be ready and waiting for you. Select the settings shown in Figure 4-7, as follows:

    - Turn on the **Preview** check box so you can see what you're doing.
    - Leave the **Mode** set to **Multiply**. This combines the black ink of the shadow with the magenta and yellow of the background, thus eliminating any trapping issues (a topic we'll discuss in more detail in Lesson 12, "Printing and Output").
    - Change the **Opacity** value to 100 percent. This results in the darkest shadow possible.
    - Enter a value of 0p1 for both the **X Offset** and **Y Offset** values to position the shadow 1 point down and to the right from the *S*. (InDesign automatically sets the Distance and Angle values according to the Pythagorean theorem. If your middle school geometry's a little rusty, don't sweat it. With a study partner like InDesign, you're covered.)
    - By default, drop shadows are fuzzy. To make the shadow sharp, reduce the **Size** value to 0p0.
    - When working with blurred shadows, the **Spread** value enlarges the core. With a Size of 0, Spread has no effect, so leave this value set to 0.
    - **Noise** affects the texture of a blurred shadow, making it more granular and crunchy looking. This value also requires blurring, so again, leave it set to 0.

    When you finish, click **OK**. Figure 4-7 shows the result.

Figure 4-7.

12. ***Select the* O.** That takes care of the *S*, now for the *O*. Click the outline of the letter with the black arrow tool to select it.

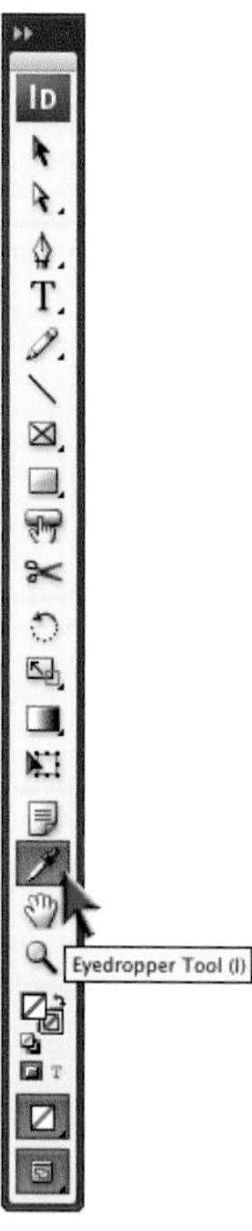

Figure 4-8.

13. ***Select the eyedropper tool in the toolbox.*** At this point, you could add the same drop shadow to the *O* that you added to the *S* by choosing the Drop Shadow command and resetting every single one of the options described in Step 11. But there's a better way: the eyedropper. Click the eyedropper icon (see Figure 4-8) or press the I key to get it.

14. ***Click the* S *to lift its attributes.*** Click anywhere in the *S* to copy the drop shadow from the first letter to the second. That's all it takes to transfer all those settings from one object to another.

One word of advice: You may notice that clicking with the eyedropper changes the cursor's appearance. This tells you the eyedropper is now loaded with the new settings and ready to apply them over and over to other objects. To load new settings—because you didn't quite click exactly on the *S*, for example—press the Alt key (or Option on the Mac) and click again. For more information on the eyedropper, see Video Lesson 8, "Duplicating Formatting Attributes" (see page 318).

15. ***Switch back to the type tool.*** The only remaining problem is that the type is spaced too closely to the drop caps. We'll remedy this with kerning. Press the T key to select the type tool. Then click the *y* in *you*, right after *SO*. You should see a short insertion marker, just the height of the word *you*. (If it appears the full height of *SO*, press the → key until the blinking insertion marker becomes shorter.)

16. ***Kern the text away from the drop caps.*** Change the kerning value in the control palette to 50. Or, assuming you changed the Kerning value in the Preferences dialog box to 5/1000 em (as I recommended in the "Formatting Shortcuts" sidebar on page 104 of Lesson 3), press Ctrl+Alt+→ (⌘-Option-→ on the Mac) twice in a row to kern *you* away from *SO*. Either way, InDesign kerns all three lines in unison away from the drop caps, as shown in Figure 4-9.

You'll probably also want to increase the spacing between the *S* and the *O*. To do so, press the ← key twice in a row to position the insertion marker between the two graphic letters. Then press Ctrl+Alt+→ (or ⌘-Option-→) to kern them apart.

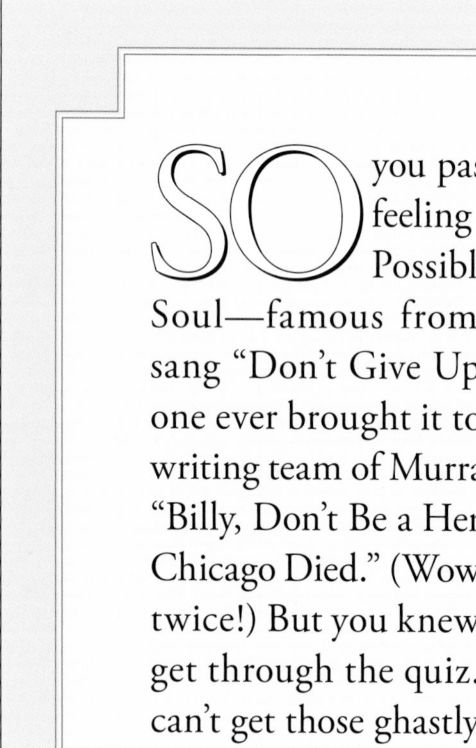

Figure 4-9.

I'm a big fan of drop caps. But despite my enthusiasm, I don't use them in this particular book. (Hey, different documents call for different solutions.) Instead, each lesson begins with what are termed *raised caps*, which are nothing more than letters set in a larger type size. Raised caps require no special paragraph-level formatting. If you decide you want to make raised caps with drop shadows, however, that takes some extra work. Fortunately, that work is identical to what we did in the "Extra Credit" portion of the preceding exercise.

Lists and Hanging Indents

As I say, drop caps are a wonderful way to begin list entries. But the more popular method of formatting is the *hanging indent*. Introduced in Video Lesson 4, "Spaces, Indents, and Tabs," a hanging indent occurs when the first line of a paragraph extends to the left of the other lines. Another way to think of it is that all lines except the first line receive an indent. Usually, this means a number or bullet hangs off to the left, as illustrated by the formatting applied to every step in this book.

In this exercise, we'll apply hanging indents to entries in a numbered list. In the "Extra Credit," we'll take a look at a special formatting option that goes by the name indent-to-here.

1. ***Open a document.*** Open the document *Look&Learn p122.indd*, contained in the *Lesson 04* folder inside *Lesson Files-IDcs3 1on1*. As you can see in Figure 4-10, this one-page document features a seven-entry list. The entries begin with blue letters, but they could just as easily start with numbers or bullets, formatted in any typeface, size, and color you like.

2. ***Select the first lettered entry with the type tool.*** Assuming that the black arrow tool is active, double-click inside the paragraph that leads off with the blue *A* to get the type tool and the blinking insertion marker.

3. ***Display the paragraph options in the control palette.*** This time, just for variety, we'll work inside the control palette (although you could just as easily use the Paragraph palette). Indents are a paragraph-level formatting attribute. So if you're working on a small screen, press F4 to move all the paragraph attributes to the left side of the palette. (This assumes that you loaded dekeKeys as instructed on page xix of the Preface; otherwise, click the ¶ icon).

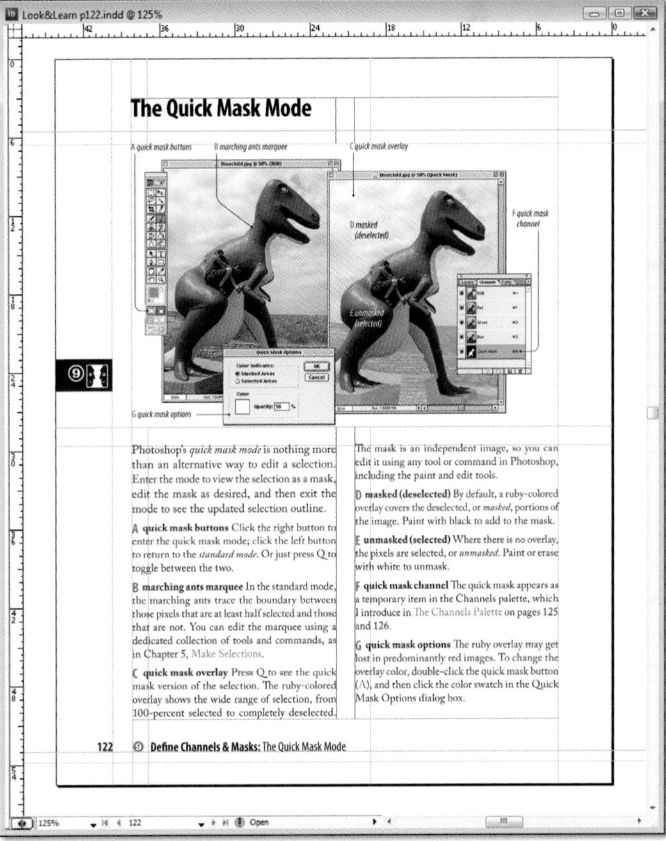

Figure 4-10.

4. *Change the left indent value to 1p3.* Note the orange guideline toward the left side of each of the two columns. If all goes according to plan—which it will, of course—the text will indent in alignment with one of the orange lines. In other words, the lines are there so we can gauge our progress.

   The guides are spaced 15 points in from the left side of each column. So click the →≣ icon in the control palette to highlight the left indent value. Enter 15 pt and press Tab. InDesign converts the value to 1p3 and indents the text 15 points to the left, in line with the orange guide.

   To highlight the first option box in the control palette from the keyboard, press Ctrl+6 (⌘-6 on the Mac). It's not the easiest shortcut to remember but, man, is it useful when you're trying to move quickly.

   ---

5. *Change the first-line indent value to –1p3.* Press the Tab key a second time to advance to the first-line indent value, identified by ⁺≣. This option controls the first line in the paragraph independently of all other lines. A positive value sends the first line rightward, resulting in a standard paragraph indent; a negative value sends the first line leftward. To align the first line with the left edge of the column, a negative first-line indent should exactly offset the left indent. So enter –1p3 and press Enter or Return. The *A* returns to the left margin, as in Figure 4-11.

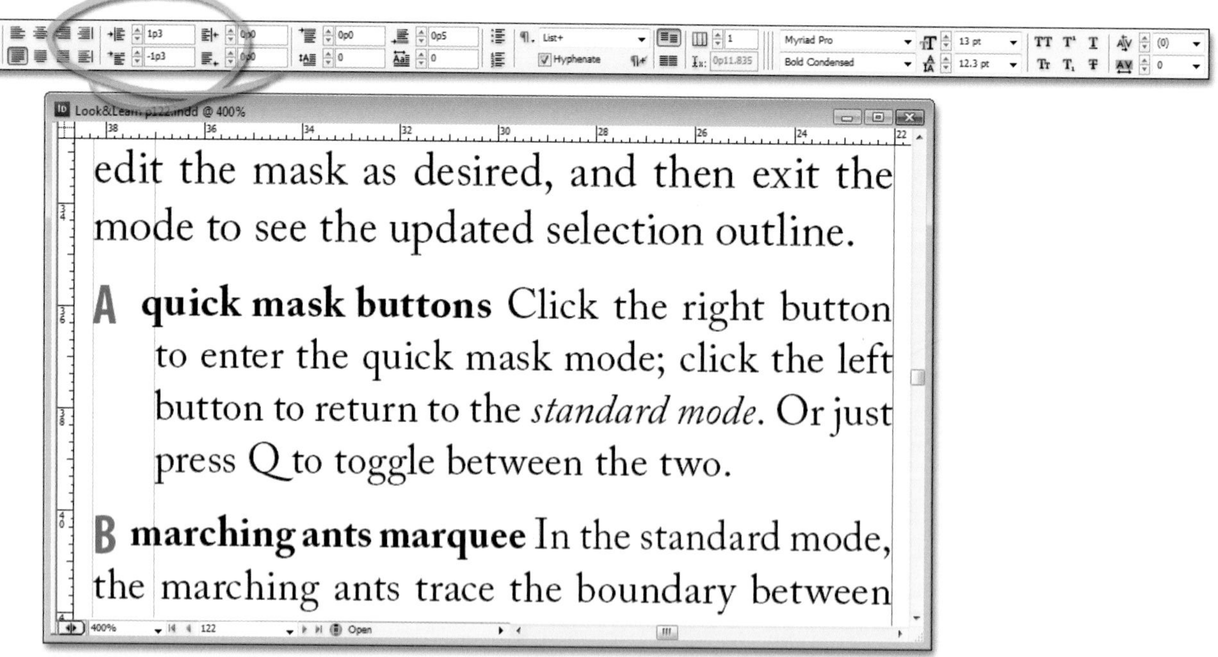

Figure 4-11.

6. ***Update the other paragraphs to match.*** All right, that takes care of one paragraph, but what about the others? Fortunately, this paragraph and most of the others are tagged with a custom style sheet called List that I designed in advance. I discuss style sheets in detail in Lesson 8, "Using Style Sheets." But for the present, just know this: A style sheet links a group of formatting attributes to a word or a paragraph. This way, if you change one paragraph, you can update the others to match.

   To take advantage of this wonderful feature, first make sure the insertion marker is blinking away in a regularly styled portion of the indented paragraph, that is, somewhere in the word *Click* or later. Then click the ¶ icon in the middle of the control palette (the one to the left of the word **List+**) to display the palette menu. Choose the **Redefine Style** command or press Ctrl+Shift+Alt+R (or ⌘-Shift-Option-R). This updates the style sheet definition and changes all other entries to match, as in Figure 4-12. (Only the last entry, *G*, is not updated. We'll fix that one manually in a moment.)

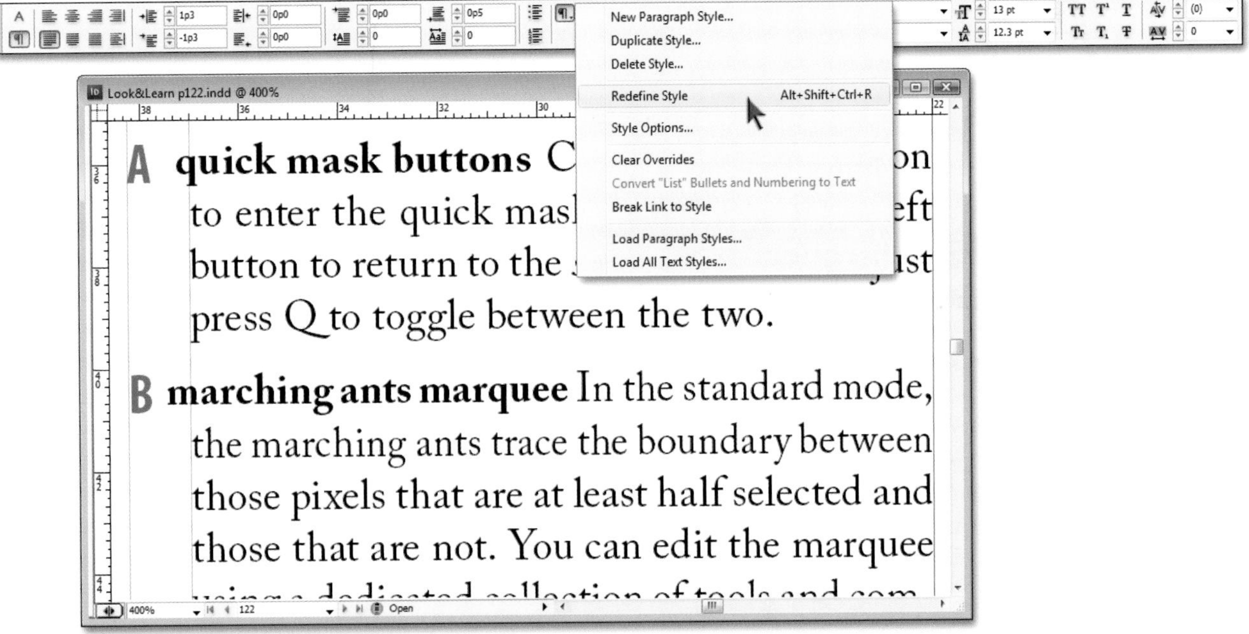

Figure 4-12.

7. ***Show all hidden characters.*** That takes care of the hanging indents, but we have some outstanding alignment problems. Ideally, the words after the big blue letters should align with the lines below them. But not only do they fail in this regard, they don't even align with each other. In Figure 4-12, for example, the bold word *quick* appears a bit to the right of *marching*.

The culprit is the spacing that I used. To see this spacing, choose **Type→Show Hidden Characters** or press Ctrl+Alt+I (⌘-Option-I). InDesign displays a series of nonprinting characters, known as *invisibles*, which include orange dots as well as ¶ and # symbols. The dots represent spaces, the ¶s are paragraph breaks, and the # marks the end of a story. Two spaces follow each blue letter. Space characters can vary in width—especially in justified paragraphs—and are therefore unpredictable spacing tools. They're great for spacing one word from the next, but that's it.

PEARL OF WISDOM

Note that the dots and ¶ symbols appear orange in this document because I assigned orange to this layer. By default, hidden characters in other documents appear light blue. To learn how to assign colors to layers, read the exercise "Creating and Using Layers" on page 389 in Lesson 9.

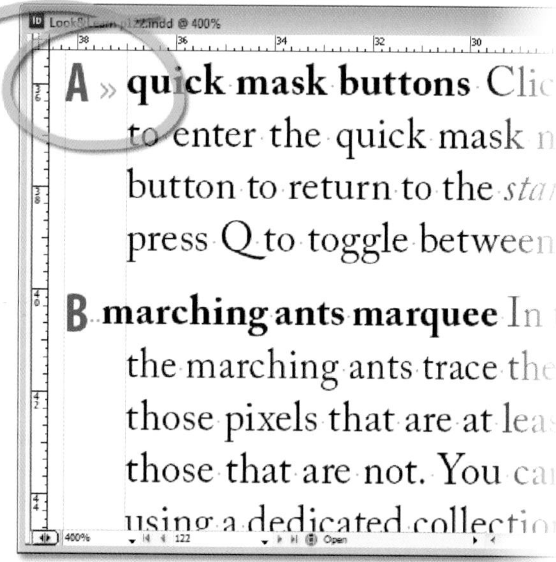

Figure 4-13.

8. ***Replace the double spaces with tabs.*** So if spaces aren't the solution, what are? Tabs. You can set the exact width of a tab character. Better yet, tabs automatically provide exactly the proper amount of spacing inside hanging-indent lists. So do this: Select the two spaces that separate the *A* and *quick*. Then press the Tab key. In a flash, InDesign inserts a tab character and fixes the spacing. Where possible, any text after the first tab character automatically aligns to the first-line indent. Hence the paragraph looks neat as a pin, as in Figure 4-13.

9. ***Choose the Find/Change command.*** Of course, just because you fix one entry doesn't mean you've fixed them all. The others still have spaces. You could fix them manually by entering one tab at a time. Or, better, save yourself labor and time by searching for the offending double spaces and replacing them with tabs.

   To begin your search-and-replace operation, choose **Edit→Find/Change** or press the shortcut Ctrl+F (⌘-F on the Mac). InDesign displays the **Find/Change** dialog box (see Figure 4-14 on the facing page), which lets you search for one sequence of characters and replace it with another, as we saw ever so briefly in Lesson 2 (see page 65). You might be wishing that hidden characters such as spaces and tabs were searchable as well, in which case rejoice for I have glad news: They are.

Better yet, if you edit the text or change its formatting, the indent-to-here character goes with the flow, shifting position along with the other characters, hidden or otherwise.

So what's the conclusion? Use the indent values to format multiple paragraphs in a long and consistent list. Use the indent-to-here character to format a single special paragraph, especially when you want the spacing to update with respect to other lines as you edit the text.

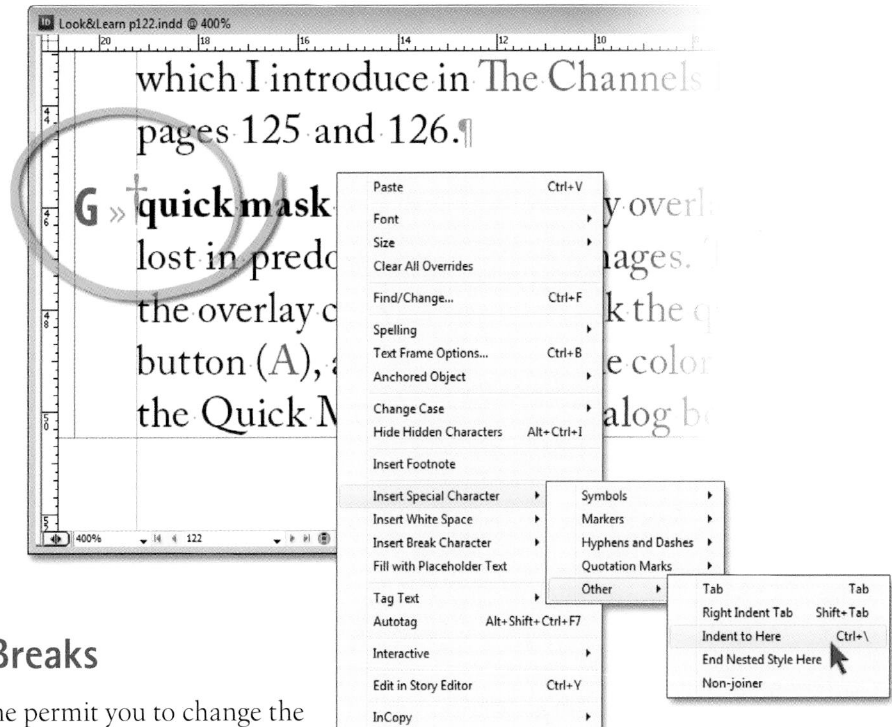

Figure 4-17.

Dashes, Spaces, and Breaks

The next functions we'll examine permit you to change the appearance of a sentence, paragraph, or longer passage of type. But this time, rather than applying formatting attributes, we'll use glyphs, like those I showed you in Lesson 3.

The length of a dash, the width of a space, even how one line of type breaks to the next—these are all qualities that InDesign expresses as special characters. Some, such as dashes, are defined by the typeface. The rest are brought to you by InDesign itself. Strange as it may sound, InDesign ships with its own glyphs, all of which you can use in combination with any typeface, type size, or type style. And they are, as a group, indispensable.

In the following steps, we'll take a three-page spread and load it up with a veritable top-ten collection of dashes, spaces, and breaks. While this may sound like a strange and remote topic, it's actually the very model of practicality. I use some of these characters—em dashes, nonbreaking spaces, and line breaks—more regularly than I use many letters in the alphabet. Such seemingly obscure characters can have a profound effect on the look of a document.

1. *Open a multipage document.* This time, I'd like you to open a revised version of the last document, called *Look&Learn three-pager.indd*, which you'll find in the *Lesson 04* folder inside *Lesson Files-IDcs3 1on1*. Most likely, you'll see the first two pages in the document window, as in

Figure 4-18. The beige page with the dinosaur is the one we created in the previous exercise. It serves as a sidebar, breaking up the content that flows from page 122 to page 124. In examining the document, you may happen to notice a few formatting flubs, including some overlapping text blocks. If so, good eye; we'll remedy all problems in the upcoming steps.

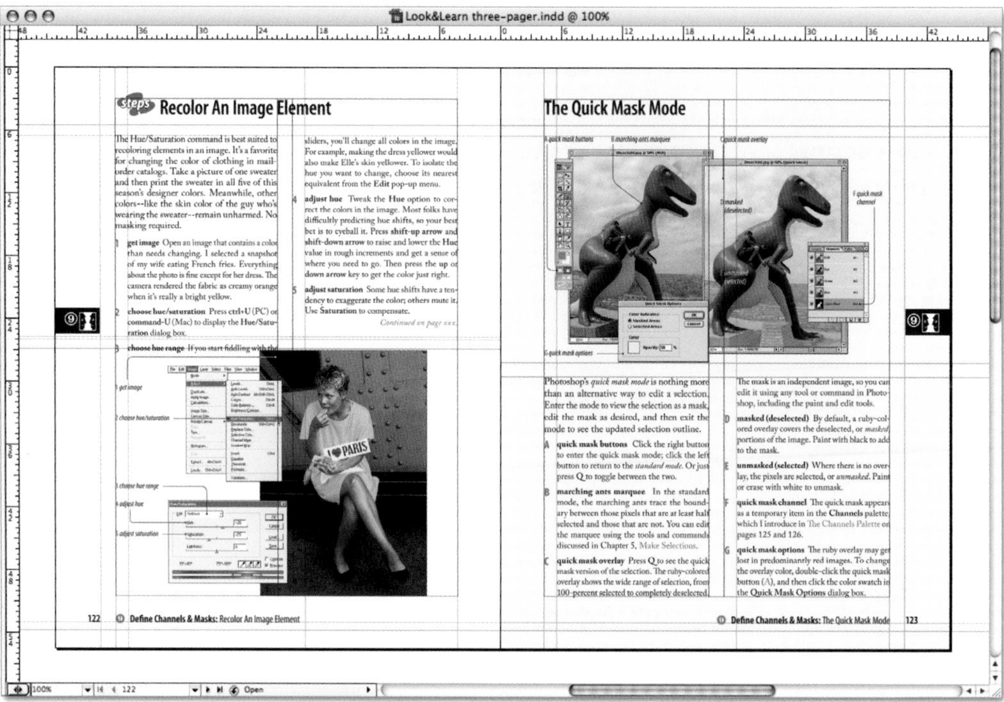

Look&Learn three-pager.indd @ 100%

Recolor An Image Element

The Hue/Saturation command is best suited to recoloring elements in an image. It's a favorite for changing the color of clothing in mail-order catalogs. Take a picture of one sweater and then print the sweater in all five of this season's designer colors. Meanwhile, other colors--like the skin color of the guy who's wearing the sweater--remain unharmed. No masking required.

1 **get image** Open an image that contains a color than needs changing. I selected a snapshot of my wife eating French fries. Everything about the photo is fine except for her dress. The camera rendered the fabric as creamy orange when it's really a bright yellow.

2 **choose hue/saturation** Press ctrl+U (PC) or command-U (Mac) to display the **Hue/Saturation** dialog box.

3 **choose hue range** If you start fiddling with the sliders, you'll change all colors in the image. For example, making the dress yellower would also make Elle's skin yellower. To isolate the hue you want to change, choose its nearest equivalent from the **Edit** pop-up menu.

4 **adjust hue** Tweak the **Hue** option to correct the colors in the image. Most folks have difficultly predicting hue shifts, so your best bet is to eyeball it. Press **shift-up arrow** and **shift-down arrow** to raise and lower the **Hue** value in rough increments and get a sense of where you need to go. Then press the **up** or **down arrow** key to get the color just right.

5 **adjust saturation** Some hue shifts have a tendency to exaggerate the color; others mute it. Use **Saturation** to compensate.

Continued on page xxx.

122 Define Channels & Masks: Recolor An Image Element

The Quick Mask Mode

Photoshop's *quick mask mode* is nothing more than an alternative way to edit a selection. Enter the mode to view the selection as a mask, edit the mask as desired, and then exit the mode to see the updated selection outline.

A **quick mask buttons** Click the right button to enter the quick mask mode; click the left button to return to the *standard mode*. Or just press Q to toggle between the two.

B **marching ants marquee** In the standard mode, the marching ants trace the boundary between those pixels that are at least half selected and those that are not. You can edit the marquee using the tools and commands discussed in Chapter 5, Make Selections.

C **quick mask overlay** Press Q to see the quick mask version of the selection. The ruby-colored overlay shows the wide range of selection, from 100-percent selected to completely deselected. The mask is an independent image, so you can edit it using any tool or command in Photoshop, including the paint and edit tools.

D **masked (deselected)** By default, a ruby-colored overlay covers the deselected, or *masked*, portions of the image. Paint with black to add to the mask.

E **unmasked (selected)** Where there is no overlay, the pixels are selected, or *unmasked*. Paint or erase with white to unmask.

F **quick mask channel** The quick mask appears as a temporary item in the **Channels** palette, which I introduce in The Channels Palette on pages 125 and 126.

G **quick mask options** The ruby overlay may get lost in predominantly red images. To change the overlay color, double-click the quick mask button (A), and then click the color swatch in the **Quick Mask Options** dialog box.

Define Channels & Masks: The Quick Mask Mode 123

Figure 4-18.

2. ***Select one of the two double-hyphen combinations.*** Zoom in on the first paragraph on page 122 (the first page). Notice that the second-to-last sentence—the one that begins *Meanwhile*—contains two pairs of consecutive hyphens, which I've circled in Figure 4-19 on the facing page. These double hyphens are stand-ins for long dashes, commonly used to offset descriptive or parenthetical phrases in a sentence. Were this a piece of plain-text email, I would regard such uses of double hyphens as the height of grammatical decorum. But it ain't, so they ain't either. In the realm of professional typesetting, the better solution is the *em dash*, so-called because it extends the full width of a capital letter *M*.

PEARL OF WISDOM

Never use a lone hyphen in place of a dash. A lone hyphen is used to hyphenate a word onto a separate line or join multiple words into a compound word. It is not designed to separate a phrase from the rest of its sentence.

Now that I've finished haranguing you on the subject of hyphenation etiquette, get the type tool and select one of the hyphen pairs so we can set about replacing it.

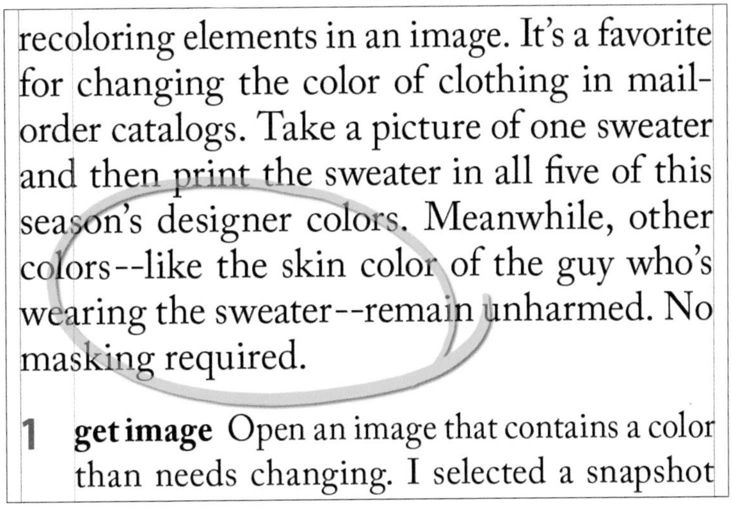

recoloring elements in an image. It's a favorite for changing the color of clothing in mail-order catalogs. Take a picture of one sweater and then print the sweater in all five of this season's designer colors. Meanwhile, other colors--like the skin color of the guy who's wearing the sweater--remain unharmed. No masking required.

1 **get image** Open an image that contains a color than needs changing. I selected a snapshot

Figure 4-19.

3. ***Replace the double hyphens with em dashes.*** Right-click in the document window to display the shortcut menu. (On the Mac, you may need to Control-click.) Then choose **Insert Special Character→Hyphens and Dashes** to display a submenu with four dash-like characters, which work like so:

   - The Em Dash command inserts a long dash, suitable for punctuating inset phrases like ours.
   - The next command, En Dash, creates a slightly narrower dash, used mainly for linking numbers, such as 1995–98. It's also sometimes used for faking minus signs (although technically the minus sign is its own, slightly narrower character).
   - Discretionary Hyphen changes where InDesign breaks a word. As explained in the upcoming Step 6, this character shows up only when it's needed. If you edit the text and the word fits completely on one line, the hyphen disappears.

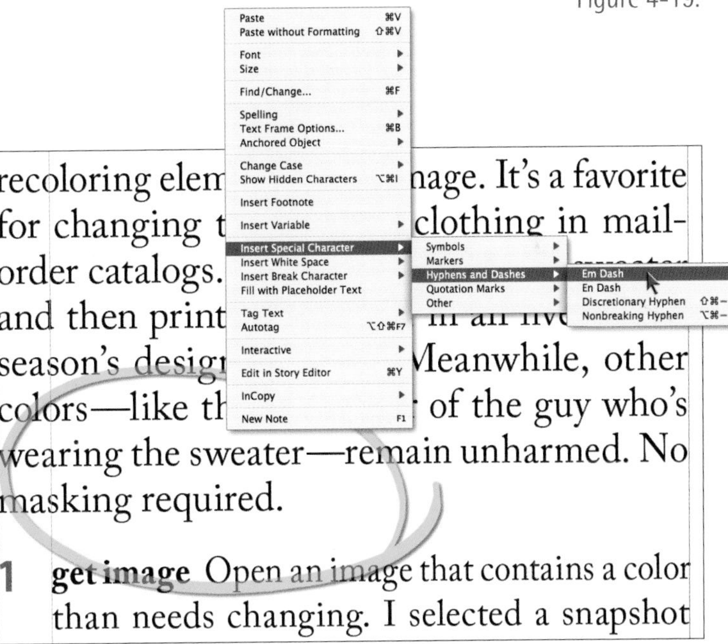

Figure 4-20.

   - Nonbreaking Hyphen prohibits InDesign from breaking a compound word at the hyphen. We'll see this one in use in the very next step.

Choose the **Em Dash** command to replace the double hyphen with a proper long dash. Then select the other double hyphen and replace it using the keyboard shortcut, Shift+Alt+- (Shift-Option-- on the Mac). Both methods deliver the em dash defined by the active font, as pictured in Figure 4-20. (You may notice that my em dashes are "closed," or tight to the text that surrounds them. This is the custom of most publications, although some prefer to surround the em dash with spaces.)

4. ***Replace the hyphen with a nonbreaking hyphen.*** Toward the top of this same paragraph—just three lines down on the right—is the compound word *mail-order* broken onto two lines. There's nothing inherently wrong with InDesign busting up a compound word, but in this case, I think it interrupts the flow. When I read *mail-* on one line, I don't expect to see *order* on the next. It makes me wonder if I skipped a line, which ultimately impairs the legibility of the text. Fortunately, we can tell InDesign to keep both parts of the word together, as follows:

   - Select the hyphen after *mail*.
   - Right-click (or Control-click) to display the shortcut menu and choose **Insert Special Character→Hyphens and Dashes→Nonbreaking Hyphen**.

   Or you could press the keyboard shortcut Ctrl+Alt+⊟ (⌘-Option-⊟). InDesign spreads the text and knocks the whole of *mail-order* to the fourth line.

5. ***Force the word* of *to the next line.*** In the previous lesson, I spoke of the wonders of InDesign's Paragraph Composer, which attempts to balance the spacing from one line of type to the next. Usually, it works splendidly. But the nonbreaking hyphen has thrown it for a loop. Now we have four loosely spaced lines followed by two rather packed lines. The solution is to balance the spacing manually.

   With the type tool, click directly in front of the word *of* at the end of the fifth line. Then press the Backspace or Delete key to delete the preceding space, so that *fiveof* runs together. Now try each of the following:

   - Press the Enter or Return key. InDesign starts a new paragraph, complete with a generous supply of paragraph spacing, as in Figure 4-21. (Note that I've turned on Show Hidden Characters so we can see the paragraph breaks and other invisibles.)
   - This is obviously the wrong solution, so press Ctrl+Z (or ⌘-Z) to undo.
   - Now for the correct solution: Right-click (Control-click) to display the shortcut menu and choose **Insert Break Character→Forced Line Break**. InDesign adds a *forced line break* that knocks the word *of* to the next line without starting a new paragraph. The appearance is therefore one of a single paragraph with more uniform spacing, as in Figure 4-22 (facing page).

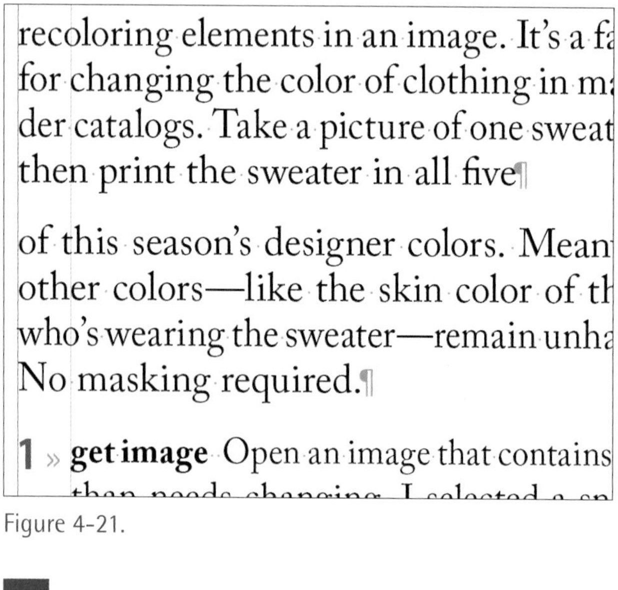

Figure 4-21.

The immensely useful line break character includes its own keyboard shortcut, one common to other page-layout and word-processing programs, and I recommend that you assign it to memory. Fortunately, it's easy: Shift+Enter (Shift-Return on the Mac).

6. ***Add a discretionary hyphen.*** Scroll down a few paragraphs to step 2 in the text. Notice the way the bold command name breaks at the end of the second line (*Hue/Satu-ration*). Personally, I'm not too fond of it, so let's move that hyphen to a different spot using a *discretionary hyphen*.

   - Click with the type tool between *ra* and *tion* at the beginning of the third line.

   - Right-click (Control-click) and choose **Insert Special Character→Hyphens and Dashes→Discretionary Hyphen**, or press Ctrl+Shift+⊟ (⌘-Shift-⊟). InDesign shifts the hyphen so the word breaks as *Hue/Satura-tion*.

   Now for a hypothetical situation. Let's say you decide to modify the sentence. Click immediately after the word *the* that precedes *Hue/Satura-tion*. Then press the spacebar and type the word "familiar." The text now reads *the familiar Hue/Saturation dialog box* without any hyphenation whatsoever. That's the beauty of the discretionary hyphen—it thoughtfully disappears when not needed so as not to leave an extraneous hyphen in the middle of a line of type.

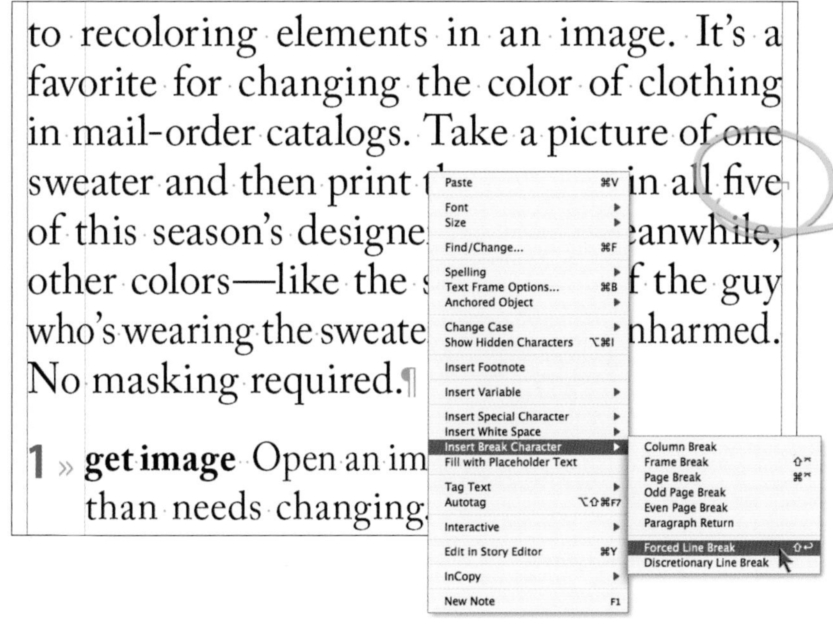

Figure 4-22.

7. ***Break step 3 to the next column.*** Notice that I've clumsily permitted the text frame to dip too low, so that step 3 overlaps the graphic below it. I could select the frame with the black arrow tool and drag the bottom handle up to force a column break. But so long as we're in the text edit mode, let's try a different solution.

   Click in front of the big blue 3 to set the insertion marker. Then right-click and choose **Insert Break Character**. The commands at the top of this submenu work as follows:

   - The Column Break command forces the text to the next column in a multicolumn text block, like the one that I demonstrated in Video Lesson 2, "Text and Frames" (see page 48).
   - The more useful Frame Break command moves the text to the next frame in the story.
   - To bypass all remaining frames on this page and send the text to the next page, you'd choose the Page Break command. Other commands move the text to the next odd or even page.

   The best way to move step 3 to the top of the next column is to choose the **Frame Break** command. (In this case, Column Break delivers the same result, but it could create problems in the unlikely event that you later decided to add columns to the text block.) Or press Shift+Enter on the numerical keypad. Either way, you end up with the results pictured in the zoomed out Figure 4-23.

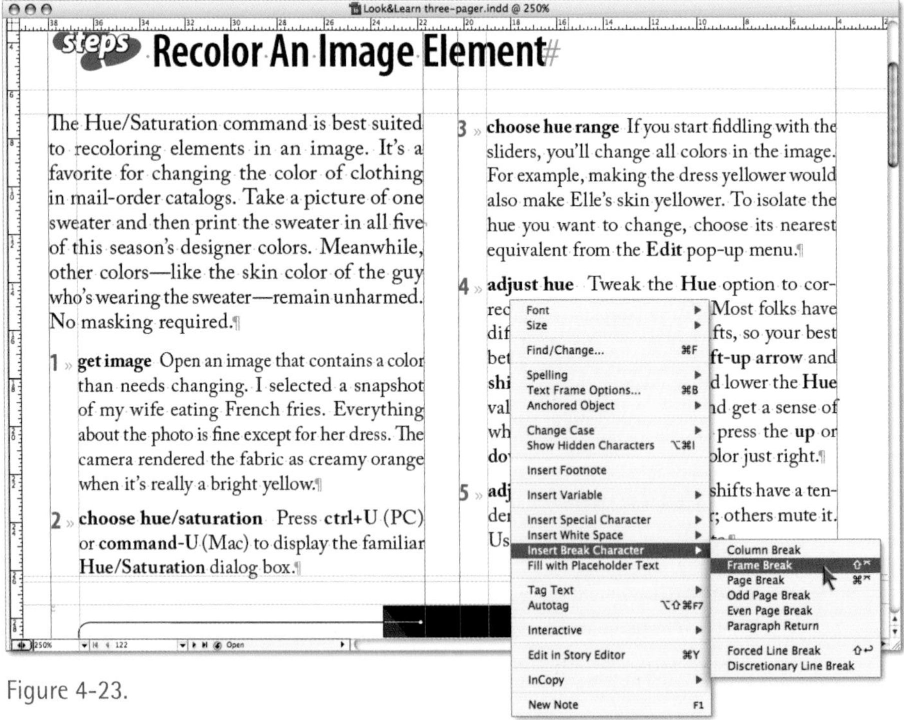

Figure 4-23.

PEARL OF WISDOM

In the sample file, notice that the bold text at the outset of each step ends with two spaces. As I've intimated, consecutive spaces are bad form. This goes even for sentence spacing. In professional typesetting, just one space character separates a sentence from its successor. The idea is that two spaces result in an exaggerated gap that impedes legibility. Besides, the sentence ends with a period; why do you need multiple spaces? But this bold text is different. Termed a *run-in head*, it demands a larger space. And a larger but more predictable space we will give it.

---

8. ***Replace a pair of spaces with an en space.*** Any two spaces are fine. I selected the pair that follow the bold text in step 3. Then right-click and choose **Insert White Space**. InDesign displays a long list of *fixed-width spaces*, which means that the program does not alter the width of the spaces to suit the alignment or spacing of a paragraph. Here's how the various spaces work:

   - You can think of an *em space* as being roughly as wide as a capital letter *M*. More precisely, it's exactly as wide as the type size is tall. It also happens to be the space on which many of the other relative-width spaces are based.
   - An *en space* is ½ as wide as an em space, making it approximately as wide as a lowercase letter.
   - InDesign CS3 introduces what it calls *sixth*, *quarter*, and *third spaces*, all named after fractions of an em space.
   - The *figure space* is exactly as wide as a tabular number, making it well suited to spacing numbers in a table. In most fonts, the figure space is equivalent to an en space.
   - The *punctuation space* matches the width of a period in the prevailing typeface. It's designed to stand in for a missing decimal point when aligning figures in a table.
   - Thinner than the punctuation space is the *thin space*, which is ¼ as wide as an en space, or ⅛ as wide as an em space. Hence, it tends to be about half as wide as a lowercase *i*.
   - If you want to shave a gap even thinner, the *hair space* is just ⅓ as thick as the thin space, or 1/24 an em space. You may find the hair space useful for offsetting an em dash or other punctuation that otherwise crowds neighboring characters.
   - The *nonbreaking space* matches the width of a standard space character and may even vary in width to suit the spacing needs of a justified paragraph. To prevent the width of the space from varying, choose the (Fixed Width) option.

- The other variable-width space character is the *flush space*, which grows to fill all the excess space in the last line of a justified paragraph. InDesign aligns the word or character that follows the flush space with the right side of the column, helpful when spacing end-of-paragraph ornaments.

I want you to choose the **En Space** command. Or press the keyboard shortcut Ctrl+Shift+N (⌘-Shift-N on the Mac).

9. ***Search for and replace the other double-space combos.*** Just as you can search for tabs and replace them, you can search for and replace every special character covered in this exercise. Choose **Edit→Find/Change** or press Ctrl+F (⌘-F). Then do the following:

    - Enter two spaces into the **Find What** option box.
    - Press the Tab key to advance to the **Change To** option.
    - Click the @ icon to the right of the option and choose **White Space→En Space**. InDesign enters the cryptic code ^>, as in Figure 4-24.
    - Click the **Change All** button. After InDesign announces that it's made 17 changes, click **OK**.
    - Click the **Done** button to exit the dialog box.

    Every step now features an en space that divides the bold run-in heads from the plain text that follows. Each en space is roughly equivalent to two standard spaces. But because the en spaces can't be flexed like word spaces during justification, they are consistent in width from one step to the next.

10. ***Prevent one or more words from breaking.*** Moving right along, scroll to the hyphenated word at the end of the first line in step 4, which should read *cor-rect*. This isn't a bad break, but it does result in overly loose spac-

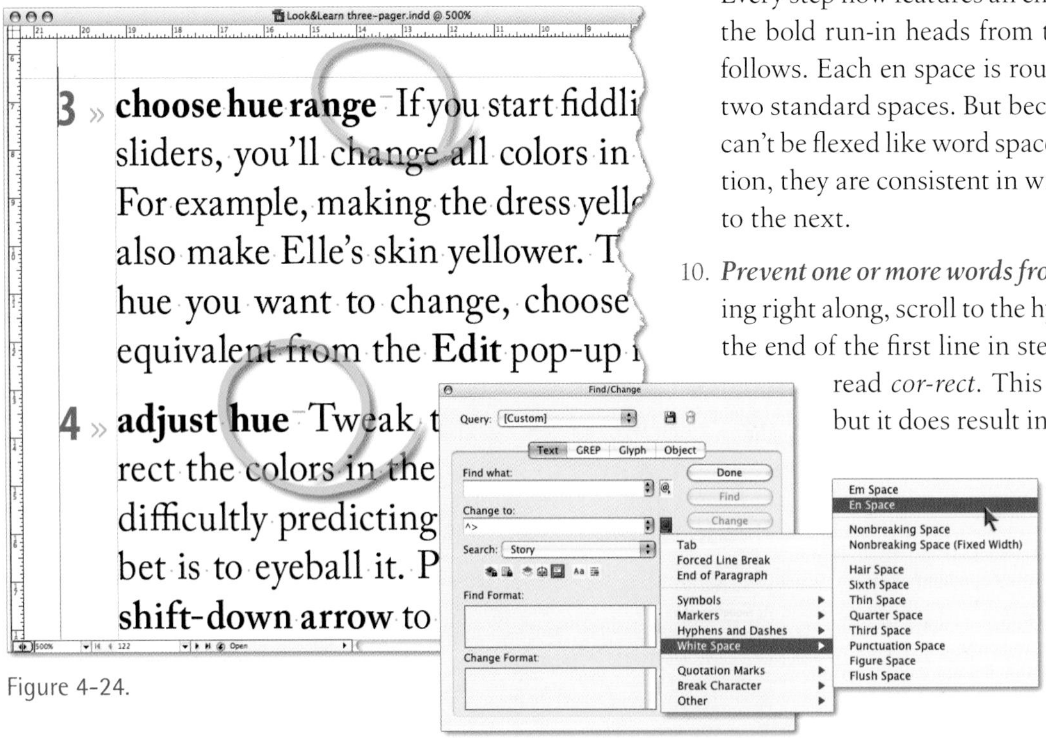

Figure 4-24.

ing in the first line. Fortunately, you can instruct InDesign not to break one or more words. And it's the one time in this exercise that we'll apply a formatting attribute:

- Double-click the word *cor-rect* to select it.
- In the control palette, make sure all the character-level attributes are visible. (If they aren't, click 🄰 or use my shortcut F4.)
- Click the ▾≡ icon on the far right of the palette to bring up the control palette menu. Then choose **No Break**. InDesign deletes the hyphen and squeezes the word *correct* onto the first line. And as fortune would have it, the word fits just fine, as you can see in Figure 4-25.

The No Break command is equally useful for binding several words. It is so useful, in fact, that I've given it a keyboard shortcut. If you loaded my dekeKeys shortcuts (see page xix of the Preface), press Ctrl+Alt+N (⌘-Option-N on the Mac).

11. ***Add a page number to the* Continued *reference.*** Scroll further down the column to the end of step 5 and the italic, blue *Continued* item. Note that the reference ends with the placeholder *xxx*, which I routinely use to stand in for page numbers that I fill in after the chapter is laid out. But InDesign is capable of updating some kinds of page number references automatically, and this turns out to be one of them.

    Double-click in the italic, blue *xxx* to select it, and then right-click and choose **Insert Special Character→Markers**. The following four commands add page number variables that InDesign will update automatically:

    - The Current Page Number command (formerly called Auto Page Number) adds the number assigned to the active page. You can use this handy command to add folios, as I explain in "Pages, Sections, and Text Variables," which begins on 380 in Lesson 9.

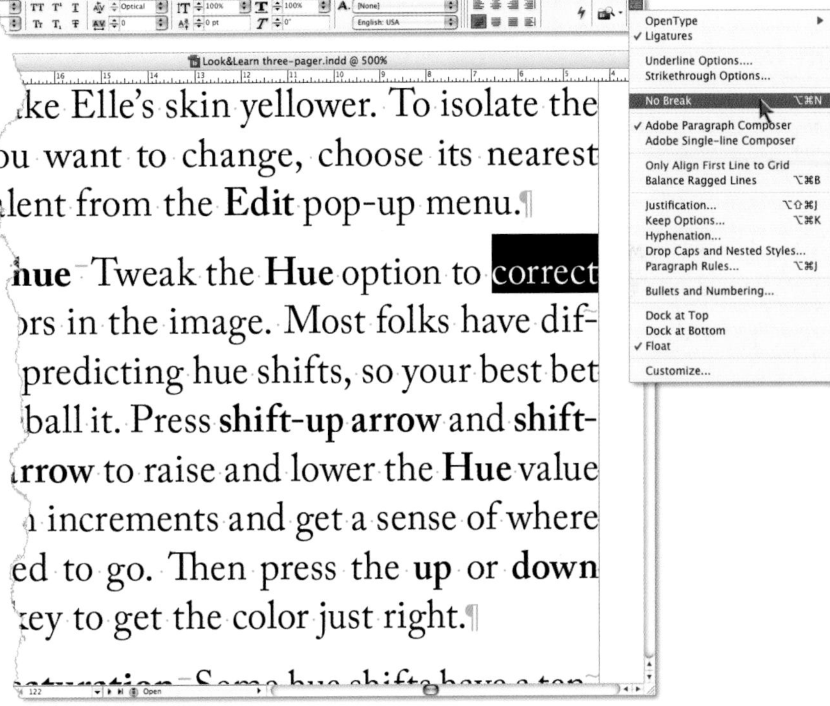

Figure 4-25.

- Choosing Next Page Number or Previous Page Number adds the number of the page that contains the next or previous linked frame in the active story. The document may or may not have an adjacent page. These are the commands you use to complete *Continued on* and *Continued from* references.
- The final command, Section Marker, inserts any Section Marker text you may have entered into the Numbering & Section Options dialog box. Again, I explain this in the "Page Numbers and Sections" exercise in Lesson 9.

Choose **Next Page Number**. As illustrated in Figure 4-26, InDesign replaces the *xxx* with *124*, which is not the next page number but the one after. Just as it should be, InDesign is smart enough to know which page contains the rest of the story.

Bear in mind, InDesign treats every one of the options we've seen in this exercise as a real, if occasionally invisible, character. (The one exception is the No Break command, which is a formatting attribute.) After you create one of these characters, you can copy and paste it in a new location, change its formatting, or even delete it. This goes not only for dashes, spaces, and breaks, but also for the tab and indent-to-here characters from the preceding exercise. Just turn on Type→Show Hidden Characters to see the invisible glyphs, and then edit away.

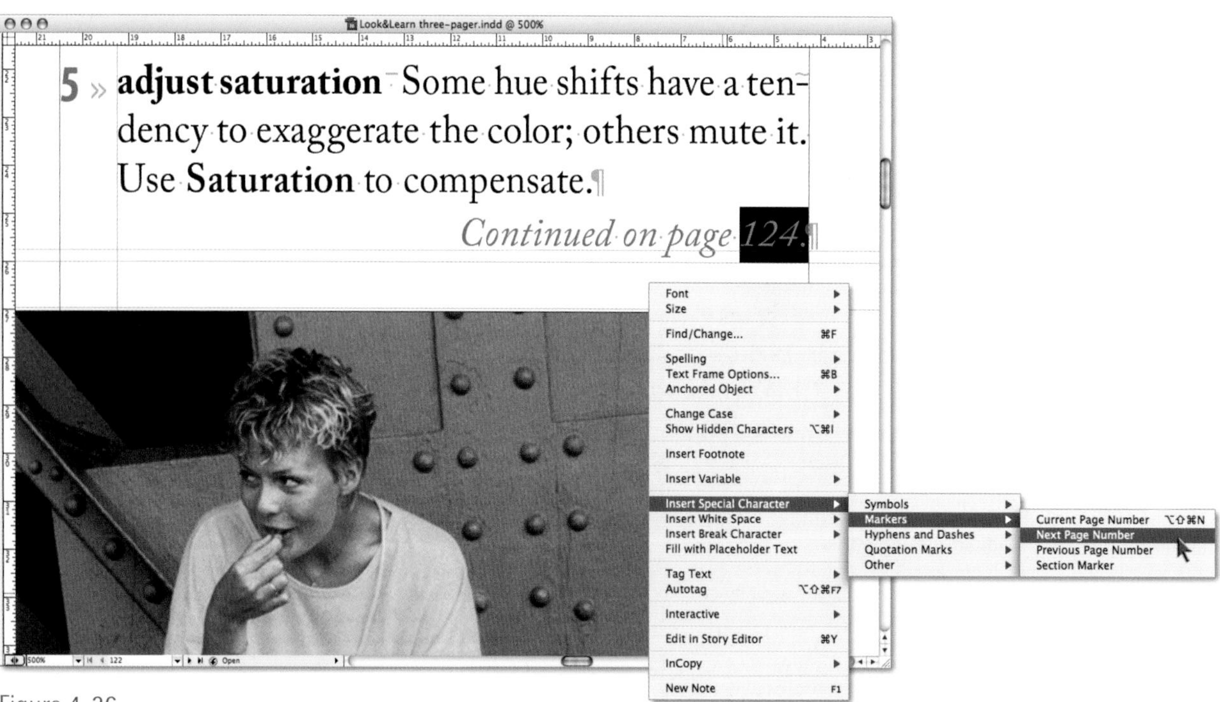

Figure 4-26.

Setting Tabs

Remember typewriters, those clattering, monitorless contraptions that were all the rage back when I was a sapling? Although about one-millionth as capable as computers, they had the distinct advantage of being input and output devices all in one. There wasn't much mystery, because what you typed was what you got. Take tables, for example. If you were an adept typist, you knew how to set tab stops on your typewriter, thereby permitting you to exactly align table entries by pressing the Tab key. If you were a novice, you could accomplish the same thing with a bit more effort by tapping the spacebar a dozen or so times in a row. It was by no means an exact science—one too many taps would throw your columns out of alignment—but it worked.

Not so in InDesign. Unless you use Courier or some other monospaced font, all characters—including spaces—are slightly different in width. And when text is justified, a space character in one line of type is different from a space character in the next. In other words, using the spacebar to align text is a recipe for disaster. And setting tab stops isn't a best practice; it's the *least* you should do. Tables set in InDesign look a heck of a lot better than tables created on a typewriter, but they require a more deliberate approach as well.

In the following steps, you'll format a table entry by setting and adjusting tab stops in the Tabs palette. Just for fun, you'll also learn how to use paragraph rules to improve the legibility of rows. Suffice it to say, if you've ever even considered aligning columns with spaces, this exercise is for you.

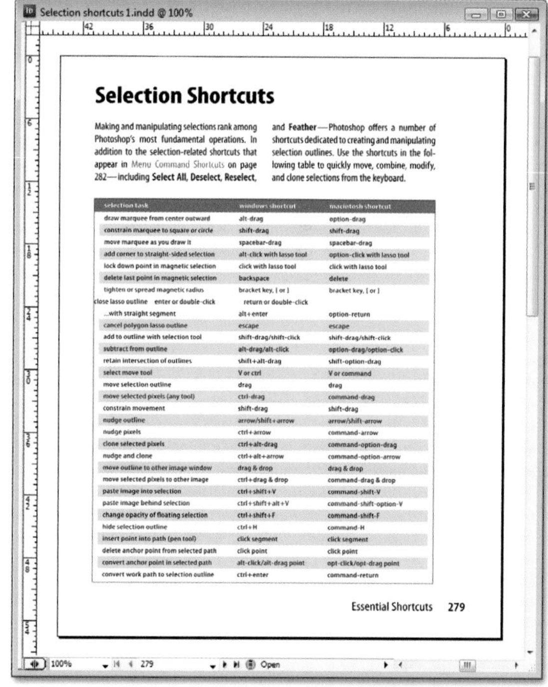

Selection Shortcuts

Making and manipulating selections rank among Photoshop's most fundamental operations. In addition to the selection-related shortcuts that appear in Menu Command Shortcuts on page 282—including **Select All, Deselect, Reselect,** and **Feather**—Photoshop offers a number of shortcuts dedicated to creating and manipulating selection outlines. Use the shortcuts in the following table to quickly move, combine, modify, and clone selections from the keyboard.

selection task	windows shortcut	macintosh shortcut
draw marquee from center outward	alt-drag	option-drag
constrain marquee to square or circle	shift-drag	shift-drag
move marquee as you draw it	spacebar-drag	spacebar-drag
add corner to straight-sided selection	alt-click with lasso tool	option-click with lasso tool
lock down point in magnetic selection	click with lasso tool	click with lasso tool
delete last point in magnetic selection	backspace	delete
tighten or spread magnetic radius	bracket key, [or]	bracket key, [or]
close lasso outline enter or double-click	return or double-click	
...with straight segment	alt+enter	option-return
cancel polygon lasso outline	escape	escape
add to outline with selection tool	shift-drag/shift-click	shift-drag/shift-click
subtract from outline	alt-drag/alt-click	option-drag/option-click
retain intersection of outlines	shift+alt-drag	shift-option-drag
select move tool	V or ctrl	V or command
move selection outline	drag	drag
move selected pixels (any tool)	ctrl-drag	command-drag
constrain movement	shift-drag	shift-drag
nudge outline	arrow/shift+arrow	arrow/shift-arrow
nudge pixels	ctrl+arrow	command-arrow
clone selected pixels	ctrl+alt-drag	command-option-drag
nudge and clone	ctrl+alt+arrow	command-option-arrow
move outline to other image window	drag & drop	drag & drop
move selected pixels to other image	ctrl+drag & drop	command-drag & drop
paste image into selection	ctrl+shift+V	command-shift-V
paste image behind selection	ctrl+shift+alt+V	command-shift-option-V
change opacity of floating selection	ctrl+shift+F	command-shift-F
hide selection outline	ctrl+H	command-H
insert point into path (pen tool)	click segment	click segment
delete anchor point from selected path	click point	click point
convert anchor point in selected path	alt-click/alt-drag point	opt-click/opt-drag point
convert work path to selection outline	ctrl+enter	command-return

Essential Shortcuts 279

Figure 4-27.

1. *Open a document that contains a table.* Open the file called *Selection shortcuts 1.indd*, which you'll find in the *Lesson 04* folder inside *Lesson Files-IDcs3 1on1*. Pictured in Figure 4-27, this page shows a bunch of keyboard shortcuts for selecting images in Photoshop. The table looks pretty nice until you get about a third of the way down, where you come to a row that begins *close lasso outline*. For one thing, this row should be blue. For another, it's out of alignment with everything in the table. Our job is to remedy these problems in the most expedient manner possible.

2. *Show the hidden characters.* The table is constructed with tabs, which are invisible characters. To view the hidden characters lurking inside the table, zoom in on the middle portion of the table and then choose **Type→Show Hidden Characters** or press Ctrl+Alt+I (⌘-Option-I). The document becomes peppered with

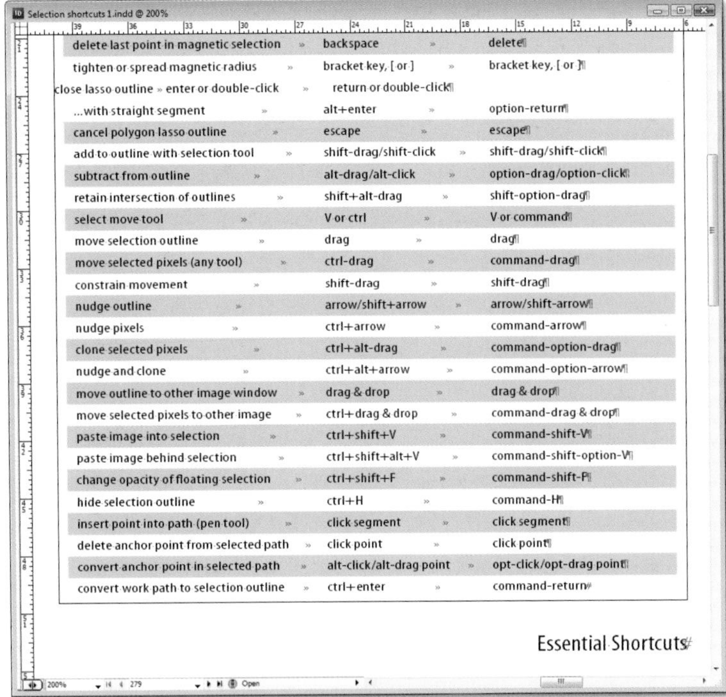

delete last point in magnetic selection	backspace	delete
tighten or spread magnetic radius	bracket key, [or]	bracket key, [or]
close lasso outline » enter or double-click	return or double-click	
...with straight segment	alt+enter	option-return
cancel polygon lasso outline	escape	escape
add to outline with selection tool	shift-drag/shift-click	shift-drag/shift-click
subtract from outline	alt-drag/alt-click	option-drag/option-click
retain intersection of outlines	shift+alt-drag	shift-option-drag
select move tool	V or ctrl	V or command
move selection outline	drag	drag
move selected pixels (any tool)	ctrl-drag	command-drag
constrain movement	shift-drag	shift-drag
nudge outline	arrow/shift+arrow	arrow/shift-arrow
nudge pixels	ctrl+arrow	command-arrow
clone selected pixels	ctrl+alt-drag	command-option-drag
nudge and clone	ctrl+alt+arrow	command-option-arrow
move outline to other image window	drag & drop	drag & drop
move selected pixels to other image	ctrl+drag & drop	command-drag & drop
paste image into selection	ctrl+shift+V	command-shift-V
paste image behind selection	ctrl+shift+alt+V	command-shift-option-V
change opacity of floating selection	ctrl+shift+F	command-shift-F
hide selection outline	ctrl+H	command-H
insert point into path (pen tool)	click segment	click segment
delete anchor point from selected path	click point	click point
convert anchor point in selected path	alt-click/alt-drag point	opt-click/opt-drag point
convert work path to selection outline	ctrl+enter	command-return

Essential Shortcuts

Figure 4-28.

delete last point in magnetic selection	backspace	
tighten or spread magnetic radius	bracket key, [or]	
close lasso outline » enter or double-click	return or double-click	
...with straight segment	alt+enter	
cancel polygon lasso outline	escape	

Figure 4-29.

delete last point in magnetic selection	backspace	
tighten or spread magnetic radius	bracket key, [or]	
close lasso outline »		enter or double-click
...with straight segment	alt+enter	
cancel polygon lasso outline	escape	

Figure 4-30.

little red symbols that indicate the various invisible characters (see Figure 4-28). The » is a tab.

3. ***Position the insertion marker after a wayward tab.*** If it's not already selected, press the T key to select the type tool. Then click between the first tab character and the word *enter* in the misaligned row. Figure 4-29 shows exactly where the insertion marker should be.

4. ***Press the Tab key a few times.*** We want to align the *enter or double-click* entry with the second column, directly below *bracket key, [or]*. Because you can align columns using tab characters, you just need to press Tab a few times to bring the text into alignment, right? So give it a try:

   - Pressing Tab once isn't far enough.
   - Pressing Tab a second time still doesn't do the trick.
   - As Figure 4-30 shows, pressing Tab a third time overshoots the column.

   Why didn't the tabs work? Because a tab character doesn't describe an exact position on the page; it merely moves the text to the next column increment, known as a *tab stop*. Although we can't see these tab stops yet, it's obvious that the neatly aligned rows in this table are obeying a different set of tab stops than the active row. Therefore, to fix the errant row, we need to adjust the tab stops, not heap on more tab characters.

5. ***Delete the three extra tabs.*** As you can see, entering excess tab characters doesn't do any good. So as a rule of thumb, don't use tab characters in series. We now have four consecutive tab characters; to delete the excess three, press Backspace or Delete three times in a row. (Don't delete all four tabs; we still need one!)

6. ***Display the Tabs ruler.*** To gain access to the all-important tab stops, we need to bring up the **Tabs** palette. To do just that, choose **Type→Tabs** or press Ctrl+Shift+T (⌘-Shift-T). Pictured in Figure 4-31, the palette features a small handful of options and a horizontal ruler. You'll be using this ruler to position your tab stops.

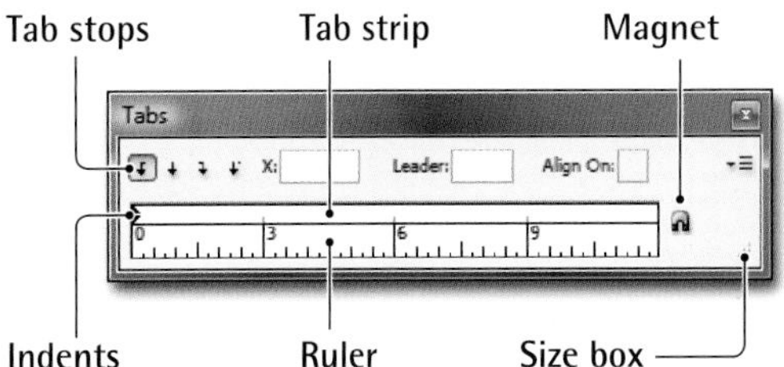

Figure 4-31.

7. ***Align the Tabs ruler to the text that you want to modify.*** InDesign tends to center the Tabs palette on screen. But to be truly useful, the palette ruler needs to line up with the text you want to modify. One way to align the ruler is to move and size the palette manually. A better way is to have InDesign align the palette automatically, which is the purpose of the magnet icon (⋒). Bad news: The magnet is notoriously finicky. Good news: It's great when it works.

   - Make sure the ⋒ icon is active. If it isn't, click in the text again with the type tool.
   - Click the ⋒ icon. Nothing happens; the Tabs palette just sits there like a slug. That's because the infuriating ⋒ needs to be able to see the top of a text block before it can align to it. Idiotic, frankly, but who can argue with an icon?
   - Turns out, the Tabs palette needs not only to see the top of the text block but also sufficient room above the block to place itself. What a diva! Scroll up so that you can see at least an inch of the document above the top of the table.
   - Click the ⋒ again. As if by magic, the Tabs ruler stretches and snaps to the top of the frame, as in Figure 4-32.

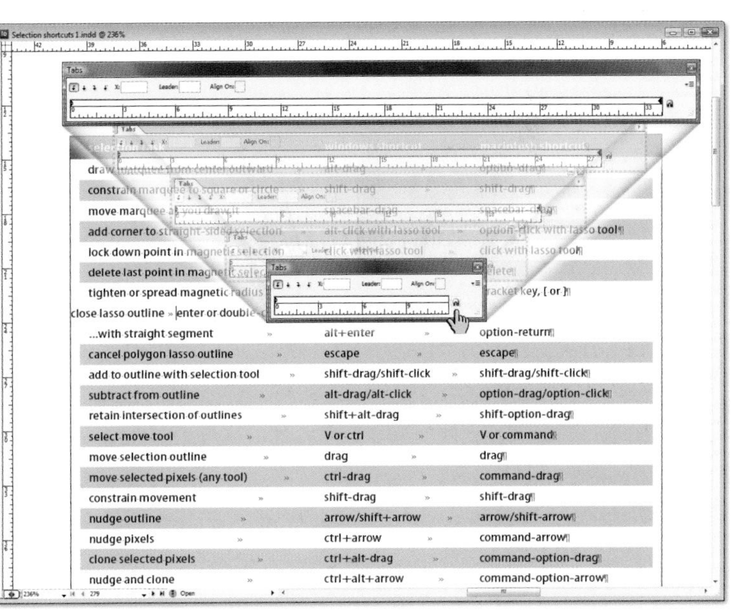
Figure 4-32.

Now that the Tabs palette is properly aligned, you can scroll up or down in the document window all you want. So remember, when auto-aligning the Tabs ruler, make the ⋒ icon happy, which will make *you* happy.

8. ***Indent the row 1 pica to the left.*** Notice the pair of triangles (▸) above the 0 in the Tabs ruler. The top triangle sets the first-line indent; the bottom triangle sets the overall left indent. In this table, every row is its own paragraph, so moving either triangle produces the same results.

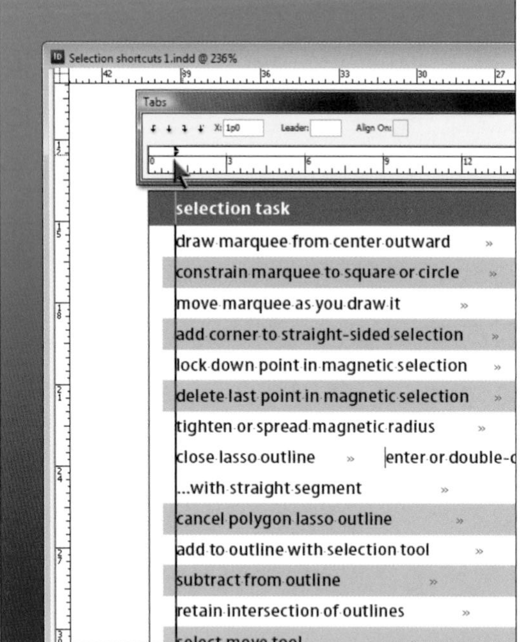

Figure 4-33.

Here's what I want you to do: Drag the bottom triangle to the right exactly 1 pica. You can track the movement on the ruler, with the help of the vertical guideline that drops down into the document window, or by keeping an eye on the X value above the ruler in the Tabs palette. Figure 4-33 shows the guideline and X value at work.

When you drag the bottom triangle (as I want you to do in this step), the top triangle travels along for the ride. However, you can drag the bottom triangle independently. Just press the Shift key and drag it. The result is a hanging indent, like the one we reviewed earlier in the exercise "Lists and Hanging Indents," which began on page 141.

---

9. ***Set a tab stop at 14p6.*** Now to set some tab stops. Click somewhere near the 12-pica point in the space directly above the ruler. A tab stop appears at this position. This specific variety of tab stop, which looks like ↓, is called a *left-justified tab* because the left side of the entry (in our case, *enter or double-click*) aligns to it. Drag the tab stop so that the entry aligns with the second column in the table; the X value should read 14p6, as in Figure 4-34.

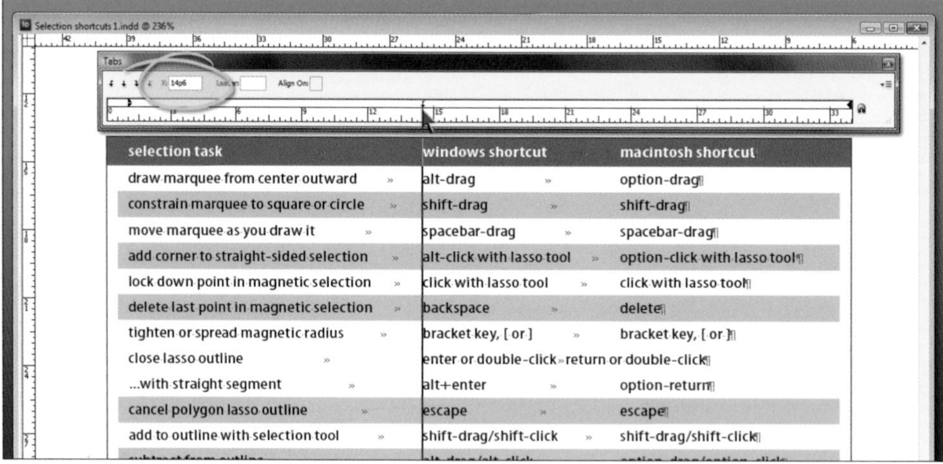

Figure 4-34.

Although we'll stick to left-justified tabs in this table, you can align columns in other ways. To apply a different alignment option, you click one of the icons in the top-left corner of the palette while a tab stop is active. Here's how they work:

- The center-justified tab (↓) centers the entry (such as *enter or double-click*) below the tab stop.
- The right-justified tab (↓) aligns the right edge of the entry with the tab.

- The decimal tab (↓̇) aligns the entry at a character specified in the Align On option box. This setting is most frequently used to align a column of numbers by decimal points, which is why the default Align On value is a period.

To cycle through the different types of tabs, Alt-click (or Option-click) the tab stop in the strip above the ruler.

---

10. ***Set another tab stop at 23p6.*** Click in the strip above the ruler to the right of the existing tab stop to create another one. The *return or double-click* entry jumps into alignment. Notice that the new stop is surrounded by a gray or colored rectangle; this indicates that the stop is selected, which permits you to reposition the stop numerically. Select the **X** value and change it to 23p6. Then press the Enter or Return key. This aligns the entry with the third row, as in Figure 4-35.

You may have noticed that you can't press Backspace or Delete to delete a tab stop, even if it's selected. Instead, you have to drag the tab stop out of the Tabs palette. To delete all tab stops, choose Clear All from the palette menu.

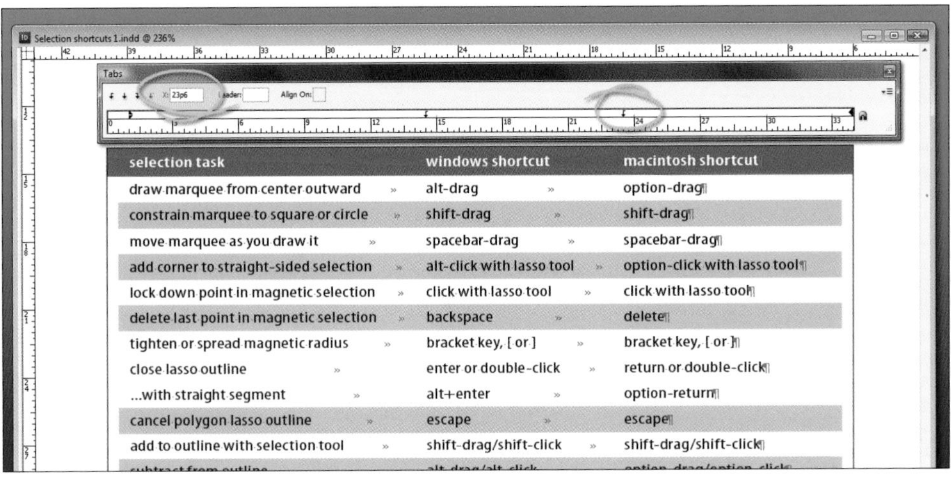

selection task	windows shortcut	macintosh shortcut
draw marquee from center outward	alt-drag	option-drag
constrain marquee to square or circle	shift-drag	shift-drag
move marquee as you draw it	spacebar-drag	spacebar-drag
add corner to straight-sided selection	alt-click with lasso tool	option-click with lasso tool
lock down point in magnetic selection	click with lasso tool	click with lasso tool
delete last point in magnetic selection	backspace	delete
tighten or spread magnetic radius	bracket key, [or]	bracket key, [or]
close lasso outline	enter or double-click	return or double-click
...with straight segment	alt+enter	option-return
cancel polygon lasso outline	escape	escape
add to outline with selection tool	shift-drag/shift-click	shift-drag/shift-click

Figure 4-35.

PEARL OF WISDOM

Before we depart the Tabs palette, you should know about one more option. The Leader option lets you specify a *tab leader*, which is a series of characters that fills the space between the entry before a tab and the entry after a tab. A common example of a tab leader is a series of repeating periods between a chapter name and page number in a table of contents. To create a tab leader, simply select a tab stop, type one or more characters in the Leader option box, and press Enter or Return.

11. *Choose the Paragraph Rules command.* Our final task is to create the blue background that should appear in the newly aligned row. Click the ▾≡ icon on the right side of the control palette and choose the **Paragraph Rules** command, or press Ctrl+Alt+J (⌘-Option-J on the Mac). InDesign responds by displaying the **Paragraph Rules** dialog box. Rather than providing a list of rules concerning paragraphs, this dialog box lets you place a straight line (or *rule*) above, below, or even behind the paragraphs in your document.

12. *Turn on the paragraph rule and adjust the settings.* Look at Figure 4-36 to see exactly how I want you to set the options in the Paragraph Rules dialog box. Here's the lowdown:

    - Turn on **Preview** so you can see what you're doing.
    - Select **Rule Below** from the top-left pop-up menu to create a rule below the active paragraph. Then turn on the **Rule On** check box. At this point, all the remaining work may be done for you, but it's worth running through the rest of the options to see how they work.
    - **Weight** controls how heavy the rule will be; set this value to 14 points.
    - The **Type** pop-up lets you select from different line patterns. Choose **Solid** for a plain, unbroken rule.
    - From the **Color** pop-up menu, choose **Pantone 285 CVU**, which is the spot color used in this document. Reduce the **Tint** value to 25 percent to create a light version of the color that won't interfere with the legibility of the table entries.
    - Turn on **Overprint Stroke** to print the black text on top of the blue rule. Technically, this setting is redundant—black is set to overprint by default in InDesign—but if the person printing my document turns black overprinting off, I want to be covered.
    - The **Width** option determines how far the rule extends across the row; set this to **Column**.
    - **Offset** determines where the rule appears in relation to the baseline of the text. Counterintuitively, positive values lower the rule and negative values raise it. Enter –0p9.5 to raise the rule so it fits behind the text rather than below it.
    - Set both **Indent** options to 0p6 to scoot the rule 6 points in on the left and right sides.

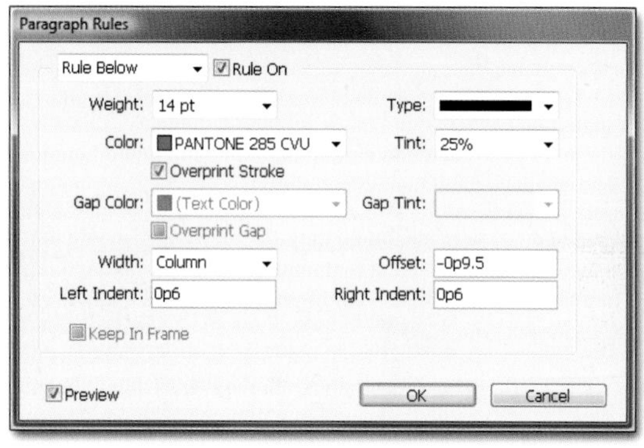

Figure 4-36.

13. ***Accept the rule and save the document.*** Click **OK** to accept the new blue rule. As Figure 4-37 shows, the wayward row has finally joined the fold. We'll continue working on this document in the next exercise, so you might as well take a moment and save your work. Choose **File→Save As**, name your document "My table.indd," and save it in the *Lesson 04* folder.

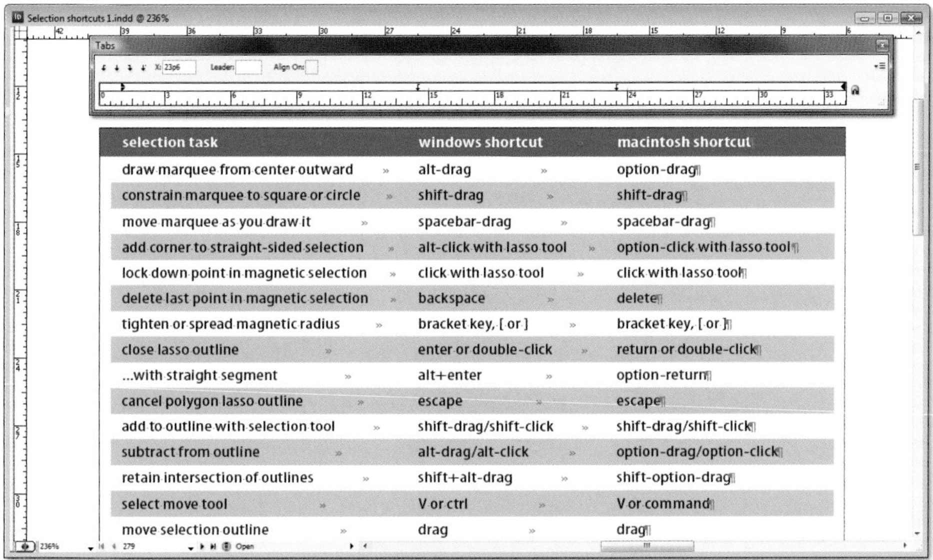

selection task	windows shortcut	macintosh shortcut
draw marquee from center outward	alt-drag	option-drag
constrain marquee to square or circle	shift-drag	shift-drag
move marquee as you draw it	spacebar-drag	spacebar-drag
add corner to straight-sided selection	alt-click with lasso tool	option-click with lasso tool
lock down point in magnetic selection	click with lasso tool	click with lasso tool
delete last point in magnetic selection	backspace	delete
tighten or spread magnetic radius	bracket key, [or]	bracket key, [or]
close lasso outline	enter or double-click	return or double-click
...with straight segment	alt+enter	option-return
cancel polygon lasso outline	escape	escape
add to outline with selection tool	shift-drag/shift-click	shift-drag/shift-click
subtract from outline	alt-drag/alt-click	option-drag/option-click
retain intersection of outlines	shift+alt-drag	shift-option-drag
select move tool	V or ctrl	V or command
move selection outline	drag	drag

Figure 4-37.

Creating a Full-Fledged Table

I didn't want to mention this in the last exercise—you seemed to be having so much fun using tabs to polish that table—but tabs aren't necessarily the best tools for creating tables. Tabs work well when all the entries fit neatly onto a single line of text, as they have so far. But in my experience, single-line tables are the exception rather than the rule. More often, at least one entry wants to break onto multiple lines, at which point a tabbed table falls apart.

So in this exercise, we're going to upgrade to the better solution, InDesign's full-fledged Table function. Specifically, you'll take the tabbed table from the last exercise and convert it to a spreadsheet-style table, in which each entry is relegated to its own private *cell*. You'll also learn how to style the table to split it over multiple pages.

1. ***Open a document with a tab-based table.*** If you still have open the *My table.indd* document that you saved in the preceding exercise, you're all set. If you didn't work through the last exercise or you neglected to save the file, open *Selection shortcuts 2.indd*, located in the *Lesson 04* folder inside *Lesson Files-IDcs3 1on1*.

2. ***Hide the tabs and the Tabs palette.*** The red tab characters and Tabs palette are now nothing more than distractions. So press Ctrl+Alt+I (⌘-Option-I on the Mac) to hide the tabs. Then go ahead and close the **Tabs** palette.

3. ***Select all the text in the table.*** Armed with the type tool, click anywhere inside the table. Then choose **Edit→Select All** or press Ctrl+A (⌘-A) to select all the text in the table.

4. ***Choose the Convert Text to Table command.*** If you were creating a table from scratch, you would draw a frame with the type tool and choose Table→Insert Table. But because we already have a tabbed table, we can convert it. Choose **Table→Convert Text to Table** to display the **Convert Text to Table** dialog box, which appears in Figure 4-38.

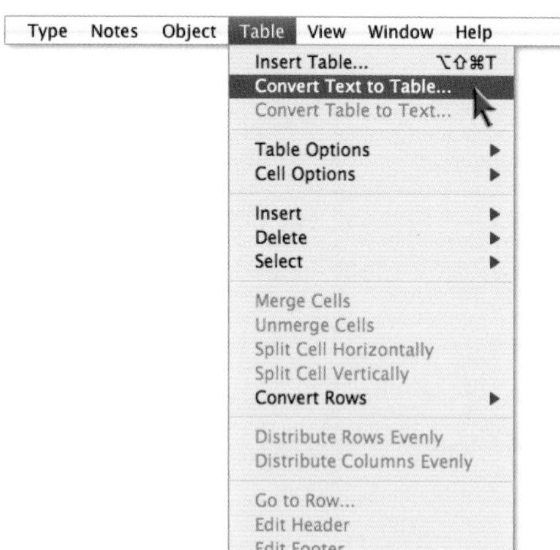

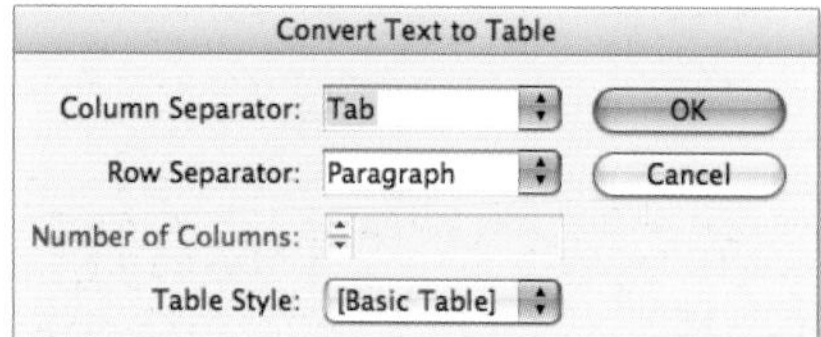

Figure 4-38.

5. ***Click OK.*** We want the columns in our table to be based on tab characters and the rows to be based on paragraph breaks, so the default settings are fine. Click **OK** to create the table shown in Figure 4-39. The automatic conversion isn't half bad. But we have some spacing problems, and the paragraph rules and cell borders are for the birds. We'll fix all that.

6. ***Fix the table indent.*** To the untutored eye, our table appears to fill the text block. But in InDesign, a table is actually an element—like a character of type—inside a frame. As things stand now, that element is indented 1 pica, as you specified back in Step 8 of the preceding exercise (see page 161). To remove that indent, click in the vertical white strip to the left of the table. You should see a table-high blinking insertion marker. Assuming that the paragraph options remain visible in the control palette, press Ctrl+6 (or ⌘-6) to highlight the first option box, which controls the left indent. Type 0 and press Enter or Return.

7. ***Add a pica to the width of the table.*** The table is a pica too narrow to fit its frame. Click a word in the table to move the insertion marker into the table text. (Make sure to click when your cursor appears as an I-beam.) Then move your cursor over the top-left rectangular cell in the table to get the ⬇ arrow and click to select the first column. Near the middle of the control palette, click the ⊟ icon under the words **At Least** to select the current column width, 13p6. Change that value to 14p6 and press Enter or Return.

8. ***Select all the text in the table.*** Now to format the table. Choose **Table→Select→Table** or press Ctrl+Alt+A (⌘-Option-A on the Mac) to select all the text inside the table.

9. ***Turn off the paragraph rules.*** Let's start by dismissing the paragraph rules. Press Ctrl+Alt+J (or ⌘-Option-J). Alternatively, you can display the Paragraph palette and choose Paragraph Rules from the palette menu. (You can no longer access the Paragraph Rules command from the control palette, because the latter now displays table options.) Inside the **Paragraph Rules** dialog box, make sure the **Rule Below** option remains active. A square or dash appears inside the **Rule On** check box. This indicates that the rule is sometimes on and sometimes off inside the selection. To get rid of the paragraph rules, click once in the check box to change the dash to a check mark and then click again to eliminate the check mark. Click **OK**.

10. ***Remove the borders from the cells.*** As shown in Figure 4-40, the disjointed blue lines are gone from the table. But the cells (the rectangular intersections of rows and columns) continue to exhibit borders, which I find obtrusive. I could get rid of these borders by choosing Table→Cell Options→Strokes and Fills and then working my way through a dialog box, but there's an easier way:

    - Note that the control palette contains a score of options that let you change how you format a table. On the far right is a grid (labeled ❶ in Figure 4-41 on the next page—I know, it's a drag, but this page is full). Check that all lines in the grid are blue. If they aren't, triple-click any line in the grid to select them all. This shows you that all borders in the table are active and ready to accept changes.
    - Click the stroke icon below the zoom tool in the toolbox (❷) to target the color of the borders. The icon should look like ⧉.
    - Click the ☒ icon near the bottom-right corner of the toolbox (❸), or press the ⁄ key. The borders are now invisible, just as they should be.

The one remaining border is a rectangle around the entire table. That happens to be an outline I applied to the text frame itself, and I want to leave it in place.

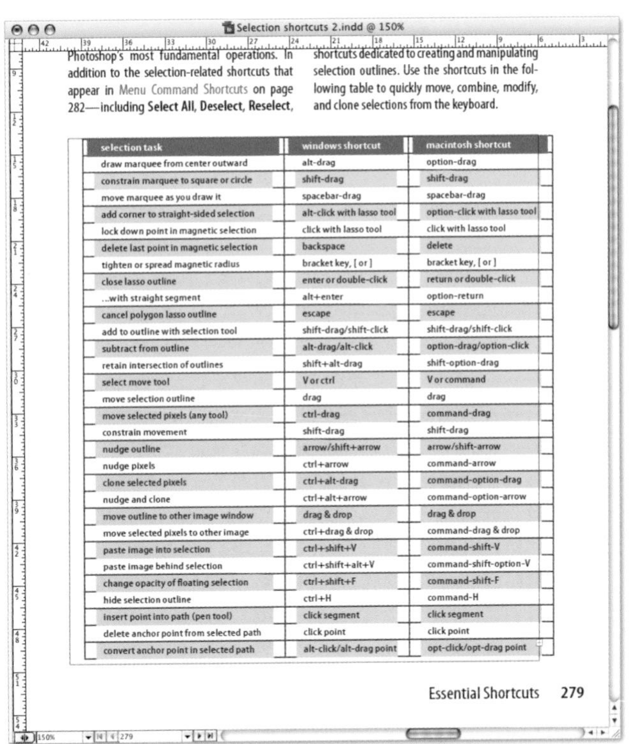

Selection shortcuts 2.indd @ 150%

Photoshop's most fundamental operations. In addition to the selection-related shortcuts that appear in Menu Command Shortcuts on page 282—including **Select All, Deselect, Reselect,** shortcuts dedicated to creating and manipulating selection outlines. Use the shortcuts in the following table to quickly move, combine, modify, and clone selections from the keyboard.

selection task	windows shortcut	macintosh shortcut
draw marquee from center outward	alt-drag	option-drag
constrain marquee to square or circle	shift-drag	shift-drag
move marquee as you draw it	spacebar-drag	spacebar-drag
add corner to straight-sided selection	alt-click with lasso tool	option-click with lasso tool
lock down point in magnetic selection	click with lasso tool	click with lasso tool
delete last point in magnetic selection	backspace	delete
tighten or spread magnetic radius	bracket key, [or]	bracket key, [or]
close lasso outline	enter or double-click	return or double-click
...with straight segment	alt+enter	option-return
cancel polygon lasso outline	escape	escape
add to outline with selection tool	shift-drag/shift-click	shift-drag/shift-click
subtract from outline	alt-drag/alt-click	option-drag/option-click
retain intersection of outlines	shift+alt-drag	shift-option-drag
select move tool	V or ctrl	V or command
move selection outline	drag	drag
move selected pixels (any tool)	ctrl-drag	command-drag
constrain movement	shift-drag	shift-drag
nudge outline	arrow/shift+arrow	arrow/shift-arrow
nudge pixels	ctrl+arrow	command-arrow
clone selected pixels	ctrl+alt-drag	command-option-drag
nudge and clone	ctrl+alt+arrow	command-option-arrow
move outline to other image window	drag & drop	drag & drop
move selected pixels to other image	ctrl+drag & drop	command-drag & drop
paste image into selection	ctrl+shift+V	command-shift-V
paste image behind selection	ctrl+shift+alt+V	command-shift-option-V
change opacity of floating selection	ctrl+shift+F	command-shift-F
hide selection outline	ctrl+H	command-H
insert point into path (pen tool)	click segment	click segment
delete anchor point from selected path	click point	click point
convert anchor point in selected path	alt-click/alt-drag point	opt-click/opt-drag point

Essential Shortcuts 279

Figure 4-39.

Selection shortcuts 2.indd @ 150%

Photoshop's most fundamental operations. In addition to the selection-related shortcuts that appear in Menu Command Shortcuts on page 282—including **Select All, Deselect, Reselect,** shortcuts dedicated to creating and manipulating selection outlines. Use the shortcuts in the following table to quickly move, combine, modify, and clone selections from the keyboard.

draw marquee from center outward	alt-drag	option-drag
constrain marquee to square or circle	shift-drag	shift-drag
move marquee as you draw it	spacebar-drag	spacebar-drag
add corner to straight-sided selection	alt-click with lasso tool	option-click with lasso tool
lock down point in magnetic selection	click with lasso tool	click with lasso tool
delete last point in magnetic selection	backspace	delete
tighten or spread magnetic radius	bracket key, [or]	bracket key, [or]
close lasso outline	enter or double-click	return or double-click
...with straight segment	alt+enter	option-return
cancel polygon lasso outline	escape	escape
add to outline with selection tool	shift-drag/shift-click	shift-drag/shift-click
subtract from outline	alt-drag/alt-click	option-drag/option-click
retain intersection of outlines	shift+alt-drag	shift-option-drag
select move tool	V or ctrl	V or command
move selection outline	drag	drag
move selected pixels (any tool)	ctrl-drag	command-drag
constrain movement	shift-drag	shift-drag
nudge outline	arrow/shift+arrow	arrow/shift-arrow
nudge pixels	ctrl+arrow	command-arrow
clone selected pixels	ctrl+alt-drag	command-option-drag
nudge and clone	ctrl+alt+arrow	command-option-arrow
move outline to other image window	drag & drop	drag & drop
move selected pixels to other image	ctrl+drag & drop	command-drag & drop
paste image into selection	ctrl+shift+V	command-shift-V
paste image behind selection	ctrl+shift+alt+V	command-shift-option-V
change opacity of floating selection	ctrl+shift+F	command-shift-F
hide selection outline	ctrl+H	command-H
insert point into path (pen tool)	click segment	click segment
delete anchor point from selected path	click point	click point
convert anchor point in selected path	alt-click/alt-drag point	opt-click/opt-drag point

Essential Shortcuts 279

Figure 4-40.

11. ***Restore the alternating pattern.*** You may have noticed that the top row of text has turned invisible. It's really white text against a white background. To see the text again, we need to restore the alternating pattern of blue and white rows.

draw marquee from center outward	alt-drag	option-drag
constrain marquee to square or circle	shift-drag	shift-drag
move marquee as you draw it	spacebar-drag	spacebar-drag
add corner to straight-sided selection	alt-click with lasso tool	option-click with lasso tool
lock down point in magnetic selection	click with lasso tool	click with lasso tool
delete last point in magnetic selection	backspace	delete
tighten or spread magnetic radius	bracket key, [or]	bracket key, [or]
close lasso outline	enter or double-click	return or double-click
...with straight segment	alt+enter	option-return
cancel polygon lasso outline	escape	escape
add to outline with selection tool	shift-drag/shift-click	shift-drag/shift-click
subtract from outline	alt-drag/alt-click	option-drag/option-click
retain intersection of outlines	shift+alt-drag	shift-option-drag
select move tool	V or ctrl	V or command
move selection outline	drag	drag
move selected pixels (any tool)	ctrl-drag	command-drag
constrain movement	shift-drag	shift-drag
nudge outline	arrow/shift+arrow	arrow/shift-arrow
nudge pixels	ctrl+arrow	command-arrow
clone selected pixels	ctrl+alt-drag	command-option-drag
nudge and clone	ctrl+alt+arrow	command-option-arrow
move outline to other image window	drag & drop	drag & drop
move selected pixels to other image	ctrl+drag & drop	command-drag & drop
paste image into selection	ctrl+shift+V	command-shift-V
paste image behind selection	ctrl+shift+alt+V	command-shift-option-V
change opacity of floating selection	ctrl+shift+F	command-shift-F
hide selection outline	ctrl+H	command-H
insert point into path (pen tool)	click segment	click segment
delete anchor point from selected path	click point	click point
convert anchor point in selected path	alt-click/alt-drag point	opt-click/opt-drag point

Figure 4-41.

Choose **Table→Table Options→Alternating Fills** to bring up the **Fills** section of the **Table Options** dialog box. Then apply the settings shown in Figure 4-42:

- Turn on **Preview** in the lower-left corner of the dialog box. Why is this check box ever off?
- Choose the **Every Other Row** option from the **Alternating Pattern** pop-up menu to set every other row as a different color.
- Choose **Pantone 285 CVU** from the **Color** pop-up menu on the left side of the dialog box. This establishes the color for the first alternating row. Set the left **Tint** value to 25 percent.
- Turn on the **Overprint** check box. As I mentioned in the last exercise, this is redundant. But backups are redundant, and backups are good.
- The right-hand **Color** option sets the color for the next row. Leave it set to **[None]**.
- Set the **Skip First** value to 1 row. I want the first row of the table to be white. That may not make sense, given that the top row has white text in it. But trust me, it all works in the end.

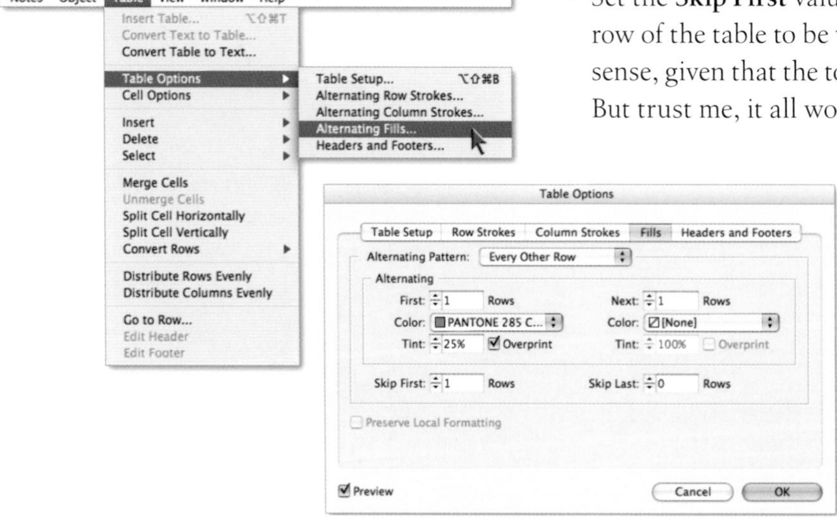

Figure 4-42.

12. ***Click the OK button.*** Click **OK** to apply the alternating row colors. You might also want to deselect the table by clicking inside it with the I-beam cursor so you can see your changes, as shown in Figure 4-43. When I created this document in 2000, back before InDesign added its Table feature, I had to color each alternating line independently. This is so much easier, it makes me cry.

13. ***Select the top row of the table.*** Our next task is to format the top row so that it's no longer invisible. Click in the top row to set the insertion marker. Then choose **Table→Select→Row** or press Ctrl+3 (⌘-3 on the Mac). InDesign selects the entire row.

14. ***Fill the cells with blue.*** Even selected, you can't see your white-on-white text. So let's set it against a different color:

    - Go to the bottom of the toolbox and select the fill icon (labeled ❶ in Figure 4-44), so it looks like ◪. Or press the X key. This targets the interior of the selected cells.
    - Choose **Window→Swatches** or press F5 to display the **Swatches** palette.
    - Select the blue swatch named **Pantone 285 CVU** (❷ in the figure).

Figure 4-44 shows the top row inverted—black against orange—because the text is highlighted. But really, the text is white against cobalt blue.

Photoshop's most fundamental operations. In addition to the selection-related shortcuts that appear in Menu Command Shortcuts on page 282—including **Select All, Deselect, Reselect,** shortcuts dedicated to creating and manipulating selection outlines. Use the shortcuts in the following table to quickly move, combine, modify, and clone selections from the keyboard.

draw marquee from center outward	alt-drag	option-drag
constrain marquee to square or circle	shift-drag	shift-drag
move marquee as you draw it	spacebar-drag	spacebar-drag
add corner to straight-sided selection	alt-click with lasso tool	option-click with lasso tool
lock down point in magnetic selection	click with lasso tool	click with lasso tool
delete last point in magnetic selection	backspace	delete
tighten or spread magnetic radius	bracket key, [or]	bracket key, [or]
close lasso outline	enter or double-click	return or double-click
...with straight segment	alt+enter	option-return
cancel polygon lasso outline	escape	escape
add to outline with selection tool	shift-drag/shift-click	shift-drag/shift-click
subtract from outline	alt-drag/alt-click	option-drag/option-click
retain intersection of outlines	shift+alt-drag	shift-option-drag
select move tool	V or ctrl	V or command
move selection outline	drag	drag
move selected pixels (any tool)	ctrl-drag	command-drag
constrain movement	shift-drag	shift-drag
nudge outline	arrow/shift+arrow	arrow/shift-arrow
nudge pixels	ctrl+arrow	command-arrow
clone selected pixels	ctrl+alt-drag	command-option-drag
nudge and clone	ctrl+alt+arrow	command-option-arrow
move outline to other image window	drag & drop	drag & drop
move selected pixels to other image	ctrl+drag & drop	command-drag & drop
paste image into selection	ctrl+shift+V	command-shift-V
paste image behind selection	ctrl+shift+alt+V	command-shift-option-V
change opacity of floating selection	ctrl+shift+F	command-shift-F
hide selection outline	ctrl+H	command-H
insert point into path (pen tool)	click segment	click segment
delete anchor point from selected path	click point	click point
convert anchor point in selected path	alt-click/alt-drag point	opt-click/opt-drag point

Essential Shortcuts 279

Figure 4-43.

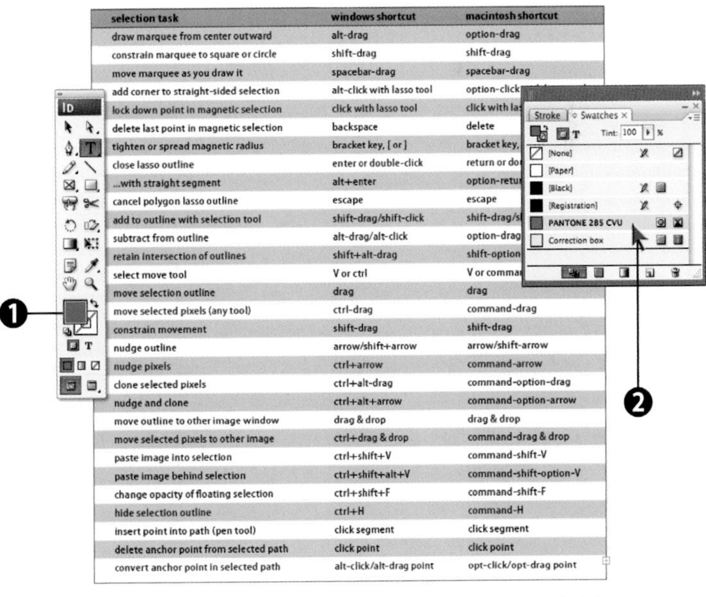

selection task	windows shortcut	macintosh shortcut
draw marquee from center outward	alt-drag	option-drag
constrain marquee to square or circle	shift-drag	shift-drag
move marquee as you draw it	spacebar-drag	spacebar-drag
add corner to straight-sided selection	alt-click with lasso tool	option-click
lock down point in magnetic selection	click with lasso tool	click with la
delete last point in magnetic selection	backspace	delete
tighten or spread magnetic radius	bracket key, [or]	bracket key,
close lasso outline	enter or double-click	return or do
...with straight segment	alt+enter	option-retu
cancel polygon lasso outline	escape	escape
add to outline with selection tool	shift-drag/shift-click	shift-drag/s
subtract from outline	alt-drag/alt-click	option-drag
retain intersection of outlines	shift+alt-drag	shift-option
select move tool	V or ctrl	V or comma
move selection outline	drag	drag
move selected pixels (any tool)	ctrl-drag	command-drag
constrain movement	shift-drag	shift-drag
nudge outline	arrow/shift+arrow	arrow/shift-arrow
nudge pixels	ctrl+arrow	command-arrow
clone selected pixels	ctrl+alt-drag	command-option-drag
nudge and clone	ctrl+alt+arrow	command-option-arrow
move outline to other image window	drag & drop	drag & drop
move selected pixels to other image	ctrl+drag & drop	command-drag & drop
paste image into selection	ctrl+shift+V	command-shift-V
paste image behind selection	ctrl+shift+alt+V	command-shift-option-V
change opacity of floating selection	ctrl+shift+F	command-shift-F
hide selection outline	ctrl+H	command-H
insert point into path (pen tool)	click segment	click segment
delete anchor point from selected path	click point	click point
convert anchor point in selected path	alt-click/alt-drag point	opt-click/opt-drag point

Figure 4-44.

PEARL OF WISDOM

Each of the entries in the first column is a title for the column under it. In other words, the first row is a *header*, which has special significance in InDesign. Notice the red ⊞ in the bottom-right corner of the text block. When you converted the tabbed text into a table, the rows expanded slightly and created one row of overflow text. You could shorten the rows by choosing Table→Cell Options→Text and reducing the Top or Bottom value. But I'd prefer to flow the table onto a second page. Naturally, if a table is going to spread over two pages, you need the header to repeat at the top of the second page. Thankfully, InDesign's headers can do exactly that.

Selection shortcuts 2.indd @ 150%

Photoshop's most fundamental operations. In addition to the selection-related shortcuts that appear in Menu Command Shortcuts on page 282—including **Select All, Deselect, Reselect,** shortcuts dedicated to creating and manipulating selection outlines. Use the shortcuts in the following table to quickly move, combine, modify, and clone selections from the keyboard.

selection task	windows shortcut	macintosh shortcut
draw marquee from center outward	alt-drag	option-drag
constrain marquee to square or circle	shift-drag	shift-drag
move marquee as you draw it	spacebar-drag	spacebar-drag
add corner to straight-sided selection	alt-click with lasso tool	option-click with lasso tool
lock down point in magnetic selection	click with lasso tool	click with lasso tool
delete last point in magnetic selection	backspace	delete
tighten or spread magnetic radius	bracket key, [or]	bracket key, [or]
close lasso outline	enter or double-click	return or double-click
...with straight segment	alt+enter	option-return
cancel polygon lasso outline	escape	escape
add to outline with selection tool	shift-drag/shift-click	shift-drag/shift-click
subtract from outline	alt-drag/alt-click	option-drag/option-click
retain intersection of outlines	shift+alt-drag	shift-option-drag
select move tool	V or ctrl	V or command
move selection outline	drag	drag
move selected pixels (any tool)	ctrl-drag	command-drag
constrain movement	shift-drag	shift-drag
nudge outline	arrow/shift+arrow	arrow/shift-arrow
nudge pixels	ctrl+arrow	command-arrow
clone selected pixels	ctrl+alt-drag	command-option-drag
nudge and clone	ctrl+alt+arrow	command-option-arrow
move outline to other image window	drag & drop	drag & drop
move selected pixels to other image	ctrl+drag & drop	command-drag & drop
paste image into selection	ctrl+shift+V	command-shift-V
paste image behind selection	ctrl+shift+alt+V	command-shift-option-V
change opacity of floating selection	ctrl+shift+F	command-shift-F
hide selection outline	ctrl+H	command-H
insert point into path (pen tool)	click segment	click segment
delete anchor point from selected path	click point	click point
convert anchor point in selected path	alt-click/alt-drag point	opt-click/opt-drag point

Essential Shortcuts 279

Figure 4-45.

Selection shortcuts 2.indd @ 150%

selection task	windows shortcut	macintosh shortcut
delete anchor point from selected path	click point	click point
convert anchor point in selected path	alt-click/alt-drag point	opt-click/opt-drag point
convert work path to selection outline	ctrl+enter	command-return

Ommy numsandiat lum exerat

Sis am velesto odolore raesse dolortionsed dolorper susci tie endigniat vulla conse tisit nos non hendreet, velenit utpatinis adigna facipit vel dolorperit lor summy num ea feu feu faciniat praesenim vulla feugait dolenim eum quat accummy nullum dolenibh exer si.

Ed tat, vero del exer alismodolore vel do commy nissim vero dolut lum vel ullut iustrud exer si bla conulput aut praessim irit ilisit niamconse velis aliquam, velesse feummod magna at. Ut elent alit wis adip ent eugait ulput velis eriureetummy num alit del ut vendre magna faci te veliquisl euguer si.

Sed dionse corem zzrilis iscinis modiam in eum volortis diat. Duipit, volorti smolessent il et delendre moloreet vulputa tumsand ionsed ming eugiam iniam, quam dui erostissim vulput enit utet, conulla feugait dolendr erostrud te et la at, quisl ut praesto odiam dignim deliquat. Ut laore del ulla feugiam quis nulputatem zzriure tet, sed magna am nonsenis ex et lor iureet lan volore duip esto dolore dip et etumsandit il utpat at lore duis aut velisi.

Del esto dolobore feugait landiat praestio commodo do odiamet ulla feugait irilla conulputpat eugait aliquis modolor eraesse elenibh eugiam incilit at. Alisi.

Ignit ilisit, velessi. Im num zzriliquat ut venibh ex eum volor augait vulputpat, conse eugiat, quam irit augiat, corem adit lore doloreet, senim euiscilla feuguero dit augiam vercili quismolortie tatum volorem quis dui ex eum quat dunt ad minim quat, vel utpat iure faci blan velenis modolesto odolorpero dolorer sismodit lutat eliquip endre voloreet laor si.

Ureet venit, velis nisim ex et velesed diam illut nissim quiscil ismolesting eraessi bla feumsan henim incilit laore dit wissi. Magnim quisi. Magnim venim quip euis at, quisismodio odolorp erillamcon hendion henis elit, si. Conseniam nostion ut wiscil dolor si exer aut et wismolore ercipis num ad enim zzrit aut alit lumsan hent augiat. Duis ad dolum vero od magna feuisi tatuerosto dolobor sequam, quismodignim del utem zzrit nis adiam, quisciliqui tem adiatue core magna alit aciliquis digniatis augait velesto consequ ismodolor sequism odolobo rperit non ese magnis ad modipsustrud magna faccum iure diam, sed esequat, cor in ulputat nisit num incilis non volum adit vel ipisis nibh et praesed molut aute te magniam vulla conse dolese tat.

Ut vent autpat adit la feum quis eumsan ulla faccum veliquam ipsumsan henisit iure duipsum nullut velisim iurerae senibh ex euissecte veros alis alisi. Rud tate diatue dolore diam, volorperat. Ut estie

Figure 4-46.

15. ***Identify the row as a header.*** InDesign doesn't recognize a header automatically; it needs to be told. Make sure the first row of the table is still selected and choose **Table→Convert Rows→To Header**. While no visible change occurs in the first row, the blue and white alternating lines reverse in all subsequent rows. Why? At the end of Step 11, we told InDesign to skip the first row. That first row used to be the top row, but now that you've designated the top row as the header, the first row becomes the one below the header, thus matching the color scheme of the original shortcuts table.

16. ***Deselect the table and show the guides.*** Assuming you loaded my dekeKeys shortcuts (see page xix of the Preface), press Enter on the keypad to deselect the table and select the black arrow tool. Or just click the black arrow tool in the toolbox. Then choose **View→Grids & Guides→Show Guides** or press Ctrl+; (⌘-;) to show all guides.

17. ***Shorten the text block.*** Make sure the frame that contains the table is selected. Then drag the bottom handle of the frame upward until it snaps to the orange guide, as in Figure 4-45. You don't want just one row of overflow text (which is what we have now). By shortening the text block, you force a couple of additional rows to flow onto the second page.

18. ***Flow the table onto the second page.*** Click the red out port (⊞) in the bottom-right corner of the text block. Press Shift+Page Down to advance to the second page. Move your cursor into the empty text frame at the very top of the page (so that the cursor looks like with a linked frame symbol and a text preview) and click. InDesign automatically tops off the three rows of overflow text with the header, as in Figure 4-46.

So ends our first look at tables, but not our last. For a more advanced application of InDesign's extensive table-creation and -editing capabilities, stay tuned for the exercise "Using Table and Cell Styles," which awaits you in Lesson 8.

WHAT DID YOU LEARN?

Match the key concept in the numbered list below with the letter of the phrase that best describes it. Answers appear upside-down at the bottom of the page.

Key Concepts

1. Drop cap
2. Hanging indent
3. Hidden characters
4. Em dash
5. Forced line break
6. Discretionary hyphen
7. Run-in head
8. Fixed-width space
9. No break
10. Tab stop
11. Cell
12. Header

Descriptions

A. One or more large characters at the beginning of a paragraph that descend below the first line of type into the lines below.

B. A boldface or an italic introduction separated from a caption or list entry by multiple spaces or, better, a fixed-width space.

C. A common formatting convention in which the first line of a paragraph extends to the left of the other lines, commonly used to set bulleted and numbered lists.

D. A ↓ or other mark on a ruler to which the text after a tab character aligns, whether to the left, right, or center, or by a period or other character.

E. This top row of a table contains the titles for the columns below it.

F. Used in place of a pair of consecutive hyphens to offset descriptive or parenthetical phrases, this specialized punctuation is roughly as long as the type size is tall.

G. This exceedingly useful command prevents the selected text from breaking between lines, even at a hyphen, dash, or space.

H. Spaces, paragraph breaks, tabs, end-of-story markers, and other nonprinting glyphs that you can display by choosing a command from the Type menu or by pressing Ctrl+Alt+I (⌘-Option-I on the Mac).

I. This specialized punctuation—which you get by pressing Ctrl+Shift+⊟ (⌘-Shift-⊟ on the Mac)—appears only when needed to break a word to the next line of type.

J. This intersection of a row and column in a full-fledged table houses a single table entry.

K. Any of several specialized space characters that InDesign cannot alter to suit the alignment or spacing of a paragraph.

L. An invisible character that knocks all text after it to the next line without starting a new paragraph.

Answers

1A, 2C, 3H, 4F, 5L, 6I, 7B, 8K, 9G, 10D, 11J, 12E

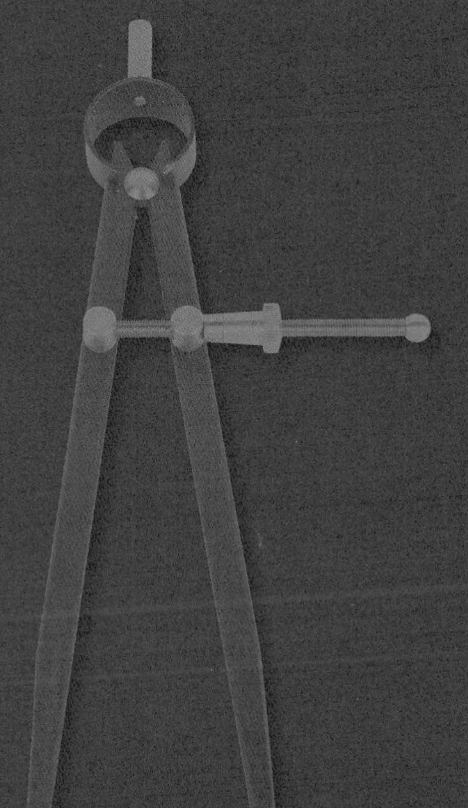

LESSON 5

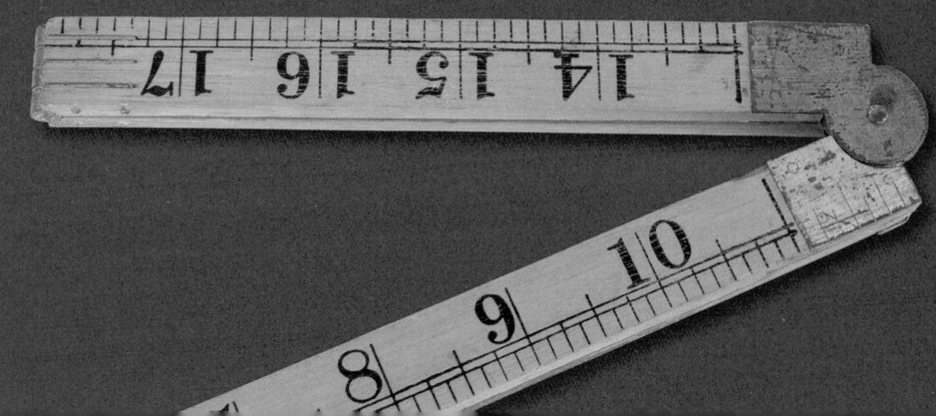

DRAWING INSIDE INDESIGN

BY NOW, WE can all agree that InDesign's text-handling capabilities are the best in the business. If not entirely beyond reproach, they are safely beyond compare. And if you ask me, that's only fitting. Great typography is integral to great design. I ask you, if the world's best layout program won't provide us with the best tools for manipulating and formatting type, what in the world will?

No, InDesign's text-handling prowess is no surprise. What's truly astounding—what knocks my socks off, tosses them in the oven, and bakes them at 450 degrees (which, were that to happen, really would surprise me)—is how much attention InDesign lavishes on graphics. Here's an application that's intended first and foremost for laying out pages, and yet it provides better illustration tools than most dedicated illustration programs. Once upon a time, for example, I might have drawn the line art in Figure 5-1 using a 2-D drawing program. Although I still use such programs—Adobe Illustrator in particular is extremely powerful—I drew these lines and shapes directly in InDesign.

Figure 5-1.

InDesign's illustration tools are devoted to the creation of *vector-based graphics*. By this, I mean mathematically defined outlines that conform to the

ABOUT THIS LESSON

Project Files

Before beginning the exercises, make sure you've copied the lesson files from the DVD, as directed in Step 3 on page xvii of the Preface. This should result in a folder called *Lesson Files-IDcs3 1on1* on your desktop. We'll be working with the files inside the *Lesson 05* subfolder.

In this lesson, we'll explore InDesign's extensive collection of drawing tools. You can draw paths, edit them, mix colors, assign a variety of solid and dashed strokes, create multicolor gradients, align objects, combine simple shapes to create more complex ones—the list goes on and on. Along the way, you'll learn how to:

- Use the line, pen, rectangle, ellipse, and polygon tools to draw graphic objects . . . . . . page 176
- Apply fill and stroke, assign dynamic corner effects, design custom stroke styles, and create linear and radial gradients. . . . . page 190
- Align and distribute text and graphic objects . . . . page 206
- Combine shapes using compound paths and Pathfinder operations . . . . page 211

Video Lesson 5: Pencil, Pen, and Shapes

InDesign lets you draw ornaments, symbols, and other art directly on the page using a wealth of line and shape tools, most of which are lifted right out of Adobe's flagship illustration program, Illustrator. Prominent among these are the pencil and pen. Use the pencil to draw freehand lines; use the pen to create precise outlines one anchor point at a time.

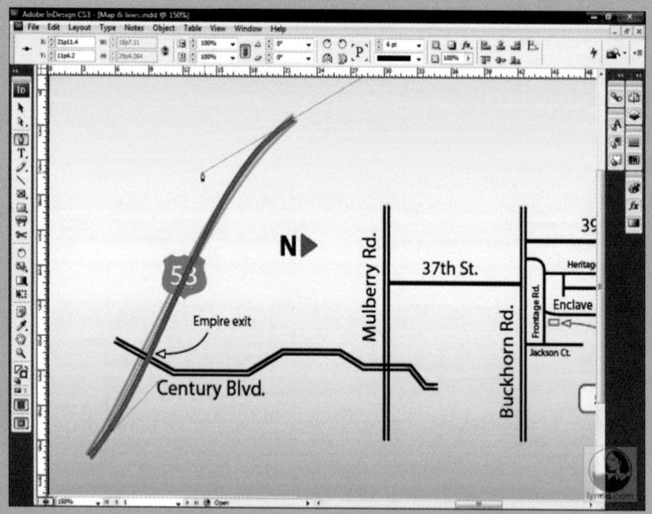

To learn how the pencil and pen tools work—as well as how to convert one shape to another—watch the fifth video lesson. Insert the DVD, double-click *IDcs3 Videos.html*, and click **Lesson 5: Pencil, Pen, and Shapes** under the **Tables and Graphics** heading. During its 20 minutes and 31 seconds, this movie covers the following operations and shortcuts:

Operation	Windows shortcut	Macintosh shortcut
Select pencil or pen tool	N or P	N or P
Connect pencil line to another segment	Ctrl while drawing path	⌘ while drawing path
Use pencil tool to smooth line	Alt-drag over line	Option-drag over line
Draw perpendicular segment with pen tool	Click, Shift-click	Click, Shift-click
Clone a path with black arrow tool	Alt-drag path	Option-drag path
Deactivate path so you can draw a new one	Ctrl+Shift+A	⌘-Shift-A
Change curvature of path	Ctrl-drag control handle	⌘-drag control handle

highest resolution of your printer, monitor, or other piece of hardware. No matter how far you zoom in or scale the outlines, they appear impeccably smooth (see Figure 5-2). Therefore, anything you draw in InDesign is said to be resolution-independent.

The technical term for a line or shape in InDesign is *path outline*, or just plain *path*. The idea is that the contour of the shape follows a mathematically defined path from Point A to Point B and so on. We'll learn how to draw paths and put them to use in the upcoming exercises. In fact, paths are what this lesson is all about.

Figure 5-2.

Homegrown Graphics

As impressed as you might be that you can draw inside a page-layout program, you may wonder why you would want to. After all, isn't drawing a great example of a task that's better handled in another program? Then there's the matter of talent. Just because you're good at designing and assembling pages doesn't mean you're an artist. What good is a bunch of drawing tools if you can't draw?

InDesign provides its drawing tools primarily for your convenience. Rather than making you go to another program to create page ornaments, symbols, maps, diagrams, and other common graphics, InDesign lets you do it right there on the page. In addition to saving you the time and effort otherwise required to swap programs and place artwork, drawing in InDesign means that you can edit in InDesign. So just as you can fix a typo without returning to your word processor, you can adjust the angle of a line without having to open, modify, and save the illustration with a separate application.

Better yet, when you draw inside InDesign, you know exactly how big and what proportions to make your graphic because you can see it interact with text and other elements as you build it. In other words, InDesign's drawing tools eliminate guesswork and make for a more intuitive page-creation experience.

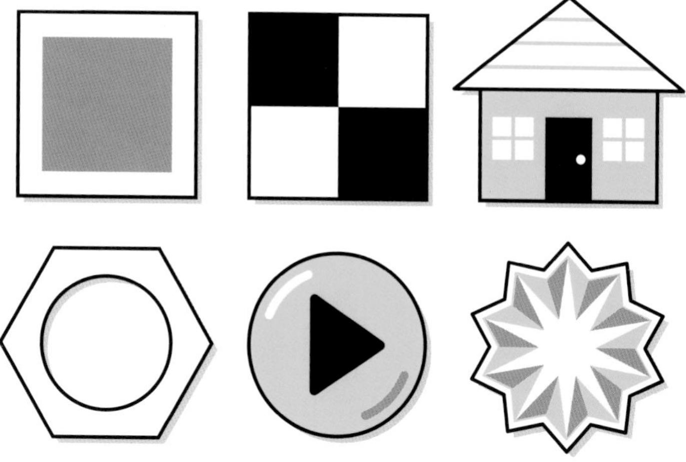

Figure 5-3.

If you doubt your drawing skills, if even the best of your stick figures makes you blush with shame, don't despair. I can't promise InDesign will have you drawing faces like the one in Figure 5-2. But the program's handful of simple line and shape tools will have you drawing, well, simple lines and shapes in no time. Figure 5-3 shows a series of ornaments crafted entirely with the simplest of the simple shapes: rectangles, ovals, and stars. None of them is the least bit difficult to draw. The success of the ornaments hinges on having a clear idea of what you want to accomplish and divining the proper means to that end. Drawing in InDesign is less about artistic dexterity and more about creative thinking. Throw in a dash of practice, and I dare say the quality of your stick figures might improve as well (see Figure 5-4).

Figure 5-4.

Drawing Lines and Shapes

You might think of InDesign's drawing tools as being organized into a kind of pyramid, with the pen tool at the top and everything else below. Introduced in Video Lesson 5, "Pencil, Pen, and Shapes" (see page 174), the pen tool is so capable that, truth be told, it can draw *anything*. In comparison, the tools at the bottom of the pyramid are very narrowly focused. For example, the rectangle tool draws rectangles and squares—that's it.

But that doesn't mean you should focus on the pen tool to the exclusion of all others. Just try drawing a circle with the pen tool and you'll quickly come to appreciate the narrow focus and utter simplicity of the ellipse tool. In fact, as with the food pyramid, the tools at the bottom are your staples, the ones you turn to on a regular basis. The pen tool is dessert and, as such, to be used sparingly.

In this exercise, we'll look at all courses in the drawing tool banquet—line, rectangle, ellipse, polygon, and pen. The only drawing tool I skip is the pencil tool; I said all there is to say about it in the video.

1. ***Open the map to the Pirate Cove theme park.*** Go to the *Lesson 05* folder inside the *Lesson Files-IDcs3 1on1* folder and open the *Pirate Cove map.indd* file. Pictured in Figure 5-5, this document features a map to the key attractions in a swashbuckler-themed amusement park.

2. ***Examine the layers.*** To keep the various elements of the map separate, I've assigned this document three layers. If you're unfamiliar with layers, don't fret; I discuss them at length in the "Creating and Using Layers" exercise in Lesson 9. For now, let's take a look at the layers and see what they hold:

    - Choose **Window→Layers** to display the **Layers** palette (see Figure 5-6).
    - The bottom layer, Map and Background Text, contains the background image (from iStockphoto contributor Peter Zelei), text, and a few other elements that I've supplied for you ahead of time.
    - The middle layer, Guide Dots, contains the color-coded dots you'll use as guides for your drawing. The dots are small, so you may have to zoom in to see the numbers and colors.
    - You can turn off either of these layers by clicking the icon next to the layer name. Click where the used to be to turn on the layer.
    - The icon next to the two lowest layers means that these layers are locked and their contents cannot be altered. Please leave them locked.
    - The top layer, named Drawing Layer, is the active layer. This is the layer on which you'll be drawing.

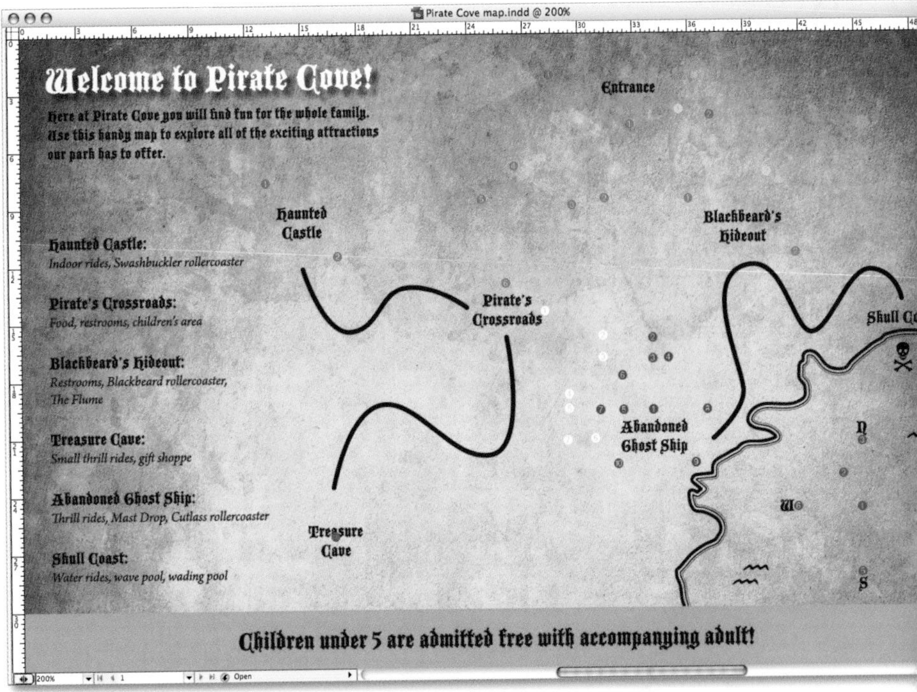
Pirate Cove map.indd @ 200%
Welcome to Pirate Cove!
Here at Pirate Cove you will find fun for the whole family.
Use this handy map to explore all of the exciting attractions
our park has to offer.
Haunted Castle:
Indoor rides, Swashbuckler rollercoaster
Pirate's Crossroads:
Food, restrooms, children's area
Blackbeard's Hideout:
Restrooms, Blackbeard rollercoaster,
The Flume
Treasure Cave:
Small thrill rides, gift shoppe
Abandoned Ghost Ship:
Thrill rides, Mast Drop, Cutlass rollercoaster
Skull Coast:
Water rides, wave pool, wading pool
Entrance
Haunted Castle
Pirate's Crossroads
Blackbeard's Hideout
Abandoned Ghost Ship
Treasure Cave
Children under 5 are admitted free with accompanying adult!

Figure 5-5.

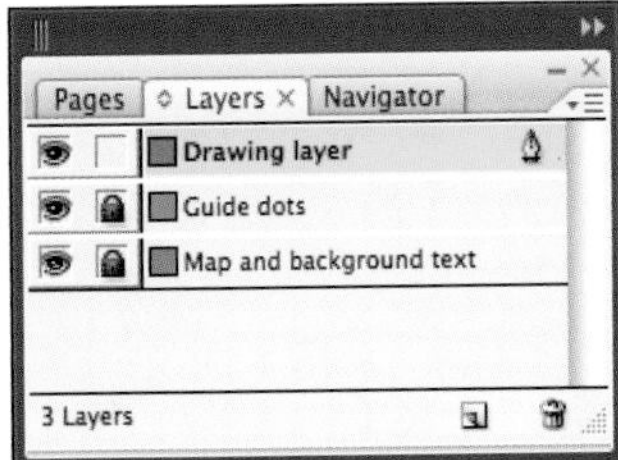
Pages
Layers
Navigator
Drawing layer
Guide dots
Map and background text
3 Layers

Figure 5-6.

If you are trying to use the drawing tools but your cursor resembles the icon, you've managed to select a locked layer. Click Drawing Layer in the Layers palette and all will be well.

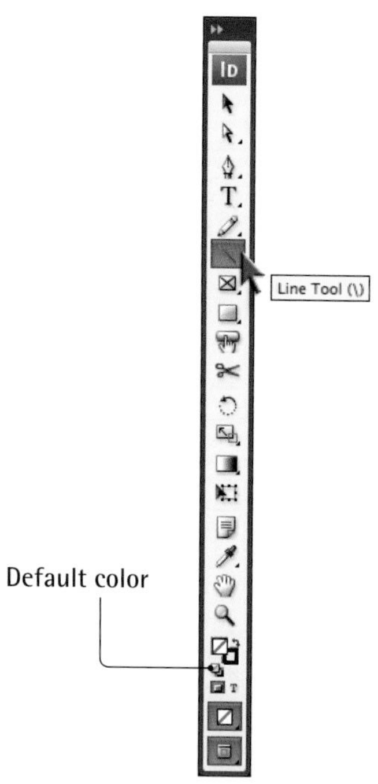

Figure 5-7.

3. ***Select the line tool in the toolbox.*** The map may appear more or less complete, but it's missing some key elements. For example, no pirate would be caught dead without a secret passageway. Let's start by drawing a line to indicate the tunnel that connects the *Entrance* to the booty-filled catacombs below *Blackbeard's Hideout*. Zoom in on the map so you can read the yellow numbered circles in the top-right region. Then click the line tool in the toolbox, as in Figure 5-7. You can also press the \ key, which is logical given that the line tool looks like a backslash.

4. ***Set the colors to their defaults.*** Before you begin, let's make sure we are working with the same tools. Press Ctrl+Shift+A (⌘-Shift-A on the Mac) to deselect everything. Now click the tiny default color icon in the lower-left region of the toolbox, as labeled in Figure 5-7, or press the D key. InDesign resets the colors so our shapes will have transparent interiors and black outlines.

5. ***Draw a line to indicate the secret tunnel.*** Click and drag from the yellow ❶ to the yellow ❷. When you release your mouse, you should see a 1-point black line inside a red bounding box, as in Figure 5-8.

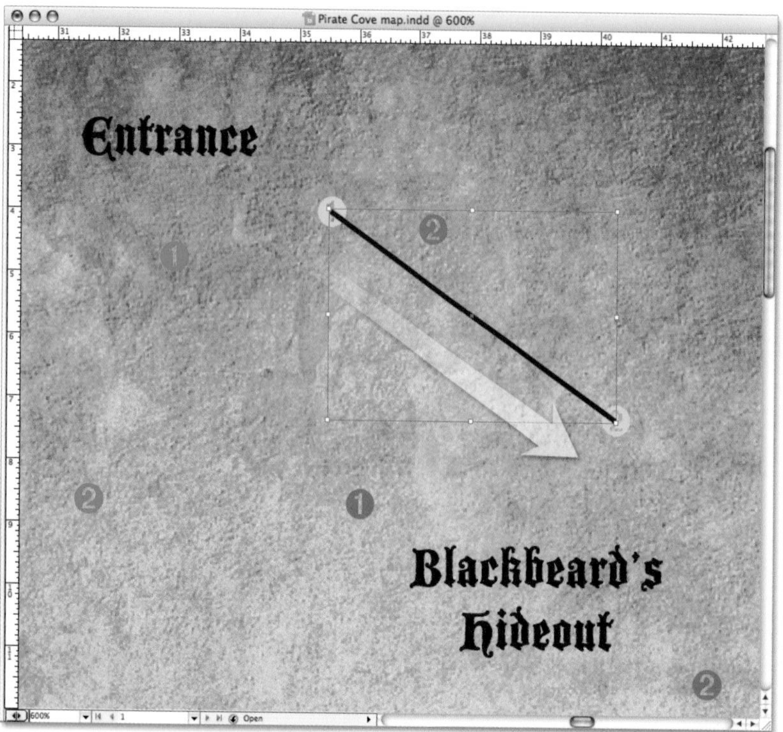

Figure 5-8.

Have you ever started drawing a line, only to realize midway that you started in the wrong place? Apparently someone at Adobe has as well, because there's no need to start over. While drawing, press and hold the spacebar. As long as the spacebar is down, moving your mouse moves the line to a different location. When you've relocated the line to your satisfaction, release the spacebar and finish drawing the line. This technique works with all drawing tools except the pencil.

6. ***Change the line weight in the control palette.*** Our tunnel looks a bit claustrophobic, so let's change the thickness of the line, known as the *line weight*. Choose **3 pt** from the weight pop-up menu on the right side of the control palette. Your line should thicken, as in Figure 5-9 on the facing page.

7. ***Set a new default line weight.*** Press Ctrl+Shift+A (or ⌘-Shift-A) to deselect the line. The bounding box disappears from the tunnel indicator line. But also notice that the line weight setting in the control palette switches back to its default, 1 pt. When an object is selected and you change the value, the change affects that object only. To change the weight of all subsequent lines, including those we are about to draw with other InDesign tools, you have to change the weight with *no* object selected. So again choose **3 pt** from the weight pop-up menu on the right side of the control palette.

8. ***Draw a perfectly upright line for the mast.*** Next, I want you to use the line tool to draw a mast for the currently nonexistent ghost ship. (Trust me, the specter will materialize later in this exercise.) Scroll down to the bottom-right region of the map, to the words *Abandoned Ghost Ship*. Press and hold the Shift key as you drag from the dark blue ❶ up to the dark blue ❷. As you can see in Figure 5-10, the ship may be vapor, but the mast is true.

Figure 5-9.

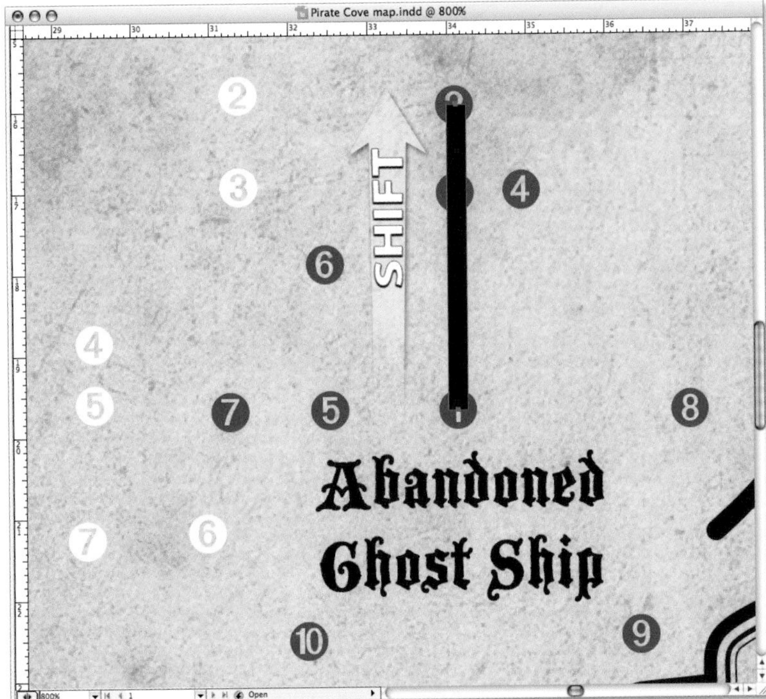

Figure 5-10.

Figure 5-11.

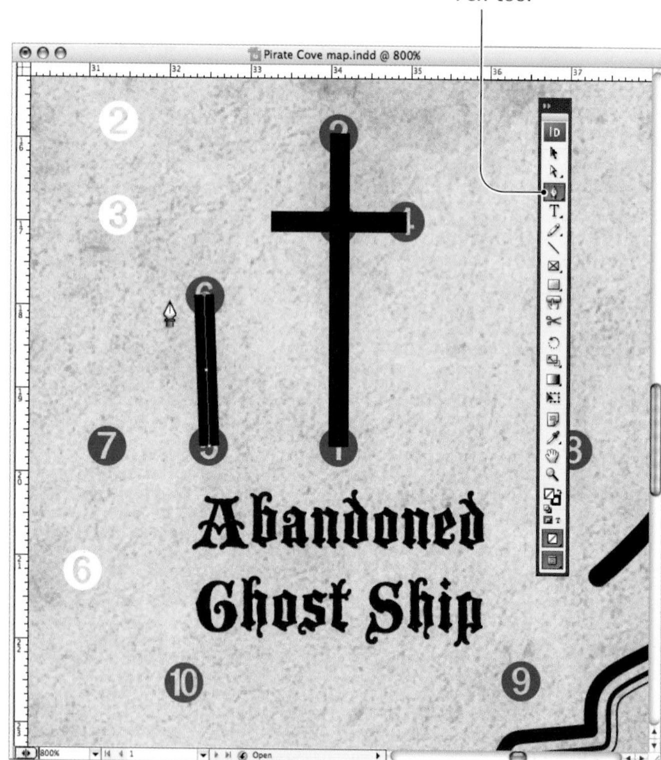

Figure 5-12.

Holding down Shift when drawing with any tool constrains the behavior of that tool. When drawing with the line tool, pressing Shift locks the angle of the line to a multiple of 45 degrees, perfect for drawing horizontal or vertical segments. You can press Shift at the outset of your drag or in the middle. Just make sure you hold down the Shift key until after you release the mouse button.

9. ***Draw a perpendicular line for the yardarm.*** For something a little bit different, press the Shift and Alt keys (Shift and Option on the Mac) and drag from the dark blue 3 (now slightly obscured by the mast) to the dark blue 4. Notice that the line moves in two directions at once, both to the right and to the left, as in Figure 5-11. This is because pressing Alt (or Option) draws the line outward from the center.

10. ***Draw a line with the pen tool.*** We're finished with the line tool; now let's turn our attention to the pen tool. As I demonstrated in the video (see page 174), the pen tool draws paths one point at a time. This means you can create free-form paths that contain lots of lines all linked together. InDesign calls these lines *segments*. The points at which they join are *anchor points*.

    Let's draw another mast for the ship. Click the pen tool (below the white arrow in the toolbox), or press the P key to select it. Click in the center of the dark blue ❺ to set an anchor point at this location. Then click the dark blue ❻ to set a second point. InDesign automatically connects the dots with a slightly skewed straight segment, as in Figure 5-12.

The control palette's L value tells you the exact length of the selected line (almost 2 picas, in my case). It even tells you the length of the line as you draw it. So you will do well to keep an eye on it.

11. ***Deselect the line.*** I want you to use the pen tool to create the rest of our as-yet-to-be-visible ship. But don't start clicking yet—if you do, you'll add more segments to the existing line. Before you

can start a new path, you must deselect the active one. Press and hold Ctrl+Shift+A (⌘-Shift-A). Or, if you'd prefer to try something new, press and hold Ctrl (or ⌘) to get the white arrow tool and then click an empty portion of the document. The pen tool is now poised to create a completely new path.

12. ***Click or Shift-click each of the other four blue guide dots.*** Next, draw a free-form trapezoid that will serve as our as-promised ship by clicking around the words *Abandoned Ghost Ship*. Draw the shape as follows:

    - Click the dark blue ❼ to set the first anchor point.
    - Press the Shift key and click the blue ❽. A horizontal line extends from one point to the other. As when drawing with the line tool, the Shift key constrains the angle of a pen segment to the nearest multiple of 45 degrees. The one difference is that you have to press Shift *before* you click. In other words, press and hold Shift, click with the pen tool, and release Shift.
    - Release the Shift key. Then click the blue ❾. InDesign adds a slanting segment to the line.
    - Shift-click the blue ❿. InDesign appends a precisely horizontal segment. The beauty of the pen tool is that you can draw paths in any shape you want.

13. ***Close the path.*** The result is an incomplete, or *open*, shape. To finish the shape, we must draw a segment between the first and last points. Notice that when you hover over the first point in the path (in the blue ❼), a tiny circle appears next to the pen tool cursor, like this: ✒ₒ (see Figure 5-13). This circle signifies that you are about to *close* the path you are drawing. Click when you see the ✒ₒ cursor and the hull of what is now a scary ghost ship will be complete and, more importantly, watertight.

Figure 5-13.

You can close a path also by choosing a command. To join two endpoints with a straight segment, choose Object→Paths→Close Path. To open a closed path like the cockeyed box you just created, choose Object→Paths→Open Path. In the latter case, the path looks the same but the point at which you closed the hull is severed in two. To verify this, grab one of the points with the white arrow tool and drag it away.

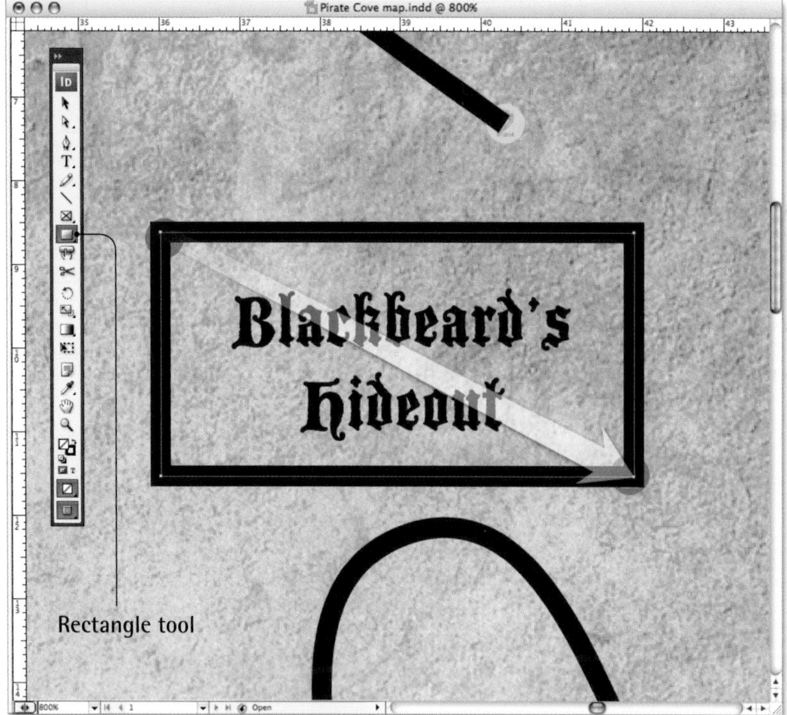

Figure 5-14.

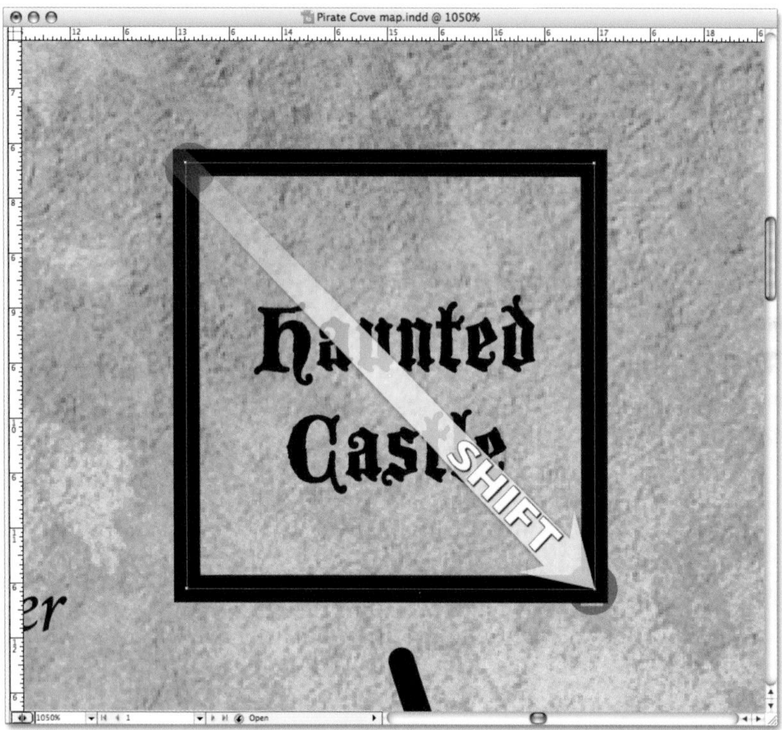

Figure 5-15.

14. ***Draw a rectangle around Blackbeard's Hideout.*** The pen tool is great for drawing free-form shapes, but InDesign also supplies tools for quickly rendering common shapes. We'll use these shapes to indicate other key areas on our map. Start by selecting the rectangle tool, the solid rectangle labeled in Figure 5-14. Or press the M key (a shortcut lifted from Photoshop, where the rectangle tool is known as the marquee.) Scroll up to *Blackbeard's Hideout* in the top-right region of the map. Drag from the magenta ❶ to the magenta ❷ to draw a rectangle that indicates the hideout building. (I cheated toward the outer edges of the magenta circles to provide the space around the text shown in Figure 5-14.)

15. ***Draw a square around the Haunted Castle.*** Move to the left and put a square around the *Haunted Castle*. Press the Shift key and drag from the red ❶ to the red ❷, as in Figure 5-15. Pressing the Shift key constrains the rectangle to a perfect square. You can press the Shift key after beginning your drag, but make sure you have the key down when you release the mouse button.

16. ***Select the ellipse tool in the toolbox.*** Scroll down and to the left to the words *Treasure Cave*. This happens to be a round area, where the littlest mates can run wild yet stay in sight of their parents, so we'll draw it with the ellipse tool. Select the ellipse tool in one of the following ways:

    - Click and hold the rectangle tool icon in the toolbox to display the shape tool flyout menu, which appears in Figure 5-16, and then choose the second tool in the list, the ellipse tool.

- Alt-click (Option-click) the rectangle tool icon.
- Press the L key.

17. ***Draw a circle by the numbers.*** Although you can draw the shape by dragging inside the document window, I'd like to take this opportunity to show you a different technique:

    - Press the Alt (or Option) key and click the brown dot in the middle of the *Treasure Cave* text to bring up the **Ellipse** dialog box, where you define the width and height of a prospective shape. (Note that the dialog box would have appeared if you had simply clicked. Pressing the key instructs InDesign to center the shape at the click point.)
    - Change both the **Width** and **Height** values to 4p3. Then click the **OK** button. The result is a perfect circle with a diameter of 4 picas 3 points, as in Figure 5-17.

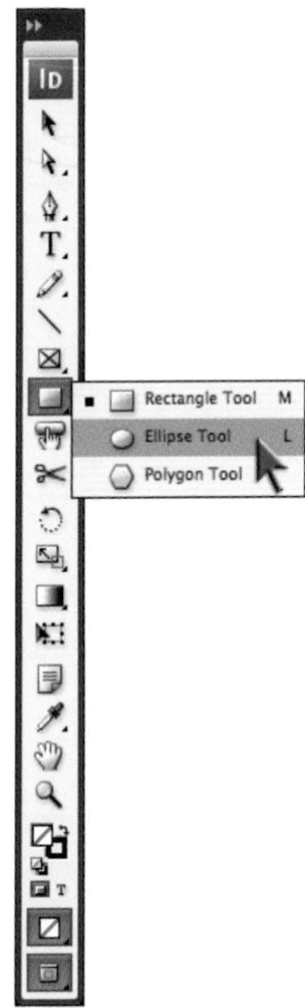

Figure 5-16.

The Ellipse dialog box always lists the dimensions of the last oval or circle you drew, even if you drew it by hand. You can repeat shapes over and over again just by clicking with the tool. This technique works with the rectangle tool and Rectangle dialog box as well.

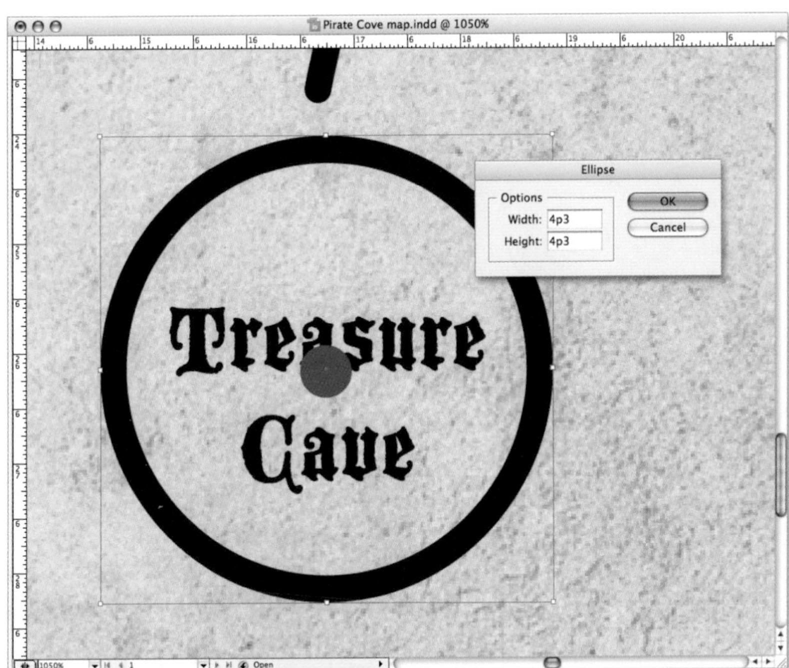

Figure 5-17.

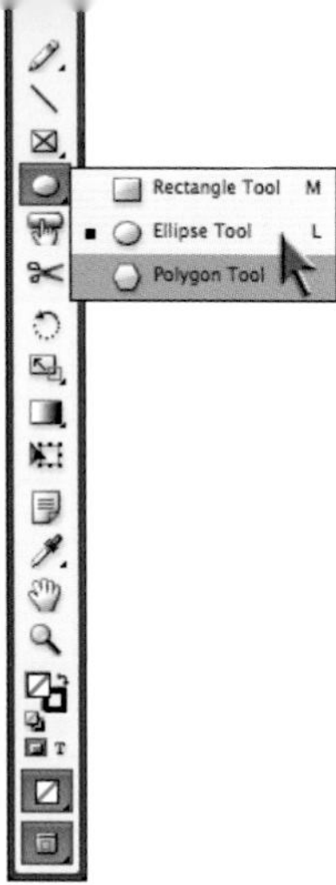
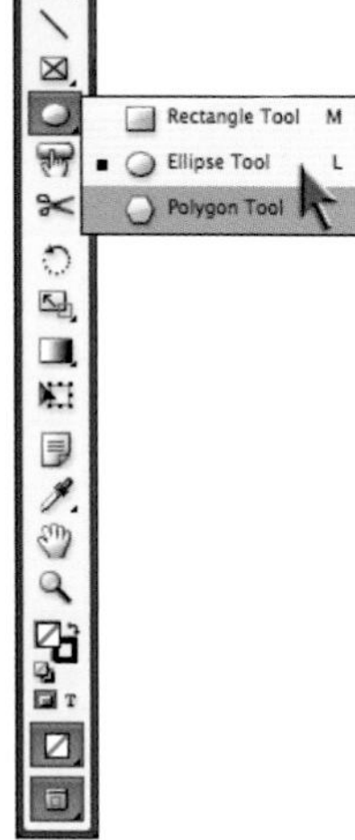

Figure 5-18.

18. ***Select the polygon tool.*** Click and hold the ellipse tool icon in the toolbox and select the polygon tool (see Figure 5-18), which draws regular polygons with three or more straight and equal sides. The polygon tool has no shortcut, but you can get it also by pressing Alt (or Option) and clicking the ellipse tool icon.

19. ***Draw a triangle to indicate the entrance.*** We're going to surround the word *Entrance* in the top-right area of the document with a down-pointing triangle. By default, the polygon tool draws a hexagon (an even shape with six sides). You can change the number of sides in the midst of drawing by pressing the ↑ or ↓ key. Each press of the key adds or deletes a side. The feature is a little flaky, however, and it works only when your mouse is in motion. So here's what I want you to do:

    - Drag from the green ❶ toward the green ❷, and keep your mouse button down.
    - Keep dragging toward the ❷. While moving the mouse, press the ↓ key three times to remove three sides and make a triangle. If it doesn't take, wiggle your mouse and try pressing ↓ again.
    - Once you arrive at a triangle like the one in Figure 5-19, release the mouse button.

Figure 5-19.

20. ***Flip the triangle vertically.*** By default, InDesign has created a triangle that points upward, out of the park and over the word *Entrance*. Show the landlubbers the correct direction by flipping the triangle vertically. We can do this from the control palette:

    - See that grid of nine tiny squares I've circled on the far left side of the control palette in Figure 5-20? That's the *reference point matrix*. Click the center box so it looks like [icon]. This ensures that the triangle flips across its center.
    - Now click the [icon] icon next to the big **P** to flip the triangle vertically. Conveniently, the icon uses triangles to

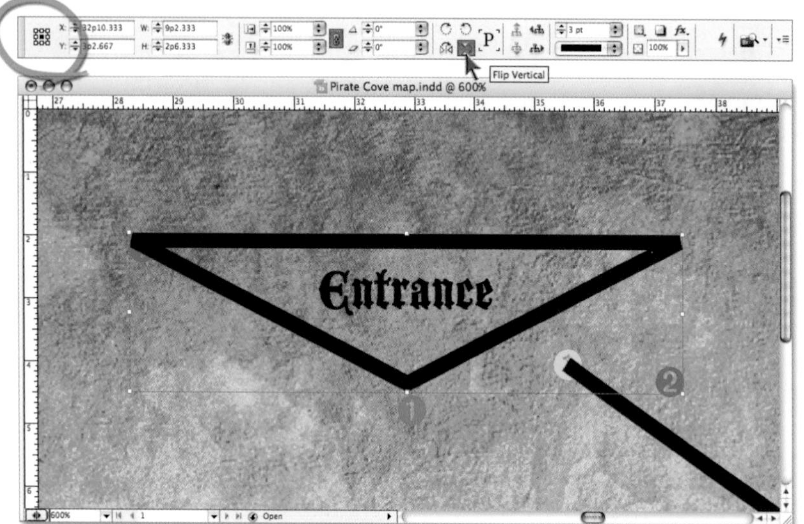

Figure 5-20.

demonstrate the command's effect, so in this case what you see is what you get. The triangle now points down into the park, as in Figure 5-20.

21. ***Set the polygon tool to make stars.*** The polygon tool can also make stars. Scroll to the bottom-right corner of the document until you find letters for the four directions in the lagoon. This is where we'll put that ages-old map element, the compass rose.

    A typical compass rose begins life as a star. Double-click the polygon tool icon in the toolbox to display the **Polygon Settings** dialog box, shown in Figure 5-21. You can specify the number of sides the tool draws by default and the "pointiness" of the spikes emitting from a star:

    - Change the **Number of Sides** value to 8. If we were to draw a polygon, this would result in an octagon. For a star, it means 8 spikes, or 16 segments.
    - You create a star by folding the sides of the polygon into the body of the shape. The Star Inset value decides how deeply the sides fold. Higher values result in spikier stars. Set the **Star Inset** value to 45 percent.
    - Click the **OK** button. The next polygon you draw will subscribe to these settings.

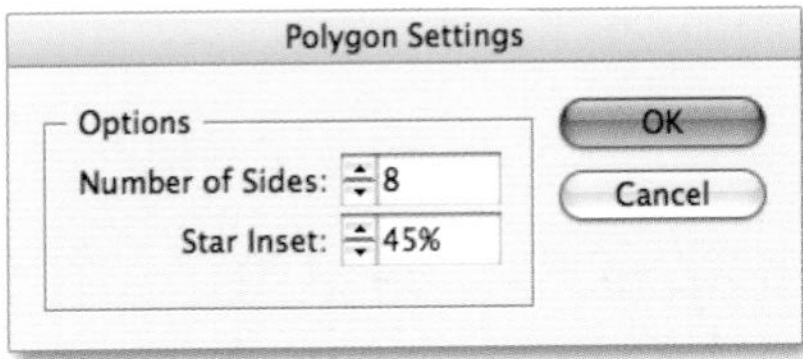

Figure 5-21.

22. ***Draw a star.*** Press Shift+Alt (or Shift-Option) and drag from the violet ❶ beyond the violet ❷ until an outside point of the star touches the ❷. This draws the star from the center out and forces all sides to be symmetrical, as in Figure 5-22.

23. ***Rotate the star 22.5 degrees.*** InDesign invariably chooses to draw its polygons upright. This means we have to rotate the star into the desired position. Click the △ icon in the middle of the control palette to highlight the rotation angle value. Type 22.5 and press Enter or Return. The star rotates into the position shown in Figure 5-23, which appears on the next page.

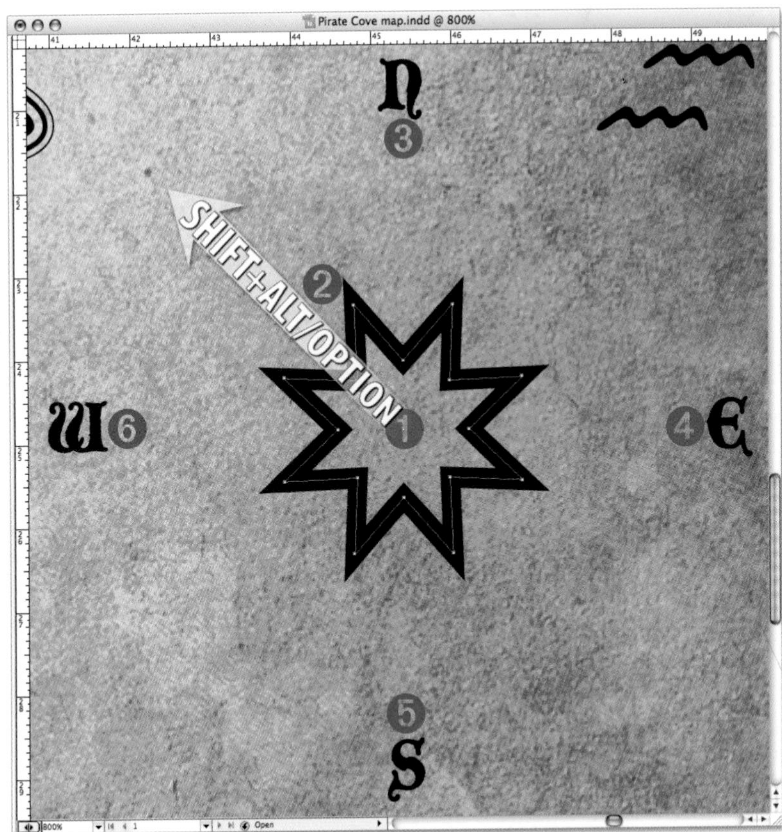

Figure 5-22.

24. ***Select the white arrow tool from the toolbox.*** Our star is currently symmetrical, with every point exactly as long as its neighbor. I want to extend the four points that point toward the letters. And to do that, we need the white arrow tool (which Adobe calls the direct selection tool). Click the white arrow icon in the toolbox (the one labeled in Figure 5-24) or press the A key.

25. ***Shift-drag the top of the star upward.*** Click the top anchor point in the star to select it. The point changes from a hollow square to a solid one. (It may be hard to see—anchor points are pretty tiny—but that's what's happening.) Press the Shift key and drag the selected anchor point up to the purple ❸. Holding down Shift constrains the movement to the closest multiple of 45 degrees—in this case, vertically.

26. ***Extend the left, right, and bottom points.*** You can repeat this same process on the left, right, and bottom points. That is, click on the anchor point to select it, and then Shift-drag the point to the nearest purple grid dot: ❹, ❺, or ❻. But that's the sucker's way. Better to move all points at once by scaling them. Here's how this wonderful technique works:

    - First, undo the last operation. Press Ctrl+Z (⌘-Z) to restore the top point to its previous position.
    - The top point should still be selected, but click it just to be sure. Then press the Shift key and click each of the other three points (left, right, and bottom). All four points should now be selected.
    - Click the icon in the control palette to highlight the horizontal scale value. Enter 224 percent and press the Enter or Return key to transform all four points.

Note that unlike the rotate value, InDesign resets the scale values to 100 percent when the operation is complete. Because you're working on a partial path, there's nothing to worry about. As long as your compass rose looks like the one in Figure 5-24, all is well.

FURTHER INVESTIGATION

InDesign's drawing tools are a capable bunch. But they're a far cry from Illustrator's. Imagine the seemingly simple task of drawing a symmetrical shape, like a heart. In InDesign, you can draw one half and then flip it to make the other, but joining the two halves together requires some work. In Illustrator, meanwhile, you have only to choose the Join command. And that's just the beginning. If you're interested in learning Illustrator—as well you should—try out my three-part, 24-chapter video series *Illustrator CS3 One-on-One*. To gain access 24/7, go to *www.lynda.com/dekeID* and sign up for your 7-Day Free Trial Account.

Figure 5-23.

EXTRA CREDIT

At this point, we've mapped out the key areas of our theme park using the line, pen, and shape tools. If that's enough mapmaking for you, skip ahead to "Fill, Stroke, Color, and Gradients," which begins on page 190. But then you'll miss out on the true power of the pen tool, drawing smooth, organic curves. Not only is this an essential part of drawing in InDesign, but the lines in the following steps are essential to getting our pirate patrons safely from one place to another. These are *children*, for goodness sake.

27. ***Begin drawing a path from* Entrance *to* Pirate's Crossroads.** In addition to drawing straight segments, the pen tool can draw curved segments. We'll use this capability to complete the pathways that connect the main areas of the park. Select the pen tool from the toolbox or by pressing the P key. Then click on the cyan ❶ at the top of the page by the entrance.

28. ***Draw the first curve.*** Continue the path by clicking the cyan ❷ and dragging (in one continuous movement) to the cyan ❸, as in Figure 5-25. The click on ❷ designates the location of the anchor point; the remainder of the drag draws forth a pair of control handles in opposite directions (witnessed by the tiny red circles at either end of the red line in the figure). This kind of point is known as a *smooth point* because it defines a smooth arc in the path. The circular handle that stretches to the right of the smooth point bends the new segment toward it, causing the segment to curve. The bottom-left handle will bend the next segment you create. Release the mouse when you get to the ❸.

Figure 5-24.

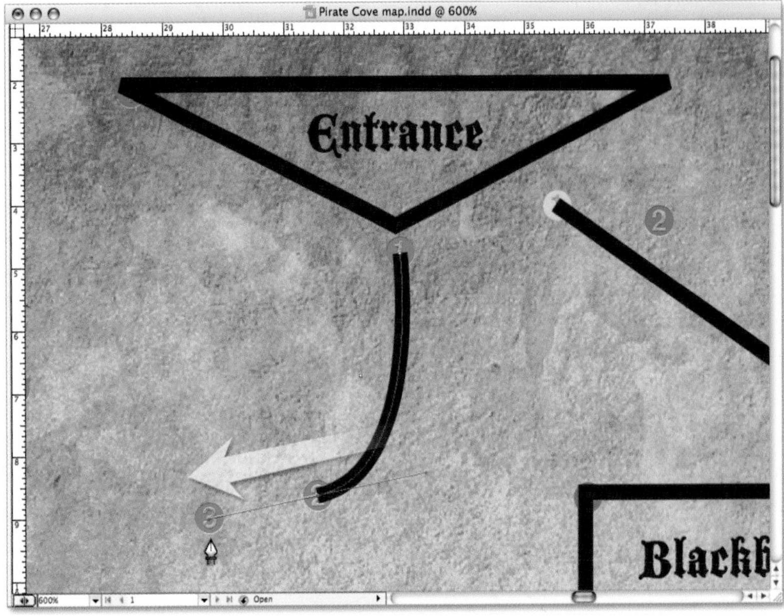

Figure 5-25.

Figure 5-26.

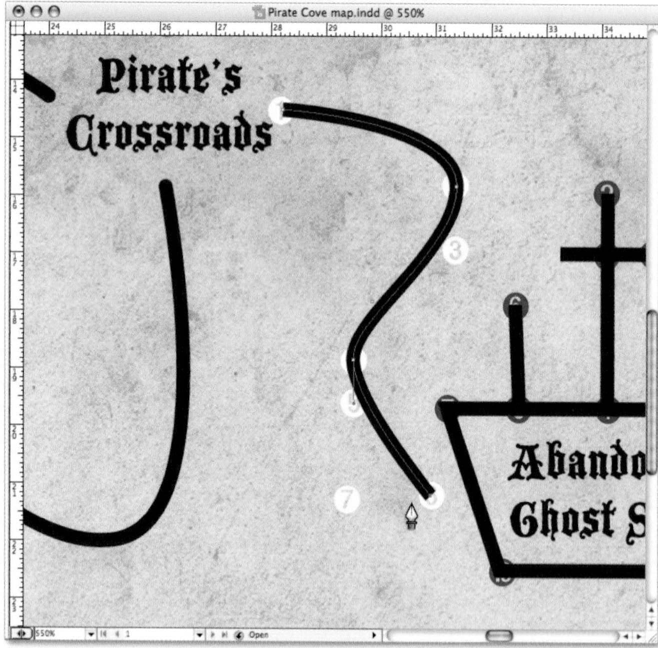

Figure 5-27.

29. ***Continue the path.*** To add segments to the route, do the following:

    - Click the cyan ❹. Clicking with the pen tool adds an anchor point with no control handle, known as a *corner point* because it creates a corner in the path. But the new segment curves anyway. It remains under the influence of the lower-right control handle from the preceding smooth point.
    - Shift-click the cyan ❺ to the left. This creates a straight corner and path. This might be useful in other circumstances, but it isn't quite the pirate's way. Press Ctrl+Z (or ⌘-Z) twice to undo our path back to the ❷ point.
    - This time, click-and-drag from the ❹ and release at the ❺ to create a looping path, apropos of childhood marauding. Click the cyan ❻ to complete the journey to Pirate's Crossroads in serpentine pirate fashion, as shown in Figure 5-26.
    - Ctrl-click (or ⌘-click) off the path to deselect it. That's the top-secret way to deselect, best suited to enemies of the Queen.

30. ***Add the final pathway.*** Finally, we'll create a path from the words *Pirate's Crossroads* to the *Abandoned Ghost Ship*. Start by clicking the white ❶ to place the first corner point. Then drag from the white ❷ to the ❸; drag from the white ❹ to the ❺; and finally click the white ❻. (We'll come to the ❼ in a moment.) The resulting path should look like the one in Figure 5-27, down to the unfortunate flat spot at the end of the curve (between ❺ and ❻).

31. ***Fix the lifeless curve.*** InDesign can help you fix the flat spot. Press and hold Ctrl (or ⌘) to get the white arrow tool. With the key down—mind you, I want you to keep it down throughout the entire step—click the anchor point positioned at the ❹. Hover your cursor over the control handle on the white ❺ so the cursor looks like

an arrow with a tiny diamond next to it, as in ↖◇. Then drag the handle to the white ❼ to smooth out the arc. You can go even further or make other adjustments if you want. As indicated by the yellow arrowheads in Figure 5-28, I ended up dragging the bottom control handle for the arc about a pica west of the ❼ and lifting the top control handle as well. This rounds out the curve in a more fanciful fashion. And pirates are nothing if not fans of fanciful fashion.

32. ***Turn off the Guide Dots layer.*** Okay, now you can release Ctrl (or ⌘). You're finished drawing. That means you don't need to see the guide dots anymore. Return to the **Layers** palette and click the 👁 icon in front of the **Guide Dots** layer. The circles disappear, revealing just the lines and the map, as in Figure 5-29.

33. ***Save the document.*** We're going to continue working on this map in the next exercise, so it's a good idea to save your work. Choose **File→Save As**, name your document "My map.indd," and save it in the *Lesson 05* folder.

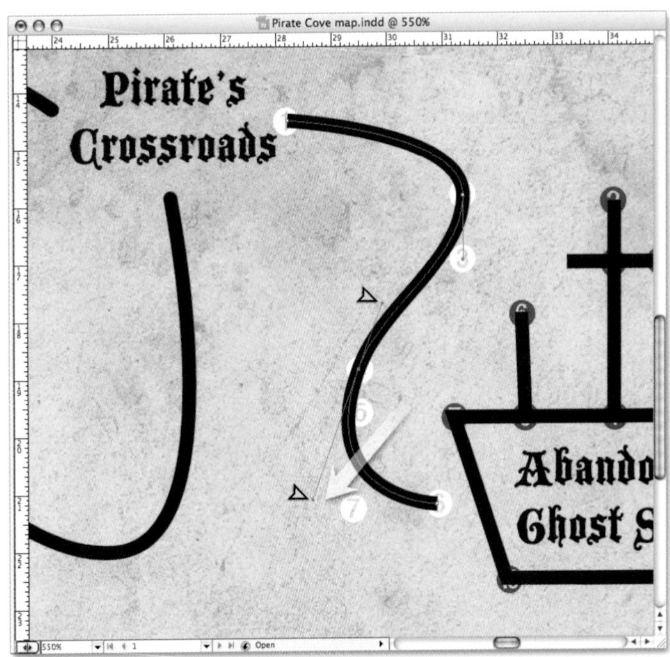
Pirate Cove map.indd @ 550%
Pirate's
Crossroads
Abando
Ghost S

Figure 5-28.

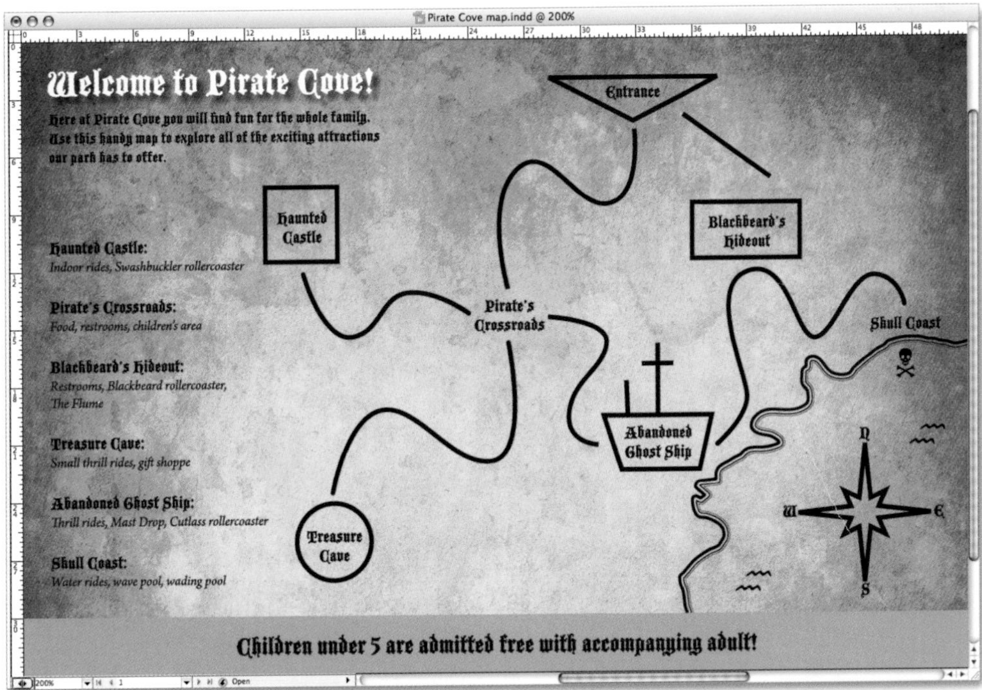
Pirate Cove map.indd @ 200%
Welcome to Pirate Cove!
Here at Pirate Cove you will find fun for the whole family.
Use this handy map to explore all of the exciting attractions
our park has to offer.
Haunted Castle:
Indoor rides, Swashbuckler rollercoaster
Pirate's Crossroads:
Food, restrooms, children's area
Blackbeard's Hideout:
Restrooms, Blackbeard rollercoaster,
The Flume
Treasure Cave:
Small thrill rides, gift shoppe
Abandoned Ghost Ship:
Thrill rides, Mast Drop, Cutlass rollercoaster
Skull Coast:
Water rides, wave pool, wading pool
Entrance
Haunted
Castle
Blackbeard's
Hideout
Pirate's
Crossroads
Skull Coast
Abandoned
Ghost Ship
Treasure
Cave
N
W
E
S
Children under 5 are admitted free with accompanying adult!

Figure 5-29.

Fill, Stroke, Color, and Gradients

One of the beauty's of InDesign's vector-based approach is that lines and shapes remain editable long after you create them. If you draw a path in the wrong color, for example, you don't have to undo the operation or redraw the path, you just apply a new color. In this exercise, we'll change some of the features of our amusement park map to give it a more interesting look. We'll be dealing with the two basic components of objects that you draw in InDesign, fill and stroke (see Figure 5-30). *Fill* affects the interior of a shape; *stroke* affects the outline. You'll learn how to select colors, apply fill and stroke, add corner effects, create gradients, and even design a custom stroke pattern.

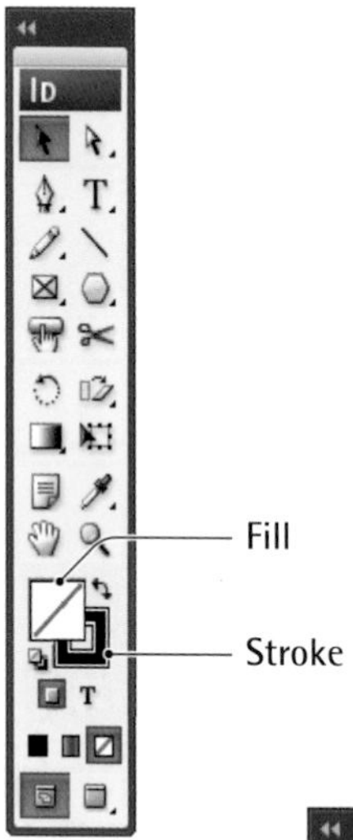

Fill

Stroke

Figure 5-30.

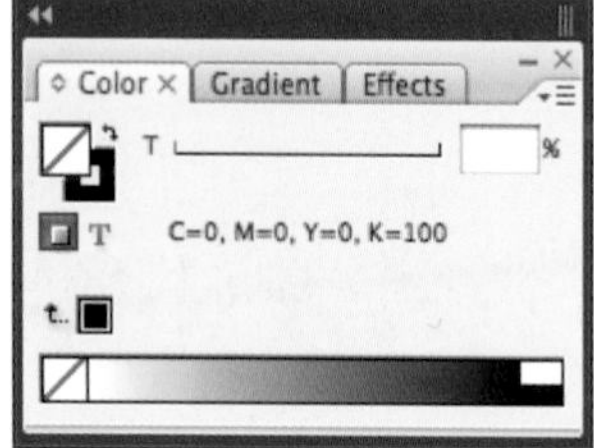

Figure 5-31.

1. ***Open a document.*** If you still have open the *My map.indd* file that you saved at the end of the last exercise, skip to the next step. If not, open my saved file, which is called *All Pirate Cove paths.indd*, so-called because all the paths have been drawn. You'll find it in the *Lesson 05* folder inside *Lesson Files-IDcs3 1on1*.
2. ***Remove the fill from the compass rose.*** Let's start things off by applying a fill to the compass rose in the lower-right region of the document. Press the V key to select the black arrow tool and then click the compass rose to select it. Next, click the fill icon in the toolbox, labeled in Figure 5-30 (which appears two columns wide to make the fill and stroke controls larger). This activates the fill of the selected object, which is currently set to None, as indicated by the red slash icon. The upshot is that the area inside the compass rose is transparent.
3. ***Display the Color palette.*** Press F6 or choose **Window→Color** to display the **Color** palette, shown in Figure 5-31. The Color palette contains the same fill and stroke icons as the toolbox, plus a few options for specifying a color. Choose **Show Options** from the palette menu or click the ⬍ arrow next to the palette name if the Color palette doesn't show all the options.
4. ***Click the far left of the tint ramp.*** Move your cursor over the *tint ramp* at the bottom of the palette. As Figure 5-32 shows, your cursor turns into an eyedropper. Click in the left side of the ramp to fill the star shape with a light gray.

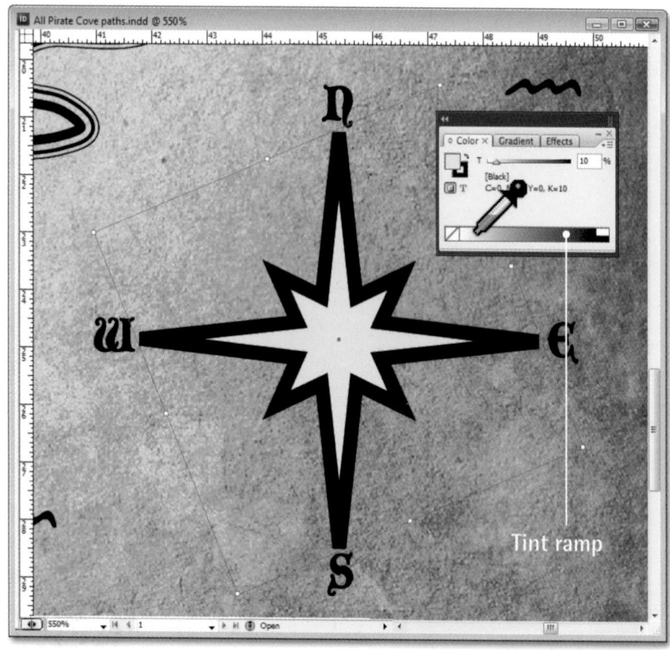

Figure 5-32.

5. ***Choose CMYK from the Color palette menu.*** When working with a predefined color such as black, the Color palette addresses the color in a vacuum. You can use the Tint slider (labeled T) to make the ink lighter or darker. To switch to a different color, you must first select a color model from the palette menu.

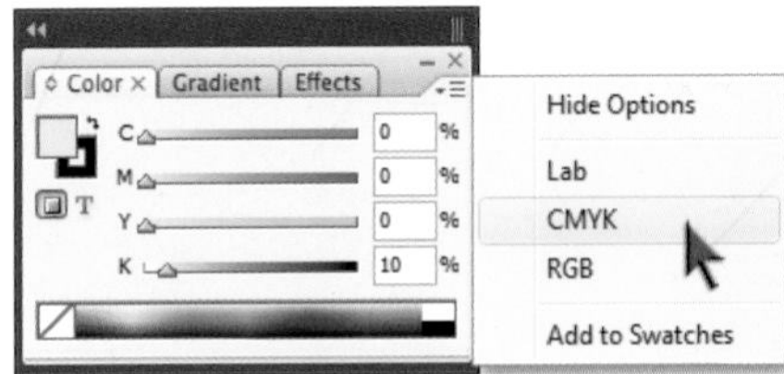

Figure 5-33.

The palette menu presents you with a choice of three *color models* (which are ways of defining colors), on display in Figure 5-33:

- Lab is a theoretical model that defines colors independently of any monitor, printer, or other piece of hardware. It's a great color space for editing continuous-tone photographs, as in Photoshop. But its use in InDesign is limited at best.
- CMYK is the color model for printing. As we explore at length in Lesson 12, "Printing and Output," full-color process printing most commonly involves four inks: cyan, magenta, yellow, and black, together known as *process colors*. If the final destination for your document is a printing press, CMYK is the obvious and best choice.
- RGB is used by devices that display and capture colors, such as monitors, scanners, and digital cameras. If your document is intended to be viewed on screen—as may be the case when exporting a PDF file—you should define your colors in RGB.

Our map is intended for printing, so choose **CMYK** from the palette menu. Or Shift-click in the tint ramp to switch from one color model to the next. The palette now contains four sliders, one for each ink color (including K for black), as in Figure 5-33.

6. ***Dial in a rich gold color.*** It takes some experience to dial in CMYK colors. To help you out, Figure 5-34 shows a collection of incremental CMYK combinations—as they appear when printed in this book. (I mention that last part because different presses render colors differently. Your experience will surely vary.) Only the last column includes black ink (the K value). The role of black is to darken colors, making them less colorful.

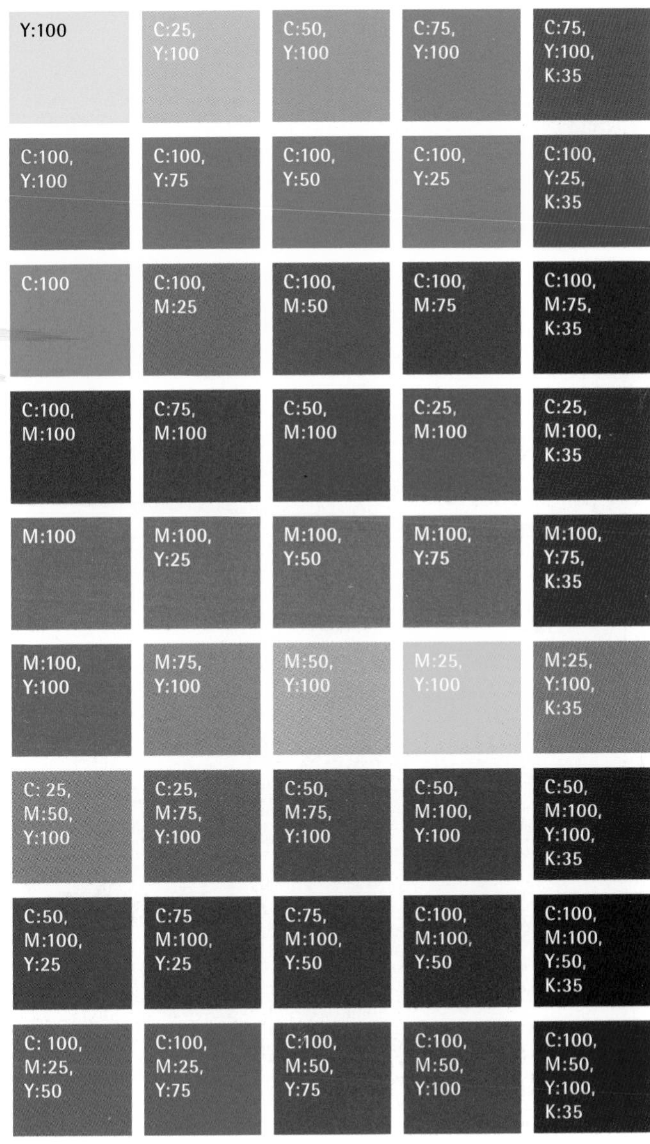

Figure 5-34.

Let's say you want to change the center of the compass rose to a rich pirate's gold. If you combine 100 percent yellow with the small amount of black we started with, we get a cold, hard yellow. Adding black makes the color darker. For gold, we need to add some magenta as well. Enter the following:

- **C**: 0 percent
- **M**: 25 percent
- **Y**: 100 percent
- **K**: 10 percent

If you find it tedious to select each value and enter a new one—goodness knows I do—try the following:

Press the F6 key twice to highlight the C value, enter a value, and then press Tab to advance to the next one. When you finish, press Enter or Return to accept the color.

---

7. ***Activate the stroke icon.*** However you got there, the interior of your compass rose should be the color of a polished doubloon. Now let's give it a more colorful stroke. You can click the stroke icon in either the toolbox or the Color palette. Or just press the X key, which toggles between activating the stroke and fill.

Pressing Shift+X switches the assigned stroke and fill colors. I don't recommend that you do this now, but if you do, you'll get a black star with a gold stroke.

Figure 5-35.

8. ***Assign a dark, ominous red stroke.*** Again, choose **CMYK** from the palette menu or Shift-click the tint ramp twice. This time, instead of dialing in a color, click a shade of dark red in the colorful *spectrum bar*, which replaces the tint ramp at the bottom of the palette, something close to the black box on the right. Don't worry about getting exactly the same color that I did in Figure 5-35; just choose one that looks dark, sinister, and very, very bloody.

Alt-clicking (or Option-clicking) in the spectrum bar sets the color of the *inactive* attribute. So if the stroke is active, Alt-clicking sets the color of the fill.

---

9. ***Save the red color as a swatch.*** Despite not wanting to think too hard about where a pirate would get such a color, I like my red so much that I want to save it for future use. Choose **Window→Swatches** or press F5 to display the **Swatches** palette. Then click the ◱ icon at the bottom of the palette to add the red color to the list. Or you can choose Add to Swatches from the Color palette menu. The dark red appears as the last item in the Swatches palette color list, as in Figure 5-36.

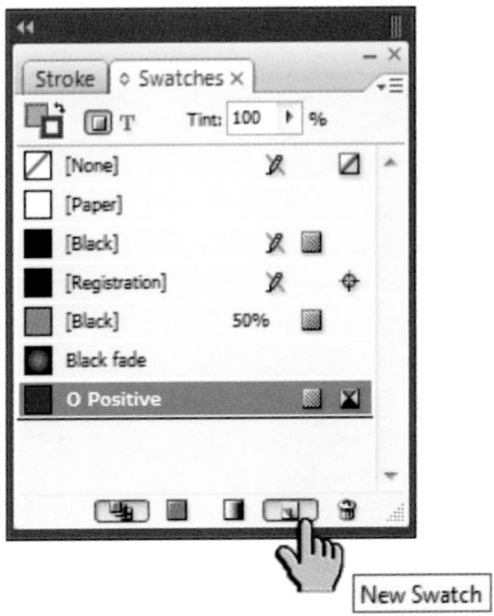

Figure 5-36.

By default, InDesign automatically names a swatch with a close numerical approximation of its CMYK values. If you want to give your swatch a more meaningful name, double-click it, turn off the Name with Color Value check box, enter a new name in the Swatch Name option box—say "O Positive"—and click OK.

---

10. ***Display the Stroke palette.*** Aside from changing the color, you can apply some other features to existing strokes. In the last exercise, we changed the thickness of a line from the control palette (see Step 6 on page 178). To access other stroke functions, choose **Window→Stroke** or press F10 to bring up the **Stroke** palette. (If this keyboard shortcut gives you problems on the Mac, change your Exposé settings as I describe on page xx of the Preface.) If you don't see all the options shown in Figure 5-37, choose **Show Options** from the palette menu or click the ♦ arrow next to the palette name.

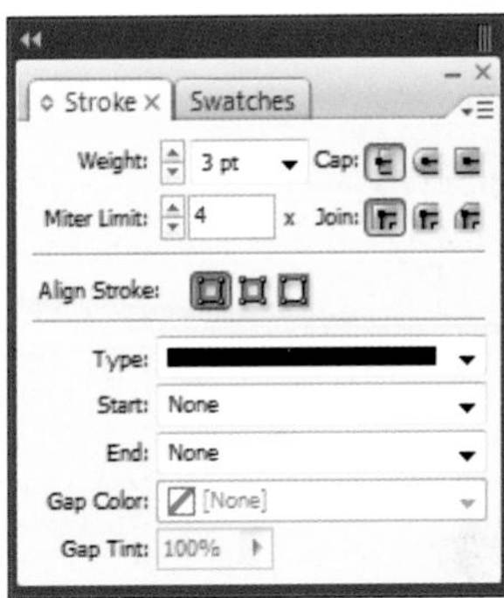

Figure 5-37.

11. ***Round off the line caps.*** Let's start by adjusting the stroke settings to change our pathways to something more dynamic. Inside the Stroke palette, the Cap settings define the appearance of the stroke at the *endpoints* (that is, the anchor points at the beginning and end of the path):

    - Currently the cap is set to my favorite attribute in all of InDesign: the butt cap. (Call me juvenile, but it makes me laugh like a giddy third-grader. Butt I digress.) The butt cap option (⊟) cuts the line abruptly at the ends of the path. It also happens to be the default setting.
    - Click the round cap icon (⊖) to end the path with a half circle, which creates a smoother finish.
    - The projecting cap (⊟) extends the stroke beyond the endpoints to a distance equal to half the stroke's width. Use this setting when you want to make sure one stroke overlaps another.

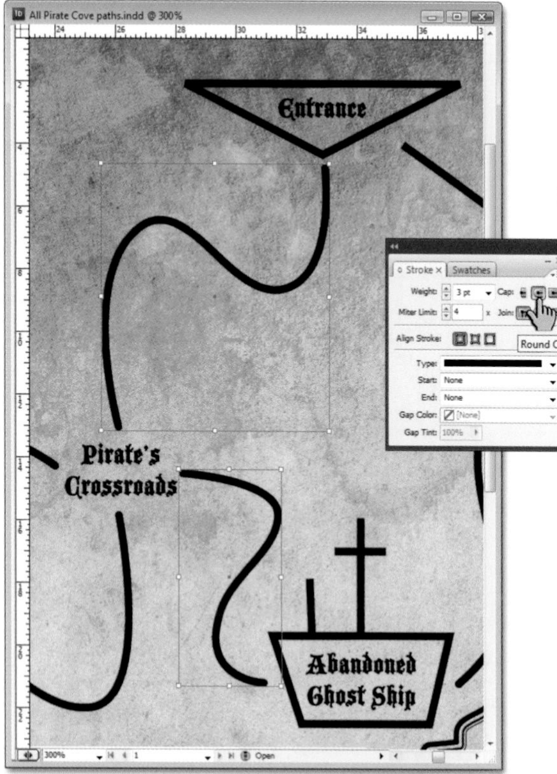

Figure 5-38.

Press V to get the black arrow tool. Click on the path toward the top of the document that extends between the words *Entrance* and *Pirate's Crossroads*. Then press the Shift key and click the lower path from *Pirate's Crossroads* to the *Abandoned Ghost Ship*. Click the second **Cap** icon (⊟) to give the lines gentle round caps, as in Figure 5-38.

12. ***Raise the Miter Limit value on the Entrance triangle.*** Click the triangle that surrounds the word *Entrance* with the black arrow tool to select it. We're going to fix a problem that may have been bothering you for some time now: The corners of the top edge points appear clipped, or *beveled*, rather than coming to a sharp point. The Stroke palette offers three Join options that determine how the stroke looks at corners in the path:

    - The first option, ⊡, creates a sharp, or *mitered*, tip.
    - The second option, ⊡, rounds the tips.
    - The final option, ⊡, bevels the tips.

    The miter option is active, and yet the three points in the triangle are obviously beveled. What gives? Mitered strokes have a habit of extending well beyond their paths, especially at acute (very sharp) corners. To counteract this, InDesign includes a Miter Limit value that keeps moderate corners sharp and bevels acute ones. The value is measured as a ratio between the miter length and the line weight, both of which I've illustrated in Figure 5-39.

    Go ahead and raise the **Miter Limit** to 5. This permits the miter length to grow to 5 times the line weight, or 15 points for our 3-point stroke. The result is that the two corners display proper Entrance-arrow sharpness, as witnessed in Figure 5-40 on the facing page.

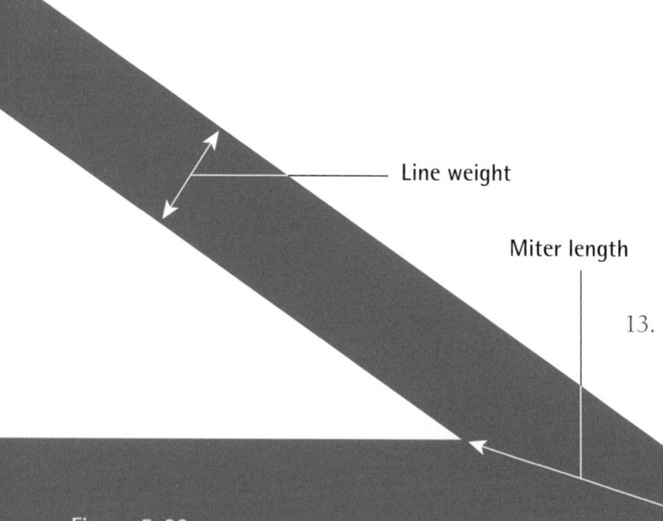

Figure 5-39.

13. ***Change the stroke pattern for the tunnel line.*** Another feature of the Stroke palette is the ability to change the type or pattern of a stroke. Let's apply a different type to the underground tunnel to differentiate it from the above-ground pathways. Select the line that goes from *Entrance* to *Blackbeard's Hideout* with the black arrow tool. Click the **Type** pop-up menu in the Stroke palette to see previews of all of InDesign's built-in stroke patterns. Select the **Thin-Thick-Thin** option for the secret passageway.

14. ***Add an arrowhead to the tunnel line.*** Toward the bottom of the Stroke palette, the Start and End options let you add arrowheads and other ornaments to the beginning and end of an open path. Let's say park management wants people to use the main path on their way out, to entice patrons with last-minute souvenirs. Our job, then, is to make the secret passage a one-way affair—you can go in, but you can't get out:

   - Assuming you drew the path from the top downward (see "Drawing Lines and Shapes," Step 5, page 178), the bottom point is the end of the path. The bottom point is where I want the arrow, so select **SimpleWide** from the **End** pop-up menu, as you see me doing in Figure 5-41.

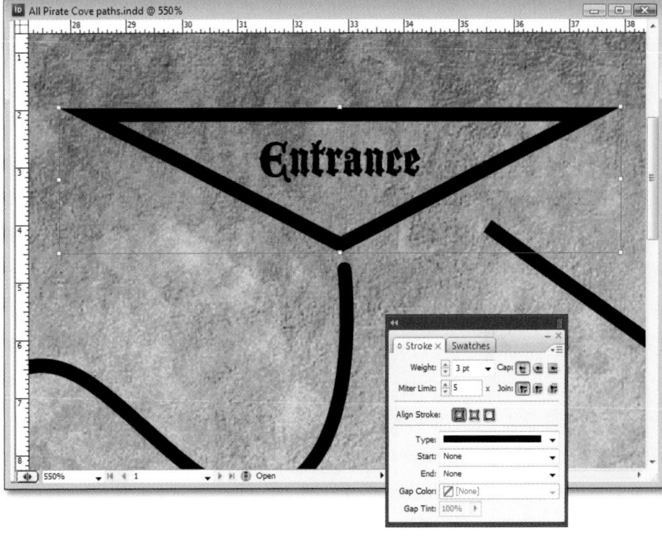

Figure 5-40.

But what if you forget which end was which? No problem. Just put the arrowhead where you guess it belongs, and if your 50-50 bet turns out wrong, choose Object→Paths→Reverse Path.

   - Change the **Cap** option to ⊟. Figure 5-42 diagrams how the arrowhead and other stroke attributes work together. The round cap setting smooths off the endpoints; the miter join ensures a nice sharp point. In other words, an arrowhead is just another path—albeit a virtual one created outside your control—as indicated by the white lines in the figure.

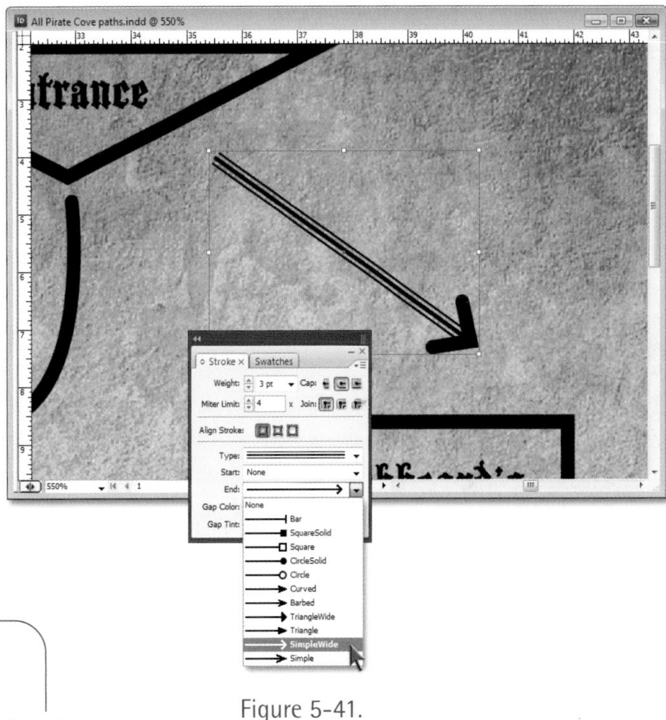

Figure 5-41.

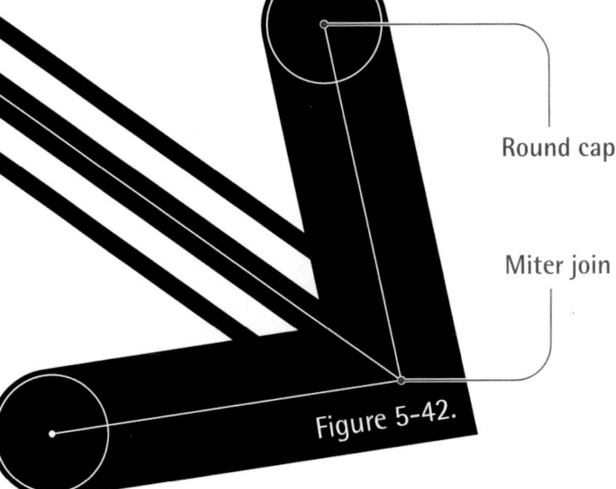

Figure 5-42.

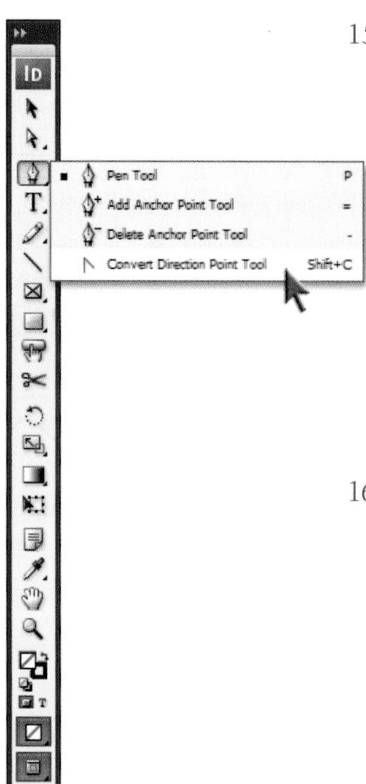

Figure 5-43.

15. ***Select the convert point tool from the toolbox.*** In actuality, the secret passageway loops back and forth a little on its way to the booty-filled catacombs of Blackbeard's Hideout. We don't have to map out every twist and turn, but a little bit of twisting seems in order. To put a few bends in the straight, triple-stroked line, click and hold the pen tool icon in the toolbox and select the convert direction point tool (*direction point* being one of Adobe's names for what I call a control handle). This tool, which I refer to as simply the convert point tool, changes the behavior of anchor points by adding or deleting control handles.

16. ***Convert the straight tunnel to a winding passageway.*** In our case, we need to change the existing corner points to smooth points, which you do by dragging them. Here's how:

    - From the top point, drag down and to the right, to the point indicated by the tiny yellow arrowhead in Figure 5-44. As you do, the convert point tool draws forth two symmetrical control handles, which arc the line downward.
    - From the bottom endpoint, drag down and to the left, past the *Blackbeard's Hideout* rectangle, as indicated by the white arrowhead in the figure. This lifts the right side of the line, pointing the rounded arrow toward the building.
    - Press and hold the Ctrl (or ⌘) key to temporarily get the white arrow tool, and then drag the bottom point a bit closer to the rectangle, as indicated by the tiny black arrowhead in Figure 5-44.

Figure 5-44.

17. ***Apply a stroke pattern to a shape.*** Now let's adjust the stroke pattern of a geometric shape. Scroll to the top-left region of the map and select the square around *Haunted Castle* with the black arrow tool. For the sake of variety, we'll adjust the stroke from the control palette:

    - Up the line weight by selecting **4 pt** from the pop-up menu in the middle of the palette.
    - Choose **Thick-Thin** from the unmarked pop-up menu directly below the line weight, as demonstrated in Figure 5-45.

18. ***Apply the Corner Effects command.*** InDesign's drawing tools are terrific and everything, but you may have noticed that one is missing: the

rounded rectangle tool. Instead, you have something better: A command that can sculpt the corners of *any* shape. We'll use it to liven up this boring square.

Choose **Corner Options** from the **Object** menu. If you loaded my dekeKeys shortcuts back in the Preface, you can also press Ctrl+Alt+Shift+R (or ⌘-Option-Shift-R) to display the **Corner Effects** dialog box. Then do the following:

- Check **Preview** so you can see what you're doing.
- Set the **Effect** option to **Inverse Rounded**.
- Change the **Size** value to 0p6 and press the Tab key to update the preview.
- Click the **OK** button.

The inwardly rounded corners appear in Figure 5-45.

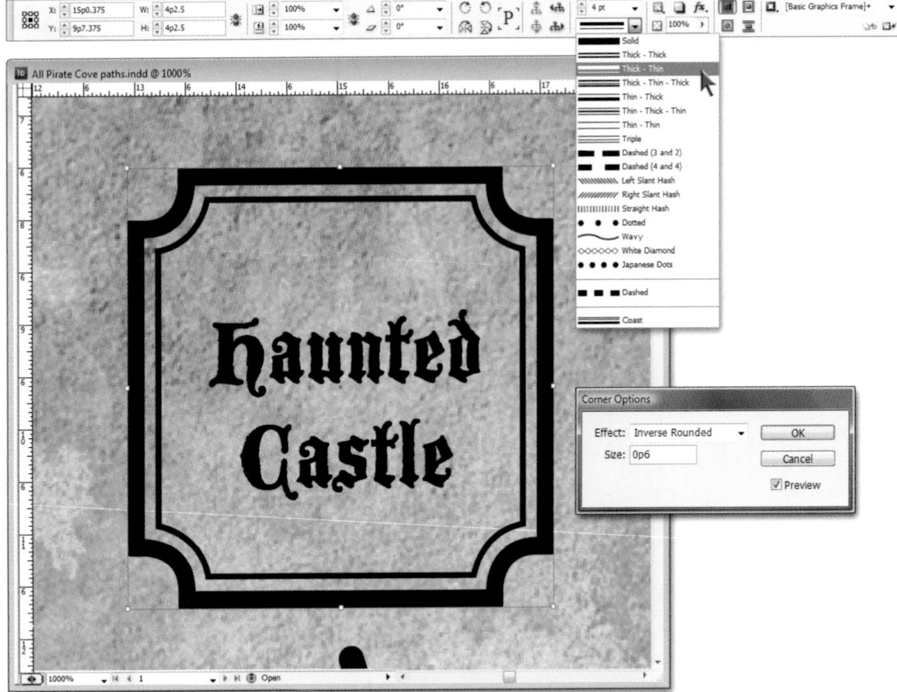

Figure 5-45.

PEARL OF WISDOM

You can apply Corner Effects to any line, shape, or frame. Plus, the command is dynamic, so you can change or remove a corner effect at any time by choosing Object→Corner Options. (To remove the effect, select None from the Effect pop-up menu.) Furthermore, if you edit an object with the white arrow tool, InDesign automatically adapts the corners to fit.

19. ***Apply a different effect to Blackbeard's Hideout.*** To see what I mean, scroll right to *Blackbeard's Hideout* and select the surrounding rectangle with the black arrow tool.

    - Choose **Object→Corner Options**.
    - Set the **Effect** to **Fancy** and the **Size** to 0p10.
    - Click **OK** and notice that the 3-point-thick line obscures the fancy effect.
    - Reduce the stroke by selecting **2 pt** in the Stroke or control palette. As you can see in Figure 5-46 on the next page, our fancy corners now open to reveal their true fanciness.

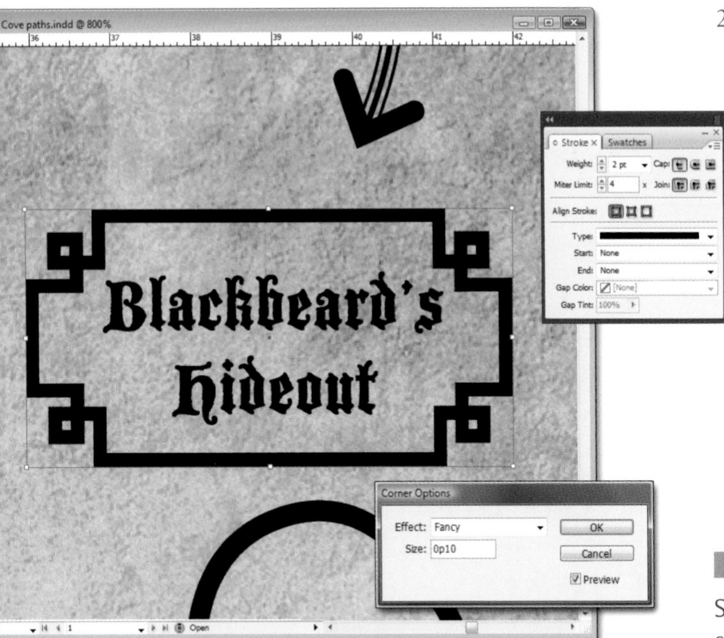

Figure 5-46.

Figure 5-47.

20. ***Set the corners of the free-form ship.*** Corner effects work on free-from shapes as well as those created with a shape tool. Select the ship path that you traced around *Abandoned Ghost Ship* in the previous exercise. Choose **Object→Corner Effects** or press that dekeKeys shortcut, Ctrl+Alt+Shift+R (⌘-Option-Shift-R). Change the **Effect** option to **Inset** and reduce the **Size** value to 0p3. As illustrated in Figure 5-47, InDesign treats the upper and lower corners differently based on the angles at which their segments meet, lending our trapezoidal path some real character. It's not rocket science—it's not even pirate ship science—but Corner Effects allows you to do some cool stuff with very basic shapes.

EXTRA CREDIT

So you've colored the compass rose and turned boring lines and shapes into more interesting ones. If you're the type who's easily satisfied, you might decide that your map is good enough and skip to "Aligning and Distributing Objects" on page 206. But be forewarned, you do so at your peril. For if you leave now, you'll miss out on a couple of InDesign's most exciting features: stroke styles and gradients, which let you define elaborate stroke and color patterns and save them for future use. But I understand. Who wants to learn some powerful techniques, lord it over friends and colleagues, probably get promoted and ultimately appointed head of the company, discover the cure for cancer, and bring everlasting peace to the world when you can save a few minutes and skip these last steps? You think I exaggerate? There's only one way to find out...

21. ***Try out a more elaborate stroke effect.*** Scroll westward to the circle around *Treasure Cave*. You may recall that this particular building is designed for the kiddos to run around in like they're insane—which, as any parent knows, they are—while staying in full view. So naturally it's surrounded by windows, which we'll simulate with a specialty stroke. Select the shape and do like the bulleted text says:

- Set the **Type** option in the **Stroke** palette to **White Diamond**, which traces the circle with a pattern of hollow diamonds.
- Raise the **Weight** value to 5 points, and you get the window-like effect pictured in Figure 5-48 across the spine.

PEARL OF WISDOM

InDesign's predefined stroke effects are a versatile bunch. But sadly, there aren't all that many of them. Which is why it comes as a relief to so many designers that you can create custom effects using *stroke styles*. Although you can't build patterns of shapes like White Diamonds, you can repeat parallel lines, dots, and dashes, as you're about to see.

Figure 5-48.

22. ***Begin a new style for the pathways.*** Pirate maps usually use dotted or dashed lines, but none of the prebuilt options in the Stroke palette look quite right. So let's create our own. Use the black arrow tool to select any of the free-form paths that emanate from the centrally located *Pirate's Crossroads*. Then click the ▾≡ icon in the top-right corner of the **Stroke** palette and choose **Stroke Styles** from the palette menu. InDesign responds with the unfriendly **Stroke Styles** dialog box that appears in Figure 5-49.

23. ***Select a dashed stroke style.*** The Styles area lists seven predefined multiline strokes and an eighth, Coast, that I created for the coastline. But the dashes, hashes, and others are missing. To create a dashed line, ignore the Styles list and click the **New** button to display the **New Stroke Style** dialog box. Near the top, the Type pop-up menu invites you to select the kind of stroke you want to create. You have three options:

    - Choose Stripe to create patterns of parallel lines. You define the relative widths of the lines by dragging the edges of the black bars in the Stripe area. Numerical controls are also available.
    - The Dotted option strokes a line with circular dots. Click below the ruler to add dots.
    - The final option, Dash, results in a repeating sequence of dashes and gaps. Click below the ruler to add a dash. You can even assign the dashes round or square ends and control whether InDesign adjusts dashes or gaps to compensate for corners in a stroked path.

    Choose the **Dash** option from the **Type** pop-up menu. InDesign produces a horizontal ruler with a single pica-long dash that starts at the 0-pica mark. Pretty boring stuff, which is why we'll be switching things a bit.

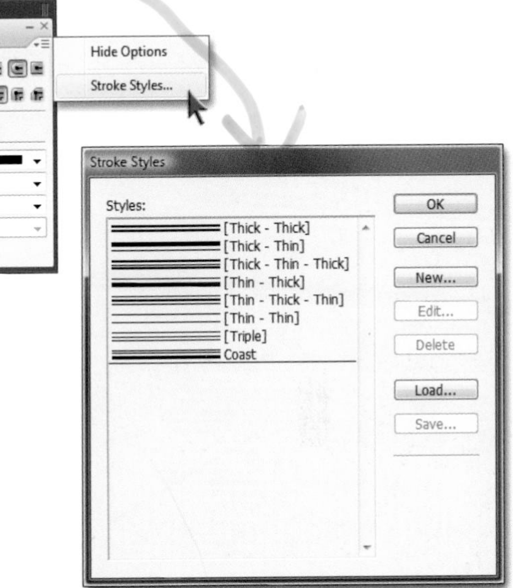

Figure 5-49.

24. ***Customize the dash stroke.*** Naturally, we don't want to settle for InDesign's default dash line settings. To that end, let's enter the settings shown in Figure 5-50, as follows:

- Click at the already-selected pointer at the 1-pica mark on the ruler and drag it back to the 4-point mark. Or just change the **Length** value to 0p4.
- Add a second dash at the 1-pica mark by clicking below the 1 in the ruler. To be sure you clicked at the right spot, confirm that the **Start** value is 1p0.
- Again type "0p4" into the **Length** option box.
- The **Pattern Length** defines the interval before the pattern repeats itself. Leave this value set to 2 picas.
- Leave the **Corners** option set to **Adjust dashes and gaps**. This tells InDesign to automatically contract or expand the gaps between dashes to make sure the dashes don't fold in on themselves at corner points.
- Change the **Cap** style to ⊟. This rounds off the ends of each and every dash in the pattern, resulting in a series of symmetrical pills.
- The rounding is not reflected in the ruler area. But you can see it at a reduced size in the Preview area at the bottom of the dialog box. To make sure the effect looks right, reduce the **Preview Weight** to 3 points, which is the line weight assigned to our free-form paths.
- Enter "Pirate Dashes" into the **Name** option at the top of the dialog box.

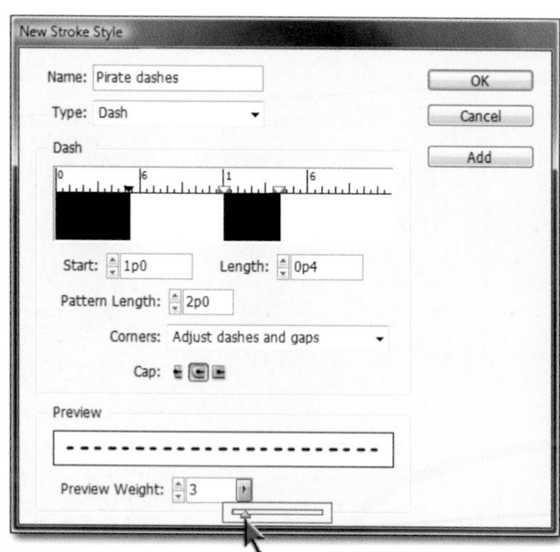

Figure 5-50.

Click **OK** to exit the New Stroke Style dialog box and add an entry to the Styles list. Click **OK** again to exit the Stroke Styles dialog box and make your new style.

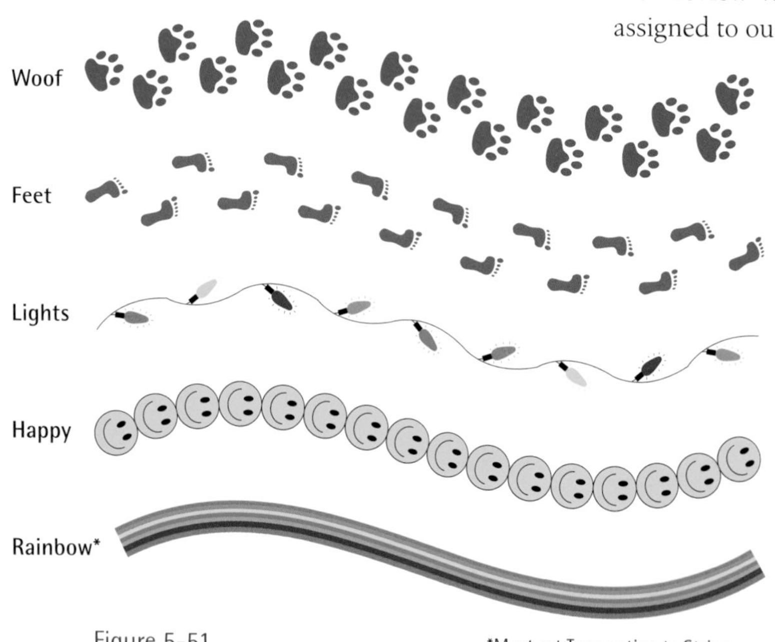

Figure 5-51.

Want something besides lines, dashes, and dots? InDesign provides a handful of hidden stroke styles that you get to by entering secret codes. Inside the Stroke Styles dialog box, click New. Then change the Name value to "Woof" and click OK. You'll get a repeating pattern of paws. Figure 5-51 shows a few other names you can try. Enter the names exactly as I've written them. Only one of the presets requires an adjustment. After entering "Rainbow," set the Type option to Stripe, and then click OK.

25. ***Apply the Pirate Dashes style.*** Apply the new stroke to the selected line by choosing **Pirate Dashes** from the **Type** pop-up menu in the **Stroke** or control palette.

26. ***Sample the stroke with the eyedropper tool.*** The easiest way to apply the new style to the other four paths, including the one that leads down to the peaceful (but deadly) Skull Coast, is to use the eyedropper tool. Select the tool from the toolbox or press the I key. Click anywhere along the pirate-dashed path. The cursor switches from empty and slanted down to the left (🖊) to full and slanting to the right (🖊).

27. ***Click the other four paths with the loaded eyedropper.*** After the eyedropper is loaded, it remains loaded until you select another tool or Alt-click (or Option-click) to load new attributes. Click each of the other paths to apply the setting. Our pathways are now rendered according to time-honored pirate map decorum, as in Figure 5-52.

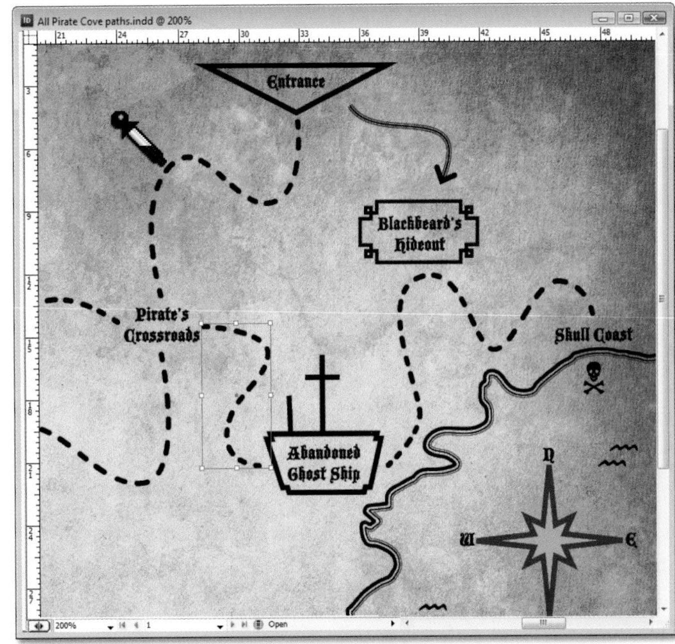

Figure 5-52.

28. ***Select the orange banner at the bottom of the map.*** A fill or stroke doesn't have to be a single solid color. You can create your own transitioning color pattern, called a *gradient*, to give some dimension to objects, backgrounds, and even text. Get the black arrow tool and click anywhere in the gold band behind the text at the bottom of the document.

29. ***Make a new gradient swatch.*** We're going to shade the existing banner with some darker colors. Go to the **Swatches** palette and make sure the fill icon is active, as in ▣. Then click the ▾≡ icon in the corner of the Swatches palette and choose the **New Gradient Swatch** command. Up pops the **New Gradient Swatch** dialog box. Type the name "Offer Background" into the Name field (see Figure 5-53) and then click **OK** to close it. That's right. InDesign adds an Offer Background item to the end of the Swatches palette.

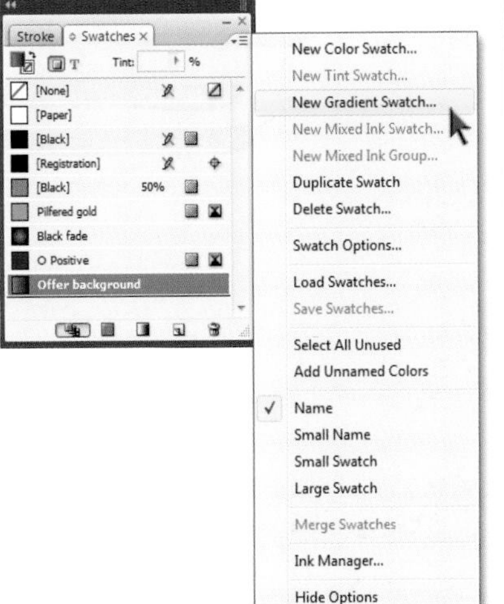

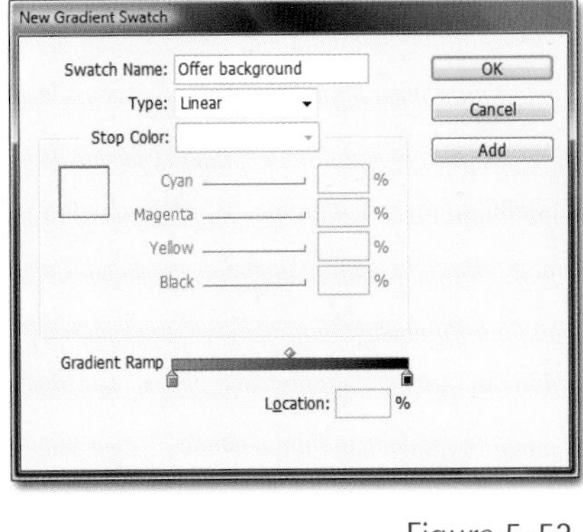

Figure 5-53.

Why did we just enter a dialog box and do nothing? Well, you can go ahead and create your gradient in the New Gradient Swatch dialog box, but there's no Preview option. Me, I like to see what I'm doing, so I close the dialog box after creating the swatch, then I reopen it, and, lo and behold, there's our old friend the Preview check box. Actually, I got this trick from a lynda.com video by none other than David Blatner. If you've never heard of him, note to you, the guy's an InDesign wiz. To quote the musical duo Flight of the Conchords, "Good one, Dave. Ooh, you're a legend, Dave." They weren't talking about InDesign tips, but if they knew Blatner, they very nearly might have been. He could've been a part-time model.

30. ***Reopen the Offer Background swatch.*** Double-click on your new swatch in the **Swatches** palette to reopen it. This brings up the **Gradient Options** dialog box, which, as I promised above and you can now see for yourself in Figure 5-54, has a **Preview** check box, which you should definitely turn on since you've gone to this much trouble. The once orange banner is a mess, but have faith, we'll fix it.

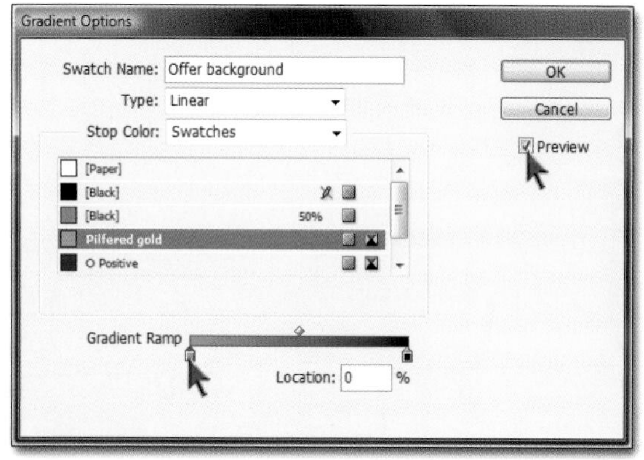

Figure 5-54.

When it comes to InDesign gradients, you have two basic types to choose from:

- Linear creates a blend of colors in a straight line, which can move horizontally, vertically, or at an angle you specify.
- Radial creates a blend of concentric circles moving out from a designated center.

In this case, we're working with a horizontal area, so I want you to choose **Linear** from the **Type** pop-up menu.

31. ***Set the left-hand stop color to orange.*** You set the colors for the gradient by clicking one of the *color stops*, indicated by a ◙ below the Gradient Ramp slider.
    - Start by clicking the ◙ on the left side of the **Gradient Ramp** slider bar. Suddenly, the entire dialog box lights up with active options.
    - Go to the third option down, the **Stop Color** pop-up menu, and choose **Swatches** (if it isn't set that way already), which gives you the choice of all the colors you would see in the Swatches palette itself. Click the **Pilfered Gold** swatch in the scrolling list.

32. ***Dial in the CMYK values for the other stop.*** We don't have a color swatch for the other color stop, so we'll dial it in manually with the help of CMYK values.

Here's the approach I recommend:

- Click the right-hand stop in the **Gradient Ramp** slider bar to select it.
- Choose the **CMYK** option from the **Stop Color** pop-up menu. As you can see in Figure 5-55, the window shifts from Swatches to something very reminiscent of the Color palette in its CMYK mode.
- Set the color values to **C**: 40, **M**: 75, **Y**: 100, and **K**: 0. You now have a nice transition from a bright orange to a darker brown across the bottom of the map.

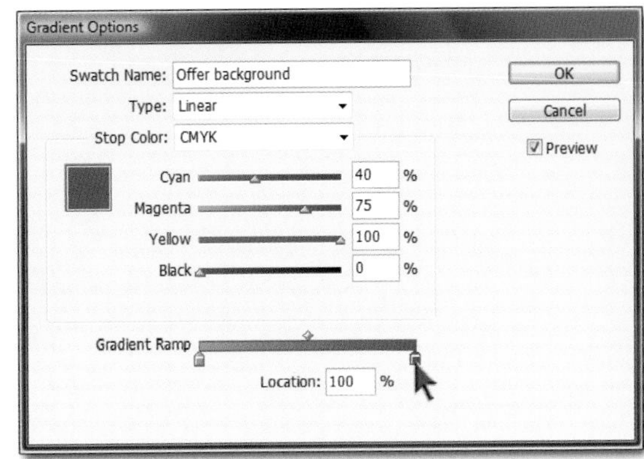

Figure 5-55.

If you want to have some fun, watch what happens to the previously orange banner as you dial in each component. With the Preview check box on, the gradient updates with each press of the Tab key, providing for some wild color combinations along the way to our desired shade.

---

33. ***Add a stop to your gradient.*** InDesign gradients are not limited to the transition between a mere two colors. You can add as many stops in as many colors as you like. For our purposes, I want you to add another stop of the darker color on the left side of the gradient so that the bright orange lands in the middle of the banner.
    - Start by dragging the Pilfered Gold stop indicator to the center of the Gradient Ramp slider bar. The **Location** value below the slider bar should ultimately read 50 percent.
    - Next, click below the Gradient Ramp slider bar on the far left to create another stop. Assign the same color values as you did for the right-hand stop (**C**: 40, **M**: 75, **Y**: 100, and **K**: 0) and click **OK** to exit the Gradient Options dialog box.

Now, as shown in Figure 5-56, our gradient not only provides a better degree of visual interest, but it subtly highlights the word *free* in the text. (Keep an eye peeled for my next title, *Subliminal Messaging One-on-One.*)

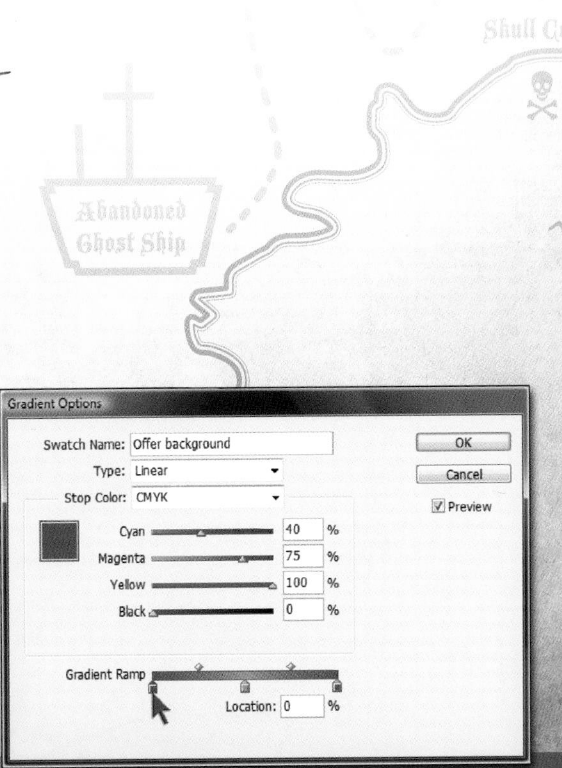

Figure 5-56.

34. ***Apply a gradient to a stroke.*** As I mentioned at the outset, you can use a gradient as you would any swatch, which means we can also apply it to the stroke that defines our compass rose. Start by selecting the compass rose object in the bottom-right area of the document with the black arrow tool. Then click the stroke icon in the toolbox, which is currently set to our lurid O Positive red.

35. ***Create a new radial gradient.*** Click the ▾≡ icon in the **Swatches** palette and choose the **New Gradient Swatch** command. Then do the following:

    - Name the new gradient "Compass Rose" and close the dialog box so you can reopen it and preview the results of your actions.
    - In the Swatches palette, double-click the **Compass Rose** item (which, for the moment, looks like the Offer Background swatch) to open the **Gradient Options** dialog box.
    - Turn on the **Preview** check box.
    - Set the **Type** setting to **Radial**, so that our transitions radiate outward from the center of the compass.

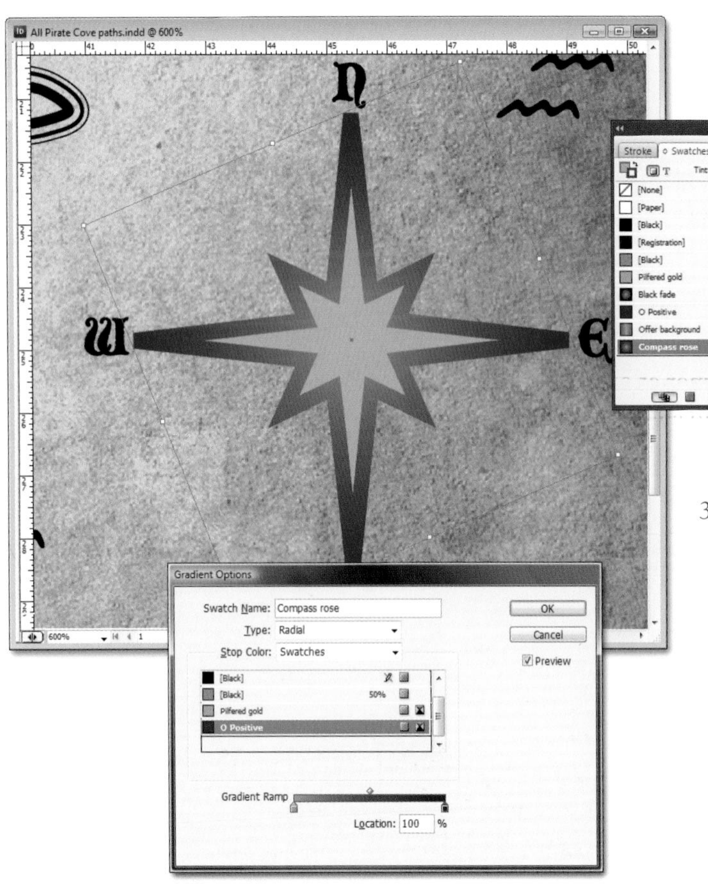

Figure 5-57.

36. ***Remove a stop and set a new color.*** You can remove any stop by dragging its ■ indicator down and away from the Gradient Ramp slider bar. I call it the "rip."

    - Rip the leftmost brown ■ away from the slider bar to delete it.
    - Move the bright orange center stop to the vacant left position, so the **Location** value reads 0 percent.
    - Click the brown stop on the right (**Location**: 100), change **Stop Color** to **Swatches**, and select the dark red we created earlier, **O Positive**.

On display in Figure 5-57, the modified compass rose radiates an inner warmth, like a star that beckons to all manner of seafaring rascals, devilish or dastardly. Don't click OK yet; we'll stay inside this dialog box for one more step.

37. ***Adjust the gradient to center the golden glow.*** The gradient is too diffused to have much impact. Let's punch it up by giving the gold center a little bit of focus:

   - Click on the red stop to activate it, after which it will look like ☗, with a dark triangle at the top.
   - Change the **Location** value to 45 percent, which moves the stop radically to the left.
   - The diamond shape (◇) above the slider bar marks the midpoint of the gradient, where the colors mix in equal amounts. Click the midpoint ◇ and change the **Location** value to 75 percent to favor the gold center and make it fade more sharply into red.
   - When the dialog box and document look like those pictured in Figure 5-58, click the **OK** button.

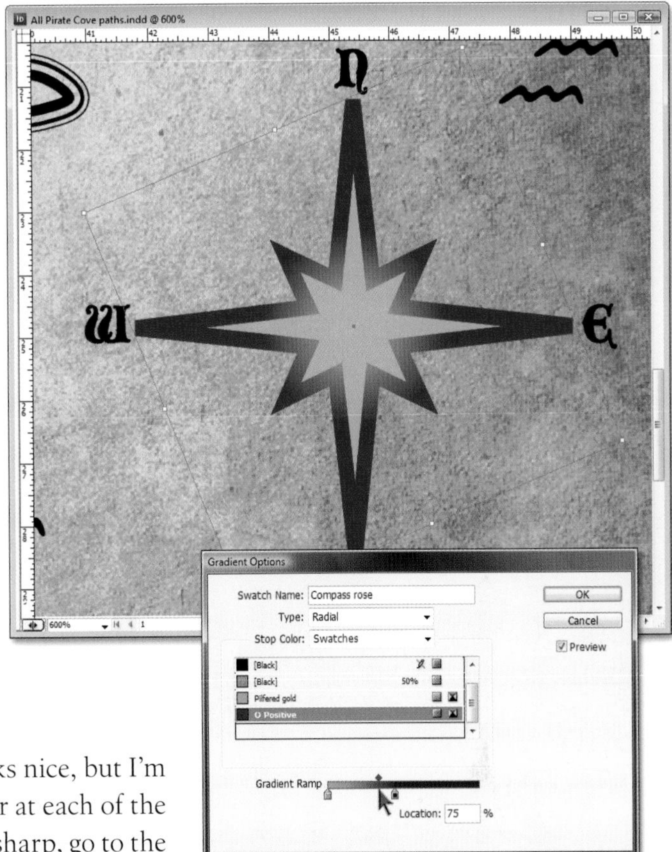

Figure 5-58.

38. ***Raise the Miter Limit value.*** The gradient looks nice, but I'm not the least bit pleased with the beveled corner at each of the four directions. To make these points nice and sharp, go to the **Stroke** palette and raise the **Miter Limit** to 10. This restores the sharp corners, all right, but it also presents a new problem. As illustrated in Figure 5-59, the farthest points of the star skewer the direction letters.

39. ***Align the stroke to the inner wall of the path.*** InDesign lets you modify the way a stroke aligns to its path. By default, the stroke is centered on the path, with half of the stroke inside the path and half out. We want it all in. So click the second **Align Stroke** icon (⌑) to tuck the stroke inward. I also reduced the **Weight** value to 2 points. The Stroke palette settings and resulting compass rose appear in Figure 5-60.

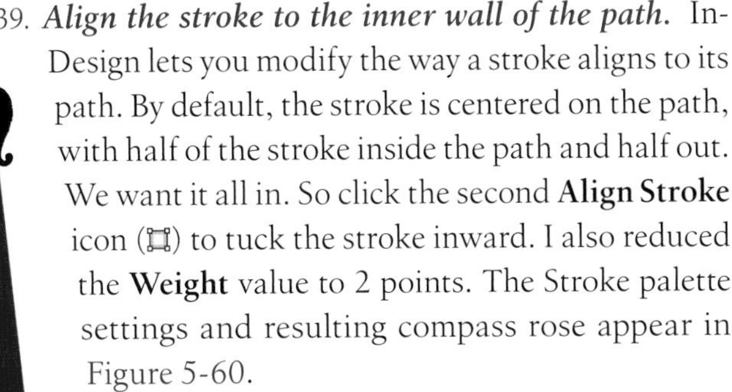

Figure 5-59.

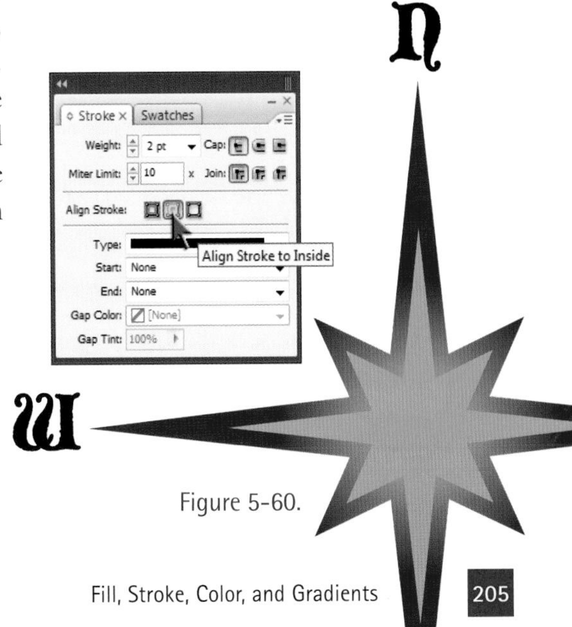

Figure 5-60.

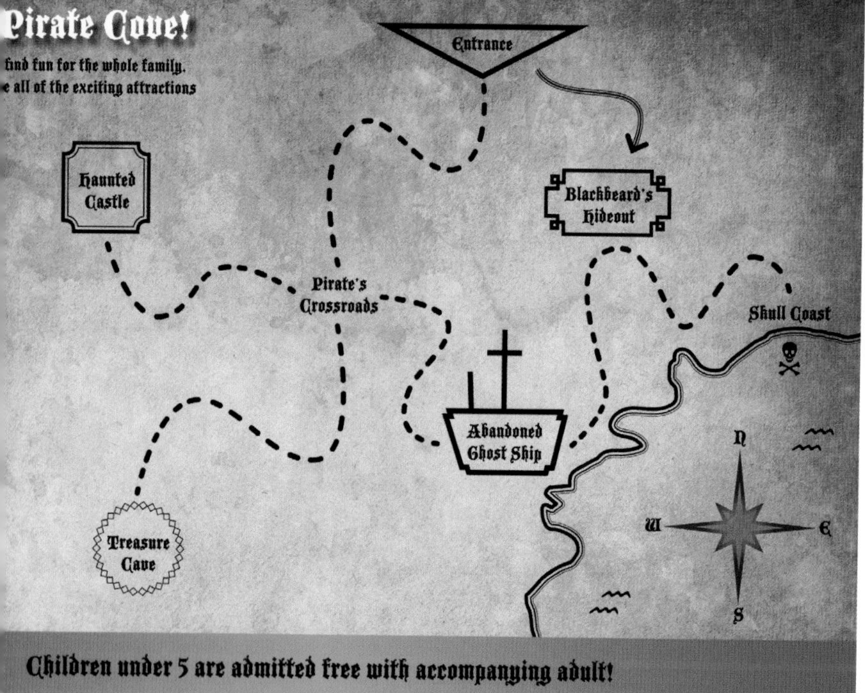

Figure 5-61.

PEARL OF WISDOM

One last word about gradients: InDesign devotes a lot of attention to gradients. Consider the gradient tool, which allows you to define the angle of a linear gradient and click to set the center of a radial gradient. But while undeniably flexible, gradients have a tendency to date a document or make it look amateurish. Used discretely, a gradient or two can add color and depth to an image. But applied in wide swaths across expansive backgrounds, your document may start to look like one big, dull PowerPoint presentation. Crazy as it may sound, when in doubt, a flat color beats a showy gradient any day of the week.

Which is why I elected to downplay the compass rose by burning it into its background. To achieve this effect, I brought up the Effects palette and selected the Multiply mode from the palette's top-left pop-up menu. For more information on Multiply and other blend modes, check out Lesson 7, "Transparency and Effects." The final map appears in Figure 5-61.

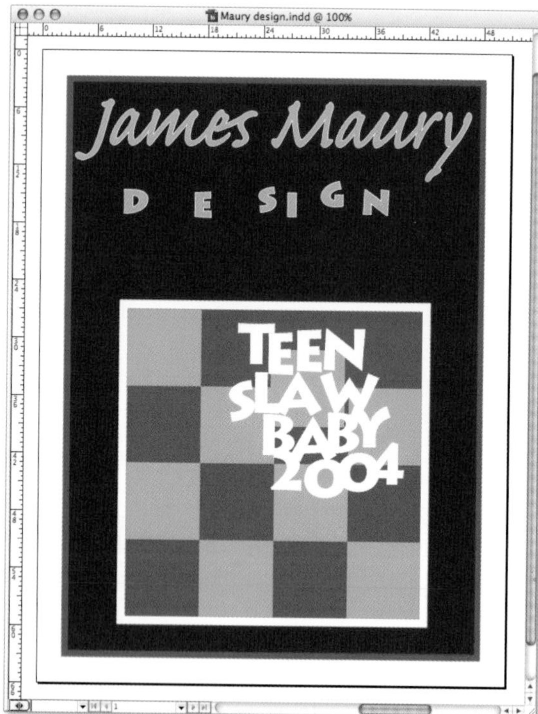

Figure 5-62.

Aligning and Distributing Objects

When bringing text blocks and graphic objects into alignment, your first move might be to drag guides from the rulers and snap the objects into place. But there's another way. InDesign's Align palette can position selected objects so that their edges or centers are in perfect alignment, all without a single guide. The Align palette can also *distribute* a row or column of objects so that they're evenly spaced. This exercise shows you how the Align palette's alignment and distribution powers work.

1. ***Open a document with objects in need of alignment.*** Go to the *Lesson 05* folder inside *Lesson Files-IDcs3 1on1* and open the file named *Maury design.indd*. Shown in Figure 5-62, this document features some randomly scattered characters—each housed inside its own frame—over a checkerboard pattern. Each character belongs inside one of the checkerboard squares,

which when put in the proper order will spell the street address for our design company. Note that some of the items are placed on a locked layer, which you won't need to select during this exercise.

2. ***Select the misplaced beige square.*** On closer inspection, one of the beige squares is out of place. Located under the heap of white characters, it should be in the top row of squares. Because the square is so thoroughly buried, you can't select it by simply clicking it with the black arrow tool. You need to use a special technique that I call "selecting down the stack."

   The trick to selecting down the stack is the Ctrl key (⌘ on the Mac). Try this: Using the black arrow tool, click the *A* in *SLAW* to select it. Then press Ctrl (or ⌘) and click the *A* again. As Figure 5-63 shows, the bounding box changes to encompass the misplaced square. You selected *down through* the *A* to the next lowest item in the stack.

3. ***Add the top-left square to the selection.*** Shift-click the top-left beige square in the checkerboard to add it to the selection. Except for the misplaced square, all the other squares are locked, meaning that you can select them but not move them. As we'll see, locked objects are great for aligning other objects.

4. ***Bring up the Align palette.*** Choose **Window→Object & Layout→Align** or press Shift+F7 to display the **Align** palette. Before you start, make sure the bottom pop-up menu is set to **Align to Selection**, as by default.

5. ***Top-align the wayward square.*** Click the fourth icon () in the **Align Objects** section of the palette. As shown in Figure 5-64, the misplaced square aligns with the top-left square. There's no chance that the top-left square will move because it's locked. Therefore, it serves as an anchor for the alignment operation.

6. ***Deselect the top-left square and select the sixth beige square.*** Shift-click the first square to deselect it, and then Shift-click the sixth beige square—the one under the 2 and *0* in *2004*—to select it.

7. ***Right-align the wayward square.*** Click the third Align Objects icon () to align the right edges of the selected objects. Because the lower of the two squares is locked, the top square moves to the right, precisely aligning to the checkerboard. Figure 5-65 shows the result.

Figure 5-63.

Figure 5-64.

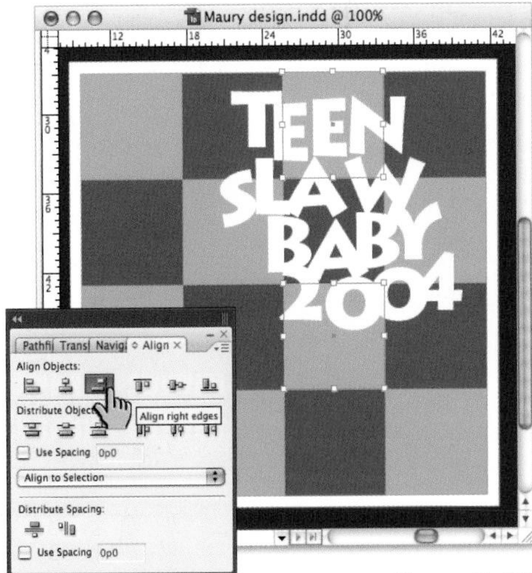

Figure 5-65.

Figure 5-66.

8. ***Lock down the formerly wayward square.*** Now that the errant square has been assimilated into its proper position, it's time to lock it down so it doesn't move again. With the squares still selected, choose **Object→Lock Position** or press Ctrl+L (⌘-L on the Mac). One of the selected squares was already locked, but it doesn't hurt anything to lock it again.

9. ***Align the* 4 *with the top-left square.*** Now we begin the somewhat arduous task of aligning the white characters with their respective squares. We'll start with the *4* in *2004*:

   - Select both the *4* and the top-left beige square by clicking one and Shift-clicking the other.
   - Click the second Align Objects icon (⊟) to center the two selected objects horizontally. The *4* scoots over into the left column.
   - Next, click the fifth alignment icon (⊪) to center the objects vertically, as in Figure 5-66.

10. ***Align an* E *to the bottom-right square.*** Click one of the *E*s in *TEEN* and then Shift-click the bottom-right beige square. Again, click the ⊟ and ⊪ icons to snap the *E* into place with the square.

    We could continue like this, aligning each letter or number to its proper square, but that wouldn't harness the full power of the Align palette. Instead, we'll move more expeditiously to finish the layout.

Figure 5-67.

11. ***Roughly position the other* E *and a* B.** Drag the other *E* and one of the *B*s in *BABY* into the approximate positions shown in Figure 5-67. Then Shift-click to select all four characters along the diagonal—that is, *4*, *E*, *B*, and *E*. We have the *4* and the bottom-right *E* exactly where they need to be, so be careful not to move them as you select them. Now let's distribute the other *E* and the *B* into place. (The *4* and bottom-right *E* will serve as the anchors.)

12. ***Distribute the four selected characters.*** This time, we'll focus on the **Distribute Objects** section of the Align palette. Click the second icon (⊟) to vertically distribute the objects so their centers are equally spaced. Next, click the fifth icon (⊪) to space the centers of the objects horizontally. Both distribution options move only the inside objects, so the *4* and the *E* remain fixed, as in Figure 5-68 on the facing page.

13. ***Lock the selected letters and position the others.*** Now that you have this diagonal line of letters exactly where you want them, choose **Object→Lock Position** or press Ctrl+L (⌘-L) to secure them in place. Congratulations, you have successfully positioned and locked a letter in each row and each column of the checkerboard. As you'll see, this will hasten the pace of the remaining alignment operations.

    Now move the twelve other characters into the rough locations shown in Figure 5-69. Don't even attempt to get them centered. As before, we'll have InDesign do this for us.

14. ***Align each of the four rows.*** Starting in the blue area outside the checkerboard, drag with the black arrow tool to draw a marquee through the objects in the first row, as illustrated in Figure 5-70. (Remember, you want to select only the first row. If you accidentally select a letter in any other row, click away from the objects to deselect them and try again. When done properly, you'll select four characters and a couple of beige squares; because the latter are locked, they won't be harmed by the operation.) Click the fifth **Align Objects** icon (⊪) to snap the *2* and the two *0*s into vertical alignment with the row.

    Next, repeat this operation—marqueeing and aligning—for each of the next three rows.

Figure 5-68.

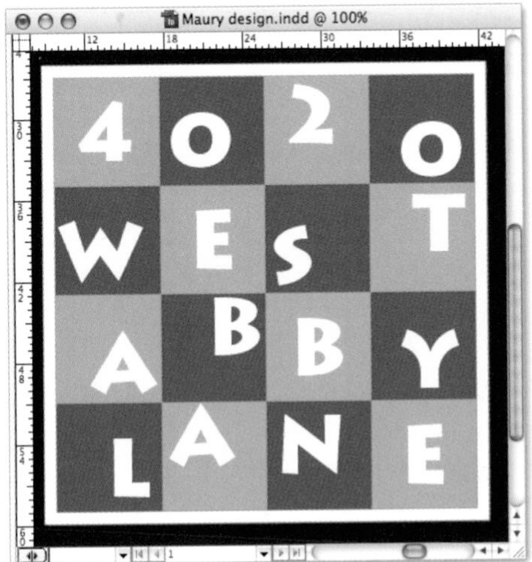

Figure 5-69.

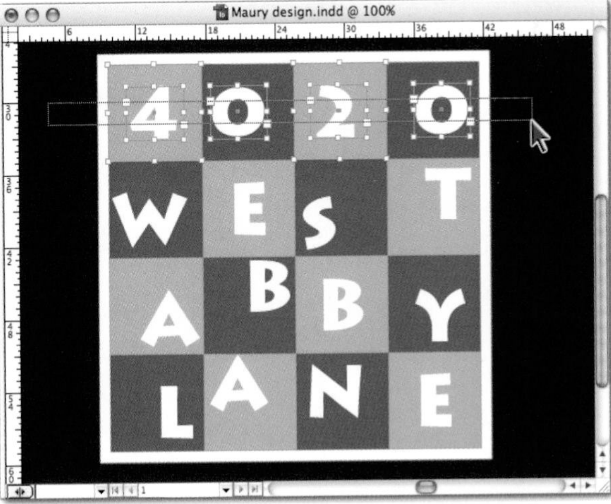

Figure 5-70.

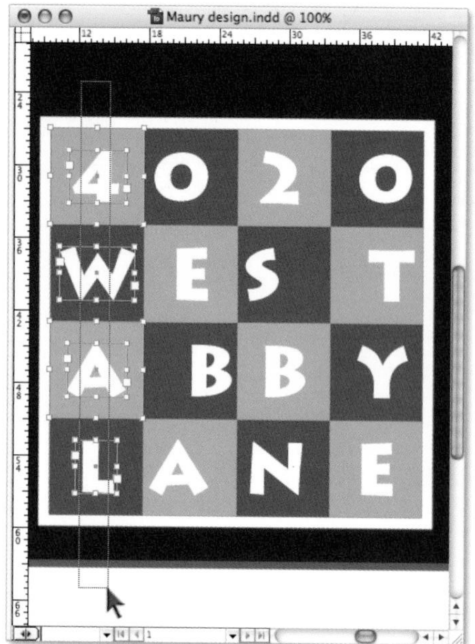

Figure 5-71.

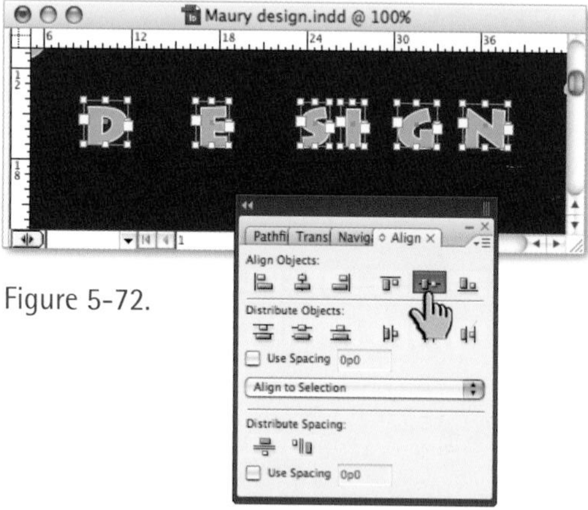

Figure 5-72.

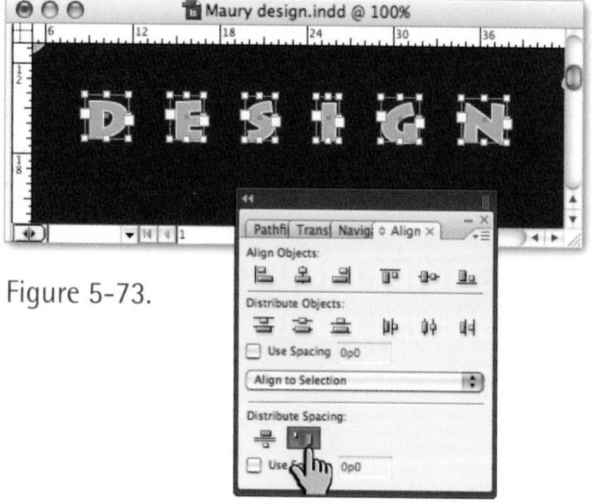

Figure 5-73.

15. ***Align each of the four columns.*** From rows we move to columns. Draw a slim marquee through the objects in the first column, as in Figure 5-71. Then click the second Align Objects icon (⊟). This makes the *W*, *A*, and *L* snap into horizontal alignment with the locked *4* above them. You might not see much of a change, but rest assured, the letters are now perfectly aligned. Marquee each of the three remaining columns and align them in a similar fashion.

16. ***Align the letters that appear above the checkerboard.*** Now that the sixteen characters are precisely aligned, we need to fix the yellow word *DESIGN*. Again, I recommend that you draw a marquee around the letters to select them. Click the fifth Align Objects icon (⊞). Note that the *D* is locked so it serves as the anchor. Figure 5-72 shows the result.

17. ***Distribute the selected letters.*** The letters are now aligned, but the distribution could use some work. Click the fifth **Distribute Objects** icon (⫴) to freeze the horizontal placement of the outside letters (the *D* and *N*) and to adjust the intermediate letters so that their centers are an equal horizontal distance apart. Problem is, that's not really what we want. There's too much space on either side of the *I*, and the *G* and *N* are jammed together. Sadly, the other distribution options don't fair any better. What's a person to do?

18. ***Even out the space between the letters.*** Situated at the bottom of the Align palette, the Distribute Spacing options ensure that there's equal space between the neighboring edges of the objects (as opposed to left or right edges or centers). Click the second **Distribute Spacing** icon (▯|▯) to create an equal amount of space between the nearest edges of neighboring letters. As Figure 5-73 shows, there's now an equal amount of space between the *I*, *G*, and *N*, resulting in a more pleasing layout.

PEARL OF WISDOM

Both the Distribute Objects and Distribute Spacing areas include Use Spacing check boxes. When active, these options permit you to distribute objects by a specified amount of space. One object remains stationary, and the others move with respect to it.

19. ***Group the word* Design *and align it to the page.*** Unfortunately, the locked *D* that we've been using as our base object for the last few steps was off-center horizontally, so now the entire word is off-center on the page.

Here's how to fix the problem:

- Choose **Object→Group** or press Ctrl+G (or ⌘-G) to treat the selected letters as a single object.
- A message tells you that a group can't include both locked and unlocked items. Click **Unlock All** to proceed.
- Rather than selecting another object to align to, choose **Align to Page** from the pop-up menu above the Distribute Spacing options, which I've circled in Figure 5-74.
- Click the second **Align Objects** icon (⊟) to align the horizontal center of the word to the page. All better.

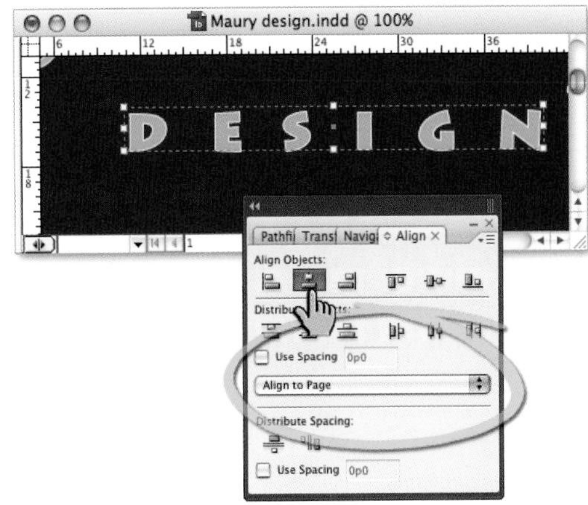

Figure 5-74.

Compound Paths and Pathfinder Operations

The pen tool is expertly suited to drawing free-form paths. But it can be a chore to use, so much so that even veteran designers admit to shying away from it. Even if you're one of the few who've taken to it like the proverbial fish takes to water, you have to admit that the pen is every bit as plodding as it is precise.

Which is why InDesign gives you other options. Instead of drawing an intricate path point-by-point with the pen, you can draw pieces of the path and then assemble those pieces into a composite whole. This not only simplifies the path-drawing ritual but also offers greater control when creating repeating or symmetrical forms.

Consider the circle cut from a square pictured at the top of Figure 5-75. Had I attempted to draw the shape with the pen tool, I'd have had to manually position nine points and eight control handles in such a way as to achieve perfect vertical and horizontal symmetry. InDesign offers many constraints (ruler guides, the Shift key, and so on), but none guarantee that one arc will be a precise mirror image of another. The better solution is to draw the base shapes using the rectangle and ellipse tools, align them as illustrated at the bottom of Figure 5-75, and finally combine them—in this case, by choosing Object→Pathfinders→Subtract. The approach is simple, the result is symmetrical, and I am happy.

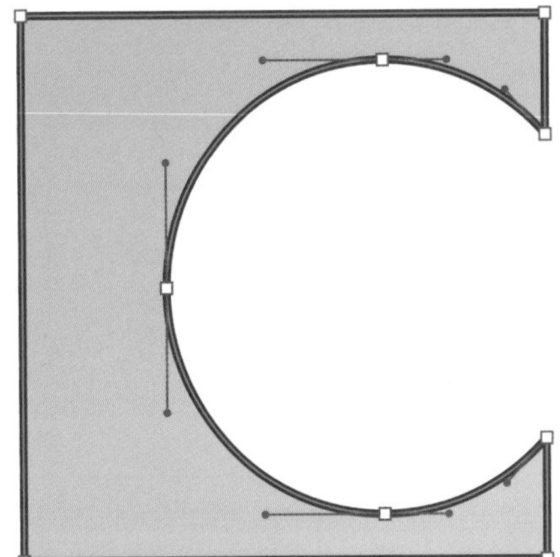

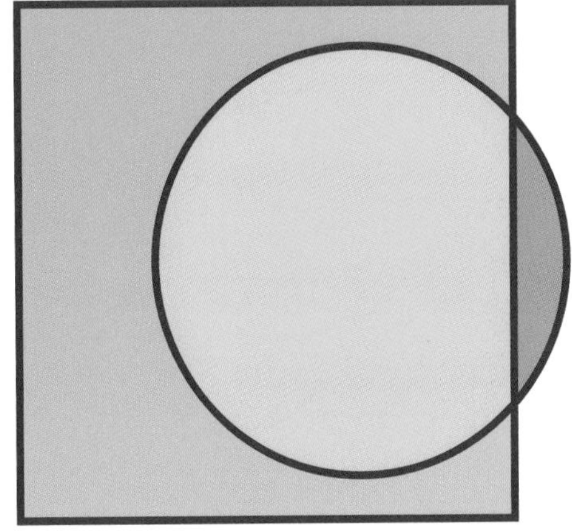

Figure 5-75.

This next exercise shows you how to combine simple paths to create more elaborate ones. You'll use paths to cut holes in one another, add paths together, and even calculate elaborate intersections. Simply put, using paths you'll learn how to do in a few minutes what would otherwise take hours to do with the pen.

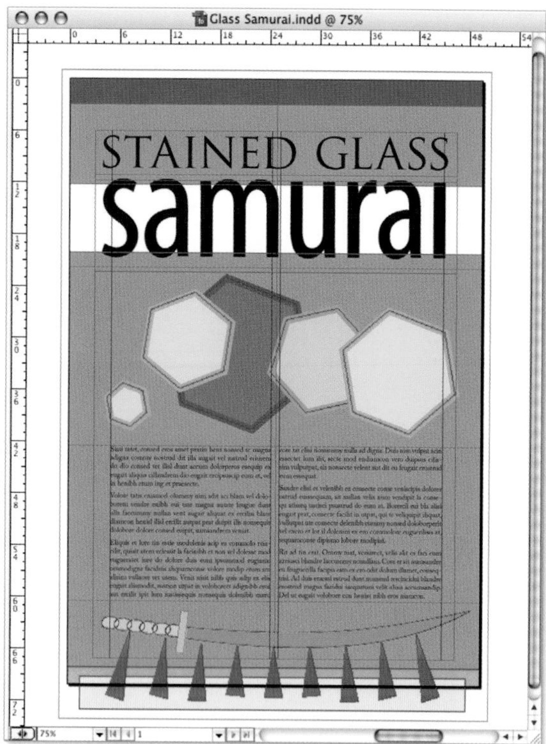

Figure 5-76.

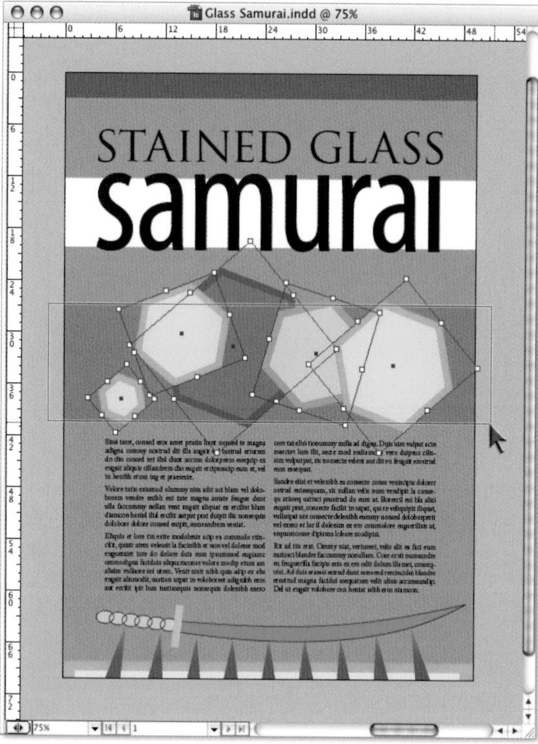

Figure 5-77.

1. ***Open a document that contains some primitive vector art.*** Open the file called *Glass Samurai.indd*, which is included in the *Lesson 05* folder inside *Lesson Files-IDcs3 1on1*. Shown in Figure 5-76, this page contains a bevy of basic shapes, including rectangles, ovals, and hexagons. In cases where basic shapes wouldn't suffice—the triangles at the bottom of the page and the blue blade of the sword—I drew some paths with the pen tool. But even these are limited to three points apiece. Such shapes are commonly called *primitives* because you can use them to build more complex artwork.

2. ***Select the hexagons.*** Using the black arrow tool, draw a marquee across the center of the hexagons to select all five shapes, as in Figure 5-77. (Note that, in the figure, I've pressed the W key to hide the guides and other nonprinting distractions.) We'll use the selected hexagons to create a stylized stained glass effect.

3. ***Combine the selection into a compound path.*** Choose **Object→Paths→Make Compound Path** or press the shortcut Ctrl+8 (⌘-8 on the Mac). InDesign converts the hexagons into a special object called a *compound path*. This special object possesses two key attributes:

   - A compound path can include only one fill and one stroke. This means all shapes now share the same color scheme, lifted from the lowest shape in the stack.
   - Areas that overlap within the compound path are treated as holes, and are thus transparent. The number 8 is the quintessential compound path, with two inner circles cutting holes out of a larger shape (hence Ctrl+8 or ⌘-8 as the keyboard shortcut). To my way of thinking, the occasional transparency heightens the stained glass effect.

Figure 5-78 verifies the first attribute and calls the second one into question. All shapes now share the blue fill and stroke originally applied to the rear hexagon. But of the three areas where the shapes intersect, only one is treated as a hole. What gives?

PEARL OF WISDOM

According to an arcane bit of PostScript printing code called the *nonzero winding fill rule*, shapes cut holes in each other only when their paths travel in opposite directions. For reasons known only to InDesign, the second hexagon to the left travels in the opposite direction of the other three, so as a result, only it cuts a hole. If we reverse the direction of the second hexagon on the right, which overlaps hexagons on both sides, we'll correct our problem.

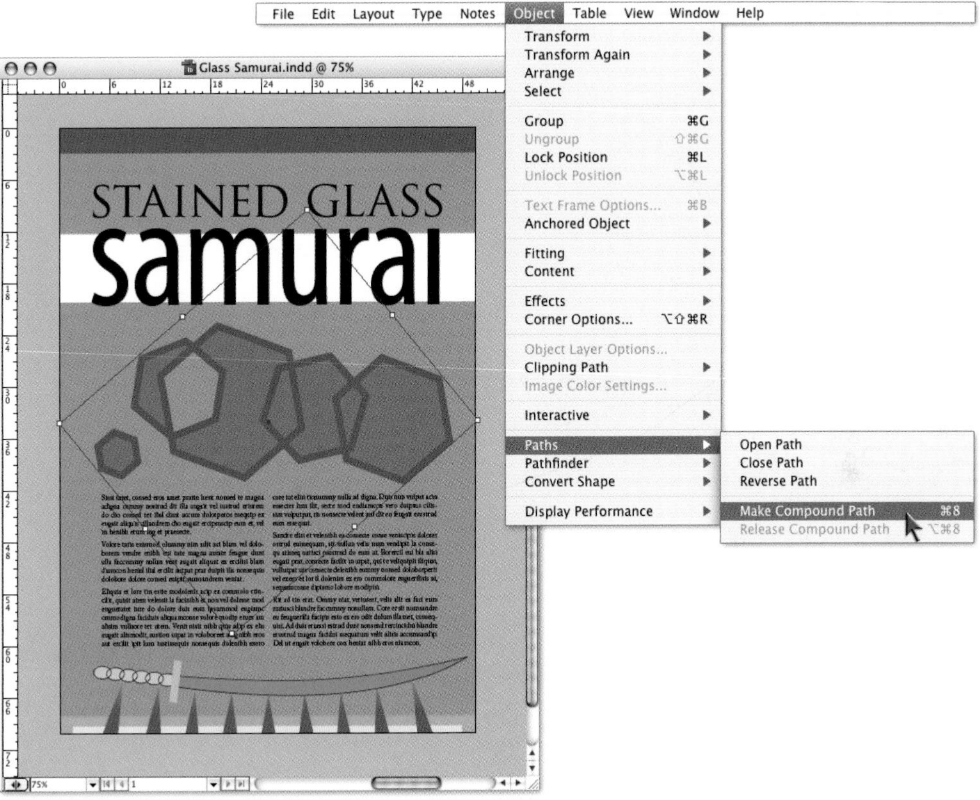

Figure 5-78.

4. ***Reverse the direction of the fourth shape.*** Based on how the hexagons interact, each of the three shapes on the right must travel in the same direction. Therefore, reversing the middle shape—that is, the fourth one from the left—should remedy our problem. Here's how to do it:

   - Switch to the white arrow tool by clicking the icon in the toolbox or by pressing the A key. InDesign selects the individual shape outlines.
   - We want to select only one shape, and the easiest way to do that is to redefine the selection. Press Ctrl+Shift+A (or ⌘-Shift-A) to deselect everything and start again.

- Press the Alt (or Option) key and click inside the fourth hexagon, the one under the *ur* in *samurai*. InDesign surrounds the shape with solid points (as opposed to the hollow ones seen elsewhere) to show that the shape is selected.

- Go to **Object→Paths** and choose **Reverse Path**. The redirected shape now cuts holes in its neighbors.

The result is a dynamic interaction of shapes, in which one shape intersects another to produce transparency. If you move or otherwise modify a shape independently of the others, the holes will update dynamically as well. So if InDesign's implementation of compound paths seems a bit weird, take heart that it's exceptionally flexible to boot.

5. ***Select the sword.*** Magnified in Figure 5-79, the sword is a collection of nine shapes. I drew the blade with the pen. Otherwise, it's all rectangles and ellipses that I rotated slightly from the control palette. (To learn about rotating, see the "Rotating, Slanting, and Flipping" exercise that begins on page 238 of Lesson 6.) In the next step, we'll combine the nine shapes into a single object. But first, we have to select them.

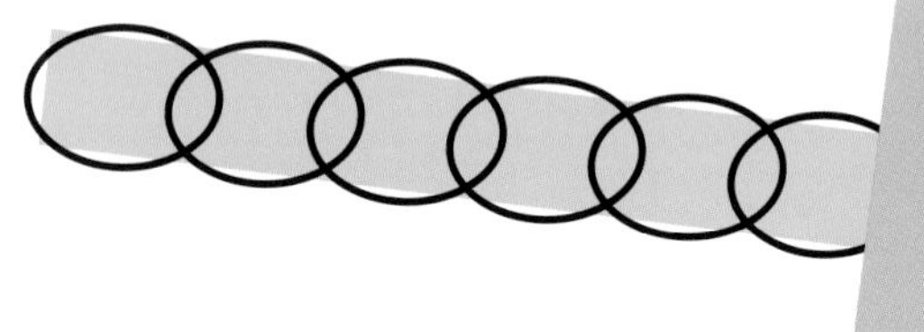

Figure 5-79.

To simplify the task of selecting the various sword elements—and eliminate the chance of selecting the triangles and other shapes that aren't part of the sword—I've relegated the salient shapes to an independent layer. Here's what you do:

- Choose **Window→Layers** or press F7 to display the **Layers** palette. You should see five layers, from Backdrop at the bottom to Sword at the top.

- Press the Alt (or Option) key and click the word **Sword** at the top of the palette. This wonderful little trick makes the layer active and selects all objects on that layer.

Just like that, the sword is selected. Of course, if you want to hone your manual selection skills, feel free to marquee or Shift-click the individual shapes. But isn't this so much easier?

6. ***Unite the nine paths into one.*** Now that you've selected the shapes, you can combine them using InDesign's foremost Pathfinder operation, Add. *Pathfinder* is Adobe's term for a collection of commands that use one path to manipulate the outline of another. The Add operation takes the selected paths and unites them all. To apply the Add command, do one of the following:

   - Choose **Object→Pathfinder→Add**.
   - Choose **Window→Object & Layout→Pathfinder** to display the **Pathfinder** palette. Then click the first icon, which looks like .

   InDesign unites the selected shapes into one continuous path, as in Figure 5-80. The path receives the fill and stroke attributes of the frontmost shape, so it now appears light brown with no stroke.

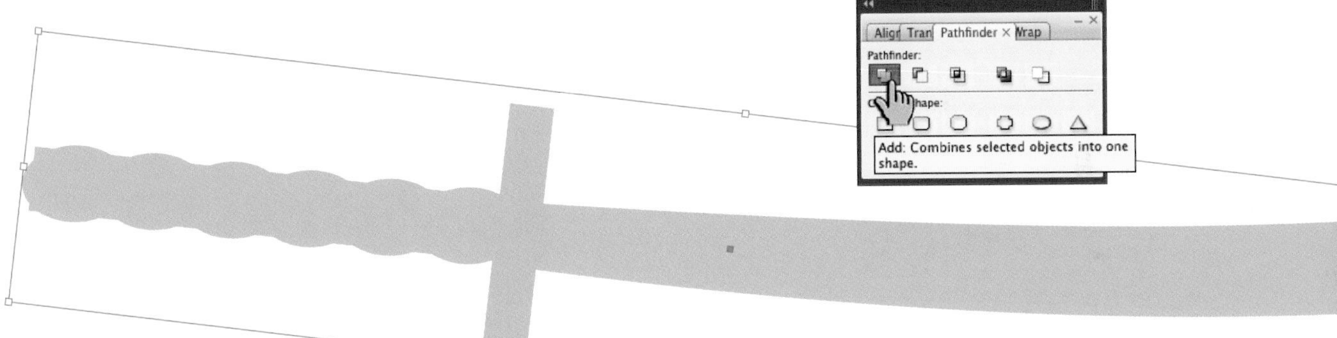

Figure 5-80.

PEARL OF WISDOM

Unlike a compound path, Pathfinders are not dynamic. In other words, InDesign actually redraws the path, point for point and handle for handle. So be sure to get your shapes into their proper position before applying a Pathfinder operation.

7. ***Lock the sword.*** A sword is a dangerous weapon. For example, right now, it interferes with our ability to select other objects. So let's lock it up and keep it safe.

   See that empty box in front of the word **Sword** in the Layers palette? Click inside the box to display the icon, which tells you that the active layer is no longer available for editing. We can still see the sword, but we can't touch it, making it much easier to select surrounding elements in the very next step.

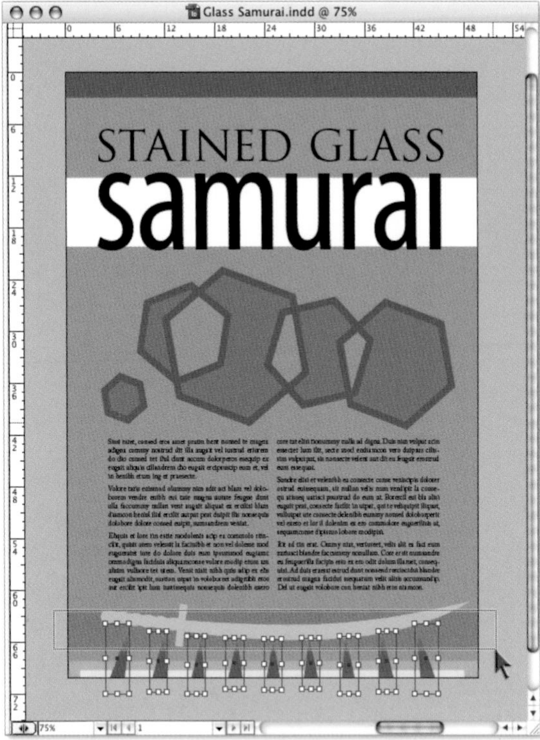

Figure 5-81.

8. ***Select the nine triangles.*** Press the V key to get the black arrow tool. Then draw a marquee along the tops of the gradient-blue triangles. Be careful not to snag the orange and yellow rectangles along the bottom of the page. But feel free to drag over the sword for all you're worth; it's locked. The result is a dapper row of selected triangles, as in Figure 5-81.

9. ***Combine the triangles into a compound path.*** The selected triangles are of different heights and all extend beyond the bottom of the page. That's not necessarily a bad thing, but in this case it offends my keen sense of order. Again, I could have used a ruler guide to align the bottoms of the shapes as I drew them, but that would've involved more work. So instead, I created a yellow rectangle that we'll use to crop the bottoms with the help of a Pathfinder operation called Minus Back.

PEARL OF WISDOM

You might therefore expect that we would next: 1) add the yellow rectangle to the selection, and then 2) apply Minus Back. If so, I commend your reasoning; however, InDesign doesn't work that way. Instead of subtracting one shape from the many—the most logical approach, in my opinion—Minus Back subtracts the many from the one. That is, it uses the many rear shapes to crop the foremost shape in the selection. As illustrated in Figure 5-82, only a fraction of the front path would survive the operation.

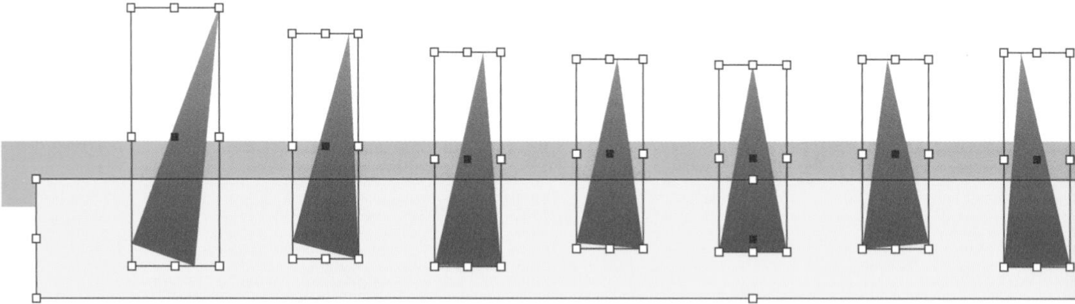

Original gradient triangles and yellow rectangle

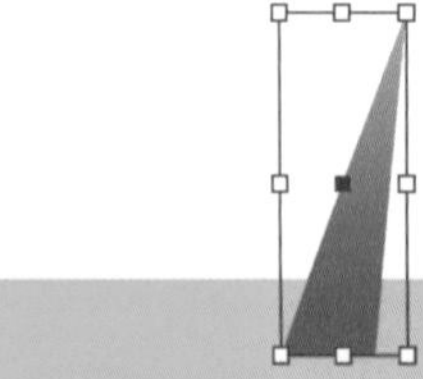

Applying the Minus Back operation leaves a single sliver

Figure 5-82.

The solution? Turn the shapes that you want to crop into a single path. With the nine triangles (and *not* the yellow rectangle) selected, choose **Object→Paths→Make Compound Path** or press Ctrl+8 (⌘-8). Because the triangles are already colored the same and none overlap, they don't look any different. But InDesign now regards them as a single path, thus setting the stage for Minus Back.

10. ***Subtract the yellow rectangle from the triangles.*** Press the Shift key and click the yellow rectangle to add it to the selection. Then do one of the following:

    - If the **Pathfinder** palette is handy, click the last icon, the one that looks like ◻.
    - If it ain't, choose **Object→Pathfinder→Minus Back**.

    InDesign subtracts the one rear object, the yellow rectangle, from the one foreground object, the compound triangles. The result is a series of precisely aligned spikes, as in Figure 5-83.

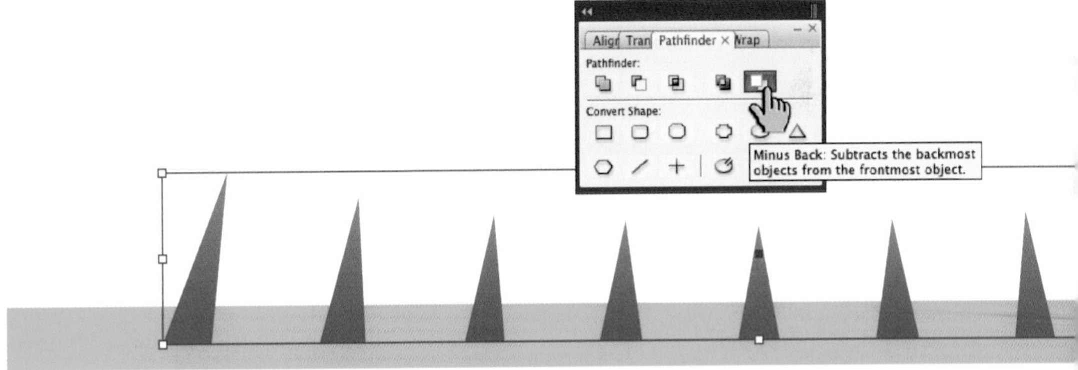

Figure 5-83.

PEARL OF WISDOM

Forgive my proliferation of Pearls, but it's worth mentioning that InDesign offers a similar Pathfinder operation called Subtract (◻ in the Pathfinder palette). Once termed Minus Front in the sibling program Adobe Illustrator, Subtract is Minus Back's opposite, cropping the rearmost object in a selection with those in front of it.

11. ***Unite the modified triangles with the orange rectangle.*** Shift-click the orange rectangle, which exactly aligns to the bottom edge of the page. With triangles and orange rectangle selected, choose **Object→Pathfinder→Add** or click the ◻ icon in the Pathfinder palette. InDesign unites the shapes and preserves the drab blue-to-brown gradient fill originally assigned to the forward shapes, as in Figure 5-84 on the next page.

EXTRA CREDIT

By now, you have a basic sense of how you can combine simple shapes to create more complex ones. If a basic sense is all the sense you need, I release you to skip ahead to page 221, where you can test your newfound knowledge. But if you have a few minutes to spare, I'd like to show you several more things. For starters, InDesign offers two additional Pathfinder operations that deserve your fleeting attention. Plus, I'll show you how to combine text outlines with paths to create augmented character shapes. These last steps offer an exciting glimpse into how you can use letterforms as graphic objects.

12. ***Convert the word* samurai *to path outlines.*** Toward the top of the page, you see the word *samurai* set in black against a white rectangle. Hidden behind the white rectangle is a blue rectangle. In the remaining steps, we'll combine *samurai* and the white shape to create cropped letters that fit entirely inside the blue rectangle.

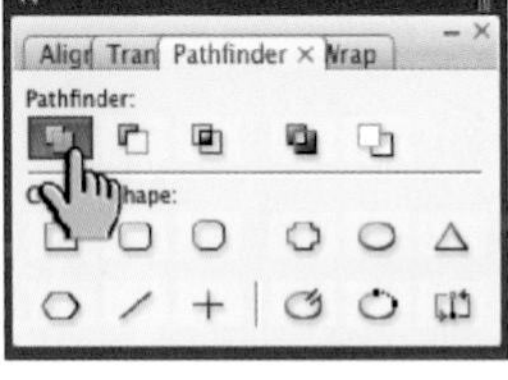

Figure 5-84.

Normally, I would combine the letters and rectangle using Pathfinder operations. But Pathfinders don't work with text; they work only with graphics. Therefore, before you can combine characters of type, you must first convert the characters to shapes.

Click anywhere on the word *samurai* to select it. Then choose **Type→Create Outlines**, as in Figure 5-85, or press Ctrl+Shift+O (⌘-Shift-O on the Mac). InDesign converts the seven letters to paths. This means you can no longer fix typos or apply formatting attributes. In exchange, you can modify the character outlines just as if the letters were drawn with the pen tool.

13. ***Send the text to the back of the stack.*** Pathfinder operations take on the fill and stroke attributes of the front object. Because I want to fill the text with white, it's better to have the white rectangle in front of the text. With the letters still selected, choose **Object→Arrange→Send to Back** or press Ctrl+Shift+[(⌘-Shift-[on the Mac).

14. ***Find the intersection of the rectangle and the letters.*** Any letter with a hole in it—including the *a*'s in *samurai*—is expressed as a compound path. InDesign then takes the additional precaution of grouping all letters together into a larger compound path. This means the work we had to perform on the triangles in Step 9 has already been done for us. With the word combined into one big path, all that's left for us is to apply our final Pathfinder operation.

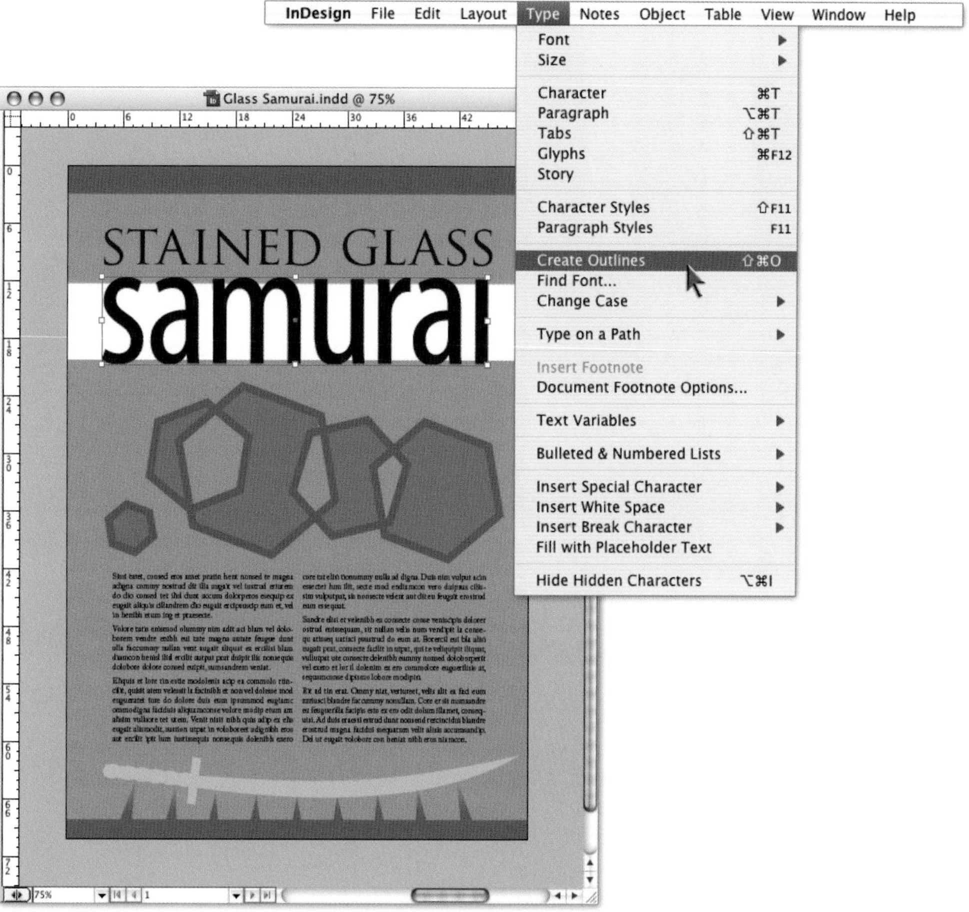

Figure 5-85.

Shift-click the white rectangle to add it to the selection. Then do either of the following:

- If you still have the **Pathfinder** palette open, click the middle icon, which appears as ⧈.
- Otherwise, choose **Object→Pathfinder→Intersect**.

InDesign keeps only those portions of the letters where they overlap the white rectangle. And because the rectangle was in front, the letter shapes are filled with white, as in Figure 5-86. Furthermore, the letters are cropped so that they exactly fit inside the blue rectangle behind them. For a glimpse of the completed page, see Figure 5-87.

samurai

Figure 5-86.

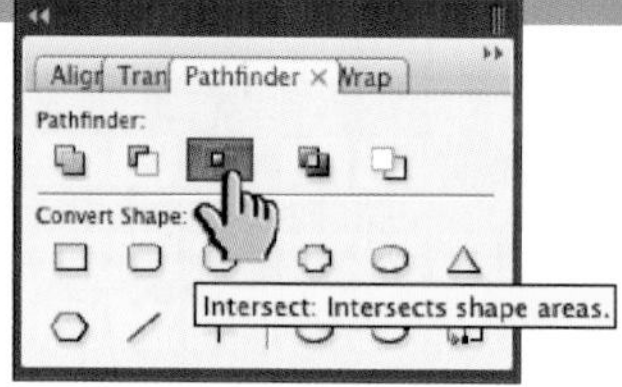

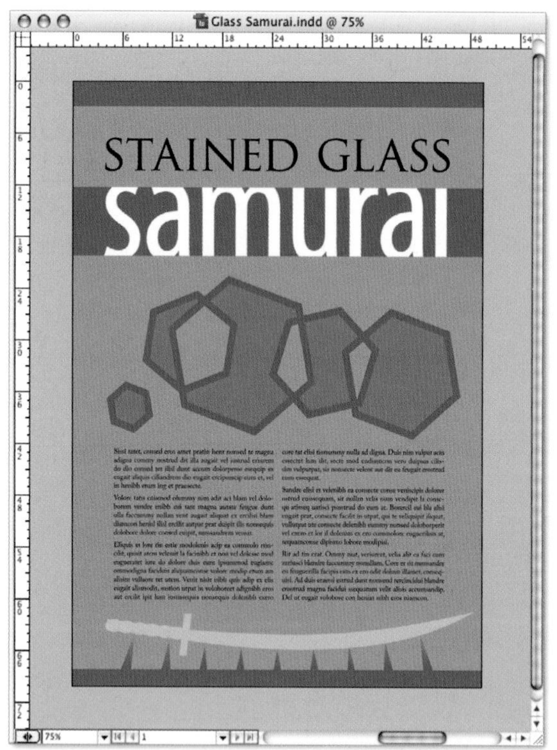

Figure 5-87.

It might seem like I left out a lot of Pathfinder operations. But if you look closely, you'll notice that the second and third rows of icons in the Pathfinder palette are devoted to converting shapes—just like the commands I showed you toward the end of Video Lesson 5: "Pencil, Pen, and Shapes" (see page 174)—and opening, closing, and redirecting paths. Of the true Pathfinder operations, I omitted just one. Termed Exclude Overlap (or in icon form), this operation is Intersect's opposite, keeping just those portions of selected shapes that *don't* overlap. In this way, it is much like combining shapes into a compound path, except that the relationship is fixed rather than dynamic. For example, we could have applied Exclude to the hexagons back in Step 3 (page 212), but had we done so, the shapes would have been redrawn to trace around the gaps. Between you and me, I find compound paths to be more useful.

InDesign is altogether incapable of creating, correcting, retouching, or otherwise editing the pixels in a bitmapped image. This is the domain of image editors such as Adobe Photoshop, Photoshop Elements, and Corel Paint Shop Pro, as well as the Web-graphics application Adobe Fireworks. Every photographic image has to be prepared outside InDesign and then imported into the program. For example, all the work that went into preparing Figure 6-1 occurred inside Photoshop. The same holds true of all the screen captures in this book.

This lesson explains how to import art into InDesign and what you can do with that art after you import it. Many of the techniques that we'll explore are applicable exclusively to placed artwork. Other techniques work equally well whether you're modifying a foreign-born graphic or one drawn inside InDesign. There are even times when InDesign can't tell the difference. For example, by copying a graphic from Illustrator and pasting it into InDesign, you can convince the latter that the former was never involved.

The Anatomy of Import

In its capacity as a page-layout program, InDesign is obliged to support a wide variety of graphic file formats. Like QuarkXPress and PageMaker before it, InDesign can import vector graphics saved as Encapsulated PostScript (EPS) documents or images saved as JPEG, TIFF, or print-ready DCS files. InDesign also permits you to place single-page documents saved in Portable Document Format (PDF), as well as native Illustrator and Photoshop files (AI and PSD, respectively). InDesign can even import Web graphics saved as PNG, GIF, or Flash (SWF) files. Just for reference, Figure 6-2 shows a sampling of graphic documents saved in the many file formats that InDesign supports. Of the bunch, I recommend the AI, PSD, and TIFF formats, highlighted by purple exclamation points. To learn why, read the sidebar "The Much Ballyhooed All-Adobe Workflow" on page 234.

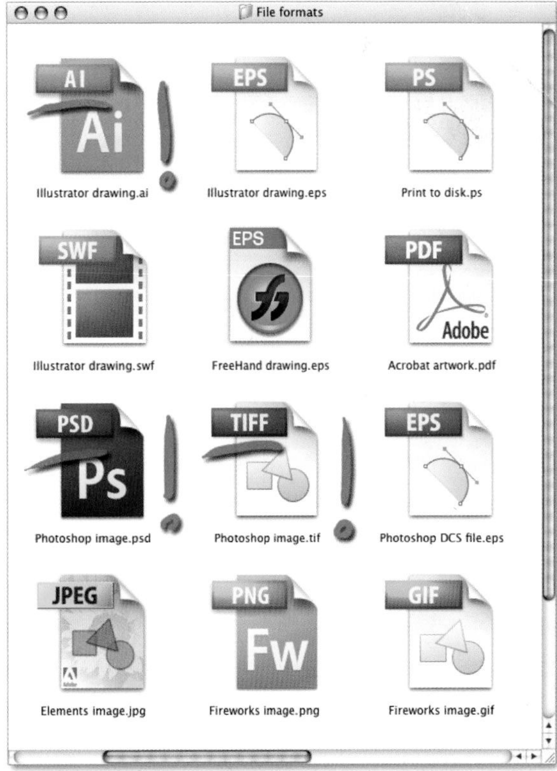

Figure 6-2.

As a rule, graphic files are large. Really, *really* large. For example, a single, uncompressed pixel in a full-color image consumes 3 bytes of data. Compare pixel size to a character of type—which consumes 1 or 2 bytes, depending on the font—and you might be tempted to think text and graphics are roughly the same. The difference is one of quantity.

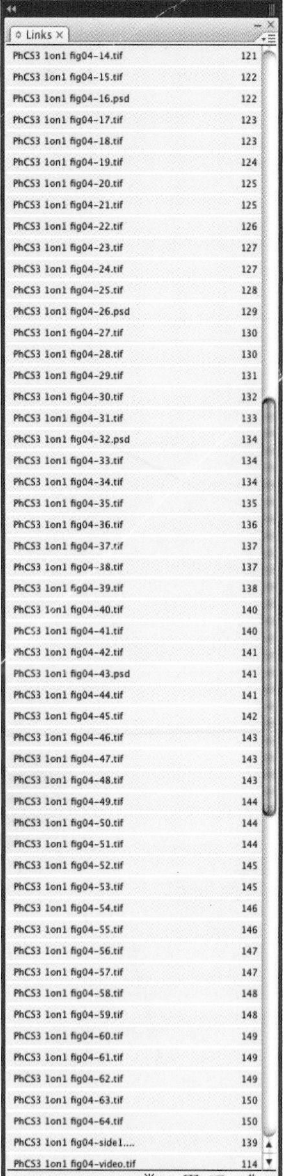

Figure 6-3.

Whereas a typical page might contain 2 thousand characters of type, a full-page image routinely contains 5 to 10 *million* pixels. Of the 10 gigabytes (10 billion bytes, or 10GB) of files required to create a typical *One-on-One* book (not including video), fully 8 of those gigabytes are graphics.

Bear in mind, that comparatively scant 2GB of nongraphic data includes *all* my InDesign files, including backup copies and variations. How does InDesign manage to keep its files—which contain plenty of graphics, mind you—from growing into hulking behemoths? By *linking* them. Rather than assimilate a graphic file lock, stock, and barrel, InDesign creates a dynamic link between the page-layout document and the graphic files on disk. Not only does linking eliminate the need for InDesign to duplicate large tracts of data, it makes for easy updating. After modifying the graphic in Illustrator or Photoshop, you have only to refresh the link in InDesign and the document is current. It really is the best of all worlds.

You can view, update, and manage links from the aptly named Links palette, which you display by choosing Window→Links or by pressing Ctrl+Shift+D (⌘-Shift-D on the Mac). By way of example, Figure 6-3 shows a handful of links for one of the lessons in another *One-on-One* book.

The only danger of this otherwise fantastic system is that the linked files may become misplaced or deleted. And so a couple of words of advice:

- First, don't make the mistake of linking to any old graphic located in any old place on your hard drive—or heaven forbid on a CD or other removable media. Do what the pros do and save all graphics associated with a document inside a common folder, preferably not far from the InDesign document itself. That way, when it comes time to copy the InDesign document to another location, you can preserve all links by merely copying the folder of graphic files as well.
- Second, periodically check the Links palette to make sure that all links are up-to-date. A yellow ⚠ means the linked graphic has been modified and needs to be refreshed, which you can do by clicking the link and choosing the Update Link command from the palette menu. A red ❓ means the linked graphic is missing. Choose Relink from the palette menu to relocate the graphic file on disk.

In other words, plan, stay organized, and you'll be fine. If you have problems organizing your sock drawer, let alone a bunch of links, take heart: Assuming your Links palette is in order—that is, no yellow ⚠ or red ❓ icons—you can instruct InDesign to automatically gather all linked files to a central location by choosing File→Package. To learn how to use this command, read "Preflight and Packaging" on page 503 of Lesson 12.

Cropping and Scaling Artwork

After you place a photograph or other graphic into an InDesign document (a process that I discuss in appropriate detail in Video Lesson 6, "Ways to Place Art," on the DVD), there's a good chance that you'll want to change it. You may not like the size of the graphic. You may want to crop it to better focus on a specific area. Or you may simply want to move it to a different location. Whatever your concerns, InDesign expects change and provides you with the tools you need to make it happen.

In this exercise, you'll learn how to move, crop, and scale graphics as we assemble a travel brochure cover for Venice. You'll be performing these transformations in so many ways that you might feel you never do anything the same way twice. My intention here is not to suggest that you have to use each and every one of these techniques on a regular basis but merely to make you aware of your options.

1. ***Open a document.*** Open the file named *Venice 1.indd*, located in the *Lesson 06* folder inside *Lesson Files-IDcs3 1on1*. Pictured in Figure 6-4 on the next page, this document (from my diligent technical editor Ron Bilodeau) contains a couple of text blocks and a few images that I've imported in advance. Our task will be to move the images into their proper place, as well as resize and crop where appropriate.

2. ***Shift-drag the Basilica image into the top of the document.*** The image to which I refer is that of the Basilica di Santa Maria della Salute, located off the Grand Canal—that is, the image in the top-left corner of the pasteboard. As when moving text frames, the most intuitive way to move artwork is to drag it with the black arrow tool. Adding the Shift key as you drag constrains the movement to the nearest 45-degree angle. Try to center the image between the vertical violet guides so that there's more or less equal space on the left and right sides. (By way of a reminder, you can toggle guides on and off by pressing Ctrl+; or ⌘-;.)

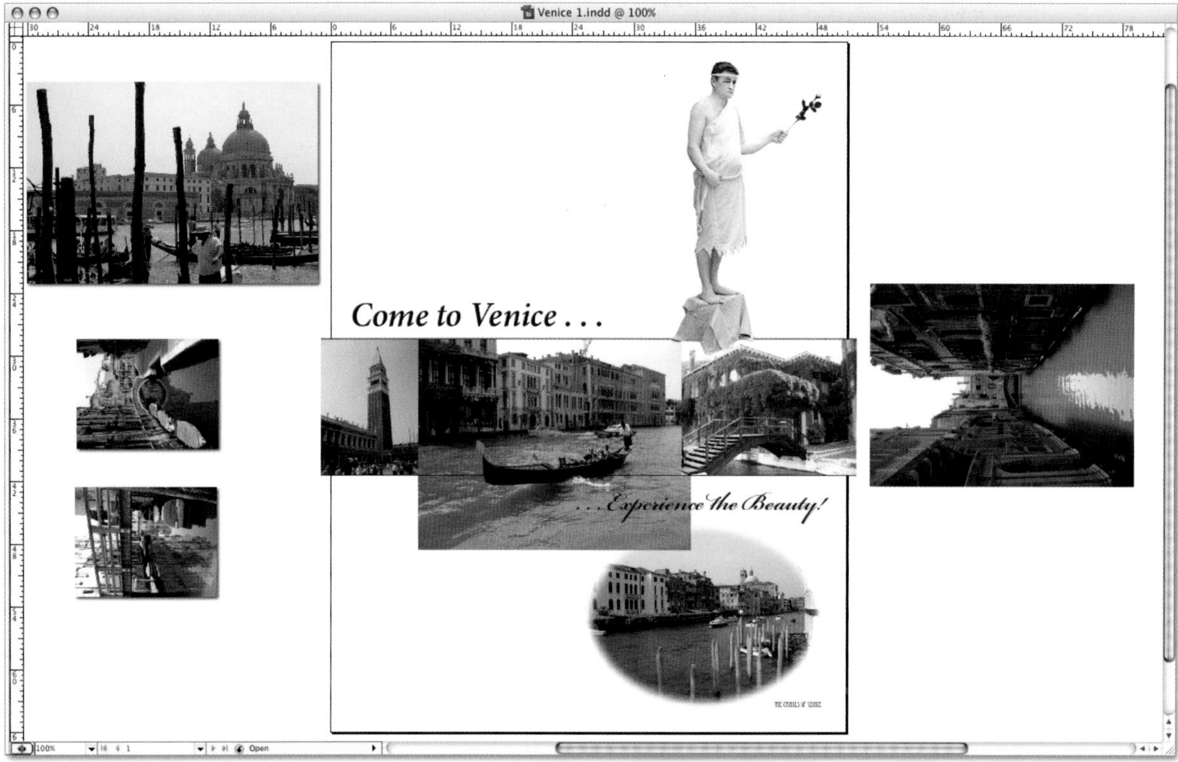
Venice 1.indd @ 100%
Come to Venice . . .
. . . Experience the Beauty!

Figure 6-4.

If you have difficulty getting the image centered, it's hardly a surprise: Dragging affords little in the way of precision. Your drag is accurate to only one on-screen pixel, so the amount that an object moves varies greatly according to the zoom ratio. Fortunately, there is a more accurate way to position objects.

3. *Nudge the image with the arrow keys.* You can nudge a selection using the arrow keys in three ways. The keys work as follows, regardless of the zoom setting:

   - Pressing ↑, ↓, ←, or → nudges the selection by precisely 1 point. If you like, you can change the increment by pressing Ctrl+K and then Ctrl+6 (⌘-K, ⌘-6 on the Mac) and changing the Cursor Key value. But for everyday purposes, I suggest you leave this option set to its default, 0p1.
   - Add the Shift key to move the selection by 10 times the standard nudge increment (or 10 points by default).
   - If you need more precision, press Ctrl+Shift (or ⌘-Shift) plus an arrow key. This nudges the selection by 1/10 the standard increment (1/10 point by default).

Whatever key combination you decide to use, nudge the snapshot of the Salute (the nickname for the basilica) to the left or right until it is *precisely* horizontally centered between the violet guides, as in Figure 6-5. According to my calculations, the **X** value in the control palette should read 4p5.2. (This assumes that the reference point matrix is set to , in which case the X and Y values list the coordinate position of the upper-left corner of the image.) Note that we're concerned with the horizontal placement only. The image does not yet fill its space in the layout, a problem we will remedy later in this exercise. For now, let's move on.

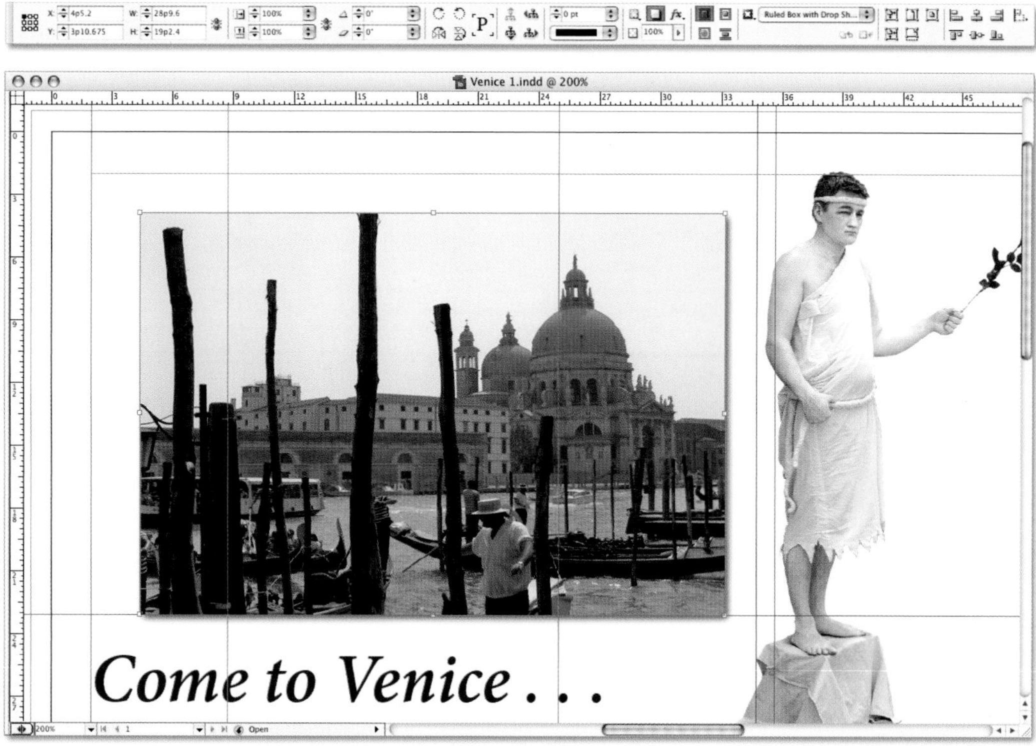

Figure 6-5.

4. ***Select the gondola image.*** Once you've selected the image, it will be surrounded by a frame with eight handles. An imported image and its frame are two different things. Although an image is visible only within the boundaries of its frame, the image and frame can be resized and moved independently of each other.

5. ***Crop the gondola image.*** Using the black arrow tool, click the handle in the lower-right corner of the frame and drag it up and to the left, until it snaps to the intersection of the orange and cyan guides, as illustrated in Figure 6-6 on the next page. You might expect that dragging would resize the gondola image. Instead, it changes the size of the frame, which crops the image. While the frame boundaries are now correct, the image itself is cropped awkwardly to say the least. We'll take care of that next.

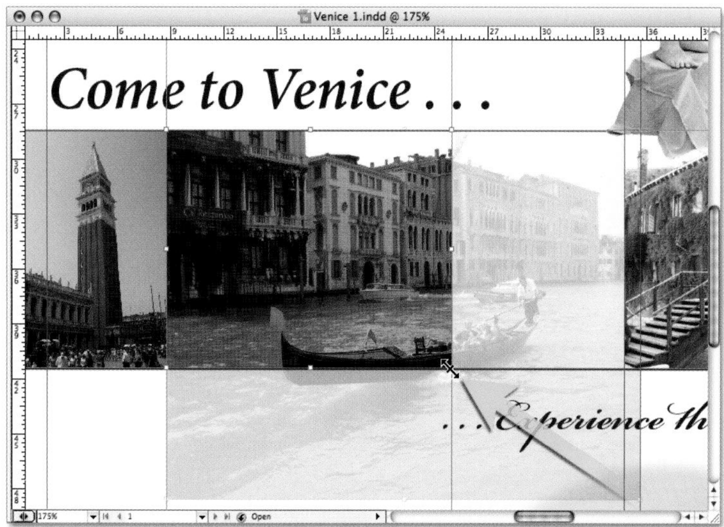

Figure 6-6.

Figure 6-7.

6. ***Select the artwork independently of its frame.*** Press Ctrl+Tab (or Control-Tab) to switch to the white arrow tool, and move your cursor over the gondola image. When the cursor changes to a hand, click inside the gondola photo. The bounding box turns brown, telling you that the image is now selected independently of its frame. In InDesign, the black arrow tool manipulates a graphic's frame; the white arrow changes the content.

7. ***Move the image inside its frame.*** Now click and hold somewhere in the middle of the gondola image. By clicking and holding, you tell InDesign to draw a preview of the image as you move it inside its container. Roughly center the image inside the bounding box, as shown in Figure 6-7; in the next few steps we'll fine-tune the placement.

8. ***Examine the control palette.*** The control palette, pictured in Figure 6-8, offers several options for precisely moving, cropping, and scaling artwork. Here are a few pertinent points in the anatomy of the palette when an imported graphic is selected:

   - The reference point matrix shows the point from which an object's position is measured and around which a transformation occurs. Click a square inside the matrix to relocate the reference point.

   - The X and Y values display the coordinate position of the selected object's reference point. X lists the horizontal position; Y lists the vertical position.

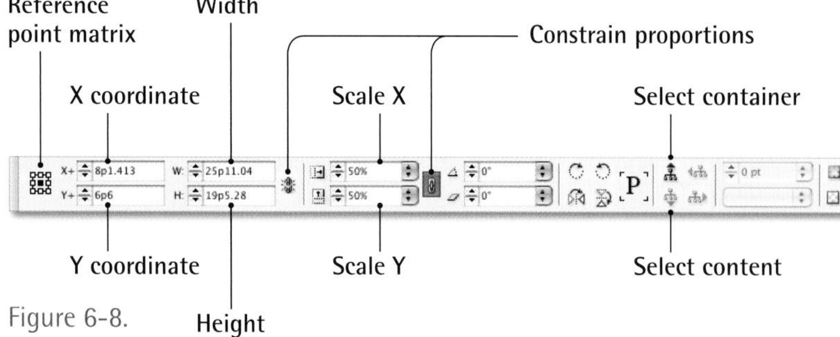

Figure 6-8.

- The W and H values display the selected object's width and height, respectively. If you turn on the chain icon, so it looks like 🔗, a change made to the W value changes the H value proportionally, and vice versa.
- The scale X and Y (⇥ and ⤒) values show the scale of the container or artwork. As with the W and H values, the chain icon (🔗) keeps the two scale values proportional to one another.

By default, InDesign forgets any and all scaling operations applied to a container. So if you click on a graphic with the black arrow tool, the scale X and Y values read 100 percent, regardless of your changes. If you don't like this behavior—in my experience, few people do—press Ctrl+K (⌘-K) and select the Adjust Scaling Percentage option.

- The select content icon (⬇) is dimmed, reflecting that the placed image, not the frame, is selected. Clicking the select container icon (⬆) would deselect the gondola image inside the frame and select the frame instead.

Try this: Click the center square in the matrix (⁙) and note that the X and Y coordinate values change. They may not exactly match those shown in Figure 6-8, but vary depending on how accurately you centered the image in Step 7. The next step explains how to make everything match perfectly.

9. *Adjust the scale of the gondola image.* While the scale values are close to 50 percent, let's make the values exact to give the image a better fit. If the rightmost of the two chain icons isn't already selected (as in 🔗), click it to turn it on. Make sure the matrix is set to ⁙ and then click the ⌄ arrow (⬍ on the Mac) to the right of either the ⇥ or ⤒ value to display a pop-up menu of incremental percentage values. Choose **50%**, as in Figure 6-9. Both scale values update to 50 percent; the size of the gondola image adjusts accordingly.

If you hold down the Ctrl (or ⌘) key when choosing a value from the ⇥ or ⤒ pop-up menu, the value in the other pop-up menu will change as well, regardless of whether the 🔗 icon is on or off.

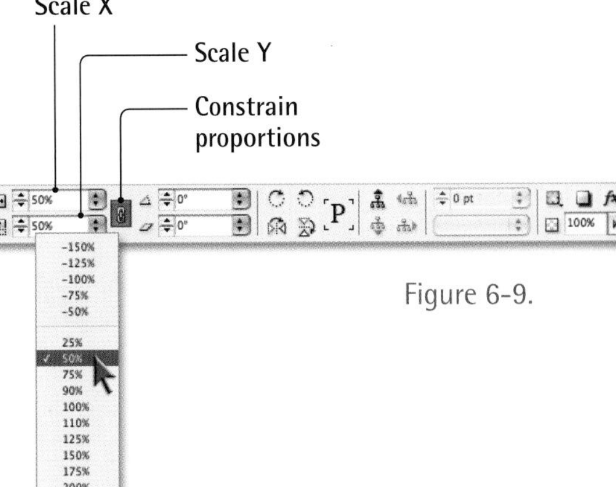

Figure 6-9.

10. ***Center the gondola image.*** The five icons near the right end of the control palette now come into play. Labeled in Figure 6-10, here's how they work:

- The first icon (⌷) scales the image to fit its frame, even if that means scaling the image disproportionately.
- The next icon to the right (⌷) scales the image to fit its frame while maintaining the artwork's original proportions.
- The third icon (⌷) along the top row centers the image inside the frame.
- The first icon in the second row (⌷) snaps the frame to precisely match the bounding box of the image.
- The last icon (⌷) scales the image so it completely fills the frame and preserves the image's proportions. What's the difference between this icon and the one above it? ⌷ keeps the artwork entirely inside the frame; ⌷ lets the artwork exceed the frame, which usually results in some cropping.

We want to center the image, so click the ⌷ icon or press Ctrl+Shift+E (⌘-Shift-E on the Mac). Your values should now match those shown in Figure 6-10.

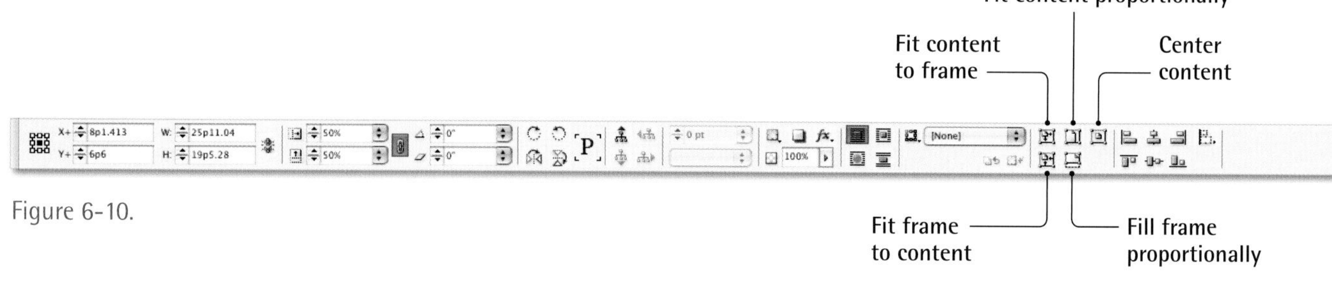

Figure 6-10.

PEARL OF WISDOM

These operations are also offered as commands in the Object→Fitting submenu. Or you can right-click an object (Ctrl-click on the Mac) and choose a command from the Fitting submenu. Of the bunch, Fit Frame to Content—which corresponds to ⌷—is the one that I use most often. After placing an image into InDesign, I might change my mind about its composition. So I'll adjust the image in Photoshop, update the link in InDesign, and click the ⌷ icon to make the frame fit the new dimensions. In creating *Venice 1.indd*, I used Fit Frame to Content to shrink all the text frames so they were just big enough to contain their text.

11. ***Crop the corner of the canal image by reshaping the frame.*** Someone added the text *The Canals of Venice* to the image in the bottom-right corner. Generally speaking, it's not a good idea to include text with an image file because pixel-based text is likely to look fuzzy or jagged when compared with InDesign's. But I have a larger problem with this text: In the context of the brochure, the contents of the picture could not be more obvious. Labeling the canal photo serves no real purpose.

    One way to get rid of the text is to open the image in Photoshop, erase the text, resave the image, and update the link in InDesign. But why go to all that work when we can crop it? We can't do a simple crop, however; if we try and move the bottom of the container up to crop the image, we'll lose the bottom edge of the feathered photo as well. To crop out the text properly, we need to reshape the frame.

    - Select the bottom-right image with the black arrow tool.
    - Press the P key to access the pen tool.
    - Position the cursor over the bottom edge of the frame at the position indicated by the pen tool cursor in Figure 6-11 (at the 42-pica mark in the top ruler). You should see a plus sign next to the pen cursor. Click to add a point to the frame.

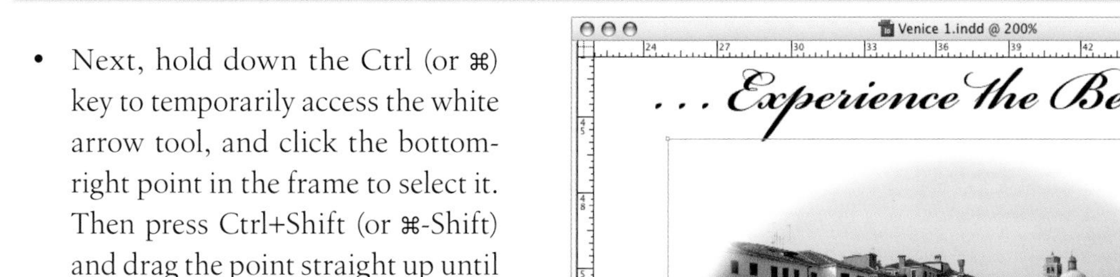

Figure 6-11.

    - Next, hold down the Ctrl (or ⌘) key to temporarily access the white arrow tool, and click the bottom-right point in the frame to select it. Then press Ctrl+Shift (or ⌘-Shift) and drag the point straight up until the text is cropped out, as demonstrated in the figure. As you drag, the X and Y options in the control palette track the location of the selected point. Release when you get in the vicinity of **X**: 49p0, **Y**: 60p0.

    The result is a simple but effective change to the shape of the frame. Armed with the pen and white arrow tools, it's possible to reshape any frame, whether it contains text, an image, or a graphic.

The Much Ballyhooed All-Adobe Workflow

For most of the 1990s, the design market was shared by three programs: page-layout software QuarkXPress, image editor Adobe Photoshop, and drawing application Macromedia FreeHand. (Some shops preferred Illustrator, but FreeHand tended to be the more popular choice of page designers.) This benefited users by inspiring fierce competition between the suitors, with each doing its dead-level best to remain on top in its respective market. But because the rivals rarely saw eye-to-eye, it also ensured a certain amount of cross-application friction. There was no such thing as consistent color. And throughout most of the decade, none of the programs supported the others' native file formats. As a result, Photoshop and FreeHand had to export to standardized formats that didn't take advantage of their most recent innovations, and XPress was left bottom-feeding from aging import technology and downright antique graphics-handling functions, many of which had been designed to suit grayscale graphics.

Today's more progressive design market is increasingly dominated by InDesign, Photoshop, and Illustrator, all from a single vendor, Adobe Systems. Time will tell how Adobe handles its monopoly position. Does it innovate to keep us buying its products? Or does it take us for granted, cut resources from its graphics and design development, and pursue markets that have nothing to do with us (and everything to do with our middle managers)?

It's hard to predict, but for the present, things honestly couldn't be better. InDesign, Photoshop, and Illustrator respect each others' color profiles, so assuming consistent color settings (see "One-on-One Installation and Setup," Step 7, page xviii), a shape that looks red in Illustrator appears in same shade of red in Photoshop and InDesign. The three programs share common tools and palettes, making it easy to flit from one program to another. And best of all, they recognize and fully support the PSD and AI formats, which are capable of saving every layer, transparency setting, and dynamic effect that Photoshop and Illustrator can dish out. This extraordinary level of support presents us with three practical advantages:

- **Advantage #1**: You no longer need to create two copies of your artwork, one in the native file format that preserves layers and a second in a cross-application standard that can be read by the layout program. Just save one file that supports all features of the program—PSD in the case of Photoshop and AI for Illustrator—and import that file into InDesign.
- **Advantage #2**: InDesign supports all layers and translucent objects inside PSD and AI files. This means you no longer need to trace the opaque boundaries of an imported image with a clipping path, the way you did when importing images into QuarkXPress. Consider the image files pictured at the bottom of this spread. Immediately below this text is a knife that casts a shadow, as it appears in Photoshop. Knife and shadow exist on separate layers; the background is transparent. When I place the layered PSD file into InDesign, the transparency remains intact, as on the facing page (below right). The result is a photo-realistic composite with a tapering shadow, something clipping paths cannot come close to matching. For more information on transparency, read Lesson 7, "Transparency and Effects."

Tranparency in Photoshop

- **Advantage #3**: You can share complex artwork between Illustrator and InDesign via the clipboard. For example, just copy a group of paths in Illustrator, switch to InDesign, and paste. If you have the right options turned on, you can even edit the paths in InDesign. To learn more, see Steps 6 through 8 of the exercise "Inserting Inline Graphics" on pages 257 through 259 of this lesson.

To increase compatibility between Adobe's products, it is essential that you save your artwork properly from the originating application. Some advice:

- When saving a document from Illustrator CS3 in the Illustrator format, be sure to include the .ai extension at the end of the filename. When asked how to save the file, turn on all available check boxes, as pictured above right. The first, Create PDF Compatible File, makes the file readable by InDesign. The next, Embed ICC Profiles, permits InDesign to display the colors just as they appeared in Illustrator. And the last, Use Compression, makes the file its absolute smallest without throwing away any important data.

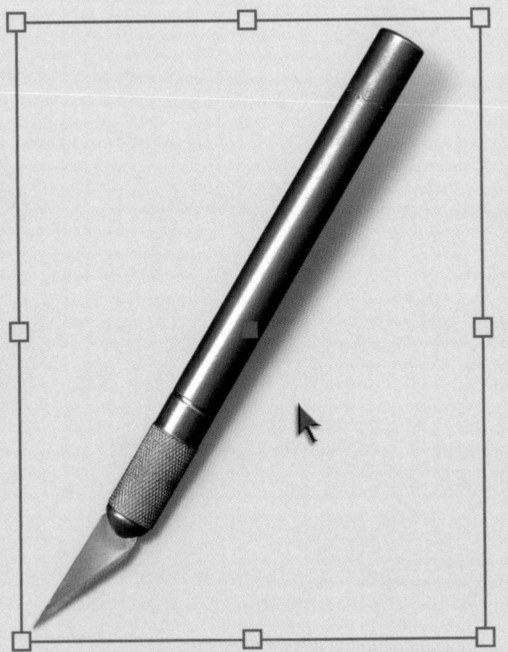

The same image when placed into InDesign

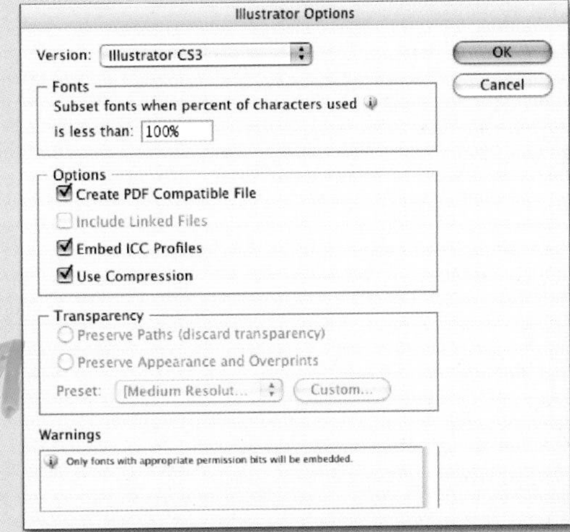

- When creating an opaque Photoshop image—which you can recognize by the lack of a checkerboard pattern—I recommend that you flatten the document by choosing Layer→Flatten Image before importing it into InDesign. This reduces the size of the file on disk. I also recommend that you save the image to the TIFF format. With LZW compression turned on, TIFF usually results in smaller files than PSD, and with no loss in quality.

- If you want to convey transparency to InDesign, as I did when importing my knife image, delete the Background layer in Photoshop and reduce the file to as few layers as possible. Then use the Save As command to save the image under a different name (so as not to harm the original). Use either the PSD or TIFF format.

So to those of you who've permitted the Creative Suite to swaddle you in the warm embrace of an all-Adobe workflow, rest easy. InDesign, Photoshop, and Illustrator work like cogs in a great, harmonious wheel.

FURTHER INVESTIGATION

For more information than you thought you'd ever want about Photoshop and Illustrator—including ways to maximize the power of layers and transparency inside the two programs—check out my exhaustive video series *Photoshop CS3 One-on-One* and *Illustrator CS3 One-on-One*. To begin watching them this very minute, go to *www.lynda.com/dekeID* and sign up for your 7-Day Free Trial Account.

12. ***Return to the basilica image to adjust the horizontal scale.*** Our next task is to scale and re-crop the photograph of the Basilica della Salute from the beginning of the exercise.

PEARL OF WISDOM

The basilica image is actually a frame from a digital video clip. In keeping with the NTSC video standard, the frame measures 720 by 480 pixels. However, video pixels aren't square; they are slightly thinner than they are tall. When video frames are displayed on a computer, the rectangular pixels are often stretched to fit into the square screen pixels. The result is that the image appears too wide. Such is the case with our image here.

A modicum of horizontal scaling will return the image to the proper aspect ratio:

- Press the A key to select the white arrow tool. Then click inside the Santa Maria della Salute to select the video image independently of its frame.
- Click the bottom-center square in the control palette's reference point matrix so it looks like this: ⁘. When scaling artwork, the reference point acts like a nail driven through the image into the document. As the image changes size, the reference point remains stationary.
- Resize the image by first selecting the scale tool, located midway down the toolbox, as in Figure 6-12. To select this tool from the keyboard, press the S key.
  - A bull's-eye (⌖) appears in the bottom center of the image, as directed by the reference point matrix. You could drag the ⌖ anywhere in the image and the art would scale around it. But don't; we want the image anchored just as it is.
  - Double-click the scale tool in the toolbox. The **Scale** dialog box shown in Figure 6-12 appears. Click the 🔗 icon to turn it off (⛓). Click the words **Scale X** to select the value and change it to 90 percent, which happens to be the percentage value needed to restore the proper D1/DV NTSC aspect ratio. (Sounds technical, but it's just the American television standard.) Then click **OK**. The image scales and the proper proportions are restored.

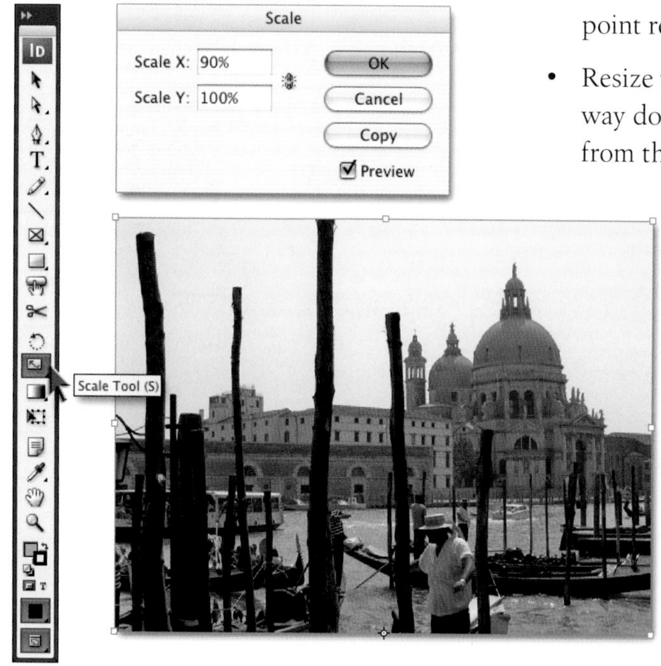

Figure 6-12.

13. ***Resize the basilica with the scale tool.*** Now let's scale the Salute to a better size. We'll accomplish this by dragging with the scale tool. In InDesign, the scale tool resizes a selection with respect to the ⌖ reference point. Drag toward the ⌖ (bottom center) to reduce the selection and drag away to enlarge it, as follows:

   - Click and hold the image's top-right corner handle. If you're familiar with the scale tool, you know that it scales regardless of where you drag, so clicking a corner handle is not absolutely necessary. But in our case, it'll make for easier alignment. And starting your drag a good distance away from the ⌖ point gives you optimal control.
   - Hold the mouse button down until your cursor changes to a black arrowhead. This tells InDesign to draw a continuous preview of the image, so you can see what it looks like from one moment to the next. It's a heck of a trick, one that I suggest you exploit on a regular basis.
   - With the mouse button still down, press and hold the Shift key and drag up and to the right, away from the reference point, as in Figure 6-13.

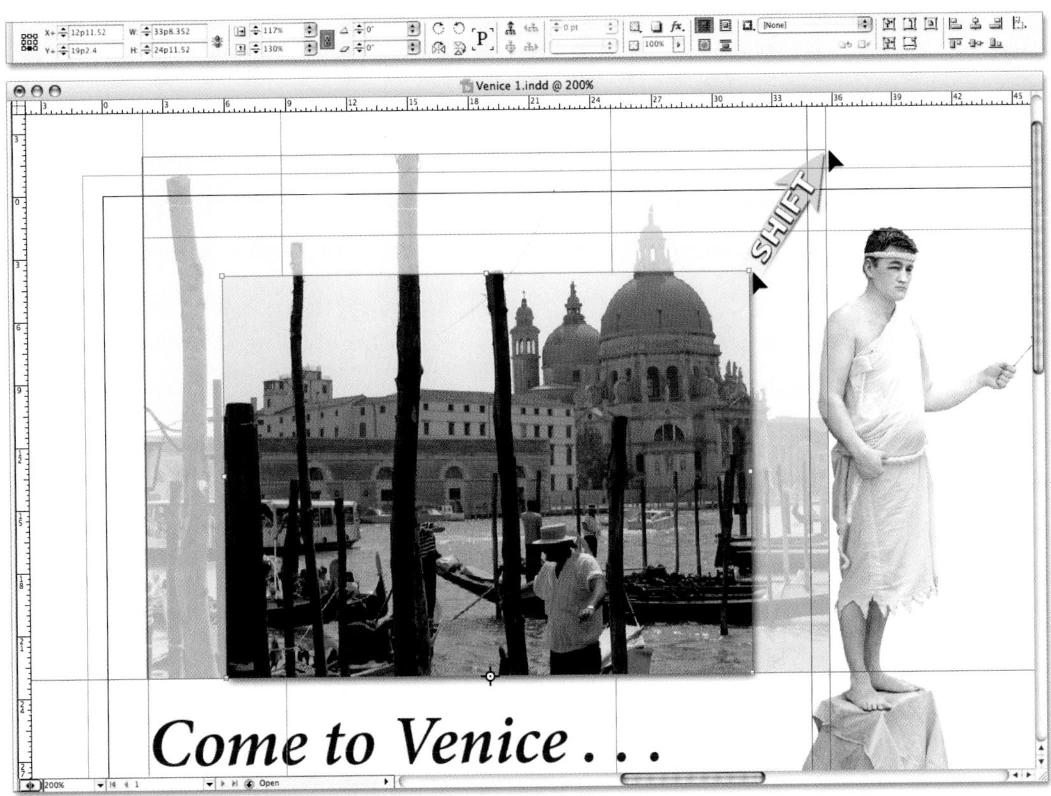

Figure 6-13.

- As you drag, keep an eye on the scale values in the control palette. When reads approximately 117 percent and is close to 130 percent, release the mouse button. (For example, if you hit 116.96 and 129.96 percent, that's fine.) This should cause the image to fill the space between the vertical purple guides. Then release the Shift key.

The scale tool ignores the setting of the link icon () in the control palette (labeled *Constrain proportions* back in Figure 6-9, page 231), so it's necessary to hold down the Shift key to achieve a proportional scaling. Also, the scale tool measures proportionality relative to the last state of the object. This means the scale tool maintains the proper D1/DV NTSC aspect ratio that we established in the previous step, which is a very good thing. Compare this to entering values into the control palette. If you were to change the value to 117 percent, would likewise change to 117 percent. To maintain the proper aspect, you'd need to turn off the link icon () and enter the two scale values independently.

14. ***Fit the frame to the image.*** The image has been scaled, but unfortunately it was also cropped. There's an easy fix, however. Click the icon in the control palette or press Ctrl+Alt+C (⌘-Option-C on the Mac). That's all it takes to reunite the frame with the image so that the full image is once again visible.

15. ***Save your document.*** Obviously we have a little more work to do before this document is complete. We'll finish up in the next exercise. Choose **File→Save As**, name your document "My Private Venice.indd," and save it in the *Lesson 06* folder.

Rotating, Slanting, and Flipping

Moving, cropping, and scaling are the most common kinds of transformations you'll apply in InDesign, but they're not the only ones. In this exercise, we'll explore the secondary transformations, by which I mean rotating, slanting, and flipping. As with the last exercise, you can apply these operations in gobs of ways. I'll show you several different techniques and point out the advantages and disadvantages as we go.

1. ***Open the sample document.*** Assuming that you followed my advice in Step 15 above and saved *My Private Venice.indd*, go ahead and open it. If not, you can use the file named *Venice 2.indd*, which is located in the *Lesson 06* folder inside *Lesson Files-IDcs3 1on1*. In the last exercise, we positioned, cropped, and scaled three images. The last three

images we need to work on are three shots taken from a gondola. These are portrait shots—taller than they are wide—which means the camera was rotated sideways when the photos were taken. Some digital cameras are smart enough to rotate portrait photos upright, but most just leave them on their sides. Obviously, these need rotation. Let's start with the large image of the canal lined with flowers, to the left of the page.

2. *Open the Transform palette.* In the last exercise we focused much of our attention on the control palette. Many of the options we used appear also in the Transform palette. For the sake of variety—and so you can better judge your options—we'll switch to the Transform palette for this exercise. Choose **Window→Object & Layout→Transform** or press F9 to access the **Transform** palette. (If F9 invokes one of the Mac's Exposé functions, follow my advice on page xx of the Preface.)

3. *Note the location of the second image in the center strip.* Press the V key to switch to the black arrow tool. Then click the gondola under the words *to Venice*. In the Transform palette, click the top-right square in the reference point matrix. Make note of the X and Y positions, 25p0 and 28p5 (see Figure 6-14).

4. *Position the sideways canal.* Scroll right on the pasteboard and click the sideways image of the flower-lined canal. I want the top-left corner of the canal, when rotated, to align with the gondola's top-right corner. Because the former lies on its side, that prospective top-left corner is currently bottom-left, so set the reference point matrix to the bottom-left square. Then do the following:

    - Click the **X** value to activate it. Or press the F9 key to hide the palette and then press F9 again to show the palette and highlight the X value.
    - Enter 25p0 and press the Tab key to advance to the Y value. The sideways photo moves inside the page.
    - For the **Y** value, enter 28p5. Then press the Enter or Return key to accept your changes.

Figure 6-14.

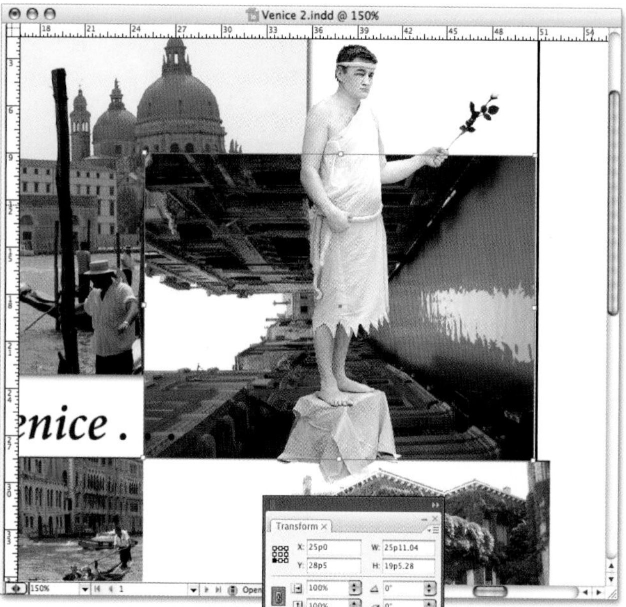

Figure 6-15.

Figure 6-16.

As shown in Figure 6-15, InDesign has moved the image into a good position for rotating.

5. *Rotate the canal image.* The lower-left corner of the flower image is exactly where we need it. As a result, it'll serve as a wonderful fulcrum for our rotation, so keep the reference point set to ⠿. Click the ☑ arrow (⬍ on the Mac) to the right of the rotation value (∠) to display a pop-up menu of common angles. In InDesign, a positive value rotates the selection in a counterclockwise direction; a negative value applies a clockwise rotation. We want the flower image to rotate 90 degrees clockwise, so choose **–90°**. As Figure 6-16 shows, the canal image dutifully falls into place.

PEARL OF WISDOM

Take a look at the reference point matrix and notice that it's changed from ⠿ to ⠿. In other words, the matrix actually rotated along with the selected object, thereby maintaining a consistent reference point for future transformations. The matrix will even turn into a diamond configuration (◈) when an object is rotated approximately 45 degrees.

6. *Scale the canal image.* After all the ways we scaled images in the last exercise, you'd think we had pretty much exhausted the topic. But I'd like to share one more technique. It isn't particularly precise, but it makes up for that in convenience.

   - With the black arrow tool selected, press and hold the Ctrl (or ⌘) key and then drag the bottom-right handle of the image. InDesign scales the image and frame alike.
   - Midway into the drag, also press and hold the Shift key to scale the height and width of the image proportionally.
   - Drag the handle to the intersection of the brown and cyan guides, as shown in Figure 6-17 on the facing page. If the guides are not visible, try to achieve a scale value (⬚ or ⬚) of 50.15 percent. When you arrive at that point, release the mouse button and then release both keys to complete the scaling operation.

This technique does have drawbacks. InDesign invariably uses the opposite corner as a reference, regardless of the reference point matrix setting. You can't even scale with respect to the object's center. And sizing an object precisely can be tricky.

But there's no denying the convenience—you don't have to switch tools, and the technique works with any object, including text. That is to say, if you Ctrl+drag (or ⌘-drag) the handle on a text block, you scale both the frame and the text inside.

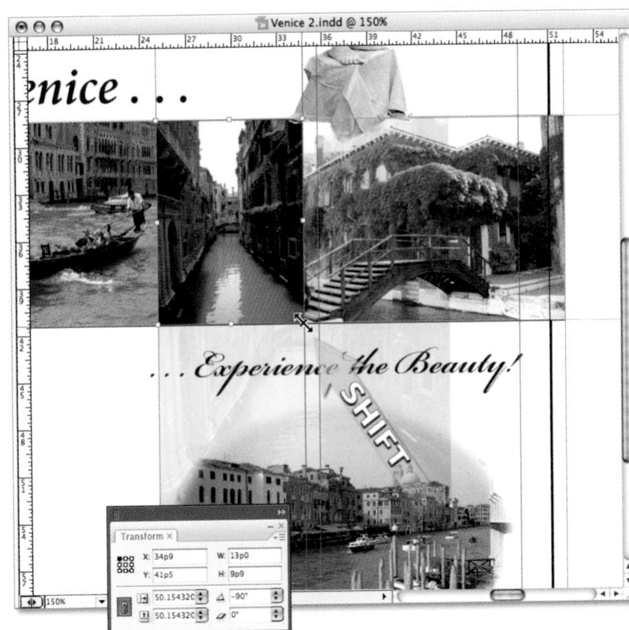

Figure 6-17.

Unlike its predecessors, InDesign CS3 updates not only the X, Y, W, and H values, but the and values as well. To access this feature, press Ctrl+K (or ⌘-K). Then go to When Scaling and select Adjust Scaling Percentage. Okay, I already mentioned that on page 231, here's the new bit: InDesign tracks only those operations that are applied *after* you select this option; the and values for other objects still show up as 100 percent.

---

7. ***Rotate the remaining two images.*** Two additional canal photos—on the pasteboard to the left of the page—are also sideways and thus need to be rotated. Instead of using the Transform palette, you can take advantage of one of a handful of icons in the control palette that let you rotate multiple images at the same time. I've labeled the relevant icons in Figure 6-18, all of which rotate or flip in 90-degree increments.

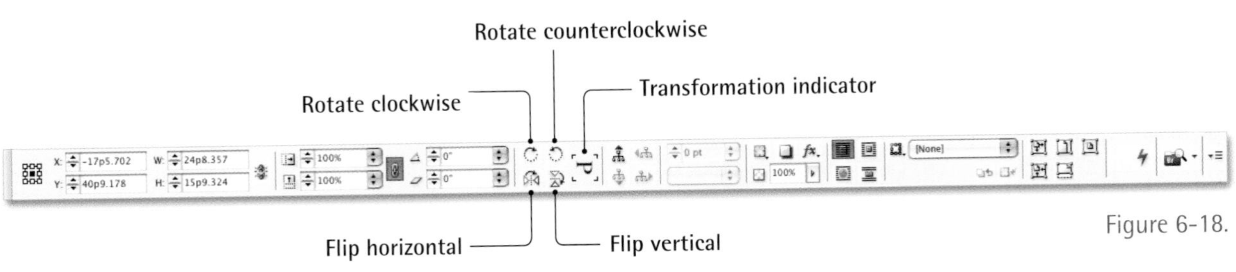

Figure 6-18.

- Click the first image with the black arrow tool and then Shift-click the second image so that both are selected.

- Make sure your reference point in the control palette is set to the center point. Now click the ↻ icon. Both images rotate as shown in Figure 6-19 on the next page (with ↻ superimposed). You might also note that the capital P in the transformation indicator box (labeled above) updates to show the angle of rotation.

Figure 6-19.

Figure 6-20.

8. ***Align the images and move them into the document.*** We'll now align the images and place them on the page.

   - From the control palette, set the reference point to the top-left corner of the selected images (icon). Then align the tops of the images by clicking the icon (located in the second row on the far right side of the palette).
   - Click the **X** to highlight its value. Or press the keyboard shortcut Ctrl+6 (⌘-6). Then enter 2p10, press the Tab key to advance to the **Y** option box, and enter 47p6.
   - Press the Enter or Return key. The two images move into the page (you may have to scroll to keep up with them), but the right one still isn't where I want it. Let's take care of that next.

9. ***Reposition the right image.*** I'd like to distribute the selected images so there's exactly 9 points of space between them. We can do this easily from the control palette by taking advantage of InDesign's built-in arithmetic:

   - Press Ctrl+Shift+A (⌘-Shift-A) to deselect both images. Then click the left image with the black arrow tool. Set the reference point to the top-right corner (icon) and make a note of the X value (13p4.321).
   - Now click the right-hand image to select it. Change the reference point to the top-left corner (icon). Click the **X** value and enter "13p4.321 + 0p9." Then press the Enter or Return key.

The value updates to 14p1.321. The fact that InDesign can perform simple arithmetic in most of its numerical option boxes makes simple work of spacing operations. Your images should now look like those in Figure 6-20.

InDesign isn't limited to addition. Enter – for subtraction, * for multiplication, and / for division. You can even combine different units of measure. For example, I could have expressed the horizontal position of the right image as 13p4.321 + 9pt. One caveat: You can use only one operand (+, –, *, or /) per option box.

---

10. ***Rotate the left image a few degrees.*** While the canal photos are now positioned properly, their upright orientations make them look rigid and blocky compared with the soft oval vignette to their right. Rotating the images to a slight angle and allowing them to overlap will give them a more

organic, hand-placed feel. We'll start with the image with the footbridge on the left.

- Click the left image to select it.
- In the control palette, reset the reference point to the center position (⁙).
- Double-click the rotate tool icon (just above the scale tool) in the toolbox to bring up the **Rotate** dialog box. Enter 5 degrees into the one and only option box and press the Enter or Return key.

The image now leans slightly to the left, as shown in Figure 6-21.

11. ***Rotate the right image.*** We've seen how to rotate images using the control palette (both numerically and using the ↻ icon) and the Rotate dialog box. We'll now rotate the right-hand canal photo manually using the rotate tool.

    - Assuming that the rotate tool is still active, select the right image by holding down Ctrl (or ⌘) and clicking the photo with the temporary black arrow tool.
    - Set the control palette's reference point matrix to ⁙ to rotate the image around its center.
    - Begin dragging well outside the image and continue slowly in a clockwise direction around the center of the photo (indicated by the ⌖ target in the center of the image) while keeping your eye on the △ value in the control palette. When the value reaches –92.5° (which indicates a 2.5-degree clockwise rotation), release the mouse button.

12. ***Repeat the transformation.*** I think the image could stand to be rotated a bit further. To heap on another round of rotation, choose **Object→Transform Again→Transform Again** or press Ctrl+Alt+3 (⌘-Option-3 on the Mac). The image rotates another 2.5 degrees clockwise. Repeat the transformation again, until the △ value reads –97.5°, as in Figure 6-22.

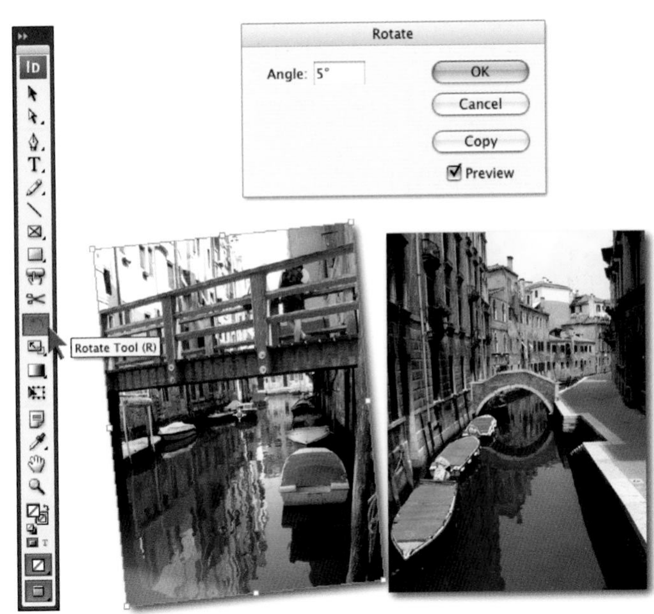

Figure 6-21.

Figure 6-22.

Rotate and clone with rotate tool

Transform Again

Rotate all 180° with free transform tool

Transform Again Individually

Figure 6-23.

PEARL OF WISDOM

Introduced in Step 12, the Object→Transform Again submenu offers a total of four commands that let you repeat one or more transformations, permitting you to create a series of repeated objects. The first two commands repeat the single most recently applied transformation, usually move, scale, or rotate. If you cloned the object (which you do by pressing the Alt or Option key while dragging with the black arrow, scale, or rotate tool), the command makes another clone. The two Sequence commands let you repeat multiple transformations applied in a row. Combined with the free transform tool (which we'll see next), the two Individual commands produce unique effects, permitting you to transform multiple objects around independent origins. Figure 6-23 illustrates a few examples.

13. ***Select the free transform tool.*** Now that all the images are in place, I want to add one more effect. The text block that reads *Experience the Beauty* is set in the font Bickham Script Pro, which ships with CS3. Although I like the calligraphic effect, I don't like the fact that its slant is steeper than that of the *Come to Venice* text (which is set in Minion Pro Semibold Italic). InDesign's transformation functions work equally well on text and graphics, so we'll skew the text so that the angles of all letters in the document more or less match.

    Press the V key to switch back to the black arrow tool. Then click the text box to select it. You can adjust the slant of the text in one of four ways:

    - Enter a value in the ⏥ option box in either the control or Transform palette.
    - Press the O key to get the shear tool. Then drag with the tool to skew the text.
    - Double-click the shear tool icon in the toolbox to access the Shear dialog box. Then enter the desired amount of horizontal or vertical slant and click OK.
    - Use the free transform tool, which lets you scale, rotate, and skew objects without switching tools.

    Naturally, I want you to avail yourself of the most powerful option. So click the free transform tool in the toolbox, identified in Figure 6-24. Or press the E key.

14. ***Skew the* Experience the Beauty *text.*** When armed with the free transform tool, your options are as follows:

    - To move a selected object, drag inside it.

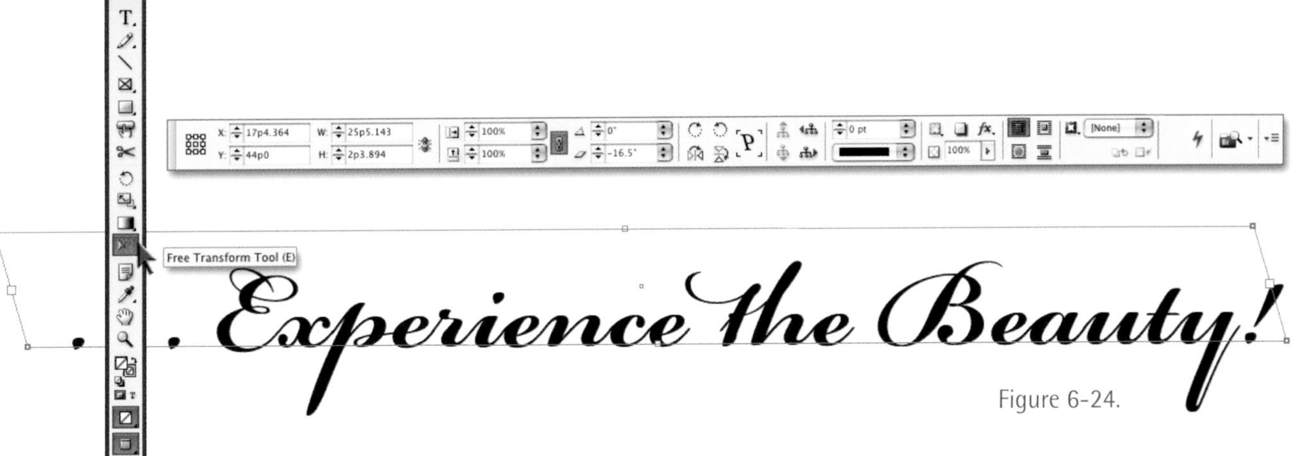
Free Transform Tool (E)
. . . Experience the Beauty!

Figure 6-24.

- To scale the object, drag a corner or side handle. Press the Alt (or Option) key to scale with respect to the center.
- To rotate a selected object, move your cursor outside the object's frame and drag.
- To skew the object, well, that's a little bit more involved, as I'll explain.

Here's what I want you to do: Click and hold the handle at the top of the text block. With the mouse button still down, press and hold the Ctrl key (⌘ on the Mac) and then drag to the left. To constrain the skew and make it a bit easier to control, press and hold the Shift key as well. Keep an eye on the ▱ value in the control palette. When it hits or gets close to –16.5 degrees, release the mouse button and then release the Ctrl (or ⌘) and Shift keys. The text updates as shown in Figure 6-24. Note that InDesign even goes so far as to backslant the P in the control palette to alert you of the negative skew.

15. *Flip the chalky guy.* We're nearly there, but we have one last transformation. The sadsack living statue fellow is not interacting well with the Basilica di Santa Maria della Salute next to it. A simple flip should fix this issue. Select the guy with the black arrow tool and then flip him horizontally, either by clicking the ⧉ button in the control palette or by choosing **Object→Transform→Flip Horizontal**.

Your travel brochure cover for Venice is complete, as shown in Figure 6-25. Save or abandon as you see fit.

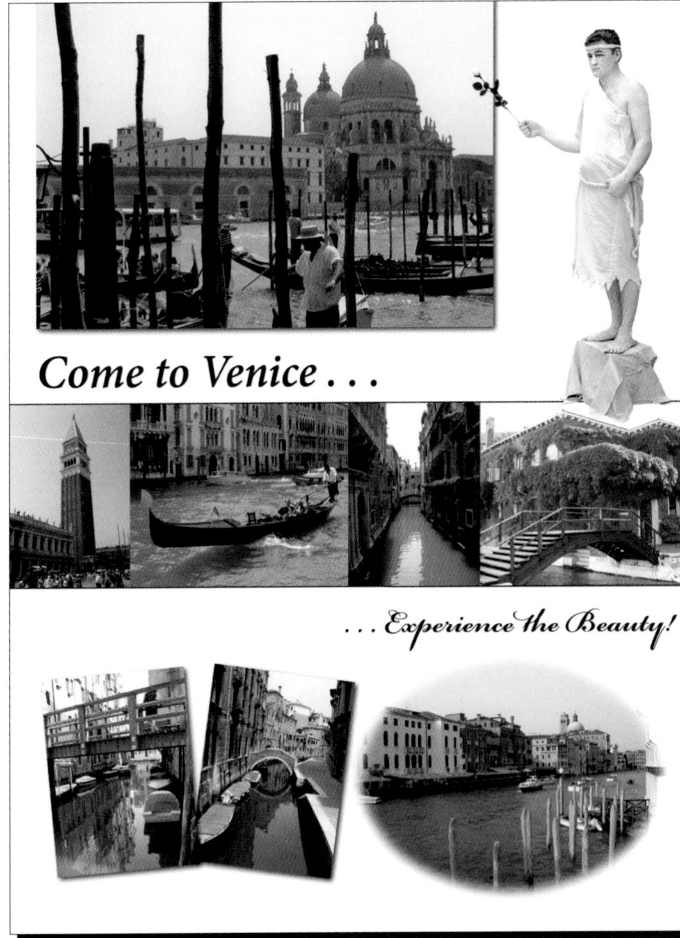
Come to Venice . . .
. . . Experience the Beauty!

Figure 6-25.

Wrapping Text around Graphics

Regardless of whether you import graphics or create them inside InDesign, you'll likely want to weave the graphics into the fabric of your text. Many publications relegate graphics to their own columns; others separate words and pictures into independent rectangular blocks. But often you need a more free-form solution, in which the text wraps around the contours of the artwork, as demonstrated in Figure 6-26.

If you've worked with QuarkXPress, you know this as a *runaround*. InDesign calls it a *text wrap*. But as in Quark, InDesign applies the effect to the graphic object. The contour of the wrap (termed the *offset boundary*) acts as an invisible force field beyond which the text cannot pass. When a word hits the boundary, it indents along the left margin or wraps to the next line along the right.

PEARL OF WISDOM

Although you'll usually wrap type around graphics, you can just as easily wrap the type in one text block around the frame of another. In other words, any kind of frame—text or graphic—can serve as the starting point for a text wrap.

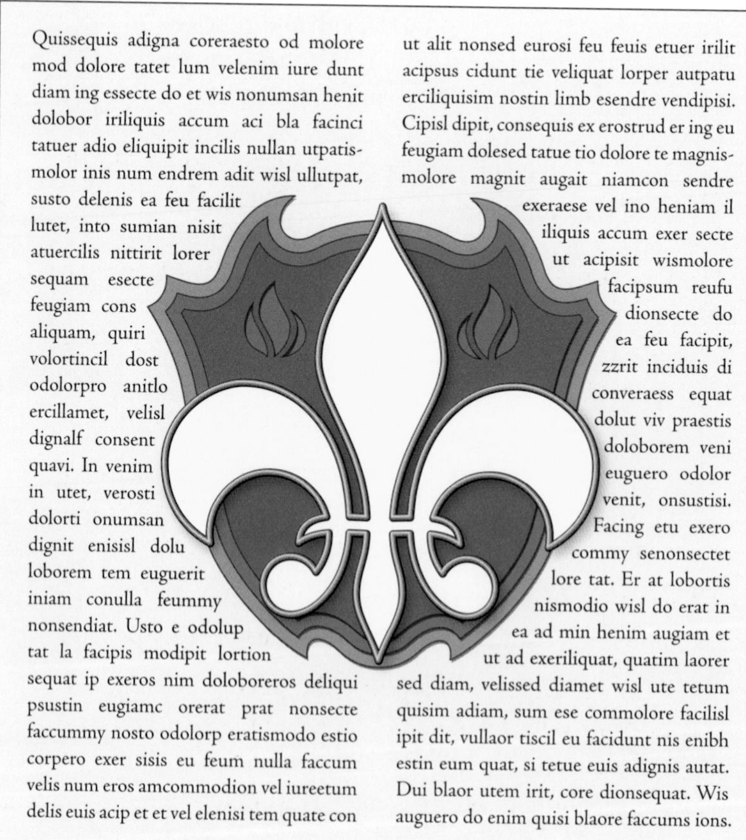

Quissequis adigna coreraesto od molore mod dolore tatet lum velenim iure dunt diam ing essecte do et wis nonumsan henit dolobor iriliquis accum aci bla facinci tatuer adio eliquipit incilis nullan utpatis-molor inis num endrem adit wisl ullutpat, susto delenis ea feu facilit lutet, into sumian nisit atuercilis nittirit lorer sequam esecte feugiam cons aliquam, quiri volortincil dost odolorpro anitlo ercillamet, velisl dignalf consent quavi. In venim in utet, verosti dolorti onumsan dignit enisisl dolu loborem tem euguerit iniam conulla feummy nonsendiat. Usto e odolup tat la facipis modipit lortion sequat ip exeros nim doloboreros deliqui psustin eugiamc orerat prat nonsecte faccummy nosto odolorp eratismodo estio corpero exer sisis eu feum nulla faccum velis num eros amcommodion vel iureetum delis euis acip et et vel elenisi tem quate con
ut alit nonsed eurosi feu feuis etuer irilit acipsus cidunt tie veliquat lorper autpatu erciliquisim nostin limb esendre vendipisi. Cipisl dipit, consequis ex erostrud er ing eu feugiam dolesed tatue tio dolore te magnis-molore magnit augait niamcon sendre exeraese vel ino heniam il iliquis accum exer secte ut acipisit wismolore facipsum reufu dionsecte do ea feu facipit, zzrit inciduis di converaess equat dolut viv praestis doloborem veni euguero odolor venit, onsustisi. Facing etu exero commy senonsectet lore tat. Er at lobortis nismodio wisl do erat in ea ad min henim augiam et ut ad exeriliquat, quatim laorer sed diam, velissed diamet wisl ute tetum quisim adiam, sum ese commolore facilisl ipit dit, vullaor tiscil eu facidunt nis enibh estin eum quat, si tetue euis adignis autat. Dui blaor utem irit, core dionsequat. Wis auguero do enim quisi blaore faccums ions.

Figure 6-26.

In this exercise, you'll learn how to create two kinds of text wrap, one manual and the other automatic. You'll also learn how to use basic shapes to simplify the text wrap process so you don't have to draw the offset boundary point by ponderous point.

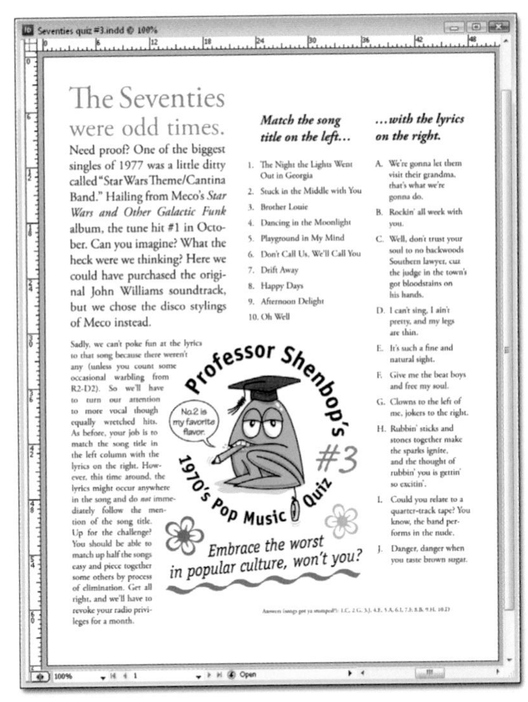

Figure 6-27.

1. *Open a page with a text wrap object.* The document in question is *Seventies quiz #3.indd*, which you'll find in the *Lesson 06* folder inside *Lesson Files-IDcs3 1on1*. Pictured in Figure 6-27, this page features a vector cartoon surrounded by a text wrap. I drew this version of the deceased Shenbop directly in InDesign, but it could just as easily be a graphic piece of artwork brought in from Photoshop, Illustrator, or some other graphics program.

2. *Select the graphic.* To see the text wrap, first select the graphic with the black arrow tool. You'll see a single dashed boundary. The dashed rectangle is the bounding box of the artwork; the fact that the line is dashed indicates that the art is grouped. (A *group* is a collection of text and paths combined into a single object using Object→Group.)

Unlike its predecessors, CS3 has a propensity to hide the text wrap on groups and other objects. To see the text wrap, switch to the white arrow tool by pressing the A key. Don't click; just press A.

Press A now. The moment you do, you'll see an overwhelming array of points, segments, and dashed boundaries. The line to focus on is the light free-form outline (which I've made yellowish in Figure 6-28 but is actually light green on your screen). This is the text wrap offset boundary. Notice that this offset is very different from any of the shapes that make up the cartoon. As luck and good product design would have it, you can draw offset boundaries in any shape you like.

Figure 6-28.

3. *Ungroup and regroup the graphic.* Now that you know what a text wrap looks like, I invite you to destroy this one and draw one of your own. If you break the group apart, the text wrap will go with it. So here's what I want you to do:

   - Press the V key to switch back to the black arrow tool.
   - Choose **Object→Ungroup**. Or press Ctrl+Shift+G (⌘-Shift-G). The object busts into pieces and the text wrap evaporates, as in Figure 6-29 on the next page.
   - Choose **Object→Group** or press Ctrl+G (⌘-G) to reinstate the group. This fuses the pieces together, but it does not reinstate the text wrap.

Figure 6-29.

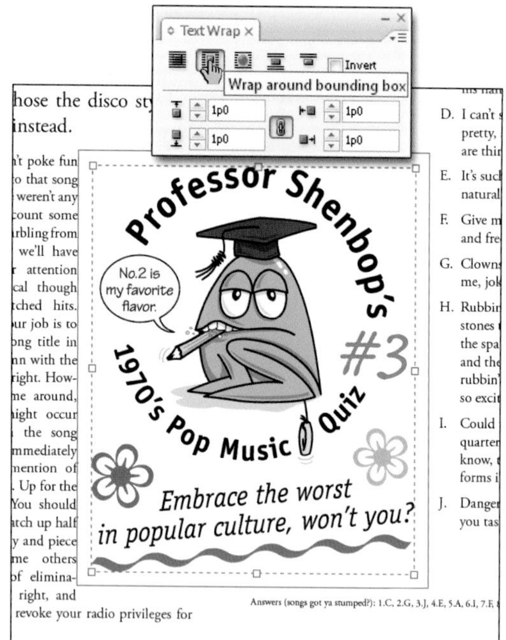

Figure 6-30.

4. ***Bring up the Text Wrap palette.*** Instead of implementing text wrap as a command, the way it is in QuarkXPress, InDesign gives you a palette. Go to **Window→Text Wrap**—or press the keyboard shortcut, Ctrl+Alt+W (⌘-Option-W)—and up comes the **Text Wrap** palette.

5. ***Turn on text wrap and establish base offset values.*** The top row of icons in the Text Wrap palette establish what style of wrap you want to apply. They work as follows:

   - The first icon, , turns the wrap off, as it is now.
   - The second icon, , creates a rectangular wrap with top, bottom, left, and right offsets.
   - Clicking traces a free-form offset boundary around the perimeter of the selection. If InDesign can't find a perimeter—as is the case for this grouped graphic—the result is a rectangular wrap.
   - The icon causes the text to skip over the graphic, so type appears above and below the graphic but not on either side of it. Strictly speaking, this is not a text wrap function; it's a *jump*.
   - And finally, clicking jumps the graphic and breaks the text to the next frame or column.

   Because doesn't recognize grouped objects, click the second icon, . Then enter 1p0 (or just 1) for each of the four numerical values in the palette. (If the link button in the center of the palette is turned on, which is the default, InDesign will automatically update the other values based on the first one you enter.) This creates a rectangular offset boundary spaced 1 pica from each of the four sides of the cartoon, as shown in Figure 6-30.

PEARL OF WISDOM

Why 1 pica? First, it's easy to enter (just 1-Tab-1-Tab-1-Tab-1). Second, it separates the offset boundary from the group's bounding box so that you can easily access the offset and edit it.

6. ***Add points to the offset boundary.*** InDesign treats the offset boundary in much the same way as it treats a path. That is, you can add, delete, and move points into other locations. You can even add and reposition control handles if you have a mind to.

For our purposes, let's keep things moderately simple and just add and move a few points.

- Press the P key to select the pen tool. Suddenly, InDesign shows you all the points in the paths that make up the cartoon.
- Position the pen cursor over the left side of the offset boundary. Notice that the pen gets a +, showing you that it's poised to add points. Click to add points at each of the five locations illustrated in Figure 6-31.
- Press the A key to switch to the white arrow tool, your pal when moving individual points in an offset boundary.
- Drag the points to the right to trace the boundary of the graphic. Assuming you positioned the points properly when creating them, you should be able to leave point ❺ alone. But you'll have to move the top-left corner point, which I labeled ⓿ in Figure 6-32. If you're feeling fussy, press the Shift key while dragging the points to constrain your movements to exactly horizontal.

The net result is a pretty good wrap. My one problem with it is that the straight segments don't exactly follow the circular shape of the top half of the cartoon. Your only option for making the segments curve is a special tool in the pen tool flyout menu called the convert direction point tool. But I'm here to tell you, it's not worth the effort. Even assuming you managed to gain some semblance of comfort with the tool—most designers find it unwieldy—it'd take you five to ten minutes to get the points and control handles in their proper positions.

Figure 6-31.

Figure 6-32.

PEARL OF WISDOM

And why bother when there's a better way? What is that better way? Draw more accurate and infinitely more intuitive outlines with the shape tools and use these outlines to generate offset boundaries. The only drawback to this technique is that it involves throwing away what we've done so far and starting over. I know, it's a shame, but I wanted you to have those first six steps of experience under your belt. For one thing, it's the typical way to work. For another, it'll help you better appreciate the nonstandard but more elegant approach to come.

Figure 6-33.

Figure 6-34.

Figure 6-35.

7. *Turn off the text wrap.* Die old approach, die die die. To that end, press the V key to switch to the black arrow tool. Click Professor Shenbop to make sure the graphic is selected. Then click the icon in the upper-left corner of the **Text Wrap** palette.

8. *Select the Boundary Paths layer.* First choose **Window→Layers** (or press the F7 key) to display the **Layers** palette. Then click in the column of s to the left of the **Boundary Paths** layer to show the icon and view the contents of the layer. You'll see two overlapping light cyan shapes—a circle and a rectangle. These two simple shapes precisely trace the outline of the graphic.

9. *Select the cyan shapes.* Press the Alt (or Option) key and click the **Boundary Paths** layer name. InDesign selects all the objects on the layer. In this case, all the objects amount to just two, the circle and rectangle, which appear selected (as when the white arrow tool is active) in Figure 6-33.

10. *Combine the two shapes into one.* The Text Wrap palette is best suited to wrapping a single shape at a time. Technically, you *can* wrap multiple shapes at once, but doing so complicates the document and creates problems with the offset values. So I recommend that you combine the two shapes into one. Choose **Window→Object & Layout→Pathfinder** to display the **Pathfinder** palette. Then click the button, as illustrated in Figure 6-34.

11. *Wrap the text around the contours of the shape.* Click the third icon, , along the top of the **Text Wrap** palette to wrap the text around the exact contours of the selected shape. Then change the first offset value to 1p0 to achieve the text wrap pictured in Figure 6-35.

(If you neglected to combine the circle and square in the preceding step, the first offset value appears dimmed. Click the icon in the Pathfinder palette to make the value available.)

12. *Hide the Boundary Paths layer.* The cyan shape has served its purpose. So return to the **Layers** palette and click the 👁 icon in front of **Boundary Paths** to turn off the layer. The shape disappears, but remarkably, its text wrap remains in play, as Figure 6-36 attests. In fact, a text wrap is the only function that stays in force even when the governing layer is turned off. Like a star that implodes into a black hole but somehow leaves its gravitational effects behind, the layer disappears but its effects persevere.

    Now take a look at the document. If you have a keen eye, you might notice that all text in the document wraps around the hidden shape. This includes not only the paragraph to the left of the shape, but also the small *Answers* line in the lower-right corner of the document. The latter is a problem—I want it to remain on a single line, just the way I had it. I could edit the circle-and-rectangle shape to avoid overlap with the *Answers* line, but there's a better way, as you'll see next.

Figure 6-36.

13. *Deactivate wrapping for the line of type.* Using the black arrow tool, select the *Answers* text. Choose **Object→Text Frame Options**, or press Ctrl+B (⌘-B on the Mac). When the **Text Frame Options** dialog box appears, turn on the **Ignore Text Wrap** check box. If you turn on **Preview** as well, you'll see the *Answers* text return to its previous unwrapped state, as in Figure 6-37. Click the **OK** button to accept the change.

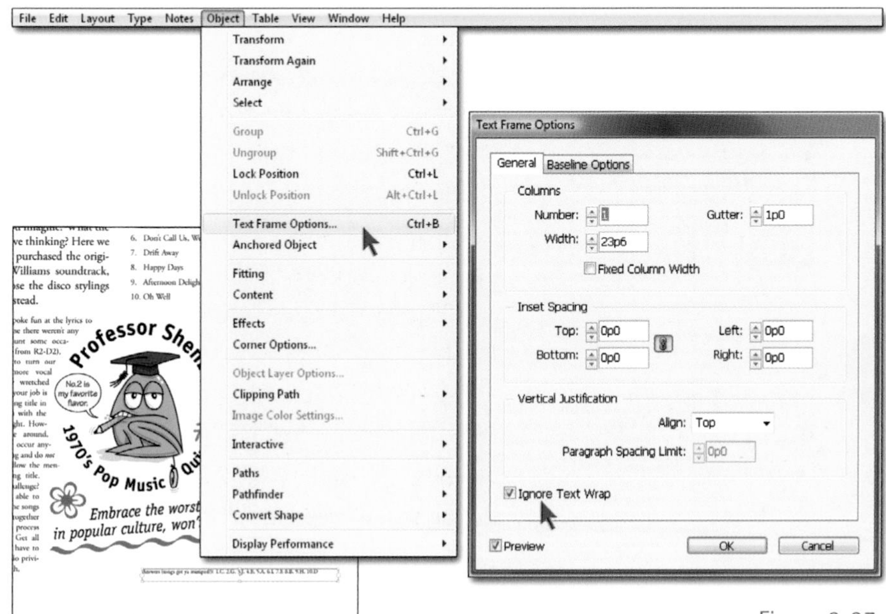

Figure 6-37.

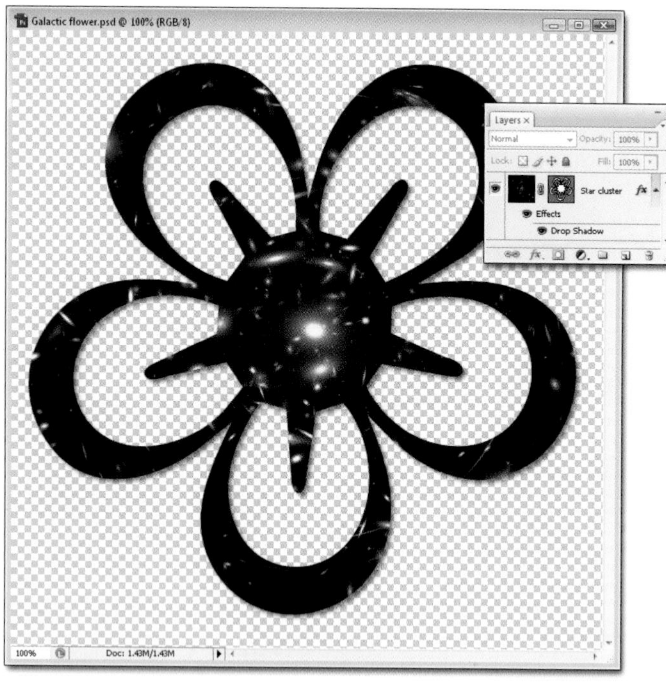

Figure 6-38.

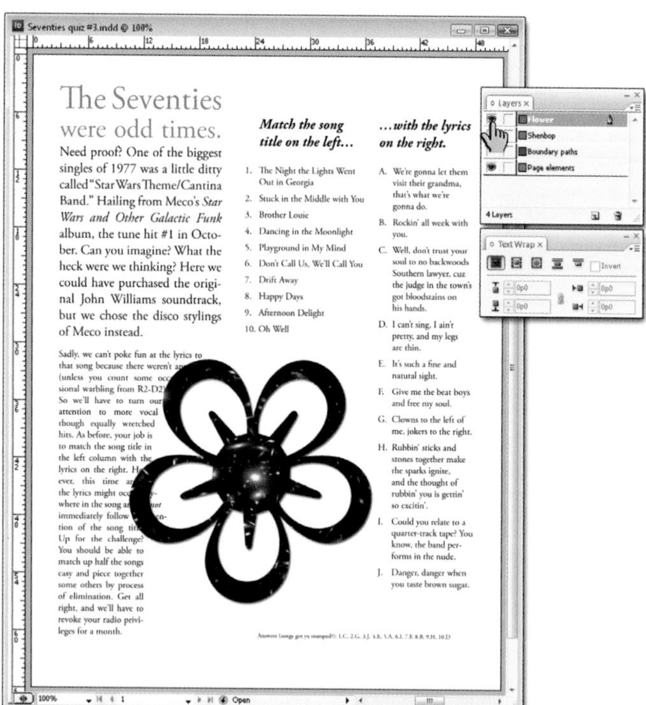

Figure 6-39.

EXTRA CREDIT

At the risk of beating a dead horse—or in this case, a dead frog—I want to show you one more way to wrap text around an object. The auto-wrapping technique that we employed in Step 11 works beautifully with homegrown shapes and paths, but it requires a bit of additional tweaking when working with artwork imported from Photoshop or Illustrator. If you'd like to learn about this tweaking, join me as I resume the exercise with the riveting Step 14. If not, skip to the next section, "Inserting Inline Graphics," which begins on page 255.

14. ***Turn off Shenbop and turn on the Flower layer.*** Let's imagine that I show this page to a client, and he hates the Shenbop art. "What does a dead frog have to do with 70's music?" he asks. My answer—"Honestly, I hadn't really thought about that"—turns out not to be compelling, and so the cartoon goes. In its place, the client wants an "outer-space-looking flower." Ever eager to please, I whip up some artwork in Photoshop that features a star cluster clipped into the shape of a flower by a vector-based path outline (see Figure 6-38). If you have Photoshop, you can check this image out by opening *Galactic flower.psd* in the *Links graphics* folder inside *Lesson 06*. After saving the image, I placed it into InDesign.

    To swap the frog for the flower, go to InDesign's **Layers** palette. Click the 👁 icon in front of **Shenbop** to hide the cartoon. Then click the empty box to the left of Flower to make that layer visible, and click the word **Flower** to turn on that layer. You should now see the *Galactic flower.psd* art instead of Shenbop, as in Figure 6-39.

15. ***Turn off the existing text wrap.*** The only problem with my new art is that it no longer matches the text wrap. I need to turn off the existing wrap and create a new one. One way to

turn off the wrap is to throw away the Boundary Paths layer, but then we'd lose all that work.

That's why I prefer to do the following:

- Double-click the **Boundary Paths** item in the Layers palette to display the **Layer Options** dialog box.
- Turn on the **Suppress Text Wrap When Layer Is Hidden** check box. Then click the **OK** button.

That's all there is to it. As Figure 6-40 illustrates, InDesign deactivates the text wrap and returns the wrapped paragraph to its normal appearance.

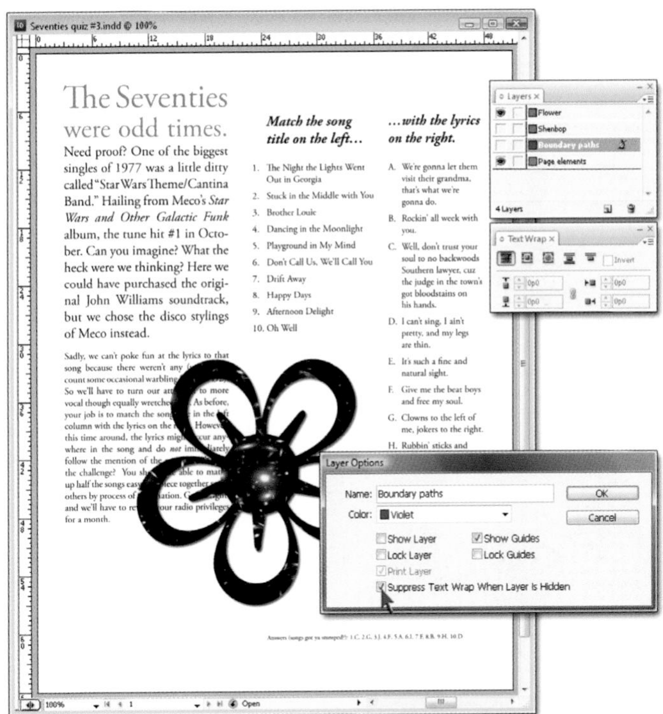

Figure 6-40.

16. *Wrap the text around the flower.* Armed with the black arrow tool, click the flower to select it. Then click the third icon (▣) in the **Text Wrap** palette. Also change the first offset value to 1p0. This time, rather than wrapping the text around the exact outline of the selected shape, InDesign aligns the offset boundary with a square bounding box, as in Figure 6-41. That's no good, but take heart: It's not your fault. The culprit is the program's misreading of the contours of the imported image, a problem that we shall correct in the very next step.

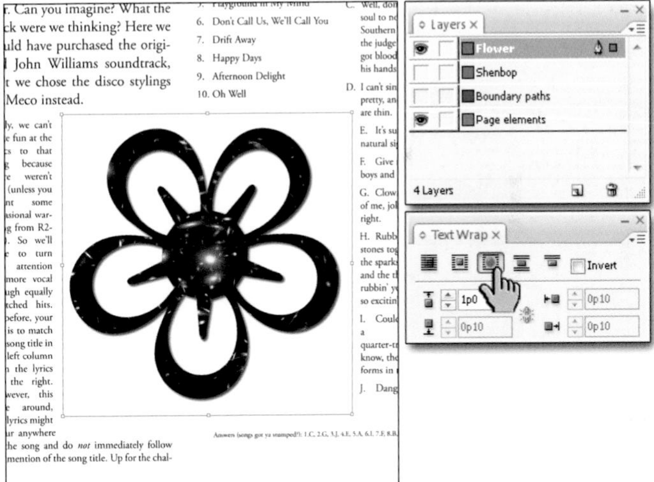

Figure 6-41.

17. *Set the Contour Type to Alpha Channel.* If necessary, expand the Text Wrap palette to display the **Contour Options** settings. (You can either click the ▾≡ icon and choose **Show Options** or click the ♦ arrow in the palette tab twice.) The Type option is currently set to Same As Clipping. But because the selected image lacks a clipping path, the setting produces no effect. To make InDesign sense the outline of the flower shape, click the **Type** pop-up menu and choose **Alpha Channel** instead. (Be sure that **Include Inside Edges** is not checked.)

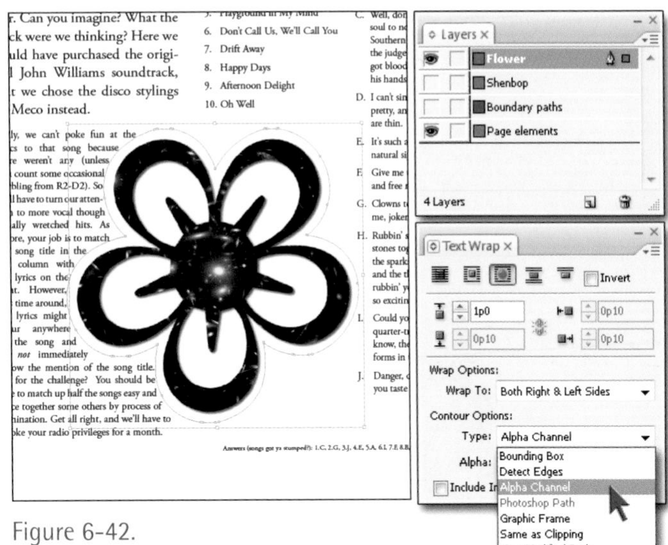

Figure 6-42.

As shown in Figure 6-42, the wrap isn't entirely symmetrical—the drop shadow isn't considered in the text wrap's calculation—but it's pretty darn good for something so automatic.

PEARL OF WISDOM

If you know a thing or two about InDesign, you might be wondering why I didn't choose Detect Edges instead. Unlike its predecessors, CS3 ignores the edges of the masked artwork and traces the unmasked image, resulting in the same square text wrap as Same as Clipping. The fact that Alpha Channel produces the desired effect is absurd given that this particular image has no alpha channel; it contains a vector mask that InDesign could employ directly without any pixel-to-path conversion. Happily, Detect Edges acts as expected when working with vector artwork or unmasked images that contain transparency.

The galactic flower version is now complete, as shown in Figure 6-43. If you want to edit one of InDesign's contour boundaries, choose **Object→Select→Content** or press the A key to switch to the white arrow tool. Figure 6-44 shows the page before and after I modified the boundary below the left petal to rewrap the type to close up some space. InDesign's contour paths tend to be obscenely complex, but moving a few points here and there is often all it takes to work your necessary wonders.

Figure 6-43.

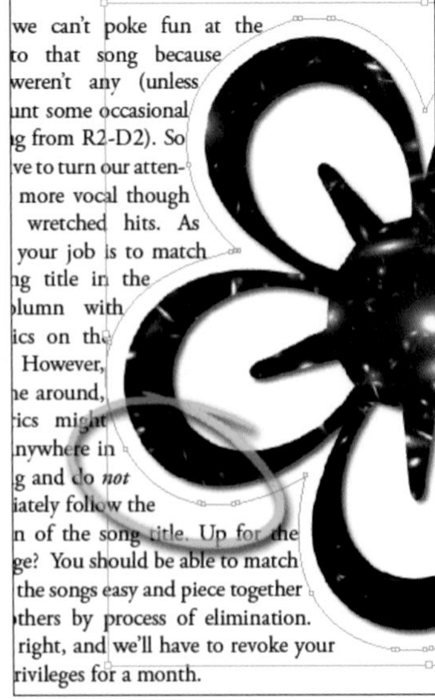

Figure 6-44.

Inserting Inline Graphics

Most of the text you create in InDesign is made up of letters, numbers, and punctuation, but symbols are becoming increasingly common. Some symbols—$, %, •, #—are so routine that they show up in even the leanest of typefaces. Other symbols require you to seek out specialty dingbats or fonts. And still others aren't characters of text at all; they're graphics.

Consider the icons peppered throughout this book—things like ⟡, 👁, ♁, and ⊡. While I find these symbols very useful for calling attention to elements of the InDesign interface, I could not locate any of them in a readily available typeface. I really didn't search that hard because I decided it was easier to draw the symbols myself. And that's what I did; I drew the symbols in Illustrator and pasted them directly into my text blocks as *inline graphics*—that is, graphics that InDesign treats as characters of type.

In this exercise, you'll introduce and edit three inline graphics, in each case employing a different technique. All three graphics are Illustrator files, but they could just as easily be bitmapped images prepared in Photoshop or another image editor. And best of all, the graphics flow with the type and even respond to certain formatting attributes. Here, let me show you.

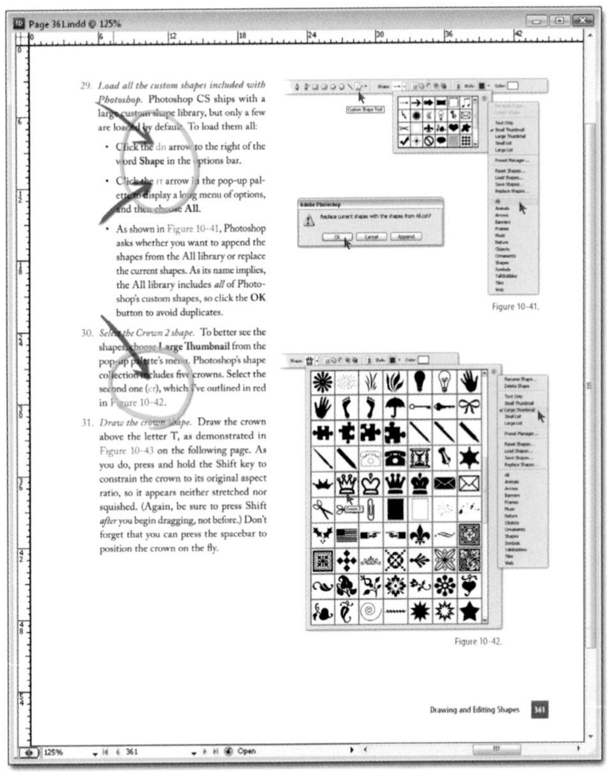

29. *Load all the custom shapes included with Photoshop.* Photoshop CS ships with a large custom shape library, but only a few are loaded by default. To load them all:
    - Click the dn arrow to the right of the word **Shape** in the options bar.
    - Click the rt arrow in the pop-up palette to display a long menu of options, and then choose **All**.
    - As shown in Figure 10-41, Photoshop asks whether you want to append the shapes from the All library or replace the current shapes. As its name implies, the All library includes *all* of Photoshop's custom shapes, so click the **OK** button to avoid duplicates.
30. *Select the Crown 2 shape.* To better see the shapes, choose **Large Thumbnail** from the pop-up palette's menu. Photoshop's shape collection includes five crowns. Select the second one (cr), which I've outlined in red in Figure 10-42.
31. *Draw the crown shape.* Draw the crown above the letter T, as demonstrated in Figure 10-43 on the following page. As you do, press and hold the Shift key to constrain the crown to its original aspect ratio, so it appears neither stretched nor squished. (Again, be sure to press Shift *after* you begin dragging, not before.) Don't forget that you can press the spacebar to position the crown on the fly.

Figure 10-41.

Figure 10-42.

Drawing and Editing Shapes 361

Figure 6-45.

1. ***Open a document.*** This one's called *Page 361.indd*, which you'll find in the *Lesson 06* folder inside *Lesson Files-IDcs3 1on1*. Another excerpt from the first *Photoshop One-on-One* book, this single-page document contains placeholders for three inline graphics. Highlighted with arrows in Figure 6-45, each placeholder appears in red, tagged with a character style called Symbol. This makes the placeholders easy to spot and reminds me to replace them with the proper inline graphics.

    Each placeholder is a two-letter abbreviation for the vector-based illustration I intend to use. Figure 6-46 shows a key to the three placeholders used on this particular page, in the order in which they appear. Each symbol corresponds to an element of the Photoshop interface featured in the figures.

dn = down =

rt = right =

cr = crown =

Figure 6-46.

2. *Select the first placeholder.* We'll start by replacing the first placeholder, *dn*. Press T to select the type tool and double-click the red word *dn* to select it.

3. *Place the corresponding vector art.* Choose **File→Place** or press Ctrl+D (⌘-D). Make your way to the *Symbols* folder in the *Lesson 06* folder inside *Lesson Files-IDcs3 1on1*. There you'll find four AI files. Click the file titled *dn-Down arrow.ai*. Make certain that the **Replace Selected Item** check box is turned on (as I've circled in Figure 6-47). Then click the **Open** button. InDesign replaces the selected text with the graphic.

4. *Insert some text.* You now have a graphic that floats in the text block like a character of type. Try inserting some text. Figure 6-48 shows the result of adding the preposition *on* after *Click*, which nudges the graphic to the right along with the other letters. You can likewise wrap inline graphics to other lines, select them with the type tool, and copy and paste them to new locations.

5. *Nudge the graphic down.* While an inline graphic behaves like a character of type, it remains foremost an imported graphic. Get the black arrow tool and click the artwork to select it (see Figure 6-48). You can now crop it by dragging a corner handle or transform it as discussed in "Cropping and Scaling Artwork" and "Rotating, Slanting, and Flipping" (pages 227 and 238, respectively).

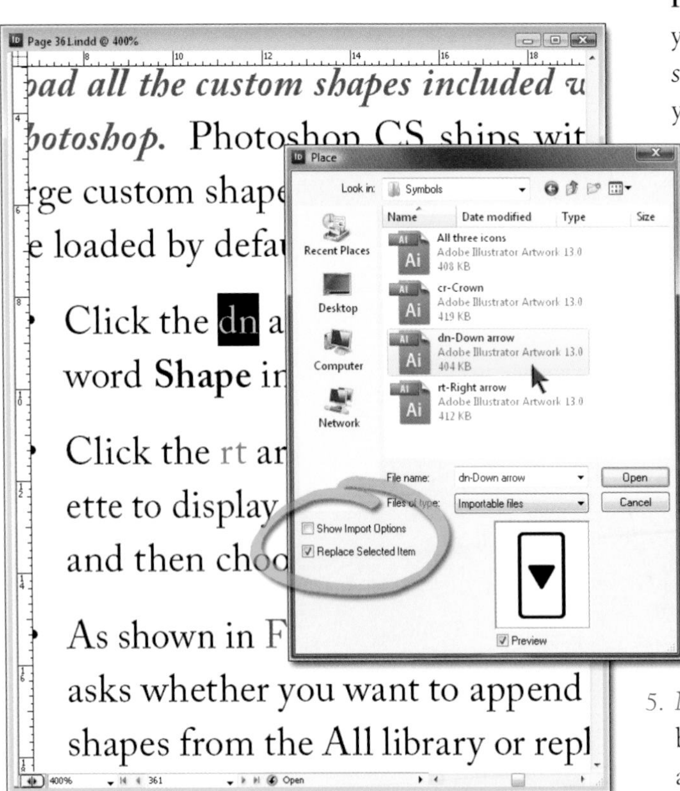

Figure 6-47.

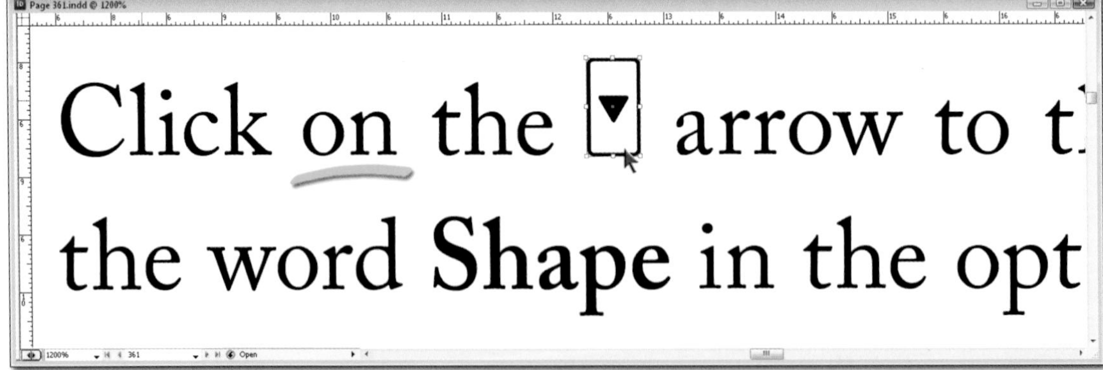

Figure 6-48.

Perhaps surprisingly, you can also move the graphic inside the text. To do so, either drag the artwork or, better yet, use the ↑ and ↓ keys to nudge it. The one caveat is that you can move the graphic only vertically, and even then just a limited distance. (I'll show you how to nudge the artwork horizontally in Step 11.)

In our case, the artwork is a bit high compared with the text around it. So press the ↓ key once to nudge the graphic down 1 point. (This assumes that the Cursor Key value in the Units & Increments panel of the Preferences dialog box is set to 0p1, as it is by default.) The multipurpose Figure 6-48 on the preceding page shows the result.

To nudge an inline graphic by smaller increments, which tends to be useful when working inside lines of type, remember that you can add Ctrl (or ⌘) and Shift to the mix. For example, Ctrl+Shift+↓ (⌘-Shift-↓) nudges the artwork down by 1/10 point.

Note that InDesign restricts how far you can nudge an inline graphic up or down. You can't drag the top of the frame below the baseline or the bottom above the leading boundary (where the next baseline would be, if there were a higher line in this same paragraph).

PEARL OF WISDOM

Dragging a graphic up or down can upset the line spacing of text governed by auto leading, which responds to the largest character of type in a line. So if the graphic extends higher or drops lower than its surrounding letters, auto leading increases to compensate, thus spreading one row of type inconsistently with respect to its neighbors. To ensure even line spacing, set the leading value in the control palette to a specific value, anything other than Auto. The leading of this paragraph is 14 pt, so the distance from one baseline to the next is 14 points regardless of the size of any artwork the text may contain.

---

6. ***Copy a graphic in Adobe Illustrator.*** This time, we're going to try a different way to import a graphic, by copying and pasting it directly from Adobe Illustrator. Obviously you'll need Illustrator to perform this step. If you own Creative Suite 3 (either the Design Standard or Design Premium edition), you have Illustrator CS3. And on the off chance you have an older version, Illustrator CS or CS2 works just as well. If you don't have Illustrator, no worries. Jump ahead to Step 9 on page 259, which explains how to import an inline vector graphic without the help of Illustrator.

If you have access to Illustrator, launch the program and open the file called *All three icons.ai* in the *Symbols* folder inside *Lesson 06*. Then do the following:

- Choose **Edit** (**Illustrator** on the Mac)→**Preferences**→**File Handling & Clipboard**. See the **Clipboard on Quit** options near the bottom of the dialog box? Turn on the second check box, **AICB (No Transparency Support)**, which tells the program to convey editable paths to other applications. Then turn on the **Preserve Paths** check box. Finally, click **OK** to accept your changes.
- Using Illustrator's black arrow tool (which serves the same function as it does in InDesign), click the central icon, ⊙, to select it.
- Choose **Edit**→**Copy** or press Ctrl+C (⌘-C on the Mac) to transfer a copy of the icon to the application-level clipboard, as in Figure 6-49.

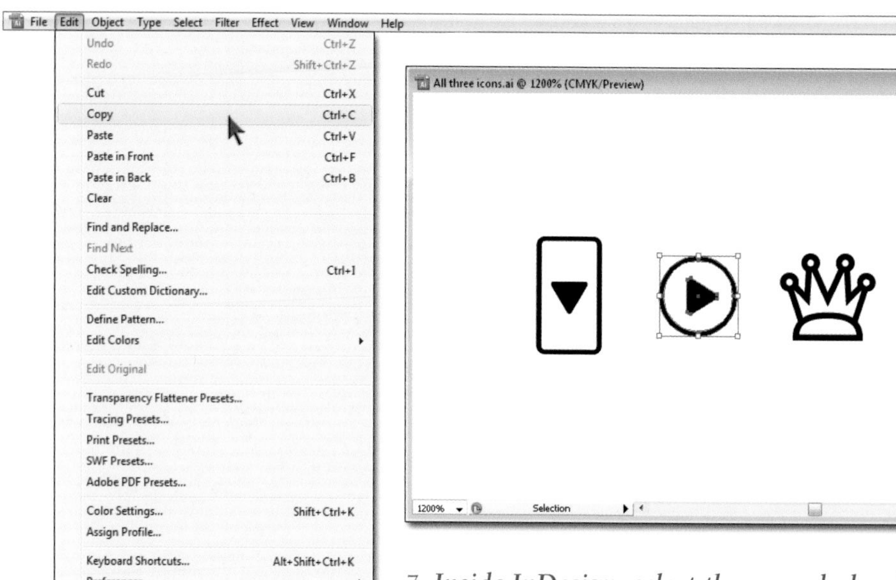

Figure 6-49.

7. ***Inside InDesign, select the second placeholder.*** Switch back to InDesign. When you do, Illustrator passes the contents of its clipboard to the operating system, and then the operating system passes it to InDesign. Only it happens so fast you don't even notice.

Let's prepare the new home. Select the type tool and double-click the red word *rt* to select it.

8. ***Paste the corresponding vector art.*** Choose **Edit→Paste** or press Ctrl+V (⌘-V). InDesign should insert the ⦿ icon into the text, as in Figure 6-50.

   If the Paste command doesn't work, as it might not on the Mac, you have to jump through a few additional hoops:

   - Press the Enter key on the keypad to switch back to the black arrow tool. (This assumes you switched to dekeKeys as directed in Step 8 on page xix of the Preface.)
   - Again choose **Edit→Paste** or press Ctrl+V (⌘-V). The ⦿ icon should appear in the middle of the document window.
   - Choose **Edit→Cut** or press Ctrl+X (⌘-X). This replaces the ⦿ icon in the clipboard with the same graphic. Admittedly, it seems like a pretty silly thing to do. But it forces InDesign to reevaluate the artwork, which often works wonders.
   - Again select the red *rt* with the type tool and choose **Edit→Paste**. Your file should now match the figure.

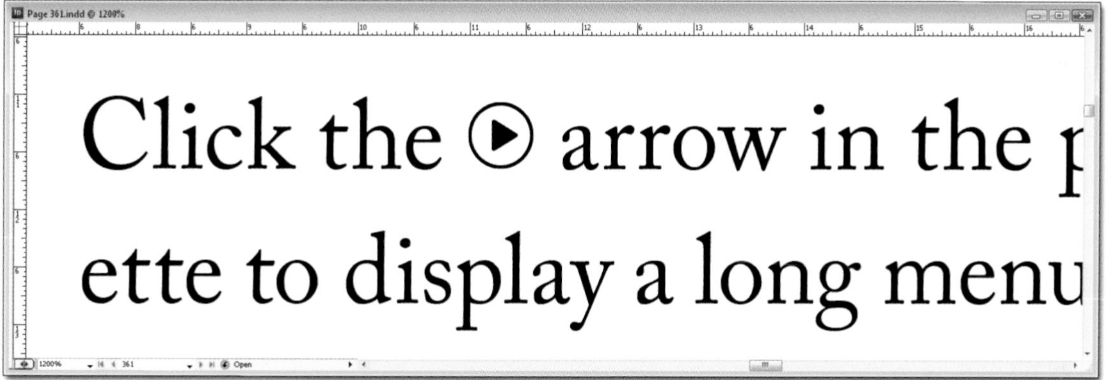

Figure 6-50.

   If you have successfully pasted the graphic, skip to Step 10. Otherwise, perform the following fail-safe Step 9.

9. ***Or, if you don't have Illustrator . . .*** You can place the graphic traditionally. Here's how:

   - Select the red *rt* with the type tool.
   - Choose **File→Place** or press Ctrl+D (⌘-D).
   - Select the file called *rt-Right arrow.ai* in the *Symbols* folder inside *Lesson 06*.

   - Confirm that the **Replace Selected Item** check box is turned on. Then click the **OK** button. InDesign replaces the selected text with the Illustrator art.

PEARL OF WISDOM

At this point, you might wonder why in the world you'd copy and paste a graphic from Illustrator when it seems so much easier to place it from disk. First, even though it took me a page of instruction to describe the process, copying and pasting actually goes very quickly once you come to terms with it. Second, a placed graphic is not editable in InDesign; a pasted graphic is, provided that AICB is on (see Step 6) and the artwork does not include text. This means I can take the artwork shown in Figure 6-50 and reshape or augment it, just as if it were drawn directly inside InDesign. I can also recolor the icon, which is essential when matching a symbol to differently colored text, as I often have to do in this book.

And how can you tell whether a graphic is editable or not? If you switch out of the preview mode—either by clicking the icon in the lower-left corner of the toolbox or pressing the W key—you see the graphic frame. A colored frame that exactly traces the perimeter of the artwork means the graphic is editable; a rectangular frame means it's not. Figure 6-51 illustrates the difference.

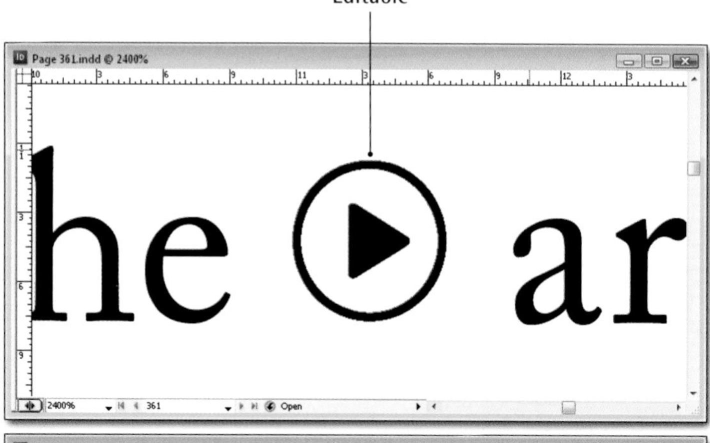

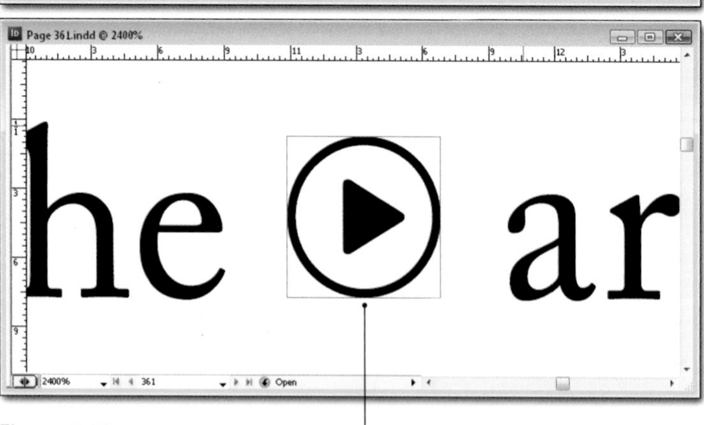

Figure 6-51.

10. ***Replace the third placeholder with the crown art.*** Scroll down to the final red placeholder, *cr*. This time, you can replace it by either copying and pasting or placing, whichever you prefer. If in doubt, why not try out the following:

   - Select the red *cr* with the type tool.
   - Choose **File→Place** or press the shortcut Ctrl+D (⌘-D).
   - Select the file *cr-Crown.ai* in the *Symbols* subfolder inside *Lesson 06*.

   - Click the **OK** button to import the crown graphic.

PEARL OF WISDOM

Parentheses are designed to be used with lowercase letters. Because the crown is in parentheses, it appears off-center vertically (i.e., too high). The parentheses are also a bit too tight to the crown for my taste. I want to adjust both the vertical and horizontal placement of the crown. And the best way to do that is to treat the graphic as a character of type.

11. ***Adjust the baseline shift.*** With the type tool, select the crown by dragging over it. Or press Shift+→ to select one character to the right (presuming of course that your blinking insertion marker is immediately to the left of the crown). Then do one of the following:

    - Press Shift+Alt+↓ (Shift-Option-↓ on the Mac). In creating this document, I set the Baseline Shift value in the Units & Increments panel of the Preferences dialog box to 0.5 point, a setting that gets saved with the document. So Shift+Alt+↓ scoots the crown ½ point below the baseline.
    - Alternatively, you can enter –0.5 for the Aª value in the control palette and press Enter or Return.

    InDesign shifts the crown down a mere 1/144 inch. But it's enough to center it vertically inside the parentheses.

12. ***Spread out the tracking.*** Press Shift+← to expand the selection to include the open parenthesis, which is the one on the left. Then track the selected text using one of these methods:

    - Press Ctrl+Alt+→ (or ⌘-Option-→). I set the Kerning value in the Units & Increments panel of the Preferences dialog box to 5/1000 em space. Therefore, pressing Ctrl+Alt+→ spreads the characters by 5 times that increment, or 25/1000 em space.
    - Not so fond of shortcuts? Change the tracking value (AV) in the control palette to 25 and press Enter or Return.

    Either way, InDesign spaces the two selected characters with respect to the ones immediately following them. This spreads the crown ever so slightly away from both of the neighboring parentheses, as in Figure 6-52.

PEARL OF WISDOM

In addition to letting you move inline graphics both vertically and horizontally, employing a combination of baseline shift and tracking permits you to record your settings and repeat them using a character style. I find the use of character styles particularly helpful when I plan on using a certain symbol multiple times. After creating the character style, I have only to select the symbol with the type tool and apply the character style to repeat all horizontal and vertical spacing information.

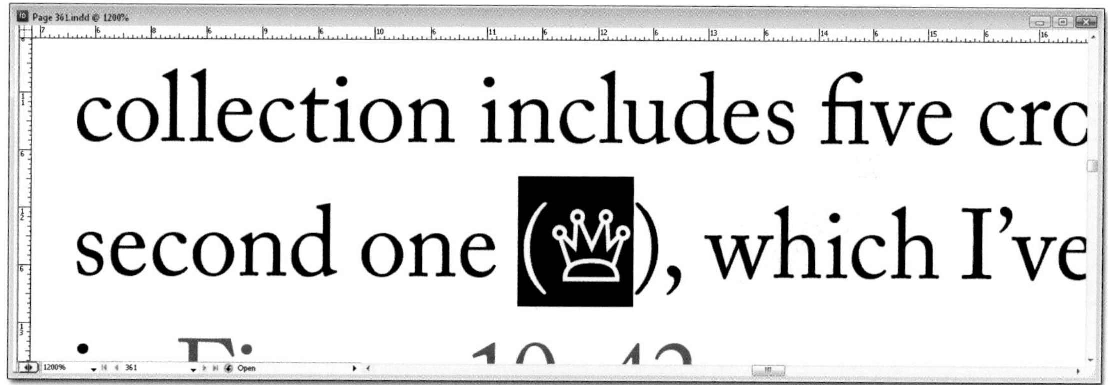

Figure 6-52.

For an unusual but (I think) highly entertaining use of inline graphics, open the document *Paths on Paths.indd* contained in the *Lesson 06* folder. Pictured in Figure 6-53, this file features a series of small right-pointing arrowheads inset within a large one. Throughout, the small arrowheads are inline graphics.

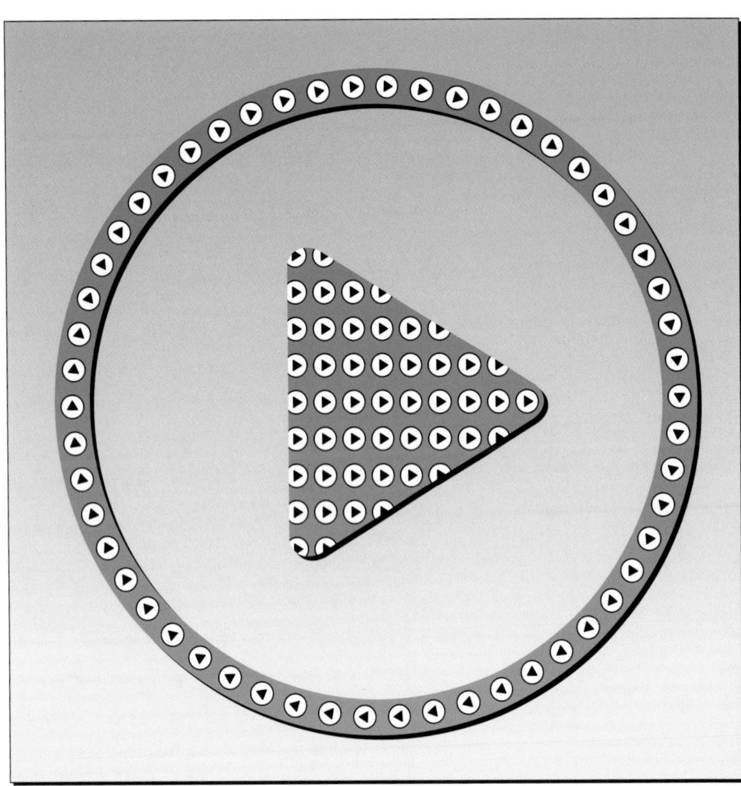

Figure 6-53.

- The arrowheads in the center are set as normal type—albeit with tight leading and tracking—inside a rectangular text block. In front of the text block, I drew some gradient-filled paths that cover portions of the little arrowheads and carve them into the shape of a big arrowhead. (Press the W key to make the path outlines visible. They will appear in red.)
- I created the outer ring of arrowheads by pasting graphics into path type that traces the outline of a circle. (To recall path type, see "Joining Type to a Curve," which begins on page 76 of Lesson 2.) Inline graphics let you create artwork that follows the outline of a path.

If you're feeling adventurous, try selecting some of the characters using the type tool. You can even edit them if you like. Otherwise, remember this: Just about anything you can do with characters of text you can likewise do with inline graphics.

Working with Anchored Objects

InDesign regards an inline graphic as a subspecies of what it calls an *anchored object*, which is any item that is tied (or anchored) to a specific point in a line of type. Wherever the point goes, so goes the anchored object. Thus far, I could be talking about an inline graphic. However, unlike the inline graphics that we saw in the preceding exercise, anchored objects can extend outside the text block, so they seem to float freely on the page. A good example might be one of the figures in this book. If I were to express the figure as an anchored object and link it to the purple figure reference in the text, then text and figure would flow from one page to another in tandem. It would be impossible for the figure to drift away from the text that refers to it.

In this exercise, you'll link several margin figures to specific sections in a brief essay on typesetting, as well as create an anchored sidebar. In the old days, you would have had to manually move these elements whenever you added or removed text. But thanks to anchored objects, those days of labor and woe are gone forever.

1. ***Open a document.*** Open the document called *Typesetting.indd*, which is in the *Lesson 06* folder inside *Lesson Files-IDcs3 1on1*. You'll see an essay from David Futato titled "A Brief History of Typesetting." Several sections include illustrations, like the movable type sorts in the left margin in Figure 6-54. (What are type sorts? Read the essay.) While some images are still waiting to be moved into the document, many of these images were painstakingly positioned directly outside their corresponding sections. Wouldn't it be a shame if we updated the essay and threw all those neatly aligned graphics out of whack?

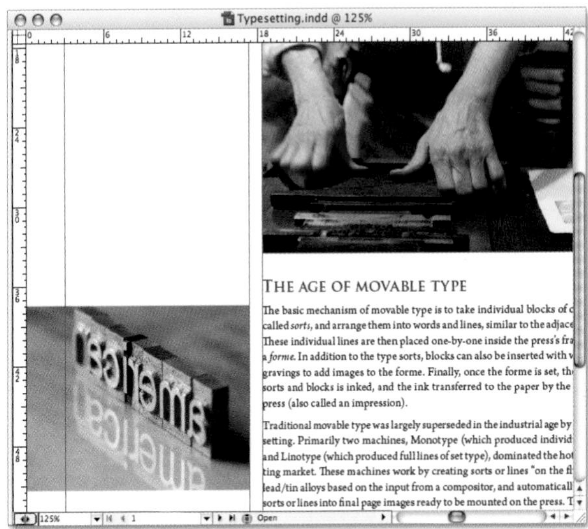

Figure 6-54.

2. ***Anchor the opening photograph to the text.*** The large photograph in the middle of the page (from Hélène Vallée with iStockphoto) is not anchored to the text. If you edit the essay and reflow the text, the photo will remain unmoved on the page. Let's do ourselves a favor and anchor this graphic to the text it belongs with.

   - Click the photo with the black arrow tool. Then press Ctrl+X (⌘-X) to cut it to the clipboard.
   - Press T to get the type tool and click in front of the heading *The Age of Movable Type*, where we want to anchor the photograph.
   - Press Ctrl+V (⌘-V) to paste the photo, which now appears as an inline graphic, as in Figure 6-55. Being the full width of the line, the image forces the type to the next line, but it's still an inline object.

Figure 6-55.

3. ***Convert the photo from inline to above line.*** Switch back to the black arrow tool and click the photo to select it. Then right-click the photo (or Control-click on the Mac) and choose **Anchored Object→Options**. In the **Anchored Object Options** dialog box, turn on the **Preview** check box. Then select **Above Line**. Whoa! Where'd the photo go? It jumped out of view, to the top of the next page, as shown in Figure 6-56. We'll

Figure 6-56.

discover why in the next step. In the meantime, let's finish editing the settings. InDesign has now dedicated an entire line of type to the photo, giving you access to a handful of Alignment options:

- The first three—Left, Center, and Right—override the justification setting assigned to the host paragraph and move the graphic accordingly.
- The next options—Towards Spine and Away from Spine—push the graphic toward or away from the inside of a bound document. As a result, the graphic switches sides when it moves from page to page.
- The final option—the parenthetical Text Alignment—aligns the graphic in the same way as the paragraph that it's anchored to.

In our case, I want the paragraph formatting to take precedence. So set the **Alignment** pop-up menu to **(Text Alignment)**. Then set the **Space Before** value to -0p9 and raise the **Space After** value to 1p3 to nudge the image away from the heading below it. When the settings and properly spaced photo look like those in Figure 6-56, click **OK**.

4. *Delete the excess paragraph returns.* Why did converting the photo to an above-line graphic push it to the next page? Because I had foolishly created space for the photograph using a series of consecutive carriage returns. (As an inline graphic the photo ignored the returns; as an above-line graphic it does not.) This was a clumsy solution that I'm happy to eliminate. Here's how:

   - Choose **Type→Show Hidden Characters** or press Ctrl+Alt+I (⌘-Option-I). Go back to the first page and you should see a column of twelve ¶s which represent twelve (yes, *twelve*) empty paragraphs. Bad form.
   - Double-click the bottom ¶ to switch to the type tool. Then press the Backspace key (Delete on the Mac) twelve times to take out all of the paragraph returns. Pictured in Figure 6-57, the space above and below the anchored photo now very nearly matches the appearance of the original document. The difference is, now you have an anchored graphic that will move with your text (as indicated by the blue ¥ symbol that precedes *The Age of Movable Type*).

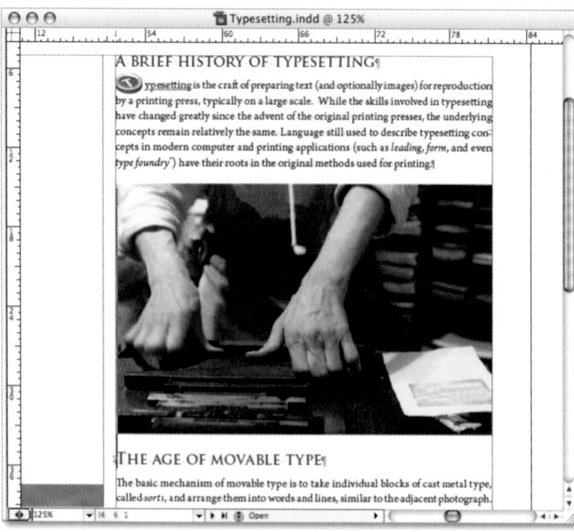

Figure 6-57.

If seeing the invisible characters bugs you, press Ctrl+Alt+I (⌘-Option-I) to make them vanish.

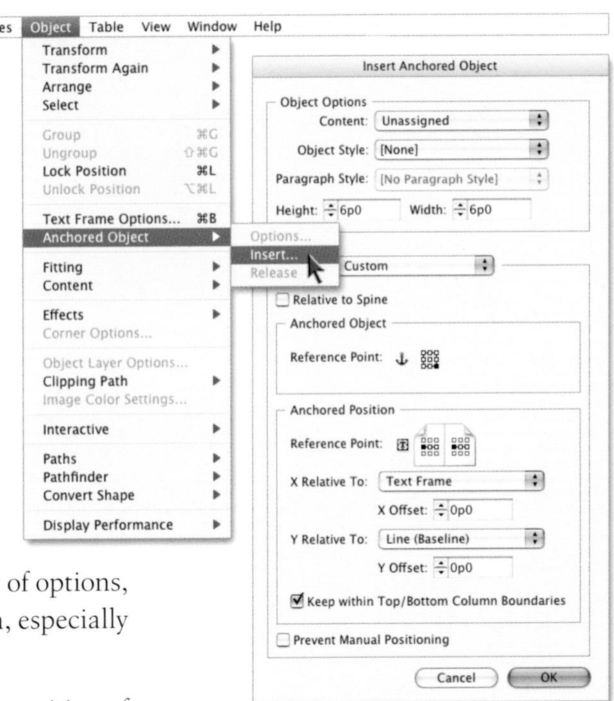

Figure 6-58.

5. *Cut the first margin illustration.* Now let's create a more flexible anchored object using InDesign's custom anchor settings. With the black arrow tool, select the letters that spell out *american* (from photographer Maurice van der Velden of iStockphoto). Then press Ctrl+X (⌘-X) to cut the image to the clipboard.

6. *Anchor a frame in the outside margin.* Switch to the type tool and click before the first character in the *The basic mechanism* paragraph. This is the point to which we'll anchor the cut photo, but first we need to create an anchored frame. To do this, choose **Object→Anchored Object→Insert**. Pictured in Figure 6-58, the **Insert Anchored Object** dialog box contains a staggering array of options, but they're not nearly as convoluted as they may seem, especially with me at your side to explain them:

   - As when creating a frame, you can specify the composition of an anchored object by setting the Content pop-up menu to Text or Graphic. **Content** is usually necessary only when overriding an existing object; for now, leave it set to **Unassigned**.

   - For the moment, leave **Object Style** set to **None**. I'll introduce you to this wonderful tool in a couple of pages.

   - Use the Height and Width options to specify the dimensions of the anchored frame you want to create. The default 6-pica **Height** value is fine for now. The outside margin (to the page edge) of the our document is 17⅓ picas wide, so change the **Width** value to 17p4.

   - This essay is meant to go in a book, with the text on the inside of the page and the illustrations on the outside. This means the illustrations need to be able to move left or right depending on the page they occupy. To make this happen, turn on the **Relative to Spine** check box.

   - InDesign adds a pair of facing pages to the **Anchored Object** box, each of which contains a small matrix icon ( ). The two matrix settings change in lock step, with one mirroring the other. We happen to be working on a left-hand page, in which we want the top-left corner of our anchored frame to align with the text entry. Click the top-right square on the left-hand matrix icon ( ) so the pair of facing pages looks like ( ), as in Figure 6-59.

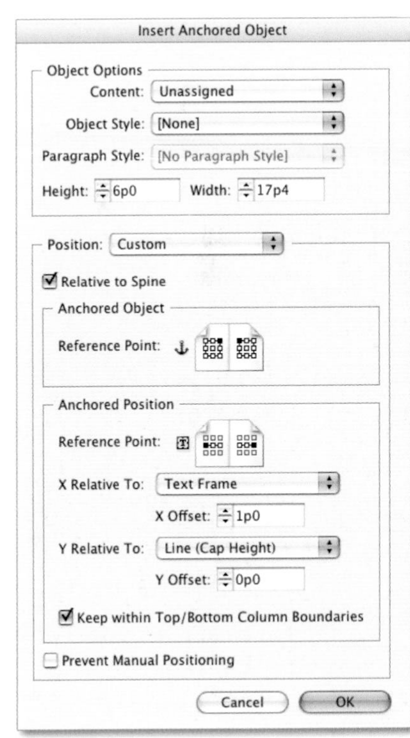

Figure 6-59.

Figure 6-60.

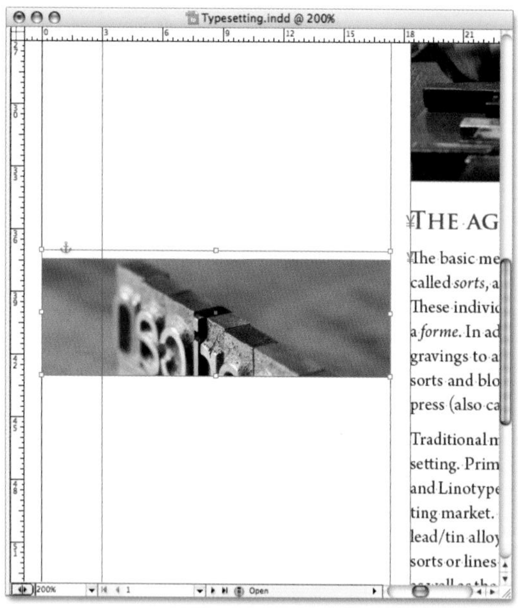

Figure 6-61.

- The **Anchored Position** box offers another pair of facing pages, which let you specify the location of the anchored frame with respect to its text entry. This time we have only three options: inside, center, and outside. We want the anchor frame toward the outside margin, so click the outermost square on the left-hand matrix icon. The facing pages should look like.
- We want to position the anchored object so that it's one gutter's width beyond the edge of the text frame that holds the glossary entries. To this end, leave the **X Relative To** option set to **Text Frame**. Then enter the width of the gutter, 12 points (or 1p0), into the **X Offset** option box.
- I want the top of the anchored frame to align with the top of the characters in the first line of the paragraph. The **Y Relative To** setting of **Line (Cap Height)** does just that automatically, so we can leave the **Y Offset** value set at 0.
- Leave the **Keep within Top/Bottom Column Boundaries** check box turned on. If off, the anchored object would be allowed to drift above or below the text frame that contains the essay body, and that would look awful.
- The final check box locks the anchored object so you don't accidentally drag it to a different position. While this sounds like a good idea, it can bind your hands when you're trying to refine your layout. So give yourself some latitude and leave **Prevent Manual Positioning** turned off.

When your dialog box looks like the one in Figure 6-59 on the previous page, click **OK**. InDesign adds an empty frame directly to the left of the cursor, as in Figure 6-60.

7. ***Paste the illustration into the anchored frame.*** Assuming you haven't cut or copied anything since Step 5, the *america* image remains in the clipboard. To place it inside the frame, choose **Edit→Paste Into** or press Ctrl+Alt+V (⌘-Option-V). The image appears too large for its frame (see Figure 6-61), a problem that's easily remedied by a tool you already know.

If you lose track of your anchored frame—which happens if you accidentally click outside the text—take heart. You can locate it again by choosing View→Show Frame Edges. Then click the frame with the black arrow tool and you're back in business. If you're not sure which frame goes with which anchor point, choose View→Show Text Threads or press Ctrl+Alt+Y (⌘-Option-Y). A dashed line connects the text and the anchored frame.

---

8. *Fit the frame to the content.* Our anchored frame isn't tall enough to accommodate the full height of the image. We could have specified the precise height of the frame back in Step 6, but there's an easier fix that doesn't require you to go around measuring your images in advance. With the newly pasted image still selected, click the icon in the control palette or press Ctrl+Alt+C (⌘-Option-C). InDesign shrink-wraps the frame around the graphic, revealing the entire image and nudging the image into alignment with the text beside it, as witnessed in Figure 6-62.

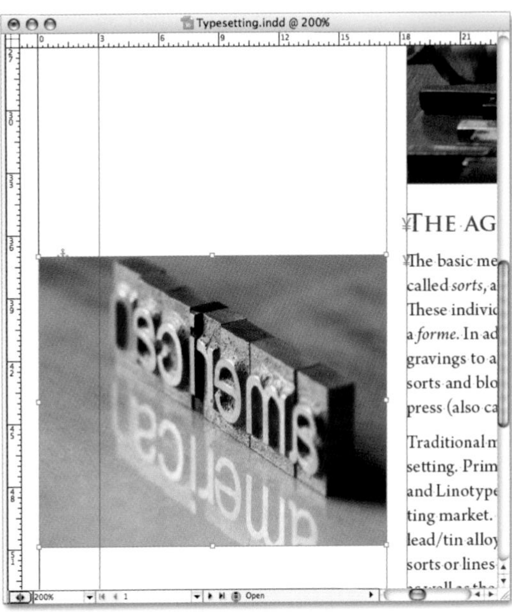

Figure 6-62.

9. *Save the anchored frame setting as an object style.* Congratulations, you've successfully established an anchored object. But while that's good news for the first image, what about all the other illustrations? Are you supposed to repeat that laborious Step 6 for each and every graphic? Of course not. With the help of an object style, you can save your anchored frame settings and apply them over and over again.

   I'll tell you all about object styles and other style sheets in Lesson 8, "Using Style Sheets." But for now, know this: An *object style* lets you save graphic attributes for later use. Make sure the anchored object is selected and do like so:

   - Choose **Window→Object Styles** or press Ctrl+F7 (⌘-F7) to open the **Object Styles** palette.
   - Click the ▾≡ icon at the top of the palette to display the palette menu, and then choose **New Object Style**.
   - The **New Object Style** dialog box (see Figure 6-63) makes everything you've seen so far look simple. Its many panels contain so much minutia, it'd make your melon go mushy. Fortunately, the options have recorded all but one thing you did in Step 6 (see the next step).
   - Just two things to do in this dialog box. First, type a new name for your style; I suggest "Margin Objects." Then, turn on the **Apply Style to Selection** check box and click **OK**. This will apply the object style to the anchored frame upon which the style is based. The new style name appears in the Object Styles palette.

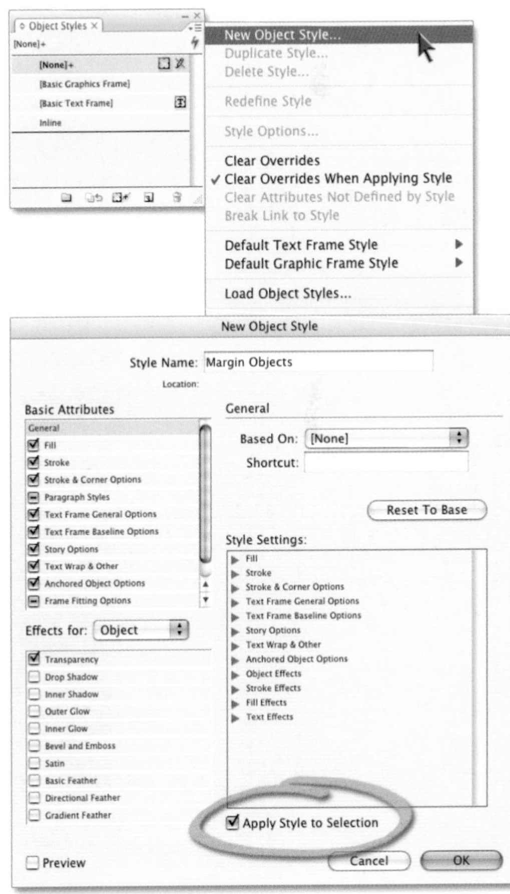

Figure 6-63.

10. *Specify the default anchored frame settings.* I mentioned that the New Object Style dialog box ignored one item; it turns out to be frame dimensions. The height and width of the anchored frame are omitted to accommodate a diverse world of differently sized anchored objects. But what do you

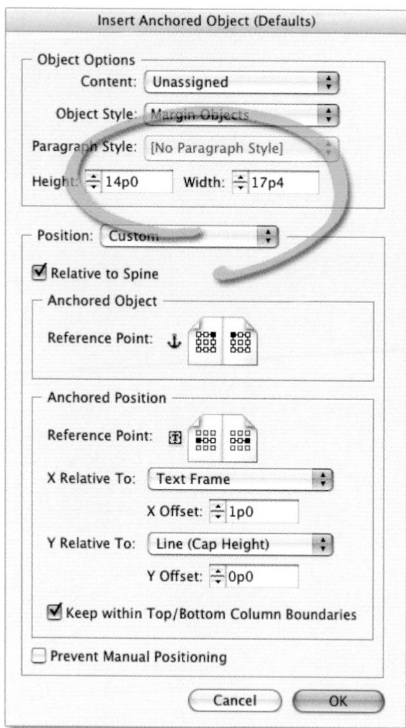

Figure 6-64.

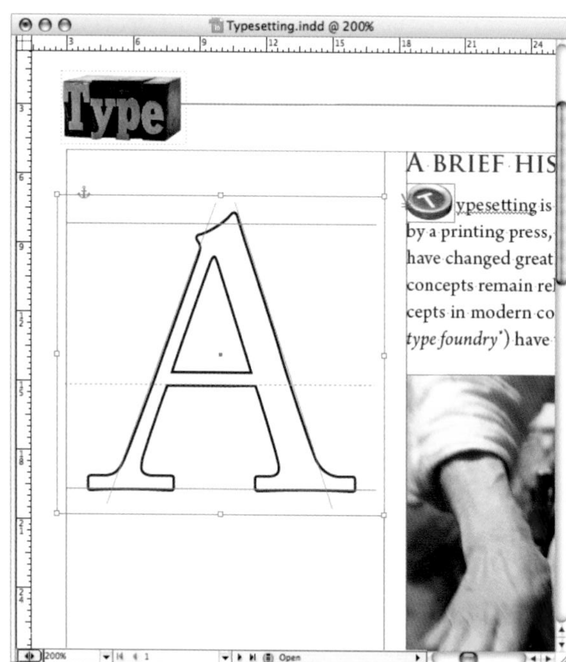

Figure 6-65.

do if you want to specify a frame size? Are you expected to reset the frame width to 17p4 manually for each and every illustration in the essay? As luck would have it, no. You can change the default frame width or height and let that guide future object dimensions:

- Click away from the anchored image or press Ctrl+Shift+A (⌘-Shift-A on the Mac) to deselect it.
- Choose **Object→Anchored Object** to see two new commands: Options (Defaults) and Insert (Defaults). Choose **Insert (Defaults)** and you're back on familiar turf.
- Select **Margin Objects** from the **Object Style** pop-up menu. Then change the **Height** value under **Object Options** to 14p0 and the **Width** value to 17p4 (see Figure 6-64) and click **OK**. (Changing the height will fix the problem of the box being too short to hold a typical graphic.) The deed is done.

11. *Anchor another graphic.* Now that you've established the ground rules, it's a routine matter to automate the addition of another anchored object:

- Get the black arrow tool and select the letterform diagram (the vector-based capital A outline on the left side of the pasteboard).
- Choose **Edit→Cut** or press Ctrl+X (⌘-X) to move the illustration to the clipboard.
- Switch to the type tool and click in front of *A Brief History of Typesetting* at the top of the page.
- Press the ↓ key to drop down to the line that contains the inline typewriter *T* key.
- Choose **Object→Anchored Object→Insert** to revisit the **Anchored Object** dialog box, which should contain the default settings that you established in the preceding step (see Figure 6-64). Assuming it does, click **OK**. The result is an anchored frame in the outside margin.
- Choose **Edit→Paste Into** or press Ctrl+Alt+V (⌘-Option-V) to paste the illustration in the anchored frame. While the height is fine, the frame is too wide. Click the icon in the control palette to fit the frame to the graphic, which pulls the art flush right with the gutter (see Figure 6-65) per our anchored object settings.

When working with anchored frames, it's usually a good idea to click the icon or press Ctrl+Shift+C (⌘-Shift-C) to "shrink-wrap" the frame to its contents. Not only does this ensure that your graphic will align properly horizontally, but it also prevents an anchored object at the bottom of a page from being forced out of vertical alignment due to excess dead space in the frame.

12. *Advance to the next page.* So much for that page. Press Shift+Page Down to advance to the next one. On this page, you'll see an unanchored image of some letters, as well as a typewriter image and a sidebar off on the right side of the pasteboard.

13. *Cut the sidebar.* Scroll to the right of the second page to see a drab violet sidebar. This sidebar is slated to go between the two paragraphs in the section titled *The Digital Revolution*. Select the sidebar with the black arrow tool. Note the dimensions of the box in the control palette, $29\frac{2}{3}$ picas (29p8) wide by $10\frac{1}{2}$ picas (10p6) tall. We'll need that info in the next step. For now, press Ctrl+X (⌘-X) to cut the frame.

14. *Anchor a frame to the column.* Switch to the text tool and click at the end of the paragraph that concludes with *enterprise computer systems*. Next, choose **Object→Anchored Object→Insert** and apply the following settings, pictured in Figure 6-66:

    - Change the **Height** and **Width** values to 10p6 and 29p8, respectively, to match the sidebar specs.
    - Confirm that the **Relative to Spine** option is checked.
    - Check that the first pair of **Reference Point** pages are set to their top-inside corners, as in . For the second pair of **Reference Point** pages, click the left square () of the right-hand page so the pair look like . This will align the sidebar to the inside edge of the larger text frame.
    - The **X Relative To** option should already be set to **Text Frame**. Lower the **X Offset** value to 0p0, so the sidebar and frame are flush left (where this right-hand page is concerned). Change the **Y Relative To** setting to **Line (Baseline)** and raise the **Y Offset** value to 1p0. This adds 1 pica of space between the sidebar and the anchoring paragraph.
    - Once everything looks the way it does in Figure 6-66, click the **OK** button.

InDesign places your new anchored frame 1 pica below the *enterprise computer systems* paragraph. But it overruns the next paragraph, a problem we'll address in the next step.

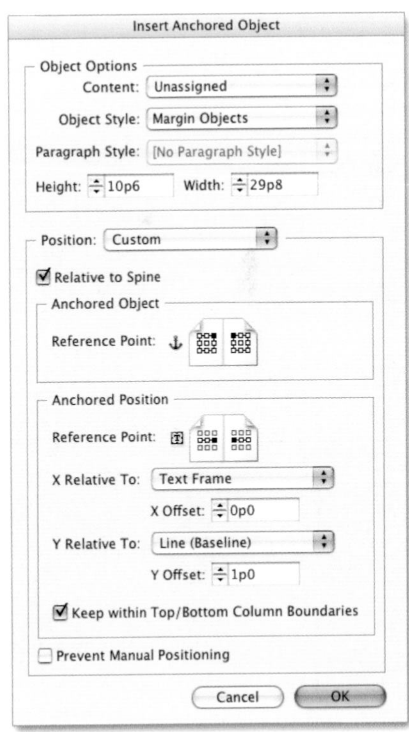

Figure 6-66.

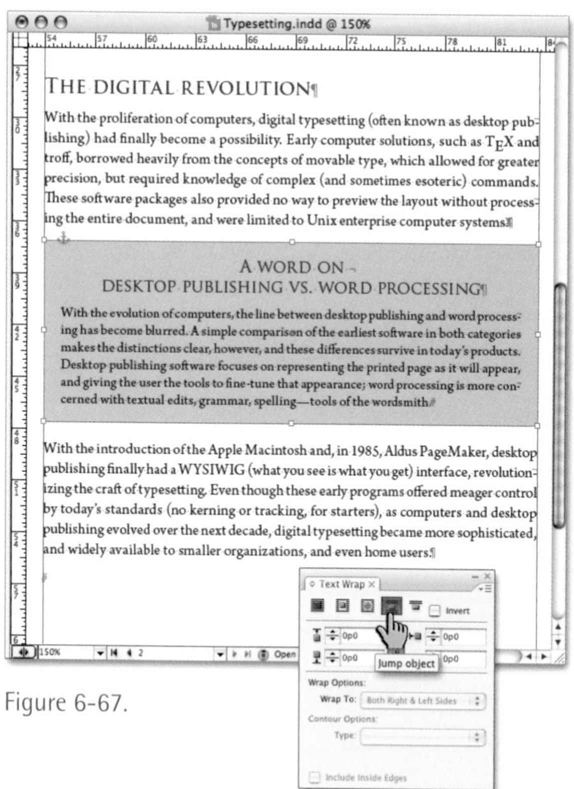

Figure 6-67.

15. ***Paste the sidebar and set the text wrap.*** Choose **Edit→Paste Into** or press Ctrl+Alt+V (⌘-Option-V) to paste the sidebar into the frame. The sidebar is now completely overlapping the second paragraph, but we can fix that by setting the text wrap on the frame. Bring up the **Text Wrap** palette by pressing Ctrl+Alt+W (⌘-Option-W) and click the fourth icon in (▤). The palette, icon, and results appear in Figure 6-67.

EXTRA CREDIT

For all intents and purposes, you're done. So if you feel like you've learned as much as a body has the right to, go ahead and skip to the quiz on page 273. But I warn you, if you do, you'll miss out on a really great technique for creating anchored objects, one that's even easier than anything you've seen so far, as well as a trick for preserving text wraps in anchored objects. Plus, I have a little more theory to share with you, and I know how much you enjoy theory. It's only five more steps—come on, join me.

16. ***Anchor yet another graphic.*** The bottom-right region of the pasteboard features a typewriter. I'd like this typewriter to end the essay, so it should be anchored near the last few paragraphs. That way it will always be at the end of the document, even if the sections are expanded. Here's how to get things started:

    - Select the typewriter photo (from iStockphoto's Frank Ferguson) with the black arrow tool. Press Ctrl+X (⌘-X) to move it to the clipboard.
    - Switch to the type tool and click at the end of the paragraph that closes with *enterprise computer systems*, after the blue ¥ symbol.
    - Choose **Edit→Paste** or press Ctrl+V (⌘-V).

    InDesign adds the typewriter to the text as an inline graphic behind the sidebar, making a general mess of everything. To fix everything, we have only to adjust its position.

17. ***Anchor the graphic to the outside corner of the page.*** Assuming you loaded my dekeKeys shortcuts, press the Enter key on the keypad to switch back to the black arrow tool. Then click on a bit of exposed typewriter to select it. Choose **Object→Anchored Object→Options** to bring up a new but strangely familiar dialog box. Figure 6-68 shows the settings I want you to use.

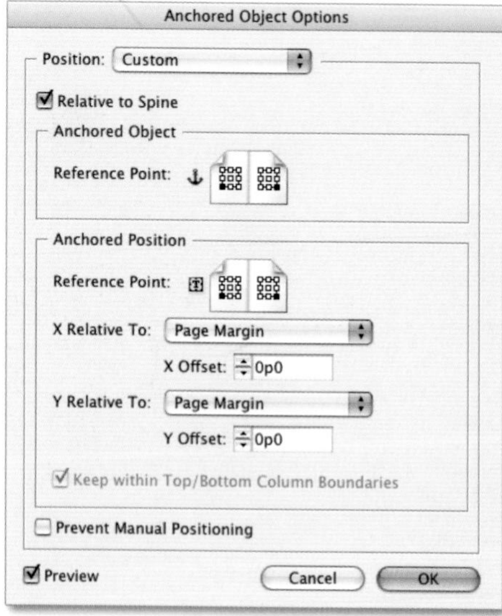

Figure 6-68.

Here, let me explain:

- Start by changing **Position** from **Inline or Above Line** to **Custom**. This establishes the graphic as a movable anchored object.
- I want the masked typewriter photo to occupy the bottom-outside corner of the document. So set both the **X Relative To** and **Y Relative To** pop-up menus to **Page Margin**.
- If necessary, change both the **X Offset** and **Y Offset** values to 0p0.
- Move to the top of the dialog box and turn on the **Relative to Spine** check box to give yourself a pair of reference points.
- Set both **Reference Point** icons to to align the image to the bottom-outside corner of the page.

Click **OK**. The typewriter shifts to the bottom-right corner of the page, as shown in Figure 6-69.

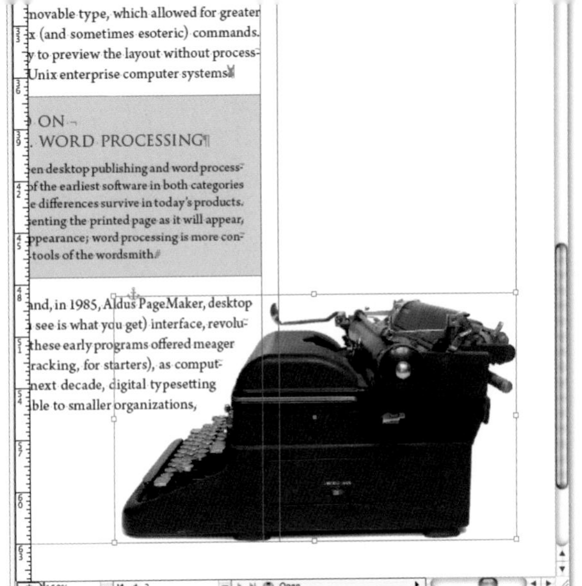

Figure 6-69.

PEARL OF WISDOM

You may be wondering why we jumped through these hoops, rather than placing the frame and pasting the image as we have in previous steps. This latest method of pasting the image as an inline graphic and then converting it to an anchored object is the only way to preserve a clipping path-based text wrap, which permits the text to wrap along the contours of the typewriter as it does above.

18. *Anchor your final graphic.* All right, there's one final approach I haven't shown you yet, and frankly, it's the best of them all. Here's how it works:

    - Scroll up to the top-right corner of the page and select the photo of the alphabet in perspective (from photographer O.C. with iStockphoto). Press Ctrl+X (⌘-X) to transfer the image to the clipboard.
    - Switch to the type tool and click at the start of the paragraph that begins *Photographic typesetting*.
    - Choose **Edit→Paste** or press Ctrl+V (⌘-V).
    - Switch back to the black arrow tool. Then click the alphabet graphic to select it.
    - See the icon near the middle of the control palette, the one that reads [None]? That's the object style pop-up menu. Click on **[None]** and choose the object style you saved back in Step 9, **Margin Objects**.

As Figure 6-70 ably demonstrates, that's all it takes to convert the image into an anchored object and snap it into place. Best of all, the frame size is defined automatically, so there's no need to fit the frame to its content as with previous techniques.

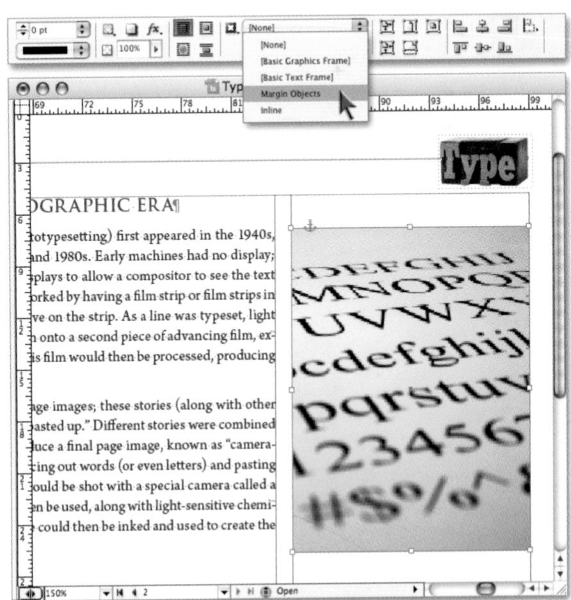

Figure 6-70.

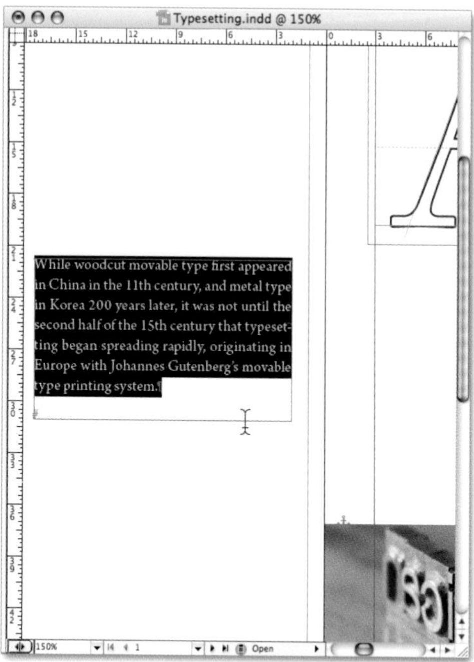

Figure 6-71.

19. ***Edit the text and watch the anchored objects do their thing.*** Suppose that my editor reviews the essay and suggests a better intro to *The Age of Movable Type* section. She writes up some text and places it on the left side of the pasteboard for my review.

    I decide that I like it, so I get the type tool and quadruple-click in the paragraph to select the whole thing, as in Figure 6-71. I press Ctrl+C (⌘-C) to copy the text. (Cutting leaves the frame behind, so I might as well copy.) Now I click at the end of the headline *The Age of Movable Type*, press → to move to the beginning of the next line, and press Ctrl+V (⌘-V) to paste the copied entry into place. The anchored frames cascade with the text, as shown in Figure 6-72. If necessary, they would even switch pages.

20. ***Save your work.*** This document can be helpful for jogging your memory on anchored objects and testing out your own anchored object scenarios, so I recommend you save it. Choose **File→Save As** or press Ctrl+Shift+S (⌘-Shift-S). Give your file a snappy name like "Edited typesetting" and click **Save**.

Nice work. Over the course of these steps, you've created a document in which text and figures can't possibly get separated. You're now ready to graduate to bigger and better things, including the world of transparency, as I discuss in Lesson 7.

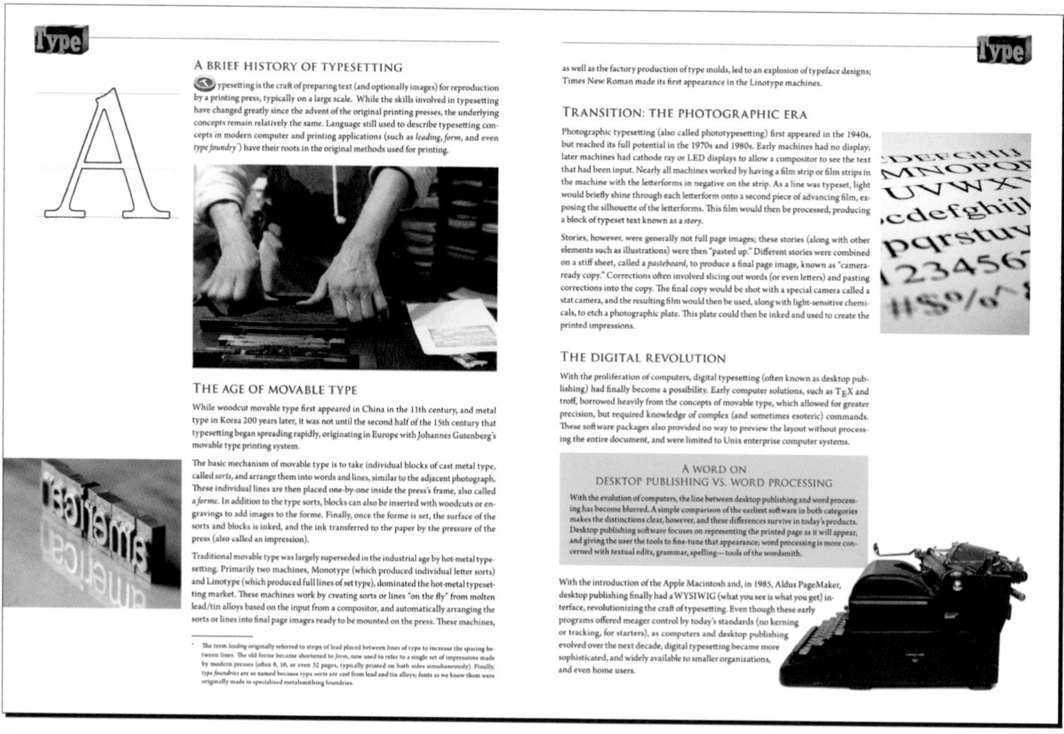

A BRIEF HISTORY OF TYPESETTING

Typesetting is the craft of preparing text (and optionally images) for reproduction by a printing press, typically on a large scale. While the skills involved in typesetting have changed greatly since the advent of the original printing presses, the underlying concepts remain relatively the same. Language still used to describe typesetting concepts in modern computer and printing applications (such as *leading*, *form*, and even *type foundry**) have their roots in the original methods used for printing.

THE AGE OF MOVABLE TYPE

While woodcut movable type first appeared in China in the 11th century, and metal type in Korea 200 years later, it was not until the second half of the 15th century that typesetting began spreading rapidly, originating in Europe with Johannes Gutenberg's movable type printing system.

The basic mechanism of movable type is to take individual blocks of cast metal type, called *sorts*, and arrange them into words and lines, similar to the adjacent photograph. These individual lines are then placed one-by-one inside the press's frame, also called a *forme*. In addition to the type sorts, blocks can also be inserted with woodcuts or engravings to add images to the forme. Finally, once the forme is set, the surface of the sorts and blocks is inked, and the ink transferred to the paper by the pressure of the press (also called an impression).

Traditional movable type was largely superseded in the industrial age by hot-metal typesetting. Primarily two machines, Monotype (which produced individual letter sorts) and Linotype (which produced full lines of set type), dominated the hot-metal typesetting market. These machines work by creating sorts or lines "on the fly" from molten lead/tin alloys based on the input from a compositor, and automatically arranging the sorts or lines into final page images ready to be mounted on the press. These machines,

* The term *leading* originally referred to strips of lead placed between lines of type to increase the spacing between lines. The old forme became shortened to *form*, now used to refer to a single set of impressions made by modern presses (often 8, 16, or even 32 pages, typically printed on both sides simultaneously). Finally, *type foundries* are so named because type sorts are cast from lead and tin alloys; fonts as we know them were originally made in specialized metalsmithing foundries.

as well as the factory production of type molds, led to an explosion of typeface designs; Times New Roman made its first appearance in the Linotype machines.

TRANSITION: THE PHOTOGRAPHIC ERA

Photographic typesetting (also called phototypesetting) first appeared in the 1940s, but reached its full potential in the 1970s and 1980s. Early machines had no display; later machines had cathode ray or LED displays to allow a compositor to see the text that had been input. Nearly all machines worked by having a film strip or film strips in the machine with the letterforms in negative on the strip. As a line was typeset, light would briefly shine through each letterform onto a second piece of advancing film, exposing the silhouette of the letterforms. This film would then be processed, producing a block of typeset text known as a *story*.

Stories, however, were generally not full page images; these stories (along with other elements such as illustrations) were then "pasted up." Different stories were combined on a stiff sheet, called a *pasteboard*, to produce a final page image, known as "camera-ready copy." Corrections often involved slicing out words (or even letters) and pasting corrections into the copy. The final copy would be shot with a special camera called a stat camera, and the resulting film would then be used, along with light-sensitive chemicals, to etch a photographic plate. This plate could then be inked and used to create the printed impressions.

THE DIGITAL REVOLUTION

With the proliferation of computers, digital typesetting (often known as desktop publishing) had finally become a possibility. Early computer solutions, such as TEX and troff, borrowed heavily from the concepts of movable type, which allowed for greater precision, but required knowledge of complex (and sometimes esoteric) commands. These software packages also provided no way to preview the layout without processing the entire document, and were limited to Unix enterprise computer systems.

A WORD ON
DESKTOP PUBLISHING VS. WORD PROCESSING

With the evolution of computers, the line between desktop publishing and word processing has become blurred. A simple comparison of the earliest software in both categories makes the distinctions clear, however, and these differences survive in today's products. Desktop publishing software focuses on representing the printed page as it will appear, and giving the user the tools to fine-tune that appearance; word processing is more concerned with textual edits, grammar, spelling—tools of the wordsmith.

With the introduction of the Apple Macintosh and, in 1985, Aldus PageMaker, desktop publishing finally had a WYSIWIG (what you see is what you get) interface, revolutionizing the craft of typesetting. Even though these early programs offered meager control by today's standards (no kerning or tracking, for starters), as computers and desktop publishing evolved over the next decade, digital typesetting became more sophisticated, and widely available to smaller organizations, and even home users.

Figure 6-72.

Did I imply this was all in the past? How silly of me. This is *still* the way transparency is handled by most vector-based applications, including all but the most recent versions of QuarkXPress, as well as the PostScript printing language, which is the industry standard for printing books, magazines, reports, and other professional-level mass-market documents. But InDesign dares to operate outside the PostScript box and deliver partial transparency, cross-fades, drop shadows, and other translucency effects. InDesign CS3 even goes so far as to let you apply an effect to an independent fill or stroke. If you cut your teeth on PageMaker or QuarkXPress, InDesign's effects options may seem like little more than a trendy grab bag of impractical tricks and gimmicks. But I guarantee that, in time, it will change the way you work.

A bitmapped image imports as a rectangle

You can then carve it into shapes using vector masks

Figure 7-2.

Gradations in Translucency

Transparency is the name Adobe gives to a group of functions that permit you to see through one object to the objects behind it. Every one of these functions is a *live effect*, which means that you can forever and for always change your mind without degrading an object or in any way modifying the original version of a placed graphic.

For example, let's say I want to make a text block or graphic translucent, so that it appears to be ghosted. Translucency is expressed as a percentage value labeled Opacity, with 100 percent being opaque and 0 percent, transparent. Every one of the orange-and-violet shapes in Figure 7-3 on the next page is a copy of the same Illustrator artwork set to a different Opacity value. This value can be especially useful when setting dimmed graphics in front of text, as in the case of the first three shapes, or behind it, as in the last one. If I decide the artwork is too light or too dark, there's no need to go back to Illustrator, adjust the fill and stroke, and replace the graphic (as I used to do routinely in the days before transparency). I have only to change one value in InDesign and the fix is made.

An Opacity setting is constant over the course of an object. But other transparency effects may vary. InDesign's drop shadows are perfect examples. The first strange humanoid in Figure 7-4 on the facing page casts a shadow onto the checkerboard pattern behind it. The shadow starts off dark and fades into nothingness a pica beyond the image. This particular shadow was created inside InDesign, but I could have just as easily imported the shadow as part of the original artwork. InDesign preserves translucent effects created in Illustrator and Photoshop. It evens goes so far as to recognize and correctly interpret the translucency of each and every pixel on each and every Photoshop layer, essential for maintaining custom blurs and articulated edges like those featured in the right-hand image in Figure 7-4.

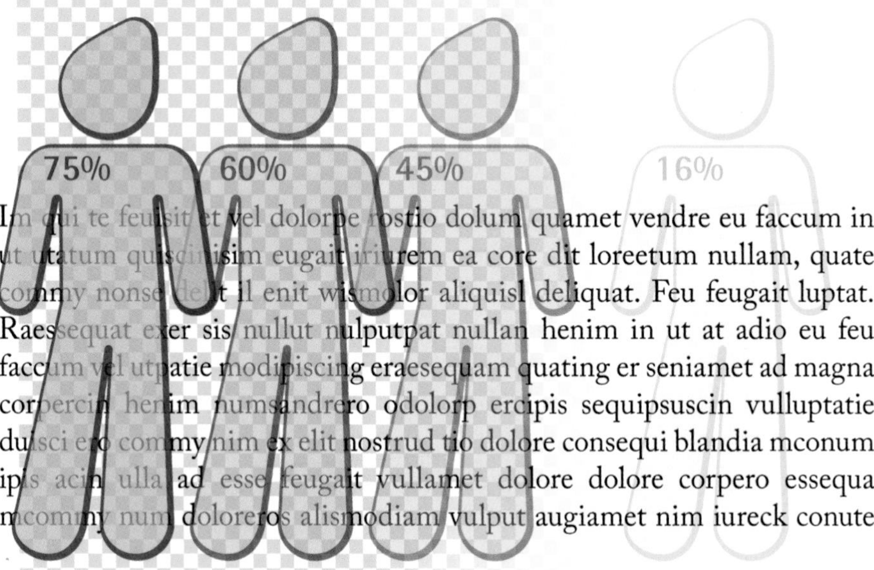

InDesign lets you make any object translucent . . .

which is ideal for dimming graphics in front of and behind text

Figure 7-3.

As a professional-level page-layout program, InDesign can't merely equip you with everything you need to create translucent objects and incremental fades; it also has to print them. This means translating every single Opacity value, drop shadow, and imported Photoshop layer to the PostScript printing language—no small feat given that translucency is strictly outside PostScript's ability to render. But translate InDesign does. I have yet to encounter a problem printing translucent objects directly from InDesign—and, as you may have noticed, this book is full of them. But if you do hit a wall, trust InDesign to give you the tools you need to make things right. And trust me to help you learn how these and other transparency functions work.

Adjusting Opacity and Blending Colors

In this first exercise, we'll take a look at the most obvious expression of transparency inside InDesign, the Transparency palette. In addition to the Opacity value I mentioned a moment ago, the Transparency palette provides you with a pop-up menu of *blend modes*, which are ways of mixing the colors of overlapping objects using prescribed mathematical equations. For instance, the Multiply blend mode multiplies the color values of overlapping objects. Turns out, this makes the colors darker, which is why Multiply is most often used to create shadows.

In the following steps, you'll learn how to use the Opacity value along with blend modes to combine the colors of overlapping objects. Rather than teach you all the blend modes—there are sixteen—I'll focus on the few that you're likely to need on a regular basis, and leave you to explore the rest (which vary dramatically in practicality). You'll be applying these functions to vector graphics that I copied from Illustrator and pasted into InDesign. But bear in mind that everything you see can be applied just as easily to homegrown lines and shapes, imported Photoshop images, and text.

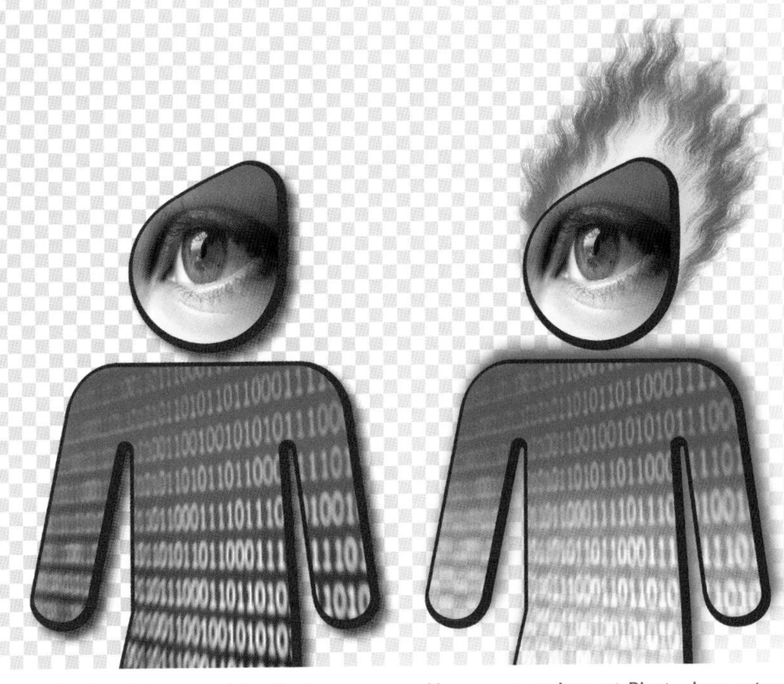

InDesign lets you add soft drop shadows to any object

You can even import Photoshop artwork with translucent layer effects

Figure 7-4.

1. *Open a document.* Open *Seventies quiz #2.indd*, located in the *Lesson 07* folder inside *Lesson Files-IDcs3 1on1*. The file includes a two-page spread, with text and artwork on the right page and a big purple rectangle on the left. We'll use this rectangle as a backdrop for our translucent, blended artwork.

2. *Turn on the Big Bopper layer.* Press F7 or choose **Window→Layers** to display the **Layers** palette. Then click in the box to the far left of **Big Bopper** to display an 👁 and reveal the enormous visage of Shenbop the cartoon frog (see Figure 7-5 on the next page). Although slightly different than the Shenbop on the other side of the document's spine, it's ultimately a repeat graphic. But thanks to transparency, it will receive a very different treatment.

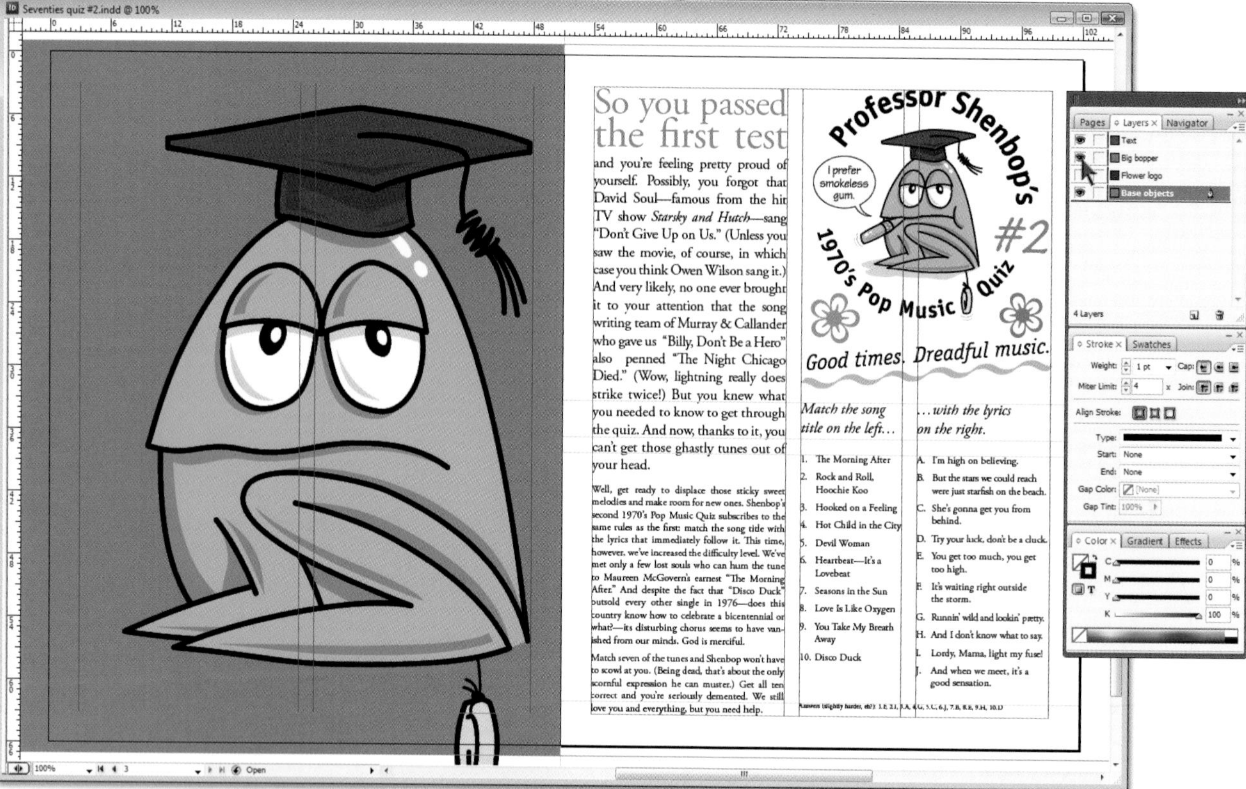

Figure 7-5.

3. ***Reduce the opacity of the large cartoon to 25 percent.*** Select the graphic by clicking inside it with the black arrow tool. Then choose **Window→Effects** or press Shift+F10 to display the modest **Effects** palette. Notice that the top item in the palette's list reads Group: Normal 100%, which tells you that you have selected a group of lines and shapes, and the group is fully opaque. You can change the opacity of the selected group in one of two ways:

   - Click the word **Opacity** to highlight the value. Enter 25 and press Enter or Return.
   - Click the ▸ arrow to the right of the Opacity value to display a slider bar. Drag the slider triangle to the left to reduce the value to 25 percent.

   Either action results in a dimmed version of the graphic. Set to 25 percent opacity, the artwork is nearing transparency with 75 percent of the background showing through, as in Figure 7-6.

4. ***Apply the Luminosity blend mode.*** Although the frog is ghosted, you can see a lot of color. And quite frankly, I don't like it. The green mixes with the purple to create a murky gray. (Shenbop appears greenish, but that's because he's set against purple and our

brains are trained to see relative rather than absolute colors. If you separate his colors from the background, as I have in the three swatches on the right side of Figure 7-6, you can see that the frog flesh is actually purplish gray.) To my eyes, the ghosted green looks terrible, so better to just trash the green entirely. To accomplish this, we'll apply the first of our blend modes, Luminosity.

Click the ▾ arrow (⬍ on the Mac) to the right of the word **Normal** at the top of the Effects palette. (The default Normal mode applies no special effect and is therefore equivalent to turning off the blend mode.) InDesign displays a pop-up menu of the 16 blend modes. Select the last mode, **Luminosity**. InDesign tosses out the colors in the frog and keeps only its lights and darks—termed *luminosity values*—as in Figure 7-7.

Figure 7-6.

PEARL OF WISDOM

Luminosity is one of the two great color-blending modes. The other is Color. As we've just seen, Luminosity maintains the lights and darks of the selected object and lets the background colors show through. Color does the opposite: It keeps the colors of the selected object and lets the lights and darks show through. Apply the Color blend mode to an object to colorize the objects behind it; use Luminosity to abandon color.

5. *Turn on the Flower Logo layer.* Click in the box to the far left of **Flower Logo** to turn on its 👁 and display a few more objects. Among these is a gray pad-like shape under Shenbop's feet. This is intended to be a shadow. Like the shadow in the illustration on the right-hand page of the document, I created this one to work against a plain white background. Now that we have a purple background, it's way too light. Let's fix that.

Figure 7-7.

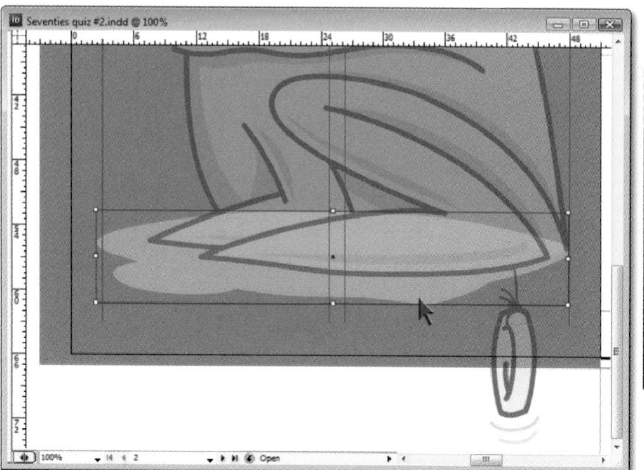

Figure 7-8.

6. ***Reduce the opacity of the shadow.*** Click the shadow to select it. The first item in the Effects palette reads Object: Normal 100%, showing that a path is selected. Click the word **Opacity** and change the value to 50 percent. The shadow blends in better, but it's still not right. The object remains substantially lighter than its background (see Figure 7-8), something that cannot be said of a shadow. No Opacity value can remedy this problem, so it's time to bring in another blend mode.

7. ***Apply the Multiply blend mode.*** As I mentioned earlier, Multiply is the mode of shadows. It drops out the whites and burns in the other colors. Still inside the Effects palette, click the word **Normal** to display the blend mode pop-up menu and then choose **Multiply**, as in Figure 7-9. The object darkens the purple beneath it, transforming the selected shape into a deep, rich, credible cartoon shadow.

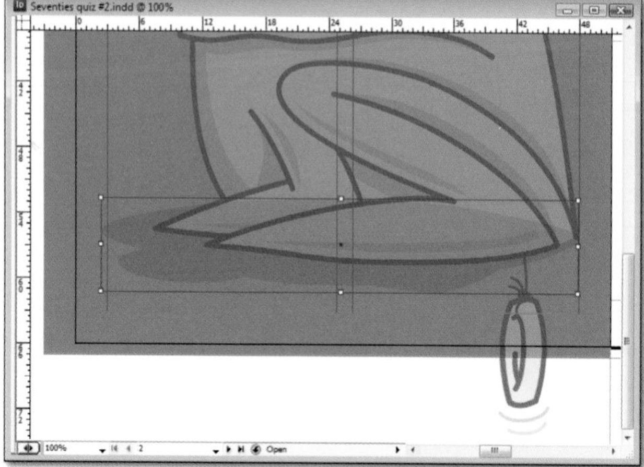

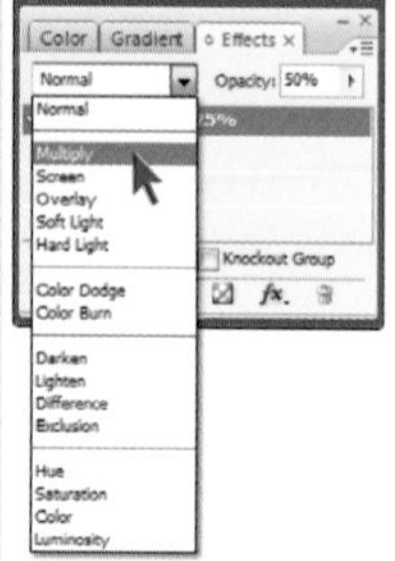

Figure 7-9.

PEARL OF WISDOM

I like math, so sometimes I find it helpful to know how InDesign calculates a blend mode. If you feel the same, read on; if not, skip to Step 8. Let's say you place one 50 percent cyan circle in front of another and set the top circle to Multiply. InDesign multiplies 50 times 50 to get 75 percent cyan where the two shapes intersect. How does 50 times 50 get you 75? InDesign converts the percentage values to decimals (which means dividing the percent by 100) and then *normalizes* the decimal by subtracting it from 1. So 0% becomes 1.0, 25% becomes 0.75, 50% becomes 0.5, 75% becomes 0.25, and 100% becomes 0, just to name a few. Thus, the resulting equation looks like the one at the top of Figure 7-10. The math for Multiply's opposite, Screen, looks more complicated in the figure, but it's actually similar, with InDesign subtracting everything from 1. (In other words, Screen is Multiply without the normalization.) This results in lighter overlapping colors, making Screen great for creating highlights.

8. ***Reduce the Opacity of the logo.*** Now to attack the logo elements in the upper-left corner of the page. Click inside the flower with the ugly dark stroke to select it and the surrounding type on a circle. Then lower the **Opacity** value for this group to 75 percent. This fades the logo, but only slightly, as Figure 7-11 confirms. We need a more powerful solution in the form of another blend mode.

9. ***Apply the Screen blend mode.*** See how the radial gradient in the flower transitions from medium violet in the center to very dark violet at the outside? I want to drop out those dark colors so the outer edge of the flower gradually fades away. And no blend mode drops out darks better than Screen. Click the pop-up menu in the Effects palette and choose the third option, **Screen**, which drops out the darkest colors and uses all others to brighten the colors in the background. As seen in Figure 7-12, the letters appear light; the flower starts light in the center and fades away at the edges; and the stroke goes white. It's the effect I want and I didn't have to recolor a thing. (To learn more about creating custom gradient effects with Screen, read the sidebar, "How Color Space Affects Blend Mode," on the next page.)

   You may notice that the Screen mode lightens colors only until it exceeds the boundaries of the rear purple rectangle. This is because InDesign blends objects only as long as there are objects to blend. When a blend mode arrives at an empty portion of a page or a pasteboard, the object returns to its normal appearance. But not to worry; our problem transition is well outside the document, outside even the bleed. Press the W key to enter the Preview mode and the wonky details disappear from view.

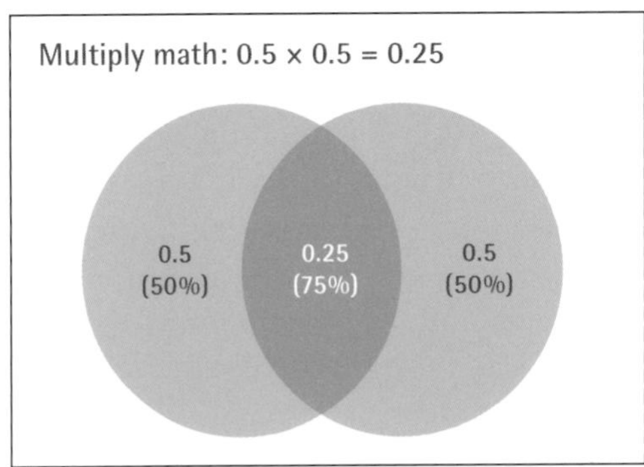

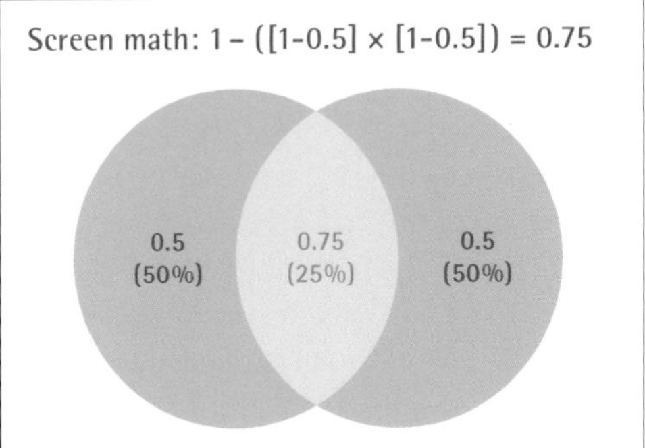

Figure 7-10.

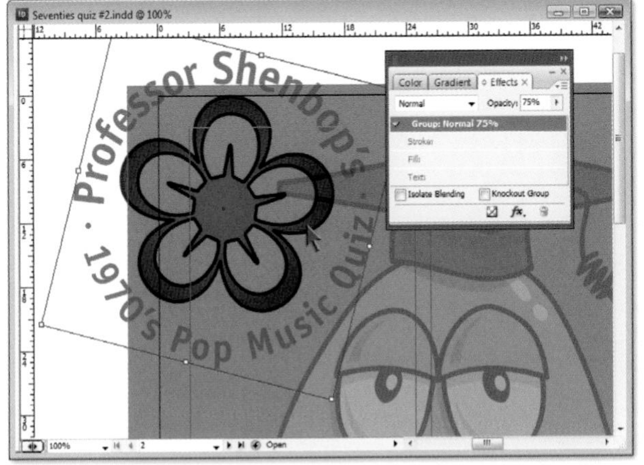

Figure 7-11.

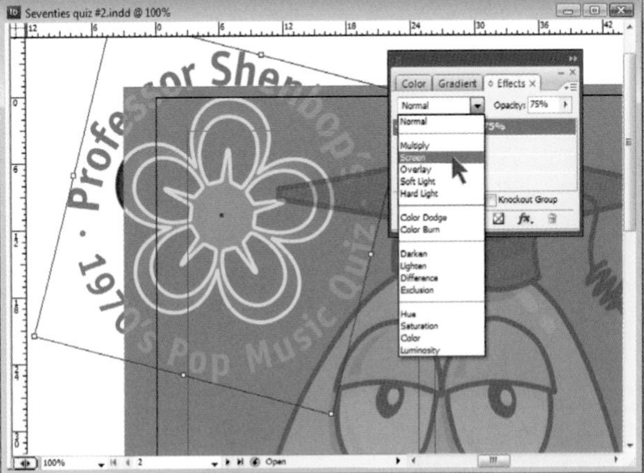

Figure 7-12.

How Color Space Affects Blend Mode

Like other varieties of transparency, blend modes—Multiply, Screen, Overlay, and the rest—grew up inside Photoshop. In fact, for an entire decade, they existed *only* in Photoshop. So it's hardly a coincidence that blend modes were specifically designed to suit digital photographs, scanned artwork, and other images stored in the RGB color space. When Adobe ported its blend modes over to InDesign, they met with a different default color space, CMYK. As a result, many blend modes behave differently in InDesign than they do in Photoshop.

To understand why this is, we have to take on a little color theory. Red, green, and blue are the primary colors of light. Cyan, magenta, and yellow are inks that absorb those lights. In this regard, the two color spaces are opposites. That turns out not to be a problem; because of the way InDesign normalizes color values, blend modes behave the same in RGB and CMY. Unfortunately, CMY*K* contains a pesky fourth ink, black. The black ink is great for filling in shadows and enhancing contrast, but it can create problems for blend modes.

By way of example, let's consider one of my favorite uses for blend modes in InDesign: creating custom gradients. I'll start by taking a rectangle and filling it with a linear gradient from bright red (C:0, M:100, Y:100, K:0) to deep blue (C:100, M:100, Y:0, K:50), as indicated by figure ❶. (The exact colors aren't important; these just happen to pop nicely on the page.) Now let's say I want to add a glow of light color to the lower-left corner of the shape. InDesign doesn't let me add colors to specific points in a filled shape, so I have to float another gradient on top. Ideally, this would be a light-to-transparent gradient—so the glow would be visible in the lower-left corner and that's it—which I could do using a gradient feather effect (see "Applying Dynamic Effects," which begins on page 287). But in this case, I'm going to combine the floated gradient with a blend mode.

❶

❷

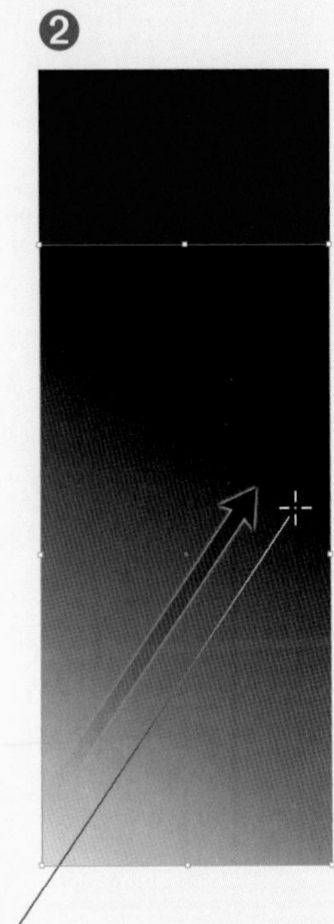

Here's my solution: I draw another rectangle on top, precisely aligned to the first but a bit shorter (because I'm trying to lighten only the bottom of the first shape). I fill this one with a white-to-black gradient and use the gradient tool to angle it up and to the right, as in figure ❷. Note the wealth of solid black at the top of the forward shape; this ensures that the top of the shape will turn transparent when I drop out the blacks.

Next I go to the Effects palette and choose Screen, the blend mode that keeps the whites and tosses out the blacks. If I were working on an RGB image in Photoshop, the blacks would drop out completely, leaving just a light highlight. But in the CMYK environment of InDesign, I'm left with a white-to-light-gray gradient that doesn't even mildly resemble what I want, as in figure ❸ on the facing page.

The culprit is the way black is represented in CMYK, which is not as the absence of all light, as in RGB, but as solid black ink. The Screen mode doesn't expect that, so it fails. One possible solution is to ask InDesign to calculate blend modes in RGB instead of CMYK. I do this by choosing Edit→Transparency Blend Space→Document RGB. Depending on the specifics of your color management settings, this may actually solve the problem. But more likely, you'll end up with a more colorful but still incorrect gradient, like the one shown in figure ❹.

The more foolproof solution is to redefine black in the white-to-black gradient as a *rich black*, filled with all four inks. With the front rectangle still selected, I bring up the Gradient palette and click the color stop for black. Then I switch to the Color palette. By default, black is defined as C:0, M:0, Y:0, K:100—

that is, solid black ink but no cyan, magenta, or yellow. The Screen mode therefore reads the front gradient as bright in the CMY space and leeches all colors but gray from the red-to-blue gradient. To remedy this, I need to crank up the CMY values to their maximums. I choose CMYK from the palette menu to see all inks. Then I change the values to read C:100, M:100, Y:100, K:100 (100 percent across the board). The blacks in the front rectangle now drop off to complete transparency, thus producing the gorgeous multidirectional gradient pictured in figure ❺.

The moral of the story? When a blend mode fails you, try choosing Edit→Transparency Blend Space→Document RGB. This solution is acceptable even when your document is ultimately bound for CMYK output. (If in doubt, consult the Separations palette, which I introduce in Video Lesson 12, "Previewing Color Separations.") Note, however, that this command affects all blend modes in a document, not just the one you're having problems with. If changing the blend space doesn't work—or you're just worried about the print-worthiness of your document—try redefining the CMYK ingredients of your blacks.

On a somewhat related note: As a rule, I discourage combining blend modes with spot colors. Multiply and Screen *sometimes* perform as expected, leaving the spot colors intact. But the other blend modes almost invariably replace overlapping inks with their nearest CMYK equivalents (which often aren't very near at all). Spot colors blended with CMYK objects may also render out to CMYK. For more information on spot colors, read "Trapping and Overprinting," which begins on page 493 of Lesson 12.

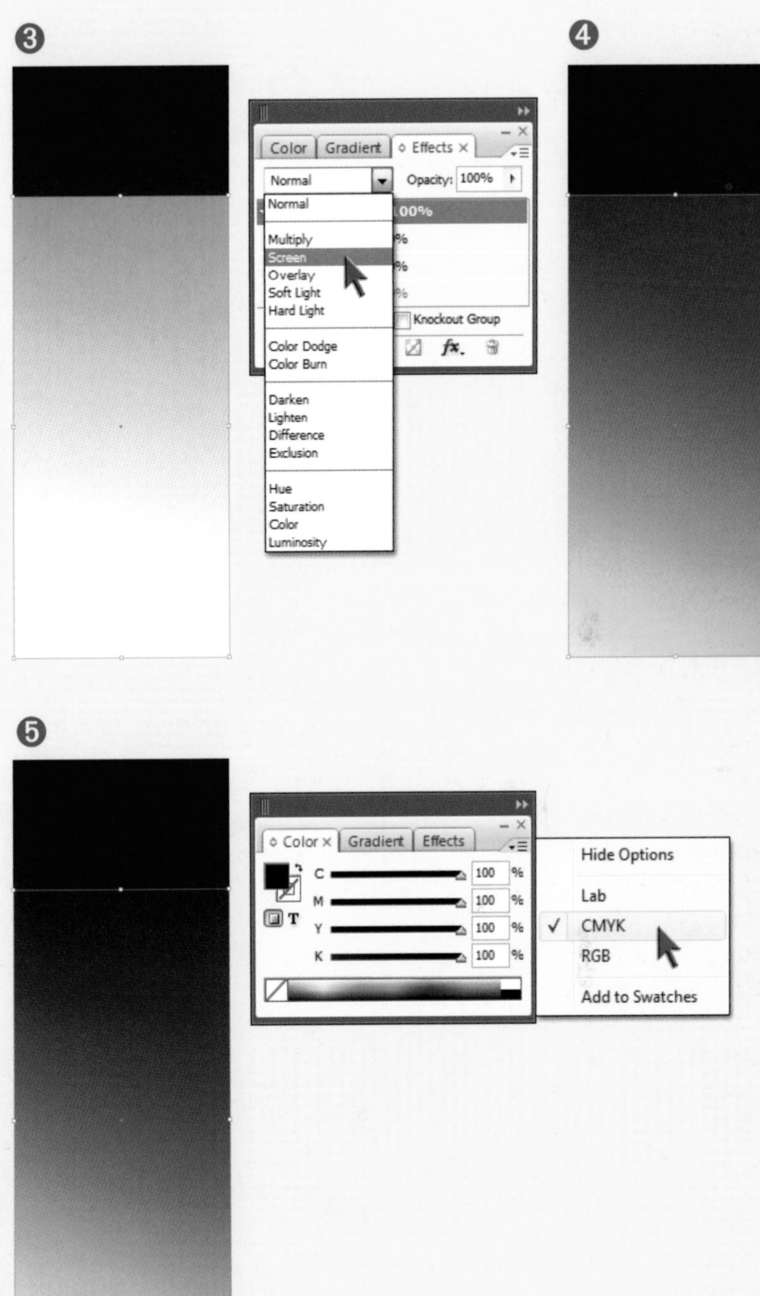

10. ***Reduce the opacity of the flower's stroke.*** The flower logo looks nice and washed out with one exception: the stroke. Fortunately, InDesign CS3 lets you adjust the opacity of an object's fill and stroke attributes independently. But because the flower is part of a group, it takes a bit of work:

Figure 7-13.

- Press Ctrl+Shift+A (⌘-Shift-A on the Mac) to deselect the logo art.
- Press the A key or press Ctrl+Tab (Control-Tab) to switch to the white arrow tool.
- Press Alt (or Option) and click on the flower to select it independently of the rest of the group. Alt-click (or Option-click) again to select all points in the flower.
- In the Effects palette, click the item that reads **Stroke: Normal 100%**. This selects the stroke independently of the fill.
- Reduce the **Opacity** value to 15 percent. With any luck, your screen should look like the one in Figure 7-13.

11. ***Assemble the artwork into a knockout group.*** The last remaining problem is to resolve the odd interactions between our blended graphics. If you look closely, you can see the edge of an *s* and a small bullet intersecting the left side of Shenbop's mortarboard. Worse, we can see through the frog's translucent feet to his shadow. That's no good, so here's what you do:

    - Press the V key to switch to the black arrow tool.
    - Select all three graphics—the logo, the shadow, and Shenbop. It's probably easiest if you click one of the items and Shift-click the other two.
    - Choose **Object→Group** or press Ctrl+G (⌘-G on the Mac) to group them all together.
    - With the massive group selected, go to the Effects palette and turn on the **Knockout Group** check box.

    Just like that, the various objects inside the group no longer show through each other. As pictured in Figure 7-14, Shenbop's feet and mortarboard hide the shadow and text behind them, and our facing-page graphics are complete.

The Transparency palette contains one more check box, Isolate Blending. Like Knockout Group, this check box controls blending inside a group. But instead of preventing blending inside the group, it prevents the group from blending with anything outside it, turning off blend modes but leaving translucency intact. If that sounds obscure, it's because it is. My recommendation is to have fun experimenting with Opacity adjustments and blend modes and not worry too much about the check boxes. If a pesky problem arises, group your blended objects and fiddle with turning the check boxes on and off. If the problem goes away, great; if not, no harm done.

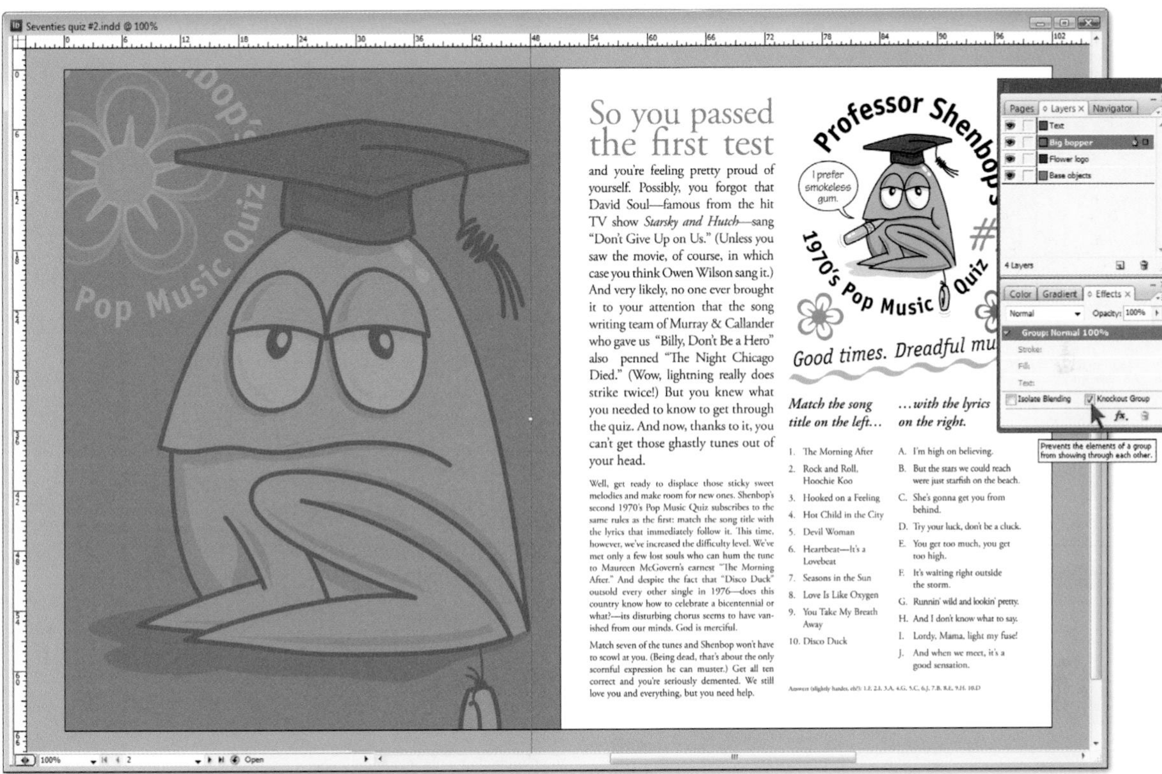

Figure 7-14.

Applying Dynamic Effects

InDesign CS3 includes a category of dynamic effects that you can apply and edit from the Effects palette. Modeled after Photoshop's layer effects, they include directional shadows, inner and outer glows, a variety of blurs, and other contour attributes that let you add dimension and softness to otherwise flat vector objects. I call them *dynamic effects* because you can edit them any time you like and even mix and match them between objects and attributes.

Dynamic effects serve two opposing purposes: to set an object apart from other page elements and to bring them together. If a headline casts a shadow, it suggests that the text hovers above its surroundings. An effect can also blend the interior or the perimeter of an object with its background. The various objects appear not as disparate objects but rather as seamless members of a cohesive whole.

In the following steps, we'll employ a handful of dynamic effects with the goal of adding a bit of depth and visual interest to a business advertisement. Some of our uses will be orthodox, others somewhat unorthodox. But all will prove illuminating and—dare I hope?—even slightly inspirational.

Figure 7-15.

1. ***Open a file in need of shadows and feathering.*** Open *Staff advertisement.indd*, found in the *Lesson 07* folder inside *Lesson Files-IDcs3 1on1*. Shown in Figure 7-15, this single-page document contains a series of independent text blocks and colored shapes (as well as a photograph from Libby Chapman of iStockphoto). As with transparency and blend modes, dynamic effects are best applied to discrete objects.

2. ***Create a traditional drop shadow.*** We'll start by adding a drop shadow to the text *Going to have a vacancy to fill?* at the top of the page. Click the white text with the black arrow tool and choose **Object→Effects→Drop Shadow** or press Ctrl+Alt+M (⌘-Option-M on the Mac) to bring up the **Effects** dialog box filled with drop shadow options, as in Figure 7-16 on the facing page. As usual, I recommend that you turn on the **Preview** check box so you can see what you're doing, at which point you should see a hint of a dark shadow behind the white text.

PEARL OF WISDOM

This document contains Chaparral Pro Semibold. While the font is not automatically installed with Creative Suite 3, it is included with the Suite on the DVD labeled Content. If you want to use the font, you will need to install it manually. See Step 11 on page xix of the Preface for more information.

Here's a rundown of the options available to you:

- The Mode pop-up menu lets you select a blend mode. Multiply is great for making a shadow because it ensures that the shadow darkens everything behind it. But the menu has plenty of other options, such as creating directional glows, as you'll see later in this exercise.

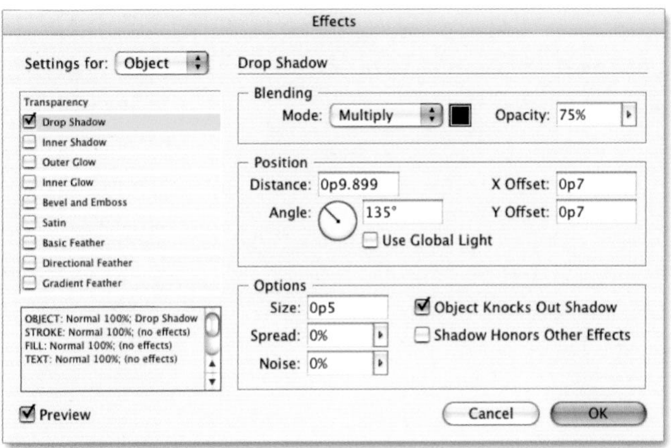

Figure 7-16.

- Click the color swatch to change the color of the shadow to something other than black. The default setting of Swatches gives you access to colors defined in the Swatches palette. You can also choose RGB, CMYK, or Lab to display sliders and dial in custom color values.
- Lower the Opacity value to create a translucent shadow.
- Use the Distance and Angle values to move the shadow a specified distance away from the object that is casting it. You also have the comparatively clunky X and Y Offset values found in InDesign CS2 and earlier. Changing the Distance or Angle value automatically changes the X and Y Offset values, and vice versa.
- Turn on Use Global Light to establish a common light source for all directional effects, including inner shadows and bevels.
- The Size value blurs the shadow. A value of 0p0 creates a hard-edged shadow that precisely matches the contours of the object casting it. Higher values result in a gradient of opacity levels that simulates an indistinct blur.
- Spread moves the midpoint of the shadow's transition from opaque to transparent within the range defined by the Size value. A high Size value combined with a high Spread value results in a sharp shadow that is bigger than the object casting it. For soft shadows, leave Spread set to 0.
- Noise adds random flecks to a shadow. A very low Noise value—typically, 5 percent or less—can be useful for matching the inherent noise in a digital photograph.
- Turn off the Object Knocks Out Shadow check box if you want to see through a translucent object to the shadow behind it. Otherwise, the shadow appears exclusively outside the object.
- Turn on the Shadow Honors Other Effects check box to trace the shadow along an edge blurred by one of the three Feather effects.

3. ***Specify the Drop Shadow settings.*** We're looking for a subtle effect that just slightly elevates the text with respect to the photograph in back of it, like so:

   - Raise the **Opacity** value to 100 percent.
   - Tab to the **Distance** value and change it to 0p3.
   - Turn on the **Use Global Light** check box and change the **Angle** value to 135 degrees.
   - A **Size** value of 0p5 works fine.
   - Raise the **Noise** value to 2 percent to more or less match the noise in the background photograph.

   Leave all other options set to their defaults, as shown in Figure 7-17. Click **OK** to apply the shadow effect. An ***fx*** icon appears to the right of Object: Normal 100% in the Effects palette, showing that the selected object includes an effect.

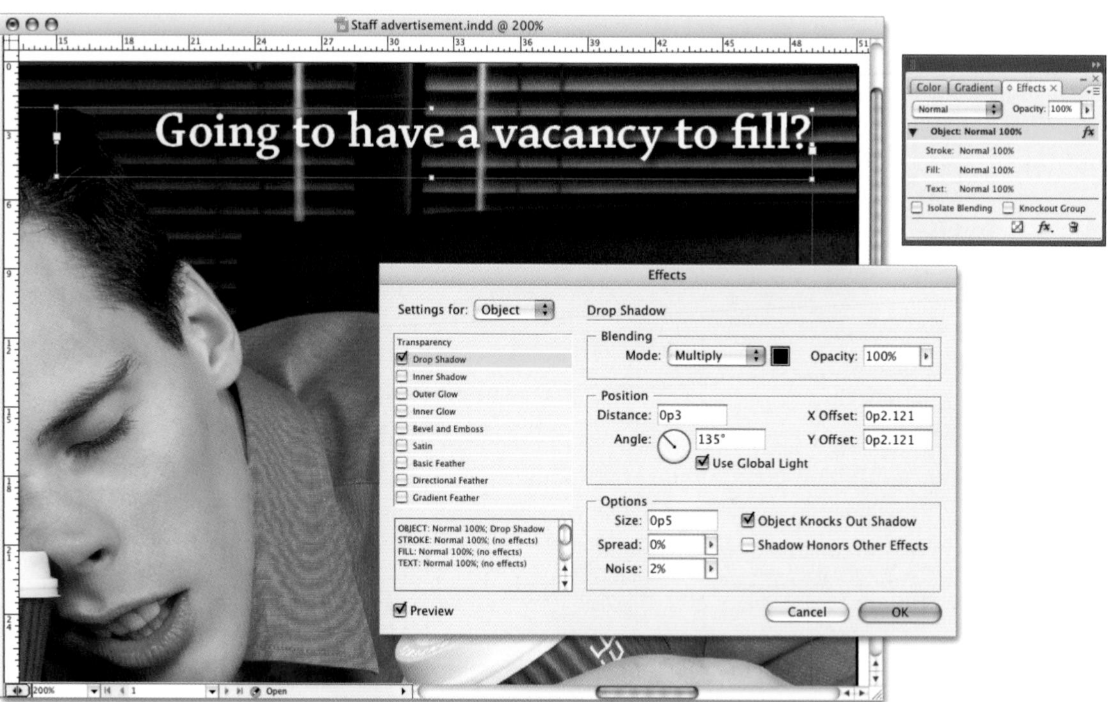

Figure 7-17.

4. ***Create a less traditional drop glow.*** By default, the Drop Shadow command results in a dark shadow. But the outcome can just as easily be a light "drop glow" or some other directional effect. Consider the nearly invisible black text toward the bottom-left corner of the photograph that reads *We've got you covered*. Here's how to make it stand out better:

- Click the black text in the bottom-left corner of the image with the black arrow tool.
- Click the *fx* icon along the bottom of the **Effects** palette and choose **Drop Shadow** or again press Ctrl+Alt+M (⌘-Option-M) to visit the **Effects** dialog box.
- I want to surround this text with a soft glow in one of the flesh tones reflected off the surface of the shiny tabletop (see Figure 7-18). To dial in such a color, click the black color swatch to the left of the word **Opacity** to bring up the **Effect Color** dialog box. Select **RGB** from the **Color** pop-up menu. Then set the **Red**, **Green**, and **Blue** values to 150, 110, and 100, respectively. Click **OK** to accept the new color.
- Back in the **Effects** dialog box, change the **Mode** option to **Screen**, which uses the new colors to lighten the colors in the background photo.

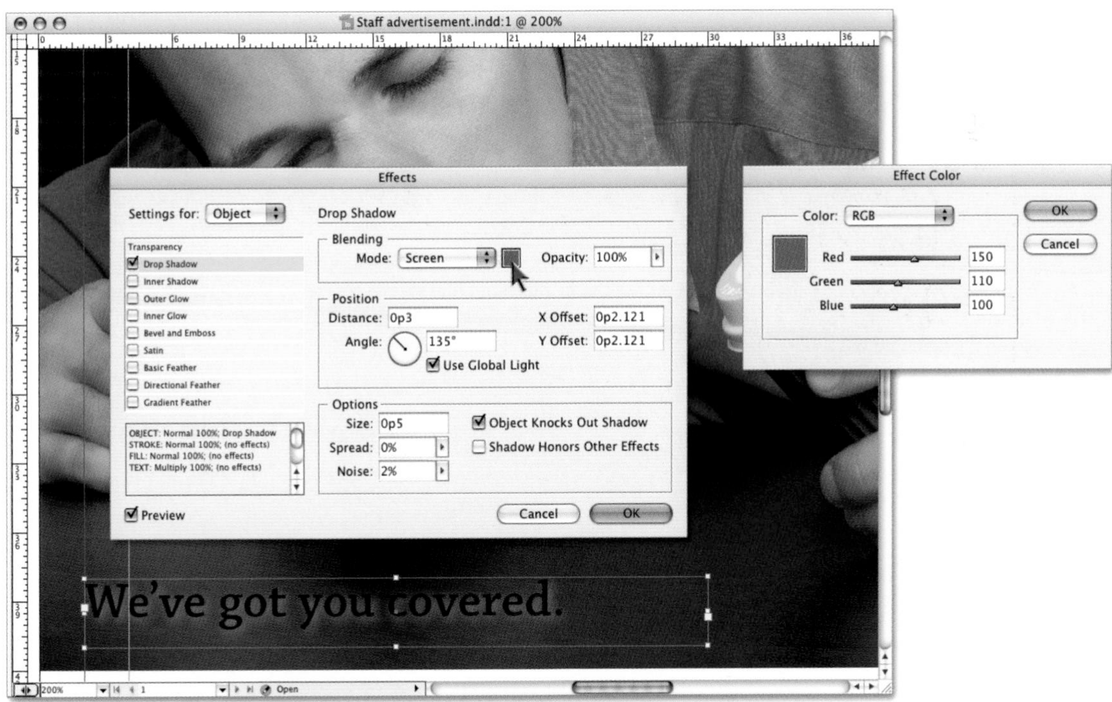

Figure 7-18.

- Adjust the other settings to match the preceding shadow effect. That is, set the **Opacity** value to 100 percent. Reduce the **Distance** value to 0p3 and turn on **Use Global Light** to match the previous angle. Confirm that the **Size** value is 0p5. And then raise **Noise** to 2 percent. When your settings look like those in Figure 7-18, click the **OK** button.

5. ***Add an Emboss effect to the*** **SuperStaffer** ***logo.*** Scroll down to the SuperStaffer logo, set inside the violet bar with the bevelled corners. The logo is set in the proper corporate font; it's even converted to path outlines to ensure that no one inadvertently edits it. However, the powers that be have decided it could use some punch. InDesign supplies that punch in the form of the Bevel and Emboss effect.

    - Click the logotype with the black arrow tool to select it.
    - Click the *fx* icon at the bottom of the **Effects** palette and choose **Bevel and Emboss**. InDesign displays a different panel in the **Effects** dialog box.
    - Set the **Style** option to **Emboss** to trace sculptural highlight and shadow effects both inside and outside the edges of the letters, as in Figure 7-19.
    - Change the **Size** value to 0p5.
    - Set the **Technique** option to **Chisel Soft** to create a more defined edge with sharply grooved corners.
    - Turn on the **Use Global Light** check box to match the angle of the drop shadows.
    - Click **OK**. The settings and effect appear in Figure 7-19.

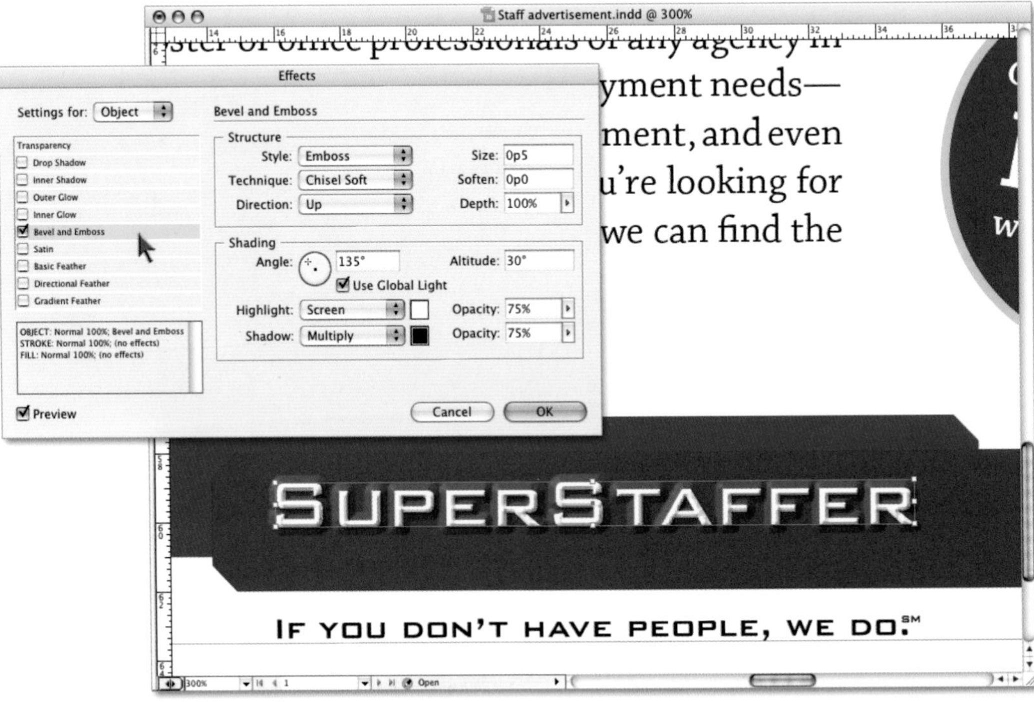

Figure 7-19.

6. ***Convert the violet bar to a translucent gradient.*** One of the best of the new dynamic effects is Gradient Feather, which turns any object into an opaque-to-transparent gradient. You can fade a graphic, text, an imported image, anything. We'll fade the violet bar:

   - Click on the violet bar behind the SuperStaffer logo with the black arrow tool.
   - Click the *fx* icon at the bottom of the **Effects** palette and choose **Gradient Feather** to display yet another panel in the **Effects** dialog box.
   - The default effect looks pretty great, fading the bar from violet on the left side to transparency on the right. But the color fades too quickly. To slow it down, click the ◇ midpoint control above the gradient ramp and drag it to the right until the **Location** value reads 75 percent, as demonstrated in Figure 7-20.
   - I want the violet bar to darken the blue bar in back of it. So click the **Transparency** item in the list on the left side of the dialog box. Then set the **Mode** option to **Multiply**.
   - Assuming your bar looks like the one pictured in Figure 7-20, go ahead and click **OK**.

If you're partial to keyboard shortcuts, you can access any effect by pressing Ctrl+Alt+M (⌘-Option-M), which adds a drop shadow. Then turn off Drop Shadow in the list of effects on the left side of the Effects dialog box and click the name of the effect you want to apply instead.

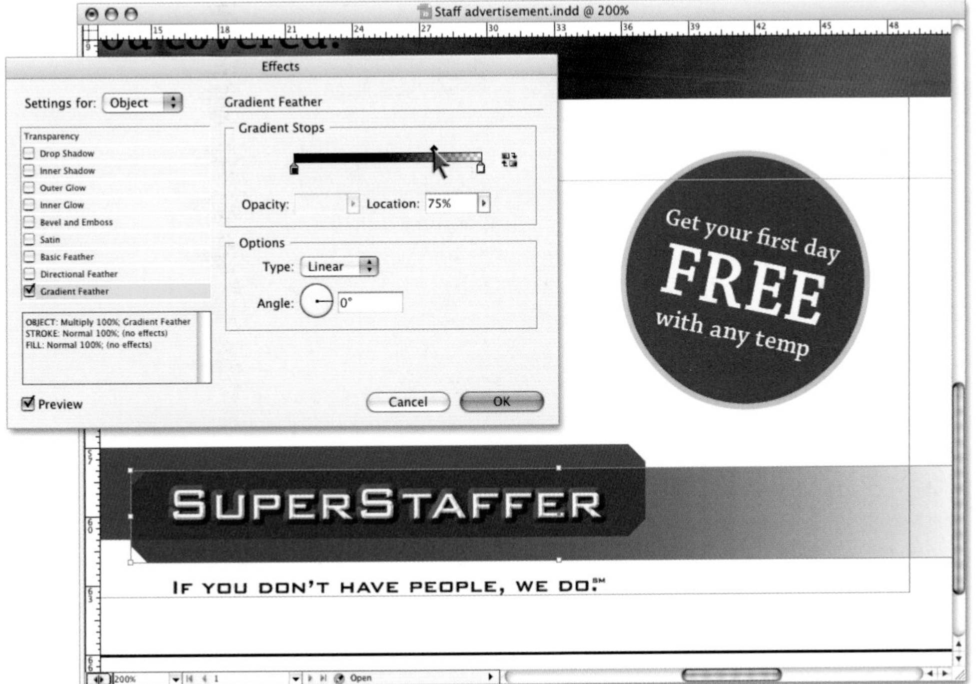

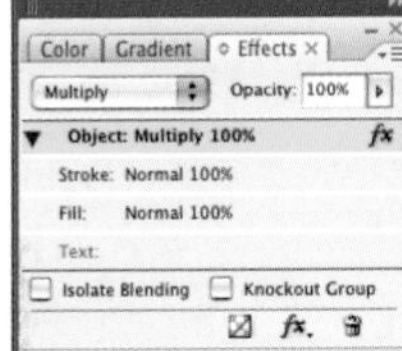

Figure 7-20.

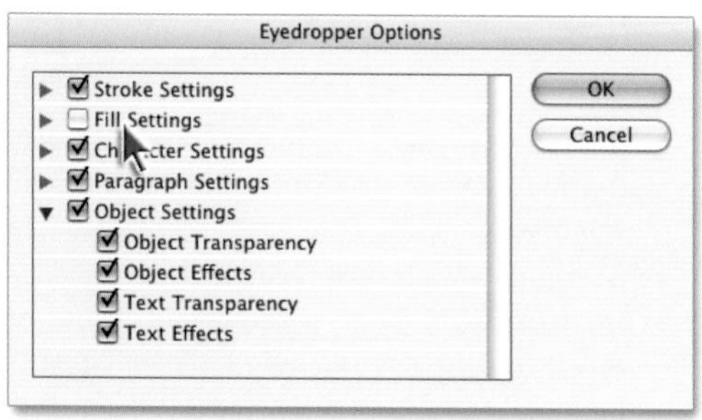

Figure 7-21.

7. ***Select and configure the eyedropper tool.*** It stands to reason that the blue bar should fade as well. And the easiest way to do that is to lift the effect from the violet bar with the eyedropper tool. Naturally, we don't want to lift the violet color, so we first need to configure the eyedropper to ignore the fill. Double-click the eyedropper tool icon in the toolbox to display the **Eyedropper Options** dialog box. Turn off the **Fill Settings** check box (see Figure 7-21) and click **OK**.

8. ***Copy the effect from the violet bar to the blue one.*** Armed with the eyedropper, click in the violet bar to lift its attributes. Then click in the blue bar with the loaded eyedropper cursor to deposit the translucent gradient effect.

9. ***Edit the Gradient Feather effect.*** Commonsense aesthetics dictate that the blue gradient should fade in the opposite direction. So edit the gradient as follows:

   - Press the V key to switch back to the black arrow tool. Then click the blue bar to select it.
   - In the **Effects** palette, double-click the *fx* icon to the right of **Object: Multiply 100%**.
   - Reverse the **Angle** value to 180 degrees and click the **OK** button. Figure 7-22 shows the result.

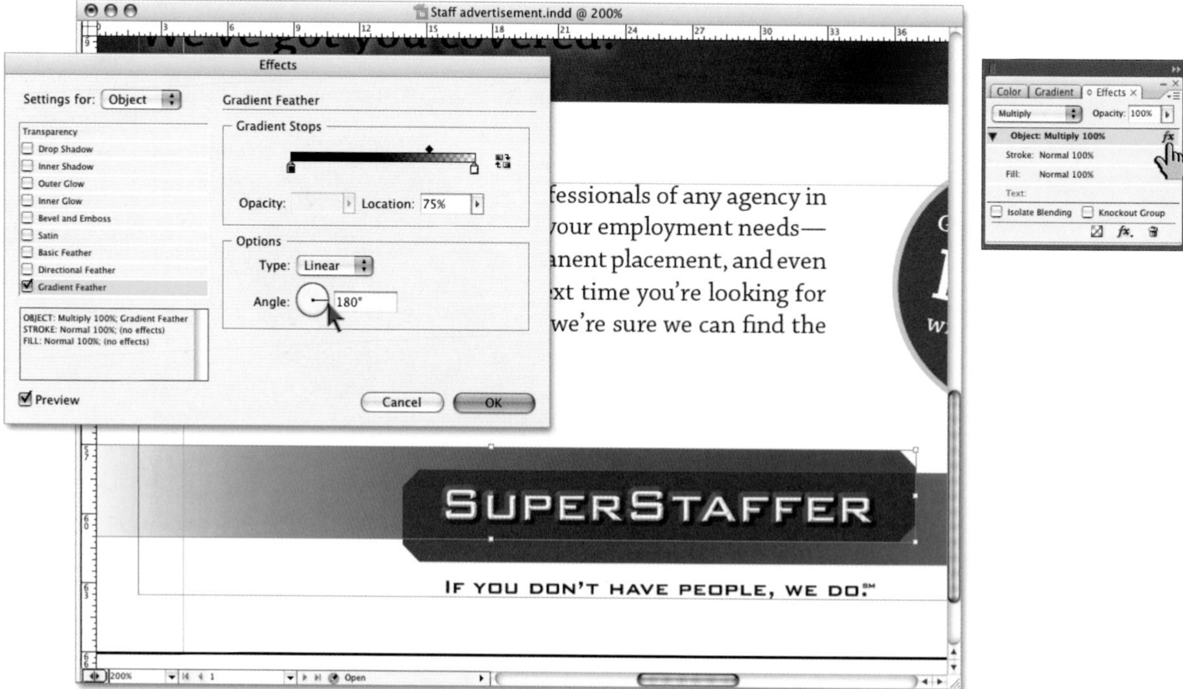

Figure 7-22.

EXTRA CREDIT

In the remaining steps, you'll turn the violet circle with a yellow stroke into an embossed button with a tangible sense of depth. In doing so, you'll learn how to apply effects to individual attributes, such as fill, stroke, and text. You'll also fade the photo with a Directional Feather effect. If you aren't interested, skip to the next exercise, "Using Clipping Paths and Alpha Channels," which begins on page 298. Or suspend your disinterest and continue.

10. ***Apply an Inner Bevel effect to the violet fill.*** Use the black arrow tool to select the rotated circle (the one with the big *FREE* inside it). I want to start things off by raising the violet fill with respect to the yellow stroke. So double-click the item that reads **Fill: Normal 100%** in the Effects palette to display the **Effects** dialog box, as in Figure 7-23. Then do the following:
    - Click the words **Bevel and Emboss** in the left-hand list.
    - Change the **Size** value to 0p8, **Technique** to **Chisel Hard**, and the **Soften** value to 0p1.
    - Turn on **Use Global Light** and raise the **Altitude** (which is the orientation to the light source in the sky) to 50 degrees.
    - Raise the **Opacity** values for the **Highlight** and **Shadow** settings to 100 percent apiece. As Figure 7-23 shows, the fill gets the effect; the stroke and text do not.

Figure 7-23.

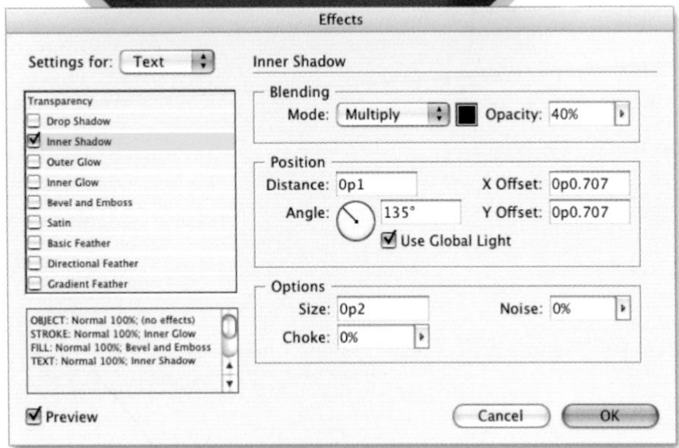

Figure 7-24.

11. *Apply an Inner Shadow effect to the text.* Next, I want to add a shadow inside the text so it looks like it's cut out of the circle. Still inside the Effects dialog box, choose **Text** from the **Settings For** pop-up menu, located in the top-left corner. (If you reflexively clicked OK and closed the dialog box, then double-click the Text: Normal 100% item in the Effects palette.) Then do this:

    - Click **Inner Shadow** in the left-hand list.
    - Lower the **Opacity** value to 40 percent.
    - Turn on the **Use Global Light** check box to change the Angle value to the usual 135 degrees.
    - Set **Distance** to 0p1 and **Size** to 0p2.

    The result appears in Figure 7-24. Don't click OK. We have another step to go.

12. *Apply an Inner Glow effect to the stroke.* Now for the yellow stroke. Choose **Stroke** from the **Settings For** pop-up menu in the top-left corner of the Effects dialog box. Here's how to soften the stroke with a violet, neon-like halo:

    - Click the words **Inner Glow** in the left-hand list to turn on the glow effect and display its options in the dialog box.
    - Click the white color swatch. In the **Effects Color** dialog box that follows, switch the **Color** setting to **Swatches**, select the Violet swatch, and click **OK**.
    - Set the **Mode** option to **Hard Light**, which infuses the inner and outer edges of the yellow outline with violet without shading or highlighting the stroke.
    - Raise the **Opacity** value to 100 percent.
    - Reduce the **Size** value to a very slim 0p2.

    Click the **OK** button to accept the result, which appears magnified and in the preview mode in Figure 7-25.

13. *Fade the photograph with a Direction Feather effect.* I'm still not entirely satisfied with the way the black text reads against Libby Chapman's photograph. The best solution, it seems to me, is to fade the area below the text to white. You could achieve such an effect using the Gradient Feather effect, which produces the smoothest

Figure 7-25.

results. But this time around, I'll have you use Directional Gradient, which sacrifices some smoothness for better control.

- Select the photograph with the black arrow tool.
- Double-click the item that reads **Object: Normal 100%** in the **Effects** palette to display the **Effects** dialog box.
- Click the words **Directional Feather** in the left-hand list.
- In the **Feather Widths** area, click the icon to break the link between the Top and Bottom values.
- Set the **Bottom** value to 8p0 to create an 8-pica fade along the bottom edge of the image. Then change the **Top** value to 3p0 to add a bit of top fade as well.
- Set the **Noise** option to 2 percent to match the slight noise inside this digital photo.
- Rotate the **Angle** value to –8 degrees. Then set the **Shape** option to **First Edge Only** to keep the rotated edges rectangular, thus fading just the corners, as in Figure 7-26.
- Click **OK** to accept the effect.

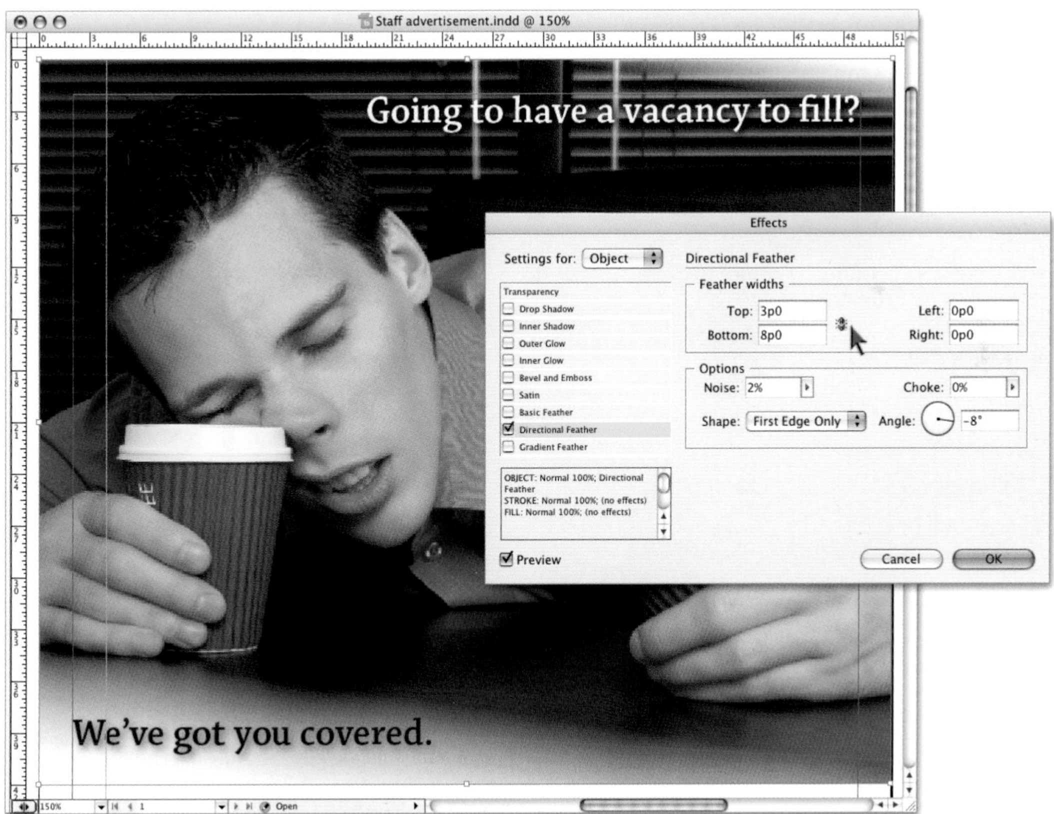

Figure 7-26.

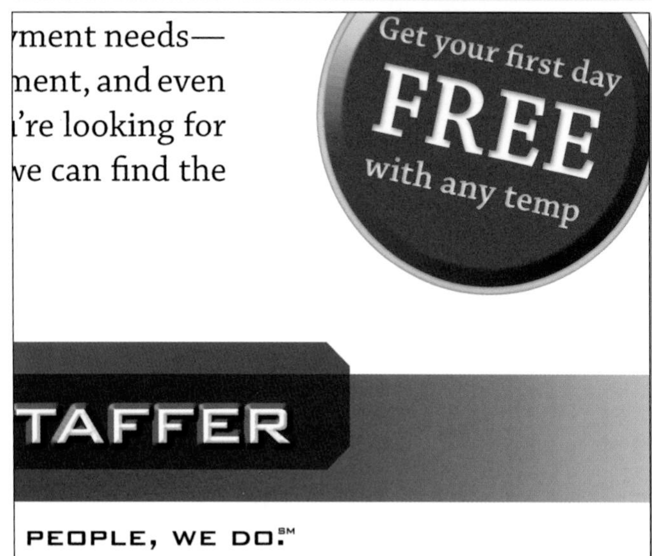

Figure 7-27.

Figure 7-27 shows a reduced version of the final advertisement, along with an actual-size detail from the letter-sized page. What's amazing is just how great the document looks in print. Although they still have a little ways to go, InDesign's dynamic effects are quickly becoming as flexible and powerful as their pixel-based brethren in Photoshop.

Using Clipping Paths and Alpha Channels

According to the rules of the PostScript printing language, vectors may convey transparency but images may not. Suppose you take a circle drawn in Illustrator and place it into a PostScript-only program such as QuarkXPress 6.0 or earlier. Because the circle is a vector, Quark knows that everything inside the circle is opaque and everything outside is transparent. But draw that same circle in Photoshop, and Quark sees it very differently. According to the sacred text of PostScript, every pixel must be opaque. So what appears as a layered circle set against a transparent background in Photoshop looks like a circle inside an opaque white rectangle in Quark.

Thankfully, the designers of PostScript came up with a clever solution: If an image can't be transparent, then by golly, let's place it inside a vector, which can. To create a circular photograph, for example, you would place a flat image file inside a circular vector-based frame. The portion of the photo inside the frame is opaque; the portion outside is transparent. Such a frame is called a *clipping path* because it's a path outline that clips an image into a custom shape.

The illustrious Photoshop introduced support for clipping paths in 1993, more than a year before it added layers. So it's hardly a surprise that InDesign supports them as well. But InDesign can also import a native Photoshop document—complete with alpha channels and layers—and recognize the exact amount of translucency applied to each and every pixel. As a result, you can import soft-edged images.

In this exercise, you'll experiment with two varieties of transparency. First, you'll import an image that contains a clipping path. Then, you'll swap the hard-edged clipping path for a soft-edged alpha channel. To perform these steps in their entirety, you'll need Adobe Photoshop (which ships with InDesign when you purchase the Creative Suite) running on your computer. If you don't have the absolute newest version of Photoshop, you should be able to get by okay with an older version, anything from Photoshop 6 on. If you don't own any version of Photoshop, *c'est la vie*. With a few minor adjustments (which I'll explain as we go), you'll still be able to complete the project just fine.

1. ***Launch Photoshop.*** Check to see that Photoshop is running. If it isn't, start 'er up. If you don't own Photoshop, continue reading for now. (In other words, no skipping—I have a couple of things to show you.) I'll switch back to InDesign in Step 7 (page 301), at which point you can take up your mouse and rejoin our elaborate game of Simon Says.

2. ***Open an image file that contains one or more paths.*** Using Photoshop's own File→Open or the Adobe Bridge, open the image called *Bird with paths.tif*, included in the *Lesson 07* folder inside *Lesson Files-IDcs3 1on1*. Pictured in Figure 7-28, this vibrant composition features a pelican-shaped trash can against an oddly colored, aqueous background.

3. ***Display the Paths palette.*** Choose **Window→Paths** (or click the Paths tab in the Layers palette cluster) to display the **Paths** palette. This palette contains vector-based path outlines that you can convert to selections inside Photoshop or employ as clipping paths outside the program. We'll be doing the latter.

4. ***Select a clipping path.*** In all, I've added three paths to this image. The first exactly traces the outline of the cartoon trash can; the second is a sun pattern; the third adds some bubbles to the trash can outline. The thumbnail icon next to each path name preview shows how the clipping path will work. The white areas are inside the path and thus opaque; the gray areas are outside the path and transparent. As you'll see in Step 10 (page 303), you can access from inside InDesign any path outline saved with an image. But it's typically a

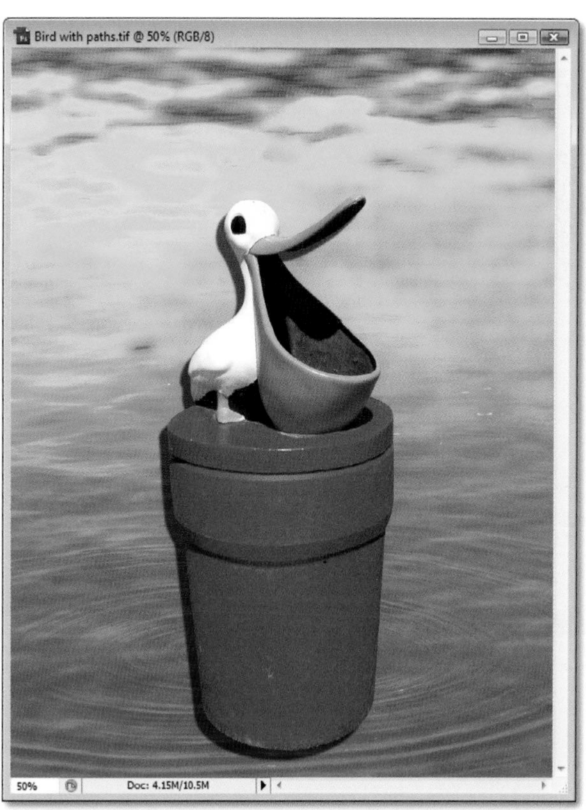

Figure 7-28.

PEARL OF WISDOM

If you read *Adobe Photoshop CS3 One-on-One*, you may recognize this pelican trash can as part of a project we created using Photoshop's pen tool and Paths palette. This time around, we'll be experiencing those same paths in a larger, cross-application context. Oh, the synergy.

good idea to identify one as a clipping path before leaving Photoshop, if only to establish a preferred setting.

Click the **Peli Can** path in the **Paths** palette. The path appears in the image window. Then click the tiny ▾≡ icon in the top-right corner of the Paths palette and choose the **Clipping Path** command from the palette menu, as in Figure 7-29. Make sure the **Path** option in the **Clipping Path** dialog box is set to **Peli Can** and then click **OK**.

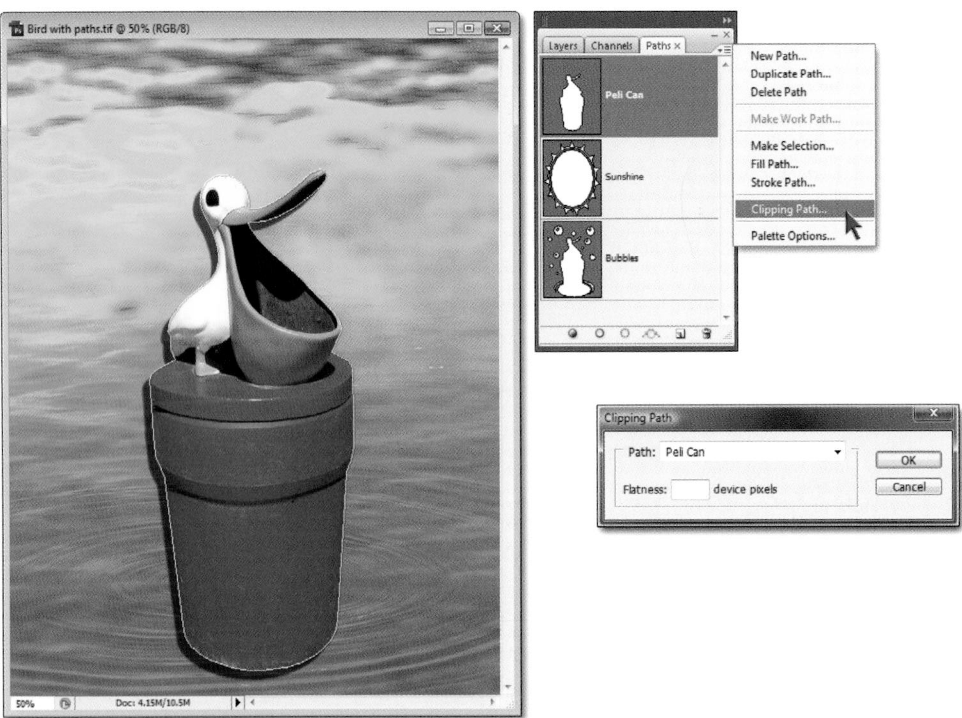

Figure 7-29.

Now press the Shift key and click **Peli Can** in the **Paths** palette to turn off the path. On the PC, the path name remains bold. On the Mac, it appears bold and outlined. Either way, you know it is now the clipping path that will be used to frame the image when you import it into InDesign, QuarkXPress, or some other page-layout program.

5. ***Take a look at the alpha channels.*** Another way to specify transparency in a Photoshop image is to add an *alpha channel*. Also known as *masks,* alpha channels distinguish opaque from transparent areas using pixels instead of vectors. To see the alpha channels that I've added to this image, click the **Channels** tab at the top of the Paths palette or choose **Window→Channels**. Photoshop displays the **Channels** palette. The palette begins

with the composite RGB image followed by the independent Red, Green, and Blue channels. The remaining channels, Silhouette through Final Mask, are the alpha channels.

The thumbnails next to each channel name preview the mask. White indicates opacity; black means transparency. You can also view the mask and image together. Click in the box to the left of the last channel, **Final Mask**, to show the 👁 icon and make the channel visible. Photoshop displays the mask as a cyan overlay, as in Figure 7-30. Any place containing cyan will turn transparent. The cyan overlay gradually fades away toward the center of the image, suggesting that under the right circumstances, this alpha channel might result in soft transitions.

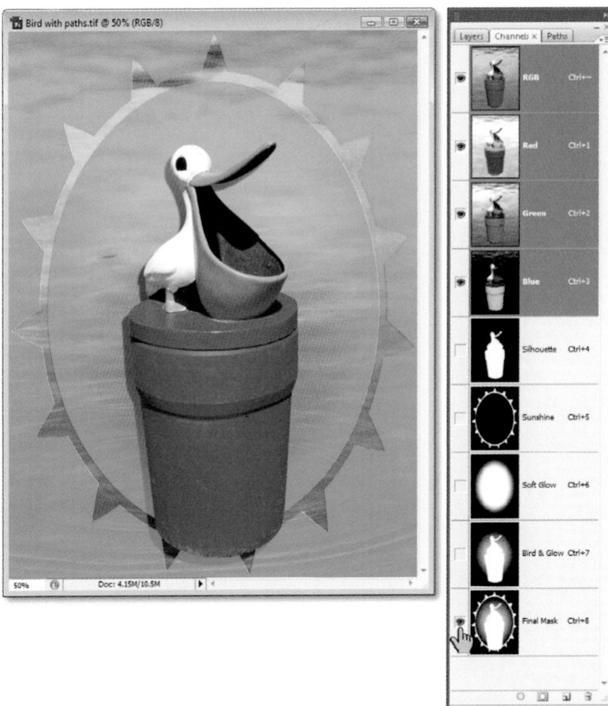

Figure 7-30.

6. ***Save your changes to the image.*** That's enough in Photoshop. But before you leave, you need to save your clipping path designation. Choose **File→Save** or press Ctrl+S (⌘-S on the Mac). In a flash, Photoshop updates the file on disk.

7. ***Open the InDesign document.*** Switch back to InDesign CS3. (Those of you who've been waiting for the Photoshop steps to end, it's time to get back to work.) Then open the document called *Pelican page.indd* from the *Lesson 07* folder inside *Lesson Files-IDcs3 1on1*. Pictured in Figure 7-31, this single-page story includes a handful of blended gradients, several text blocks, and a large empty frame for the Photoshop image.

Figure 7-31.

8. ***Place the trash can image.*** With the black arrow tool in hand, click the big frame with the X through it to select it. Then choose **File→Place** or press Ctrl+D (or ⌘-D). Select the *Bird with paths.tif* file in the *Lesson 07* folder. Make sure the **Replace Selected Item** check box is turned on, and then click **Open**. If you successfully completed Steps 1 through 6, the pelican trash can appears separated from its background inside the selected frame, as in Figure 7-32 on the next page. If not, you see the entire image, complete with its toxic yellow-orange background. Either way is okay—we'll all end up with the same result in just a few steps.

9. ***Add a slim drop shadow.*** To provide the pelican with some additional definition, double-click the **Object: Normal 100%** item in the **Effects** palette and then click the words **Drop Shadow** in the **Effects** dialog box. Or press that excellent (but unmemorable) shortcut Ctrl+Alt+M (⌘-Option-M). Then do the following:

   - Leave the **Mode** option set to **Multiply**. And raise the **Opacity** value to 100 percent.
   - Set the **Distance** value to 0p3 and the **Angle** to 45 degrees. This nudges the shadow down and to the left.
   - Reduce the **Size** to 0p2 to slightly undercut the Distance.

   Assuming the **Preview** check box is on, you'll see the shadow in the document window. If the shadow looks like the one shown in Figure 7-33, click the **OK** button to apply it. (If you see the entire Photoshop image, your shadow overlaps slightly into the text. We'll fix that shortly.)

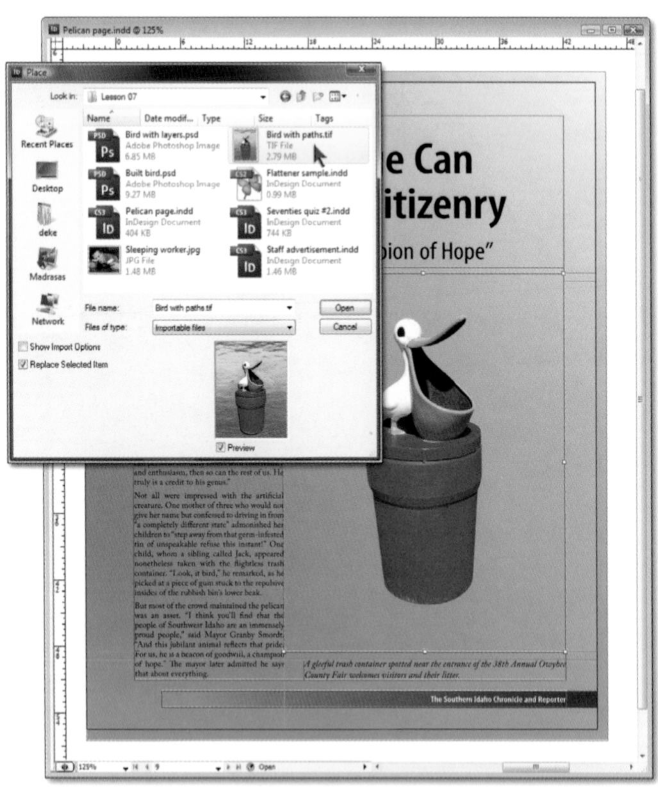

Figure 7-32.

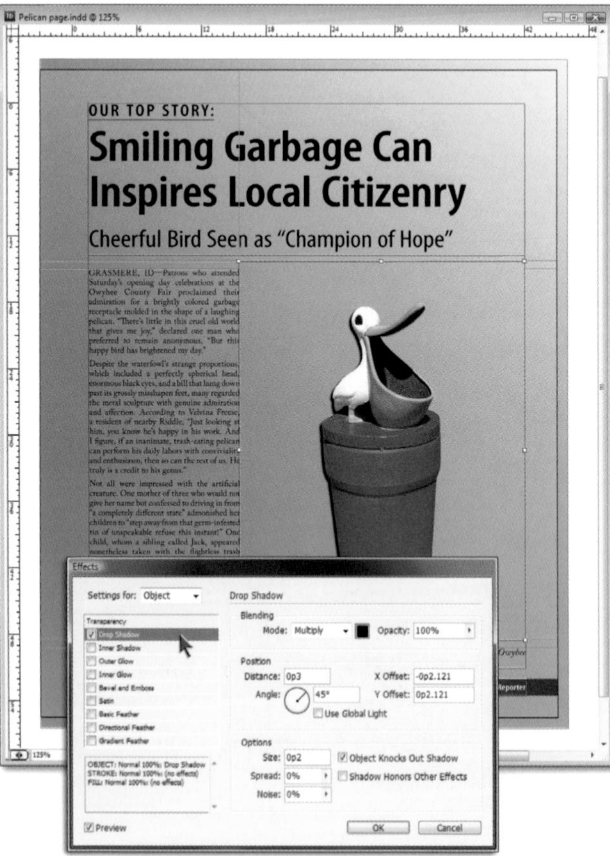

Figure 7-33.

PEARL OF WISDOM

As a result of the active clipping path, the pelican is too small to fill the space I've allotted it. Therefore, the active clipping path might strike you as a bad idea. Fortunately, InDesign gives you ample opportunity to change your mind. Just because you import an image with a clipping path doesn't mean you have to use that clipping path. You can turn off the clipping path, turn on a different path, or even generate one from an alpha channel.

10. *Swap one clipping path with another.* To exercise any the options mentioned in the above Pearl, choose **Object→Clipping Path→Options**. InDesign displays the **Clipping Path** dialog box, which lets you extract a clipping path from an image.

    While inside this dialog box, here are a few tricks you might like (though you should not feel obligated) to try:

    - To turn off the active clipping path, choose None from the Type pop-up menu. Then turn on the Preview check box to see the restored background in the document window.

If the image appears off-center, with the top 2 picas or so cropped away, click the OK button to exit the dialog box. Click the icon in the control palette or press Ctrl+Shift+E (⌘-Shift-E) to center the selected image inside its frame. Then choose Object→Clipping Path to revisit the Clipping Path dialog box.

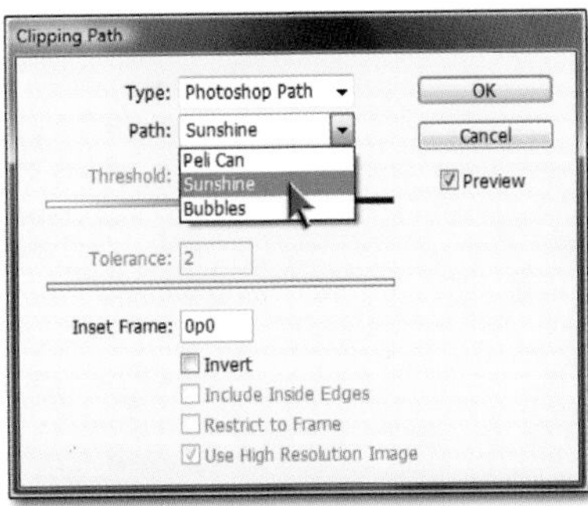

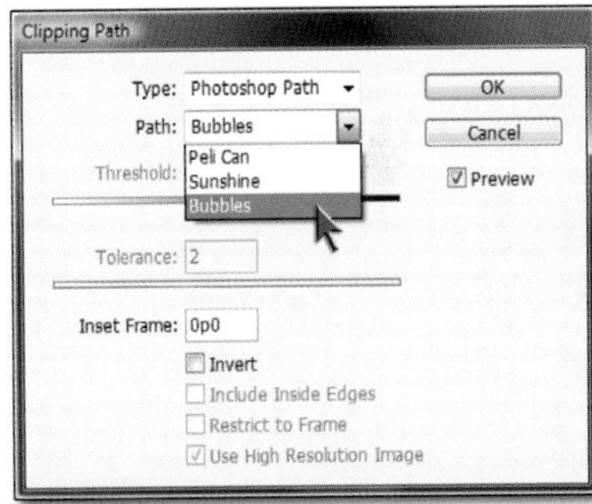

Figure 7-34.

- If you don't own Photoshop and therefore have yet to see the original clipping path in play, set Type to Photoshop Path. Then choose Peli Can from the Path pop-up menu.
- To try out other paths saved with the image, make sure Type is set to Photoshop Path. Then select either Sunshine or Bubbles from the Path menu. Figure 7-34 shows the effect each setting has on the placed graphic.

- If you would rather work from one of the soft masks saved with this image (the ones we saw in Step 5), choose Alpha Channel from the Type menu. Then select the desired mask's name from the Alpha pop-up menu, which lists each of the five alpha channels pictured in the thumbnail previews back in Figure 7-30 (see page 301).
- Choose Final Mask from the Alpha pop-up menu to load the most elaborate of the masks, which I created by combining elements of the four previous alpha channels.
- Surprisingly, InDesign ends up tracing only the outermost perimeter of the mask, as witnessed by the first example in Figure 7-35. To remedy this peculiar oversight, turn on the Include Inside Edges check box, which carves out the inner portion of the Sunshine shape (which seems to me to be the more logical default behavior, but I digress). Then raise the Threshold value to 160, which expands the size of the inner ellipse, as shown on the right side of the figure.

PEARL OF WISDOM

If you've been following events closely, you might notice a disconnect. Back in Step 5, I said that alpha channels permit soft transitions. And yet the edges in Figure 7-35 are every bit as sharp as those associated with clipping paths. That's because these *are* clipping paths. The Clipping Path dialog box cannot load a mask with its softness intact; instead, it traces a clipping path around the mask. The Threshold value determines where along the softness that trace occurs; raising the value spreads the path outward, and lowering the value chokes it inward. (You can also use the Tolerance value to smooth rough edges, though I generally leave this value unchanged.)

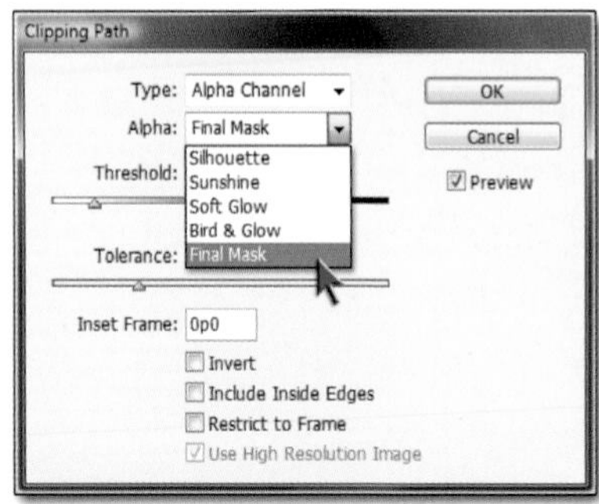

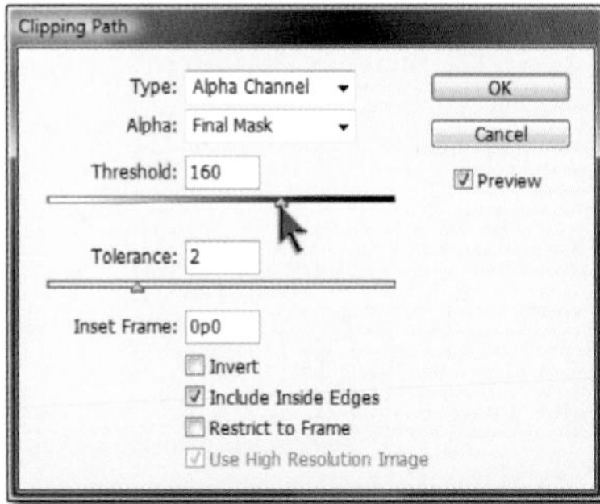

Figure 7-35.

In the final analysis, the Clipping Path dialog box is the cat's meow when it comes to loading predefined clipping paths and something of a hairball when tracing alpha channels. If the alpha channel is really what you want, you're better off reimporting the image, as I discuss in Step 13.

11. ***Set the clipping path to Bubbles.*** That last step was essentially a minute or two of educational playtime. Now, let's make a choice. Set the two pop-up menus at the top of the Clipping Path dialog box to **Photoshop Path** and **Bubbles**, respectively. Then click **OK**. Figure 7-36 shows the resulting graphic.

12. ***Edit the clipping path.*** Let's say you're not quite happy with the clipping path. No problem, you can edit it right here inside InDesign. The Clipping Path command should automatically switch you to the white arrow tool, but if not, press the A key. Then click anywhere on the pelican. InDesign displays all the anchor points and segments that make up the clipping path. You can make whatever adjustments you like, but here's what I recommend:

    - Press the Alt (or Option) key and click the outline for the bubble directly to the left of the pelican's fanny. This selects the entire circle, as in the left example of Figure 7-37.

OUR TOP STORY:

Smiling Garbage Can Inspires Local Citizenry

Cheerful Bird Seen as "Champion of Hope"

GRASMERE, ID—Patrons who attended Saturday's opening day celebrations at the Owyhee County Fair proclaimed their admiration for a brightly colored garbage receptacle molded in the shape of a laughing pelican. "There's little in this cruel old world that gives me joy," declared one man who preferred to remain anonymous, "But this happy bird has brightened my day."

Despite the waterfowl's strange proportions, which included a perfectly spherical head, enormous black eyes, and a bill that hung down past its grossly misshapen feet, many regarded the metal sculpture with genuine admiration and affection. According to Velvina Freese, a resident of nearby Riddle, "Just looking at him, you know he's happy in his work. And I figure, if an inanimate, trash-eating pelican can perform his daily labors with conviviality and enthusiasm, then so can the rest of us. He truly is a credit to his genus."

Not all were impressed with the artificial creature. One mother of three who would not give her name but confessed to driving in from "a completely different state" admonished her children to "step away from that germ-infested tin of unspeakable refuse this instant!" One child, whom a sibling called Jack, appeared nonetheless taken with the flightless trash container. "Look, it bird," he remarked, as he picked at a piece of gum stuck to the repulsive insides of the rubbish bin's lower beak.

But most of the crowd maintained the pelican was an asset. "I think you'll find that the people of Southwest Idaho are an immensely proud people," said Mayor Granby Smordt. "And this jubilant animal reflects that pride. For us, he is a beacon of goodwill, a champion of hope." The mayor later admitted he says that about everything.

A gleeful trash container spotted near the entrance of the 38th Annual Owyhee County Fair welcomes visitors and their litter.

The Southern Idaho Chronicle and Reporter

Figure 7-36.

Figure 7-37.

- Press Shift and Alt (or Shift and Option) and click the outline of the inset circle to select it as well.
- Drag the outline of one of the two selected circles up and slightly to the right to fill in the gap toward the top of the image, as illustrated on the right side of Figure 7-37.

If you see other things you want to change, by all means, soldier on. Clipping paths behave like paths drawn with InDesign's pen tool, so feel free to apply any of the path-editing techniques you learned in Lesson 5, "Drawing inside InDesign." For example, you can move independent anchor points, drag control handles, and even add or subtract points using the pen tool. When you finish, press the V key (or Enter on the keypad) to exit the path edit mode and return to the black arrow tool.

Figure 7-38.

EXTRA CREDIT

At this point, you've seen just about everything there is to see on the topic of creating, importing, and modifying clipping paths. But that's just one method for assigning transparency to an image—and a relatively narrow method at that. The remaining steps in this exercise document another means of communicating transparency from Photoshop to InDesign: alpha channels. Rather than converting an alpha channel to clipping paths, as illustrated back in Figure 7-35, we'll instruct InDesign to ignore clipping paths altogether and respect all levels of translucency in the mask, something QuarkXPress and others can't do.

13. ***Replace the trash can image.*** The only time you can tell InDesign to lift an alpha channel from an image file is when you import it. In other words, we have to reimport the pelican trash can art. Make sure the black arrow tool is active and the image remains selected. Choose **File→Place** or press Ctrl+D (⌘-D) and again select the file *Bird with paths.tif* in the *Lesson 07* folder. However, this time, I want you to turn on the **Show Import Options** check box (highlighted in Figure 7-38), which is your doorway to InDesign's support for alpha channels. Then click the **Open** button to proceed.

14. ***Select the desired alpha channel.*** Because you selected Show Import Options, InDesign displays the **Image Import Options** dialog box, which permits you to modify clipping path and mask settings. We

won't be needing a clipping path this time around, so turn off the **Apply Photoshop Clipping Path** check box to ignore the Peli Can path that you assigned back in Step 4 (see page 299). Select **Final Mask** from the **Alpha Channel** option. Click the **OK** button to replace the previous version of the pelican graphic with the new one.

Unfortunately, as shown in Figure 7-39, the artwork looks terrible. If you're thinking that it looks like some sick, twisted combination of both an alpha channel and a clipping path, you're absolutely right. Even though you specifically requested that InDesign lay off the clipping path, the previous path (our customized variation of Bubbles) remains in force. I'm afraid it's up to you to manually eliminate it.

15. ***Turn off the clipping path.*** Choose **Object→Clipping Path→Options**. Select **None** from the **Type** pop-up menu. Then click **OK**. InDesign shows the image masked only by the alpha channel, complete with gradual transitions between opacity and transparency, thus imparting the hundreds of incremental levels of translucency that we see on display in Figure 7-40.

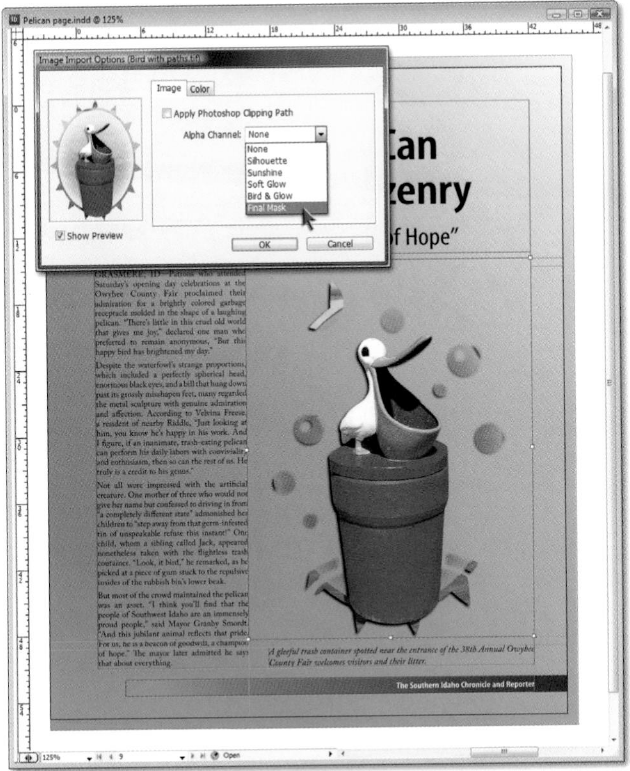

Figure 7-39.

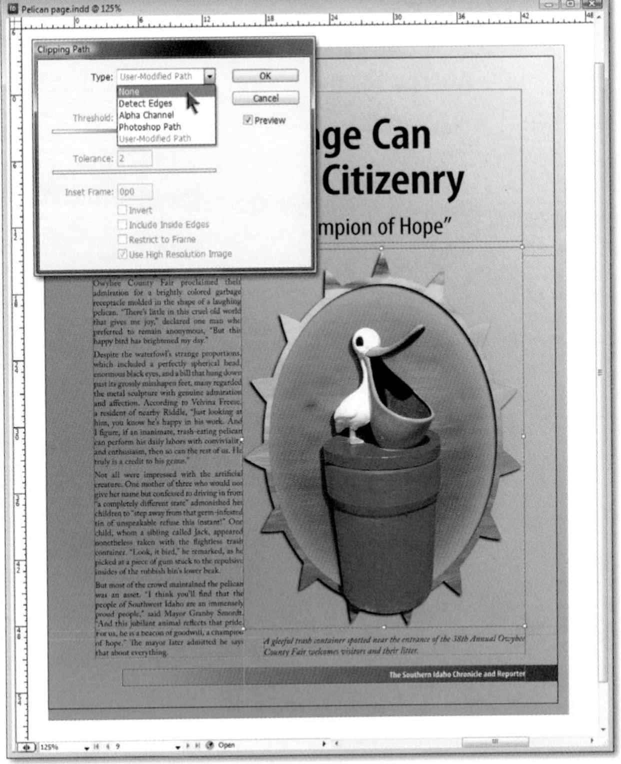

Figure 7-40.

16. ***Turn off the drop shadow.*** Compare Figure 7-40 to the likes of Figure 7-35 and earlier, and you may notice a moody darkness settling over the previously joyful pelican, especially toward the center of the image. This is a function of the drop shadow you applied in Step 9. Although just 2 points in size, it has a pronounced effect on the soft transitions. Because translucent pixels simultaneously cast effects and reveal them, translucency actually magnifies a drop shadow. Turn off the effect as follows:

    - Press the V key to switch to the black arrow tool. Then click the image to select it in its entirety.
    - Go to the Effects palette and double-click the ***fx*** icon to the right of **Object: Normal 100%**.
    - Turn off the **Drop Shadow** check box and then click **OK**.

For the sake of reference, Figure 7-41 compares the placed pelican with a drop shadow to the same image without.

Figure 7-41.

Importing Layered Photoshop Artwork

There's no denying that clipping paths and alpha channels are powerful tools, ones that remain in prevalent use to this day. But neither is the best way to convey transparency from Photoshop to InDesign. Clipping paths are too circumscribed, alpha channels are too obscure, and both are too much work. They are decades-old answers to a thoroughly modern question.

The best solution is the simplest. Create the desired combination of translucent layers and effects in Photoshop, save your artwork in Photoshop's native PSD format, and then import that same layered image into InDesign. We'll explore these steps using a variation on the pelican image and newspaper article from the preceding exercise. This time, the trash can composition is more elaborate, involving a degree of transparency that would be impossible to achieve with clipping paths and exceedingly difficult (if not likewise impossible) with alpha channels. And yet, the procedure involves less work and fewer steps.

Figure 7-42.

Again, we'll start inside Photoshop. Follow along if you can; just read the text if you can't.

1. ***Open a layered image in Photoshop.*** If Photoshop is still open, switch to it; otherwise, launch the application. Then open *Bird with layers.psd* in the *Lesson 07* folder inside *Lesson Files-IDcs3 1on1*. Pictured in all its trashy avian glory in Figure 7-42, this PSD file contains a total of five layers, which you can see by choosing **Window→Layers** or pressing F7 to display the **Layers** palette.

2. ***Hide all but the bottom layer.*** Just so you're clear on exactly what you'll be placing inside Photoshop, let's take a moment to walk through the layers and change the composition to bring in some transparency. For starters, press the Alt key (Option on the Mac) and click the 👁 icon in front of the last layer, **Tide**. This hides all but the bottom layer, which is nothing more than a photo of some water.

3. ***Mask the bottom layer.*** See the white-on-black oval with a red X through it to the left of the word *Tide* in the Layers palette? That's a kind of alpha channel that controls the opacity of a single layer, called a *layer mask*. Currently, it is off, hence the red X. To turn it on, press the Shift key and click the oval. The layer becomes transparent where the layer mask is black—that is, outside the oval—as shown in Figure 7-43.

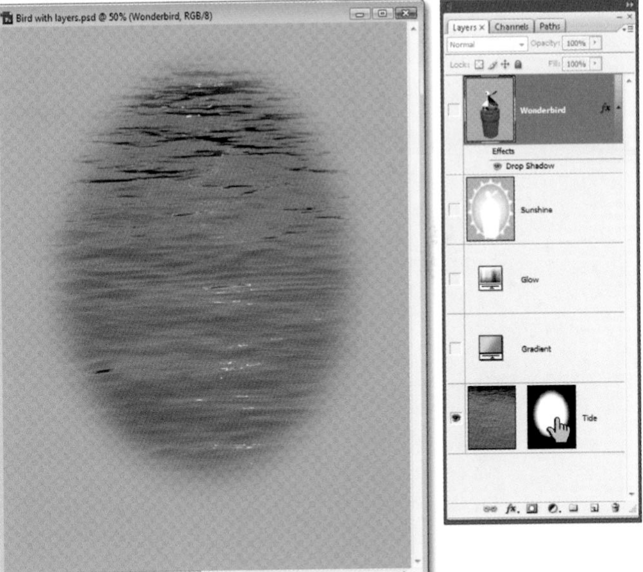

Figure 7-43.

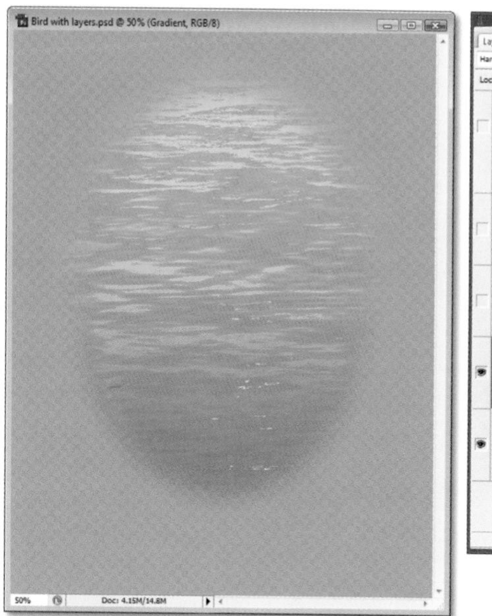

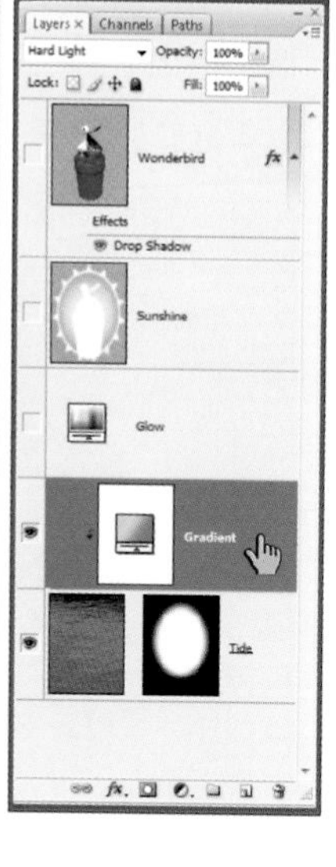

Figure 7-44.

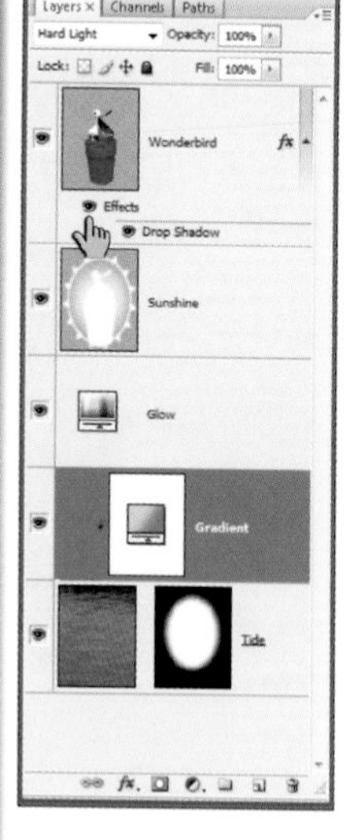

Figure 7-45.

The checkerboard pattern behind the oval water layer represents the void of transparency. Your checkerboard is probably gray and white, as it is by default. I've edited mine to give me a better sense of what the image will look like against the blue-green background in InDesign. To make your checkerboard match mine, press Ctrl+K and Ctrl+6 (⌘-K, ⌘-6) to display the Transparency & Gamut options. Click the white and gray squares in the Grid Colors option to change the colors. The H, S, and B values for my colors are 220, 30, 90 and 160, 30, 85, respectively. Mind you, these colors have no effect on the final appearance of the image; they merely help you better gauge the results of your edits.

4. ***Group the Gradient and Tide layers.*** Click the word **Gradient** in the Layers palette and then click the empty gray square to the left of it to display the layer and make it active. This yellow-to-red gradient fills the frame, but we want it to appear only inside the oval. To mask the gradient with the layer behind it, choose **Layer→Create Clipping Mask**. Photoshop combines the two layers into a *clipping mask*, in which the bottom layer masks the one above it. A clipped layer appears indented in the Layers palette, as in Figure 7-44.

5. ***Turn on the other layers.*** Click the empty boxes to the left of the **Glow**, **Sunshine**, and **Wonderbird** layers to display the 👁 icons and make the layers visible. The Glow layer brightens the colors; Sunshine contains a silhouette of white pixels; and Wonderbird gives us the bird. Lastly, click the 👁 icon next to the word **Effects** to unveil the drop shadow. The finished composition appears in Figure 7-45. If it looks a little pale, don't worry; it'll pop nicely on the InDesign page.

6. ***Turn on Maximum File Compatibility.*** Before saving the revised composition, we have to visit a special saving preference that helps InDesign interpret layered Photoshop files. Choose **Edit** (on the Mac, **Photoshop**)**→Preferences→File Handling** or press Ctrl+K followed by Ctrl+3 (⌘-K, ⌘-3). Midway down, you'll see a **Maximize PSD & PSB File Compatibility** option. Set it to **Ask** (see Figure 7-46 on the facing page) and click the **OK** button.

7. ***Save the image under a new name.*** Choose **File→Save As** or press Ctrl+Shift+S (⌘-Shift-S). Change the filename to "Bird with MFC.psd" and make sure the **Save in** option is trained on the *Lesson 07* folder. Turn on the **Layers** and **ICC Profile** check boxes (see Figure 7-47) and click the **Save** button. Photoshop displays an alert message. Make sure **Maximize Compatibility** is turned on and click **OK**. This option tells Photoshop to create two versions of the image in a single file: The first contains all layers so that you can open and edit them in Photoshop; the second collapses the layers to reduce InDesign's overhead.

8. ***Open the InDesign document.*** Switch back to InDesign CS3 and open the document *Pelican page.indd* in the *Lesson 07* folder inside *Lesson Files-IDcs3 1on1*. If you still have the document open from the previous exercise, choose **File→Revert** to restore the original version of the file.

9. ***Place the layered trash can image.*** With the black arrow tool, select the empty frame with the X through it. Choose **File→Place** or press Ctrl+D (⌘-D). Select the *Bird with MFC.psd* file in the *Lesson 07* folder. (If you don't own Photoshop, select the image that I built for you, *Built bird.psd*.) Make sure the **Replace Selected Item** check box is turned on and **Show Import Options** is off. Then click **Open**. The Photoshop image fills the selected frame, with all layers, effects, and relationships intact.

10. ***Manipulate the visible layers.*** It's hard to imagine an improved vision of pelican pulchritude. But there's no accounting for a client's taste. Let's say ours doesn't like the orange water behind the creature. You might assume this would mean a trip back to Photoshop. But InDesign lets you turn on and off layers in an imported PSD image.

    Choose **Object→Object Layer Options**. Turn on the **Preview** check box in the **Object Layer Options** dialog box to monitor the effects of your changes. Scroll down to the bottom of the **Show Layers** list

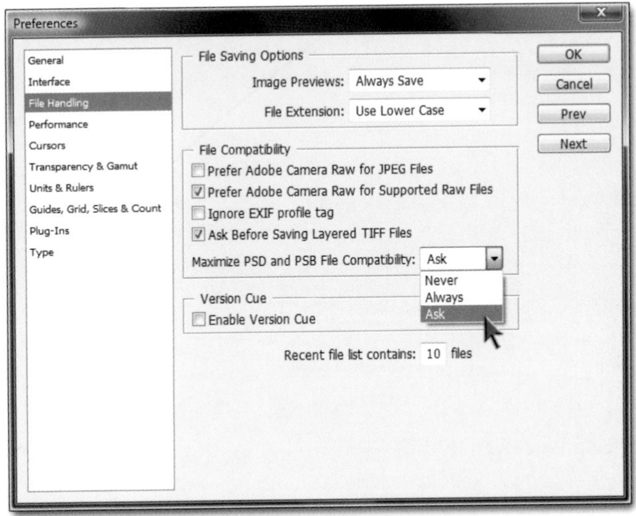

Figure 7-46.

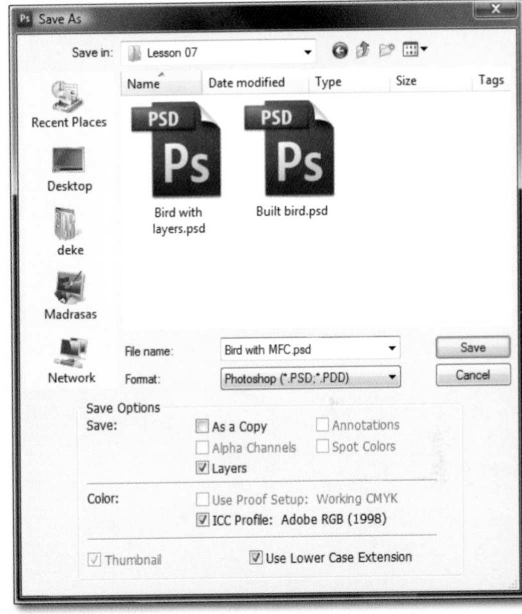

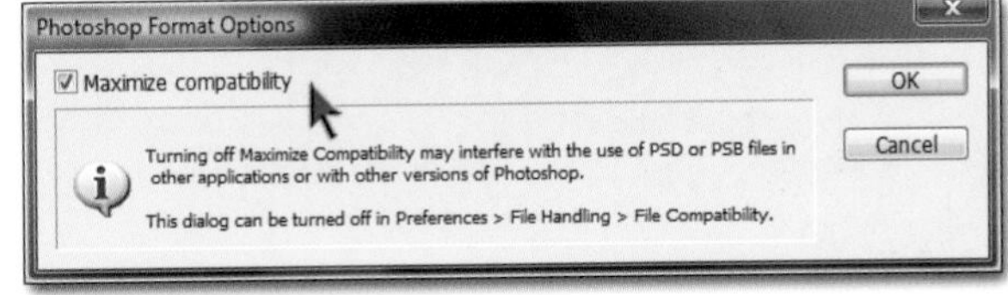

Figure 7-47.

Rasterization and the Flattener Preview Palette

InDesign's wealth of effects and transparency functions are a marvel to behold. But as beautiful as your pages may look on screen, there's always the nagging issue of output. Given that the industry-standard PostScript printing language doesn't support a single one of InDesign's transparency functions—including Opacity settings, blend modes, drop shadows, and imported Photoshop layers—how can we have any confidence whatsoever that this stuff is going to print?

The answer lies in InDesign's ability to translate something that PostScript can't possibly understand into something that it can. Consider that every line, shape, and character of text eventually gets converted to printer dots. These dots are tiny, densely packed squares—in other words, pixels. So a printed page is ultimately just another bitmapped image, albeit one that contains a hundred times as many pixels as a typical digital photograph. For example, the page spread you're looking at now contains more than a billion printer dots.

The act of converting vectors to pixels is called *rasterization*. When printing to a PostScript printer, the rasterization is performed by a *raster image processor*, or *RIP* (pronounced *rip*) for short. The RIP may be a piece of hardware or software, the latter being easier to update. In the normal course of printing, InDesign conveys its text and graphics as mathematical objects and lets the RIP convert them to pixels. But when InDesign comes across something that the RIP won't understand, such as translucent or blended objects, it simplifies the objects by *flattening* them. When expedient, InDesign flattens objects by breaking them into lots of little vector objects (as when rendering a gradient to a few hundred bands of color). Otherwise, it converts the objects into a high-resolution image. In this regard, InDesign is capable of serving as its own software RIP.

By way of example, take a look at the modified pelican article on the right. (To inspect this page more closely, open the file *Flattener sample.indd* in the *Lesson 07* folder.) The background is a single rectangle filled with a gradient. Among the translucent objects:

- The footer in the lower-right corner of the page features a gradient set to the Multiply blend mode.
- The white headline includes a drop shadow.
- The graphic is a layered Photoshop image.

To see how InDesign plans to flatten the document, choose Window→Output→Flattener Preview to display the Flattener Preview palette. Then choose an option from the Highlight pop-up menu. Any setting but None grays out the document and adds red to call attention to areas that require special treatment. The Highlight menu contains lots of options, but you need to concern yourself with only two:

- Choose All Affected Objects to see all the objects that are slated for flattening. Because the background contains a gradient—which has to be broken into smaller vectors—all but the opaque text turns red.
- To see just those areas InDesign intends to rasterize, choose All Rasterized Regions. As illustrated on the facing page, only the three translucent areas—the multiplied footer gradient, the drop shadow, and the placed Photoshop art—turn red.

Lest you regard the red highlights as rough approximations, rest assured that you are seeing the precise boundaries between vector and raster art. PostScript requires images to be rectangular, so InDesign rasterizes in rectangles. In the case of the pelican page, InDesign is showing us that it means to put the gradient at the bottom of the stack, the three raster rectangles above that, and the vector-based text on top.

Although InDesign rasterizes portions of a page to assist the printer, it doesn't do so at the full resolution of the printer. That would lead to long print times or possibly print failure. Instead, InDesign rasterizes paths and text at about half the resolution of a high-end PostScript device and sets drop shadows and gradients to 300 pixels per inch (ppi). These are good settings; if you decide to change them, I recommend doing so only slightly. For example, in printing this book, I adjusted the path and text resolution a bit higher and the drop shadow and gradient resolution a bit lower. Here's how I did it:

- I chose Transparency Flattener Presets from the palette menu (as indicated by ❶ in the figure below right).
- Inside the Transparency Flattener Presets dialog box, I selected the best of the flattener settings, High Resolution, as a base for my changes and then clicked the New button (❷ in the figure) to display the Transparency Flattener Preset Options dialog box.
- I named my new preset "Best Resolution" and then tabbed down to the Line Art and Text Resolution value (❸).
- While the resolutions of professional-level PostScript imagesetters vary, one of the more prevalent standards is 2540 dots per inch (dpi). So I increased the Line Art and Text Resolution value from 1200 ppi to precisely half the printer resolution, 1270 ppi. It's unlikely anyone will notice the difference, but the higher value can smooth out the appearance of very high-contrast raster edges.
- Drop shadows and rasterized gradients (like the one behind the footer) are so soft that the resolution makes little difference. You might as well lower the value a bit. I reduced my Gradient and Mesh Resolution value to 254 ppi (❹), or 1/10 the printer resolution.
- I clicked OK in each of the two dialog boxes to accept my changes and create the new preset. Then I chose Best Resolution from the Preset pop-up menu in the Flattener Preview palette. I also clicked the Apply Settings to Print button to make my new preferences the default settings when printing the document.
- Finally, I clicked the Refresh button to confirm that my rasterized areas remained intact, which they had.

When you're satisfied that you understand what will flatten during output, choose None from the Highlight pop-up menu to return the document to its normal appearance. Then close the Flattener Preview palette, safe in the knowledge that InDesign is fully capable of converting your bold experiments in transparency to the buttoned-down world of PostScript.

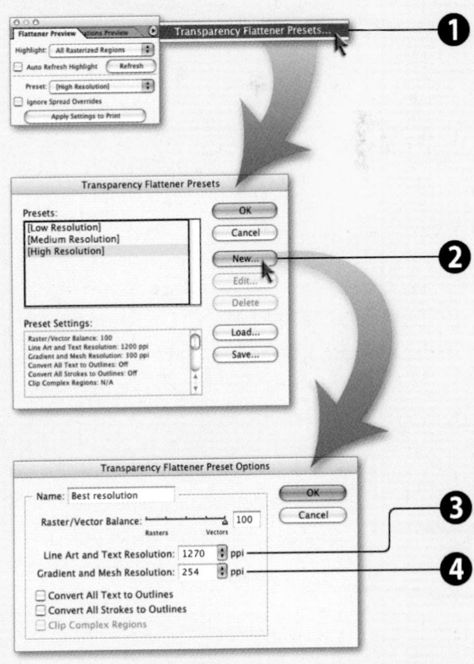

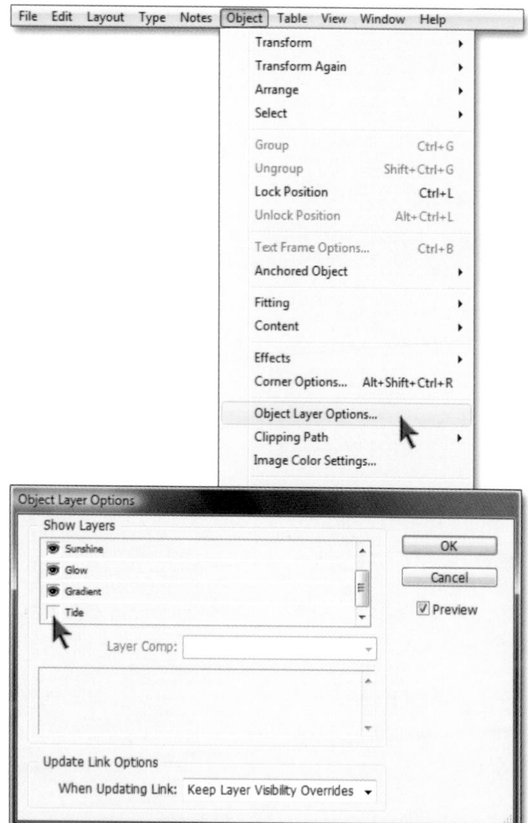

Figure 7-48.

and click the 👁 icon in front of the **Tide** layer to hide it, as in Figure 7-48. A moment or two later, the water disappears, taking the yellow-to-red fountain from the Gradient layer along with it. (Hiding a clipping mask hides the clipped layers above it as well.) Click **OK** to accept the change.

If the pelican art never updates and you see a yellow ⚠ symbol below the Preview check box, it means the preview timed out and InDesign canceled it. Just turn the Preview check box back on. In my experience, the preview always succeeds the second time around.

The layered Photoshop image looks great in its new home, but not perfect. The image crowds the body copy to the left and doesn't appear centered over its caption. To fix this, press Shift+→ six times to nudge the image 60 points to the right. Figure 7-49 shows the final product in the preview mode, with the image blending seamlessly with its gradient background. If you decide later to bring the water layer back, choose Object→Object Layer Options and turn on the Tide layer. It's entirely dynamic.

OUR TOP STORY:

Smiling Garbage Can Inspires Local Citizenry

Cheerful Bird Seen as "Champion of Hope"

GRASMERE, ID—Patrons who attended Saturday's opening day celebrations at the Owyhee County Fair proclaimed their admiration for a brightly colored garbage receptacle molded in the shape of a laughing pelican. "There's little in this cruel old world that gives me joy," declared one man who preferred to remain anonymous, "But this happy bird has brightened my day."

Despite the waterfowl's strange proportions, which included a perfectly spherical head, enormous black eyes, and a bill that hung down past its grossly misshapen feet, many regarded the metal sculpture with genuine admiration and affection. According to Velvina Freese, a resident of nearby Riddle, "Just looking at him, you know he's happy in his work. And I figure, if an inanimate, trash-eating pelican can perform his daily labors with conviviality and enthusiasm, then so can the rest of us. He truly is a credit to his genus."

Not all were impressed with the artificial creature. One mother of three who would not give her name but confessed to driving in from "a completely different state" admonished her children to "step away from that germ-infested tin of unspeakable refuse this instant!" One child, whom a sibling called Jack, appeared nonetheless taken with the flightless trash container. "Look, it bird," he remarked, as he picked at a piece of gum stuck to the repulsive insides of the rubbish bin's lower beak.

But most of the crowd maintained the pelican was an asset. "I think you'll find that the people of Southwest Idaho are an immensely proud people," said Mayor Granby Smordt. "And this jubilant animal reflects that pride. For us, he is a beacon of goodwill, a champion of hope." The mayor later admitted he says that about everything.

A gleeful trash container spotted near the entrance of the 38th Annual Owyhee County Fair welcomes visitors and their litter.

The Southern Idaho Chronicle and Reporter

Figure 7-49.

FURTHER INVESTIGATION

If interacting with Photoshop's transparency functions has got you wondering how you can use paths, alpha channels, and other tools to carve images out of their backgrounds with such deadly accuracy, then make your way to my two-part, 32-hour video series *Photoshop CS3 Channels and Masks*. Its more than 300 movies make it the longest, most exhaustive series in the lynda.com Online Training Library. For immediate access, go to *www.lynda.com/dekeID* and sign up for your 7-Day Free Trial Account.

Assembling a Custom Style

Style sheets break into five camps. *Paragraph styles* affect entire paragraphs at a time; *character styles* affect individual letters or words; *object styles* affect entire frames; *table styles* affect entire tables; and *cell styles* affect individual cells, rows, or columns. And here, as luck would have it, Adobe and the countless designers who rely on its graphics and publishing software use the same terms.

The most common of the bunch, the paragraph style, may contain all formatting attributes, from font to alignment to tabs. Figure 8-1 shows four paragraph styles applied to a passage from the ever-cheerful *Macbeth*. In each case, the style sheet changes both the character- and paragraph-level attributes, making it useful for formatting all kinds of text, from body copy to captions to headlines. When people talk generally about style sheets, this is what they mean.

A character style is a subset of a paragraph style that is limited to character-level attributes and may define as many or as few attributes as you like. On the next page, Figure 8-2 shows the result of creating a character style that has two attributes—18-point size and italic style—and applying it to four words at the outset of each of the paragraphs. The character style changes what little formatting it can and leaves the rest intact.

An object style is applied not to individual characters or paragraphs of text but to the frame that contains the text. An object style may include a paragraph style definition, as well as frame-level attributes such as fill, stroke, transparency, frame margins, text wrap, and anchored object settings. And it can be applied just as easily to a frame that contains an imported graphic or a drawing created inside InDesign.

New to CS3, a table style saves the basic attributes of a table that you can specify with the Table→Table Options commands, including borders as well as alternating strokes and fills. (Sadly, a table style does not track row-height and column-width information.) The more useful cell style lets you format a header, footer, or cell entry, and may include a paragraph style definition, as well as stroke, fill, and inset parameters.

Paragraph style 1: Bernhard Modern, 12.5/16, flush left

Out, out brief candle! Life's but a walking shadow, a poor player, that struts and frets his hour upon the stage, and then is heard no more; it is a tale told by an idiot, full of sound and fury, signifying nothing.

Paragraph style 2: Chaparral Light, 11/16, flush left

Out, out brief candle! Life's but a walking shadow, a poor player, that struts and frets his hour upon the stage, and then is heard no more; it is a tale told by an idiot, full of sound and fury, signifying nothing.

Paragraph style 3: Rotis Serif Italic, 11.5/16, justified

Out, out brief candle! Life's but a walking shadow, a poor player, that struts and frets his hour upon the stage, and then is heard no more; it is a tale told by an idiot, full of sound and fury, signifying nothing.

Paragraph style 4: Silentium Roman 9/13.5, centered

Out, out brief candle!
Life's but a walking shadow, a poor player,
that struts and frets his hour upon the stage,
and then is heard no more; it is a tale told by
an idiot, full of sound and fury,
signifying nothing.

Figure 8-1.

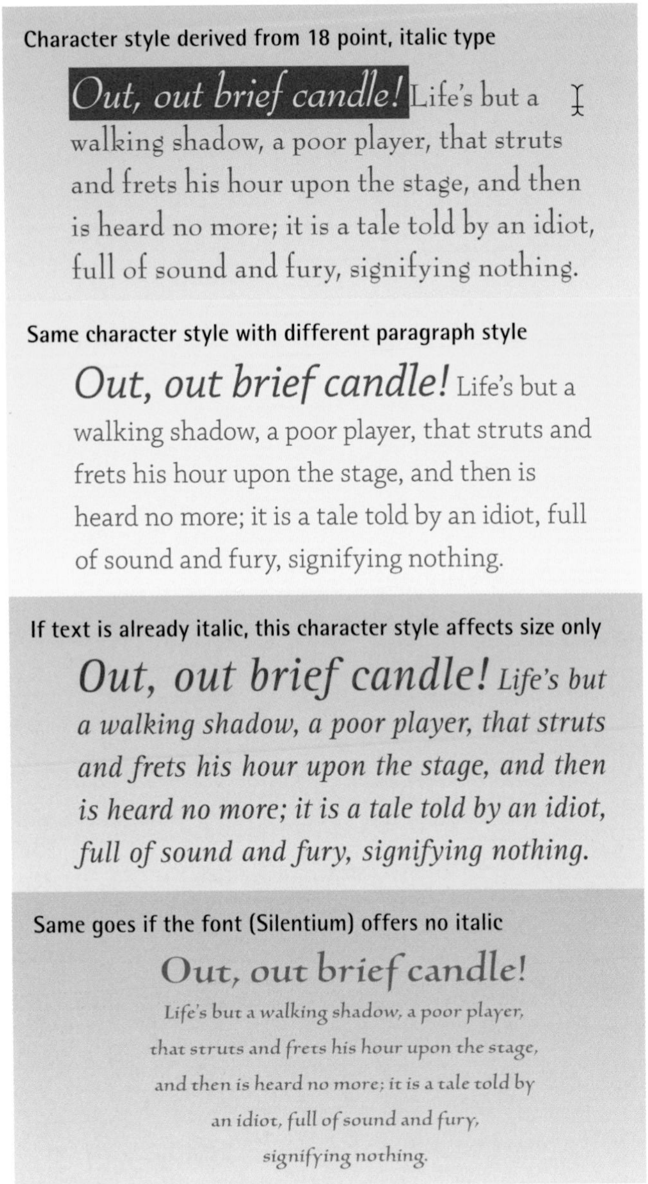

Character style derived from 18 point, italic type

Out, out brief candle! Life's but a walking shadow, a poor player, that struts and frets his hour upon the stage, and then is heard no more; it is a tale told by an idiot, full of sound and fury, signifying nothing.

Same character style with different paragraph style

Out, out brief candle! Life's but a walking shadow, a poor player, that struts and frets his hour upon the stage, and then is heard no more; it is a tale told by an idiot, full of sound and fury, signifying nothing.

If text is already italic, this character style affects size only

Out, out brief candle! Life's but a walking shadow, a poor player, that struts and frets his hour upon the stage, and then is heard no more; it is a tale told by an idiot, full of sound and fury, signifying nothing.

Same goes if the font (Silentium) offers no italic

Out, out brief candle!

Life's but a walking shadow, a poor player, that struts and frets his hour upon the stage, and then is heard no more; it is a tale told by an idiot, full of sound and fury, signifying nothing.

Figure 8-2.

In addition to facilitating the formatting of a document, style sheets make quick work of changes. If your client switches to a different typeface, just change the style definition and all styled frames, paragraphs, letters, or cells update in kind. You can even create dependent styles, so that changing one style affects others.

Also worth noting, InDesign can import and override style sheets from a word processor. This makes it possible for the content provider—the person writing the text—to work independently of the content designer—you—and still have all the pieces fit together seamlessly. For example, I initially wrote this text in Microsoft Word. The text was set in a paragraph style that I named Body, which was 10-point Verdana, making it easy to read on screen. In InDesign, Body is 10.5-point Birka. Thanks to style sheets, InDesign imported the text and converted it automatically.

Creating and Applying Paragraph Styles

We'll begin our exploration of style sheets with the most commonly used variety: paragraph styles. In this exercise, you'll learn how to create paragraph styles based on the formatting of selected text and assign shortcuts to the styles so you can apply them in a flash. You'll even learn how to base one style on another and specify the next style that InDesign applies when you begin a new paragraph. If you think that's slick, you'll be bowled over when you apply three different styles to three different paragraphs with a single click. Enjoy.

1. ***Open a document.*** Open the file named *Table of Contents 1.indd* located in the *Lesson 08* folder inside *Lesson Files-IDcs3 1on1*. Pictured in Figure 8-3 on the facing page, this is a table of contents (known as *TOC* in the biz) for a gardening magazine.

PEARL OF WISDOM

This document contains Myriad Pro Light. While it isn't automatically installed with Creative Suite 3, it is included with the Suite on the DVD labeled Content. See Step 11 on page xix of the Preface for more information.

2. ***Open the Paragraph Styles palette.*** Choose **Type→Paragraph Styles** or press F11 to display the **Paragraph Styles** palette, shown in Figure 8-4. Each TOC entry consists of three paragraphs. The first is the page number and title, the second is the byline, and the third is the article description. The first TOC entry is already formatted, which is helpful because the easiest way to create a style is to base it on existing text, which is what we're going to do.

3. ***Activate the first line of type.*** Press T to select the type tool and click in the word *Editorial*, which belongs to the first line in the formatted entry. This is enough to tell InDesign which paragraph's formatting we want to use.

4. ***Create a new style sheet.*** Click the ⧉ icon at the bottom of the Paragraph Styles palette. As Figure 8-5 shows, a new style called Paragraph Style 1 appears in the palette. This style contains all the character and paragraph formatting that has been applied to the active paragraph of text, including the font, color, alignment, and drop-cap settings for the page number (*18*).

5. ***Apply the new style sheet.*** Although the first paragraph is styled exactly as Paragraph Style 1 dictates, the paragraph doesn't have the style applied to it. How do we know this? Because the default [Basic Paragraph] remains selected (subject to a few additional formatting attributes, known as *local overrides*, as indicated by the + sign). So click **Paragraph Style 1** in the Paragraph Styles palette to establish a link between the text and the paragraph style.

This is one of the easiest things to forget when working with style sheets: After you create a style based on a formatted paragraph, you must turn around and apply that style to the same paragraph. Otherwise, text and style are not linked, which means the text won't reflect any changes you make to the style later.

---

6. ***Edit the new style sheet.*** A style sheet is a dynamic collection of formatting attributes. You can edit the style—and any text linked to it—at any stage in the development of a document. To modify the style sheet you just created:

   - Click the ▾≡ icon at the top of the Paragraph Styles palette and choose the **Style Options** command.
   - Or more simply, double-click the **Paragraph Style 1** item in the palette list.

Figure 8-3.

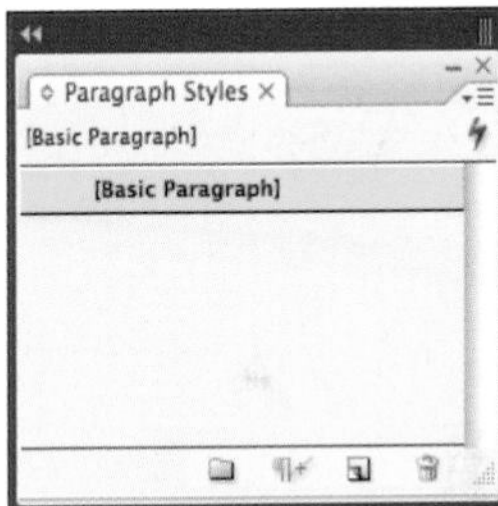

Figure 8-4.

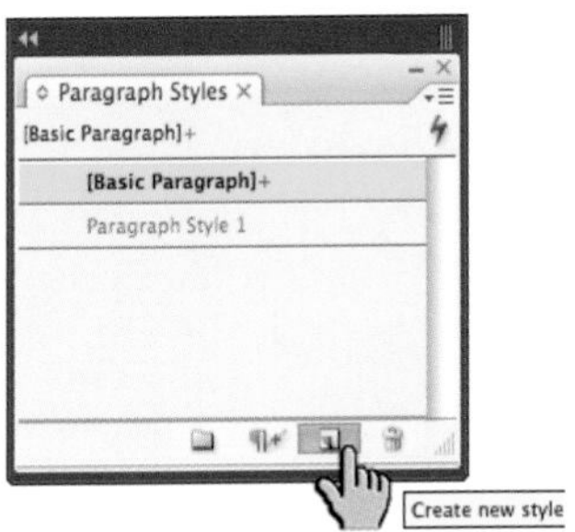

Figure 8-5.

InDesign displays the **Paragraph Style Options** dialog box shown in Figure 8-6. This dialog box lets you view and edit the various formatting attributes contained in your paragraph style. Click the options on the far left side of the dialog box and then press the ↓ or ↑ key to change panels.

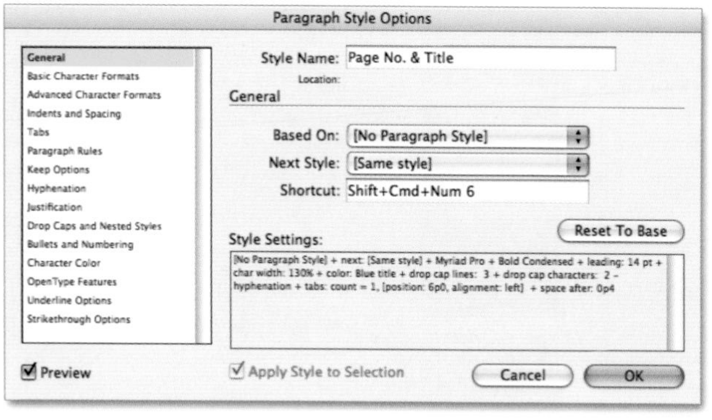

Figure 8-6.

7. ***Name the style sheet.*** Our first task is to give this style sheet a more descriptive name. In the **Style Name** option box, type "Page No. & Title," which is apt for the line that contains the big page number and the article title. We'll use this style sheet to format the first line of the other TOC entries.

I cannot stress enough the importance of giving your style sheets descriptive names. Name the style after its function—not its formatting—so that you (or someone working after you) can easily identify the style.

---

8. ***Assign a keyboard shortcut.*** Let's next assign a shortcut to our paragraph style so that we can apply it from the keyboard. InDesign requires that style shortcuts include one or more modifier keys—Ctrl, Alt, or Shift (⌘, Option, or Shift on the Mac)—combined with a number on the numeric keypad. That's right, it has to be a number, [0 Ins] through [9 PgUp], on the keypad only, and the Mac's Control key is out of bounds.

PEARL OF WISDOM

One problem with this restriction is that not all keyboards have keypads. To activate the keypad equivalent on many laptops—Apple's MacBooks come to mind—you must press the Num Lock key, which overrides a dozen or so letter keys. After you enter the shortcut, press Num Lock again to turn off the function and continue typing as usual. It's hideously inconvenient.

Assuming your keyboard includes a keypad, click the **Shortcut** option box. Then press Ctrl+Shift+[6] on the numeric keypad (⌘-Shift-[6]). If InDesign beeps at you or does nothing, press the Num Lock key and try again. If successful, InDesign spells out the sequence of keys in the Shortcut option box.

If you can't make this step work, skip it. Keyboard shortcuts are just one of many options. We investigate all kinds of ways to apply style sheets in the Extra Credit portion of this exercise, which begins on page 325.

---

9. ***Inspect the drop cap settings.*** The Style Settings area at the bottom of the dialog box provides a summary of the attributes conveyed by the paragraph style. You can see that the

font is Myriad Pro, the style is Bold, the type size is 14 points, and so on. To investigate a setting, click the corresponding item in the left-hand list.

For example, let's say you're curious about *drop cap lines: 3 + drop caps characters: 2*. Click **Drop Caps and Nested Styles** on the left side of the dialog box to switch to the settings pictured in Figure 8-7, which call for a drop cap 3 lines tall and 2 characters wide, hence the big two-digit page number at the outset of the TOC entry.

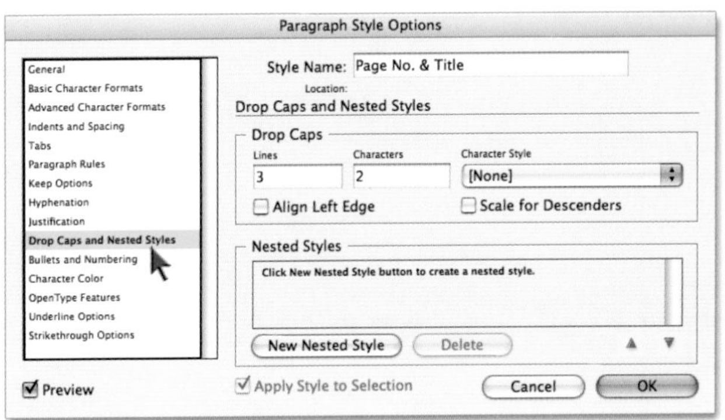

Figure 8-7.

You could change the settings and update the style sheet. But for this exercise, the current settings are fine. I point them out just so you know how the paragraph is formatted and what the Style Settings notations mean.

10. *Accept your changes.* Click **OK** to close the Paragraph Style Options dialog box and accept your changes. As Figure 8-8 shows, the style formerly named Paragraph Style 1 now appears as Page No. & Title, and with a shortcut to boot.

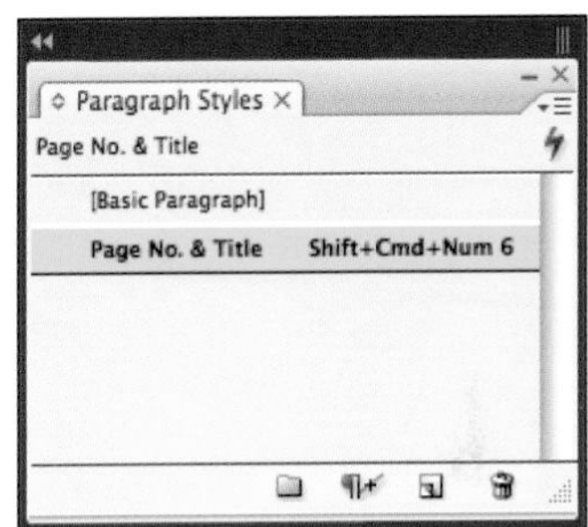

Figure 8-8.

11. *Create a style sheet for the byline.* Press the ↓ key to move the insertion marker to the second line of type. Again, [Basic Paragraph] becomes highlighted in the **Paragraph Styles** palette, indicating that you haven't assigned a style sheet to the active paragraph. Press the Alt (or Option) key and click the icon at the bottom of the Paragraph Styles palette to display the **New Paragraph Style** dialog box, which lets you edit a style sheet as you create it. In the **Style Name** option box, enter "Byline."

12. *Base the style sheet on Page No. & Title.* The Based On option establishes a parent-child relationship between two style sheets. Any changes made to the parent style will affect formatting attributes shared in the child style. In this way, you can modify multiple styles at a time.

Choose **Page No. & Title** from the **Based On** pop-up menu, as in Figure 8-9. This may seem like an odd thing to do, given that the Byline style isn't really based on Page No. & Title at all. And switching Based On settings often creates problems, as witnessed in gruesome detail in the very next step. But it also affords you greater control in the future, as we will explore in "Updating a Paragraph Style," which comes up next. In the meantime, trust me, I won't steer you wrong.

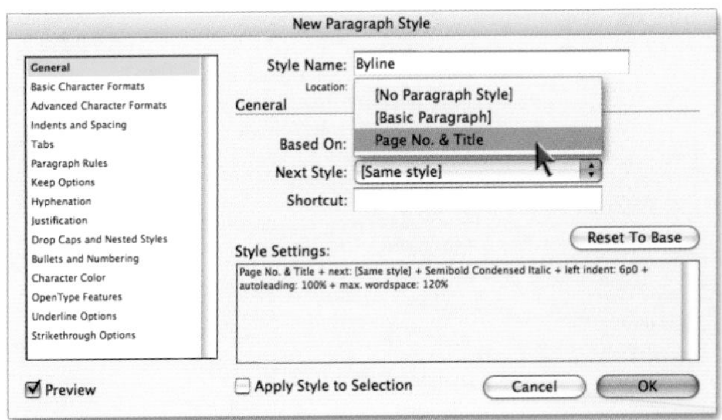

Figure 8-9.

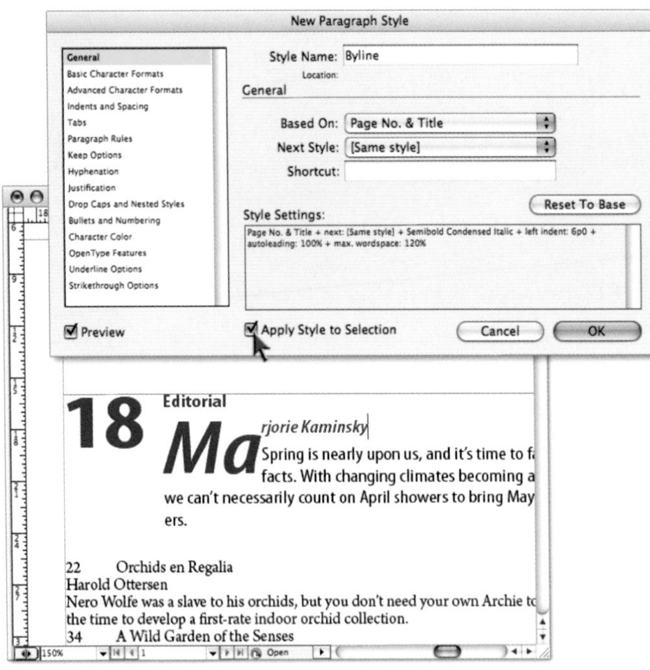

Figure 8-10.

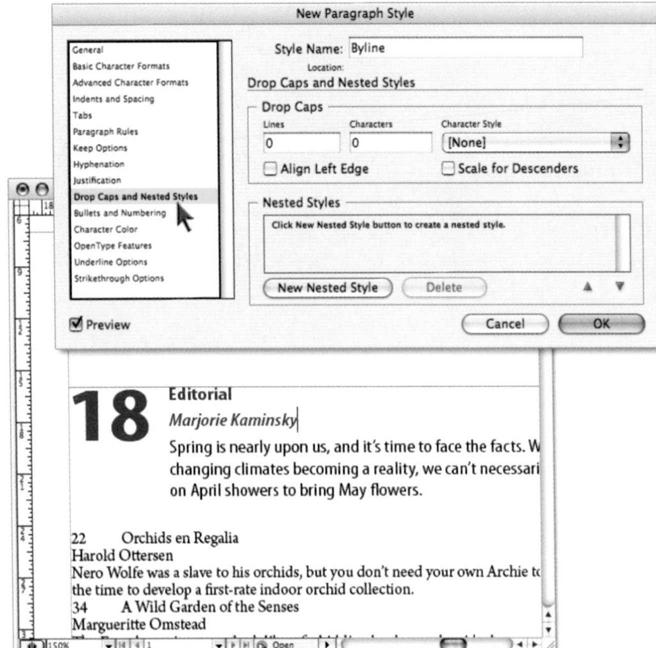

Figure 8-11.

13. *Apply the style and click OK.* This time, don't worry about assigning a keyboard shortcut. But I would like you to turn on an option that was dimmed the last time we saw this dialog box, **Apply Style to Selection**, which applies the style to the active paragraph. Assuming that the Preview check box is on, you'll see that the child style has inherited some unwanted traits from its parent, leaving us with a hybrid mutant that combines the font and type style from the original byline text with the color and drop caps of the paragraph above it (see Figure 8-10). Nothing to do but roll up our sleeves and set things right.

14. *Kill the drop caps.* Click **Drop Caps and Nested Styles** in the list on the left side of the dialog box. Set the **Lines** value to 0 and press Tab. InDesign automatically changes both values to 0 and cancels the drop cap effect, as in Figure 8-11.

15. *Restore the character color to black.* Select **Character Color**, which is a couple of items down in the left-hand list. Scroll to the top of the color list and click the swatch labeled [**Black**]. Now that the proper formatting has been restored, click the **OK** button to accept the results.

16. *Create a style sheet for the description.* The third paragraph of each TOC entry features a description of the article. As before, use the ↓ key to move the blinking insertion marker down one line and Alt-click (or Option-click) the icon at the bottom of the **Paragraph Styles** palette to open the **New Paragraph Style** dialog box. Name the style sheet "Description." Then change the **Based On** setting to **Byline**. The new style is similar enough to Byline that Based On won't create any problems.

17. *Set the Next Style to Page No. & Title.* The Next Style option allows you to choose a style sheet that automatically becomes active when you begin a new paragraph. For example, when creating a newspaper article, you could set the Body Copy style to follow the Headline style. That way, pressing Enter or Return after typing a headline

would not only drop the insertion marker to the next line but also switch to the Body Copy style. Better still, the Next Style option lets you format multiple paragraphs with a single command, as you'll experience firsthand in just a few steps.

In the TOC, the article description is followed by a new page number and title. So choose **Page No. & Title** from the **Next Style** pop-up menu, as it is in Figure 8-12.

18. *Assign the style and click OK.* Before you close the dialog box, confirm that the **Apply Style to Selection** check box is active; thanks to Step 13, it should be on by default. (Note that this check box appears only inside the General panel.) Then click **OK** to create your third style sheet.

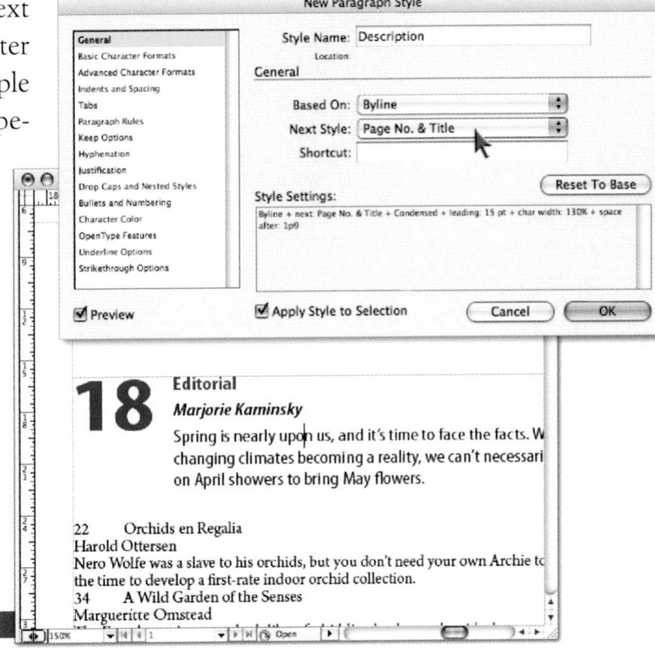

Figure 8-12.

EXTRA CREDIT

Congratulations. You have created and applied three style sheets in InDesign, as well as established relationships between them. Frankly, that last part makes you more adept at using style sheets than most working designers. Now I want to show you how the Next Style option can make life a whole lot easier for you when typing new text or formatting existing pages or stories. (Or you can skip this next task and go directly to "Updating a Paragraph Style" on page 327.)

19. *Complete the style loop.* We've established that the style after Description is Page No. & Title. But which styles follow the other styles? To answer that question, do the following:

    - Press Ctrl+Shift+A (⌘-Shift-A) to deselect all the text. This helps us avoid applying style sheets as we edit them.
    - Double-click the **Page No. & Title** item in the Paragraph Styles palette. Set the **Next Style** pop-up menu to **Byline** and click the **OK** button.
    - Next double-click the **Byline** style. Change **Next Style** to **Description** and click **OK**.

    The three styles now reference each other in a continuous, repeating sequence. The result is a closed *style loop.*

20. *Apply the style sheets to the other lines of type.* Now that our style sheets are finalized, let's put them to use:

    - Click with the type tool anywhere in the line of type that contains 22 and *Orchids en Regalia*.

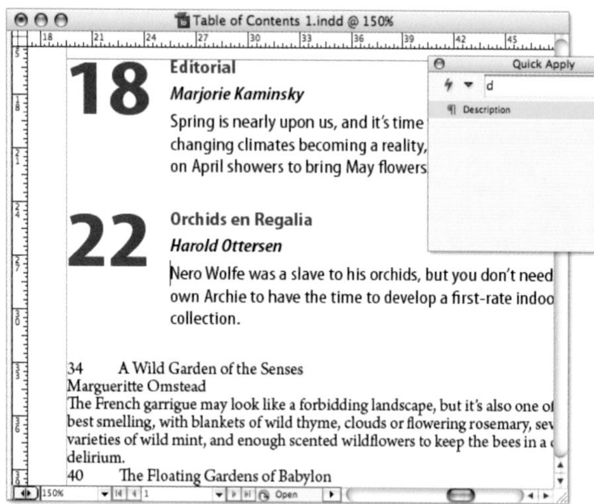

Figure 8-13.

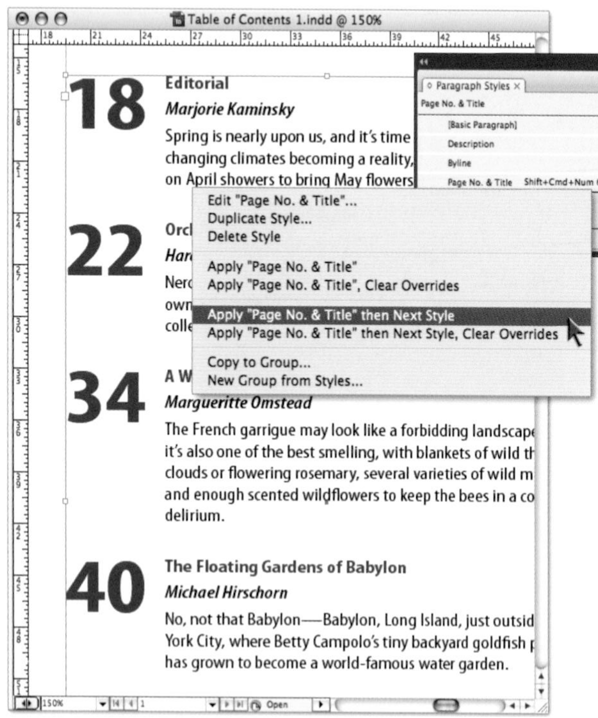

Figure 8-14.

- Press the keyboard shortcut for the Page No. & Title style, Ctrl+Shift+6 on the numeric keypad (⌘-Shift-6 on the Mac). If you weren't able to assign a keystroke back in Step 8, click the Page No. & Title style in the Paragraph Styles palette.

- Press ↓ to move the insertion marker to the next paragraph, which is a byline. We never assigned a keyboard shortcut to the Byline style, so we'll avail ourselves of a different shortcut, *quick apply*. Choose **Edit→Quick Apply** to display a list of styles and menu commands in the top-right corner of the screen. Then click the **Byline** style.

You can also invoke quick apply by clicking the ϟ icon in the Paragraph or control palette. Problem is, you could just as quickly click the Byline style in the Paragraph Styles palette. That's why quick apply includes shortcuts. Press Ctrl+Enter—that's the standard, not keypad, Enter key—(or ⌘-Return) to display the Quick Apply list. Type the first few letters of the desired style name and press Enter or Return.

- Let's give that shortcut a try. Press ↓ yet again. Then press Ctrl+Enter (⌘-Return), type the letter D, and press Enter or Return. The only style that starts with D is Description (see Figure 8-13), so InDesign applies it to the active text.

Note that quick apply remembers the last characters you entered (in our case, D). So you can repeat the application of a style by pressing Ctrl+Enter, Enter (⌘-Return, Return).

---

21. ***Format the rest of the TOC with one command.*** You might think that this is a pretty time-consuming way to save time, and you'd be right. But as you're about to see, the payoff is worth it:

    - Press Ctrl+A (⌘-A) to select all the text in the text block. Or switch to the black arrow tool and click the text frame to select the whole thing.

    - Right-click (or Control-click) the **Page No. & Title** style in the Paragraph Styles palette. Then choose the **Apply "Page No. & Title" then Next Style** command, as in Figure 8-14. With one command, InDesign formats the entire text block. Hard to beat that.

22. ***Add another TOC entry.*** Most magazine editors are organized, but let's assume this one spent too much time smelling the roses and forgot to add an article to the table of contents. We'll add it for him, all the while applying style sheets without ever touching the Paragraph Styles or quick apply palette:

    - With the type tool, click at the end of the TOC text, after the words *water garden*. If the text is already active, press Ctrl+End (or ⌘-End).
    - Press Enter or Return and type "44," the two-digit page number for our next article. It automatically appears in big blue drop caps, subject to the Page No. & Title style.
    - Now press the Tab key and invent an article title such as "Our Gardens, Our Selves."
    - Press the Enter or Return key again and type your name. With each new paragraph, InDesign obediently applies the next style from the loop you completed in Step 19, in this case, Byline.
    - Press Enter or Return once more and add a short description of the article. Make it a few lines long just to prove beyond a shadow of a doubt that the Description style really has taken hold. Figure 8-15 shows what I came up with.

23. ***Save your work.*** Nicely done, you budding style sheet wizard. We will continue working on this document in the next exercise, so choose **File→Save As**, name your document "My formatted TOC.indd," and save it in the *Lesson 08* folder.

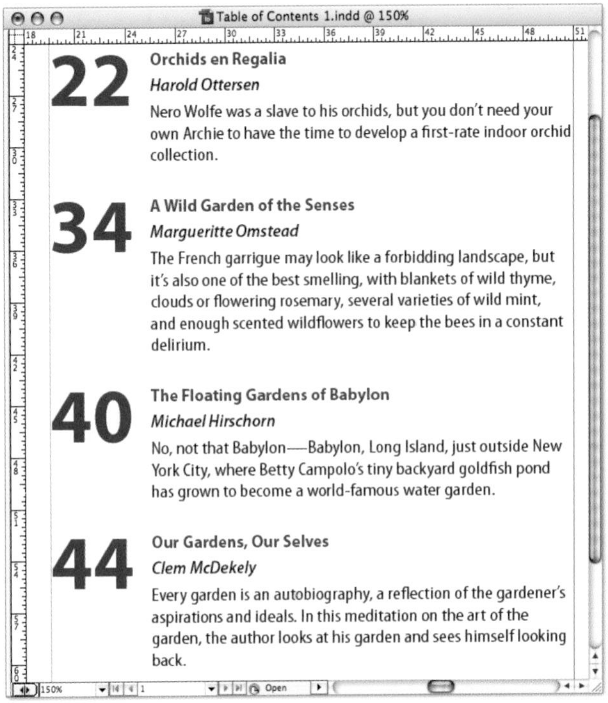

Table of Contents 1.indd @ 150%

22 **Orchids en Regalia**
Harold Ottersen
Nero Wolfe was a slave to his orchids, but you don't need your own Archie to have the time to develop a first-rate indoor orchid collection.

34 **A Wild Garden of the Senses**
Margueritte Omstead
The French garrigue may look like a forbidding landscape, but it's also one of the best smelling, with blankets of wild thyme, clouds or flowering rosemary, several varieties of wild mint, and enough scented wildflowers to keep the bees in a constant delirium.

40 **The Floating Gardens of Babylon**
Michael Hirschorn
No, not that Babylon—Babylon, Long Island, just outside New York City, where Betty Campolo's tiny backyard goldfish pond has grown to become a world-famous water garden.

44 **Our Gardens, Our Selves**
Clem McDekely
Every garden is an autobiography, a reflection of the gardener's aspirations and ideals. In this meditation on the art of the garden, the author looks at his garden and sees himself looking back.

Figure 8-15.

Updating a Paragraph Style

In addition to automating the application of many formatting attributes at a time, style sheets are dynamic. InDesign creates a live link between the style and the text (or frame, in the case of an object style) to which it's applied. So when you make a change to a style sheet, the text updates to match your changes.

In this brief exercise, you'll make a couple of changes to an existing paragraph style and see firsthand how those changes affect your text. You'll also see exactly how changes to a parent style get passed down to the children.

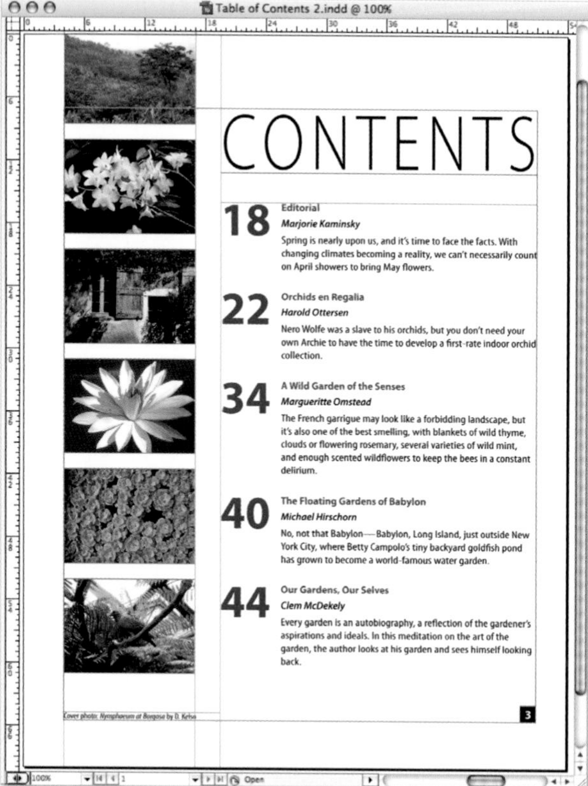

Figure 8-16.

1. ***Open the table of contents document.*** This exercise picks up where the last one left off. If you still have open the *My formatted TOC.indd* file that you saved in the preceding exercise, super. If not, open the file named *Table of Contents 2.indd* in the *Lesson 08* folder inside *Lesson Files-IDcs3 1on1*. You should see the document pictured in Figure 8-16.

2. ***Deselect any active text.*** If you are reading this on the heels of the last section, the insertion marker might still be blinking away at the end of the last line you typed. I don't want you to harm that pristine line of type, so choose **Edit→Deselect All** or press Ctrl+Shift+A (⌘-Shift-A on the Mac) to deselect any and all text.

3. ***Edit the Page No. & Title style sheet.*** I like the basic design, but I'm not all that thrilled with my choice of fonts. For one thing, I used Myriad Condensed for the article descriptions, which meant I had to stretch the letters 130 percent horizontally to make them look standard. For another, three out of five descriptions end in widows. I'd like to switch to a serif font that better fits the design, and thanks to our style linking in the previous exercise—remember the Based On option?—I can do most of the work by changing a single style sheet.

   Double-click the **Page No. & Title** style in the **Paragraph Styles** palette to display the familiar **Paragraph Style Options** dialog box.

4. ***Confirm that Preview is checked.*** When editing a style, it's a good idea to turn on the **Preview** check box so you can observe your changes as you make them.

5. ***Change the typeface.*** Select the **Basic Character Formats** category on the left side of the dialog box or press Ctrl+2 (⌘-2). Then choose **Adobe Garamond** from the **Font Family** pop-up menu. (The font is alphabetized under *G* for *Garamond*.) Alternatively, you can click the words Font Family to highlight the font name, type "gar" to select Garamond Premier Pro, and press the ↓ key to advance to Adobe Garamond Pro. Then press Tab to preview the results in the document window.

   The Byline and Description styles take their cues from their parent and update accordingly, even if they do so with difficulty. Your page should fill with the pink bars that represent InDesign's missing font warnings. Adobe Garamond lacks Semibold and Condensed styles, so the type styles will need to be modified.

6. ***Change the other formatting attributes.*** The reformatted numbers look great, but the titles are too small. To make them larger, tab to the **Size** value and raise it to 14 points. Click **OK** to close the dialog box and apply your changes to the Page No. & Title style and its progeny, thus causing the Byline and Description text to grow so it exceeds the bottom of the page (see Figure 8-17).

7. ***Select all the text in one of the bylines.*** All right, that was one way to update a style sheet. Now let's look at a potentially easier and certainly more intuitive way. Get the type tool and triple-click one of the five names on the TOC page to select it. I happened to select *Harold Ottersen*, but any name will do.

8. ***Change the type style.*** Click the A icon in the control palette to display the character-level formatting attributes. Then change the second pop-up menu from [Semibold Italic] to **Bold Italic**.

9. ***Lean the letters upright a bit.*** I'm not fond of Garamond Italic. It's too narrow, scripty, precious, and just plain fragile. I suggest we rough it up with the help of two subtle adjustments:

   - Click the *T* icon to highlight the skew value and change it to –8 degrees. This leans the letters to the left so that they're more upright. While the letters remain quite obviously italic, the negative skew opens up the letterforms and makes the text more legible (in this reader's opinion, anyway).

   - Click the AV icon to select the tracking value. Then enter 20 to loosen the letter spacing, as in Figure 8-18.

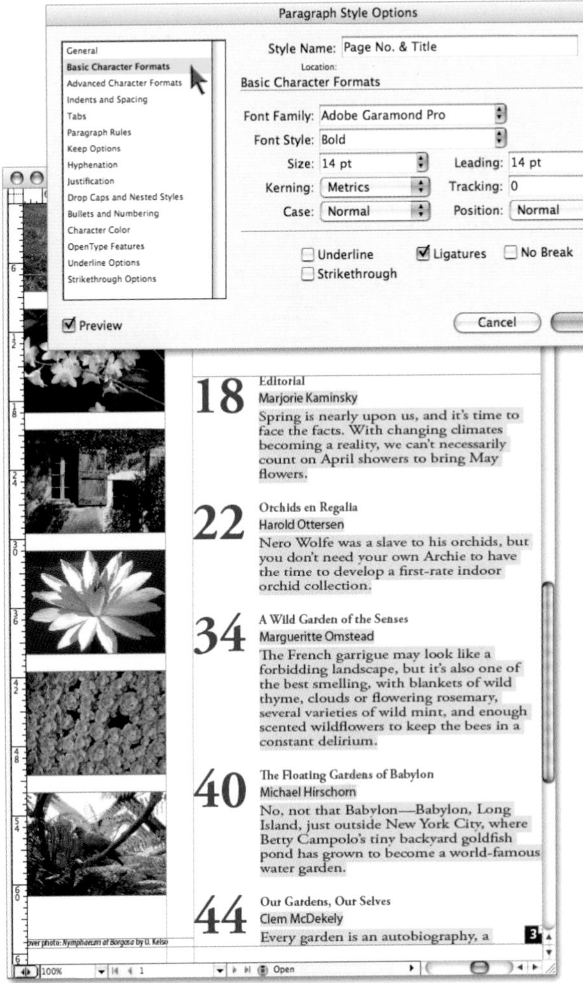

Figure 8-17.

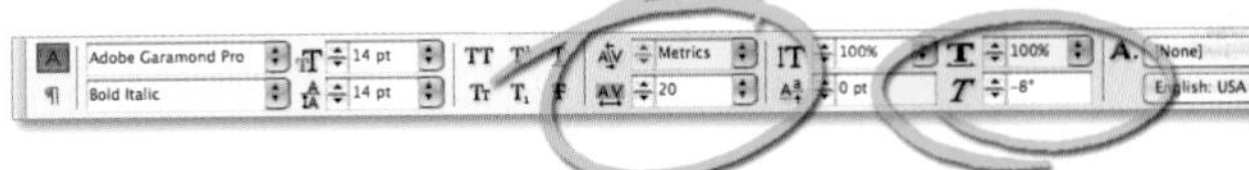

Orchids en Regalia

Harold Ottersen

Nero Wolfe was a
you don't need yo

Figure 8-18.

PEARL OF WISDOM

The Byline style in the Paragraph Styles palette ends in a +, which shows that you made changes to this particular paragraph so it no longer exactly matches the Byline specifications. The active paragraph enjoys what are called *local overrides*. If you were to change the font or type size associated with the Byline style, the selected text would update in kind. But if you changed Byline's type style, skew, or tracking settings, your local overrides would remain in place. We need to fold the overrides into the style sheet, as the next step explains.

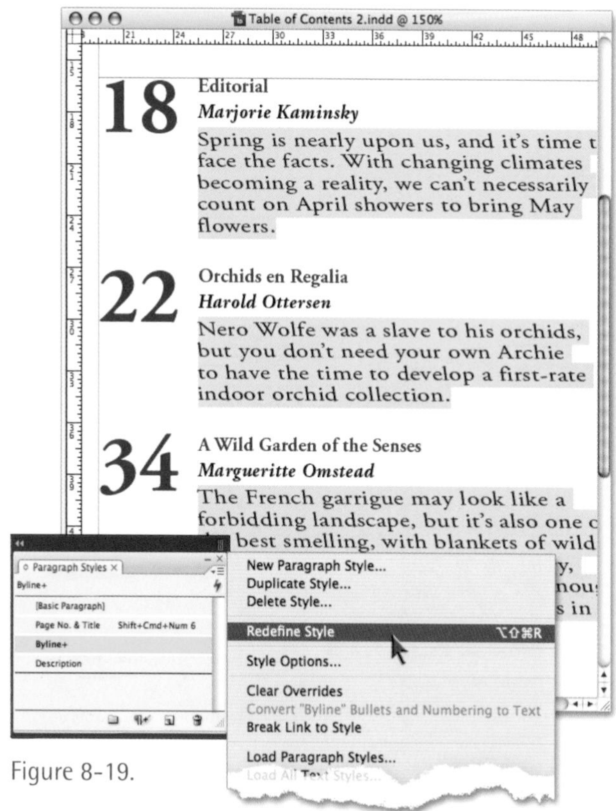

Figure 8-19.

10. ***Redefine the Byline style.*** Click the ▾≡ icon at the top of the **Paragraph Styles** palette and choose the **Redefine Style** command. Or press the keyboard shortcut, Ctrl+Alt+Shift+R (⌘-Option-Shift-R). All paragraphs that use the Byline style update to reflect the new type style. In the Paragraph Styles palette, the + next to Byline disappears. Because the article descriptions are set in a different type style, their style doesn't change. But the skew and tracking do, causing the letters to lean backward as in Figure 8-19.

11. ***Reformat a word in an article description.*** You don't need to select an entire paragraph to update a paragraph style. Try double-clicking any word in a still-pink article descriptions. Then do the following:

    - Choose **Regular** from the type style pop-up menu in the control palette, or press Ctrl+Shift+Y (⌘-Shift-Y).
    - Change the AV and *T* values back to 0.
    - Click the T icon to select the horizontal scale value and change it to 100 percent. Then press Enter or Return to apply the style.

All this causes the Description style in the Paragraph Styles palette to get a +. You can see a list of local overrides just by hovering your cursor over the style name. If you wanted to delete all local overrides and return the selected text to the style sheet specifications, you'd Alt-click (or Option-click) the style name or click the ¶+ icon at the bottom of the Paragraph Styles palette. If you hold down the Ctrl (or ⌘) key while clicking the icon, InDesign resets the character-level overrides only. Ctrl+Shift-clicking (⌘-Shift-clicking) resets just the paragraph-level overrides.

12. ***Balance the lines.*** To avoid any potential for widows, click the ▾≡ icon in the control palette and choose **Balance Ragged Lines** from the palette menu on the right side of your screen.

13. ***Redefine the Description style.*** With the word still selected, choose **Redefine Style** from the Paragraph Styles palette menu or press Ctrl+Alt+Shift+R (⌘-Option-Shift-R). All article descriptions update to reflect the new formatting attributes, as in Figure 8-20. Your document is finished.

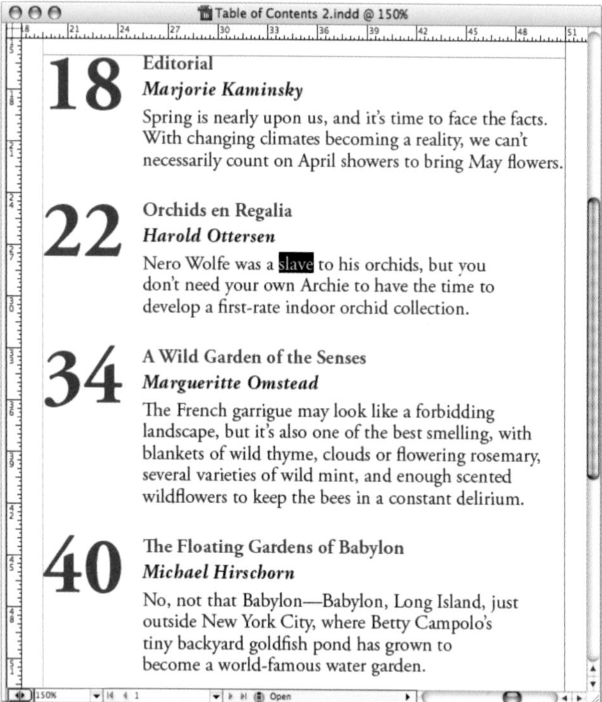

Figure 8-20.

Augmenting Text with Character Styles

Ask a room full of professional designers what they think of style sheets, and they'll tell you that they assign paragraph styles to just about every line of type they create. Formatting a few pages of text is just too tedious and time-consuming without them.

But ask those same designers about character styles, and you'll get a different response. Sure, they use them, just not as much. And with good reason. Paragraph styles permit you to assign dozens of formatting attributes to entire blocks of text—or sequences of blocks—with a single click. Character styles typically convey far fewer attributes and affect only a few words or letters at a time. Simply put, applying character styles takes more effort and produces a smaller effect. (For an exception to this—a Great Big Exception, as it just so happens—see "Employing Nested and Number Styles" on page 336.)

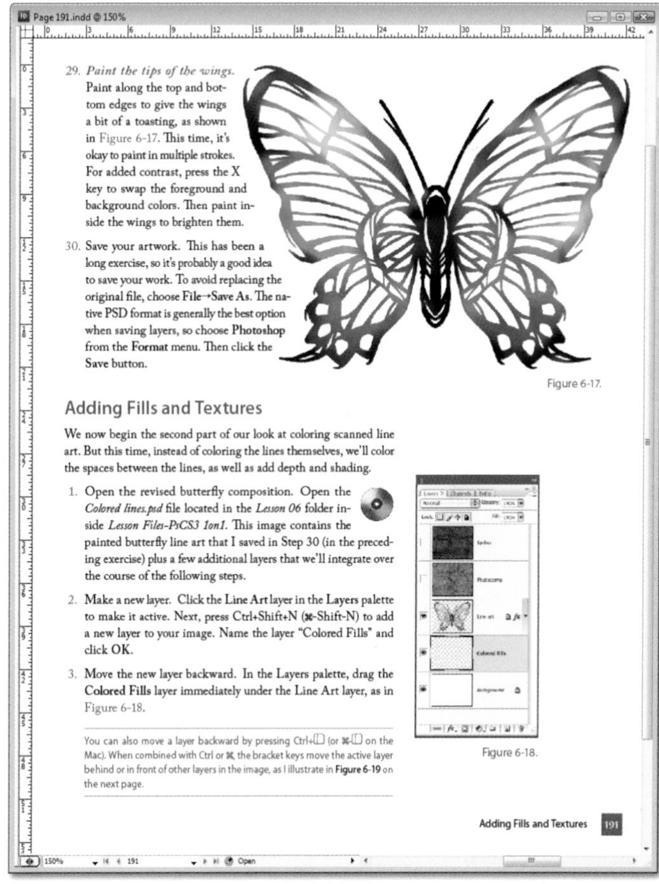
Page 191.indd @ 150%

29. *Paint the tips of the wings.* Paint along the top and bottom edges to give the wings a bit of a toasting, as shown in Figure 6-17. This time, it's okay to paint in multiple strokes. For added contrast, press the X key to swap the foreground and background colors. Then paint inside the wings to brighten them.
30. Save your artwork. This has been a long exercise, so it's probably a good idea to save your work. To avoid replacing the original file, choose **File→Save As**. The native PSD format is generally the best option when saving layers, so choose **Photoshop** from the **Format** menu. Then click the **Save** button.

Figure 6-17.

Adding Fills and Textures

We now begin the second part of our look at coloring scanned line art. But this time, instead of coloring the lines themselves, we'll color the spaces between the lines, as well as add depth and shading.

1. Open the revised butterfly composition. Open the *Colored lines.psd* file located in the *Lesson 06* folder inside *Lesson Files-PsCS3 1on1*. This image contains the painted butterfly line art that I saved in Step 30 (in the preceding exercise) plus a few additional layers that we'll integrate over the course of the following steps.
2. Make a new layer. Click the **Line Art** layer in the **Layers** palette to make it active. Next, press Ctrl+Shift+N (⌘-Shift-N) to add a new layer to your image. Name the layer "Colored Fills" and click **OK**.
3. Move the new layer backward. In the Layers palette, drag the **Colored Fills** layer immediately under the Line Art layer, as in Figure 6-18.

You can also move a layer backward by pressing Ctrl+[(or ⌘-[on the Mac). When combined with Ctrl or ⌘, the bracket keys move the active layer behind or in front of other layers in the image, as I illustrate in **Figure 6-19** on the next page.

Figure 6-18.

Adding Fills and Textures 191

Figure 8-21.

The primary strength of character styles is editability. When you assign a character style—a process made slightly easier if you add your own keyboard shortcut—you tag the styled text. From that point on, changing a character style updates all the tagged text as well. Several pages of underlined words, for example, can be changed to italic in a matter of seconds. In the following steps, we'll create a character style and apply it to several sentences in different paragraphs. Then we'll update an entirely different style and watch the results cascade up and down the page in the blink of an eye. It's the usual style sheet miracle, just on a more microscopic level.

1. *Open the sample document.* This time around, we'll start with the document *Page 191.indd*, which is found in the *Lesson 08* folder inside *Lesson Files-IDcs3 1on1*. Pictured in Figure 8-21, this slightly modified excerpt from my *Adobe Photoshop CS3 One-on-One* comprises a total of eight paragraphs, five of which are styled as steps. The remaining three are styled, respectively, as a headline, introductory body text, and a tip. Feel free to inspect these styles from the Paragraph Styles palette, as explained in the previous exercise.

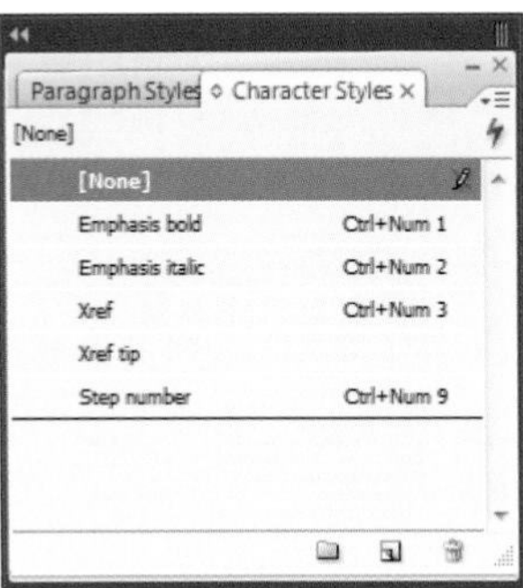

Figure 8-22.

2. ***Open the Character Styles palette.*** Assuming the Paragraph Styles palette is open, you can switch to the Character Styles palette by clicking the **Character Styles** tab. Alternatively you can choose **Type→Character Styles** or press Shift+F11. InDesign displays the palette pictured in Figure 8-22, which contains five character styles that I've defined for you in advance. Diagrammed in Figure 8-23, these styles control the appearance of individual words, such as vocabulary terms and option names. Most of the style sheets are simple, applying a bold or an italic variation. But by relying on a character style instead of a type style, I make it possible to modify the formatting attributes of multiple words at a time, something you'll do in just a few moments.

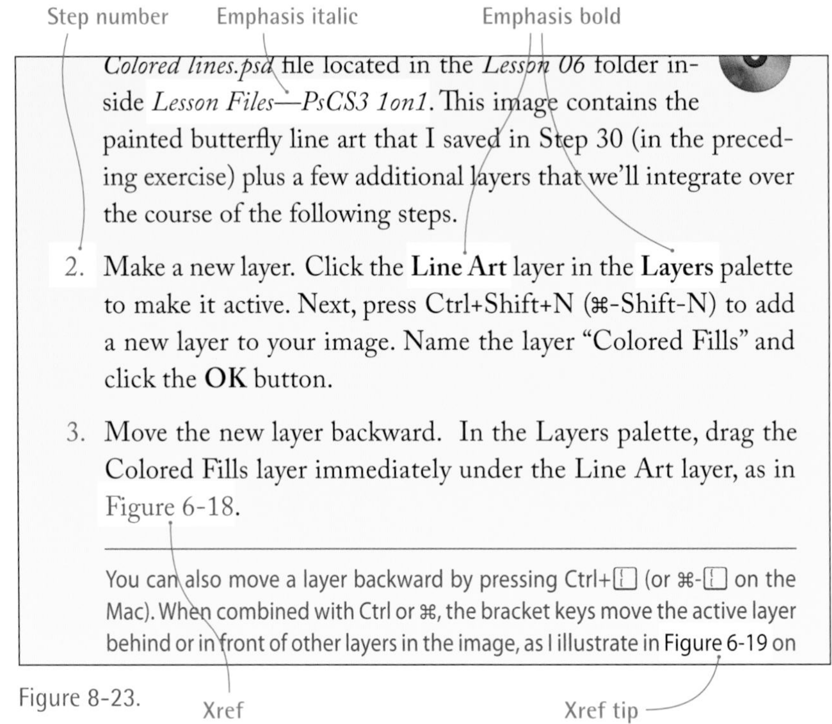

Figure 8-23.

But first, let's create a style. Among the many specially formatted strings of characters in the figure, you may notice that one—the first sentence of the first paragraph—goes unlabeled. This text is not yet tagged with a character style. Nor, it so happens, do you find its style repeated in subsequent steps. We'll remedy both omissions in the next steps.

3. ***Select the first sentence on the page.*** Start by selecting the characters on which you intend to base your style—in this case, the

turquoise sentence. Among its many selection shortcuts, InDesign lacks a keystroke that selects an entire sentence. Instead, you must select the type tool and use one of the following methods:

- Double-click the first word, *Paint*; on the second click, drag to the end of the sentence, into the butterfly, so that you include the period and the en space.
- Click in front of the *P* in *Paint*. Then press Ctrl+Shift+→ (or ⌘-Shift-→) seven times in a row, once for each word plus the punctuation and the en space after it.
- Click in front of the word *Paint*, and then hold down the Shift key and click just before the *P* that begins the next line.
- Don't cotton to such fancy tricks? Select the sentence the old-fashioned way by dragging from one end of the sentence to the other.

However you decide to approach it, your selection should appear as it does in Figure 8-24.

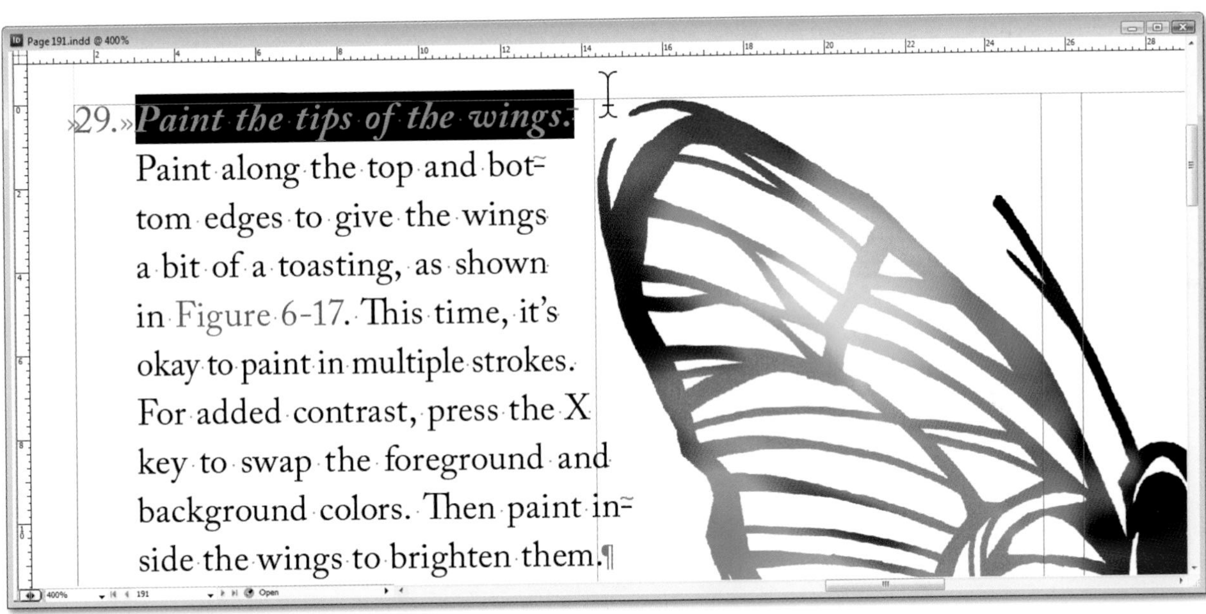

Figure 8-24.

4. *Create a new character style.* Choose **New Character Style** from the **Character Styles** palette menu. Or press the Alt key (Option on the Mac) and click the icon at the bottom of the palette. InDesign displays the **New Character Style** dialog box, which lists all special formatting attributes applied to the highlighted text, most importantly *Bold Italic + size: 11pt + color: Autumn Brown*.

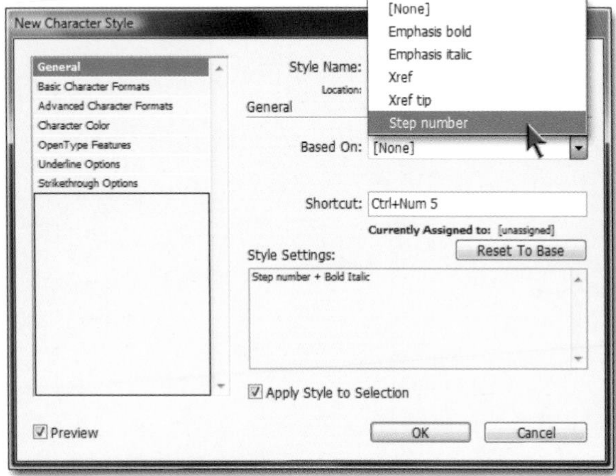

Figure 8-25.

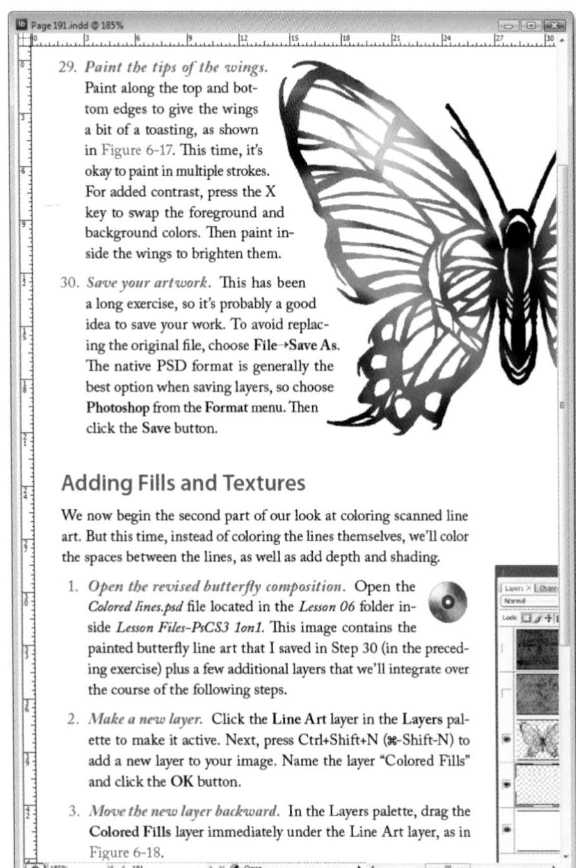

29. *Paint the tips of the wings.* Paint along the top and bottom edges to give the wings a bit of a toasting, as shown in Figure 6-17. This time, it's okay to paint in multiple strokes. For added contrast, press the X key to swap the foreground and background colors. Then paint inside the wings to brighten them.

30. *Save your artwork.* This has been a long exercise, so it's probably a good idea to save your work. To avoid replacing the original file, choose **File→Save As**. The native PSD format is generally the best option when saving layers, so choose **Photoshop** from the **Format** menu. Then click the **Save** button.

Adding Fills and Textures

We now begin the second part of our look at coloring scanned line art. But this time, instead of coloring the lines themselves, we'll color the spaces between the lines, as well as add depth and shading.

1. *Open the revised butterfly composition.* Open the *Colored lines.psd* file located in the *Lesson 06* folder inside *Lesson Files-PsCS3 1on1*. This image contains the painted butterfly line art that I saved in Step 30 (in the preceding exercise) plus a few additional layers that we'll integrate over the course of the following steps.

2. *Make a new layer.* Click the **Line Art** layer in the **Layers** palette to make it active. Next, press Ctrl+Shift+N (⌘-Shift-N) to add a new layer to your image. Name the layer "Colored Fills" and click the **OK** button.

3. *Move the new layer backward.* In the Layers palette, drag the **Colored Fills** layer immediately under the Line Art layer, as in Figure 6-18.

Figure 8-26.

5. *Name the style and give it a shortcut.* Change the **Style Name** to "Step Leader." Then Tab to the **Shortcut** option and press Ctrl (or ⌘) and 5 on the numeric keypad. The Shortcut option reads *Ctrl+Num 5* (or *Cmd+Num 5*).

   Remember, if InDesign beeps or ignores you when you try to enter a shortcut, tap the Num Lock key and try again. As I mentioned earlier, not all keyboards have keypads; if yours does not, don't worry about the shortcut.

PEARL OF WISDOM

Style shortcuts are a matter of taste. But for my part, I keep my character style shortcuts simple—just Ctrl or ⌘ and a number—and add other modifier keys to the paragraph styles. In this document, for example, Ctrl+Alt+1 applies the essential Headline paragraph style; the simpler shortcut Ctrl+1 applies the discretionary Emphasis Bold character style. If this sounds counterintuitive, consider this: I apply my paragraph styles in big swaths, to many paragraphs at a time. Character styles are finishing effects, so I apply them to small sequences of letters at a time. Because I spend more time applying character styles, they get the quicker shortcuts. You should design your shortcuts to suit your work habits.

6. *Select a Based On style.* Set the **Based On** option to **Step Number**, as shown above in Figure 8-25. This establishes a parent-child relationship between the two style sheets and changes the Style Settings info to *Step Number + Bold Italic*. Now any change made to the parent, Step Number, will affect the shared attributes of the child, Step Leader. I'll show you how this works in Step 10.

7. *Apply the new style sheet to the text.* Confirm that the **Apply Style to Selection** check box is on to link the first sentence to the style. As always, this ensures that any changes made to the style will affect the highlighted text in kind. Then click **OK** to make the new character style.

8. *Apply the character style to the other first sentences.* Select the sentence at the outset of step 30, being sure to select the period and the en space. Then apply the **Step Leader** style sheet, which—depending on your success in Step 5—you may be able to do by pressing Ctrl+5 (⌘-5). Repeat this process for each of the first sentences from steps 1 through 3 in the bottom half of the page. Figure 8-26 shows how the finished styles should look. (Note that I've deselected the text and pressed the W key to hide all guidelines.)

9. ***Deselect the text.*** The remaining step explains how to modify a character style. Unless you want to apply the style as you edit it (which for purposes of this exercise, you don't), you need to first deselect all text. For the sake of variety, here's another way to do that: Press Ctrl (or ⌘) to temporarily access the black arrow tool. Then with the key pressed, click in an empty portion of the document window.

10. ***Edit the Step Number style.*** Now let's say you show your design to a client, and the client is me. I love it except for one thing—I want the number and the lead-in text to match the rest of the colored items on the page. Every lesson has an overarching color, and where the lesson you're editing and the lesson you're reading are concerned, that color is blue. The nice thing is, you can change brown to blue in one operation.

    - Double-click the recently established parent style **Step Number** in the **Character Styles** palette. This displays the **Character Style Options** dialog box.
    - If it's not selected, turn on the **Preview** check box so you can see the effects of your changes.
    - Click the **Character Color** item on the left side of the dialog box. InDesign displays a panel of options that assign color attributes to the active style.
    - Click the fill icon in the center portion of the dialog box so that it looks like ■.
    - The right side of the dialog box features a short list of colors that I created in the Swatches palette. (To learn how to create your own, see the "Fill, Stroke, Color, and Gradient" exercise, which begins on page 190 in Lesson 5.) Click the officiously named **Pantone DS 203-1C** to apply it.
    - Click the **OK** button to accept your changes and exit the dialog box.

    Because color is a shared attribute of Step Number and its progeny Step Leader, both the numbers and the bold, italic sentences change to a medium navy blue. All other attributes remain unchanged. Likewise unchanged are all words that are tagged with style sheets that are not children of Step Number. Figure 8-28 shows the result.

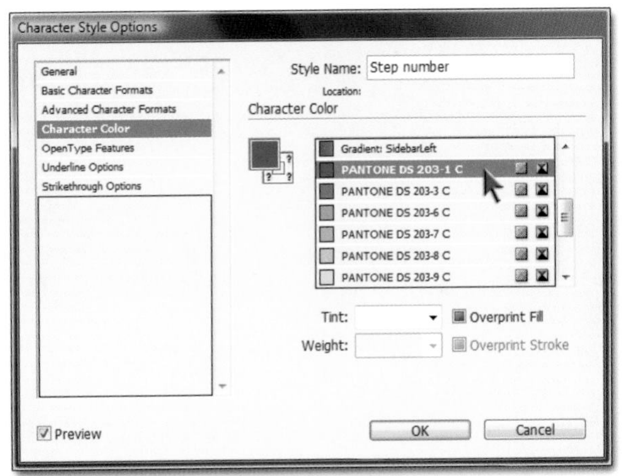

Figure 8-27.

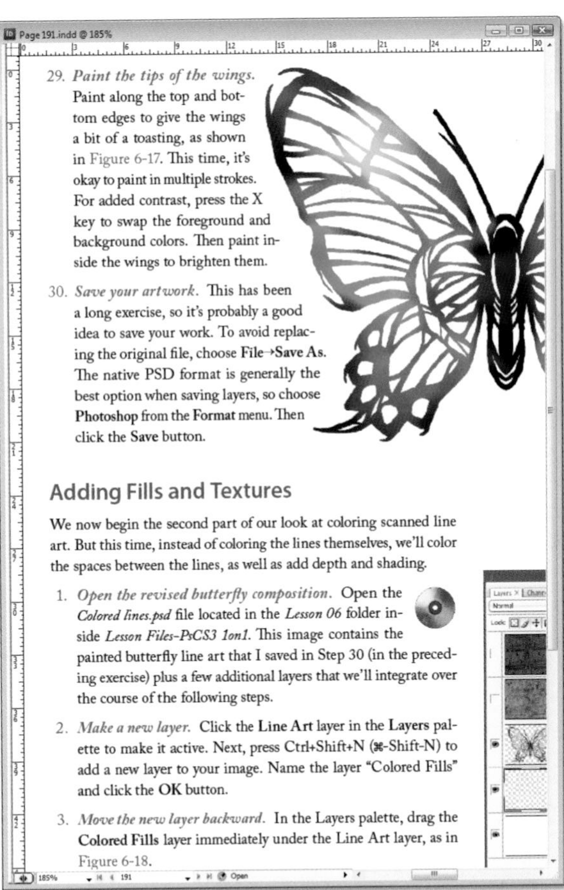

29. *Paint the tips of the wings.* Paint along the top and bottom edges to give the wings a bit of a toasting, as shown in Figure 6-17. This time, it's okay to paint in multiple strokes. For added contrast, press the X key to swap the foreground and background colors. Then paint inside the wings to brighten them.

30. *Save your artwork.* This has been a long exercise, so it's probably a good idea to save your work. To avoid replacing the original file, choose File→Save As. The native PSD format is generally the best option when saving layers, so choose **Photoshop** from the **Format** menu. Then click the **Save** button.

Adding Fills and Textures

We now begin the second part of our look at coloring scanned line art. But this time, instead of coloring the lines themselves, we'll color the spaces between the lines, as well as add depth and shading.

1. *Open the revised butterfly composition.* Open the *Colored lines.psd* file located in the *Lesson 06* folder inside *Lesson Files-PsCS3 1on1*. This image contains the painted butterfly line art that I saved in Step 30 (in the preceding exercise) plus a few additional layers that we'll integrate over the course of the following steps.

2. *Make a new layer.* Click the **Line Art** layer in the **Layers** palette to make it active. Next, press Ctrl+Shift+N (⌘-Shift-N) to add a new layer to your image. Name the layer "Colored Fills" and click the **OK** button.

3. *Move the new layer backward.* In the Layers palette, drag the **Colored Fills** layer immediately under the Line Art layer, as in Figure 6-18.

Figure 8-28.

Employing Nested and Numbered Styles

By now, you've seen how creating and employing styles in InDesign can save you time and reduce repetitive stress, both physical and psychological. In this next exercise, I'm going to show you a couple of recent developments in InDesign that add even more automation to the formatting of recurring text elements.

The first of these beauties is *nested styles*, which allow you to embed character styles into a paragraph style definition, saving you the tedium of applying them to a mere few letters or words at a time. Let's say you find yourself repeating a series of character styles over and over again within a specific kind of styled paragraph. The steps in this book are a perfect example. In each and every case, the number is colored; the leading sentence is colored, bold, and italic; and the second through last sentences are black and Roman (just as in the previous exercise). This is exactly the sort of formatting pattern that nested styles are designed to facilitate. Using spaces, periods, and other delineators, nested styles tell InDesign exactly when to start applying a character style and when to stop.

The second innovation is InDesign CS3's new automatic numbering and bulleting feature. I introduced this feature in the last blue lesson, Lesson 4 (see "Automating Bulleted and Numbered Lists," page 146), but now you'll have a chance to apply it firsthand to a series of starting and stopping steps. On its own, the Bullets and Numbering command makes quick work of managing numbered entries such as lists and even figure captions. But combined with a paragraph style, Bullets and Numbering affords you an unprecedented level of control over what is already a highly automated process.

In this exercise, you'll nest the Step Leader character style inside the Step paragraph style. You'll also apply the Step Number style to a series of automatic step numbers and alternate a list between numbered and inset bulleted entries. Don't be surprised if, by the end of this lesson, your head is spinning with ideas for ways to put nested and numbered styles to work in your own documents.

1. ***Open yet another sample document.*** Open *Pages 194–195.indd* from the *Lesson 08* folder inside *Lesson Files-IDcs3 1on1*. As shown in Figure 8-29 on the facing page, this is another excerpt lifted from the pages of *Adobe Photoshop CS3 One-on-One*, with two important differences: First, the document contains the necessary character styles, Step Number and Step Leader, but I haven't applied them yet.

Second, I've removed all manually typed numbers and bullets to clear room for the automatic ones. I saved the document in the preview mode so we can focus on the text without sifting through the guides and other folderol.

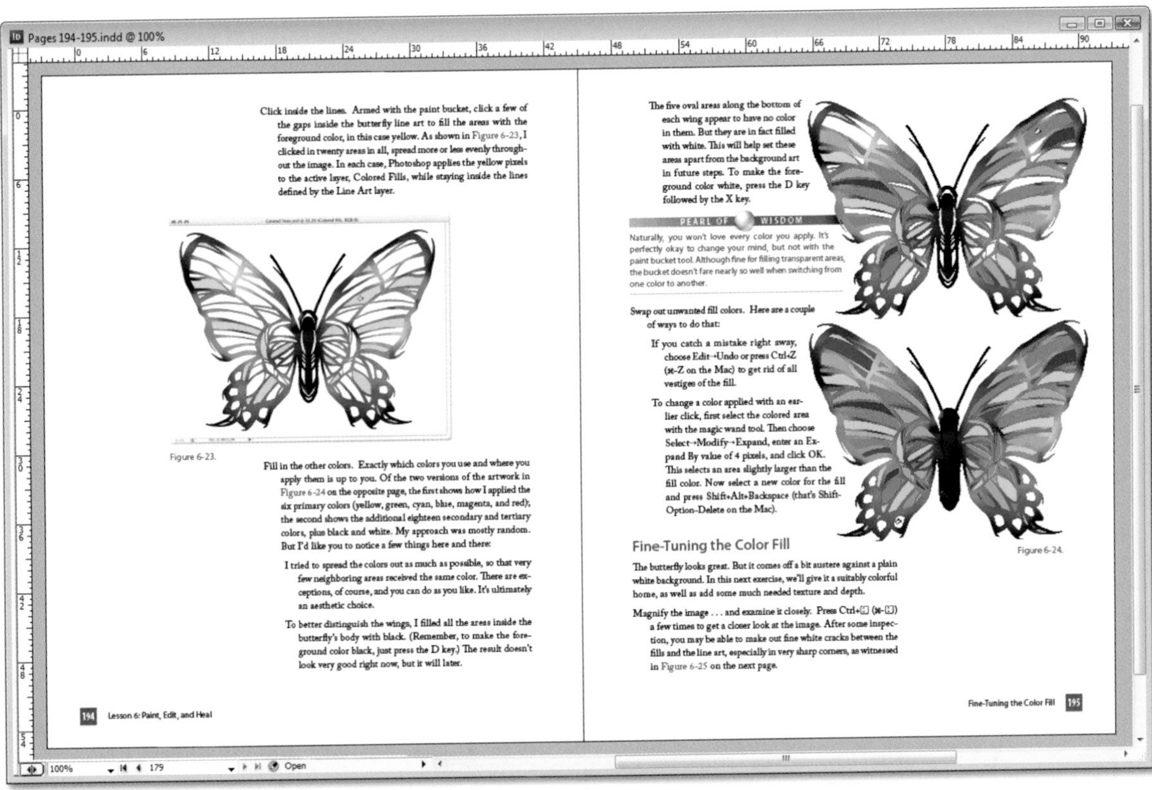

Pages 194-195.indd @ 100%

Click inside the lines. Armed with the paint bucket, click a few of the gaps inside the butterfly line art to fill the areas with the foreground color, in this case yellow. As shown in Figure 6-23, I clicked in twenty areas in all, spread more or less evenly throughout the image. In each case, Photoshop applies the yellow pixels to the active layer, Colored Fills, while staying inside the lines defined by the Line Art layer.

Figure 6-23.

Fill in the other colors. Exactly which colors you use and where you apply them is up to you. Of the two versions of the artwork in Figure 6-24 on the opposite page, the first shows how I applied the six primary colors (yellow, green, cyan, blue, magenta, and red); the second shows the additional eighteen secondary and tertiary colors, plus black and white. My approach was mostly random. But I'd like you to notice a few things here and there:

I tried to spread the colors out as much as possible, so that very few neighboring areas received the same color. There are exceptions, of course, and you can do as you like. It's ultimately an aesthetic choice.

To better distinguish the wings, I filled all the areas inside the butterfly's body with black. (Remember, to make the foreground color black, just press the D key.) The result doesn't look very good right now, but it will later.

194 Lesson 6: Paint, Edit, and Heal

The five oval areas along the bottom of each wing appear to have no color in them. But they are in fact filled with white. This will help set these areas apart from the background art in future steps. To make the foreground color white, press the D key followed by the X key.

PEARL OF WISDOM

Naturally, you won't love every color you apply. It's perfectly okay to change your mind, but not with the paint bucket tool. Although fine for filling transparent areas, the bucket doesn't fare nearly so well when switching from one color to another.

Swap out unwanted fill colors. Here are a couple of ways to do that:

If you catch a mistake right away, choose Edit→Undo or press Ctrl+Z (⌘-Z on the Mac) to get rid of all vestiges of the fill.

To change a color applied with an earlier click, first select the colored area with the magic wand tool. Then choose Select→Modify→Expand, enter an Expand By value of 4 pixels, and click OK. This selects an area slightly larger than the fill color. Now select a new color for the fill and press Shift+Alt+Backspace (that's Shift-Option-Delete on the Mac).

Fine-Tuning the Color Fill

The butterfly looks great. But it comes off a bit austere against a plain white background. In this next exercise, we'll give it a suitably colorful home, as well as add some much needed texture and depth.

Magnify the image . . . and examine it closely. Press Ctrl+⊞ (⌘-⊞) a few times to get a closer look at the image. After some inspection, you may be able to make out fine white cracks between the fills and the line art, especially in very sharp corners, as witnessed in Figure 6-25 on the next page.

Figure 6-24.

Fine-Tuning the Color Fill 195

100% 179 Open

Figure 8-29.

PEARL OF WISDOM

Before we go any further, I'd like you to play a quick visualization game with me. After manually applying the Step Number and Step Leader character styles to page 191 ("Augmenting Text with Character Styles," page 331), you switch to page 194 only to find you have all that work to do over again. And then there's the rest of the book to look forward to—12 lessons in all with roughly 100 steps per lesson. Can you imagine having to apply these character styles 2,400 times (1,200 times each) over the course of a single book-length document? Prior to InDesign, that's what you had to do. I just want you to appreciate how much time you're about to save.

2. *Display the Paragraph Styles palette.* Although nested styles are technically character styles, you apply them within the context of paragraph styles. So click the **Paragraph Styles** tab or press F11 to bring up the **Paragraph Styles** palette. Of the nine styles, we are concerned with just the two applied to the step copy, Step and Step Bullet, as illustrated in Figure 8-30 on the next page.

3. ***Open the Nested Styles options for the Step style sheet.*** We'll start by assigning character styles to the Step style sheet. And to do that, we need to open one of InDesign's most well-hidden collections of options, like so:

   - Double-click the **Step** item in the Paragraph Styles palette to display the **Paragraph Style Options** dialog box.
   - Click **Drop Caps and Nested Styles** on the left side of the dialog box.

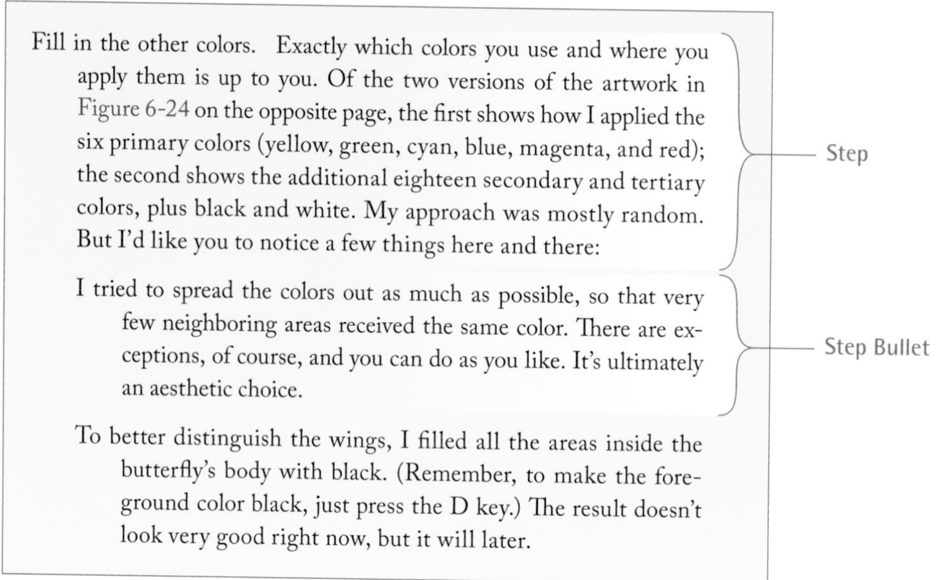

Figure 8-30.

Perhaps InDesign has chosen to couple its nested styles options with drop caps because they both affect the first few characters in a paragraph. Whatever the reason, we'll be giving drop caps the slip and focusing exclusively on the Nested Styles options toward the bottom of the dialog box.

4. ***Add the Step Leader character style.*** The first step is to apply the Step Leader style to the first complete sentence in the paragraph. Here's how you do it:

   - Click the **New Nested Style** button. This adds an entry that reads *[None] through 1 Words*. While hardly grammatical, this strangely worded entry is editable.
   - Click the ☑ arrow (⬍ on the Mac) to the right of [None] and choose **Step Leader** to make it a nested style.
   - The modified entry, *Step Leader through 1 Words*, tells InDesign to apply the Step Leader character style to the first word of each tagged paragraph. (Think of *through* as

being short for *through and including*.) To style the entire sentence, click **Words** to activate this option and then click the ⊡ (or ⊡) arrow and choose **Sentences**, which changes the first full sentence to the Step Leader style.

To preview the effect of this addition in the document window, turn on the **Preview** check box. If Preview is already turned on, press Enter or Return, or click an empty portion of the dialog box. Either action deactivates your choice of character style and invokes the preview.

PEARL OF WISDOM

Choosing the Sentences option ends the character style at a period, question mark, or exclamation point. Happily, a period goes unnoticed within a filename because the Sentences option is smart enough to demand that a space follow the punctuation. But my manual ellipsis creates a problem. We need a more foolproof (i.e., Deke-proof) solution.

After you update the preview in the document window, you'll see strings of blue, bold, italic text all over the document. Of the handful of problems, the most glaring occurs in the final paragraph: Circled in Figure 8-31, the phrase *and examine it closely* is part of the lead-in sentence. In keeping with prevalent journalistic conventions, I expressed the triple-dot ellipsis not as a single character (…) but as a sequence of periods and spaces. While this pleases my editors, it confuses InDesign and cuts the sentence prematurely short.

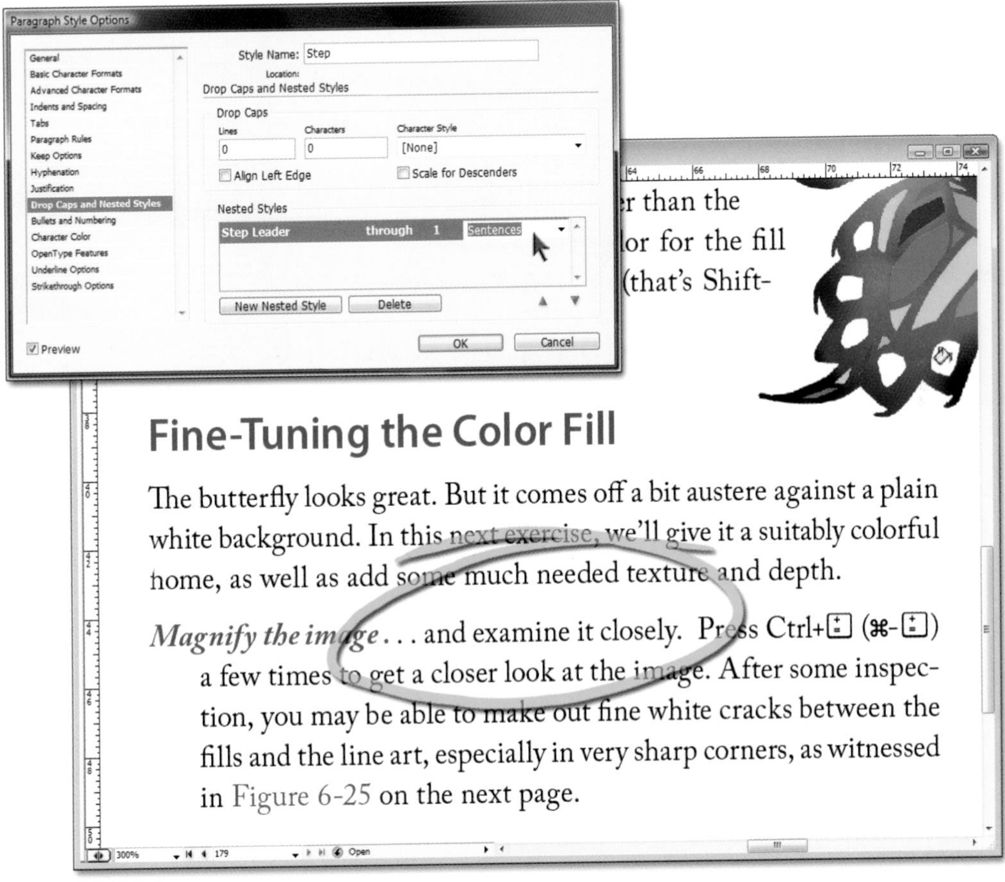

Figure 8-31.

5. *Change the ending point for Step Leader.* I separated the initial sentence from the text that follows with an en space. Fortunately, this is a character that InDesign has chosen to identify:

   - Click the word **Sentences** to activate the option.
   - Click the ⌄ (or ⇕) arrow next to Sentences and choose **En Spaces** from the pop-up menu.
   - Click the word **through**, and then click its ⌄ and choose **up to**. This tells InDesign to apply the character style to everything up to (but not including) the en space.

   Press Enter or Return to see the preview in Figure 8-32. (We still have more to do, however, so stay inside the dialog box.) From now on, InDesign will style the first sentence without regard to punctuation, as I've highlighted with a yellow underline in the figure.

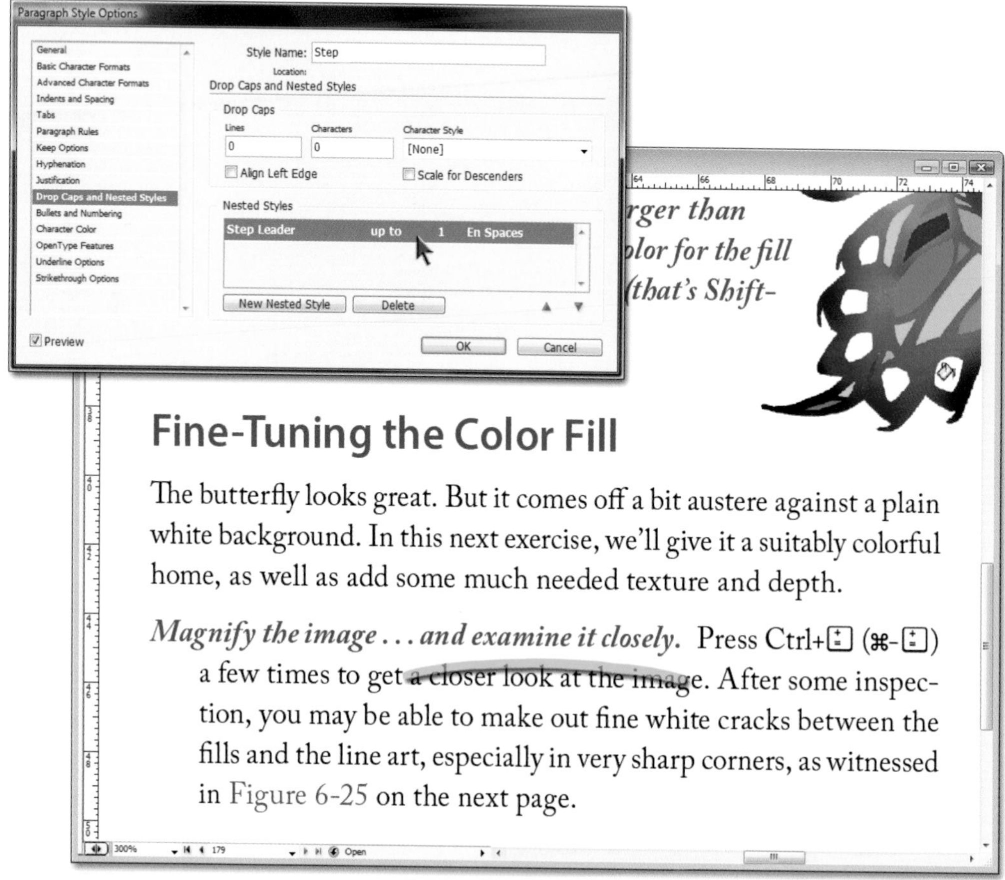

Figure 8-32.

6. ***Add an automatic number to the Step style.*** Having made it about two-thirds through this book—and thus having witnessed several hundred paragraphs formatted like the one you're reading now—you will have noticed that the steps in the *Pages 194–195.indd* document are missing a prime ingredient: enumeration. In InDesign CS3, you can add numbers or bullets as routine elements of a paragraph style. Start by clicking **Bullets and Numbering**, the next item down in the list on the left-hand side of the Paragraph Style Options dialog box. Then do the following:

   - Select **Numbers** from the **List Type** pop-up menu.
   - The **List** option permits you to continue numbering across multiple stories or even from one document to another. For more information about using this option, read the sidebar "Auto-Numbering Elements across Stories" on page 342. For now, leave List set to **[Default]**.
   - Set the **Format** to **1, 2, 3, 4...**, which produces Arabic-style numbers, as opposed to Roman numerals or letters.
   - The **Number** option should read **^#.^t**, which is InDesign's code for a number (^#) followed by a period (.) and a tab character (^t).
   - Leave the **Mode** option set to **Continue from Previous Number** so the number for each paragraph continues from the previous paragraph that's tagged to the Step style.

7. ***Fix the color and placement of the number.*** InDesign has filled our spread with automatically enumerated paragraphs, but we have a few problems. As exhibited in Figure 8-33, one problem is that the numbers are black, but they should be in color. That's where the Step Number character style comes in. We also need to adjust the spacing of the tabs to accommodate either one- or two-digit numbers. Here's how:

   - Set the **Character Style** option to **Step Number**. The numbers become blue.
   - Drop down to the Bullet or Number Position options and set **Alignment** to **Right**. This aligns the right side of the numbers to the left side of

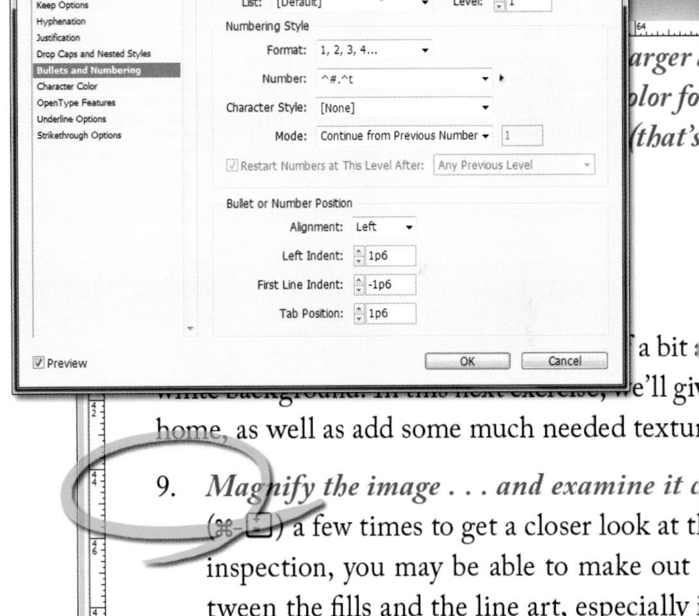

Figure 8-33.

Auto-Numbering Elements Across Stories

InDesign's auto-numbering feature has really changed the way I and my team work on the *One-on-One* books. In the past, I had to manually type each and every step number and my editor Carol was constantly fixing my mistakes. The same was true for the hundreds of captions that appear below the figures. But now that InDesign lets you create a numbered style that keeps accurate count across stories or even documents, steps and figure captions are addressed automatically. We still have to manually reference the figures and page numbers from the main text, but otherwise, numbering is InDesign's job.

If you want to follow along with this sidebar, open up another sample spread from *Adobe Photoshop CS3 One-on-One*, this one titled *Pages 198-199.indd* and found in the usual *Lesson 08* folder. You'll see that the top-left illustration sports one of our old manual figure numbers. Double-click the blue caption below the image to switch to the type tool and place the blinking insertion marker. Then Alt-click (or Option-click) the ⊡ icon at the bottom of the **Paragraph Styles** palette. In the **New Paragraph Style** dialog box, name the style "Figure Number," select **Bullets and Numbering** from the left-hand list, and choose **Numbers** from the **List Type** pop-up menu.

InDesign adds a number to the beginning of the caption in the document window. This isn't what we want at all, so let's switch things out a bit. Below Format, the Number field currently reads *^#.^t*, which is great for steps but bad for captions. Click **Number** to select the text and replace it as follows:

- Type the word "Figure" and then press the spacebar to insert a standard space character.
- Click the ▶ arrow to the right of the Number field and choose **Insert Number Placeholder→Chapter Number**. InDesign adds the code *^H*.
- In my captions, chapter and figure numbers are separated by a hyphen, so press the - key to add one here.
- The last item we'll add is the number that uniquely identifies each figure. Click the ▶ arrow again and choose **Insert Number Placeholder→Current Level**. The Number field now reads *Figure ^H-^#* without the closing period that actually appears at the end of each caption.

Why no period? InDesign requires some sort of manual text to accompany the frame; if the frame contains no text, it gets no numbering. So we'll be entering that one character (.) manually. Thankfully, we need do it only once, as you'll see.

Because we'll be expecting InDesign to track figure numbers from one caption to another—without us resorting to threading the captions, which would be a pain in the neck—we need to establish a list. Go up a couple of options to the **List** pop-up menu and choose **New List** to display a small dialog box. Enter the name "Figures," turn on **Continue Numbers across Stories**, and turn off **Continue Numbers from Previous Document in Book**. This restarts the figure numbering at the beginning of each lesson. When your settings look like those shown below, click **OK** in each of the two dialog boxes to create the new style.

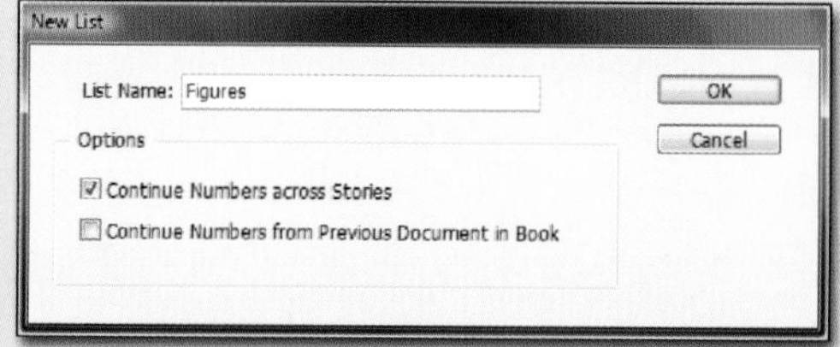

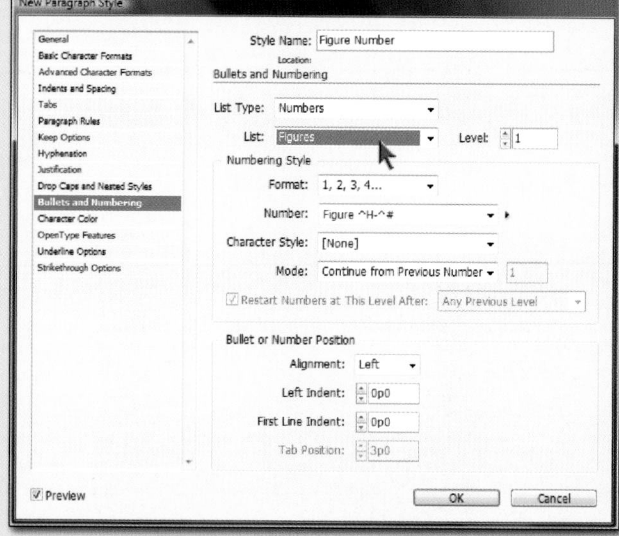

The figure caption now reads *Figure 1-1Figure 6-1*, which is both repetitive and wrong. Here's how to fix it:

- Delete the hand-typed *Figure 6-1*, leaving just the final period as a placeholder. You'll know you got it right if all that's left is *Figure 1-1*.
- To fix the chapter number, choose **Layout→Numbering & Section Options**, set the **Chapter Number** value to 6, and click **OK**.

Now we have a caption worth duplicating. Get the black arrow tool and Alt-drag (or Option-drag) the caption text block to directly below the image in the bottom-left portion of the page. (If you press W, you'll see that I've provided guides to help you with alignment.) The new text updates automatically to read *Figure 6-2*. Duplicate the caption to the spot below the top-right image on page 199 and you get *Figure 6-3*.

The great news is, these numbers will automatically update to reflect other changes. For example, the first image is really Figure 6-30. Double-click in the caption to activate it with the type tool. Then click the ▾☰ icon in the control palette and choose **Bullets and Numbering**. Set the **Mode** option to **Start At**, enter a value of 30, and click **OK**. With no additional effort, all three figure captions update automatically, as I've circled in violet below.

Auto-numbering progresses in the order that frames are added to the page. Moving a text block to the front or back has no effect. So if the numbers get out of order, cut and paste a text block to move it into the last position.

The bad news is, you have to enter all cross-references to the figures manually. I've provided three blue placeholders in the document. To update the placeholders, you will have to manually change the items that read *Figure 6-X*, *Y*, and *Z* to "Figure 6-30," "31," and "32," as I've circled in yellow. That's too bad, but there is a silver lining: Because we have the automatically numbered captions to serve as fact checkers, I rarely referenced a figure by the wrong number.

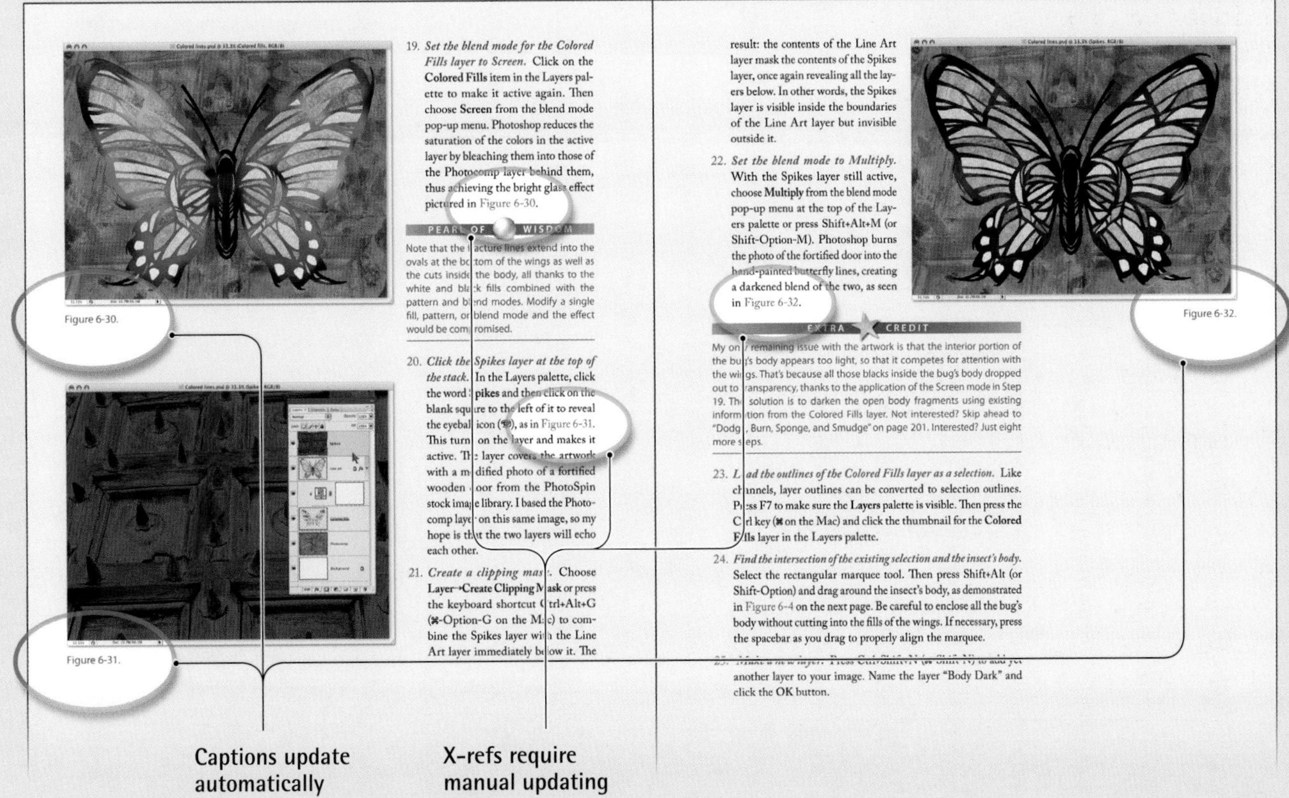

19. *Set the blend mode for the Colored Fills layer to Screen.* Click on the **Colored Fills** item in the Layers palette to make it active again. Then choose **Screen** from the blend mode pop-up menu. Photoshop reduces the saturation of the colors in the active layer by bleaching them into those of the Photocomp layer behind them, thus achieving the bright glass effect pictured in Figure 6-30.

PEARL OF WISDOM

Note that the fracture lines extend into the ovals at the bo tom of the wings as well as the cuts inside the body, all thanks to the white and bla k fills combined with the pattern and blend modes. Modify a single fill, pattern, or blend mode and the effect would be compromised.

20. *Click the Spikes layer at the top of the stack.* In the Layers palette, click the word **Spikes** and then click on the blank square to the left of it to reveal the eyeball icon, as in Figure 6-31. This turns on the layer and makes it active. The layer covers the artwork with a modified photo of a fortified wooden door from the PhotoSpin stock image library. I based the Photocomp layer on this same image, so my hope is that the two layers will echo each other.

21. *Create a clipping mask.* Choose **Layer→Create Clipping Mask** or press the keyboard shortcut Ctrl+Alt+G (⌘-Option-G on the Mac) to combine the Spikes layer with the Line Art layer immediately below it. The result: the contents of the Line Art layer mask the contents of the Spikes layer, once again revealing all the layers below. In other words, the Spikes layer is visible inside the boundaries of the Line Art layer but invisible outside it.

22. *Set the blend mode to Multiply.* With the Spikes layer still active, choose **Multiply** from the blend mode pop-up menu at the top of the Layers palette or press Shift+Alt+M (or Shift-Option-M). Photoshop burns the photo of the fortified door into the hand-painted butterfly lines, creating a darkened blend of the two, as seen in Figure 6-32.

EXTRA CREDIT

My only remaining issue with the artwork is that the interior portion of the bug's body appears too light, so that it competes for attention with the wings. That's because all those blacks inside the bug's body dropped out to transparency, thanks to the application of the Screen mode in Step 19. The solution is to darken the open body fragments using existing information from the Colored Fills layer. Not interested? Skip ahead to "Dodge, Burn, Sponge, and Smudge" on page 201. Interested? Just eight more steps.

23. *Load the outlines of the Colored Fills layer as a selection.* Like channels, layer outlines can be converted to selection outlines. Press F7 to make sure the **Layers** palette is visible. Then press the Ctrl key (⌘ on the Mac) and click the thumbnail for the **Colored Fills** layer in the Layers palette.

24. *Find the intersection of the existing selection and the insect's body.* Select the rectangular marquee tool. Then press Shift+Alt (or Shift-Option) and drag around the insect's body, as demonstrated in Figure 6-4 on the next page. Be careful to enclose all the bug's body without cutting into the fills of the wings. If necessary, press the spacebar as you drag to properly align the marquee.

another layer to your image. Name the layer "Body Dark" and click the **OK** button.

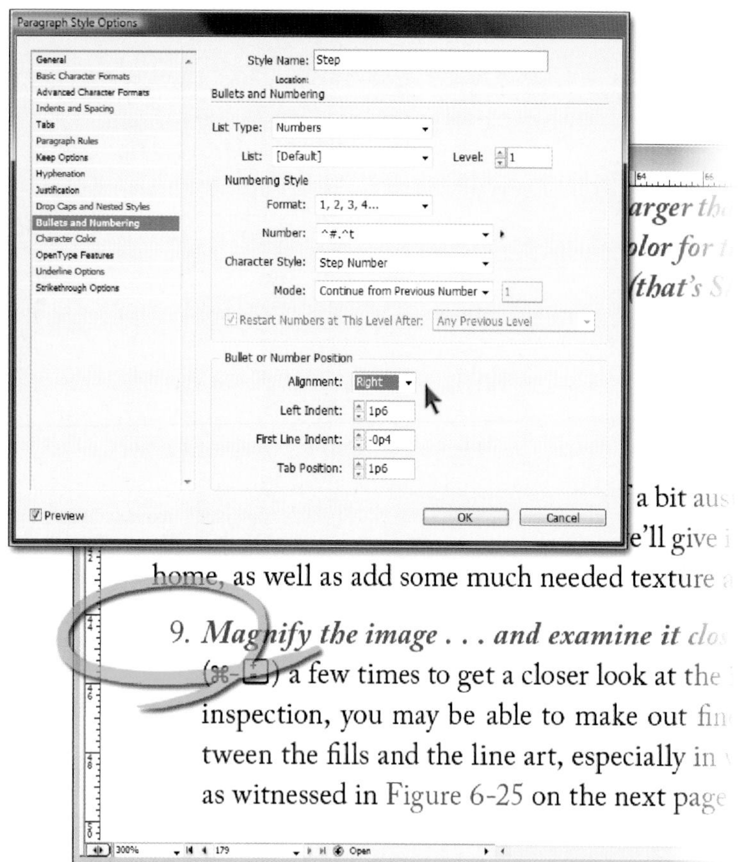

Figure 8-34.

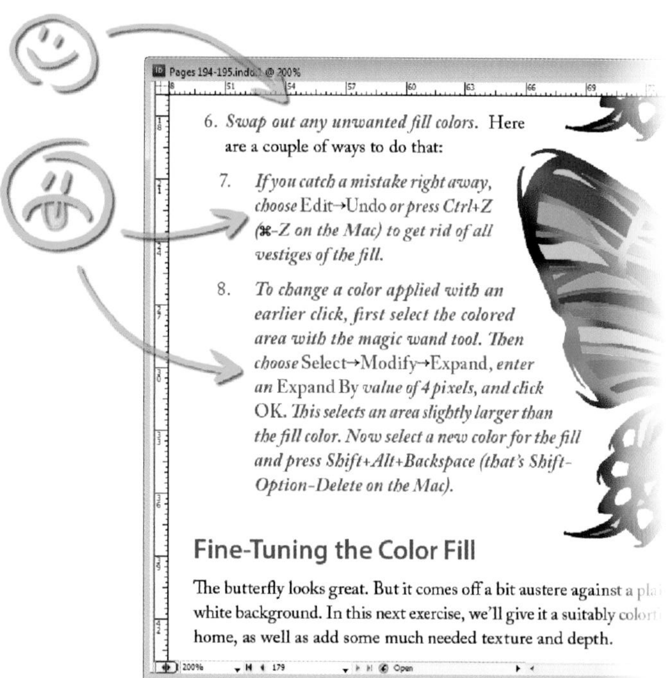

6. *Swap out any unwanted fill colors.* Here are a couple of ways to do that:

7. *If you catch a mistake right away, choose* Edit→Undo *or press Ctrl+Z (⌘-Z on the Mac) to get rid of all vestiges of the fill.*

8. *To change a color applied with an earlier click, first select the colored area with the magic wand tool. Then choose* Select→Modify→Expand, *enter an* Expand By *value of 4 pixels, and click* OK. *This selects an area slightly larger than the fill color. Now select a new color for the fill and press Shift+Alt+Backspace (that's Shift-Option-Delete on the Mac).*

Fine-Tuning the Color Fill

The butterfly looks great. But it comes off a bit austere against a pl white background. In this next exercise, we'll give it a suitably colo home, as well as add some much needed texture and depth.

Figure 8-35.

the first-line indent marker. It's an unusual approach—I don't know of any other way in InDesign to right-align a character to the first-line indent marker—but it works.

- Currently, the First Line Indent value is set to –1p6, which would put the right-aligned numbers outside the text frame. But InDesign doesn't let text fall outside its frame, so the numbers in the document window look the same as they did when they were left-aligned. To change that, tab to the **First Line Indent** value and press the ↑ key several times to incrementally raise the value. (Don't press the ↓ key or InDesign will scold you in a highly irritating fashion.) You'll see the numbers in the document window begin to scoot at around –0p9. The value that I used to format the numerals in this book is –0p4. This gives you 4 points of space between the punctuation after the number and the text to the right of it.
- For a proper hanging indent, the **Left Indent** and **Tab Position** values must be equal. By default, both options are set to 1p6. Leave them that way. (Note that, regardless of the Alignment setting, the Tab value always indicates a left-aligned tab stop.)

Once you arrive at the settings and the document-window preview shown in Figure 8-34, you have my permission to click **OK** and exit the Paragraph Style Options dialog box.

8. ***Delete the nested character style from the Step Bullet style.*** The top-level steps—the ones that are currently numbered 1, 2, 6 and 9—and their nested character styles are looking just as they should. But the substeps—3, 4, 5, 7, and 8—are a mess. As illustrated in Figure 8-35, the substeps are formatted almost entirely in blue, bold, and italic. Steps and substeps are also numbered sequentially, as if steps and substeps are equals, neither of which is the case.

This problem arises because the Step Bullet style that oversees the substeps is a child to the Step style and has therefore adopted its nested character styles and numbers. Solution: Rid the Step Bullet style of its offending blue, bold italics, as follows:

- Still in the Paragraph Styles palette, double-click the **Step Bullet** item to again visit the **Paragraph Style Options** dialog box.
- Click the **Drop Caps and Nested Styles** item in the left-hand list to display the character style that you added in Step 4. We don't want the blue leader style on these substeps, so click the **Step Leader** entry in the **Nested Styles** area and then click the **Delete** button to make it go away.

Just like that, InDesign replaces the blue, bold italic text in the substeps with black, Roman characters, just as we see in Figure 8-36.

9. *Change the list style to Bullets.* I suppose I could have chosen to number my substeps using a series of subordinate Roman numerals or the like, but that degree of formality strikes me as somewhat oppressive. So I chose the less formal route, bullets. They look and work like the following:

- Click **Bullets and Numbering** on the left side of the dialog box to revisit the automatic numbering options.
- Change the **List Type** setting to **Bullets**, which adds bullets to the subsets and resequences the top-level steps.
- The default bullet character, the round and elevated •, is fine for our purposes. Anything fancier would be too much, IMHO. But if you like fancy, or you want to get away from the plain, everyday bullet, feel free to select another character from the Bullet Character list.
- Among the **Bullet or Number Position** options at the bottom of the dialog box, change the **Alignment** setting to **Center** and the **First Line Indent** value to -0p9. This centers each bullet 9 points away from the text to the right of it.

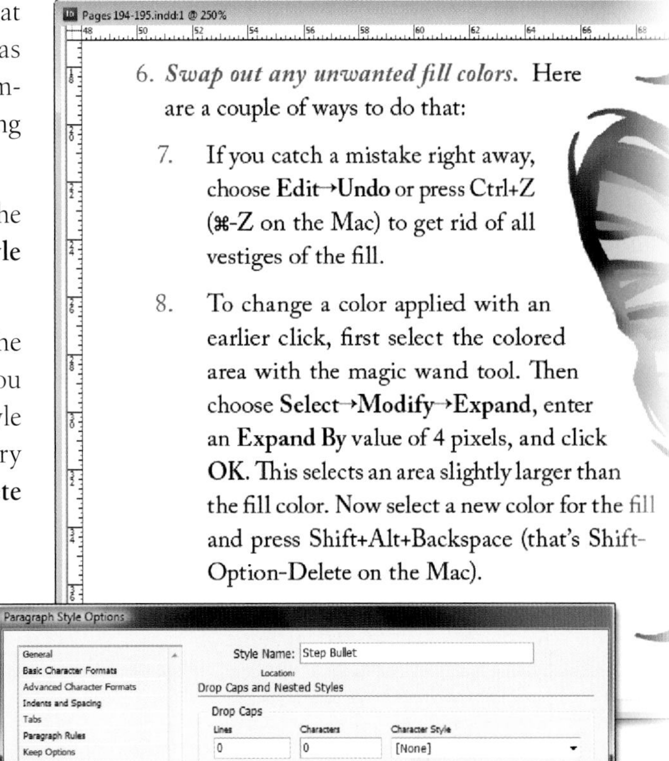

Figure 8-36.

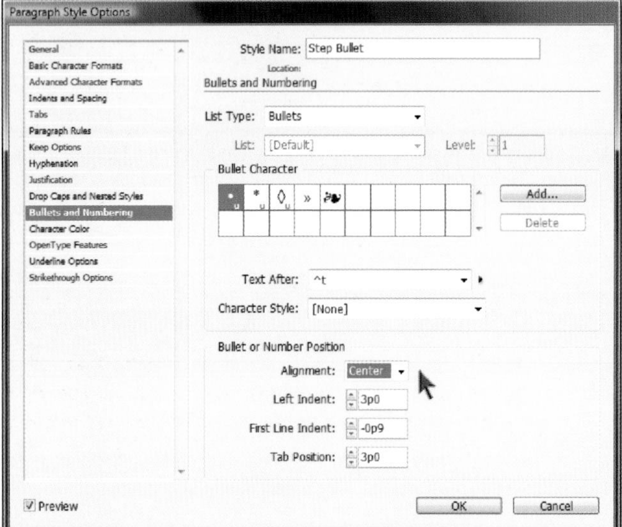

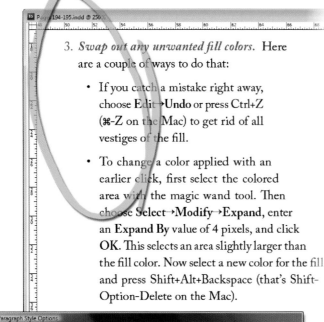

Figure 8-37.

Click the **OK** button. Our Step Bullet style is back in shape. I've circled some bullets and an updated number from a leading top-level step in Figure 8-37.

PEARL OF WISDOM

If you were to take in the entire page spread, you'd see that the numbers now range from 1 to 4, maintaining continuity against several interruptions—including not just substeps but also two figures, a Pearl of Wisdom, and a headline. Such continuity would not be possible without the help of style sheets.

10. ***Begin the first step at 9.*** This document is an excerpt from a large lesson that started much earlier and ended much later than the few steps and substeps we see before us. So it's hardly a surprise that what currently professes itself to be step 1 is actually a later step in the exercise. It is, in fact, step 9. We could address this problem by making a global modification to the paragraph style, but that would mess up future exercises. And it's flat out impossible to select the step number directly and change it from a 1 to a 9. (Like runes projected onto a waterfall, automatic numbers and bullets are inconstant, untouchable phantoms.) This is a job for a local override, as I will describe in these informal, phantasmic bulleted substeps:
    - Double-click somewhere in the first paragraph in the top-left corner of page 194 to switch to the type tool and activate the paragraph for editing.
    - Click the ▾≡ icon on the far right side of the control palette and choose the **Bullets and Numbering** command to display a by-now-familiar set of options.
    - Change the **Mode** option (in the middle of the dialog box) to **Start At**. This kills all natural continuity and puts you in charge of the numbering.

- Select the numerical value to the right of the Mode setting and change it to 9.
- Click the **OK** button to confirm your change.

The first paragraph now bears the single-digit number 9; the last bears the double-digit 12. Regardless of digits, all numbers ascribe to an absolute and, it must be said, *intelligent* authority of aesthetic conformity, to which Figure 8-38 calls testament.

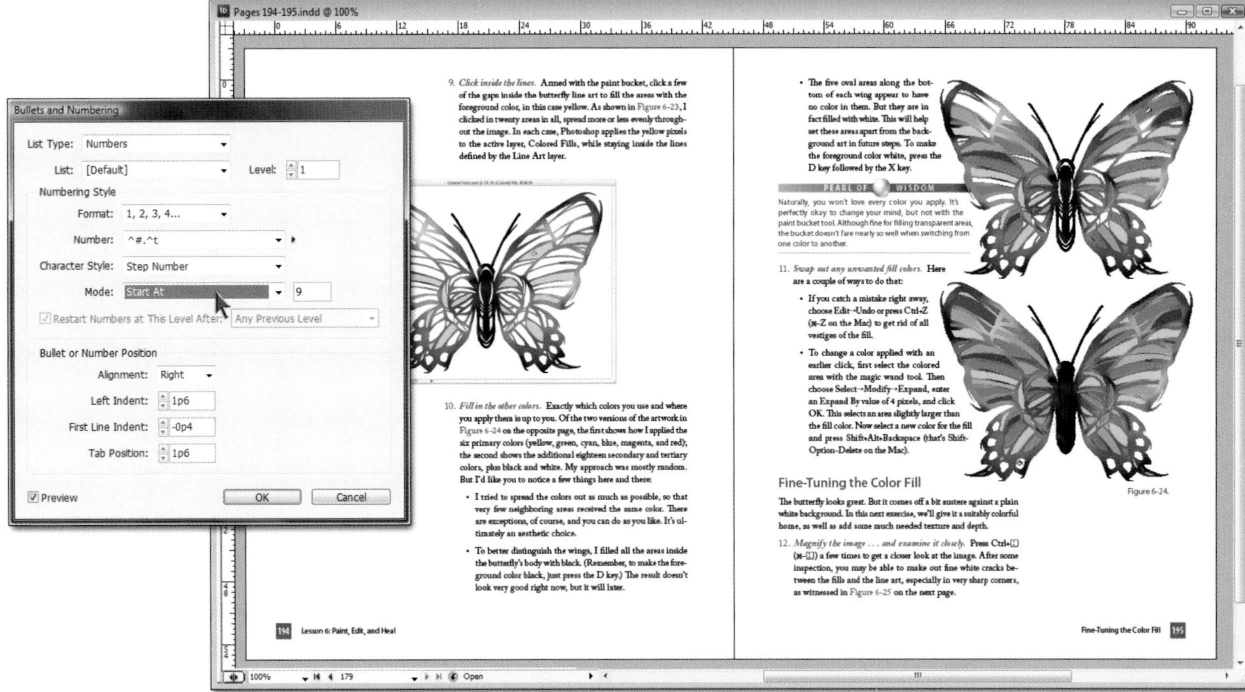

Figure 8-38.

11. ***Set the next exercise to begin at Step 1.*** Just one problem remains: The final paragraph on page 195 represents the beginning of a new exercise, and should therefore be numbered 1. To reset the numbering pattern for this new exercise, click in that final paragraph with the type tool. Then right-click (or Control-click) and choose **Restart Numbering** to begin the list afresh, as illustrated in Figure 8-39 on the next page.

I continue to be amazed by the variety of things you can do with style sheets in InDesign. With the exception of the first few title pages, there isn't a word in this book that isn't tagged to at least one paragraph style, and many are tagged to character styles as well. And while this ends our discussion of character and paragraph styles, we still have table, cell, and object styles to explore in the remaining two exercises.

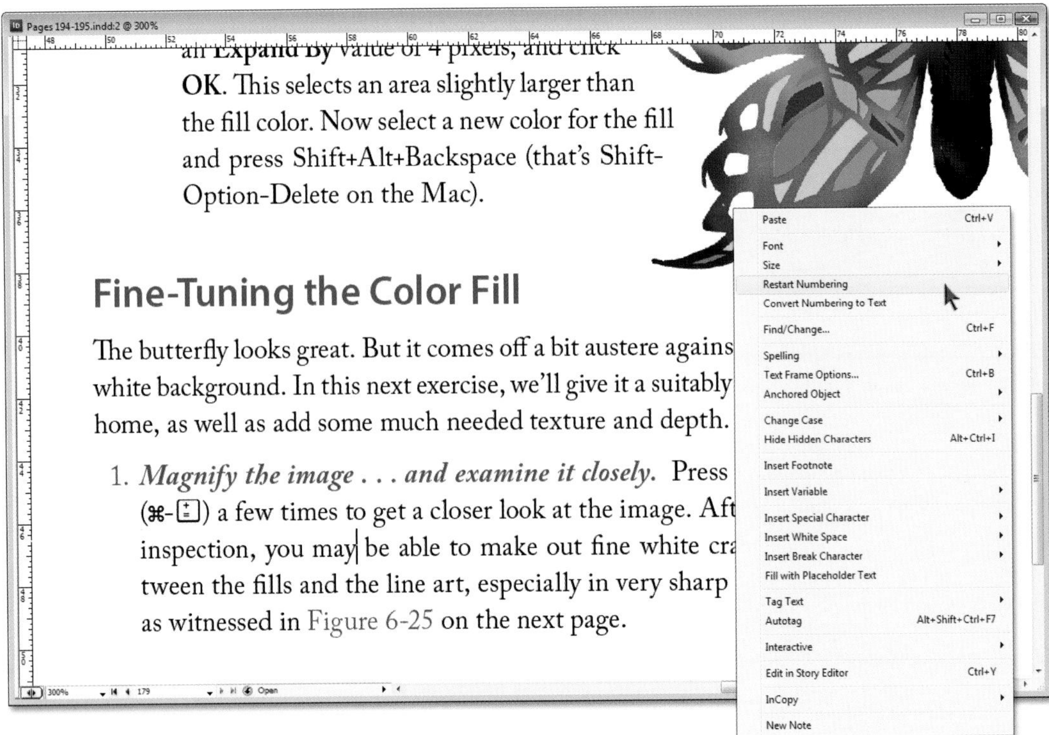

Pages 194-195.indd:2 @ 300%
OK. This selects an area slightly larger than
the fill color. Now select a new color for the fill
and press Shift+Alt+Backspace (that's Shift-
Option-Delete on the Mac).
Fine-Tuning the Color Fill
The butterfly looks great. But it comes off a bit austere agains
white background. In this next exercise, we'll give it a suitably
home, as well as add some much needed texture and depth.
1. Magnify the image . . . and examine it closely. Press
(⌘-[+]) a few times to get a closer look at the image. Aft
inspection, you may be able to make out fine white cra
tween the fills and the line art, especially in very sharp
as witnessed in Figure 6-25 on the next page.
Paste Ctrl+V
Font
Size
Restart Numbering
Convert Numbering to Text
Find/Change... Ctrl+F
Spelling
Text Frame Options... Ctrl+B
Anchored Object
Change Case
Hide Hidden Characters Alt+Ctrl+I
Insert Footnote
Insert Variable
Insert Special Character
Insert White Space
Insert Break Character
Fill with Placeholder Text
Tag Text
Autotag Alt+Shift+Ctrl+F7
Interactive
Edit in Story Editor Ctrl+Y
InCopy
New Note
300%
179
Open

Figure 8-39.

Using Table and Cell Styles

Back in Lesson 4, I showed you how to create a table and make it look spiffy. That process took some effort if you recall. New to InDesign CS3 is the ability to save cell and table styles, which—like the other style sheets we've seen—can save you ages worth of repetitive and tedious work. In this exercise, I'll show you how to use cell and table styles to refine the formatting of one table and transfer that formatting goodness to another table. If you're like me, you'll be flat-out amazed by what you can automate—and what you can't.

1. *Open the file.* Open the file *55-word review.indd* in the *Lesson 08* folder inside *Lesson Files-IDcs3 1on1*. Pictured in the facing page's Figure 8-40, the document features a miniature review of a selection of popular music commissioned by the British radio station, Radio 1. The legal-sized document contains some nice eye candy—all homegrown in InDesign, by the way—but it lacks even the slightest vestige of a table. Let's remedy that.

2. *Turn on the tables layer.* Press F7 to display the **Layers** palette. Then turn on the 👁 for the topmost layer, **Text & Tables**. (Leave the Highlights layer off for now.) As shown in Figure 8-41, the

layer contains a pair of tables that outline the 40 songs on the CDs. (They're all cover tunes. Each artist was assigned a specific year from 1967 to 2006 and allowed to pick a song from that year. Many songs represent Radio 1 landmarks, such as "Flowers in the Rain," which was the first song officially played by the station, and "Teenage Kicks," which was so beloved by DJ John Peel that he famously played it twice in a row and awarded it 28 out of 5 stars.) I've formatted the first table close to the way I want it. The second table, disc two, is a tabbed list. I adjusted the tab stops so I could see what I was doing; otherwise, the formatting is entirely arbitrary.

Where style sheets are concerned, this document contains a handful of paragraph styles but nothing more. In this exercise, we'll be creating cell and table styles and applying them to various elements of the tables.

Figure 8-40.

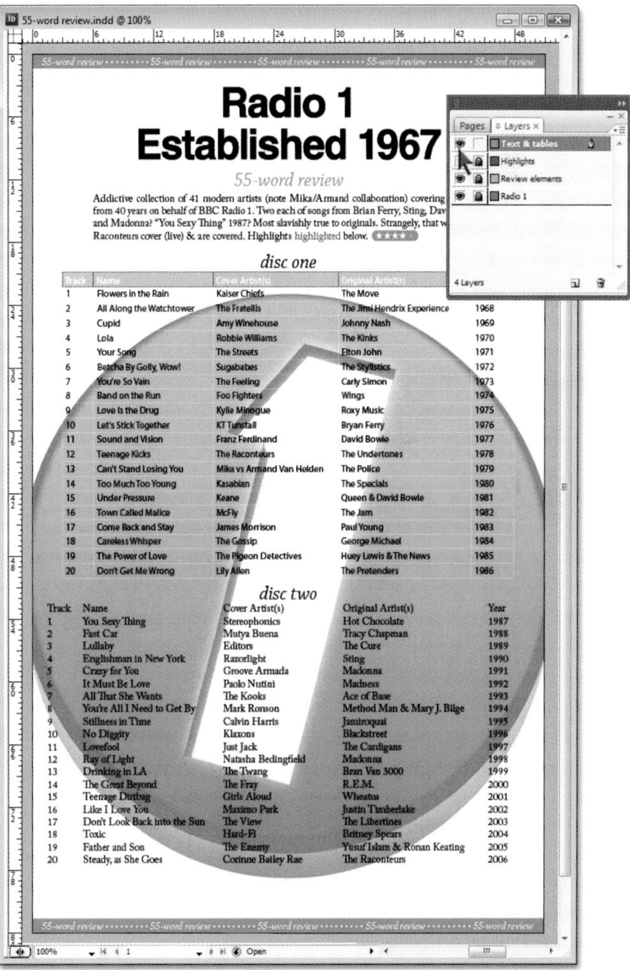

Figure 8-41.

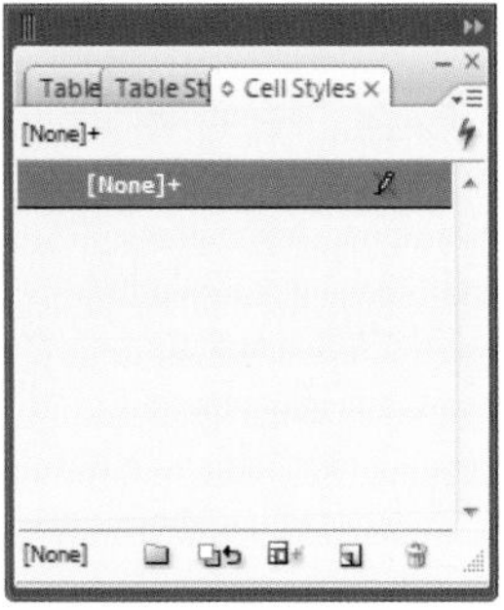

Figure 8-42.

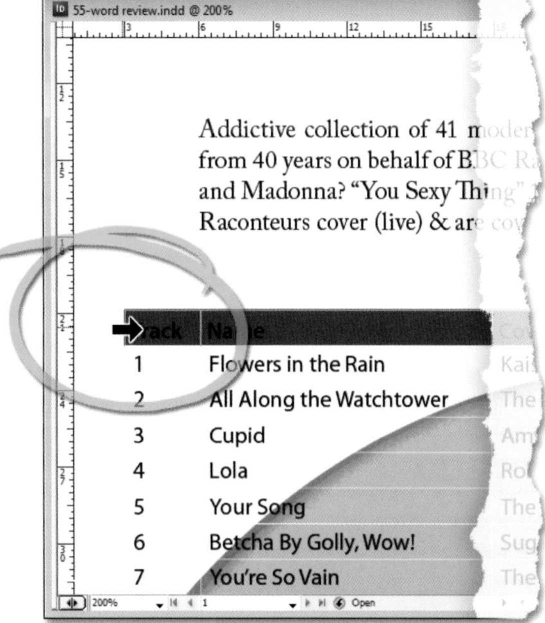

Figure 8-43.

PEARL OF WISDOM

The relationship between cell and table styles is similar to that between character and paragraph styles, with cell styles providing finer control and table styles capable of including nested cell styles. Because of this nested relationship, and the fact that a table style can accomplish little without nested cell styles, it makes the most sense to create a handful of cell styles first and then wrap them up into an overarching table style. Which is precisely what we'll be doing.

3. ***Open the Cell Styles palette.*** There is no shortcut for the **Cell Styles** palette, so you have to choose the laborious **Window→Type & Tables→Cell Styles**. On a positive note, by default, that command offers the bonus arrival of the Table and Table Style palettes (see Figure 8-42), which we'll need as well.

4. ***Select the top row of the built table.*** I've already formatted the header row of the disc one table, so we can lift its formatting attributes to serve as our first cell style. Press the T key to get the type tool, and hover your cursor at the top-left corner of the table, over the *T* in *Track*. When your cursor changes to the thick black ➡, click to select the top row, as I've done in Figure 8-43.

   If you can't get the ➡ to appear reliably—which is unfortunately common given that InDesign requires you to get your cursor inside a zone just 5 pixels wide—click anywhere in the table and choose Table→Select→Header Rows.

5. ***Make a new cell style.*** Press the Alt key (Option on the Mac) and click the ◱ icon at the bottom of the Cell Styles palette to display the **New Cell Style** dialog box, which lists all the formatting attributes applied to the highlighted text. Call your new style "Table Head" typing exactly that into the **Style Name** field.

6. ***Set a paragraph style for the cell style.*** Review the information in the **Style Settings** list and you'll see lots of cell properties, but nothing in the way of character- or paragraph-level formatting attributes. To communicate text formatting, you have to link a paragraph style to the cell. So go to the **Paragraph Style** pop-up and choose **Table Title**, as in Figure 8-44.

7. ***Adjust the insets and alignment.*** At the moment, the header entries appear a little too close to the bottom-left corners of their cells. We can fix that by adjusting some spacing values. Click the **Text** item on the left-hand side of the dialog box to

display a collection of inset and alignment options. Note that because you can't apply a cell style to a table until after you create it, no link exists between the selected header and the active style. There's no advantage to selecting the Preview check box (I don't even know why that darn thing's there), so we'll be working blind. Fortunately, I've already sussed things out, so trust in me and make the following changes, all of which appear in Figure 8-45.

- Click the icon in the **Cell Insets** area to turn it off and unlink the inset values.
- To change the amount of room between a cell entry and the edges of the cell wall, set the **Top** value to 0p0, **Bottom** to 0p1, and **Left** to 0p6. The **Right** value is fine at 0p3.
- On their own, those values would actually have the effect of moving the text down even farther. To center the entries vertically—so the tiny Bottom value has the effect of raising the header entries from their current positions—set the **Align** pop-up menu to **Align Center**.

Now click **OK** to create the style.

For those who may be wondering, "C'mon, there has got to be a way to preview these settings," you're right, there is, but it involves more steps. You'd have to make a new style, click OK, apply the style to the desired cells, and then edit the style with the Preview check box on.

8. *Apply the new style to the header row.* Making a new cell style does not apply that style to the active text. But apply it we should. So Alt-click (or Option-click) on the **Table Head** style in the **Cell Styles** palette. The Alt (or Option) key ensures that InDesign replaces any potential overrides with your modified style settings.

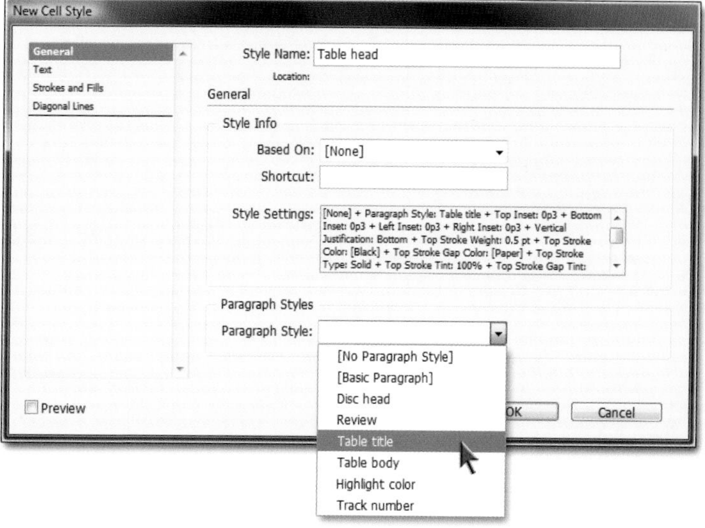

Figure 8-44.

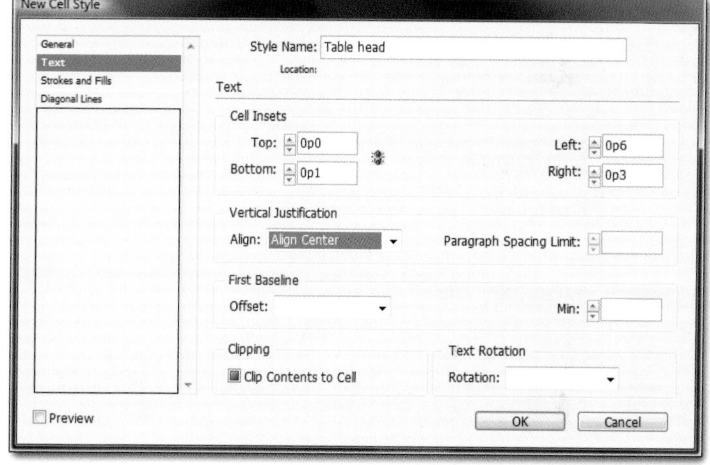

Figure 8-45.

9. *Select the body rows.* Our next cell style is going to be based on the existing body rows. To conveniently select all of them in one operation, choose **Table→Select→Body Rows**.

10. *Create a cell style for the body rows.* Alt-click (or Option-click) the icon at the bottom of the **Cell Styles** palette. To make simple work of the inset and alignment settings, set the **Based On** option to **Table Head**. Then make the following changes:

    - Name the new style "Songs & Artists."
    - Change the **Paragraph Style** option to **Table Body** to ensure that the text in our table remains black.
    - Click the **Text** item in the left-hand list or press Ctrl+2 (⌘-2) to switch panels. Check to make sure the icon is off (it should be) and set the **Right** value to 0p1.
    - As it stands, this style is set to leave the outlines around the cells white (from the current cell formatting) and fill the cell with beige (from the Table Head style), which is the reverse of what I want. Click **Strokes and Fills** or press Ctrl+3 (⌘-3) to avail yourself of the options needed to change these settings.
    - Change the **Color** option in the **Cell Stroke** section to the preset swatch **[Black]**.
    - Then change the **Color** option in the **Cell Fill** area near the bottom of the dialog box to **[None]**, as in Figure 8-46.

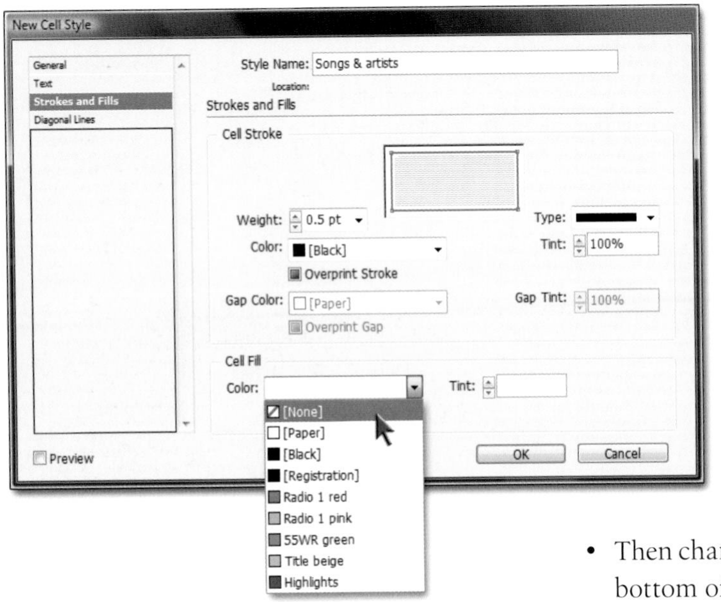

    If you switch back to the General options—Ctrl+1 (⌘-1)—the Style Settings should read *Table Head + Paragraph Style: Table Body + Right Inset: 0p1 + Fill Color: [None]*. Assuming they do, click the **OK** button.

Figure 8-46.

11. *Apply the new style to the body rows.* Press Alt (or Option) and click the **Songs & Artists** item in the **Cell Styles** palette to apply the style to the selected cells and avoid any overrides. A few resulting body cells appear, deselected, in Figure 8-47 on the opposite page.

12. *Create a style for the cells in the last column.* I don't want a stroke on the right edge of the table, and the best way to get rid of it is to create another cell style. Drag across the years in the table to select all 20 body cells in the last column. (Avoid selecting the word *Year* at the top of the column; you don't want

to modify the header.) Then Alt-click (or Option-click) the ◲ icon at the bottom of the Cell Styles palette. The **New Cell Style** dialog box comes up with the Based On option automatically set to Songs & Artists, after the style applied to the active cells. You just need to make a couple of changes:

- Name the new style "Last Column."
- Press Ctrl+3 (⌘-3) to switch to the **Stroke and Fills** panel.

disc one

Name	Cover Artist(s)	Original Artist(s)
Flowers in the Rain	Kaiser Chiefs	The Move
All Along the Watchtower	The Fratellis	The Jimi Hendrix Experie
Cupid	Amy Winehouse	Johnny Nash
Lola	Robbie Williams	The Kinks
Your Song	The Streets	Elton John
Betcha By Golly, Wow!	Sugababes	The Stylistics
You're So Vain	The Feeling	Carly Simon
Band on the Run	Foo Fighters	Wings
Love Is the Drug	Kylie Minogue	Roxy Music
Let's Stick Together	KT Tunstall	Bryan Ferry
Sound and Vision	Franz Ferdinand	David Bowie
Teenage Kicks	The Raconteurs	The Undertones
Can't Stand Losing You	Mika vs Armand Van Helden	The Police

Figure 8-47.

Year
1967
1968
1969
1970
1971
1972
1973
1974
1975
1976
1977
1978
1979
1980
1981
1982
1983
1984
1985
1986

Figure 8-48.

- Click on the top, bottom, and left edges of the blue rectangle below the words **Cell Stroke** to turn off all but the right edge. (Alternately, you can click the right edge three times in a row.) Then change the **Weight** value to **0 pt** to delete the right stroke.

Click **OK** to make the new style. Then Alt-click (or Option-click) the Last Column item in the **Cell Styles** palette to apply the style sheet to your selected cells. The newly formatted fifth column appears deselected and without a right border in Figure 8-48.

13. ***Create a style for the first column.*** The track numbers in the first column need to be right-aligned, and if the table has no right stroke, I reckon it shouldn't have a left stroke either. Drag across all the track numbers (without including the header word *Track*) to select the first column. Then, as ever, Alt-click (or

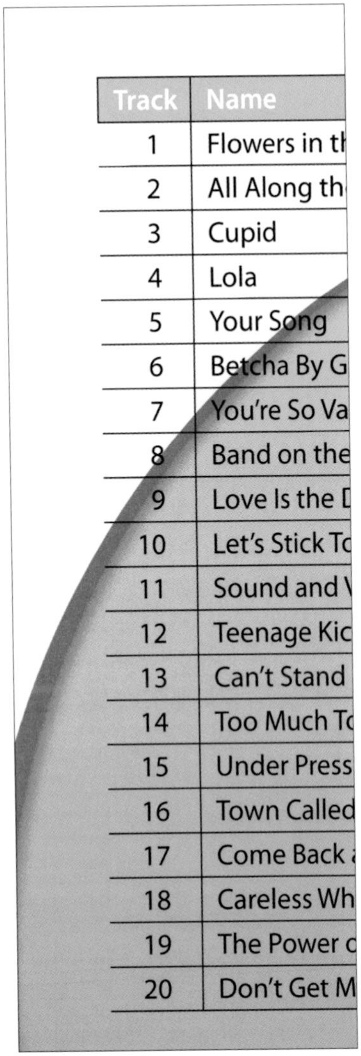

Track	Name
1	Flowers in tl
2	All Along th
3	Cupid
4	Lola
5	Your Song
6	Betcha By G
7	You're So Va
8	Band on the
9	Love Is the [
10	Let's Stick Tc
11	Sound and \
12	Teenage Kic
13	Can't Stand
14	Too Much Tc
15	Under Press
16	Town Called
17	Come Back ;
18	Careless Wh
19	The Power c
20	Don't Get M

Figure 8-49.

Option-click) the icon at the bottom of the Cell Styles palette. Confirm that the Based On option reads Songs & Artists and then do the following:

- Name the new style "First Column."
- Choose **Track Number** from the **Paragraph Style** pop-up menu to select a style sheet that calls for right alignment.
- Press Ctrl+2 (⌘-2) to switch to the **Text** panel.
- Check that the icon is nice and broken, and set the **Right** value to a full pica, 1p0.
- Press Ctrl+3 (⌘-3) to switch to the **Stroke and Fills** panel.
- Double-click the left edge in the blue rectangle below **Cell Stroke** to make the blue go away, and then click again to bring the left edge back. Change the **Weight** value to **0 pt** to make the corresponding stroke go away.

Click the **OK** button to create the style. And finally, Alt-click (or Option-click) on the **First Column** item in the Cell Styles palette to apply the cell style to the selection. Figure 8-49 shows the result.

14. ***Select the entire table.*** For those of you who really get off on making cell styles, I have some bad news: We're done for the present. We'll make another cell style later, but first we're going to make a table style that brings together the four cell styles we've made thus far. Let's start by selecting the entire table, either by choosing **Table→Select→Table** or pressing Ctrl+Alt+A (or ⌘-Option-A). If the command is dimmed or the shortcut doesn't work, click in the table with the type tool and try again.

15. ***Create a new table style.*** The Table Styles palette should be open, nested behind the Cell Styles palette. Click the **Table Styles** tab to bring it to the front. Or, if you can't find it, choose **Window→Type & Tables→Table Styles**. By now, creating a new style sheet should be old hat, but in the name of full disclosure, press the Alt (or Option) key and click the icon at the bottom of the palette. Predictably, InDesign delivers you to the **New Table Style** dialog box. Name your new style "Disc Contents" and await further instructions.

16. ***Set the cell styles you want to include in your table style.*** One glance at the bottom of the dialog box tells you why I made you create all those cell styles prior to making the table style. The

Cell Styles options allow you to assign cell styles to each part of your table. Figure 8-50 shows you how to fill out this section; the following substeps add narration:

- Set the **Header Rows** option to the **Table Head** style.
- The one option we don't need is **Footer Rows** for the simple reason we don't have any. Leave this option set to **[Same as Body Rows]**.
- Set the **Body Rows** option to **Songs & Artists**.
- Set **Left Column** to the **First Column** style.
- Set **Right Column** to the **Last Column** style.

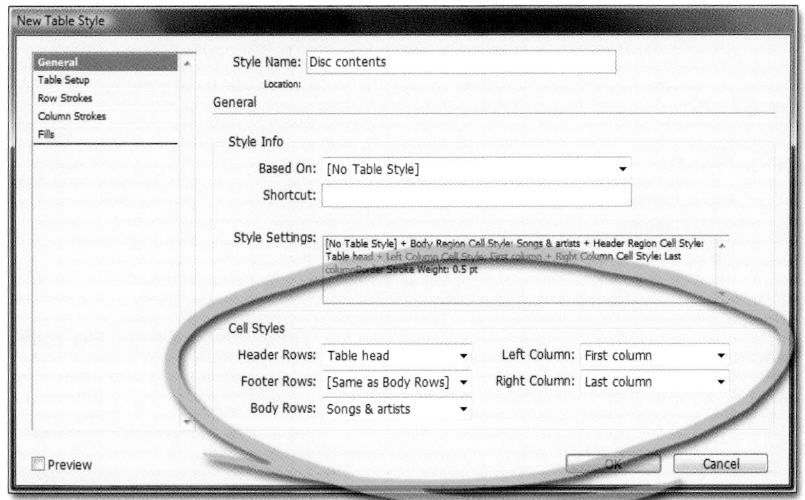

Figure 8-50.

17. ***Turn off any table stroke.*** Click **Table Setup** in the left-hand list or press Ctrl+2 (⌘-2) to switch panels. Then change the **Weight** value in the **Table Border** section to **0 pt**, thereby leaving the stroking to our meticulously crafted cell styles. You can ignore the Row and Column Strokes panels because they, too, will be controlled by our cell style specifications. Just click **OK** and you are done. Cell styles can be a lot of work, but when properly constructed, they make table styles a breeze.

18. ***Apply the newest style to the table.*** Let's make sure that we've created the table style properly. The best way to accomplish that it to apply the style to the existing table. With the table active, Alt-click (or Option-click) the **Disc Contents** item in the **Table Styles** palette. If the table doesn't change at all, your table style is a success.

19. ***Convert the tabbed text to a styled table.*** We still have an unformatted table to style. Fortunately, we now have the table and cell styles we need to make the job easier and faster (although as you'll see, not entirely perfect). Select all of the paragraphs below *disc two*, taking care, of course, not to select *disc two* itself. Then do the following:

    - Choose **Table→Convert Text to Table** to convert the text from tabbed text to a full-fledged table.
    - Leave the **Column** and **Row Separator** options set to **Tab** and **Paragraph**, respectively.
    - Choose the **Disc Contents** style from the **Table Style** pop-up menu and click the **OK** button.

    You would think that'd be all there was to it. But you'd think wrong. In fact, as seen in Figure 8-51, our newly formatted table looks terrible. Styling a table is just a first step to making it look it's very best.

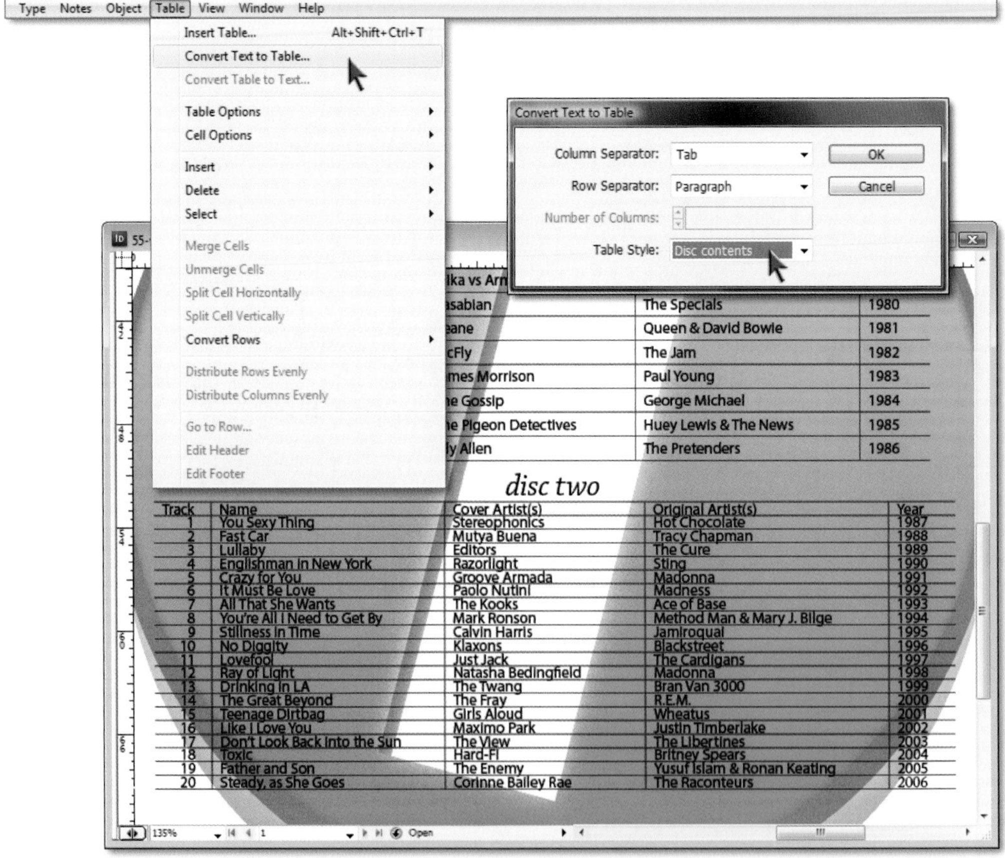

Figure 8-51.

20. ***Convert the top row to a header.*** The first step in fixing this mess of a styled table is easy. Still armed with the type tool, click anywhere in the first row, the one that starts with *Track*. Then choose **Table→Convert Rows→To Header**. This tells InDesign that you want the top row to be a header, and the program styles the row accordingly.

21. ***Adjust row heights and column widths.*** Quite mysteriously in my opinion, table and cell styles don't provide any specific control over the cell dimensions, so you have to fix the row heights and column widths manually from the **Table** palette. These are the steps I suggest:

    - Press Ctrl+Alt+A (⌘-Option-A) to select the entire table.

    - Click the **Table** tab to switch to the Table palette, which should be clustered with Cell and Table Styles. Or just press Shift+F9.

    - The third numerical value in the palette affects row height. Select this value (which reads 0p3), change it to 1p4.7, and press Enter or Return. The height of the table expands to fill the bottom half of the page.

    - Position your cursor over the word *Name* in the header row to see the ⬇ arrow. Then drag across the tops of the middle three columns—*Name*, *Cover Artist(s)*, and *Original Artist(s)*—to select them. Enter a value of 13p0 into the fourth numerical field in the Table palette (which starts off blank) and press Enter or Return.

    - Use the ⬇ cursor to select the *Track* column and then change its column width in the Table palette to 3p0. Do the same for the *Year* column.

    - The table is now the right width, but it's flush left inside its text frame. To remedy this, click just slightly to the right of the table to drop in a very tall blinking insertion marker. Then click [center icon] in the control palette to center the table. The result is two tables in perfect alignment, as seen in Figure 8-52.

disc one

Track	Name	Cover Artist(s)	Original Artist(s)
1	Flowers in the Rain	Kaiser Chiefs	The Move
2	All Along the Watchtower	The Fratellis	The Jimi Hendrix
3	Cupid	Amy Winehouse	Johnny Nash
4	Lola	Robbie Williams	The Kinks
5	Your Song	The Streets	Elton John
6	Betcha By Golly, Wow!	Sugababes	The Stylistics
7	You're So Vain	The Feeling	Carly Simon
8	Band on the Run	Foo Fighters	Wings
9	Love Is the Drug	Kylie Minogue	Roxy Music
10	Let's Stick Together	KT Tunstall	Bryan Ferry
11	Sound and Vision	Franz Ferdinand	David Bowie
12	Teenage Kicks	The Raconteurs	The Undertones
13	Can't Stand Losing You	Mika vs Armand Van Helden	The Police
14	Too Much Too Young	Kasabian	The Specials
15	Under Pressure	Keane	Queen & David B
16	Town Called Malice	McFly	The Jam
17	Come Back and Stay	James Morrison	Paul Young
18	Careless Whisper	The Gossip	George Michael
19	The Power of Love	The Pigeon Detectives	Huey Lewis & The
20	Don't Get Me Wrong	Lily Allen	The Pretenders

disc two

Track	Name	Cover Artist(s)	Original Artist(s)
1	You Sexy Thing	Stereophonics	Hot Chocolate
2	Fast Car	Mutya Buena	Tracy Chapman
3	Lullaby	Editors	The Cure
4	Englishman in New York	Razorlight	Sting
5	Crazy for You	Groove Armada	Madonna
6	It Must Be Love	Paolo Nutini	Madness
7	All That She Wants	The Kooks	Ace of Base
8	You're All I Need to Get By	Mark Ronson	Method Man & M
9	Stillness in Time	Calvin Harris	Jamiroquai
10	No Diggity	Klaxons	Blackstreet
11	Lovefool	Just Jack	The Cardigans
12	Ray of Light	Natasha Bedingfield	Madonna
13	Drinking in LA	The Twang	Bran Van 3000
14	The Great Beyond	The Fray	R.E.M.
15	Teenage Dirtbag	Girls Aloud	Wheatus
16	Like I Love You	Maximo Park	Justin Timberlake
17	Don't Look Back into the Sun	The View	The Libertines
18	Toxic	Hard-Fi	Britney Spears
19	Father and Son	The Enemy	Yusuf Islam & Ror
20	Steady, as She Goes	Corinne Bailey Rae	The Raconteurs

5-word review • • • • • • • • • 55-word review • • • • • • • • • 55-word review • • • • • • • • • 55-word review

Figure 8-52.

EXTRA CREDIT

Before we put this project to bed, there's one more thing I'd like to have you do. The review promises, and I quote, "Highlights highlighted below," meaning that I need to call out what I consider to be the most successful songs from the compilation inside the table. This requires the hand-styling of specific cells using a custom cell style that we'll create and apply in the remaining steps.

---

22. ***Create a drop-in cell style.*** Press Ctrl+Shift+A (or ⌘-Shift-A) to deselect the table and surrounding text. Switch to the **Cell Styles** palette, select the **Songs & Artists** style to serve as a base, and Alt-click (or Option-click) the ◲ icon at the bottom of the palette to display the **New Cell Style** dialog box. Then create the style like so:

    - Name the style "Best Songs."
    - Set the **Paragraph Style** option to **Highlight Color**, which features dark red, semibold text.
    - Because you'll be assigning the style sheet to a few cells at a time, you'll need to be able to access it quickly and easily. So click in the **Shortcut** option and press Ctrl+1 (or ⌘-1) to assign the style about the most brain-dead shortcut possible.
    - Press Ctrl+3 (or ⌘-3) to open the **Strokes and Fills** panel.
    - With the entire perimeter of the **Cell Stroke** rectangle blue, set the **Weight** value to **1 pt** and the **Color** to a swatch that I created for you in advance called **Radio 1 Red**, as featured in Figure 8-53.

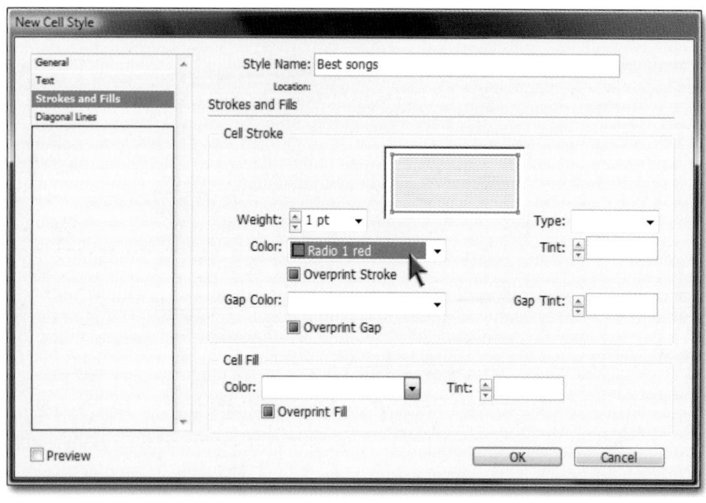

Figure 8-53.

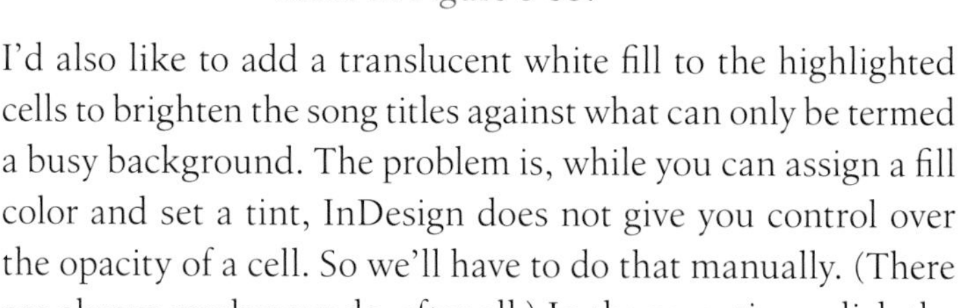

I'd also like to add a translucent white fill to the highlighted cells to brighten the song titles against what can only be termed a busy background. The problem is, while you can assign a fill color and set a tint, InDesign does not give you control over the opacity of a cell. So we'll have to do that manually. (There are always workarounds, after all.) In the meantime, click the **OK** button to make the style.

23. ***Apply the newest cell style to the best songs.*** If you decide to go along with my reasoning (which is the only way the translucent backgrounds will align properly), you'll be assigning the

Best Songs style to two to six cells at a time. For example, start by dragging with the type tool from *Lola* (track 4) down two and to the right one to the girl group *Sugababes* (a UK-based trio who, while they haven't made much of a splash State-side, have racked up more hits in the twenty-first century than any other female act, including Madonna, Pink, and Britney Spears). Then press Ctrl+1 (or ⌘-1) or click **Best Songs** in the Cell Styles palette. (No need to press Alt or Option for once!)

After that, it's a matter of styling the cells across both the *Name* and *Cover Artist(s)* columns for these tracks:

- Tracks 12 and 13 of the first disc, which includes what has to be the best Police cover I've heard.
- Tracks 18 and 19, same disc. The British Isles are up to their ears in cool acts, and Radio 1 invites The Gossip, from Portland, Oregon.
- On disc two, track 3, a feel-good ditty about a guy being consumed by a spider.
- Still on two, tracks 9 and 10. Calvin Harris is the new king of mindless, infectious disco. (And, yes, there is a place for such things.)
- Track 13, the cover of an antidrinking song that went to No. 3 in the UK thanks to a beer commercial.
- Tracks 15 and 16 on two, about which I have little to say, except that Maximo Park exhibits an unexpected grasp of funk.
- Close to the end, tracks 18 and 19, in which Britney Spears meets The Clash and Cat Stevens (Yusaf Islam) has a brief encounter with Chaka Khan.

24. ***Turn on the Highlights layer.*** Now for the translucent white fills that I lamented I couldn't make at the end of Step 22. Return to the **Layers** palette and click where the 👁 should be in front of the **Highlights** layer to display a collection of translucent rectangles. Pictured in Figure 8-54, the white fills highlight the red cells nicely. The problem is, were we to edit the table or change our collective minds about the top songs, we would have to hand-edit the white rectangles. Hopefully, support for transparency will extend to tables and other objects in future versions of InDesign. For now, though, we're done.

Radio Establishec

55-word revie

Addictive collection of 41 modern artists (note Mika/Arma from 40 years on behalf of BBC Radio 1. Two each of songs f and Madonna? "You Sexy Thing" 1987? Most slavishly true to Raconteurs cover (live) & are covered. Highlights highlighte

disc one

Track	Name	Cover Artist(s)
1	Flowers in the Rain	Kaiser Chiefs
2	All Along the Watchtower	The Fratellis
3	Cupid	Amy Winehouse
4	Lola	Robbie Williams
5	Your Song	The Streets
6	Betcha By Golly, Wow!	Sugababes
7	You're So Vain	The Feeling
8	Band on the Run	Foo Fighters
9	Love Is the Drug	Kylie Minogue
10	Let's Stick Together	KT Tunstall
11	Sound and Vision	Franz Ferdinand
12	Teenage Kicks	The Raconteurs
13	Can't Stand Losing You	Mika vs Armand Van Helden
14	Too Much Too Young	Kasabian
15	Under Pressure	Keane
16	Town Called Malice	McFly
17	Come Back and Stay	James Morrison
18	Careless Whisper	The Gossip
19	The Power of Love	The Pigeon Detectives
20	Don't Get Me Wrong	Lily Allen

disc two

Track	Name	Cover Artist(s)
1	You Sexy Thing	Stereophonics
2	Fast Car	Mutya Buena
3	Lullaby	Editors
4	Englishman in New York	Razorlight
5	Crazy for You	Groove Armada
6	It Must Be Love	Paolo Nutini
7	All That She Wants	The Kooks
8	You're All I Need to Get By	Mark Ronson
9	Stillness in Time	Calvin Harris
10	No Diggity	Klaxons
11	Lovefool	Just Jack
12	Ray of Light	Natasha Bedingfield
13	Drinking in LA	The Twang
14	The Great Beyond	The Fray
15	Teenage Dirtbag	Girls Aloud
16	Like I Love You	Maximo Park
17	Don't Look Back into the Sun	The View
18	Toxic	Hard-Fi
19	Father and Son	The Enemy
20	Steady, as She Goes	Corinne Bailey Rae

55-word review • • • • • • • • • 55-word review • • • • • • • • • 55-word review • • • •

Figure 8-54.

Creating and Using Object Styles

The previous version of InDesign broke through the style barrier with the introduction of object styles. Now any combination of effects and graphic attributes that you can apply to an object or a frame—even an empty frame—can be saved as a style sheet that you can apply again and again. If you've been working through the book in order, you first experienced object styles in the "Working with Anchored Objects" exercise in Lesson 6 (see page 262). But that introduction merely scratched the surface. In this exercise, you'll learn how to create object styles that include embedded paragraph styles, so you can create precise text-frame effects and format the text inside the frames in one fell swoop.

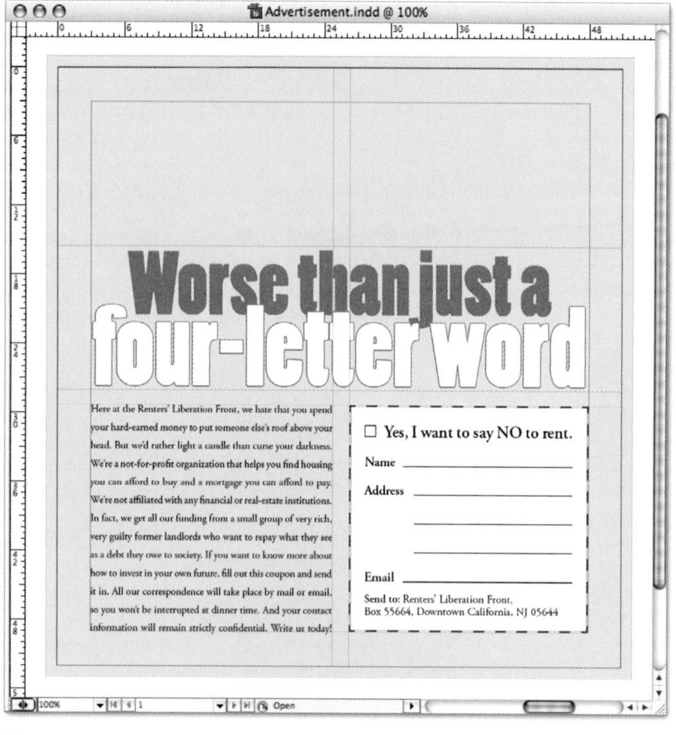

Figure 8-55.

1. ***Open a document.*** Open the file called *Advertisement.indd*, located in the *Lesson 08* folder inside *Lesson Files-IDcs3 1on1*. Featured in Figure 8-55, this spot advertisement will eventually appear inside a larger document. Back in the bad old days, circa 1985, this is what I used to do for a living. Day in, day out, I created spot ads for a newspaper. Only I was cursed with a beta version of PageMaker 1.0, three fonts, and a really slow first-generation LaserWriter. Fortunately, I was blissfully ignorant of how good you would have it today. Otherwise, I would have cried a lot.

   Let's relish in your good fortune by creating a headline in the form of a series of Scrabble tiles. You'll make the first tile by hand. Then you'll make an object style to automate the creation of the other tiles. Finally, you'll embed a paragraph style inside the object style to format any text in the tiles. It may sound complicated, but it's really not that much work.

2. ***Make a frame for the first tile.*** You'll create four tiles in a row, each of which will measure 10 by 10 picas:

   - Click the rectangle frame tool (just below the line tool in the single-column toolbox) or press the F key.

- Click near the top-left corner of the ad to open the **Rectangle** dialog box. Enter 10p0 for both the **Width** and **Height** values, as in Figure 8-56.
- Click **OK**. InDesign creates an empty square frame.
- Press the D key to assign the default fill and stroke attributes (transparent and black, respectively), as pictured in the figure.

3. ***Position the first tile.*** Press the V key to switch to the black arrow tool. Then drag the new frame to the top-left corner of the document, as formed by the violet and magenta guides. The frame should snap into place.
4. ***Clone three more tiles.*** Mind you, you *could* draw three more frames manually. But as always, there's an easier way. With the frame still selected, choose **Edit→Step and Repeat** to created a series of evenly spaced squares across a specified distance.

   Had you measured the page in advance, you might be able to calculate the spacing so that the final frame lands exactly on the right margin. But we didn't, so let's wing it:

   - Let's start with the offset values. Change the **Horizontal Offset** value to 11p0 to move the square 11 picas to the right. The squares are 10 picas wide, so 11p0 provides for a 1-pica gap between shapes.
   - We want the frames to align in a perfect horizontal row. So tab to the **Vertical Offset** value and enter 0.
   - Now return to the **Repeat Count** value and set it to 3 to create three cloned frames.

   Now click **OK**. Figure 8-57 shows the Step and Repeat values and the result.

Figure 8-56.

Figure 8-57.

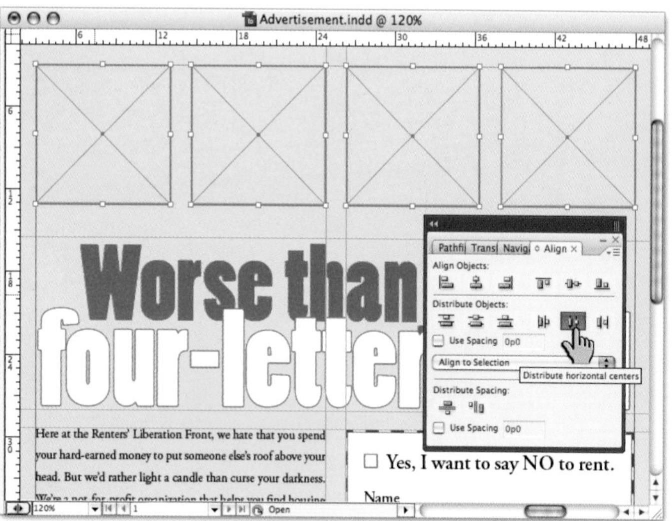

Figure 8-58.

5. ***Distribute the tiles across the page.*** The right-hand frame falls a couple of picas short of the page margin. So drag the frame into place and distribute the other frames to fix the spacing:

   - Get the black arrow tool and drag the selected frame to the right until its right edge snaps into alignment with the right margin guide.
   - Select all four frames either by marqueeing them or Shift-clicking them.
   - Press Shift+F7 or choose **Window→Object & Layout→Align** to open the **Align** palette.
   - Make sure the pop-up menu is set to **Align to Selection**. Then click the second-to-last **Distribute Objects** icon (⌷⌷) to balance the horizontal spacing, as in Figure 8-58.

   That's it for the Align palette.

6. ***Add text to the frames.*** We want to spell *RENT* with our tiles and give the letters little value numbers, like in a real Scrabble game. Problem is, in Scrabble, the letters *RENT* are worth 1 point apiece. Fortunately, few folks are going to know that, so we'll spice things up with some random values.

   - Press T to get the type tool. Then click anywhere inside the top-left frame.
   - Type a capital *R*, press Enter or Return, and then type 3. The text appears formatted with Times or some other generic font. Don't worry that it looks ugly; we'll format the text in a few steps.
   - Click in the next frame to set the blinking insertion marker. Then type a capital *E*, press Enter or Return, and type 1.
   - Click in the third frame, and type a capital *N* followed by a 5 on the next line.
   - Finally, click in the fourth frame, type a capital *T*, press Enter or Return, and type 2.

   Press Ctrl+Shift+A (⌘-Shift-A) to deactivate the text. You should be facing the underwhelming display pictured in Figure 8-59.

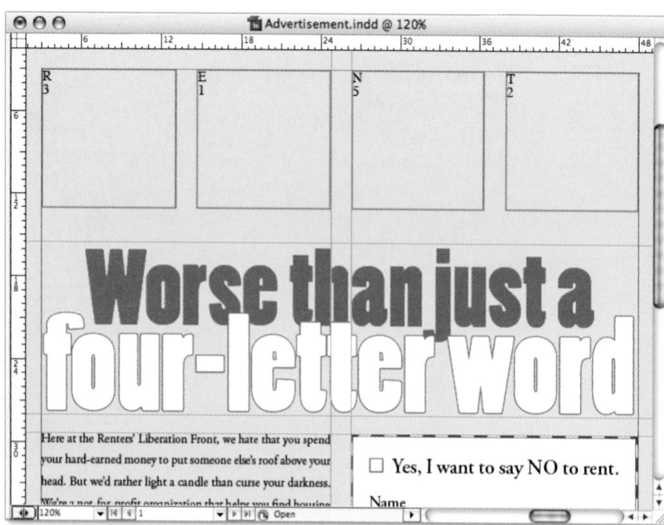

Figure 8-59.

7. ***Fill and stroke the first frame.*** As with a text style sheet, you can base an object style on an existing object. So let's format the first tile and build a style based on it. Switch to the black arrow tool—rather miraculously, it's the only tool we'll need from here on—and select the top-left frame. Then do the following:

   - Press F5 to show the **Swatches** palette.
   - Click the fill icon at the top of the palette so the icon looks like ⧉. Then click the **Tile Beige** swatch to fill the frame.
   - Press the X key to switch to the stroke. Click the swatch called **Tile Brown** to assign a brown stroke.
   - Press F10 to bring up the **Stroke** palette. Change the **Weight** value to 2 points. Then select the ⌑ icon from the **Align Stroke** settings to keep the stroke inside the margins. The result appears in Figure 8-60.

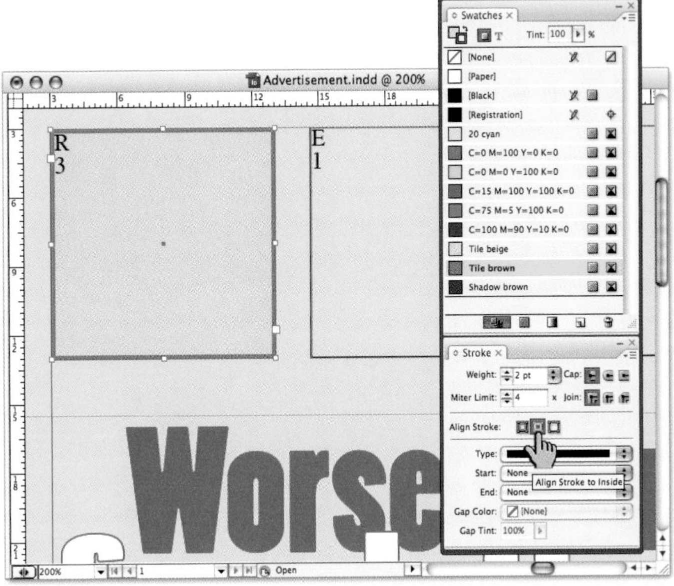

Figure 8-60.

8. ***Round the frame's corners.*** We're not after photorealism here, but rounding the tiles' corners might make them look more Scrabbley. So choose **Object→Corner Options** or, if you loaded my dekeKeys shortcuts (see page xix of the Preface), press Ctrl+Shift+Alt+R (⌘-Shift-Option-R). Select **Rounded** from the **Effect** pop-up menu and change the **Size** value to 0p6. Click the **OK** button to replace the frame's right-angle corners with 6-point-radius arcs.

You may notice that the *R* in the tile has taken on a slight indent. As shown in Figure 8-61, the R is essentially ducking out of the way in reaction to the new shape of the corner of the frame. Any corner effect that impinges on the text frame will have a similar result. Naturally, we'll fix this.

Figure 8-61.

9. ***Add a drop shadow.*** The last step in prepping the tile is to fake a 3-D effect with the help of a drop shadow. Choose **Object→Effects→Drop Shadow** or press Ctrl+Alt+M (or ⌘-Option-M). The **Effects** dialog box opens set to the **Drop**

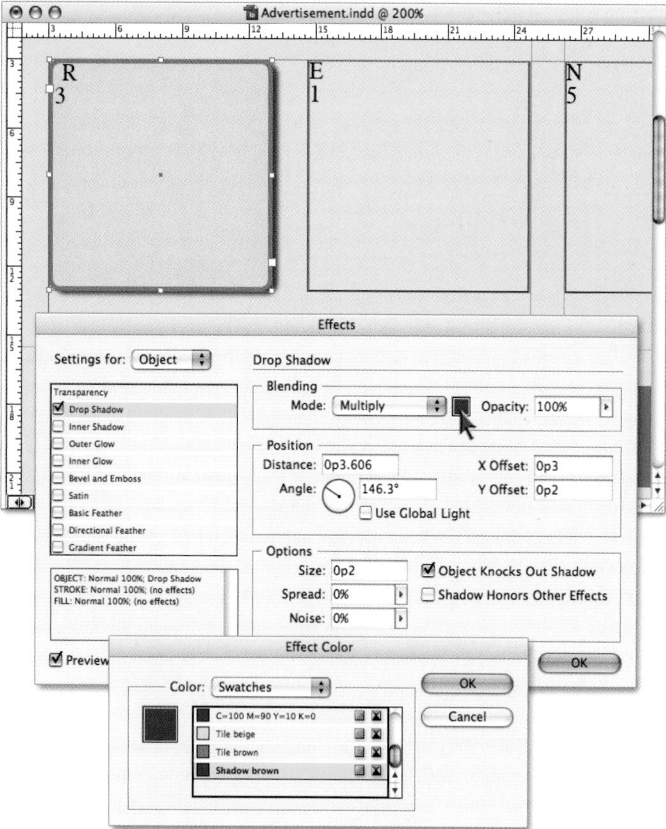

Figure 8-62.

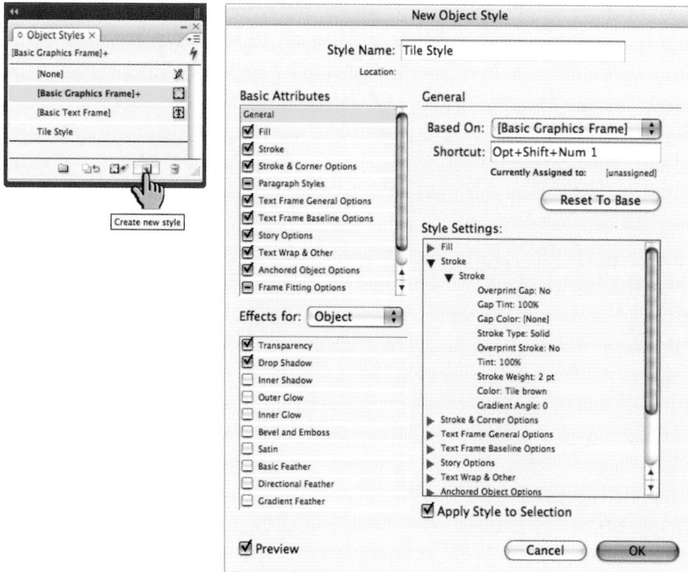

Figure 8-63.

Shadow panel. Adjust the values and settings as shown in Figure 8-62:

- Leave **Mode** set to **Multiply** and raise the **Opacity** value to 100 percent.
- Click the swatch to the right of the Mode setting to bring up the **Effect Color** dialog box. Choose **Swatches** from the **Color** pop-up menu, select **Shadow Brown** from the list, and click **OK**.
- Back in the **Effects** dialog box, change the **X Offset** and **Y Offset** values to 0p3 and 0p2, respectively.
- To apply a slight blur, set the **Size** value to 0p2.

Click the **OK** button to apply the shadow.

10. *Create a new object style.* Now that the tile is formatted, you can create a style sheet based on those settings. Choose **Window→Object Styles** or press Ctrl+F7 (⌘-F7 on the Mac) to open the **Object Styles** palette. Then press Alt (or Option) and click the icon in the bottom-right corner of the palette to open the **New Object Style** dialog box. Name the style sheet "Tile Style." Give it a shortcut if you like. For no particular reason, I decided on Shift+Alt+1 (Shift-Option-1). Leave the check boxes on the left side of the dialog box as is. You can review the specific formatting attributes saved with an object style in the Style Settings list. For example, I twirled open the **Stroke** item in Figure 8-63.

11. *Apply and accept the new object style.* When you're satisfied with your new style, turn on the **Apply Style to Selection** check box to link the style and the *R* tile. Then click the **OK** button to finish creating your style.

12. *Create two placeholder paragraph styles.* The tile looks good, but the text remains squalid and homely. Instead of formatting the text directly, we'll create a couple of para-

graph styles from scratch and apply them to the tiles via the object style. Believe it or not, this approach tends to be quicker.

To try it out for yourself, press Ctrl+Shift+A (⌘-Shift-A) to deselect the frame. Then press F11 to bring up the **Paragraph Styles** palette. We'll need two style sheets, one for the big tile letter and another for the tiny score number. Click the icon at the bottom of the palette to make a new style sheet named Paragraph Style 1. Click the icon again to create a second style sheet named Paragraph Style 2.

13. ***Define the first paragraph style.*** Double-click **Paragraph Style 1** to open the **Paragraph Style Options** dialog box. Then establish these settings:

   - Name the style sheet "Big Letter" and set the **Next Style** option to **Paragraph Style 2**.
   - Click **Basic Character Formats** in the list on the left side of the dialog box. Change **Font Family** to **Myriad Pro** and **Font Style** to **Condensed**. Then set the **Size** and **Leading** values to 100 points each.
   - Select **Advanced Character Formats** from the left-hand list. Change **Horizontal Scale** to 120 percent to compensate for the Condensed style. Lower **Baseline Shift** to –14 (see Figure 8-64) to scoot the letter down in the frame. (I would normally prefer to offset the text with Object→Text Frame Options, but the tile's rounded corners limit this function's utility.)
   - Select **Indents and Spacing** from the left-hand list and set the **Alignment** option to **Center**.

   Click the **OK** button to complete the Big Letter style.

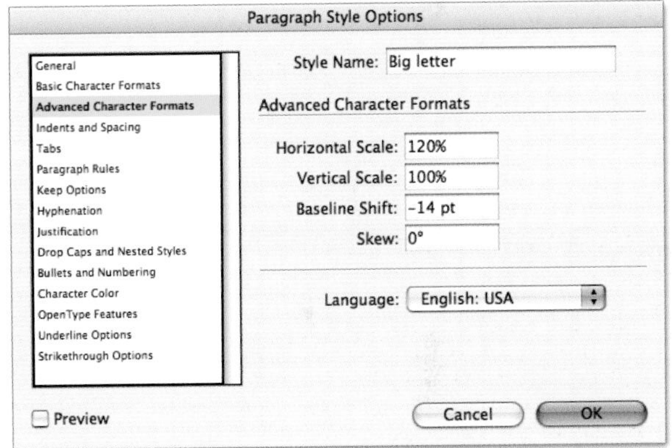

Figure 8-64.

14. ***Define the second paragraph style.*** Double-click **Paragraph Style 2** in the **Paragraph Styles** palette and specify the settings for the letter scores.

   - Name the style sheet "Tiny Score."
   - Set the **Based On** option to **Big Letter**. Then click **Basic Character Formats** in the left-hand list and see how the essential formatting attributes are already filled in.
   - Change the **Size** value to 36 and the **Leading** to 20.
   - Select **Advanced Character Formats** from the list on the left and reset the **Baseline Shift** value to 0.

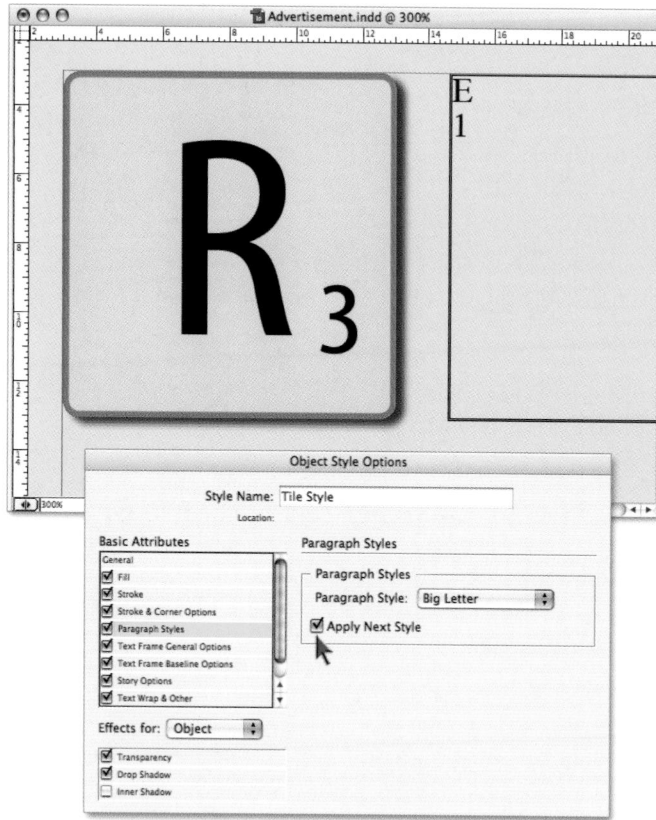

Figure 8-65.

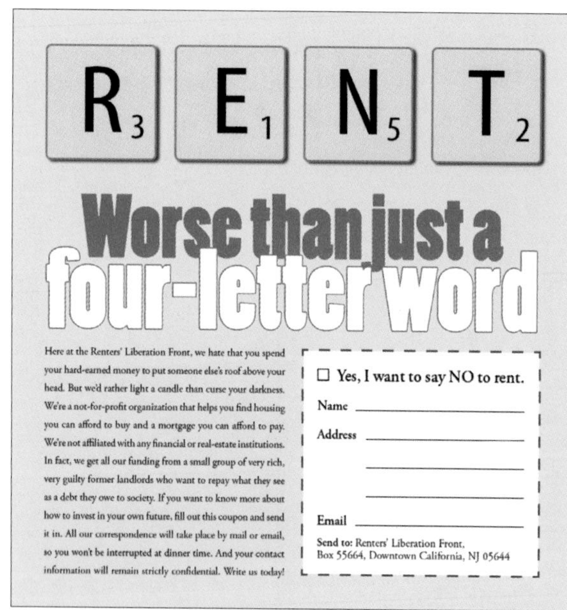

Figure 8-66.

- Select **Indents and Spacing** from the left-hand list. Set the **Alignment** option to **Right**. Change **Right Indent** to 0p9 to nudge the score away from the right edge of the frame. Then click the **OK** button to accept your changes.

15. ***Embed the paragraph styles into the object style.*** Your text is ready to format at the click of a mouse. Ditto for the frames that contain it. But two clicks is one click too many, so let's embed the new paragraph styles into Tile Style and establish a formatting grand slam:

    - Double-click **Tile Style** in the **Object Styles** palette to open the **Object Style Options** dialog box.
    - Turn on the **Preview** check box to watch the first tile update in response to your edits.
    - Click **Paragraph Styles** on the left-hand side of the dialog box to turn on this check box and display its options.
    - Choose **Big Letter** from the **Paragraph Style** pop-up menu. InDesign formats the *R* in the first tile.
    - Turn on the **Apply Next Style** check box and watch InDesign format the number 3, as in Figure 8-65.
    - Click **OK** to approve your changes.

16. ***Format the remaining frames.*** Select the three unformatted tile frames. Then click the **Tile Style** item in the **Object Styles** palette. InDesign assigns all text and graphic attributes to the three tiles in one fell swoop. The strokes remain black because InDesign regarded them as local overrides. To format them as well, press the Alt (or Option) key and click **Tile Style** again. Figure 8-66 shows the final document in the preview mode.

WHAT DID YOU LEARN?

Match the key concept in the numbered list below with the letter of the phrase that best describes it. Answers appear upside-down at the bottom of the page.

Key Concepts

1. Style sheet
2. Paragraph Styles palette
3. Based On
4. Next Style
5. Quick apply
6. Local override
7. Redefine Style
8. New Character Style
9. Nested style
10. Sentences
11. Table style
12. Object style

Descriptions

A. A formatting change applied to a word or paragraph so that it no longer exactly matches its corresponding style sheet.

B. A collection of formatting attribute settings that you can save, reapply, and even assign a keyboard shortcut.

C. A tool for storing a selection of strokes, fills, paragraph styles, and cell styles that is unfortunately insensitive to row height or column width, leaving you to do much work manually.

D. You create this special kind of style sheet by embedding a character style into a paragraph style definition.

E. Your primary means for creating, modifying, and applying style sheets, which you can show and hide by pressing the F11 key.

F. An option that establishes a parent-child relationship between two style sheets, after which any changes made to the parent style will affect shared formatting attributes in the child style.

G. This option lets you choose a style sheet that will become active when you begin a new paragraph or format an entire story in one operation.

H. This command updates a style sheet to include any local overrides applied to the selected text, and includes the keyboard shortcut Ctrl+Alt+Shift+R (⌘-Option-Shift-R on the Mac).

I. A way to save graphic attributes—such as fill, stroke, drop shadow, and text wrap—that you can use to format entire frames at a time, whether they contain graphics or text.

J. This option in the Drop Caps and Nested Styles panel of the Paragraph Style Options dialog box ends the nested character style at a period, a question mark, or an exclamation point followed by a space.

K. Accessed by pressing Ctrl+Enter (⌘-Return), this palette lets you apply a style sheet by typing the first few letters of the style's name.

L. This command creates a special kind of style sheet that affects single words or characters of type at a time.

Answers

1B, 2E, 3F, 4G, 5K, 6A, 7H, 8L, 9D, 10J, 11C, 12I

LESSON 9

PAGES, LAYERS, AND XML

THE BULK OF what we've discussed so far has centered on creating, importing, and modifying the content of your documents. In other words, we've spent a whole lot of time with type and graphics. But with the exception of the exercises in Lesson 1, we've given precious little attention to the documents themselves. This paragraph marks the point at which we shift our collective focus. From here on out, it's all document all the time.

In this lesson, I introduce you to the big S word in the realm of page design, *structure*. If content is the heart, lungs, and brains of a document, the stuff that makes it work and gives it life, structure is the skeleton, the part that gives it form and holds it all together. It is structure's job to arrange, organize, and prioritize information (see Figure 9-1). Structure confines content, so that it's easier for you to edit and your reader to interpret. And it can aid in the assembly of a document, bringing pieces together and even automating repetitive tasks. Blessed with structure, your document becomes a walking, talking thing of beauty.

Content

Structured content

Figure 9-1.

Structure, Structure, Structure

In InDesign, structure takes three forms. First there are the pages, the physical containers that hold everything. Pages may correspond to real, tangible pieces of paper emitted from a printer. Or they may translate to virtual pages displayed on screen in a PDF document (as we'll explore at great length in Lesson 11, "Hyperlinks, Bookmarks, and PDF").

Project Files

Before beginning the exercises, make sure you've copied the lesson files from the DVD, as directed in Step 3 on page xvii of the Preface. This should result in a folder called *Lesson Files-IDcs3 1on1* on your desktop. We'll be working with the files inside the *Lesson 09* subfolder.

ABOUT THIS LESSON

In this lesson, we look at the three structures of a document: pages, master pages and layers, and XML. You'll learn how to:

Video Lesson 9: Managing Your Pages

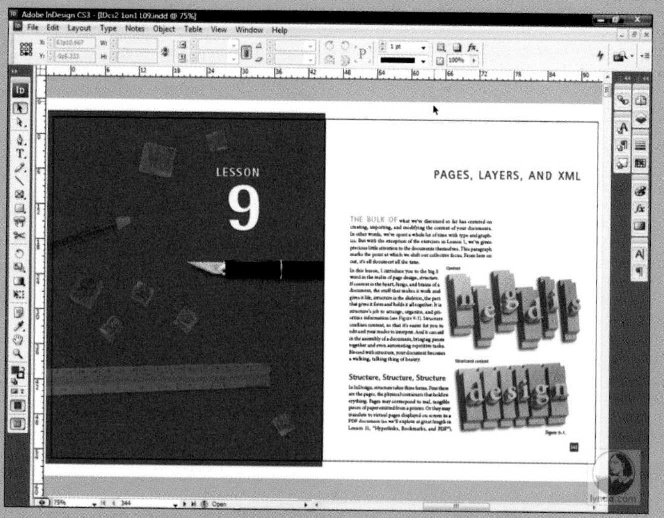

Creating a multipage document in InDesign means coming to grips with the Pages palette. This humble collection of page icons lets you navigate between pages; add, move, duplicate, and delete pages; assign relationships between document and master pages—in short, it lets you manage the fundamental holding cells for the elements of your publication.

To acquaint yourself with this deceptively powerful feature, watch the ninth video lesson on the DVD. Insert the DVD, double-click the file *IDcs3 Videos.html*, and click **Lesson 9: Managing Your Pages** under the **Dynamic Effects, Styles, and Pages** heading. Lasting 15 minutes and 36 seconds, this movie introduces you to the following shortcuts and techniques:

Operation	Windows shortcut	Macintosh shortcut
Show or hide Pages palette	F12	F12
Select a range of pages	Click one page, Shift-click another	Click one page, Shift-click another
Select multiple nonsequential pages	Ctrl-click page icon	⌘-click page icon
Center page in document window	Double-click page icon	Double-click page icon
Add multiple pages at specific location	Alt-click ◻ icon	Option-click ◻ icon

But they always result in rectangular collections of text and artwork, modeled after pages in those old-fashioned content containers with which we've communicated for hundreds of years, books.

Next come master pages and layers. These are virtual containers that let you separate and organize key elements of your document. A *master page* supplies the base elements for a group of pages, much as a piece of preprinted corporate stationery provides the base elements for a series of letters or memos. *Layers* let you group and separate objects so that you can more easily select, lock, hide, edit, stack, and just plain keep track of them. And because InDesign makes a given layer available to all pages and master pages, you can use layers to send objects forward or backward throughout an entire document.

InDesign's third and final structural cohort is XML, the *Extensible Markup Language*, developed by the World Wide Web Consortium (W3C). InDesign's support for XML is twofold: First, you can create and assign XML tags, which identify bits and pieces of your content according to the functions that they serve. Second, you can partition a page into different XML elements and pair XML tags with style sheets. The result is an intelligent template that enables InDesign to import, position, and format all varieties of content—from individual characters of text to entire text blocks and graphics—in one breathtaking operation.

Conceptually, each form of structure is more challenging than the one before it. Pages are straightforward; XML is at best intimidating. One might argue that each is less essential as well. You can hardly lay out the simplest of documents without pages; meanwhile, most designers don't know what XML is, let alone how to put it to use inside InDesign. But if you take the time to learn how each feature works, InDesign will reward you several times over, saving you time, effort, and a whole lot of busy work. And what better way to learn than to create structured documents for yourself with the help of a series of practical hands-on exercises? Seriously, right now, I wouldn't blame you if the very idea of taking on XML makes you break out in a cold sweat. I recall feeling the same way myself. But after you finish this lesson, you'll be busting your buttons over all that XML—and, in turn, you—can do. And you won't just have read about it; you will have actually *done* it.

Pages, Sections, and Text Variables

Some types of documents, such as books, manuals, and newspapers, are divided into *sections*, which are groups of pages that have their own page-numbering schemes. For example, in this book, the table of contents and Preface employ lowercase Roman numerals while the rest of the book uses more typical Arabic numbers. Meanwhile, technical documents such as owner's manuals and contracts may be divided into lettered or numbered sections that are paginated independently, perhaps beginning A-1, 1-1, or what have you.

In this exercise, we'll put the finishing touches on a brief excerpt from my late, lamented *Look & Learn Photoshop 6*, which I believe was the first computer book laid out in InDesign, ever. The file contains a handful of replacement pages for a second printing of the book. Our job is to ensure that the pages are correctly numbered and include the proper title information where appropriate. In doing so, you'll learn how to implement multiple sections in an InDesign document and specify unique numbering options for each one. You'll also learn how to use *text variables* to make a chapter title or subhead appear automatically in a chapter opener or footer.

1. ***Open a multipage document.*** Open the file named *Look&Learn 7 pages.indd*, which is located in the *Lesson 09* folder inside *Lesson Files-IDcs3 1on1*. The document should open to the page spread shown in Figure 9-2, which consists of the final page of the table of contents and the first page of chapter 1. The large black rectangle below the billiard ball is intended to frame the chapter title, which we will insert later in the exercise.

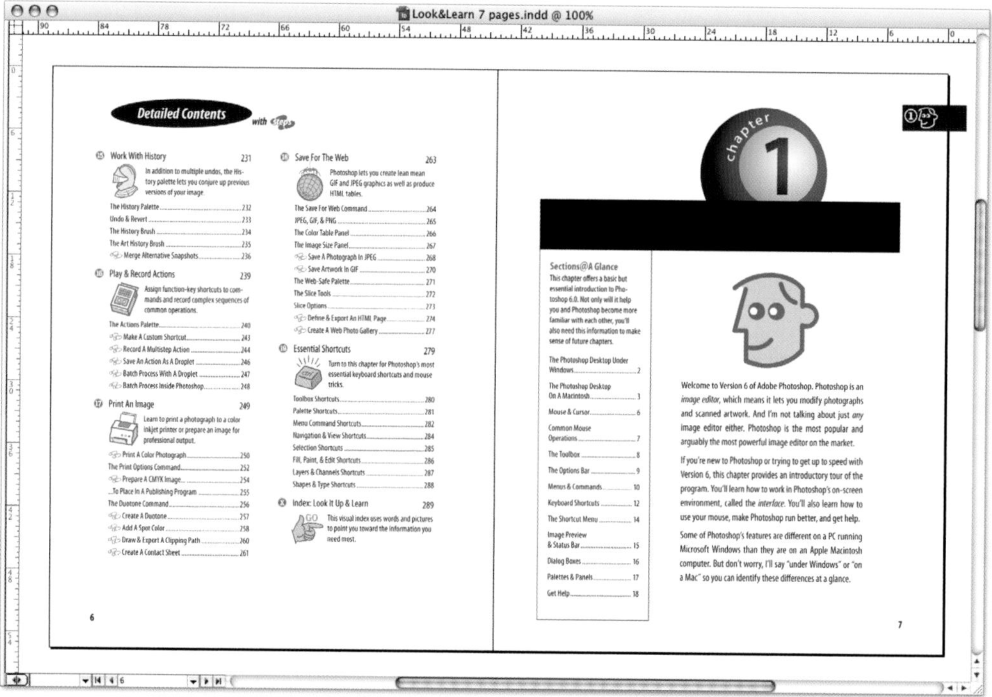

Figure 9-2.

PEARL OF WISDOM

If InDesign greets you with a warning about "hyphenation exceptions," click User Dictionary to acknowledge the message and move on. This is InDesign's way of telling you that the document contains its own built-in dictionary. To see it, choose Edit→Spelling→Dictionary and then select Look & Learn 7 pages.indd from the Target pop-up menu. You can add or remove words as you like. When you finish, click the Done button.

2. ***Open the Pages palette.*** Choose **Window→Pages** or press F12 to display the **Pages** palette, diagrammed in Figure 9-3. I have my palette options set to show the pages on the top and master pages on the bottom, as I recommend in Video Lesson 9, "Managing Your Pages" (see page 370). But feel free to use any configuration that suits your needs. The letter in the top-outside corner of a page icon indicates the assigned master page. We visit master pages in the next exercise, "Setting Up Master Pages."

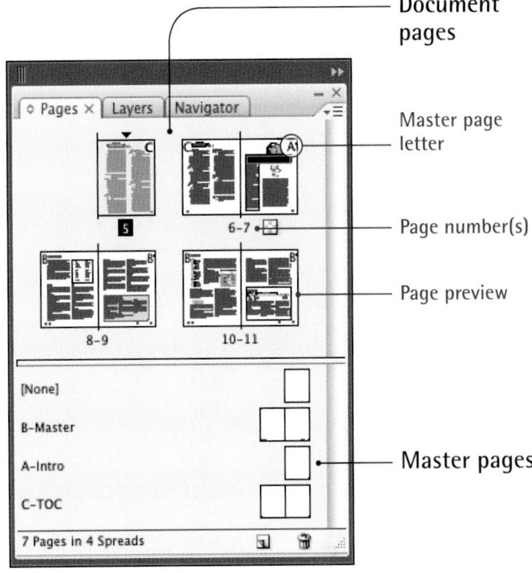

Figure 9-3.

3. ***Switch the active page.*** Notice that the 5 below the first page thumbnail in the Pages palette is highlighted, yet the document window shows pages 6 and 7. Also notice that the vertical ruler along the left side of the document window is dimmed. This tells you that the document window pages are inactive, which means they are unavailable for editing. If you ever wonder which page or spread *is* active, the highlighted page numbers in the Pages palette provide the answer.

   If you ever try to perform a common layout technique—such as, say, drag a guide from the horizontal ruler—and that something refuses to happen, the page or spread you're looking at may be inactive. To remedy the situation, just click the document window.

   Click anywhere in the document window. The vertical ruler darkens and the Pages palette shows a highlighted 6-7. Now the page spread that you see also happens to be active.

4. ***View pages 8 and 9.*** In the top half of the Pages palette, double-click the numbers **8–9** below the pair of miniature pages to skip ahead one page spread in the document, as in Figure 9-4 on the next page. At the bottom of these and subsequent pages in the document is a small graphic featuring the number 1 in a blue circle. This is part of the *footer*, which is recurring information that runs along the base of a typical multipage document. By the end of the exercise, we'll make the chapter title part of the footer.

5. ***Open the Numbering & Section Options dialog box.*** As is customary with books, the pages from the table of contents should be numbered using lowercase Roman numerals. Then the numbering should switch to regular Arabic numerals starting with the first page of the first chapter. We'll start by applying Roman numerals to the table of contents:

   - Select page 5 by clicking its page thumbnail in the **Pages** palette. Although pages 8 and 9 remain active in the document window (as indicated by the black-on-white vertical ruler and highlighted 8–9 in the palette), page 5 is now active in the Pages palette. This permits you to modify one set of pages in the document window and another in the Pages palette. It's a bit weird, but it makes sense after a while.

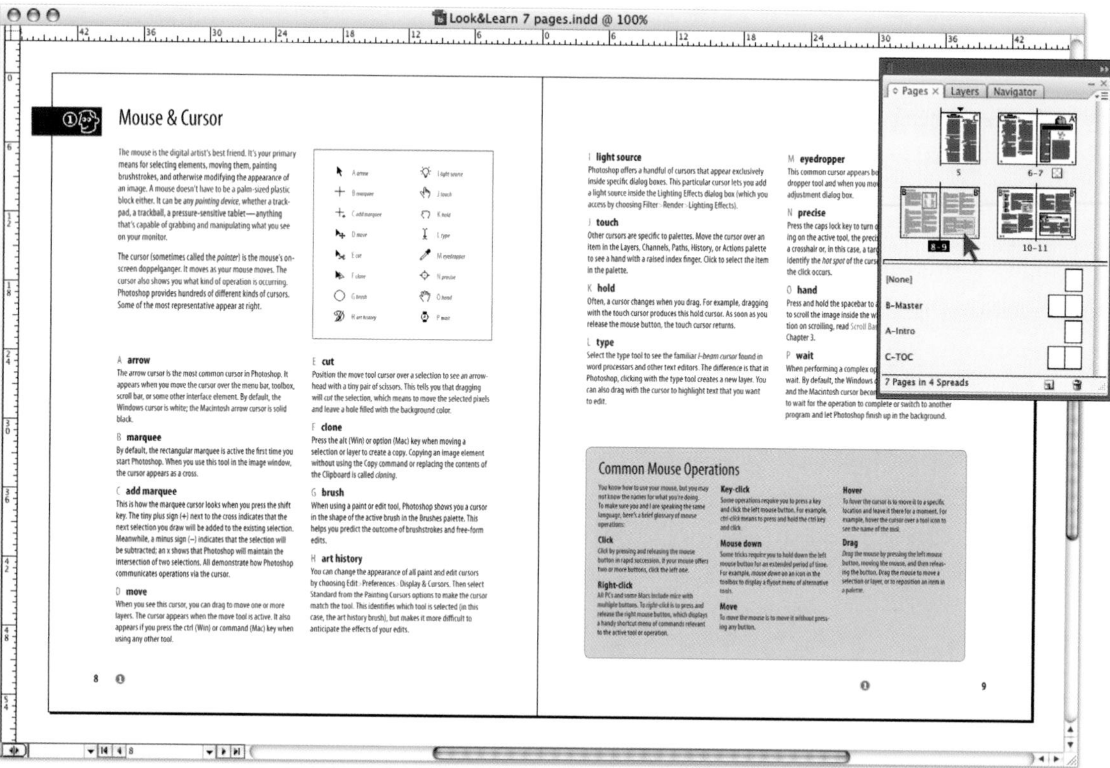

Figure 9-4.

   - Choose **Numbering & Section Options** from either the Pages palette menu or the Layout menu. Alternatively, you can double-click the tiny black triangle (▼) above page 5 in the Pages palette. That triangle indicates the beginning of a section—in this case the only section in the document thus far. InDesign responds with the **Numbering & Section Options** dialog box.

6. ***Set the numbering to start at page xxi.*** As I mentioned earlier, imagine that we are preparing a handful of pages for a reprint of the book. A total of 20 pages precede what is currently page 5, so we need to change the page numbering to start at Roman numeral xxi (that is, 21). Enter 21 in the **Start Page Numbering at** option box. Then from the **Style** pop-up menu, choose the third option, **i, ii, iii, iv...**, and click **OK**. As Figure 9-5 shows, the first page in the document is now number xxi.

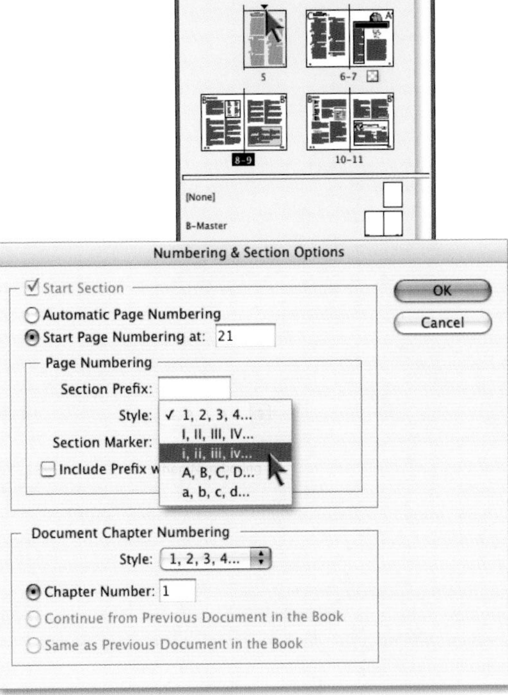

Figure 9-5.

7. ***Create a new section.*** The two pages from the table of contents are now numbered correctly, but we've created a problem: The Roman numerals continue into the first chapter, which is no good. We need to create a new section in the document, starting with what is currently page xxiii.

   Click the thumbnail for page **xxiii** in the Pages palette. (Be sure to click just that one page, not the spread.) Then choose **Numbering & Section Options** from the Pages palette menu. If you loaded dekeKeys as directed in the Preface, you also have a shortcut, Ctrl+Shift+Alt+N (⌘-Shift-Option-N on the Mac). Either way, you get the **New Section** dialog box. Here's a rundown of the changes you should make (all of which I feature in Figure 9-6):

   - We want to start a new section, so keep the **Start Section** check box turned on.
   - Select the **Start Page Numbering at** option, which allows you to start the new section at a unique page number. Then enter 1 in the associated option box.
   - The Section Prefix option is useful primarily when creating technical documents. We don't want a prefix, so click the words **Section Prefix** and press the Backspace or Delete key to make the option box blank.
   - Click the **Style** pop-up menu and choose the first option, **1, 2, 3, 4...**, to restore Arabic numerals.
   - The **Section Marker** option lets you enter text that you can easily recall and insert within the pages of the section. Section markers may accompany page numbers or serve as chapter names. Press the Tab key and enter the title of this chapter, "Get to Know Photoshop," into the Section Marker field.
   - Leave the **Chapter Number** set to 1.

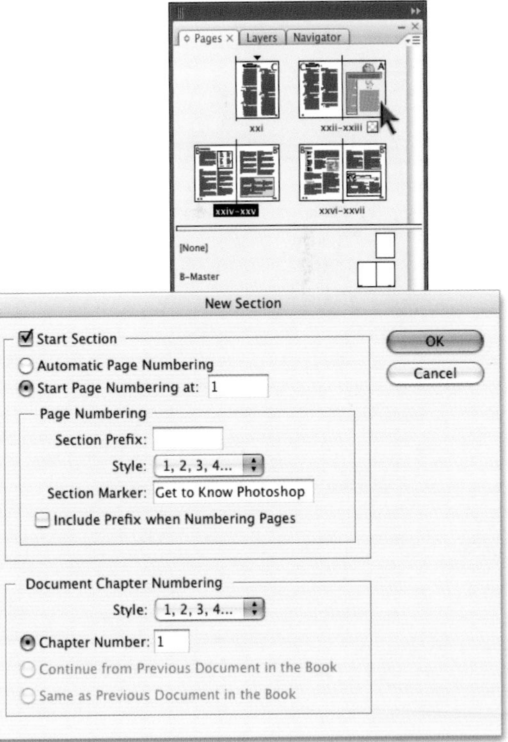

Figure 9-6.

After you specify these settings, click **OK**. You should notice a few changes at the bottom of the page spread in the document window. First, the page numbers have changed from xxiv and xxv to 2 and 3, respectively. Also, the chapter title that we typed in the Section Marker option box now appears in the footer at the bottom of each page, as in Figure 9-7. I'll show you how this ended up happening in the next steps.

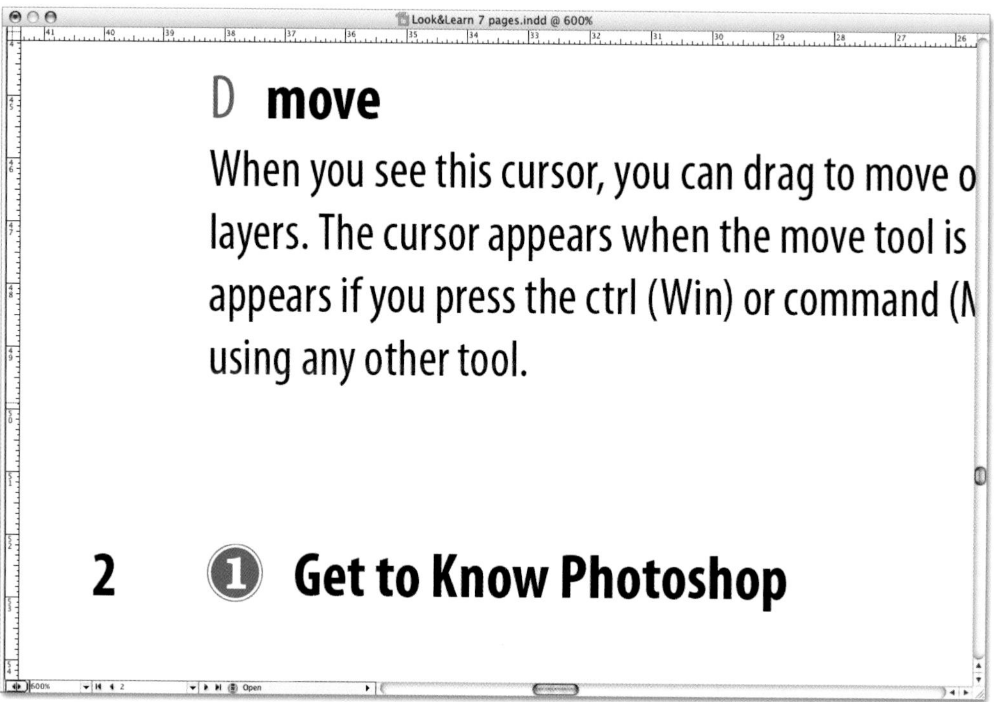

Figure 9-7.

8. ***Place the chapter title on page 1.*** Our next task is to insert the chapter title on the first page of the chapter:

   - Double-click the page 1 thumbnail in the **Pages** palette. This activates the page and centers it in the document window.
   - Notice the horizontal black rectangle that appears in front of the blue billiard ball near the top of the page? Click in it with the black arrow tool. A cyan text frame (which I created in advance) appears in front of the rectangle.
   - Double-click the text frame to switch to the type tool. The text is formatted flush right, so the insertion marker blinks on the right side.
   - Finally, right-click (or Control-click on the Mac) inside the text frame to display the shortcut menu. Choose **Insert**

Special Character→Markers→Section Marker. The section marker that you entered in the preceding step appears inside the black rectangle, as in Figure 9-8.

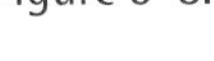

Figure 9-8.

9. ***View the B-Master master pages.*** I used this same technique to add the chapter name to the footers. The only difference is that I added the section marker to the master page spread instead of to the title page. To see for yourself, double-click the **B-Master** item in the bottom portion of the Pages palette and scroll to the bottom-left corner of the left page. The word *Section* marks the spots where the section marker text will appear. Try selecting the word *Section* with the type tool and note that it's actually a single, special character (see Figure 9-9).

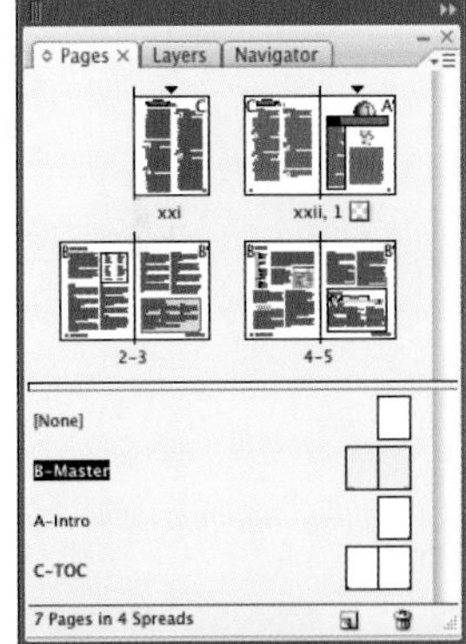

PEARL OF WISDOM

The letter *B* at the bottom of each master page is an automatic page number character. You insert such a character by creating a text block and choosing Type→Insert Special Character→Markers→Current Page Number or pressing Ctrl+Shift+Alt+N (⌘-Shift-Option-N). (This is a context-sensitive shortcut, which is why it's identical to the custom shortcut that performs a different function, mentioned on page 375.) Any pages that have this master applied to them automatically display the correct page number. For more information on master pages, see the next exercise.

Figure 9-9.

10. ***Define a new text variable.*** A section marker is a kind of *text variable*—that is, a text entry that can vary according to a single, central definition. If I were to revisit the Numbering & Section Options dialog box and replace the Section Marker text with something else, all instances of the section marker—on page 1 and the B master pages—would update in kind.

    InDesign CS3 adds several more text variables. For example, let's say we want to make a variable that automatically lists the most recent subhead in the footer of the right-hand page (which, as you may have noticed, is the way things work in this book). Here's how to define the variable in the first place:

    - Choose **Type→Text Variables→Define** to display the **Text Variables** dialog box, which lets you manage variables.
    - Click the **New** button to display another dialog box.
    - Enter "Subhead Title" into the **Name** field.
    - All of the subheads in the *Look & Learn* book are formatted in a paragraph style called Head 1. Choose **Running Header (Paragraph Style)** from the **Type** pop-up menu. Then set the **Style** option to **Head 1**, as in Figure 9-10.
    - The Use option allows you to distinguish between many lines of styled text that may occur on a single page or page spread. To track the final subhead set in the Head 1 style on any given spread, set **Use** to **Last on Page**.

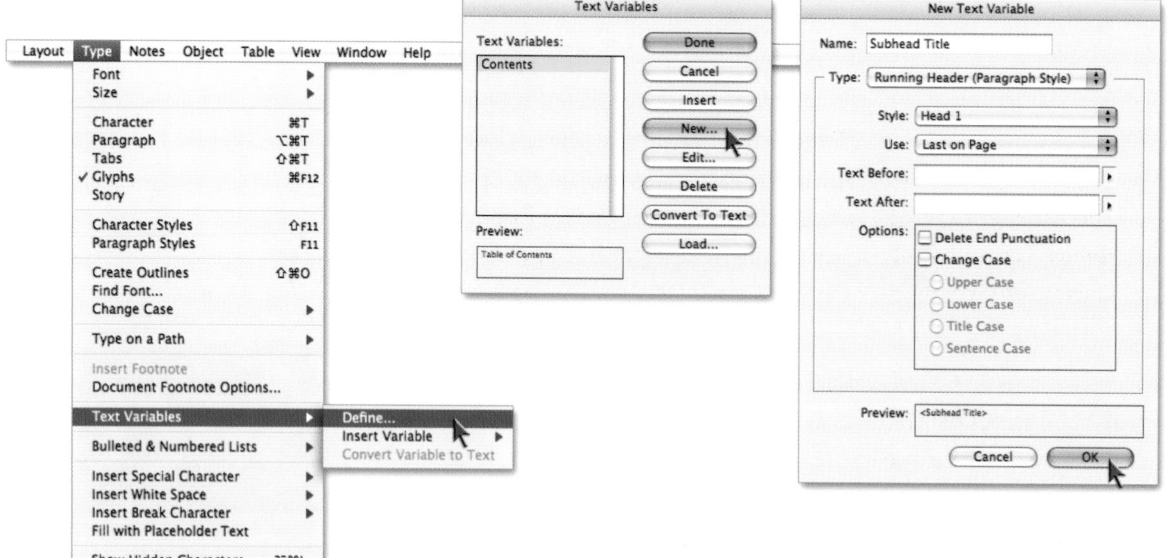

Figure 9-10.

When your settings match those pictured in the far right dialog box in Figure 9-10, click the **OK** button. Then click the **Done** button in the **Text Variables** dialog box. Congratulations, you have made a text variable. In just a moment, you will see what a wonderful thing it is.

11. ***Add the variable to the master page.*** Assuming that you're still working on the B-Master page spread, scroll over to the bottom of the right-hand page. You'll see that the footer currently reads *Section*. Select that lone section marker character with the type tool. Then right-click and choose **Insert Variable→Subhead Title**. *Section* goes away, to be replaced by *<SubheadTitle>*. If you don't see *<SubheadTitle>*, confirm it works like so:

    - Double-click the thumbnail for page 3 in the **Pages** palette. Zoom out for a wide view of the entire spread and see that the bottom-right footer reads *Mouse & Cursor*, which matches the subhead at the top of page 2.
    - Now double-click the page 5 thumbnail in the Pages palette and see how the right-hand footer reads *The Toolbox*, diligently matching its most recent subhead. Amazingly, no more work is required from you because it all happens automatically.

    Both of our subhead-and-footer pairs can be seen in Figure 9-11.

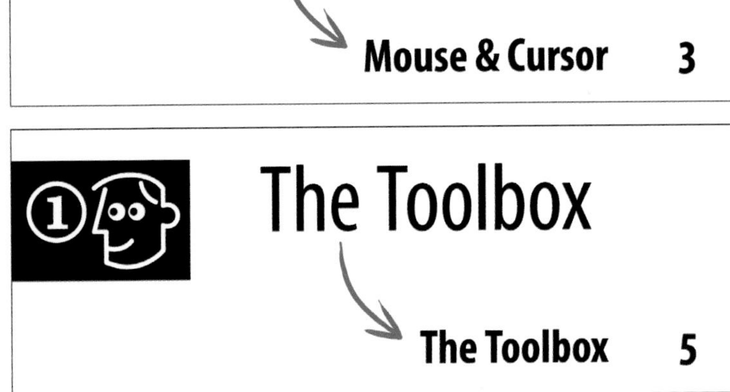

Figure 9-11.

12. ***Modify the* Table of Contents *head.*** InDesign lets you select between several kinds of text variables, including the current chapter number, the date a document was last modified, and the last page of the document (so you can automatically number a page, say, *23 of 48*, where *48* is the last page). But one of the most useful variables, the *custom text variable*, can be anything you want it to be. To see this variable in action:

    - Go to page xxi or xxii (either one), both of which list the contents of the book. Notice that the white headline inside the black ellipse at the top of the page reads *Table of Contents*. This is a custom text variable.
    - Let's say you want to change the headline for all contents pages in one operation. Choose **Type→Text Variables→Define** to display the **Text Variables** dialog box.

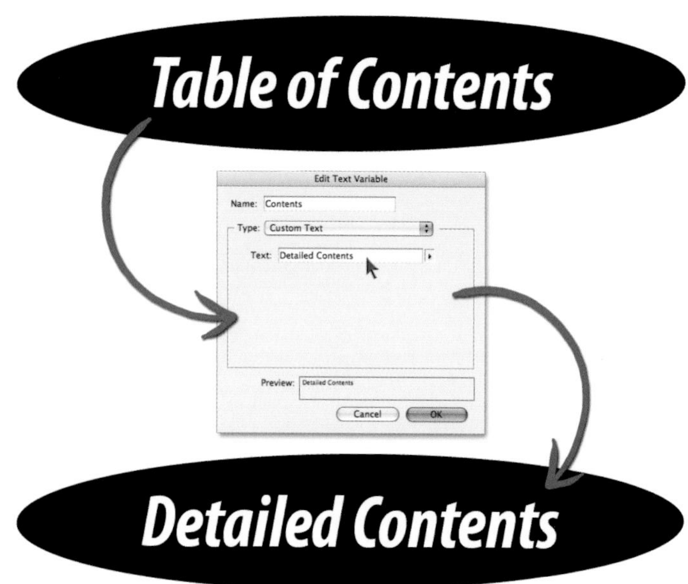

Figure 9-12.

- Select the **Contents** variable, which I've defined for you in advance. To edit the variable, either double-click it or click the **Edit** button.
- In the **Edit Text Variable** dialog box, notice that the **Type** option is set to **Custom Text**, which is the setting for a custom text variable. Change the **Text** variable to "Detailed Contents" and click the **OK** button.
- Click the **Done** button. Regardless of which of the contents pages you're looking at—and bear in mind, this could be happening over the course of tens or even hundreds of pages—the headline changes from *Table of Contents* to *Detailed Contents*, just like that. Figure 9-12 shows one man's interpretation of the transformation.

Setting Up Master Pages

Master pages are one of the seminal efficiency functions of page-layout software. Like a puppet master who directs the behavior of a stage full of marionettes, the master page dictates the content of many pages at a time. A change made to an object on a master page affects how that object looks and prints on all linked pages. But between you and me, the term *master* and, by association, my analogy are a bit overwrought. Without the puppet master, the marionette would lie in a silent and inert heap; without its master page, a given page of your document might be missing an object or two. Out of all the stuff on the page you're reading now, for example, only the elements at the bottom of the page—the page number (or *folio*) and footer text—along with a few guides hail from the master page. The body copy, headlines, figures, captions, and sundry icons appear on this page and this page only.

But while a master page is less master than servant, it is nonetheless an exceedingly helpful one. As a rule, publications are rife with repeating page elements: headers, footers, folios, borders, copyright statements, logos, contact information, and everything else that tells you where you are in a document and who brought it to you. Even single-page documents such as flyers, transparencies, and handouts contain objects that repeat from one file to the next. Rather than constructing these objects manually for each and every page, you create the object once, place it on a master page, and forget about it. This avoids tedium, minimizes the potential for inconsistencies and errors, and even reduces file size. Master pages may also contain nonprinting elements, such as frames and guides, which help you size and align nonrepeating objects.

In this exercise, you'll use master pages to repeat a pair of footers over the course of multiple pages. You'll make a master page, assign that master to a sequence of document pages, base one master page on another, and replace a master-page placeholder with a headline that is unique to the active document page. In other words, you'll learn everything there is to know about master pages and, in doing so, discover the identity of the *real* master in this relationship: you.

1. ***Open a document that contains repeating elements.*** Locate and open *Pages 62 through 67.indd* in the *Lesson 09* folder inside *Lesson Files-IDcs3 1on1*. Upon opening, you should land in the middle of the six-page document, with a distant elephant on the left page and cookies on the right, as in Figure 9-13. If you find yourself someplace else, double-click 64–65 below the second spread in the **Pages** palette.

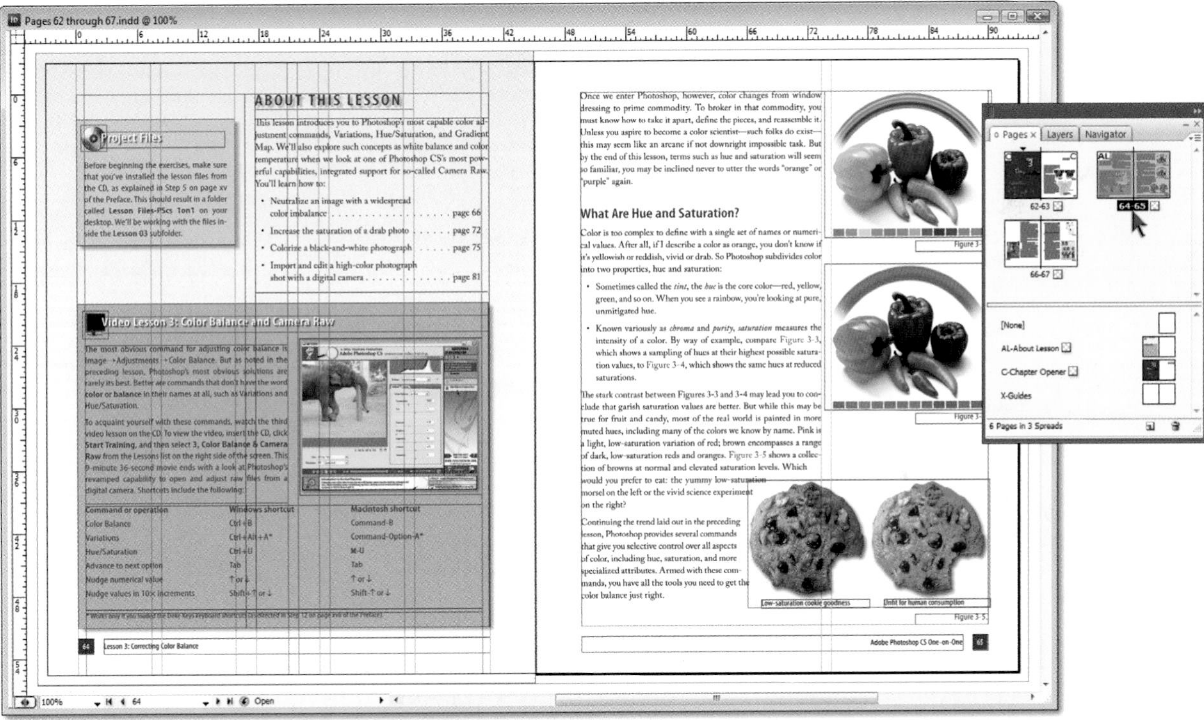

Figure 9-13.

2. ***Inspect the Pages palette.*** You create and manage master pages from the Pages palette. So if the palette is not already on screen, choose **Window→Pages** or press F12 to make it available. Expand the palette so that you can see the six document page icons and seven master page icons. If you followed my advice in Video Lesson 9, "Managing Your Pages," the pages appear on the top; by default, they're on the bottom.

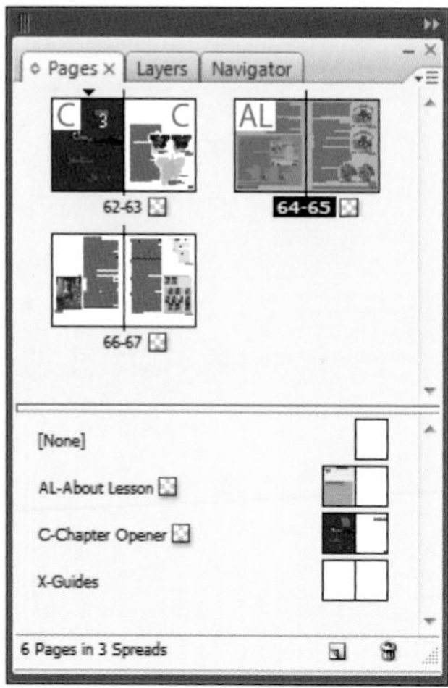

Figure 9-14.

Enhanced with red master page letters in Figure 9-14, the Pages palette conveys the following information:

- The document contains six pages, 62 through 67.
- It also contains six master pages organized into three spreads. (The [None] item is not a master page; it's just there to disable links to master pages.)
- The label for each master spread begins with one or two letters. Any page to which a master has been applied displays those letters, which I've colored red in the figure. So pages 62 and 63 link to the C-Chapter Opener master, page 64 uses AL-About Lesson, and the others use none. X-Guides is not yet associated with any page.

3. ***Select the footers.*** Setting up a master page is first and foremost a matter of deciding what portions of the page you want to repeat. Zoom out to take in the entire spread (see Figure 9-13), and you'll see that the only elements these two pages share in common are the footers and folios. Presumably, you want these to appear on other pages as well, so you should relocate them to a master page.

   I've grouped each footer in advance to make it easier to select. Using the black arrow tool, click the left footer and then Shift-click the right one to select them both.

4. ***Cut the footers to the clipboard.*** The easiest way to move items to a master page is to cut and paste them. (You can also duplicate one or more pages as masters, but that copies *all* elements on the page, which is not what we need.) Choose **Edit→Cut** or press Ctrl+X (⌘-X on the Mac). This deletes the footers and transfers them to InDesign's clipboard.

5. ***Create a new master spread.*** Click the ▾≡ icon in the upper-right corner of the Pages palette to display the palette menu and then choose **New Master**. When the dialog box comes up, click the **OK** button to accept the default settings and generate the new master spread.

To bypass the command and dialog box, press the Ctrl key (⌘ on the Mac) and click the ◲ icon, as demonstrated in Figure 9-15 on the facing page. Just like that, a new master spread with default settings appears in the Pages palette.

---

6. ***Apply the X-Guides master.*** One of the irritating things about new master pages is that they subscribe to the settings you entered in the New Document dialog box when you first conceived the file. This particular document is based on a design that began to take shape more than a year ago, and I've changed my mind a lot since then. As a result, the narrow inside margins, glut of columns, and complete absence of ruler guides are all wrong.

   Fortunately, I have us covered. Because I'm so unhappily familiar with this issue, I created the X-Guides master, which is based on the settings we applied in the "Adjusting Margins and Guides" exercise way back in Lesson 1 (see page 15). Thanks to this bit of planning, you can apply the X-Guides settings to the new master spread using one of the following techniques:

   - Choose **Master Options for "A-Master"** from the Pages palette menu. Then select **X-Guides** from the **Based on Master** pop-up menu in the **Master Options** dialog box and click **OK**.
   - In the **Pages** palette, drag the **X-Guides** entry—the words, not the thumbnails—and drop it on the **A-Master** entry. (Dragging a thumbnail copies a single master page only.)
   - Check that the A-Master spread is highlighted. Then press the Alt (or Option) key and click the name **X-Guides**.

   However you do it, you will have applied a master page to another master page. The Xs that appear inside the A-Master thumbnails show that the X-Guides master holds sway. Even better, the margins, column guides, and ruler guides are restored to X-Guides perfection, as in Figure 9-16.

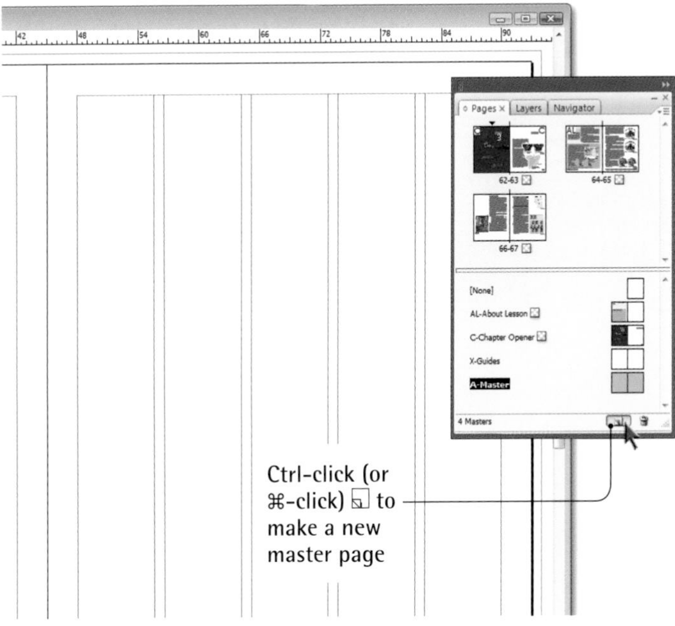

Figure 9-15.

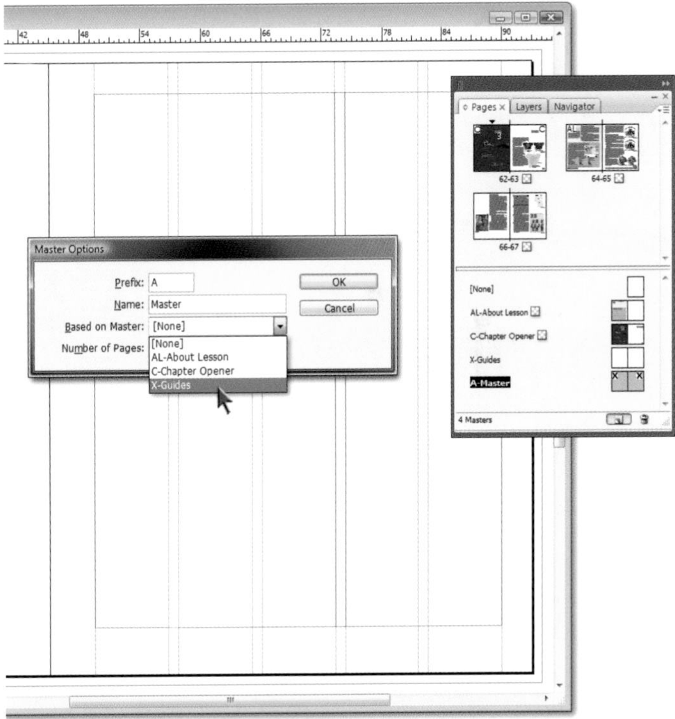

Figure 9-16.

7. ***Paste the footers in place.*** Now it's time to paste the footers and folios you cut in Step 4. If you choose Edit→Paste, InDesign drops the objects in the center of the document. To put them back right where you found them, choose **Edit→Paste in Place** or press Ctrl+Shift+Alt+V (⌘-Shift-Option-V).

   As shown in Figure 9-17, InDesign replaces the automatic page number character in the folio with an *A*. (As you may recall, you create this character by choosing Type→Insert Special Character→Markers→Current Page Number.) This tells us we're on the A-Master page. When you return to the document pages, the *A* will update to reflect the page number.

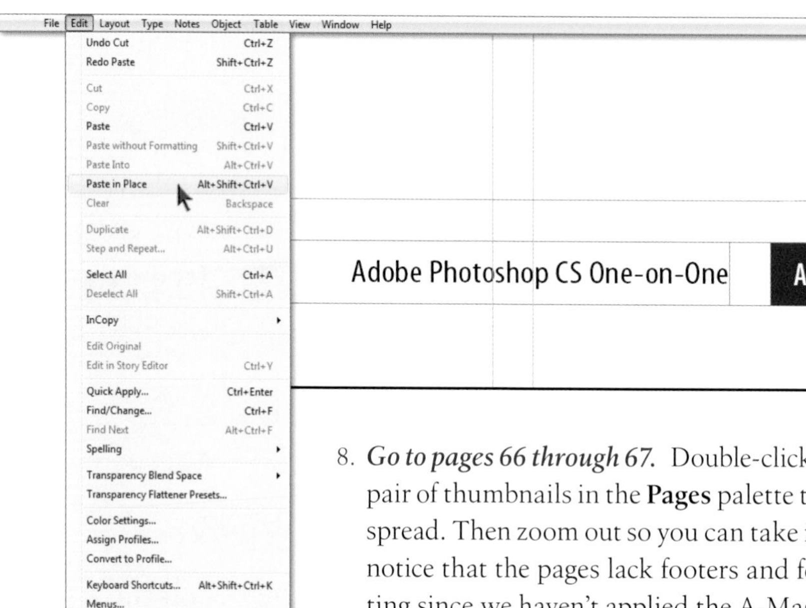

Figure 9-17.

8. ***Go to pages 66 through 67.*** Double-click **66–67** below the third pair of thumbnails in the **Pages** palette to display the final page spread. Then zoom out so you can take in both pages. You may notice that the pages lack footers and folios, which is only fitting since we haven't applied the A-Master pages yet.

9. ***Apply A-Master to pages 65 through 67.*** Still inside the Pages palette, Shift-click the thumbnail for page 65. Pages 65 through 67 should now be active. Next, Alt-click (or Option-click) **A-Master**. An *A* appears in each of the highlighted page icons, which tells us that InDesign has applied the associated footers, folios, and guides to the active pages, all witnessed in Figure 9-18.

PEARL OF WISDOM

At this point, A-Master is the master page for pages 65 through 67, and X-Guides is the master page for A-Master. This makes X-Guides a kind of master^2 to pages 65 through 67. Rather than calling it something nutty like "grand master" or "master once removed," InDesign terms X-Guides the *parent* master and A-Master the *child*. As it so happens, X-Guides could be based on another master, resulting in a grandparent master. But for the sake of sanity, most designers limit their discussions to parent and child.

10. ***Advance to the first page spread.*** Double-click **62–63** below the first thumbnail spread in the Pages palette to go to the first pair of pages in the document. As shown in Figure 9-19, these pages use a different master spread, C-Chapter Opener, which features a full-page opening graphic on the left and a folio on the right. The right master also includes a placeholder for the lesson name, which reads *Chapter Title*. In the last exercise, we added a chapter title using a section marker. This time, we'll try a different way.

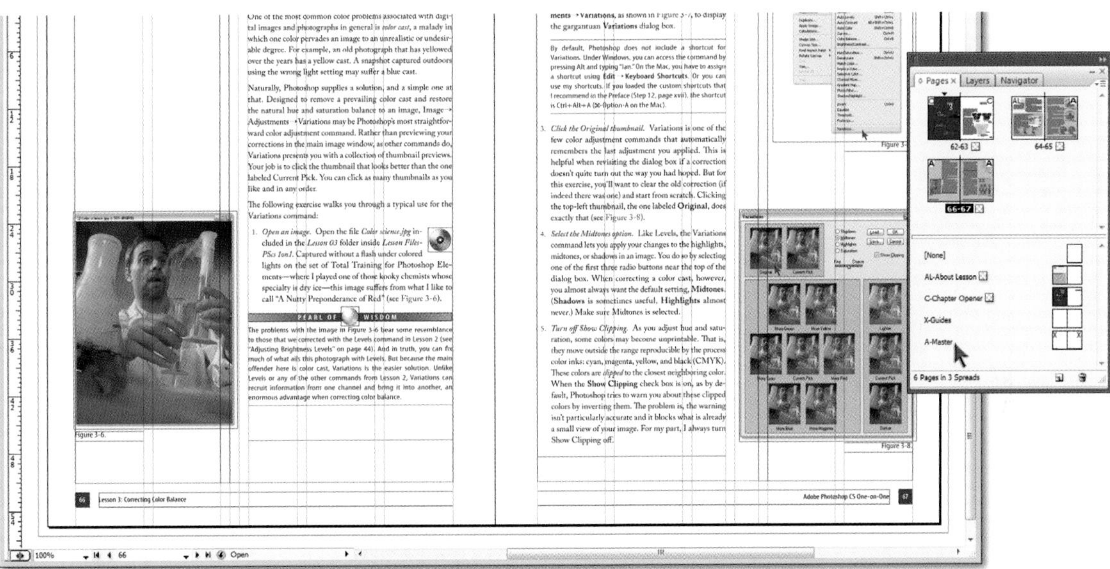

Figure 9-18.

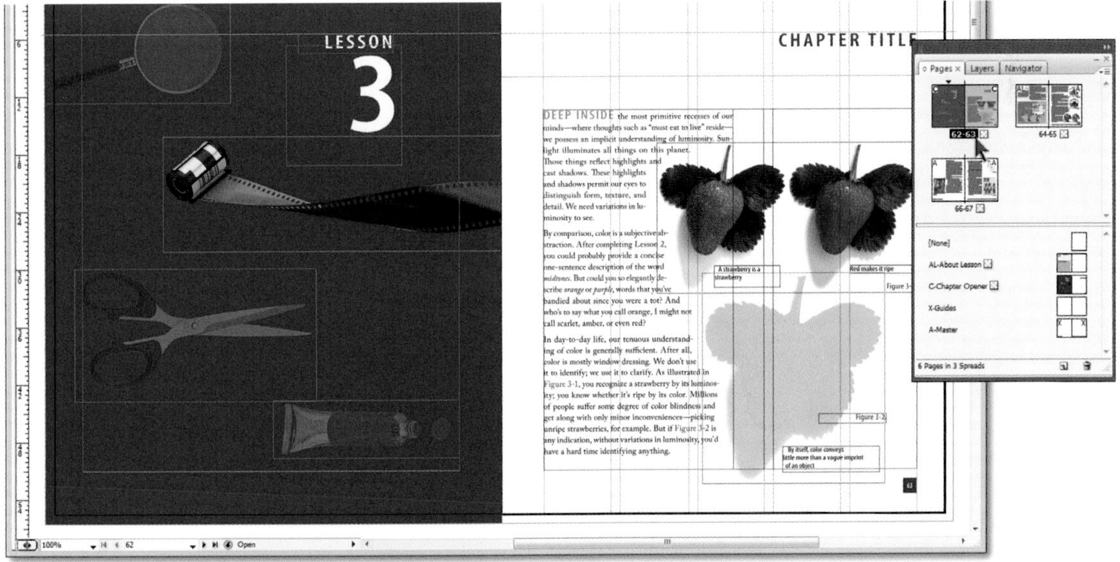

Figure 9-19.

11. ***Enter the proper lesson name.*** By default, InDesign prevents you from accessing master-page elements while working on a document page. This protects the master page and ensures that you don't end up moving objects, editing text, and otherwise making a mess of things by accident. To override this protection, you perform this top-secret, shortcut-only action:

To edit a master-page object from a document page, press Ctrl and Shift (⌘ and Shift on the Mac) and click the object in the document window. InDesign copies the master object to the document page and hides the master object so you don't end up with two overlapping items. You can now edit the object.

Using the black arrow tool, Ctrl+Shift-click (or ⌘-Shift-click) the *Chapter Title* text block. InDesign transfers the text block from the master page and selects it. Double-click inside the text block to activate it. Then press Ctrl+A (⌘-A) and change the text to "Correcting Color Balance," the proper name for Lesson 3 of *Adobe Photoshop One-on-One*. Then (assuming you loaded my dekeKeys shortcuts) press Enter on the keypad to complete your edit. The revised text appears in Figure 9-20.

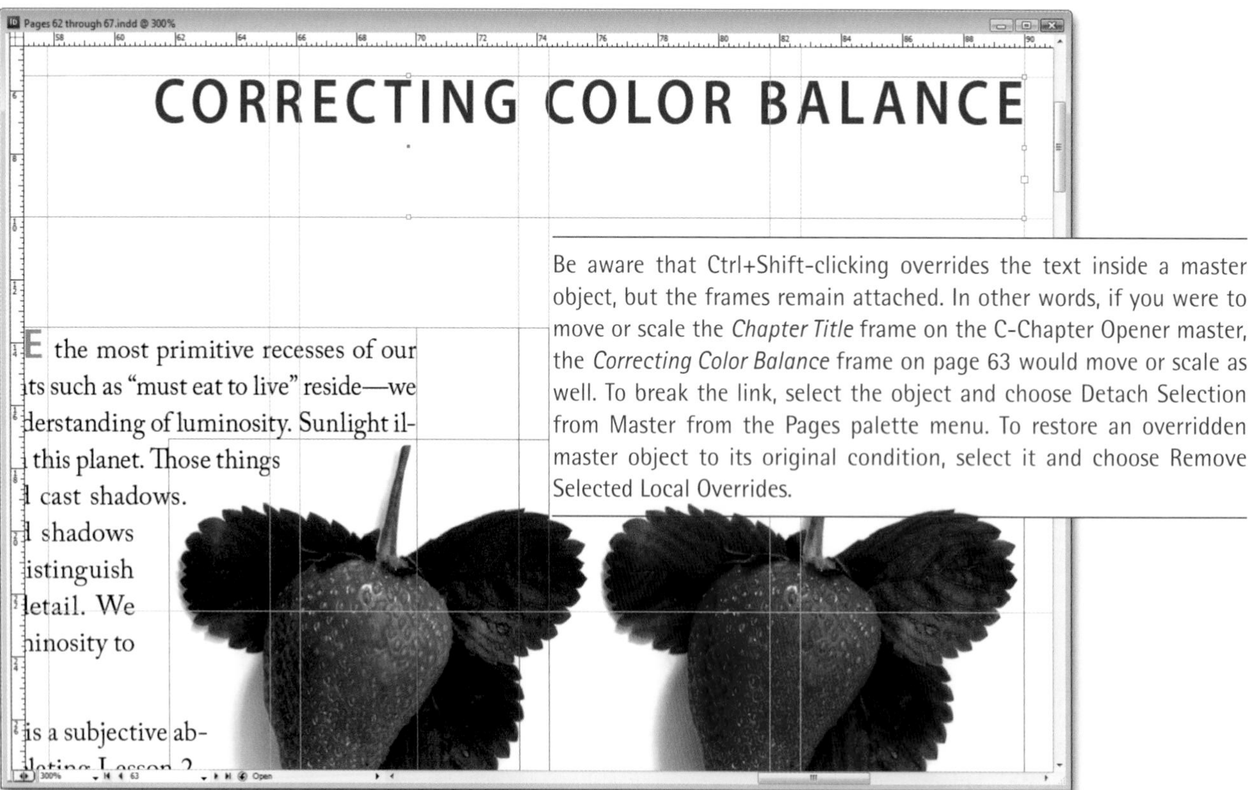

Be aware that Ctrl+Shift-clicking overrides the text inside a master object, but the frames remain attached. In other words, if you were to move or scale the *Chapter Title* frame on the C-Chapter Opener master, the *Correcting Color Balance* frame on page 63 would move or scale as well. To break the link, select the object and choose Detach Selection from Master from the Pages palette menu. To restore an overridden master object to its original condition, select it and choose Remove Selected Local Overrides.

Figure 9-20.

EXTRA CREDIT

That pretty much covers how master pages work. You've seen how to create master pages, apply them to document pages or other masters, transfer objects between pages and masters using the Paste in Place command, and modify a master-page placeholder. That leaves just one more thing: how to use layers to share items between master pages. For complete information on layers—including their effects on master pages—read the exercise "Creating and Using Layers," which begins on page 389. In the meantime, here's how to create a layer that transfers a folio from one master page to another.

---

12. ***Return to pages 64 and 65.*** Double-click **64–65** below the second spread in the Pages palette. Notice that page 65 is blessed with both footer and folio, but page 64 contains neither. This is because page 64 relies on AL-About Lesson, a master page that does not yet include a footer. This problem can be solved in three ways, listed in order of increasing likelihood of success:

    - Apply A-Master to page 64 instead. This would solve the footer problem, but we'd lose all the elements specific to the About This Lesson page, such as the background gradient and the light violet box. Very bad idea; let's not do it.
    - Copy the left footer and folio from A-Master and paste them in place in the AL-About Lesson master page. The problem with this approach is that if I ever want to change the even-page footer—as when laying out Lesson 4 or another book, for example—I'd have to update the info twice, both on A-Master and AL-About Lesson, increasing my labor and the odds of introducing typos or other errors.
    - Make A-Master the parent of AL-About Lesson. With any luck, this will carry over the footer text while permitting you to edit it from a single location.

    Having weighed the pros and cons, let's give the third method a try and see whether it works.

13. ***Base the AL-About Lesson master on A-Master.*** Double-click **AL-About Lesson** in the Pages palette to go to that master spread. Then press the Alt (or Option) key and click **A-Master**. This shifts the column guides and copies the footer elements to the right page. But the footer remains absent on the left page. All things being equal, an object from a master or parent master appears below any objects on the document page or child master. Thus the footer is hidden by the big gradient rectangle that covers the left page, and no combination of Bring to Front or Send to Back is going to fix the problem.

14. ***Switch to the A-Master spread.*** Note that I prefaced my preceding remarks with, "all things being equal." I'm for democracy and all, but in this particular case, equality is our enemy. To bring the footer forward—and further mix our metaphors—we need to jury-rig the playing field.

    Double-click **A-Master** in the Pages palette to go to the parent master. This is the spread that contains the footers, so this is the spread you need to edit.

15. ***Go to the Layers palette.*** Click the **Layers** tab or press F7 to display the **Layers** palette. It contains two layers: The active one is called Main Layer; the one above it is Top Objects. As you'll learn in the next exercise, all layers exist across all pages and master pages. And the front layer is the front layer throughout all pages. Therefore, moving the footers and folios to the top layer moves them to the front of the stack on all pages.

16. ***Move the footer elements to the Top Objects layer.*** Here's what I want you to do:

    - The 🔒 icon in front of **Top Objects** shows that the layer is locked. Click the 🔒 icon to make it go away and thereby unlock the layer.
    - Select the footers on both pages of the spread. Because these are the only objects on the spread, you can press Ctrl+A (or ⌘-A) to select them. (If that doesn't work, press Enter and then press Ctrl+A again.)
    - Notice that a tiny blue square (■) appears on the right side of the Layers palette. This ■ represents the selected objects. Drag the square up, so it's even with Top Objects, and release. As shown in Figure 9-21, the square turns red, showing that the selection now rests on the frontmost layer.

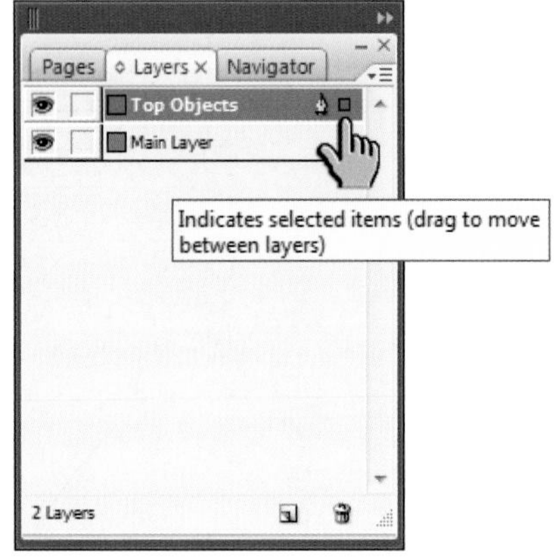

Figure 9-21.

17. ***Return one last time to pages 64 through 65.*** Click the **Pages** tab or press F12 to switch back to the **Pages** palette. Then double-click **64–65** below the middle thumbnail pair to display the two-page spread where we began this exercise. As celebrated in Figure 9-22 on the facing page, the footer and folio appear on both pages and all is well in the world.

Incidentally, if you're ever curious about which objects are part of the current document page and which objects hail from the master page, choose Hide Master Items from the Pages palette menu. Choose Show Master Items to bring the master objects back.

After all this talk about transferring objects from one master page to another, the next logical step is to transfer entire master pages from one document to another. Happily, InDesign CS3 makes this possible. To import the master pages of another document, click the ▾≡ icon in the top-right corner of the Pages palette and choose Load Master Pages from the Pages palette menu. Then select the document that contains the master pages you want to use. For this user, anyway, it's been a godsend.

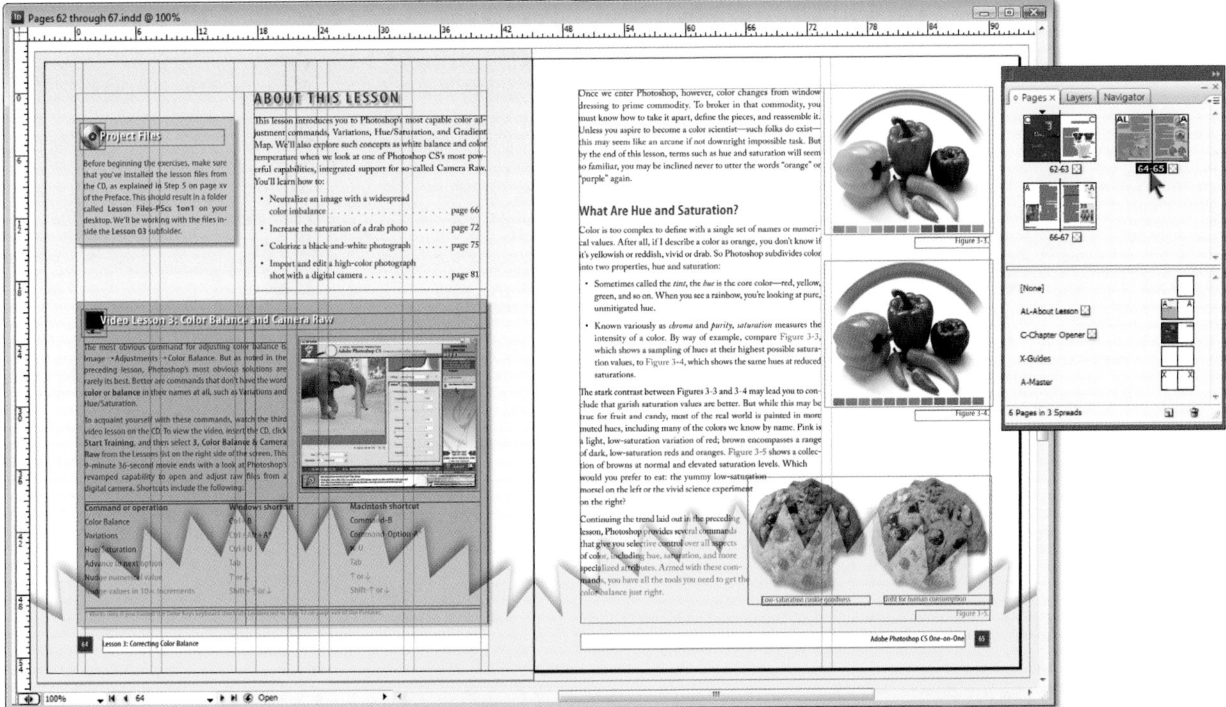

Figure 9-22.

Creating and Using Layers

If you use other Adobe products, you're probably well aware of the power and flexibility that layers can bring to your work. Separating the various elements in your document onto layers gives you the ability to select, hide, lock, and arrange those elements with enormous freedom. But in InDesign, layers are perhaps even more pervasive than they are in other Adobe apps. For starters, layers can hold *anything*, including text, images, drawn objects, and even guides. Furthermore, layers extend not just to the page you're currently working on, but to every page in the entire document, including master pages.

In this exercise, we'll use layers to craft a bilingual flier for a fictional bank. In the process, you'll learn a few different ways to create layers and experience firsthand how they can expedite your progress as you develop a design. You'll also see how you can use layers to organize guides and minimize on-screen clutter.

1. ***Open a document.*** Open the file named *MetroBanco bilingual.indd*, which is located in the *Lesson 09* folder inside *Lesson Files-IDcs3 1on1*. Pictured in Figure 9-23 on the next page, the document includes a three-column text block, a couple of logo elements, and images from Heinz Linke

(the service desk), Tomaz Levstek (the advisor with clients), and Maciej Korzekwa (the bank exterior), all of iStockphoto. And yet, if you try to select any of these elements, you'll find that you can't. The next step explains why.

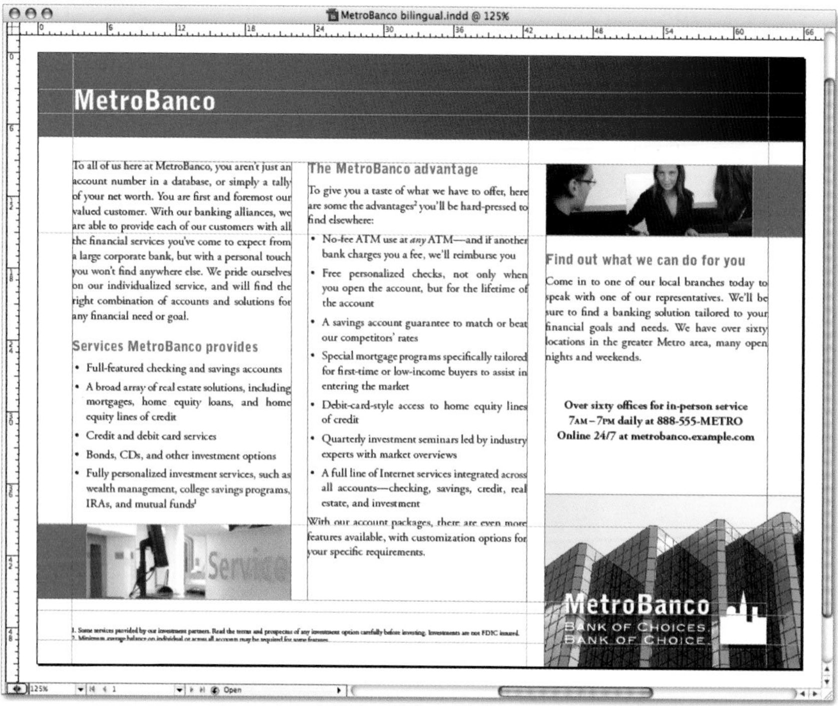

Figure 9-23.

2. ***Open the Layers palette.*** Choose **Window→Layers** or press F7 to bring up the **Layers** palette. As shown in Figure 9-24, this document consists of just two layers. The white logo elements in the top-left and bottom-right corners of the document exist on the Logos layer. The other objects are placed on the rear layer, Layer 1. Some other things to note:

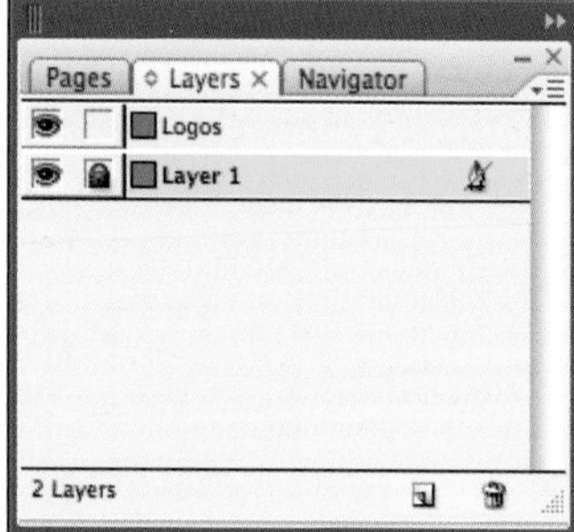

Figure 9-24.

- The 👁 icons in front of the layer names show that both layers are visible.
- Layer 1 sports a 🔒 icon, which tells you that the layer is locked and its contents can't be selected.
- Meanwhile, you can tell that Layer 1 is active by the fact that it's highlighted and followed by a ✎ icon. The red slash through the icon reminds us that the layer is locked.
- The Logos layer is not locked, and yet its objects are similarly unavailable for selection. From this, we can infer that the logos exist on a master page (which is indeed the case).

- The Logos layer is stacked in front of Layer 1, so the white logo elements appear in front of the red gradient bar at the top of the page and the blue bank photograph at the bottom (both of which are located on page 1). As you saw in the previous exercise, layers are effective tools for moving master-page elements to the top of the stack.
- The colored swatch to the left of each layer name shows the color assigned to the layer. If you could select a frame on that layer, it would appear in that color.

3. ***Create a new layer for the English-language text.*** To create a bilingual document that's alternately English and Spanish, we need to be able to isolate text and graphics to independent layers. (Being language-independent, the graphics can be shared.) Let's start by making a new layer for the existing text, which is English:
   - Press the Ctrl (or ⌘) key and click the icon at the bottom of the Layers palette. Pressing the key ensure that the new layer appears directly in front of the existing one.
   - Double-click the new **Layer 3** item to display the **Layer Options** dialog box. The Color is set to a vivid green, meaning that objects on this layer will exhibit a green frame when selected. Leave this setting as is.
   - Type "English Text" in the **Name** option box (see Figure 9-25), and click the **OK** button.

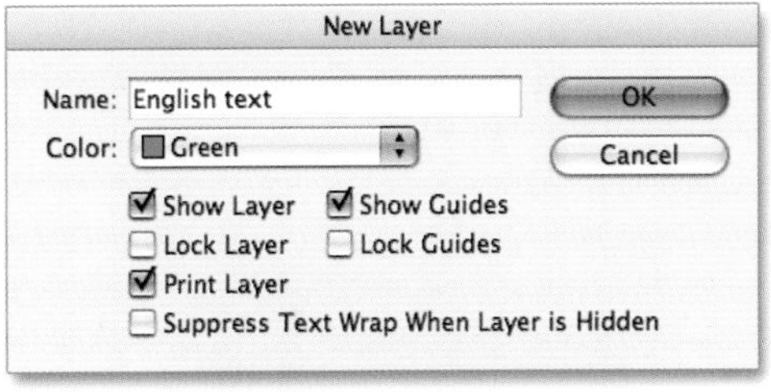
New Layer
Name: English text
Color: Green
OK
Cancel
Show Layer
Show Guides
Lock Layer
Lock Guides
Print Layer
Suppress Text Wrap When Layer is Hidden

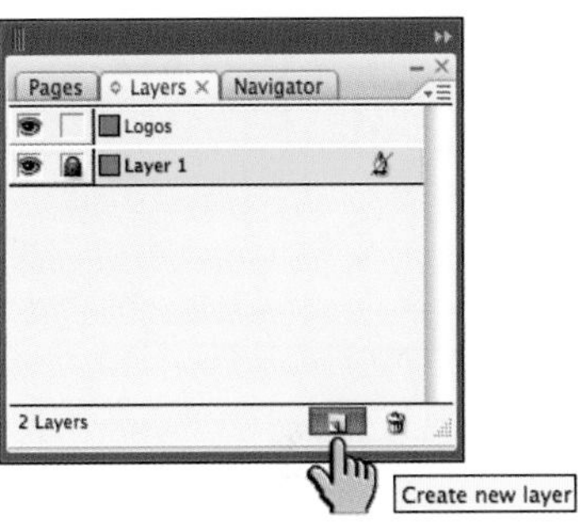
Pages
Layers
Navigator
Logos
Layer 1
2 Layers
Create new layer

Figure 9-25.

4. ***Select the text blocks.*** To move the text to the new layer, you must first unlock its existing layer. So click the icon in front of **Layer 1** to make its objects accessible. Back in the document window, use the black arrow tool to select both the three-column text block and the 7-point, legalistic footnote text at the bottom of the page.
5. ***Move the text to the new layer.*** In the **Layers** palette, note the tiny blue ■ to the right of the icon, which represents any and all selected objects in the document window. Note also that the selected text frames are blue, which tells you that they are part of Layer 1. To move the frames up the stack, drag the tiny blue ■ from **Layer 1** up to the **English Text** layer. As shown in Figure 9-26, the rectangle's bounding box turns green, which indicates that the shape now resides on its self-named layer.

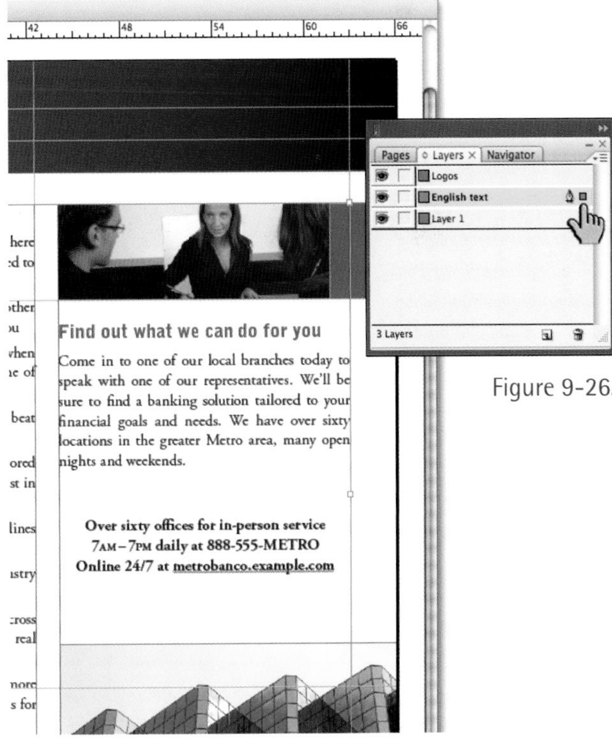
Find out what we can do for you
Come in to one of our local branches today to speak with one of our representatives. We'll be sure to find a banking solution tailored to your financial goals and needs. We have over sixty locations in the greater Metro area, many open nights and weekends.
Over sixty offices for in-person service
7AM–7PM daily at 888-555-METRO
Online 24/7 at metrobanco.example.com
Pages
Layers
Navigator
Logos
English text
Layer 1
3 Layers

Figure 9-26.

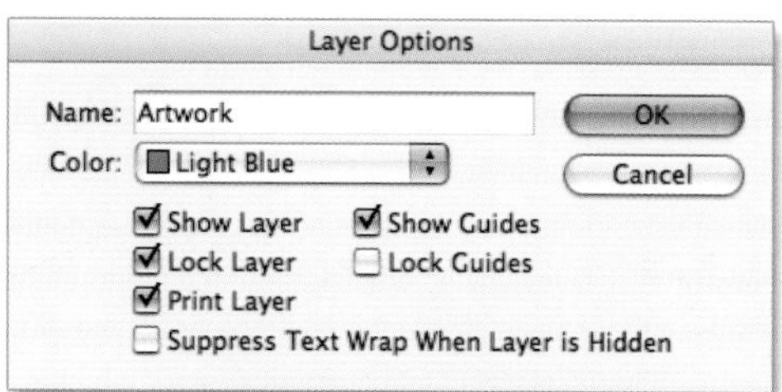

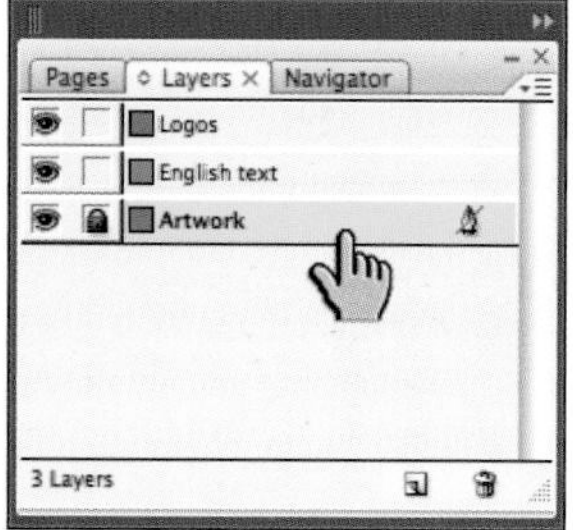

Figure 9-27.

To duplicate one or more selected objects from one layer to another, press the Alt (or Option) key as you drag the tiny selection ■ to a different layer. The clone moves to the new layer; the original stays put.

---

6. ***Rename and lock Layer 1.*** If you click the 👁 for the English Text layer to turn it off, you'll see that Layer 1 is now reduced to artwork and the guidelines. So we might as well call it that. Double-click **Layer 1** to display the **Layer Options** dialog box. Change the **Name** option to "Artwork" and turn on the **Lock Layer** check box. Then click **OK**. The layer is now more meaningfully named as well as locked to protect its contents.

7. ***Duplicate the English Text layer.*** If you hid the English Text layer, turn it on to make it visible again. For the simple reason that its easier to work from existing text frames than create new ones, this layer will serve as the basis for the Spanish-language text. Click on **English Text** to make it active. Then duplicate the layer as follows:

   - Click the ▾≡ icon in the top-right corner of the **Layers** palette and choose **Duplicate Layer "English Text"** from the palette menu.
   - Change the **Name** option to "Spanish Text."
   - For some obvious contrast, choose **Gold** from the **Color** pop-up menu, as shown in Figure 9-28.
   - Click **OK** to return to the **Layers** palette, and then drag the new **Spanish Text** layer below English Text, as on the far left side of Figure 9-28.

8. ***Replace the English text with the Spanish document.*** Turn off the **English Text** layer by clicking its 👁. Then double-click in the three-column text block to switch to the type tool and position the blinking insertion marker. Press Ctrl+A (or ⌘-A) to select all the text and choose **File→Place** or

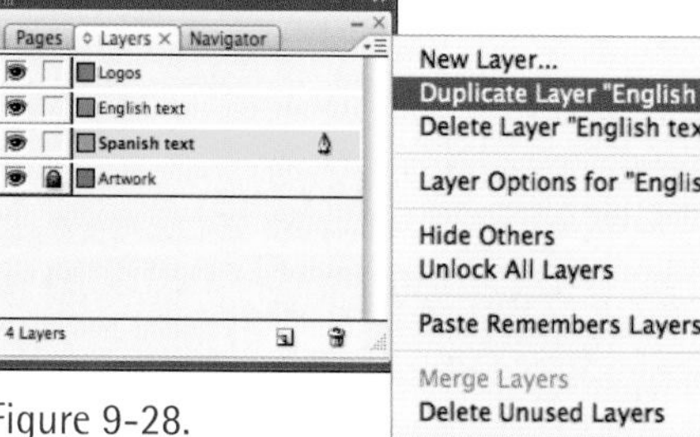

Figure 9-28.

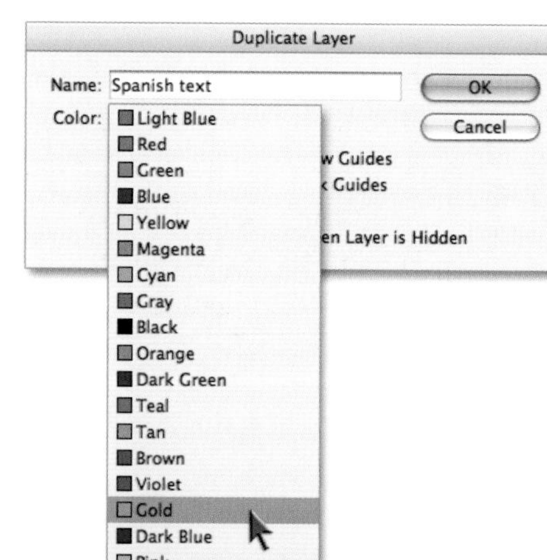

press Ctrl+D (or ⌘-D) to display the **Place** dialog box. Navigate to the *MetroBanco assets* subfolder inside the *Lesson 09* folder and select the *MetroBanco copy (Spanish).doc*. Then click the **Open** button to replace the selected text with the placed Word document, as in Figure 9-29.

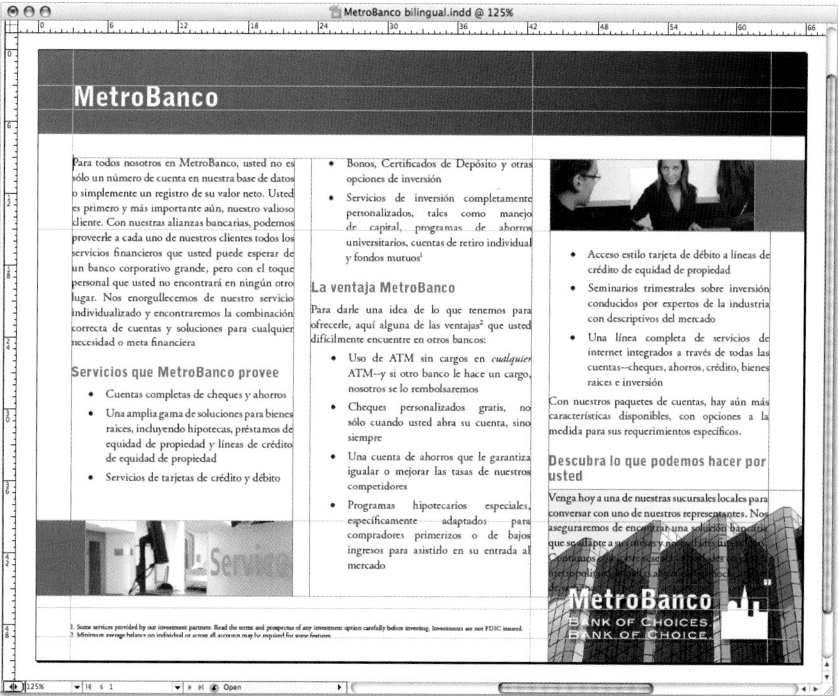

Figure 9-29.

9. ***Copyfit using revamped paragraph styles.*** The text in the Word document automatically maps to the style sheets included in the InDesign file. But the Spanish text is much longer, so it doesn't fit as nicely into the columns and it overflows the end of the final column. Fortunately, I created some alternate styles in advance. Here's how to switch them out:

   - Choose **Edit→Find/Change** or press Ctrl+F (or ⌘-F) to display the **Find/Change** dialog box. Make sure the **Text** panel is active.

   - Let's start by taking care of a slight punctuation problem with this particular document. Enter "--" (two hyphens) into the **Find What** field. Then click the @ icon to the right of the **Change To** field and choose **Hyphens and Dashes→Em Dash** from the pop-up menu to access the em dash character. Click **Change All** to replace two instances of the double hyphen. When the alert comes up, click **OK** to dismiss it.

- Now to replace the styles. Delete the contents of the **Find What** and **Change To** fields. Next, click the icon to the right of the **Find Format** field in the lower half of the dialog box to display the **Find Format Settings** dialog box. Set the **Paragraph Style** option to **Body**—that's it, nothing more—and click **OK**. Then click the icon to the right of **Change Format** and set **Paragraph Style** to **Body (Spanish)**. Again click **OK** and then click the **Change All** button. InDesign tells you it made six changes. Click **OK** to say, "Yeah, whatever."
- We have one more change to make. Click the icon for **Find Format** to display the **Find Format Settings** dialog box. Change **Paragraph Style** to **Bullet** and click **OK**. Now click the for **Change Format** and set **Paragraph Style** to **Bullet (Spanish)**. Click **OK** and then click **Change All**. This time you find out that InDesign made two changes, which happens to mean several bulleted items clustered into two groups were changed. Click **OK** because it's the only thing you can do. Then click the **Done** button to exit the Find/Change dialog box. The very large Figure 9-30 illustrates the resulting document.

Figure 9-30.

10. ***Activate the Spanish hyphenation dictionary.*** The text wraps better than before, but there are still plenty of inconsistent gaps. The text needs hyphenation that subscribes to the rules of Spanish:

   - We'll change the hyphenation via a paragraph style. To avoid assigning the style to any text, press Ctrl+Shift+A (⌘-Shift-A).
   - Go to the **Paragraph Styles** palette and double-click **Body (Spanish)** to display the **Paragraph Style Options** dialog box.
   - Click the word **Hyphenation** in the left-hand list or press Ctrl+8 (⌘-8). Then turn on the **Hyphenate** check box and reduce the **Hyphen Limit** value to 1. (Hyphenation reduces legibility, which is a premium for ad copy. So fewer hyphens are better.) Assuming the **Preview** check box is on, you'll see all body copy, including the bulleted items (which rely on a child style), hyphenate on the page.
   - Click **Advanced Character Formats** on the left side of the dialog box, or press Ctrl+3 (⌘-3). Switch the **Language** setting from English: USA to **Spanish** and watch the hyphens update.

The text hyphenates in keeping with the conventions of Spanish-language text. As Figure 9-31 shows, the text wraps better as well. To accept your changes, click **OK**.

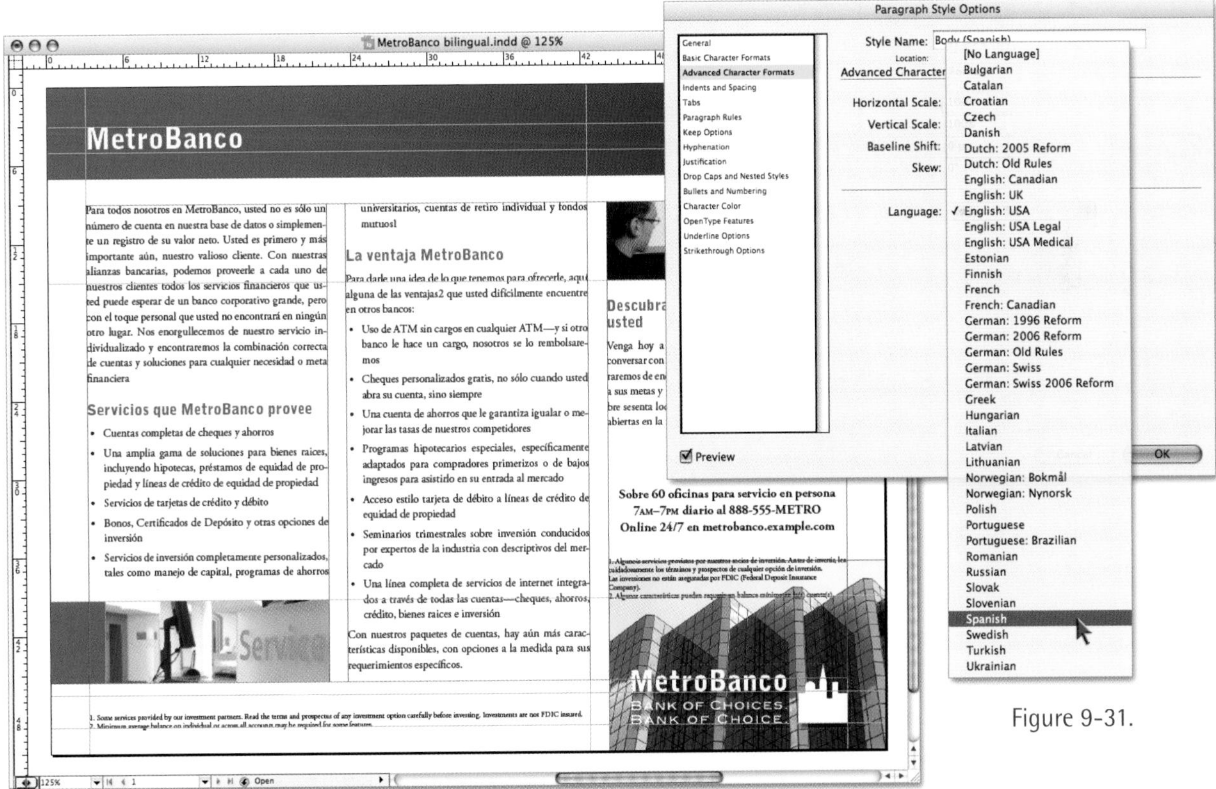

Figure 9-31.

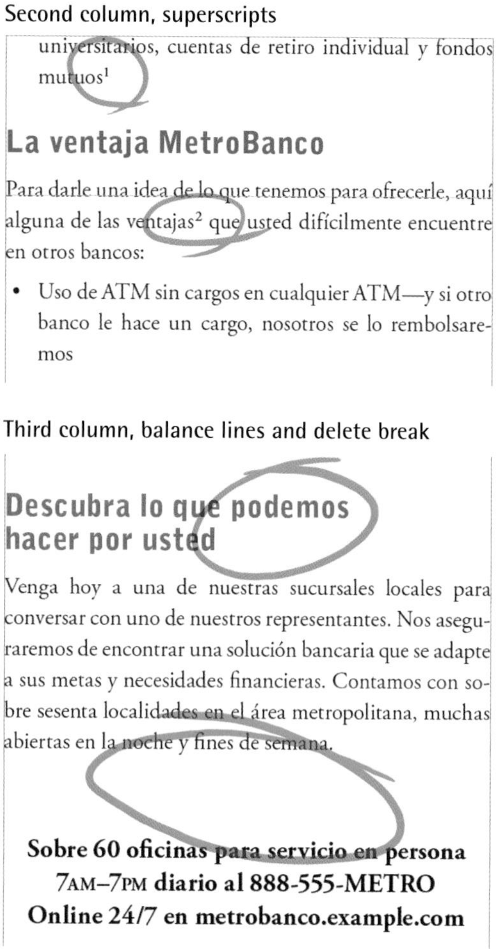

Second column, superscripts

universitarios, cuentas de retiro individual y fondos mutuos[1]

La ventaja MetroBanco

Para darle una idea de lo que tenemos para ofrecerle, aquí alguna de las ventajas[2] que usted difícilmente encuentre en otros bancos:

- Uso de ATM sin cargos en cualquier ATM—y si otro banco le hace un cargo, nosotros se lo rembolsaremos

Third column, balance lines and delete break

Descubra lo que podemos hacer por usted

Venga hoy a una de nuestras sucursales locales para conversar con uno de nuestros representantes. Nos aseguraremos de encontrar una solución bancaria que se adapte a sus metas y necesidades financieras. Contamos con sobre sesenta localidades en el área metropolitana, muchas abiertas en la noche y fines de semana.

Sobre 60 oficinas para servicio en persona
7AM–7PM diario al 888-555-METRO
Online 24/7 en metrobanco.example.com

Figure 9-32.

11. ***Make a few small text modifications.*** The text needs some additional work before we achieve perfection. It's all housekeeping stuff, so I'm lumping it into one step:

    - At the top of the column, you should see a couple of lines of text that end *y fondos mutuos1*. That *1* should be subscripted. To do it properly, select the 1 with the type tool, click the ▾≡ on the far right side of the control palette, and choose **OpenType→Superscript/Superior**.
    - Repeat the operation for the 2 a few lines down, in the text that reads *de las ventajas2*.
    - Click with the type tool in the third column headline, the one that reads *Descubra lo que podemos hacer por usted*. Click the ▾≡ on the right side of the control palette and choose **Balance Ragged Lines**. If you loaded my dekeKeys, you can press Ctrl+Alt+B (⌘-Option-B) as well.
    - To eliminate the excess vertical spacing near the end of the third column text, click at the end of the paragraph of body copy—after the period that follows *muchas abiertas en la noche y fines de semana*—and press the forward delete key, labeled Delete on the PC (⌦ on the Mac). This deletes the paragraph break. Figure 9-32 shows this and the previous three edits, all circled in blue.
    - Now to replace the English footnote with the Spanish version. Select the five lines of 7-point text at the end of the third column. (The most effective way is to quadruple-click on the first paragraph and, on the fourth click, drag down to include the other paragraphs.) Then press Ctrl+X (⌘-X) to cut the text to the clipboard. Next click in the second text block, the one at the bottom of the page. Press Ctrl+A (⌘-A) to select all the English copy and then Ctrl+V (⌘-V) to replace it with the Spanish equivalent.

That's the majority of the text trimming, anyway. The text includes a handful of widows, but given my complete and utter ignorance of Spanish, I think I'll leave well enough alone.

EXTRA CREDIT

Although powerful compositional tools, layers can get a little ponderous at times. Astonishing only in their dullness, if you prefer. If you're nodding off, you can skip ahead to "Assigning XML Tags and Structure," which begins on page 400. Or grab a cup of Joe with an espresso shot and stick with me as we explore customizing layers, isolating text wraps, relegating guides, and other zany, madcap, increasingly ponderous topics. Honest, it's interesting stuff.

12. ***Move the service desk image to a higher position.*** I'm not crazy about how the final bulleted entry in the first list breaks to the second column. But short of editing the text (which would require a Spanish-speaking copywriter), there's nothing to do about it. However, we can minimize the interruption by moving the service desk image above the first red subhead. Meanwhile, I want to keep the image in place for the English text. That's going to take some effort, but the results are worth it:

    - Switch to the black arrow tool. As a precaution, press Ctrl+Shift+A (⌘-Shift-A) to deselect everything.
    - Click on the **Artwork** layer to make it active. Then click its 🔒 icon to unlock it.
    - Drag a new horizontal guideline out of the top ruler. Drop it any old place. It should appear blue to show that it's still selected (so colored because the Artwork layer is blue). Change the **Y** value on the left side of the control palette to "23p9" and press the Enter or Return key to move the guide to the desired location.
    - Select the service desk artwork by clicking the red area to the left of the photo and beyond the left edge of the text block. (The text block is in front, so clicking it will select it.) This selects a group with a text wrap around it.
    - Back in the **Layers** palette, click the empty square to the far left of the **English Text** layer to display its 👁 and turn on the layer. The document window will look a mess, what with one language overlapping the other. Call it an occupational hazard—we have to see the layer to edit it.
    - Drag the tiny blue ■ to the right of the **Artwork** layer up to the **English Text** layer to move the service art to the same layer as the English marketing copy.
    - Now let's make a duplicate of that same artwork for the Spanish layer. Press the Alt (or Option) key and drag the tiny green ■ from the **English Text** layer to the **Spanish Text** layer, as pictured in Figure 9-33.
    - Click the 👁 in front of the **English Text** layer to turn it off again. Make sure that the **Spanish Text** layer is active and the service image is selected. Then drag the selected artwork until the top edge snaps into alignment with the new horizontal guide. (The artwork is in front of the text so don't worry about where you start your drag.) While dragging, press and hold Shift to constrain the angle of your drag to exactly vertical.

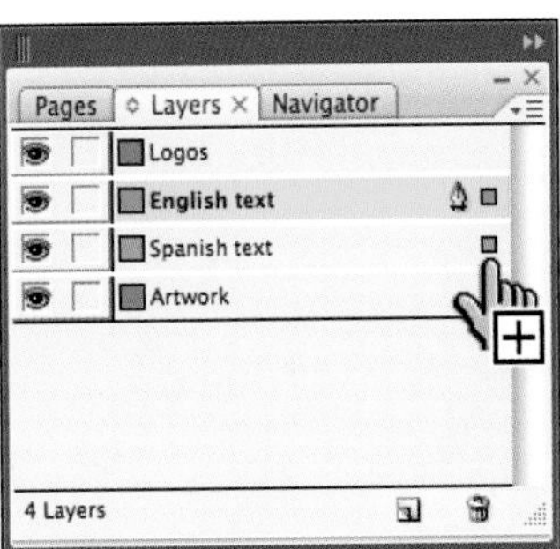

Figure 9-33.

13. ***Suppress the hidden text wraps.*** The graphic no longer breaks the text, but now we're left with a big gap at the bottom of the first column. You might suppose that the text frame needs to be expanded to the bottom of the page. But the frame fills the entire area within the magenta margin boundaries. The real culprit is the text wrap from the hidden artwork on the English Text layer. We'll solve the problem using an option that we first visited in the "Wrapping Text around Graphics" exercise in Lesson 6 (see page 246):

   - Double-click the **English Text** layer in the Layers palette to display the **Layer Options** dialog box. Turn on the **Suppress Text Wrap When Layer Is Hidden** check box to prevent an invisible English layer from affecting a visible Spanish one. Then click **OK**. The first column of text stretches down to the bottom of the frame, as shown in Figure 9-34.
   - Repeat the operation for the Spanish layer. Double-click **Spanish Text** in the Layers palette, turn on the **Suppress Text Wrap When Layer Is Hidden** check box, and click **OK**. Now the Spanish layer won't affect the English one when it's invisible either.

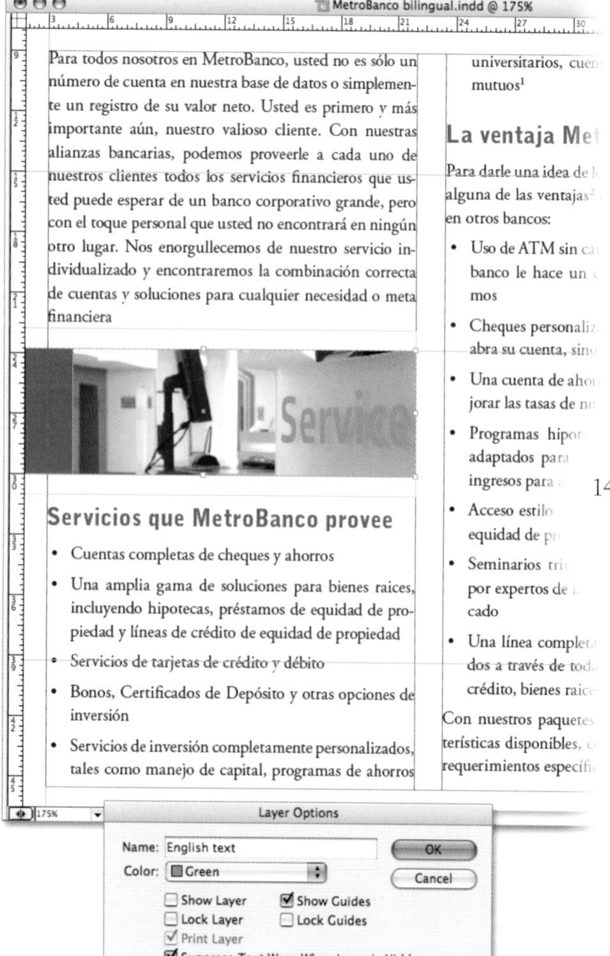

Figure 9-34.

14. ***Move the corporate logo to the language layers.*** It may have occurred to you that one object remains untranslated: the logo in the bottom-right corner of the page. It's English, so it belongs on the English Text layer:

   - Because the logo elements exist on the master page, we're going to have to go there. Press the F12 key to switch to the **Pages** palette and then double-click the **A-Master** thumbnail.
   - Locate the white letters and stylized city silhouette with drop shadows in the bottom-right corner of the document. Click the logo with the black arrow tool to select it.
   - Press F7 to return to the **Layers** palette. Click the empty box to the far left of **English Text** to again turn on the layer and then drag the red ■ to the right of the **Logos** layer down to English Text.
   - Alt-drag (or Option-drag) the green ■ from **English Text** to **Spanish Text** to make a copy of the logo.
   - Click the 👁 in front of **English Text** to turn it off.

15. ***Import the Spanish-language logo.*** With the English logo still selected in the document window, choose **File→Place** or press Ctrl+D (⌘-D on the Mac). With any luck, the **Place** dialog box will still be targeted on the *MetroBanco assets* subfolder in the *Lesson 09* folder. Locate the *Logo Spanish.eps* file, confirm that the **Replace Selected Item** option is checked, and click the **Open** button. We now have a Spanish logo on the Spanish layer.

16. ***Return to page 1.*** Choose **Layout→Go Back** to return to page 1 of the document. You can also press the keyboard shortcut Ctrl+Page Up (or ⌘-Page Up). The alternate logo appears against the bank photo in Figure 9-35.

Similarly, you can press Ctrl+Page Down (or ⌘-Page Down) to bounce back to the master page. You might think of Ctrl+Page Up and Ctrl+Page Down (⌘-Page Up and ⌘-Page Down) as the equivalents of the Back and Forward buttons in a Web browser. Bear them in mind when you need to move back and forth between pages in a document.

Figure 9-35.

17. ***Isolate the ruler guides on their own layer.*** By way of a farewell tip, I'll show you how to create a special guides layer. The advantage of such a layer is that it permits you to hide ruler guides while keeping margin and column guides visible:

    - Press Ctrl+Alt+G (⌘-Option-G) to select all the guides.
    - Alt-click (or Option-click) the icon in the **Layers** palette, type "Guides" in the **Name** option box, set the **Color** to **Ochre** (for contrast), and click **OK**.

Clicking the icon creates a new layer at the top of the stack. To create a layer directly above the active layer, press Ctrl (or ⌘) and click the icon. To create a layer below the active layer, Ctrl+Alt-click (or ⌘-Option-click) the icon. To display the New Layer dialog box during either operation, press Ctrl (⌘) or Ctrl+Alt (⌘-Option) and click the ▾≡ icon in the top-right corner of the Layers palette. The first command in the palette menu will change to New Layer Above or New Layer Below depending on the keys pressed.

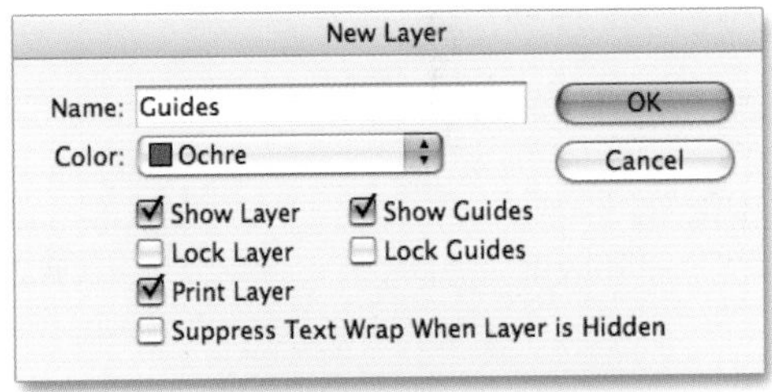

    - Drag the blue ■ from the **Artwork** layer up to the **Guides** layer, as in Figure 9-36.
    - Click the icon in front of **Guides** to hide the new layer.

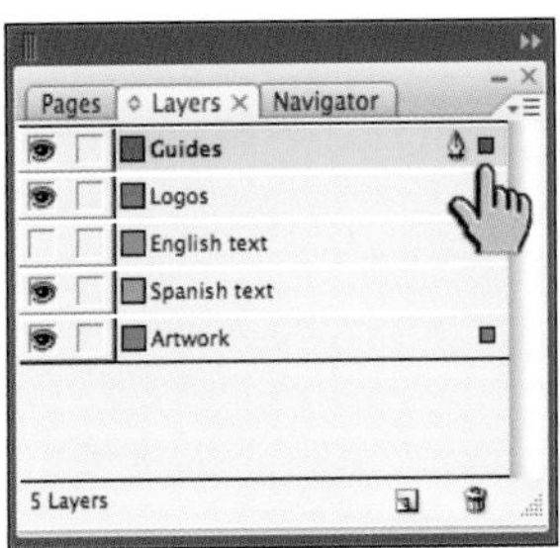

Figure 9-36.

Unfortunately, we were only partially successful in hiding the ruler guides; the orange guides are gone, but the cyan guides are still there. The cyan guides reside on the master page.

18. ***Move the master-page ruler guides to the Guides layer.*** Press Ctrl+Page Down (or ⌘-Page Down) to return to the master page with logos and cyan guides. Then do like so:

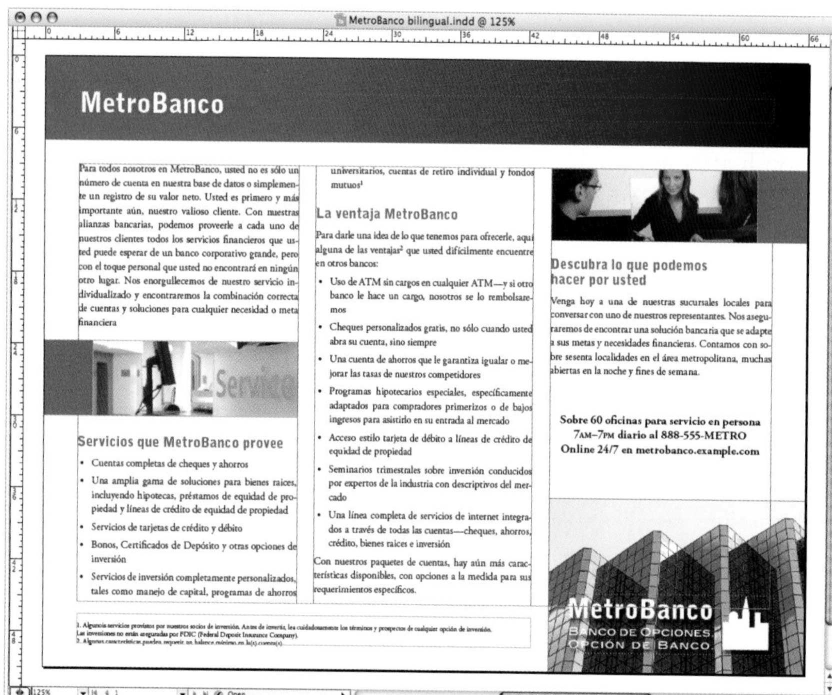

Figure 9-37.

- Press Ctrl+Alt+G (⌘-Option-G) to select the guides.
- Back in the **Layers** palette, click the empty 👁 box to turn on the **Guides** layer.
- Again drag the blue ■ from the **Artwork** layer to the **Guides** layer to transport the selected guides. The guides turn ochre, indicating that they now reside on the Guides layer.

Click the 👁 icon for the **Guides** layer to hide all the ruler guides, whether they're on the page or the master page. Then press Ctrl+Page Up (or ⌘-Page Up) to go back to page 1. Figure 9-37 shows the final, Spanish-language page design.

PEARL OF WISDOM

The upshot of the final MetroBanco document (the exercise above) is that you can now easily flit between two-documents-in-one, each localized for a different market. But beware: Thanks to Steps 12 and 13, the layers influence each other in ways you might not expect. Turn on the English Text layer and the document turns into a mess of weird wraps and unresolved conclusions. Turn off Spanish Text, and suddenly English Text is all better. The English text negatively affects the Spanish text as well. As InDesign is currently wired, the two languages can't quite coexist. No, I don't like the implications either.

Assigning XML Tags and Structure

Text variables, master pages, and layers are great organization and efficiency tools. But it still takes a lot of time, patience, sweat, tears, and good old-fashioned designer stamina to assemble a document from beginning to end. For my part, I quite enjoy it. Laying out pages is very zen. And I'm a big believer that where results are concerned, the manual approach is invariably the best approach. But it's not always practical. Maybe time is short, or you're understaffed, or your client is just plain cheap. That's when it's time to automate the design process with the help of three powerful letters, XML.

Like its cousin, HTML (the underlying framework for most Web pages), XML is a *document-processing language*, meaning that it enables you to create and format documents by writing relatively simple computer code. The difference is that XML is *extensible*, allowing you to create and define your own code words, called *tags*.

If you've never written a line of computer code, rest assured that I'm not about to change that. InDesign can read and write XML without sharing any of the unpleasantness with you. For those of you who have some coding experience, InDesign generates efficient and comprehensible XML that you can edit as easily as your own.

InDesign CS3 employs XML for three purposes:

- First, XML automates the layout of documents that contain a consistent collection of elements. Suppose you publish a newsletter that is always 12 pages long. Page 1 carries the masthead, an article, and a photo; Page 2 contains a member roster and a list of upcoming events; and so on, month after month. Using a text editor, you can prepare an XML file that contains all the text for the upcoming newsletter and lists the locations of the graphics. Import that file into InDesign and every object goes into its proper place. A few tweaks and the layout is complete.
- Second, XML lets you separate the content from the design. Then you can place the content into different templates to achieve different results. Placing the newsletter XML file into one template makes it a printed newsletter. Another template turns it into an online PDF file. And a third excerpts a single story and adds it to the annual report. XML facilitates the repurposing of material and permits you to better appeal to the changing needs of your target audience.
- Third, you can further automate the design process by creating an *XML rule set*. Most commonly scripted in the cross-platform JavaScript, an XML rule set is a file of coded instructions that you can apply to a tagged document from the Scripts palette (Window→Automation→Scripts). The rule set looks for certain conditions inside a document and, if and when a condition is met, applies a specific action. So in the case of our newsletter, every issue can vary in structure and length based on its content.

In return for its promise of timesaving automation, XML demands that you spend a hefty amount of time in the up-front planning phase. As a result, I devote a total of three exercises to this topic. In this first exercise, you'll assemble a collection of tags, assign those tags to everything from entire frames to individual words of text, and define the structure of your XML-savvy document. In the second exercise, you'll export your text links and graphic links to an XML file and then strip out all content until you're left with a bare-bones, XML-structured template. And finally, you'll overhaul your XML content and place it into the structured template. Then all you have to do is sit back and watch the fireworks.

FURTHER INVESTIGATION

Scripting falls outside the scope of this book. But if you have some experience with JavaScript and you're inclined to push the envelope, you can learn more about scripting and applying rule sets at *www.adobe.com/products/indesign/scripting*. The site contains documentation, white papers, and other detailed information.

1. ***Open a file that will serve as a template for future documents.*** Our model document is yet another in the Shenbop-the-dead-frog series, *Seventies Quiz #4.indd* in the *Lesson 09* folder inside *Lesson Files-IDcs3 1on1*. Pictured in Figure 9-38, this single-page document sports a thick column of narrative text up top, a flanking piece of imported line art, and three columns of hanging indents below. XML can be a daunting topic, so I've purposely selected a short, simple, goofy design. But bear in mind, everything we'll be doing throughout the remainder of this lesson works just as well for long, complex documents, including newspapers, magazines, and books.

You know, it's really not fair to stigmatize an entire generation of music because of a few awful songs. In our last test, The Rockets' "Oh Well," Sugarloaf's "Don't Call Us, We'll Call You," and Dobie Gray's "Drift Away" are all respectable pop tunes, each a modest classic in its own right.

But the rest of the songs range from lackluster to excruciatingly awful. "The Night the Lights Went Out in Georgia" tells the story of a girl who murders two people, gets a third hung, and yet reckons it's all the fault of ignorant law enforcement officials. "Afternoon Delight" draws a frisky analogy between lovemaking and fish baiting. And "Playground in My Mind" is the stupidest song ever.

Which brings us back to the quiz. As before, match the song title with the lyrics, which might occur at any point in the song. This is the hardest test yet—with 5 more songs than usual!—so prepare to dig back into the darkest recesses of your memory.

Answers: 1.L, 2.E, 3.O, 4.H, 5.D, 6.I, 7.M, 8.J, 9.C, 10.G, 11.B, 12.F, 13.A, 14.K, 15.N

Match these song titles…

1. Rock On
2. Undercover Angel
3. Heaven on the 7th Floor
4. Couldn't Get It Right
5. Radar Love
6. Moonlight Feels Right
7. I'd Really Love to See You Tonight
8. The Night Chicago Died
9. One Tin Soldier
10. Saturday Night
11. Rock Me Gently
12. Brand New Key
13. Come and Get Your Love
14. The Cover of the Rolling Stone
15. You Sexy Thing

…with the lyrics below.

A. Cuz you're fine in your mind and you look so divine.
B. Don't you know that I have never been loved like this before?
C. Turned the stone and looked beneath it. "Peace on Earth," was all it said.
D. No more speed, I'm almost there. Gotta be cool, now, I gotta take care.
E. I never had a dream that made sweet love to me.
F. Some people say I done all right for a girl.
G. We're gonna rock it up, roll it up, do it all, have a ball.
H. I kept on lookin' for a sign in the middle of the night.
I. I play the radio on Southern stations, cuz Southern belles are hell at night.
J. In the heat of the Summer night, in the land of the dollar bill.
K. We sing about beauty and we sing about truth at $10,000 a show.
L. Jump up and down in blue suede shoes.
M. Hello. Yeah, it's been a while. Not much. How 'bout you?
N. I believe in miracles. Where ya from?
O. I thought I was out of luck, and ten seconds later, somehow we got stuck in the elevator.

Figure 9-38.

2. ***Open the Structure bay.*** Click the ◆ icon in the lower-left corner of the document window to open the **Structure** bay. Alternatively, you can choose View→Structure→Show Structure or press Ctrl+Alt+1 (or ⌘-Option-1 on the Mac). Shown on the left side of Figure 9-39, this clandestine subwindow permits you to manage the underlying structure of the XML document that you'll eventually export from InDesign.

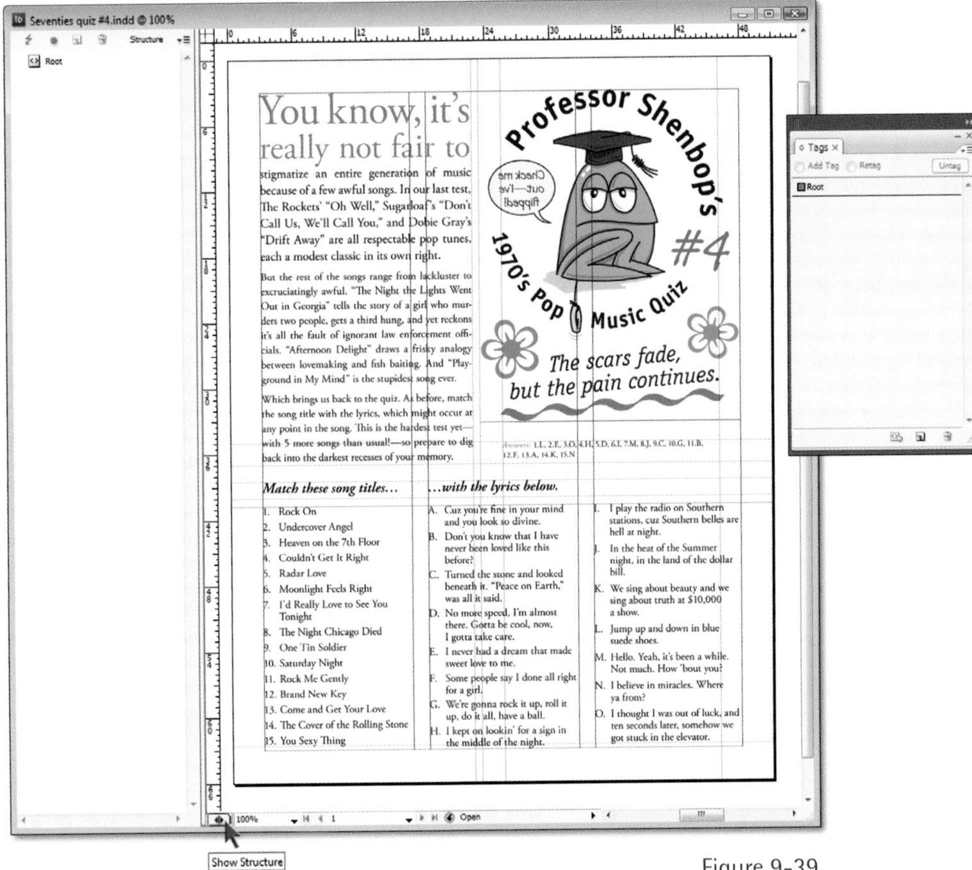

Figure 9-39.

Although this might be the first time you've stumbled across it, the Structure bay is lying in wait inside every document you create. Drag the vertical bar to the left of the ruler to adjust the width of the bay. If you ever find yourself wanting to get rid of the bay, again click the ◂|▸ icon or press Ctrl+Alt+1 (⌘-Option-1).

---

3. ***Open the Tags palette.*** Choose **Window→Tags** to display the **Tags** palette, which lets you create and apply XML tags. Although it lacks a keyboard shortcut, the Tags palette is every bit as important as the Structure bay. The fact is, you need both to create an XML-formatted document in InDesign.

PEARL OF WISDOM

Like style sheets, *tags* identify paragraphs and words so that you can format them automatically. You can even apply tags to entire text blocks and graphics to control the placement of imported objects. Unlike style sheets, tags do not by themselves convey formatting attributes. They merely label objects; you then use InDesign to define what those labels mean. For more information on tags, read the sidebar "XML, Tags, and Elements," which begins on page 410. Or just hang in there and all will become clear.

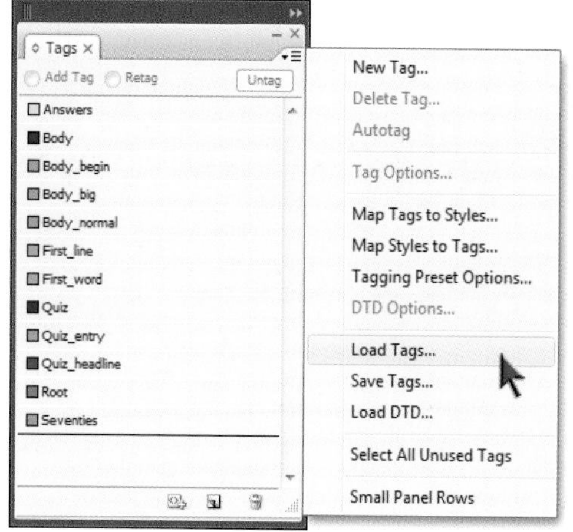

Figure 9-40.

By default, both the Structure bay and Tags palette contain one tag apiece, Root, which represents the base level of XML content. You need do nothing with Root; just leave it as is and everything will work fine.

4. ***Load a file of predefined tags.*** The Tags palette lets you create single tags at a time or import a group of previously saved tags from disk. To cut down on the tedium, we'll start with the latter and then try out the former. Click the ▾≡ icon in the top-right corner of the Tags palette and choose **Load Tags** from the palette menu. Select the file *Quiz tags.xml* in the *Lesson 09* folder and then click the **Open** button. Eleven new tags appear in the Tags palette, as in Figure 9-40.

At this point, you may have some questions: For example, how did I create the *Quiz tags.xml* file that you just loaded? What's with the underscores in the newly imported tag names? And what made me select *these* particular tag names? My answers:

- To generate *Quiz tags.xml*, I started by manually creating each of the eleven tags in the Tags palette. Then I chose the Save Tags command from the palette menu and named the file *Quiz tags.xml*. InDesign stored all the tags (including Root) to disk. You can likewise load XML documents scripted inside a text editor. For reference, the contents of *Quiz tags.xml* appear in Figure 9-41. (The red and blue coloring is imposed automatically by Internet Explorer, which I used to view the code. The actual file is composed of plain, unformatted text.)
- Your XML tags can be as long or short as you want, but by the laws of XML, they should contain only letters and numbers. Slashes, colons, quotes, and most other punctuation are illegal. Also steer clear of spaces. If you need a space, use one of the two sanctioned dashes, which are an underscore (_) and a hyphen (-).
- Beyond that, you can name your tags anything you want. Just bear in mind that you'll have to reference them again, which may involve entering the tag names with all underscores and capitalization precisely intact. For the most part, I rely on tags that match the names of my style sheets. We'll see why in Step 8 (page 406).

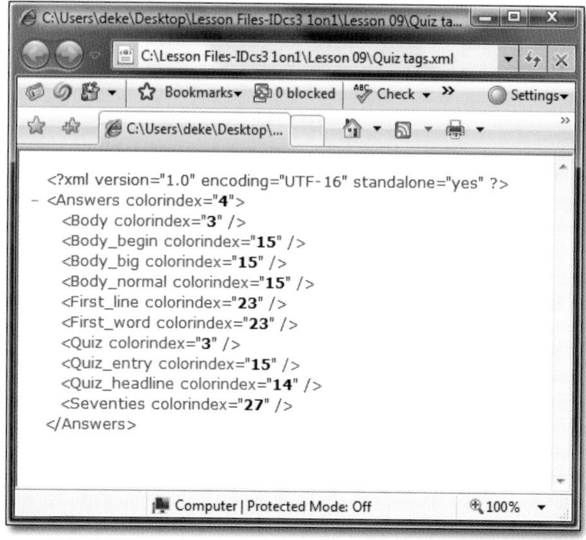

Figure 9-41.

5. ***Create a Cartoon tag.*** As we'll see, the tags make up all but one element of the page, namely the imported Shenbop graphic. So we need to create a tag for the graphic manually. To do so:

   - Press the Alt key (Option on the Mac) and click the ◻ icon at the bottom of the Tags palette. Pressing the key while clicking the icon forces the display of the **New Tag** dialog box, shown in Figure 9-42.
   - Enter "Cartoon" into the **Name** field. Be careful to spell the word correctly, start it with a capital *C*, and make the word singular. Proper naming of this item will affect the success of future steps.
   - Change the **Color** to **Red**. (It's okay to use another color if you like, but your screen will look different from mine.)
   - Click the **OK** button to accept the new tag.

   The word *Cartoon* preceded by a red box appears in alphabetical order inside the Tags palette.

Figure 9-42.

6. ***Apply the Cartoon tag to the graphic.*** Now to put the tags in play. Let's begin with the tag you just created. Select the Shenbop graphic with the black arrow tool and click **Cartoon** in the **Tags** palette.

To highlight tagged objects so that you can tell one from the other, choose **View→Structure→Show Tagged Frames**. The selected graphic will appear red, as in **Figure 9-43** on the next page. This command is merely a display function; it does not represent how the document will print, nor does it affect the export or execution of the XML script.

Notice that the Structure bay now contains a Cartoon entry. In XML lingo, this entry is called an *element*. An XML element may in turn contain an *attribute*, which often defines the content of the tagged object. Click the ▶ triangle to the left of **Cartoon** in the **Structure** bay to reveal this attribute, which begins with *href* (the very same *hypertext reference* attribute employed in HTML). The selection is an imported graphic, so InDesign adds a line of *href* code to document the location of the linked vector illustration on disk.

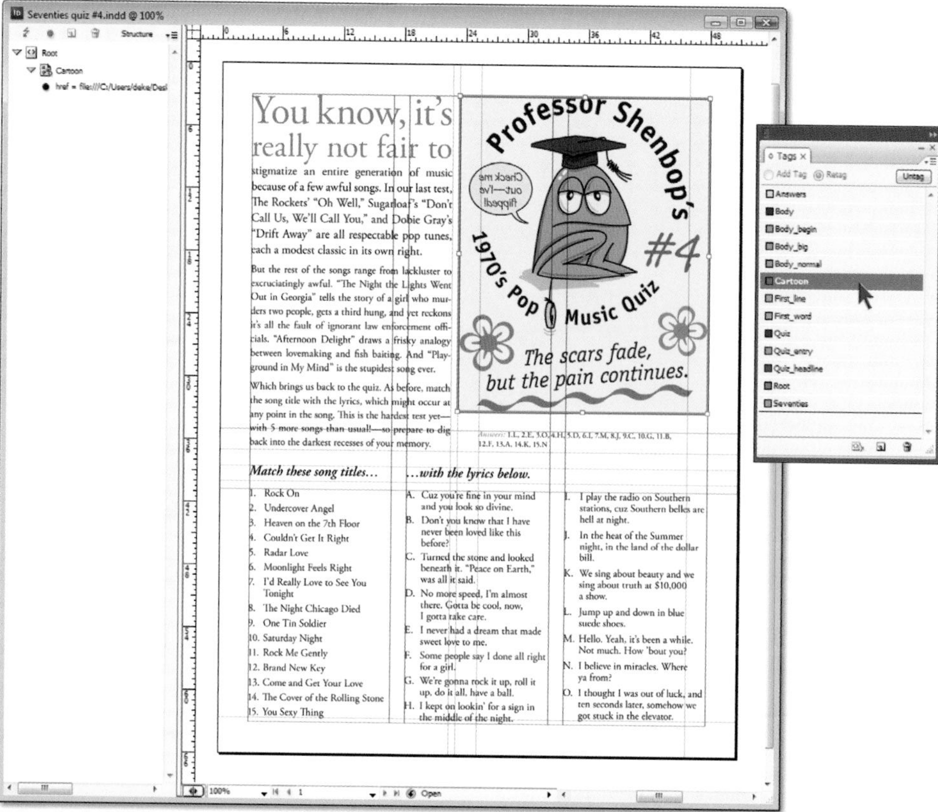

Figure 9-43.

7. ***Apply tags to the text elements.*** All told, this document contains seven text blocks. Here's how I want you to tag them, and the exact order I want you to use:

    - Select the large upper-left frame with the black arrow tool, and then click the blue **Body** tag in the **Tags** palette.
    - Select the two bold, italic subheads and apply the violet **Quiz_headline** tag.
    - Select the column of numbered song titles and click **Quiz_entry**. Then select the second column and click **Quiz_entry** again to tag the entire lettered list.
    - Click the small text block below the graphic—the one that begins with the red word *Answers*—and apply the yellow **Answers** tag.

    Assuming you turned on Show Tagged Frames, you should see a fully color-coded document like the one in Figure 9-44.

8. ***Compare the tags to the style sheets.*** It's important to tag all frames in a document so that InDesign knows where to position imported XML text and referenced graphics. But while

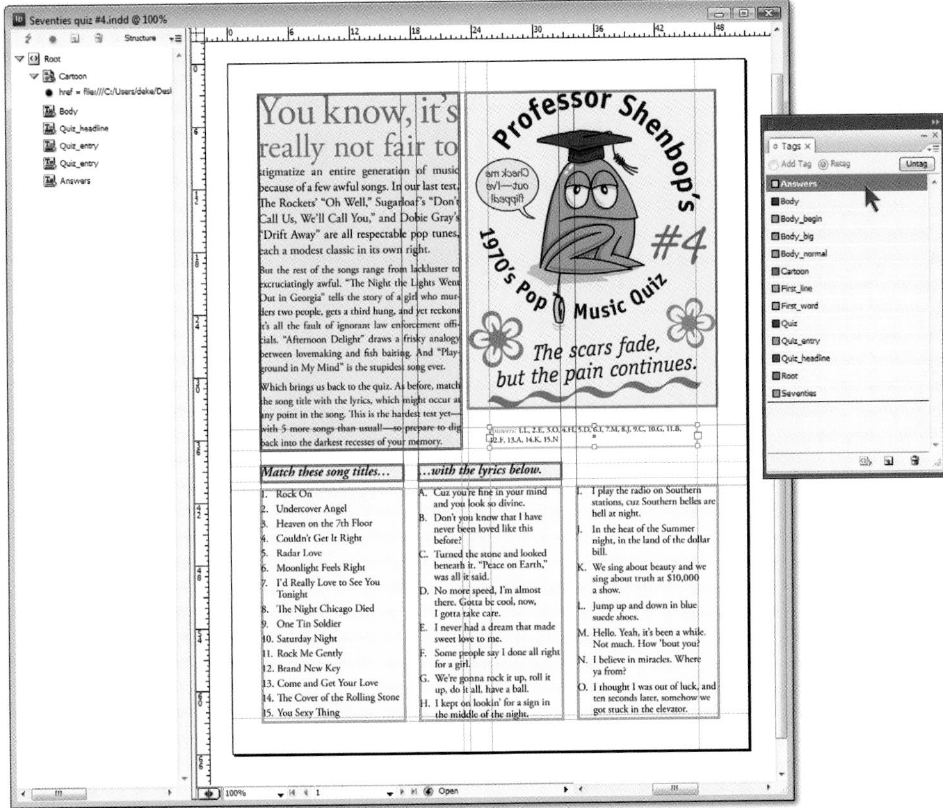

Figure 9-44.

tagging addresses placement, it does nothing for formatting. To preserve the formatting of individual characters and paragraphs, you have to select and tag text with the type tool, a potentially long and dull process. Fortunately, there's a better way. If you first take the time to apply style sheets to all formatting distinctions, you can map those styles to tags lickety-split.

To see the styles assigned to this document, bring up both the **Paragraph Styles** and **Character Styles** palettes (F11 and Shift+F11, respectively). As illustrated in Figure 9-45, every style—paragraph and character styles alike—corresponds to an identically named tag. How? I defined the style sheets first, and then I created tag names to match, just as I recommend you do when building your own XML-savvy documents.

9. *Map the style sheets to tags.* To assign the remaining formatting tags, choose **Map Styles to Tags** from the **Tags** palette menu. (You can also get to the command from the Structure bay menu.) The ensuing dialog box lists every style sheet in the document, both paragraph and character,

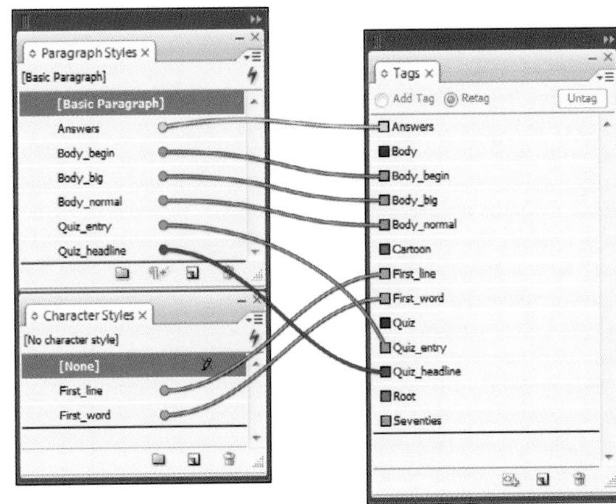

Figure 9-45.

followed by a corresponding tag (most likely [Not Mapped] because no style has yet been mapped). Here are your options:

- Because the style sheets and tags share names, you can click the **Map by Name** button under the list in the dialog box to set each style to its corresponding tag. The problem with this simple approach is that you already assigned three of these tags—Answers, Quiz_entry, and Quiz_headline—to text frames. Mapping these tags to every paragraph of text inside the styled frames would duplicate the tags and clutter the code, which is sloppy and pointless.
- The better solution is to figure out which tags you haven't applied and select them manually. To do so, click a tag name on the right side of the dialog box to display a pop-up menu of available tags. We need to map five tags in all: those that correspond to the character styles, namely First_line and First_word, as well as the three Body variations. To make the tags easier to find, I colored them red in Figure 9-46.

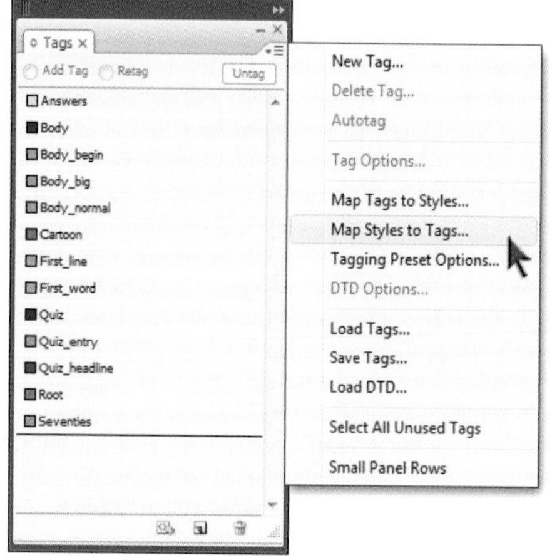

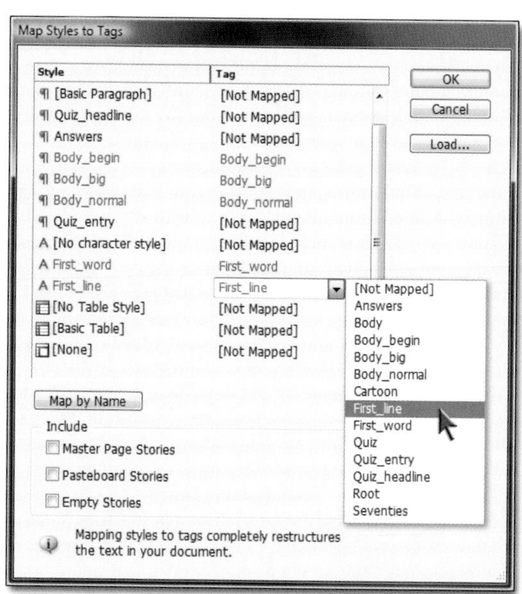

Figure 9-46.

Select the proper tags for the red items in the figure. Then click **OK**. In the document window, InDesign highlights the formatting tags with subtle colored brackets. The orange brackets in the blue text block are the easiest to see, but you can spot green tags in the blue and yellow blocks if you look carefully.

10. ***Fully expand the element tree.*** The hierarchy of entries in the Structure bay is the *element tree*, so termed because it branches into elements and subelements. To expand the tree so you can

see all the subelements, do like so: First, click the ▼ triangle to the left of the word **Root** to collapse the tree and hide all the elements. Now, press the Alt key (Option on the Mac) and click the ▶ to expand the tree, this time revealing all elements.

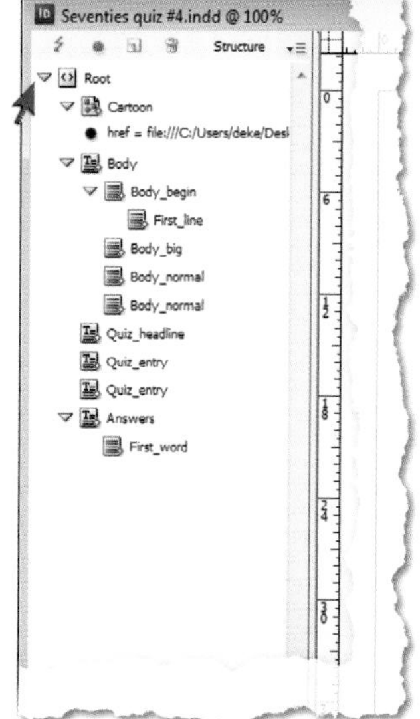

Figure 9-47.

Pictured in Figure 9-47, the expanded tree reveals how elements are grouped. The character tags—First_line and First_word—are nested inside their paragraphs. The Body text tags—the ones with the underscores—are nested inside the Body text block. That still leaves some work. I'd like to see the Quiz subelements grouped together. And then I'd like to shuffle the elements into a more logical order. We'll do both tasks in the next steps.

11. ***Create a new Quiz element.*** Click **Root** to select it. Then click the icon to create a new element inside Root. InDesign displays the **Select Tag for Element** dialog box, which lets you assign a tag to the element. Choose **Quiz** from the **Tag** pop-up menu (see Figure 9-48) and click **OK**. A new Quiz element appears at the bottom of the tree.

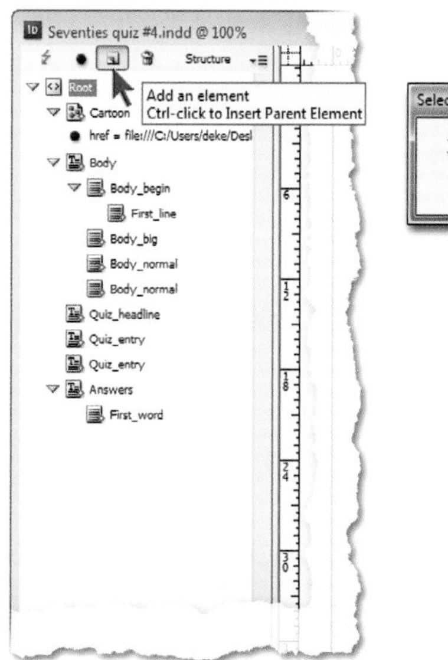

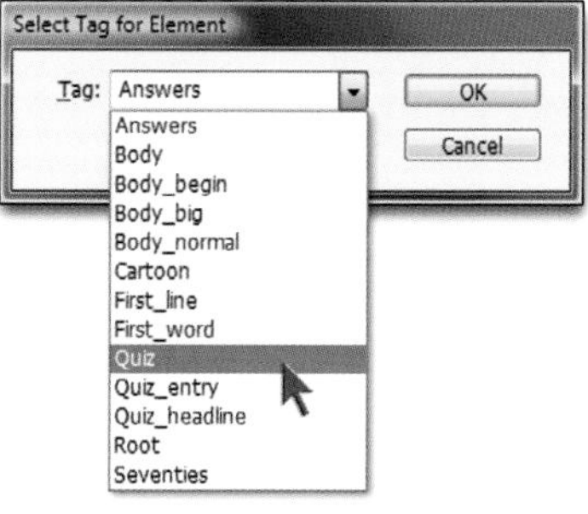

Figure 9-48.

12. ***Reorganize and group elements.*** Now to change how the elements are ordered and grouped:

   - Drag the new **Quiz** element above and slightly to the left of Quiz_headline. (This ensures that Quiz is even with Body, not nested inside it.) Wait until you see a long horizontal bar before releasing the mouse button.

   - Click **Quiz_headline** and Shift-click the second of the two **Quiz_entry** elements to select all three items. Then drag them onto the **Quiz** icon and release. This makes

XML, Tags, and Elements

Computer languages are a foreign concept to most designers. So when I say that you can use a computer language, XML, to automate page layout, most designers conjure up images of a scripting language, in which one line of code says *put Item A here* and another says *put Item B there*. The script explains a sequence of operations to the application—in our case, InDesign—and the application does as it's told.

Scripting can be an intimidating prospect. To be a successful scripter, you have to understand the syntax, plan a logical approach, verify whether your script works, and troubleshoot when it fails. It's a unique discipline, and it takes time to master.

Thankfully, XML is not a scripting language. As its last two initials suggest, XML is a *markup language*, which means that it uses *tags* to identify elements in a document. InDesign uses these tags to decide where the elements should go and how they should look. I wouldn't necessarily characterize XML as easy—it's a complex language with its own syntax, standards, and oversight committee. But happily, InDesign doesn't require you to know anything about that stuff. So far as InDesign is concerned, XML is a method for assigning tags and nothing more.

The X in XML stands for *extensible*, which for our purposes means that you can name your tags anything you want. You can call one line of type *Headline*, another *Subhead*, and a third *Caption*. Or you can call them *head-1*, *head-2*, and *cutline*. As long as you subscribe to XML's naming conventions—start with a letter; stick with letters and numbers; and use underscores and hyphens instead of spaces—then you can call them *Tom*, *Dick*, and *Hermione* for all anyone cares.

To give you a sense of how tags work, the figure on the right shows a few lines of XML code. The red labels encased by blue angle brackets (called *delimiters*) are the tags. An opening tag begins an *element*, a closing tag (which starts with a slash) ends it. An element usually contains text, but it may also contain other elements. For example, in the figure, the *headlines* element includes both the *mainhead* and *subhead* elements. The black text inside the *mainhead* and *subhead* elements and elsewhere is the actual text that will appear in the laid out InDesign document.

If XML's tags remind you of style sheets, it's no coincidence. After all, both tags and style sheets define passages of text, and you can assign them custom names. The big difference is that styles convey formatting attributes, but tags do not. In fact, tags have no intrinsic meaning at all; they are merely labels waiting for definitions, the very definitions that style sheets are eager to supply. Thus, to format the *mainhead* tag in the figure, you have only to create a corresponding *mainhead* style sheet. It's a match made in heaven.

You can also associate tags with InDesign's frames. For example, I might assign the *headlines* tag from the figure to a text frame that's large enough to contain both the *mainhead* and *subhead* text. Assuming that I've defined *mainhead* and *subhead* style sheets, the layout and formatting operations become automatic. As illustrated at the top of the facing page, the *headlines* tags tell the text where to go; the *mainhead* and *subhead* tags define how the text should look. Thus with the help of XML, you can place, position, and format text in one operation, using no more coding than a few simple tags.

Opening tag
<headlines>
<mainhead>All of Humankind's Amassed Knowledge Now Understood to Be Wrong</mainhead>
<subhead>Toss Those Books in the Dumpster, Say Experts, They Ain't No Good No More</subhead>
</headlines>
<lead>GOTHAM CITY, NY—A hastily assembled forum of scientists, philosophers, and theologians met Monday to take it all back. "We don't know quite what the Earth revolves around," admitted Jonathan Leahy, PhD, a Senior Research Fellow at the Astro-Zeitgeist Institute, "But it sure as heck isn't the Sun." According to Dr. Sarah Weidenbach of the Epicurean Foundation, "We now realize that every time Rene Descartes opened his mouth, he excreted utter and complete nonsense." When asked to comment, Rev. Peter Górecki of the National Ecclesiastical Society said, "Honestly, folks, I don't know where to begin."</lead>
Tagged element
Closing tag

You can use XML tags to place and position graphics as well. To do so, you create what's called an *empty element* that contains no text and no closing tag. The opening tag ends with a slash, making it self-closing. The tag, which

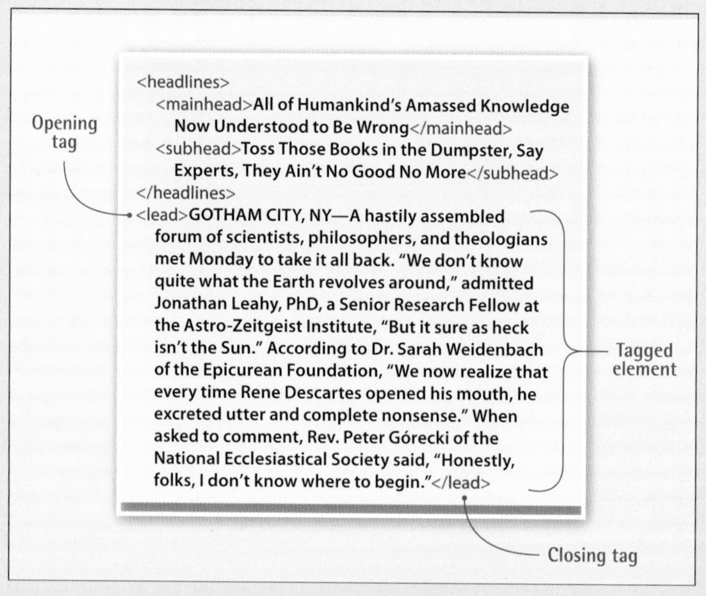

I've named *scientist_photo* in the illustration at the bottom of the page, is immediately followed by *href*, an attribute borrowed from the Web-page language HTML, which is commonly used to reference external graphics. The *href* attribute is followed by an equal sign, quotes, *file:///*, and the location and name of the graphic on disk.

This is all a lot to remember, which is why it's fortunate you don't have to. Based on the line of code pictured in the figure below-right, do as follows:

- Replace the red text with your own tag name.
- Replace the black text with the location and name of the graphic file.
- Enter the blue text exactly as shown, including spaces around the *href*, around the equal sign, and before the final slash.

In InDesign, assign your tag to a frame large enough to hold the graphic. If the frame is not large enough, the graphic will be cropped along the right and bottom edges. In other words, InDesign aligns the graphic to the upper-left corner of its frame. InDesign offers no means to include scaling or other transformation data in an XML document, so the graphic comes in at the full size and resolution specified in the originating graphics application. (If only we had graphic style sheets, you could create a style that specified custom cropping, scaling, and rotating info. But for the present, you have to perform these operations by hand after importing the XML content.)

One last note: When specifying the location of a graphic on disk, you should enter all folders relative to the location of the XML file separated by slashes. In the example to the right, the XML file and the *Links* folder must reside together in the same folder or volume, and the file *Nutty Guy.tif* must reside in the *Links* folder. This is not the only way to specify file locations, but it is usually the best way because it permits you to move the XML file and all associated graphic links to another hard drive or shared volume without confusing the *href* attribute.

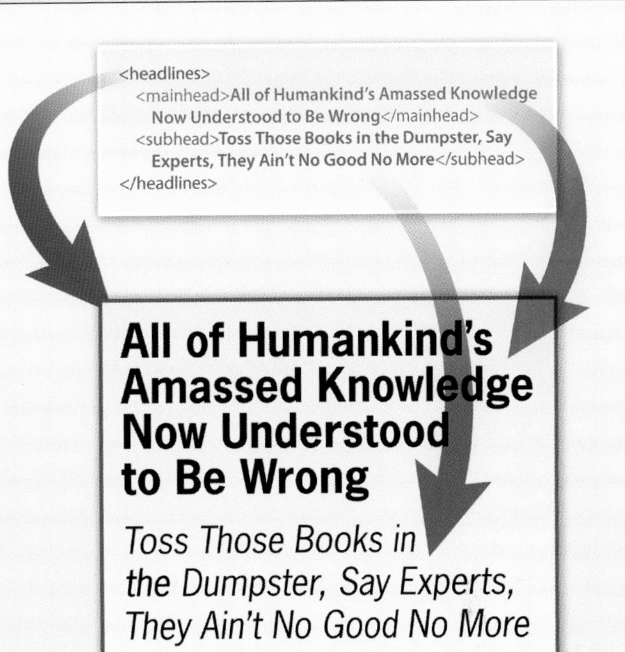

photo by Brian Maffitt

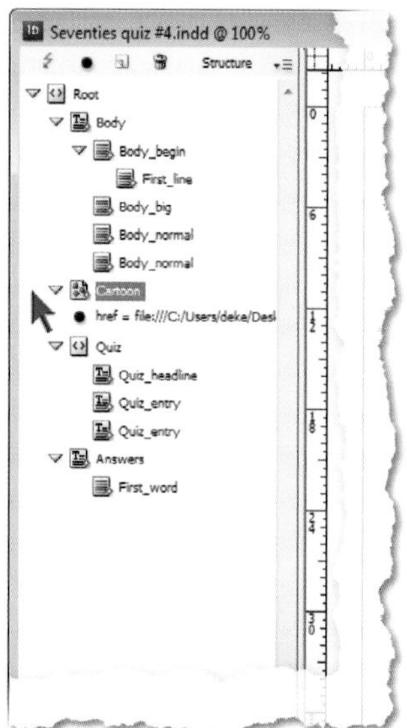

Figure 9-49.

Quiz_headline and Quiz_entry subelements of Quiz. Click the ▶ triangle next to **Quiz** (if it's not already pointing downward) to expand the element and see its contents.

- Drag the **Cartoon** item to just above and slightly to the left of Quiz. (Again, we're trying to ensure that Cartoon is even with Body, not inside it.) The resulting list of four elements and nine subelements should look like Figure 9-49.

13. ***Add a document-level element.*** This step is not absolutely necessary, but it's a good habit to get into. Currently, we have a series of elements organized under the banner of Root, the XML base. But what's to distinguish these tags—with common names such as Body and Cartoon—from similarly named tags in different documents? As it currently stands, someone could import this XML content into the wrong template and watch the content go completely haywire.

PEARL OF WISDOM

The solution is to gather all elements (except Root) into a document-level element that serves as a project identifier. If a template doesn't include the document element, the XML content is ignored and no harm is done. If the template does include the element, the template is confirmed as a match and the import goes forward.

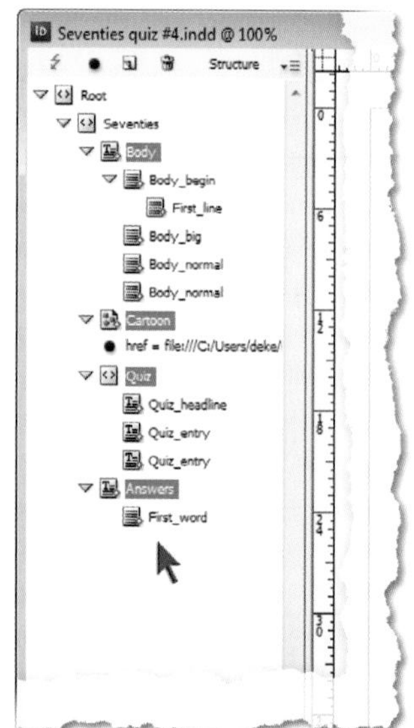

Figure 9-50.

I know, it all sounds dense. Fortunately, it's easy to pull off:

- Select the **Root** item and click the icon.
- Inside the **Select Tag for Element** dialog box, select **Seventies** from the **Tag** pop-up menu and click **OK**.
- Click **Body** and Shift-click **First_word** (below Answers) to select all elements except Root and Seventies. Then drag the selected elements onto **Seventies** and release.
- If the ▶ triangle in front of **Seventies** is pointing to the right, click it to expand the outline. When the triangle is pointing down, you'll see the outline as pictured in Figure 9-50. This outline comprises every element—not to mention, every word of text and link information for every imported graphic—in the document.

14. ***Save your structured document.*** Choose **File→Save As.** Name your XML-savvy document "Seventies quiz #4-xml.indd" and save it in the same *Lesson 09* folder inside the directory *Lesson Files-IDcs3 1on1*. Your saved file will serve as the starting point for the next exercise.

Separating XML Content and Design

Having arrived at a highly organized and structured InDesign document, our next task is to separate the content from the design. In these steps, you'll export the text from the Shenbop quiz as a tagged XML file. This file will also contain information about the linked Illustrator graphic. Next you'll strip out all text and graphics while leaving the style sheets, tags, and XML elements intact. Then you'll save the result as a super-powerful structured template.

1. ***Open the document you saved in the last exercise.*** If the file is still open, great. If not, open the *Seventies quiz #4-xml.indd* file that you saved to the *Lesson 09* folder inside *Lesson Files-IDcs3 1on1*. If you neglected to save the file, you can open my version of the file, *Structured Shenbop.indd*, also inside *Lesson 09*.

   Whichever file you use, make sure that the **Structure** bay is available. If it isn't, click the ◂▸ icon or press Ctrl+Alt+1 (⌘-Option-1 on the Mac). Then Alt-click (or Option-click) the ▶ triangle next to **Root** to expand the entire element tree.

2. ***Add an attribute.*** In addition to elements, the Structure bay may contain *attributes*, which qualify an element. As I mentioned earlier, the Cartoon element includes an *href* attribute that tells us the location of the graphic on disk. While *href* has a specific meaning in InDesign—if you add an *href* to an XML element, InDesign will attempt to load a linked graphic—the meaning of other attributes is entirely up to you.

   Although custom attributes do not change the behavior of an XML file, they are useful for imparting background information. For example, you can create an attribute to credit the document's author, add a copyright statement, or report the date the document was last updated. I'd like you to credit the author, which in this case is you:

   - To make it easy to locate, basic information such as author credit is usually assigned to the document element. So select the **Seventies** element in the Structure bay.
   - Click the ● at the top-left corner of the window to display the **New Attribute** dialog box, as in Figure 9-51.

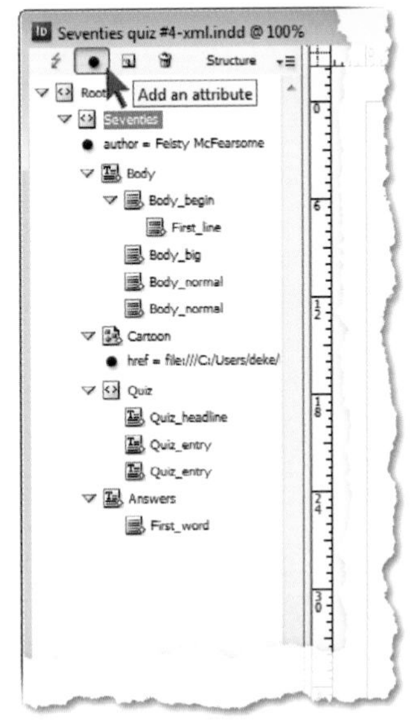

Figure 9-51.

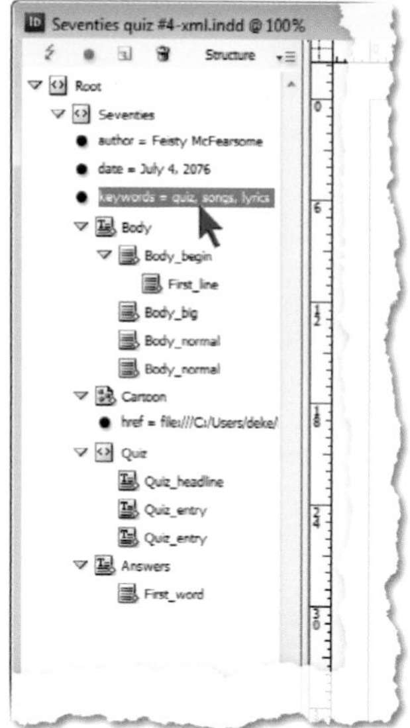

Figure 9-52.

- Type "author" for the **Name**. For the **Value**, type your name (complete with capital and lowercase letters, periods, and whatever else you have going). Then click **OK**.

InDesign adds the attribute as a bullet point below the word *Seventies* that reads *author* = you.

PEARL OF WISDOM

A few words of advice about attributes: First, you can add multiple attributes to an element, but they must all have different names, like the three attributes (*author*, *date*, and *keywords*) that I added to Seventies in Figure 9-52. If you want to assign multiple values to an attribute—as when crediting multiple authors—go for it. Customarily, values are separated by commas or spaces, but you can use any punctuation you like. In the figure, I added a *keywords* attribute that includes three values, each separated by a comma. You can also use punctuation inside a single value. In my *date* attribute, I used a comma to separate the date from the year, but it's all one date.

3. ***Change the* href *value to a relative pathname.*** Take a look at the *href* attribute for the Cartoon element. Most likely, it reads *href = file:///* followed by an *absolute pathname*, meaning that it explains every hard disk, folder, and subfolder that you have to open to get to the linked graphic. The problem with an absolute pathname is that it doesn't work when you transfer the graphic to another computer. Assuming that all your files are collected in a central folder—in our case, the *Lesson 09* folder—you're better off using a *relative pathname*, which explains the location of the graphic relative to that of the XML file. Copy the central folder to a different computer and the relative pathname remains accurate.

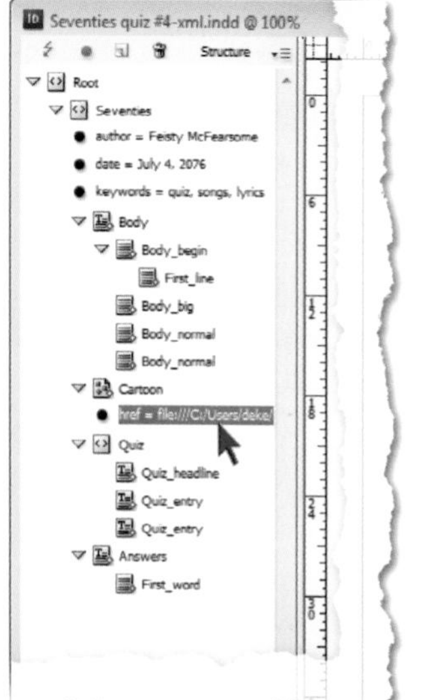

Figure 9-53.

Here's how to change the absolute pathname for the Shenbop cartoon to a relative one:

- Double-click the **href** item to display the **Edit Attribute** dialog box.
- In the **Value** option, delete everything from the hard drive through and including the *Lesson 09* folder (shown highlighted in Figure 9-53). The Value string should now read *file:///Cartoons/Shenbop_4.ai*. (Note that the word *file*, the colon, and the three slashes must remain intact.)
- Click **OK** to accept your changes.

4. ***Export the XML data.*** Having fixed the graphic attribute, we are ready to export the content of this structured document as an XML data file:

   - Choose **File→Export** or press Ctrl+E (⌘-E).
   - Inside the **Export** dialog box, set the **Save As Type** pop-up menu (which goes by the name **Format** on the Mac) to **XML**. Make sure *Lesson 09* is the active folder. Name the file "Structured Shenbop.xml" and click **Save**.
   - Next the **Export XML** dialog box appears. Turn on the **View XML Using** check box and choose **Internet Explorer** (or **iexplore.exe**, as in Figure 9-54). The other options—including Encoding, which by default is set to UTF-8 (the widely supported 8-bit-per-character Unicode Transformation Format)—are fine as is. Click **Export** to save the XML file.

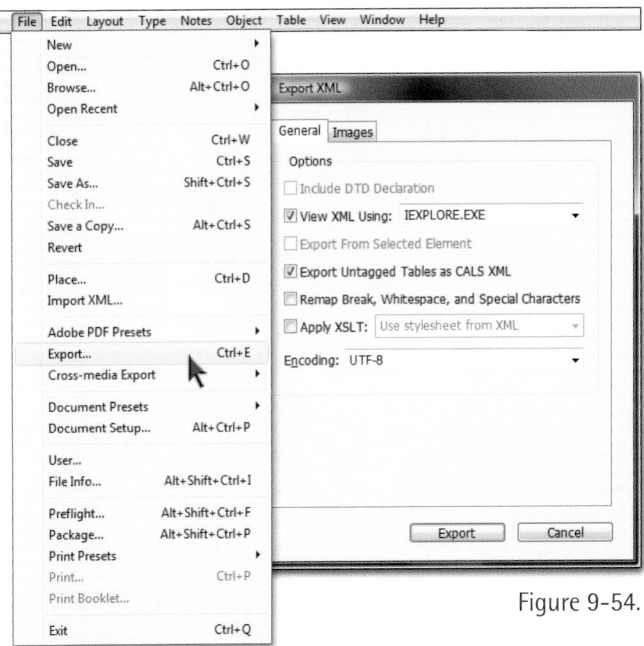

Figure 9-54.

In the blink of an eye, InDesign writes the XML data and opens it in Internet Explorer. The result appears in all its color-coded glory in Figure 9-55. Explorer formats the tags and attribute names in red, special scripting in blue, and all document text and attribute values in black.

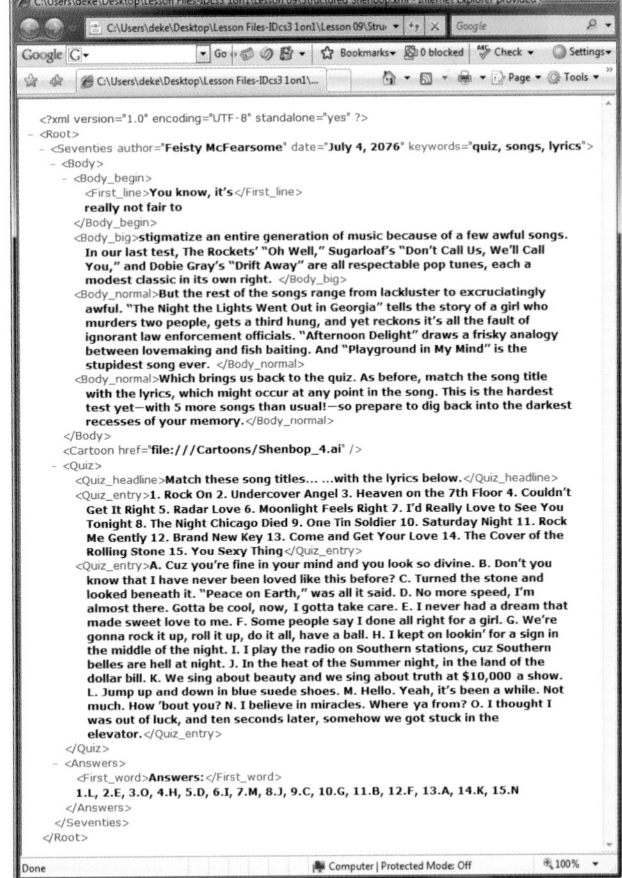

Figure 9-55.

PEARL OF WISDOM

If you're a Macintosh user, you may wonder why I don't use Apple's Safari. As I write this, the most recent version of Safari (2.0.4) lacks the ability to color-code and indent XML tags. And knowing the sometimes counterproductive brand of enlightenment that permeates Apple, it never will. You might try another browser, such as Mozilla's flexible and practical Firefox (*www.mozilla.com*), which deserves a space on every Mac. Or, if you plan on doing a lot of scripting, you might want to invest in a sophisticated text editor such as Bare Bone Software's BBEdit (*www.barebones.com*).

5. ***Switch back to InDesign.*** Thanks to File→Export, the XML content has been set free from the clutches of its design. With the content thus safe and sound, we are able to convert the InDesign document into a template. Go ahead and return to InDesign so we can get started.

6. ***Delete the cartoon from the graphic frame.*** To successfully convert an XML-savvy document into an XML-savvy template, you must delete the content without removing the frames or the structure. The best way to accomplish this varies depending on whether you're removing an imported graphic or text.

   We'll start with the graphic. First, select the white arrow tool. (Assuming no text is active, you can do this by pressing the A key.) Then click inside the Shenbop cartoon to select the imported graphic independently of its frame. Press the Backspace or Delete key. The cartoon goes away but the frame remains.

7. ***Delete the* href *attribute.*** InDesign is an astute application. But every once in a while, even it misses a beat. In this case, InDesign has succeeded in deleting the graphic, but it forgot to delete the *href* attribute, which could create problems when placing other graphics into this container. Click **href** in the **Structure** bay to select it; then press Backspace or Delete.

8. ***Delete all type from the text frames.*** To extract text from its frame, you have to first select the text with the type tool. With seven frames to choose from, this might take a while. So it's fortunate that InDesign provides a slight shortcut.

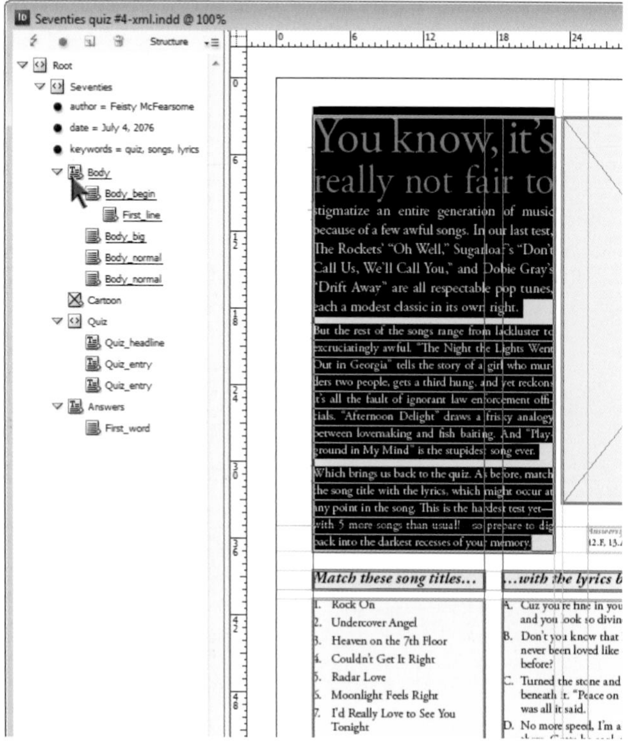

Figure 9-56.

To select the contents of a tagged text frame, double-click its element in the Structure bay. For example, double-click the top-level **Body** element to select all text in the upper-left frame, as demonstrated in Figure 9-56. Then press Backspace or Delete to get rid of it.

Repeat this process for the other text elements:

- Double-click the **Answers** element to select the text below the graphic frame. Then press the Backspace or Delete key.
- The Quiz tag is not assigned to a specific frame, so we have to address the Quiz subelements independently. Double-click **Quiz_headline** to select the text inside the violet frames, and then press the Delete key. Next, double-click a **Quiz_entry** element and press Delete. Repeat for the other **Quiz_entry** element.

Now that all the frames are empty, press Enter on the keypad to deactivate the frames and return to the black arrow tool. (If you didn't load my dekeKeys CS3 shortcuts, click the black arrow tool in the toolbox.)

9. ***Detach all character-level style sheets.*** A couple of tiny, subtle formatting problems remain. Each blue and yellow text frame begins with a character-level style sheet. If we neglect to turn off these style sheets, they will haunt us when we import the XML data in the next exercise. Here's the fix:

   - Press Ctrl+A (or ⌘-A) to select all the frames in the document.

   - Display the **Character Styles** palette (by pressing Shift+F11, if necessary). Then click the **[None]** option, as you see me doing in Figure 9-57. This deactivates the character styles but leaves all paragraph styles intact.

10. ***Save the document as a template.*** Choose **File→Save As**, or press Ctrl+Shift+S (⌘-Shift-S), and navigate to the *Lesson 09* folder. As demonstrated in Figure 9-58, change the **Save as Type** setting (**Format** on the Mac) to **InDesign CS3 template**. Rename the file "Structured template.indt" and click the **Save** button.

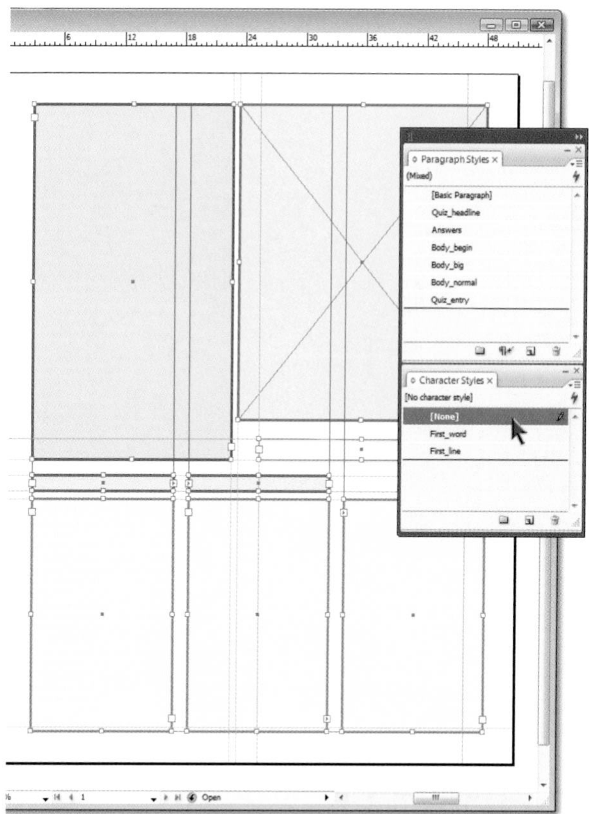

Figure 9-57.

Importing XML-Formatted Text

Congratulations, you have successfully accomplished a feat that precious few professional designers have dared attempt: You have created an XML-compatible template. In this final exercise, you'll see how this one magical document enables InDesign to assemble a complete page design—one that originally took me more than an hour to create—in a few minutes.

1. ***Close all open InDesign documents.*** In particular, be sure to close the document that you saved as a template file in Step 10 of the preceding exercise. This prevents you from accidentally damaging or overwriting your template document.

2. ***Open your XML-savvy template.*** If you successfully completed the last exercise, open the document you saved in Step 10, *Structured template.indt*, presumably found in the *Lesson 09* folder inside *Lesson Files-IDcs3 1on1*. Otherwise, open my version of the template, *My template.indt*, also inside *Lesson 09*.

Figure 9-58.

Before leaving the **Open a File** dialog box, make sure the **Normal** option (on the Mac, **Open Normal**) in the lower-left corner is turned on, as highlighted in Figure 9-59. This opens the template as an untitled document.

Make sure that the Structure bay is visible. Then Alt-click (or Option-click) the ▶ next to **Root** to expand the element tree.

3. ***Import an XML file.*** Choose **File→Import XML**, which imports the file and implements the XML code. (By comparison, File→Place would flow all text—content and tags alike—into columns.) Then do the following:

   - Navigate to the *Lesson 09* folder and select the *Structured Shenbop.xml* file that you saved in Step 4 of the preceding exercise (see page 415). If you can't find it, you can use my version of the file, *Seventies quiz #4.xml*.
   - Turn off the **Show XML Import Options** check box.
   - Select the **Merge Content** option to match the tags in the XML file with the elements in the template.
   - Click **Open** to import the file. A heartbeat later, InDesign places the document, arranges all the text and graphics into their allotted frames, and attempts to apply the appropriate style sheets. Not all the styles come out right (witness the headline in the blue frame in Figure 9-60), but we can fix that.

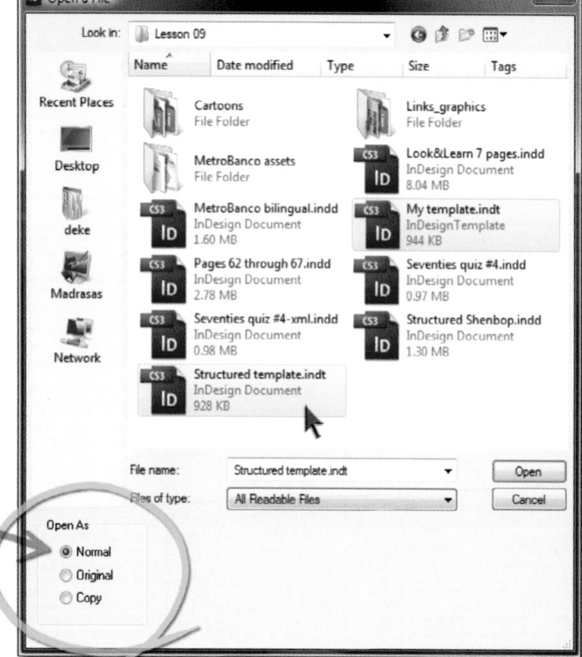

Figure 9-59.

PEARL OF WISDOM

If the Shenbop cartoon appears out of frame or cropped incorrectly, it's because your graphic import options are messed up. To fix them, press Ctrl+Z (or ⌘-Z) to undo the XML import. Choose File→Place and select the *Shenbop_4.ai* file inside the *Cartoons* subfolder in *Lesson 09*. Turn on the Show Import Options check box and click Open. In the Place PDF dialog box, set the Crop To option to Bounding Box. Make sure Transparent Background is on and click OK. Instead of clicking with the place cursor, press Ctrl+Z (or ⌘-Z) to abandon the operation. The preference now is reset and you're ready to go. Once again, choose File→Import XML and place the *Seventies quiz #4.xml* file to get the results in Figure 9-60.

4. ***Map the tags to style sheets.*** To properly format the imported text, choose **Map Tags to Styles** from either the **Tags** palette or the Structure bay menu. Modeled after the Map Styles to Tags command that we chose in Step 9 of "Assigning XML Tags and Structure" (see page 407), this command uses XML tags to select style sheet definitions. And this

time, we can do it entirely automatically. Click the **Map by Name** button to assign a style sheet to every applicable tag (highlighted red in Figure 9-61), and then click **OK**. Just like that, InDesign applies all style sheets exactly as we had them before.

5. ***Choose Undo twice.*** "All right," say the skeptics among you. "That's nice, but so what? What possible purpose does it serve to import text and graphics that we already had in place two exercises ago?" Fair enough, we'll call that a test—one that went over fabulously, but a test nonetheless. Choose **Edit→Undo** or press Ctrl+Z (⌘-Z) twice to undo the formatting and placement of the XML content. And now, let's replay these steps with a different XML document that contains completely new content.

6. ***Open the XML document for Quiz #5.*** Open the *Lesson 09* folder inside *Lesson Files-IDcs3 1on1*. Then double-click the file *Seventies quiz #5.xml*, which is the next edition of the Shenbop song quiz. With any luck, it'll open inside Internet Explorer. (If not, switch to Internet Explorer, choose **File→Open**, and then click the **Browse** button and locate the file on your hard disk. On the Mac, choose **File→Open File** or get a copy of BBEdit.)

   This XML document is largely different from the one we saw back in Figure 9-55 (page 415), but it uses the same tags and conforms to the same structure. In Figure 9-62 on the next page, I've highlighted the modified portions of the document in yellow. Notice that only the black text—i.e., the content—has changed, and not quite all of that. The quiz headlines and the word *Answer* are the same. And the only change made to the *href* attribute is the number at the end of the filename. I was careful not to modify a single red tag, nor did I change the sequence of the tags in the document.

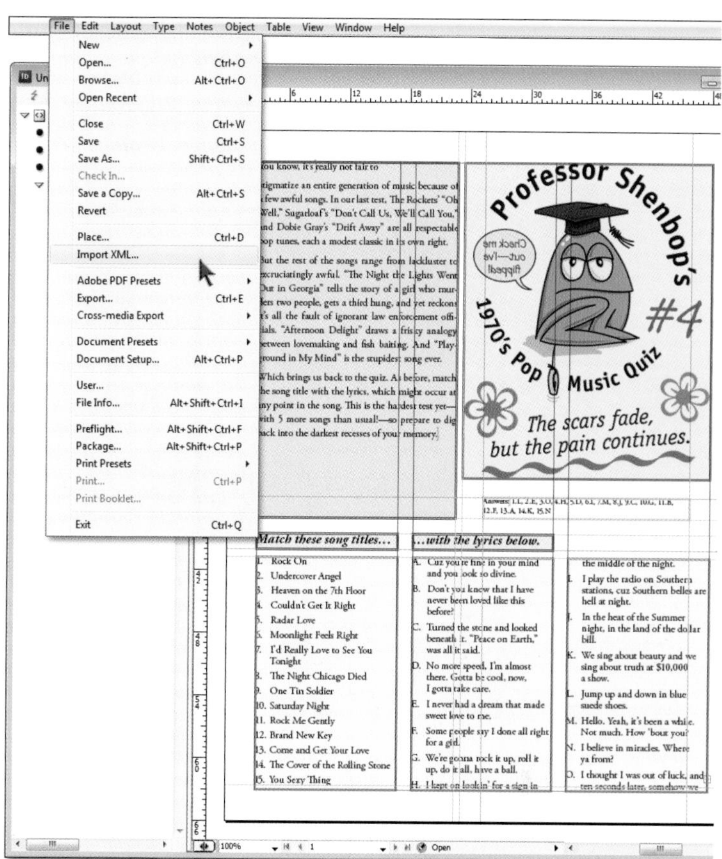

Figure 9-60.

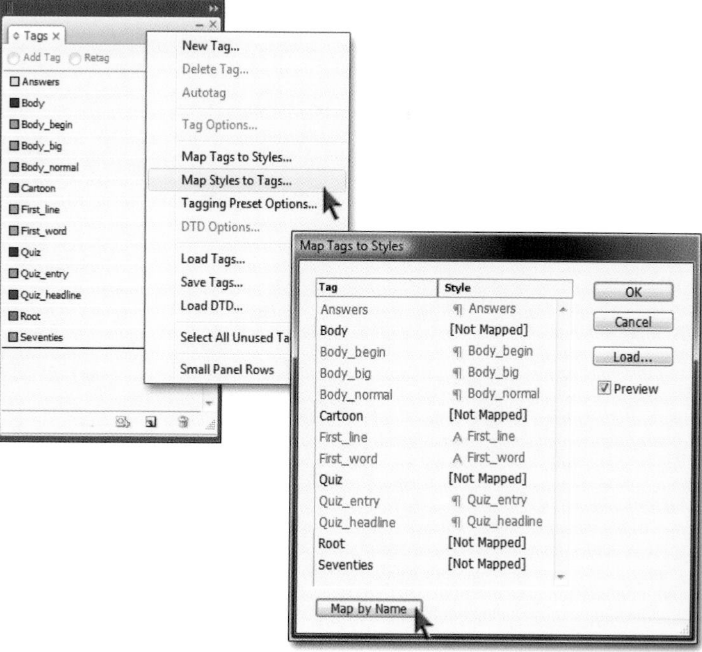

Figure 9-61.

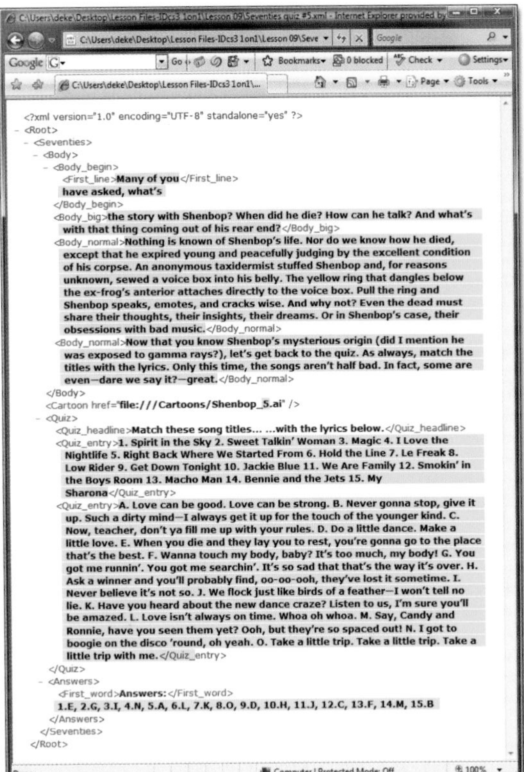

Figure 9-62.

PEARL OF WISDOM

You may wonder what program I used to make my edits. If you own the full Creative Suite (anything but the Design Standard or Production Premium variation), you can edit an XML document in Dreamweaver. Or you may prefer to cut down on the overhead and use a run-of-the-mill text editor. On the PC, you can use Notepad, which ships with Windows. I advise against using WordPad, which doesn't properly handle UTF-8 encoding (applied back in the preceding exercise in Step 4 on page 415). To keep your text inside the boundaries of the Notepad window, turn on Format→Word Wrap. On the Mac, I use TextEdit, included with OS X, or the more capable BBEdit. By way of example, Figure 9-63 shows details of the *Seventies quiz #5.xml* document open inside Notepad on the left and TextEdit on the right. Unlike Dreamweaver and BBEdit, neither of these free programs highlights the XML code, so you have to keep an eye out for the angle brackets, < and >, which surround all tags.

7. ***Return to InDesign and import the revised XML file.*** In InDesign, choose **File→Import XML**. Select *Seventies quiz #5.xml* in the *Lesson 09* folder and click **Open**. The program automatically lays out the fifth of the music quizzes (see Figure 9-64), filling each of the colored frames according to the specifications of the template and XML file. As before, the text in the blue frame needs help.

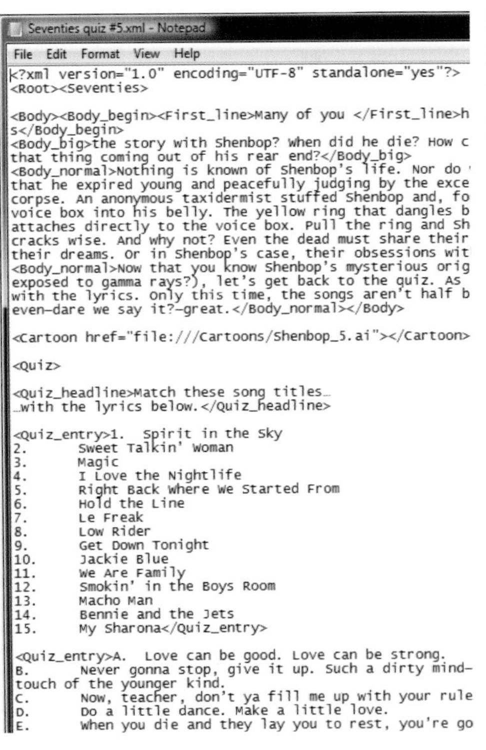

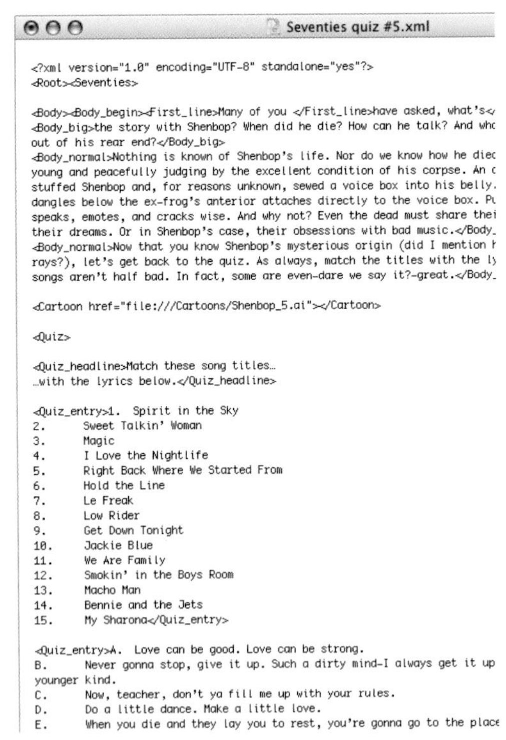

Figure 9-63.

8. ***Map the tags to style sheets.*** Choose **Map Tags to Styles** from the **Tags** palette or the Structure bay menu. Click the **Map by Name** button, and then click **OK** to apply all the proper style sheets to the document. The blue text block is by no means perfect, exhibiting enormous gaps in the first three lines, as illustrated on the left side of Figure 9-65. This is a common problem when placing XML content. Despite my best efforts to anticipate how much text I needed to fit the space, manual adjustments must be made.

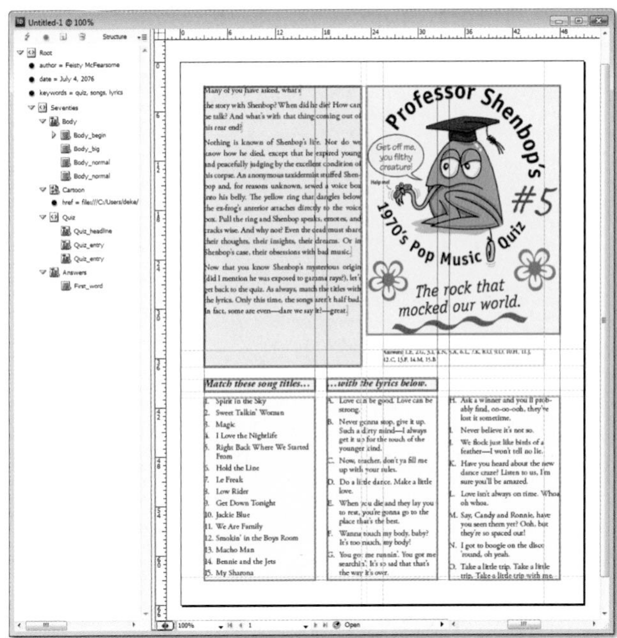

Figure 9-64.

9. ***Adjust the type size for the Body_begin style.*** The paragraph of large, crimson type is governed by the Body_begin style sheet. Let's make a one-time edit to this style as follows:

   - Double-click **Body_begin** in the **Paragraph Styles** palette to display the **Paragraph Style Options** dialog box.
   - Click **Basic Character Formats** in the left-hand list or press Ctrl+2 (⌘-2) to switch to the second panel of options.
   - Click the word **Size** to highlight the type size value. Then press the ↓ key four times to reduce the type size to 34 pt.
   - Click **OK**. The crimson type fits on two lines, as on the right side of Figure 9-65.

10. ***Add some paragraph spacing to the Quiz_entry style.*** The other slight problem with the text is the unevenness of the orange columns in the quiz, and the way the *H* entry splits between the second and third columns. Again, this can be remedied by adjusting a style sheet:

    - Double-click **Quiz_entry** in the **Paragraph Styles** palette.
    - Click **Indents and Spacing** in the left-hand list or press Ctrl+4 (⌘-4) to switch to the fourth panel.
    - Tab to **Space After** and raise it to 0p4.
    - Click **OK** to accept your changes.

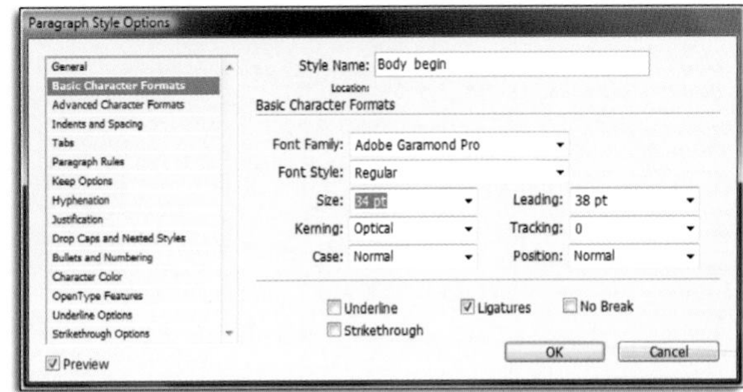

Figure 9-65.

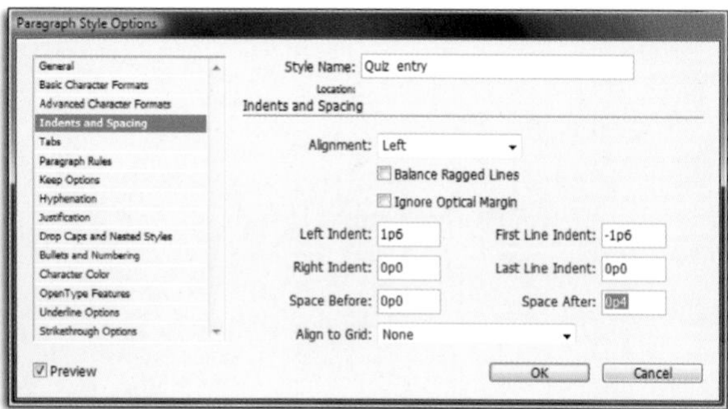

1. Spirit in the Sky
2. Sweet Talkin' Woman
3. Magic
4. I Love the Nightlife
5. Right Back Where We Started From
6. Hold the Line
7. Le Freak
8. Low Rider
9. Get Down Tonight
10. Jackie Blue
11. We Are Family
12. Smokin' in the Boys Room
13. Macho Man
14. Bennie and the Jets
15. My Sharona

A. Love can be good. Love can be strong.
B. Never gonna stop, give it up. Such a dirty mind—I always get it up for the touch of the younger kind.
C. Now, teacher, don't ya fill me up with your rules.
D. Do a little dance. Make a little love.
E. When you die and they lay you to rest, you're gonna go to the place that's the best.
F. Wanna touch my body, baby? It's too much, my body!
G. You got me runnin'. You got me searchin'. It's so sad that that's the way it's over.

H. Ask a winner and you'll probably find, oo-oo-ooh, they've lost it sometime.
I. Never believe it's not so.
J. We flock just like birds of a feather—I won't tell no lie.
K. Have you heard about the new dance craze? Listen to us, I'm sure you'll be amazed.
L. Love isn't always on time. Whoa oh whoa.
M. Say, Candy and Ronnie, have you seen them yet? Ooh, but they're so spaced out!
N. I got to boogie on the disco 'round, oh yeah.
O. Take a little trip. Take a little trip. Take a little trip with me.

Figure 9-66.

This adjustment fills the orange frames and nudges answer *H* to the third column, as in Figure 9-66.

11. ***Save the finished document.*** In the last four steps, you've managed to lay out a page that comprises eight frames, eight style sheets, and dozens of formatting variations. It was a cakewalk, but that's no reason not to save your changes. Choose **File→Save** or press the shortcut Ctrl+S (⌘-S). Then name the file "Seventies Quiz #5.indd" and click the **Save** button.

I made a couple of additional adjustments. The middle column in the quiz struck me as a bit short, so I selected paragraphs *A* through *G* with the type tool and raised the ≡ value in the Paragraph palette from 0p4 to 0p5. I also changed the size of the first crimson line of text in the upper-left corner of the page from 47 pt to 48 pt.

I mention this because I'm one of those designers who tends to fuss over a document long after I should probably let it go. But in this case, there's just not much for me to fuss over. Pictured in the preview mode in Figure 9-67, my final document is every bit as clean and polished as the one we saw way back in Figure 9-38 (see page 402). The difference is that I laid out that document manually, while this one laid out itself. With a little planning, you too can automate your way out of a whole lot of work.

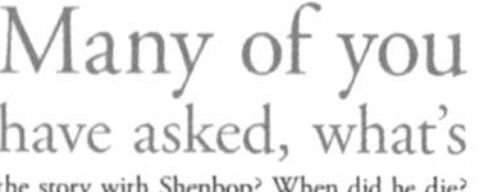

the story with Shenbop? When did he die? How can he talk? And what's with that thing coming out of his rear end?

Nothing is known of Shenbop's life. Nor do we know how he died, except that he expired young and peacefully judging by the excellent condition of his corpse. An anonymous taxidermist stuffed Shenbop and, for reasons unknown, sewed a voice box into his belly. The yellow ring that dangles below the ex-frog's anterior attaches directly to the voice box. Pull the ring and Shenbop speaks, emotes, and cracks wise. And why not? Even the dead must share their thoughts, their insights, their dreams. Or in Shenbop's case, their obsessions with bad music.

Now that you know Shenbop's mysterious origin (did I mention he was exposed to gamma rays?), let's get back to the quiz. As always, match the titles with the lyrics. Only this time, the songs aren't half bad. In fact, some are even—dare we say it?—great.

Answers: 1.E, 2.G, 3.I, 4.N, 5.A, 6.L, 7.K, 8.O, 9.D, 10.H, 11.J, 12.C, 13.F, 14.M, 15.B

Match these song titles...

1. Spirit in the Sky
2. Sweet Talkin' Woman
3. Magic
4. I Love the Nightlife
5. Right Back Where We Started From
6. Hold the Line
7. Le Freak
8. Low Rider
9. Get Down Tonight
10. Jackie Blue
11. We Are Family
12. Smokin' in the Boys Room
13. Macho Man
14. Bennie and the Jets
15. My Sharona

...with the lyrics below.

A. Love can be good. Love can be strong.
B. Never gonna stop, give it up. Such a dirty mind—I always get it up for the touch of the younger kind.
C. Now, teacher, don't ya fill me up with your rules.
D. Do a little dance. Make a little love.
E. When you die and they lay you to rest, you're gonna go to the place that's the best.
F. Wanna touch my body, baby? It's too much, my body!
G. You got me runnin'. You got me searchin'. It's so sad that that's the way it's over.
H. Ask a winner and you'll probably find, oo-oo-ooh, they've lost it sometime.
I. Never believe it's not so.
J. We flock just like birds of a feather—I won't tell no lie.
K. Have you heard about the new dance craze? Listen to us, I'm sure you'll be amazed.
L. Love isn't always on time. Whoa oh whoa.
M. Say, Candy and Ronnie, have you seen them yet? Ooh, but they're so spaced out!
N. I got to boogie on the disco 'round, oh yeah.
O. Take a little trip. Take a little trip with me.

Figure 9-67.

WHAT DID YOU LEARN?

Match the key concept in the numbered list below with the letter of the phrase that best describes it. Answers appear upside-down at the bottom of the page.

Key Concepts

1. XML
2. Section
3. Footer
4. Automatic page number
5. Master page
6. Folio
7. Tag
8. Structure bay
9. href
10. Delimiter
11. Relative pathname
12. Map Tags to Styles

Descriptions

A. A fancy name for a page number, usually added to the top or bottom of a document.

B. A code word that identifies a passage of text, a frame, or an imported graphic so that it can be positioned and formatted automatically.

C. Recurring information that runs along the bottom of most pages, such as the lesson names and section titles in this book.

D. This subwindow permits you to manage elements and attributes in an XML document or a template.

E. An angle bracket, < or >, used to separate a tag from its contents in an XML document.

F. A special character that tracks and records the order of pages in a document, which you can insert from the keyboard by pressing Ctrl+Shift+Alt+N (⌘-Shift-Option-N on the Mac).

G. Borrowed from the Web-page language HTML, this attribute specifies the location of a linked illustration or image file on disk.

H. An extensible document-processing language that enables you to create and format pages by writing relatively simple computer code.

I. A collection of pages that subscribe to their own independent page-numbering scheme.

J. This command automatically assigns style sheets according to the element specifications in an imported XML document.

K. The location of a linked graphic or other file on disk, as expressed in relation to the location of an XML or InDesign file.

L. This provides the base elements for a series of pages, much as a corporate letterhead provides the base elements for a series of memos.

Answers

1H, 2I, 3C, 4F, 5L, 6A, 7B, 8D, 9G, 10E, 11K, 12J

LESSON 10

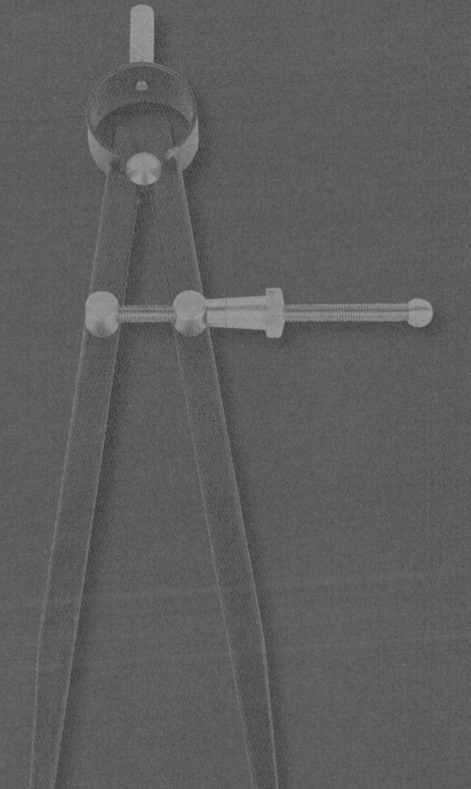

WORKING WITH LONG DOCUMENTS

THIS LESSON, as well as the eleven other lessons in this book, lives most of its life as a single InDesign CS3 document. It was written, illustrated, and edited as its own individual entity, separate from its eleven siblings. But to bring all these documents together into the completed work you hold in your hands, I had to import the lessons into an InDesign *book file*, as symbolically illustrated in Figure 10-1.

Despite its name, a book file isn't restricted to building a book. You can use book files to assemble any type of long document, including catalogs, manuals, reports, and the like. In short, if the easiest way to work on a publication is to break it into separate documents, then by all means do it. You can always use a book file to assemble the pieces into a unified whole.

An InDesign book file manifests itself as a palette, into which you add the documents that you need to bring together. Of course, you can add new documents to a book at any time, delete documents you don't need anymore, and drag documents around in the palette until you have them in the perfect order. (And by the way, a single document can belong to more than one book.) But as essential as the book palette is, it only scratches the surface of InDesign's bookmaking capabilities.

Figure 10-1.

ABOUT THIS LESSON

Project Files

Before beginning the exercises, make sure you've copied the lesson files from the DVD, as directed in Step 3 on page xvii of the Preface. This should result in a folder called *Lesson Files-IDcs3 1on1* on your desktop. We'll be working with the files inside the *Lesson 10* subfolder.

This lesson examines InDesign's long-document functions, which help you collect multiple files, synchronize style sheets and swatches, and create navigational aids such as a table of content and an index. In these exercises, you'll learn how to:

Video Lesson 10: Making a Book

You might reckon that you need InDesign's book palette only when editing, say, a book. But in fact, I recommend you use it anytime you opt to divide a publication across more than one file. The book palette lets you automatically number pages across multiple documents, as well as synchronize style sheet definitions and generally keep things in order. And it's a great leaping off point for opening files.

For a quick look at the book palette, watch the tenth video lesson on the DVD. Insert the DVD, double-click *IDcs3 Videos.html*, and click **Lesson 10: Making a Book** under the **Books, Hyperlinks, and Output** heading. As you watch this 15-minute 36-second movie, bear in mind the following shortcuts:

Operation	Windows shortcut	Macintosh shortcut
Enter and exit the Bridge's compact mode	Ctrl+Enter	⌘-Return
Select a range of documents	Click one, Shift-click another	Click one, Shift-click another
Select nonadjacent documents	Click one, Ctrl-click another	Click one, ⌘-click another
Open a document from the book palette	Double-click document name	Double-click document name
Change the page number options	Double-click page number	Double-click page number
Close a document	Ctrl+W or Ctrl+F4	⌘-W

Binding, Synchronizing, and Indexing

Regardless of the individual page-numbering schemes your documents may employ, a book file lets you coordinate or even override them to make one group of pages flow evenly into the next. You think that chapter in the middle of the book might work better as an appendix? No problem—a book file's page numbers will adjust on-the-fly to accommodate any last-minute adjustments.

As you develop the various documents that make up a publication, your style sheets, color swatches, and other presets are likely to evolve and change. Once again, InDesign has the answer. After you've imported all the documents into a book file, just designate one document as the style source. Then you can synchronize the style sheets and swatches of all the other documents to match the style source, creating a cohesive, consistent look from one page of a publication to the next.

If your documents happen to combine into a lengthy work—say, 50 pages or more—your readers might reasonably hope for a little guidance so they can find their way around. InDesign's book function includes tools for generating the most common kinds of publication maps: tables of contents and indexes. Creating a table of contents is largely automatic, a function of properly defining style sheets and assigning them to headlines and subheads. Creating a quality index, on the other hand, requires some effort. InDesign's Index palette does a fine job of making the process as painless as possible, but expect to put in a few hours or even days of work. The good news is that once you have a table of contents or index established, it is a simple matter to update. You define the entries; InDesign keeps track of the page numbers and sorting.

The four exercises in this lesson take you step by step through importing documents into a book, synchronizing styles, generating a table of contents, and creating an index. It's essential that you work straight through this lesson starting with the first exercise. There's a lot to know about assembling a book, but stick with me and you're bound to succeed.

Assembling Documents into a Book

If you watched Video Lesson 10, "Making a Book," you saw how to assemble documents into a book file and put InDesign in charge of the pagination. Now's your chance to try it out for yourself. In this exercise, you'll assemble three chapters and the table of contents from an old book of mine into an InDesign book file. You'll see how simple it is to import and arrange the various documents. And you'll witness how, regardless of your previous page-numbering settings, the book palette lets you sync the numbering for all your documents.

1. *Create a book file.* Choose **File→New→Book** to display the **New Book** dialog box. Navigate to the *Lesson 10* folder inside *Lesson Files-IDcs3 1on1*. Name the new book file "Look&Learn book 1.indb," and click **Save**. The palette shown on the right side of Figure 10-2 appears.

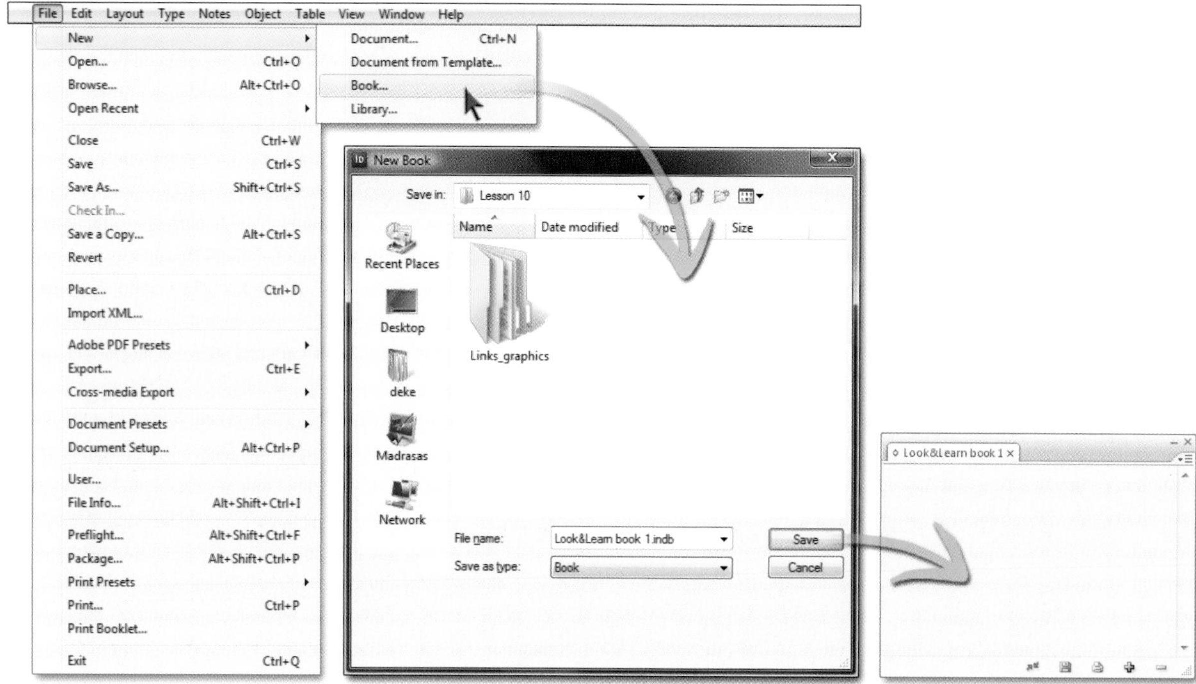

Figure 10-2.

2. *Add documents to the book.* Click the ✢ icon at the bottom of the palette to bring up the **Add Documents** dialog box, as illustrated in Figure 10-3. Navigate to the *Lesson 10* folder, if it doesn't come up automatically. We want to bring the four files with names that begin with "Look&Learn" into the book. Click *Look&Learn Ch01.indd*, Shift-click *Look&Learn TOC vii.indd*, and then click **Open**.

   InDesign confronts you with the warning message shown at the bottom of Figure 10-3. This warning notifies you that fonts are missing in the *Look&Learn Ch09.indd* document, but it also conveys a larger message: Importing these chapter files into the book has prompted InDesign to begin applying a page-numbering scheme to the documents. I've already corrected the font problems in Chapter 1, but Chapters 9 and 11 do indeed have missing fonts. We'll use the book palette to take care of this problem in the next exercise, and everything will work out fine. For now, just click the **Don't Show Again** check box, and then click **OK**.

3. *Rearrange the order of the documents.* The **Look&Learn book 1** palette now displays four imported documents. The documents in the book palette need to be arranged in the order in which they will appear in the book. The TOC file, which stands for Table of Contents, came in last but it should be first. Drag the **Look&Learn TOC vii** item in the palette to the top of the stack. When a thick black line appears above the top item, as in Figure 10-4, release the mouse button. The Look&Learn TOC vii item moves to the top of the palette, where it belongs. Be prepared for InDesign to take several seconds to complete the operation.

4. *Set the page numbering for Chapter 1.* Now let's take a look at the page numbering. The one-page table of contents file is numbered vii, which is fine. But Chapter 1 starts on page 8, which is no good. Chapter 1 should start on page 1, so we need to change that:

   - Click the **Look&Learn Ch01** item in the book palette. Then click the ▾≡ icon and choose **Document Numbering Options** from the palette menu, as in Figure 10-5. Or better yet, just double-click the page numbers, **8–25**.

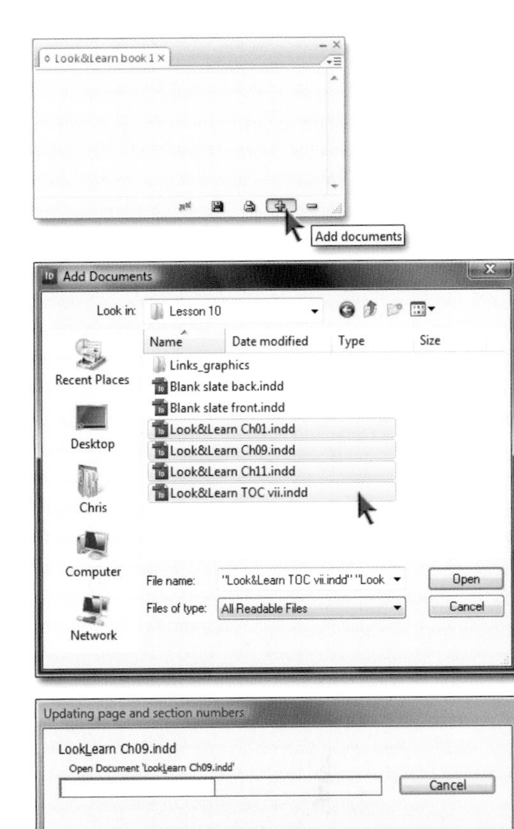

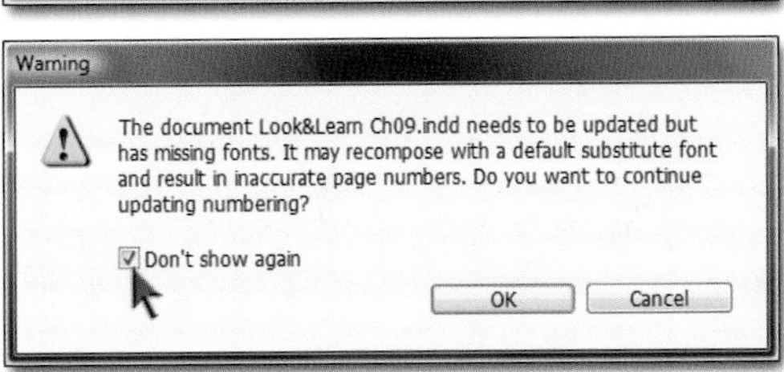

Figure 10-3.

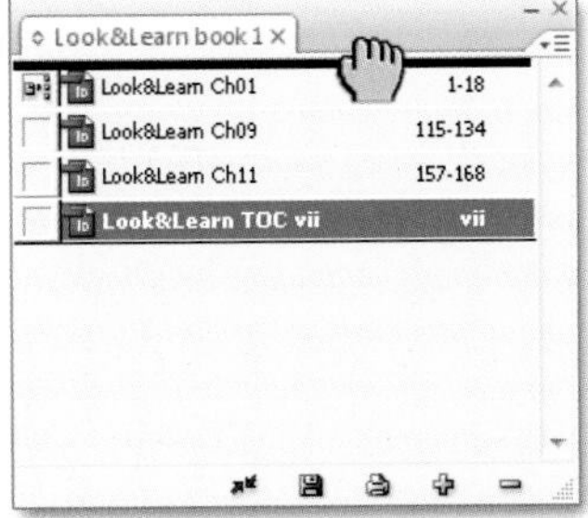

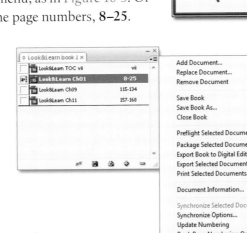

Figure 10-4.

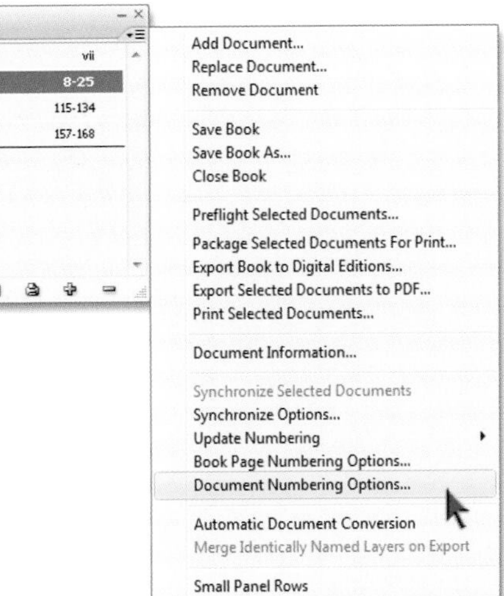

Figure 10-5.

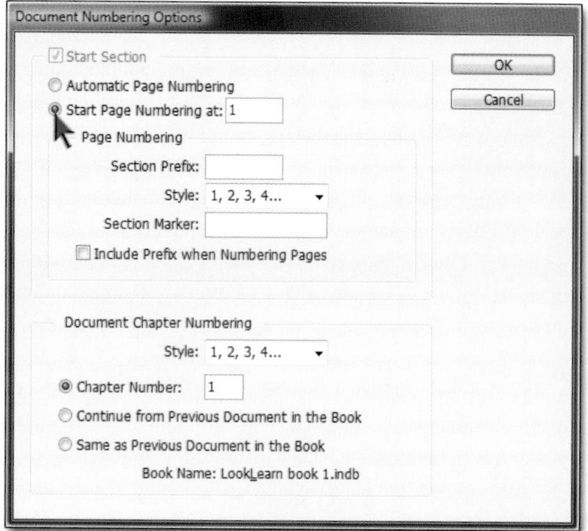

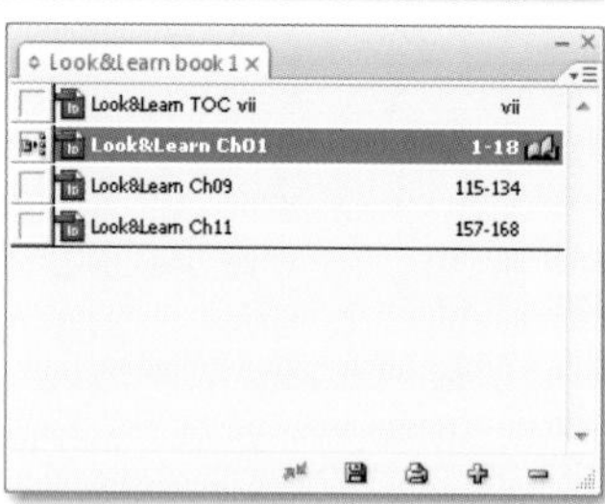

Figure 10-6.

- If you get a hyphenation warning, click the User Dictionary button. If you get a missing links error, click Fix Links Automatically. Next, InDesign opens the Chapter 1 document. And after that, you are greeted by the **Document Numbering Options** dialog box.
- Here's why Chapter 1 was starting at page 8: Automatic Page Numbering is turned on, which numbers the document immediately after the preceding file in the book palette, which is the TOC. Click the **Start Page Numbering At** option, enter 1 in the option box, and click **OK**. As Figure 10-6 shows, Chapter 1 now starts on page 1.

5. ***Automatically number Chapter 9.*** Let's say, for whatever kooky reason, we want the page numbering for Chapter 9 to begin where Chapter 1 leaves off. (Okay, I confess. Every so often I have to bend logic for the sake of demonstration.)
   - Select the **Look&Learn Ch09** item in the book palette. Again choose **Document Numbering Options** from the palette menu or double-click the item's page numbers.
   - As the Chapter 9 file opens, InDesign may or may not display a complaint about the hyphenation dictionary. If it does, click User Dictionary.
   - InDesign will next deliver a warning message about missing fonts. (If you don't see the warning, you're luckier than most.) We'll take care of this problem in the next exercise, "Synchronizing Book Documents." For now, click **OK** to close the **Missing Fonts** dialog box.
   - When you get a message about missing links, click **Fix Links Automatically** or press the F key.
   - Finally the **Document Numbering Options** dialog box appears. Chapter 9 starts on page 115 because that's what its numbering settings are telling it to do. Select the **Automatic Page Numbering** option and click **OK**. The book palette now shows Chapter 9 as starting on page 19, immediately after Chapter 1.
6. ***Automatically number Chapter 11.*** Now we need to bring Chapter 11 in line. Again, for the sake of demonstration, I want it to follow directly on the heels of Chapter 9:
   - No need to even select the **Look&Learn Ch11** item. Just double-click its page numbers, **157–168**.

- If InDesign bugs you about hyphenation, click User Dictionary. When it bugs you about missing fonts, click **OK**. And if you get the missing links message, click Fix Links Automatically. So many alert messages, so little patience.
- Turn on **Automatic Page Numbering** and then click **OK**.

As Figure 10-7 shows, Chapters 1, 9, and 11 are all numbered sequentially. At last, the documents are in the right order, and their page numbering is correct.

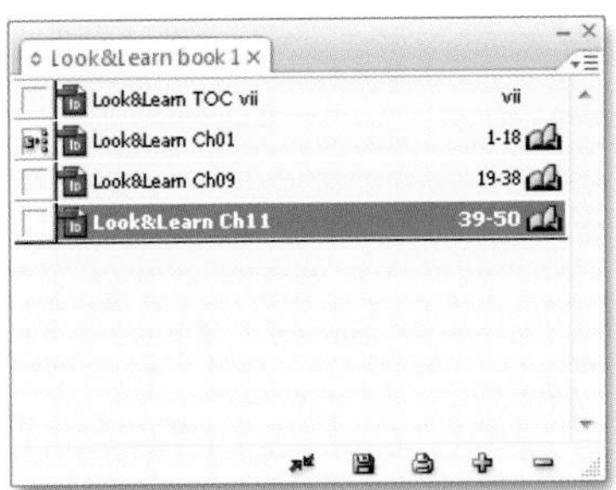

Figure 10-7.

7. ***Save and close the open documents.*** See those open book icons (📖) next to each chapter name in the book palette? They indicate that the corresponding documents are open. By changing the pagination options, we've made changes to the documents themselves. Naturally, we need to save those changes. So for each document, press Ctrl+S to save it and Ctrl+W to close it (⌘-S and ⌘-W on the Mac).
8. ***Save the book.*** Click the ▾≡ icon in the top-right corner of the book palette and choose **Save Book As** from the palette menu Name the file "Look&Learn book 2.indb" and then save it in the *Lesson 10* folder. You'll need the current version of this file in the next exercise.

Synchronizing Book Documents

By assembling documents into a book file and adjusting their pagination, you can combine multiple documents into a single unit. But the book palette provides other ways to connect disparate documents. In this short exercise, we'll synchronize the style sheets between the documents in the book file from the preceding exercise so that all three chapters share a common set of formatting attributes.

As you discovered in the preceding steps, Chapters 9 and 11 contain fonts that are missing from our systems. Chapter 1, however, has no missing fonts; I modified its styles to contain only those fonts that are automatically installed with InDesign. By synchronizing the style sheets from Chapters 9 and 11 to match those in Chapter 1, we'll fix the missing fonts problem and unify the formatting attributes throughout the book.

1. ***Open the book file.*** If you're coming straight from the previous exercise, the book is already open. If not, use **File→Open** to open the *Look&Learn book 2.indb* file that you saved in Step 8 of the last exercise. You should find the file in the *Lesson 10* folder inside *Lesson Files-IDcs3 1on1*.

2. *Designate Chapter 1 as the style source.* The icon to the immediate left of a document name in the book palette identifies the source document to which all other files will sync. As I mentioned, I fixed the font problems in Chapter 1, so click in the box to the left of **Look&Learn Ch01** in the book palette to set it as the style source.

3. *Specify the styles that you want to synchronize.* Before we synchronize the other documents with Chapter 1, we need to specify exactly what it is we want to synchronize. Choose **Synchronize Options** from the book palette menu to bring up the **Synchronize Options** dialog box, as in Figure 10-8. You can synchronize all kinds of things in InDesign CS3, including color swatches, master pages, numbered lists, text variables, and trapping presets (all of which we've covered by now except the last; for information on trapping presets, read "Trapping and Overprinting," Lesson 12, page 493). But we're interested only in the style sheets. So do the following:

   - Click the **Other** check box twice to turn off all of its options.

   - Turn off the **Style and Swatches** check box. (This requires just one click.) Then turn on **Object Styles**, **Character Styles**, and **Paragraph Styles**, as in the figure.

   Clicking the Synchronize button would synchronize any selected documents with the designated style source. If no document is selected, the synchronization applies to all files in the book, which is what we want. Given that you might have a document selected (as I do in Figure 10-8), the best course of action is to click the **OK** button to save your sync preferences without actually applying them. We'll sync the files in the next step.

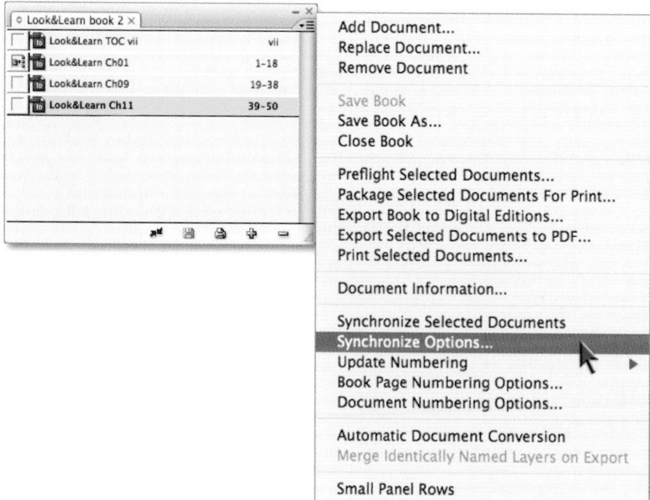

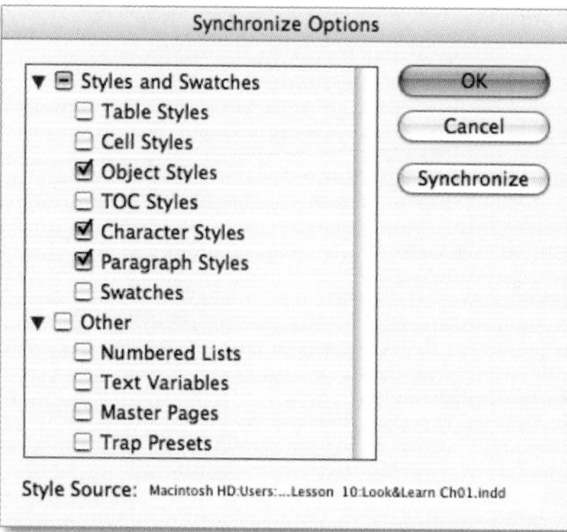

Figure 10-8.

4. *Synchronize all documents with Chapter 1.* Click in the blank space below the last document in the book palette to deselect all files. Then, with no document selected, choose **Synchronize Book** from the book palette menu.

5. *Address the missing fonts warning.* InDesign's first response is to deliver the cautionary missive shown in Figure 10-9. As the message warns, "these documents *may* be recomposed using a default substitute font" (my emphasis). But in our case, they won't. This is because we're recomposing the documents using specific fonts installed on your computer, not some random and patently awful default substitutions. Trust me and click **OK**.

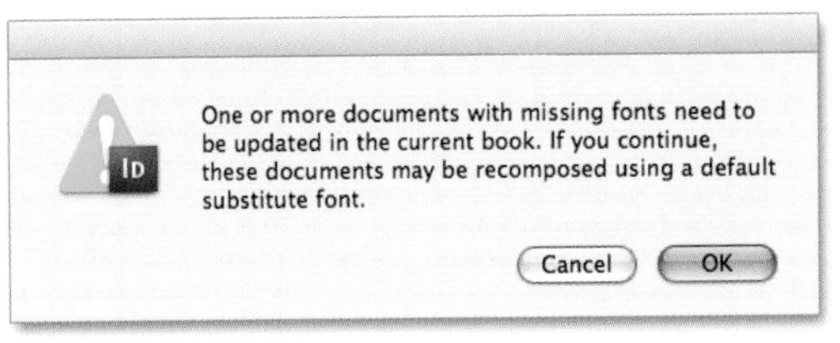

Figure 10-9.

6. *Address the overset text warning.* After displaying a progress bar for a few moments, you may encounter another warning (see Figure 10-10) alerting you to the dangers of "overset text" becoming "non-overset." Overset text is what I call overflow text—that is, text that doesn't fit inside its frame. So the message is saying the text may shrink and actually fit inside the four walls of the document. That sounds like a good thing but it could present problems if a document includes hidden text that you don't want to reveal. If you see the message, click **OK**; if not, consider yourself lucky and move on.

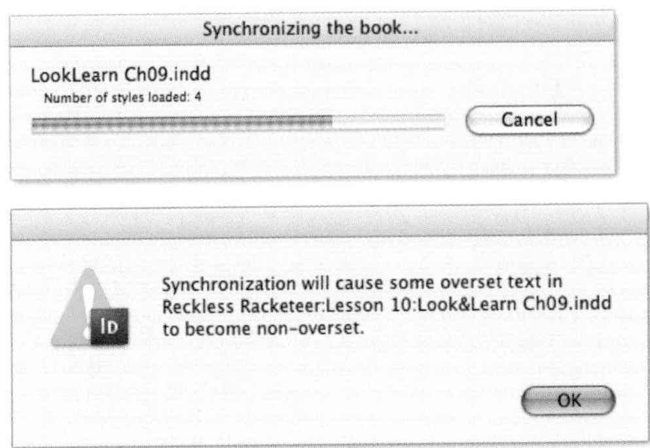

Figure 10-10.

7. *Dismiss the final message.* Next, you are presented with the alert message shown in Figure 10-11. As if InDesign hadn't been perfectly clear during its previous barrage of warnings, this message notifies you that your documents may have changed. Specifically, the synchronization has solved the missing fonts problem in Chapters 9 and 11. This truly is a good thing, so smile as you click **OK**.

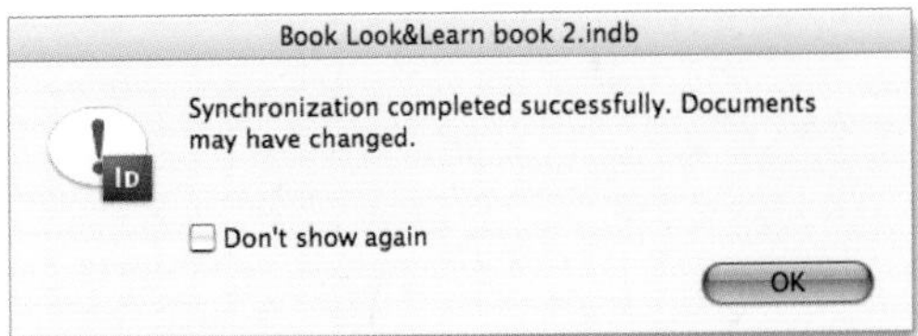

Figure 10-11.

8. *Open a synchronized document.* According to InDesign, the documents are synced. But we humans need confirmation. Double-click on **Look&Learn Ch09** to open the Chapter 9 file. No font warning—in fact, if you've been following along faithfully, no warnings at all. That's a good sign, but perhaps we should dig deeper, just to be safe.

9. *Inspect the fonts.* To check out exactly which fonts are used in the document, choose **Type→Find Font**. InDesign displays the **Find Font** dialog box, with a total of seven fonts. The first three are OpenType fonts that ship with InDesign. The remaining four are crazy fonts such as MyriadMM-It_480_wt_500_wd. I assure you, these numbered typefaces (all multiple master fonts, varieties of yesterday's cutting-edge technology) are not included on your system. And yet InDesign does not complain. What gives? To see, select the first of the numbered fonts in the list. Note that the standard Find First button changes to **Find Graphic**. Give this button a click. InDesign scrolls to the

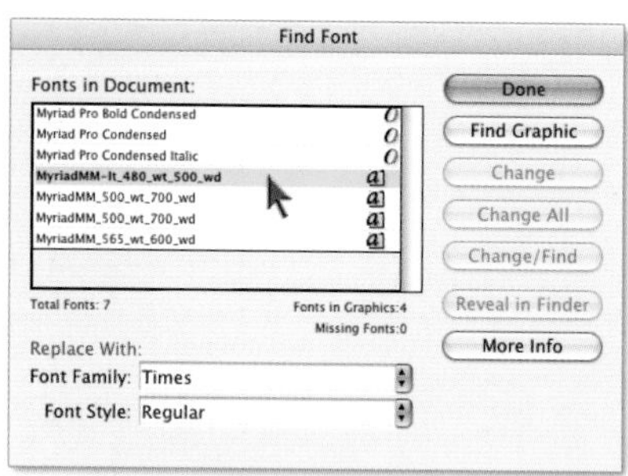

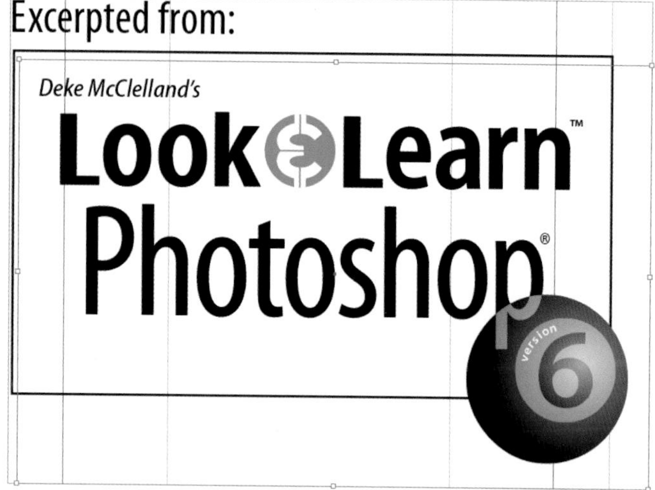

Excerpted from:
Deke McClelland's
Look&Learn
Photoshop
version
6

Figure 10-12.

graphic pictured in Figure 10-12. And therein lies your answer. The numbered fonts are not part of the InDesign text, but rather part of the imported Illustrator graphics. Illustrator embeds font definitions when saving files, so the fact that your system doesn't include these fonts is no problem whatsoever. Click the **Done** button, safe in the knowledge that you are covered.

10. *Save the book.* Press Ctrl+W (or ⌘-W) to close the Chapter 9 file. If InDesign asks you to save your changes, press the N key (D on the Mac) to decline. Then go to the book palette and choose **Save Book As** from the palette menu. Target the *Lesson 10* folder, name the file "Look&Learn book 3.indb," and click **Save**. You'll need this file in the next exercise, so leave it open.

Creating a Table of Contents

After you've assembled various documents into a book, InDesign can examine those documents and automatically generate a table of contents based on how you set up your style sheets. In this exercise, you'll create a table of contents for the three chapters in the book file we've created so far. You'll tell the program exactly which styles to look for, and you'll set paragraph styles for the table of contents itself.

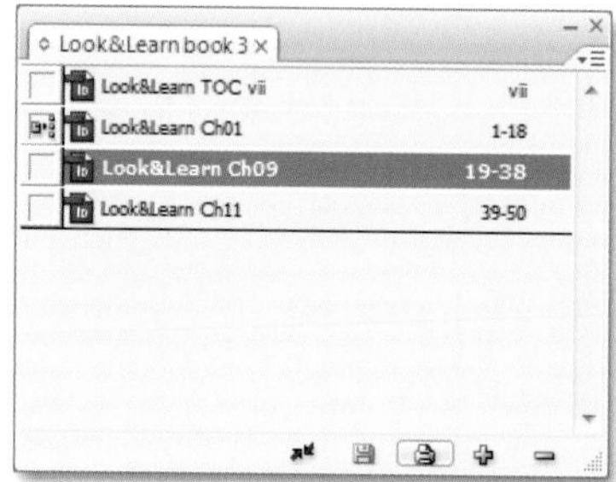

Figure 10-13.

1. *Open the book file.* If your ongoing book file is already open in the book palette, great. If not, open the *Look&Learn book 3.indb* file that you saved in the *Lesson 10* folder at the end of the last exercise. Your book palette should look like the one in Figure 10-13.

2. *Open the table of contents document.* As you may recall from the previous exercises, this book file already includes a table of contents. To open it, double-click the **Look&Learn TOC vii** item in the book palette. When you get the links warning, click **Fix Links Automatically** or press the F key. As shown in Figure 10-14, this is but a single page from the full table of contents for the book. I include it simply so you

can see the styles I used to create the document. Note that the file contains certain elements—such as the one-sentence summaries of each chapter—that InDesign's automatic table of contents function can't generate without employing complicated tricks. But that's okay; we don't need them. The table of contents we're going to generate will include the name of each chapter, the sections therein, and the page number on which each chapter and section begins.

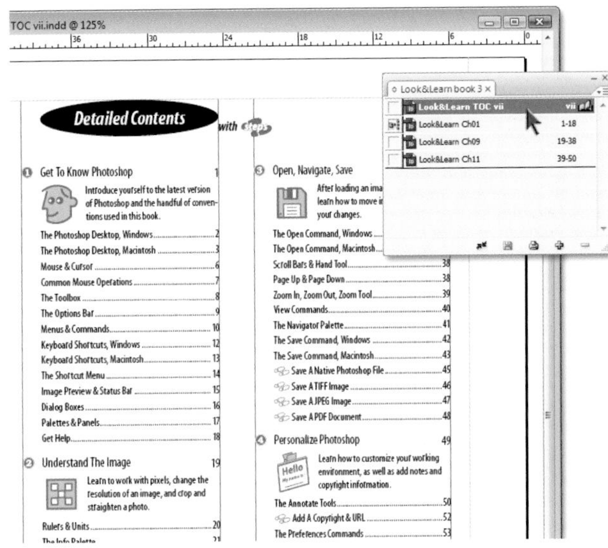

Figure 10-14.

3. *Examine the paragraph styles.* Press the F11 key or choose **Type→Paragraph Styles** to access the **Paragraph Styles** palette. Select the type tool and click somewhere in the first chapter title, *Get To Know Photoshop*. A glance at the Paragraph Styles palette reveals that this title was formatted using the TofC Chap Name style (see Figure 10-15).

   Now click to set the insertion marker in the first section name, *The Photoshop Desktop, Windows*. Another glance at the Paragraph Styles palette tells us that this line was formatted using the TofC Section style. (The style includes a + because I modified the leading to make the text fit better.) The upshot: I gave each of the two main elements—the chapter name and the section name—a unique paragraph style. These styles will come in handy in future steps.

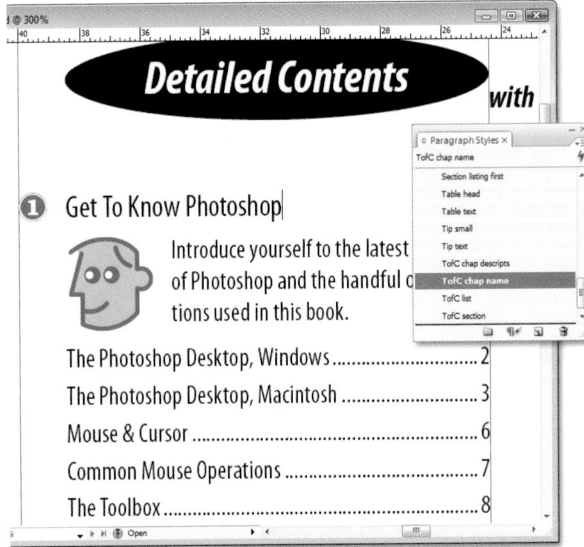

Figure 10-15.

4. *Close the file and remove the TOC from the book.* Press Ctrl+W (⌘-W) to close the table of contents file. If InDesign asks to save changes, click **No** (**Don't Save** on the Mac). Make sure **Look&Learn TOC vii** is selected in the book palette. Then click the ▭ icon at the bottom of the palette, as in Figure 10-16, to delete the TOC file from the book. This prevents InDesign from referencing the TOC file along with the chapter documents when you generate the new table of contents.

5. *Add a blank document to the book.* It's good that we deleted the old table of contents. But we need a reservoir for our new table of contents. Click the ✚ icon at the bottom of the book palette to bring up the **Add Documents** dialog box. Navigate to the *Lesson 10* folder, select the file named *Blank slate front.indd*, and click **Open**. The new, empty document appears as the last file in the palette.

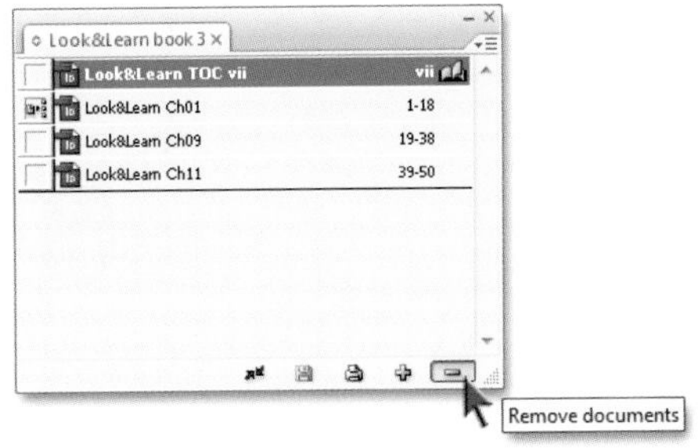

Figure 10-16.

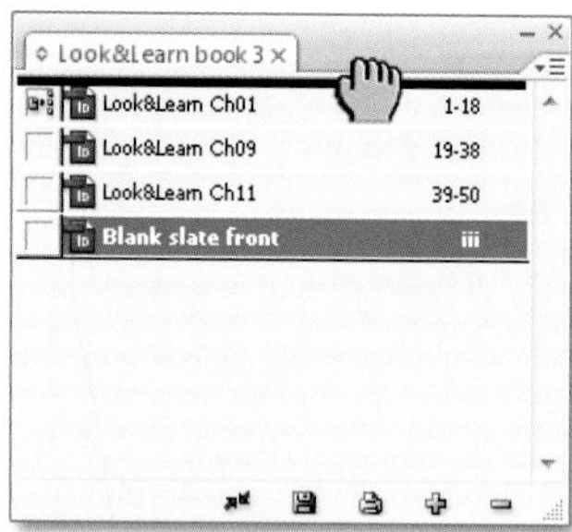

Figure 10-17.

6. *Move the newly added file to the top of the palette.* This document will serve as our new table of contents, so it needs to be placed at the top of the stack. Drag the **Blank Slate Front** item to the top of the book palette, as in Figure 10-17. Because Chapter 1 is set to begin on page 1, and Chapters 9 and 11 have automatic page numbering turned on, no pagination shifts occur.

7. *Examine the paragraph styles in the blank document.* In the book palette, double-click the **Blank Slate Front** item to open the document. It's entirely empty, but as Figure 10-18 shows, it includes two paragraph styles similar to the ones we examined in Step 3: TofC Chapter and TofC Section. You'll use these styles to format the new table of contents.

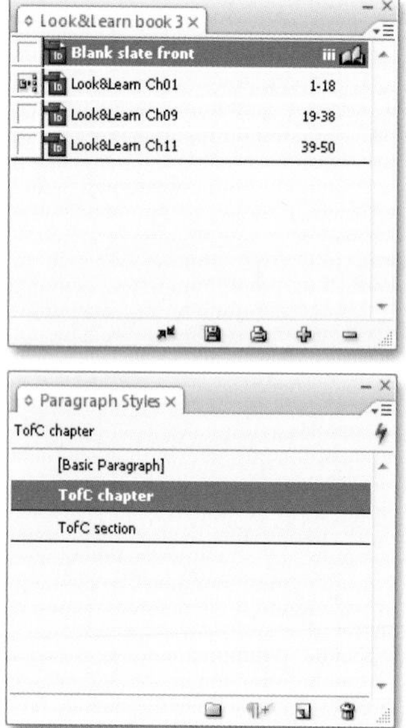

Figure 10-18.

8. *Create a new table of contents style.* Now it's time to decide which portions of the chapters are included in the table of contents, based on how they're styled. Choose **Layout→Table of Contents Styles** to display the dialog box shown at the top of Figure 10-19. Click the **New** button to bring up the **New Table of Contents Style** dialog box, also pictured in Figure 10-19.

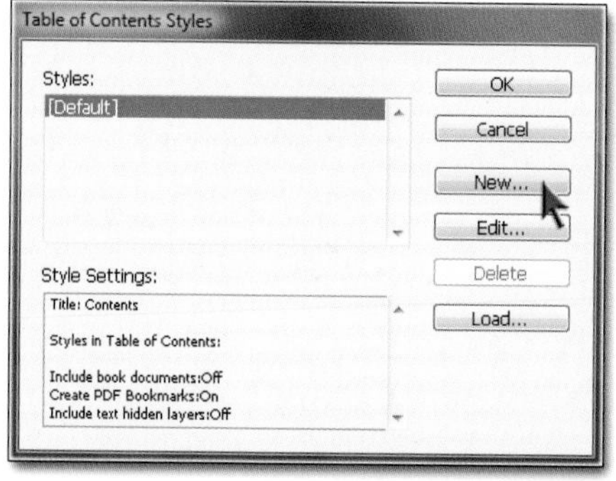

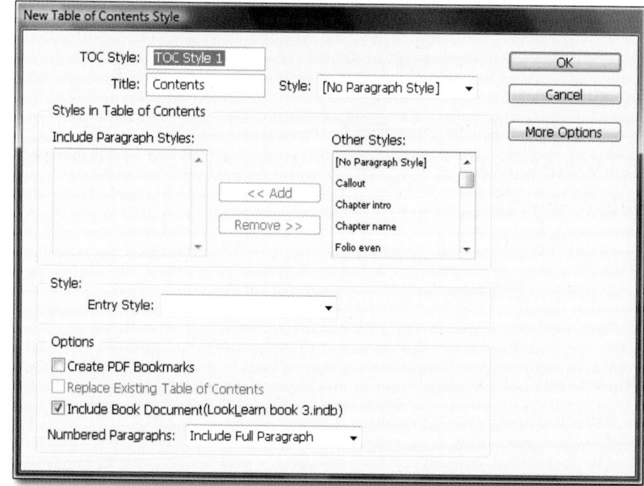

Figure 10-19.

9. ***Specify a title for your table of contents.*** Change the first few options in the dialog box as follows:

   - Type "L&L TOC Style" in the **TOC Style** option box. This is the name that will appear in the Styles list in the Table of Contents Styles dialog box.
   - The next option, **Title**, designates the title that will appear at the outset of the finished table of contents document. Press Tab to advance to this option and type "Detailed Contents."
   - The **Style** setting allows you to apply a style sheet to the title. The options include the two styles currently contained in the document plus a third style that InDesign has created specifically for this purpose. Choose this last option, **TOC Title**.

10. ***Select the styles you want to include in the table of contents.*** InDesign generates a table of contents by looking at the documents in your book file and lifting text formatted with the style sheets that you specify. Select the style sheets that you want InDesign to draw upon from the middle section of the dialog box (the part labeled Styles in Table of Contents). Here's what I want you to do:

    - In the **Other Styles** list on the right, select **Chapter Name**, which is the style applied to the chapter title in each document, and click the **Add** button. The Chapter Name style appears in the Include Paragraph Styles list on the left.
    - You also need to include the subheads, or section names, in the table of contents. These are assigned the Heading 1 and Heading 2 styles. So select **Heading 1** in the Other Styles list and then Shift-click on **Heading 2**. Then click the **Add** button to add both styles to the Include Paragraph Styles list.

11. ***Select styles to be applied to the table of contents entries.*** Now InDesign knows which style sheets to search for inside the book's documents to generate the table of contents. But after the table of contents is generated, what will it look like? To answer that question, do like so:

    - Select **Chapter Name** in the Include Paragraph Styles list, and choose **TofC Chapter** from the Entry Style pop-up menu in the bottom portion of the dialog box.
    - Select **Heading 1** in the Include Paragraph Styles list, and then choose **TofC Section** from the Entry Style pop-up menu.
    - Then select **Heading 2** in the left-hand list, and again choose **TofC Section** from the Entry Style pop-up menu.

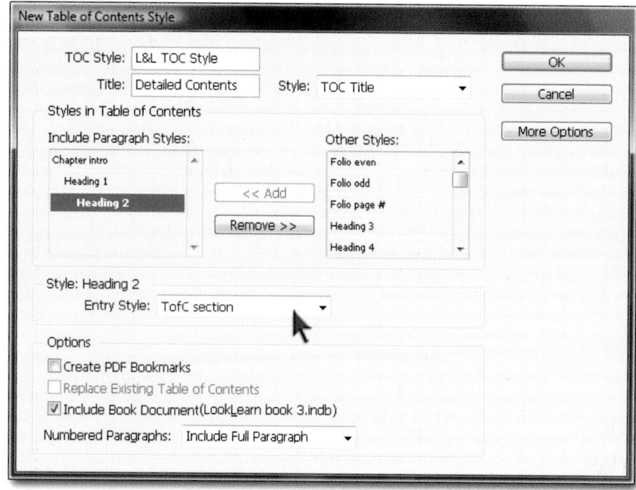

Figure 10-20.

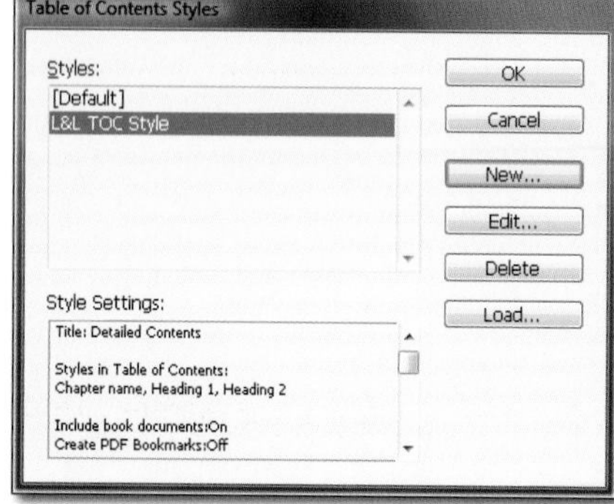

Figure 10-21.

The options in the New Table of Contents Style dialog box should now appear as shown in Figure 10-20.

12. *Close the two open dialog boxes.* Make sure that the last check box, **Include Book Document**, is selected so that InDesign includes all documents within your book file in the table of contents. Then click **OK**. As Figure 10-21 shows, the newly created L&L TOC Style is now selected in the Table of Contents Styles dialog box. Click **OK** to accept it.

13. *Generate the table of contents.* Now to generate the table of contents. Choose **Layout→Table of Contents** to display the **Table of Contents** dialog box shown in Figure 10-22. Weren't we just here? Well, no. While this dialog box is virtually identical to the one we saw a couple of steps back, there is a difference: You can select and edit any table of contents styles you've created. Make sure the first option is set to **L&L TOC Style** and then click **OK**. InDesign starts to create a table of contents and then presents you with a loaded text cursor.

14. *Place the table of contents.* Press the Shift key and click at the top of the first column in the *Blank slate front.indd* document. This places all table of contents entries in one fell swoop. And there it is, a table of contents, automatically extracted from our three-chapter excerpt, as in Figure 10-23.

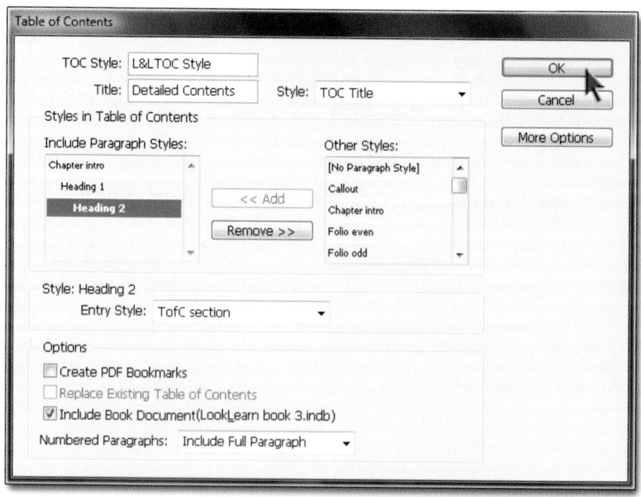

Figure 10-22.

15. ***Eliminate the inline graphics.*** All in all, InDesign did a great job of extracting the chosen paragraph styles from the chapter files and compiling them in one document, replete with page numbers. But InDesign also included the inline "steps" graphics anchored in some of the section names, and frankly, it just doesn't look right. Let's get rid of them:

    - Choose **Edit→Find/Change** or press Ctrl+F (⌘-F on the Mac) to bring up the **Find/Change** dialog box.
    - To let InDesign know what you want it to find, click the @ symbol to the far right of the **Find What** option box and choose **Markers→Anchored Object Marker** (fifth option down) from the pop-up menu. A ^*a* appears in the option box, which is InDesign's code for an anchored object.
    - Not only do we want to eliminate each inline graphic, but we also want to delete the space after the graphic. Press the spacebar once to enter a space character after the ^*a*.
    - Leave the **Change to** option box blank so that InDesign replaces everything it finds with nothing. When your settings look like those in Figure 10-24, click **Change All**.

    An alert appears to tell you that InDesign deleted 10 inline graphics. Click **OK** to dismiss it. Next, click **Done** to close the Find/Change dialog box.

    The modified table of contents appears in Figure 10-25 on the next page. If you were going to publish this document, you'd want to adjust the text frames to eliminate the orphan at the top of the second column, but otherwise things look great.

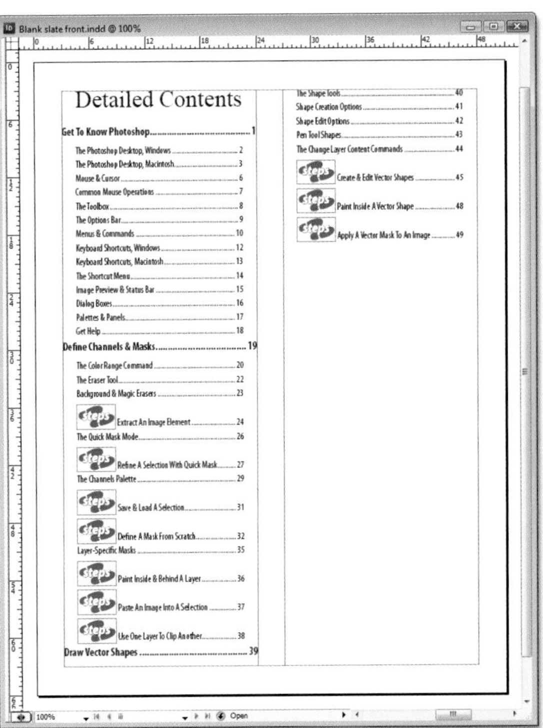

Figure 10-23.

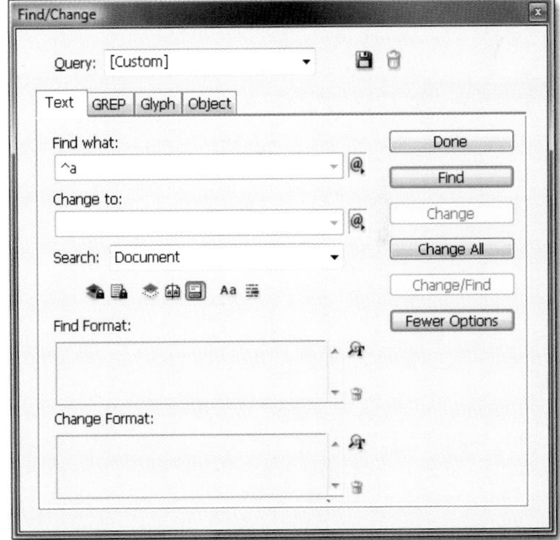

Figure 10-24.

PEARL OF WISDOM

If you ever need to update a table of contents to account for changes made to the documents in your book, select the text in the TOC and choose Layout→Update Table of Contents. Note, however, that you will lose any manual changes you may have made. This means you'll have to repeat the deletion of the inline graphics that you performed in the last step.

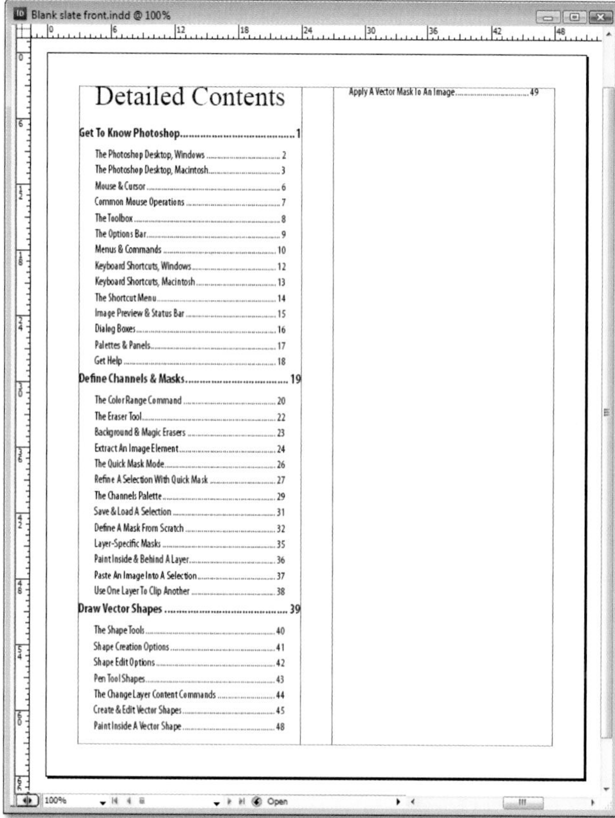

Figure 10-25.

16. ***Save your work.*** Press Ctrl+S and Ctrl+W (⌘-S and ⌘-W) to save and close your newly created TOC file. Then click the ▾≡ icon in the book palette, choose **Save Book As** from the palette menu, name the file "Look&Learn book 4.indb," and click **Save**.

Generating an Index

When generating a table of contents, you can count on InDesign to do most of the heavy lifting. But when it comes time to make an index, InDesign puts a 500-pound barbell in front of you and says, "Go get 'em, Tiger!" That's why indexing books isn't really a task; it's a profession. People make their living solely out of creating indexes, and while they regard InDesign as a useful tool, it provides only slim automation. Given the current state of technology, indexing is a job for humans, not machines.

Rather than create a complete index—a process that would take about 1,000 steps, 980 of which would bring new meaning to the words "staggeringly dull"—the goal of this exercise is to give you a sense of how indexing works. You'll create a handful of entries and address a few special-case scenarios such as cross-references and proper names. In the end, you'll place the partial index—complete with page numbers (InDesign's best automatic contribution)—into a new document. I can't promise you a roller coaster ride, but with some luck we might have a smidgen of fun along the way.

PEARL OF WISDOM

Word of warning: InDesign CS3 originally shipped with a faulty index feature for which the InDesign community had to create special workarounds. Adobe has fixed the problem, but you'll need to make sure you've updated your software to the latest version of InDesign (it should be 5.0.1 or later) for your indexing to work properly.

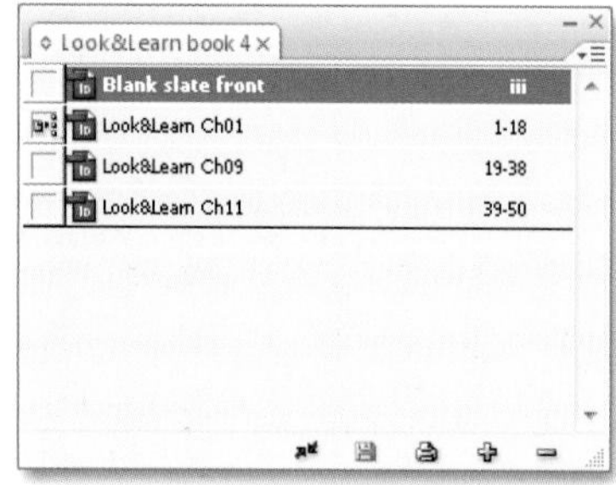

Figure 10-26.

1. ***Open the book file.*** If the most recent version of the book file is open, advance to the next step. If not, open the *Look&Learn book 4.indb* file that you saved in the *Lesson 10* folder at the end of the last exercise. You should see the palette shown in Figure 10-26.

2. ***Open the Chapter 1 document.*** Double-click the second file in the book palette, **Look&Learn Ch01**. InDesign opens the Chapter 1 file, which makes an appearance in Figure 10-27. Our rollicking adventure in indexing will begin with this chapter.

3. ***Open the Index palette.*** Choose **Window→Type & Tables→Index** or press Shift+F8 to display the **Index** palette. Pictured in Figure 10-28, this sparse palette is the central headquarters for indexing in InDesign. Make sure the **Reference** option is selected, as it is by default. This permits us to see all index entries as well as the page numbers on which these entries are found. Then turn on the **Book** check box. We want our index to cover all the documents in the book palette, not just a single chapter.

4. ***Go to page 2.*** At present, you should see some portion of the first page in the document, page 1, which is featured in Figure 10-27. Assuming you do, press Shift+Page Down to advance to page 2, which appears in Figure 10-29. We'll create our first index entry here.

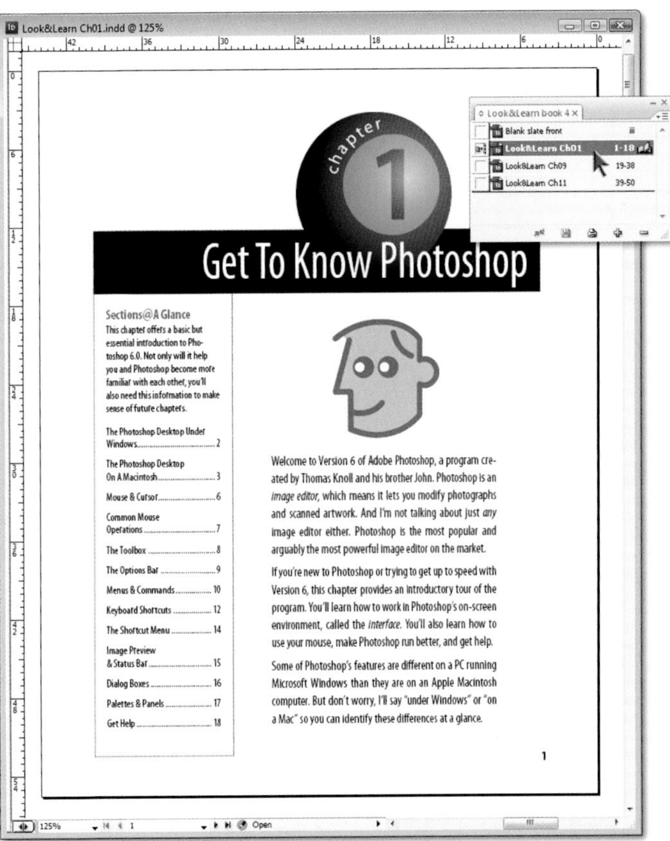

Figure 10-27.

Figure 10-28.

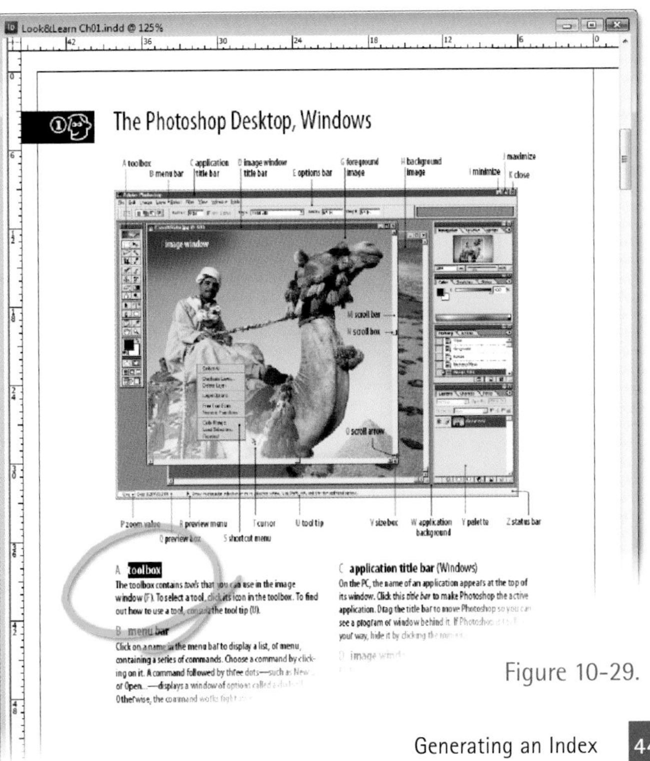

Figure 10-29.

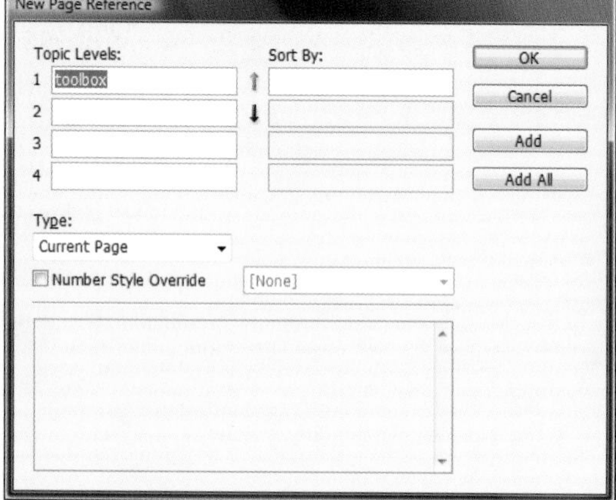

Figure 10-30.

5. ***Begin an index entry for the word*** **toolbox.** Press T to get the type tool and then double-click the word *toolbox*, circled in Figure 10-29. Then click the icon at the bottom of the Index palette or press Ctrl+U (⌘-U on the Mac). The **New Page Reference** dialog box appears with *toolbox* thoughtfully entered in the first **Topic Levels** option box, as in Figure 10-30.

6. ***Specify the topic level.*** Numbered 1 through 4, the **Topic Levels** option boxes let you determine where within the index you want the entry to appear. Here we have a few options (don't do them, just read for now):

   - Were we to keep *toolbox* as a top-level topic—as it is by default—InDesign would alphabetize it with the *T*s.
   - However, it's conceivable that you might want to make *toolbox* subordinate to another entry, perhaps one for *interface*. In this case, *interface* would be alphabetized under *I*, and *toolbox* would be listed as a subcategory. To make this happen, you would click the ↓ arrow to move *toolbox* to option box 2, and then type "interface" in option box 1.
   - InDesign lets you build entries four levels deep, so you could conceivably categorize the entry as, for example, *applications→Photoshop→interface→toolbox*.

   But why make things complicated? I much prefer to stick with first- and second-level entries and keep most entries at the top level. So let's leave *toolbox* as is, as a first-level entry.

PEARL OF WISDOM

It's not necessary to fill out the Sort By option boxes. They exist so you can sort an entry by something other than its first letter. For instance, if you were writing a book on the proud history of modern puppetry and wanted the entry *The Great Muppet Caper* to appear as written but have it alphabetized under the letter *G*, you would enter "The Great Muppet Caper" in the Topic Levels option box and "Great Muppet Caper" (sans the article *The*) in the associated Sort By option box.

7. ***Choose a page range option.*** Next you need to choose a page range option for your entry. Midway down the dialog box, the **Type** pop-up menu gives you a plethora of choices, all of which determine the range of pages that will be indexed for the entry. We'll stick with the default option, **Current Page**, which references page 2 and page 2 alone.

PEARL OF WISDOM

In addition to indexing a single page, you can choose to index a range of pages that extend to a change in style sheet styles or until the next use of a matching style sheet. You can even extend a range until the end of the story, section, or document. But I recommend that you use these options sparingly. Put yourself in the reader's position: When you look up a word in an index, you want to find the exact page on which that entry is discussed, not some nebulous page range. Specific is always better.

8. *Leave Number Style Override off.* The Number Style Override check box lets you apply a different style sheet than the default to the page number that follows an index entry. For instance, references that include illustrations are sometimes set in bold type, in which case you might want to employ a specific character style that you created for this purpose. Our entry doesn't require any special styling, so leave this option turned off.

9. *Add the entry to the index.* To add the *toolbox* entry to the index, click the **Add** button. Suddenly, the entire alphabet appears in the large field at the bottom of the dialog box. Scroll down to the *T*'s and click the ▶ arrow to reveal the *toolbox* entry, as in Figure 10-31.

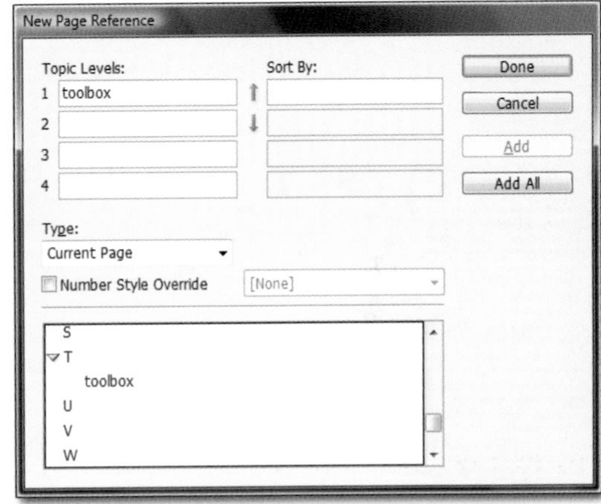

Figure 10-31.

PEARL OF WISDOM

Alternatively, you could click Add All, which would cause InDesign to search all open documents for occurrences of the selected term. This may sound like a great timesaving idea, but it rarely is. In truth, you don't want *every* instance of a term indexed, especially a common term like *toolbox*. Furthermore, if the term appears multiple times on a single page, Add All will usually give each instance its own page reference, rendering your index bloated and useless. That's what I meant when I said that creating an index is a job for humans, not computers. You need to decide which occurrences of the term are worthy of inclusion in the index on a case-by-case basis.

10. *View the index entry.* Click the **Done** button to exit the dialog box. The Index palette now contains an alphabetized index. If you scroll down and Alt-click (or Option-click) the triangle next to the T (to completely expand the reference), you'll see the page 2 reference for *toolbox*, as in Figure 10-32.

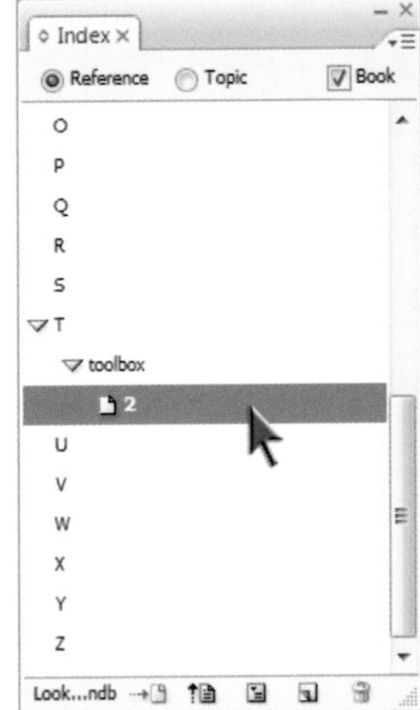

Figure 10-32.

11. *Show hidden characters.* InDesign tracks an index entry by inserting an invisible character into the text. To see this character, first deselect the text by pressing Ctrl+Shift+A (⌘-Shift-A on the Mac). Then choose **Type→Show Hidden Characters** or press Ctrl+Alt+I (⌘-Option-I). The ‸ character,

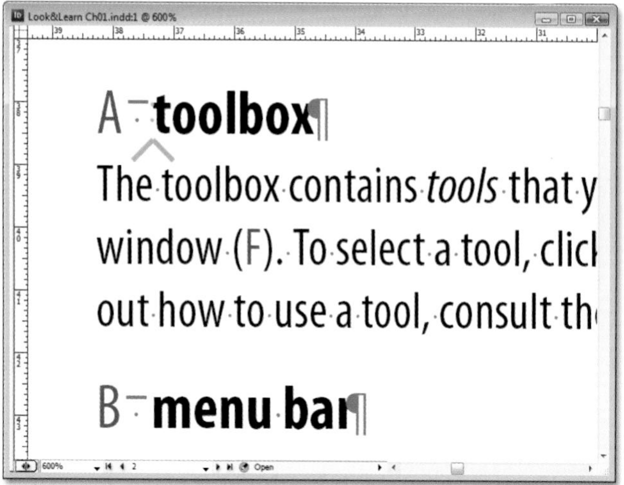

Figure 10-33.

which I've colored orange in Figure 10-33, indicates the occurrence of an *index marker*, which tracks the location of the word *toolbox*. If you bump the word to a different page, the index marker moves with it and updates the entry in the Index palette. (In case you're curious, that ˉ character before the ‸ character is an en space.)

12. ***Add another entry to the index.*** Press Shift+Page Down to go to page 3. Select the words *options bar*, as in Figure 10-34. Then instead of clicking the ◰ icon in the Index palette, press Ctrl+Shift+Alt+[(⌘-Shift-Option-[). InDesign adds the *options bar* entry to the index preview in the Index palette according to the default settings, so it's a first-level topic that references the current page only.

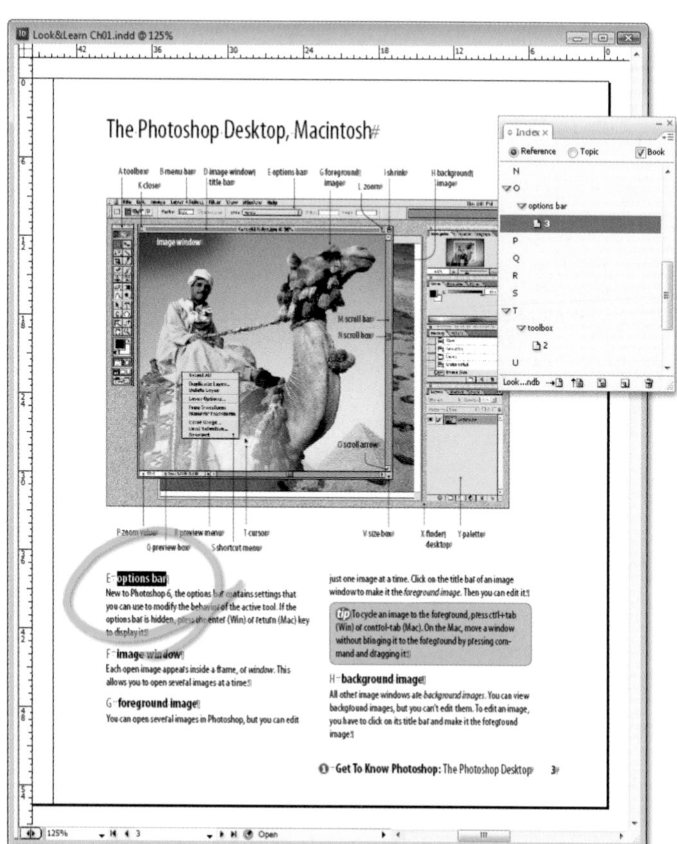

Figure 10-34.

EXTRA CREDIT

By now, you have a pretty good idea of how you add index entries to an InDesign document. But there's so much more—page ranges, subentries, cross-references, and name sorting, to mention a few. Plus, we really haven't seen the fruits of our indexing, have we? To experience these many options for yourself, I strongly urge you to complete the remaining steps in this exercise. If you prefer to suffer a life of index ignorance, skip to the "What Did You Learn?" quiz on page 449.

13. ***Add another* toolbox *reference.*** Press Shift+Page Down five times in a row—or press Ctrl+J (⌘-J), enter 8, and press Enter or Return—to advance to page 8, which begins a two-page spread devoted to the toolbox. We really owe it to our readers to add the spread to our index. You might be tempted to select the word *Toolbox* in the heading at the top of the page, but don't. By default, doing so would create a new entry for *Toolbox* with a capital *T*, and that's hardly what we want. Instead, do the following:

    - Double-click to select the word *toolbox* in the first full sentence on page 8, circled in Figure 10-35.
    - To reference the entire page spread, we need to extend the entry into page 9. So click the ◰ icon at the bottom of the Index palette to bring up the **New Page Reference** dialog box.

- Choose **To End of Story** from the **Type** pop-up menu, and click **OK**. InDesign adds the page range to our existing *toolbox* entry, as shown in the Index palette in Figure 10-35.

14. ***Add a subentry to the index.*** Next let's add a reference to the words *quick mask* at the top of page 9:

    - Select the words *quick mask* (circled in Figure 10-36) and click the icon at the bottom of the **Index** palette.

    - Since Photoshop's quick mask control resides in the toolbox, it makes sense to make *quick mask* a subentry under *toolbox*. Inside the **New Page Reference** dialog box, click the ↓ arrow to the right of Topic Levels option box 2 to send *quick mask* down a level.

    - Next, find the T in the index preview at the bottom of the dialog box and click the ▶ arrow to twirl the letter open. Then click in option box 1 at the top of the dialog box and double-click the word *toolbox* in the preview area. (You could also type the word "toolbox," but double-clicking the existing entry eliminates the chance of typos.)

    - Click **Add** to add *quick mask* as a subentry under *toolbox* Then click the ▶ arrows in front of the *T* and *toolbox* to see the subentry, as in Figure 10-37.

15. ***Create a cross-reference.*** Before we leave this dialog box, I reckon we ought to create a cross-reference so that a reader who looks up *quick mask* under the letter Q will be directed to the recently added *toolbox* entry (as in "*See* toolbox"):

    - Click the *quick mask* topic level entry, and then click the ↑ arrow to the right of option box 1. The *quick mask* and *toolbox* entries switch places.

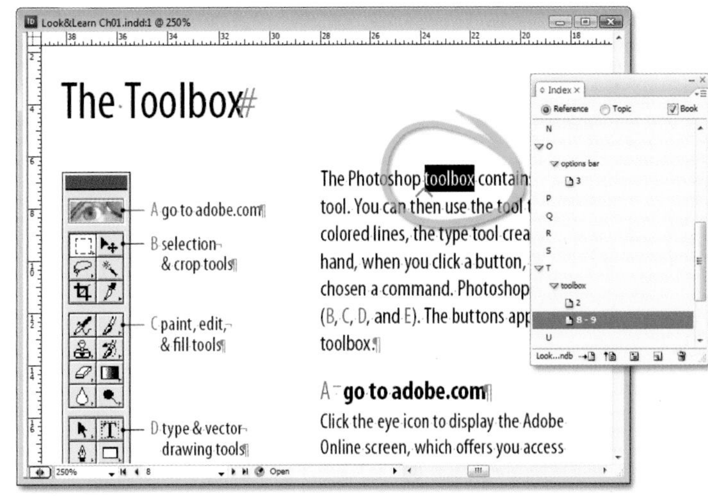

Figure 10-35.

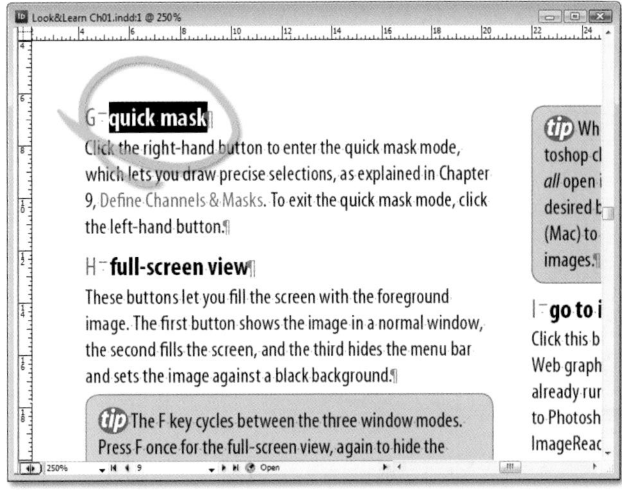

Figure 10-36.

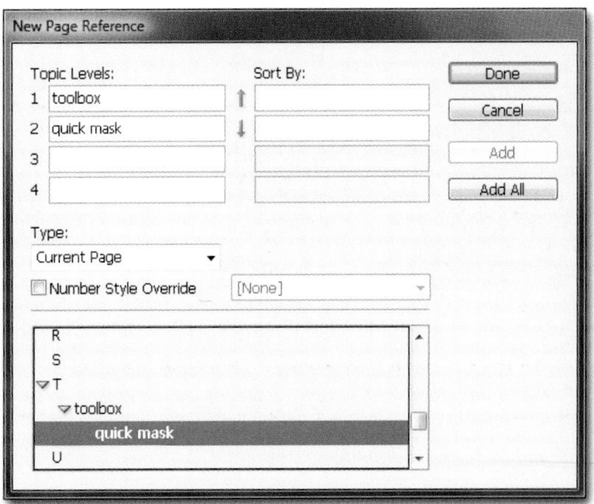

Figure 10-37.

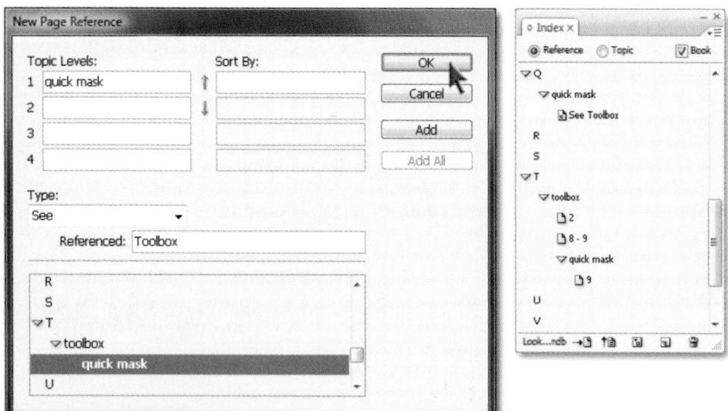

Figure 10-38.

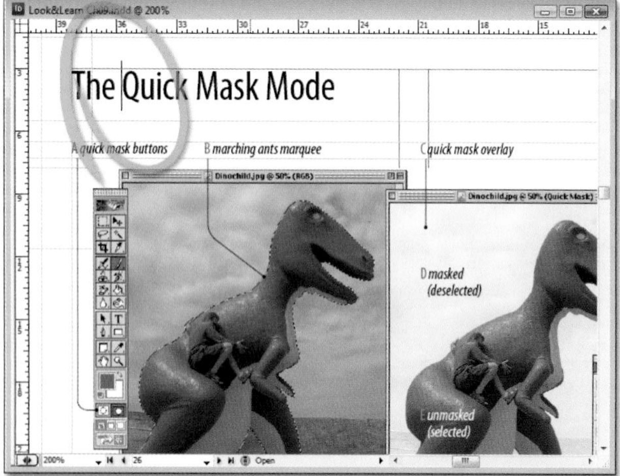

Figure 10-39.

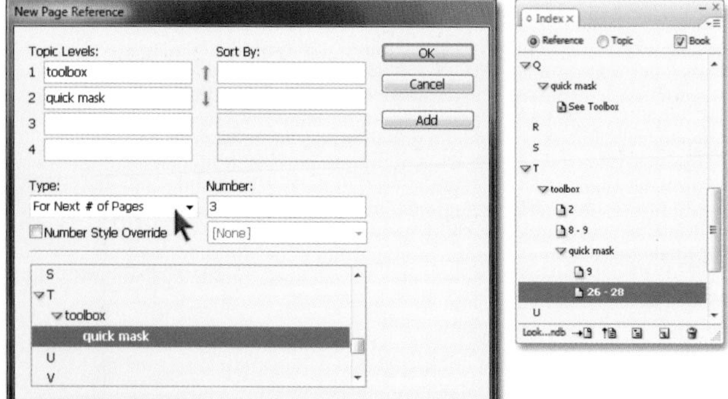

Figure 10-40.

- Select the *toolbox* subtopic entry and delete it.
- Choose **See** from the **Type** pop-up menu. Then type "toolbox" in the neighboring **Referenced** option box. (You have to type it manually—no double-clicking this time around.)
- Finally, click the **OK** button. As you can see in Figure 10-38, InDesign adds the *quick mask* cross-reference to the Index palette. Clicking the OK button both adds the word and exits the dialog box.

16. ***Add a* quick mask *entry from Chapter 9.*** Double-click the **Look&Learn Ch09** item in the book palette to open the Chapter 9 file. Then press Ctrl+J (⌘-J on the Mac), enter 26, and press Enter or Return to advance to page 26 of the document, which contains a one-page introduction to the quick mask mode. The page is followed by a two-page step-by-step exercise on this same feature. We could list these different treatments as two separate entries, but to streamline the index, I suggest we create a single entry for all three pages instead:
    - Click with the type tool to place the insertion marker immediately in front of the word *Quick* in the headline, which I circled in Figure 10-39.
    - Then click the ◻ icon at the bottom of the **Index** palette. Scroll the index preview at the bottom of the dialog box until you come to the *T*, and then twirl it and the *toolbox* entry open by clicking the ▶ arrows so you can see the *quick mask* entry.
    - Double-click the words *quick mask* in the preview area to display *toolbox* and *quick mask*, in that order, in the Topic Levels list.
    - Choose **For Next # of Pages** from the **Type** pop-up menu, and enter 3 in the **Number** option box, as shown in Figure 10-40. Then click the **OK** button. The Index palette updates to include the new three-page reference.
17. ***Add a final entry from Chapter 1.*** Switch back to Chapter 1, which should still be open. Press Ctrl+Shift+Page Up (⌘-Shift-Page Up) to retreat to the first page in the document, page 1. I want to show you one other keyboard

shortcut, which involves indexing names of people. Select the name *Thomas Knoll* in the second line of the text (circled in Figure 10-41). Because it's a proper name, an index entry for this person should be alphabetized under *K*. While you could do this by creating a new entry and manually replacing the topic entry with *Knoll, Thomas*, there's a quicker way.

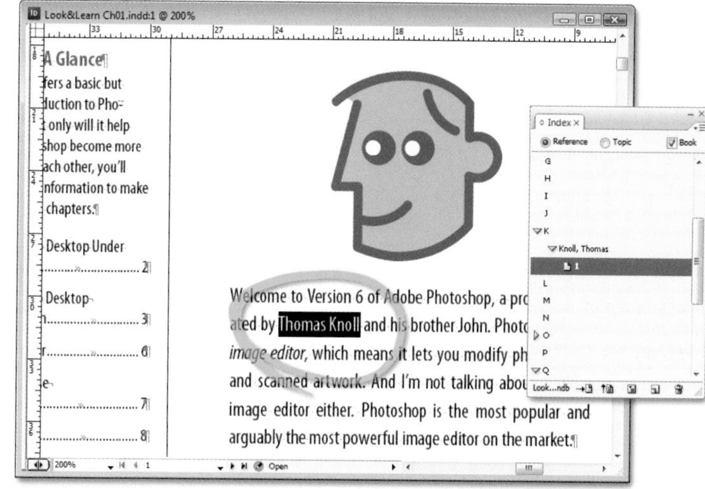

Figure 10-41.

Press Ctrl+Shift+Alt+] (⌘-Shift-Option-]). Just like that, InDesign adds an entry under K in the Index palette. Thanks to this spiffy keyboard shortcut, InDesign created the entry from the last selected word, *Knoll*, rather than the first.

If a proper name ends with *Jr.* or another suffix, you don't want to create the entry from the last selected word. Fortunately, there's a workaround: Enter a nonbreaking space between the last name and the *Jr.* by choosing Type→Insert White Space→Nonbreaking Space or by pressing Ctrl+Alt+X (⌘-Option-X). This forces InDesign to read the word before the nonbreaking space as the last name.

18. ***Save and close the two open documents.*** Close Chapter 1 and Chapter 9. Make sure to save your changes when prompted so you preserve the special index markers that InDesign has placed in the documents. After you close the documents, do not be alarmed that the Index palette is now blank. The palette displays the index markers for open documents only.

19. ***Add a document to the book.*** Click the ✚ icon at the bottom of the book palette. In the **Add Documents** dialog box, navigate to the *Lesson 10* folder and select the file *Blank slate back.indd*. Then click **Add** (**Open** on the Mac). Drag the document to the bottom of the stack so that your book palette looks like the one in Figure 10-42.

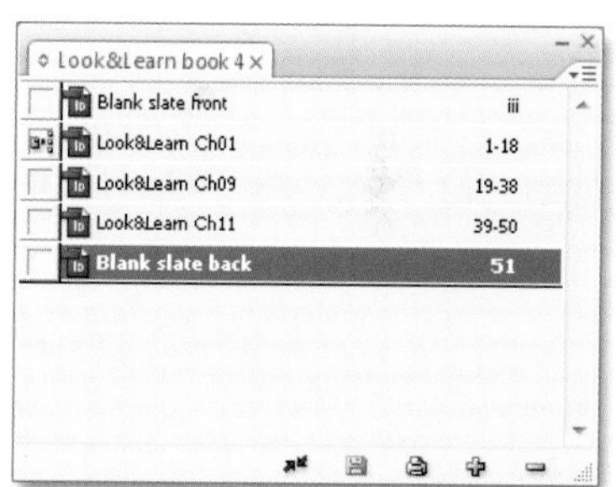

Figure 10-42.

20. ***Prepare to generate the index.*** Double-click the **Blank Slate Back** item in the book palette to open this empty document. A book's index can be generated only in a document that's already part of that book; that's why we had to import this blank document into the palette.

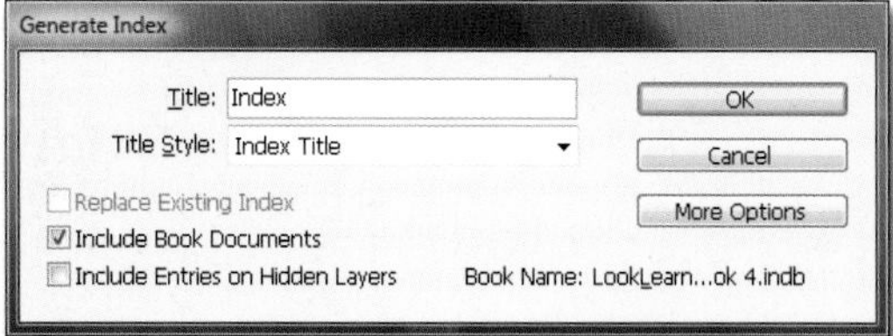

Figure 10-43.

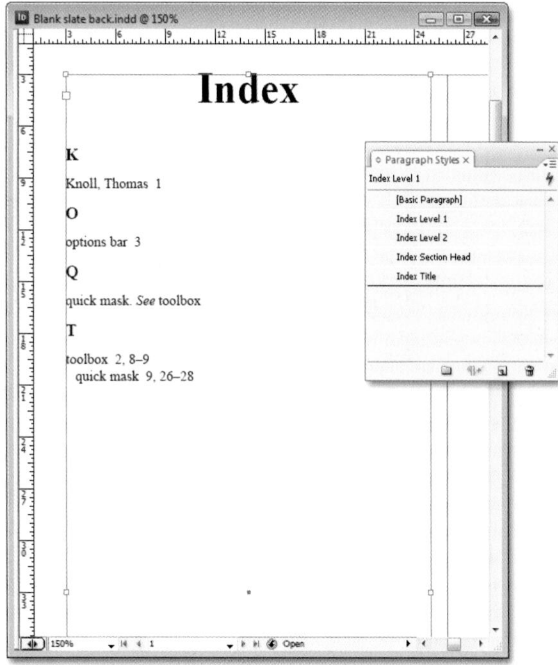

Figure 10-44.

21. ***Specify index options.*** Click the icon at the bottom of the **Index** palette to bring up the **Generate Index** dialog box, as in Figure 10-43.

    - The Title option lets you specify the title that will appear at the top of the index. The default title, Index, is fine for our purposes.
    - The Title Style option lets you choose a style to apply to the title. I haven't created any styles for this document, so the default Index Title style is fine.
    - Turn on the **Include Book Documents** check box to instruct InDesign to search every document in the book palette for index entries.
    - The documents in this book have no hidden layers, so leave the Include Entries on Hidden Layers check box turned off.

22. ***Generate the index.*** Click the **OK** button to dismiss the Generate Index dialog box. Moments later, you are presented with the loaded cursor. Click at the top of the left column in the *Blank slate back.indd* document to place the index, as in Figure 10-44.

And here's a great feature: Even though this document didn't have any style sheets before you created the index, it has style sheets now. A glance at the Paragraph Styles palette (shown in Figure 10-44) reveals that InDesign has automatically created paragraph styles for the topic levels in the index. If you want to adjust the formatting attributes, simply change the paragraph styles and the index updates. So while building an index is a lot of work, laying out and formatting the index goes very quickly.

WHAT DID YOU LEARN?

Match the key concept in the numbered list below with the letter of the phrase that best describes it. Answers appear upside-down at the bottom of the page.

Key Concepts

1. Book file
2. Automatic Page Numbering
3. Open book icon
4. Style source
5. Synchronize Options
6. Table of contents
7. Find/Change
8. Index entry
9. Sort By
10. Number Style Override
11. Add All
12. Cross-reference

Descriptions

A. This option lets you apply a character style other than the default setting to the page number for a specific index entry.

B. When you create one of these, InDesign inserts a hidden character ( ) to monitor the item and its page number.

C. InDesign can generate one of these automatically by examining the style sheets used throughout the documents in a book.

D. Use this command to specify exactly which attributes you want to match to those in the style source document.

E. This command lets you search for a string of characters or inline graphics and either replace them with a different string or delete them.

F. Marked with a , a document with this designation becomes the model according to which InDesign synchronizes all other documents in the book palette.

G. This option numbers the pages in a document starting at the point where the preceding document in the book palette leaves off.

H. Use this option to alphabetize an index entry by something other than its initial letter.

I. An index entry that begins with *See* or *See also* and points you to a different entry in the index.

J. This button instructs InDesign to reference every occurrence of a term within every open document.

K. This function tracks multiple InDesign documents so you can evaluate and modify them as a group.

L. If you see the icon next to a document's name in the book palette, you know that the document is open and ready to accept changes.

Answers

1K, 2G, 3L, 4F, 5D, 6C, 7E, 8B, 9H, 10A, 11J, 12I

LESSON 11

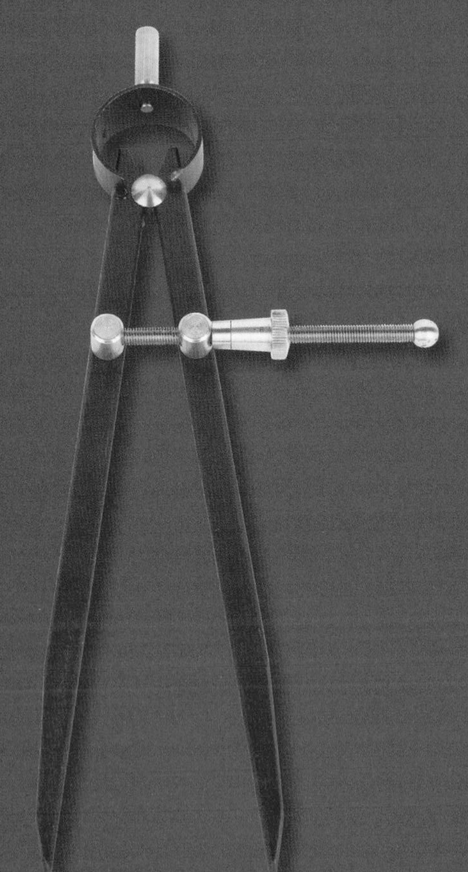

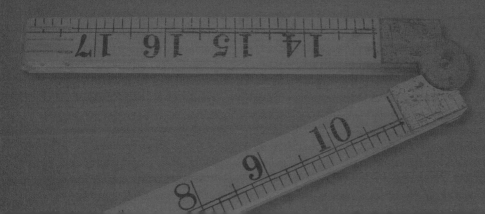

HYPERLINKS, BOOKMARKS, AND PDF

BOOKS AND OTHER printed documents can be many things. They can be instructive. They can be entertaining. They can be thought-provoking. They've even been known to shape events. But one thing printed documents can't be is interactive. Whatever you can say in their defense—and certainly a lot comes to mind—printed pages are static. If you're searching for a particular topic, you might find aid in the form of an index or a table of contents, but you have to thumb through the document to locate the page yourself.

If you want to craft a more interactive reading experience, you might turn to the World Wide Web, which lets you express a document as a dynamic and nonlinear site. You can create links that define or explain a topic, take you to a related topic, or reference an entirely new one. If you want to convert an InDesign document to a Web site, you can export the document to a collection of files that can be read by GoLive, the Web-site-creation application that Adobe includes with the Premium edition of the Creative Suite. Exporting to GoLive is an interesting and powerful solution, but it requires you to learn yet another application, which is rarely what I would call quick or easy.

The better medium for outputting an interactive InDesign document is the Portable Document Format, or *PDF* for short. A PDF file may be self-contained or it may reference external files. It can be viewed on screen or printed, either with or without Internet access. Some operating systems, such as Apple's OS X, can view PDF files without additional software. Otherwise, you need a utility called Adobe Reader, which you can download for free (*www.acrobat.com*) and without registering any personal information. And finally, a PDF file can be static like a book document or interactive like a Web site, or even an amalgam of the two. It all depends on the kinds of elements you add to your document.

ABOUT THIS LESSON

Project Files

Before beginning the exercises, make sure you've copied the lesson files from the DVD, as directed in Step 3 on page xvii of the Preface. This should result in a folder called *Lesson Files-IDcs3 1on1* on your desktop. We'll be working with the files inside the *Lesson 11* subfolder.

This lesson explores InDesign's little-known multimedia capabilities. You can compose a fully interactive document—with bookmarks, hyperlinks, buttons, sounds, and movies—and export your creation to a PDF file that can be played on any modern computer. In the following exercises, you'll learn how to:

- Generate bookmarks automatically from a table of contents . . . . page 454
- Create hyperlinks that take the reader to other pages within a document or to entirely different documents . . . . page 458
- Design graphic buttons that animate when the reader moves the cursor over the button or clicks . . . . page 463
- Import and define the appearance of sound and movie files . . . . page 468
- Output your bookmarks, hyperlinks, buttons, sounds, and movies to an interactive PDF document . . . . page 472

Video Lesson 11: The Final PDF File

This time around, I'm going to do something different. Instead of introducing you to the larger concepts of hyperlinks, bookmarks, and PDF, I'm going to start at the end. Over the course of the many exercises in this lesson, I'll be showing you how to create a multimedia PDF file. Problem is, I can't really show you the results of your efforts–complete with bookmarks, rollover buttons, sounds, and even an embedded movie–on the printed page. Which is why I'll be showing you all that stuff here in this video.

To join me in my exciting interactive PDF tour, watch the eleventh video lesson included on the DVD. To watch it, insert the DVD, double-click the file *IDcs3 Videos.html*, and click **Lesson 11: The Final PDF File** under the **Books, Hyperlinks, and Output** heading. The video lasts 7 minutes and 30 seconds. And for once I don't mention a single shortcut.

Tools for Interactivity

What varieties of interactivity does InDesign support? For starters, you can create a series of *bookmarks*, which behave like a live table of contents. Click a bookmark and you're whisked away to the corresponding headline. You can also create *hyperlinks*, which are hot spots built into the pages of a document. A hyperlink can be any text or graphic object, including a single word or character of type. Clicking the hyperlink might take you somewhere inside the same PDF file or transport you to a different file, including a file posted on the Internet. To give a hyperlink more visual impact, you can upgrade it to an animated *rollover button* that changes appearance when the reader's cursor passes over it. Buttons can trigger the same actions as bookmarks and hyperlinks, plus perform tasks like opening and closing files, quitting Adobe Reader, and playing embedded sounds and movies.

Did I say "sounds and movies?" Why, yes I did. Although InDesign hardly qualifies as a full-fledged multimedia program, it does let you implant audio and video files into a PDF document. As long as you're creating a publication for the screen, you might as well take advantage of all the benefits the screen has to offer (see Figure 11-1). The truth is, InDesign lets you create PDF documents with so many bells and whistles—literally—that your audience will swear the initials PDF stand for "Pretty Darn Fun."

Figure 11-1.

You've made it through these opening credits, and you'll be sitting next to me for the duration of this feature. So relax, turn off your cell phone, and don't kick the seat in front of you.

PEARL OF WISDOM

As in the last lesson, you should work your way through each exercise in sequence. Sadly, I can't provide you with intermediate documents—if I did, some links would not perform as advertised.

Before you settle in for the feature presentation, I invite you to watch the short-subject Video Lesson 11, "The Final PDF File," which shows you how your bookmarks, hyperlinks, rollover buttons, and embedded movies will work when the project is done. Otherwise, prepare to delay an awful lot of gratification before arriving at the stirring conclusion, "Exporting to PDF" (page 472).

Creating Bookmarks

Adobe's use of the word *bookmark* is a little misleading. In the real world, a bookmark is placed by the reader to indicate where he or she stopped reading. In a PDF document, bookmarks are placed by the document's creator to aid in navigation and highlight sections that the creator thinks are important. It's like buying a Stephen King thriller and finding it laced with bookmarks put there by Mr. King himself, bookmarks that turn the pages for you as if by an unseen hand.

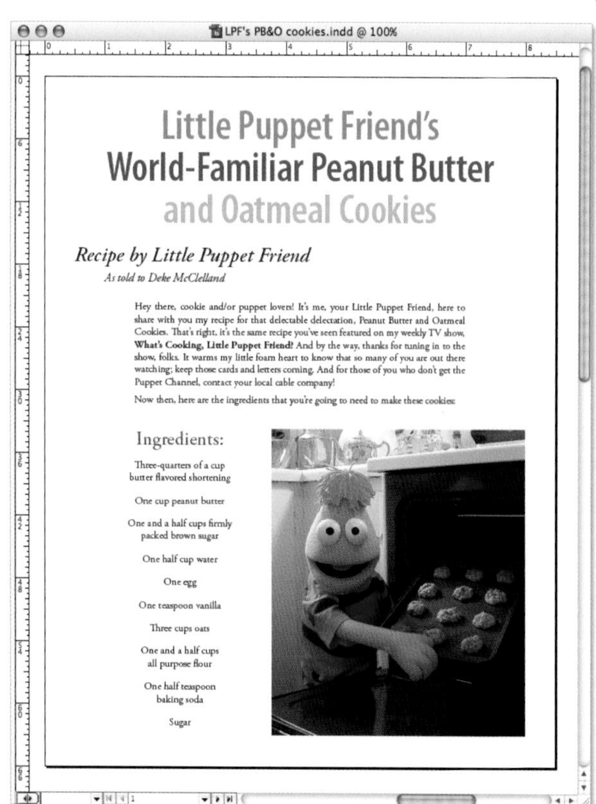

Figure 11-2.

In this exercise, you'll start with a formatted version of a document we created back in Lesson 2 and add bookmarks that will make the document easier to navigate when we export it as a PDF file. If you're consistent in your use of style sheets, adding PDF bookmarks is as easy as making a table of contents (see "Creating a Table of Contents, which begins on page 434 of Lesson 10). In fact, generating a table of contents is one of the first things we'll do.

1. ***Open a document in need of bookmarks.*** Open *LPF's PB&O cookies.indd*, which is located in the *Lesson 11* folder inside *Lesson Files-IDcs3 1on1*. As in Lesson 2, we are greeted by LPF and his oven-fresh cookies (see Figure 11-2). Lest you think I'm shamelessly repurposing a sample file, rest assured I have plenty of new stuff to keep the weary InDesign student entertained. In fact, at the risk of subjecting you to a pun, you're in for a treat.

2. ***Examine the style sheets used in the document.*** Choose **Type→Paragraph Styles** or press F11 to access the **Paragraph Styles** palette. Press the T key to get the type tool. Click in the multicolored headline (circled yellow in Figure 11-3) and check out its settings in the Paragraph Styles palette. Then click the *Ingredients* subhead (circled orange) and check out its settings. The headline uses a modified variation of the Title style; the subhead uses the Ingredients style.

   Repeat the process for the subheads on pages 2 and 3. You'll find that the *Reviewing the Ingredients*, *Making the Cookies*, and *Finishing the Cookies* subheads are formatted with the Heading style. Page 3 features a subhead called *The Joke*, but I neglected to assign a paragraph style to it.

Figure 11-3.

3. ***Open the Bookmarks palette.*** Choose **Window→Interactive→Bookmarks** to open the **Bookmarks** palette. At this point, the palette is empty, but it won't be for long.

4. ***Generate a table of contents.*** Just as InDesign can create a table of contents using paragraph styles, it can create PDF bookmarks from a table of contents. In fact—and I think somewhat bizarrely—that's the *only* way to automate the creation of bookmarks. So choose **Layout→Table of Contents** to summon the **Table of Contents** dialog box. We want to include the title and all subheads in our TOC.

   - Click **Title** in the **Other Styles** list. Then click the **Add** button. Title becomes the first-level head.
   - Click **Ingredients** in the right-hand list and then Shift-click **Heading**. Next click the **Add** button. The three styles appear in the left-hand list, as shown in Figure 11-4.
   - Turn on the **Create PDF Bookmarks** check box, as I've circled in the figure. This tells InDesign to automatically make bookmarks for each item in the TOC.

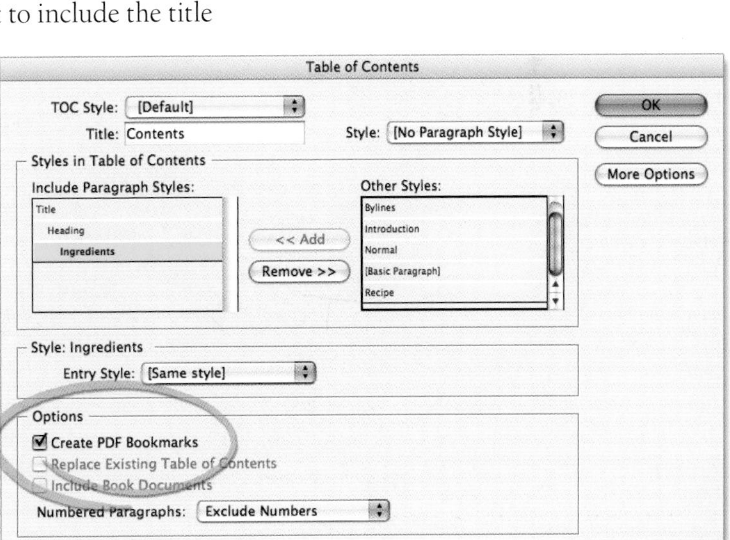

Figure 11-4.

- Click the **OK** button. Your cursor is now loaded and ready to place text.

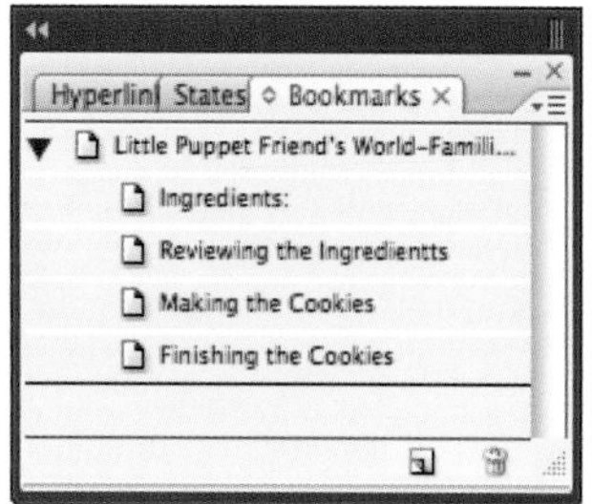

Figure 11-5.

5. ***Examine the bookmarks.*** Before you click with the cursor, take a look at the **Bookmarks** palette, which now contains bookmarks for the title and headings, as in Figure 11-5. (If you see only one item, click the ▶ arrow on the left to reveal the others.)

6. ***Place the table of contents.*** Now to place the table of contents. The question is, where do you put it? We don't want to print the darn thing—what do we need with a TOC for a three-page document, for crying out loud?—so I recommend you throw it on the pasteboard. Armed with the cursor, draw a text frame in the pasteboard next to page 1, as indicated by the text block on the left side of Figure 11-6. The formatting looks pretty ugly, but we don't care. We're keeping it around only to retain the PDF bookmarks. And out there in the pasteboard, it won't print or export to a PDF file, so nobody but you will see it.

PEARL OF WISDOM

Even after you place the table of contents, it remains inextricably linked to the bookmarks. In other words, if you were to delete the table of contents at this point, the bookmarks would be deleted as well. It's exceedingly weird—there's no bookmark marker in the TOC text and the relationship between TOC and bookmarks is largely static—but that's the way it works.

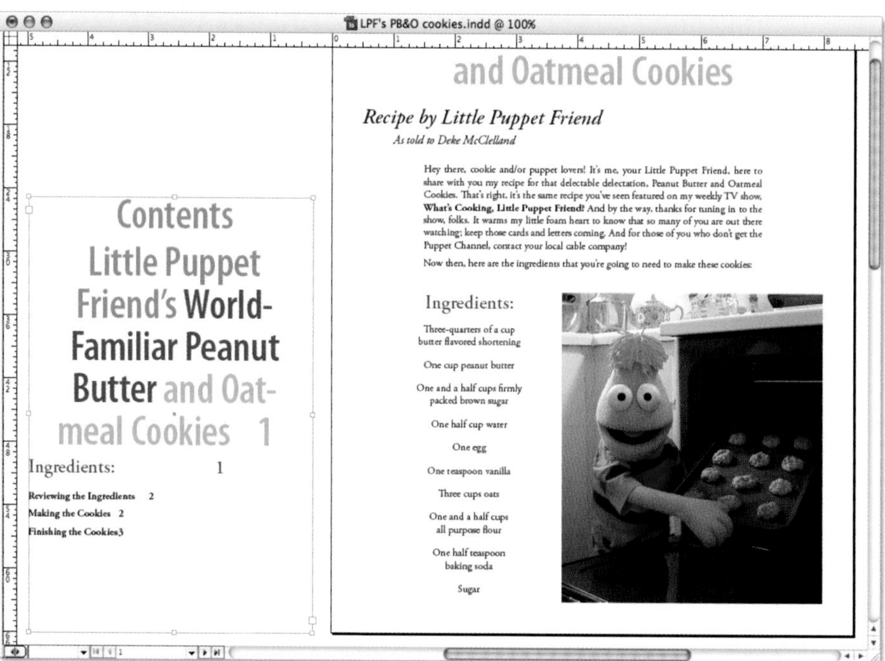

Figure 11-6.

7. ***Test a couple of bookmarks.*** Let's preview some bookmarks to make sure they work. You can test a bookmark by double-clicking it in the Bookmarks palette. Double-click the **Making the Cookies** bookmark to advance to page 2. Then double-click **Finishing the Cookies** to jump to page 3.

Should you be so inclined, you can rearrange bookmarks by dragging them up or down in the Bookmarks palette. Drag a bookmark on top of another bookmark to create a subcategory bookmark. To rename a bookmark, select it and choose Rename Bookmark from the palette menu. Or just click a bookmark that you've already selected and wait a second. (Think of it as a very slow double-click, as when renaming a file at the desktop level.)

---

8. ***Create a new bookmark.*** I'd like you to add one more bookmark, this time for the subhead that reads *The Joke* in the first column of page 3. This paragraph doesn't have a style sheet applied, so it wasn't included in the table of contents. But no worries, you can add bookmarks manually any time you like:

   - Get the type tool and select the heading *The Joke*. Be sure to select the entire line of text so that InDesign names the bookmark properly.
   - Click the **Making the Cookies** bookmark in the Bookmarks palette so that the next bookmark you create appears below it as a subcategory.
   - Click the icon at the bottom of the Bookmarks palette. As Figure 11-7 shows, InDesign automatically adds the bookmark and names it after the selected text. Press the Enter or Return key to accept the name.

   Notice that the new bookmark name has a icon beside it in the Bookmarks palette. This indicates a *hyperlink anchor*, or just plain *anchor*, embedded into the text of the document. You'll learn more about hyperlink anchors in the next exercise.

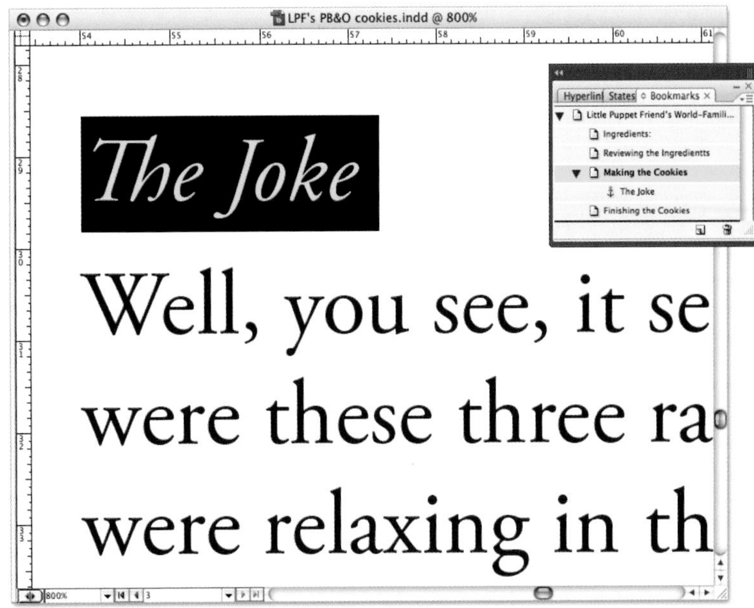

Figure 11-7.

PEARL OF WISDOM

There are a few more things you should know about creating bookmarks manually. If you want a bookmark to take the reader to the top of a page (rather than to a specific anchor on a page), double-click the page in the Pages palette to select it, and then create a new bookmark. You can also bookmark a graphic by selecting it and then clicking the icon. InDesign will suggest the name *Bookmark*, but you can (and, what the heck, should) give it a more descriptive name.

9. ***Save your work.*** If you're going to continue on to the next exercise, you'll need this document in its current state, so it's a good idea to save your work. Choose **File→Save As**, name the document "LPF's PB&O cookies 2.indd," and click **Save**.

Setting Up Hyperlinks

Bookmarks are terrific for helping readers get around inside a document, but hyperlinks offer more flexibility. InDesign lets you create hyperlinks that take readers to different locations within a document or to external documents, including other PDF files and Web pages. Put it this way: If bookmarks are the table of contents, hyperlinks are the index.

In this exercise, you'll add three hyperlinks to the cookie recipe document that you saved at the end of the last exercise. First, you'll create a hyperlink that jumps to a different section of the document. Next, you'll create a hyperlink that leaps to a Web page available only if you have an Internet connection. And finally, you'll create a hyperlink that opens a *future* PDF file, one that won't exist until the end of the final exercise in this lesson.

1. ***Open the cookie recipe document.*** If it's not already up on the screen, open the *LPF's PB&O cookies 2.indd* file that you saved in the last step of the last exercise. If you didn't work through the last exercise, please go back and do so now. These exercises must be performed in order.

2. ***Open the Hyperlinks palette.*** If the palette is not already visible, choose **Window→Interactive→Hyperlinks** to display the **Hyperlinks** palette.

3. ***Create a hyperlink destination.*** Let's turn one of the ingredients in the list on the first page into a hyperlink that takes readers to the paragraph describing that ingredient. First, we need to define the destination of the link by adding a hyperlink anchor. Then we can create the link.

- Go to the second page of the document and locate the second paragraph under the heading *Reviewing the Ingredients* in the first column (the one that begins *Then you're going to need one cup of peanut butter.*) Click in front of the first letter in this paragraph with the type tool to set the blinking insertion marker.
- Click the ▾≡ icon in the upper corner of the **Hyperlinks** palette and choose **New Hyperlink Destination** to bring up the dialog box shown in Figure 11-8.
- The Type option lets you specify whether you want to create a link to a specific page in the document (Page), a hyperlink anchor (Text Anchor), or a Web page (URL). We've already determined that we want to use an anchor, so choose **Text Anchor** from the **Type** pop-up menu.
- Enter "PB paragraph" in the **Name** option box and click **OK** to close the New Hyperlink Destination dialog box.

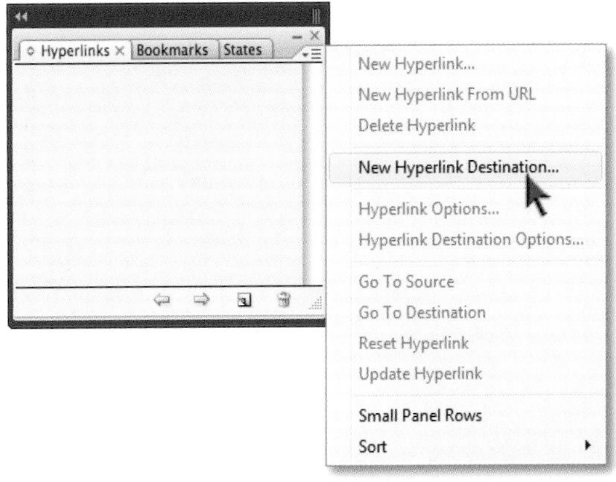

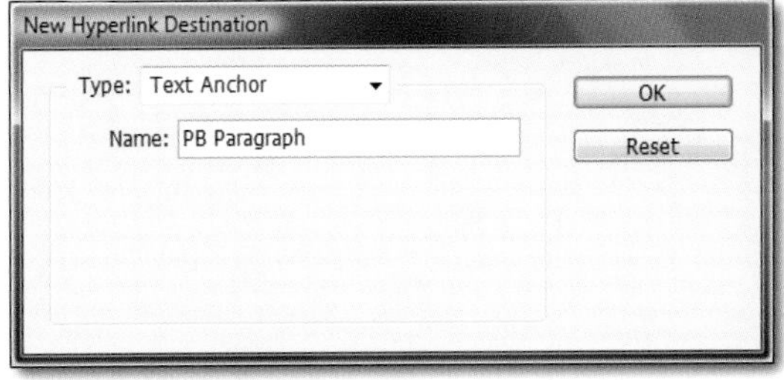

Figure 11-8.

PEARL OF WISDOM

Nothing appears in the Hyperlinks palette yet because we've created only the destination for the hyperlink, not the hyperlink itself. The only way to confirm that anything whatsoever has happened is to choose Type→Show Hidden Characters or press Ctrl+Alt+I (⌘-Option-I). A light blue colon (:) appears in front of the first letter in the paragraph. That is your new hyperlink anchor.

4. ***Create a hyperlink.*** Go to the first page and triple-click the second ingredient in the ingredients list, *One cup peanut butter*, to select the entire line of text. Then click the ◰ icon at the bottom of the **Hyperlinks** palette to display the **New Hyperlink** dialog box. Enter "Peanut Butter" in the **Name** option box. Then set the Destination options as shown in Figure 11-9:

    - Leave **Document** set to the default, **LPF's PB&O cookies 2.indd**, which is the document that contains the link destination. Note that when we update this document and save it under different names, InDesign will update this reference.
    - Choose **Text Anchor** from the **Type** pop-up menu.
    - Leave the **Name** option set to **PB paragraph**, which is the destination we set up in the preceding step.

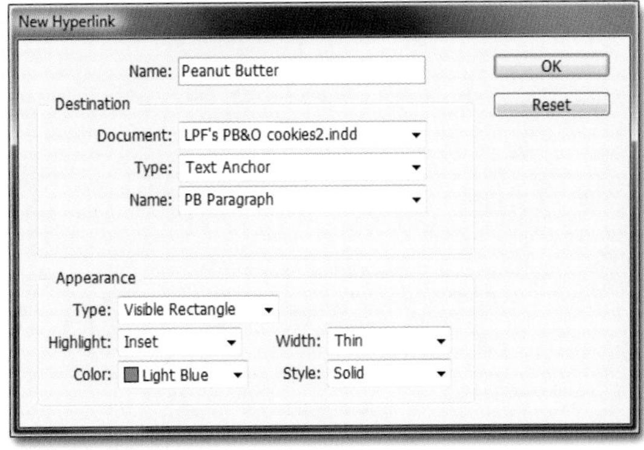

Figure 11-9.

- A hyperlink is useless if no one knows to click it, so it's best to visually distinguish it from other text. The options in the Appearance section of the New Hyperlink dialog box let you do just that. A rectangle is the only visual clue available for hyperlinks, so choose **Visible Rectangle** from the **Type** pop-up menu (if it's not set that way already).
- The Highlight option determines what a link looks like when it's being clicked. None makes no change in the link's appearance. Invert creates an inverted rectangle, Outline draws a hollow rectangle, and Inset adds a shadowed effect like a button being pushed. Choose **Inset** from the **Highlight** pop-up menu.
- Set the **Color** pop-up menu to **Light Blue**.
- The **Width** setting determines the thickness of the rectangle outline. Stick with the default option of **Thin**.
- The **Style** option lets you choose between a solid or dashed outline; choose **Solid**.

When you're through, click **OK**. Then press Ctrl+Shift+A (or ⌘-Shift-A) to deselect the hyperlink so you can see what it looks like. As Figure 11-10 shows, a blue rectangle now appears around the link, and a hyperlink named Peanut Butter appears in the Hyperlinks palette with a little ‡ to the right of it.

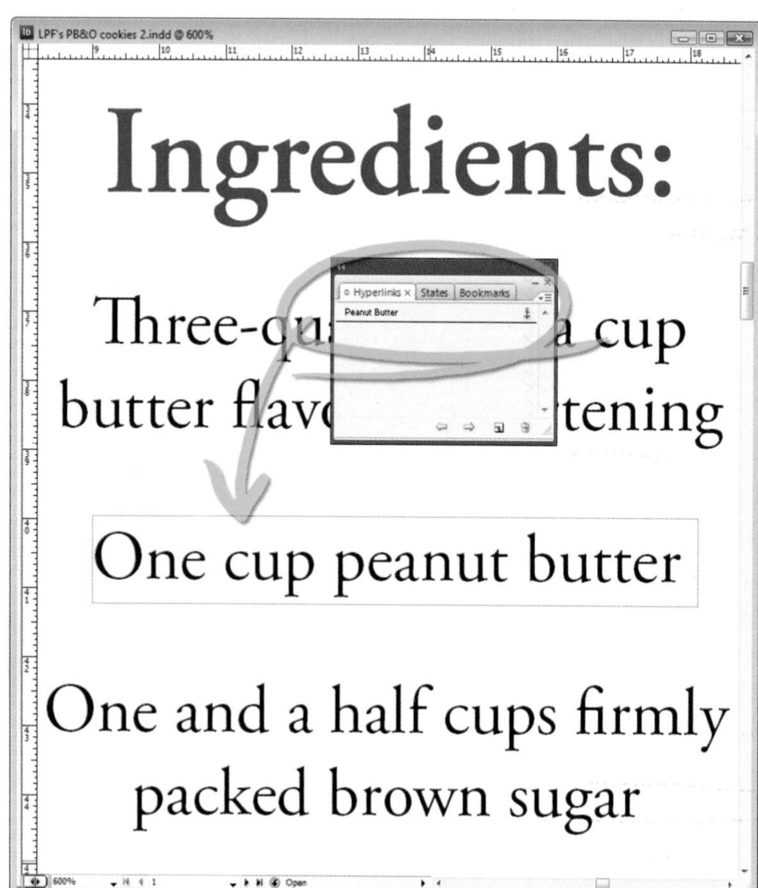

Figure 11-10.

If you wish InDesign would imbue a hyperlink with some visual identifier other than a rectangle (and I concur, incidentally), keep in mind that you can format the link text however you want. For instance, say you want *One cup peanut butter* to appear blue and underlined, which would make it look more like a standard hyperlink on the Web. Double-click the link in the Hyperlinks palette and change the Type option in the Appearance area to Invisible Rectangle. (You might also want to change the Highlight option to Invert or None.) Click OK to leave the dialog box. Then use the type tool to select the link text in the document window, and color the text blue and underline it using InDesign's character-level formatting controls.

---

5. ***Test the hyperlink.*** To test a bookmark, all you had to do was double-click it in the Bookmarks palette. Not so with hyperlinks; double-clicking a hyperlink opens the Hyperlink Options dialog box, where you can edit the settings for the link. To test the hyperlink, select it in the **Hyperlinks** palette, and then click the ⇨ arrow at the bottom of the palette. In our case, the document jumps to page 2, and the insertion marker is set at the beginning of the peanut butter paragraph.

Select the link name again and click the ⇦ arrow at the bottom of the Hyperlinks palette to go back to the peanut butter ingredient link on page 1.

---

6. ***Create a URL hyperlink.*** Now let's create a hyperlink to a Web site. We'll do this by entering a URL (Uniform Resource Locater), which is the address of a Web page. Note that a URL can just as easily point to an image or a movie on your hard drive, another PDF document, or some other file. And that's just fine by InDesign. So long as you enter a valid URL, the PDF file can link to it.

   Unlike in Step 3, there's no need to specify a destination because the URL *is* the destination. So we'll just make the hyperlink:

   - Navigate to the final paragraph in the lower-right corner of page 3 and select the entire italicized book title, *Baking Cookies One-on-One*.
   - Next, click the ◰ icon at the bottom of the Hyperlinks palette to bring up the **New Hyperlink** dialog box. InDesign names the link after the book title, so you can leave the **Name** option as is.
   - Choose **URL** from the **Type** pop-up menu. Then enter "http://oneonone.oreilly.com" in the **URL** option box. (Note that there's no "www" in the URL.) This is the URL for info on my *One-on-One* books.
   - Ignore the Document and second Name options, neither of which apply. Also ignore the Appearance settings; we'll use the same ones we applied last time. Your settings in the New Hyperlink dialog box should match those in Figure 11-11. When they do, click **OK**, and then press Ctrl+Shift+A (⌘-Shift-A) to deselect the text and view the new hyperlink.

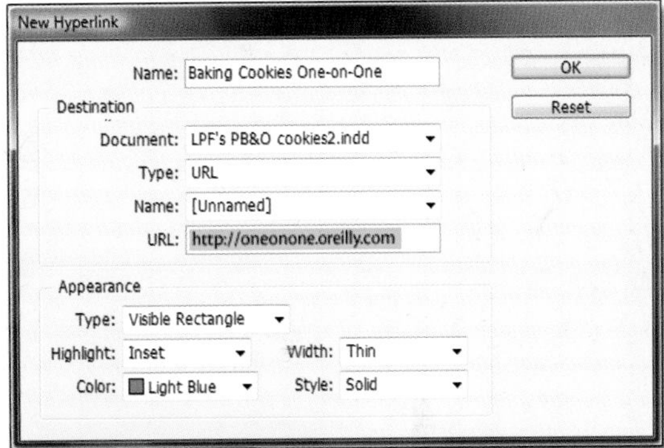

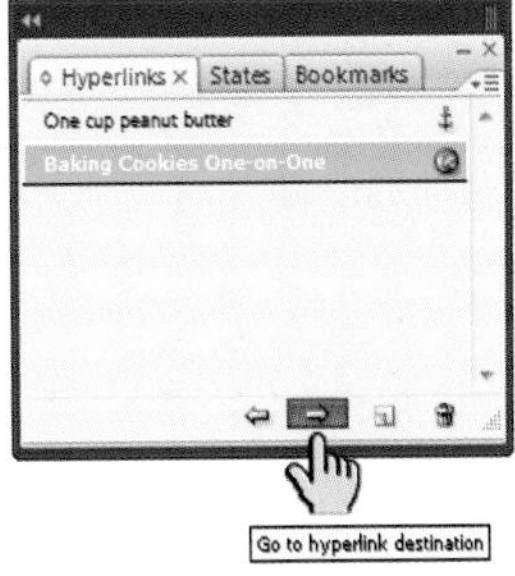

Figure 11-11.

Figure 11-12.

7. ***Test the URL.*** To preview the hyperlink and make sure it works, select the link name and click the ⇨ arrow at the bottom of the palette. This time InDesign launches your default Web browser and then loads the *One-on-One* Web site, pictured in Figure 11-12. Note that you'll need an active Internet connection. If the site looks different than it does in the figure, it just means the site has been updated. (If the link fails, it's probably because you entered it incorrectly. Double-click the link in the Hyperlinks palette and confirm the URL in the Hyperlink Options dialog box.)

8. ***Create yet another hyperlink.*** We have one last hyperlink to add. This time we'll create a link that opens another document. Go to page 1, and select the boldface *What's Cooking, Little Puppet Friend?* (including the question mark) in the main text. Oh, and as long as we're making a new hyperlink, let's try our hands at a new technique:

   - Right-click in the document window to display the shortcut menu. (If your Mac mouse has just one button, press Control and click.) Then choose **Interactive→New Hyperlink**. This brings up the familiar **New Hyperlink** dialog box, shown in Figure 11-13 with the settings I want you to enter.
   - Go ahead and accept the default name, which is derived from the selected text.
   - Choose **Browse** from the **Document** pop-up menu to bring up the **Locate InDesign File** dialog box. Navigate to the *Lesson 11* folder inside *Lesson Files-IDcs3 1on1*, select the file named *What's cooking.indd*, and click **Open**. Back in the New Hyperlink dialog box, the Document pop-up menu now lists What's cooking.indd.
   - Next, choose **Page** from the **Type** pop-up menu. The Name option is irrelevant for our purposes. The Page option is set to 1 and can't be changed, because *What's cooking.indd* is a single-page document. For the **Zoom Setting** option, choose **Inherit Zoom**, which will open the linked file at the viewer's current zoom setting.

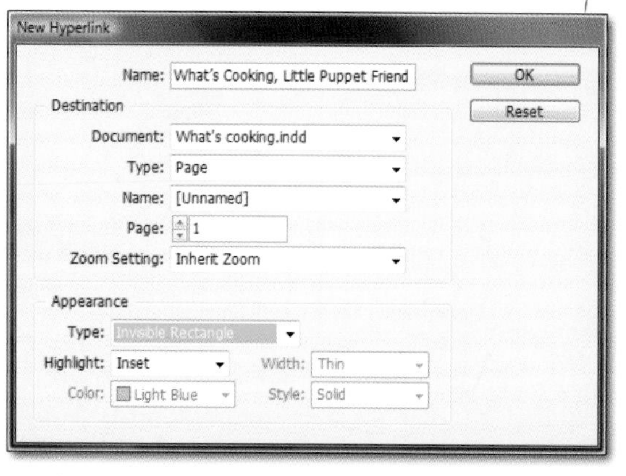

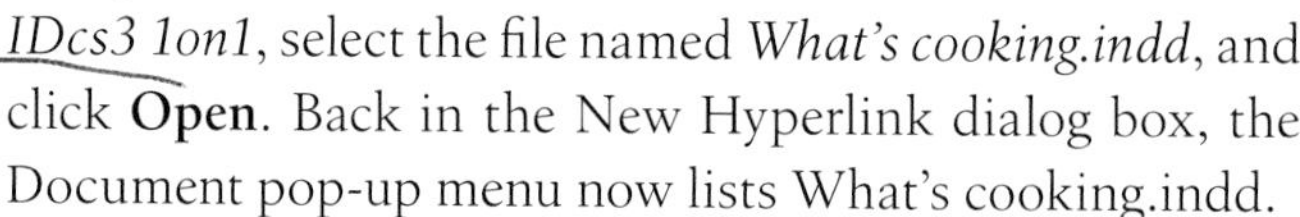

Figure 11-13.

- Under Appearance, change the **Type** option to **Invisible Rectangle**. The link text is already bold, so the rectangle is overkill. Besides, we'll create a more compelling way to launch the *What's cooking* document in the next exercise; this link is just a backup.

When your settings look like those in Figure 11-13, click **OK**. Then press Ctrl+Shift+A (⌘-Shift-A) to deselect your text. No rectangle. Nice.

9. ***Test the latest hyperlink.*** Click the newest link item in the **Hyperlinks** palette, and then click the ⇨ arrow at the bottom of the palette. The *What's cooking.indd* document window opens, as pictured in Figure 11-14. If the page appears magnified, press Ctrl+1 (or ⌘-1) to zoom out to 100 percent.

PEARL OF WISDOM

When we export *LPF's PB&O cookies.indd* to a PDF file in the final exercise, this hyperlink will automatically update to look for a file named *What's cooking.pdf*. This means we'll need to export *What's cooking.indd* as a PDF file as well. Otherwise the link won't work.

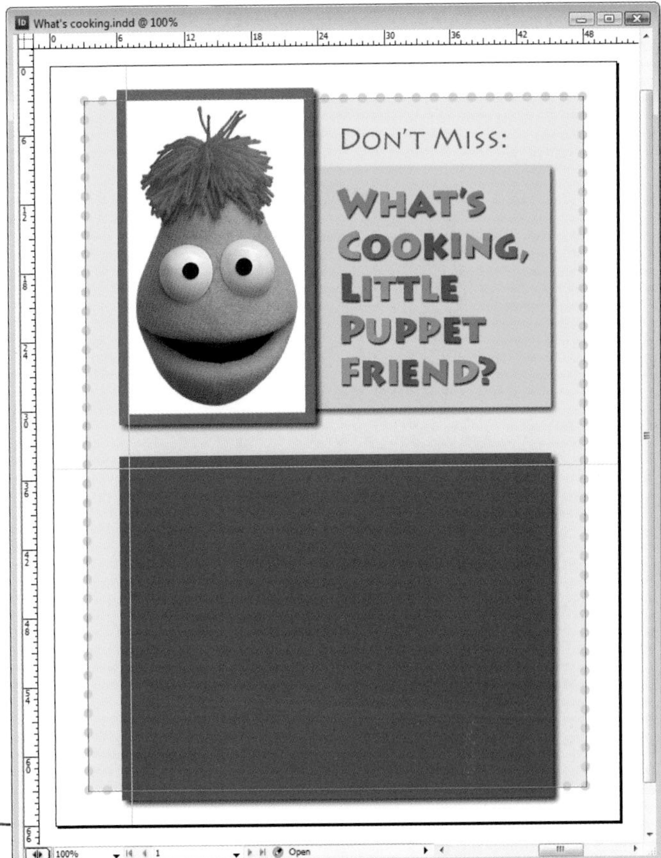

Figure 11-14.

10. ***Close one document and save the other.*** Go ahead and close *What's cooking.indd*. If InDesign asks whether you want to save changes, click **Yes** (or **Save** on the Mac). We'll see this document again in a couple of exercises.

We're not finished with the cookie recipe, so keep it open. Choose **File→Save As**, name the document "LPF's PB&O cookies 3.indd," and click **Save**. You'll need this document in the next exercise.

Making Buttons

Our next task is to create a rollover button. A button can link to an anchor, a URL, or another PDF file, just like a hyperlink. It can also exhibit different visual states when you click it or roll over it. In addition to offering a Convert to Button command (which we put to use in the next exercise), InDesign even goes so far as to provide you with a dedicated button tool. In this exercise, you'll learn how to create a button using the button tool, trigger a change in the button's appearance relative to a mouse action, and set up a behavior for the button so that it performs an action.

Figure 11-15.

1. ***Open the cookie recipe document.*** If it's not already smack dab in front of you, open the *LPF's PB&O cookies 3.indd* file that you saved in the *Lesson 11* folder in Step 10 of the last exercise.

2. ***Turn on the hidden layer.*** Press F7 or choose **Window→Layers** to open the **Layers** palette. There you'll find a hidden layer called Word Balloon. Click in the empty box to the left of the **Word Balloon** layer to show its 👁 icon and display a cartoon word balloon in the document window. The message in the word balloon directs the reader to click a link that we haven't yet created. To make this link, we'll need a little guidance.

3. ***Show the guides.*** Choose **View→Grids & Guides→Show Guides** or press Ctrl+; (⌘-; on the Mac) to turn on the guides. As Figure 11-15 shows, four gray guides intersect to create a rectangle around Little Puppet Friend's eyes. We'll use these guides to help in drawing the button.

4. ***Draw a button.*** Before drawing a button, you need to make sure that both the fill and stroke icons in the toolbox are set to none, as in . Then select the button tool, the one right above the scissors tool in the single-column toolbox. Or you can press the B key. See that rectangle around the eyes created by the four gray guides? Drag from the upper-left corner of that rectangle to the lower-right corner, as in Figure 11-16. The corners of the button should snap into alignment with the guides. If you don't get the button exactly aligned, use the black arrow tool to adjust the corner handles.

Figure 11-16.

5. ***Name the button.*** Choose **Window→Interactive→States** to open the **States** palette. In the **Name** option box at the top of the palette, type "Button Eyes" and press Enter or Return. This button currently has one state, labeled **Up** in the States palette (see Figure 11-17). This indicates how the button will look when the mouse button is not pressed, or "up." We'll see how to add other states in just a moment. The States palette also offers an Appearance pop-up menu, which offers access to a few prefab effects, useful for creating raised or glowing buttons. But LPF would look weird with raised or glowing eyes, so we'll create our rollover button manually.

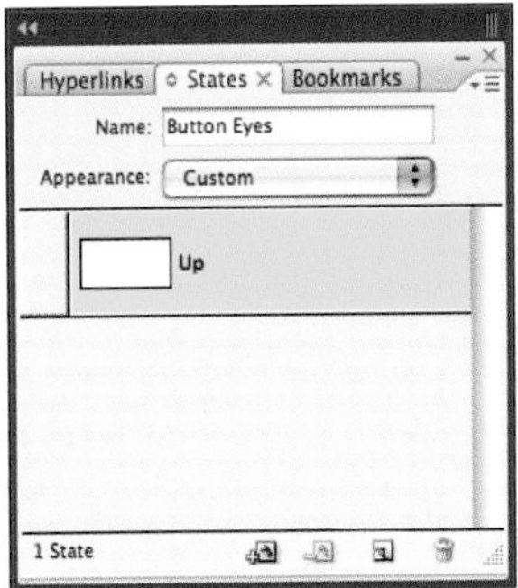

Figure 11-17.

6. ***Create two additional states.*** Click the icon at the bottom of the States palette twice to create two new states, **Rollover** and **Down**. The Rollover state defines how the button looks when you move your mouse over it; the Down state defines how it looks when the mouse button is down, which happens when you click. Note that you can't click the icon more than twice; a button is limited to a maximum of three states.

7. ***Assign the button a Rollover appearance.*** Click the **Rollover** state and then click the first icon at the bottom of the States palette. The **Place** dialog box opens. Go to the *Links* subfolder in the *Lesson 11* folder. Then select the *Puppet-eyes-rollover.jpg* file and click **Open**. As Figure 11-18 shows, the JPEG image loads into the button's Rollover state, giving Little Puppet Friend a startled appearance. (You'd look that way, too, if someone was about to poke you in the eye.)

Those with keen eyes will notice that the palettes in the figures sport larger thumbnails than they do by default. To scale your thumbnails to this larger, more helpful size, click the icon in the top-right corner of the States palette and choose Panel Options from the palette menu. Then select the largest of the Thumbnail Size options and click the OK button.

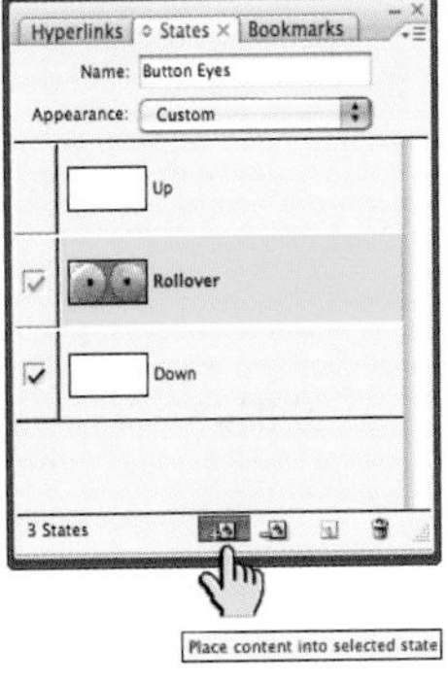

Figure 11-18.

8. ***Give the button a Down appearance.*** Now we need to load an image for the button's Down state. Click the **Down** state in the **States** palette and again click the icon. In the **Place** dialog box, select the file called *Puppet-eyes-down.jpg* located in the same *Links* folder as in the last step, and then click **Open**. Figure 11-19 shows how LPF looks when the Down state is active.

Figure 11-19.

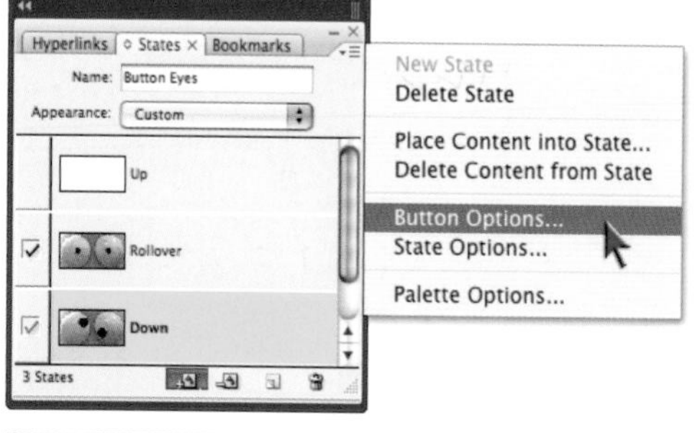

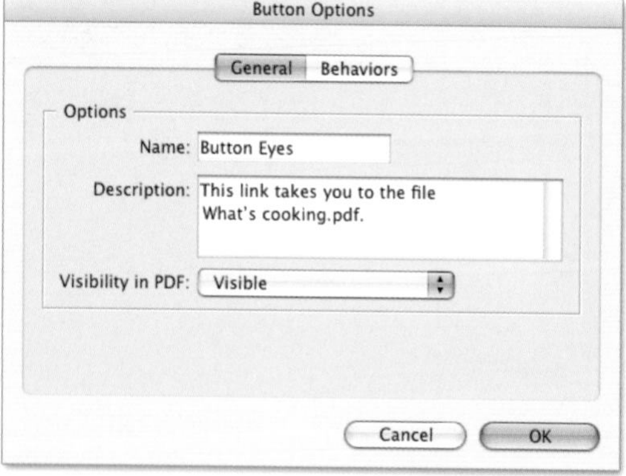

Figure 11-20.

9. ***Specify general button options.*** Now that we have the button's appearance taken care of, let's make it do something useful. Choose **Button Options** from the **States** palette menu, or just double-click the button in the document window with the black arrow tool. Either way, you get the **Button Options** dialog box shown in Figure 11-20. The options in this dialog box affect the entire button, not just the selected state.

   In the **Description** area, enter the following: "This link takes you to the file What's cooking.pdf." This text will appear when a cursor passes over the button. It may also be read by text-to-speech software used by the visually impaired. The **Visibility in PDF** pop-up menu lets you specify whether the button will be visible in the PDF file on the screen and when the PDF document is printed. You can leave the option set to **Visible**.

10. ***Assign an event and a behavior.*** Click the **Behaviors** button at the top of the dialog box to switch to a second panel

of options. This is where we'll assign an action to our button and specify the event that triggers it:

- The Event pop-up menu lists the various things a reader can do to activate the button. The beginning of a click is Mouse Down, the end of the click is Mouse Up. A cursor moving over a button is Mouse Enter, a cursor moving out of the button is Mouse Exit. The final two options, On Focus and On Blur, apply when a button is selected (focused) or deselected (blurred) by pressing the Tab key. We want to initiate the event *after* the reader clicks the button, as is standard, so leave the **Event** option set to **Mouse Up**.
- The Behavior pop-up menu lets you select whether a button jumps you to an anchor or a page, opens or closes a document, or triggers a movie or a sound file. We want this button to open *What's cooking.pdf*. So choose **Go To Anchor** from the **Behavior** pop-up menu. Then click the **Browse** button (called **Choose** on the Mac) to bring up the **InDesign Format File** dialog box. Select the file named *What's cooking.indd*, and click **Open**.
- I've created a hyperlink anchor called **What's Cooking, Little Puppet Friend?**, which should appear by default in the **Anchor** pop-up menu. If it doesn't, choose it.
- Set the **Zoom** option to **Inherit Zoom** so that the viewer's current zoom factor will be maintained.

11. ***Put the button options into play.*** Assuming that you have all your Behavior options set as in Figure 11-21, click the **Add** button in the lower-right portion of the dialog box. This adds a new event and behavior in the left-hand list. Click **OK** to accept your changes and dismiss the dialog box. The button is now complete. Unfortunately, we can't preview it until we actually export the PDF document in the last exercise. The good news is, that's just one more exercise from now. So hang in there.

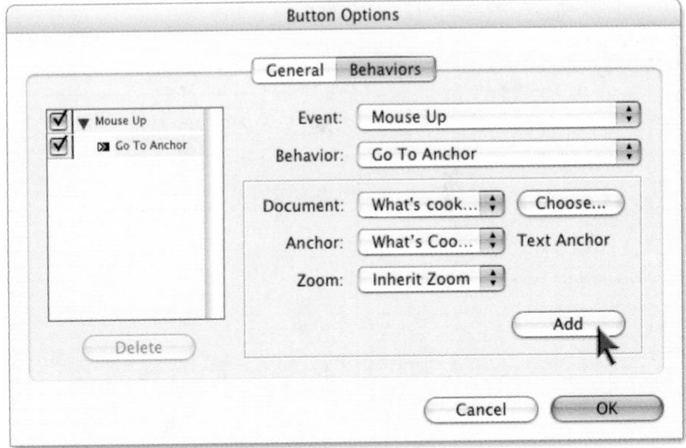

Figure 11-21.

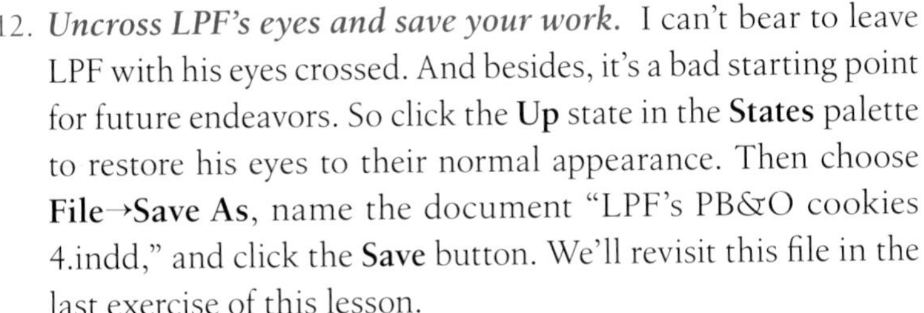

12. ***Uncross LPF's eyes and save your work.*** I can't bear to leave LPF with his eyes crossed. And besides, it's a bad starting point for future endeavors. So click the **Up** state in the **States** palette to restore his eyes to their normal appearance. Then choose **File→Save As**, name the document "LPF's PB&O cookies 4.indd," and click the **Save** button. We'll revisit this file in the last exercise of this lesson.

Embedding Sounds and Movies

InDesign CS3 lets you embed audio and video files inside your PDF documents to enhance the reader's experience. You can import audio clips stored in the WAV, AU, and AIF formats, as well as videos saved as MOV, MPEG, SWF, and AVI files. In this exercise, we'll use WAV for our audio and MOV for our video. You can play a WAV file with just about any sound or music software, including Windows Media Player and Apple's iTunes. To watch the MOV file, you'll need to have Apple's QuickTime installed on your computer. All versions of Macintosh OS X come with QuickTime installed; it's also relatively common on the PC. However, if you don't have QuickTime, please take a moment to download and install it from *www.apple.com/quicktime/download*.

In the following steps, you'll embed sound and movie files into a document. You'll set various options that determine when the files play and how they are displayed in the document. You'll also build upon the skills you learned in the last exercise by creating a button that triggers the embedded files to play.

Figure 11-22.

1. ***Open a document.*** Go to the *Lesson 11* folder inside *Lesson Files-IDcs3 1on1* and open *What's cooking.indd*. (If you get a modified links warning, be sure to click the Fix Links Automatically button; otherwise you'll get an error message when you export this document to PDF in the next exercise.) First witnessed back in Figure 11-14 (see page 463), this document is the target of the button we created in the preceding exercise as well as one of the hyperlinks we created in the exercise before that.

2. ***Place a sound file.*** Make sure nothing is selected. Then choose **File→Place** or press Ctrl+D (⌘-D on the Mac). In the **Place** dialog box, select the file named *Hi folks.wav*, located in the *Links* subfolder inside the *Lesson 11* folder, and click the **Open** button. Your cursor changes to a little speaker, as in 🔊. Click in the top-left corner of the document to place the audio file, as shown in Figure 11-22. This audio file contains an introductory message from LPF. Now we need to set options for playing and displaying the file.

3. ***Set the placed file to play when the document opens.*** Choose **Object→Interactive→Sound Options** or just double-click the placed audio file with the black arrow tool. In either case, the upshot of your efforts is the **Sound Options** dialog box. When it appears, here's what I want you to do:

   - Midway down the dialog box, the Poster option determines what the audio file looks like in the PDF file. The default setting of Standard displays a speaker icon. You can also assign an independent image file. But we want our sound file to be heard and not seen, so choose **None** from the **Poster** pop-up menu.
   - Turn on the **Play on Page Turn** check box to play the sound file when the document first appears on screen. This way, LPF will greet visitors when they open the document.

   Leave the Description field empty; otherwise, a message might spring to life when the reader hovers a cursor over the invisible sound file. When your dialog box looks like the one in Figure 11-23, click **OK**. The speaker icon will disappear from the upper-left corner of the document.

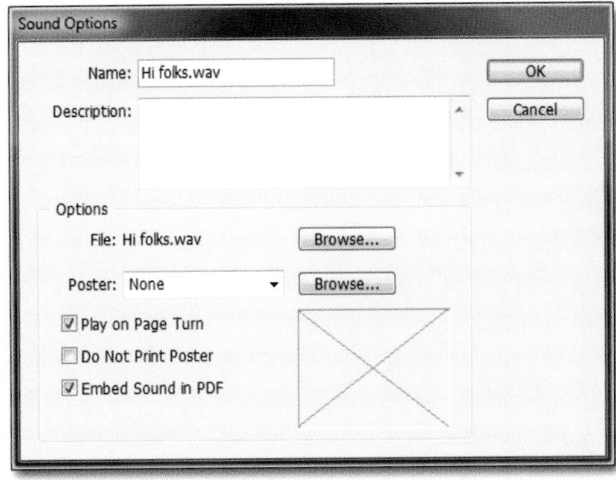

Figure 11-23.

4. ***Place another sound file.*** To avoid replacing the selected sound file, press Ctrl+Shift+A (⌘-Shift-A) to deselect it. Then again choose **File→Place**. This time, select the file named *Click me.wav* inside the *Links* subfolder in *Lesson 11*, which features a brief instruction from LPF. Click the **Open** button and then click with the cursor to place the sound file in the upper-right corner of the document. If necessary, drag the file until it snaps into alignment with the corner, as in Figure 11-24.

5. ***Make the sound file invisible.*** Double-click the sound file to open the **Sound Options** dialog box. Choose **None** from the **Poster** pop-up menu. Leave the other options alone. (For example, do *not* turn on the Play on Page Turn check box or enter a Description.) Then click **OK**.

6. ***Place the movie file.*** Once again press Ctrl+Shift+A (⌘-Shift-A) to deselect the sound file. Then choose **File→Place**, select the file named *WCLPF promo.mov* inside the *Links* folder, and click **Open**. InDesign equips you

Figure 11-24.

Figure 11-25.

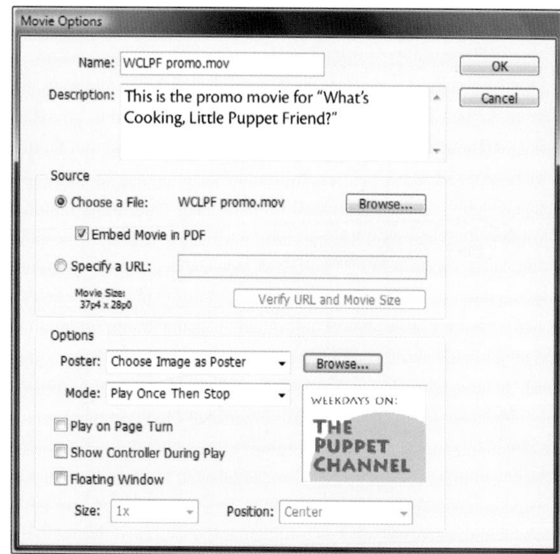

Figure 11-26.

with the cursor. Use it to click at the intersection of the cyan guides on the left side of the page below the photo of LPF. As Figure 11-25 shows, this centers the now-black movie against the blue background at the bottom of the page.

7. *Set the options for the movie file.* Double-click the movie file with the black arrow tool to open the **Movie Options** dialog box. Here's how you should set the options:

   - Tab to the **Description** area and enter the text pictured in Figure 11-26 (or words to that effect). This description will appear in a pop-up when the reader hovers a cursor over the movie.

   - The **Source** options let you select a different movie or play an online movie by entering its URL. We already have a movie, so you should leave most of these options alone. However, I do want you to turn on the **Embed Movie in PDF** check box, which saves the movie as part of the PDF file. This makes the PDF file larger, but it also ensures that the link between document and movie is never broken.

   - The **Poster** pop-up menu lets you choose the image that will display in the document when the movie isn't playing. The Default Poster setting displays the first frame of the movie, which—being completely black—serves as a poor representative. Instead, click the **Browse** button (called **Choose** on the Mac) just to the right of the pop-up menu. Then select the file named *TPC logo.psd* in the *Links* folder inside *Lesson 11* and click **Open**. The selected image appears in the preview window.

   - The **Mode** pop-up menu lets you choose options for playing the movie. Play Once Then Stop plays the movie once through, and then goes back to displaying the poster frame. Play Once Stay Open is a viable option if you activate the Show Controller During Play or Floating Window option below; rather than displaying the poster frame after the movie has played, the movie controls or floating window (or both) will stick around so that the viewer can watch the movie again. Repeat Play makes the movie loop. Keep this option set to **Play Once Then Stop**.

Leave the check boxes at the bottom of the dialog box turned off. When your settings match those in Figure 11-26, click **OK**. The specified poster image appears at the bottom of the document window, as in Figure 11-27.

Figure 11-27.

8. ***Convert the photo of LPF into an interactive button.*** The movie file will play if the poster frame is clicked in the PDF document. But I also want you to create a button that will trigger both the movie and the *Click me.wav* sound file:

   - If the **States** palette isn't still open, choose **Window→Interactive→States**.
   - Select the large photo of LPF's head with the black arrow tool and choose **Object→Interactive→Convert to Button**. A new button appears in the States palette.
   - Change the **Name** to "Big Puppet Head" and press Enter or Return. The result appears in Figure 11-28.

   This time around, we'll forgo adding a rollover or down state to the button. But we do need to apply a few behaviors to it.

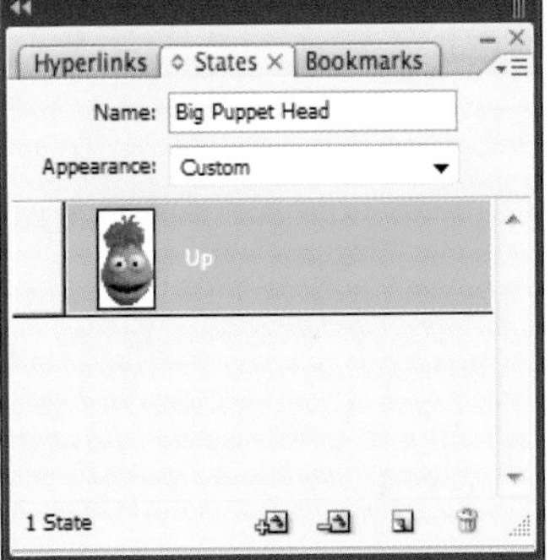

Figure 11-28.

9. ***Set options for the button.*** Double-click the button in the document to open the **Button Options** dialog box. Enter "Click to play the promo movie" in the **Description** area. Then switch to the **Behaviors** panel and do the following:

   - First, I want the *Click me.wav* file to play when the cursor rolls over the button. Choose **Mouse Enter** from the **Event** pop-up menu. Then choose **Sound** from the **Behavior** option and **Click me.wav** from the **Sound** option. Check that the last option is set to **Play** and click the **Add** button.

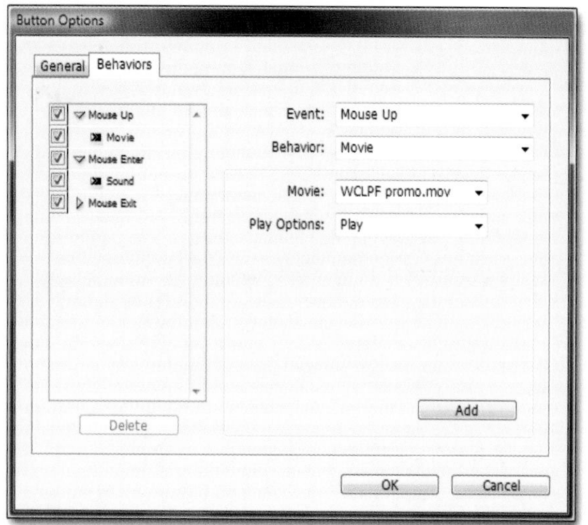

Figure 11-29.

- Next, let's add a behavior that makes the *Click me.wav* file stop playing when the cursor leaves the button area. Choose **Mouse Exit** from the **Event** pop-up menu and **Click me.wav** from the **Sound** pop-up menu. Set the **Play Options** to **Stop**. Then click the **Add** button.
- Our last behavior will make the *WCLPF promo.mov* file play when the reader clicks the photo. Set the **Event** option to **Mouse Up**. Choose **Movie** from the **Behavior** pop-up menu. Make sure the next two options are set to **WCLPF promo.mov** and **Play**, and then click **Add**.

The settings from the last bullet item appear in Figure 11-29. Assuming that you and the figure match, click **OK** to close the dialog box.

10. ***Save your work.*** Congratulations, you have successfully created a multimedia file in InDesign. Granted, you've experienced scant evidence of your labors so far, but that will change in the next exercise. In the meantime, choose **File→Save As**, name the document "What's cooking 1.indd," and click **Save**.

Exporting to PDF

My only complaint with InDesign's bevy of interactivity functions is that you have to wait until you export a document as a PDF file to see the functions interact. As a result, you've amassed an entire lesson of delayed gratification, and that's just not healthy. The good news is, now that you've done all that work, it's finally time to sit back and reap the rewards. In this final exercise, you'll export your interactive InDesign documents to the widely acclaimed Portable Document Format. Then you'll click a few buttons and smile. Honestly, I can't imagine a more satisfactory way to end a lesson.

PEARL OF WISDOM

Before you can perform these steps, you'll need a working copy of the free Adobe Reader or the commercial Adobe Acrobat (6 or later) installed on your computer. Adobe Reader is available gratis at *www.acrobat.com*; just click the graphic Get Adobe Reader button near the bottom of the page. Acrobat ships with the Premium edition of the Creative Suite.

1. ***Open both of your interactive documents.*** Open the latest versions of the two documents we've been working on throughout this lesson: *LPF's PB&O cookies 4.indd* and *What's cooking 1.indd*. Your two documents should look like the ones pictured in Figure 11-30. (I switched both of my documents

to the preview mode—by pressing the W key, as you may recall. This hides the guides and the light blue rectangle around the *One cup peanut butter* entry.)

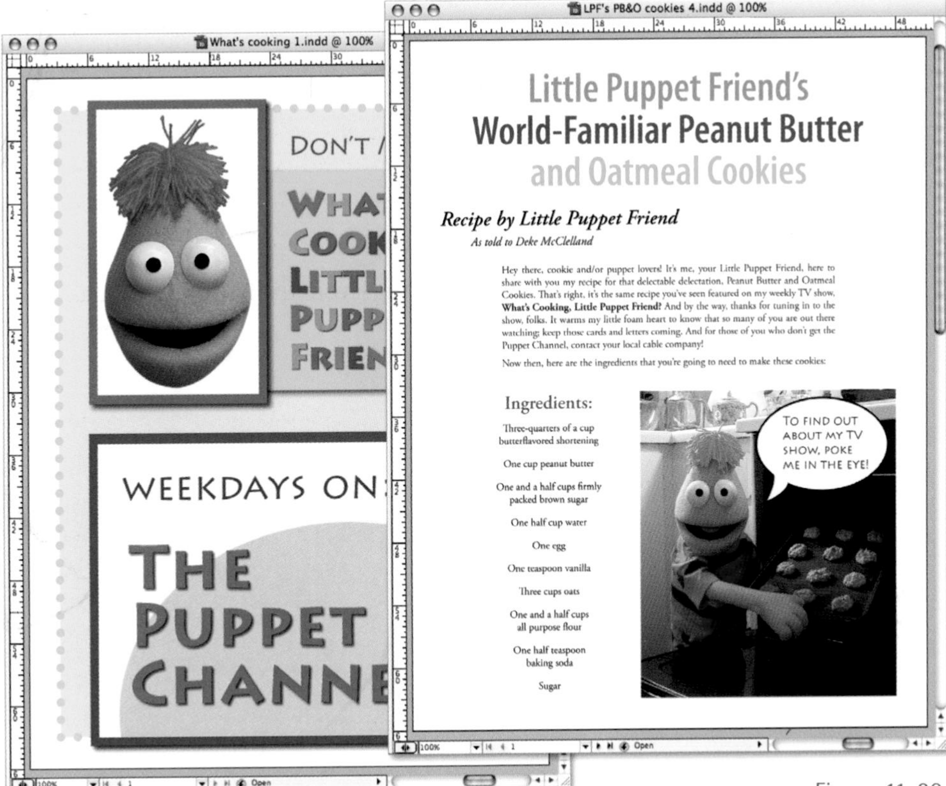

Figure 11-30.

2. *Bring the Peanut Butter and Oatmeal document to the front.* The cookie recipe (*LPF's PB&O cookies 4.indd*) contains more interactive elements, so we'll start with it.

3. *Choose the Export command.* Choose **File→Export** or press Ctrl+E (⌘-E). InDesign displays the **Export** dialog box, which asks you to name the file and select a format. Navigate to the *Lesson 11* folder inside *Lesson Files-IDcs2 1on1*. Make sure the **Save as Type** option (**Format** on the Mac) is set to **Adobe PDF**. Change the name of the file to suit your tastes. (I removed the number.) Then click the **Save** button.

4. *Load a preset.* InDesign presents you with the capacious **Export Adobe PDF** dialog box, which contains seven panels of options designed to overwhelm and intimidate. Fortunately, we need to concern ourselves with relatively few of them. Start by selecting **[High Quality Print]** from the **Adobe PDF Preset** pop-up menu. None of the presets gets us very close to our ideal settings, but at least we're all starting from a common point.

5. ***Set Compatibility to Acrobat 6.*** To permit embedded sounds and movies, set the **Compatibility** option to **Acrobat 6 (PDF 1.5)**, as in Figure 11-31. This particular document doesn't have a movie, but the next one does. We might as well establish one group of settings that works for both. This limits compatibility to Adobe Reader 6 or Acrobat 6 (or later), but such is the price of progress.

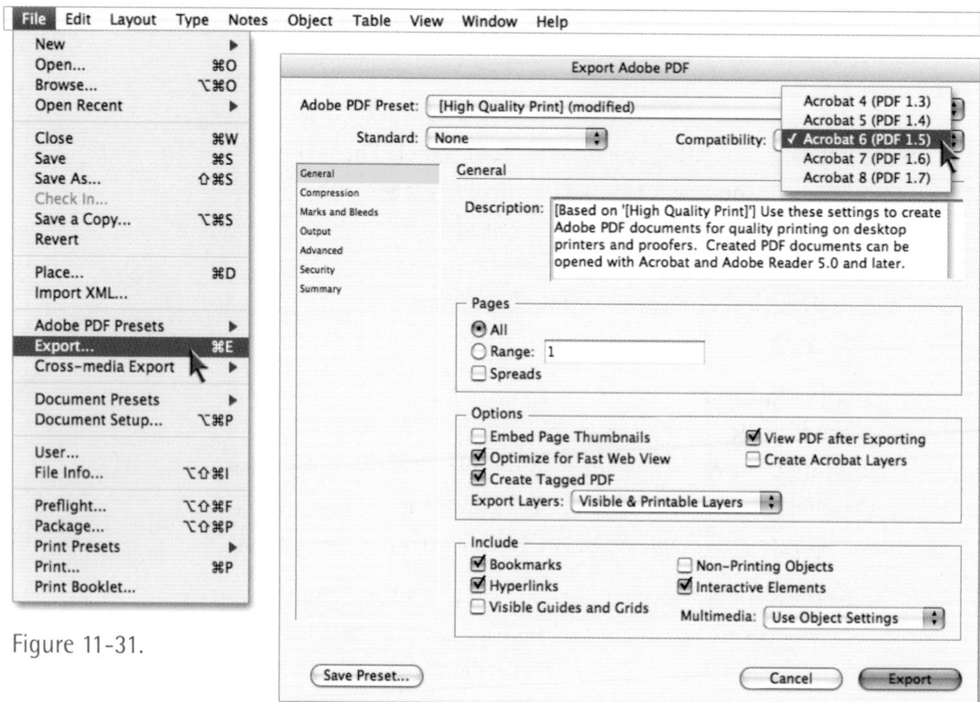

Figure 11-31.

6. ***Make sure All and Optimize are on.*** We want to export all three pages, so check that the **All** option is selected. You should also see check marks in front of **Optimize for Fast Web View** and **Create Tagged PDF**. The first setting organizes the PDF data so it can be read as soon as the first page is downloaded from a Web site or a server. The second check box assigns a predefined collection of XML-style tags, like those we learned about in Lesson 9, "Pages, Layers, and XML." (If you own Adobe Acrobat, you can view eBook tags by choosing View→Navigation Tabs→Tags. The free Adobe Reader does not support them.)

7. ***Tell InDesign to open the PDF file when you finish.*** I imagine that you'll want to see your PDF file after you finish creating it. You've been waiting all this time, after all. So turn on the **View PDF after Exporting** check box to instruct InDesign to automatically launch Adobe Reader or Acrobat and open the PDF file the moment it gets finished exporting the document.

8. ***Include the bookmarks and hyperlinks.*** Turn on the **Bookmarks**, **Hyperlinks**, and **Interactive Elements** check boxes near the bottom of the dialog box to ensure that InDesign saves the results of our labors in the first three exercises. Without them, we'd wind up with just a plain-vanilla, static PDF file. Then confirm that the **Multimedia** option is set to **Use Object Settings**, which embeds the sounds (as by default) and movie (according to our directions in Step 7 on page 470) in the PDF file. Your settings should look like those in Figure 11-31.

9. ***Prevent the downsampling of placed images.*** Click **Compression** in the left-hand list to advance to the next panel. These options let you reduce the resolution of imported images and specify how InDesign compresses them. Pictured in Figure 11-32, the panel is divided into three sections, which control color, grayscale, and black-and-white images. Within each section, you'll find two or more of the following options:

   - The first pop-up menu lets you reduce the resolution of imported images by averaging pixels, a process called *downsampling*. Lower resolutions make for a smaller PDF file, which is faster to download, email, and transmit over a network. But that's a big compromise, as I explain in a moment.

   - *Compression* is a means of reducing the size of the image data saved with the PDF file. InDesign may choose to eliminate redundant data (so-called *lossless* compression), restructure the image to reduce its complexity (*lossy*), or both. My tests suggest that InDesign is very smart about how it applies compression; therefore, I advise leaving **Compression** set to **Automatic (JPEG)** so it can work its magic without interference.

   - When saving color and grayscale images, InDesign applies lossy compression according to rules published by the Joint Photographic Experts Group, or *JPEG*. The Image Quality setting determines how much compression is applied. More compression results in lower quality images and a smaller PDF file. If file size isn't a concern, you can leave the Image Quality at Maximum. Otherwise, set it to Medium (which is as low as I dare go).

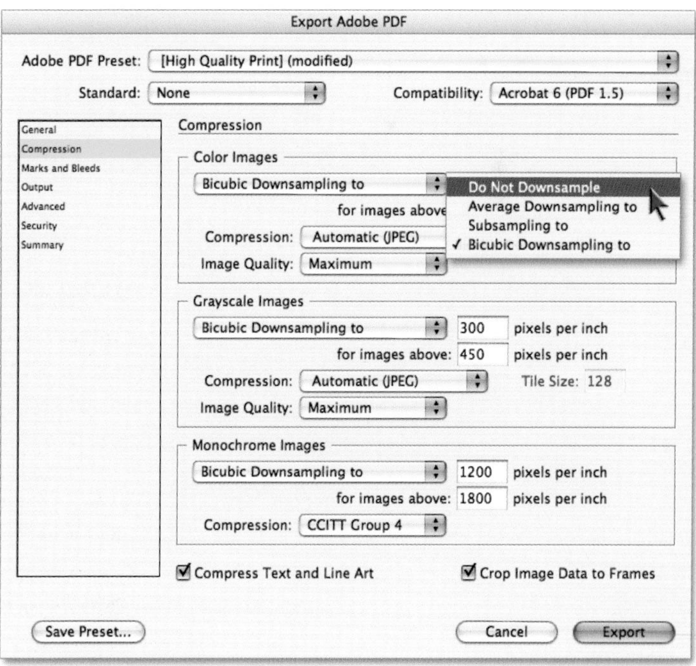

Figure 11-32.

PEARL OF WISDOM

I am an enthusiastic supporter of JPEG compression, which may reduce the size of an imported image by a factor of 50 to 80 percent with only a slight loss in quality. I am less enthusiastic about downsampling, which provides comparatively small reductions in file size in return for sometimes obvious losses in quality, especially in the case of high-contrast images.

The cookie recipe contains a total of four color images—two photos plus LPF's alternative eyes used for the Over and Down button states in the "Making Buttons" exercise. There are no grayscale or black-and-white images, so the second and third sections in the dialog box don't apply. Click the first pop-up menu and choose **Do Not Downsample**. Leave all other settings as you found them.

10. ***Adjust the color space.*** Click **Output** in the left-hand list. This takes you to the Color options, circled in Figure 11-33. Assuming you followed my advice in the Preface (see Step 7, page xviii), your document is set up for commercial output, not screen display. To change that, do the following:

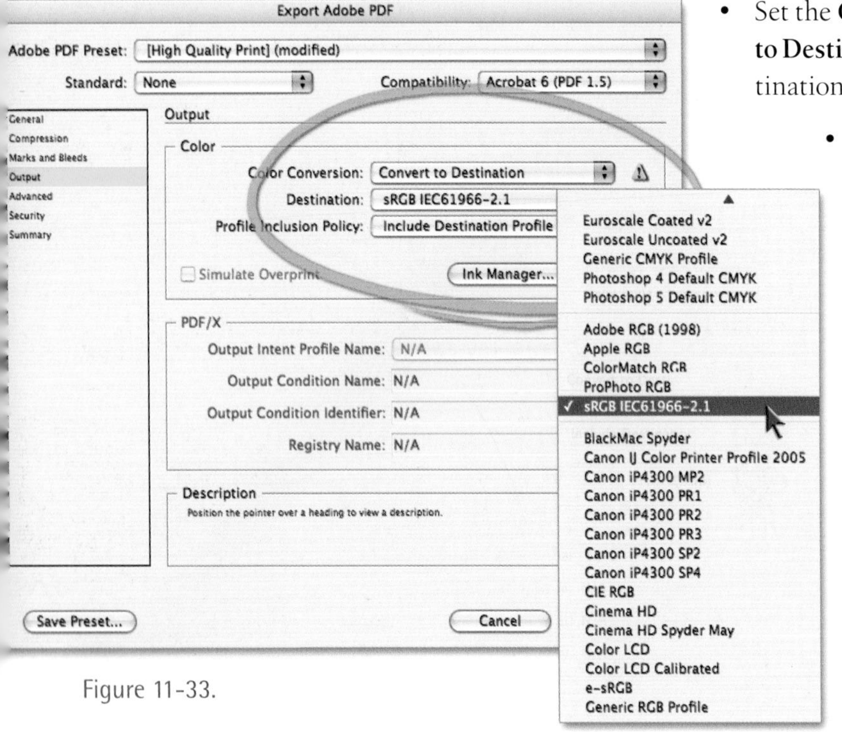

Figure 11-33.

- Set the **Color Conversion** pop-up menu to **Convert to Destination**, which converts the colors to the destination that you specify in the next option.
  - Both Adobe Reader and Acrobat can read profiles, interpret them, and adjust colors accordingly. But these aren't the only programs that can open PDF files, and most programs aren't always so clever. To convert the colors in your document so they look halfway decent with or without color management, set the **Destination** option to **sRGB IEC61966-2.1**. (As Figure 11-33 shows, you may have to look carefully; this is likely one of several dozen color profiles available to your system. Have faith: It's there, somewhere.) The sRGB color space best anticipates the display capabilities of a consumer-grade computer monitor. A ⚠ icon warns you that some colors may go awry. Not true in our case; ignore it.
- To embed this color profile so that Acrobat and other color-savvy programs can read it, set the **Profile Inclusion Policy** option to **Include Destination Profile**.

11. *Save your settings for later use.* Click the **Save Preset** button in the bottom-left corner of the dialog box. Enter "Interactive Document" and click **OK**. This saves all the settings you assigned in Steps 5 through 10 so that you can retrieve them again without going to all that effort. In a stroke of brilliance, all CS3 applications share PDF export presets, which are stored in a common library. Because of its interactivity features, the preset you just created may not be entirely useful in nonlayout applications. But you could use the general screen-output specs as the basis for consistent output across other CS3 programs.

12. *Create and test the PDF document.* Now for the moment of ultimate truth. Click the **Export** button. InDesign displays a progress bar as it generates the PDF file. Then it launches Adobe Reader or, if you have it, Adobe Acrobat and opens the spanking-new document, as in Figure 11-34. Here are some things to try:

    - Click the icon along the left edge of the window (as you see me doing in the figure) to display the tags you created in the first exercise, "Creating Bookmarks." Click a bookmark name to go to the corresponding entry in the text.
    - Click the hyperlink *One cup peanut butter* to advance to the peanut butter paragraph on page 2. Press the Page Down key a couple of times to go to the bottom of page 3, and then click the *Baking Cookies One-on-One* link. Assuming you're connected to the Internet, this should load the *oneonone.oreilly.com* Web page. (If you get a Specify Weblink Behavior dialog box, select In Web Browser and click OK.)
    - Go back to the beginning of the document and hover your cursor over LPF's eyes. They should get beady. Don't click, however—our destination page isn't done yet.
    - Get the zoom tool and click a few times inside one of the photos to zoom into it. Thanks to the compression settings you established in Step 9, the high-resolution photographs look great.

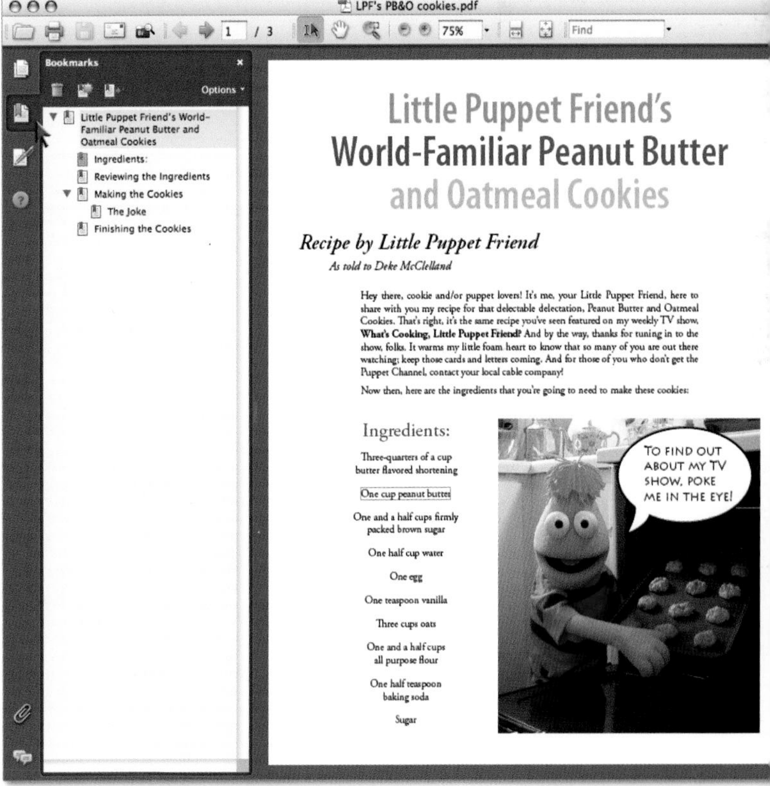

Figure 11-34.

Figure 11-35.

13. ***Return to InDesign.*** We still have another document to export. So switch back to InDesign and bring the document that contains the movie and sound files to the front.

14. ***Choose the Export command.*** Because you saved a preset in Step 11, things are considerably easier this time around:

    - Choose **File→Adobe PDF Presets→ Interactive Document**, as in Figure 11-35.
    - On the PC, check that **Save as Type** is set to **Adobe PDF**. (On the Mac, InDesign knows you're saving a PDF file.)
    - Name the PDF file "What's cooking.pdf." This ensures that the links function as specified in the previous exercises.
    - Click **Save** to open the **Export PDF** dialog box.
    - This time, turn off **View PDF after Exporting**. Better to load the PDF doc by following the links in the recipe file.
    - Click the **Export** button. If you get a missing links warning, just click OK to move on. InDesign generates the PDF file, but does not switch to Reader or Acrobat.

15. ***Load, listen, and watch.*** Return to the *LPF's PB&O cookies.pdf* file that you have open in Reader or Acrobat. Make sure your computer's speakers are on. Then click and hold for a moment on LPF's eyes to see them cross. Release the mouse button to load *What's cooking.pdf.* If you're using Adobe Reader 7 or higher, you may encounter a security warning, in which case, click the **Play** button. (If you encounter other errors, choose **Help→Check for updates now** to update your Reader software.) You should hear LPF welcome you to the page. Hover over LPF's image to hear another message. Then click anywhere on his face to start the movie, which I show playing in Figure 11-36.

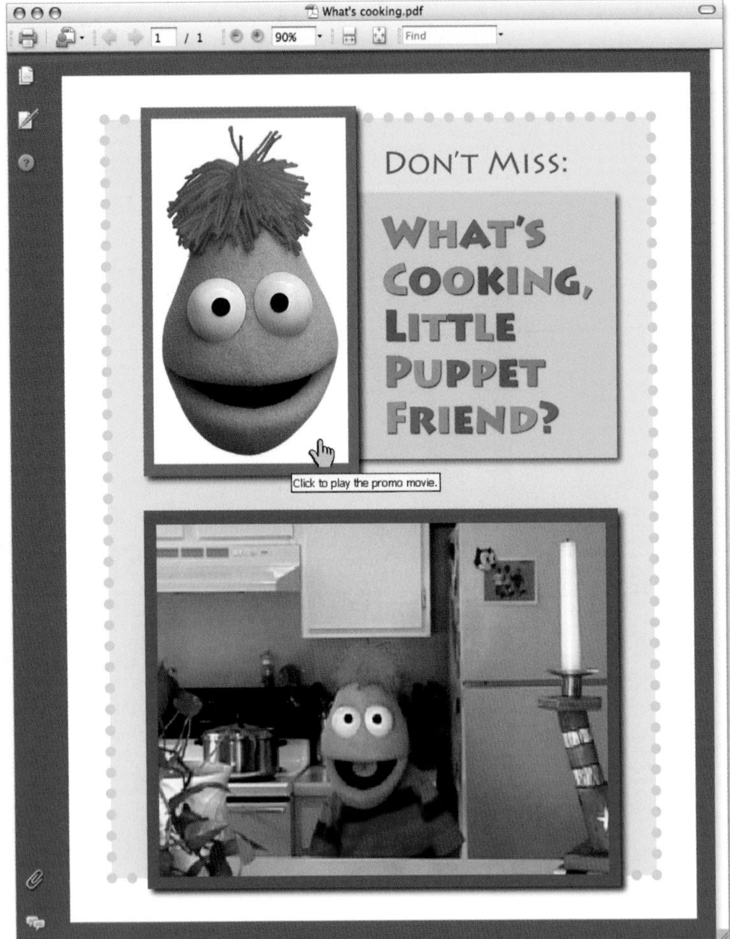

Figure 11-36.

As a backup, I've included copies of my PDF files inside the *Final PDFs* folder in the *Lesson 11* folder. If you encounter a problem with getting something to work in your documents, try loading mine and see if they work any better. And if you decide to make the cookies, let me know how they turn out. I'm really curious how they taste.

This is no small task, what with all the differences in the way professional and consumer printers work. Consider the PostScript *imagesetter*, which is a monstrously expensive device that service bureaus and print houses use to output pages to film or other media before loading the inks and plates onto the press. An imagesetter prints at resolutions of several million dots per square inch, but it can render just two colors: black and white. Given that every one of the full-color pages in this book was output by an imagesetter, you may find this difficult to believe. That's because the imagesetter fools us into seeing a rich array of colors. Here's how:

- First, the imagesetter prints the document in multiple passes, known as *separations*. When placed on the press, each separation is coated with a different ink, which imparts a different primary color to the printed page. Most color documents are printed using four separations, one for each of the four *process inks*: cyan, magenta, yellow, and black.
- The inks are translucent and thus blend with each other. But at most, this results in eight color variations. (I say "at most" because black mixed with one ink doesn't look all that different from black mixed with another.)
- So where do all the other color variations come from? The imagesetter simulates shades by assembling printer dots into a grid of *halftone cells*. A single, roughly circular halftone cell may contain more than 100 printer dots. Large, closely packed halftone cells translate to dark colors; small cells with lots of white space around them read as light colors.

By way of example, take a look at the book cover in Figure 12-1. Although I've confined my artwork to a small range of purples and oranges with occasional bands of muted green, it nevertheless comprises several thousand unique colors. On the next page, Figure 12-2 shows

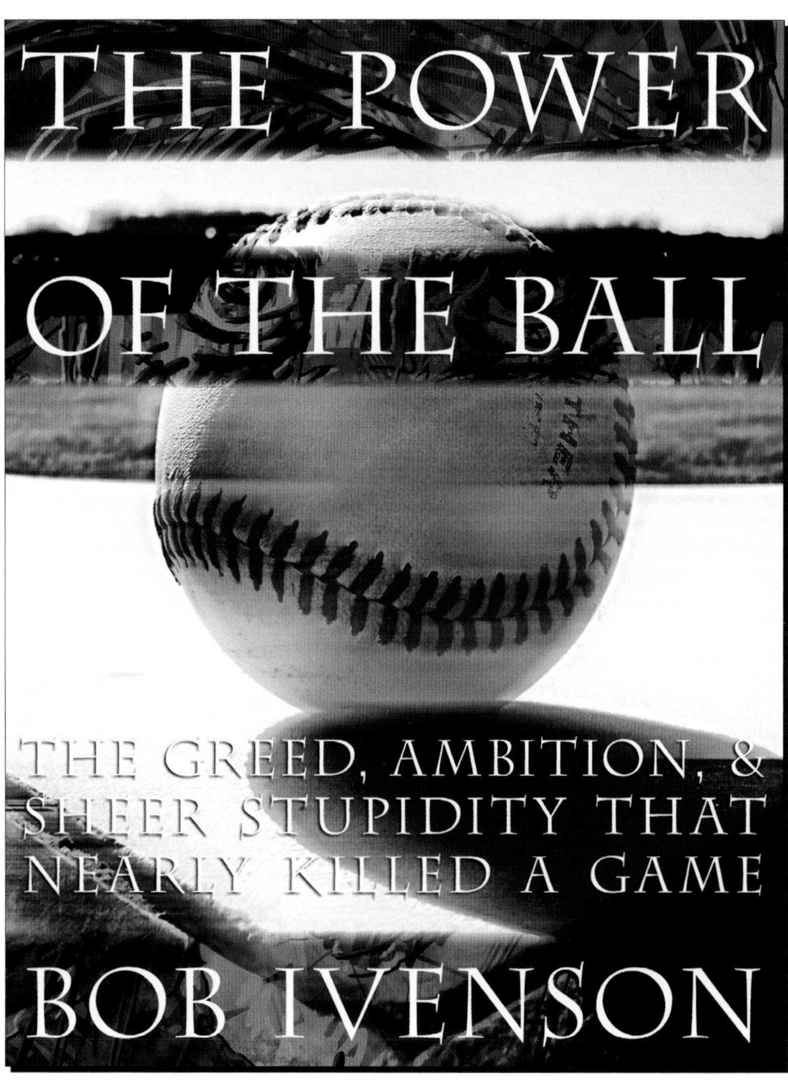

Figure 12-1.

a detail from the cover magnified by a factor of 10. At this size, you can make out the individual halftone cells. The top portion of the figure shows the four layers of halftone cells interacting with each other; the bottom area shows each process color by itself. The right-hand circle zooms in on a sampling of black halftone cells. The cells contain just two colors, black and white, with no tonal variation between them.

Figure 12-2.

A typical inkjet printer uses six or more inks and organizes its dots in a much tighter pattern. Even when separated and magnified by a factor of 50, as in the circle on the right side of Figure 12-3, the dots remain remarkably small and intricately woven. As a result, remarkable as it may sound, an inkjet device is able to print artwork with a wider color range, smoother variations, and better detail than the stuff we see reproduced in this book. The downside it that inkjet output is not commercially reproducible—except by scanning the page and separating it, which would defeat the purpose. This limits inkjet printers to proofing pages and printing drafts, as explained in the exercise "Printing a Draft of Your Document," which begins on the very next page.

PostScript and inkjet printers also differ in how they process data. A PostScript printer is capable of rendering type and vector objects on its own. InDesign conveys the page as a series of mathematical equations; the printer renders the math, even going so far as to adjust curves and character outlines to better suit specific size and resolution ratios. The result is razor-sharp text and graphics that print quickly and efficiently, without slowing down the computer or other hardware. (It's worth noting that InDesign limits its support to PostScript Levels 2 and 3, which account for most devices sold since 1990. Comparatively ancient Level 1 printers are out of luck.)

Figure 12-3.

In contrast, printing to a consumer inkjet device requires InDesign to render the entire document to pixels and communicate the colored pixels to the printer. This means everything prints roughly the same as it looks on screen. It also means more work for InDesign and more processing effort on the part of your computer. Hence inkjet documents take longer to print and may slow your computer's performance.

The consequence of all this is that most of InDesign's printing capabilities are designed to support PostScript and generate professional-level color separations. Fortunately, this is precisely the way you want it to be, assuming that you intend to mass-reproduce a document in quantities of one hundred or more copies. But InDesign also gives passing attention to non-PostScript devices, permitting you to proof colors, gauge layout and composition, and otherwise monitor the development of a document.

Printing a Draft of Your Document

With the exception of interactive PDF files (like those you made in Lesson 11), the world's ever-growing supply of InDesign documents are most commonly bound for the printed page. So regardless of what a document looks like on the screen, the printer is the final arbitrator, the medium where the pages succeed or fail. Back when I was a thin scrap of a lad, when monitors were black and white and screen renderings were at best rough approximations of a document, I had to print lots of test pages. These *drafts* were often my only reliable means of gauging how a design was coming together—and sadly for a forest or two, I went through a lot of them.

Thankfully, InDesign previews pages a heck of a lot more dependably than the meager applications available when I was growing up. With its sophisticated color management, high-quality image display, and Separations Preview palette (see Video Lesson 12, "Previewing Color Separations"), InDesign is just plain terrific at accurately translating type and graphics to a color monitor. Even so, it never hurts to print a draft of your document just to be sure. I'm not suggesting that you print one every ten minutes, the way I used to. But one complete printout at the end is a great way to hunt down typos, confirm the placement of page elements, and assess the appearance of imported graphics. A draft is your opportunity to experience the document from a reader's perspective.

The quality of your draft depends on the quality of the printer itself. In all likelihood, you have an inkjet printer (assuming you have a printer at all). Inkjets are inexpensive, they print a wide range of colors, and they're great at rendering photographic images. On the downside, they're relatively slow, they consume a lot of ink, and you have to use them regularly or the heads clog. If you're feeling flush, you can purchase a more expensive color laser printer. Although these workhorse devices aren't as good at rendering photographs, they are fast, reliable, efficient in their use of toner, and better at printing text and line art (see Figure 12-4 on the next page). If you want to make a serious investment in your future, look into a PostScript-equipped laser printer. Color PostScript printers cost upwards of $2,000, but they do the best job of matching commercial output, which also relies on PostScript. A PostScript laser printer is also well-suited to small print runs, in the neighborhood of a hundred or fewer copies. The upshot is that you can print your document yourself rather than visit a commercial print house.

Figure 12-4.

Despite my recommendations, it's my job to help you make the printer you have now work. Because you'll be printing a draft, there's no sense in throwing a lot of expensive paper at this project. For my part, I load the printer with a 20-pound bond in the 80 to 90 brightness range, which is cheap stuff that you can buy in bulk at a warehouse store. If you're trying to impress a boss or client, look for something closer to 26-pound with a brightness rating of 94 or higher. But don't use glossy photo paper or the like—that's just a waste of money and it doesn't provide any better indication of how the job will look when it comes off the press.

PEARL OF WISDOM

Obviously, I have no idea what printer you're using, so your experience may diverge from mine (though I try to give you hints as to when divergences might occur). And I leave it up to you to make sure your printer is set up properly and in working order. This means that the power is turned on, the printer is connected to your computer, print drivers and other software are installed, the printer is loaded with plenty of ink or toner, and the print head nozzles are clean. For more information on any of these issues, consult the documentation that came with your printer. Finally, it's possible that your default settings are set to something different from what I suggest in the steps. Afford me the usual leap of faith, do as I direct to the best of your printer's ability, and all will be fine.

1. ***Open a test document.*** Open the document called *Pages 62-67 reprise.indd*, found in the *Lesson 12* folder inside *Lesson Files-IDcs3 1on1*. If InDesign warns you about missing or modified links, click the Fix Links Automatically button to find the graphic files in the *Lesson 09* folder. (These links are more important than in the past; without them, the pages won't print correctly.) Eventually, you'll see the document pictured in Figure 12-5, which is the file you created by the end of the "Setting Up Master Pages" exercise in Lesson 9. Blessed with six pages and lots of color, this document will serve you well in your exploration of printing.

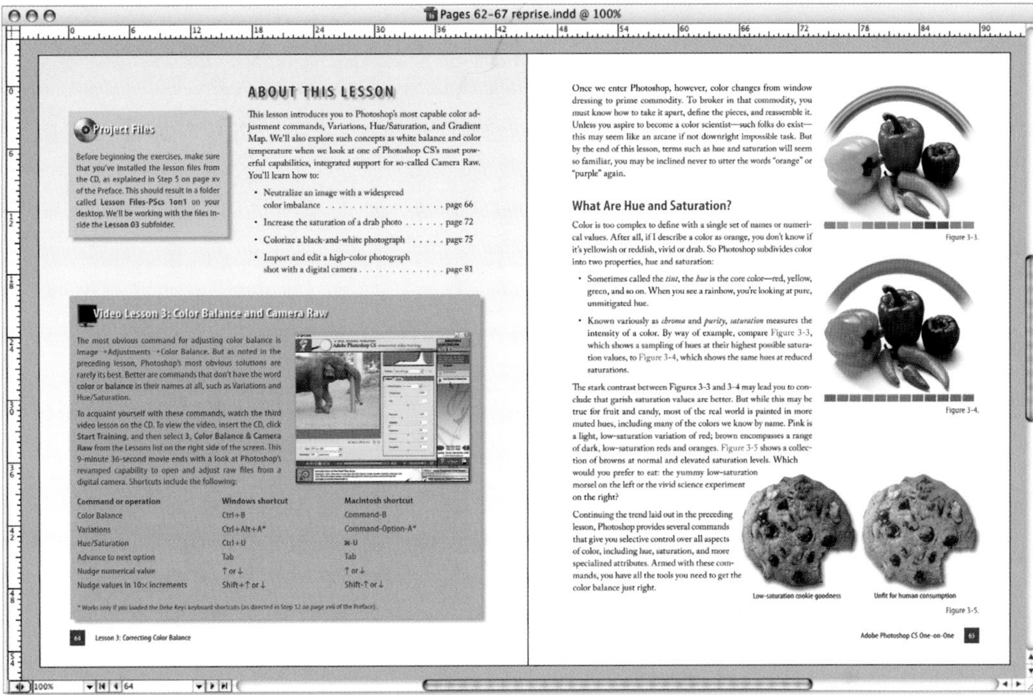

Figure 12-5.

2. ***Choose the Print command.*** Choose **File→Print** or press Ctrl+P (⌘-P on the Mac). InDesign displays its highly specialized **Print** dialog box. As you'll see, this dialog box is a mixed bag. On one hand, it provides you with a vast array of options not found in competing programs. But it also hides many of your printer's unique capabilities, which can prove a bit frustrating if you're using an inkjet printer.

3. ***Select your printer model.*** Choose the model of printer that you want to use from the **Printer** pop-up menu. Figure 12-6 on the next page finds me choosing my color PostScript laser printer, a Tektronix Phaser 750N. But I could just as easily choose my consumer inkjet device, the Epson Stylus Photo 1280, or one

of the other printers networked to my computer. If you select a PostScript printer, the PPD setting will be updated to reflect the associated *PostScript printer description* file. Otherwise, the PPD option is blank.

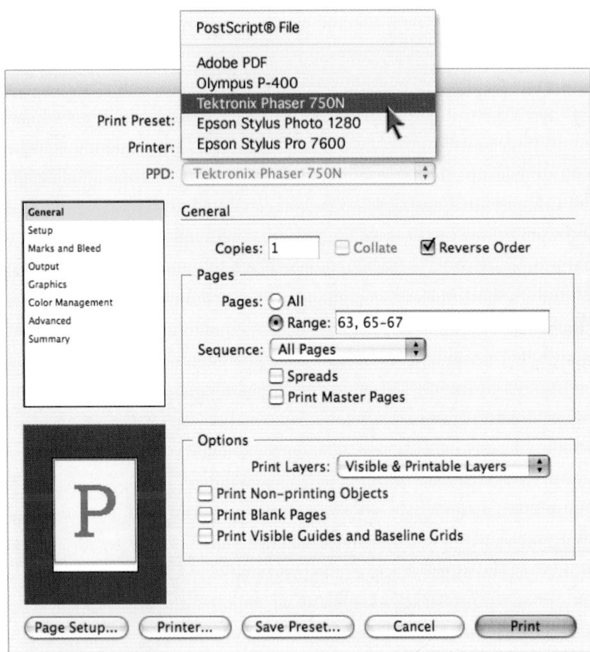

Figure 12-6.

4. *Set the page order.* The Print dialog box is divided into eight panels, only a few of which we'll look at. The first panel, **General**, includes the most basic controls. Here's how I'd like you to set them:

   - Leave Copies set to 1. When printing drafts, one copy of each page is enough.
   - Suppose you want to print just those pages that are set against a white background. In our case, this means page 63 as well as pages 65 through 67. Click in the **Range** option box. Then enter "63, 65–67." A comma separates independent pages, a hyphen indicates a range. Spaces are irrelevant.

   When printing to the end of the document, you can omit the final page number, as in "63,65–." If you don't know how a document is numbered, you can enter a + followed by a relative page number, as in "+2,+4–+6" or just plain "+2,+4–" because the sixth page is the last page.

   - To print all pages in the range in the opposite order in which they appear in the document, so the pages are stacked properly when they come out of the printer, select the **Reverse Order** check box.
   - The other check boxes let you output an entire spread on a single page, output master pages independently of their print pages, and print such nonprinting elements as guides. Leave these options turned off.

5. *Specify the paper size.* In most other programs, you use the Page Setup command to define the size and orientation of the printed page. But in InDesign, you click the **Setup** option along the left side of the Print dialog box. Set the **Paper Size** pop-up option to match the size of the paper you have loaded in your printer (most likely Letter). Then select the first **Orientation** icon, which prints each page upright rather than on its side. Other options let you scale the pages to fit the paper, useful when printing drafts of an oversized document. Leave each of these options set as is.

6. *Turn on all printer marks.* Click the **Marks and Bleed** option to switch to the third panel, which allows you to print a collection of marks and labels around the perimeter of the page. Select the **All Printer's Marks** check box. This turns on all marks used by professional printers to trim, identify, and gauge pages, which I've labeled for your viewing pleasure in the symbolic Figure 12-7. Frankly, this is overkill for draft prints. But it's easier than picking and choosing just those check boxes that you absolutely need: Page Information, which adds filename and date labels, and Crop Marks, which prints trim lines that you can use to cut the paper down to size. (In Figure 12-7, the dark orange represents the page size; the light orange represents the bleed.)

   Also make sure that **Use Document Bleed Settings** is turned on. The slug is too big to fit on a letter-sized page, so go ahead and turn off **Include Slug Area**.

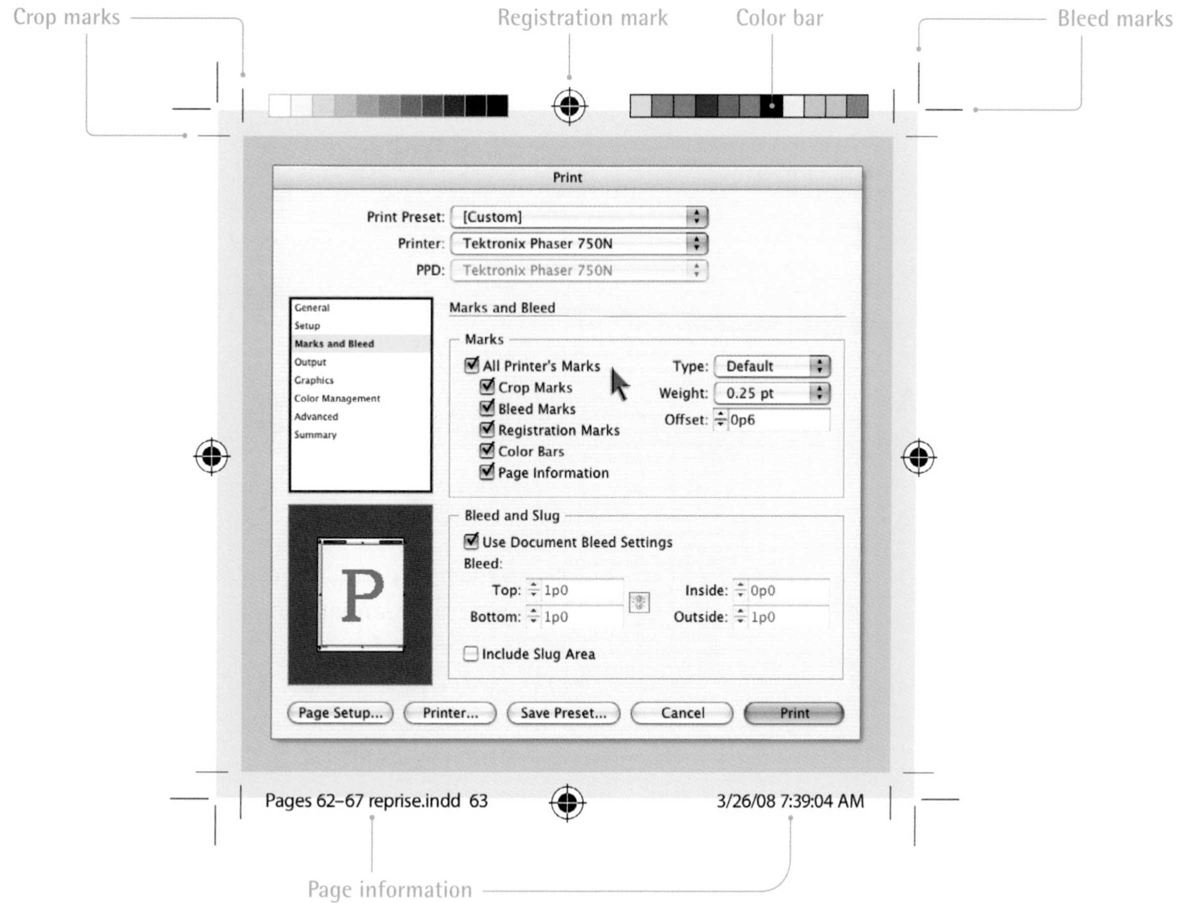

Figure 12-7.

7. ***Select the proper color output settings.*** Click the **Output** option on the left side of the dialog box to enter the first of two areas that let you control how InDesign outputs color. The proper settings in this panel vary depending on whether you're printing to a PostScript printer or not:

   - When printing to a typical inkjet or laser printer that does not understand PostScript, set the **Color** option to **Composite RGB**. This leaves the printer driver in charge of translating the document colors from RGB to the printer's native color space. Most inkjet printers offer more inks than the standard CMYK, so limiting yourself to CMYK would produce inaccurate results.

   - When printing to a color PostScript device, set **Color** to **Composite CMYK**. This puts PostScript in charge of the color calculations and thus stands the best chance of matching your final press colors.

   This document contains lots of colored text that I want to print in color, so turn off the **Text as Black** check box. Finally, turn on the lower-right **Simulate Overprint** check box, as I have in Figure 12-8. This blends colors to simulate the effect of any manual traps and overprints you may have established. To learn more, read the next exercise, "Trapping and Overprinting," which begins on page 493.

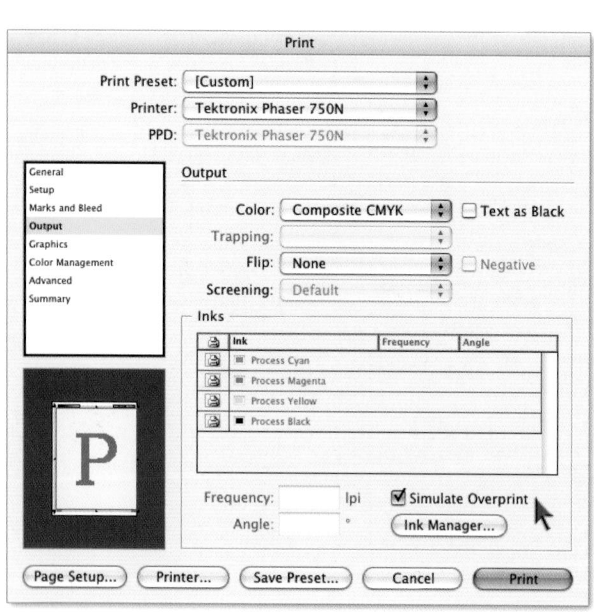

Figure 12-8.

8. ***Turn off the downsampling of graphics.*** As I mentioned in an exercise in the preceding lesson ("Exporting to PDF," Step 9, page 475), I'm strongly opposed to the idea of InDesign or any other layout program automatically reducing the number of pixels in imported images. While it may speed up print times, it does so only very slightly and at an obscenely high price: Downsampling can harm the definition of high-contrast, high-resolution imagery. To confirm that no downsampling will occur:

   - Click the **Graphics** option along the left side of the dialog box.

   - Make sure that the **Send Data** option is set to **All**, as circled in Figure 12-9. This setting prints every pixel in every placed image, which is presumably what you want. You can shave a few seconds by choosing Optimized Subsampling, but unless *all* your images are photographs—that is, no high-contrast Photoshop art, text, or the like—I recommend against it.

The other options in this panel will be dimmed when printing to a non-PostScript printer. If you're using a PostScript device, leave the options set as is.

9. *Adjust the Color Management settings.* Click the **Color Management** option on the left side of the dialog box to control how InDesign conveys colors to your printer. Color is a subjective concept, and conditions and software vary wildly from one printer to the next. In other words, you may have to experiment to come up with the best settings. But I can offer some advice:

   - When working with a PostScript printer, the easiest solution is to set the **Color Handling** option to **PostScript Printer Determines Color**. Also make sure the **Preserve CMYK Numbers** check box is turned on to avoid any changes to your document's carefully defined CMYK values.
   - If you don't like the results, or you're working with a non-PostScript printer and the Document option reads *Profile: U. S. Web Coated (SWOP) v2*, set **Color Handling** to **Let InDesign Determine Colors**. Then choose your printer from the **Printer Profile** pop-up menu. If your printer isn't there, cross your fingers and hope. Regardless, leave **Preserve CMYK Numbers** checked.
   - If you're working with an inkjet printer, the Document option reads *Profile: Adobe RGB (1998)* and your only option for Color Handling is Let InDesign Determine Colors. I have the most luck setting **Printer Profile** to **sRGB IEC61966-2.1** (see Figure 12-10) and letting InDesign reconcile the other details on its own. Critics of this approach point out that the colors get converted twice, once by InDesign and again by the printer software. But because most inkjet printers are factory-calibrated to work with the ubiquitous sRGB, your output will likely benefit from this repeated attention.

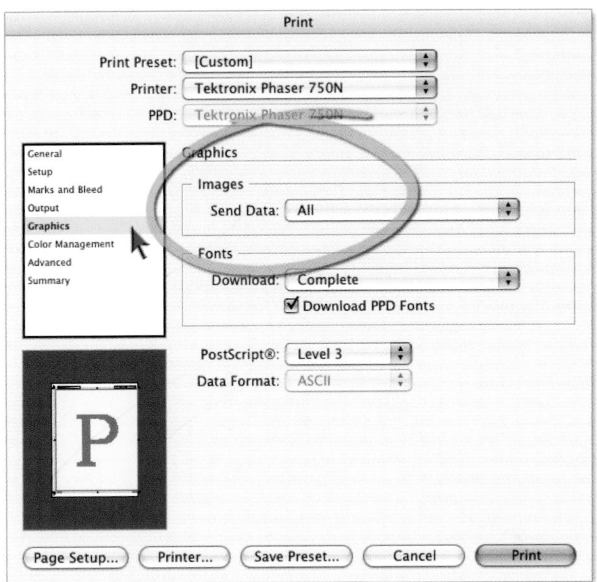

Figure 12-9.

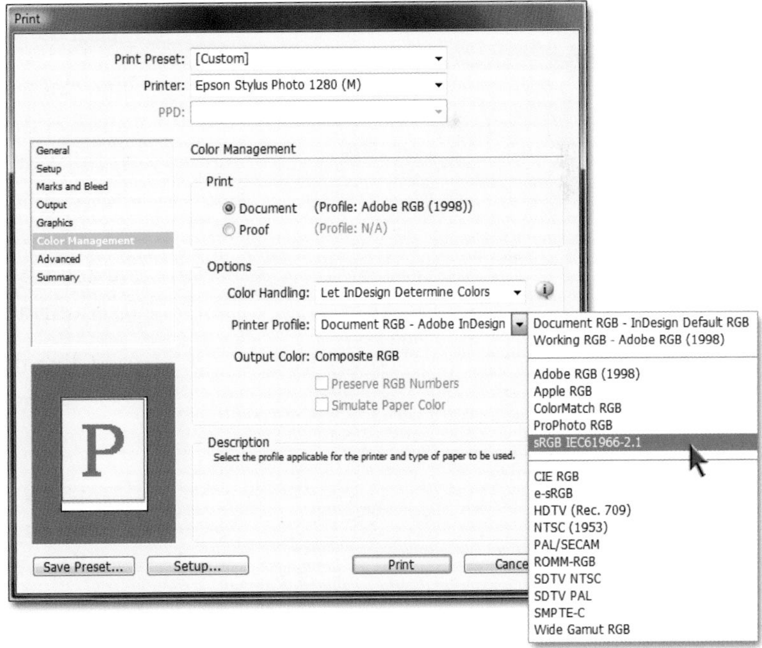

Figure 12-10.

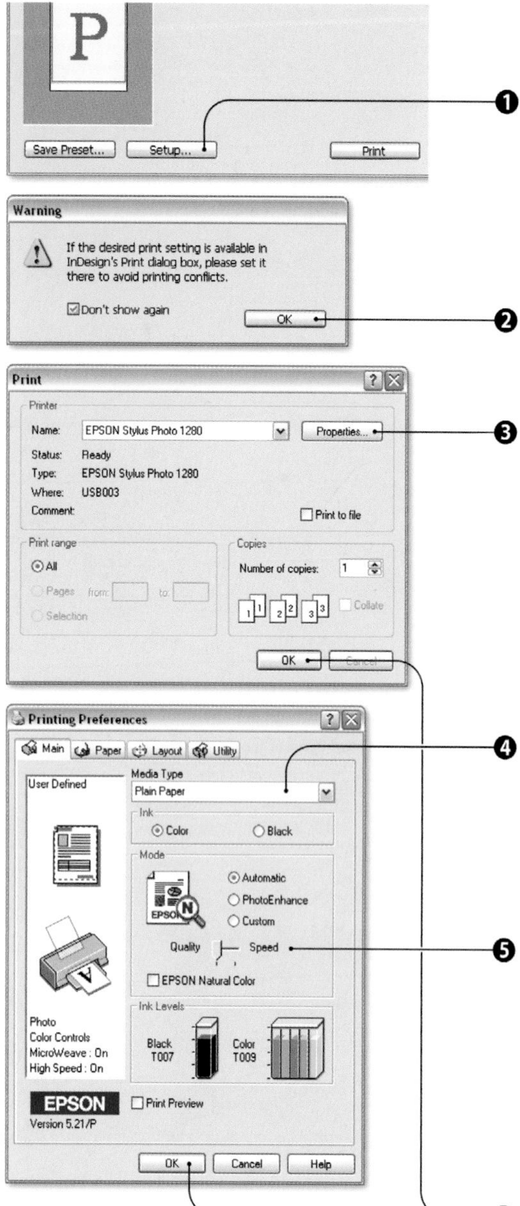

Figure 12-11.

- If your inkjet output doesn't benefit from double-color management, select your specific combination of printer, paper, and inks from the **Printer Profile** pop-up menu. This will require you to turn off the printer software's color management, as I'll explain shortly.

10. ***Select the paper and quality settings for your inkjet printer.*** If you're using a PostScript laser printer or another CMYK device, skip to Step 11. You inkjetters, stick with me. You see, inkjet printers permit you to adjust the paper quality and ink standards. That's part of what makes them so versatile. But if you get the combination wrong, it can make a mess of your output. So it's always worth checking to make sure everything's in order. The exact process for doing so varies fairly significantly between the PC and the Mac, as well as from one model of printer to another. Diagrammed for Windows in Figure 12-11 and for the Mac in Figure 12-12, the following is a walk-through based on the behavior of my Epson Stylus Photo 1280:

    - Click the **Setup** button (labeled ❶ in the figures) at the bottom of the Print dialog box. (On the Mac, click the **Printer** button.)
    - InDesign alerts you that it doesn't approve of you adjusting print settings outside the Print dialog box. Turns out, you have no choice. So turn on the **Don't Show Again** check box and click **OK** (❷ in the figures).
    - This dumps you into yet another Print dialog box. On the PC, click either the **Preferences** or **Properties** button (❸ in Figure 12-11), whichever is available. On the Mac, choose **Print Settings**, **Quality & Media**, or an equivalent option from the third pop-up menu (❸ in Figure 12-12).
    - Look for an option called **Media Type** or the like, and set it to **Plain Paper** (❹) or something equally prosaic. Feel free to raise the quality setting (❺), but unless you're using special paper, you'll probably want to steer clear of any Advanced or Custom settings.
    - If you specified the printer profile in the previous step, as documented in the last bulleted item (top of this page), you'll need to hunt down and turn off any color management or adjustment functions.
    - Click **OK** twice on the PC or click **Print** once on the Mac (❻). This returns you to InDesign's Print dialog box.

11. *Save your settings as a preset.* You don't want to go through these steps every time you print a file. So save yourself some effort by clicking the **Save Preset** button. Name the preset "One-on-One draft" and click **OK**. From now on, you can retrieve all your settings except the page range and the inkjet settings applied in Step 10 by choosing this preset from the Print Preset pop-up menu at the top of the dialog box.

12. *Print the document.* Click the **Print** button to send the document on its way. InDesign displays a few progress bars explaining that it's flattening the file (i.e., reconciling the transparency) and so on. It all happens on-the-fly; no change is made to your document. InDesign hands off the document to the operating system, which spools it to the printer. A few minutes later, the pages you requested should be waiting in your printer's tray, stacked in the proper order.

If this were a real-world document, you would read it to catch any typos, gauge the quality of the graphics, and perhaps even hand it off to others for approval. If you like the printed colors, you might also consider submitting the pages along with the electronic version of the document to your commercial print house. This way, the press technicians have a benchmark that they can use to compare the output. If they're sufficiently conscientious, they may even use your output to tweak a press setting or two.

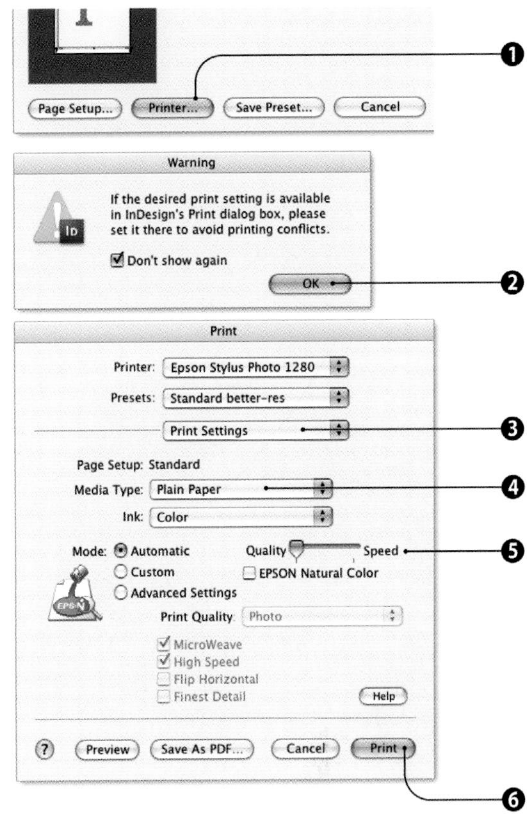

Figure 12-12.

Trapping and Overprinting

The publishing industry has long been divided into two camps—the designers who create the documents and the technicians who print them. So if InDesign's printing controls strike you as a bit over-the-top, bear in mind that they weren't intended for you. Adobe made InDesign's Print command to conform to the specialized needs of service bureaus, commercial print houses, and other companies that make printing their primary business. The fact that the command just so happens to work with your inkjet printer is literally an afterthought; InDesign couldn't print reliably to non-PostScript devices until Version 1.5.

When it comes time to commercially reproduce your document, you no longer have to worry about the Print command and its many complexities. Happily, that becomes someone else's responsibility. But tempting as it may be, you can't expect to ignore the printing process entirely. Your commercial printer will expect you to turn in a document that's ready for output. And that means predicting what can go wrong and accounting for it in advance.

PEARL OF WISDOM

Having spent my formative years working at a PostScript service bureau—where we rendered PageMaker and QuarkXPress files to film in advance of commercial reproduction—I strongly urge you to seek the counsel of a kind, knowledgeable representative from your print house. If no such representative exists, bid that establishment *adieu* and move along to the next one. The people who manage printers for a living know the demands and rigors of their equipment far better than you or I ever will. And if they're wise, they'll be more than happy to warn you about the most frequent problems and tell you what to do to avoid them.

In this exercise, we'll take a look at one of the most common pitfalls of commercial printing, misregistration. We'll also examine two popular solutions, trapping and overprinting. Be forewarned, these may or may not turn out to be issues you have to contend with. Some print houses trap files automatically; others do not. Either way, you'll be familiar with the process and ready to have a moderately intelligent conversation on the topic.

Tight (good) registration

Loose (bad) registration

Figure 12-13.

Tight registration with trapping

Loose registration with trapping

Figure 12-14.

Because inks are laid down in separate passes (see the sidebar "The Commercial Printing Process" on page 498), each ink must precisely align, or *register*, with the next to accurately reproduce the colors in your text and graphics. But this is not as easy as it may sound. With paper flying through the press at breakneck speeds, some degree of misregistration is bound to occur. And when it does, you end up with gaps between neighboring objects that do not share common inks. Figure 12-13 compares the tight registration in this book with the loose registration that may occur if press conditions are not closely monitored, as is often the case at bargain print shops. Note that the crown is made up of cyan and black inks, while the background is exclusively magenta and yellow.

Fortunately, you can fill in potential gaps using *trapping*. The easiest way to trap an object is to create a *spread*. First add a stroke that matches the color of the fill. Then set the stroke to *overprint* its background. As pictured in Figure 12-14, overprinting mixes the cyan and black inks with the magenta and yellow inks. The result isn't perfect—the right crown remains out of sync with its background—but it's better than a gap. The other way to trap an object is to stroke the background behind the object. Called a *choke*, this is a harder effect to achieve, as you'll see in the exercise.

PEARL OF WISDOM

Bear in mind, trapping is necessary only when two neighboring objects do not share common inks. Why? Because when as much as a single ink travels from one object to another, it fills in the gap. A great example of an object that never requires trapping is a full-color photograph. Virtually every pixel contains a mixture of CMYK inks, hence no gaps. This is not to say misregistration doesn't hurt a photo—it does. But trapping doesn't help.

In the following steps, we will focus on those objects that benefit from trapping: vector art and text. In addition to learning how InDesign's trapping controls work, you'll learn how to identify the mercifully few kinds of objects that require trapping and which of two trapping solutions (manual or automatic) to use. If later it transpires that your print house provides trapping as part of its standard service, all the merrier. Instead of scratching your head in bewilderment, you'll know to be grateful. Then again, if you're getting a good deal, and your printer has never heard of trapping (many small printers haven't), you'll recognize which objects might give you trouble and be raring to fix them.

1. ***Open a document in need of trapping.*** Typically, I try to present you with documents that have at least one foot in the real world. But this time, I present you with one that's purely instructional in nature. The document in question: *Trapping turtles.indd* in the *Lesson 12* folder inside *Lesson Files-IDcs3 1on1*. Pictured in Figure 12-15, it includes four variations on a turtle set against a multicolored background. As it just so happens, two of these reptiles require trapping and two do not.

2. ***Inspect the colors of the first turtle.*** With the black arrow tool, select the upper-left turtle. Then press F6 to display the **Color** palette. Like all the other turtles, this one offers no stroke. Its chartreuse fill is made up of 20 percent cyan

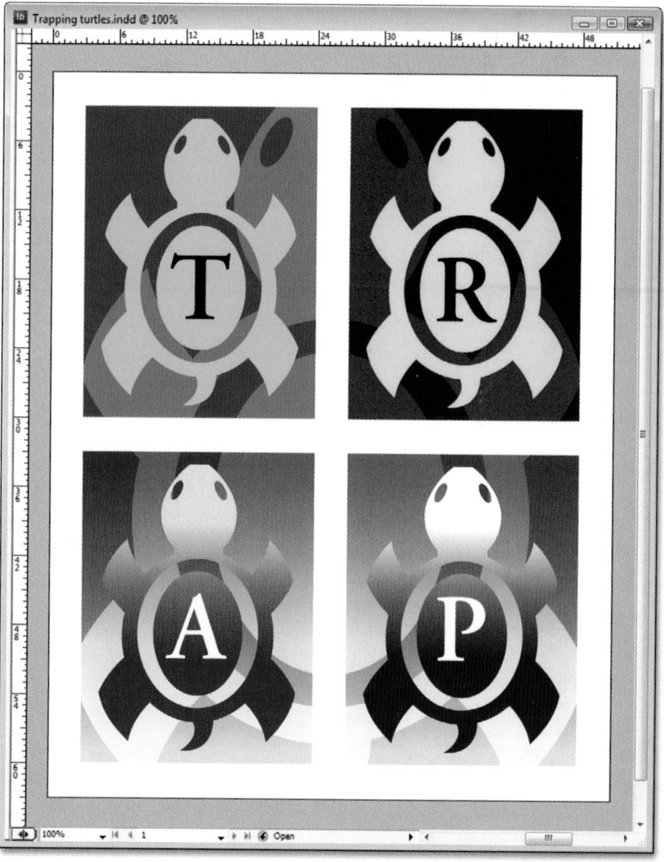

Figure 12-15.

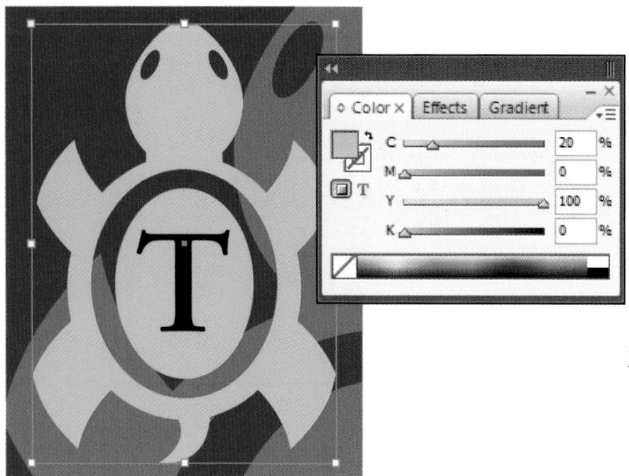

Figure 12-16.

and 100 percent yellow, as shown in Figure 12-16. (If you don't see the color values, press the X key to switch focus to the fill.) Although the background exists on a locked layer—making it difficult to confirm its exact colors—we can reasonably assume by its appearance that it contains lots of cyan. I can also tell you that it contains some yellow. So given that the turtle and its background share common inks, I know that there's no need for trapping.

3. *Inspect the second turtle.* Now click the upper-right turtle to select it. This guy is 100 percent yellow with no other ink. Meanwhile, its deep blue background contains equal parts cyan and magenta with a bit of black. The objects share no common color, so we should apply some trapping.

4. *Assign a yellow stroke.* The best way to trap the yellow turtle is to surround it with a yellow stroke. Click the stroke icon (◪) in the Color palette or press the X key. Then change the **Y** value to 100 to exactly match the fill. (You may be able to get this color by clicking the swatch in the bottom-left corner of the Color palette.) By default, the stroke is 1-point thick, which is about right for most press scenarios. But I want you to display the **Stroke** palette and then increase the **Weight** value to 8 points. This exaggerates the trap so you can better see what's going on.

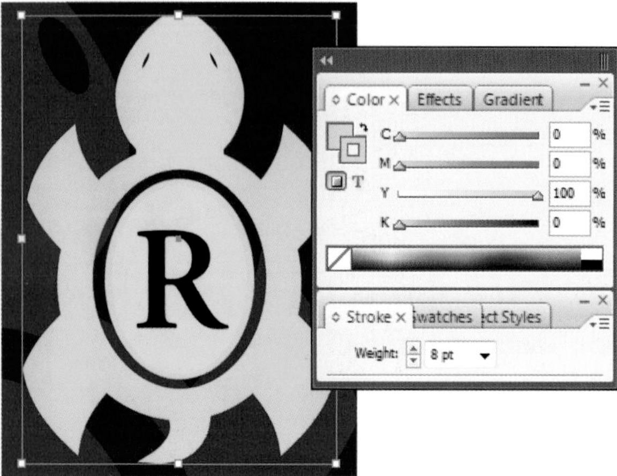

Figure 12-17.

PEARL OF WISDOM

The stroke is centered on the path outline. This means the turtle grows out half the line weight, or 4 points, as shown in Figure 12-17. If you're clever, it might occur to you that you could also align the stroke to the outside of the path and reduce the Weight value to 4 points. But if you did that, you wouldn't trace the inside of the eyes, which need trapping as well. A centered stroke set to twice the thickness of the intended trap is your best bet.

5. *Overprint the stroke.* So far, we haven't really accomplished anything. The yellow turtle spreads outward 4 points, but the background retreats those same 4 points. Without overprinting, the inks don't overlap and therefore you have no trap.

   To apply overprinting, choose **Window→Attributes** to display the tiny **Attributes** palette. Then, with the yellow turtle still selected, turn on the **Overprint Stroke** check box.

6. *Turn on the overprint preview.* If you were to print this document to a PostScript printer, the yellow stroke would

mix with the deep blue background. But the document doesn't look any different on screen because, by default, you can't see overprints on screen. Why this is, I can't tell you. Hiding overprints doesn't speed things up and is highly misleading. Even so, you have to ask to see them. To do just that, go to the **View** menu and choose the first command, **Overprint Preview**. Or press the inconvenient shortcut, Ctrl+Shift+Alt+Y (⌘-Shift-Option-Y on the Mac). The yellow turtle collapses to its previous size, and the intersecting inks appear very dark, as in Figure 12-18.

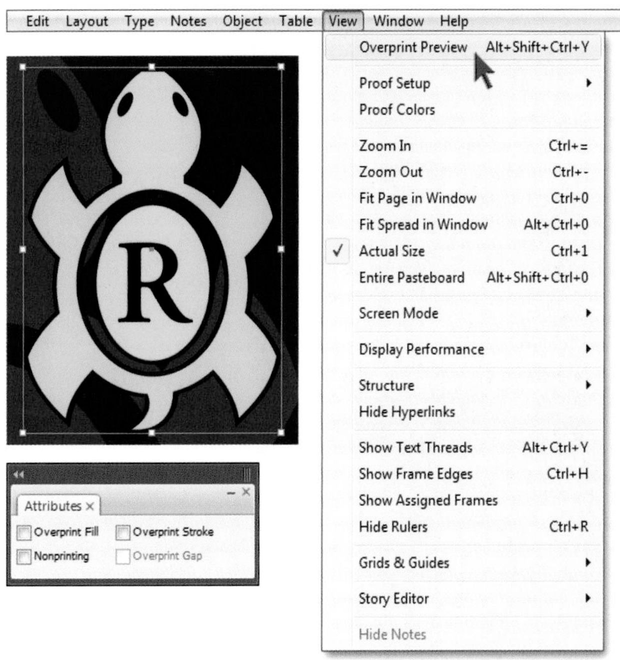

Figure 12-18.

7. ***Reduce the stroke to 1 point.*** Now that you know what the trap looks like, restore the **Weight** value in the **Stroke** palette to 1 point. This may seem awfully thin—after all, it makes for a narrow ½-point trap. But given that you don't want to see your trap—you just want it to fill in the gaps—it makes sense to keep it as small as possible. And most professionally minded printers are willing to guarantee their registration within ½ point. I recommend going higher—say, 2 points—only when printing to newsprint, which is more liable to stretch on the press, or when working with a bargain quick-print outfit whose standards may be lax.

8. ***Select and inspect the first gradient turtle.*** Click the lower-left turtle to select it. As witnessed in Figure 12-19, this graceful terrapin is filled with a gradient. Press the **X** key to activate the fill icon at the bottom of the toolbox (as in ◪). Then bring up the **Gradient** palette and click either of the color stops. The recipe for the first stop is C: 5 and M: 20; the second includes all four inks. The background not only includes lots of magenta but also is filled with the same gradient as the turtle; the direction is merely reversed. With so many shared colors, no trapping is warranted.

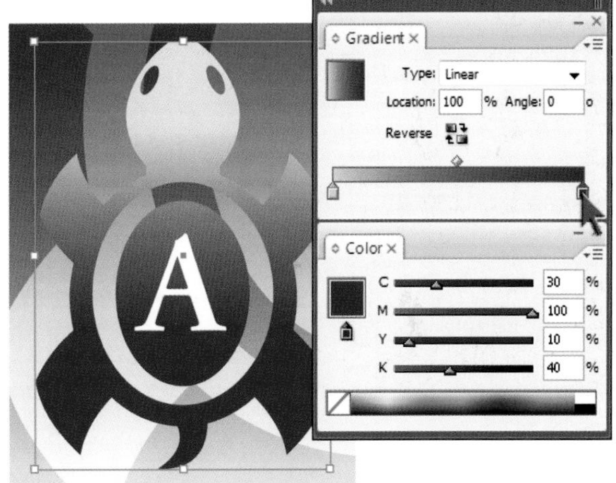

Figure 12-19.

9. ***Take a gander at the last turtle.*** As it just so happens, you rarely need to trap gradients. One exception is when the gradient contains a *spot color*, which is an ink that will print to a separate plate. Select the lower-right turtle. Then click the second color stop in the Gradient palette. Sure enough, this color stop calls for a spot color from the Pantone ink library. The spot color will print to a separate plate, so it should be trapped.

The Commercial Printing Process

Commercial printing is an elaborate, expensive, resource-intensive process. A large printing press costs millions of dollars, is longer than your house, and weighs as much as 50 elephants. And as you might imagine, it's more complicated to operate than an inkjet or a laser printer. Many steps that occur automatically when you print a document in your home or office have to be performed manually by your service bureau or press technician. For example, technicians never output a document directly to the printer. Instead, they create independent pages for each ink, known as *color separations*. The figure at the bottom of this page shows a detail from a full-color document, followed by four separations, one for each of the CMYK inks.

Technicians may render the separations to film and then burn the film to flexible, usually aluminum, *lithographic plates*; or they may print to the plates directly. The plates are then wrapped around cylinders and installed on the press. For large print runs—a few thousand copies or more—the most popular press technology is *web-offset lithography*, or just plain *offset printing*. Diagrammed in the simplified illustration at the top of the opposite page, offset printing uses the plate cylinders to transfer ink to continuous rolls of paper. (The term *web* refers to these rolls; it has nothing to do with the World Wide Web.) Water rollers clean the excess ink off the plates. The plate conveys the ink to a rubber *blanket*, which in turn shuttles the ink to the paper. The result is that the plate never touches the paper, hence the term *offset*. Each of the roller groups in the illustration is called a *printing unit*. One printing unit exists for each ink. Standard process-color printing requires four units, one each for cyan, magenta, yellow, and black, as in the illustration. Each spot color adds another unit. Most presses can accommodate at least six printing units, enough for CMYK and two spots.

Each rotation of the plate and blanket lays down what's known as an *impression*, which is typically equal to anywhere from four to twelve pages. The big presses—the ones that print newspapers, magazines, and books—can print as many as a dozen impressions per second. No kidding, the paper speeds through the press so rapidly that it manufactures its own breeze and the printed pages look like one big blur. The high-speed snapshots at the bottom of the opposite page show my *Look & Learn Photoshop* (the first project I laid out in InDesign)

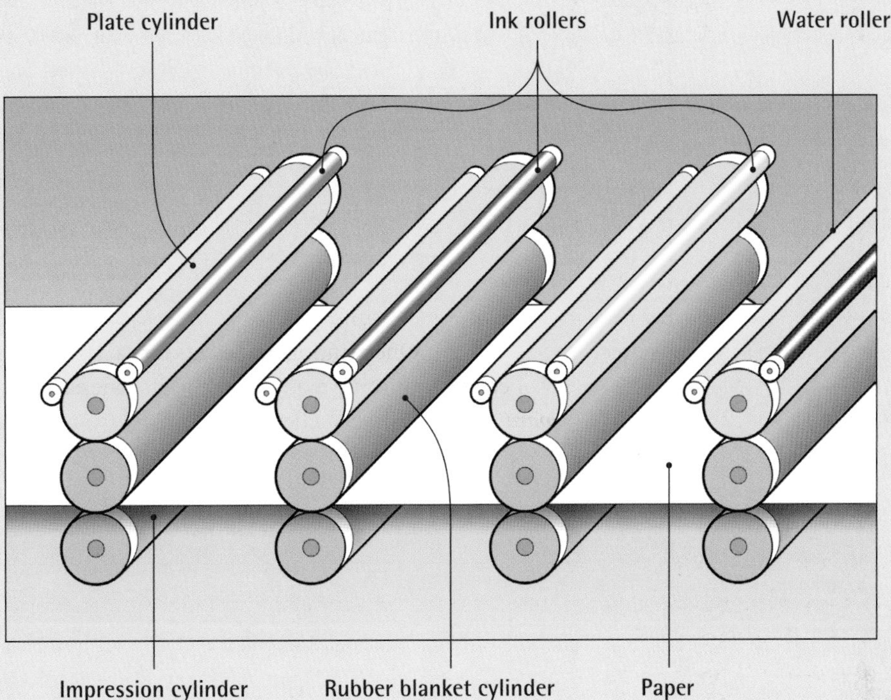

whizzing through the press and rolling off as cut, folded pages called *signatures*. Incidentally, this was a two-color job, black and Pantone 285 blue; so it required just two printing units, which resulted in lower press costs.

Smaller print runs are better served by a *sheetfed press*. As with offset printing, a sheetfed press relies on color-separated lithographic plates that convey ink to paper by way of blanket cylinders. But instead of using a web roll, a sheetfed press prints to individual sheets of paper. The process is a little slower, but it's still faster than you might think, with overlapping pages traveling by in a steady stream. A *registration board* ensures that one piece of paper precisely aligns with the next. As a result, a sheetfed press may enjoy tighter registration than its web-offset counterpart and thus require little or no trapping. But as always, this is an issue for you to discuss with your good-natured printer representative.

Figure 12-20.

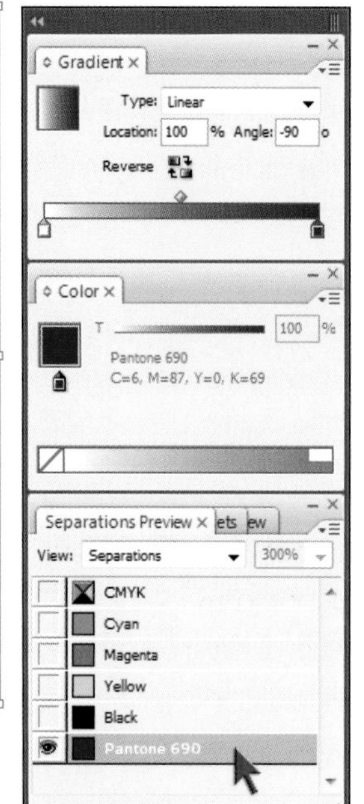

PEARL OF WISDOM

To see just how isolated this poor turtle is, choose **Window→Output→Separations Preview** or press Shift+F6 to display the **Separations** palette. Choose **Separations** from the **View** pop-up menu and then click the last option in the palette, **Pantone 690**. As you may recall from Video Lesson 12, "Previewing Color Separations" (see page 482), the Separations palette lets you view each ink independently or in combination with others. So when you click Pantone 690, you see only those objects that will print on the Pantone 690 plate, which means the bottom-right gradient turtle and nothing else (see Figure 12-20). If you click one of the other inks in the Separations palette, you'll see a white turtle-shaped hole, called a *knockout*. In other words, the gradient turtle exists on the Pantone 690 plate and nowhere else, which means it's just begging for trapping.

10. ***Create a custom trap preset.*** You could trace the turtle with a gradient stroke, but you may find it difficult to exactly align the fill and stroke gradients. The more convenient solution is to create a customized trap preset and apply it to the entire page. This leaves InDesign in charge of making the trapping decisions automatically, which you may prefer in the long run anyway.

    Choose **Window→Output→Trap Presets** to display the **Trap Presets** palette (by default, clustered with the Separations Preview palette). Then press the Alt key (Option on the Mac) and click the icon at the bottom of the palette. This displays the **New Trap Preset** dialog box, pictured in Figure 12-21.

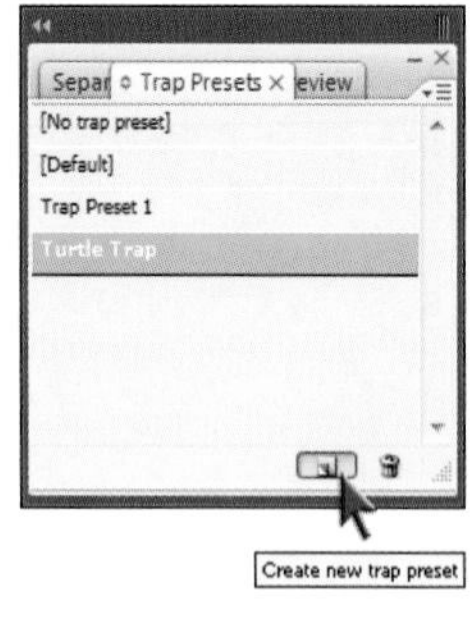

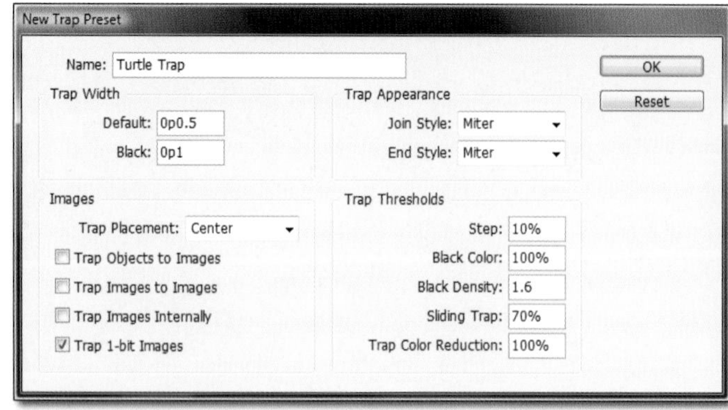

Figure 12-21.

11. ***Enter your preferred trap settings.*** InDesign's trapping controls are nothing if not comprehensive. I could fill another twelve pages with a discussion of this dialog box alone. But I'm not going to for two simple reasons: 1) That discussion would be the most boring thing you would ever read, and 2) it would end with the conclusion, "And that's why most of the settings are fine as is." I recommend you change just five options, so let's save ourselves a lot of tedium and focus on those:

    - Name the new preset "Turtle Trap."
    - Notice that InDesign offers two Trap Width values. The first, **Default**, affects the size of traps that do not involve black ink. InDesign measures the trap in one direction only, so the value should be half as thick as you would use for an overprinting stroke. To match the trap thickness that you established back in Step 7 (see page 497), raise this value to 0p0.5, or ½ point.
    - Very wisely, InDesign does not spread objects on the black plate. First, any such spreading would be overly obvious. Second, most text appears on the black plate, and spreading text can ruin its legibility. Instead, InDesign spreads other inks into black according to the second Trap Width value, **Black**. Because black ink does a better job of covering the others, you can set this value higher. I recommend a value of 0p1 (1 point).
    - As I mentioned in the introduction to this exercise, you don't need to trap images. In fact, doing so takes a lot of time and may even harm your imported photos. So turn off the **Trap Objects to Images** check box, which would otherwise spread vector objects into imported images.
    - Also turn off the exceedingly unwise **Trap Images to Images**, which would attempt to spread overlapping images into each other. The only worse setting is Trap Images Internally, which spreads neighboring pixels inside an image. Fortunately, this one is off by default; leave it that way.

    The other settings are set the way they ought to be set. You now have my permission to click the **OK** button.

12. ***Apply the new trap preset to the page.*** InDesign adds a Turtle Trap item to the **Trap Presets** palette. But just because you made it doesn't mean that it's in force. To apply the preset to the current page, do the following:

   - Click the ▾≡ in the upper-right corner of the palette and choose **Assign Trap Preset**, as shown in Figure 12-22.
   - Select **Turtle Trap** from the **Trap Preset** pop-up menu.
   - Click the **Assign** button to apply the preset to all pages in the document (which happen to be just this one).
   - Click the **Done** button. Note that the document won't look any different. I explain why in just a moment.

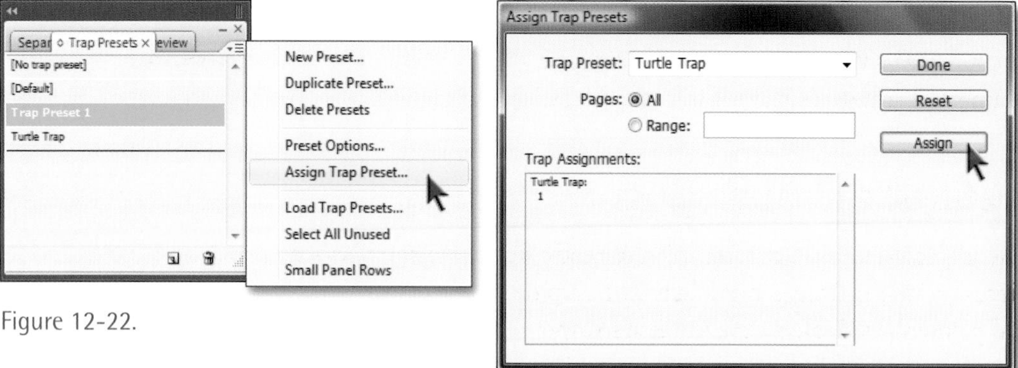

Figure 12-22.

13. ***Set the text to overprint.*** At this point, the document is entirely trapped with one exception. Click the **Yellow** plate in the **Separations Preview** palette and you'll see white knockouts in the shape of the *T* and *R* in the yellow turtles. As I mentioned before, the trapping preset will not spread the letters, but it will choke the yellow turtles into the letters. Turns out, this is not the ideal solution. Given that the letters are 100 percent black, it makes the most sense to overprint them in their entirety against the turtles. This way, you eliminate any chance of misregistration gaps and no trapping is needed.

    To overprint all black objects on the page, press Ctrl+K (or ⌘-K) to display the **General** panel of the **Preferences** dialog box. In the list on the left, click **Appearance of Black**, which presents the options shown in Figure 12-23. Then turn on the **Overprint [Black] Swatch at 100%** check box, which I've circled. This sets all objects that contain 100 percent black ink without any C, M, or Y to overprint the colors behind them. Click **OK** to accept your changes. The knockouts in the yellow turtles vanish.

Although your head may be swimming, I must ask you to keep in mind two more points: First, there's no way to preview the trapping preset you established in Steps 10 through 12. InDesign's automatic trapping functions come into play only when printing color separations. Second, even though you specifically assigned your Turtle Trap preset in Step 12, InDesign will *not* trap the document until it is specifically told to do so during the printing process. I recommend that you include a little note for the press technicians telling them to set the Trapping option in the Output panel of the Print dialog box to Application Built-In. Or better yet, read the final exercise, "Preflight and Packaging," where I'll tell you how to communicate this and much more as you prepare your document for its ultimate destination, the commercial press.

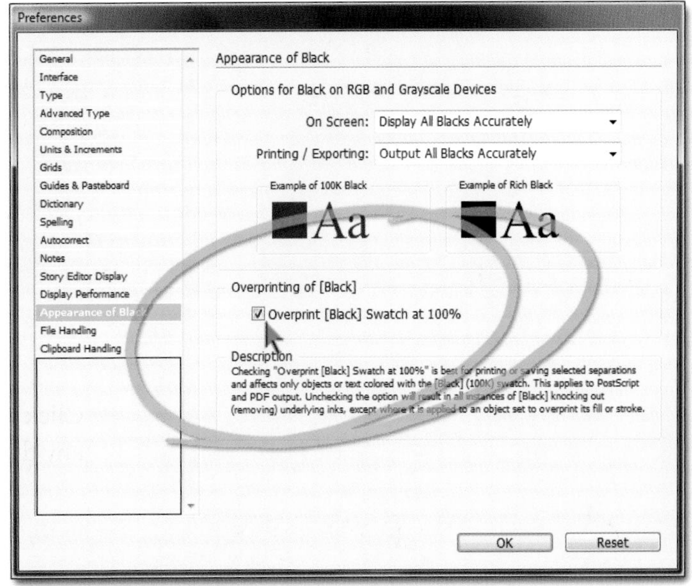

Figure 12-23.

Preflight and Packaging

The glorious day has arrived. You're ready to collect the various pieces of your InDesign document and ship them off to a commercial printer. It's finally someone else's responsibility to worry over your document while you fret about something else for a change. But only if your document is really—and I do mean *really*—rock-solid ready to go. Failing to include so much as a single linked graphic or font file can result in the dreaded phone call from your print rep. It starts with, "Uh, we seem to have a problem," and ends with you making a mad dash across town to avoid getting bumped off the press. Because many printers book far in advance, missing a press date can throw you a week or more off your deadline.

Fortunately, InDesign provides two tools that help calm some of this last-minute frenzy:

- Before you submit any print job, you can run what's known as a *preflight* inspection. Like the aviation test for which it's named, preflighting is a safety check. But rather than confirming a plane's airworthiness, it examines a document's readiness for professional output.
- Once preflighting is complete, you *package* the document, which involves hunting down all links and fonts—no matter how far-flung—and collecting them inside a single folder. Copy that folder to a CD or server, and your job is ready for takeoff.

InDesign lets you initiate these two distinct operations by choosing either of two commands under the File menu. The Preflight command inspects the document and then offers you the option of packaging it. The Package command starts with a preflight check and then copies the links and fonts to a common location. The upshot is that you have to choose just one command to both preflight and package a document.

Of the two, I prefer File→Package. It interrupts you only if the preflight check finds a problem. Then it automatically moves on to the essential task of packaging. In this final exercise, you'll use the Package command to confirm the press-worthiness of a real-world document, assemble its pieces, and copy the resulting folder to a jump drive, CD, or some other medium.

1. *Open the reprise document.* As in the first exercise, open *Pages 62-67 reprise.indd* in the *Lesson 12* folder inside *Lesson Files-IDcs3 1on1*. You've output this file to your own printer; now let's get it ready for commercial reproduction. The document happens to link to a total of seventeen graphics that are contained in the *Lesson 09* folder. Although InDesign should be able to locate the graphics easily enough, this is poor long-term organization because it means I have to copy the entire *Lesson Files-IDcs3 1on1* folder to preserve the links. Better to package the document and collect the files in a central, tidy location, independent of the other lesson files.

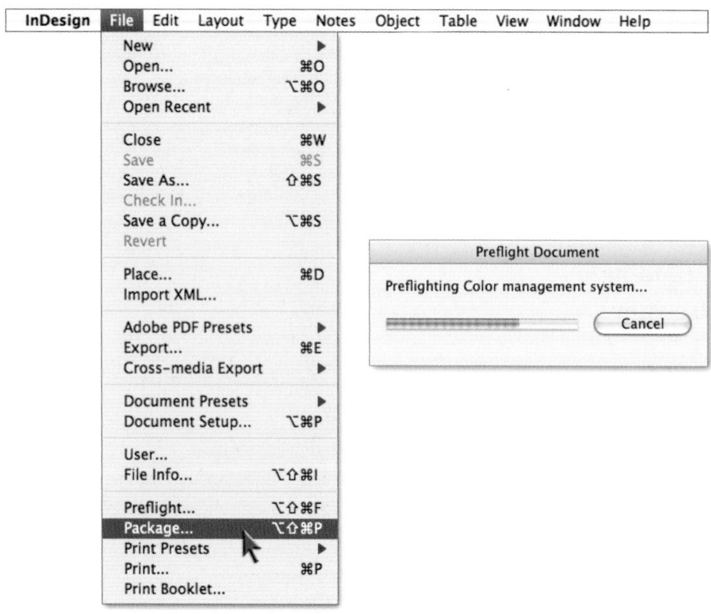

Figure 12-24.

2. *Choose the Package command.* Choose **File→Package** or press Ctrl+Shift+Alt+P (⌘-Shift-Option-P). Depending on the speed of your system and the condition of your document, the program may flash a few progress messages, telling you that InDesign is rounding up images, looking for fonts, and evaluating the color settings, as in Figure 12-24. (If you don't see a message, it just means these processes occur too quickly for InDesign to document.)

3. *View the potential preflight problems.* A moment later, you'll see an alert message warning you that InDesign has encountered "possible problems." Click the **View Info** button to see what those problems might be. InDesign displays the multipaneled **Preflight** dialog box.

Pictured in Figure 12-25, the first panel provides a summary of all preflight issues, including fonts, imported graphics, color settings, and transparency.

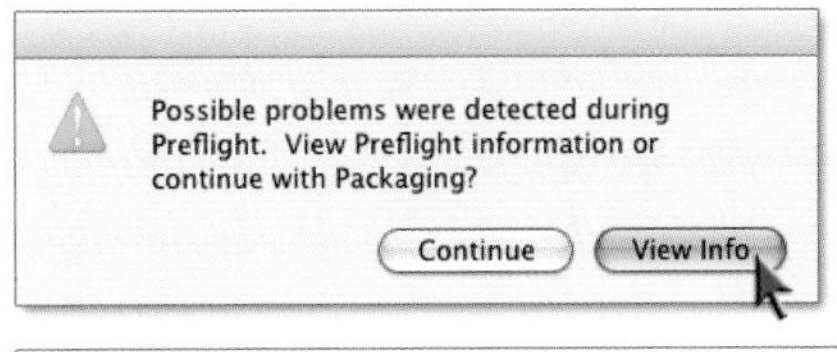

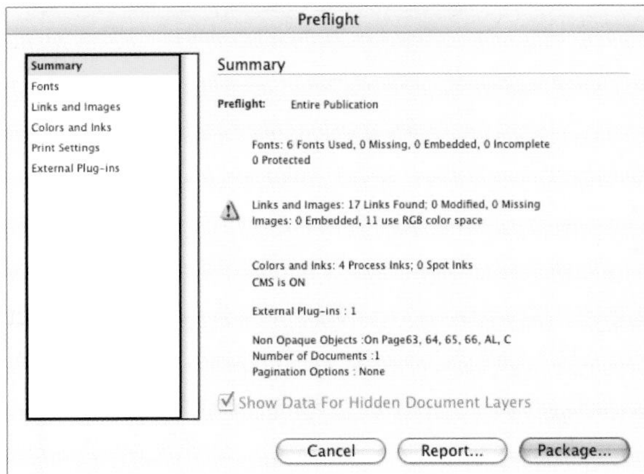

Figure 12-25.

4. ***Repair all broken links.*** InDesign highlights its "possible problems" with yellow ⚠ icons. In our case, a single ⚠ appears in front of the information about imported graphics. But what is InDesign's concern? To figure that out, we have to dig a little deeper, as follows:

   - Click the **Links and Images** option along the left side of the dialog box or press Ctrl+3 (⌘-3 on the Mac). This brings up the **Links and Images** panel, which contains detailed information about all imported graphics. The scrolling list below the ⚠ icon chronicles the sixteen Photoshop images linked to the document. (An image is repeated, which is why InDesign lists a total of seventeen links.)
   - To refine the list to just the problem graphics, turn on the **Show Problems Only** check box, as in Figure 12-26. This should reduce the list to eleven images. (If not, keep reading; I explain a solution.)
   - Click a graphic in the list to explore it in detail. You'll see the date it was last modified, its original resolution, and the effective resolution after factoring in any scaling performed inside InDesign.

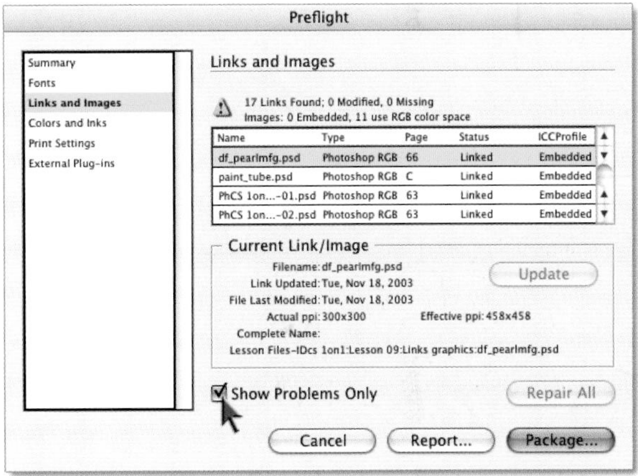

Figure 12-26.

The Update and Repair All buttons permit you to refresh outdated links and locate missing files, respectively. If available, click **Repair All** to establish links with the graphic files on disk. For those of you who still saw seventeen images in the list, now you have eleven.

What exactly *is* the problem with the outstanding pages? Take a peek at the entries in the second column of Figure 12-26, all of which read *Photoshop RGB* or *TIFF RGB*. We're poised to submit a document to a CMYK press, and yet most of our linked images are saved in the RGB mode. Conventional wisdom says that the way to maintain accurate color is to convert an image to the CMYK mode in Photoshop before importing it into InDesign. Therefore, InDesign flags the files as potential problems.

FURTHER INVESTIGATION

To learn how to convert an RGB image to CMYK—and maintain accurate colors in the translation (a huge source of frustration if not addressed properly)—consult another book in this series, *Adobe Photoshop CS3 One-on-One* (Deke Press/O'Reilly Media, 2007). See the exercise "Preparing a CMYK File for Commercial Reproduction," which begins on page 486 of Lesson 12, also named "Printing and Output."

PEARL OF WISDOM

I'm as much a fan of conventional wisdom as the next guy, but in this case, it's only half true. If I were printing an image from PageMaker or QuarkXPress, I'd make darn certain I converted the image to CMYK before saving it in Photoshop. But InDesign is more flexible. RGB images work just as well as CMYK, provided that 1) you set up InDesign's color management function as directed in Step 7 on page xviii of the Preface, and 2) your press technician prints the document directly from InDesign or from a PDF document generated by InDesign. Because Photoshop and InDesign share a common color engine, a conversion made in one program is identical to a conversion made in another.

Need proof? Look no further than these very pages. Every screen shot and photograph in this book is an RGB image that InDesign converted on-the-fly during the print process. The advantage of this approach is threefold:

- Photoshop works more quickly when you edit RGB images rather than CMYK images.
- RGB images take up less room on disk than their CMYK counterparts.
- In its capacity as the end-of-the-road output program, InDesign is the better program for making the tricky conversion from RGB to CMYK. Because your technicians can fine-tune the CMYK conversion to best suit their particular brand of press, an RGB image is actually *more* likely to provide accurate color than its CMYK equivalent.

5. ***Click the Package button.*** With all that in mind, InDesign's "possible problems" turn out to be no problems at all. Click the **Package** button at the bottom of the dialog box to say goodbye to preflighting and move on to the more important process of packaging. If InDesign asks you to save the document, go ahead and do so.

6. ***Enter your printing instructions (if any).*** Rather out of the blue, the **Printing Instructions** dialog box invites you to construct a Read Me file for your press technician. Fill in the various options according to your personal tastes and click the **Continue** button to create a plain text file that can be read on any computer.

   - If you have nothing to communicate, do *not* click Cancel. Instead, click the Continue button to close the dialog box and move on. But be aware: This causes InDesign to create a file called *Instructions.txt* that lacks any meaningful instructions. Before submitting your project to a commercial printer, I recommend that you delete the empty *Instructions.txt* file to avoid confusion.

- Better yet, take a few moments to fill out the print instructions, line for line. Figure 12-27 shows my filled-in dialog box followed by the resulting text file. If you don't like how InDesign organizes your printing instructions, you can modify the text later using a text editor such as NotePad on the PC or TextEdit on the Mac.

7. ***Specify a folder name and location.*** InDesign next asks you what you want to name the folder that contains the packaged files and where you want to put it. Just so we're all on the same page, change the folder name to "My Project" and navigate to the *Lesson 12* folder (see Figure 12-28). Then turn on the first three check boxes (some or all of which may already be on), which do the following:

   - The first check box copies all font files required to print the document. The *(Except CJK)* moniker excludes Chinese, Japanese, and Korean fonts, which may contain tens of thousands of characters and weigh in at many megabytes.

   - The next check box copies all imported graphics. In our case, it copies the image files from the *Lesson 09* folder.

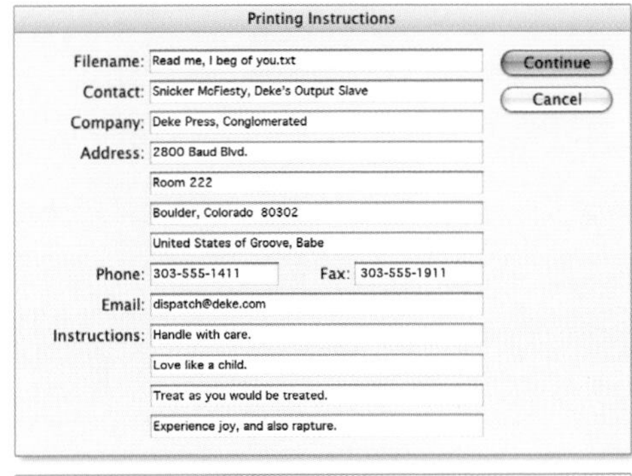

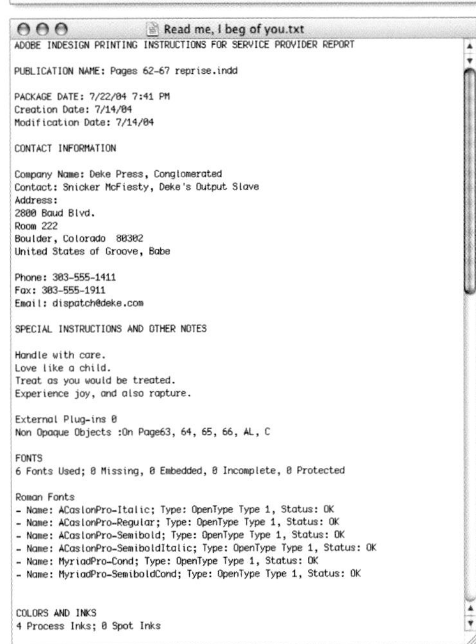

Read me, I beg of you.txt

```
ADOBE INDESIGN PRINTING INSTRUCTIONS FOR SERVICE PROVIDER REPORT

PUBLICATION NAME: Pages 62-67 reprise.indd

PACKAGE DATE: 7/22/04 7:41 PM
Creation Date: 7/14/04
Modification Date: 7/14/04

CONTACT INFORMATION

Company Name: Deke Press, Conglomerated
Contact: Snicker McFiesty, Deke's Output Slave
Address:
2800 Baud Blvd.
Room 222
Boulder, Colorado 80302
United States of Groove, Babe

Phone: 303-555-1411
Fax: 303-555-1911
Email: dispatch@deke.com

SPECIAL INSTRUCTIONS AND OTHER NOTES

Handle with care.
Love like a child.
Treat as you would be treated.
Experience joy, and also rapture.

External Plug-ins 0
Non Opaque Objects :On Page63, 64, 65, 66, AL, C

FONTS
6 Fonts Used; 0 Missing, 0 Embedded, 0 Incomplete, 0 Protected

Roman Fonts
- Name: ACaslonPro-Italic; Type: OpenType Type 1, Status: OK
- Name: ACaslonPro-Regular; Type: OpenType Type 1, Status: OK
- Name: ACaslonPro-Semibold; Type: OpenType Type 1, Status: OK
- Name: ACaslonPro-SemiboldItalic; Type: OpenType Type 1, Status: OK
- Name: MyriadPro-Cond; Type: OpenType Type 1, Status: OK
- Name: MyriadPro-SemiboldCond; Type: OpenType Type 1, Status: OK


COLORS AND INKS
4 Process Inks; 0 Spot Inks
```

Figure 12-27.

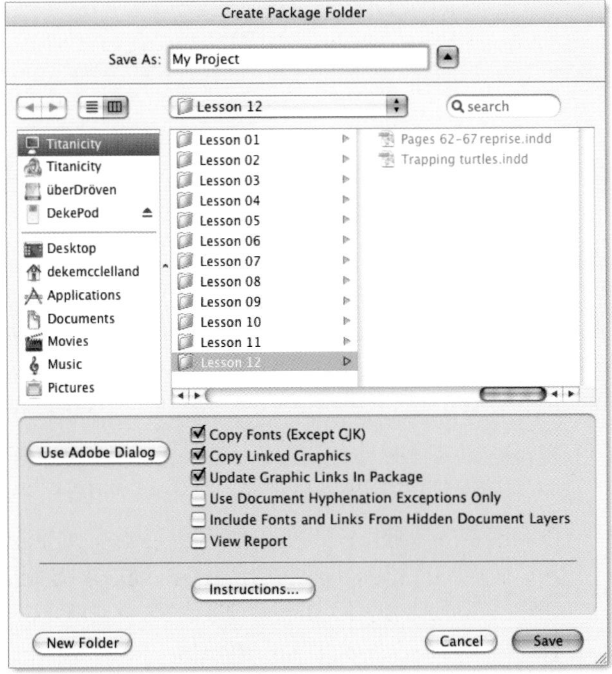

Figure 12-28.

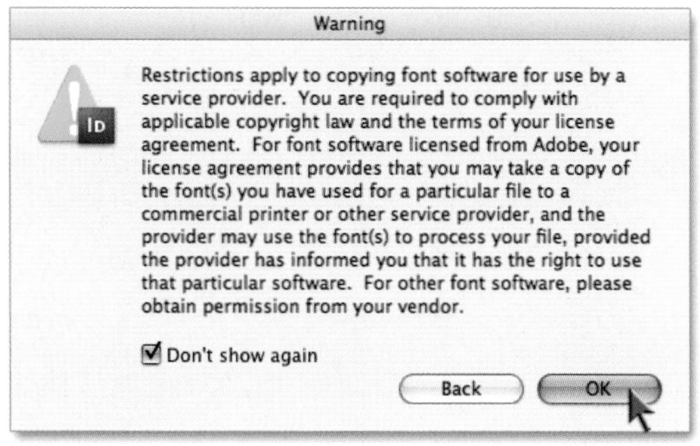

Figure 12-29.

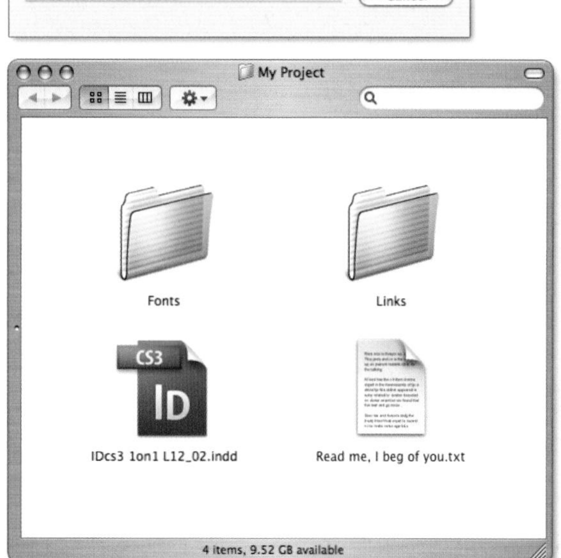

Figure 12-30.

- The third check box links the InDesign document to the graphic files copied by the preceding check box. This option must be on to create a self-contained print job.

When you finish, click **Package** (or **Save** on the Mac) to accept your settings and continue.

8. *Acknowledge the legal statement.* Like all modern contrivances, fonts are copyrighted. And as a font vendor, Adobe is keen to make you aware of this fact. So the first time you copy font files, InDesign displays the legal statement pictured in Figure 12-29. If you're curious about what it says, read it. (Summary: Where Adobe's fonts are concerned, it's okay for you to send the font files to your print house as long as they already have the right to use the fonts. As for the other vendors, your guess is as good as InDesign's.) Assuming you don't want to see the infernal warning again, check **Don't Show Again** and click **OK**.

9. *Examine the packaged folder.* Once again, InDesign flashes a series of progress messages. When the progress bar disappears, the package is complete. Switch from InDesign to the desktop level of your computer. Open the *Lesson 12* folder inside *Lesson Files-IDcs3 1on1*. Then open the *My Project* folder to view the newly packaged items pictured in Figure 12-30:

   - The *Fonts* subfolder contains all typefaces and type styles used in the document.
   - The *Links* subfolder contains the sixteen imported images, both CMYK and RGB.
   - *Pages 62–67 reprise.indd* is a duplicate of the InDesign document that has been saved with all external artwork relinked to the files inside the *Links* subfolder.
   - The remaining document is the instructions file that you created in Step 6. If you didn't include any instructions, delete this file. Otherwise, leave it where it is.

10. *Copy the folder to a jump drive, CD, or other medium.* The files are now ready to hand off to a commercial print house. If I were handing this project off to a local print house, I'd copy the *My Project* folder—which contains about 41MB of files—to a USB jump drive. If the print house were remote, I'd try to avoid shipping costs by uploading the files to a server or FTP site, just as we do with this book. To find out what options are available, consult your friendly print representative.

WHAT DID YOU LEARN?

Match the key concept in the numbered list below with the letter of the phrase that best describes it. Answers appear upside-down at the bottom of the page.

Key Concepts

1. Imagesetter
2. Color separation
3. Halftone cells
4. Composite RGB
5. Misregistration
6. Trapping
7. Spread
8. Overprint Stroke
9. Web-offset lithography
10. Sheetfed press
11. Preflight
12. Package

Descriptions

A. Service bureaus and print houses use this monstrously expensive PostScript device to output pages to film or some other medium before loading the inks and plates onto the press.

B. A check box that mixes the outline of an object printed on one plate with an underlying fill or stroke from another plate; to preview the effect, press Ctrl+Shift+Alt+Y (⌘-Shift-Option-Y on the Mac).

C. This process hunts down all links and fonts contained in a document and collects them inside a single folder, which you can copy to a CD or upload to your print house's FTP site.

D. One of the many passes rendered by an imagesetter when printing a full-color document; each pass receives a different ink.

E. Smaller print runs are better served by this press technology, which outputs to individual sheets of paper.

F. This pesky output problem occurs when paper slips or plates don't line up perfectly during the commercial reproduction process.

G. The art of filling in the tiny gaps between colors that may occur as a result of misregistration.

H. An imagesetter simulates shades of color by assembling printer dots into a grid of these.

I. This press technology prints on continuous rolls of paper and is the most popular choice for magazines, books, and other large print runs.

J. This trapping technique adds an overprinting stroke that matches the fill of a foreground object.

K. This rigorous if occasionally overzealous inspection examines a document's readiness for professional output.

L. When printing to an inkjet printer or other non-PostScript device, this option leaves the printer driver in charge of translating colors.

Answers

1A, 2D, 3H, 4L, 5F, 6G, 7J, 8B, 9I, 10E, 11K, 12C

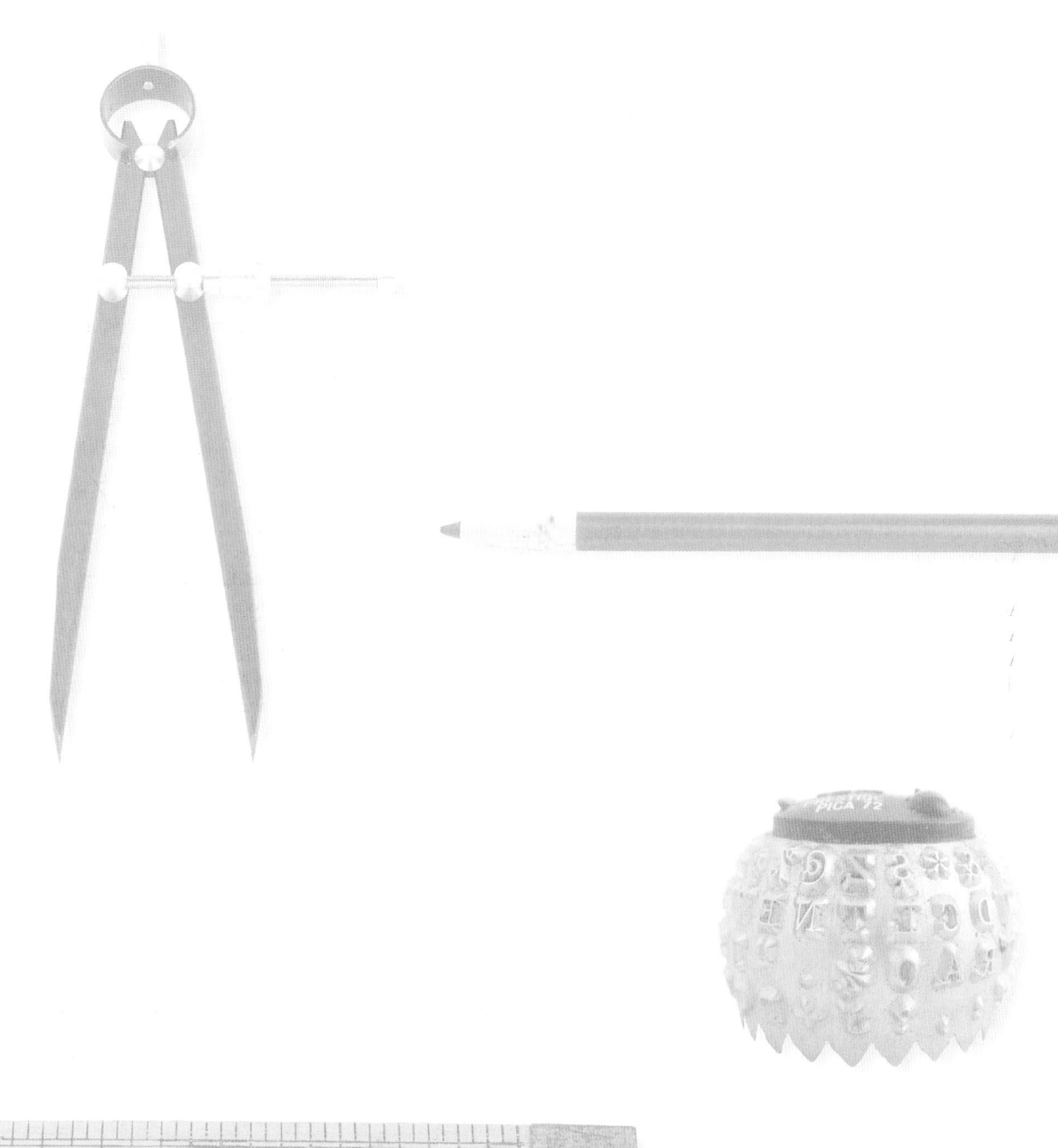
PICA 72

INDEX

D

E

F

L

M

N

O

P

Q

R

S

T

U

V

W

X

Z

THE STORY OF
A MUSICAL LIFE

Da Capo Press Music Reprint Series
General Editor
FREDERICK FREEDMAN
Vassar College

THE STORY OF A MUSICAL LIFE

An Autobiography
by
GEORGE F. ROOT

DA CAPO PRESS • NEW YORK • 1970

A Da Capo Press Reprint Edition

This Da Capo Press edition of
The Story of a Musical Life
is an unabridged republication of the
first edition published in Cincinnati in 1891.

Library of Congress Catalog Card Number 70-126072

SBN 306-70031-X
Published by Da Capo Press
A Division of Plenum Publishing Corporation
227 West 17th Street, New York, N.Y. 10011

Manufactured in the United States of America

THE STORY OF A MUSICAL LIFE

Geo. H. Root

THE STORY

OF

A MUSICAL LIFE.

AN AUTOBIOGRAPHY

BY

GEO. F. ROOT.

CINCINNATI:

PUBLISHED BY THE JOHN CHURCH CO. 74 W. 4TH ST.

——Chicago——
Root & Sons Music Co.
200 Wabash Ave.

——New York——
The John Church Co.
13 East 16th St.

PREFACE.

OCTOBER 1, 1888, was the fiftieth anniversary of my leaving home to commence my musical life. On that occasion we had a family gathering, at which were commenced the series of narrations which have grown into this book.

They were mostly written in 1889, and that will account for the mention of the names of some people who have died since that time.

Special prominence could have been given in this work to the orderly arrangement of such musical statistics and items of musical history as come within its scope, but such a plan would have interfered with my story, as such, so those matters have been allowed to come in as wanted, without reference to their chronological order.

I do not like the appearance of self-praise that I have to assume while recording in this book certain sayings and events which refer to myself and my career. I hope the reader will see that my story would not be complete without them, and on that ground excuse the apparent egotism.

G. F. R.

TABLE OF CONTENTS.

CHAPTER V.

CHAPTER VI.

CHAPTER VII.

CHAPTER VIII.

CHAPTER IX.

CHAPTER X.

CHAPTER XI.

CHAPTER XII.

CHAPTER XIII.

CHAPTER XIV.

CHAPTER XV.

CHAPTER XVI.

CHAPTER XVII.

CHAPTER XVIII.

CHAPTER XIX.

APPENDIX.

MUSIC.

THE STORY OF A MUSICAL LIFE.

CHAPTER I.

1820–1838—BIRTH—LEAVING HOME—HARMONY HALL—FIRST PIANO LESSONS—EARLY MUSICAL CONDITIONS—TWO TUNES FOR PRAYER-MEETING—THE ODEON.

I WAS born in Sheffield, Mass., August 30, 1820, but my father moved to North Reading, not far from Boston, when I was six years old, and there my youth was spent.

I was always very fond of music—not singing at all as a boy, but playing a little upon every musical instrument that came in my way. At thirteen I figured that I could "play a tune" upon as many instruments as I was years old. Such an achievement in the light of to-day looks entirely insignificant, but in our isolated village, and in those days, it was regarded as something rather wonderful. There was a chronic curiosity in the village choir as to what instrument the boy would play upon next.

The dream of my life was to be a musician. I did not know exactly what kind, or how to get started. I thought, perhaps, I could make a beginning as second flute in some theater orchestra. It wasn't reputable, I knew (as people regarded the matter then), and relatives and friends were all opposed to it. Indeed, any line of music, as a business, in those days was looked down upon, especially by the more religious and respectable portion of the community. So I knew I should have to fight my way. I ought to except my mother. It was either an unaccountable faith in my ability to succeed, or so much love in her tender heart that she could not bear to thwart me, and she said, "Go, my son, if you find the opportunity; I'll get along in some way." I knew well what that meant—my father and the brother next younger than myself being both in South America, and six younger children to care for—hard times certain—possibly privation; but I had the hardihood of the inexperienced youngster that I was, and said, "Mother, just let me get a start and you shall never want for anything." I thank the Lord that I was able to make that promise good.

But to go on with my story: During the summer of 1838 a member of Mr. A. N. Johnson's choir in Boston spent a few weeks in our village. She had a great deal to say in praise of her teacher as leader and organist, and of his great success as the conductor of the Musical Education Society, to which she also belonged. She described Harmony Hall, on Tremont Row, where the society met and where Mr. Johnson taught, and enlarged generally upon musical matters in that connection until I thought it would be heaven on earth to be in the midst of such opportunities. I did not see how that could ever happen for me, but it did.

Just after the departure of this much-envied member of a Boston choir, a neighbor (a young man a few years older than myself) invited me to go with him to a little town near Worcester, where, as I afterward ascertained, some negotiations of a particular and very interesting nature to him were pending. These, I am happy to say, terminated to his entire satisfaction.

That journey was to me also a very important event. The only railroad going west from Boston then, ended at Worcester. The hardy traveler who would go farther in that direction must climb hills and descend into valleys and wind along by the streams in the old-fashioned stage-coach. It was my first railroad ride, and the luxury of it, and the wonder of it, I shall never forget.

On our return, it was owing to what then seemed a serious dilemma that I was enabled so soon to go to Boston to live. My friend must be at home on the morning of a certain day. To accomplish that, we must be driven from the place of our visit to Worcester to take an afternoon train to Boston, where we were to be met and taken to North Reading at night. Had that program been carried out I should have gone through Boston without stopping, but in Worcester, where we had an hour to wait, my friend went to attend to some matters in which he did not need my company, and I went to the music store, where I became so much absorbed in the instruments and music that when I came to myself the train was gone. There would not be another until the next morning, and I had no money. I was in great trepidation, but soon bethought myself that my mother had a second cousin, who was a theological student, somewhere there. So I trudged out to the seminary, and fortunately found him. He was very kind—"glad to do anything for a son of cousin Sarah"—so he kept me till morning and then gave me money enough to take me home. It is unaccountable that I did not think at the time of that money as anything to be returned. I suppose I associated it with supper, lodging and breakfast as a matter of hospitality, and soon the whole affair passed from my mind. It was perhaps twenty years afterward, on hearing my mother speak of "Cousin Edwin" and his ministry, that I recalled the event, and then came a realizing sense of my delinquency.

It did not take long to figure double compound interest on the amount he gave me, and send him the money.

On my way to Boston I determined to call on Mr. Johnson at Harmony Hall, and see if, by any possibility, there could be an opening for me there. How well I remember ascending the stairs, and knocking at the door. How well I remember the somewhat astonished countenance of the blonde gentleman who let me in. What he said afterward of that interview, not being very complimentary either to my personal appearance or my modesty, I omit, but he did happen to want some one to stay in the room while he was out—to see to the fires and the general order of the place, to answer questions about his engagements, and to make himself generally useful, and he said I might come. He questioned me as to what I could do. Could I sing? No. Could I play at all upon the piano? No. I had seen the keyboard of piano or organ but a few times in my life, but I could play the flute pretty well, and some other instruments a little. Well, the first thing would be to learn to play the piano, and I could practice while he was out, which was most of the time, as the private lessons he then gave were nearly all at the houses of his pupils. I could board at his house, and he would for the present give me three dollars a week beside. This was munificent. Three dollars was a great deal of money. If I could get fitted out with suitable clothes I could save some of my "salary" from the very start, and I knew well what I wanted to do with it.

I have thought many times since how extraordinary it was in Mr. Johnson to take me as he did, for, from his own representation, I could not have been a very promising subject. I do not understand it now, but am glad to think that I could, and did, in some measure, repay his kindness to a friendless boy in the immediate years which followed.

On my way home from Boston, in the old stage-coach,

after the interview and agreement with Mr. Johnson, I was in another world. The ride in the wonderful cars was nothing to this. That was on iron rails, this was in the golden air. The dusty old towns through which we passed were beautiful as never before; even the mulleins by the wayside were transformed into more gorgeous flowers than ever bloomed in garden or conservatory. How often had I felt cramped in the limited surroundings and opportunities of the old home. How many times I have walked, after the day's work was over, through dreary forest roads, to neighboring towns to exercise my musical powers with some embryo performer like myself, or, late "in the stilly night," as a lone serenader, unknown, unexpected and unchallenged, to breathe my sighs for freedom through the old four-keyed flute. But no more of this. I was going where the air was filled with music, and pent-up desires and ambitions could have unlimited freedom.

There was great excitement when I reached home. I was really going to Boston to study music—must be at my post on the first day of the next month. On the strength of my prospects I borrowed a little money of my grandmother for an outfit, and went around telling the good news to interested and sympathizing neighbors. All met me with good words. "Go ahead!" they said; "we'll lend a hand on the farm if we're needed." They believed in me musically, and as for my mother there was not a person in the town who would not do her a kindness if he had the opportunity.

At last the important first day of October arrived. I wheeled my trunk down the willow lane to the main road, about a quarter of a mile (our place was called "Willow Farm"), to wait for the old stage-coach that lumbered by every morning on its way to the city. An hour passed and no stage. I forget how I found out that it had been taken off—had made its last journey the day before. The new railroad from Lowell to Boston had taken so many of its passengers that it would no longer pay to run it. But I must get to Boston that day. What was I to do? Our nearest neighbor, "Uncle Mike," as everybody called him said: "Why, we'll make that very railroad carry ye there. Old Pete and I'll take ye over to Wilmin'ton, and you'll catch the cars afore night." So Uncle Mike harnessed up and took trunk and me six miles to the new railroad, where, by good fortune, I had not long to wait for a train. Then, with thanks and a good-bye to the old neighbor, I left for aye the old life, and in due time arrived in the city, and at Mr. Johnson's house at the "North End."

The next morning I commenced the duties and pleasures of my new vocation in Harmony Hall, as Mr. Johnson's music-room was called. This place was leased by the Musical Education Society, but Mr. Johnson had the use of it for conducting the society once a week. It was a light, cheerful room, up one flight of stairs; a platform, with a piano on it at one end, and a little curtained office, with a desk, at the other. After being told what my duties in regard to fires and care of room would be, I went with eagerness to the piano for my first lesson. The idea of calling it drudgery—this making musical sounds upon a pianoforte—nothing could be more absurd, as it seemed to me. It was a delight, even though my large, clumsy fingers would go right in the simplest exercises of Hunten's Instruction book only by the most laborious practice. But that was cheerfully given. Every minute when Mr. Johnson was out, or when I was not answering a call at the door, I was at work, and during Mr. Johnson's lessons in the room, while I was out of sight at the curtained desk, I was trying to get some flexibility into my stubborn fingers, while looking over some music-book. I had learned to read the notes of simple music both on treble and base staffs by the various instruments I had played.

When I say I had never sung, I do not mean that I had never used my voice at all in that way. I had occasionally joined in the base of simple church tunes, but was never encouraged by listeners to continue my performances long, or to make them prominent. It was always:—"George, you'd better take your flute." But Mr. Johnson said that if I was going to teach I ought to be able to use my voice correctly, and sing at least enough to give examples of tone and pitch. I dare say he saw then, what I realized after awhile, that I had begun too late to make much of a player upon piano or organ, and that if I developed any gift for teaching, my success must be in singing-classes and other vocal work. So I went at it. I sang in the Musical Education Society and in Mr. Johnson's choir at the Odeon, and often growled a base to my five-finger exercises while practicing.

But here I ought to say something about the condition of music in our part of the country in those days. Not many years before, a singing-school had been held in the old red school-house, where "faw, sol, law, faw, sol, law, me, faw," were the syllables for the scale—where one must find the "*me* note" (seven) to ascertain what key he was singing in, and where some of the old "fuguing tunes," as they were called, were still sung. I well remember how, shortly after, we heard that a new system of teaching music had been introduced into Boston, in which they used a blackboard and sang "do, re, mi," etc., to the scale. But how silly "do" sounded. We thought it smart to say that the man who invented that was a *dough*-head, and how flat were *fa* and *la*, in comparison with the dignified "faw" and "law." Later, however, when some tunes connected with the new movement came, we changed our minds about the man who was at the head of it. Nothing before, so heavenly, had been heard as the melody to "Thus far the Lord hath led me on" (Hebron); and one of the great things in going to Boston was that I should probably see LOWELL MASON.

It is an interesting fact that some music, at every grade, from lowest to highest, has in it that mysterious quality which makes it live, while all the rest fades away and is forgotten. Sometimes I think the more we know the less keen are our perceptions in regard to that divine afflatus. We understand better the construction of the music we hear, but do not feel, as in more unsophisticated states, the thrill of that mysterious life—at least I do not, and I put it forth as a possibly true theory in general, because every tune that produced that enchanting effect upon me then, lives in the hearts of the people now, while those that did not have dropped out of use.

Certain it is, if music writers and publishers could know of every composition whether it had in it that mysterious vitality or not, there would be far less music issued, for but few musical compositions in proportion to the number printed have in them the elements even of a short life.

I worked steadily at my piano lessons, and got on well, considering the obstacles I had to overcome in my grown-up hands. But piano playing was not then what it is now, by a difference that it would be hard to describe. A piano in a country town was a rarity, and a person even in Boston who could play as well as hundreds of young people all over the country now play, would have attracted universal attention.

I think I could not have been practicing more than two weeks before Mr. Johnson started me in the playing of chords by the method that has since been so well known under the name of Johnson's Thorough Base. By this means I was to learn to play Hebron and Ward and Hamburg and Boylston, and all those tunes that had moved me as no music had ever done before. I need not say that I worked with a will, but I remember well that I was in a chronic state of astonishment that my hands would *not* do what I saw so clearly should be done, and that I must play a succession of chords over so many, many times before they would go without a hitch.

It was not long after this that Mr. Johnson said to me one day; "I wish you would learn two of those tunes to play at the Wednesday night prayer-meeting." "What! play for the people to sing?" "Yes; you can do it; you need not play the tune through first; just play the first chord, and then start, and they'll all go with you. It will be all the more sure if you sing the first word or two." "But I shall make some mistakes, I'm afraid." "Well, if you do they won't be noticed." "But I may run against a stump and stop." "Well, they'll go on, and you can catch up at your leisure." Talk about courage! I mean on Mr. Johnson's part. He would take more and greater risks of that sort than any man I ever knew. But he knew I would strain every nerve to accomplish what he wished, and he always said he could rely on my—I think "self-confidence" was the term he used, but there is a much shorter word now coming into our vocabulary which would perhaps have expressed his meaning more forcibly. However, I went through it, and after that, for some months, prepared my two tunes every week for the prayer-meeting.

This church arrangement was peculiar. It was a Congregational church, under the pastoral care of Rev. Wm. M. Rogers, then one of the most popular clergymen of Boston. Its services were held in what had been the Federal St. Theater (corner of Federal and Franklin Streets), but was now called the "Odeon." It was owned or leased by a new organization called the "Boston Academy of Music," and used exclusively by that association and this Congregational church. It had been somewhat remodeled, though it had still the theater look. The stage was fitted with raised seats for a large chorus. There was a large organ at the back, and a conductor's platform in front, occupied on Sundays by the minister's pulpit. Lowell Mason was at the head of the Boston Academy of Music, and the conductor of its large chorus, and George James Webb was the organist, but on Sundays Mr. Johnson was the organist, and his choir the performers. The prayer-meetings were held in a long room over the front entrance, called "The Saloon." I don't think that word was then used at all as the name of a drinking place. It had more the signification of drawing-room or parlor. I don't know how it came to be applied to that little hall, but as I remember the notices, they would sound strangely now:—"The Sunday-school after service in the *saloon;*" "The ladies' meeting Tuesday afternoon in the *saloon;*" "The prayer-meeting Wednesday evening in the *saloon;*" and there we had our choir rehearsals, and later, singing classes, so that in those days that word became connected in my mind with all that was "pure and lovely and of good report," instead of bearing the bad signification which attaches to it now.

CHAPTER II.

1838–1839, BOSTON—MY FIRST PUPIL—A NEW BARGAIN—THE FLUTE CLUB—FIRST VOICE LESSONS—SOME OF THE PROMINENT TEACHERS, AUTHORS, AND CONCERT PERFORMERS OF EARLY DAYS—DAVID AND GOLIATH—SOME REMARKS ABOUT SIMPLE MUSIC—MY FIRST SINGING CLASS—MR. WOODBURY—MY VENERABLE PUPIL FROM MAINE—THE "OLD CORNER BOOKSTORE."

I DO not think it could have been more than six weeks from my beginning with Mr. Johnson that I had another surprise. One day a young man called to inquire about taking lessons upon the piano. He was a mechanic —an apprentice to a jeweler I think. Mr. Johnson asked him if he could play at all. No, he knew nothing about music whatever. Mr. Johnson reflected a moment and then said, as if it were the result of very serious and important deliberation: "I think my assistant here, Mr. Root, would be best adapted to your case." My astonishment was unbounded, but if this young man knew nothing I was a little ahead of him, and it would be a delight to help him over the road I had just traveled. That was my first pupil, and what I lacked in experience I made up in good will and attention. At any rate he was well satisfied, as I had good reason to know afterward. It was not long before others came and inquired for me instead of Mr. Johnson, on account of young Slade's recommendation.

About this time, certainly not more than seven weeks from the beginning of my connection with Mr. Johnson, he proposed a new bargain. The first had not been for any definite time—we were "to see how we liked," as he said, but of course the seeing was wholly on his side. He had now evidently made up his mind, and an agreement was made for a year at a very considerable increase in pay. That I was glad and thankful goes without saying. The news flew to the old farm as fast as Uncle Sam's machinery in those days could take it (there was no dream yet for years of telegraph), and at "Thanksgiving," toward the end of November, when I made my first visit home, we had a happy time, as you may imagine.

About this time Mr. Mason advertised that new members would be admitted to the Boston Academy's Chorus. Those who wished to join must be at a certain place at a certain time, and have their voices and reading ability tested. Mr. Johnson said I had better go; that the Academy's work was more difficult than that of the Musical Education Society, and that the practice would be good for me in every way. I shook in my shoes at the suggestion, but Mr. Johnson's courage was equal to the occasion, and I went. That was my first sight of Lowell Mason, and also of Geo. Jas. Webb, who did the trying of the voices, while Mr. Mason looked on. I passed, and was much surprised when Mr. Mason came to where I was sitting and asked me to join his choir—that famous Bowdoin Street Choir, the like of which has rarely been equaled, in my opinion, in this or any other country. I told him why I could not—that I was with Mr. Johnson, etc., but that invitation settled the voice question in my mind. I was going to sing. Lowell Mason had wanted me in his choir, and that was as good as a warranty that I could succeed.

Meanwhile I did not neglect my flute. I was so well along on that that Mr. Johnson thought something might come of it. So I took some lessons and gave some lessons on that instrument, and some time in the following year I organized a flute club of my pupils and others. There were some pretty good singers in it, and we called it the "Nicholson Flute and Glee Club." "Nicholson's Flute Instructor" was my delight, both for method and music, hence the name. We had music arranged in six parts for our ten flutes. Simon Knaebel, a good orchestra and band musician, I remember, did the arranging. We had marches, quicksteps, waltzes, etc., all simple but popular then. We gave some concerts in the neighboring towns, and on one grand occasion played at some performance in the Odeon, and, what is better, were encored. It was rather absurd to have harmony, the base of which could go no lower than middle C; but it was a novelty, and to us a source of great enjoyment.

One important day, soon after my admission to the Boston Academy's Chorus, Mr. Johnson said I had better take some voice lessons of Mr. Webb; that private voice teaching was very profitable, and he thought I could fit myself to do that work. Mr. Johnson never flinched from what he thought I ought to do. I was glad enough, however, to take lessons of Geo. Jas. Webb, the best vocal teacher in Boston, an elegant organist, an accomplished musician, and a model Christian gentleman. He received me with great kindness, and after trying my voice in various ways, gave me some exercises to work upon. At my next lesson, after I had sung what he had before given me to practice, he looked up with an expression of pleased surprise and said: "Well, Mr. Root, I believe you *will* learn to sing." I replied, "Of course; that is what I fully intend to do." "Ah, but," he responded, "at your first lesson I thought it extremely doubtful whether it would be worth your while to try." Of course he had reference to solo singing, and not to joining with the bases in a chorus, which I could then do fairly well.

My lessons went on with him for months—a year, perhaps, and I came not only to delight in them, but in the friendly atmosphere of his pleasant home. I used always to be glad when I could see his little Mary—four or five years old perhaps; she was so bright and so full of music. Once I remember she came into the teaching room, where I was waiting for my lesson, and said: "Papa will come pretty soon, but I've been to the 'Rainers.'" The Rainers were a family of Swiss Yodlers, the first, I think, to come to this country, and were singing in costume and in their native language their pretty Swiss songs. Everybody went to hear them. "I've been to the Rainers," she went on, as she climbed upon the piano stool, "and wasn't it funny what they said?" Here she piped up with a comical motion of her head, but with accordant tones on the piano:—

Take a piece a yarn, Take a piece a yarn.

Mr. Webb, coming in at that moment, laughed and explained that Mary was very fond of giving her imitation of Simon Rainer's manner and her translation of his German. I thought often of this little incident in after years, while listening to her splendid rendering of "I know that my Redeemer liveth," or some other oratorio classic, and later, while enjoying her gracious hospitality as the wife of Dr. William Mason, in their lovely home in Orange, New Jersey.

Speaking of foreign performers, it was about this time that we heard Herwig, who was, I think, the first really great violinist to come to this country. His harmonic playing—making his violin sound like a fine high wind instrument, caused great astonishment, and filled his houses to overflowing. It was some years afterward that we heard Vieuxtemps, Sivori, and Ole Bull on his first visit, but Artot came soon after Herwig. About that time also came the first pianists that much excelled the best we had heard. Jane Sloman was first, and in a few months Rakemann. They had great success then, but such playing now would be considered only mediocre—I mean as concert playing. Every large city in the country has better players.

But a matter of greater interest to me was the advent in those days of Braham, who had been for a generation the greatest English tenor. He was an old man, and it was said his voice was not what it had been, but no one who then heard him sing "Thou shalt dash them in pieces like a potter's vessel" probably ever heard anything before or since to compare with his tone upon the word "dash"—so large and at the same time so terrifically intense. Marcus Colburn, one of our resident tenors, came the nearest to him in power, and would have made as great a singer probably, if he had had the opportunity, for his voice excelled Braham's in a certain sweet and ringing quality.

That brings to my mind a rather ludicrous scene in which Mr. Colburn and I were chief actors. Mr. Colburn was a giant in size, over six feet in height, and very portly —weighing probably near to three hundred pounds. After I came to be regarded as a promising base singer it came about —I don't remember whether through Mr. Johnson's courage or that of some one else — that I was appointed to sing with Mr. Colburn from Neukomm's Oratorio of "David" the duet between David and Goliath, at a concert at the Odeon. It was absurd enough when we went forward together to begin, for this giant was David, and I, a stripling in comparison to him, was Goliath; but when I had to sing, in the most ponderous tones I could assume, "I can not war with boys," the audience broke out into irrepressible laughter, in which Colburn, who had the most contagious laugh in the world, joined, and that "broke me all up," as they say nowadays. We went through our performance, however, though we did not consider it an unqualified success.

But the most important event to me, in the way of public performances, in those days (1839), was the singing of Henry Russell, an English Jew, who composed and sang "The Ivy Green," "Our Native Song," "A Life on the Ocean Wave," "The Old Sexton," "Wind of the Winter Night," and many other songs of that grade. He had a beautiful baritone voice and great command of the keyboard—played his own accompaniments, gave his concerts entirely alone, and in a year in this country made a fortune. Songs of his, like "The Maniac" and "The Gambler's Wife," were exceedingly pathetic, and always made people cry when he sang them. He looked so pitiful and so sympathetic—"he felt every word," as his listeners would think and say—and yet, when he retired to his dressing room, he was said to have been much amused at the grief of his weeping constituents, showing that he had not really the heart in his song that he appeared to have.

Of course it is a part of the singer's art to assume emotions that he does not really feel, and that is all right if the emotions he assumes are healthful and good. For instance, a man may sing of the delights of a farmer's or a sailor's life in such a way as to make his hearers think he likes that life best, when, in point of fact, he may much prefer some other. But good taste requires that the singer should treat respectfully the emotion he excites.

I was so taken with Russell's songs that I worked harder than ever before to be able to play and sing them as he did. When the accompaniments were too much for me, or the pitch too high, I modified and simplified and transposed, and in a few months had them at my tongue's and fingers' ends, and I have sung certain of them ever since — more than fifty years. While Russell was in this country, Joseph Philip Knight came over and gave us "Rocked in the Cradle of the Deep," which Russell added to his repertoire, and I, with certain modifications, to mine.

This is a good place to speak of the absurdity of saying that simple music keeps the tastes and musical culture of the people down. You might as well say that a person is kept in addition, subtraction, multiplication and division by having around him more examples in elementary arithmetic than he needs. If he is interested in the subject, he'll go on after he has mastered the simpler to that which is more difficult, if the examples or books that he needs are within his reach. You can not keep him in the lower grade by multiplying elementary books. If he is not interested, or is more occupied with other things, he may never go beyond those elementary mathematics which are needed for the common duties of life; but since he can not get higher *without going through them*, it is useless to put that which is higher before him *until they are mastered.*

For a few months Russell's songs filled me with delight. They were just what I needed to help me out of my elementary condition. Before a year was over they had done their work, and I craved something higher. Schubert's songs came next. Is it supposed for an instant that songs of the Russell grade, had they been multiplied a hundred-fold, would have had any effect in keeping me back, if I could get what I wanted? Certainly not; and Schubert's songs, and others of that grade, were, and are, plenty, and more easily obtained, because, being non-copyright, they are free to all publishers. Those not in music, or not so musical naturally, do not get through the elementary state so soon; in fact, many business and professional people, giving very little time or thought to the subject, never get through; they prefer the simpler music to the end of their days. But there is no royal road for such. They must get their fill of the simple—must hear it until they crave something higher—before that which is higher can be of any use to them. It is an axiom that emotional or æsthetic benefit by music can come to a person only through music that he likes. By that alone can he grow musically.

Just as the elementary departments of mathematics are the foundations of that great subject, so tonic, dominant and sub-dominant (the simplest harmonies) are foundations in all music—the highest as well as the lowest. No one derides or looks with contempt upon the elements of mathematics, or upon the thousand ways by which those simpler things are made interesting to the learner. On the contrary, the most learned mathematicians appreciate their importance and delight in their success. So it should be in our science and art; and, without apologizing for what is incorrect or untasteful in the simple music of the day, I say, unhesitatingly, that all correct musical forms, however elementary, find some one to whom they are just what is needed, either for practical or æsthetic benefit, or both. Since, therefore, there are always so many grown-up men and women, learned and strong in other things, who are still in elementary musical states, I keep, ready for use, the simple songs that helped me, and am always glad to sing them where they will do any good.

I do not quite remember where my first "singing-school" was taught, but I think an experimental class was held in Harmony Hall during my first winter (1838–9), under the guise of helping some young ladies and gentlemen to "read notes," who were desirous of joining the Musical Education Society. I had seen Mr. Johnson teach a few times, but I had no orderly method, and my work must have been exceedingly desultory and crude. Something carried me through, however, and the next autumn I had a large class at the North End, which lasted nearly through the winter, and which, on the closing night, made me very proud and happy by the gift of a silver goblet, suitably engraved, and which now occupies a place among my treasures.

About this time I became acquainted with I. B. Woodbury. He was two or three years older than myself, and had commenced his musical work a year or two before me. He had a small room, also, in Tremont Row. He was a most indefatigable student and worker. I think it was during my first winter in Boston that he taught a singing-school in Beverly, and often walked back to Boston, fifteen miles, after nine o'clock at night, to be ready for his lessons in the morning. We who were inured to the hardships of New England country life in those days did not think of such things as they would be thought of now. Mr. Woodbury was very economical, and in a year or two had saved enough money to go to London and take lessons for a few months. Soon after he came home he began to write, and it was not long before he published his first book of church music. He was prosperous and very ambitious. He said to me once, "When I die I shall surprise the world," and he did. He was not strong constitutionally, and the flame burned so fiercely that the end for him came early. It was then found that he had left almost his entire estate to found a Musical Institution—the money to be used for that purpose after it had been invested long enough to produce a certain sum. But the law stepped in and changed this disposition of his fortune in favor of his wife and children. Mr. Woodbury was a genial, pleasant gentleman, and because he wrote only simple music, never was credited (by those who did not know him) with the musical ability and culture that he really possessed.

Speaking of Mr. Woodbury's long walk, and the hardihood of New England country boys, reminds me of what I used sometimes to do to be home on Thanksgiving Day. That was then by far the greatest day of the year in New England, viewed in a social or religious way. Christmas was hardly noticed. Everybody would be at the father's or grandfather's home for "Thanksgiving," if within the bounds of possibility. If I had a singing-school the night before, I would start, after a short sleep, perhaps at two or three o'clock in the morning, and walk homeward, somebody starting from there at the same time in a wagon to meet me, so that I might be at home for breakfast. Once, after my father returned from South America, a young man from North Reading, who was learning a trade in Boston, took this walk with me. We were in the highest state of boyish exhilaration, and when my companion suggested that it would be a good scheme to be on the lookout for the wagon, and, when we heard it, to conceal ourselves and surprise horse and rider in highwayman fashion, I agreed. It was my father whom we met, and it was a lonely part of the road. We sprang out at the horse, and he said: "Hullo! what are ye about?" and immediately added when he saw who we were: "Boys, this would have been anything but a Thanksgiving Day for us if I had been armed as I was in South America." We saw at once how foolish we had been, although, as no one carried arms in those days, no idea of risk came to our minds. We did not tell of our exploit at home, but I have often thought how my father "stood fire," and what crestfallen highwaymen we were for the rest of the journey.

I must not omit to speak of one most interesting pupil that I had during my second year in Harmony Hall. One day I answered a gentle rap at the door, and a large, fine-looking old gentleman entered. He said: "I suppose you will think it strange that an old man like me should wish to learn to play upon the organ, but I have a small one in my house (there were no reed organs then), and if I could learn to play a few of my favorite tunes upon it I should be very glad. I live in Farmington, Maine, but am spending a few days with my son in the city here." I told him that he could not do much in a few days, but that I would do my best for him if he decided to try. He did so decide, and seemed to enjoy the lessons, as I certainly did his acquaintance, although he did not accomplish all he had hoped in the way of learning his favorite tunes. He was a typical New Englander, of the best kind of those days—one who had lived a long, blameless life, practicing all the virtues of the Puritans without their hardness. His quaint, shrewd remarks were a constant source of pleasure and benefit, for they were from the "innocence of wisdom."

I mention this circumstance, first, because this lovely old gentleman was the father of the brothers Abbott, the oldest of whom was Jacob Abbott, the author of "The Young Christian" and "The Corner Stone," and later of the "Rollo" books, and grandfather of Dr. Lyman Abbott, the present pastor of Plymouth Church, Brooklyn, and editor of the *Christian Union*, and of Benjamin V. and Austin Abbott, distinguished lawyers and legal authors in New York City. I also mention this circumstance because it led to an important change in my life and prospects four years later.

I must not omit to speak of the "Old Corner Bookstore," which still stands at the corner of School and Washington Streets. It was a bookstore then as now, only at that time, on one side, with one counter, was the sheet-music and music-book establishment of "Parker & Ditson." I went there often for music, and was often waited upon by the handsome, dark-eyed junior partner of the concern—the man who then was making the beginning of what is now one of the largest music houses in the world.

CHAPTER III.

1840–1844, BOSTON—PARTNERSHIP—FIRST EFFORTS AS ORGANIST AND CHOIR LEADER—THE FIRST TEACHING OF MUSIC IN PUBLIC SCHOOLS—THE TEACHERS' CLASS OF THE BOSTON ACADEMY OF MUSIC AND MY FIRST EFFORTS AT VOCAL TRAINING IN CLASSES—THE OLD MARLBORO' AND MY UNINTENTIONAL CRITIC—BOWDOIN ST. CHOIR AND MY INTENTIONAL CRITIC—BOSTON'S FIRST BOAT CLUB—CALL TO NEW YORK.

A GREAT change for me, in fact for both of us, took place before my first year's agreement with Mr. Johnson was out. He proposed a partnership for five years, in which he should have two-thirds and I one-third of what we both should earn, he to have the privilege of spending one of the years in Germany, the division of profits to be the same during his absence. I agreed, and the plan was carried out, and now I can not be quite sure of the dates of certain things, for the Chicago fire destroyed my records of those days, and of many years after. But I shall be near enough for the purposes of this story.

It was not long after our partnership agreement (probably about 1840) that Mr. Johnson was called to take charge of the choir and play the organ in Park Street Church—the first church then in point of size and importance in the Congregational denomination of the city. I had long before commenced my organ performances by playing the "last tune" at the Odeon services, in which all the people joined, and which was always well known and simple, and then, as soon as Mr. Johnson's courage was equal to it, I supplied an organist's place for six months at Mr. Buddington's church in Charlestown, just across the bridge. This was my first organ engagement. Mr. Johnson still had the choir at Mr. Rogers' church, and now was to play half a day at each place, I playing the other half. Whether the Odeon church (the Central Congregational) had yet moved to its new edifice in Winter street, built near the spot where the Music Hall now stands, I am not certain; but if not yet, it was accomplished soon after. Then all went smoothly in regard to the two choirs—they were near neighbors and often met together for general practice. There were about thirty voices in each choir.

Mr. Johnson had had a rigid business training in a large hardware store in Boston before he made music his entire occupation, and always had the idea of making ours a business establishment, modeled strictly on business principles. I was his first "apprentice;" I became afterward "confidential clerk," and later, partner, and he would now have others coming along in the same way. So, soon after the arrangement with the Park Street Church, he decided to give up Harmony Hall and take three rooms in the fine basement of that church facing the Common. I remonstrated gently, for the new rooms would cost us $600 a year, and $600 then was as much for most purposes as twice that sum would be now. But he said we could there have a fine sign out; that we could raise our prices, take a new student or two, and increase the business generally, enough to more than pay the extra expense. We certainly did have our hands full, but we probably should have had that at the old place. Nothing, however, could be more convenient for our purposes than those rooms, and the outlook under the great trees of the Common was most picturesque and beautiful.

About the time I went to Boston, Lowell Mason told the public school authorities of the city that he believed vocal music could be successfully taught in the schools as a regular branch of education, and that if they would allow him he would teach in one or two for a year without pay, to show that it could be done. Music in public schools was then an unheard-of thing in this country, but Mr. Mason's experiment was tried, and it resulted in the introduction of music into the entire school system of the city, with Mr. Mason for musical superintendent. The first year Mr. Mason and Mr. J. C. Woodman (of whom I will speak more at length later) taught in all the schools. The second year Mr. Mason employed Mr. Johnson and myself to help, and taught less himself. I taught in five of the schools, and I think Mr. Johnson had the same number. A course was marked out which took a year, each school receiving two half-hour lessons a week.

One of my schools was on Fort Hill, an elevation, as I remember it, of eighty or a hundred feet above the surrounding houses. I had no occasion to go into that part of the city for many years after I left it, and not very long ago, when I thought I would climb the old hill again, not a vestige of it remained. It was as flat all about there as Chicago. But when I meet Mr. Haines, the partner and now practical head of the great Ditson establishment, it is the same face that used always to give me a friendly greeting from behind his desk at the Mason street school, when I appeared there for the singing lesson; so of a distinguished banker in Cincinnati whom I occasionally see; and a successful Chicago merchant who is a near neighbor—all were boys in the Mason street school.

If my getting on so fast in a city like Boston seems unaccountable, I must explain again that music was in a very different condition then from what it is now. It was just emerging from the florid but crude melodies and the imperfect harmonies of the older time. Lowell Mason had but just commenced what proved to be a revolution in the "plain song" of the church and of the people, and his methods of teaching the elementary principles of music were so much better and so much more attractive than anything that had before been seen that those who were early in the field had very great advantage. We had no competition and were sought for on every hand. To be sure there were organists then who would be considered fine organists now, but such very moderate players as we were, got on, because our choirs produced the new kind of simple, sweet music that went to the hearts of the people and the people connected the organ, little as there was in the playing, with the general effect they so much enjoyed. It was very much like the success of an early dealer in pianos in Chicago, who used to sell a great number of instruments by sitting down to them and singing a song while playing two or three simple chords. It must be a fine piano to be connected with such soul-stirring music.

One of the things that spurred me up from the first to do my best to succeed was the consciousness that if my father should return from South America and find my experiment a failure—having left mother and the children as I did, that I should not feel entirely comfortable in the paternal society, for his own effort to better the family fortunes had not been very successful. But during my second year with Mr. Johnson he returned and no fault was found. On the contrary, he went back to the old farm and enjoyed my prosperity with the rest of us. My brother (E. T. Root, who, years afterward, with C. M. Cady, started the firm of Root & Cady in Chicago) came home from South America, where he had gone for his health, a few months before my father, and soon found a situation in Boston where he could devote a part of his time to music. It was not long, however, before he decided to make music his business, as I had done. So we sent a piano up to the old red house, and he went home and gave himself wholly to practice. He was always the singer of the family. Before his voice changed it was a beautiful soprano, and after the change a smooth, sympathetic tenor; but more of that later. My sisters, too, practiced whenever they could get at the piano, and all played and sang, much to their enjoyment and advantage in following years. Indeed, my youngest sister, who was a baby when I left home, has been for some years one of the best and most successful voice teachers in the profession, as all the musical people of Chicago will testify.

It was perhaps the year before I went to Boston that Lowell Mason and Geo. Jas. Webb held the first "Musical Convention," but they did not call the gathering by that name. It was for some years "The Teachers' Class of the Boston Academy of Music." Its sessions continued for ten days, and brought together teachers of music and choir leaders from city and country. These being mostly men, the Academy's chorus, Mr. Mason's choir and other singers of the city joined for the afternoon and evening practice and performances. The mornings were spent by Mr. Mason in showing his new method of teaching and in giving his ideas of church music; the afternoons with Mr. Webb in part-song, glee and madrigal singing, and in the evening, when all could come, the choruses of the great masters were sung, Mr. Mason conducting and Mr. Webb accompanying upon the organ. Mr. Mason was a strong conductor and an intelligent interpreter of those great works, and Mr. Webb, the most refined and delightful teacher of the English glee and madrigal that I have ever known.

It was at the Teachers' Class of 1841, I think, that I began to figure as an instructor in that kind of work. It came about in this way: — I noticed that the voices, especially the bases, were, many of them, pinched and hard, and I thought I would see if I could help them. There had been no voice training in classes then; that work had been done entirely by private instruction. So, in pursuance of my plan, I told some of the men of the class privately to meet me during the noon recess in the saloon (the small hall of the Odeon of which I have spoken) and we would see if our voices were all right. Singers, especially those in elementary states, are always interested in that subject, so the proposition met with a hearty response. There were perhaps twenty present at that first meeting. I took each one separately, all the rest looking on or occasionally joining, and sang a tone with him either an octave higher or an octave lower, and showed him and all how much more resonance and blending there was when the tone was produced with the throat more open, and when he could not readily change from the way to which he had been accustomed, I devised such means as I could think of to help him, much to the interest of the class and sometimes to their great amusement. When I got through there was a good deal of favorable excitement in the little company. "This is what we want. Can't we have this every day?" was heard on all sides. I said I was willing enough, but they would have to go to Mr. Mason about it; we certainly could not meet at this time every day, for some of us had then lost our dinners.

When the class came together for Mr. Webb's exercise in the afternoon, these men gathered about Mr. Mason and told him what they wanted. They were so close to him, and so clamorous I remember, that he jumped up into a chair, and when he fully understood the situation, announced that the last hour of the morning would be devoted to vocal training under the instruction of Mr. Root. This was my first appearance in vocal training class-work. Of course I could not hear voices alone so much after this as I had done in the smaller and more informal gathering, but it was better than nothing, and as there was no previous work of the kind to compare it with, it was popular, and continued as one of the features of teachers' classes and conventions during my long connection with Mr. Mason, and has been an integral part of normals and conventions ever since.

It may be worth mentioning that in the Spring of my third year in Boston the first Boat Club of that city was formed. It consisted of twenty-four young men (two crews), mostly members of Park Street and Winter Street Churches. We had a boat house on Beacon street, where now are magnificent residences, and used often to row up near to the Common where the Public Garden now is. All was open water where Commonwealth avenue and those finest buildings of Boston now are; the only obstructions were the railroads on piles and bridges that ran across the back bay. There was then, as to-day, the "mill dam," and the long bridge to Cambridge, and the bridges to Charlestown, to pass, when we wanted to row down the harbor. Ours was a ten-oared boat that had belonged to the Yale College Club at New Haven. We named it the "Shawmut" (the old Indian name for Boston), and our club was called the "Shawmut Boat Club." There was room enough in the boat for six guests, and in her we had many pleasant excursions up the rivers and down among the islands of the harbor, and much delight and advantage from the open air and the rowing. I take pleasure in recalling that I was the first president of the club.

After everything was well under way at the Park Street and Winter Street Churches (about 1841), and all my time was occupied in teaching, Mr. Johnson went to Germany. During his absence I taught both choirs, and Mr. S. A. Bancroft, who had taken some lessons from us, and who afterward became one of the prominent organists of Boston, played the "other half-day." I now took up my quarters at the Marlboro' Hotel, on Washington street, opposite the head of Franklin street. This was a temperance and religious house, our excellent landlord, Mr. Nathaniel Rogers, conducting family prayers in the public parlor every morning. Church and temperance people from all over the country gathered there, and I made many valuable acquaintances from among them during the two years that I was one of the family. One friend was made in a rather curious way. I was standing at one of the parlor windows, looking down Franklin street one Sunday afternoon after service, observing the people pouring up from the principal Catholic church, which was then on Franklin near Federal street, and talking with some of my young fellow-boarders, when a gentleman joined us and asked where all the people were coming from. I answered him, and then he asked about other churches of the city, and, finding I could tell him what he wanted to know, he began to ask about the music of the different denominations and then about the organists of the city. Presently he said, "I was at Park Street Church this afternoon, and I found it there as almost everywhere—the organist seemed to think the organ was everything. He played so loud that the voices of the choir were almost drowned." Here my companions, who stood about, became suddenly interested and glanced mischievously at each other and at me. I replied that in the summer it was often the case in chorus choirs that the leading voices were away and the organist had to play louder than he liked, to bolster up the others. He did not seem to think that was a very good excuse, and soon came the question I dreaded: "Do you know who the organist is at Park Street Church?" If my mischievous companions had not been there I should have spared him and myself in some way, but as it was I could not flinch, and answered that I was the individual. He was a good deal embarrassed, but I helped him out by saying that the reasons

I had given were the real ones in my case, and that if he would come and hear us at our best he would not have to find that fault with the accompaniment. It turned out that he was a lawyer from Troy, very fond of music and something of an organist. He seemed to appreciate my efforts to relieve his embarrassment, and the interview terminated in a very pleasant way. The next day we went to see some of the fine organs of the city, and two or three years afterward, when Messrs. Mason and Webb held a musical convention in Troy, in which I did my usual voice work, this gentleman was an interested and helpful friend to us throughout the session. But this incident taught me a lesson in regard to saying unpleasant things about a person unless I know to whom I am talking.

In due time Mr. Johnson returned. He had studied harmony a year or more under Schneider von Wartensee, at Frankfort, and once when he went for his lesson had heard Mendelssohn play one of his new compositions to the old harmonist. I was much impressed with Mr. Johnson's description of the way the old man said "schön" at the close of the performance, and of Mendelssohn's pleasure at the approval of the man who almost never spoke a word of praise. I do not remember anything very eventful in our affairs for a while after Mr. Johnson's return.

Mr. Mason used occasionally to call at our rooms, sometimes leading a small boy who was then practicing his first lessons upon the piano. That boy was his son William, the now well-known and distinguished pianist and composer, and the strong and true friend of musical education in this country.

Mr. Jacob Abbott used to stop at the "Marlboro" when he came into the city, and I remember once taking him out for a boat ride in the "Shawmut." He was greatly interested in the working of the boat, and especially in the nautical terms employed in directing the ten oarsmen and the bowman. We went through all the maneuvers we knew for his especial benefit. All of these appear in "Uncle George's" directions to Rollo and the boys on the formation of their boat club, in one of the "Rollo Books" published not long after.

Something less than a year remained of my engagement with Mr. Johnson when a change took place in our church matters. For some reason Mr. Mason decided that he would rather be at Winter Street (Central) Church, and what he wished was generally accomplished in those days, so it was arranged that he should come there where Mr. Johnson and I had had charge, and that I should go to Bowdoin street, Mr. Johnson remaining at Park street. It was hard for me to follow Mr. Mason and his magnificent choir with any hope of success, but all the people who were interested realized my difficulty and were very considerate and kind. If there were complaints or unpleasant comparisons they never came to my ears. It was thought best that my headquarters should be Bowdoin street, the convenient rooms that Mr. Mason had used for teaching being placed at my disposal, so I made an amicable arrangement with Mr. Johnson for the balance of my five years' agreement and commenced on my own account. Most of Mr. Mason's choir went with him. Of those who remained my memory dwells most upon one of whom I have often thought since that he denied himself the advantages and enjoyment of his place in the best choir in the country to help me in my difficult undertaking, but his way was so peculiar (so good in some respects) that I mention it here. He was one of Mr. Mason's best base singers, both in the Academy's chorus and in the choir, considerably older than myself, a prosperous business man, prominent in the church and in the Sunday-school, opinionated, decided and outspoken on every question in which he took an interest, but with clear-cut ideas of subordination which had been intensified by his long course of training under the best musical disciplinarian that this country has ever seen. I did not know all this then, although I had been acquainted with him for two or three years, so was in some anxiety when I learned that he was going to stay at Bowdoin street, lest I might find it difficult to be master of the situation. It was with considerable trepidation that I went to the first rehearsal, but instead of greeting me in his outspoken way or patronizing me as I feared he would, my friend was seated in his place, not saying a word to any one. It was time to begin, but I had been delayed by one thing and another and was a little behind time in starting. I knew how exact everything had been there, and thought that perhaps Mr. Benson might take me to task on the spot, but not a word did he say, and during the evening, when I appealed to him on some musical point, or asked him some questions concerning their customs, his answers, given with an almost timid, downcast look, were in a subdued and most respectful tone of voice. To say that I was astonished is to put it mildly. Could this be the man who, although kind enough, had always treated me in his bluff way like a boy? But before the evening was out I had a glimmering of his purpose, and after all were gone I was not left in the least doubt. First he looked carefully around to see that no one was in sight or hearing, and then went through a list of my shortcomings in his off-hand, decided way. First, I was behind time in beginning—how was I to expect promptness on the part of the choir if I was not prompt myself?—then there was this fault and that fault in the singing that I did not correct; and he did not believe my making the choir laugh now and then would wear well in the long run, etc. I have often been thankful that I did not resent these criticisms, for, although I did not always take his advice, I received much help from him in the months that followed, and his personal example of subordination and ready obedience in the choir was invaluable in getting it into order.

After I had been at Bowdoin street a few months, Mr. Jacob Abbott, on one of his visits to Boston, asked if he could go with me to one of my class singing lessons. Yes, he could go to one of the public school lessons or to an evening class of ladies and gentlemen. I think he went to both, but remember particularly his visit to the evening class. I knew that he was a great educator, and that his "Mt. Vernon School for Young Ladies" in Boston had been famous a few years before. Mr. Mason taught in it (before the public school work began), and, when one of the young ladies died, composed a tune for the hymn "Sister, Thou wast Mild and Lovely," which was written for the occasion, and called it "Mt. Vernon." I think both hymn and tune are well known now. I was very glad when Mr. Abbott seemed pleased with my classes and my teaching, but had no idea what that approval would lead to. I found out soon after, however. He and his brothers, John S. C., Gorham and Charles, had just started a young ladies' school in New York City, and he wrote them that he thought he had found the teacher they wanted for the music of their institution. Upon their answering, Mr. Jacob spoke to me on the subject of going there. I hesitated; I was doing well, had a large circle of good friends, was near my old home, etc., but Mr. Abbott said: "There is a great field in New York—nothing like Mr. Mason's work and yours has been done there. Here Mr. Mason and Mr. Webb are at the head, and you must for a long time occupy a subordinate place. There you will have a clear field, and I think you can sustain yourself in it. We want such work as you can do in our school, and we think other institutions will want the same when they know what it is." He offered a generous price for a daily class lesson five days in the week, I to have the entire amount I could make from private instruction. He thought, also, that at Mercer Street Church—Dr. Skinner's—where he attended church, they were considering a change, and he believed they would like our kind of large choir. After talking with the folks at home and my good friends in Boston about the matter, I finally said: "If the church position can be secured, I will go." "Well, come and stay a few days with us, and let the people see and hear you, and we believe it will be brought about." I went, gave a lesson or two to the young ladies in class assembled, talked with the church people, played the organ a little, and, at a company assembled at Mr. Abbott's for the purpose, sang my repertoire of songs from Russell's "Ivy Green" to Schubert's "Wanderer." The next day the matter was settled for church and school, and I went back to Boston to arrange for a speedy commencement of my work in the great city of New York. It was some time in 1844 that I left Boston for my new field of labor.

CHAPTER IV.

1844–1847. NEW YORK—ABBOTT'S SCHOOL FOR YOUNG LADIES—RUTGERS FEMALE INSTITUTE—MISS HAINES' SCHOOL—THE UNION THEOLOGICAL SEMINARY—THE NEW YORK INSTITUTION FOR THE BLIND AND THE MERCER ST. PRESBYTERIAN CHURCH—MY MARRIAGE—MY QUARTET AND PERFORMANCE AT THE PHILHARMONIC—SUMMER CONVENTION WORK WITH MESSRS. MASON AND WEBB—MR. JACOB ABBOTT'S ADVICE ABOUT THE WAY TO KEEP A DIARY.

ABBOTT'S school for young ladies at that time was in one of the fine houses in the white marble row in Lafayette Place, New York, spacious and convenient beyond anything I had before seen. I found the work delightful. Our methods were new, as Mr. Abbott had said they would be, and no one having made class teaching and singing tedious and unpopular in the school it was not difficult to arouse and keep up an interest in the lessons. We had frequent visitors—parents and friends of the young ladies, and other persons interested in seeing the new work, and later on in hearing the pleasant part-singing. This singing in parts came along astonishingly soon, for three-quarters of an hour every school day with those bright, interested girls was very different from the two half hours a week that I had been accustomed to in the Public Schools of Boston.

The work had been going on but a few weeks when I observed one day a large, benignant-looking old gentleman, accompanied by two younger men, looking on and apparently taking an unusual interest in the lesson I was giving. This was Dr. Isaac Ferris, then pastor of Rutgers Street

Church, and President of the Board of Trustees of Rutgers Female Institute, and afterward Chancellor of the New York University, and two of the Rutgers Institute trustees. They came to see if the new Yankee music teacher would do for their celebrated old Knickerbocker institution, of which Prof. Charles E. West, LL. D., was then Principal. The result was that I soon added a daily lesson at Rutgers to my work. This institution then occupied a large, commodious building on Madison street, which had been erected for its use. Here I met four hundred girls and young ladies five days in the week, giving three-quarters of an hour at each session. Of my ten years' work in this institution I shall have frequent occasion to speak, as my story goes on.

My duties at Mercer Street Church commenced very soon after my arrival in New York. The chapel of the church was just back of the main building, and facing on Greene street. Here were lecture room and Sunday-school rooms; and over the main entrance a fine octagonal room, which had been especially prepared as a study for the pastor, but Dr. Skinner preferred his home study, which was next door, and this most convenient room for my purposes was turned over to me. I met the choir every Saturday night in the lecture room, but heard individual voices and gave some private lessons in this smaller room, which was my pleasant musical home during my entire New York life.

I remember well my first lesson at a pupil's home in New York. She was one of the young ladies of the Abbott School, and lived on University Place near Twelfth street. I mention it because it will seem strange to those who know New York now, that this point should even then have been so far "up town." I was a few minutes too early when I reached the house, and thought I would walk on to an opening I saw ahead at Fourteenth street. It was rough ground where Union Square now is, and only scattered houses and blocks around and beyond. A further showing of the great change in New York since those days is seen in the fact that Miss Haines' celebrated School for Young Ladies, in which I commenced teaching soon after, was then on Chambers street near Broadway. It was some years after that that Mason Brothers moved from Park Row to Duane street, because they needed larger quarters, and could get a large building there at a very low rent, because it was so far up town, and so near the residence portion of the city. The business sagacity of the house was, however, shown there as it was in many other "moves" in following years. They had a long lease, and sold the balance of it for a good sized fortune after they had occupied the place two or three years.

In my choir were some students of the Union Theological Seminary, then near by, on University Place, between Eighth street and Waverly Place. Two of the names, Jessup and Harding, are known to all persons interested in foreign missions, those men having been at the head of missionary work in India for many years. In due time it was brought about that I should give two lessons a week to the students in the Seminary, and the year after I commenced daily class lessons in the New York State Institution for the Blind. This establishment occupied a large, fine building facing Ninth avenue, and owned the entire block of ground between Thirty-second and Thirty-third streets, and Eighth and Ninth avenues, then far up town. In walking over from Twenty-fourth street and Fourth avenue, as I sometimes did, I crossed corn and potato fields, and remember occasionally being much disgusted at soiling my clean shoes in a muddy ditch where Madison Square now is.

Within six weeks after the commencement of my work in New York I was fully occupied. I had not all the class teaching then that came to me afterward, but all my spare time was filled with private lessons. As the class-work increased I turned the private lessons over to others.

In Mr. Mason's choir in Boston were several members of a very musical family by the name of Woodman. One of the sons, Mr. J. C. Woodman, had a fine baritone voice, and was one of the soloists in the Boston Academy of Music. He was a teacher of music, and, as I have mentioned, was Mr. Mason's first assistant in the introduction of music into the Public Schools of Boston. He was also a good composer and organist. He is the author of "State Street," which, according to the law of "the survival of the fittest," has come down to us with the tunes which are still the standards in our churches where worship, and not musical display, is the object. His son, R. Huntington Woodman, of Brooklyn, N. Y., is now one of the most promising young organists of this or any other country, having recently received endorsements to that effect from the highest musical authorities of London and Paris, where he played in 1888.

Within a year after I went to New York (in August, 1845) I married J. C. Woodman's sister, Mary Olive. She was an accomplished singer, and if my children inherit musical qualities they get quite as much from her side of the house as from mine.

During my first winter at Mercer Street Church I often said to the officers of the church that I could make the choir much better if they would have the key-board of the organ brought out to the front of the gallery so that the choir could be before me (between me and the organ), instead of behind me while I was playing—that my voice would help more, and my directions be better understood and observed, if I could see all the choir and they could see me. I also suggested that while they were about it they might make some much-needed improvement in the organ itself. This was done the next summer. A judicious expenditure of two thousand dollars made a great change in the fine old instrument. I was married during the vacation, and when I returned and put the new soprano and the other leading voices in front of me, with the remaining members of the choir, thirty or forty in number, at their sides, but all in sight, I felt like a king upon his throne, certain of his ability to control and take care of his entire kingdom.

And now my sisters came along, one after another, and went to school either at Rutgers or Abbott's, and under greater advantages pursued their musical studies. My brother, of whom I have previously spoken, and Mr. Henry T. Lincoln, a noble base, who began his musical career in my first singing school at the "North End" in Boston, in '39, also came, both to sing in my choir and to assist me in my teaching. A little later my youngest brother, William A. Root, also came, and went to a commercial school and then into a business office. One of my sisters had an excellent contralto voice, and we now had a well-balanced home quartet—wife, sister, brother and self, and adding Mr. Lincoln, a good quintet. We took great delight in practicing some of the Mendelssohn part-songs, then comparatively new, and such old madrigals and glees as were set for soprano, alto, tenor, baritone and base. William Mason, then a very young man, had written a serenade, entitled "Slumber Sweetly, Dearest," that we greatly delighted in. (See page 228.)

After a while we found we were singing with a balance and blending sometimes heard in very simple music by such singers as the Hutchinson family (then in the zenith of their success), but rarely if ever (in our experience) in music of a higher grade, and this encouraged me to strive for the highest perfection possible in every point that I could think of for my quartet. In one of our summer vacations we all went to the old home in North Reading, and practiced together every day for six weeks—some days hours at a time on a repertoire of about five numbers. At last I, who was the leader, had no more to think of the others while we were singing together than if I had been singing alone. I could carry out every conception I had in the way of expression —increasing, diminishing, accelerating or retarding, sudden attack or delicate shading, with the utmost freedom, being sure that all would go exactly with me. I had for some time been feeling that a musical demonstration might have to be made in New York, and on their own ground, musically, to some of the chronic contemners of simple music, and of our New England way of teaching it. I knew that as soloists none of us would be regarded as anything more than mediocre, but I believed that as a quartet, with the work we had done, we should at least close their mouths as to our musical competency.

Fortunately, at the previous Commencement of the Rutgers Female Institute, Theodor Eisfeld, the then conductor of the New York Philharmonic Society—the most important musical association in the country—was one of a committee of three to examine the singing class. He pronounced the work good, and so reported. So, soon after the autumn work commenced, I asked Mr. Eisfeld to come and hear us sing a quartet. He was evidently not at all elated by the musical prospect before him, but he was good-natured and came. We began with Mendelssohn's "Hunting Song." Perhaps it was because of his surprise, but his praises were extravagant; so much so that I will not repeat them here. We sang other quartets at his request, and then came the invitation that I had been working for: "Will you sing two numbers at the next Philharmonic concert?" "Oh, yes, with pleasure," and we did. We sang the "Hunting Song" and Wm. Mason's "Serenade." We were somewhat abashed on that occasion at the first sound of our voices—it was such a musical atmosphere as we had never been in before as performers, but we soon pulled ourselves together, and when at the end of the first quartet the musicians of the orchestra laid down their instruments and joined the audience in hearty applause we knew our object had been accomplished. The "Serenade" was encored, and the next day the papers said only pleasant things of our performances. We heard nothing more, in a disagreeable way, about the Yankee singing master. We had passed the ordeal successfully at the highest musical tribunal, and that ended the matter. From that time on I had the good will and friendship of the best musicians in New York, to the end of my stay in that city.

The summer vacations in New York were longer than those of Boston, so I could continue my connection with the great Teachers' Classes of the Boston Academy of Music and of similar gatherings under the direction of Messrs. Mason and Webb in other parts of the country. This was from 1845 onward. It was also a great delight to go with Mr. Mason, when I could, to the day school Teachers' Institutes, which were conducted by Horace Mann and other great educators of that day. They prized Mr. Mason's lessons exceedingly. Mr. Mann said he would walk fifty miles to see Mr. Mason teach if he could not otherwise have that advantage.

That work helped me greatly, for there the principles of teaching as an art were more clearly set forth than they were in our musical work. Once, I remember, at an Institute in Chelsea near Boston I had the pleasure of seeing and hearing Louis Agassiz, the great naturalist—the man who never forgot anything that he had once seen from a beetle to a human being. He was one of the model teachers on that occasion, and it was beautiful to see the facility and accuracy with which he drew upon the blackboard every kind of insect of which he spoke, and most interesting and instructive to listen to his clear Pestalozzian teaching in regard to them. I met him but for a moment as a hundred others did at that time, but many years after, on being presented to him in a literary gathering in Chicago, he said, "Ah, I have met you before—at an Institute in Chelsea, I think." This is mentioned only to illustrate one faculty possessed by that great man, the extent of which may not be generally known.

Rochester, N. Y., was a favorite place for a week or ten days' musical convention right after the Boston meeting. The vocal training class had succeeded so well that they decided to try harmony, and Mr. Johnson went along for that. I remember one lovely summer day when we were thirty or forty miles from Auburn on our way tc Rochester, that we found ourselves almost the only occupants of a large car. The windows were open to the sweet air of the harvest fields and we were enjoying to the full the change from the hot and dusty city to this lovely country. Presently at a station an hour or so from Auburn, fifteen or twenty young ladies, evidently all acquainted with each other, entered, and seated themselves around us. They were in an unusually merry mood and after awhile began to sing. Their selections were all from the Boston Glee Book, by Messrs. Mason and Webb, and were sung from memory. We also knew every piece, and I felt inclined to join, but Mr. Mason looked dignified, and Mr. Webb, I feared, might not think it quite proper, so I kept silent, but when they began Mornington's Glee, "Here in cool grot," Mr. Mason and I evidently thought of the same thing at the same time—"what will they do when that bit of base solo comes in?" A glance from him was sufficient, and when the time came I supplied it:—"Nor yet for artful strains we call," then Mr. Johnson joined, and, I think, the older gentlemen assisted, so that before the glee was through there was quite a little chorus effect. The young ladies were evidently astonished, but as evidently pleased. They said nothing to us, nor we to them, but went on singing, and we continued to supply some tenor and base. At last Mr. Johnson said to the young lady nearest to him, "Do you know who those two gentlemen are?" She answered that she did not. "Well, they are Lowell Mason and George James Webb, the authors of the book you have been singing from." That was to her a tremendous piece of information. The young singers of the country then regarded those two men as most exalted beings. Almost the only books used were theirs, and their influence and fame were unbounded. The word flew from one to another and not another note was sung. Presently one of the older ones explained to Mr. Webb that they were all attending a young ladies' school in Auburn, and two or three hours before had come in a body to the station at Auburn to to see a school-mate off, and that the conductor had invited them to take this ride, and now they were returning. I remember that we did not go on from Auburn until the next morning (there was no thought of sleeping cars in those days), and that, at this young lady's invitation, Mr. Webb and I called upon her at her father's house in the evening.

My Quintet went once during a summer vacation with Mr. Johnson on a short convention tour into New York State, and that was about the last of both Quartet and Quintet for concert singing, for my sister became engaged to a New York gentleman who objected to that sort of publicity for her. Once I remember that I so far overcame his scruples that he gave his consent to her singing at a concert that Gottschalk was to give in Dodworth's Hall, but when the time came she was too ill to sing and some other performance took our place. I mention it because we were to sing there a quartet that Mr. Eisfeld composed for us soon after our advent at the Philharmonic, and which we had sung, I think, at one of his chamber concerts, and with great delight in our practice and to friends. It begins, "On the lake's unruffled surface," and I presume may still be found. It will repay careful study. (See page 229.)

I ought to say something more here of that remarkable family with whom it was my good fortune to be connected during my ten years in New York. The published works of Jacob Abbott and of John S. C. Abbott are known. In the legal profession the works of Benjamin Vaughan Abbott and of Austin Abbott are, I am told, regarded as standards, and in the theological and editorial world Lyman Abbott is one of the most eminent men of the present time. These three last mentioned are sons of Jacob Abbott, and were boys at the time of which I write. That, however, which is not "known and read of all" is the home and school-life of these admirable men. In their homes and in their school-rooms, with each other and with all who were connected with them, either as pupils or teachers, their intercourse was characterized by a sincerity and a gentle friendliness so steady and so constant that breaking over it into roughness of any kind or into disobedience seemed impossible. I saw no outbreak or case of "discipline" in all the years that I was with them. That their excellent methods and great skill and attainments as teachers had something to do with the result will of course be understood. They were called in the school by no other names than "Mr. Jacob," "Mr. John," "Mr. Gorham," and "Mr. Charles," and I was always "Mr. George," and my brother "Mr. Towner."

As larger buildings were needed the school was moved, first to Houston street, then to Bleecker, both near Broadway. I can not remember just when the brothers decided to have two schools, and now I miss my diary again. In fact, as I go on, I miss it more and more. That book, by the way, and the circumstances that caused it, are worth speaking of.

Early in my New York life Mr. Jacob said to me one day: "Did you ever keep a diary?" "Yes," I answered, "I have begun a half dozen at least." "You haven't any of them now?" "No." "You burned each one after writing a few weeks or a few months in it." "Yes." "Was it because you had been so sentimental that you gradually grew tired of what you had written, and at last ashamed to have any one see it?" I laughed and said it was exactly so. "Well," he said, "that is a very common experience. I will tell you what kind of a diary you will never wish to burn. Get a good sized, substantially bound blank-book and record in it simply facts of your every-day life; first, every event of your past life, with its date, that you think you would like to remember years hence, then begin where you are now and do the same thing every day. Speak of pupils, letters, people you see, concerts, classes, journeys—in short, every occurrence of any prominence that is connected with your work or home. Do not give an opinion or admit a word of sentiment in regard to any of the records you make, but let them be stated in the briefest and most concise manner possible. They may look dry to you now, but years hence they will be full of associations of the successful and pleasant life you are now living, and instead of growing tiresome as you read them, they will become more and more interesting and valuable."

I saw at once how good this advice was, and went right off to Mr. Ivison (who was then a member of Mercer Street choir) and had the book made. It was as large as a good-sized ledger, was bound in strong leather, and so arranged that it could be locked. As soon as it was done I asked Mr. Jacob to come and see it. He came, and when he had looked and approved I asked him to begin it for me. He did, and this is about what he wrote:

"Mr. George has brought me in here to see his new book. This is his music room. It is octagonal in shape, two corners being cut off for closets and two for doors of entrance. The wood-work is oak. An octagonal table occupies the center, and book-cases with glass doors are on the side between the doors. There is a piano and a lounge here, and several easy chairs in convenient places. Twenty years hence, Mr. George, when you read this in some totally different scene let it remind you of your New York music room and

"MR. JACOB."

I did as he advised—began with my early life, and found I could recall almost everything of importance before going to Boston, and while there, then started from that time (early in 1845) to make short daily records. This went through my New York life, my first stay in Europe, and my early convention work to 1871, when we were in full tide of successful business in Chicago—more than twenty-five years of brief, close record. The book was but little more than half full, and how true were Mr. Jacob's ideas about the memories and associations it recalled. "Closing exercises at Rutgers to-day" was not merely the record of a musical exercise twenty years before. About that commonplace event were now summer flowers, bright skies and dear friends—and the flowers grew sweeter, the skies brighter, and the friends dearer as the years rolled on. But a memorable day came when my big journal shared the fate of its little predecessors. It was burned! But not by my hand. It went up, with many other mementos of my former life, in the flames of the great Chicago fire.

Somebody may be as much obliged to me as I was to Mr. Jacob for this suggestion about the way to keep a diary.

CHAPTER V.

1848–1849, NEW YORK—SPINGLER INSTITUTE—ADDING DIFFICULTIES TO THE MUSICAL WORK OF MY CLASSES—REFERENCE TO DR. MASON'S FIRST "SINGING SCHOOL"—MY FIRST EFFORTS AT COMPOSITION AND BOOK-MAKING—DIFFERENT MUSICAL GRADES—JENNY LIND.

IT must have been about 1848 that the heirs of the Spingler estate in New York city erected a fine stone building on Union Square, between Fourteenth and Fifteenth streets, for Mr. Gorham Abbott's school. On the corner of Fifteenth street, where Tiffany now is, had already been built a large church for Dr. Cheever. Mr. Gorham Abbott's school was called the "Spingler Institute," and the church was called the "Church of the Puritans." Mr. Spingler was a dairyman, who some years before had kept his cows thereabout. His little farm took in some acres from where Union Square now is, to near Sixth avenue, and from Fourteenth street upward a block or two.

People were disposed to be humorous about the name "Spingler" at first. It was suggested that "Spinster Institute" would be more appropriate, but the result was a good illustration of the fact that a name, whether of a person, or a town, or a street, or an institute, takes on the character of what it names. If that is excellent or beautiful, the name soon becomes so to those interested, however lacking it may be in euphony or beauty in the abstract. "Spingler" soon lost its odd sound to us and came to be just the word to mean an elegant structure, fitted in a costly manner for its purposes, and filled with young ladies of culture and refinement.

Mr. Abbott was constantly adding to the attractiveness of the institution by various means. One of his most important purchases was the original "Voyage of Life," by Thomas Cole—four large pictures—which he hung on the walls of the Chapel where the daily singing lessons were given, and where were enjoyed many fine concerts and literary entertainments.

Connected with the Abbott school I often think of a bright, vivacious girl, who was always conspicuous in the school entertainments, especially in those that had any fun in them. She was an excellent scholar and a great favorite. This was Helen Fiske, now known the world over as Helen Hunt Jackson (H. H.).

One of the first troubles that I met in the classes at Rutgers and Abbott's was that the course which took the whole year in the Boston public schools here lasted but a couple of months, the difference being between two half-hour lessons a week to children, and daily lessons of three-quarters of an hour to young ladies and bright, interested girls. When I saw the end of my usual course approaching I did not know exactly what to do for exercises, but finally decided to work in the more remote keys, major and minor (from the blackboard), and to have the class transpose the scales, both major and harmonic minor, through all the keys. Understand, when I say transpose the *scales* I mean just that. Singing one exercise or tune in one key, and then a different exercise or tune in another, is not transposing the scale—it is not transposition at all. What my classes did was to sing the scale in the key of C, ascending and descending, and then the same in G, then in D, and so on through the enharmonic change from the key of F-sharp to the key of G-flat, back to the key of C—out through the sharps (so to speak), and back through the flats, or *vice versa*. First the major scales, then the minor, then each major, followed by its relative minor in a series, as, C, A, G, E, D, B, etc. I thought this for exercise practice would occupy the year, but it did not take three months to do the work well, without an instrument, and to read pretty difficult diatonic lessons in all the keys, major and minor. Then I began upon the practice of the chromatic scale, feeling sure that that would last through the term, but it did not. In two months, or thereabout, the classes at Rutgers and Spingler could sing that series in any key to syllables, or "la," or "ah," rapidly and accurately. All this is not wonderful now, but it was then. At the annual examinations of the classes at Rutgers three of the best musicians of the city were regularly chosen to pass upon the work, and the Principal and Trustees of the Institute, and all concerned, greatly enjoyed their surprise and unlimited praise.

About the time we had accomplished the work of singing the chromatic scale, as above described, I had occasion to go to Boston for a day, and told Mr. Mason what we had done. "What! four hundred girls sing the chromatic scale in the way you describe? I can't believe it." I assured him that it was so, but left him in evident doubt. At the next summer vacation, when we met for the usual Teacher's Class and Convention work, he said "That chromatic scale singing is not so difficult after all. I have tried it in one of the schools here, and they do it fairly well already." I make this record in the belief that the musical exercises above described were the first ever undertaken in class-teaching in this country.

If this seems strange, it must be remembered that we were then in the early times of class-teaching as we know it now. It was not many years before that Wm. C. Woodbridge (who may be remembered as the author of a once popular geography and atlas) called Mr. Mason's attention to Nageli & Pfeiffer's method of adapting Pestalozzi's idea of teaching to vocal music. Mr. Mason liked what he could see of it very much; then Mr. Woodbridge said to him: "If you will call together a class I will translate and write out each lesson for you (the work was in German) as you want it, and you can try the method; it will take about twenty-four evenings." This was done, and the class was held in the large lecture room of Park Street Church, Boston. Dr. Mason has often described how he took Mr. Woodbridge's translation in one hand and his pointer in the other, and developed, as well as he could, what was afterward embodied in the "Teacher's Manual of the Boston Academy of Music," as the Pestalozzian method of teaching vocal music in classes. The class was composed largely of prominent people of the city who were interested in musical education, and all were greatly delighted with the new way.

That was undoubtedly the first class of its kind ever taught in the English speaking world, and its essential principles exist now wherever the ideas of key relationship and the movable "do" prevail. Speaking to Dr. Mason once about this remarkable class, I asked him what those ladies and gentleman paid for that course of twenty-four lessons. "Oh, they arranged that among themselves," he replied. "They decided that five dollars apiece would be about right." "And how many were there in the class?" He smiled as he answered: "About five hundred."

Up to this time I had not written anything to speak of. I did put together some simple tunes while in Boston, one of which (Rosedale) has come along down in a modest way with its more popular companions, being occasionally sung and asked for at the present time. After I was well under way in New York Mr. Bradbury and Mr. Woodbury used to say: "Root, why don't you make books; we are doing well in that line,"—but I had no inclination that way. I am ashamed to say it, but I looked then with some contempt upon their grade of work. My ladies' classes and choirs were singing higher music, and my blind pupils were exciting the admiration of the best musical people of the city by their performances of a still higher order of compositions. There was a well-balanced choir of sixty good voices in this institution for the blind, and they worked with an interest and enthusiasm that was wonderful to see. We sang, eventually, Romberg's setting of Schiller's "Song of the Bell," "Morning," by Ries, several of Mendelssohn's Part-songs, and several choruses from his and other oratorios. "Thanks be to God, He laveth the thirsty land," from "Elijah," I remember they liked best of all, and sang extremely well.

After a while I began to find it difficult to get proper music for my girls at Rutgers and Spingler to sing, and it took so much time to select what was needed and cost so much to get copies enough, that I felt that something must be done in the way of preparing music especially for them. There was also a strong pressure from classes and teachers —at Rutgers especially—for new music for opening and closing religious exercises. So I got together the material for my first book. It was called "The Young Ladies' Choir." I did not ask anybody to publish it, but just had copies enough made for my own use. I don't think I even copyrighted it, for I had no thought then in regard to composition and book-making beyond supplying my own needs. This book was used two or three years for devotional exercises, but its secular music lasted but a few months, and then my brother and I began the plan of getting up pamphlets of such music as I needed, still seeking no publisher, and thinking only of my own wants. At this time, too, I began to write and arrange music for my choir in the same way, only I did not need so many copies, and so did not go to the expense of having it printed. I had manuscript books for each part, and had each part copied in, or, if I found something printed that I liked, had it cut out and pasted in.

The first book that I had anything to do with that sought a publisher was made with and at the suggestion of the organist of Dr. Cheever's church, then on the corner of Fifteenth street and Broadway, J. E. Sweetser. It was called "Root & Sweetser's Collection." It contained the music we had been gathering for our choirs, with such other material as we could collect and purchase, and an elementary department which, for scientific but uninteresting exercises, could not be excelled; they were taken largely from elementary works that Hullah was then using in England. A few choirs adopted the book, and some of the music is still sung; but, as a whole, it was not at all adapted for popular use. I did not then realize what people in elementary musical states needed.

How true it is that to every music lover and learner there is a grade of music in which he lives, so to speak—where he feels most at home and enjoys himself best. When he hears or studies music that is above that grade, if he is sensible he simply says: "That is above me; I am not there yet." If he is not sensible, he is liable to say: "There's no music in that." The conversation of two gentlemen at one of our recent Thomas concerts is a good illustration of that condition of things. One says: "Do you call that music?" The other answers: "Yes; and the best there is—it is a composition by Wagner." To which his friend responds: "Well, for my part, I think Wagner had better stick to his sleeping cars, and let music alone."

People change their musical homes, or rather add to them, as they progress in musical appreciation. At first they care only for the little way-side flowers and simple scenery of the land of tonic, dominant and subdominant. They regard the musical world outside of that boundary as a kind of desert, entirely unfit to live in, and I may add once more, what has often been said in substance, that many people remain in this musical condition all their lives. But those who progress, begin, by and by, to see some beauty in the sturdier growths and the more varied scenery, and after awhile realize that the still unexplored regions beyond may be yet more beautiful when they are reached.

But here there is a danger. People in this state are apt to grow conceited, and to despise the simple conditions they once enjoyed. "Unworthy, narrow and bigoted" are the proper terms to apply to such. The way-side flower has its place in the economy of God's creation as truly as the oak, and the little hill and the brooklet are as truly beautiful as the mountain and torrent are grand.

"But," some one says, "there is so much trash in the simple music of the day." There is trash at every musical grade, even to the highest. How much that is grotesque and senseless is seen in the ambitious attempts of those who follow Wagner, or would rival him in new paths, but have nothing of his transcendent genius. Such are usually among the despisers of the elementary conditions through which all must pass, and in which a majority of the music-loving world must always be. "Trash" of course; so there are offensive plants and flowers and disagreeable scenes, but the proportion is small, and I contend that most of the simple music that *lives* is no more trash than Mozart's "O dolce concento" or "Rousseau's Dream," than which nothing is written that is simpler or more perfect.

In returning to my story I must not omit to speak of the great musical sensation of 1849—the advent of Jenny Lind. P. T. Barnum had engaged her for a certain number of concerts in this country at what was then considered an enormous price. With consummate skill he had seized upon the fine reputation which she had among musicians and extended it among all the people. He manufactured and manipulated public opinion until the excitement was intense.

An angel could not have met the expectation he raised in many minds.

There was then no hall in New York large enough to hold the people that wanted to see this wonderful being on the occasion of her first concert, so Castle Garden was prepared. I think it was arranged to seat about ten thousand people. Even then the lowest priced seats were in the neighborhood of three dollars, if I remember rightly, and a large sum was realized by selling the choice of seats at auction. An enterprising hatter, by the name of Genin, captured fame and fortune by paying six hundred dollars for first choice.

What a breathless hush rested upon the vast audience when the time came for her first song, and what a burst of welcome greeted her swift coming forward. She was simply dressed in white, and was most statuesque in her apparent calmness as she waited for the orchestra to finish the prelude to "Casta Diva." It was daring in her, under the circumstances, to risk a first impression on the long, soft tone with which that aria commences, but it was a great success. While you wondered at its extreme pianissimo you were distinctly conscious that its fine, steady intensity penetrated to the remotest corner of the hall. All were filled with wonder and delight, excepting those victims of the great advertiser, who were bound to be disappointed if her tones were anything like those of a human being.

She had a long and very successful career in this country, making a large fortune for herself and a much larger one for her enterprising manager. A small financial transaction of my own, in connection with her concerts, comes freshly to my mind with a good deal of satisfaction. I thought I was commissioned to get a lot of tickets for one of the schools, but it proved I was not, and the tickets were on my hands—about twenty, if I remember rightly. But I "speculated" with them, and made money enough by the operation to pay for all my Jenny Lind concerts. I heard her first note and her last, both in Castle Garden, and spent nearly nine months abroad between them.

CHAPTER VI.

1850–1851, NEW YORK AND PARIS—GETTING READY FOR A TRIP ABROAD—THE VOYAGE—ARRIVAL IN PARIS—A FEW WORDS ON THE STUDY OF A FOREIGN LANGUAGE—THE SINGING AT THE MADELEINE—LESSONS FROM ALARY AND POTHARST—A MUSICAL COMPATRIOT—GOTTSCHALK—MEMORABLE CONCERTS.

ABOUT this time I began to feel the effects of my reckless treatment of a naturally strong and healthy constitution. For years I took a hasty breakfast before other people were up, in order to be with my blind class, nearly two miles off, at half past seven in the morning. Then every working hour through the day was filled with other classes and private lessons, and some nights in the week with evening work, and if a new pupil wanted my dinner hour I gave it and snatched a lunch as I could get it in place of the regular meal. This, with the Sunday work, gradually sapped my vitality and brought on the usual trouble of overworked people—dyspepsia.

I think it was early in November of 1850 that Mr. Jacob Abbott said to me one day, "Mr. George, you should stop work for a while. Go to Paris. (He made nothing of picking up his satchel and going across, writing on his books during the voyage, and while there.) The trip will do you good, and Paris is a good place to rest and amuse yourself in, and, if you feel like it when you get there, you can study the language and anything more about music that you wish to know; for the best teachers of the world congregate there." My wife was considerably astonished when I told her what Mr. Jacob had said, and that I believed I should go. However, she agreed that if it could be managed it would be a good plan.

The first thing was to see how the church people would feel about it, and how the organ and choir could be attended to during my absence. This was soon ascertained and settled. One of the elders of the church and the chairman of the music committee was John P. Crosby, an older brother of the present Dr. Howard Crosby. He was one of the noblest gentlemen I have ever known, and one of the truest and dearest friends I ever had. He was very musical —entirely competent to teach the choir and play the organ, and in a day or two after I told him my plan I was not surprised when he said: "It is all arranged. Leave Mrs. Root to be our leader, and I'll meet the choir and play the organ for you until you return, and your salary shall go on all the same." I ought to have said that there was no thought of my wife's going with me, partly because that would have been too great a strain on our finances, but more, perhaps, because we then had two little children, F. W., four years old, and Charlie, three years younger.

I engaged Richard Storrs Willis (a brother of N. P. Willis, an author of considerable celebrity in those days) to teach for me at Rutgers and Spingler Institutes, and Sigismund Lasar to carry on the work at the Institution for the Blind during my absence. Much of my work would naturally have fallen to my brother, but he had a little while before accepted an offer to teach for the winter in Alabama. I took my passage for the fifth of December, 1850, on the Franklin, a new steamer of a new line just established between New York and Havre, and then went to Boston and to the old home to say good-bye. A few days before sailing I decided to get my life insured. I mention it because it was one of the early risks of the "N. Y. Mutual

Life," now the largest institution of the kind in the world. When I see their present magnificent building I contrast it mentally with the little office in Wall street where I arranged to have a certain moderate sum paid to my wife in case of my death. Although not a large amount it has improved considerably since that day, more than forty years ago.

The "Splendid Steamer Franklin" was a small affair in comparison with the present ocean liners, but, notwithstanding she bowed and rolled as gracefully as she could at every wave of that wintry sea, and made nearly all of us very seasick, she carried us safely across and landed us in due time (thirteen days, I think) at Havre. I had some letters which enabled me to settle myself pleasantly in Paris almost immediately on my arrival.

One of my plans was to learn as much of the language as possible while there, and I asked a son of my landlady—a young collegian who could speak English a little—if he would give me lessons. He was timid and hesitated about undertaking it, but I told him he would not have any responsibility; that I would be the teacher and he would have only to obey orders. He agreed, and I commenced with the then popular "Ollendorf."

I had seen a good deal of the teaching of French in the schools in New York, and thought I saw why so few learners were willing to try to speak even short phrases in that language. They were like piano pupils, who know how their exercises ought to go, but can not make the proper movements of their fingers at the proper time—they have continually to stop or stumble for want of muscular control, which simply means want of practice.

I saw that in French there were new adjustments of the vocal and articulating organs for certain sounds which are not in our own language, and that there were constantly successions of familiar sounds in an entirely new way. It seemed to me also that just as new and difficult successions of finger movements could only be rendered smooth and certain by much repetition and practice, so the new sounds of a strange language could only be made to follow each other fluently by the same means.

So, when my youthful teacher would have passed my imperfect pronunciation and hesitating utterance of a phrase because I had all the words right, I said, "No, we have only begun—have only laid out the work for this phrase; now you say it, and I will say it after you, not only until it goes smoothly and unhesitatingly, but has just the right vowel and consonant sounds." I tired that young man dreadfully, but he was rather proud of his pupil after a while. Only once, I remember, I undertook too much. The phrase was: "*un peu plus haut*" (a little higher), and I said: "Now I am going to repeat that after you until there is no foreign accent in it at all, and you say you could not tell it from a Frenchman." But in vain; he was too honest, and the exact shades of difference between the vowels of "*peu*" and "*plus*," or some other subtle peculiarity of utterance always caused the same result. "Is it like a Frenchman now?" "*Non, monsieur.*" Again and again I tried. I asked him to show or tell me what caused the difference between his utterance and mine. This he could not do. Each word alone after him he seemed to think right, but when put together it was to his ears a foreigner speaking. All he could say was: "*N'entendez vous pas la difference, monsieur?*" And I had to answer that I did not.

On reflection, I saw that this might be so; for all foreigners who learn our language after they are grown up, although they may have the entire vocabulary, and for practical purposes may speak as well as a native, are still readily perceived to be foreigners. It is only as children, when the organs are tender and can be moulded, that we learn to speak a foreign language without accent.

If an educational word on this subject would not be considered out of place here, I would say to the piano teacher: When your pupil is not willing to play for friends under proper circumstances, it is generally because he is afraid his fingers will not go right, and that he will be mortified by hesitations or blunders at certain places—in short, he does not want to play because he has not practiced enough to get that muscular control which gives confidence. To the teacher of the foreign language I say the same thing. If your pupil is not willing to speak in the language you are teaching him, it is in most cases because the muscles of the articulating organs will not obey his will—he has not practiced his *five-finger exercises* enough, so to speak.

People like to do what they can do well. If they play the piano well, even though the pieces be simple, they like to play to those who enjoy their music; if they speak readily and smoothly in a foreign language they like to exercise their powers in that way, even though they may know but a few phrases and may make many mistakes in construction or grammar. If a piano teacher allows a new exercise or piece before the previous one is perfectly learned, or a French teacher goes on to a second phrase while there is the least hesitation in the utterance of the one at which the pupil is at work, trouble, and, in the end, failure and dissatisfaction will be the certain result.

I studied the language and looked about the city for two or three weeks before commencing the more regular work that occupied me later. The first thing in a musical way that interested me very much was the singing and organ playing at Christmas time in the Church of the Madeleine. A boy with a wonderful voice sang the melody of the "Adeste Fideles" (" Portuguese Hymn," as we know it) at the priests' end of the church, the choir, which was also there, coming in with the ending of each verse, the organ, which was situated with the singers, giving a different harmony with each verse, and then another organ, several times larger, four hundred feet off, over the front entrance, rolled out an interlude between the verses. It was a strange effect to me and very impressive.

About this time I began taking voice lessons. I forget who it was in New York who told me to go to Giulio Alary, but when I got to Paris I found that he was the great man in that line outside of the Conservatoire. It shows how large the world is, and how fast it moves, that perhaps no one who reads this will ever have heard of this man, who was so conspicuous as a composer and teacher a generation ago in Paris and London. I sang a good deal with him from an oratorio of his called "La Redemption," and while I was with him his opera "Les Trois Marriages" was performed at the Italian opera-house there, with Sontag, Lablache, and Gardoni in the cast.

At the close of my lesson one day he said: "I am going to the last rehearsal of my opera. You can come with me and hear these people sing if you like." I was in trouble, for I knew I could not make him conceive how there could be any conscientious scruples against accepting his invitation, but at that time, in the church to which I belonged, it was thought wrong to go to opera or theatrical representations, and I determined when I left home that I would do nothing in Paris that I would not do in New York. So I explained as well as I could why I could not go. He did not understand it at all, as I knew he could not, and evidently regarded me as a kind of fanatic—an opinion in which I coincided a few years later. I never felt quite comfortable with him after that scene, but he soon had to go to London where his opera was next performed, and I went to another teacher.

Jacques Potharst was some kind of a northman by birth, but he had lived in Italy and France nearly all his life, and had been a successful tenor in the Italian Opera. He was a good teacher, and I took lessons of him during the rest of my stay in Paris. One day he said, "I have another American pupil, a baritone, whom you must meet. I have some duets that will just suit your two voices." That was soon brought about. My compatriot proved to be a young man by the name of Mann. He was the son of one of our government officials, who was, in pursuance of his diplomatic duties, sometimes in one European country and sometimes in another. Just then he was living in Paris. Young Mann had an exceptionally fine baritone voice, and we sang together a good deal, not only at our lessons, but in musical companies, where Signor Potharst seemed to take a good deal of pride in parading his American pupils.

This young gentleman was a good illustration of what I was saying about the way to speak a foreign language without accent. His father began his diplomatic career when this son, his only child, was very young—about ten years of age I think. He went to school in every country where they made any stay, and was left long enough in each one to acquire the language. His French, German and Italian were absolutely without foreign accent, as I was told by those who knew. I extend this remembrance of my friend because one of those curious happenings that sometimes take place has brought him freshly to my mind. Last year one of my neighbors said, "I have rented a house on this street for the summer, to a gentleman by the name of Mann, who says that he knows you—that you were together in Paris forty years ago." I called on him, and instead of the slender youth of eighteen, found a portly gentleman of fifty-eight, now Judge Mann, of Florida, who, with his wife, formerly a Chicago lady, was going to pass the summer by Lake Michigan. I need not say that we renewed our acquaintance, music and all, with much pleasure.

Before leaving New York a gentleman of my acquaintance said to me, "My daughter will arrive in Paris soon after you. The family with whom she is going are not musical, and I shall take it as a great favor if you will see that she has a good piano teacher while she is there. This I readily undertook to do. By good fortune Gottschalk, the great pianist, was passing a few months in Paris, and I found him willing to give some lessons to my young friend, who already played well for an amateur. This was the beginning of an acquaintance with that distinguished man, which continued up to that fatal journey to South America, from which he never returned.

I say "*great* pianist" of L. Moreau Gottschalk advisedly. Critics and some prominent musicians did not call him a *great* player—all agreed that he was an exquisite player, and all admitted that he was the most popular and successful concert pianist that ever played in America, but those who knew him well could testify to his wonderful repertoire of classic music. He could play all of Beethoven by heart, and he delighted in Bach, but he was too honest to play such music to any extent at his popular concerts, and too strong in the consciousness of his own merit to heed those critics who, if they could have their way, would never give the people any music that they could understand and enjoy.

It was particularly exasperating to hear unfavorable criticisms of Gottschalk's compositions, for they are not only understandable and useful to the people, but elegant and musicianly in a high degree. I think it may be said that his are among the most original and characteristic of all American compositions for the piano-forte.

My daily life was now pretty regular. Ollendorf, voice and piano practice, lessons and recitations until afternoon;

then the picture galleries, museums, libraries, palaces, cathedrals, parks, gardens, and endless objects of interest until five or six o'clock. Then dinner, and afterward gathering in the parlor for conversation or music. One evening a week at the Protestant Chapel, where I always went on Sunday, and occasionally a concert, occupied my time.

Two concerts I remember with special interest: One was at a small hall connected with Henri Herz's piano establishment, at which Madame Sontag, Madame Viardot Garcia, Lablache, and Gardoni, a young tenor of great promise, sang. I do not know that these names will excite the interest now that they did then, and for some years after, over the entire musical world. Sontag was the soprano of her time. Viardot Garcia was not only a great mezzo-soprano and accomplished pianist, but being the sister of Malibran, one of the greatest singers that ever lived, and then recently deceased, excited great interest wherever she appeared. But Lablache was the king. He had been the greatest basso of the world for a quarter of a century or more. He was a giant in size, his magnificent head crowned with a thick mass of white hair, towering far above his companions as they stood together upon the stage. It had been my greatest desire for years to hear this man, whose fame was greater then than that which any singer enjoys now, that I know of. His voice was proportionate to his size, and had the advantage of being trumpet-toned like a tenor, or rolling out like the sub-base of an organ, at his pleasure. It was said that at C-sharp or D above, no orchestra, however large, could be more than a fair accompaniment when he chose to put forth all his power, and I could readily believe it. I heard his D-flat below, in a concerted number in which all joined, and the ponderous solidity of the long-sustained tone could only be compared to a grand sub-base, though it was much richer in quality than any instrument could produce.

Madame Viardot played a difficult waltz by Chopin, to which had been added, in a most musicianly manner, a melody which she sang. It was a curious and wonderful performance. Madame Sontag and Lablache sang a humorous duet—an Italian singing master giving his favorite pupil a lesson. He was so large and she so *petite* by comparison, that when he nodded his great bushy head in admiring approval of her brilliant execution he brought to mind the old story of the lion who found a congenial companion in a canary bird.

I came near meeting this great man once, but, much to my regret, did not quite succeed. It was while I was taking lessons from M. Alary. He was one day looking for a song that he wished me to practice, when at last he said, "now I remember; Lablache has it; I will send for it." I asked him to let me call for it on my way home, and he readily consented. He gave me a note which described what was wanted, and I took it to the great basso's apartments, but he was at dinner. I heard his ponderous voice and jovial laugh in the next room, but did not see him; his daughter brought me the book.

The second concert to which I referred was in the Italian Opera-house. It was Rossini's "Stabat Mater," and was the only occasion while I was in Paris that I entered an opera-house or theater. Sims Reeves came over from London to sing the tenor solos. Down deep in the French heart there is a national animosity to English people, but they could not resist the charm of that performance. At the "Cujus animam" they were wild with delight, and recalled the great tenor again and again.

The first English tenor of this generation is Edward Lloyd. In the last generation Sims Reeves was the acknowledged best, and in the generation before, Braham. When, therefore, at a recent Musical Festival in Cincinnati

(May, 1888), I heard Lloyd, I had heard the three great tenors of the three generations, and what greatly increased the interest of this fact was, that I heard Braham sing Handel's "Sound an alarm," Sims Reeves the "Cujus animam," and Edward Lloyd both of those songs.

Two other concerts I now remember that are perhaps worth mentioning. At one was a new composition by Felicien David, conducted by himself. I forget what it was, but at that time he was very famous as the composer of "The Desert," a kind of cantata, founded largely upon Arabian melodies. The new piece was good, but not striking, and verified what Auber was reported as having said: "When David descends from his camel you will find he is not at all remarkable." But what was more especially in my mind when I began to speak of that concert was the performance on that occasion of the "Hallelujah chorus." It was so fast as to be ridiculous. Colossus had lost all his dignity and strength by crossing the channel.

The other concert that I think of with special interest was an orchestral performance of new compositions by Hector Berlioz, conducted by himself. That pale, wild face, surmounted by shaggy locks, black as night, haunted me for months. He was a disappointed man. His works, now taking so high a rank, did not find much recognition in his life-time.

CHAPTER VII.

1851, PARIS AND LONDON—FOURTH OF JULY—THE CONVERSATIONAL MODE OF LEARNING FRENCH, AND THE ROMANCE THAT FOLLOWED—TWO CONCERTS AT EXETER HALL, LONDON—THE LOYALTY OF THE ENGLISH TO OLD FAVORITES—THE FIRST WORLD'S EXPOSITION—AMERICAN FRIENDS—THE M'CORMICK REAPER—THE SEWING MACHINE—THE DAY & NEWELL LOCK—THE YACHT AMERICA—THE NARROW ESCAPE ON THE HOME VOYAGE.

MY stay in Paris was just before the famous *coup d'etat* of Louis Napoleon. He was then simply President, but there was a half-concealed anxiety in the community lest they might be on the eve of some outbreak or calamity, as indeed they were.

When the fourth of July came, six of us Americans decided to make a day of it in honor of the fatherland. We went out to Enghien, a pretty suburb a few miles from Paris, and celebrated in various ways, much to our enjoyment and somewhat to the surprise of the natives. We came home for dinner at five o'clock, and then adjourned to the parlor for a grand wind-up. We made speeches and sang songs—the " Star-Spangled Banner," "America," and whatever else we could think of that would be appropriate. At last I started " The Marseillaise "—" Ye sons of freedom, wake to glory," etc. I had not proceeded far when good Madame Maffit, our landlady, came rushing in. " O, gentlemen, stop, I beg of you," she said; " a crowd is collecting in the street—the *gendarmes* will come—my house will be ruined;" and she flew to the windows, which had been open, and shut them violently. "Oh, we are only celebrating our American Independence," one of us said. "Well, we are not independent enough yet to sing 'The Marseillaise,'" she answered.

That song had been interdicted some time before, and although France was then nominally a Republic, the Government was still afraid of its effect upon that inflammable people. An old officer, who had served under the first Napoleon, and had been decorated by the great Emperor himself, was one of Madame Maffit's boarders. He went down to the street, and in some way induced the crowd to disperse. Our landlady assured us that if we had continued five minutes longer we might have had to make our explanations at the *Prefecture*—an ending to our celebration that we certainly should not have enjoyed.

In pursuance of my plan to improve myself all I could in the French language, I entered into conversation with the natives whenever I had an opportunity. The first Napoleon's old soldiers were always to be found in the parks and gardens on pleasant days. They had nothing to do, and were always ready for a talk as soon as they found I was an American. One word about *Le grand Empereur*, whose memory they worshiped, was enough to see them off, and much practice their garrulous enthusiasm gave me, both in listening to rapid utterances and in framing questions to bring them out.

But my most important opportunities in this way were in the parlor of our *Pension*, where all the household assembled for a while after dinner. I talked a good deal with two sisters from Metz, whose business it was to copy pictures in the Louvre and other galleries, mostly for the churches of the provinces. A pretty romance came from this acquaintance, which is worth relating.

They were intensely interested in all I could tell them

of America, about which their ignorance was surprising. Was New York in North or South America? was *La Nouvelle Orleans* near New York? were there many white people? had we to be constantly on our guard against the Indians? etc. They were greatly interested in the daguerreotypes of my wife and children (there were no photographs then), and utterly astonished at my description of American social life. Could it be possible that a young lady could go to a concert or to the theater alone with a young man, or receive him at her home without the presence of a third person? Did they decide upon and arrange their marriages themselves? It seemed incredible. They did not see why good girls might not do all that, but it would not be thought of in France. In fact, nice girls in France could not marry at all unless they had a "portion" (*dot*). Men they would marry would not have them, and men that would marry them they would not have. I expatiated upon the self-reliance of our girls—how young people married when they fell in love, and of their happy married lives. I grew eloquent in very ungrammatical French on the advantages of our ways, and volunteered a good deal of information as to probable results if they were in America instead of in France. I would think of something to say that I thought would interest them, and then see if I could say it, not realizing the full signification that it might bear to their minds. In fact, it did not seem as if the kind of French I was speaking could mean much of anything, but I should have been considerably astonished if I could have known then how I was making America, and especially New York, appear to them the veritable land of promise. This feeling grew stronger as we became better acquainted.

I sometimes saw them at their copying in the Louvre, but, mindful of the proprieties as there regarded, never accosted them while they were at their work. I was not much of a judge of painting, but what they did seemed to me good. Adèle, the older sister, was exceptionally fine looking, the younger something of an invalid, and the good heart of the former was constantly shown in her tender care of her less favored sister. I admired Adèle greatly, and if I thought of some sentence like "I think you would do well in your profession in New York," or, "You would not be long in America without marrying," I would say it as best I could, thinking mainly of its construction and very little of its meaning; and this was not insincerity—what I said was true enough, but I should have made some further modification of my sentences if I could have foreseen what they would lead to.

To finish this little story I shall have to transfer the scene to New York, then I will return and finish the account of my Paris visit. I had not been long at home when the *coup d'etat* took place. A few weeks after that I received a letter from Adèle, saying that they had lost nearly all their little property, and that there was then nothing for them to do in France—that their only hope now was America, which, from my representation, was exactly the place for them to go to. She said she should go first alone, and when she had established herself, her sister would join her. She wrote to me because I was the only person in America that she knew—would write again when she had decided what ship to go in, and then would tell me when I might expect her. There was a situation! I had told her I thought she would do well in New York, but I could not know. How I despised then that conversational mode of learning French. I wrote her at once that perhaps I had been extravagant in my praises of my native land—that I did not know enough about painting to be *sure* of her success—that in our conversations the wish had been the father of the thought, etc., etc. But she never received that letter. Before it reached the other side she had started. She had written me again about when to expect her. Then I set about making inquiries and preparations. On all sides they said, "If she is a good artist she will succeed; it all depends on that. She can be profitably employed either in teaching or in painting pictures, if she is really competent.'' As I did not know whether she answered that description or not I was naturally anxious, but the next thing was to get a pleasant home for her. We were still at the boarding-house where my family had stayed during my absence. It was, however, full, much to our regret, for my wife was now deeply interested in the success of my new *protegée*. However, I found a very pleasant place for her near by, and not knowing what condition her finances would be in at first, assumed all necessary responsibility.

In due time I received a note from a little French hotel in Murray street: "I have arrived; please come for me." I went at once, and found her none the worse for her voyage. I took her first to see my wife. The two had heard much of each other, but as one could speak no English and the other no French, their meeting was exceedingly amusing. They smiled sweetly on each other, and said all sorts of pleasant and complimentary things, which I interpreted to the best of my ability. I believe my wife did manage to say "thank you" in French for some gloves that Mademoiselle had brought her. Then we all went to the boarding-place that had been arranged for her. She was much pleased with it, and the landlady was evidently much prepossessed in favor of her new lodger. Next we went to the Spingler Institute, where I introduced her to the French teacher, who was a French lady, and to Mr. and Mrs. Abbott. In a day or two she was introduced to the wife of one of the most distinguished physicians of New York, a Swiss lady from one of the French-speaking cantons, and by her to some other important people of the city. Everybody was delighted with her grace and beauty, and she *was* a good artist. Some pictures that she brought with her were exhibited in Williams & Stevens' window (they were the great picture-sellers of New York then), and were much admired. She began by teaching and painting some portraits, and in a very short time was fully occupied. It proved that she brought some money with her, but she would not have needed any assistance if she had not, for she was soon in receipt of a much larger income than she had ever enjoyed in France. She sent for her sister in a few weeks, but the younger lady, who was still in delicate health, found our climate so uncongenial that she soon returned to France.

And now for the *dénouement.* The second year after Miss Adèle's arrival a rich Fifth avenue family, with whom she was a great favorite, invited her to spend the summer with them at the White Mountains. There a wealthy gentleman from Cuba fell in love with her, and in the autumn they were married. A year afterward I received a letter from her, filled with praises of her beautiful boy, and calling down blessings upon my head as the cause, to some extent, of her happiness. So the conversational mode of improving in French did not turn out so badly after all. At all events, it was permitted that the promises I made in so careless and unthinking a fashion should all be fulfilled.

And now to return to Paris. After the first of May, 1851, the Americans that came from London were in a state of great mortification and disgust at the United States exhibit in the great Crystal Palace Exposition—the first affair of the kind in which all nations united. They said that the United States Commissioners had insisted upon a large space, and that it was not half filled, and that the chief things there were some plows, and a barrel of shoe-pegs. That was extravagant, of course, but the American department did look plain and uninviting in comparison with the elegant profusion of things from the older and nearer nations; but more of that later.

Soon after the fourth of July one of my American friends and I started for London *en route* for home. This gentleman was Levi P. Homer, a young Bostonian, who had been studying music abroad for a year or two, and had been with us at Madame Maffit's for a few weeks. He was afterward Professor of Music in Harvard College, and was, I think, the immediate predecessor of the present occupant of that office. He died many years ago. We left Paris on a Friday morning, and arrived in London that afternoon. The first thing that attracted my attention there was an announcement of the "Messiah" at Exeter Hall. It was to be given that evening. My friend was too much shaken up by that abomination of all travelers—the passage across the channel—to go, and I was scarcely better, but I could not miss that opportunity. It was a magnificent performance—six hundred in the chorus, a large orchestra and organ, Clara Novello, Miss Dolby, Sims Reeves and Carl Formes (at his best) taking the solos, and all under the direction of Sir Michael Costa. The oratorio was not "cut," and took four hours in performance. The alto was sung mostly by men, and one reason of the great perfection of the chorus work was that a large proportion of the singers on all the parts knew the music by heart, and could keep their eyes upon the conductor.

An incident illustrating the loyality of the English people to their old favorites comes freshly to my mind in connection with that concert. I was early, and found myself seated by a stout, plainly dressed man, who, with myself, was evidently much interested in seeing the audience gather. After a while the members of the orchestra began to take their places, and when an old man with a violoncello entered, the audience applauded, my neighbor joining heartily. The old man bowed and quietly took his seat. I said: "What is that applause for?" "Oh, that's Mr. Lindley," responded my neighbor, with a strong Yorkshire accent; "he used to be a great solo player, and we always give him a hand in remembrance of old times." I remembered then to have heard that name as the famous 'cellist of the previous generation. This led to further conversation with the good-natured Yorkshireman, who was much interested to learn that I was an American. He introduced a young lady who was sitting by his side by saying: "My daughter and I always come up to London when they sing the 'Messiah.'" A week from that night the same company precisely gave "Elijah." The value of those two performances to me in after years was very great. They were authentic and authoritative, both for tempos and style. Of the "Messiah" the tradition was in a direct line from its great author, and "Elijah" had been conducted by Mendelssohn himself but a few years before in Birmingham.

The day after we arrived in London we went to the Crystal Palace, the same magnificent building that is now in Sydenham. It was then in Hyde Park. As we approached we noticed an odd-looking machine on one side of the entrance, evidently not thought worthy a place inside. The papers made a good deal of fun of it, as they had of several other "Yankee notions," not realizing what a commotion that weather-beaten apparatus would make when the time for test and trial came. It was a McCormick Reaper.

When I entered the United States Department I went up to a short, thick-set man, with a most jovial and contented expression of countenance, who was sitting on a high box, swinging his feet in true Yankee fashion. "Why, Hobbs, what are you doing here?" was my first greeting. I had not seen him since the old Musical Education Society days in Boston, where he was one of my cronies on the base. He was a machinist by trade, and I knew him then as a bright, pushing fellow. "Oh, I'm representing the Day & Newell lock." "Well, how are you getting along?" "First-rate; look in the papers to-morrow and you'll see." I told him I had but just come, and did not know what was going on. Would he tell me all about it? "Well, the Bramah lock has been the great lock of England for a long time. It is on the vaults and safes of the Bank of England, and is used everywhere here as the best. There has been a safe in the window of its sales-room for years with this legend upon it: 'There are twenty pounds within this safe which will be given to any one who can pick this lock.'" "And are you going to do it?" "Yes; I have been to see it to-day, and have told them that I should open it to-morrow." "And are you sure you can do it?" "Yes; I don't like the idea of picking a lock, but that is the best way to introduce mine, and, besides, that twenty pounds will come in handy." And he did it. It took him just as many minutes as there were pounds that went into his pocket, and it made a great sale for his lock. I think it was subsequently used in the bank and other public places.

The first sewing machine was there in charge of two brothers who had been members of Park Street choir. A Philadelphia chairmaker had a new reclining chair that could be adjusted in many ways. Prince Albert, who was the projector of the great enterprise, and Queen Victoria, used often to go in and look about early in the day, before the public was admitted. The Prince was especially interested in everything that saved labor, or that made in any way for the welfare of the people. One day this Philadelphian, who, by the way, was originally from Vermont, was in great spirits. He said: "I've had the Queen in that chair this mornin'. I put her into all the positions I could think of, and the Prince he laughed well, and now I'm goin' to put a sign up: 'The Queen has set in that chair, and anybody else who wants to set in it has got to pay a shillin'.'" We left our enterprising countryman anticipating great results from his scheme.

Of the general and costly magnificence of the Exposition it is not worth while to speak, for the world is familiar with such things now. One thing, however, that was there has not been seen in any other country, and that was the "Kohinoor," the enormous diamond belonging to the British crown jewels. In this case it was the real article, and not the paste substitute which has sometimes been shown. It was in an octagonal glass and iron case, on an iron pedestal, and was surrounded by a strong railing that prevented people from getting within two or three feet of it, and to further protect it was guarded day and night by four soldiers.

When the time came for examining the exhibits and awarding the prizes a great change took place in the public mind in regard to the American Department. The rusty, weather-beaten machine, that had been the butt of so many jokes at the expense of the Yankees, was taken out onto a smooth English grain field and set going. The effect was magical. Could this be the ungainly thing they had laughed at? Such reaping had not been dreamed of. The Englishman loves fair play, and we got full credit for that, and many other things that had not seemed to be of much account until they were put to use. To crown all, about the same time the new yacht "America" beat the English yacht squadron in a race off the Isle of Wight. The Americans held up their heads after that, and were a little ashamed that they had distrusted the ability of Uncle Sam to hold his own in this contest of nations.

We stayed in London about four weeks, and then went to Southampton, where the Havre steamers touched, and took the Humboldt for home. It was a remarkably smooth voyage, though one incident as we neared our coast I shall never forget. I was a little seasick all the way—just enough to be nervous and apprehensive, especially after hearing stories of running into icebergs or fishing craft, and the marvelous things about the density of the fog banks off Newfoundland. But one night I went to bed quite peaceful, for the moon was bright and the air clear, and the ocean almost as calm as a mill-pond. About midnight, however, I was awakened by sudden orders and hurried footsteps overhead, and felt immediately that the ship's side had hit against something, for she heeled over in a most perceptible and alarming way. I sprang out of my berth and called to Mr. Homer, who occupied the upper one, that the ship had struck something. I thought of fishing smacks and icebergs, and was in a state of great nervous excitement while trying to get into my clothes. I feared every moment that something worse would happen. My friend started to get out of his berth, but, being but half awake, lost his balance and came down on my back as I was stooping over to put on my shoes. I thought the ship had gone to the bottom. I believe I was never so frightened before, or have ever been since. As soon as I recovered I rushed upon deck, and found we were within a hundred yards of the rocks of Cape Race, the eastern point of Newfoundland. Strange as it may seem, the officers of the ship had made a mistake in their reckoning, and did not suppose they were within a hundred miles of the cape. They took the wall before them for a fog bank, and if every man had not been at his post when they discovered their error, and had not obeyed the sudden orders instantly, we should have crashed straight on to the rocks and gone down like a broken egg-shell. We afterward learned that our captain had been on the Havre packets (sailing vessels) many years, but that this was his first voyage on a steamer. He said it was a receding wave that made the ship heel over, but she went into dry-dock when we arrived in New York, and was there some weeks, so we knew she was hit.

It was a hot August morning when we landed, and I remember thinking that everybody we met on Broadway looked sick—they were so pale and thin. The contrast to the ruddy English people we had just left was striking. New Yorkers and the American people generally are healthier looking now than they were in those days. The women wear thicker shoes and take more exercise, and both men and women know better about eating, drinking, and the laws of health generally.

CHAPTER VIII.

1851–1853, NEW YORK—"THE FLOWER QUEEN" AND THE FIRST "ROSE"—"WURZEL" AND "THE HAZEL DELL"—MY BEST PIANO PUPIL—THE FIRST NORMAL MUSICAL INSTITUTE—"DANIEL" AND EARLY BOOKS—THE NEW HOUSE AT WILLOW FARM, AND THE SINGING IN THE VILLAGE CHURCH—MY FIRST MUSICAL CONVENTION—THE VALUE OF A SPECIALTY—THE OLD VIOLIN—EARLY ORCHESTRAS.

I FOUND my family at the old home in North Reading. We had a week or so more of vacation, and then I went back to New York and resumed my work. The first need I felt was for something new for my classes, especially at Rutgers and Spingler Institutes, to sing. This was in the autumn of 1851. Mr. Bradbury had given some floral concerts with children at the Broadway Tabernacle, and at a recent one had introduced some selections in a connected series. This gave me the idea that a little musical play might be made for girls and young ladies that would be useful. I cast about for a subject. It was not difficult to find one; the whole world was open to me, for nothing of the kind had been done. I soon decided that the subject should be flowers choosing a queen, and that the little play should be called "The Flower Queen."

At the Institution for the Blind there was at that time a lady who had been a pupil there, but was now a teacher, who had a great gift for rhyming, and, better still, had a delicate and poetic imagination. The name of Fanny Crosby was not known then beyond the small circle of her personal friends, but it is now familiar, especially wherever

Gospel songs are sung. I used to tell her one day in prose what I wanted the flowers or the Recluse to say, and the next day the poem would be ready—sometimes two or three of them. I generally hummed enough of a melody to give her an idea of the meter and rhythmic swing wanted, and sometimes played to her the entire music of a number before she undertook her work. It was all the same. Like many blind people her memory was great, and she easily retained all I told her. After receiving her poems, which rarely needed any modification, I thought out the music, perhaps while going from one lesson to another, (the distances were so great that I had to spend a good deal of time every day in omnibuses or street cars,) and then I caught the first moment of freedom to write it out. Sometimes this was a half hour before dinner or supper, sometimes a little while between lessons, and sometimes an hour at night. This went on until the cantata was finished.

I can truly say that I had no other thought in this work than my own needs. I did not know that it would ever be heard outside of the walls of the institutions in which I was teaching. I had to have it printed because I needed so many copies myself, and this time it fell into good hands. The two older sons of Dr. Mason were then book-sellers and publishers in New York, under the firm name of Mason Brothers. They willingly undertook to supply me with copies, and they said, "We'll publish it regularly—others may want what you want," and so it proved.

I have often been glad that I did not begin earlier to write for publication. It was not a noble motive that restrained me, but our foolishness is often overruled to our advantage. By delaying I had become better equipped. I had heard a good deal of good music, and had been obliged to teach some of a high order. Everything that my blind pupils sang I had to know in the most thorough manner.

My acquaintance with some of the best musicians of the day was such as to bring me into close contact with what they performed and liked, and in my family we were familiar with music of a grade considerably above that of the popular music of the day. The reservoir was, therefore, much better filled than it would have been if I had commenced when urged to do so by the friends of whom I have spoken, and the comparatively simple music that I have written from that time to this has included a greater variety of subjects, and has been better in quality in consequence.

I saw at once that mine must be the "people's song," still, I am ashamed to say, I shared the feeling that was around me in regard to that grade of music. When Stephen C. Foster's wonderful melodies (as I now see them) began to appear, and the famous Christy's Minstrels began to make them known, I "took a hand in" and wrote a few, but put "G. Friederich Wurzel" (the German for Root) to them instead of my own name. "Hazel Dell" and "Rosalie, the Prairie Flower" were the best known of those so written. It was not until I imbibed more of Dr. Mason's spirit, and went more among the people of the country, that I saw these things in a truer light, and respected myself, and was thankful when I could write something that all the people would sing.

"The Flower Queen" served an excellent purpose, both as an incentive to work on the part of the classes, and as an entertainment for the friends of the schools. I served in the double capacity of Recluse and stage manager in the first performances, and fear the latter character appeared sometimes during the performance of the former much to the detriment of that dignitary. However, we always rehearsed thoroughly, and the success of those first representations was all that could be desired. The first "Rose" is worth telling about.

Two or three years before, I noticed one day a strange voice among my four hundred at Rutgers. It did not seem loud, but it pervaded the whole room and was exceedingly rich in quality. It seemed so mature that I looked among the young ladies for it at first, but there was no stranger among them. Then I stepped down from the platform and walked back among the younger girls and soon discovered her, a small brunette, twelve or thirteen years old, with laughing eyes and a profusion of dark, wavy hair hanging unconfined about a handsome, dark face. That was her first day at the school, but she soon became our *prima donna,* and the name of Annie Thomas will not soon be forgotten by those who heard her during those years at Rutgers, and afterward in her more prominent musical life in New York.

I used to take my pupils occasionally to hear the blind people sing. Annie was a great favorite there. She not only captivated the class, but in a special and particular way a young gentleman who not only could hear her voice, but see her face. He was a theological student, temporarily teaching there. He had a younger brother who was a part of the time in the Institution, I think, as an office boy. This theological student sought an introduction to my young lady and I introduced him. A few years after he married her. He is now the Rev. Wm. Cleveland, of Forestport, N. Y., and the office boy was, not long ago, President of the United States.

Speaking of my best singer in New York, on account of her connection with a well-known personage, brings to my mind my best piano pupil, a lovely young girl of thirteen or fourteen. If you will read Charles Dudley Warner's "My Summer in a Garden," you will be much amused at his allusions to his wife who was this young girl. I hope she has not forgotten the Cramer's studies she played so well.

With every Teacher's Class and Convention that I attended with Mr. Mason and Mr. Webb I became more interested in the improvement of the teachers who came to be instructed. I saw how inadequate the time was for much improvement, not only in my department (the voice), but in the art of teaching and in harmony and general musical culture. Early in 1852 I conceived the idea of having a *three months'* session for this work. It must be in the summer, because then the teachers had more leisure. It must be in the city of New York, for I must be there where my work was. I knew the expenses of advertising and place of meeting would be large, but I believed that from all the States and Canada enough teachers, and those who wished to become such, would come, to save the enterprise from pecuniary loss.

I went immediately to Boston, where Mr. Mason still lived, and told him my plan. It did not strike him at first as feasible. He did not believe any considerable number of persons could be induced to come, especially from a distance, on account of the great expense of traveling and of such a stay in New York City, in addition to the cost of instruction. I said, "Well, I am going to have such a class. You are the proper person to appear at the head of it, and to be the real head when it comes to the teaching, but I do not expect you to do any of the work of getting it up; I'll see to that. It will be a better opportunity than you have ever had to make your ideas of notation, teaching, and church music really known, for you will have time enough thoroughly to indoctrinate people with them, and that you know you never have had in Teachers' Classes and Conventions."

I knew this would move him if anything would. No word of money or remuneration for his services passed between us, and I take this opportunity to say that Lowell Mason was the most misjudged man in this respect that I ever knew. He had plenty of money. It came in large sums from his works, but I do not believe he ever made a plan to make money, unless when investing his surplus funds. In his musical work it was always "Is this the best thing—will it be received—will it do the most good?" It was a clear case in its sphere of seeking first what was right and finding that all other things were added. And now that I am about it, I will say further of this remarkable man, that although great in every way, intellectually and morally as well as musically, he was like a child if any error could be pointed out in his works or defect in his teaching. It was not often that either thing happened, but when it did, it was "Is that so? Let us see," and prompt correction took place whenever he saw he was wrong. A favorite saying with him was, "Error makes us weak—truth makes us strong."

As I am writing these recollections I open my morning paper and the following item catches my eye. It is worth inserting here, but first I will explain that Mr. Mason was a Massachusetts man by birth, but lived for a while in Savannah, Ga. From there he was induced to return to Boston, by some prominent citizens who knew of his gifts, and believed that he could inaugurate the musical reform that they felt was needed. "Missionary Hymn" was, I am quite sure, his first publication.

When Bishop Heber's famous missionary hymn, "From Greenland's Icy Mountains," which he wrote in 1824 when in Ceylon, first reached this country, a lady in Savannah was much impressed with the beauty of it, and was particularly anxious to find a tune suited to it. She ransacked her music in vain, and then chancing to remember that in a bank down the street was a young clerk who had considerable reputation as a musical genius, she decided to ask him to write a tune to fit it. He readily complied with her request, and the melody thus dashed off is to-day sung all over the world, and is inseparably connected with the hymn. The young bank clerk was Lowell Mason.

Mr. Mason finally agreed to be at the head of the enterprise, which I decided to call "The Normal Musical Institute," but he said he had promised to go to England for a short visit. "When did I wish to commence?" "In June," I told him—June, July and August, I thought, should be the months. Well, he would be back in time without doubt. Then I went back to New York, and with Mason Brothers, the publishers, I took a different line of argument. I said: "It will be a great thing for the sale of your father's books to have his methods and music better understood than they can be in the shorter gatherings. (I had no books of my own then for such work.) Will you do the work of making the right people know of this all over the country?" They said they would, and they did. The responses were most encouraging, but a change took place in our plans. A few weeks before the time set to begin, Mr. Mason wrote that he could not be back until in the summer, perhaps not until the autumn. He had found work to do in England that delighted him, and that he felt was useful, and we must go on with the Institute without him, or defer the opening until the next summer. The brothers said, "We believe this is going to be a success, and if you will put it off we will not only pay all the expenses incurred thus far, but all the expenses of advertising it for next year. To this I readily agreed, as I did not wish to begin without the "master." So the notice of postponement, with explanations, was sent wherever the Institute had been advertised, and to all who wrote about coming, and the matter rested.

It will be of interest to mention that Mr. Mason's work in England had reference principally to congregational singing, although he gave some lessons in his incomparable way in the elementary principles of music. The Rev. John Curwen, father of the present Messrs. Curwen, and founder of the tonic-sol-fa method of notation, was present at many of Mr. Mason's lectures and lessons, and was greatly interested in both. Tonic-sol-fa was in its infancy then. Mr. Mason spoke of it as a simple notation for the poor people of Mr. Curwen's congregation. He had no idea that its use would extend much farther than that. It is certain that these two men—the one having exercised a vast influence for good on the singing of the people in America, and the other destined to perform a similar use in England—were sincerely attached to each other.

In the summer of 1853 the first Normal Musical Institute was held. Its sessions were in Dodworth's Hall, Broadway, New York, and continued three months. The principal teachers were Lowell Mason, Thomas Hastings, Wm. B. Bradbury and myself; assistant teachers, John Zundel, J. C. Woodman, and some others, for private lessons, whose names I do not now recall. The terms were $25 for the normal course; $50 if private lessons were added. There were upwards of a hundred from abroad, and enough singers from the city to make a good chorus. I think we met but one evening a week for chorus practice; certainly not more than two. Working as we did all through the day in the hot city, we did not think it safe to add much evening work. We gave no concerts. It was years before the "Normal" thought of deriving any revenue in that way. In fact, it was not exactly business to any of us (excepting to those who gave private lessons). Each had his regular occupation in other ways. As the years went on, modifications in many things were made, and improvements in some of the studies introduced, but the main objects of the institution and the program of daily work have remained in this, and have been adopted in the other institutes that have sprung up since, essentially as in that first memorable session.

About this time I gathered the best of the material together that we had been using in Rutgers and Spingler

Institutes, and with some new music, and an elementary course taken from Mr. Mason's books, embodied all in the "Academy Vocalist," my first work of any pretension for schools. Through the energy of the publishers, and the fact that other teachers and schools experienced the same needs that we felt, the book had considerable success. The "Flower Queen" quickly became popular, and "Hazel Dell" began the run which was not to end until the boys whistled it and the hand organs played it from Maine to Georgia, and no ambition for a song-writer could go higher than that.

These successes gave me a new inclination to write, and I decided that I would next make a cantata for my choir. At this time one of the students in the Union Theological Seminary was C. M. Cady, who, afterward, with my brother E. T. Root, started the firm of Root & Cady in Chicago. I decided on "Daniel" as the subject, and Mr. Cady and Fanny Crosby helped me in preparing the words. About the time the cantata was completed I was approached with reference to making a church-music book with Mr. Bradbury. This I was very glad to do, and "The Shawm" was the result. All interested thought it would be a good plan to print the new cantata at the end of the book—that many of its choruses could be used as anthems, and that some of its solos and quartets might also find a place in church service. So that was done; but in order that Mr. Bradbury's name might rightfully appear as joint author, I took out two of my numbers from the cantata, and he filled their places. "The Shawm" was a succcss, but the cantata was so much called for, separate from the book, that it was not bound up with it after the first or second edition. Its place was filled with set pieces, and "Daniel" has been printed as a book by itself ever since.

And now I decided to build a new house on the old place at North Reading, not only better to accommodate the clan which assembled there every summer, but for the greater comfort of the dear people who stayed there all the time. So one of my boy friends, then a prosperous carpenter in the town, came to New York, and we agreed upon a plan which on his return met the approval of the home folks and was speedily carried out. The delight with which we went into the new and completed house at Willow Farm at our next vacation can not be described. No palace ever gave kingly occupants greater pleasure. In the old red house the swaying branches of the great elm did not reach our windows; now we were right up under them. There, close by, at the end of a long, graceful bough, was where the oriole, in his gorgeous red costume, swung his hammock every year, and there it was, as we looked, rocking as of yore in the summer breeze.

It was not only delightful for us to be at the old home in the summer, but a great gratification to give some extra pleasure to the old friends of the little town. This was principally done by singing in church on Sunday, though we sometimes gave a concert on a week evening, to which everybody was invited. There were so many of us, and always some musical friends to swell the number, that we had an excellent choir—one that would have been acceptable anywhere. We all remember well a tall, shy boy, who then was an apprentice to a farmer in the town, who used to listen with wonder and delight to our music, and who has told me since that he could not have looked upon princes with greater awe than he did upon us in those days. He is now one of Chicago's millionaires. One of his "deals" on the Board of Trade will ever be memorable in the history of that institution. Six hundred and fifty thousand dollars clear in one day, not to mention the enormous profits of other days during the operation! His name is B. P. Hutchinson. A few years ago we rode up from Boston one summer day, to see the old friends. He enjoyed greatly being where people called him " Ben," and treated him as if he were no more than common folks.

My life now went on very pleasantly in New York, but I began to be asked to conduct musical conventions in the neighboring states. My connection with the Teachers' Classes, and the " Normal" recently held, and with Mr. Bradbury in " The Shawm," had brought me more before the singers of the country. I declined at first, partly because I did not like to take the responsibility of the entire conduct of one of those gatherings, and partly because I did not care to break into my regular work. But finally I decided to try it, and accepted a call from Sussex county, New Jersey, and now I miss again my lost diary. With that I could have told exactly when and where I had my first convention experience; who employed me; who the clergymen and prominent musical people of the section were; where I stayed, and who invited me to dinner or tea; who were the solo singers; what books I used, and how much I received. But as it is I can only recall a pleasant scene in a hilly country, with a crowd of happy people, who took kindly to my way of teaching and entertaining them.

My first successful song ("Hazel Dell") was published in 1852 by Wm. Hall & Son, who then occupied a store on the corner of Broadway and Park Place. This was followed by a contract with this house, by which I was to give them all my sheet music publications for three years. My brother had returned from the South, and becoming tired, as he said, of being, as a teacher, only " Mr. Root's brother," decided to learn the music business, and was then a clerk in the Hall establishment.

The Messrs. Hall were the publisher's of Gottschalk's and Wm. Vincent Wallace's music at that time, and I frequently met those gentlemen there. Wallace, who may be remembered as the author of "Maritana," an opera quite popular at one time, and still somewhat sung, and of many fine songs and pianoforte compositions, was a distinguished pianist and a fine violinist. As a concert player upon *either* instrument he would have been a success, but undertaking to give concerts upon *both*, he failed. It is a curious fact that the public will not give a musician a high place in its esteem if he makes himself prominent in two or more specialties, however excellent he may be in them.

I remember once seeing a great conductor step down from his platform and play a solo upon the violin. It was done, of course, extremely well, but everybody felt that he had "stepped down" in more senses than one. Carl Zerrahn, the able and popular conductor of the Handel and Haydn Society of Boston, and of the Worcester and other Festivals, came over to this country with the Germania orchestra as a solo flute player, but I dare say that not a dozen people of the tens of thousands who have placed him, in their estimation, upon the highest round of the ladder in his specialty, know that he plays that instrument at all, and were he to take his flute some day instead of his baton, and give them a solo, he might astonish them, but he would have to pay for that pleasure by "stepping down" a round, musically, in their estimation. Mr. Zerrahn sings well, but he never sings a song. He understands perfectly the value of having but one specialty in the public mind.

"Hall's" was a famous rendezvous for musical people. A frequent visitor was Captain Brooks, who owned and ran a little steamboat from New York to Bridgeport, Conn. He was an enthusiastic and indefatigable collector of old violins. He would often rush in and want some one to go down to his boat with him and see a new violin—"a real Stradivarius" or "Guarnarius," or something of the kind. He could not play much, but through his great interest in the subject he had become a pretty good judge of the instrument, and if he was sometimes deceived as to the maker he had no poor ones in his collection. One day he was particularly excited, and wanted some of us to go with him and see a violin that he had just paid some hundreds of dollars for. A slight, smooth-faced, decidedly handsome young fellow, who was known to play the violin well, was there, and Captain Brooks induced him to go and try it. I could see that the young violinist was skeptical as to the great merits of the instrument, as claimed by the excited Captain. But when he took it into his hand, before he touched bow to string, his whole manner changed (though what he could see in that glance I could not imagine), and when he tucked it lovingly under his chin the rest of the world was nothing to him for half an hour or more. He was entranced, and so were we. It was a rare and beautiful instrument, and the young player was Theodore Thomas.

Speaking of the "Germania" reminds me of the delight with which we listened to the first fine orchestra that came to this country. It was called the Steyermarkische orchestra. It was not large, about twenty players, if I remember rightly, but they played *in tune*, and the smoothness so produced was a revelation. Their shading and pianissimo playing were also new and delightful. They had a successful tour and went home. This must have been about 1846. Then came the Germania orchestra, with Carl Bergmann for conductor. They gave concerts in our principal cities, and finally disbanded here, most of its members remaining on this side of the water.

The only other foreign orchestra to come to this country was Jullien's; I forget whether just before or just after the Germania, but probably at about the same time. Jullien was a talented man and an able conductor, but he was much laughed at for his flashy taste in dress and his funny affectations. He brought with him a gorgeous conductor's stand and platform, and a magnificent chair, all apparently of ebony and gold. After each number he would sink into this great chair and let his arms fall as if the splendid performance had entirely exhausted him, for the performances, although of the sensational order, were fine. Bottesini, the great contra-bass player, was in this company. I see he is prominent in Europe now as an author and conductor.

But it was the oboe player who created the greatest sensation. He was the first one here to continue a tone while taking breath. I shall never forget the curious effect upon the audience when, at a cadenza, the accompaniment ceased and a long tone commenced. After it had continued to the utmost bounds of the longest breath there was a distressed holding of breath by the audience, and when it still went on, strong and clear, the excitement was intense. A little longer and everybody saw he must have taken breath somehow, and the relief and applause were tremendous. The instrument requires but little breath, and he could supply it from the mouth on the principle of a bellows, while filling his lungs through the nostrils.

We do not now have to get orchestras from the other side of the water, nor to go over there to hear the best. Theodore Thomas has rendered both unnecessary by the impulse he has given to the formation of first-class orchestral combinations in this country.

CHAPTER IX.

1853-1855, NEW YORK—A FRANK STATEMENT—GENIUSES IN MUSIC—"THE SHINING SHORE"—EARLY BOOKS—THE FIRST AMERICAN-MADE DOCTOR OF MUSIC—EARLY CONVENTIONS AT RICHMOND, VA., AND IN THE WEST—PREPARING TO LEAVE NEW YORK—HOW THE NORMAL WENT TO NORTH READING.

BEFORE going on to speak more at length of my compositions and books, I desire to make a frank statement with regard to myself and my work in that line; and my first remark is, that I never felt in the least that I had a "call" to be a musical composer. My first efforts, as I have shown, were made to supply my own wants, and it was only on finding that they were in a good degree successful for myself and others that I continued them.

I can truly say I never dreamed of eminence as a writer of music, and never had fame for an object. Some of my friends who knew who "Wurzel" was, used to say: "Aim high; he who aims at the sun will reach farther than he will who has a lower object for a mark." But I saw so many failures on the part of those who were "aiming high" in the sense intended, and trying to do useless great things, that I had no temptation in that direction, but preferred to shoot at something I could hit.

I did, on two or three occasions, write what I knew would not be needed, but in every case had an object. Once, two prizes were offered by the publishers of a musical paper in New York—fifty dollars for the best four-part song, and twenty-five dollars for the second best. I sent in two, anonymously, (as all had to do,) and took both prizes. Two of the judges were loud despisers of "trash," as they indiscriminately called all simple music, and were much disgusted when they learned who had taken the prizes.

Friends used to say: "Root, why don't you do something better than 'Hazel Dell,' and things of that grade?" I used to answer: "If you and other musicians wished to use songs of a higher grade, either for teaching or for your own singing, do you suppose you would take mine when you could get Schubert or Franz, or even Abt, at the same price or less?" They were generally silent at that, and then I would tell them that in the elementary stages of music there were tens of thousands of people whose wants would not be supplied at all if there were in the world only such music as they (the critics) would have; but

> "Convince a man against his will—
> He's of the same opinion still."

So they continued harping upon the well-worn subject. At last I thought I would publish a song or two above the grade of the "People's song." It was much easier to write where the resources were greater; where I did not have to stop and say, "That interval is too difficult," or "That chord won't do," and I produced two or three that I knew would never be wanted to any extent. But they gave me the opportunity, when the old question came, "Why don't you do something better?" to say "Have you ever seen or heard of 'Gently, Ah, Gently,' or 'Pictures of Memory?'" To which they would have to answer "No," and I could say "That is why I do not write 'something better,' as you call it. Neither you nor any one else would know anything about my work on that grade, and I should be wasting my time in trying to supply the wants of a few people, who are already abundantly supplied by the best writers of Europe." Then they would say, "Well, it is nothing to write those little songs." I remember one, especially, then an eminent musician in New York, who said: "I could write a dozen in a day," and, thinking there might be money in it, he did try under a *nom de plume*. But his dozen or less of "simple songs" slumbered quietly on the shelves of a credulous publisher until they went to the paper mill. It is easy to write correctly a simple song, but so to use the material of which such a song must be made that it will be received and live in the hearts of the people is quite another matter.

Geniuses among musical composers, that is, those who invent and give to the world new forms and harmonies *that live*, are rare—but two or three appear in a century. Of such, Beethoven in his day and Wagner in this, are conspicuous examples. Then there are great composers, who, although not inventors in the above sense, make use of existing material in such new and wonderful ways that their music not only delights and benefits the world, but is regarded in an important sense as original. Of such it seems to me that Mendelssohn is in the highest rank.

In all grades from the simplest to the highest—from Stephen C. Foster to Wagner, and in every kind of instrumental music, compositions divide themselves into two classes in another way. In one class are the comparatively few compositions having that mysterious vitality of which I have spoken; that power to retain their hold upon the hearts of the people after their companions of the same grade, and by the same composer perhaps, are forgotten. In the other class are those which create a temporary interest if any, and soon pass away. I do not think a composer ever knows when that mysterious life enters his work. If I may judge by my own experience, successes are usually surprises, and the work that we think best while we are doing it, is liable to be considered in a very different light by the public.

That applies, however, to single compositions and not to

books. One may think he is making a good instruction book, or putting together a good collection of music, without being mistaken. I should like to enlarge upon this point when I come to speak of particular compositions. All I want seen now is, that I am simply one, who, from such resources as he finds within himself, makes music for the people, having always a particular need in view. This, it seems to me, is a thing that a person may do with some success, without being either a genius or a great composer.

My next book, I think, was the "Musical Album." It was on the plan of the "Academy Vocalist," and followed that work when my classes wanted something new. I now wrote some every day, taking the intervals between lessons and occasionally an evening for that purpose. I also took a course of lessons during one of those winters from an excellent harmonist and teacher, a Frenchman by the name of Girac.

Mason Brothers published a musical monthly called *The Musical Review*, and at one time I undertook to supply music for each number. I remember once when the boy came for copy I had none ready, but looking into the drawer of my desk I found a piece that I had written some months before and thrown aside as not being of much account. I sent this for want of something better. It was "There's Music in the Air," and illustrates what I was saying a little while ago about not knowing when we do that which will touch the popular heart.

But it was at Willow Farm that I enjoyed my writing and book-making most. However we might be confined in New York by the summer Normal, we always had two or three weeks before the autumn work commenced at the old place, or, I might say now, the new place. With the dear mother about the house, and father attending to farm matters, with children or grand-children always around one or the other, an atmosphere was there which was very favorable to the work I was doing. One day, I remember, I was working at a set of graded part-songs for singing classes, and mother, passing through the room, laid a slip from one of her religious newspapers before me, saying: "George, I think that would be good for music." I looked, and the poem began, "My days are gliding swiftly by." A simple melody sang itself along in my mind as I read, and I jotted it down, and went on with my work. That was the origin of "The Shining Shore."

Later, when I took up the melody to harmonize it, it seemed so very simple and commonplace that I hesitated about setting the other parts to it. But I finally decided that it might be useful to somebody, and completed it, though it was not printed until some months afterward. When, in after years, this song was sung in all the churches and Sunday-schools of the land, and in every land and tongue where our missionaries were at work, and so demonstrated that it had in it that mysterious life of which I have spoken, I tried to see why it should be so, but in vain. To the musician there is not one reason in melody or harmony, scientifically regarded, for such a fact. To him, hundreds of others now forgotten were better. I say so much about this little song because it is a particularly good illustration of the fact that the simplest music may have vitality as well as that which is higher, and that the composer knows no more about it in one case than in the other.

The newspaper slip containing this hymn which my mother handed me had no author's name attached. It was some years before I learned that it was the Rev. David Nelson who wrote it, and it was but recently that the following sketch of his life, taken from "Asa Turner and His Times," was sent to me:

David Nelson was born in East Tennessee in 1793; graduated from Washington College in 1809. He at first studied medicine, but afterward entered the ministry and preached in Tennessee and Kentucky, and finally removed to Missouri. He was six feet and two inches high, and had a voice of great power and melody, which he used with great success, anticipating the singing evangelist of to-day.

He opened a plantation in Missouri in true southern style, but an address by Theodore D. Weld changed his sentiments and led him to say, "I will live on roast potatoes and salt before I will hold slaves." He became an advocate of colonization, and, in 1831, at the close of a camp-meeting, read a notice calling people to meet to discuss the project. Disorder followed, and Dr. Nelson was driven from his home by a body of armed men. After three days and nights of wandering he came to the great river, and made known his condition to friends in Quincy, Illinois, on the opposite side—there, far away.

Hiding in the bushes, with the Mississippi at the foot of the bluff "gliding swiftly by," and "friends passing over" to and from a free state—a safe landing on which he could "almost discover," he wrote on the backs of letters the Christian psalm of life, "My days are gliding swiftly by."

Two members of the Congregational Church in Quincy, at dusk paddled a "dug-out" across the river and fished in the slough near the western shore. Learning by signs just where Dr. Nelson was, they let their boat float down toward the Missouri "strand." With huge strides the fugitive evangelist came down, and the slaveholding scouts were foiled.

Dr. Nelson, well-nigh starved, asked if they had brought him anything to eat. "Something in the bag," replied one of the brethren, rowing with all his might. The brave but famished man brought up from the bag at the stern only dried codfish and crackers. Laughing heartily he said, "Well, I'm dependent on Yankees, and shall have to be a Yankee myself after this, and I may as well begin on codfish and crackers."

The chivalry crossed the river and demanded that Dr. Nelson should be given up, but were told that he was under the laws of Illinois, and slaveholders could not have him.

Dr. Nelson was commissioned by the Home Missionary Society in Illinois, and, in addition to his regular work, made powerful and touching anti-slavery addresses. He died in October, 1844.

From 1853 to 1855 inclusive the Normal Musical Institute was held in New York city, but every year my convention work, and, consequently, my knowledge of what the singers throughout the country needed, and could do, increased, and every year it became more and more apparent that the city was not a good place for Normals, not only on account of the heat but the expense. So, in 1855, I decided to give up my city work as soon as it could be brought about, and devote myself wholly to conventions, Normal and authorship. Meanwhile Mr. Mason had come to like New York, and his sons, who had prospered greatly there, induced him to leave his Boston home and settle in the great city. They had some picturesque and valuable acres on the mountain side, in Orange, New Jersey, and soon the three families built and occupied fine residences there.

One day, soon after Mr. Mason came to New York to live, I called on Dr. Ferris, with whom I had been connected for some years at Rutgers Institute, and who was now Chancellor of the New York University, and said to him, "Could your institution confer the degree of Doctor of Music?" "Certainly." "Well, I think that that title has never been conferred upon an American by an American institution. S. Parkman Tuckerman, of Boston, is the only American Doctor of Music that I know of, and his degree is from an English university." I then said, "you know of Lowell Mason, and what he has done for church music and musical instruction in schools and among the people of this country." "Yes." "Well, what would you think of having your University the first in America to confer the title of Doctor of Music, and that that distinction should fall upon America's greatest musical educator?" He thought so well of it that it was promptly done.

I said nothing to Mr. Mason about it until it was accomplished. When it was, and was announced in one of the morning papers, I took a copy and went to his house. He was in his library, and as I entered I saluted him with "Good morning, *Doctor* Mason," emphasizing the title. He looked up, evidently wondering a little that I should be making a cheap joke of that kind, but immediately resumed his usual manner, and said, "I want to show you a tune that I have just made for this hymn." He was very full of that tune. I forget now what it was, but I remember that I had considerable difficulty in getting the idea of the title fully into his mind. I mention this as illustrating the fact, well known to Dr. Mason's friends, that he never sought honors or distinctions any more than he did wealth. He gave himself wholly to his work, and if other things came they must come without any effort on his part.

Among the early normals was Wm. C. Van Meter, then a typical far-westerner, a preacher, exhorter, singing-master, and I don't know what else. Eloquent and magnetic as a speaker in his strange western way, he created a great interest in the class. He stopped at the Astor House the night he arrived, and said that when he got up in the morning and saw such crowds going down toward a church that he saw a little way off (Trinity) he thought there must be a revival there, and he reported that he did not wait for his breakfast, but hurried down to join in the exercises. It took him some time to realize that that was the ordinary flow of humanity at the "down town" hour.

Mr. Van Meter was great for engineering musical conventions. He made up his mind that my talents were being wasted in New York and the East, and that I must go to the South and West to be properly appreciated. So he prepared the way, to begin with, in Richmond, Va. Let Mr. Van Meter get an audience together and there was no resisting him. He could make people laugh or cry at will, and paint in more glowing colors whatever he described than any man I ever knew. He always induced a large number of people to attend conventions, but he made it particularly hard for the conductor to meet the expectations that he raised.

I went to Richmond first to conduct a convention of Mr. Van Meter's getting up, and then some months after to conduct some performances of "The Flower Queen." On this latter occasion my home was the hospitable mansion of the father of "Marion Harland." She was then a young lady, writing her second book, her first, "Alone," having been a great success, making her famous at a bound. The Rev. Dr. Terhune, whose wife she now is, then a young man, was also a guest in that charming home. At the close of "The Flower Queen" class I was presented with my first gold-headed cane. In after years I had good reason to believe the donors would have been glad to break it over the head of the man who wrote war songs for the northern army. I hope and think that feeling has now entirely passed away. On both sides we did what we thought was right.

Speaking of Richmond reminds me that I conducted two conventions in Washington, not far from that time, one alone, and one assisted by Mr. Bradbury. I mention them because the second one was in the Smithsonian Institute when Prof. Henry was at its head. It was an effort to secure a more general attendance than such gatherings usually have, and was located at Washington to be near the southern states. I remember well the hearty welcome that Prof. Henry gave us, and the kind interest he took in the exercises. Nothing in the nature of popular education appealed to him in vain. He was a man of whom the nation is justly proud.

Under Mr. Van Meter's management I conducted two conventions in Quincy, Ills., and held a sort of short Normal in Jacksonville. A part of the program of this manager seemed always to be a present for the conductor at the close of the session. A silver cup, or a cane, or something for the table, always appeared at the closing concert, and I used to get Mr. Van Meter to help me return thanks, which he always did in the most eloquent manner. This remarkable man worked afterward, for some years, in and for the Five Points Mission in New York, and was for a still greater number of years in evangelistic labors in Rome, Italy.

It was hard to leave the work and the friends in New York. The work had been pleasant and the friends most kind and generous. Not a year of the ten that I had been there did the "commencements" fail to bring some token of remembrance, often costly, always useful, from schools or church. The last, and most valuable, was a solid silver tea-service to my wife when we left Mercer Street Church. We have all these gifts now, excepting some volumes of rare old English music, one of the annual presents from Rutgers. They were in my working room at the store at the time of the great fire, and shared the fate of my diary. Thinking of the presents, a beautiful silver cup reminds me of a class I had in those days at the "Brick Church" in Orange, New Jersey. I mention it because I think it will interest some of the many hundreds who now go daily to New York from there, to know that then three persons constituted the daily quota from that station.

As soon as I decided to leave New York I said to my old friends in North Reading, "If you will prepare a suitable place for us, I will have the Normal Musical Institute here next summer." They called a town meeting, at which was explained that the school would probably bring a hundred strangers there for three months, which would mean to the town some money and a good deal of music. Both ideas were well received and prompt action was taken. The building that was prepared for us is worth telling about.

When I was a boy there stood in the center of the village one of the old colonial "meeting houses." Its pews were square, its pulpit twelve or more feet high, with a "sounding board," like a huge bell, hanging above it, under which the minister stood. When at last the old building became too dilapidated for further use it was decided to tear it down and replace it with a modern structure. In the olden times all had worshiped there together with no dissensions, but, gradually, differences of opinion had arisen, and had been maintained as usual in such cases with a good deal of rancor. The "orthodox," as they were called, although not the most numerous, had the most money, and were the most willing to spend it for church purposes, so they had minister and service pretty much their own way. This did not tend to conciliate the other side, among whom were quite a number of Universalists, and who, in consequence, did not go much to "meeting."

Still they went on and put up the new building, nominally all together as a society, but it was really by the energy, and mostly by the money, of the first named party that it was accomplished. When the new edifice was completed, and a minister settled, the Universalists asked permission to have service there occasionally on Sunday afternoons. I don't think it was bigotry, so much as conscience, that led the orthodox party to refuse this request, but it was refused. Then the opposing elements got together and said, "This building belongs to the society, and a majority of the society can say what kind of preaching shall be in it." They probably would not have ignored the fact that they did very little toward building it if they had been kindly treated, but, as it was, they called a meeting of the society and managed to have a majority there to vote that a Universalist minister should occupy the new pulpit all the time.

I was but a boy then, but I remember how sad my old grandfather, one of the deacons of the church, looked the next day. However, he went immediately to work to get the names of those who would form a new society, specifically "orthodox," and build a new church. This was speedily done, but, as was foreseen, the Universalists, and those who sympathized with them but did not care much about "going to meeting," could not, or would not support a minister, and carry on Sunday services. So, in a short time, all such efforts were abandoned, and the building was useless for years, excepting as it was wanted for an occasional public gathering.

When, therefore, my proposition came, all differences ceased. Music and some general advantage to the town were grounds for a general amnesty, and it was voted unanimously to give up the building to the town, and then the town voted to prepare it for our use. This they found would make it just what was wanted for a convenient town hall.

CHAPTER X.

1856–1859, NORTH READING, MASS.—A GREAT SCHOOL IN A SMALL TOWN—A VISIT FROM HENRY WARD BEECHER AND MRS. STOWE—NATHAN RICHARDSON AND "ROSALIE, THE PRAIRIE FLOWER"—WRITING AT WILLOW FARM—THE "HAYMAKERS"—THE BEGINNING OF EAR TRAINING IN CLASSES FOR HARMONY—"EXCEPT YE BECOME AS LITTLE CHILDREN"—DISTINGUISHED VISITORS—RELATIVE PROFITS OF CANTATA MAKER AND CANTATA GIVER—COMPOSITIONS AS PROPERTY.

THE Normal Musical Institute commenced in North Reading in 1856. The faculty then was Dr. Mason, Mr. Webb, Mr. Bradbury and myself—August Kreissman, of Boston, assisting in private lessons. The attendance was large, and the difference between the city and this dear old place delightful. As may readily be seen, so long as this was the only institution of the kind in the country it not only attracted people from afar, but it brought the prominent ones--those who at home were the principal teachers or singers of their sections. All liked North Reading—the place, the people and the arrangements for work. It *is* a picturesque old town. Few views are more beautiful than that which is seen from a hill near the village, of the Ipswich River, there a small stream, winding in and out among the trees that fringe its sides, far away in the meadows below; and the walk over this hill and through the woods beyond to Willow Farm was a great delight, especially to the western contingent, to whom the "rocks and rills and wooded hills" of New England were a novelty.

The people of the town were always ready to do anything in their power to further the interests of the school and to make the stay of the strangers pleasant. The building, as it had been prepared for us, was very comfortable and convenient. Up one flight of stairs was the room where all assembled for the opening exercises, and where Dr. Mason's and other lessons to the whole Institute were given. On the ground floor was a larger hall, and below that a light basement. An additional room in a neighboring building was also used for some of the smaller classes. We had one evening rehearsal in the week in the hall, and one evening when the friends and neighbors could come and hear us sing.

It was a strange thing to hear such a chorus under such conductors as Dr. Mason and Mr. Webb in so small a place as our little village, but we never lacked an audience. Indeed, as the Normal did not then seek to derive any revenue from public performances, it was not long before we were troubled for room on our public evenings. We invited the neighbors, but we did not limit the neighborhood, and that gradually extended until it took in the neighboring towns, which were Andover on the north, Middleton and Lynnfield on the east, the other two Readings on the south, and Wilmington on the west. Every pleasant Friday, at five or six o'clock in the afternoon, vehicles of all sorts could be seen coming from one or more of these places to be in time for the evening sing. Those were happy times. How Dr. Mason's grand chorus work and the exquisite glee singing under Mr. Webb did ring and float out at the open windows of our pleasant hall, and away upon the summer air! Almost incredible stories were told of the distance at which our music was heard when the evenings were still.

One of the most prominent members of the Institute at North Reading was W. W. Killip, of Geneseo, N. Y. He was a man of excellent abilities, musical and otherwise, and he had a hearty, whole-souled way of meeting people that was very attractive. Mrs. Harriet Beecher Stowe then lived at Andover, near the Theological Seminary, seven miles from our town. Henry Ward Beecher generally spent a week or two with his sister there in the summer. The boys, or, I should say, all the members of the Institute, wanted to see Mr. Beecher, and Dr. Mason and I intended to ask him to spend a day with us, but Mr. Killip wouldn't wait. He said: "I'm not going to have any uncertainty about this; I'm going to see him and get him to set a day to come soon." Ordinarily, such a messenger, going on his own account, would not have fared so well as a simple bearer of an invitation from Dr. Mason, whom Mr. Beecher highly esteemed; but I knew Mr. Beecher, and was sure Mr. Killip's bluff, hearty way would interest him. He went, and came back triumphant. "Yes, he's coming next Tuesday." "Did he consent readily?" I asked. "He hesitated some," Mr. K. replied, "but I told him I'd vote for his candidate for Governor if he would come, and that settled it."

Not only Mr. Beecher, but Mrs. Stowe and the old father, Dr. Lyman Beecher, and Mr. Charles Beecher came. After the opening exercises and Dr. Mason's inimitable teaching lesson, the great desire of the class to hear Mr. Beecher speak was gratified. His beginning was most characteristic. He said: "I like the way your seats are arranged to bring the class near the platform and into close connection with the teacher, and your platform is just the right height. The devil always looks on when they are building a church to see how far they get the pews from the minister." Then Mr. Beecher, supposing a case, paced slowly the long way of the platform, to represent the wide space that was being left between minister and people, counting his steps in a crescendo of satisfaction, and bringing his fist down into his open palm at the close—all to represent what his satanic majesty would do and say under the circumstances: "One, two, three, four, five, six, seven; good! he'll never hit 'em!" Then he talked for half an hour on the relations of music to the church and the home, as only Mr. Beecher could talk. The whole party dined at Willow Farm and attended the afternoon chorus and glee singing, which they greatly enjoyed.

About the time that I began to be known as a successful song-writer Nathan Richardson (afterward author of "The Popular Piano Instructor") started a music publishing house in Boston. He had lived some years in Germany, and had come home filled with a strong desire to improve the musical tastes of the benighted people of his native land. This sounds like laughing at my old friend. Well, it is so; but not so much as I have done to his face many a time. The saying of the boatswain in "Pinafore" of the Admiral would have applied exactly here: "He means well, but he don't know." As it was, he determined that he would publish nothing but high-class music. I doubt if there was an American then whose compositions he would have taken as a gift. He had an elegant store on Washington street, fitted and furnished in an expensive manner through the generosity of an older brother, who had plenty of money, and who seemed delighted to aid Nathan in his praiseworthy efforts for the fatherland.

All went well for a few months. Musicians met there and greatly enjoyed a chat amid the luxurious surroundings, and they occasionally bought a piece of music when they found what their pupils could use. Some of the comparatively few amateurs of the city, who were advanced, also patronized the establishment, but it did not pay. At length both Nathan and the rich brother became convinced that they could not make people buy music, however fine, that they could not understand nor perform, and they found that calling the music that the common people liked, "trash," did not help the matter at all.

So the question came up between them of getting something to publish that the people would buy. In this dilemma my friend came to me and asked me if I would write him six songs. I laughed at him a little, but was very happy to do it, my three-years' engagement with Wm. Hall & Son being just out. The songs were finished during vacation, and we tried them over at Willow Farm in manuscript. There were six of us, and I said: "Let us choose from these six songs the one that we think will become most popular. The oldest shall choose first, then the next shall choose from the remainder, then the next, and so on down to the youngest." The youngest was my sister Fanny, then a young girl, and when the choice came to her the only song left unchosen was "Rosalie, the Prairie Flower."

When I took the songs to my friend he said he would prefer to buy them outright. What would I take for the "lot"? There was a bit of sarcasm in the last word. "Well," I replied, "as you propose a wholesale instead of a retail transaction, you shall have the "lot" at wholesale prices, which will be one hundred dollars apiece—six hundred dollars for all." He laughed at the idea. His splendid foreign reprints had cost him nothing. The idea of paying such a sum for these little things could not be thought of. "Very well," I said, "Give me the usual royalty; that will suit me quite as well." This was agreed to, and when he had paid me in royalties nearly three thousand dollars for "Rosalie" alone, he concluded that six hundred for the "lot" would not have been an unreasonable price, especially as all the songs of the set had a fair sale, for which he had to pay in addition. But he learned wisdom by experience as to what people in elementary states must have, and he showed himself an able man and a good musician in the great instruction book that bears his name.

Willow Farm was now headquarters. From there I went to musical conventions in all parts of the country, and there I worked at books and songs. I have said that I never considered that I had a "call" to be a musical composer—that my efforts in that way began by trying to supply my own needs. I can say the same in a still more emphatic way in regard to writing words for music. I presume I should never have attempted to do that if I could always have found some one to do what I wanted. But this I could not do. Sometimes the trouble was with the meter, sometimes with words that followed each other roughly, jolting, like a wagon over a rocky road; sometimes a thin vowel for a high soprano tone, and sometimes wrong emotional expression for the music I had in mind.

My efforts at writing words began in New York, and I well remember how laborious the somewhat mechanical matter of rhyming was at first, and how gradually it grew easier with practice. At North Reading there was no one near to go to for words, but that kind of work was not now so formidable, thanks to the practice I had had, and I enjoyed greatly turning into rhyme for lessons and songs the thoughts that came amid the pleasant scenes that surrounded me there.

The beginning of this kind of work is seen in the "Sabbath Bell," which was the first book to grade carefully lessons and part-songs for singing classes. This was my first venture alone for choirs, singing classes and conventions, and I attribute its success largely to these words, which were written as needed for the grade wanted. The same scenes and surroundings contributed to the singing class department of the "Diapason," which followed. My first sight of the West impressed me strongly, and some songs about the prairies naturally followed. Among the lessons and songs written as above described, some have continued in use to the present time. I mention a few of them here: "By the brooklet clear," "Music everywhere," "High in the summer sky," "O'er prairie, green and fair," "Autumn winds," "O'er the calm lake," "Don't you see me coming?" (song of the bobolink), "Up in the morning so early," "Have you seen my Lillie?" "Ha! ha! ha! Laughing is contagious," "Out on the prairie," "Happy New Year," "Softly she faded," "To the mountain," "On the heather," "Thoughts of childhood" and "Merry May."

While North Reading was headquarters, I was often in New York on my way to or from conventions, and of course in constant communication with my publishers. On one occasion, during the year 1856, Lowell Mason, Jr., the senior partner of the house of Mason Brothers, suggested that I should write a cantata for mixed voices, but on some secular subject. After some consideration haymaking, as it was then carried on, was chosen, and "The Haymakers" decided upon as the title. Mr. Mason (L. M., Jr.) took a great interest in this work, and to a great extent planned it, not only as to characters and action, but as to what, in a general way, each number should be about.

Taking his plan I wrote both words and music—sometimes the words first, sometimes the music first, and sometimes both together. I did most of the work in my new library at Willow Farm, where, by stepping to the door, I could see the very fields in which I had swung the scythe and raked the hay, and in which I had many a time hurried to get the last load into the barn before the thunder-storm should burst upon us. In fact, nearly every scene described in the cantata had its counterpart in my experience on the old farm not many years before, always excepting "Snipkins," the city man who found himself so much out of place in the country and among the haymakers. That was a purely imaginary character. This cantata was published in 1857, and began to be sung immediately. During the following year I conducted it twenty times in Boston and the neighboring cities.

The second year of the Normal at North Reading had a still larger attendance. To find boarding-places within a reasonable distance for all, and to get pianos enough up from Boston to supply the increasing number who wished to take private lessons, became a difficult matter, but it was managed, and the work generally improved with experience. About this time I tried teaching elementary harmony in classes, requiring the pupils to know chords through the ear before writing them. There had been, as I thought, too much *eye* harmony—deciding that certain harmonies were wrong because they did not look right. Pupils had received the kind of training that leads to condemning the consecutive fifths that a skillful composer might use, because, to the eye, they violated a rule. I had also observed that many harmony papers that had been given to pupils to fill out with proper chords were so much Greek to them, so far as hearing in their minds the chords they were writing; not but that the teacher might have played the lesson to them as it should be, but there was no such ear training as made the harmony a part of the musical life of the pupil.

I found that twenty or thirty could hear and answer as well as one alone, so I played and they listened until they could tell promptly and accurately what they heard, beginning, of course, with the simplest combinations. In this training they had nothing to look at, and they wrote only what had entered their musical minds by the proper avenue, viz., the ear. I think the idea of working in this way came to me from teaching the blind. I found they knew and enjoyed harmony far more thoroughly than seeing pupils did, and the result of my experiment was very satisfactory. Instead of getting tired of harmony and giving it up because they could not understand it (really because they did not get it), the class grew more and more interested in their harmony lessons. I do not remember any approval of Dr. Mason and Mr. Webb that gave me so much satisfaction and pleasure as that which came to me on account of this work. Both were pleased that harmony, which had been a dull and heavy study, now promised to be a bright and cheery one.

It was interesting to observe the changes that came over the new pupils during their first three or four weeks in the Institute. Many of them were great men at home—had been praised and looked up to until they hardly liked to appear as if they came as learners. Not infrequently, on being introduced, one would give me a friendly slap on the shoulder and say: "Well, Root, I thought I would come and see how you do things here," or, "I should like to show you my way of teaching," etc. The old hands standing by would look on mischievously or compassionately, as the case might be, but generally said nothing to the new-comers about the trials and tribulations and the "valley of humiliation" which they would be pretty sure to find before them when they came to Dr. Mason's searching examination and work, to say nothing of what would happen to them if their voices or style of singing were out of true. It was interesting to see how their self-assertion began to fade out under the criticisms of the teachers' class, or when they and all in the voice class could see that the tone they had been producing was wrong.

It was very hard for some of them at first to refrain from standing on their dignity and arguing the matter, but a few words from Dr. Mason on the attitude that the true learner assumes soon opened their eyes. He was very fond of saying: "Except ye become as little children, ye can not enter into the kingdom of heaven, nor the kingdom of sound, nor any other kingdom." He used also to say: "Do not waste time in argument. You are here to get what we have to give you. Take what you think will be useful; what you think will not be, you can reject without saying anything about it." It was very common to see the self-satisfied faces of this kind of new-comers change, first to perplexity, then to anxiety, and finally to discouragement. They were almost certain then to say: "We thought we knew something about music and teaching when we came, but now we see we did not know anything worth speaking of." Then they were told that they had learned the hardest and most important lesson of the session, and from the valley the way would now be pleasant to the sunlight. Dr. Mason often said what he continually exemplified: "Do not be afraid to say 'I do not know.' The teacher who says that to his class will always be believed when he says he does know. Nothing is so dangerous to a teacher's reputation as conceit, and nothing so shuts him out from progress."

All sorts of people came to see us during those summer sessions. Sometimes it was one of Dr. Mason's co-workers in general education, and sometimes musical celebrities, native or foreign. Of the former, Governor Boutwell and Mr. Wm. Russell, the foremost elocutionist of those days, were prominent. These men gave the class many valuable ideas, as well as much enjoyment. A very pleasant gentleman was Mr. Littleton, one of the firm of Novello & Co., of London, who had met Dr. Mason in England, and, being in this country, strayed up to our little town to give him a call.

I took a great deal of interest in those days in the success of my cantatas, which had become so unexpectedly popular. But I remember once thinking that Justice was not the even-handed female she was represented to be, when a gentleman came during one of our sessions to talk with me, as he said, about "The Flower Queen." He was from New England somewhere, but had been teaching in St. Louis, and wound up his year's work by giving that little work. He said: "I have come some miles out of my way to tell you that I have just cleared a thousand dollars by two performances of your 'Flower Queen' in St. Louis, and the money is here in my pocket." Then he went on to describe the decorations of the hall, the enthusiasm of the audience, etc. "How many singers did you have?" I asked. "Nearly two hundred." "How many books did you use?" "Oh, they had to commit everything to memory, so I taught the choruses by rote. I did not need many books—perhaps nine or ten." He spoke of that as also a matter of credit to himself and of pleasant interest to me. It evidently did not occur to him that, while he had made a thousand dollars, the author of the work had realized the munificent sum of sixty cents, or thereabout, as his share of the profits. I became used to that after a while, but this first experience made a strong impression upon my mind. A law was passed a year or two later which enabled an author to control the performance of such works, if he chose to take advantage of it. I tried it awhile with "The Haymakers," but it was more trouble than it was worth to enforce it, and I soon gave up the effort.

How true it is that it is only those laws which are upheld by public opinion that are of real use to us; or, in other words, it is only those rights that our neighbors say are ours that we can make available.

The New England boy of fifty years ago remembers that many of the natural products of the old farm—berries, nuts, wild fruits, etc.—were practically common property. The neighbors helped themselves to them as freely as they drank the water of the springs or breathed the air of the pastures. Their owners had as undoubted rights to their berries as to their corn, potatoes or bank notes, and often wished to exercise those rights, but custom and public opinion did not admit them, and they were helpless—unless, indeed, they went to law, which the average citizen would rather suffer than do. After a while the cranberry began to have a merchantable value, and slowly public opinion changed, until at last it accorded to owners the same rights to their cranberry meadows that they had to their corn-fields; but to this day it is not considered half so bad to gather nuts and huckleberries without the owner's knowledge and consent as it is to take his corn or money.

So it was in early days in regard to music. We had each other's compositions for the asking, rather considering that we were complimenting the author by using them. We did not consider that we might be placing an author's works in injurious competition with himself, and that by advertising his music in our books we were seizing upon his "good-will" for our advantage. It is better now, though the rights to musical property are not yet as clearly defined as to more tangible things.

The prominent singers of Boston visited the Normal at North Reading occasionally, but I do not recall any name that would be of special interest, unless it would be that of a large, quiet young man, who was then just beginning his musical studies, and who, with his teacher, a prominent choir leader in Boston, passed part of a day with us. Nobody dreamed that that modest and farmer-like person would become America's greatest basso, but so it was to be. I presume I hardly need mention the name of Myron W. Whitney.

We had many invitations, on one pretext or another, to go to neighboring towns and sing. Carriages would be sent for us, and we should be treated like princes, if we would consent. It was pretty hard to resist the pressure from the inviters on the one side and the invited on the other, for a majority of the class were always ready for an outing of that sort. But we feared the breaking in upon our work and the distraction that such excursions would cause, and consented but once. That was at a "commencement" of the Andover Theological Seminary. The professors were great friends of Dr. Mason, and when they urged us to do them this favor we yielded. The procession of all sorts of conveyances that took us the seven miles, up and down half a dozen hills to the mile, our prairie friends will never forget. It is said that the name Andover came from the description people gave of the way there from every point—" over andover andover the hills."

I doubt if such a chorus as we then had is ever heard where people only meet for practice once or twice a week. In the first place, they were practically picked voices. The people who came to us had generally taken to music as a business because they were especially gifted by nature in that way. Then the daily practice of the chorus for so many weeks produced a blending and unanimity that can not be reached in any other way.

The commencement exercises were in the largest church there, and Mr. Webb played the organ. We sang mostly "Messiah" choruses, but a number from the cantata of "Daniel." "How lovely is Zion" came in for a large share of admiration, chiefly, as it seemed to me, because the solo was sung by the best woman that I have ever had the pleasure of being acquainted with. This was the first time that the Normal ever sang away from home, unless upon some of our Saturday excursions to Swan Pond, or some other picnic ground.

CHAPTER XI.

1859–1861, NORTH READING AND CHICAGO—PROMINENT MEMBERS OF THE NORMAL INSTITUTE—WRITING AT WILLOW FARM—OUR SIMPLE MUSIC IN ENGLAND—ROOT AND CADY—THE CURRENCY—THE GREATER THE REFINEMENT, THE SMALLER THE COIN—CHICAGO IN 1858—THE "CAMERADERIE" IN A NEW COUNTRY—CONVENTIONS ON THE PRAIRIE—LAND SHARKS—FIRST ORGAN BOOK—THE FIRST GUN OF THE WAR.

THE Normal continued its sessions in North Reading until 1859, and among its members up to this time were Geo. B. Loomis, for some years superintendent of music in the public schools of Indianapolis, Theodore E. Perkins, T. M. Towne, Chester G. Allen, J. M. North, authors and convention conductors, and Luther W. Mason, for a long time prominent in the primary department of the public schools of Boston as musical superintendent and principal teacher. A few years ago this Mr. Mason went to Japan, by the invitation of the Japanese government, to inaugurate there the system of teaching music to children that had been in use in the Boston schools. He remained in Tokio about two years, if I remember rightly.

Another member of the North Reading Normal was Theo. F. Seward, the present energetic leader of the tonic-sol-fa movement in America. Have you ever received a letter from Mr. Seward, or read one of his editorials, when he had his war-paint on for tonic-sol-fa? If so, did not the handwriting of the one, or the sledge-hammer blows of the other, give you the idea that he was a giant in size, with the voice of a stentor? Then have you met him afterward? If so, you found a rather small, delicate-looking man, with a soft voice and a sweet smile, with gentle and refined manners, and one of the kindest hearts in the world—in most respects probably entirely different from your idea. I admire Mr. Seward greatly, but this contrast between his strong, aggressive work and his gentle ways has always to me a humorous side.

Two other members of the Normal Institute in those days, of whom I shall have occasion to speak more at length later, were James R. Murray, the present editor of *The Musical Visitor*, and Chauncey M. Wyman, from Keene, N. H., then just beginning his musical career.

I can not name all the Normals who were successful in their work, for that would include nearly every member from the first session up to the time of which I am writing. They were invariably the strong men and women of their widely varied localities, and their new equipments of methods of teaching and singing gave them great popularity and success.

My time now, from Normal to Normal, was passed in writing at Willow Farm or in conducting musical conventions in various parts of the country. I could easily have occupied every week of the year in the latter work, Mr. Bradbury and I being almost the only prominent people in it for a while. Dr. Mason was occasionally tempted to conduct some of the larger gatherings in New England, but he confined his outside work in those days mostly to the Normal. Mr. Webb was also fully occupied with work in Boston, which he rarely left, but there was now a constant pressure for a book, or a cantata, or songs, so I spent about half the time at my desk. I now began to hear from Mr. Curwen, the elder. He had found my little lessons and part-songs for singing classes helpful in his tonic-sol-fa enterprise in England, and wrote very kind and appreciative letters of acknowledgment for the same. He was accustomed to say, "We have in England plenty of high-class music, and more than enough of the Captain Jinks kind of songs, but there is a wholesome middle-ground in regard to both words and music in which you in America greatly excel," and soon my cantatas and songs were issued there to an extent that I was not fully aware of until a recent visit, when I saw the list of them in the catalogue of the British Museum; but I will speak more fully of that further on. My acquaintance with Mr. Curwen, thus commenced, was kept up by correspondence until his death, and every year revealed to me more and more of his noble and beautiful character.

These were ideal days—writing until noon, and then driving to a neighboring town, or fishing in some of the pretty ponds that were all about us. The favorite fishing ground was a little lake in North Andover, about eight miles away, and many a time have we spent until dark, after our return, distributing to the neighbors the surplus fish of our afternoon's catch.

In 1858 my brother, E. T. Root, and Mr. C. M. Cady started a music business in Chicago—nearly the "far west" in those days—under the firm name of Root & Cady. My convention work brought me occasionally to their neighborhood, and it was an odd and very pleasant sensation to find in this new section a kind of business home. This was not so much on account of the small pecuniary interest I had in the enterprise as the great interest I took in everything my brother did. This brother and myself were nearly of the same age. We had been much together all our lives. He had married the lovely "Lily" of the Rutgers Institute "Flower Queen," and was now preparing for himself a home in the comparatively new city of Chicago. So, whatever applications for conventions I declined, none from the West were refused, and I appeared more and more frequently at the little store.

It was very pleasant to see the new business grow, and it was not long before the partners said: "Come, put in some more capital, and join us; we need the capital, and your name will help us." I was delighted with the idea, not that I thought of giving up my professional work—I did not dream of that, nor of living in Chicago; but to have this connection with my brother, and this business for a kind of recreation, was extremely attractive. So it was soon brought about, and I became a partner in the house of Root & Cady.

Some things that I came in contact with in those days are worth speaking of. One is the currency. Not only you could not use an Illinois bank note in New England, but in going from Boston to New York, or *vice versa*, you had to change your money into that of the state to which you were going. A bank note of either city would be closely scrutinized in the other, and only taken at a discount. As for a western bank note I might almost say it would not be taken in the East at any price. So the returns of my western conventions were always carried home in gold, which it was sometimes hard to get.

To those to whom this seems strange, in the presence of our present national currency, it may be of interest to say that I remember well when there were no such things as dimes and half-dimes, but, instead, the smallest silver coins were in New England "nine-pence" (12½ cents), and "fourpence-half-penny" (6¼ cents). In New York the same coins were called "shilling" and "six-pence." That came from the plan of having a succession of half values from the dollar—50 cts., 25, 12½, and 6¼. Then there were cents and half cents, which were large copper coins.

It is not wonderful that the trouble the fractions caused compelled the present excellent decimal plan. For a year or two perhaps after dimes came in, a difference in value was made between the 10-cent piece and the 12½-cent piece, (and the 5 and 6¼,) but that difference was so troublesome that either by a law or by common consent it was ultimately given up and both were put on a level. Then the old coins, as if mortified and disgusted at being undervalued, retired from public life. For a few years a stray one, looking lonely and antiquated by the side of the bright, new usurper, would occasionally be seen, but they are all gone now, excepting the few, perhaps, that are in the hands of the old coin collectors.

The eagerness with which gold and silver were sought in those times of trouble with bank notes made people anxious and interested in a high degree in regard to the resumption of specie payment, which was suspended during the war and for a time afterward. How good the gold and silver looked in prospect! But when the time for resumption came, everybody waked to the fact that one need of the old times was entirely gone. The new national banking system was in successful operation, and the national bank note of one state was just as good in other states as at home, and at the resumption those who at first loaded themselves with coin soon found that bank notes were far more convenient to carry, and now that they were just as "good as gold," were much to be preferred for the ordinary uses of business. So the millions in coin that were made ready to redeem the national bank notes were practically untouched, and resumption, excepting as it established the value of bank notes, was something of a farce. It was a pretty clear case of the old story of the foreigner and the shaky bank: "If you can pay me, I don't want it; but if you can't pay, I must have it."

It was curious to observe, when specie payment was suspended, how soon all the little coins, as well as the large ones, fled to hiding places. Then what trouble for change! But that seemed the beginning of success for the horse-car lines, then recently established in Chicago. People had not become used to them; they had not been well patronized, and were looking rather discouraged—horses, cars and rails. Then the company issued five-cent tickets, which were used for change, not only on the cars but in the stores, and people having a good many of these tickets in their pockets doubled or trebled their car-riding and set the enterprise on its feet.

Then came that most excellent scheme—the government fractional currency—so neat to carry, so very convenient to send by mail; in fact, as much better in every way for ordinary business than the small coin, as bank notes are better than silver dollars. They would have all the advantage now that they had then, and their wearing out and loss by fire, and in other ways, would be a large revenue to the government; but the comparatively few men who sell silver for coinage are powerful enough to deprive us of these advantages, even in the face of the hoarded millions of silver dollars that can not be forced out among the people.

An amusing little incident comes to my mind in connection with this fractional currency. It was several years that there were practically no coins in Chicago—time enough for a small merchant in newspapers to establish a flourishing business without ever having seen one. He came into the car to sell his evening papers, and a Californian, sitting next to me, took one and gave him a silver half dime. The little fellow looked at it, and at the man, and supposing that it was a joke that was being played upon him, thrust the coin back, seized his paper and ran out of the car. He did not know that the little silver disk was money. All the five-cent piece he knew was the little paper note for that amount, bearing the government stamp.

Speaking of the five-cent newspaper brings to my mind the fact that for years after I came to Chicago there were no copper coins here. The smallest sum that you could use in paying was five cents. Several efforts to start penny or two-cent papers failed because there were no pennies to pay with, and, of course, no change for a five-cent piece. This fact with regard to new sections of our country is well known, but the deduction from that fact may not be so readily thought of, namely, that where such business conditions exist, society is in a crude and not in a refined state. It is an axiom that the higher the refinement in business transactions the smaller the coin. While in Chicago a half dime was the smallest, in Boston and New York the cent was in common use, in London the half penny, and in Paris the sou, and even the centime. But Chicago has greatly improved. At the present time we are refined enough to have excellent penny and two-cent papers, and no reputable citizen now goes about without copper coins in his pocket.

Looking upon the solid and magnificent streets and drives of Chicago to-day, it is hard to realize their condition in 1858. The first level of the city was but little above the lake, and it was not until some large buildings and blocks of brick and stone had been erected that it was seen that at that level there could be no proper drainage, and that the city—buildings and streets—must be raised several feet. This process was going on when we came. In all the principal thoroughfares some of the buildings were at the new level and some at the old, and progress through them on the side-walk was a constant succession of up and down stairs. Many of the streets were yet unpaved, and although not so bad as a few years before, when in muddy weather the ladies had to be backed up to the stores on carts, the horses or oxen wading knee-deep in mud, still they were sometimes almost impassable. Wood, gravel, stone, and brick all being so far away it was slow and costly work to make the improvements required by the peculiar location of this extraordinary city. After the fire, the opportunity was taken to raise the grade still higher in rebuilding, so that now it is entirely satisfactory in that respect.

The *camaraderie*, or "hail fellow well met" feeling in a new country is one of its most striking features. People from different social grades in the older settled places of the East meet here on a level. Social distinctions are in nobody's way, for there are none, and the best man wins. One of my early conventions in the West was in such a community. On one of Illinois' great prairies, where eighteen months before there was but a railroad shanty, there were now fifteen hundred people.

They were all young and energetic—just the kind to leave the quieter East and enjoy the excitement of starting a new town. An unusual proportion were from cities where they had been members of choirs and musical societies, and they thought a musical convention in the midst of their bustle and building would be a pleasant novelty. We held our sessions in a hall over a large store, and our final concert in an unfinished church edifice, seats being improvised of the building material for the occasion. A few "prairie schooners" (as certain long wagons were called) brought singers from distant prairie homes, and a few came on the railroad from places still farther away, but from the town itself was a larger proportion of cultivated and refined singers than I ever found in a country convention at the East. L. W. Wheeler, who has been for some years one of Boston's most popular voice teachers, was one of the tenors of that convention, and, although just beginning then, gave unmistakable signs of the voice and talent which have since made him so successful.

This town was Kewanee, now one of our finest inland places. I was laughing at one of the men of that convention about the way they were hurrying up their houses, when he said: "Oh, that's nothing to the way they did at first in Chicago. There a man would say to the only carpenter they had, 'I believe I'll settle here; when can you build me a house?' and the answer would be, 'Well, there's Smith, Monday; Jones, Tuesday; Brown, Wednesday; Johnson, Thursday; I'll put yours up Friday.'" Of course this was all burlesque, but it does not give a bad idea of the way things are done while people are roughing it in a new country.

I have often thought that a romance might be written, embodying some of the early real estate transactions of Chicago that would be of intense interest. The only trouble would be that some of the events would be considered too extravagant even for fiction. One story is told of an emigrant—a Hollander, who, with his family, landed in Chicago from a sailing craft before the first railroad had reached so far, and was immediately set upon by "land sharks," as some of the early real estate dealers were called, and finally persuaded to give six hundred dollars for some low land by the river that would then have been considered dear at one-fifth the price. Some of the less hardened of the real estate brotherhood were disposed to protest against the outrageous swindle, but the old fellow seemed satisfied. He took some gold and silver from his pouch and leather belt, and his wife and children cut out coins that had been sewed up in their clothing, and he paid the money. He put up a shanty at once, and then commenced preparing his land for vegetables by processes that he had been familiar with at home. His wife and children helped. He sold his produce readily, and had no difficulty in getting a living after his fashion. Pretty soon people began to build around him, and he was occasionally asked if he did not want to sell his place. No; what should he want to sell for?—he would only have to go and get another place for a vegetable garden, and that was too much trouble. By and by the pressure grew stronger, and the offers got up into the thousands. No; he had built a frame house now, and wasn't going to move. Then the increased taxes, and some assessments for town improvements were too much for his little savings, and he sold a small end of his domain. But this brought him so much money that the surplus made him feel that he should never need any more, so he resisted all offers and importunities, and kept on with his vegetable garden as long as he lived. Then his heirs sold the place for nearly a million dollars.

This playing at business (for I did nothing of the buying or selling), and the new and adventurous life of Chicago were so attractive to me that early in 1859 I took a room in the building in which the store was, and occupied it as a library and working-room between convention engagements. Not long before, Mr. Henry Mason, the youngest brother of my publishers, had formed a copartnership with Mr. Hamlin, under the firm name of Mason & Hamlin, for the manufacture of melodeons. They prospered, and soon called their larger instruments harmoniums, and not long after, cabinet organs. Some time in 1862 the Masons asked me if I thought I could make an instruction book for these instruments. I said I would try, and the result was "The School for the Harmonium and Cabinet Organ." This was my first work of importance in my new quarters. It was published by Mason Brothers, and had a large sale. It inaugurated a much better graded method than any previous book had contained, and I have sometimes thought that the copyright laws would be more just if they included the plan as well as the contents of a book of that kind. But there being no such protection, my plan has been generally adopted by reed organ instructors ever since.

In 1860 the Normal was held in Chicago, Dr. Mason, Mr. Bradbury, and myself principal teachers. By this time other Normals were started by those who had been with us, and we no longer occupied the entire field. Still, the interest in that kind of school having increased, our attendance continued to be large. I have no list of that class, but I recall that among its successful members was N. Coe Stewart, the present superintendent of music in the public schools of Cleveland, Ohio.

My family was still at Willow Farm, excepting F. W., who was now old enough to be away at boarding school, and I had no thought, yet, of another home. However, the little business was improving and I enjoyed more and more being in the neighborhood of its small whirl. I might, perhaps, have foreseen that if it continued to increase, the whirl might eventually grow large enough to include me in its round of hard and confining work, but I did not. I went and came —was free to work in my pleasant room or to be off at conventions, now in New England, now in New York or Pennsylvania, or the West—not a moment hung heavily on my hands. Then we began to publish a little. First a song or two, and some instrumental pieces in sheet form. After a while we decided to venture on a book, and put in hand one that I was then working on for day-schools; but now the WAR burst upon us!

What a change came over the whole country when that momentous event was announced! How the bustling, cheery life of Chicago became suddenly grave and serious. With what different eyes we saw everything about us. It was not the same sunshine that made the city so bright yesterday, and these were not the same faces of neighbors that then nodded so light-heartedly as they passed. The old flag had been fired upon, and that act had waked into stern determination the patriotism of every loyal heart.

CHAPTER XII.

1861–1870, CHICAGO—WRITING THE WAR SONGS—SOME INCIDENTS CONCERNING THEM—HENRY C. WORK—P. P. BLISS—"THE SONG MESSENGER OF THE NORTH-WEST"—THE ORIGIN OF "TRAMP"—GROWTH OF BUSINESS—JAMES R. MURRAY AND "DAISY DEANE"—B. R. HANBY—CARYL FLORIO—DR. MASON'S LAST NORMAL—THE NORMAL AT SOUTH BEND, IND.—THE ORIGIN OF "NATIONAL NORMAL"—CARLO BASSINI.

IN common with my neighbors I felt strongly the gravity of the situation, and while waiting to see what would be done, wrote the first song of the war. It was entitled "The first gun is fired, may God protect the right." Then at every event, and in all the circumstances that followed, where I thought a song would be welcome, I wrote one. And here I found my fourteen years of extemporizing melodies on the blackboard, before classes that could be kept in order only by prompt and rapid movements, a great advantage. Such work as I could do at all I could do quickly. There was no waiting for a melody. Such as it was it came at once, as when I stood before the blackboard in the old school days.

I heard of President Lincoln's second call for troops one afternoon while reclining on a lounge in my brother's house. Immediately a song started in my mind, words and music together:

> "Yes, we'll rally round the flag, boys, we'll rally once again,
> Shouting the battle-cry of freedom!"

I thought it out that afternoon, and wrote it the next morning at the store. The ink was hardly dry when the Lumbard brothers—the great singers of the war—came in for something to sing at a war meeting that was to be holden immediately in the court-house square just opposite. They went through the new song once, and then hastened to the steps of the court-house, followed by a crowd that had gathered while the practice was going on. Then Jule's magnificent voice gave out the song, and Frank's trumpet tones led the refrain—

> "The Union forever, hurrah, boys, hurrah!"

and at the fourth verse a thousand voices were joining in the chorus. From there the song went into the army, and the testimony in regard to its use in the camp and on the march, and even on the field of battle, from soldiers and officers, up to generals, and even to the good President himself, made me thankful that if I could not shoulder a musket in defense of my country I could serve her in this way.

Many interesting war incidents were connected with these songs. The one that moved me most was told by an officer who was in one of the battles during the siege of Vicksburg. He said an Iowa regiment went into the fight eight hundred strong, and came out with a terrible loss of more than half their number; but the brave fellows who remained were waving their torn and powder-stained banner, and singing

> "Yes, we'll rally round the flag, boys."

Some years after, at the closing concert of a musical convention in Anamosa, Iowa, I received a note, saying, "If the author of 'The Battle-cry of Freedom' would sing that song it would gratify several soldiers in the audience who used to sing it in the army." I read the request to the audience, and said I would willingly comply with it, but first would like to relate an incident concerning one of their Iowa regiments. Then I told the above about the battle near Vicksburg. When I finished I noticed a movement at the end of the hall, and an excited voice cried out, "Here is a soldier who lost his arm in that battle." I said, "Will he come forward and stand by me while I sing the song?" A tall, fine-looking man, with one empty sleeve, came immediately to my side, and I went through it, he joining in the chorus. But it was hard work. I had to choke a good deal, and there was hardly a dry eye in the house. He was teaching school a few miles from there, and was quite musical. I sent him some music after I returned to Chicago, and kept up the acquaintance by correspondence for some time.

The following from *The Century*, published a year or two ago, will be of interest in this connection:

UNION WAR SONGS AND CONFEDERATE OFFICERS.

The reading of Mr. Brander Matthews' "Songs of the War," in the August number of *The Century*, vividly recalls to mind an incident of my own experience, which seems to me so apt an illustration of the effect of army songs upon men that I venture to send it to you, as I remember it, after twenty-five years.

A day or two after Lee's surrender in April, 1865, I left our ship at Dutch Gap, in the James river, for a run up to Richmond, where I was joined by the ship's surgeon, the paymaster and one of the junior officers. After "doing" Richmond pretty thoroughly we went in the evening to my rooms for dinner. Dinner being over, and the events of the day recounted, the doctor, who was a fine player, opened the piano, saying: "Boys, we've got our old quartet here; let's have a sing." As the house opposite was occupied by paroled Confederate officers no patriotic songs were sung. Soon the lady of the house handed me this note:

"Compliments of General —— and staff. Will the gentlemen kindly allow us to come over and hear them sing?"

Of course we consented, and they came. As the General entered the room, I recognized instantly the face and figure of one who stood second only to Lee or Jackson in the whole Confederacy. After introductions and the usual interchange of civilities we sang for them glee and college songs, until at last the General said:

"Excuse me, gentlemen; you sing delightfully; but what we

want to hear is your army songs." Then we gave them the army songs with unction—the "Battle Hymn of the Republic," "John Brown's Body," "We're Coming, Father Abraham," "Tramp, Tramp, Tramp, the Boys are Marching," through the whole catalogue to the "Star-Spangled Banner"—to which many a foot beat time as if it had never stepped to any but the "music of the Union"—and closed our concert with "Rally Round the Flag, Boys."

When the applause had subsided, a tall, fine-looking fellow, in a major's uniform, exclaimed: "Gentlemen, if we'd had your songs we'd have whipped you out of your boots! Who couldn't have marched or fought with such songs? We had nothing, absolutely nothing, except a bastard 'Marseillaise,' the 'Bonny Blue Flag' and 'Dixie,' which were nothing but jigs. 'Maryland, My Maryland' was a splendid song, but the old 'Lauriger Horatius' was about as inspiring as the 'Dead March in Saul,' while every one of the Yankee songs is full of marching and fighting spirit." Then turning to the General, he said: "I shall never forget the first time I heard 'Rally Round the Flag.' 'Twas a nasty night during the 'Seven Days' Fight,' and if I remember rightly it was raining. I was on picket, when, just before 'taps,' some fellow on the other side struck up that song and others joined in the chorus until it seemed to me the whole Yankee army was singing. Tom B——, who was with me, sung out, 'Good heavens, Cap, what are those fellows made of, anyway? Here we've licked 'em six days running, and now on the eve of the seventh they're singing, 'Rally Round the Flag.' I am not naturally superstitious, but I tell you that song sounded to me like the 'knell of doom,' and my heart went down into my boots; and though I've tried to do my duty, it has been an uphill fight with me ever since that night."

The little company of Union singers and Confederate auditors, after a pleasant and interesting interchange of stories of army experiences, then separated, and as the General shook hands at parting, he said to me: "Well, the time *may* come when we can *all* sing the 'Star-Spangled Banner' again." I have not seen him since.

The following extract from a letter recently received also belongs here:

I was lately much interested in an incident, as given in "Bright Skies and Dark Shadows," Dr. Henry M. Field's last book, just published. This incident took place on the day of the great battle of Franklin, near Nashville, Tenn., and was told Mr. Field on the battle-field by a Mr. McEwen, an old resident of Nashville, at whose house General Kimball made his headquarters, and from whose front door Mr. McEwen witnessed the whole battle, which was fought during the latter part of the day.

"About four o'clock, after the General had left for the field, there lingered a Colonel, from Indianapolis, in my parlor, who asked my daughters to sing and play a piece of music. My daughters asked what they should play. He replied that he did not know one piece of music from another, except field music. I spoke and asked the young ladies to sing and play a piece which had recently come out, 'Just before the battle, mother.' At my request they sat down and sang, and when about half through, as I stepped to the door, a shell exploded within fifty yards. I immediately returned and said, 'Colonel, if I am any judge, it is just about that time now!' He immediately sprang to his feet and ran in the direction of his regiment, but before he reached it, or about that time, he was shot, the bullet passing quite through him. He was taken to Nashville, and eighteen days after, I received a message from him through an officer, stating the fact of his being shot, and that the piece of music the young ladies were executing was still ringing in his ears, and had been ever since he left my parlor the evening of the battle. In April, four months later, after the war was over, he had sufficiently recovered to travel, when he came to Franklin, as he stated, expressly to get the young ladies to finish the song, and relieve his ears. His wife and more than a dozen officers accompanied him. He found the ladies, and they sang and played the piece through for him in the presence of all the officers, and they wept like children."

If you have made any music that will ring for four months in the ears of a person that doesn't know one tune from another, I thought you ought to know it.

As I have said, when anything happened that could be voiced in a song, or when the heart of the Nation was moved by particular circumstances or conditions caused by the war, I wrote what I thought would then express the emotions of the soldiers or the people. Picturing the condition and thoughts of the soldier on the eve of an engagement, I wrote "Just before the battle, mother" and "Within the sound of the enemy's guns." When our brave Colonel Mulligan fell, his last words were "Lay me down and save the flag." The day after the news of that event reached us, the song bearing that title was issued. It was much sung at the time in remembrance of that distinguished and lamented officer. I tried to help the enlistments by "Come, brothers, all, 'tis Columbia's call," and to hit the copperhead element of the North by "Stand up for Uncle Sam, boys." I voiced the feeling of the people in regard to the treatment of prisoners by "Starved in prison," and gave a more hopeful view in "Tramp, tramp, tramp, the boys are marching." "O, come you from the battle-field?" and "Brother, tell me of the battle" represented the anxiety of those who had fathers or sons or brothers in the army, and "The Vacant Chair" the mourning for the lost one. One of the thrilling scenes of the war is described in "Who'll Save the Left?" and the grief of the Nation at the death of President Lincoln by "Farewell, father, friend and guardian." This is a partial list of the songs that I wrote during the war. Only a few had an extended use and popularity, but none was entirely useless.

One day early in the war a quiet and rather solemn-looking young man, poorly clad, was sent up to my room from the store with a song for me to examine. I looked at it and then at him in astonishment. It was "Kingdom Coming,"—elegant in manuscript, full of bright, good sense and comical situations in its "darkey" dialect—the words fitting the melody almost as aptly and neatly as Gilbert fits Sullivan—the melody decidedly good and taking, and the whole exactly suited to the times. "Did you write this—words and music?" I asked. A gentle "Yes" was the answer. "What is your business, if I may inquire?" "I am a printer." "Would you rather write music than set type?" "Yes." "Well, if this is a specimen of what you can do, I think you may give up the printing business." He liked that idea very much, and an arrangement with us was soon made. He needed some musical help that I could give him, and we needed just such songs as he could write. The connection, which continued some years, proved very profitable both to him and to us. This was Henry C. Work, whose principal songs while he was with us were "Kingdom Coming," "Babylon is Fallen," "Wake, Nicodemus," "Ring the Bell, Watchman," "Song of a Thousand Years," "Marching Thro' Georgia" and "Come Home, Father."

Mr. Work was a slow, pains-taking writer, being from one to three weeks upon a song; but when the work was done it was like a piece of fine mosaic, especially in the fitting of words to music. His "Marching Thro' Georgia" is more played and sung at the present time than any other song of the war. This is not only on account of the intrinsic merit of its words and music, but because it is *retrospective.* Other war songs, "The Battle-cry of Freedom" for example, were for exciting the patriotic feeling on *going in* to the war or the battle; "Marching Thro' Georgia" is a glorious remembrance on coming triumphantly out, and so has been more appropriate to soldiers' and other gatherings ever since.

It must have been some time in 1863 that I received a letter from somewhere in Pennsylvania that interested us all very much. It accompanied the manuscript of a song. Would we give the writer a flute for it, was the substance of the letter, expressed in a quaint and original way, and in beautiful handwriting. We were on the lookout for bright men, and we felt sure that here was one. The song needed some revising, but we took it and sent him the flute. After a while he wrote again, saying he would like to come out to Chicago if he could find anything to do. He gave an account of his accomplishments in his droll way, and we all became much interested in having him come. I think it was he who finally made the plan that was agreed upon, namely: He would go as our representative to the towns that would naturally be tributary to Chicago, and hold conventions, or give concerts, or do something musical, whenever he could get the opportunity, (his wife being his accompanist,) and so turn people's attention to us for whatever they might want in the way of music. For this service we guaranteed him a certain annual sum. If the proceeds of his concerts and conventions did not reach that amount we were to make it up. While engaged in this work he was constantly sending in words and music of various kinds for revision and correction. It was not long before I saw that here was a man who had a "call" especially as a poet. His musical training and experiences were too limited to permit safe flights on his part beyond simple harmonies, although it was easily seen that he had a natural vein of true melody. What a wonderful use his songs have performed now for more than a score of years. I presume it is seen that I am writing of the beloved and lamented P. P. Bliss.

When Mr. Moody, from being a simple, hard working but devoted city missionary in Chicago, began to come to the front as an evangelist, Mr. Bliss's songs, and some that I wrote, were of much use to him. He used to say of my first gospel song, "Come to the Savior," that it was the "Rally Round the Flag" of the gospel work. It was indeed stirring when Mr. Bliss's magnificent voice gave it forth, for it then came from a heart and soul in deepest sympathy with the work to which he ultimately devoted himself—the writing and singing of gospel songs. He remained with us until the breaking up caused by the great fire, and we published all the songs and other music that he wrote up to that time.

The growth of our business after the war commenced was something remarkable. The name of Root & Cady went all over the land on our war songs, and on our little musical monthly, *The Song Messenger of the Northwest.* Those among the people and in the army who liked our publications seemed to turn to us for everything they wanted in our line when it was possible. We kept everything in the way of musical merchandise from pianos and organs to jewsharps, and all the music of the day in book or sheet form. My brother attended to the business detail in all the departments, Mr. Cady to the finances and general management, and I to the publications. My brother William was also with us in the office.

Speaking of *The Song Messenger* reminds me of an incident that may be worth mentioning. We published a New Year's extra in those days which we sent broadcast from Maine to—I was going to say Georgia, but that section was barred out then. We sent from the North and West as far South as we could. I think we were the first to send "To the principal singer," etc., and the plan being new the little missives were not thrown into the waste basket to any extent, either by postmasters or recipients, but produced great results. I used to write a song for this extra. The year previous to the time of which I am speaking, "Just before the battle, mother," was the song. December was now approaching, and I was very much interested in something I was working at—"The Curriculum," I think it was—and had put off the song for the coming extra. One day my brother said, "We must have that song or we can not get the paper into the hands of the people by New Year's Day; go write it now while it is on your mind." In two hours I brought him the song. We tried it over and he said, "I must confess I don't think much of it, but it may do." I was inclined to agree with him about the music, but after all was a little disappointed, because I had grown quite warm and interested in writing the words. They were on a subject that was then very near the hearts of the loyal people of the North. The song was "Tramp, tramp, tramp, the boys are marching," and was not only an illustration of the advantage of my blackboard training, but was a further confirmation of what I have said before, that in my case successes were usually surprises.

In 1863, having outgrown our quarters on Clark street, we moved into the Crosby Opera-house building, then just erected on Washington street, near State. This store and basement were one hundred and eighty feet long by thirty in width, to which was eventually added a building just across the alley in the rear, which aggregated a still larger floor area. The basement in this rear building was occupied by our printing-office and steam presses, and the main floor by pianos and organs. The second story had rooms for band and orchestra instruments and "small goods," and one fitted up for my use. Here I made my books and songs, and looked after the publishing interests of the house. This large amount of room was necessitated by the buying out of various small musical establishments, culminating in the purchase of the extensive catalogue, with all its music plates, of the entire stock of Henry Tolman & Co., of Boston—two or three car loads. This catalogue included that of Nathan Richardson, afterwards Russell & Richardson, and afterwards Russell & Tolman. So the songs of mine that they had published came back to me, and I was now their publisher as well as author.

When "The Battle-cry of Freedom" came out I sent, as usual, the first copy to my wife, who was still at North Reading. Soon after she received it she learned that James R. Murray, one of our Normal boys, to whom we were much attached, had volunteered, and was then in camp at Lynnfield, the next town east, so she and my father determined to go and give him a "God speed" before he went to the front. They did so, and gave him the new song, which he introduced into that section of the army. While in Virginia, in his second year of service, Mr. Murray wrote and sent us "Daisy Deane," a beautiful song, which, doubtless, some of my readers will remember. It was one of the marked successes of the day. We kept up a constant correspondence, and I saw not only his musical abilities, but unmistakable signs of his editorial capabilities. So when he left the army he came to us as editor of *The Song Messenger*, and assistant in the writing and publishing department of our business.

There came to us in those days a very interesting and talented man by the name of Hanby. He was educated for the ministry, but was so strongly inclined to music that he decided to try to make that his life's work. He had already written "Darling Nelly Gray," which was published by O. Ditson & Co., and which had a large sale. He was also the author of "Ole Shady," which is famous still. He wrote while with us some beautiful Sunday-school songs, some of which are in use yet. But he died almost at the commencement of his career.

I must not omit to speak in this connection of Chauncey M. Wyman, whom I have mentioned as one of the North Reading normals, and who cast in his lot with us in those days. He had used my books in his convention work in the East, and had attended some conventions that I conducted in Vermont and New Hampshire. In one he was assistant conductor, and I saw that he was one of the coming men. So when he decided that he would have a book of his own I asked him to come out to Chicago and make it, and we would publish it. This he did, and "The Palm" was the result. What he would have done as a composer can hardly be told by this one effort, but as a conductor I have no hesitation in saying that he would have stood in the highest rank had he lived. His magnetism was wonderful, and his control of a chorus absolute. What he wished to accomplish he did, if the capacities of the singers were equal to his conceptions. I have a very tender feeling when I think of the great Normal (of which I will speak later), where he was our oratorio conductor, and from which he went to his New England home never to leave it alive. His calm exterior gave no hint of the intense strain he was under on that memorable occasion in the introduction and use of his first book and the conducting of our great chorus. We also published the early, if not the first works of H. R. Palmer—"The Song Queen," "The Song King," "The Normal Collection," and "Palmer's Concert Choruses."

Among the incidents in regard to people who became connected with us in those days I must not omit this: One day a delicate and refined looking, but poorly clad young man came to the office, which was in the center of the store and where I happened to be, and said: "I am a musician, and wish employment. I have been in a theatrical company which has disbanded in Indiana, and my trunk is detained there. I am entirely without means, but I can play, I can read well at sight, and I can compose, as I will show you." All this was said with the utmost fluency, after which he stepped lightly to a piano and played an Etude elegantly. He then asked for pen and music paper, and wrote without the slightest hesitation or delay a song, words and music. I do not know why I did not think that last performance a pretense, for the work was as elegant as his playing, but I did not. There was something about him that made us all feel that under that airy manner there was solid musical attainment, and that he was all he pretended to be. That proved true, and he was with us a year or two. He was then W. J. Robjohn, but is at present known as Caryl Florio, one of New York's most accomplished musicians.

When our business began to assume the large proportions that it afterward reached, I saw that it could no longer be regarded as a secondary matter or a recreation. It was clear that I was to be absorbed in its whirl as my hard-working brother had been from the beginning. My department now demanded nearly all the time I could spare from writing, and to attend to that properly I must give up conventions, and, consequently, Willow Farm as home. So in 1863 I moved my family to Chicago. It consisted then of wife, two sons, and three daughters. F. W., the oldest, had taken lessons upon the piano from Mr. B. C. Blodgett, now one of the most prosperous musical men of Massachusetts, and then he had studied for a while with Mr. William Mason in New York. He took an organist's situation as soon as he arrived in Chicago, and divided his time between the store and practice. When my second son finished his school studies in Chicago both boys went to Europe, and studied music and languages in Germany and Italy for a year or more. On their return, F. W. decided to make music his profession, and Charles went into the store.

Early in the war, probably in 1862, the last Normal in which Dr. Mason taught was held in Wooster, Ohio. Dr. Mason, myself, and Geo. B. Loomis were the principal teachers, and the work continued six weeks. There was a good attendance, but the recruiting officers around us, and an occasional war meeting kept up an excitement that worked against us, not only in other people's minds but in our own. We were deeply interested in the struggle, and always ready to help at the war meetings. The new war-songs contributed not a little to rouse the enthusiasm of the people and help the recruiting, sung as they were by our fine chorus. Phillip Phillips, I remember, was one of the normals of that session.

When the war began no one thought it would last long —a year was the outside limit in most minds, but in the second year the magnitude of the undertaking began to appear. So many young men of the North were in the army that I made no more attempts to hold the Normal until the war was over. Then I think the first one was in Winona, Minnesota. I was the principal, but the younger men were now coming to the front, and I had excellent assistants in Bliss, Towne, F. W. (before he went abroad), and O. D. Adams. J. R. Murray was left in charge of my department of the business in Chicago. At the next Normal H. R. Palmer and I joined forces. It was held in Janesville, Wis., and was a large and interesting gathering.

But the most memorable Normal session of those days was held in South Bend, Indiana, in 1870. Dr. Mason and Mr. Webb had left the work to younger hands. Mr. Bradbury had passed away, and I was alone of the original four. I secured the services of Carlo Bassini, then well known and extremely popular throughout the United States, as the voice teacher, and William Mason, the distinguished pianist, not only to give lessons to advanced pupils, but to give recitals and lectures twice a week to the entire Institute. These recitals inaugurated a new department in Normal work, which has been kept up ever since. Chauncey M. Wyman, of whom I have spoken, was our chorus and oratorio conductor, and Bliss, Towne, and F. W. Root (just returned from Europe) assisted in various departments. W. S. B. Mathews, of Chicago, was Mr. Mason's assistant in piano teaching. I think it was here that C. C. Case and James McGranahan made their first appearance as Normal pupils. S. W. Straub was also a member this year.

Schuyler Colfax, then Vice-President of the United States, lived in South Bend, and was very fond of looking in upon us, and on one occasion I asked him to say something to the class. He first wanted to know how many were in attendance. I told him about two hundred from abroad. (I believe there were one hundred and eighty actual teachers and those intending to teach.) He then wanted to know how many States were represented, and asked the members from the different States to raise their hands as he named their State. This was done, and it was found that *seventeen* States and Canada were represented in the membership of the Institute. Then Mr. Colfax commenced his speech by saying: "This should be called 'The National Musical Institute,' since the nation is so largely represented in it," and I was glad to adopt that designation, as "Normals" had now sprung up all over the land.

The evening chorus was a noble one, numbering nearly three hundred singers. The oratorio was the "Creation," and at the first rehearsal Mr. Wyman tried several of the choruses, among them "The Heavens are Telling," to ascertain the reading ability of his class. The choruses were not well sung, but there was no breakdown. They were read straight through. Mr. Bassini, who was present, expressed some surprise that people from such widely varied localities should have all sung the "Creation." I told him they had probably never seen it before. This he could not believe. I then asked all who had sung "The Heavens are Telling" before to rise, and four persons stood up. "Ah," said Mr. Bassini, in his demonstrative way, "I was for many years chorus master for the Italian opera in different countries of Europe and in South America, and I never found people who could read like that." "How did you teach them?" I asked. "Oh, I played the part they were to sing over and over on my violin until they learned it. It was great drudgery." Recalling that incident reminds me that Mr. Bassini came to this country as a solo violinist. I heard him in that capacity in New York in '46 or '47. He did not succeed in that line, although he played finely, and for a time he went out of sight. Then he began to be known as a teacher of singing, and from that time no one ever heard of him as a violinist. He knew well the value of having but one specialty. In this he became famous, and made a great deal of money. He cleared over a thousand dollars in his six weeks with us at South Bend. But he was a delicate man. It was only his indomitable will that kept his frail body up to the work he did. He went to Chicago from South Bend to teach in a short Normal that Mr. Palmer was holding, and was there my guest. But he could not stay through. He left the second week, and went home to die. He was a most lovable man, and is remembered with warm affection by us all.

CHAPTER XIII.

1871–1873, CHICAGO—THE HEALTH LIFT AND THE ASTONISHED PIANO MOVERS—THE GIGANTIC LOTTERY SCHEME—OUR SUCCESSFUL PUBLICATIONS, INCLUDING DR. PALMER'S AND MR. BLISS'S EARLY WORKS—HEAVY STOCK—THE GREAT FIRE—MY GREEN BOX—MR. CURWEN'S GIFT—NEW BUSINESS ARRANGEMENTS—THE NORMAL OF '72—THE SAD TELEGRAM.

WHEN my convention work was at its height, and I about thirty-eight years of age, I used to have occasionally a nervous re-action at the close of my four days' work that affected my head unpleasantly. When our increasing business confined me more, and some large obligations that were upon us made me anxious, the trouble came oftener and each time remained longer. Finally it came to stay. The doctors said it was a trouble of the brain, and I must quit business—had better go to Europe, or somewhere away. About that time Mr. Curwen (the elder), hearing that I was out of health, invited me to make him a visit. He wrote that if I would come they would welcome me to London with a chorus of five thousand voices singing my music. But I had not the courage to face the sea voyage and declined.

Being near Boston not long after, a medical friend said: "Try Butler; they say he has done wonders for such cases as yours." "Who is Butler?" "Oh, he is a man who has an apparatus for lifting—says he can make people so strong that they can lift away all troubles that flesh is heir to." I could see that my friend had not unqualified confidence in the scheme, or, rather, that he had the usual professional distrust of anything out of the regular line; but drowning men catch at straws, so I tried it. I booked myself for three months of lifting iron weights. I went once a day, occupying about half an hour each time in making four lifts. Nothing could be more simple—standing erect upon a table, bending the knees, grasping a handle which was attached to a bar, upon which weights were hung under the table, and then straightening up. The act was a matter of a few seconds, but it sent the blood to every capillary of the body. As the strength increased the weights were increased. The third week I was inclined to be discouraged, for I did not feel any better. If anything, my troubles were sharper and more pronounced; but Mr. Butler smiled his imperturbable smile, and said: "Can you lift more than you could last week?" "Yes." "Are you absolutely sure of that?" "Yes; there can be no doubt about that; there are the iron weights to prove it." "Then, no matter how you feel, you are better." This bolstered me up and I went on. I required this kind of help several times before the three months were out. My troubles had been years in coming on, and were not to be driven away in a few weeks. But before the three months were out I saw that I was on the right track, so I purchased a set of the apparatus and had it sent to my house in Chicago. There I continued its use, and in six months I began to work a little.

After a while it got noised about that I was lifting heavy weights. Our piano movers were specially interested in what was said. I was still rather pale, and certainly did not look like a person who could lift such weights as they prided themselves upon lifting, so they were entirely skeptical on the subject. They said nothing to me, but were disposed to be facetious about the matter among themselves, as I was told. One day they had occasion to move a piano to my house, and I said, "Boys, would you like to try the lift?" They assented eagerly, and followed me up into the attic, where I had a room arranged for the apparatus. I showed them what to do, and put on a moderate weight which they all lifted in turn. There were three of them. Then I added more, and continued until they began to give out. The youngest, who was a very strong lad of twenty, just struggled up with six hundred. Then I added another hundred and lifted it without difficulty. Their astonishment and consternation were amusing. There must be some trick about it. But no; there were the iron disks, weighing fifty pounds each, which they could take into their hands, and fourteen of them were on the bar. I did not explain to them that I probably could not have lifted in a stooping position what they did, nor that while certain of their muscles used in that position were very strong, certain others, when they stood straight, were not up to the mark, and when the strain came equally on all, the weak ones gave way, just as a chain in use would only be as strong as its weakest link. They never could understand it, and looked at me with awe and wonder after that, whenever I passed them in the store or on the street.

In a year and a half I could lift more than a thousand pounds, and my troubles were gone. Meanwhile my partners and others tried it and were benefited, and we furnished the capital to start a room where the system could be administered to the public, and Dr. Frank W. Reilly was placed in charge. He called the establishment the "Health Lift," and made some important improvements in the apparatus, and gave a clear and rational statement of the reasons for its success. This was among the prosperous enterprises swept away by the great fire.

A curious episode in our opera-house life is worth relating. Somewhere about '69 Mr. Crosby, under some financial pressure, put up his magnificent building as the prize in a gigantic lottery scheme. One hundred thousand tickets at five dollars apiece were to be sold, and the holder of the successful one was to own the opera-house—one chance in one hundred thousand. Tickets were sold all over the United States, and it was almost a national affair when the time for drawing came. At all events the excitement in and about the building was intense. I was not present when the drawing took place, but I think it was done by a child blindfolded, the tickets having been thoroughly stirred up in a revolving cylinder. The winner was a miller in southern Illinois, but he was immediately induced, under the fear that the whole proceeding might be found to be illegal, to take a much less sum than five hundred thousand dollars for his prize. But what he did receive made him a rich man. He came into the store after the matter was all settled, and, looking about, remarked, "I owned all this for half an hour." In the course of the conversation he said, "I knew I should win; I always do." Then he gave some account of his successes at fairs and raffles in St. Louis, near which city he lived, which, if true, were certainly very remarkable. I think the building went back into Mr. Crosby's hands.

Up to 1871 we had published of my composition the war songs before mentioned, and a good many others on various subjects, and of books "The Silver Lute," "The Bugle Call," "Chapel Gems," "The Musical Fountain," "The Forest Choir," "The Prize," "The Coronet," "The Triumph," and "The Musical Curriculum." On my works we had both author's and publisher's profit. On those of other authors, for whom we published, we had only the publisher's profit, as on them we paid royalties.

When the war closed the war songs stopped as if they had been shot. Everybody had had enough of war. "Tramp" was the last successful one, and had but a short life—less than a year, but in that time our profit on it was ten thousand dollars. All the songs by Mr. Work and myself, that have been mentioned, had large sales, the above giving some general idea of the profit of each to author and publisher. Of "The Silver Lute" (for day schools) were sold more than a hundred thousand copies. "The Prize," for Sunday schools, was still more successful. "The Triumph," which was the last successful large-sized book for choirs and conventions ($13.50 a dozen), sold ninety thousand copies the first year, at a profit to us of thirty thousand dollars. H. R. Palmer made the first successful smaller-sized books for singing classes and conventions—the "Song Queen" and the "Song King," both of which had very large sales, and contributed proportionately to our profits. All the other books by Mr. Palmer and myself, as well as those by Mr. Bliss, that we published, were fairly successful. My largest work, "The Musical Curriculum," had been but recently issued, and at this date was just getting under way.

In pianos, organs, band instruments and general musical merchandise we had a large trade and carried a heavy stock. The two floors in the opera-house, 180 by 30 feet each, and as much room in the rear building, were filled to overflowing, beside the basement, in which was the type-setting and printing department. One can get some idea of the space required simply for a fair stock of books for such a trade as we had by considering how much room twenty-five cords of wood would take, and then, by figuring, ascertain that the ninety thousand "Triumph," spoken of above, would make more than twenty-five cords of books.

And now the memorable autumn of 1871 had come. Our presses had been at work all summer, and great piles of books filled the basement of the main building, ready for the fall trade. They would all be gone in a few weeks, so we did not take out a special insurance upon them, but assumed the risk for that short time ourselves. I lived then in Groveland Park, near the Chicago University, about four miles south from our place of business. Between three and four o'clock in the morning of the ninth of October some one waked me and said Jerome Beardslee was at the door in a buggy and wanted to see me. What could Jerome want at that time in the morning, and why should he come in a buggy, since he lives next door but one? I got up and tried to light the gas, but there was none. I hurried on my clothes and went down. "What is the matter, Jerome?" "There's a great fire down town, and it is spreading fearfully. Our store is gone, but I got the books out, and have just brought them home. I am going back, and if you would like to ride with me you can. I think you'll be in time to see your place go." I went, and when we got within a mile of the fire we began to see signs of the great disaster. Groups of men, women and children (some scantily clad) were standing by such household goods as they had brought to where they supposed they were out of the reach of the flames. Team after team added to the number until the streets were lined with the fugitives and such of their belongings as they could save.

The wind blew fiercely from the south-west, so the flames spread less rapidly our way, but on the north side nearly all the people who thought their goods were out of danger had to move again and again, and finally see them burn for the want of means to get them out on to the prairie beyond the farthest houses, four miles from the center. Some who placed their goods on the lake shore where there was a beach, not only had to see them burn, but had to get into the water to save their lives. The heat of the fire, maddened by the tornado it had caused, was beyond conception. I saw delicate looking tongues of flame shoot across an open space twenty or thirty feet wide, and a marble building dissolve under their touch as if it had been of sand. The action of a gigantic compound blow-pipe was the only thing to which one could liken those streams of flame and their effect. Nothing could stand before them. In the presence of miles of such intense heat our firemen and their steam engines were as impotent as children with toy watering-pots would have been. To get hose near enough at any point to be of any use would be to see it curl and shrivel as if it had been made of paper. In fact, much of the fire apparatus was destroyed before it could be got out of the way. No complete idea of this scene can be had without keeping before the mind the fierce wind, filled with keen cutting sand and cinders that hurled great flaming brands for blocks over the yet unburnt houses. When the fire had done its work but few walls were standing as landmarks. We could not tell, in the business part of the city, where the streets were. Localities that two days before were as familiar to us as the rooms of our own houses were now a strange, wild desolation.

I was in time to see the costly and elegant opera-house go. I could not get near enough to see the rear building in which was my working-room and library. I wondered if my green box was safe. The young men in the store had laughed among themselves a good deal because I often said, "If there's a fire, save that green box." It was an old paper affair, but it contained my daily work and all my unpublished manuscripts. We had built a large brick vault in the cellar of the rear building, but a few months before, to make a safe place for the plates of our now very large catalogue. It was the duty of the porter to put the green box in the vault with the other valuables at night. He had not done so at this time, and Mr. Murray's brother Robert, who slept near, and was hastily looking about just before the fire reached there, saw it, and remembering my injunction, saved it. All our important plates were in the vault, excepting those of the "Song King" and the "Curriculum." They were in use at the printing office, and were destroyed. New plates of the "Song King" were immediately made in Cleveland, but I revised the "Curriculum," and its present form is the result.

One of the noticeable things at the opera-house, as the fire approached it, was the announcement that Theodore Thomas' "unrivaled orchestra" would give a concert there that evening. When the flames enveloped the beautiful building I thought of their fine instruments, some of which had been left there, and my mind also ran over a list of the familiar and valuable objects belonging to us that were then being offered up in that fearful holocaust—the costly counters, desks, and general fittings of oak and maple, the long lines of shelves of sheet music, the cords of books in the basement, the hundreds of elegant pianos and organs, fine violins, guitars and band instruments, the still greater number of accordeons, and other small instruments, strings, reeds, etc., the printing office and presses, and the fine room in which F. W., Mr. Murray and myself had done so much pleasant and successful work. In a few minutes all were gone. It was sad, but the calamity was so general and so overwhelming that individual losses seemed insignificant in comparison, even though they reached the sum of a quarter of a million, as ours did.

The days immediately following the fire were passed in anxious waiting to see if the vault and safes had protected our plates and account books. It was some days before they were cool enough to open; when they were, their contents were found to be safe, though some of the papers were scorched. Every mail, too, brought business letters that had to be attended to. I think the first orders for goods were sent to Cleveland and Cincinnati to be filled, but it was not long before we had a large dwelling house on Michigan avenue fitted up and stocked, and business went on. The nights at first were filled with anxious forebodings. The city was in total darkness, and reports were rife that incendiaries were about and would set fires for pillage. So for weeks a patrol was organized to keep watch all night, and in this all had to take part. Then the generous letters began to come. The event was unprecedented, and the feeling it awoke in friend for friend, and in the whole world for the city was also unprecedented; we were overwhelmed with kindness; but all that is too well known to need repetition here. I will reprint from the *Song Messenger* but one after the fire, the following:

"So the smoke clears away, and the sun shines again, and from every side sympathy and aid pour in. Read this from good Mr. Curwen, the extensive publisher of the tonic-sol-fa system in England:

"LONDON, November 10, 1871.

"*Dear Mr. Root:* Our agent, at 8 Warwick Lane, says he knows Chicago well, and that there can be no doubt that your fine premises are burned. Even if you are fully insured this interruption of business must cause you heavy loss and much care. I am very sorry.

"Will you kindly accept the enclosed cheque for Twenty Pounds, to be used for the help of your people or any other sufferers by the fire? Kindly let them know that it is from one who has delighted in your music and has spread it abroad in England.

"My sons and I wish to be kindly remembered to your two sons.

"Hoping to hear of your welfare, I am, dear Mr. Root, yours, with cordial respect, JOHN CURWEN."

The paper goes on to say: "The £20 realized $107.44, and are now on their mission of blessing." It continues: "I ought to say that my sons visited Mr. Curwen during their late stay in Europe, and were delighted with the excellent working of his system; and I may add that we are really tonic-sol-faists in this country as to the matter of key relationship, the difference being in notation."

As soon as it could be brought about, our business plans for the future were adjusted. We had lost all our stock, but the plates and copyrights remained, and if I would give up some unencumbered real estate that I had, Mr. Cady and my brother would, with the above and the insurance money they hoped to get, undertake to pay the debts in full and go on with the business. I finally agreed to this proposition, and then two firms were formed. The first consisted of my brother E. T., Mr. Cady, and Mr. William Lewis, the well-known violinist, who had been with us for some years in charge of the "imported goods" department. They continued under the name of Root & Cady, and proposed to deal only in pianos, organs, and the merchandise of Mr. Lewis' department. The other firm consisted of my two sons, my brother William and myself. We took the name of Geo. F. Root & Sons, and started with the expectation of confining ourselves to sheet music, music books, and music publishing. In this arrangement I need not say it was clearly understood that I was to be free to resume my professional life untrammeled by business cares. My son F. W. also provided for himself much in the same way. William and Charles were to manage the business, whatever it might be.

One of Root & Cady's first acts was to sell the book catalogue, plates and copyrights to John Church & Co., of Cincinnati, and the sheet music plates and copyrights to S. Brainard's Sons, Cleveland. These sales realized a large sum—in the neighborhood of one hundred and thirty thousand dollars, if I remember rightly—but so many insurance companies failed that they did not get half their insurance, and when the hard times, which followed the fire, came on, could not meet the great liabilities they had assumed, and were obliged to close up. With the assistance of a wealthy friend we purchased their stock. They went through bankruptcy, and Mr. Cady left the city. My brother E. T. and Mr. Lewis then started in again, under the firm name of Root & Lewis, and we (Geo. F. Root & Sons) formed a connection with John Church & Co., of Cincinnati. The last named arrangement came about naturally, because this Cincinnati firm were now the owners and publishers of our former books, which were still successful, and they desired to continue the works of the same authors on their list.

From the re-adjustment after the fire I was in my old life again—the Normal in the summer, conventions at various times and in various places, and at my desk making books and songs the rest of the time. The Normal of 1872 was held during the vacation of the Chicago University, in their fine building overlooking Lake Michigan, with Carl Zerrahn, Robert Goldbeck, F. W. Root, P. P. Bliss, James Gill, O. Blackman, C. A. Havens, and others, as my co-workers. We had also at this session Miss Cornelia Walker, now at the head of one of the Normal schools of California, as teacher of the "art of teaching." The University had shortly before conferred upon me the degree of Doctor of Music, and I speak of it here to remark that in this country that title is only a matter of courtesy. No examinations are required before it is given, and therefore it does not necessarily imply high musical attainments on the part of the recipient. I know of but two or three American-made Doctors of Music that I think could pass the examination required for that degree in England, and I regret to say I am not one of them.

From an account in the *Song Messenger* of this Normal, the following item comes in properly:

> "Another day toward the close of the session is memorable as bringing to our knowledge an event of deep and sad interest to us all. A telegram was brought which read:
>
> "'Father died peacefully last night at ten o'clock.
>
> HENRY MASON.'"

How subduing was the effect, and how spontaneous and unanimous was the passage of the following resolution:

"*Resolved*, That in the death of Dr. Lowell Mason we recognize the loss of one who in matters of church music and musical education in this country is the great reformer of the century."

All felt that as teachers, choir leaders or writers of people's music we owed a debt of eternal gratitude to the man whose long life and noble work and powerful influence had done so much to place the musical profession in the honorable position it occupies at the present time.

CHAPTER XIV.

1873–1886, CHICAGO — BUSINESS RE-ADJUSTMENTS — VARIOUS NORMAL INSTITUTES AND CONVENTIONS—THE MEMORABLE CENTENNIAL YEAR—PARK CHURCH AT ELMIRA—GRASSHOPPERS—A FURTHER LIST OF BOOKS—ENGLISH EDITIONS—PASSAGE TAKEN TO CROSS THE WATER AGAIN.

AFTER the purchase of the stock of the old firm in 1873, Geo. F. Root & Sons went on doing a general music business, John Church & Co. and ourselves being the publishers of our works. It was a time of great business depression, but we had a "tower of strength" in the Cincinnati house, and Mr. Church's wise counsels guided us safely through. We still published the *Song Messenger*, and in its list of those who then worked more or less with us are the names of Palmer, Bliss, Straub, Matthews, Murray, Case, McGranahan, Gill, Blackman and Whittemore. Mr. Matthews, F. W. Root and myself were, in turn, editors of the *Messenger*, but all connected with us reported in it in regard to what they were doing.

The Normal of '73 was also held in the Chicago University, with Faculty as in '72, excepting that Florence Ziegfeld, the present head of the Chicago College of Music, was the principal piano teacher, Louis Falk, organist, and Elias Bogue, with F. W. Root, in voice teaching. The Normal of '74 was held in the U. P. College, in Monmouth, Ill.; F. W. Root, Carl Wolfsohn and myself, principals; Bliss, Oscar Mayo and Mrs. Cooley (model lessons), assistants. The Normal of '75 was in Somerset, Pa.; G. F. R., principal, C. C. Case, James McGranahan, T. P. Ryder, Frank Walker. C. C. Williams and myself, teachers.

In 1864 my home in Chicago was at the corner of Wabash avenue and Van Buren street. I sold the place in '69. In '71 the fire swept it away. In '72 some fine brick stores were built on the lot, one of which we occupied, but we did not stay there long. When the old business center was rebuilt we went back near to where the opera-house formerly stood. In '74 a second great fire visited Chicago. If the first had not been so vast, this one would have made some noise in the world, for it burned many acres of houses and stores, and destroyed millions of property. It reached just far enough to take the building we had just left, and so the site of my former home was burned over for the second time.

In '74 important changes took place. My son Charles sold his interest in our publications to John Church & Co., and went into other business, and the Root & Sons Music Co. was formed. In '75 the firms of Root & Lewis and Chandler & Curtiss joined us. John Church & Co. were the principal owners of the stock of the new company, and their abundant resources at once gave it standing and security. At the suggestion of my brother, E. T. Root, Charles C. Curtiss was appointed manager. I had been nominally free from business cares since the fire, but really had not been without some anxiety consequent upon starting again with so small a capital. But now our interests were in safe and strong hands, and, to adapt Mr. Longfellow's famous lines to my case—the cares that had infested *my* day, folded their tents like the Arabs and as silently stole away, and I gave myself once more, with whole-hearted freedom, to my professional work.

All who had been connected with us as Normal students, and afterwards as teachers and authors, now looked to the Cincinnati house as publishing headquarters, and in '76 the *Song Messenger* was merged into *The Musical Visitor*, which from that time became our medium of communication with the musical public. Ah, memorable '76! We went to the great Centennial celebration in Philadelphia, and then to our pleasant Normal in Towanda, Pa.; Case, McGranahan, Ryder, Coffin, Williams, Bliss, F. W. Root and myself, teachers. We then separated for our autumn and winter work. Toward the close of the year our beloved Bliss and his wife went down into that valley of fire and death at Ashtabula, disappearing from the earth as completely as did Elijah in his flaming chariot. Not a shred or vestige of them or their belongings was ever found. Mr. Bliss' unselfish devotion to his work made for him such friends while he lived and such mourners when he died as few men have ever had. It was also in '76, at Christmas time, in Delaware, O., that the National Music Teachers' Association held its first session. I was glad to aid at the beginning of that important enterprise, but have not participated since, as the subsequent meetings have been in the summer when Normal or something else demanded my attention.

Normal had now settled down into four weeks' sessions, beginning always on the first Monday after the Fourth of July. In '77 it was held in Warren, O.; in '78 in Richmond, Ind.; in '79 and '80 in Jamestown, on Chautauqua Lake, New York; in '81, Erie, Pa.; in '82, Kittanning, Pa., and a short term in Brookville, Pa.; in '83 in Erie again, and a short session in Eau Claire, Wis., and in '85 in Elmira, N. Y.

This Institution usually goes to a town because some musical person in it, in whom the people have confidence, represents its advantages to prominent citizens who bring about the necessary offer of buildings and the guarantee of a certain number of scholarships. All other things being equal, the coolest towns have the preference. We delight in being by Lake Michigan, or Erie, or lovely Chautauqua, though Kittanning and Brookville, Pa., and Eau Claire, Wis., were on pleasant rivers, which answered a good purpose. Elmira, N. Y., could not offer much in the way of a river, but she could give us the most beautiful and convenient place for our work that we have ever had.

Picture to yourself a long stone structure on one side of a small park, with great trees in front and almost bending over it. At one end a large auditorium with a fine organ; in the center a Sunday-school room below, and a lecture and entertainment room above, each capable of seating four hundred persons, and at the other end the "church home," consisting of parlors, library, some lodging rooms, and all the conveniences of a well-ordered house, all connected and under one roof, and you have PARK CHURCH, the home of the Normal of '85. It must have been more than thirty years ago that Thomas K. Beecher, nearly the youngest member of that celebrated family, was settled over that society in Elmira. He gradually got his people to look to the day when a building should be reared which should contain not only a suitable audience room for Sunday worship, but rooms and conveniences for the enjoyment of the young people, and a home for the poor wayfarer who might need temporary shelter from poverty or evil influences. This was done, but not until all the money was raised or pledged to pay for it—one hundred and thirty-two thousand dollars. Mr. Beecher had constantly urged that there be no debt to be a drag upon them when their magnificent plan went into operation.

It was characteristic of pastor and people to say, as they did to us: "Your work is calculated to improve and help people. That is what this building is for. Use it during our church vacation. The whole of it is freely placed at your disposal." It was a delightful session—the perfection of the building for the various exercises of the class, the interest of the people as shown in the attendance upon recitals and concerts, and the assurance of a welcome if we would return, no one who was there will ever forget. We should have returned the next summer, but I went to England, of which visit I will speak later.

The general scope and work of the Institution may be seen in the subjoined daily program of one of the above named sessions:

MORNING.

Preliminary, from 8:15 to 8:55, *Intermediate Harmony Class.*

9:00. Opening Exercises (devotional), followed by G. F. Root's specialties—*Vocal Drill* and *Notation* for *Elementary Singing Classes.*

10:10. Recess.

10:20. *Voice Culture* in *Class*, Frederic W. Root.

11:05. Recess.

11:15. *Harmony* and *Composition*—in two classes. *Elementary*, G. F. Root; *Advanced*, F. W. Root.

AFTERNOON.

2:00. Clubs for the practice of conducting and of giving class lessons, called, respectively, the "Conducting Club" and the "Teachers' Club." Each member acts as conductor or teacher in turn, and is criticised at the close of his work.

3:00. *Sight Reading* and *Drill* in Anthems, Glees and Part-Songs.

3:50. Recess.

4:00. Monday and Wednesday, Emil Liebling's *Pianoforte Recitals.* Tuesday and Thursday, *Vocal Recitals*, bringing out the Soloists and Members of the Institute in individual performances.

4:45. Close.

EVENING.

7:45. Monday, Tuesday, Wednesday and Thursday evenings, CHORUS and ORATORIO practice, CARL ZERRAHN, conductor. Concerts every Friday evening, closing with "THE MESSIAH" on the 31st.

PROGRAMS OF PIANOFORTE RECITALS.

First Recital.

MONDAY, JULY 6TH, AT 4 P. M.

1. Andante, Op. 32 . . . . . . *Thalberg*
2. *a.* Solitude . . . . *Hoffman*
   b. Cricket Polka . . *L. De Meyer*
3. *a.* Barcarolle . . . . . . *Rubinstein*
   b. Fantasie "Lucrezia Borgia" *Bendel*

Second Recital.

WEDNESDAY, JULY 8TH, AT 4 P. M.

1. *a.* Gavotte, B minor . . . . . *Bach*
   b. Andante, A major . . . . *Mozart*
   c. Perpetuum Mobile . . . . *Weber*
2. *a.* Menuet, A-flat . . . *Boccherini*
   b. Albumblatt, E minor . . *Grieg*
   c. The Two Skylarks . *Leschetitzky*
3. *a.* Feu Follet . . . . *Liebling*
   b. Nocturne, Op. 17 . . . . *Brassin*
   c. Polonaise . . . . . . *Scharwenka*

Third Recital.

MONDAY, JULY 13TH, AT 4 P. M.

1. Recollections of Home . . . . *Mills*
2. *a.* Scherzino, Op. 18 . . *Moszkowski*
   b. Nocturne, A major . . . . *Field*
   c. Gavotte, E minor . . . . . *Silas*
3. *a.* Silver Spring . . . . . . *Bendel*
   b. La Cachoucha . . . . *Raff*

Fourth Recital.

WEDNESDAY, JULY 15TH, AT 4 P. M.

1. *a.* Sonata, G minor . . . . *Scarlatti*
   b. Prelude and Fugue, D major, *Bach*
2. Sonata Pathetique, Op. 13, *Beethoven*
3. *a.* Soirée de Vienne, No. 7 . . *Liszt*
   b. Nocturne, Op 9, No. 2 . . *Chopin*
   c. Gavotte Moderne . . . *Liebling*

Fifth Recital.

MONDAY, JULY 20TH, AT 4 P. M.

1. Rondo Capriccioso, Op. 14, *Mendelssohn*
2. *a.* Albumblatt . . . . *Liebling*
   b. Le Tourbillon . . . . . *Goldbeck*
3. *a.* Valse Caprice, Op. 29 . . . *Mills*
   b. Melody in F . . . . . *Rubinstein*
   c. Polka Fantastique . . *Brandeis*

Sixth Recital.—Historical Program.

WEDNESDAY, JULY 22D, AT 4 P. M.

1. *a.* Sonata, A major, *Scarlatti*, 1683–1757.
   b. Prelude and Fugue, C minor, *Bach*, 1685–1750.
   c. Variations, E major, *Haendel*, 1684–1759.
   d. Turkish March, *Mozart*, 1756–1791.
2. Moonlight Sonata, *Beethoven*, 1770–1827.
3. *a.* Rondo Brillante, *Weber*, 1786–1826.
   b. Menuet, *Schubert*, 1797–1828.
   c. Songs Without Words, *Mendelssohn*, 1809–1847.
   d. Ende vom Lied, *Schumann*, 1810–1856.
4. *a.* Marche Funèbre, *Chopin*, 1809–1849.
   b. La Fileuse, *Raff*, 1822.
   c. Kammenoi-Ostrow, . *Rubinstein*, 1830.
   d. Polonaise, E major, *Liszt*, 1811.

Seventh Recital.

MONDAY, JULY 27TH, AT 4 P. M.

1. *a.* Impromptu, Op. 29,
   b. Étude, Op. 10, No. 5,
   c. Mazurka, Op. 33, No. 4,
   d. Valse, Op. 34, No. 1,
2. *a.* Nocturne, Op. 37, No. 2,
   b. Scherzo, Op. 31,
3. *a.* Berceuse, Op. 57,
   b. Polonaise, Op. 53,

Chopin

Eighth Recital.

WEDNESDAY, JULY 29TH, AT 4 P. M.

1. G minor Fugue . . . . . *Bach-Liszt*
2. *a.* Flashes from the West, *Goldbeck*
   b. Silver Spring . . . . . . *Mason*
   c. Hungarian Melody . . . . *Liszt*
3. *a.* Romanza, Op. 5 . . *Tschaikowsky*
   b. Marche Héroique . . *Saint-Saens*

In looking over the list of Musical Associations that I have conducted since the fire, I find it too long even to mention. As I glance at the list, however, my eye catches the line: "Centennial celebration of the settlement of Sheffield, Mass., June 19, '76." This is my native town, and the musical exercises there were of peculiar interest to the people who knew my parents, and to myself on their account. I was a small boy when we moved to North Reading, but I remembered well the beautiful Berkshire mountains that looked so near and were so far, the lovely Housatonic which flows through the valley, and the wide street and magnificent elms of the dear old village which I am proud to claim as my birthplace. Among the kinfolk that welcomed me on this occasion was Dr. Orville Dewey, one of America's eminent divines, who was there also at his birthplace. That brings to my mind that Dr. Dewey and Wm. Cullen Bryant, who was also a native of Berkshire County, were both school-mates of my father, and a few years before, while I was engaged in some musical work in Great Barrington (the next town), Mr. Bryant was there, and I had the pleasure of a few kind words from him in remembrance of his old school-fellow.

As I look along the list, the word "grasshoppers" catches my eye and brings to mind a wagon ride from a convention in Clarinda, Ia., to another at College Springs, fifteen miles distant, and a description that the driver gave me of the ravages of those terrible pests. During the convention I was introduced to one of the large farmers who had suffered by them, and was greatly interested in his graphic description of what had befallen him: "We had had two years of light crops," he began, "and I needed some good wheat and a lot of it the worst way, so I put in six hundred acres, and you never saw anything so fine as that was when it was about half grown. I was happy! That crop was going to fix me all right. Well, I drove in here to church one Sunday morning—I live about four miles out—and when I got back there wasn't a spear of my wheat standing; the ground where it stood was as black as if it had been burnt over, and the 'hoppers had traveled on." "But you lived through it," I said. "Oh, yes," he answered, "I'm all right now."

In '81 Mr. E. V. Church, Mr. John Church's nephew, took the management of the business, Mr. Curtiss having left for a trip to Europe. Mr. Lewis had already made other business arrangements, and now my brother, E. T., sold his stock in the company to go into business with his sons. The arrangements thus described remain to the present time, with the exception that John Church & Co. became tired of the inconvenience of occupying stores owned by other people, and bought the white marble building at the corner of Wabash avenue and Adams street, which fine premises we occupy now.

My books, after the fire and up to my second trip abroad in '86, were: "The New Curriculum," "The Glory," "The Hour of Praise," "The Guide to the Pianoforte," "The Cabinet Organ Companion," "The Normal Musical Hand-Book," "The New Song Era" (with my son F. W.), "The Choir and Congregation," "The Männerchor," "The Trumpet of Reform," "The Model Organ Method," "The Palace of Song," "The Realm of Song," "The Chorus Castle," "The Teachers' Club," "The Organist at Home," "First Years in Song Land," "Our Song World" (with C. C. Case), "Pure Delight" and "Wondrous Love" (also with Mr. Case), and the following cantatas: In the first one, "The Song Tournament," I was assisted in preparing the libretto by Palmer Hartsough, one of our Normals, who has great ingenuity in adapting words to music, and then I made the valued acquaintance of Hezekiah Butterworth, of Boston, the well-known author and poet, who prepared the librettos to "Under the Palms," "Catching Kriss Kringle," "David, the Shepherd Boy," "The Name Ineffable," "The Choicest Gift," and "Faith Triumphant." Then followed "Flower Praise" and "Santa Claus' Mistake," with librettos by my daughter, Clara Louise Burnham. Of the Sunday-school and Gospel songs, not before mentioned, the following are best known: "Why do you wait, dear brother?" "Jewels," "Ring the bells of heaven," "Knocking, knocking, who is there?" "Along the river of time," "Where are the reapers?" "We are watching, we are waiting," "The beacon light," "Because He loved me so," "Altogether lovely," "Never give up the right way," and "Behold, the Bridegroom cometh."

"Under the Palms" was the first cantata to unite adults and children (the choir and Sunday-school) in a connected performance, and its success was immediate. Not long after its publication in 1880 I received a letter from the London Sunday-school Union, saying that they had issued that work, and that it was being extensively sung throughout the kingdom. The letter enclosed a gratuity in the shape of an English bank-note, and further said if I would write them another cantata of the same kind they would pay a regular royalty on it. "The Choicest Gift" was the result of that request, but in the meantime the firm of John Curwen & Sons (consisting now only of the sons, the father being dead) wrote me that I should soon receive an English copy of "David, the Shepherd Boy," and that they proposed to pay a voluntary royalty on all copies of it that they sold. This was a purely friendly and generous act on their part, as all American compositions were as free to them as theirs are to us. They issued it in both notations, and an excellent English musician added a harmonium accompaniment, which is printed in a separate book. They also had it arranged for a large orchestra.

About this time I received a letter from Messrs. Bailey & Ferguson, of Glasgow, Scotland, to know if I would write a cantata for them. My publishers soon arranged the matter, and "Faith Triumphant" was the result. An arrangement was made to furnish the Glasgow house a set of plates by duplicating them as the book went through the press in Cincinnati.

I had long desired to go to England once more, and it now occurred to me that it would be pleasant to get to Glasgow soon after my cantata, and perhaps do something in the way of helping it start in Scotland. So when I found my publishers thought it a good plan I decided to go. After I had secured my passage I received a third letter from the London Sunday-school Union about a third cantata for them, to which I replied that I would call in a few days and talk it over.

CHAPTER XV.

ON BOARD THE STEAMSHIP ETHIOPIA—GLASGOW—FIRST SUNDAY IN LONDON — ST. MARTIN'S-IN-THE-FIELDS — INTERLUDES— THE LONDON SUNDAY-SCHOOL UNION—THE CURWENS — VOLUNTARY ROYALTIES — HERNE HOUSE — MR. EVANS AND THE LONDON PUBLIC SCHOOLS.

ON July 17, 1886, I found myself on board the steamship *Ethiopia*, of the Anchor Line, bound for Glasgow, Scotland.

It is interesting to observe the change that comes over *some* people at the beginning of a sea-voyage, as the billows, which at first seem to them so grand or so graceful, gradually become objects of utter aversion and disgust—but I will not enlarge. It is sufficient to say that in our case on the fourth day out two-thirds of the sick ones were back to their rations, and we had an excellent voyage.

We had a good deal of music as we steamed along, there being there a piano and organ, and several good players and singers among the passengers. One evening the program was varied by a mock trial. A nice old gentleman of decidedly patriarchal appearance, who had paid a good deal of attention to the ladies, "without distinction of age or previous condition of servitude," as the indictment read, was accused of being a Mormon elder, seeking proselytes. Being conducted in good taste by real lawyers, the trial afforded much entertainment. The jury was composed entirely of ladies, who rendered a unanimous verdict in the prisoner's favor.

Sunday divine service was conducted by a clergyman

from Toronto. There is an opening from the main cabin to the room above called the music-room, in which is an excellent organ and a good piano. The choir, composed of a few of the best singers among the passengers, was up there, and the effect was good, the only trouble being that the player had to be guarded lest the rolling of the ship should send him off his seat.

On Sunday evening at twilight the organist began playing quietly some of the older tunes, gradually coming nearer those of modern times. The passengers gathered round, and when he got to "Nearer, my God, to Thee" and "The Shining Shore," began to join in. This led to one of the most genuine Sunday night sings that I have ever heard. One after another called for his or her favorite, until about all the well-known tunes and gospel songs had been sung. The roar of the winds and dash of the waves outside mingling with our music would have perhaps carried our thoughts back to the Pilgrims' "Songs on the Sea," but for the beat of the engine and the knowledge that the Pilgrim fathers would not have given our gospel songs a place in their stern devotions.

The last day of our voyage. All day along the northern coast of Ireland. "Emerald" is the word, as we look on the beautiful fields and hills, and here comes the Giant's Causeway. "Don't you see the giant?" says an old sailor. "No," I answer. "Why, there, leaning his arm on the rock, so, and his feet down in the water." I couldn't see him, but all could see the wonderful pillar-like structure stretching along for miles like gigantic organ pipes.

And now up the Clyde. Fields, lawns, forests, hills, towns, country seats, castles, and then ship-yards as we near Glasgow, where the great iron steamers and ships of the world are made. Such a clang and clatter as the thousands of hammers rang out upon the iron ribs and plates as we passed!

Glasgow at last. To the hotel and then to Messrs. Bayley & Ferguson's to see if the plates of the new cantata had come. As they had not yet arrived I went back to the hotel and waited until Mr. Bayley should have leisure to show me about the town.

Glasgow is emphatically a stone city. Not a wooden structure in it, and I think Mr. Bayley said there was none of brick—at any rate, I saw none. I was not prepared to find Glasgow the second city in the empire, but so it is.

We went at evening to a park just out of the city, to hear a band play—a beautiful place of hills and valleys, fine trees and flowers. "Here," said Mr. Bayley, "where the band are now playing, was fought the battle that lost Queen Mary her kingdom. She watched it from the hill over there (a half mile or so off), and when she saw the day was against her, fled, and was never again seen in Scotland."

Many such things of historic interest came up, but I will not inflict guide-book talk upon my readers. It is sufficient to say that I passed a memorable and most pleasant day with our Glasgow publisher—a long one, too, light as day at nine o'clock at night, with twilight until ten or after.

As the plates of the cantata were delayed I did not wait, but took the "Midland" to London the next day. Tremendous speed, but so smooth that one could read or write without difficulty. I fell into conversation with an intense Englishman, who had been in our country, and who was loud in his preference for everything English. Speaking of the compartment in which we were locked, he said: "Now, if there is anybody on the train that I don't want to see, he can't get in here." I did *not* answer, "If there is anybody in here that I don't want to see, I can't get out," but I thought it.

I enjoyed some nice children that were in the compartment, and at one of the stations bought a basket of strawberries for distribution. It was a good sized basket, and, noticing that the bottom of the basket was not half way up to lessen its size, I said to myself, "How much more honest they are over here in these matters," but some cabbage leaves at the bottom of the basket threw some doubt on the superior honesty of these neighbors across the water.

My first Sunday in London I attended Argyle-square Church in the morning and "St. Martin's-in-the-fields" in the evening. Fine organs and fine organists. Excellent singers. In "St. Martin's" a surpliced choir of men and boys in the chancel, and admirable music. The hymn tunes ecclesiastical, but sung in quick time, so nothing heavy about them. All this, to say that in the five hymns heard in the morning and evening, *there was not one interlude.* There certainly was no more need of interludes in those hymns than there would have been in the chants, which were so freely sung. How inspiriting they were! The glow that commenced at the beginning of the hymn did not die out at the end of each verse, but increased steadily to the end of the song.

In this connection I may mention that I was in Lancashire for a few days soon after my arrival in England, and on the occasion of a religious gathering heard some hymns sung by a congregation of perhaps six hundred people. The tunes were modern English ("Barnby," "Smart," etc.), excellent in every way, and sung heartily and well. Fine, strong voices the Lancashire people have—the high tones good and in tune. But what struck me especially there, also, was that *not one interlude* was played during the evening. I was a good deal interested in the remark of a friend there, who said: "To use an Americanism, interludes are 'played out'—they are only used occasionally to lengthen the hymn during a collection." I am sure if our people could once hear how a hymn of five or six long verses, with a good tune, can go through, not only without weariness but with positive satisfaction, they would not put up with the *interruptions*, or worse, of interludes.

How they hold on to old names over there! I suppose St. Martin's *was* in the "fields," but there isn't a field within miles of it now. It is in the very heart of London. In its old neighbor, Westminster Abbey, I was much attracted by the new marble bust of Longfellow, especially as some admirer had placed a delicate bunch of flowers in the folds of the marble, making a sort of button-hole bouquet. Its contrast to the blackened and grim surroundings was striking. But to return to musical matters.

The London Sunday-school Union publish "Under the Palms" and "The Choicest Gift." The week before I left home I received a letter from them, saying they would like another cantata of that grade. I called upon them and arranged for future publications. My readers doubtless know that the English people have been using our American music for many years. All Foster's songs, and, in fact, pretty much all the music of a simple and medium grade that has been popular in America, have had a corresponding popularity in England. The first American cantata printed in England was "The Flower Queen." Since then nearly, if not quite, all our cantatas have appeared there, soon after their issue in America, proving not that we are better composers than the English, but that we are nearer and more in sympathy with those for whom we write. I think I do not violate any principle of propriety if I say that a high official in the Sunday-school Union added that the American cantatas that they had published had in their music a "go" (to use his expression) that they did not find elsewhere. This induces the Union to offer a royalty for what they want, although there is no international copyright.

I had word from Messrs. Bayley & Ferguson, of Glasgow,

at this time, that the plates of "Faith Triumphant" had arrived, and that the work would be issued promptly in the standard and tonic-sol-fa notations.

Years ago, when Rev. John Curwen was commencing the tonic-sol-fa enterprise he used a great deal of our American singing-school music, which is free there, there being no international copyright law. After he passed away his sons continued publishing from American works such music as suited their purpose, but since the tonic-sol-fa movement has grown stronger, and its adherents have made higher attainments, it is not the simpler music they take so much as the cantatas—that is, so far as I am concerned. These, beginning with "The Flower Queen" and ending with "Florens, the Pilgrim"—fourteen in all—are printed by them in the staff notation as well as in "tonic-sol-fa."

I say all this to explain why I, who neither teach nor write in tonic-sol-fa, was the recipient of such unbounded kindness from those friends, especially from Mr. J. Spencer Curwen, the present head of the movement, at whose home I stayed. The father made a substantial recognition of what he was pleased to consider his obligations to us at the time of the Chicago fire, as I have previously mentioned, and the present firm of their own accord proposed the royalty on "David, the Shepherd Boy," of which I have spoken.

Explaining thus how it happened that I was a guest at "Herne house," Mr. Curwen's residence, and to some extent why Mr. Curwen took so much trouble to help me to hear the representative music of the English people, I will state briefly what we did. Of course it was results that I sought—to know how the people sang as compared with ourselves, and how the reading and understanding of music compared with the same things on our side, as Mr. Evans, the superintendent of music in the public schools of London (1,100 schools, 300,000 children), told me the first time I met him:

"I say to the teachers, take what method you please; I shall report you according to *results*. If they are good we have no fault to find with the method." This, of course, is eminently just. Let the teacher do his work in his own way; simply hold him responsible for results. (As a matter of fact, a large majority of the London schools have adopted tonic-sol-fa.)

In this spirit I tried to listen to such singing as I had an opportunity to hear in England. First the voices, how they were used, then the words and expression, then the reading and comprehension of principles (where I could ascertain about the latter things).

CHAPTER XVI.

THE WORK OF THE TONIC-SOL-FA COLLEGE—MR. BEHNKE'S LIGHT TO THE THROAT—ENGLAND AND DICKENS—THE BOYS OF THE MEDWAY UNION—DON—THE STAFFORDSHIRE POTTERIES AND THE BURSLEM SINGERS—EPPING FOREST AND THE LAWN PARTY AT FOREST GATE—REV. JOHN CURWEN'S GRAVE—THE CHOIR OF THE CHAPEL ROYAL—MR. J. A. BIRCH AND "THE HAYMAKERS."

THE Normal term at the Tonic-sol-fa College was near its close when I arrived in London. It was like being at home to be there, for they have our plans for their work—teaching class, voice class, harmony class, etc., but with some improvements not dependent upon tonic-sol-fa notation which we might well adopt. The first work that I heard was Mr. McNaught's—teaching the students to teach children. For this purpose a class of children from a neighboring school was brought in, and *real work* was done, the students trying their hand at it after the model was given. We have sometimes had juvenile classes at our Normals, but not just in this way. Capital teacher, Mr. McNaught. Criticisms keen and incisive, but given with such vivacity, and at the same time with such evident kindliness and desire for the students' welfare, that the severest comments were received not only without mortification but with evident enjoyment. Normal workers know well the great importance of such an ability.

Next, Mr. Proudman's voice class. Admirable work. Mr. Proudman will be remembered as the conductor who took to Paris the English choir, which created such enthusiasm in an international competition a few years ago. There were some new points in Mr. Proudman's work which seemed to me very important and useful.

The harmony work by Mr. Oakey and Mr. McNaught interested me much. Some exercises in the way of noting harmonies as they were heard were especially good. The idea and value of "ear harmony" as distinguished from "eye harmony" they fully understand in this institution.

I had been much interested for two or three years in reading of the investigations and researches of Mr. Emil Behnke in matters pertaining to the voice, so it was with much pleasure that I found he was to lecture here, and that I could hear him. When I was introduced he said: "Ah! I have read your articles on the voice with great pleasure. They abound in good sense and valuable ideas." I had to say that the articles were not written by myself, but by my son, F. W. Root (but I dare say there was some pride in the emphasis with which I uttered the words "my son").

Think of applying an electric light of thirty thousand candle power to the throat to see what is going on inside! But let me repeat how he explained the experiment as well as I can remember it. He began by saying: "Hold your open hand close to a strong light and you can see something of the light through where the fingers join together; or hold a light behind the ear and the same transparency may be observed. So I thought a very powerful light might be so brought to bear upon the outside of the throat that the vocal cords inside would get light enough to be reflected in a mirror, and in that way reveal their different positions for the different registers of the voice. I applied to Sir Wm. Siemens (a distinguished electrician of London) for the use of apparatus to try my experiment. This was kindly granted, and I arranged the light in a box with a tube to the throat which concentrated and directed the light to the point to be investigated." Without going further into particulars, I will only say his experiment was successful, and he showed photographs of the vocal cords in various positions caused by different pitches of the voice.

They do know how to treat boys' voices in England, at least the teachers whose work I have seen, do. But I ought to say that Mr. Curwen, sparing no trouble nor expense, arranged for me to hear the best. Our first trip was to Chatham and Rochester, which practically form one town, being on either side of the river Medway, about forty miles from London. The first thought on arriving there was of one of Mr. Pickwick's early adventures. It is surprising how strong a hold Dickens' stories have upon the American mind. I found I was not alone in thinking of Dickens the first thing when I came across a name, or place, or scene that he has mentioned or described. We might almost say that it is not so much that Dickens describes England as that England illustrates Dickens. There were the ruins of Rochester Castle, "the lonely field near Fort Pitt" where Mr. Winkle and Lieut. Tappleton met for the duel which did not take place, and the bridge where "dismal Jemmy" so excited Mr. Pickwick's sympathies in the early morning. We saw them all, though the gentleman who pointed them out knew little or nothing of Dickens.

But to continue my subject:—We went to see and hear the boys of the "Medway Union." You would hardly suppose that that means a work-house, but such is the fact. It is a large establishment, with people of all ages in it. The children are, of course, of the lowest grade, many of them the veriest waifs of community, but they have excellent school privileges, and the head master, Mr. James A. Price, fortunately for them, not only loves music, but understands it and knows how to teach it as very few professional teachers do. Indeed, to his rare skill the extraordinary results that we listened to are due. What did it matter how they expressed or noted what they sang? It was, in point of fact, a tonic-sol-fa choir, but I did not think about that at all at first. It was the *singing* that struck me and delighted me as no boys' singing up to that time had ever done. There were about forty of the little fellows in the choir, carrying three well-balanced parts—the sopranos beautifully sweet and clear, and the altos of admirable quality—not a harsh voice in the whole number, nor one chest-tone forced beyond its proper place. They sang without accompaniment, but there was no flatting nor singing out of tune in any way.

They sang one or two songs of German origin, if I remember rightly, at first, and then four or five of mine. It is the same everywhere here. Wherever the tonic-sol-faists have worked, American music has found a use and a home. Mine would naturally be sung where I went, as a complimentary attention.

After the singing Mr. Price had a few of the boys play violins and violas while he played the 'cello, and after that a large drum and fife corps, also composed of the choir boys, performed admirably; only, as it was damp weather, the performance was in a room and the din almost deafening. I must not omit to mention a very prominent member of this happy company—for happy it is, as the beaming faces of the little fellows abundantly testify. This individual is "Don," a monstrous dog of the St. Bernard persuasion. Wherever the boys are, there is Don. Whenever they assemble for singing he brings up the rear and stretches his huge bulk in the aisle as near to them as he can get. During the stunning fife and drum performance, which would have set wild any other dog I ever knew, Don walked around among the instruments and players, placidly waving his great plume of a tail, the picture of contentment and benevolence. And after the music, out in the paved court where some little boys were at play, I shall never forget the affection manifested on both sides—how the little chaps clung to the great fellow, and how he seemed to feel the care of the entire group.

It will be a great pleasure always to call to mind the friends and events of that day: Mr. and Mrs. Price, and her mother (who has been the matron of the institution for many years), and the assistant teachers, and their noble work. The difference for good that in all probability they will have caused in the lives of those children can not be estimated by any earthly standard.

I now come to another most interesting event connected with my English visit. It was a journey to Burslem, in Staffordshire, by the kind arrangement of Mr. Curwen, and, as his guest, to hear one of the most celebrated choirs in the kingdom. Staffordshire is the great pottery county of England. It was in Burslem that Wedgewood lived and died. Wedgewood Hall, a beautiful building, is there erected to his memory, in which are wonders of the art which has made his name celebrated the world over. The choir is composed almost entirely of men, women and children who work in the potteries or are connected with that industry. On the way Mr. Curwen said: "I do not know whether there is something especially favorable to singing in their occupation, but it is certain that they have exceptionally good voices."

We were met at the station by Mr. Thomas Hulme, a prominent citizen and former mayor of the city, who took us to his fine residence on a commanding eminence in the suburbs. From there we went at seven to the Town Hall, where the performance was to take place. The hall which would hold a thousand or more people was packed on our arrival. On either side and in front of a good-sized organ were raised seats for the choir, already there, one hundred and seventy strong. The fact that this choir had sung my music a good deal in former years, and that the papers had announced our coming—Mr. Curwen's and mine—in a very kind and appreciative way, caused a hearty greeting on the part of both choir and audience as we entered.

I ought to say that this was a kind of public rehearsal of music to be performed at a competition of choral societies (they call them "choirs" in England) to take place at Liverpool the following week. The great competition piece was a double chorus by Bach, called "Be not afraid"—twenty-seven pages long in the Novello edition, and taking exactly ten minutes in performance. When I say that it is in eight parts, filled with the peculiar intricacies and difficulties of this great composer's music, and that it was sung magnificently *without notes and without accompaniment*, I think my readers will agree with me that it was a remarkable performance, well worth a long journey to hear. Mr. Curwen's remark about the voices was fully justified. They were not only beautiful in quality but of great power. Indeed, when the chorus began, the burst was so grand that I could hardly realize that only one-half the choir were singing.

There were other highly interesting performances during the evening, among which was a part-song by Pinsuti, most delicately sung; but I will not further particularize; yes, I must mention a test that Mr. Curwen, by request, gave to show the musical knowledge of the younger members of the choir. Two blackboards were brought on to the platform and two children called up to write what Mr. Docksey, the conductor, sang, he using the syllable *la*. The music in two parts had been prepared by Mr. Curwen before entering the hall, and was, of course, entirely unknown to the choir. The work was promptly and correctly done in the tonic-sol-fa notation, and then six other children—three on a part—were called up to sing what had been written, which was easily and well done, much to the delight of the audience. I presume they could have used the staff notation, but this was shorter.

I shall not soon forget the Burslem choir and its able conductor, and the pleasure that evening gave me.

Who has not read of that bold outlaw, Robin Hood, and his adventures in Epping Forest, then far away from London, but now near by? The forest did not go to London, but London came to the forest, the eight or nine miles out to "Forest Gate," where Mr. Curwen lives, being now a continuous city, a most pleasant and safe ride, the railway going sometimes over the streets and houses and other railways, sometimes under them, but never on their level. No "crossings," with flagmen whose best efforts can not prevent accidents, and no delays—everything like clock-work; a consummation devoutly to be wished for on our side of the water.

But I started to tell about a party—a lawn party on the borders of Epping Forest. An English lawn is something to see—the thick, soft grass, so level and green, is like cut velvet, and for bowls, ten-pins, croquet, and other outdoor games as good as a floor. The lawn at Mr. Curwen's place is of this kind, and is rendered more picturesque by being thickly bordered on the sides by fine trees, some old enough, perhaps, to have sheltered the bold outlaw and his merry men. Here the students of the sol-fa college, with the teachers and their ladies, assembled one lovely afternoon near the close of their term.

Right here let me say that if any one has an impression that these tonic-sol-fa people and their accomplished teachers do not know the staff notation, they are wonderfully mistaken. I only wish our people knew it as well. Why, the Curwen house prints everything it issues in the staff notation as well as in tonic-sol-fa. It is a curious fact that at first the other houses, Novello's, for instance, printed no tonic-sol-fa and the Curwens printed no staff. Now the Curwens print staff and Novello a great deal of tonic-sol-fa music. I am quite sure I am right in saying that all sol-faists look forward to a knowledge of the staff notation as their crowning acquirement.

Somehow or other the impression has been extensively created in America that "Sol-fa" was to sweep all other notations out of existence. I don't know who did it—Mr. Seward says he didn't; but I do know that that is not the way the matter is regarded in England, and it is much to be regretted that there should be any misunderstanding about it, for the usefulness of the work as done there can not be denied, and the teaching that has grown with it that may be applied to the staff notation is of a very superior order.

The afternoon was delightful; groups playing games, others chatting, two long tables decked with flowers, near the trees, for supper, or, I should say, tea. They do nothing there without a cup of tea. At almost any kind of meeting having at all the social element in it the first thing is a cup of tea—a discussion, a speech meeting, a singing meeting. They don't seem to get on with any of them without first getting inspiration from the cup which "cheers," etc. I do not wonder, though, that it is so popular a beverage there. It is quite another thing from the article we know as tea. "Tea meetings" would never thrive on the kind we generally get on our side of the water.

After tea a photographer appeared on the scene and placed the assembled company in a group, with the fine old "ivy-mantled" house for a background. "Come, doctor," they called. I was talking with some one a little way off. "You don't want me," I answered; "I'm not in the charmed circle." "But your music is, and we must have you." So there I am, in the excellent picture then taken.

I had the pleasure of meeting here Mr. Spedding Curwen,

the other member of the firm of J. Curwen & Sons, and its business manager, whose fine residence is not far away. Nothing could be more complete than the combination of these two men for the success of their important business enterprises; nor more delightful than the intercourse of their two families for the enjoyment of their home life.

After the picture, singing. There were too few lady students to have a mixed choir, but the men's choir, under the leadership of Mr. McNaught, was admirable. Mr. Proudman's voice work showed its rare excellence, especially in the upper tenors. Their tones were of beautiful quality, easily produced and true to pitch. Then Mr. Kestin, the teacher of elocution, gave some recitations. I wish some of our howling ranters could have heard him. The quiet sincerity with which he made every character his own, made me think of the answer a country friend once gave when asked how he liked Jefferson's acting in "Rip Van Winkle." "Why, I didn't see any *acting*. I saw a shif'less Dutchman that got druv off into the mountains, but he was such a good-natur'd feller I liked him fust rate." So Mr. Kestin was for the time whatever he assumed to be, carrying us all with him, in the same way. The drawing-room being on a level with the lawn, with windows opening out upon it, all could enjoy the solos—instrumental and vocal—with which the afternoon closed.

In connection with the romantic interest I felt in Epping Forest, a deep impression was made upon my mind about this time by a visit to Rev. John Curwen's grave. It is nearer what was the forest center, in a spot selected, I think his son said, by himself. A fine shaft bears an appropriate inscription, but his great monument is the reverence in which his memory is held by hundreds of thousands who have been the better for his modest and unselfish work.

My kind host knowing my desire to hear the representative music of England as far as possible, suggested, on a Sunday soon after, that we go to the Chapel Royal, St. James Palace, the worshiping place of royalty and nobility when in London. Arriving in due time we were ushered by a solemn functionary—I forget his title—into some seats that we might occupy. It is a small chapel, long and narrow, but rich and elaborate in decorations, particularly the part devoted to the royal family—but I won't go into guide-book talk. The first curious thing was the dress of the choir boys before they donned their white surplices (we saw them about the corridors of the palace). It was of red and gold, very elaborate and costly, more military than religious-looking, but a distinguishing uniform that they must wear all the time. But the little fellows can sing! Nothing but the severest of the English ecclesiastical music allowed—extremely difficult in all respects, and I should say only made tolerable to untrained ears by the beauty of the voices and the ease with which all difficulties were overcome. The alto was sung by men. We were invited to dinner by Mr. J. A. Birch, an acquaintance of Mr. Curwen, whose speaking voice indicates a fine, resonant base, but who is one of the altos, not only of this choir but of that of St. Paul's Cathedral, the services being at different hours. I need not say that these positions mean exceptional gifts and attainments on the part of those who hold them. The men of this particular choir are called "gentlemen of the chapel royal." Mr. Birch is a highly successful conductor and teacher in London, and gratified me much by his hearty greeting. In the course of conversation he said: "I have given your cantatas a great deal for many years; indeed, one of them has been more remunerative than any other work of the kind that I have ever had to do with—I mean 'The Haymakers.' I have given it seventeen times."

On coming out of service we were just in time to see the

change of the Queen's guard in the court-yard of the palace, and to hear two numbers from one of the two best bands in the kingdom. A Thomas orchestra performance was the only thing I could liken it to for finish and elegance.

CHAPTER XVII.

THE PARISH CHURCH—TRADITIONAL CHANTING—THE "SWANLEY BOYS"—THE HALL OF PARLIAMENT—A RECEPTION ON MR. CURWEN'S LAWN—FORTY CONDUCTORS—THE BRITISH MUSEUM—A MUSICAL CATALOGUE—ONE OF THE LONDON "CHOIRS"—THE SOUTH LONDON CHORAL INSTITUTE—DR. ALLON'S CHURCH AT ISLINGTON—MY SIXTY-SIXTH BIRTHDAY—THE CRYSTAL PALACE AND "AUTUMN WINDS"—THE CONCERT ON THE "CITY OF ROME."

GOING to "church" in England means but one thing—the Church of England. Going to other religious gatherings is called going to "chapel," or something of that kind. One Sunday morning my kind host said, "Let us go to the parish church to-day; the music will interest you." It was a walk of perhaps a mile and a half from Forest Gate, but when we got there it was indeed the parish church of old England as immortalized in descriptions innumerable: low, gothic, massive, ivy-clad, the old, gray tower rising like the chief monument of the church-yard in which it is placed. Groups of grown people and children, wending their way among the grave-stones, realized in every particular the picture so familiar to us all of this peculiarly English scene.

We entered at a side door, stepping upon the uneven stone floor that had been worn by the footsteps of many generations. The surpliced organist, in full sight, had just commenced his voluntary. Soon the ministers and choir of surpliced men and boys filed in, and service commenced. I will not go into particulars, but would simply speak of the excellent choir-singing there, as I have had occasion to do of all the surpliced choirs I heard while in England, and of the fine tunes and hearty singing of the congregation, in *all* the hymns. I did not hear one by choir alone, and *not an interlude* during the entire time.

I think my readers will bear witness that I have not sought the adverse side in my descriptions, but I must say that chanting there, judged by every consideration excepting tradition, is poor—more than that, it is to me irreverent. I will not judge others, but how any one who thinks the words of the Bible should be read or intoned deliberately, can be devotionally impressed by the unseemly haste and inevitable confusion that this mode of chanting compels, I do not understand. And it is passing strange, that while the "chapels," and dissenters generally, who have broken off from the Church of England, repudiate mostly the modes of that church, they stick to this race-horse chanting—that is, so far as I have heard them. The power of tradition is astonishing. It still holds sway over the Episcopal churches of our country, but we have reason to be thankful that Dr. Lowell Mason, a half a century ago, inaugurated the better mode that prevails in our other churches; that is, the chants so arranged that the words are uttered about as fast as the reverent reader reads.

On the Monday following we went to the Swanley Orphan's Home, one of those noble institutions for the care and training of children of which there are several about London. This place is about twenty miles out, if I remember rightly, delightfully situated on a breezy hill, and is remarkable for its boy choir, known as the "Swanley Boys." I wish you could see the photograph before me—two hundred or more of these little fellows—taken in the Institution (they teach the boys there all sorts of useful occupations); a ruddier, happier set of little faces it would be hard to find.

I say "remarkable for its boy choir." I ought to say it is remarkable for its excellence in everything that relates to the welfare of the boys, but I will confine myself to the one thing that we went especially to observe.

The whole number sang first in two parts—just soprano and alto—but such music! I am sorry I did not take a note of what was done first—I think something by Mendelssohn, but what was most prominent was the Hallelujah chorus! As music, without tenor and base, it was of course lacking, but as a performance showing the musical attainments of the boys, and especially the masterly training of their voices, it was a great success. Every time the sopranos approached the high places that every conductor so much dreads, I thought "now they can not keep up that perfect pitch and sweetness," but they did, and when the sopranos gave the high A at "And he shall reign," although on the thin vowel e, I know of no better word than "angelic" to express the impression made upon the minds of the visitors present.

I said to Mr. W. H. Richardson, their teacher and conductor: "Can these be ordinary boy voices? If so, I do not quite see how you get these results." "In the first place," he replied, "we take all the care of their voices that we can. The little fellows are not allowed to shout or talk boisterously at their play or at any time, and we are constantly on the watch to keep their tones soft and sweet, and in the proper registers." "I can not think you have much trouble in that way now," I continued. "We should have trouble enough if we were to relax our watchfulness for even a few days, I assure you," he replied. I mention this conversation to show that what seemed so easy—almost spontaneous, was really the result of hard work and constant watchfulness.

After this performance came the "Swanley Boys" proper, that is, the large chorus was sent away all but about forty boys. These form the famous choir. They go about a good deal giving concerts which result in considerable pecuniary aid to the Institution. And now came beautiful part-songs in three parts, and then some blackboard "tests." Mr. Curwen gave some excellent examinations in tonic-sol-fa, and I followed with a moderately difficult three-part exercise on staffs. After they had sung it I only wished it had been three times as difficult—they made no more of it than if it had been the scale. It was another proof that tonic-sol-fa and staff notations go hand in hand in England, whatever may be thought about the matter in America.

After much kind attention from Mr. Gregory, the governor of the Institution, Mr. Richardson accompanied us to the station, where we bade him a warm farewell, and turned our faces toward the great city.

This is not the proper place to describe the great sights of London, but I will say that after much difficulty I got "into Parliament"—one day too late to hear Mr. Gladstone, but other speakers were well worth hearing. I think all strangers wonder first why the hall is so small, and second, why there is so little room for visitors. My good friend enlightened me on these points. He said: "You observed first that the speakers used the conversational tone. [This was especially observable.] That is an important factor in English oratory, and they will not have a room that requires shouting. Second, when exciting questions are up, they will not have an audience whose size would be a moral power on one side or the other, so they planned to have but few visitors at a time."

I can only hope to be excused for so much of the personal pronoun—first person, singular number—as will appear in what remains to be related of my English visit, on the ground that some of the facts, particularly those that have a bearing upon an international copyright law, will be of general interest. For the rest, I hope my readers will not be sorry to learn more particularly of the attention and kindness shown me across the water.

The day after my arrival in London a public reception was suggested, but I preferred a less formal way of meeting the musical friends, and so expressed myself to Mr. Curwen, who had the matter in charge. This resulted in an invitation, which included the conductors in and about London, who desired to meet me, to a lawn or garden party at Mr. Curwen's residence. Some were away for their vacation, but all who were accessible came, about forty in number.

I expected to be well received in England, but the reality far exceeded my expectations. All to whom I was introduced not only greeted me as an old friend, but expressed themselves in regard to my works, and their usefulness, in a way that was as unexpected as it was gratifying. Particularly was this the case on this occasion. All these gentlemen had taught and conducted my music, more or less, from the beginning of their work—indeed, as one said, some of them "had been brought up on it" before they became teachers and conductors. I did not forget, however, while these gentlemen were speaking so kindly of what I had done, and of what was still useful to them in their more elementary work, that many of their choral societies had outgrown my music and were occupied with the higher grades. An instance of this I will speak of later.

Short interviews with the friends who had so honored me was the order of the afternoon. From Mr. John Evans, superintendent of music in the public schools of London, and Mr. J. Westwood Tosh, his able assistant, I received much interesting and valuable information concerning their work; from Mr. Robert Griffiths, secretary of the tonic-solfa college, who remembered Dr. Mason's visit thirty-six years ago, many items of interest concerning the educational movement that he had so much to do with, and from the Venables brothers something of their work; but I leave that to an account of a visit to their Institute, which took place a few days later.

As the twilight drew on we adjourned to the drawing-room (whose windows open like doors upon the lawn) and had some music. The first number was my first song, "Hazel Dell," sung by Mr. Sinclair Dunn, a graduate and medalist of the Royal Academy, and a fine tenor, who sang it in a way that made me think of Nilsson's singing of "Way Down upon the Suwanee River." Other music, vocal and instrumental, followed. The hearty applause which followed a song by the writer was, he felt, simply a compliment to the way an old man had preserved his voice. My pleasure was greatly increased on this occasion by the presence of one of my daughters who had been on the continent some months with the family of a beloved nephew. She also participated in the birthday surprise spoken of further on.

One day about this time Mr. Curwen said: "Come; I want to show you a list of your compositions in the British Museum." We went; and through Mr. C.'s application (he is a member there), and by my signing a declaration that I was more than twenty-one years of age, I became a member for one day, with all the rights and privileges of the grandest reading-room in the world.

We went first to a row of large books, which constitute the musical catalogue of the place. Taking out one with "R" on the back he turned to my name. But I should first say that the titles of the works (songs or larger works) on these pages are mostly written, and are pasted in with spaces between, that, as they come, they may be put in alphabetical order. There are, I should say, from four to six entries on a page. First, the full name of the author, then the entire title of the work, and by whom published. What was my astonishment, on counting, as we turned the leaves, to find *twenty-three* pages and a part of the *twenty-fourth* occupied entirely with my compositions. I ought, perhaps, first to have explained that every publisher in the kingdom is expected to send a copy of everything he publishes to the British Museum, where it is catalogued and kept for reference.

"Now," said Mr. Curwen, "to show you how orderly and convenient their methods are here, decide what you would like to see of these works, and I will have it brought." I had been much interested to observe that "Just Before the Battle" was entered twelve times. It had been published by six different publishers, and there were six instrumental arrangements of it, so I chose an instrumental duet on that melody. ("Vacant Chair" had been entered eight times; "Tramp," seven, and others two, three, and four times.) Mr. C. then filled out a printed form, putting on it the numbers of two seats by a table, on which he left his gloves to show that the seats were taken. "Now," he said, as he handed the order to an attendant, "we will go and get lunch, and when we come back we shall find the book, with the music you want, there."

Let my reader see this picture:—a vast rotunda—the largest reading-room in the world, with hundreds of people sitting at tables, reading, studying, or copying, and scores of attendants in the alcoves or galleries getting books or returning them, and more than a million different works to be kept in their places and selected from, and he will have some idea of the perfection of the machinery necessary to keep everything running smoothly in the reading-room of the British Museum.

We had a fine lunch in the grand buffet of the building, and when we returned there was the book. It contained the duet—a good arrangement, by Brinley Richards (if I remember rightly)—and several others of my compositions, enough to fill it. Mr. Curwen fully believes in the justice of an international copyright law, and said, before I left, "You should publish a letter in some prominent paper when you return to America, stating these facts, for you are undoubtedly the greatest sufferer among the musicians there for the want of this law."

Mr. Curwen said I ought to hear one of the London choirs (choral societies). To say that, meant, with my kind host, that it should be done, if within the bounds of possibility. I think it was planned on the afternoon of the conductors' gathering, mentioned previously, with the brothers Venables. At any rate, a short time afterward I was told that, although not yet time for the gathering of the musical forces for the autumn, one of the three choirs that competed at the Crystal Palace the previous June, under the conductorship of Mr. Leonard C. Venables, would assemble to meet me at the South London Choral Institute, an institution owned and managed by the brothers.

At the time appointed we went. Although only going from one part of London to another, we had to take two trains to get there—about fifteen miles, I should judge. While the choir were gathering we were shown by Mr. George Venables the excellent appointments and many conveniences of the building, which the brothers with indomitable energy and perseverance have partially built and entirely arranged for their musical purposes. When we returned to the large hall the choir, numbering perhaps a hundred and fifty, were singing a lovely part-song. Then came one of Mendelssohn's Psalms—the one in which the solo part is taken by an alto voice. Although out of practice, as the conductor said, the performance was admirable. The young lady's voice was like Cary's, and her method charming, and the choruses were sung as only those sing who thoroughly comprehend what they are doing. The voices here, as in all the tonic-sol-fa choirs that I heard in England, were excellently taught—true and of beautiful quality.

At the conclusion of this Psalm, Mr. Venables spoke at length and most kindly of the individual whom they had gathered to meet; of the use his music had been to them; of their familiarity with it in their earlier work, etc. This gave me my key-note. Some people can talk against time—can say something interesting when they have nothing particular to say. I envy them—it is a great gift—but I can't do it. (This is no reflection upon Mr. Venables, who *had* something to say, and said it well.) I could, however, seize upon the idea that this fine choir had been in musical conditions in which my music was just what they needed and liked, and so said that I could only account for the reception they had given me on the ground that there are always pleasant memories connected with what we have enjoyed in earlier states, whether in social or musical life. When I alluded to their having outgrown my music, cries of "No! no! no!" came from all parts of the room. Of course that was being polite to a stranger, but I allude to it to speak of two things that interested me much in English audiences. One is that when their agreement with, or approval of, the speaker is not up to the applause point, they cry "Hear! hear!" and the other is that when the disagreement is of a friendly kind, or not up to the hissing point in an unfriendly way, they cry "No! no!" There is something more supporting and encouraging in these approving utterances than even in applause, it seems to me, probably because the sound of the human voice has in it more sympathy than that of hands or canes. I only regret that I did not say on that occasion what was in my heart regarding the noble enterprise which has been brought to so successful a point by the Messrs. Venables; but I was a good deal embarrassed, and my wits did not stay by me as they should have done.

Then came a song from my "Pilgrim Fathers" by this lovely alto voice, and the double-theme chorus, "Blessed is the Nation whose God is the Lord," by the whole choir. Those interested will find the latter in "Chorus Castle," but better in Mr. McPhail's "Crown of Song," where it has an accompaniment written at Mr. McPhail's request.

We had so far to go that we were obliged to leave before the exercises closed, but the kindness of these warm-hearted friends again manifested itself by applause, which lasted until we were out of sight and hearing.

One Sunday, toward the close of my stay, Mr. Curwen proposed that we should go where we could hear what he considered the best congregational singing in London—Dr. Allon's "church," I was going to say, but I believe they call it chapel—in Islington. We again had to take two trains to get there. It is a large, fine church, as we should call it, with organ behind the pulpit and galleries on three sides converging toward the organ, without quite coming to it. These galleries were filled with people, so that the two large choirs which occupied the ends nearest the organ could not in the least be distinguished from the rest of the audience. Everybody had the same books, upstairs and down, and when "Anthem twenty-four" was given out the burst was so general and so full that no one could have told that a choir of eighty voices or more was taking part. I should not have known there was a choir at all, either by sight or sound, if Mr. Curwen had not apprised me of the fact. Chants, hymns (without interludes), and a still more difficult anthem were sung heartily and all well but the chants, which had the traditional fault before spoken of. I think the choir *do nothing alone*. They do not believe in "performing" to the people, but in singing with them.

I had a birthday while staying at Mr. Curwen's—one I shall never forget. Early on that lovely August morning the strains of Mendelssohn's "Morning Prayer" came up to my window from the lawn below. On looking out, what was my surprise to see a choir of thirty or more boys and men under the leadership of one of the conductors whom I had previously met, Mr. H. A. Donald. After this opening piece, there followed three of my little songs. When they commenced the last one I said to myself, "That's rather pretty," but did not immediately recognize it as mine. It never came to the front in America, and I had almost forgotten it. "Down where the harebells grow" is its title.

When I thanked them for the trouble they had taken, and the honor they had done me, Mr. Donald said: "Oh, we are all delighted to give you a birthday greeting—the boys, especially, have been in great excitement for a week. They sing your music a good deal, and you have come so far." I soon saw another reason for the boys' enjoyment. My kind friends, Mr. and Mrs. Curwen, of whose delicacy and attention I can not speak in adequate terms, had invited the boys, and the gentlemen who accompanied them, to breakfast. A caterer appeared as soon as the singing was over and set a table on the lawn for the boys, the gentlemen breakfasting with us in the house. The lovely grace which the boys sang before they sat down, and the three cheers they gave when they went away, will always ring in my memory when I think of that morning.

On visiting the Crystal Palace, of whose vastness words can hardly convey an adequate idea, every one is impressed with the magnitude of the arrangements for chorus performances. The great organ in the center is named "Handel," and at its sides and in front are seats in crescent form for five thousand singers, with room in the center for an orchestra of five or six hundred. I forget whether it was

Mr. Proudman, Mr. McNaught, or Mr. Venables who, when speaking of the different effects they had produced there, told me that they once gave my "Autumn Winds" in that place with forty sopranos singing the solo, and the balance of the five thousand humming the accompaniment—the vast audience being greatly excited over the result.

The only remaining thing to note was a concert, with "readings," on the steamship *City of Rome* coming home. It was for the benefit of some seamen's charitable association, and given by such musical people and elocutionists as happened to be on board. I tried to keep out of the way and let the younger people do the performing, but they found me out, and I had to take part. When my turn came I sang "The Sea," as appropriate to the occasion. The applause which followed brought the chairman to his feet, who, in a very kind and complimentary speech, gave a list of my principal songs, beginning "way back." When he came to naming and speaking of the war songs, one by one, there was a manifest commotion in the thronged cabin and gangways, and when he wound up with "Battle-Cry" and "Tramp," the whole company gave three ringing cheers. It turned out that there were quite a number of army people among the crowd of returning Americans. After the great kindness of my English friends, it was pleasant to find, after all, that "a prophet" may have some "honor in his own country."

CHAPTER XVIII.

HOME AGAIN—THE "PILLAR OF FIRE" AND OTHER CANTATAS—THE IDEA OF "CANTATAS FOR THE PEOPLE"—MR. AND MRS. J. S. CURWEN'S VISIT TO AMERICA—"WAR-SONG" CONCERTS—THE LOYAL LEGION—THE USUAL HISTORY OF MUSICAL SOCIETIES—HOW "THE HAYMAKERS" HELPED OUT—FAMILY MATTERS, "ROOTS AND BRANCHES"—THE HYDE PARK YACHT CLUB AND THE SUMMER CONGREGATION ON THE LAKE.

MY first work on my return was to carry out a plan for a cantata suggested by Mr. Hall, of the London Sunday-School Union—the return of Israel from the captivity in Egypt. Mr. Butterworth helped in the words, and "The Pillar of Fire" was the result, though they call it "Cloud and Sunshine" in England.

I made the acquaintance of Mr. John Stuart Bogg, a poet and author, while attending a New Church conference in Lancashire, and on my return he sent me a libretto for a Sunday-school and choir cantata, called "The Building of the Temple"; then followed librettos by other well-known English librettists—"Bethlehem," by Frederic E. Weatherly; "Florens, the Pilgrim," by David Gow; and "Jacob and Esau," by A. J. Foxwell. These I have set to music, and they are published in London in connection with the Cincinnati house.

For Christmas, 1886, my daughter, Clara Louise Burnham, and I wrote "The Waifs' Christmas," and for Christmas, 1887, "Judge Santa Claus." In 1888 we wrote "Snow White and the Seven Dwarfs," a cantata in which the choruses are for children and the solo parts for adult voices; and for Christmas, 1889, "Santa Claus & Co." These cantatas are also published in England, though in some cases under different names.

My other works since my return are "The Repertoire," for High-Schools; "The Empire of Song," and "The Arena of Song," (the latter with Mr. C. C. Case,) for musical conventions; "The Glorious Cause," for temperance work, and a little cantata for Sunday-schools called "The Wonderful Story," the libretto by Mrs. Mary B. Brooks, of Arkansas.

It is interesting to note the popularity of the idea of "cantatas for the people." We know at once what is meant when we say "songs for the people." In that sense I use the term "cantatas for the people." They began with "The Flower Queen," "Daniel," and "The Haymakers," as representatives of the three kinds—juvenile, scriptural and secular. They have multiplied greatly of late years, especially in England. Mr. Curwen spoke to me while I was at his house about sending me librettos when he should find those that he thought would suit me. This he has done, as above mentioned, and I am now at work upon others. This brings the record of my principal compositions up to 1890.

In the autumn of 1887 we had a visit from Mr. and Mrs. J. S. Curwen, and no one who met them wondered at their popularity and success as leaders of a great musical movement in England. I mention Mrs. Curwen's name in this connection, because to his general culture and remarkable gifts as a leader she adds such attainments, both musical and literary, as must count for much in the success of their enterprises. It was a great pleasure to return some of their kindness, and to note their friendly and unprejudiced interest in our American ways. That visit is a theme of which my family never tire.

I have said that when the war closed all interest in the

war songs ceased. For years they were out of sight, but now that time has changed the terrible realism of the march and the battle-field into tender and hallowed memories, the songs that were then sung have come back with redoubled interest. Their melodies are heard on all patriotic occasions and the most deeply stirred and enthusiastic audiences of the present time are those of the "war-song concerts." I have especially in mind a concert of this kind that was given not long ago by the Apollo Club of Chicago, under the direction of Wm. L. Tomlins. I directed the performance of "Yes, we'll rally round the flag, boys," (The Battle-Cry of Freedom) on that occasion, and as I came forward, said: "Here is the man [J. G. Lumbard] who twenty-five years ago sang that song on the court-house steps before the ink of the manuscript was dry. He will sing it now. Will all join in the chorus?" Jule's magnificent voice rang out just as it had done a quarter of a century before. The immense audience rose and, impelled by their intense emotion, joined with the band and the grand chorus of the Apollo Club, producing an effect never to be forgotten.

Soon after that demonstration I was elected a member of the Loyal Legion, but I will let Mr. Murray's article, in *The Musical Visitor* which followed, tell the story. Being in the war himself, he was in a condition to write it from a soldier's standpoint.

THE LOYAL LEGION AND DR. ROOT.

The readers of the *Visitor* will be interested in the following notes concerning Dr. Root's initiation into the "Loyal Legion," a society of noble men who have in this case honored themselves as well as the recipient of their very exclusive favors.

The "Loyal Legion" is the highest of the military and patriotic organizations of the country. The people eligible to membership in it are, in the first class—Commissioned officers who were in the war, and whose record then and since is satisfactory; second class—Their oldest sons on arriving at the age of twenty-one; third class—Civilians who rendered "important service" during the war. This last membership is limited. There are but six in the Illinois Commandery, which has over two hundred members. (General Sheridan was the commander-in-chief of the Order at the time of his death.)

A little over a year ago the former president of the Illinois Sanitary Commission died, and a month ago Dr. George F. Root was elected to fill the vacancy caused by his removal.

If there is any civilian who performed "important service" for the Union during the war, Dr. Root is that man. The editor of the *Visitor* was in the field during all the hardest fighting of the war, and had abundant opportunity to prove the above assertion true. The late testimonials in *The Century* magazine from men and officers concerning the wonderful effect of Dr. Root's "War Songs" also fully substantiate our claim. But then this fact is heartily acknowledged everywhere, and nowhere more completely than in the "Loyal Legion," as may be seen from the fact that a single objection to a candidate of this class, by a line drawn through the name on the ballot, settles the question and excludes the candidate. In this case the election was, as the senator from Kansas in his late celebrated speech said of another election, "more than unanimous."

A member has said that seldom if ever has a name been received by the Order with so much enthusiasm as greeted this one. Those familiar with the customs of the Order can very well see why this would be so. After the business and "refreshments" of the evening are through, the members gather together to sing the old war songs. Staid generals, colonels, majors, captains, chaplains, and all, become boys again, and, with the intense sphere of the old days about them, pour forth such a volume of patriotic earnestness as can only be appreciated by those who connect those melodies with camp, the march, and the battle-field. It is easy to see why the man who had to do with the making of those songs was so kindly received and heartily welcomed.

Of course the Doctor was asked to sing. He responded with "Yes, we'll rally round the flag," undoubtedly the strongest of his war lyrics. The editor of the *Visitor* heard this song once, when in the outer line of intrenchments before Petersburg, within talking distance of the Confederate line of battle. He never expects to hear it sung again as it was sung at that time, but the nearest approach to it would be to hear it sung by the "boys" who were there, who now compose these patriotic societies. Here are the men who shouted that line when the next minute they might have to give their lives for the Union they were fighting to maintain. It is not to be wondered at that their interest in the old songs is so strong. They were the companions of their camp-fires, their cheer on many long and weary marches, and their inspiration sometimes on the very field of battle.

The attachments and associations of the war are all very strong. While the animosities have nearly all disappeared between Union and Confederates, we can see very clearly how each still retains love and affection for its leaders and for each other and for the old songs, and for those who wrote them. We congratulate the "Loyal Legion" on making so worthy an addition to its membership. The *Visitor* is inclined to indulge in a little personal pride in the matter, as Dr. Root is so prominent a member of its family.

Speaking of the Apollo Club brings to mind the musical organization that I found when I came to Chicago in 1859. It was called the Musical Union, and was conducted by Mr. Cady; but soon business required all of Mr. Cady's time, and the conduct of the society passed into other hands. The history of musical societies is pretty uniform. A few insist in the outset upon practicing music beyond the ability of the chorus to perform, and of the audience to enjoy, and both drop off. Then come debt and appeals to the consciences of the chorus, and the purses of the patrons, to sustain a worthy (?) enterprise. Then follows a lingering death—and all because a few leading members will not give up the difficult music they like best, for the simple music that can be well sung and so enjoyed. The Musical Union was no exception to this rule, only it did not reach the extremity mentioned above. It traveled the usual path until it had become nearly a thousand dollars in debt, and then it stopped to think. Some one suggested that instead of appealing to the people for help, that it might be a good plan to try to please them, and so get them to pay because they desired to, and not because they ought to. In this exigency they asked me to give "The Haymakers," which I was very happy to do

Two performances cleared off the debt, and left a small balance in the treasury. A musical organization of some kind has existed ever since—sometimes two or three of them, but with no marked success until Mr. Tomlins came in 1875 and started with the Apollo Club. This was at first a male-voice chorus; after a while women's voices were added. With some of the usual mistakes, and with some fluctuations, it has held on; and under Mr. Tomlins' fine leadership has become one of the best choruses in this or any other country.

When I started out in 1838, more than fifty years ago, I was the oldest, and my sister Fanny, then a baby, the youngest, of a family of eight—three boys and five girls. There are eight still, and we still say "the boys" and "the girls"; but considering the grandfathers and grandmothers among us, others might not regard those terms as quite appropriate. My father died in 1866, and then came a contest for the dear mother. All wanted her, and she, wishing to gratify all, was sometimes with one or another of her sons, and sometimes with one of her daughters. I do not know how many journeys she made from Boston or New York to Chicago, but a good many. Finally, as she approached the age of four score, she decided upon the house of her oldest daughter in Orange, N. J., as her home, and here she lived most happily, passing away in 1881, in the eighty-fifth year of her age. If any of her children could have settled down in North Reading she would have stayed at Willow Farm, but as that could not be, she decided that the old place had better be sold, which was done soon after she left it. She was so inexpressibly dear to her children that to "rise and call her blessed" is ever in our minds, when we think of her loving and unselfish life.

My branch of the family consists of wife, two married sons, three married daughters and one unmarried, and eleven grandchildren. All live near, excepting Charles, my second son, and family, who are in the neighborhood of New York, into which city the young man goes daily to superintend certain publications of which he is proprietor.

My oldest son, Frederic W., and family live, as do all the rest of us, in Hyde Park, near Chicago. If this young man is better equipped musically and otherwise than his father was at his age, there is more need now than there was then, of higher attainment. In these days of greater demand, one only reaches the position that he occupies as a musician, teacher and writer, by beginning in advance of the previous generation and then super-adding to his inheritance, years of close study and hard work. It would be pleasant to give some account of his very successful and remunerative work, but that would hardly be proper here. I will, however, say that he teaches and writes ten months in the year, and then in the summer, when he is not at Normal, is the bold and hardy navigator of a cat-boat on the broad waters of Lake Michigan, where he stores up air and sunshine for his winter campaign.

My children were all inclined more or less to music as a profession as they were growing up, and all are considerably above mediocrity as players or singers; but F. W. is the only one who has persisted in the original inclination. My oldest daughter, Mrs. Clara Louise Burnham, is not unknown to fame as a writer of good books of fiction, and I venture to speak further of this member of my family, because her career illustrates a point in my own case to which I have two or three times alluded.

After her marriage, Mrs. Burnham, having a good deal of leisure and no family cares, felt a desire for some especial occupation. One day her brother F. W. said: "Write a book, Clara; anybody who can write so good a letter as you can, can write a good story." She certainly never felt that she had a "call" in that direction, but she tried it, and has had no heavy hours upon her hands since that time.

My younger daughters are much interested in art, in which they are fairly successful, not neglecting, however, their musical studies.

Of the clan in general, including brothers and sisters, nephews and nieces, and the families with which they are connected, living near, it is only necessary to sound the call and more than thirty respond. All are musical—the children of my brother E. T. conspicuously so. They occupy some of the best choir positions in the city, and one of the young ladies is one of Chicago's best amateur pianists. One of our modes of enjoyment is worth mentioning: Nearly all are members of the Hyde Park Yacht Club, whose fine boat-house is close by. On calm summer evenings a small fleet drifts out a half mile or so from shore, and a song commences—

"Sweet and low, sweet and low,
Wind of the western sea,"

or some other in which all can join. Then the congregation begins to assemble. Boats shoot out from all along the coast until we are surrounded by a sympathetic and appreciative audience. The whole fleet is then held together by lines or hands, and we drift, sometimes up toward the city, sometimes down toward the great park, and sometimes farther out into the "saltless sea," just as the current or the light breeze may take us, but "making music as we go," and enjoying to the full the luxury of the lovely scene. Our boats and the companionship of the club are a great resource in the summer.

CHAPTER XIX.

THE JOHN CHURCH CO.—THE PRINCIPALS OF THE HOUSE—THEIR HOMES—ANCESTRAL DESCENT—THE MEMORABLE CELEBRATION AT THE HYDE PARK HIGH-SCHOOL—MR. JOHN CHURCH'S DEATH—PREPARATIONS FOR THE WORLD'S COLUMBIAN EXPOSITION—MY PIANO TRADE—MY SEVENTIETH BIRTHDAY—*VALE!*

THERE are some people who seem to have been forced by circumstances into the wrong niche in this world, and whose work, in consequence, is a dread in the anticipation and a drudgery in the performance. I am humbly thankful that that has not been my lot. My work has always been my greatest pleasure, and still is. If I was for a time crowded into a niche that belonged to somebody else, all that passed away when we arranged with the John Church Co., as already described. From that time, as I have said, my business cares vanished, and I have been occupied in the congenial work of making such books, cantatas, songs or numbers for their Annuals (Christmas and Easter Selections, etc.) or *The Musical Visitor*, as are thought needful, while they attend to all the business matters connected with these works—copyrights, arrangements with English publishers, permissions, etc.

Mr. Church, the founder of this house, and Mr. Trevor, his long-time partner, may well be proud of its success, for that success, as I have abundant reason to know, is founded upon the most honorable business principles and the most upright business transactions. I may not speak in detail of their arrangement with me, nor of the many generous acts which have characterized our years of relationship, but I should be recreant to my sense of right if I did not take this opportunity to record my appreciation of their unvarying kindness and consideration, and of my great satisfaction in doing all in my power for their interests.

When the May Festival, or other errand, calls me to Cincinnati, it is a great pleasure to enjoy the hospitality of Mr. Trevor's beautiful home on Mt. Auburn, or in the summer to be a guest at Mr. Church's old colonial residence in Rhode Island. Ancestral descent is not a strong point with the majority of American people, nor are many situated in localities of historic interest; but in Mr. Church's case both these conditions obtain in a remarkable degree. Not far away from his residence is Mt. Hope, where King Philip, of the Narragansetts, lived and fought, and back from Mr. John Church, in an unbroken line, is Capt. Benjamin Church, who defeated the great chief and brought the famous war called "King Philip's War" to a close.

The present house stands on ground deeded to the family in 1674, and in the establishment rare skill and taste have been shown in combining modern elegance and convenience with the old colonial architecture and surroundings. In plain sight from Mr. Church's residence is also the spot where John Alden and his wife Priscilla Mullins lived. This Priscilla, it will be remembered, was the maiden made famous in Longfellow's poem, "The Courtship of Miles Standish." Both she and John came over in the *May Flower*. In the village church-yard are the grave and monument of their daughter Elizabeth, who was the first white female child born in the colony. She married William Peabody, and died at the age of 94 in 1717.

And now I am approaching the end of my story, but I can not close without recording a recent event which was as unexpected as it will ever be memorable. We have in Hyde

Park one of the finest high-schools in the state, not only as to building, but equally as to faculty and pupils. They use there one of my books for their musical studies, and one day one of the teachers asked me if I would come some afternoon and listen to a program to consist entirely of my works. I said I should be glad to do so, and the 8th of March, 1889, was fixed upon for the event. It would be hard to find a more astonished individual than the writer, on arriving at the scene of action. It was a series of surprises from beginning to end. First the crowd, then the decorations, then the performances, then the letters and speeches of distinguished people, winding up with the congratulations of neighbors and friends; but I will let the published reports describe the occasion. If it is thought that I am printing too much praise of myself, I have only to say that I can not otherwise record the great kindness of the friends who so honored me. Beside, the event took on something of a public character, from the fact that the Associated Press despatches made it known all over the land, as the letters from many states, which followed, abundantly testified. Chicago papers the next day said:

At the Hyde Park High-School Dr. George F. Root was the recipient, yesterday afternoon, of all the honor the two hundred students and their teachers and two hundred more friends and admirers could well bestow. The spacious hall of the building was profusely decorated with flags and banners, and on its walls were tablets in a variety of colors, bearing the names of his best-known compositions, each with an appropriate design. On the platform were stacked old army muskets in threes, and in the cradles formed by the bayonets rested birds' nests, emblematical of a united and peaceful country. At the left of the platform was a war relic in the shape of an army tent, in front of which burned a miniature campfire; bunches of swords here and there, and an excellent portrait of Dr. Root, draped in national colors and hung over the platform, completed the ornamentations. The musical exercises consisted of the performance of vocal and instrumental numbers selected from Dr.

Root's compositions, and of the ode printed below, which last was composed by one of the teachers of the school. These exercises were interspersed by papers composed and read by members of the school on various subjects connected with the Doctor's life and works, and by the following letters from distinguished individuals, which were in response to invitations to the celebration, sent by one of the teachers of the school. That from James Russell Lowell is as follows:

No. 68 BEACON ST., BOSTON, MASS.

It is impossible for me to be present at your interesting celebration, but I remember too well the martial cadences of Dr. Root's songs, and how vividly our hearts beat in tune to them, not to add gladly my felicitations to yours. I prize gratitude highly, and you could not have chosen a fitter creditor to whom it should be paid, or a better form in which to pay it. Pray add mine to your own.

Yours faithfully,

J. R. LOWELL.

The present Governor of Illinois writes:

I count it a privilege to be permitted to join the scholars of the Hyde Park High-School in a tribute to Dr. George F. Root. Only those who were at the front, camping, marching, battling for the flag, can fully realize how often we were cheered, revived and inspired by the songs of him who sent forth the "Battle-Cry of Freedom." The true and correct history of the war for the maintenance of the Union will place George F. Root's name alongside of our great generals. While others led the boys in blue to final victory, it was his songs that nerved the men at the front and solaced the wives, mothers, sisters, and sweethearts at home, while more than a million voices joined in the chorus, "The Union forever."

Will you please convey to your distinguished guest my kindest regards and best wishes. Sincerely yours,

J. W. FIFER.

Col. Fred. Grant writes:

The author of "Rally round the flag, boys," and "Tramp, tramp, tramp, the boys are marching," should have as hearty a welcome as it is possible to extend to any living man. His songs were a great comfort to the soldiers during the war, and helped to lighten the fatigues of many a weary march. Tell Dr. Root that I am grateful for the service he rendered.

F. D. GRANT.

Rev. S. F. Smith, D. D., author of "My country, 'tis of thee," says:

It gives me unalloyed pleasure to speak a word or two in honor of the man whose genius has given to his countrymen, and to the world, the inspiring lays, "Rally round the flag, boys," "Tramp,

Tramp, Tramp," and "Shining Shore." There is no greater honor or privilege than to have attuned the harp of the nation to words and tunes of patriotic zeal, and the harps of the world to a music which beats time to the march of a redeemed race to a holy and happy heaven.

May your honored guest long listen to the music of that march, and find his path ever growing more luminous with the light from that Shining Shore.

With assurances of sincere respect and honor to him, and the best wishes for your pupils, that some of them may rise up in his spirit to carry forward his work, I am,

Very sincerely yours,

S. F. SMITH.

Edward Everett Hale, whose response came too late to be read on that occasion, wrote from Washington as follows:

Dear Sir: Your note has followed me here. I hope this may be in time for me to join with the rest of the world in thanking Dr. Root for the strength, courage and life he has given to us all.

Very truly yours,

EDWARD E. HALE.

The response of J. G. Lumbard, Esq., now of Omaha, whose magnificent voice was the first to give utterance to the "Battle-Cry of Freedom," was also too late to be read on the day of the celebration, but was subsequently published in one of our local papers.

Dear Sir: I am most certainly and most sincerely in sympathy with the movement inaugurated at Hyde Park, looking to an appropriate recognition of the good service and unusual desert of our mutual friend and *confrère*, Dr. Geo. F. Root, and I very much regret that the delayed arrival of your invitation prevents its acceptance or any timely response. It came to hand on the day of the event.

No words of mine can add anything to the glory and beauty of a well-spent life, nor give increased lustre to the shining character of one whose career has been that of a universal benefactor.

It is not alone the community in which he has lived and exercised the rights and discharged the responsibilities of citizenship, that owes a debt of honor and gratitude to Dr. Root: the whole people have been educated to a nobler patriotism and higher citizenship by the illustrated virtues of his life, and the beneficent influence of his character and teachings.

We honor the great soldier by whose genius and prowess the way has been carved to victory and peace; but greater than the soldier is he who prevents appeal to arms, and preserves our green fields for lawns instead of devoting them to grave-yards for the brave. All this, without noise and without pretense, has been done by the gentleman to whom it is honorable to pay honor and homage.

If opportunity offers, please express from me the kindest remembrance to Dr. Root, and regret at my inability to be present in accordance with the terms of your invitation.

Yours very truly,

J. G. LUMBARD.

Several other communications, including a few words from Generals Sherman and Alger, were also received. Some war reminiscences from Dr. H. H. Belfield, formerly Adjutant of the Iowa Cavalry Volunteers, now principal of the Chicago Manual Training School, were listened to with great interest and with general surprise, for but few of those present knew that he had been a soldier and a prisoner during the eventful time of which he speaks. He said:

It affords me great pleasure to unite in this testimonial to our neighbor, Dr. Root, whose character as well as whose life-work commands our admiration.

The overthrow of the enemies of the Republic in the late war was a stupendous undertaking, demanding the supreme effort of the loyal North, not only of the men who took the field, but of the men and women who remained at home. Not men alone were needed, but arms, ammunition, clothing and food; not material support only, but sympathy as well. The Union soldier was cheered by many kind and loving messages from the yearning, often aching, hearts of wives and children, of parents and friends. How precious was the consciousness of this remembrance can be known only by those who tore themselves from the fond embrace of loved ones to endure the hardship of the march, and face the grim terrors of the bloody field.

Among the friends who, in those awful years, served his country effectually, more effectually by his pen than any man could have done by his sword, was Dr. George F. Root. You have heard to-day how his songs encouraged our troops even in that frightful campaign near Richmond. Permit me to tell briefly how they cheered the prisoners of war.

It was the 31st day of July, 1864, in Newnan, Georgia. The starry banner with which you, my young friends, have so beautifully decorated this room, had gone down in blood and death; the hated rebel rag was flying in triumph over the heads of a small company of Union soldiers, who, having obeyed the orders that they well knew would sacrifice them, had saved hundreds of their comrades, and were now prisoners of war. Their appearance showed the effects of hard campaigning—bronzed faces, torn and ragged garments, with here and there a rough bandage stained with blood. But their spirits were undaunted, and as the populace gathered around them, curious to see the hated Yankees, and, perhaps, to exult over their ill fortune, the little band sang the patriotic songs which had been wafted from "God's Country."

When we sang, with all the emphasis of which we were capable,

"Rally round the flag, boys;
Down with the *traitor!*"

I fully expected marked symptoms of disapproval; but the increasing crowd seemed to enjoy the novel spectacle, and, when we ceased singing, shouted for more songs. Then we said, "We are tired; we are hungry; we have had no food for many hours. Give us something to eat, and we will sing for you." Food was soon brought, and I now take this opportunity, long delayed, to thank *you*, Doctor Root, for what, while it could not be called "a square meal," is well and gratefully remembered after these many years.

The latter part of the summer of 1864 I spent, together with several hundred Union officers, at the sea-side, at the expense of the Southern Confederacy. The place selected for our temporary retirement from active life was Charleston, S. C. Three hundred of us were in the work-house prison, in what particular part of the city located I never knew, since the wishes of our hosts, expressed in high walls and southern muskets, prevented our exploring the town. But we knew that the sea was near, for the huge, fifteen-inch shells of the "Swamp Angel," screaming over our heads, scattered brick and mortar over the grass-grown streets of the hot-bed of the Rebellion.

Late one afternoon in September our attention was directed to the entrance of men into the adjoining prison-yard. We rushed to the windows on that side of the prison-house, and anxiously inspected the new comers. With faces blacked by sun and stained with dirt, their clothing scant and torn, they wearily dragged themselves into the prison-pen. Before they came within speaking distance the faded army blue of their uniforms suggested the truth. "Who are you?" we asked. "Andersonville prisoners." May I never behold another such sight. Their piercing eyes, their emaciated features, their shrunken limbs, now concealed, now revealed by their ragged uniforms, their bloody bandages, told the awful story of slow starvation. We shared with them our scanty rations, and after a frugal meal on each side of the wall, which neither party could cross, we did all we could for them; we sang Doctor Root's songs, and cheered their hearts with our sympathy. Never had poor performers so attentive an audience. Long into the night we sang, and in the early morning we dismissed them, Doctor Root, with your ringing chorus, in which their feeble voices were heard—

> "Tramp, tramp, tramp, the boys are marching,
> Cheer up, comrades, they *will* come;
> And beneath the starry flag we shall breathe the air again
> Of the free-land in our own beloved home."

The following Ode was most effectively rendered by a semi-chorus of the students, all the school coming in, after the first verse, with the chorus of "There's music in the air," after the second, with the chorus of the "Battle-Cry," and after the third, with the chorus of the "Shining Shore."

THE SINGER OF HOME.

Happy is he
Whose ears have heard the sound
Of music from glad voices singing
Songs himself has made.
From sea to sea,
Wherever home is found,
His loved refrains are ever ringing
Clear in grove and glade.

Chorus: There's music in the air.

THE MAKER OF WAR SONGS.

Proud is the man
Whose words can nerve the arm
Of freemen to their noblest trying,
And urge them on;
From rear to van
His war songs' loud alarm
Inspired the living, cheered the dying,
Till war was gone.

Chorus: The Union forever!

THE WRITER OF HYMNS.

How nobly best
Is he who puts to song
The comfort of the weary; driving
Sorrow's tears away.
Sweet peace and rest
Unto his lays belong
Which sing of end to toil and striving
Some glorious day.

Chorus: For oh, we stand on Jordan's strand.

Then came a toast to which I was obliged to respond. I could not make much of a speech. The difference between "Come down some afternoon and hear us sing," and this magnificent demonstration, was too much for me. However, I could say that such an occasion was a great reward, and a great encouragement for me in my work, and that I should never forget the young people and their teachers who had so honored me.

To Mr. Ray, the principal of the school, and to Mr. McAndrew, whose invitations called forth the foregoing responses, and who composed the Ode, and to Mr. Stevens, whose artistic hand was seen in the beautiful decorations of the hall, I could express more fully my surprise at the amount of work that teachers and pupils had done, and the deep and thankful pride I felt at being so honored by my neighbors.

It is now 1891. Most of this story, as I have said, was written in 1889. Of the persons mentioned, who have died since that time, the most important in its connection with these records was the death of Mr. John Church, which took place April 19, 1890.

In connection with what is said of Mr. Church in its proper place, I would like to add here the few words I wrote for *The Musical Visitor* at the time of the sudden bereavement. We heard of his illness one day, and of his death the next.

> One of Nature's noblemen has gone; and gone with such suddenness that we gaze after his vanishing form as in a dream. It does not seem possible that we shall not see again that stalwart form, nor feel again the friendly grasp of that strong hand. We could not readily connect death with him, he was so full of vigor as he carried on, in his masterful way, the important enterprises in which he was engaged.
>
> From the dark days that followed the great fire, when the strong house of which Mr. Church was chief, took hold of and sustained us in the crippled state in which the great disaster left us, to the time of his death he was a true friend—kind without pretension, and generous without ostentation; a wise counselor and a safe guide. Among my most valued memories will be those of this noble man.

The wisdom of the house in forming itself into a stock company three or four years ago, was clearly seen at the time of this sad event. Not a ripple disturbed the onward flow of its business; all goes as before, so far as I can see.

Chicago is a very interesting place just now. We are getting ready for the World's Fair, or better, as it is beginning to be called, "The World's Columbian Exposition." The inner and the outer world here—the world of mind and the world of matter, are intensely alive, devising plans of use and enjoyment, which are beginning to ultimate themselves in visible forms.

Among the new plans is "The Auxiliary Commission of the World's Columbian Exposition," which has for its motto "Not Things, but Men." I will let its prospectus state its object:

As is now well known, the four hundredth anniversary of the discovery of America by Christopher Columbus will be celebrated at Chicago in 1893, under the sanction of the Government of the United States, on a scale commensurate with the importance and dignity of the occasion.

The measures already taken give satisfactory assurances that the exposition then to be made of the material progress of the world will be such as to deserve unqualified approval.

But to make the exposition complete and the celebration adequate, the wonderful achievements of the new age in science, literature, education, government, jurisprudence, morals, charity, religion, and other departments of human activity, should also be conspicuously displayed, as the most effective means of increasing the fraternity, prosperity, and peace of mankind.

It has therefore been proposed that a series of *World's Congresses* for that purpose be held in connection with the World's Columbian Exposition of 1893, and THE WORLD'S CONGRESS AUXILIARY has been duly authorized and organized, to promote the holding and success of such congresses.

It is impossible to estimate the advantages that would result from the mere establishment of personal acquaintance and friendly relations among the leaders of the intellectual and moral world, who now, for the most part, know each other only through the interchange of publications, and, perhaps, the formalities of correspondence.

And what is transcendently more important, such congresses, convened under circumstances so auspicious, would doubtless surpass all previous efforts to bring about a real fraternity of nations, and unite the enlightened people of the whole earth in a general co-operation for the attainment of the great ends for which human society is organized.

This organization is intended to promote the success of the exposition of the material products of civilization, science and art, but will confine its own operations to the exposition, in appropriate conventions, of the principles of human progress.

CHARLES C. BONNEY, *President.* LYMAN J. GAGE, *Treasurer.*
THOMAS B. BRYAN, *Vice-President.* BENJAMIN BUTTERWORTH, *Secretary.*

These congresses will be held at such times, during the Exposition, as will be most convenient to each.

Considerable importance has been attached to the assembling of a Musical Congress on this occasion, which shall include prominent musicians and musical educators of this and other countries. I am one of the five members of the commission chosen for the furtherance of this object.

One of the greatest causes of excitement at present in Chicago, in view of the coming World's Exposition, is the real estate "boom" now upon us. The land romances, as they might almost be called, of earlier times, are being re-enacted every day. Every old resident has one or more to tell.

In the "earlier times" a man took a piece of ground out on the prairie for a small debt, or he let a friend have a piano or other article of merchandise for a lot or two. Such property was regarded as of little consequence. Almost every business man had some. While for one reason or another (the great fire a prominent one) I have failed to hold on to the large amounts of money which have been realized from my music, some of these small patches of Chicago ground that had been in my possession many years, when the decision in regard to the World's Fair was made known, came to the front, and were disposed of in a way to entitle the transaction to a place in the romances referred to.

I will not enlarge upon my seventieth birthday celebration, farther than to say it was intended to be simply and wholly a family affair, but my friends of the Chicago papers got wind of it, and the reporters and the Associated Press despatches did the rest. Gifts and congratulations from home and abroad poured in most generously, and the autograph stream, which, if small is, in general, remarkably steady, grew into a freshet, which did not subside for three or four weeks.

Of all the communications received on that occasion a poem by Mr. Murray, which was printed about that time in *The Musical Visitor*, moved me most. I do not deserve it, and it pushes the appearance of self-praise, of which I have spoken, to the very verge of propriety for me to print it, but it is so fine in itself, and is so pleasant an event in my story, that I decide it must go in with the other kind and generous things which have done so much toward making my life a happy and thankful one.

TO DR. GEO. F. ROOT.

ON HIS SEVENTIETH BIRTHDAY.

Dear Master and friend, I salute you!
The sapling bends low to the oak-tree,
And I am but one in a forest
Of those who would fain do you homage.
Your years have been many and blessed,
Though mingled with sunshine and shadow,
The life spent in service for others
Dwells not in the regions of darkness.

How grand are the gifts of the singer,
Whose voice tuned to thoughts that are noble
Sends out to the world in its sorrow
The music that lightens its labor.
How brightens the eye of the lover
When song in sweet notes tells his story.
How firm is the tread of the soldier
When song nerves his soul for the battle.
So far o'er the wastes of the waters
The wanderer sings of his homeland,

And cheered by the music of childhood,
Forgets all the pain and the toiling.

Thus up from the labor of earthland
He gazes whose home is in Heaven,
And sings as he works, as he wanders,
Of those who await his home-coming.

All these, dearest master, salute you,
And hosts of the sweet little children,
Whose studies your music made easy,
As climbing the hill of Parnassus
They leaned on the staff you provided.

How noble, how grand was the mission
The Master of Music assigned you,
To tune all the tongues of the people
To strains that were helpful and holy.
To guide like a voice in the darkness
The feet of the lonely and straying,
To cheer the forlorn and the weary,
To sing away tears from the weeping.

And what shall the end be, and guerdon,
For years full of blessing and beauty?
"Well done, faithful servant, come higher;
Come up to the music eternal!"

Pass on to the Land of the Singers,
O sweetest of all the Musicians.
Afar from the Valley of Shadows,
Up, up to the Brightness and Glory.
Away o'er the Mountains of Beauty,
Whose tops all aglow with the shining
And sheen of the Gates of the City,
Make light all the way of the journey.
Sing on to the close of the journey,
Sing ever when it shall be ended,
For they who have lessened earth's sorrows
Have songs in their hearts through the ages.

Dear Master and friend, I salute you!

JAMES R. MURRAY.

To conclude, I can not imagine a pleasanter life for myself than the one I now live. When not at normals or conventions, I work at home, because in the city I should be liable to frequent interruptions. My working-room is at the top of the house, to be as far from the parlor and the piano as possible, but the view from this elevation is an abundant compensation for the trouble of reaching it. I have only to raise my eyes to look east over the ever-changing waters of the lake, or north over one of its bays to the city center, seven miles away. Mr. E. V. Church, of whom I have spoken, is still manager of the Chicago house, and I am at my pleasant quarters in his establishment at a certain hour every day, in case any one wishes to see me, and at other times if I am wanted, or need a rest from my work. More than fifty trains pass each way every day, and the lovely ride by the lake can not be equaled, I think, in the world.

My wife and I would be glad to be permitted to see our golden wedding-day, which will be in 1895, and still more, to look over into the twentieth century, which will be five years later; but if that can not be, we will be thankful for the pleasant life we have lived here, and hope for a pleasanter and still more useful life hereafter.

APPENDIX.

FOLLOWING are lists of my books and of nearly all my sheet-music compositions. Then come the two part-songs spoken of in my story as having been sung by my Quartet. Then two of my compositions of a medium grade of difficulty (there is not room for a specimen of the more difficult ones, "The Storm Chorus" in "The Haymakers" for example), then the best known of my "People's Songs."

BOOKS.

The Young Ladies' Choir . 1847
Root & Sweetzer's Collection, 1849
Academy Vocalist 1852
The Flower Queen 1852
The Shawm (with W. B. Bradbury) 1853
Daniel 1853
The Pilgrim Fathers . . . 1854
The Young Men's Singing Book 1855
The Musical Album 1855
The Sabbath Bell 1856
The Haymakers 1857
The Festival Glee Book . . 1859
Belshazzar's Feast 1860
The Diapason 1860
The Silver Chime 1862
The Christian Graces . . . 1862
The Silver Lute 1862
School for Cabinet Organ . 1863
The Bugle Call 1863
The Musical Curriculum . . 1864
The New Coronet 1865
The Cabinet Organ Companion 1865
The Guide to the Pianoforte 1865
Our Song Birds (4 small pamphlets) 1866
The Forest Choir 1867
The Musical Fountain . . . 1867
Chapel Gems 1868
The Triumph 1868
The Prize 1870
The Glory 1872

The Hour of Praise 1872
The Normal Musical Handbook 1872
The New Musical Curriculum 1872
The Männerchor 1873
The Model Organ Method . 1873
The Trumpet of Reform . 1874
The Song Era 1874
The National School Singer 1875
The Choir and Congregation 1875
The New Song Era 1877
The Song Tournament . . 1878
First Years in Song-Land . 1879
The Palace of Song 1879
The New Choir and Congregation 1879
The Young Organist at Home 1880
The Chorus Castle 1880
Under the Palms 1880
The New Flower Queen . . 1880
The Teachers' Club 1881
David, the Shepherd Boy . 1882
The Realm of Song 1882
Pure Delight (with C. C. Case) 1883
Catching Kriss Kringle . . 1883
The Choicest Gift 1883
Our Song World (with C. C. Case) 1884
Santa Claus' Mistake . . . 1885
Wondrous Love (with C. C. Case) 1885
The Name Ineffable 1886
Flower Praise 1886
The Waifs' Christmas . . . 1886
Faith Triumphant 1886
The Empire of Song . . . 1887
The Repertoire 1887
Judge Santa Claus . . . 1887
The Pillar of Fire 1887
The Glorious Cause 1888
Snow White and the Seven Dwarfs 1888
Building the Temple . . 1889
Santa Claus & Co. 1889
Bethlehem 1889
The Arena of Song (with C. C. Case) 1890
Florens, the Pilgrim 1890
The Wonderful Story . . . 1890
Jacob and Esau 1890
Christmas and Easter Selections annually from 1878 to 1890.

SHEET MUSIC.

Annie Lowe.
Away on the Prairie Alone.
Away! Away! the Track is White.
Battle-cry of Freedom.
Beautiful Maiden Just Over the Way.
Be Sure You Call as You Pass By.
Birds Have Sought the Forest Shade.
Bright-eyed Little Nell (Arranged).
Brother, Tell Me of the Battle.
Blow de Horn.
Can the Soldier Forget?
Columbia's Call.
Comrades, All Around is Brightness.
Come to Me Quickly.
Come, Oh! Come With Me.
Day of Columbia's Glory.
Dearest Spot of Earth to Me is Home.
Don't You See Me Coming?
Dreaming, Ever Dreaming.
Down the Line.
Dearest Brother, We Miss Thee.
Early Lost, Early Saved.
Eyes That are Watching.
Flying Home.
Father John.
Fare Thee Well! Kitty Dear.
Father Abraham's Reply.
Farewell! Father, Friend and Guardian.
First Gun is Fired.
Forward! Boys, Forward!
Fling Out the Flag!
Good Bye! Old Glory.
Glad to Get Home.
Gather up the Sunbeams.
God Bless Our Brave Young Volunteers!
Glory! Glory! Or the Little Octoroon.
Grieve not the Heart that Loves Thee.
Gently Wake the Song.
Greenwood Bell.
Hazel Dell.
Hasten on the Battle-field!
Hear, Hear, the Shout!
Hear the Cry that Comes Over the Sea!
Health is a Rosy Maiden.
He's Coming Again.
Home's Sweet Harmony.
Home Again Returning.
Honeysuckle Glen.
Have Ye Sharpened your Swords?
How it Marches, the Flag of Our Union!
Honor to Sheridan.
Homeless and Motherless.
He Giveth His Beloved Sleep.
Here in My Mountain Home.
Hunting Song.
Hundred Years Ago.
I'm Married.
I Ask No More.
Independent Farmer.
If He Can.
If Maggie Were My Own.
In the Storm.
I Dreamt an Angel Came.
I had a Gentle Mother.
Johnny, the Little Cripple's, Song.
Jenny Lyle.
Just before the Battle, Mother.

Just after the Battle.
Just over the Mountain.
Kind Friends, One and All.
Kiss Me, Mother, Kiss your Darling.
Kittie Ryan.
Liberty Bird.
Lay Me Down and Save the Flag!
Let Me Go!
Let Me Carry your Pail, Dear.
Laughing Song.
Love Thy Mother, Little One.
Love Lightens Labor.
Lo! The Clouds are Breaking.
Look on the Bright Side.
Mary of the Glen.
Mabel.
May Moore.
May of the Valley.
Music Far Away.
Mother, Sweet Mother, Why Linger Away.
Music of the Pine.
Mr. and Mrs. Williams.
My Cottage Home, Dear Mother.
My Mother, She is Sleeping.
My Beau that Went to Canada.
My Father's Bible.
My Heart is Like a Silent Lute.
My Weary Heart is All Alone.
No Section Lines.
North and South.
Never Forget the Dear Ones.
Nobody Cares.
New Voice in the Heavenly Choir.
O! Blow de Horn.
On, On, On, the Boys Came Marching.
On the Shore.
O! Are Ye Sleeping, Maggie? (Arranged.)
On Old Potomac's Shore.
Only Four.
Our Protective Union.
One Word.
Old Friends and True Friends.
On the Eve of Battle.
Only Waiting.
O! Will my Mother Never Come?
On! Boys, On!
O! Mother, Sing to Me of Heaven.
Pictures of Memory.
Poverty Flat.
Pity, O Savior! (Arranged.)
Poor Robin's Growing Old.
Poor Carlotta!
Rosalie, the Prairie Flower.
Reaper on the Plain.
Rock Me to Sleep, Mother.
Rosabel.
Rock, Rock the Cradle!
Sing, Birds and Brooks and Blossoms.
Sing Me to Sleep, Father.
See, the Sky is Darkling, Boys.
She has Told it to the Winds.
Softly, She Faded.
Somewhere.
So Long as Love is Left.
Scenes of Happiness, I Love Ye.
Starved in Prison.
Stand up for Uncle Sam, Boys!
Sweet Morn, How Lovely is thy Face!
Swinging All Day Long.
The Way is Long, My Darling.
They Have Broken up Their Camps.
The Liberty Bird.
The Mason's Home.

The Quiet Days When We Are Old.
The Road to Slumberland.
The Church Within the Wood.
The Father's Coming.
The Hidden Path.
The Forest Requiem.
The Hand that Holds the Bread.
The Miner's *Protegé.*
The New Voice In the Heavenly Choir.
The Price of a Drink.
The Star of Bethlehem.
The Old Canoe.
The Old Folks Are Gone.
Tramp! Tramp! Tramp!
The Trumpet Will Sound in the Morning.
The Time of the Heart.
There's Music in the Air.
They Sleep in the Dust.
That Little German Home. (Arranged.)
Touch the Keys Softly.
The Voice of Love.
The World as it is.
Turn the Other Way, Boys! (With J. R. Murray.)
Vacant Chair.
Voices of the Lake.
Wake! Lady, Wake!
We'll Fight it Out Here on the Old Union Line.
Within the Sound of the Enemy's Guns.
Who'll Save the Left?
What will People Say?
Where are the Wicked Folks Buried?
Where Earth and Heaven Meet.
When the Mail Comes in.
We are Going Away from the Old Home.
We can Make Home Happy.
We'll Meet in Heaven, Father.
Will you Come to Meet Me, Darling?
Yes, We'll be True to Each Other

My principal instrumental compositions are in the instruction books mentioned. Besides these there are two series in sheet form called respectively "Camps, Tramps, and Battle Fields" and "Home Scenes." There are besides—

The March of the 600,000
Italia Grand March.

SLUMBER SWEETLY, DEAREST.

Andante. Sempre e piano legato.
Wm. Mason.
Slum - ber sweet-ly, dear-est, Close . . . thy
sweet - ly, Close thy
weary eyes, Guardian an-gels round thee hover Till the morning's
eyes, . . .
rise. Then may love on air-y pinions Bear thy heart in
trans-port bound To its own do-min-ions, Where no

Rit.
Dim.
earth-ly care is found. Maiden, sleep, sleep in peace.

A VOICE FROM THE LAKE.

Written for Geo. F. Root's Quartett
in 1847 by THEODOR EISFELD.

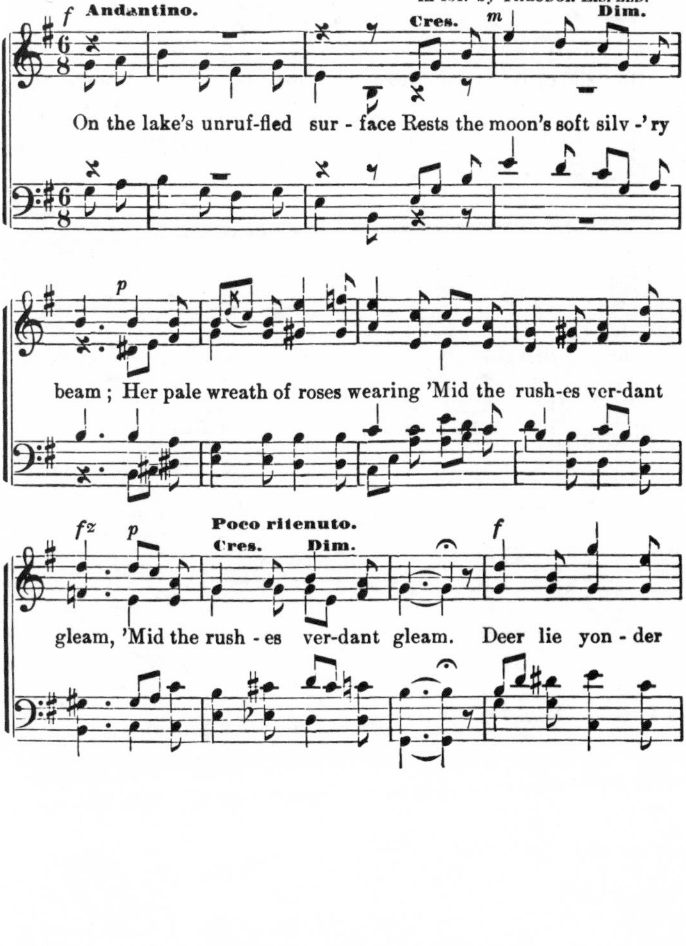

f Andantino. Cres. *m* Dim.

On the lake's unruf-fled sur - face Rests the moon's soft silv -'ry

p

beam ; Her pale wreath of roses wearing 'Mid the rush-es ver-dant

fz *p* Poco ritenuto. Cres. Dim. *f*

gleam, 'Mid the rush - es ver-dant gleam. Deer lie yon - der

p
Cres.
Dim.
near the mount-ain In the si - lent night a - wake,

Cres.
mf
pp
m
Here and there the slen-der rushes Dreami-ly the birds will

f
pp
Con dolore.
shake, Dream-i - ly the birds will shake, While the

Ad lib. Dim.
f
eyes are dim'd with weeping Deep within my soul I bear.

p
Ten.
Thoughts of thee, sweet re-collection, Floating o'er me like a prayer,
Thoughts of thee

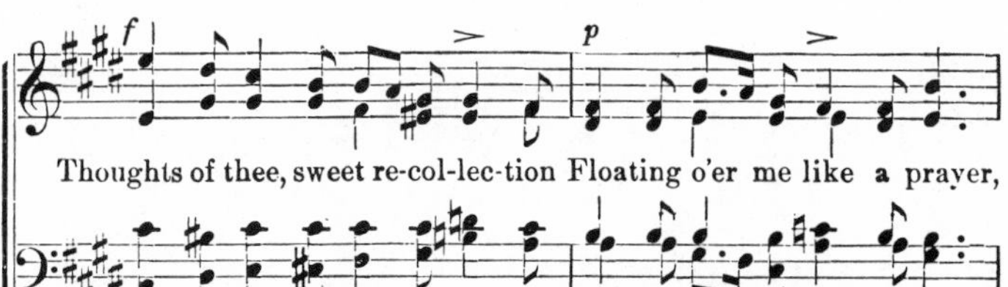
f
p
Thoughts of thee, sweet re-col-lec-tion Floating o'er me like a prayer,

p Molto cres. e stringendo.
Thoughts of thee, sweet recol - lection, Tho'ts of thee, sweet recollection,

Dolce a tempo.
Rall. e morendo.
Floating o'er me
Float - ing like a prayer, Floating o'er me like a prayer.
Float - ing like a

I WILL LAY ME DOWN IN PEACE.

G. F. Root.

p Moderato.
Dim.
mf
p
I will both lay me down in peace and sleep, For thou, Lord, for
thou, Lord, on-ly makest me to dwell in safe - ty.
I will both lay me down in peace . . .
pp
I will both lay me down in peace and sleep, and
I will both lay me down, will lay me down in peace
p
Cres.
Dim.
sleep, For thou, Lord, on-ly makest me to dwell in safe - ty.

G. F. ROOT.

Andantino grazioso.
There is a stream whose gen - tle flow Supplies the cit - y of our God. Life,
love and joy.... still glid - ing through, And
wa - t'ring our...... di - vine ..... a - bode.

THE HAZEL DELL.

WURZEL.

Moderato.
In the Ha - zel Dell my Nelly's sleep - ing, Nel-ly loved so

long; And my lone - ly, lone-ly watch I'm keep - ing,

Nel-ly lost and gone; Here in moon-light oft - en we have

wan - dered Thro' the si - lent shade, Now where
leaf - y branches drooping down - ward, Little Nel - ly's laid.
CHORUS. 2d time pp
All a-lone my watch I'm keeping In the Hazel Dell, For my
All a-lone my watch I'm keeping In the Hazel Dell, For my

dar-ling Nel-ly's near me sleep - ing,— Nelly dear, fare-well.
dar-ling Nel-ly's near me sleep - ing,— Nelly dear, fare-well.

2. In the Ha - zel Dell my Nel-ly's sleep-ing, Where the flow-ers
3. Now I'm wea-ry, friendless and for - sak - en, Watching here a-

wave, And the si - lent stars are nightly weep-ing O'er poor Nel-ly's
lone Nelly, thou no more will fondly cheer me With thy lov - ing

grave; Hopes that once my bosom fondly cherished Smile no more on
tone; Yet for-ev - er shall thy gentle im - age In my mem-'ry

me; Ev'ry dream of joy, a-las, has perish'd, Nelly dear, with thee.
dwell; And my tears thy lonely grave shall moisten, Nelly dear, fare-well.

ROSALIE, THE PRAIRIE FLOWER.

WURZEL. (G. F. R.)

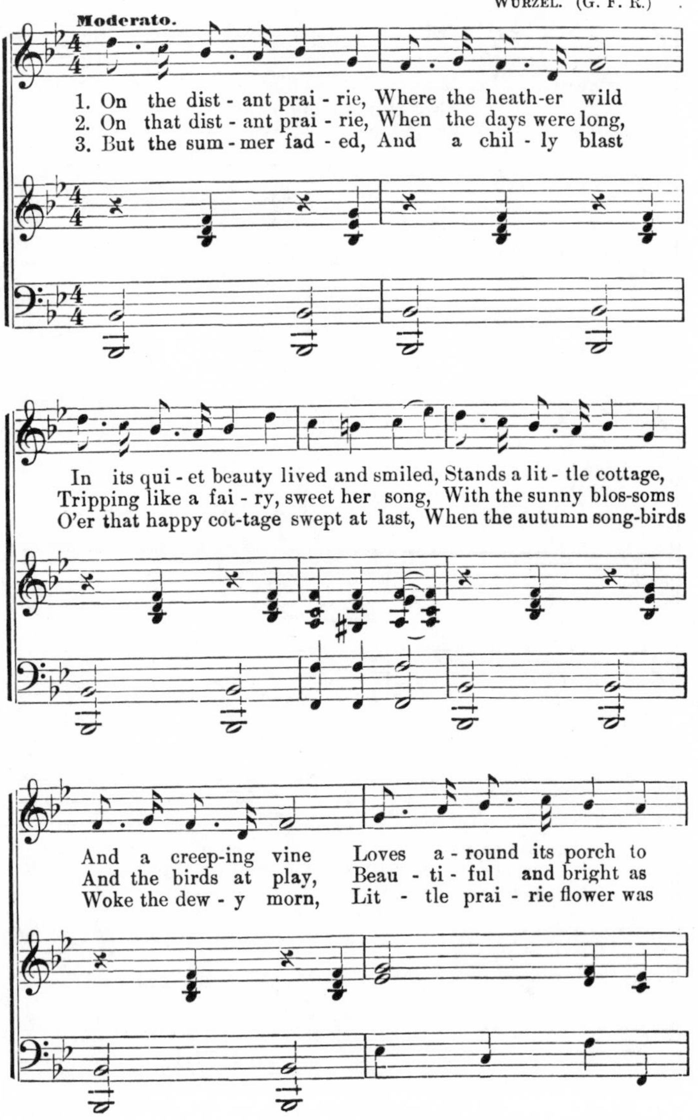
Moderato.
1. On the dist - ant prai - rie, Where the heath-er wild
2. On that dist - ant prai - rie, When the days were long,
3. But the sum - mer fad - ed, And a chil - ly blast
In its qui - et beauty lived and smiled, Stands a lit - tle cottage,
Tripping like a fai - ry, sweet her song, With the sunny blos-soms
O'er that happy cot-tage swept at last, When the autumn song-birds
And a creep-ing vine Loves a - round its porch to
And the birds at play, Beau - ti - ful and bright as
Woke the dew - y morn, Lit - tle prai - rie flower was

twine; In that peaceful dwelling was a love-ly child,
they; When the twilight shadows gathered in the west,
gone; For the an-gels whispered soft-ly in her ear,
With her blue eyes beaming soft and mild, And the wav-y ring-lets
And the voice of nature sunk to rest, Like a cherub kneeling
"Child, thy Father calls thee, stay not here," And they gently bore her,
of her flax-en hair, Waving in the sum-mer air.
seemed the lovely child, With her gentle eyes so mild.
robed in spotless white, To their blissful home of light.

CHORUS. (Repeat pp).
1 & 2. Fair as a li - ly, joyous and free, Light of that prairie home was she.
3. Tho' we shall never look on her more, Gone with the love and joy she bore,
Ev'ry one who knew her, felt the gentle pow'r of Rosalie the prairie flower.
Far away she's blooming in a fadeless bower, sweet Rosalie the prairie flower.

THE BATTLE CRY OF FREEDOM.

GEO. F. ROOT.
Maestoso.
1. Yes, we'll ral-ly round the flag, boys, we'll ral-ly once a - gain,
2. We are springing to the call of our brothers gone be - fore,
3. We will wel-come to our numbers the loy - al, true and brave,
4. So we're springing to the call from the East and from the West,
Shouting the bat-tle cry of Freedom, We will ral - ly from the hill-
Shouting the bat-tle cry of Freedom, And we'll fill the vacant ranks
Shouting the bat-tle cry of Freedom, And al - tho' they may be poor,
Shouting the bat-tle cry of Freedom, And we'll hurl the reb-el crew
side, we'll gather from the plain, Shouting the battle cry of Freedom.
with a million freemen more, Shouting the battle cry of Freedom.
not a man shall be a slave, Shouting the battle cry of Freedom.
from the land we love the best, Shouting the battle cry of Freedom.

CHORUS. ff
The Un - ion for - ev - er, Hur-rah! boys, Hur-rah!
The Un - ion for - ev - er, Hur-rah! boys, Hur-rah!
Down with the trai - tor, Up with the star; While we
Down with the trai - tor, Up with the star; While we

ral - ly round the flag, boys, ral - ly once a - gain,
ral - ly round the flag, boys, ral - ly once a - gain,
Shout - ing the bat - tle cry of Free - dom.
Shout - ing the bat - tle cry of Free - dom.

JUST BEFORE THE BATTLE, MOTHER.

GEO. F. ROOT.

Tenderly.
1. Just before the battle, Mother, I am thinking most of you,
2. Oh, I long to see you, Mother, And the loving ones at home,
3. Hark! I hear the bugles sounding, 'Tis the signal for the fight,
While upon the field we're watching, With the en - e-my in view—
But I'll never leave our banner, Till in honor I can come
Now may God protect us, mother, As he ev-er does the right.
Comrades brave are round me ly-ing, Filled with tho'ts of home and God; For
Tell the traitors all around you, That their cruel words we know, In
Hear the "Battle-Cry of Freedom,"* How it swells upon the air, Oh,

* In some of the divisions of our army the "Battle-Cry" is sung, when going into action, by order of the commanding officers.

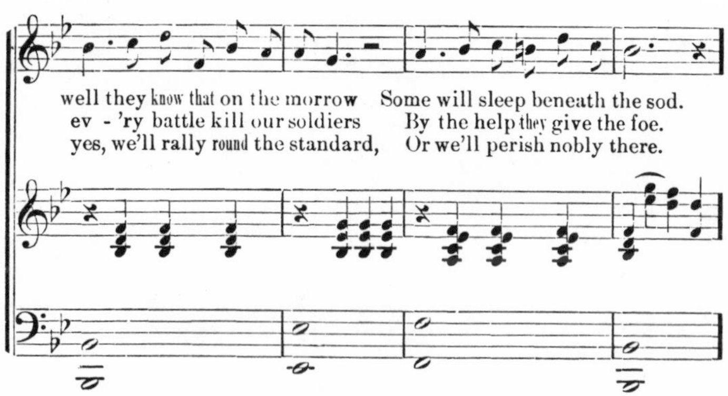
well they know that on the morrow Some will sleep beneath the sod.
ev - 'ry battle kill our soldiers By the help they give the foe.
yes, we'll rally round the standard, Or we'll perish nobly there.

CHORUS.
Fare - well, Mother, you may nev - er
you may nev - er, Mother,
Fare - well, Mother, you may nev - er, you may nev - er, Mother,

Press me to your heart a - gain; But oh, you'll not forget me,
Press me to your heart a - gain; But oh, you'll not forget me,
Rit.
Repeat pp
Mother, If I'm numbere'd with the slain.
you will not forget me,
Mother, you will not forget me, If I'm numbere'd with the slain.

TRAMP! TRAMP! TRAMP!

GEO. F. ROOT.

Tempo di Marcia.
1. In the pris-on cell I sit Thinking Mother dear, of
2. In the bat-tle front we stood When their fiercest charge they
3. So with-in the pris-on cell We are wait-ing for the
you, And our bright and happy home so far a-way, And the
made, And they swept us off, a hundred men or more, But be-
day, That shall come to o-pen wide the i-ron door. And the
tears they fill my eyes Spite of all that I can do, Tho' I
fore we reached their lines They were beaten back dismayed, And we
hol-low eye grows bright, And the poor heart almost gay, As we

try to cheer my com-rades and be gay.
heard the cry of vic - t'ry o'er and o'er.
think of see - ing home and friends once more.
When the chorus is sung, this may be omitted after the first verse.
Tramp, tramp, tramp, the boys are march-ing, Cheer up, comrades,
Tramp, tramp, tramp, the boys are march-ing, Cheer up, comrades,
Tramp, tramp, tramp, the boys are march-ing, Cheer up, comrades,
they will come, And be-neath the star - ry flag We shall
they will come, And be-neath the star - ry flag We shall
they will come, And be-neath the star - ry flag We shall

When the chorus is not sung, end here.

breathe the air a-gain, Of the free-land in our own beloved home.
breathe the air a-gain, Of the free-land in our own beloved home.
breathe the air a-gain, Of the free-land in our own beloved home.
CHORUS.
Tramp, tramp, tramp, the boys are march - ing, Cheer up, comrades,
marching on, O cheer up, com -
Tramp, tramp, tramp, the boys are march-ing on, O cheer up, com -

they will come, And beneath the star-ry flag We shall
rades, they will come,
rades, they will come, And beneath the star-ry flag We shall
breathe the air a-gain, Of the free-land in our own beloved home.
breathe the air a-gain, Of the free-land in our own beloved home.

THE VACANT CHAIR.

N. S. W. GEO. F. ROOT.

With expression.
1. We shall meet, but we shall miss him, There will be one vacant
2. At our fire - side, sad and lonely, Often will the bo-som
3. True they tell us wreaths of glo-ry Ev-er more will deck his
chair; We shall lin - ger to ca - ress him While we
swell, At re-mem - brance of the sto - ry How our
brow, But this soothes the an-guish on - ly Sweeping
breathe our even-ing prayer. When a year a - go we
no - ble Wil-lie fell; How he strove to bear our
o'er our heart-strings now. Sleep to-day, oh, ear - ly

gathered, Joy was in his mild blue eye, But a
ban-ner Thro' the thick - est of the fight, And up-
fall - en, In thy green and nar-row bed, Dirg-es
gold - en chord is severed, And our hopes in ru - in lie.
hold our country's honor, In the strength of manhood's might.
from the pine and cypress Mingle with the tears we shed.
CHORUS.
We shall meet, but we shall miss him, There will be one vacant
We shall meet, but we shall miss him, There will be one vacant
8
8

chair ; We shall lin-ger to caress him, When we breathe our evening
chair ; We shall lin-ger to caress him, When we breathe our evening
prayer.
prayer.

THERE'S MUSIC IN THE AIR.

FOR MENS' VOICES.* G. F. Root.

Moderato.
1. There's music in the air, When the infant morn is nigh, And
2. There's music in the air, When the noontide's sul-t'ry beam Re-
3. There's music in the air, When the twilight's gen-tle sigh Is
faint its blush is seen On the bright and laughing sky.
flects a gold-en light On the distant mount-ain stream.
lost on evening's breast, As its pensive beauties die.

* If sung by mixed voices, let the alto be an octave lower.

Many a harp's ec - stat - ic sound With its thrill of
When beneath some grateful shade Sorrow's ach-ing
Then, O then the loved ones gone Wake the pure ce-
joy pro-found, While we list en - chant-ed there To the
head is laid, Sweetly to the spi - rit there Comes the
les - tial song, An-gel voic - es greet us there In the

2d time pp
mu - sic in the air.
mu - sic in the air.
mu - sic in the air.

256 THE SHINING SHORE.

Rev. DAVID NELSON. G. F. ROOT.

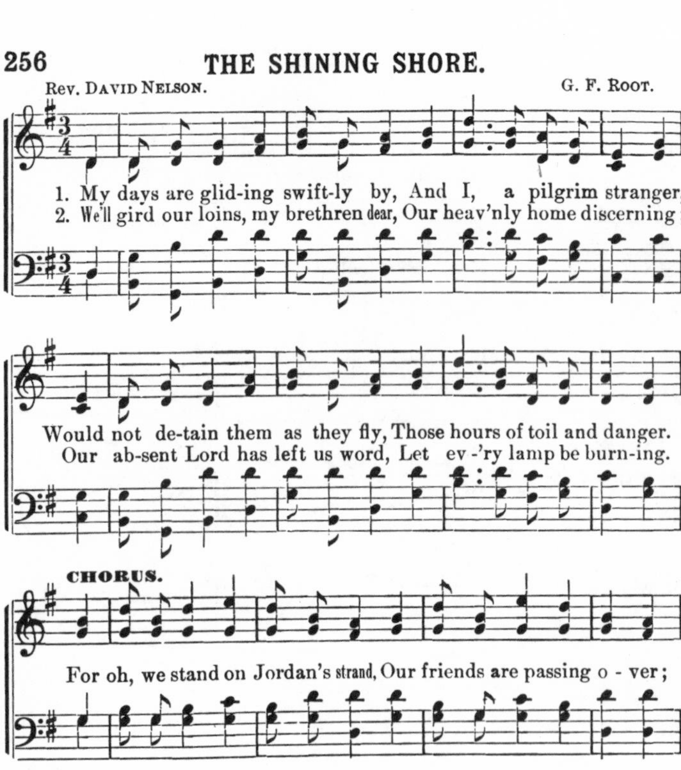
1. My days are glid-ing swift-ly by, And I, a pilgrim stranger,
2. We'll gird our loins, my brethren dear, Our heav'nly home discerning;
Would not de-tain them as they fly, Those hours of toil and danger.
Our ab-sent Lord has left us word, Let ev-'ry lamp be burn-ing.
CHORUS.
For oh, we stand on Jordan's strand, Our friends are passing o - ver;
And just be - fore the Shining Shore We may almost discov - er.

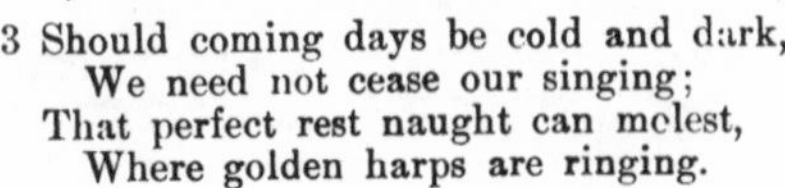

3 Should coming days be cold and dark,
We need not cease our singing;
That perfect rest naught can molest,
Where golden harps are ringing.

4 Let sorrow's rudest tempests blow,
Each chord on earth to sever;
Our King says, Come, and there's our home,
Forever, oh, forever.